Beginning JavaServer Pages™

Larry Lindbloom
Elizabeth Hedberg
1106 8th St
Golden CO 80401-1009

Beginning JavaServer Pages™

Vivek Chopra
Sing Li
Rupert Jones
Jon Eaves
John T. Bell

Wiley Publishing, Inc.

Beginning JavaServer Pages™

Published by
Wiley Publishing, Inc.
10475 Crosspoint Boulevard
Indianapolis, IN 46256
www.wiley.com

Copyright © 2005 by Wiley Publishing, Inc., Indianapolis, Indiana

Published by Wiley Publishing, Inc., Indianapolis, Indiana

Published simultaneously in Canada

ISBN: 0-7645-7485-X

Manufactured in the United States of America

10 9 8 7 6 5 4 3 2 1

1B/QT/QS/QV/IN

For general information on our other products and services or to obtain technical support, please contact our Customer Care Department within the U.S. at (800) 762-2974, outside the U.S. at (317) 572-3993 or fax (317) 572-4002.

Wiley also publishes its books in a variety of electronic formats. Some content that appears in print may not be available in electronic books.

Library of Congress Cataloging-in-Publication Data

Beginning JavaServer pages / Vivek Chopra ... [et al.].
    p. cm.
 Includes index.
 ISBN 0-7645-7485-X (paper/website)
 1. JavaServer pages. 2. Web sites--Design. 3. Web site development. I. Chopra, Vivek.
 TK5105.8885.J38B45 2005
 006.7 6--dc22

2004024591

About the Authors

Vivek Chopra has over ten years of experience as a software developer, architect, and team lead, with extensive experience with Web services, J2EE, and middleware technologies. He has worked and consulted at a number of Silicon Valley companies and startups and has (pending) patents on Web services. Vivek actively writes about technology and has coauthored half a dozen books on topics such as open-source software, Java, XML, and Web services. He contributes to open source, too, and has developed parts of the uddi4j library, an open-source Java API for UDDI.

Sing Li, first bit by the microcomputer bug in 1978, has grown up with the microprocessor age. His first personal computer was a do-it-yourself Netronics COSMIC ELF computer with 256 bytes of memory, mail-ordered from the back pages of *Popular Electronics* magazine. Currently, Sing is a consultant, system designer, open-source software contributor, and freelance writer. He writes for several popular technical journals and e-zines and is the creator of the *Internet Global Phone*, one of the very first Internet phones available. He has authored and coauthored numerous books across diverse technical topics, including JSP, Tomcat, servlets, XML, Jini, and JXTA.

Rupert Jones is a Technical Lead for J2EE projects at Internet Business Systems. Over the past six years, Rupert has provided software development and consulting services for blue-chip companies, both in Australia and internationally. He lives and works in Melbourne, Australia. Rupert can be contacted at rup@rupertjones.com.

Jon Eaves has been developing software in a variety of languages and domains for over 15 years. He is currently employed by ThoughtWorks, developing large-scale enterprise systems using J2EE. When he can find spare time, he develops J2ME/MIDP applications and works on the BouncyCastle Crypto APIs (www.bouncycastle.org). Jon can be reached at jon@eaves.org.

John T. Bell has more than 20 years of software development experience and currently serves as the lead software architect for the Web site of a major hospitality company based in Bethesda, Maryland. He is also an adjunct professor, teaching server-side Java technologies for the Center for Applied Information Technology at Towson State University. He has a master's degree in Computer Systems Management and a bachelor's degree in Electrical Engineering, both from the University of Maryland. This is Mr. Bell's third contribution to a Wrox title. He is also the author of *The J2EE Open Source Toolkit*.

Credits

Acquisitions Editor
Robert Elliott

Development Editor
Sydney Jones

Technical Editor
Wiley-Dreamtech India Pvt Ltd

Production Editor
William A. Barton

Copy Editor
Luann Rouff

Editorial Manager
Mary Beth Wakefield

Vice President and Executive Group Publisher
Richard Swadley

Vice President and Publisher
Joseph B. Wikert

Project Coordinator
April Farling

Graphics and Production Specialists
Jonelle Burns
Carrie A. Foster
Lauren Goddard
Denny Hager
Joyce Haughey
Amanda Spagnuolo

Quality Control Technicians
Jessica Kramer
Susan Moritz
Carl William Pierce
Charles Spencer

Media Development Specialist
Kit Malone

Proofreading and Indexing
TECHBOOKS Production Services

Acknowledgments

Vivek Chopra

I'd like to thank my coauthors and all the folks at Wrox for the effort and the long hours—thank you, Rupert, Sing, Jon, John, Sydney, James, and Bob! I'd especially like to thank my wife, Rebecca, for her patience and support, especially since I spent most weekends working on this book.

Sing Li

Thanks to the virtual *Beginning JavaServer Pages* team, top professionals from all corners of the globe. It was wonderful working with you throughout 2003 and 2004.

To my wife, Kim—your inspiration and support are the high-octane fuel that keeps me running, looking joyfully forward to each brave new day.

Rupert Jones

First of all, I'd like to thank my coauthors for their dedication to this book. It's not easy holding down a full-time job in this industry and fitting in time for such a venture. I am constantly amazed we all still have friends and family who will talk to us, let alone recognize us. It's been a pleasure undertaking this task with a group of such consummate professionals.

To the Wrox crew—in particular, Sydney Jones, our developmental editor, and our tech reviewers at DreamTech—thanks for all your hard work in getting us across the line. I know its difficult working with technical people at the best of times, especially when they are geographically remote.

Thanks also to my colleagues at Internet Business Systems: Steve Hayes, Rob Mitchell, and Shane Clauson. These guys provided me with much-needed help, advice, and encouragement, even in my grumpier moments. It really is a pleasure to work with each of you.

And last but certainly not least, thanks to my loving family: Julia, Michael, Nick, and Caroline.

Jon Eaves

I'd like to thank my coauthors and the team at Wrox for the hard work they put in while creating this book. Closer to home, I'd like to thank my family for their encouragement, patience, and support. Mum and Dad, everything I can do is because of your love. My wonderful wife, Sue, you rock my world more and more every day. Boo and Maddy, your purring late at night kept me going when the words wouldn't come. Thank you, all.

John T. Bell

To Tammy, my loving and patient wife, maybe someday I will write a book that you can read, and to my grandmother, Valmai Locklair, who slipped away from us as I was writing my chapters.

Contents

Contents

Contents

Contents

Describing servlets to containers in the deployment descriptor   495
The servlet declaration   497
Using servlets when JSP is available   503
Specifying initialization parameters   504
Accessing initialization parameters within the ControllerServlet   506
Custom forwarding of incoming requests via the controller servlet   508
The forwarding targets   509
Summary   **510**
Exercises   **510**

Chapter 16: The Role of JSP in the Wider Context: Web Applications   **511**

What Is a Web Application?   **512**
Directory Structure for a Web Application   **512**
The Deployment Descriptor   **513**
Deployment descriptor elements for a JSP developer   513
Using a Web Archive   **523**
Development and Deployment Strategies   **523**
Packaging and Deploying for Tomcat   **524**
Introduction to Web application security   528
Summary   **529**
Exercises   **530**

Chapter 17: Model View Controller   **533**

What Is MVC?   **534**
MVC and Web Applications   **534**
Summary   **546**
Exercise   **547**

Chapter 18: Web Frameworks   **549**

What Is a Framework?   **549**
Why Frameworks Are Good   **550**
Types of Frameworks   **551**
Application frameworks   551
Persistence frameworks   552
Utility frameworks   553
WebWork   **554**
Components of WebWork   554

Contents

Contents

Contents

Contents

Contents

Contents

Contents

Contents

Introduction

JavaServer Pages (JSP) was first introduced in 1999, and since then numerous books have been written about it. This book aims to introduce JSP in a new way, different from existing titles.

A lot has been learned in the past five years about what constitutes good practices for developing Web applications, and what should be avoided. Much of this has been learned by developers the hard way, at the cost of Web sites with bad performance or unmaintainable code. While this was understandable when these technologies were new, beginning JSP developers shouldn't have to repeat these mistakes.

As the title suggests, the book is targeted toward developers who are new to JSP development, though not to Java, or even to Web development itself. This book is *not* a second or even a third edition of an older JSP book. It has been written from scratch by experienced developers, who are eager to share their insights with you.

This book covers JSP 2.0, the latest specification, as well as how JSP interacts with other Enterprise Java technologies. JSP 2.0 introduces many new features that aid good Web development practices, and this book covers them in great detail.

The Right Way to Do Web Development

This book covers JSP development techniques in great detail. However, a central theme in the book is an emphasis on the right way to do Web development. These ideas are generally accepted "good development practices" and draw upon the authors' own experiences in this area. Some of these practices include the following:

❑ **JSP is a presentation technology:** JSPs should be used for presentation only and should not have code for control flow and application logic mixed in it. The book emphasis this and other good JSP development practices.

❑ **Use the right tools, effectively:** Use tools to assist in your Web development tasks, such as development and debugging environments, build and deployment tools, version-control tools, and profiling tools. The book provides a tutorial introduction to tools that should be in every Web developer's tool box.

❑ **Use design patterns where appropriate:** Many of the problems that you solve as a software developer have already been faced by others before you. Instead of trying to reinvent a solution to a certain class of problems over and over again, it is wiser to use a tried and tested solution. A *design pattern* is a solution to a type of a problem. Where appropriate, this book illustrates the use of common design patterns in Web applications, such as Model View Controller (MVC), front controller, Data Access Object (DAO), etc.

❑ **Use frameworks for developing applications:** Frameworks implement generic solutions to common problems faced by developers. Using a framework enables developers to focus on the business problem at hand, rather than reinventing the wheel for every application. This book introduces a number of frameworks, such as MVC (Struts, Spring, WebWork, JSF), persistence (Hibernate), testing (jUnit, HttpUnit), logging (log4j, Java Logging API), and templating (Tiles) frameworks.

❑ **Iterative development methodologies:** These cover a range of techniques, but the common theme is writing test cases early in the development cycle, often even before the actual code, testing frequently during development, having early build and integration cycles, and *refactoring* your code.

If some of these terms are not familiar to you right now, don't worry; they will be by the time you are done with this book!

Approach

We believe that the best way to learn, especially for beginners, is by first reading about a concept, seeing how it is implemented, and then finally by writing some code.

This is the approach we've followed in the book. Each chapter first introduces important concepts and then illustrates them with hands-on examples in the "Try It Out" sections. Following each "Try It Out" section is a "How It Works" section that explains the example in detail.

At the end of each chapter, we have included coding exercises for you to try yourself. These exercises build upon examples introduced earlier in the chapter and help reinforce concepts you learned in it. The solutions for the exercise are listed at the end of the book in Appendix D.

How This Book Is Structured

The book is divided into four parts.

The first part, "JSP Fundamentals," represents the bulk of the book. This part, as the name suggests, introduces the fundamentals of JSP programming. Some of the topics it covers include JSP syntax and directives, the JSP Expression Language, JSP Tag libraries, JavaServer Pages Standard Tag Library (JSTL), and techniques for testing and debugging.

The second part, "JSP and Modern Web Server Software Development," builds upon the first part and explores the Web applications and environments that most production JSP code will be deployed in. It covers the following topics:

❑ Popular Web frameworks, such as Struts/Tiles, WebWork, and Spring

❑ Persistence frameworks, such as Hibernate

❑ Enterprise Java technologies, such as Java Database Connectivity (JDBC) and Java Naming and Directory Interface (JNDI)

❑ Emerging presentation technologies such as JavaServer Faces

❑ Issues relating to security, performance, and internationalization

❑   Modern software methodologies and development tools such as Ant, JUnit, HttpUnit, jMeter, Log4j, and CVS

This part provides you with a tutorial-style introduction to these technologies. The focus of this book is JSP development, and even though these frameworks and tools are important, covering each of them in detail would have resulted in a much bigger book!

In the third part, "Spreading Your New Wings: Applying JSP in the Real World," you will be challenged to apply your new JSP programming skills to real-world projects. These projects reinforce concepts explained earlier in the book with concrete examples that you can try out on your own.

The fourth and final part consists of the four appendixes for the book, providing you with three references and exercise solutions.

The chapters are organized as follows:

Chapter 1, "Getting Started with JavaServer Pages," introduces JSPs and explains why they were needed and describes how to download and install chapter samples and projects.

Chapter 2, "JSP Basics 1: Dynamic Page Creation for Data Presentation," gives you a taste of JSP programming using simple examples. The examples presented here teach the right way to do JSP programming, without scripting elements and using JSTL, EL, and actions only.

Chapter 3, "JSP Basics 2: Generalized Templating and Server Scripting," covers embedding Java scriptlets in JSP files. This is how JSP was used originally, and even though this practice is now deprecated, developers often have to maintain and extend such code.

Chapter 4, "CSS, JavaScript, VBScript, and JSP," illustrates JSP's capability to generate not only dynamic HTML Web page content, but also Web pages with JavaScript or VBScript code.

Chapter 5, "JSP and EL," covers the JSP Expression Language (EL) in great detail and with a lot of example code.

Chapter 6, "JSP Tag Libraries and JSTL," introduces the basics of the tag library extension mechanism in JSPs. It also covers the standard tag library, JSTL, along with examples.

Chapter 7, "JSP Directives," covers the standard JSP directives and all their properties.

Chapter 8, "JSP Standard Actions," provides an item-by-item introduction to the available standard actions in JSP. Each action is introduced as a part of an actual hands-on example.

Chapter 9, "JSP and JavaBeans," discusses the important role of JavaBeans in JSP operations. It focuses on the ability of JavaBeans to act as a container of data to be presented, as well as to extend the data manipulation and transformation capabilities of JSP.

Chapter 10, "Error Handling," reveals the interpretation-time and runtime errors that can occur and how to handle them. It also discusses the application-level JSP exception-handling mechanism, as well as the Java programming language exception-handling mechanism.

Chapter 11, "Building Your Own Custom JSP Tag Library," shows you how to create a custom tag library, encapsulating a reusable piece of JSP code in a JSP tag file.

Chapter 12, "Advanced Dynamic Web Content Generation," emphasizes that the utility of JSP extends beyond the generation of HTML. JSPs can be used to generate any dynamic content for Web-based consumption, such as client-side scripting elements and XML.

Chapter 13, "Internationalization and Localized Content," explains internationalization concepts and demonstrates how JSP can be used to generate localized Web pages.

Chapter 14, "JSP Debugging Techniques," covers logging mechanisms and debugger-supported techniques. The chapter also covers the debugging of a production system and thread safety issues.

Chapter 15, "JSP and Servlets," presents Java servlets, their relationship with JSPs, servlet configuration, and the servlet context.

Chapter 16, "Role of JSP in the Wider Context: Web Applications," introduces the details of Web applications, including creating and deploying them.

Chapter 17, "Model View Controller," covers the popular Model View Controller (MVC) pattern.

Chapter 18, "Web Frameworks," describes what frameworks are, why they are needed, and what they do. This chapter covers the WebWork and Spring frameworks.

Chapter 19, "Struts Framework," provides detailed coverage of the popular Struts framework.

Chapter 20, "Layout Management with Tiles," covers the Tiles frameworks for Web page layout and its use with Struts.

Chapter 21, "JavaServer Faces," introduces JSF 1.1, with examples. This chapter also compares JSF with Struts and how they can be used together in Web applications.

Chapter 22, "JSP in J2EE," provides an overview of important J2EE components that JSP would need to interact with in Web applications.

Chapter 23, "Access to Databases," covers details of database access from Web applications, including JDBC and Hibernate.

Chapter 24, "Security," introduces security issues for Web applications, such as authentication, access control, data integrity, and privacy.

Chapter 25, "Performance," covers performance concepts for Web applications, including how to measure performance as well as performance-tuning techniques.

Chapter 26, "Best Practices and Tools," details development-time best practices and methodologies and provides a tutorial introduction to developer tools for build, version control, and testing.

Chapter 27, "JSP Project I: Personalized Portal," demonstrates how to integrate content from other Web sites using RSS and Web services. This project reinforces concepts covered earlier in the book—namely, use of tag libraries, JSTL, and EL—and emphasizes the use of design patterns.

Chapter 28, "JSP Project II: Shopping Cart Application," shows how to develop an online storefront Web application. This project reinforces Struts and Tiles concepts and database persistence from Web applications using Hibernate.

Appendix A, "JSP Syntax Reference," as the name suggests, is a handy reference to the JSP syntax.

Appendix B, "JSP Expression Language Reference," lists the JSP EL syntax, with examples.

Appendix C, "JSTL Reference," provides a reference to the JSTL tag library, including the core, XML, formatting, and SQL tags.

Appendix D, "Exercise Solutions," has the answers to all the exercise problems listed at the end of the chapters.

Conventions

To help you get the most from the text and keep track of what's happening, we've used a number of conventions throughout the book.

> *Hints, tips, and additional notes regarding the current discussion are offset and placed in italics like this.*

As for styles in the text:

❑ Important terms are *italicized* when introduced for the first time.

❑ Classes, filenames, URLs, directories, interfaces, utilities, parameters, and other code-related terms within the text are presented as follows: WEB-INF\web.xml.

Code is presented in two different ways:

```
Code that is introduced for the first time, or an important code fragment, has a
gray background.
Code that is less important to the discussion, or that has been introduced earlier,
is shown without a background.
```

Try It Out

The "Try It Out" sections are exercises that you should work through, following the text in the book.

1. They usually consist of a set of steps.

2. Each step has a number.

3. In most cases, you can follow the steps with your copy of the downloaded code.

How It Works

After each "Try It Out," the code you've typed is explained in detail.

Source Code

As you work through the examples in this book, you may choose either to type in all the code manually or to use the source code files that accompany the book. All of the source code used in this book is available for download at www.wrox.com. Once at the site, simply locate the book's title (either by using the Search box or by using one of the title lists) and click the Download Code link on the book's detail page to obtain all the source code for the book.

> *Because many books have similar titles, you may find it easiest to search by ISBN; this book's ISBN is 0-764-57485-X.*

Once you download the code, just decompress it with your favorite compression tool.

Errata

We have made every effort to ensure that there are no errors in the text or in the code. However, no one is perfect, and mistakes do occur. If you find an error, such as a spelling mistake or a faulty piece of code, we would be very grateful for your feedback. By sending in errata, you may save other readers hours of frustration, and you will be helping us provide even higher quality information.

To find the errata page for this book, go to www.wrox.com and locate the title using the Search box or one of the title lists. Then, on the book details page, click the Book Errata link. On this page, you can view all errata that has been submitted for this book and posted by Wrox editors. A complete book list, including links to each book's errata, is also available at www.wrox.com/misc-pages/booklist.shtml.

If you don't spot your error on the Book Errata page, go to www.wrox.com/contact/techsupport.shtml and complete the form there to send us the error you have found. We'll check the information and, if appropriate, post a message to the book's errata page and fix the problem in subsequent editions of the book.

p2p.wrox.com

For author and peer discussion, join the P2P forums at p2p.wrox.com. The forums are a Web-based system for you to post messages relating to Wrox books and related technologies and interact with other readers and technology users. The forums offer a subscription feature to e-mail you topics of interest of your choosing when new posts are made to the forums. Wrox authors, editors, other industry experts, and your fellow readers are present on these forums.

At http://p2p.wrox.com, you will find several different forums that will help you not only as you read this book, but also as you develop your own applications. To join the forums, just follow these steps:

1. Go to p2p.wrox.com and click the Register link.
2. Read the terms of use and click Agree.

3. Complete the required information to join as well as any optional information you wish to provide and click Submit.

4. You will receive an e-mail with information describing how to verify your account and complete the joining process.

You can read messages in the forums without joining P2P, but in order to post your own messages, you must join.

Once you join, you can post new messages and respond to messages that other users post. You can read messages at any time on the Web. If you would like to have new messages from a particular forum e-mailed to you, click the Subscribe to this Forum icon by the forum name in the forum listing.

For more information about how to use the Wrox P2P, be sure to read the P2P FAQs for answers to questions about how the forum software works as well as many common questions specific to P2P and Wrox books. To read the FAQs, click the FAQ link on any P2P page.

Part I: JSP Fundamentals

Chapter 1: Getting Started with JavaServer Pages

Chapter 2: JSP Basics 1: Dynamic Page Creation for Data Presentation

Chapter 3: JSP Basics 2: Generalized Templating and Server Scripting

Chapter 4: CSS, JavaScript, VBScript, and JSP

Chapter 5: JSP and EL

Chapter 6: JSP Tag Libraries and JSTL

Chapter 7: JSP Directives

Chapter 8: JSP Standard Actions

Chapter 9: JSP and JavaBeans

Chapter 10: Error Handling

Chapter 11: Building Your Own Custom JSP Tag Library

Chapter 12: Advanced Dynamic Web Content Generation

Chapter 13: Internationalization and Localized Content

Chapter 14: JSP Debugging Techniques

Getting Started with JavaServer Pages

JavaServer Pages (JSP) is a Java-based technology that is run on a server to facilitate the processing of Web-based requests. Many of the Web sites that you visit daily may be using JSP to format and display the data that you see. This chapter reveals what JSP is, how it works, and why it is important.

The evolution of request processing using Java-based server logic is also presented in this chapter. JSP plays a vital role in this evolution. This role, along with how JSP assists in Web request processing, will be discussed. This overview serves as a foundation upon which to build new JSP concepts and to introduce new JSP features in later chapters.

Every chapter in this book contains hands-on JSP coding examples. Starting from this very first chapter you will be working immediately with JSP coding. This chapter shows in detail how to set up JSP code on your own Windows-based PC or Linux/UNIX workstation.

In particular, this chapter:

❑ Provides a historical review of the Web technology evolution that leads to JSP

❑ Discusses why JSP is needed

❑ Reveals how JSP works

❑ Shows where to download chapter code examples and the JSP Project examples

❑ Shows where to download a server for executing JSP code on your PC or workstation

❑ Reveals how to set up the open-source Tomcat server for running your JSP code

Creating Applications for the Internet

Before looking at a server that supports JSP, think of what happens under the hood when you use your browser to access a Web site. It's likely you're using one of the popular Web browsers, such as Netscape, Microsoft Internet Explorer, Firefox, Konquerer, or Opera. Figure 1-1 illustrates the sequence of events that occurs when the browser accesses a URL.

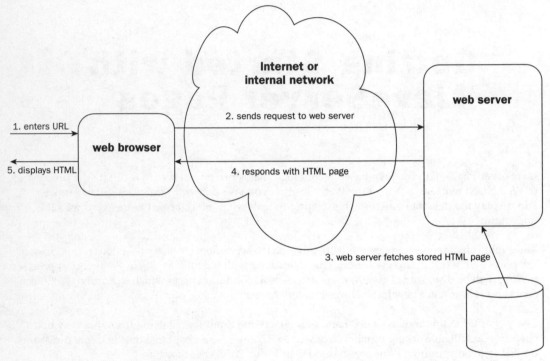

Figure 1-1: Web browser accessing a URL

The following steps correspond numerically with the numbered steps in Figure 1-1:

1. Enter the URL of a Web page into your browser. This URL tells the browser to contact a specific machine on the Internet.

2. The browser then sends the request to the specified machine on the Internet. The machine specified runs a piece of software called a *Web server*. The Web server receives the request and examines it. Popular Web servers include Apache, Microsoft Internet Information Services (IIS), Netscape Enterprise Server, Sun Java System Web Server (formerly Sun ONE), Oracle HTTP Server, and Zeus Web Server.

3. Depending on the request received, the Web server retrieves from its storage a Web page encoded in HTML.

4. The page acquired in Step 3 is passed back to the requesting browser as a response.

5. The browser, after receiving the response Web page, displays it to the user.

Of course, the Web page can contain graphical elements such as GIF files (the browser will have to issue additional requests to the server for these files), as well as hyperlinks to other URLs that the user can click.

> *HTML (Hypertext Markup Language)* **is the standard format in which Web pages are coded. HTML files are text-based files that can be edited in any text editor. An HTML page consists of tagged sections such as a header and a body, and formatted layout elements such as paragraphs and tables. All browsers understand HTML and will display (called** *rendering* **in HTML lingo) the page according to the formatting tags. For more information on HTML, check out** *Beginning Web Programming with HTML, XHTML, and CSS* **(Wrox Press; ISBN 0-7645-7078-1).**

In the preceding process, the browser talks to the Web server over the Internet. This conversation is carried out via a standard network protocol. This particular protocol is appropriately called *HTTP (Hypertext Transfer Protocol)*. HTTP is built on top of TCP/IP, the protocol suite that ties all the computers in the Internet together.

Limitations of the basic Web server model

The basic function of the Web server restricts it to serve a finite number of static Web pages. The content of each page remains the same. There is no easy way to show information that may change, such as today's weather, the latest news, or the current product list offered by an online store. A new set of static pages needs to be created to show new information.

Creating new static pages for every minute change of the underlying information is tedious. Obviously, a lot of time and effort could be saved if there were some way for the server to automatically generate portions of the HTML page. Doing so would eliminate the need to repeatedly create new static pages as information changes. This generation should happen dynamically when the request is processed. For example, it could generate the portion of the HTML page that displays the current date and time.

Internet software engineers quickly turned their attention to the Common Gateway Interface (CGI) to provide this dynamic generation capability.

Dynamic HTML generation via CGI

CGI provides a way to execute a program on the server side. This may be on the same machine running the Web server, or it may be on another machine connected to it. The CGI program's output is the HTML page that will be sent back to the Web browser for display. Figure 1-2 illustrates basic CGI operations.

1. First the browser is instructed to access a URL. You may be entering this URL by hand. More likely, a CGI URL is accessed after you fill out an online form or click a hyperlink on a page already displayed. For example, the URL may be `http://www.wrox.com/beginjsp/ch1test.cgi`. This URL tells the browser to contact a specific machine on the Internet called `www.wrox.com`.

2. The browser then sends the request to the specified machine on the Internet. This is identical to the non-CGI case in Figure 1-1. In addition to the machine, the URL also specifies a specific CGI program location. The portion of the URL that specifies the location is `beginjsp/ch1test.cgi`. The Web server examines the incoming request's URL and forwards the incoming request to the specified CGI program (`ch1test.cgi`).

3. The CGI program is executed on the server side.

4. The CGI program's output is captured by the Web server.

5. This CGI program's output is passed back to the requesting Web browser using the HTTP protocol.

6. The client Web browser finally displays the output from the CGI program as an HTML page.

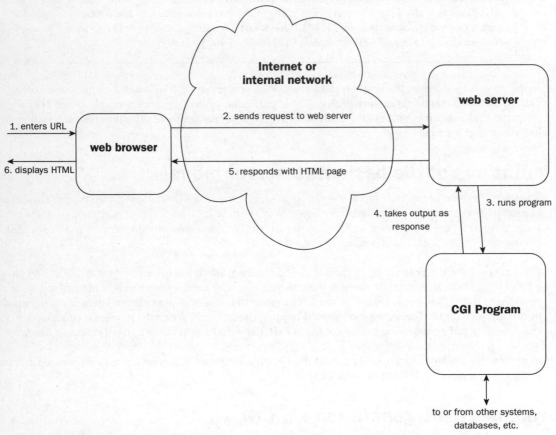

Figure 1-2: Basic CGI operations

The CGI program can be programmed using any computer programming language (the most popular CGI languages are Perl or a shell script, but C, C++, or Java can also be used). The output that the CGI program generates is not limited to a finite set of static pages. Furthermore, the CGI program can access additional resources in generating the output. For example, a CGI program displaying the available quantity for a product sold over the Internet may access a relational database containing current inventory information.

Elegant as CGI seems to be initially, it has major shortcomings. These shortcomings, described in the following section, are evident when a single CGI program is accessed by many users.

Shortcomings of CGI

The major shortcomings of basic CGI are as follows:

❑ The overhead of starting an operating system process for each incoming request

❑ The overhead of loading and running a program for each incoming request

❑ The need for tedious and repetitive coding to handle the network protocol and request decoding

The first two operations consume a large number of CPU cycles and memory. Because both operations must be performed for each incoming request, a server machine can be overloaded if too many requests arrive in a short period of time. Because each CGI program is independent of the other, and often reflect incompatible programming languages, it is not possible to share code used in networking and decoding.

The Java programming language can be used to create CGI programs. Unfortunately, using the Java programming language for CGI amplifies some of the shortcomings of basic CGI described in the preceding list. Early attempts to use the Java programming language to create CGI programs created servers that were extremely slow and inefficient, and crashed frequently due to overloading.

Java-based CGI is not suitable for handling CGI requests because Java is inherently an interpreted language. Because of this, a very large program called the Java Virtual Machine (JVM) must be started to handle an incoming request. The cycle of starting a system process, then a JVM within the process, and then running the Java CGI code within the JVM just for processing a single request is very expensive in terms of both computing cycles and resources. Worse, the whole process needs to be repeated for each incoming request. When compared to the time it takes to process the request and generate the output, this overhead can be significant. If the server needs to handle many incoming requests, the overhead can overwhelm the system.

Improving Java-based CGI: servlets

The Java-based CGI scenario can be improved if the overhead can be eliminated. If some way exists to process all incoming requests by initially starting a single operating system process with a single JVM image, the overhead can be eliminated.

Because the Java platform can load new classes during runtime dynamically, this capability can be used to load new Java code (classes) to handle incoming requests. In order words, a server-side process is started once and loaded with the JVM once, but additional classes are loaded by the JVM to process incoming requests. This is significantly more efficient. In this scenario, the following can be observed:

❑ The overhead of starting an operating system process for each request is eliminated.

❑ The overhead of loading a JVM for each request is eliminated.

❑ Java classes are loaded by the JVM to process incoming requests; if more than one request requires the same processing, the already loaded class can be used to handle it, eliminating even the class loading overhead for all but the first request.

❑ Code that handles the networking protocol and decodes incoming requests can be shared by all the dynamically loaded request processing Java classes.

The Java Web Server from Sun Microsystems released in the late 1990s worked exactly in this way. This Web server, written in the Java programming language, started up a JVM to handle all incoming requests and in turn loaded additional Java classes as needed to process specific requests.

In order to ensure that the Java classes loaded for handling requests do not step over one another, or stop the entire Web server altogether, a coding standard was created, which these classes must follow. This standard is called the *Java Servlets API (Application Programming Interface)*. The dynamically loaded classes for processing are known as *servlets*.

The portion of code that manages the loading, unloading, reloading, and execution of servlets is called a *servlet container*. Servlets may need to be unloaded if the system is running out of memory and some servlets have not been used for a very long time. A servlet may need to be reloaded if its code has been modified since it was last used.

There are many different ways to configure the Web server and servlet container. The next section discusses the most popular scenarios.

Web server configurations: integrating servlet containers

Depending on the Web server and servlet container used, very different configurations are possible. Some popular configurations include the following:

❑ The same JVM runs the Web server as well as the servlets; in this case, the Web server is coded in Java, as is also the case with the Java Web Server mentioned earlier. This is often called the *standalone configuration*. Figure 1-3a illustrates the standalone configuration.

❑ The Web server is not written in the Java programming language, but it starts a JVM within the same operating system process; in this case, the information is passed directly from the Web server into the JVM hosting the servlet container. (Some versions of both the Apache Web server and Microsoft IIS can work in this way.)This is often called the *in-process configuration*. Figure 1-3b illustrates the in-process configuration.

❑ The Web server is not written in the Java programming language and runs in a separate operating system process from the servlet container; in this case, the Web server passes the request to the servlet container, using either a local network or operating–system–specific interprocess communications mechanism (a typical configuration for the Apache or Microsoft's IIS Web server). This is often called the *independent configuration* or *networked configuration*. Figure 1-3c illustrates this configuration.

The first two configurations in the preceding list have the advantage that the JVM runs within the same OS process as the Web server. This enables rapid transfer of request information and processing output to and from the CGI code. Conversely, if the servlet container or one of its servlets crashes, the entire Web server may crash because they are in the same process.

The third configuration is less efficient when it comes to the transfer of request data between the Web server and the servlet container. However, the servlet container can crash and restart without affecting the operation of the Web server. This form creates a more robust system for handling Web requests.

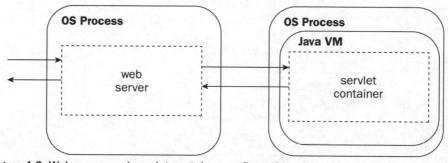

a. standalone configuration

OS Process

Java VM

web server → servlet container

b. in-process configuration

OS Process

Java VM

web server → servlet container

c. independent/networked configuration

OS Process

web server

OS Process

Java VM

servlet container

Figure 1-3: Web server and servlet container configurations

Each of the three configurations described exhibit superior performance characteristics when compared to the basic CGI operation introduced earlier.

Optimizing servlet development: JavaServer Pages

Servlets can be viewed as an efficient way of performing CGI operations using the Java programming language. Java classes representing the servlet are dynamically loaded by the servlet container when they are needed. Bear in mind, however, that each servlet can be composed of several compiled Java classes. This means that a programmer will first write the Java code, then compile it, and then register and execute (or *deploy*) the code via the servlet container. Should there be any need to modify the servlet, the Java source code must be modified, recompiled, and then re-deployed via the servlet container. Figure 1-4 illustrates the steps in the servlet development process.

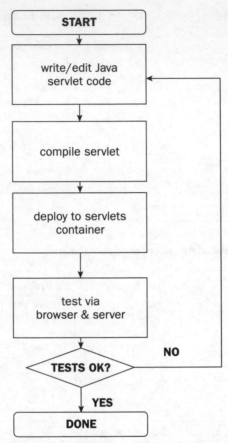

Figure 1-4: Steps in servlet development

Refer back to the basic CGI mechanism presented earlier, and it is evident that the main purpose of most servlets is to generate an HTML page. As a result, you may see servlet Java source code that looks like the following:

```java
public class HelloWorldExample extends HttpServlet {
    public void doGet(HttpServletRequest request,
                      HttpServletResponse response)
        throws IOException, ServletException
    {

        String msg = "Hello, world!";
        response.setContentType("text/html");
        PrintWriter out = response.getWriter();
        out.println("<html>");
        out.println("<head>");
        out.println("<title>JSP 2.0 Hello World</title>");
        out.println("</head>");
        out.println("<body>");
        out.println(msg);
```

```
            out.println("</body>");
            out.println("</html>");
        }
    }
```

Aside from the servlet programming details, note the repeated use of the `PrintWriter.println()` method to generate the output HTML page. You can see that every time you need to make a minor change to the HTML, the Java source code must be modified, recompiled, and re-deployed. This created a lot of tedious work for early servlet developers. In fact, this process hopelessly bound together the work of Web page design with the work of server logic design and made the programmer responsible for both!

JavaServer Pages (or *JSP*) was introduced to solve these problems. Specifically, JSP provides the following benefits:

❑   A templating mechanism whereby Java-based logic can be embedded within HTML pages

❑   Automatic detection and recompilation whenever the JSP is changed

When using JSPs, it is not necessary to write or compile any code in Java programming language. The development cycle can be very quick. Modifications to the JSP can be viewed immediately because the *JSP container* (or *JSP engine*, or *JSP runner*, as it is sometimes called) will automatically recompile the JSP.

Unlike servlets, JSPs are not written in the Java programming language (although some JSPs may contain embedded Java coding). Instead, they are text-based templates. This is best illustrated with an example. The following JSP will display the same output as the servlet presented previously:

```
<%@ taglib prefix="tags" tagdir="/WEB-INF/tags" %>
<html>
  <head>
    <title>JSP 2.0 Hello World</title>
  </head>
  <body>
    <tags:helloWorld/>
  </body>
</html>
```

Note that the preceding JSP is essentially an HTML page with some special markup tags. JSPs are typically stored in source files with a `.jsp` file extension. When the JSP is accessed by an incoming request, the JSP container will parse the special tags and replace them with dynamic output. For example, the preceding JSP may produce the following output (just as the previous servlet) after processing by the JSP container. The examples later in this chapter explain in detail how this JSP works.

```
<html>
  <head>
    <title>JSP 2.0 Hello World</title>
  </head>
  <body>
    Hello, world!
  </body>
</html>
```

In most cases, the JSP container is actually a servlet, enabling JSPs to work within a basic servlet container. However, this detail is not important to the operation of JSP, and need not concern the beginning JSP developer.

It should be clear from this discussion that JSP greatly simplifies the development and construction of server-side Java-based CGI. JSP enables the rapid development of server-side applications that create dynamic output. There is one additional benefit to JSP that may not be immediately evident. Take a second look at the JSP template. Note that although the JSP tags are embedded in the HTML file, the general HTML page structure is still completely intact. In fact, it is possible to have professional Web page designers (typically graphic design professionals with little or no programming skills) design the template. This enables the task of Web site graphics and layout design to be decoupled from the application development task. The page designer can work on the HTML portion of the template, while the JSP developer can work on the tags used and their placement.

Now is a good time to set up a system and try some actual JSP code.

Try It Out   Getting Tomcat Up and Running

This section provides step-by-step download and setup instructions for a servlet container and JSP engine called Tomcat. Instructions are provided for both a Windows-based system and a Linux or UNIX-based operating system, such as Red Hat Linux or FreeBSD.

As with all Try It Out sections, this section focuses on the hands-on aspects. If you come across questions during the procedure, it is likely that they are answered in the next "How it Works" section. You may want to read ahead if you cannot wait for the answer.

Checking your system for Java

Before downloading Tomcat, you should ascertain that you have the Java platform installed and running. This book requires version 1.4.2 or later. To determine if you have Java platform installed and running, type in the following command: On either Windows or a Linux/UNIX system, open a command prompt and type in the `java –version` command. Figure 1-5 shows Java version `1.4.2_04-b05` running on a Windows system

```
C:\>java -version
java version "1.4.2_04"
Java(TM) 2 Runtime Environment, Standard Edition (build 1.4.2_04-b05)
Java HotSpot(TM) Client VM (build 1.4.2_04-b05, mixed mode)

C:\>_
```

Figure 1-5: Verifying the Java platform version on a Windows system

If you do not get the Java version information, contact your system administrator to obtain the configuration for running Java programs. If it is your own machine, install the latest JDK. After the JDK is installed you should ensure that the JAVA_HOME environment variable is set to the Java installation directory, and that the bin directory under JAVA_HOME is added to your PATH environment variable.

Downloading Tomcat

You need to determine the latest version of Tomcat before downloading it. The latest version of the Tomcat container can be determined by checking the following URL:

```
http://jakarta.apache.org/tomcat/
```

Figure 1-6 shows a recent version of this page. Notice the table in the center of the page. This table indicates that 5.0.28 is the latest version that supports JSP Standard 2.0 (and Servlet standard 2.4). This book will make extensive use of features in JSP 2.0.

The ongoing updates of Tomcat server will transition to the Tomcat 5.5.x version. The configuration, deployment procedures, and level of support for JSP are identical between Tomcat 5.0.28 and Tomcat 5.5.x. All of the examples in this book will work with Tomcat 5.5.x.

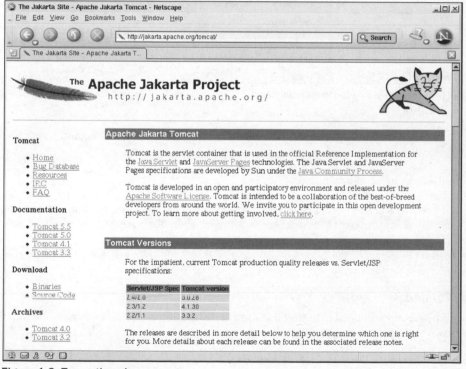

Figure 1-6: Tomcat's welcome page

Click the Binaries link under the Download heading on the left side of the Tomcat index page. Figure 1-7 shows this page.

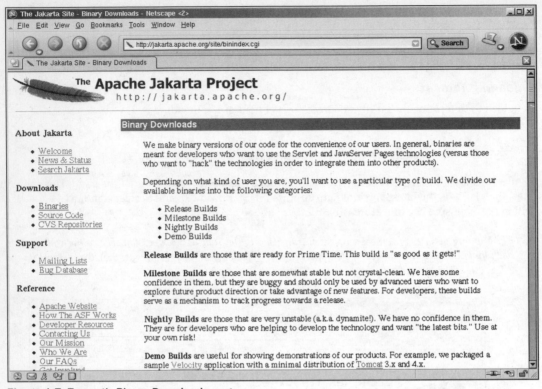

Figure 1-7: Tomcat's Binary Downloads page

From the Binary Downloads page, you will need to scroll down to the bottom and locate the latest Tomcat 5 version. In our case, it is Tomcat 5.0.28.

Now you have a choice of downloads:

❑   If you are working with Linux or another UNIX operating system, click and download the
    `.tar.gz` file (`jakarta-tomcat-5.0.28.tar.gz` in our case).

❑   If you are working with a Windows operating system, click and download the `.exe` file
    (`jakarta-tomcat-5.0.28.exe` in our case).

Installing Tomcat

After downloading, you need to extract the Tomcat installation on a Linux system. The following code shows how this is done:

```
tar zxvf jakarta-tomcat-5.0.28.tar.gz
```

This will extract Tomcat 5 into a subdirectory called `jakarta-tomcat-5.0.28` under the current directory. You may wish to rename this directory to one with a shorter name.

> *This directory will be referred to as* `<Tomcat Installation Directory>` *in future chapters.*

This completes the Linux-based installation.

On a Windows system, execute the downloaded file (by selecting Open or by double-clicking the downloaded `jakarta-tomcat-5.0.28.exe` file). This will start the wizard-based windows installer. Keep in mind the following during installation:

- ❑ When the installer asks you to choose components, choose the Normal install, which is the default.

- ❑ When the installer asks you to choose an installation location, change the default folder to `c:\tomcat5` or a similar directory of your choice.

  > *This will be referred to as the* `<Tomcat Installation Directory>` *in future chapters.*

- ❑ When the installer asks you to enter configuration options, enter the administrator login username of **tomcat**, and choose a password that you can remember for the administrator user. The discussion following assumes that you used the password **tomcat**. *User Name = admin*

Accept the default for all other prompts during installation. Tomcat 5 will start up at the end of the installation.

You can also install on Windows using the ZIP file version of Tomcat. In this case, the installation is similar to that on UNIX/Linux, as all you have to do is to extract out the ZIP file in a directory of choice.

Adding an administrative user and password on a Linux system

If you are on a Linux/UNIX system, or have installed Tomcat using the ZIP file, and not the Windows installer executable, you will need to add the administrative username and password manually.

To do so, go to the `<Tomcat Installation Directory>/conf` directory. Using a text editor, make the following highlighted modifications to the file called `tomcat_users.xml`:

```xml
<?xml version='1.0' encoding='utf-8'?>
<tomcat-users>
  <role rolename="tomcat"/>
  <role rolename="role1"/>
  <user username="tomcat" password="tomcat" roles="tomcat,manager"/>
  <user username="both" password="tomcat" roles="tomcat,role1"/>
  <user username="role1" password="tomcat" roles="role1"/>
</tomcat-users>
```

The `manager` role has been added to the user named `tomcat`. This will add the user `tomcat` to the *access control list* for the Manager utility. This utility can be used to add applications to a running Tomcat server; the "Deploying Chapter Examples" section shows how this is done. An access control list specifies which users are allowed to use the utility, and which password needs to be entered.

Save the changes to the `tomcat_users.xml` file.

Starting and shutting down Tomcat 5

On a Windows system, you should see the *Apache Process Runner* (Tomcat Launcher) running on your system tray (lower right-hand corner), with a green arrow indicating that Tomcat 5 is running. Alternatively, you can always start Tomcat 5 by clicking the Start button and choosing Programs (or All Programs with Windows XP) ⇨ Apache Tomcat 5 ⇨ Start Tomcat.

To shut down Tomcat 5 on a Windows system, right-click the Apache Process Runner on your system tray and select Shutdown ⇨ Tomcat5. Tomcat will be shut down and the Apache Process Runner will disappear from the system tray.

To start the Tomcat 5 server on a Linux/UNIX installation, change directory to the *<Tomcat Installation Directory>*/bin. From the shell, run the `startup.sh` script via the following command:

sh startup.sh

In the same directory is a `shutdown.sh` script. To shut down the Tomcat 5 server on a Linux system, issue the following command:

sh shutdown.sh

Note that even on Windows systems, there are two batch files, `startup.bat` and `shutdown.bat`, in the <Tomcat Installation Directory>/bin directory. These files can be used from a command prompt with the proper environment setup to start or shut down Tomcat 5. If you wish to use these command-line batch files, make sure you have the environmental variable JAVA_HOME set to point to the installation directory of your Java SDK.

Verifying your Tomcat 5 installation

To verify that your version of Tomcat is installed properly, try to start a browser and access the following URL:

```
http://localhost:8080/index.jsp
```

Figure 1-8 shows the resulting HTML page that you should see in your browser: the Tomcat 5 welcome page.

How It Works

Tomcat, often referred to as the *Tomcat server*, is an open-source servlet container and JSP engine. Both the servlet API and JSP specification have undergone many revisions. At this time, multiple versions of the servlet API and JSP specifications are in use. Very large bodies of applications have been written on these different versions. While each new version brings many new features and improvements, older versions tend to be well tested and more stable — two features greatly appreciated by business application developers.

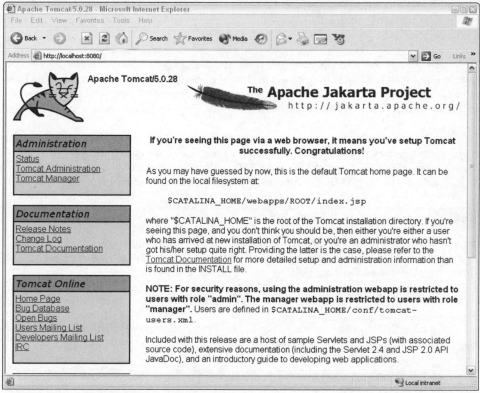

Figure 1-8: The Tomcat 5 server welcome page

The Tomcat server is the *reference implementation* for the servlet API and JSP specifications. This means that every facet of the API specification is implemented and validated against Tomcat. Because there are multiple versions of these specifications, there are also multiple versions of Tomcat servers. The following table shows the correspondence between the Tomcat server and servlet API and JSP specifications.

Tomcat Version	Servlet API Version, JSP Spec Version
3.*x.x*	2.2, 1.1
4.*x.x*	2.3, 1.2
5.*x.x*	2.4, 2.0

The servlet API and JSP specification designers aim to create, as much as possible, new versions that are *backward compatible*. This means that applications based on older versions should be able to run in newer version containers. However, in practice, this is not always possible. With new versions, there are often APIs that are *deprecated* (no longer supported) and new APIs and formats that must be utilized.

For example, this book focuses on the *JSP 2.0* specification. The JSP engine for this specification is part of the Tomcat 5.*x.x* series of servers. Products of most commercial vendors have all updated to this version of the JSP specification.

When you first start up the Tomcat server, it is operating in *standalone mode*. In this mode, Tomcat is functioning in accordance with the first configuration presented earlier (in Figure 1-3a). Tomcat has a built-in Web server that is used to handle the incoming request from your browser. Along with the Web server, the JSP engine is also started. However, the servicing of this initial welcome page does not involve the JSP engine.

The JSP page that you see in your browser is stored under the `<Tomcat Installation Directory>/` `webapps/ROOT` directory. You may want to examine the source code of this file. Note that even though the page being accessed is a JSP page, there are no JSP tags (for dynamic elements) within the file. In other words, it is mainly a static HTML file. A static HTML file with no dynamic element can be a JSP file.

Try It Out   An Initial JSP Experience

Having verified that Tomcat 5 is correctly installed, it is time to try out some JSP coding. The initial `index.jsp` that is displayed is not too exciting; it has no dynamically generated element. Using the same browser, access the following URL:

```
http://localhost:8080/jsp-examples/jsp2/tagfiles/hello.jsp
```

This time, the page that you see should be similar to the one shown in Figure 1-9, which shows the `hello.jsp` example from the Tomcat 5 distribution.

Figure 1-9: The hello.jsp example from the Tomcat 5 distribution

You can see the source code to this JSP by accessing the following URL:

```
http://localhost:8080/jsp-examples/jsp2/tagfiles/hello.jsp.html
```

The content is represented by the following code:

```
<%@ taglib prefix="tags" tagdir="/WEB-INF/tags" %>
<html>
  <head>
    <title>JSP 2.0 Examples - Hello World Using a Tag File</title>
  </head>
  <body>
    <h1>JSP 2.0 Examples - Hello World Using a Tag File</h1>
    <hr>
    <p>This JSP page invokes a custom tag that simply echos "Hello, World!"
    The custom tag is generated from a tag file in the /WEB-INF/tags
    directory.</p>
    <p>Notice that we did not need to write a TLD for this tag.  We just
    created /WEB-INF/tags/helloWorld.tag, imported it using the taglib
    directive, and used it!</p>
    <br>
    <b><u>Result:</u></b>
    <tags:helloWorld/>
  </body>
</html>
```

In Figure 1-9, the "Hello, World!" message after the "Result:" label is dynamically generated via the <tags:helloWorld/> tag in the preceding code.

To see how JSP is automatically and dynamically compiled, make some modifications to the hello.jsp file. You will find the hello.jsp file in the <Tomcat Installation Directory>/webapps/jsp-examples/tagfiles directory. Using a text editor, make the following highlighted modifications and then save the resulting file in the same directory named hello2.jsp:

```
<%@ taglib prefix="tags" tagdir="/WEB-INF/tags" %>
<html>
  <head>
    <title>Presenting JSP 2.0</title>
  </head>
  <body>
    <h1>My First JSP 2.0 Template</h1>
    <hr>
    <p>All I want to say is <tags:helloWorld/></p>
  </body>
</html>
```

Now use your browser to load the new JSP file using the following URL:

```
http://localhost:8080/jsp-examples/jsp2/tagfiles/hello2.jsp
```

The resulting HTML output is shown in Figure 1-10.

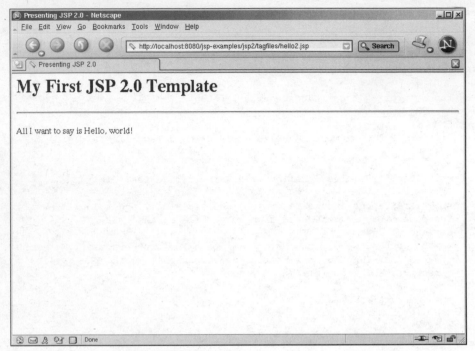

Figure 1-10: Customized hello2.jsp template

> If you get an error when attempting to access `hello2.jsp`, **your installation may not have set the required environment for compiling JSP pages. This can happen with certain versions of the Windows installer. To fix this, you need to stop Tomcat 5. Next, you need to copy the** `tools.jar` **file from the** `<java SDK installation>`/lib **directory to the** `<tomcat 5 installation>`/common/lib **directory. Start Tomcat 5 after copying this file and** `hello2.jsp` **should then display without any error.**

Edit the `hello2.jsp` page again, this time making the following highlighted modifications, and save the file under the same name:

```
<%@ taglib prefix="tags" tagdir="/WEB-INF/tags" %>
<html>
  <head>
    <title>Presenting JSP 2.0</title>
  </head>
  <body>
    <h1>My First JSP 2.0 Template</h1>
    <hr>
    <p>I am so excited, I want to scream "<tags:helloWorld/> <tags:helloWorld/>
<tags:helloWorld/>"</p>
  </body>
</html>
```

In this case, the dynamically generated text is repeated. Reload the JSP page by clicking the Reload (or Refresh) button on your browser. This time, your page should look like the one shown in Figure 1-11.

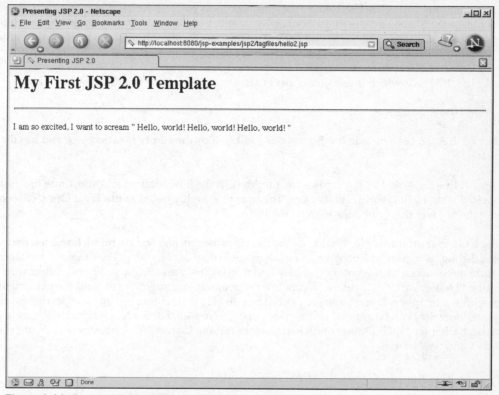

Figure 1-11: Customized hello2.jsp with repeated tag

How It Works

The Tomcat 5 distribution includes many JSP examples. Instead of creating a JSP from scratch, the preceding examples utilize one of the simple examples in the distribution.

The different JSP examples included with Tomcat are located under the `<Tomcat Installation Directory>/webapps/jsp-examples` directory. The preceding example is located under the `<Tomcat Installation Directory>/webapps/jsp-examples /jsp2/tagfiles` subdirectory.

Tags and taglib

This JSP makes use of a special custom tag that simply outputs the text "Hello World!" Custom JSP tags are collected in a *tag library*, or *taglib* for short. To notify the JSP container of the location of the custom tag, a special JSP tag (called the *taglib directive*) needs to be included:

```
<%@ taglib prefix="tags" tagdir="/WEB-INF/tags" %>
```

This directive, explained in detail in Chapter 11, tells Tomcat 5 that the tags can be found in the `/WEB-INF/tags` directory. In this case, the path is relative to the `<Tomcat Installation Directory>/webapps/jsp-examples` directory. In addition, the preceding `taglib` directive also tells Tomcat that all of the tags in this library are prefixed by the word *tags*. This prefix is very useful in production code, where a single JSP page may use tags from many different tag libraries. By having this prefix, two libraries may have tags with the same name and Tomcat will not get them confused. The prefix that is added to the tag to distinguish which library it originates from is often called the *namespace*.

Within the JSP body, which is essentially an HTML page here, the tag is embedded as follows:

```
<tags:helloWorld/>
```

Note that this `helloWorld` tag has no body, as indicated by the empty notation `</>`, and has the namespace *tags*.

Wherever this `helloWorld` tag is placed within the JSP, the JSP container will substitute the dynamically generated text "Hello, World!" in its place. This was thoroughly tested in the Try It Out section earlier, where the tag was duplicated throughout the JSP page.

Using a tag that prints "Hello, World" all the time is rather boring. Bear in mind, however, that you can create the tag using the Java programming language to do most anything. For example, the tag could perform a lookup on the inventory database and display the remaining quantity of an item instead of printing "Hello, World". Therefore, the craft of JSP programming revolves around the placement of JSP tags within a template. If you're already familiar with HTML, learning JSP involves learning a set of new tags and how they can be applied on the pages that you design. For readers who want to create their own tags, Chapter 11, "Building Your Own Custom JSP Tag Library," describes how to create your own JSP tags and tag libraries.

JSP's rapid development cycle

In the preceding Try It Out section, the `hello2.jsp` page is checked for modification every time the URL containing the JSP is accessed. This should not be surprising. Each access from a browser is a separate request, and recall that the server-side CGI mechanism (in this case, the JSP container) handles each request independently.

Because each request is independent, the JSP container is given a chance to determine whether the JSP has been modified since it was last accessed. If the JSP container detects that the JSP has been modified, the page is recompiled before being used to handle an incoming request. This makes the JSP development cycle quite straightforward; just modify the JSP file and the changes take effect immediately.

Try It Out   Deploying Chapter Examples

Now let's take a look at how to deploy the examples from this book to our Tomcat container.

If you have not yet downloaded the chapter examples, you can download the latest version of the examples from www.wrox.com. Once at the site, simply locate the book's title (either by using the Search box or by using the title lists) and click the Download Code link on the book's detail page to obtain all the source code for the book.

After extracting the example code, you should have a directory structure similar to what is shown in Figure 1-12.

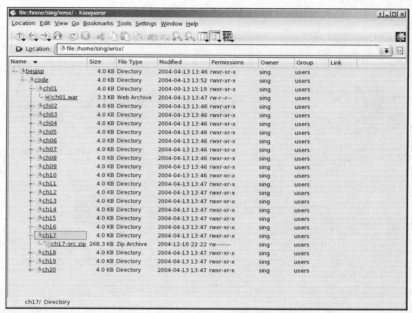

Figure 1-12: Directory structure of example code distribution

In Figure 1-12, all of the code and associated files for each chapter is stored under its own directory. For example, the code and associated files for this chapter is stored under the ch01 subdirectory.

Note that each directory contains a similarly named file with the .war extension. For example, a ch01.war file is under the ch01 subdirectory. A WAR file is a Web ARchive file. It contains a deployable Web application in a format that is accepted by all standard complaint JSP/servlet containers (such as Tomcat). In other words, the WAR file contains JSP along with other applications components that can be loaded and executed immediately on a JSP/servlet container.

Some of the later chapters contain examples with large body of code. These examples require an automated tool, called Apache Ant, in the creation of the WAR file. Unlike the earlier chapters, the code for these chapters is distributed as zip files. For example, the source code for Chapter 17 is in ch17-src.zip.

Using a Tomcat utility called *Manager*, deploying a WAR file can be quite a simple process.

Authentication for Manager access

Now try to access the Manager utility using the following URL:

```
http://localhost:8080/manager/html
```

At this point, the Manager utility should ask you for your user ID and password. This process is known as *authentication*. Figure 1-13 illustrates a typical authentication screen that you may see.

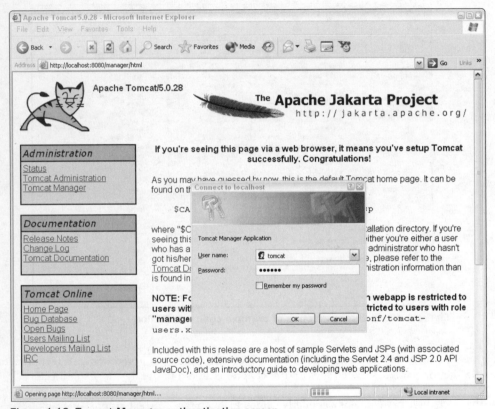

Figure 1-13: Tomcat Manager authentication screen

In the authentication screen, enter the username and password you have set up for administration during installation. Once successful, you will see the Manager utility's main screen, as shown in Figure 1-14.

In Figure 1-14 you can see the WAR files that are already deployed on the running Tomcat server. Now try to deploy the ch01.war file. Scroll down the page if you need to, until you see the box entitled WAR File to Deploy. Click the Browse button next to the Select WAR File to Upload prompt. Browse to the ch01.war file and select it. Next, click the Deploy button.

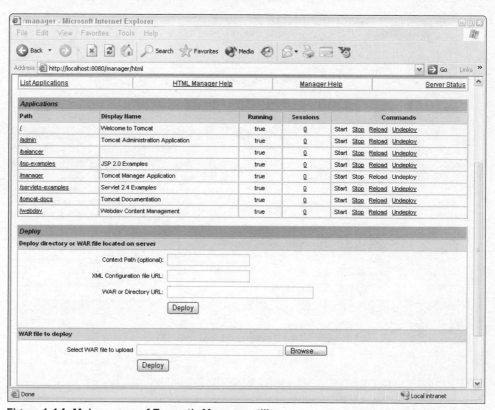

Figure 1-14: Main screen of Tomcat's Manager utility

This should start our final Chapter 1 example Web application. Looking at the list of Web applications deployed on the server, notice that the ch01 Web application is now running on the server, as shown in Figure 1-15.

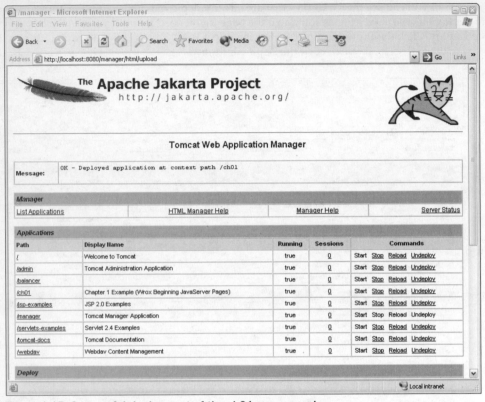

Figure 1-15: Successful deployment of the ch01.war example

You can try out the deployed ch01 example by accessing the following URL:

```
http://localhost:8080/ch01/index.jsp
```

The page displayed should be similar to what is shown in Figure 1-16.

This JSP page displays information about this book.

How It Works

This Manager application enables you to deploy, start, stop, or undeploy server-side *Web applications*. A Web application is a deployable unit represented by the WAR file. When the ch01.war file is selected using the Browse button and the Deploy button is clicked, the file is uploaded from the local directory to the Tomcat server. The WAR file is placed into the server's webapps directory. Tomcat is programmed to scan for new Web applications in this directory. When Tomcat detects the newly uploaded ch01.war file, it will deploy the ch01 Web application. This results in the retrieval of the WAR file from the webapps directory, creating a new ch01 directory holding all of the application files (JSP, servlets, tags, descriptors, and so on).

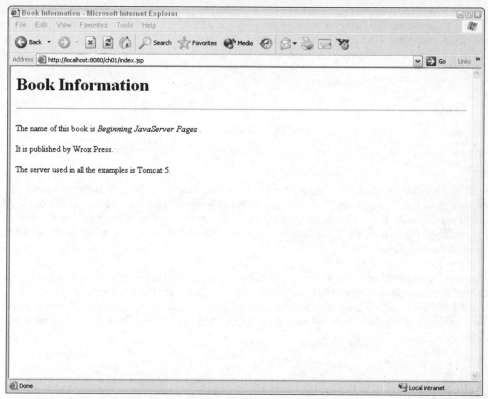

Figure 1-16: Book information presented by the ch01.war JSP example

The index.jsp file from ch01.war can be relocated to the *<Tomcat Installation Directory>*/webapps/ch01 directory. Using a text editor to view this file, you should see the following:

```
<%@ taglib prefix="wroxtags" tagdir="/WEB-INF/tags" %>
<html>
  <head>
    <title>Book Information</title>
  </head>
  <body>
    <h1>Book Information</h1>
    <hr>
    <p>The name of this book is <i><wroxtags:bookTitle/></i>.</p>
    <p>It is published by <wroxtags:publisher/>.</p>
    <p>The server used in all the examples is <wroxtags:containerName/>.</p>
  </body>
</html>
```

Again, this is an HTML template with embedded JSP tags. The first tag at the top, the taglib directive, looks familiar. It is almost exactly the same as the one in hello.jsp from the second example. This directive associates the wroxtags namespace with the tag files in the WEB-INF/tags directory.

If you take a look at the `<Tomcat Installation Directory>`/webapps/ch01/WEB-INF/tags directory you will see several `.tag` files there. Each of these files is associated with an available tag. The following table describes the tags that are used in `index.jsp`.

Tag Name	Description
bookTitle	Displays the title of the book
publisher	Displays the publisher for the book
containerName	Displays the name of the JSP container used in the book

These tags are embedded inline with the HTML within `index.jsp`. Note that the resulting JSP is independent of how these tags work. For example, if the tags were designed to look up the book information from a library database, the very same `index.jsp` file can be used to display the book information without any change. By editing the JSP file and modifying the HTML, it is easy to create the exact look required to present the information.

In other words, the presentation of the information, captured in this JSP, is completely independent of and separated from the information itself (and the method used to retrieve or synthesize this information — the tags). JSP technology is considered to be most suitable for use in the Web-based presentation of business information. Often, one will hear that "JSP is for presentation," or that JSP is a *presentation-layer* technology.

Summary

This chapter provided an introduction to JSP technology, described its intimate relationship with servlets and CGI, and provided two actual hands-on examples that enabled you to work with the technology. You now have

❑   Examined the historical evolution that lead to the development of JSP

❑   An appreciation of why JSP is necessary in addition to CGI and servlets

❑   An understanding of what JSP is and how it works

❑   An understanding of Java-based server-side Web request processing in general

❑   Downloaded and installed the Tomcat server for executing JSP code on your own PC or workstation

❑   An understanding of how to modify a JSP page to dynamically generate Web output

The next chapter explores the basic tags used in JSP programming.

Exercises

1. Modify the `index.jsp` file in the third example to display a page similar to the one shown in Figure 1-17. Make sure you use the tags to generate the book title, publisher, and container name information.

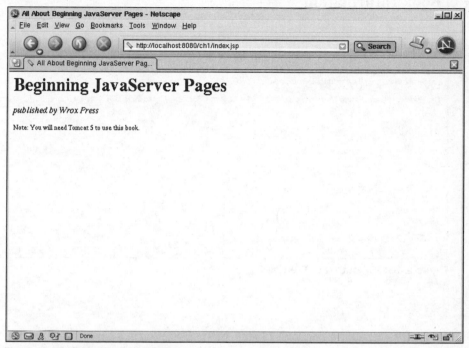

Figure 1-17: JSP output of Exercise 1

2. The `ch01.war` file contains a JSP example that displays information about this book, as well as the server used in the examples. Modify this JSP, and add JSP coding if necessary, to render a page that displays the information shown in Figure 1-18. The last line in the page should identify the browser that you are using, and will vary depending on whether you are using Internet Explorer, Netscape, or another browser. You should examine the available tags in the tag library carefully.

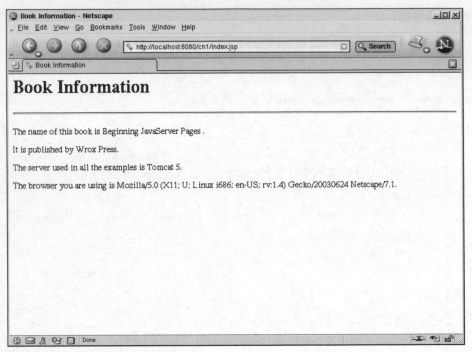

Figure 1-18: JSP output of Exercise 2

JSP Basics 1: Dynamic Page Creation for Data Presentation

Many of the most popular Web sites in the world are running JSP technology. JSP enables the flexible and dynamic creation of Web pages. For example, in an online community, JSP may be used to create highly personalized pages containing only information that is relevant to a community member. As another example, an online store could use JSP to dynamically create a checkout form with the products in a customer's shopping cart. The possibilities are limited only by the designer's imagination.

This chapter formally introduces the components that make up a JSP page, and thoroughly explores the role of JSP as a dynamic Web page creation technology.

This chapter covers the following topics:

- ❑   The anatomy of a typical JSP page
- ❑   Processing HTML forms with JSP
- ❑   Incorporating the output of JSP fragments
- ❑   Creating a JSP that generates different HTML depending on input
- ❑   Using JSP to create a personalized Web site

Three hands-on examples are presented in this chapter. They introduce new concepts and techniques in JSP programming.

The Anatomy of a JSP Page

Figure 2-1 shows a typical JSP page, with all of its visible elements explicitly labeled.

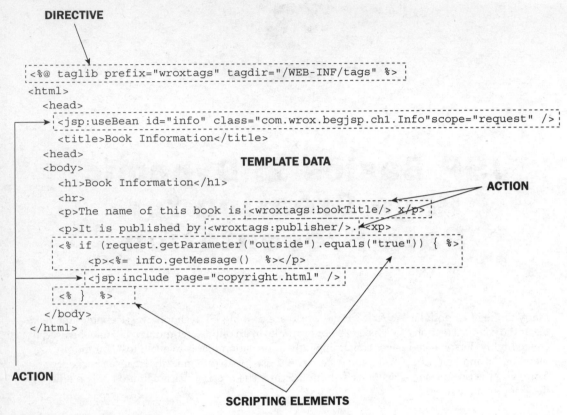

Figure 2-1: Anatomy of a JSP page

The visible elements that make up a JSP page can include the following:

- ❑ Directive elements
- ❑ Template data
- ❑ Action
- ❑ Scripting elements

A JSP page does not need to have all of these visible elements, but you will very likely encounter all of them if you look into any moderately complex JSP project. The following sections briefly describe each visible element.

Directives

Unlike other JSP elements, *directives* are not used to generate output directly. Rather, they are used to control some characteristics of a JSP page. Directives may be used to give special instructions to the JSP container about what to do during the translation of the page. You can always tell a directive from other elements because it is enclosed in a special set of braces:

```
<%@  ...  directive ...  %>
```

Three directives are allowed in JSP:

- ❑   `page` directive
- ❑   `taglib` directive
- ❑   `include` directive

Chapter 1 already demonstrated the use of the `taglib` directive. Although the examples in this chapter use the `page` directive and the `include` directive, Chapter 7, "JSP Directives," provides a thorough exploration of how to use these directives.

XML-compatible syntax

A directive — for example, a `taglib` directive — typically appears in a JSP as follows:

```
<%@ taglib ....    %>
```

The same element can also appear in a JSP as follows:

```
<jsp:directive.taglib .... />
```

This is an XML-compatible syntax for expressing the JSP directive. There are many advantages to expressing a JSP page in XML. For example, many developer tools can work with XML documents directly. Enterprise technologies, such as Web services, also make extensive use of XML. The emerging new XHTML standard is also XML-based. Because JSP works intimately with these technologies and the standard `<%@ ... %>` syntax is not valid XML, this alternative notation is necessary.

All professional JSP developers are trained in the `<%@ ... %>` notation. There are millions of lines of existing JSP code in this notation, so it will likely be supported for the foreseeable future.

Template data

Template data is static text. This static text is passed directly through the JSP container unprocessed. For example, it may be text that provides static HTML. In Figure 2-1, the template data is the static HTML.

In fact, the example in Chapter 1 demonstrated that an HTML page with no other JSP elements is considered a valid JSP page. This is because such a page consists of all template data — an allowed element on a JSP page.

Although most JSP pages are used in generating HTML pages, JSP is not specific to HTML generation. For example, JSP can be used to generate XML output or even arbitrary text-based reports for direct printing.

A helpful way to see the value of template data in a JSP page is to remember that template text is used to specify the static portion of a page, while other JSP elements are used in generating the dynamic portion of the page.

If a JSP page is expressed in XML syntax, typically contained in a .jspx *file, the template data portion may have characters that need to be escaped. For example, the characters* < *and* > *are not allowed directly in an XML document and must be expressed as* < *and* >, *respectively.*

Action

Action elements are JSP elements that are directly involved in the processing of the request. In most cases, action elements enable you to access data and manipulate or transform data in the generation of the dynamic output. For example, an online store may have a JSP page that displays a shopping cart. This cart JSP shows the products that you have purchased. Action elements may be used to generate the listing of the products (dynamic content) on the page and to calculate the cost and shipping (dynamic content), while template data (static HTML) is used to display the logo and shipping policy statements.

Action elements can be either *standard* or *custom*. A standard action is dependably available in every JSP container that conforms to the JSP 2.0 standard. For example, <jsp:useBean>, <jsp:getProperty>, <jsp:setProperty>, and <jsp:include> are standard actions that appear within the examples in this chapter. A custom action is an action created using JSP's tag extension mechanism. This mechanism enables developers to create their own set of actions for manipulating data or generating dynamic output within the JSP page.

> **Actions are synonymous with tags because every action is an XML tag. The terms are used interchangeably in this book, just as they are in the JSP developer community.**

Every XML tag has a name, optional attributes, and an optional body. For example, the standard <jsp:include> action can be coded as follows:

```
<jsp:include page="news.jsp" flush="false"/>
```

The name of this tag is jsp:include, the attributes are page and flush, and this <jsp:include> instance does not have a body. The XML empty notation is used.

An XML tag can also have a body containing other tags, of course:

```
<jsp:include page="news.jsp" flush="false">
     <jsp:param name="user" value="${param.username}"/>
</jsp:include>
```

In this tag, the name is still jsp:include and the attributes are still page and flush, but now the body is no longer empty. Instead, the body contains a <jsp:param> standard action.

After template data, actions are the next most frequently used elements in JSP coding. You will become very comfortable working with action elements by the end of this chapter.

> It was noted earlier that non-XML JSP elements such as directives have an XML-compatible alternative syntax. Actions are XML-based from the earliest version of JSP, and there is no need to have an alternative syntax.

Scripting elements

The practice of embedding code in another programming language within a JSP page is called *scripting*. Scripting elements are embedded code, typically in the Java programming language, within a JSP page. There are three different types of scripting elements:

- ❏ Declarations
- ❏ Scriptlets
- ❏ Expressions

> While the JSP specification allows the embedding of non-Java code within a JSP page, only very specialized containers may have such support. In almost all cases, the code embedded in scripting elements will be in the Java programming language. Java is the assumed scripting language throughout the discussions in this book.

Declarations are Java code that is used to declare variables and methods. They appear as follows:

```
<%!  ...  Java declaration goes here... %>
```

The XML-compatible syntax for declarations is:

```
<jsp:declaration> ... Java declaration goes here ... </jsp:declaration>
```

Scriptlets are arbitrary Java code segments. They appear as follows:

```
<%    ... Java code goes here ...    %>
```

The XML-compatible syntax for scriptlets is:

```
<jsp:scriptlet> ... Java code goes here ... </jsp:scriptlet>
```

Expressions are Java expressions that yield a resulting value. When the JSP is executed, this value is converted to a text string and printed at the location of the scripting element. Expression scripting elements appear as:

```
<%=   ... Java expression goes here ... %>
```

The XML-compatible syntax for expressions is:

```
<jsp:expression>  ... Java expression goes here ...  </jsp:expression>
```

Chapter 3, "JSP Basics 2: Generalized Templating and Server Scripting," provides a comprehensive discussion of how to use scripting elements when coding JSP.

> *Note that while the capability to embed Java code within JSP may initially appear to be a very powerful feature, that power can be abused. In actual practice, this powerful and flexible feature has been found to be the main contributor to difficult-to-maintain JSP coding in large projects. The JSP designers have concluded that removing the dependency on scripting is the only way to mend this problem moving forward. This is the primary reason why JSP 2.0 has implemented an Expression Language (EL). Using a combination of the JavaServer Pages Standard Tag Library (JSTL, described later in this chapter) and EL, it is possible to code JSP that is free of scripting elements. One desirable side effect of this is that you can become an expert JSP developer without learning Java. Beginners to JSP should adopt this style of programming and avoid the use of scripting elements whenever possible. Almost all of the examples in this book favor JSTL and EL over scripting elements. However, it is also true that many JSP developers may need to maintain legacy projects that made heavy use of scripting elements. Chapter 3 caters to these developers and explores the scripting capabilities thoroughly.*

Handling HTML form submission with JSP

One of the most frequently occurring activities within a Web-based application is the handling of data submitted from an HTML form. JSP is designed to make this frequently occurring activity easy. This section describes the elements and built-in support that enable you to handle form submission.

Consider the simple HTML form shown in Figure 2-2.

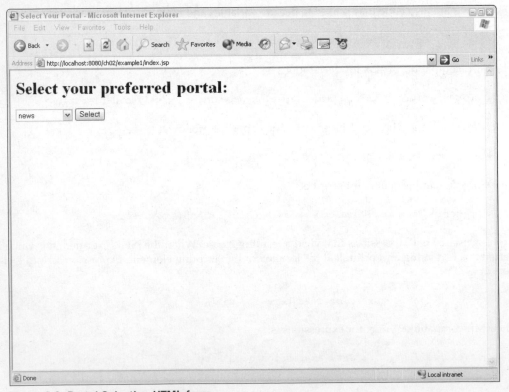

Figure 2-2: Portal Selection HTML form

In Figure 2-2, the user can select a portal (news, weather, or entertainment) from the drop-down list. When the Select button is clicked, the form is submitted to the server for processing.

Under the hood, the browser performs the following steps:

1.   Examines the HTML code to determine the server URL that will handle the form

2.   Gathers the data entered by the user in the form and creates parameters attached to the request to be sent to the browser; for example, if the user selected the news portal, the string news is sent to the server as an attached request parameter.

3.   Encodes the parameters, if necessary, for safe delivery to the server

4.   Sends the request to the server URL and waits for a response

Steps 2 and 3 need further explanation. Chapter 1 revealed that the request sent to the server uses the HTTP protocol. Under this protocol, there are two ways to attach parameters to a request: the GET method and the POST method.

GET versus POST

One way to attach parameters with a URL request is called the GET method, and the parameter data is sent inline with the main URL. For example, suppose the URL handling the form is called

```
http://localhost:8080/ch02/example1/showportal.jsp
```

and assume the user has selected the news portal. Using the GET method, the URL sent to the server will contain the following:

```
http://localhost:8080/ch02/example1/showportal.jsp?portchoice=news
```

If there is another parameter called username and it has the value admin, then the URL sent will be as follows:

```
http://localhost:8080/ch02/example1/showportal.jsp?portchoice=news&username=admin
```

Note that because the parameter is actually a part of the URL, there are at least two limitations:

❏   The length of the parameter value cannot exceed the maximum URL length.

❏   Certain characters, such as the ampersand (&) and equal sign (=), have special meanings, and must be encoded (changed to another representation) if they're to be used as part of the URL.

It is the second limitation that makes encoding parameters necessary. For example, if the username were deliberately entered as a&dm=in, the resulting URL will be sent to the server:

```
http://localhost:8080/ch02/example1/showportal.jsp?portchoice=news&username=a%26dm%
3Din
```

The good news is that the browser will know how to encode the parameters. On the server side, the JSP container will know how to decode the encoded parameter if necessary. In other words, before attaching a parameter to the URL, developers need to be aware only that a GET method may encode the parameter, but they may never need to work with the encoded parameter directly.

The other way of attaching parameters to a URL request is via the POST method. The POST method uses the HTTP message body to send the parameter information. All this is done by the browser, and the developer doesn't need to do anything extra on the client end to make it happen. The JSP container understands this method of parameter passing and will enable you to access the parameters directly on the server side. The POST method has the following advantages:

❑   The length of a parameter value sent is not limited.

❑   The parameters are not sent as part of the visible URL and are, therefore, less prone to tampering by malicious users.

Yet another difference between GET and POST relates to their intended use. Try refreshing a page that has a POST action in it, and you will promptly get a warning message from your browser. The message for Internet Explorer describes the reason very well: "The page you are trying to view contains POSTDATA. If you resend the data, any action the form carried out (such as a search or online purchase) will be repeated. To resend the data, click OK. Otherwise, click Cancel."

As designed, GET was supposed to be used for sending data that could be resent without any change in the system. For example, the GET action shown in the URL http://localhost:8080/ch02/example1/ showportal.jsp?portchoice=news shows the news portal, and reloading the page multiple times will cause no change. The POST action, on the other hand, could be used to send data that results in sending an e-mail or purchasing an item. Refreshing the result of a POST could cause the e-mail to be sent twice, or multiple items to be purchased. Of course, this was just the intent, and nothing stops Web developers from developing Web applications that behave differently.

The following exercise shows how JSP can handle HTML form submission.

Try It Out   Handling HTML Form Submission

Deploy the ch02.war file on your Tomcat 5 server. (See Chapter 1 if you are not sure how to do this.)

Access the first example by pointing your browser to the following URL:

```
http://localhost:8080/ch02/example1/index.jsp
```

The form displayed is exactly that of Figure 2-2. First, select News for the portal choice, and then click the Select button.

This will send the request to the server, and the news portal page will be displayed, as shown in Figure 2-3. Note that both the title of the page and its content indicate that it is the news portal.

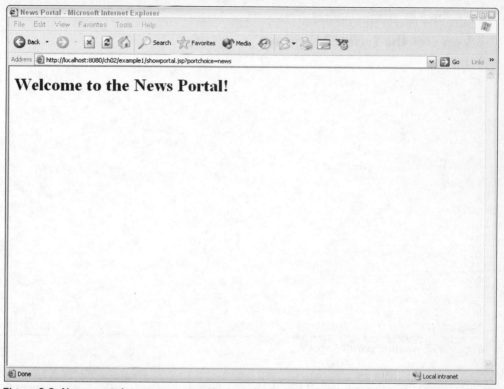

Figure 2-3: News portal page

Enter the URL again. From the portal drop-down menu, this time select Weather for the portal choice and click Select. The weather portal page will be displayed, as shown in Figure 2-4. Note that both the title of the page and the content of the page indicate that it is the weather portal.

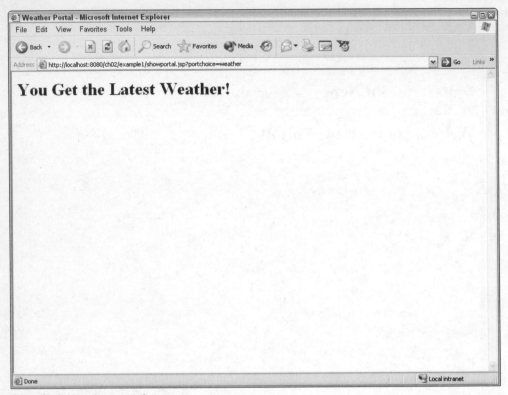

Figure 2-4: Weather portal page

Finally, enter the URL one more time. From the portal drop-down menu, select Entertainment for the portal choice and click Select. The entertainment portal page will be displayed, as shown in Figure 2-5. Again, both the title of the page and the content of the page indicate that it is the entertainment portal.

At first glance, it appears that the JSP form submission handler sends you to a different portal Web page depending on your selection. However, if you were paying attention to the URL that is displayed at the top of the browser after you click the Select button, you realized that all three portal pages are generated from the same JSP page — dynamically. The URL you will see and the JSP page that generates the portal pages is as follows:

```
http://localhost:8080/ch02/example1/showportal.jsp
```

The next section reveals how this is done.

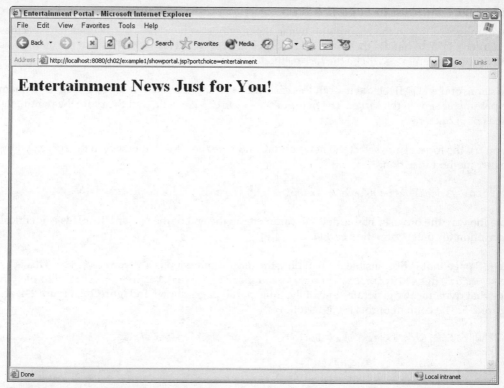

Figure 2-5: Entertainment portal page

How It Works

The index.jsp page, found in the <Tomcat Installation
Directory>\webapps\ch02\example1\index.jsp file, contains the following:

```
<html>
  <head><title>Select Your Portal</title></head>
  <body>
    <h1>Select your preferred portal:</h1>
    <form action="showportal.jsp" method="get">
      Your First Name: <input name="username" type="text" size="40"/>
      <select name="portchoice">
        <option>news</option>
        <option>weather</option>
        <option>entertainment</option>
      </select>
      <input type="submit" value="Select"/>
    </form>
  </body>
</html>
```

One thing to note immediately is that this is a pure HTML page. Our earlier analysis of the anatomy of a
JSP page reveals that this is just a special case of a JSP page in which the entire page is template data.

Using the GET method to submit a form

The highlighted line in the example shown in the previous section, the <form> open tag, specifies that the server's URL to handle the form will be showportal.jsp. It also specifies that the method used to send request parameters will be the GET method.

The name of the HTML element — in this case, the <select> element — will be used as the name of the parameter sent to the server. The name of the <select> element, and therefore the parameter, in this case is portchoice.

If you try the form again, select the news portal, and note the URL that is sent to the server, you will see the GET method in action:

```
http://localhost:8080/ch02/example1/showportal.jsp?portchoice=news
```

Note the way the browser has added the parameter to the end of the server URL. This is identical to our description for the GET method earlier.

The JSP page that is responsible for handling the form submission is showportal.jsp. This is located in the <Tomcat Installation Directory>\webapps\ch02\example1\showportal.jsp file. This is the page that dynamically generates one of the three portal pages shown in Figure 2-3, Figure 2-4, and Figure 2-5. The content of this JSP is as follows:

```
<%@ taglib prefix="c" uri="http://java.sun.com/jsp/jstl/core" %>
<html>
  <c:choose>
    <c:when test="${param.portchoice == 'news'}">
      <head><title>News Portal</title></head>
      <body>
        <h1>Headline News Just For You!</h1>
      </body>
    </c:when>
    <c:when test="${param.portchoice == 'weather'}">
      <head><title>Weather Portal</title></head>
      <body>
        <h1>Accurate Weather Around the Clock!</h1>
      </body>
    </c:when>
    <c:when test="${param.portchoice == 'entertainment'}">
      <head><title>Weather Portal</title></head>
      <body>
        <h1>The Most Popular Reality TV Shows!</h1>
      </body>
    </c:when>
    <c:otherwise>
      <head><title>System Portal</title></head>
      <body>
        <h1>Application logic problem detected!</h1>
      </body>
    </c:otherwise>
  </c:choose>
</html>
```

You should recognize the JSP directive element on this JSP page. It is the very first line, the `taglib` directive, reproduced here:

```
<%@ taglib prefix="c" uri="http://java.sun.com/jsp/jstl/core" %>
```

The `taglib` directive enables you to specify a tag library to be used within this JSP. A tag library adds custom action elements that can be used throughout the page. The attributes of a `taglib` directive are described in the following table.

Attribute	Description
`prefix`	Indicates the string prefix that is used by all the tags in this tag library. The namespace notation in XML is used to prefix the tags. For example, if the prefix is `c`, and the tag name is `out`, the full tag name is `<c:out>`. Some prefixes are reserved and cannot be used, including `jsp:`, `jspx:`, `java:`, `javax:`, `servlet:`, `sun:`, and `sunw:`.
`uri`	A URI that uniquely identifies a tag library. The JSP container will examine the available tag libraries in its `classpath` and locate the corresponding tag library. In this case, the `uri` specifies JSTL 1.1. In the example in Chapter 1, a `tagdir` attribute is used instead of `uri`. The `tagdir` attribute was used to specify the location of the custom tag files that was used. The `tagdir` and `uri` attributes are mutually exclusive; only one may be used in any `taglib` directive.

Working with JSTL 1.1

JSTL (JSP Standard Tag Library) is a standard set of tags designed for use specifically within JSP to perform most common Web application programming tasks. The set of tags includes conditional flow control, iteration, data output, internationalization, and working with XML documents and databases. The latest release of the reference implementation is open source and can be located at

```
http://jakarta.apache.org/taglibs/doc/standard-doc/intro.html
```

The version of JSTL that is designed to work with Tomcat 5, Servlets 2.4, and JSP 2.0 is JSTL 1.1.

The `taglib` directive specifies a URI that matches JSTL 1.1. This tag library contains many different tags (custom actions). You can find the JAR files for JSTL 1.1 in the application's `lib` directory. In our case, it can be located in the `<Tomcat Installation Directory>\webapps\ch02\WEB-INF\lib` directory and consists of `jstl.jar` and `standard.jar`.

One specific JSTL 1.1 tag construct that is used in the JSP is the `<choose>` tag construct:

```
<c:choose>
  <c:when test="...expression...">
...
  </c:when>
  <c:when test="...expression...">
      ...
```

```
  </c:when>
  <c:otherwise>
    ...
  </c:otherwise>
</c:choose>
```

Specifically, this construct will choose and execute only the body of one of the <c:when> or <c:otherwise> tags. During the execution of the JSP, the expression in the test attribute of the <c:when> tag will be evaluated, and the very first test expression evaluated to be true at execution time will have the associated tag body executed. In our case, the actual construct is coded as follows:

```
<c:choose>
  <c:when test="${param.portchoice == 'news'}">
    <head><title>News Portal</title></head>
    <body>
      <h1>Headline News Just For You!</h1>
    </body>
  </c:when>
  <c:when test="${param.portchoice == 'weather'}">
    <head><title>Weather Portal</title></head>
    <body>
      <h1>Accurate Weather Around the Clock!</h1>
    </body>
  </c:when>
  <c:when test="${param.portchoice == 'entertainment'}">
    <head><title>Weather Portal</title></head>
    <body>
      <h1>The Most Popular Reality TV Shows!</h1>
    </body>
  </c:when>
  <c:otherwise>
    <head><title>System Portal</title></head>
    <body>
      <h1>Application logic problem detected!</h1>
    </body>
  </c:otherwise>
</c:choose>
```

The highlighted code is the actual JSTL 1.1 <choose> construct. It should be clear that only one of the nonhighlighted bodies will be executed, depending on the value of the expression in the test attributes of <c:when> tags. The HTML code for the different portal pages is located here (the nonhighlighted bodies of the <c:when> tag). For example, if the user selected the weather portal, the incoming portchoice parameter has the value 'weather' and the weather portal's HTML code will be rendered. Chapter 6, "JSP Tag Libraries and JSTL," has significantly more detailed coverage of JSTL 1.1.

Working with the JSP 2.0 Expression Language (EL)

Take a closer look; the three EL expressions used in the preceding example are:

❑ ${param.portchoice == 'news'}

❑ ${param.portchoice == 'weather'}

❑ ${param.portchoice == 'entertainment'}

These are all EL (Expression Language) expressions. EL expressions are easily identifiable in a JSP page because they are always bracketed as follows:

```
${... EL expression ...}
```

The three expressions above are comparing using the "equals" comparative operator (==). You may also use greater than (>), less than (<), greater or equal (>=), less or equal (<=), and not equal (!=).

EL expressions are always evaluated at runtime, meaning that they are run as JSP is actually executed (while processing an actual incoming request) and not at the time when the JSP is processed by the JSP container. This distinction is important because form parameters such as portchoice will have a value only during runtime and not any time before the processing of the request.

EL expressions can be used as follows:

❑ Anywhere template data may be placed

❑ Within attributes of an action that can take an expression, such as the test attribute of the JSTL's \<when\> action

If you look at the expressions used in the \<choose\> tag again, you see that it makes use of an object with the name param. This is an *implicit object* in EL. EL *implicit objects* are described in the next section.

EL implicit objects

EL implicit objects are objects that are made available to EL expressions by the JSP container during runtime. There is no need to create or initialize these objects. They can be simply referred to by name within your EL expression.

These useful objects were designed to facilitate your JSP programming activity. The following table briefly describes the available EL implicit objects. Chapter 5, "JSP and EL," provides more in-depth coverage of each of the available implicit objects.

EL Implicit Object Name	Description
pageContext	This is the same as the pageContext implicit object in JSP. It has many properties associated with the processing of the current JSP page. Chapter 5 provides details of this object.
pageScope	Used to access any attributes attached to the page scope. *Attributes* are objects provided by Java or business logic programmers that a JSP programmer may use in generating dynamic content. Typically, attributes are attached by servlets in a framework. Chapters 5 and 19 explore this fully.
requestScope	Used to access any attributes attached to the request scope. Attributes attached to a request scope have one instance per incoming request.

Table continued on following page

sessionScope	Used to access any attributes attached to the session scope. Attributes attached to a session scope have one instance across multiple requests belonging to the same user session.
applicationScope	Used to access any attributes attached to the application scope. Attributes attached to an application scope have only one instance across multiple JSPs belonging to the same Web application (i.e., deployed WAR file). All requests, sessions, and JSPs will share the same instance.
param	Used to access parameters passed in with the request. This is typically from a form submission. Any parameter can be accessed by name through this implicit object. This is the only EL implicit object used in this chapter.
paramValues	Used to access parameters passed in with the request. It enables access to parameters that may have multiple values.
header	Used to access the HTTP header information.
headerValues	Used to access the HTTP header information and enable access to a header that may have multiple values.
cookie	Used to access cookie information available with the incoming request. Cookies are typically used to establish user sessions across different requests. See Chapter 5 for more information.
initParam	Used to access the initialization parameters for the Web application. Chapter 5 demonstrates the use of this implicit object.

In a nutshell, our portal example uses only the implicit `param` object to access the incoming parameter called `portchoice` from the form submission. The EL expression to access the value of the `portchoice` parameter is as follows:

```
${param.portchoice}
```

In general, any incoming parameter from a form submission may be accessed as follows:

```
${param.<name of parameter>}
```

In summary, the combination of JSTL 1.1's `<choose>` tag construct and EL's `param` implicit object enables the `showportal.jsp` page to generate one of three portal pages dynamically, depending on the user's portal selection.

Try It Out   Including JSP Pages

This second example is built upon the first example. Using the technique in the first example to dynamically generate a portal home page can present one major problem: All the HTML content of the portal must be coded within the one and only `showportal.jsp` page. This presents a problem if

❑ You have a large number of portals, in which case the page can become unmanageable

❑ The individual portal pages are maintained by different people or groups that will have to coordinate the update of the single `showportal.jsp` page

To resolve this problem, the `showportal.jsp` page must be rewritten to be independent of the content of the portal pages. This second example demonstrates the solution.

With the `ch02.war` deployed, try out the following URL:

```
http://localhost:8080/ch02/example2/index.jsp
```

The form displayed should be similar to the one shown in Figure 2-6.

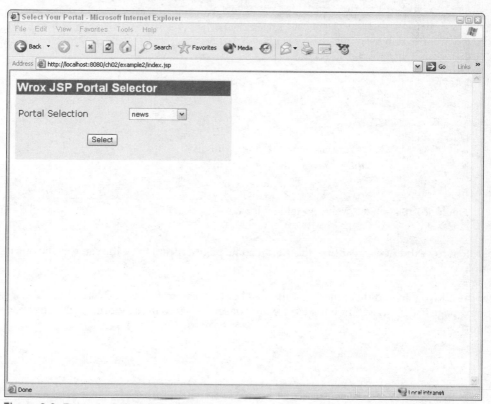

Figure 2-6: Example 2 Portal Selection form

Select the news portal and click the Select button. The news portal home page is shown, and a news headline is displayed. Figure 2-7 illustrates the news portal home page for this example.

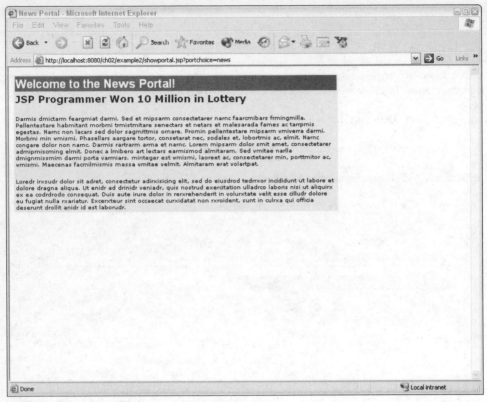

Figure 2-7: Example 2 News portal home page

Other than the extra news headline, this portal home page appears to be the same as the one in the first example.

Enter the URL again and this time select the weather portal and click the Select button. The weather portal home page is displayed, showing the weather of several cities in the world. This portal page is shown in Figure 2-8.

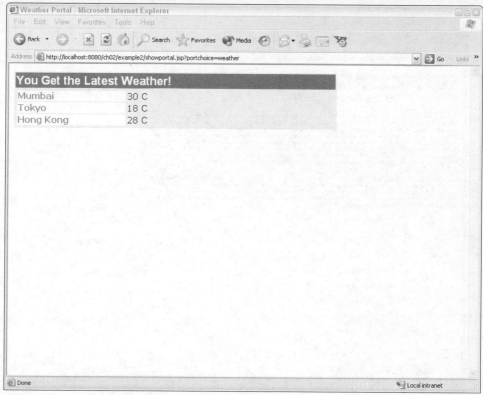

Figure 2-8: Example 2 Weather portal home page

Finally, enter the URL again, select the entertainment portal, and click the Select button. The entertainment home page is displayed with an entertainment headline, as shown in Figure 2-9.

All of these portal pages appear to be similar to those in the first example, with the exception of some additional information displayed. Bear in mind, however, that the showportal.jsp in this example no longer generates the portal pages directly behind the scenes. But this fact is completely transparent to us, the users.

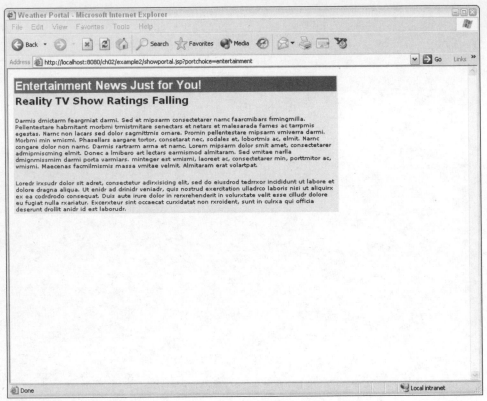

Figure 2-9: Example 2 Entertainment portal home page

How It Works

Figure 2-10 contrasts the construction of the first example against the construction of this example.

In Figure 2-10, note that in the first example, `showportal.jsp` is solely responsible for generating the portal pages. Contrast this with the case in the second example. Here, the individual portal pages reside within their own independent `.jsp` files. For example, the weather portal page resides in `weather.jsp`. In the second example, the sole purpose of the `showportal.jsp` page becomes the selection of the `.jsp` file to display. It is completely independent of what is contained within these portal pages.

EXAMPLE 1

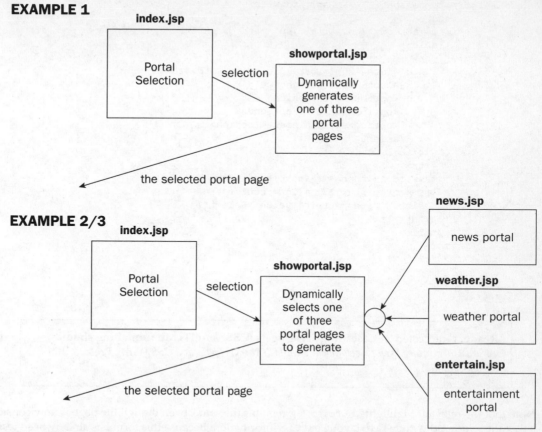

EXAMPLE 2/3

Figure 2-10: Removing dependency on portal content in the second example

The new form, index.jsp, which is located at `<Tomcat Installation Directory>\webapps\ch02\example2\index.jsp`, has been improved with added HTML layout and a CSS stylesheet. This index.jsp is reproduced as follows:

```
<html>
  <head>
    <link rel=stylesheet type="text/css" href="portal.css">
    <title>Select Your Portal</title>
  </head>
  <body>
    <table class="mainBox" width="400">
      <tr>
        <td class="boxTitle" colspan="2">
          Wrox JSP Portal Selector
        </td>
      </tr>
```

```
<tr><td colspan="2"> </td></tr>
<tr><td>
  <form  action="showportal.jsp" method="get">
    <table>
      <tr>
        <td width="200">Portal Selection</td><td>
          <select name="portchoice">
            <option>news</option>
            <option>weather</option>
            <option>entertainment</option>
          </select>
        </td>
      </tr>
      <tr><td colspan="2"> </td></tr>
      <tr><td colspan="2" align="center">
        <input type="submit" value="Select"/>
      </td></tr>
    </table>
  </form>
</td></tr>
    </table>
  </body>
</html>
```

> **Readers interested in Cascading Stylesheets (CSS) and HTML formatting should
> consult** *Beginning Web Development with HTML, XHTML, and CSS* **(Wrox Press; ISBN
> 0-7645-7078-1).**

Note that the relevant highlighted `<form>` tag remains the same, even though the page is now considerably more cluttered with HTML layout and CSS information. Because this form has already been tested in the first example, you can confidently add the layout and formatting. While this improves the appearance, the JSP logic (in this case, form submission logic) remains the same.

The CSS stylesheet is called `portal.css`. It contains styles for the major visual elements of the portal, such as boxes, a headline, and news text. `portal.css` is reproduced here:

```
.tableCell
  {   font-family : Verdana, Geneva, Arial, Helvetica, sans-serif;
    font-size : 16;
    font-weight : bold;
    color : #0f7fcf;
    background-color: #ffffff;
  }

.valueCell
  {
    font-family : Verdana, Geneva, Arial, Helvetica, sans-serif;
    font-size : 16;
```

```
        color : #000000;
        background-color: #fefefe;
    }

.headLine
    {
        font-family : Verdana, Geneva, Arial, Helvetica, sans-serif;
        font-size : 18;
        font-weight : bold;
        color: #000000;
    }

.newsText
    {
        font-family : Verdana, Geneva, Arial, Helvetica, sans-serif;
        font-size : 10;
        color: #000000;
    }
.boxTitle
    {
        font-family : Arial, Helvetica, sans-serif;
        font-size : 22;
        font-weight : bold;
        color : #ffffff;
        background-color: #0F7ACA;  }
.mainBox
    {
        font-family : Verdana, Geneva, Arial, Helvetica, sans-serif;
        font-size : 12;    color : #ffffff;
        background-color: #eeeeee;
    }
```

JSP best practices

Throughout this book, and specifically in Chapter 26, "Best Practices and Tools," JSP best practices are emphasized. Best practices are commonly accepted wisdom originating from documented industry experience. The difference between the first example and the second illustrates a best practice when designing JSP applications. The concept is quite simple:

❑ Use the simplest HTML to prototype your application before adding style and layout.

❑ Separate JSP development from HTML layout and formatting if possible.

In our case, the pages of the first example used minimal HTML. This allowed testing of the JSP elements without the clutter of HTML layout and stylesheets. Once the JSP elements are tested, HTML layout and stylesheets can be added.

If you are working in a team environment, the designer of the look and feel of the application may be a graphics designer. In this case, you may be responsible only for the putting together the JSP elements on a page. JSP development and HTML layout are typically separate activities.

Using the <jsp:include> standard action to select portal rendering

The showportal.jsp page in the second example, located at <Tomcat Installation Directory>\webapps\ch02\example2\showportal.jsp, is reproduced here:

```
<%@ taglib prefix="c" uri="http://java.sun.com/jsp/jstl/core" %>
<html>
  <c:choose>
    <c:when test="${param.portchoice == 'news'}">
      <jsp:include page="news.jsp" />
    </c:when>
    <c:when test="${param.portchoice == 'weather'}">
      <jsp:include page="weather.jsp" />
    </c:when>
    <c:when test="${param.portchoice == 'entertainment'}">
      <jsp:include page="entertain.jsp" />
    </c:when>
    <c:otherwise>
      <head><title>System Portal</title></head>
      <body>
        <h1>Application logic problem detected!</h1>

    </c:otherwise>
  </c:choose>
</body></html>
```

Changes from the showportal.jsp in the first example are highlighted in the preceding code. The <c:choose> logic of the custom JSTL action is well tested in the first example. The only new element here is the <jsp:include> standard action. Instead of having the HTML render the portal pages right inside showportal.jsp, the <jsp:include> standard action is used to import other independent JSP pages. The task of displaying (called *rendering* in JSP development) the portal page is passed on to (or *delegated* to) the individual portal pages: news.jsp, weather.jsp, and entertain.jsp.

The main function of the <jsp:include> standard action is to include the output of another JSP page at the location where the <jsp:include> tag is placed. This action is not limited to JSP, but will work with other Web files, including HTML pages. Several attributes may be added to the <jsp:include> tag; the one used in the example is described in the following table.

Attribute	Description
Page	Specifies the JSP (or HTML page, etc.) whose output is to be included at the current location of the tag

Chapter 8, "JSP Standard Actions," offers a more comprehensive exploration of the standard actions, such as <jsp:include>.

If you have selected the news portal, the news.jsp page will be included in the showportal.jsp page and rendered. The source of news.jsp, which is located at <Tomcat Installation Directory>\webapps\ch02\example2\news.jsp, is reproduced here:

```
<head>
  <link rel=stylesheet type="text/css" href="portal.css">
```

```
          <title>News Portal</title>
       </head>
       <body>
         <table class="mainBox" width="600">
           <tr><td class="boxTitle" >
             Welcome to the News Portal!
           </td></tr>
           <tr><td>
             <span class="headLine">
               <jsp:useBean id="newsfeed" class="com.wrox.begjsp.ch2.NewsFeed"
       scope="request" >
                 <jsp:setProperty name="newsfeed"  property="topic" value="news"/>
                 <jsp:getProperty name="newsfeed" property="value"/>
               </jsp:useBean>
             </span>
             <span class="newsText">
               <jsp:include page="dummytext.html" />
             </span>
           </td></tr>
         </table>
```

This page uses a simulated newsfeed to fetch a headline and then display it to the user. This is indicated by the highlighted code.

The second line of highlighted code includes a simple HTML page, called dummytext.html, that provides the simulated news article text. This demonstrates that the <jsp:include> action is not limited to the rendering of included JSP but also works with HTML pages.

The first set of highlighted code uses another three JSP standard actions to work with the newsfeed object: <jsp:useBean>, <jsp:setProperty>, and <jsp:getProperty>. How this works is explained in the next section.

Manipulating JavaBeans with JSP standard actions

A *JavaBean* is an object coded in the Java programming language that follows some rigid conventions. For example, all JavaBeans expose their capabilities through the following:

❑ **Properties:** Valued attributes of the bean; these can be read/write, read only, or write only.

❑ **Methods:** Functional procedures that can be invoked.

❑ **Events:** Notifications that can be caught.

JavaBeans are reusable software components that can be very useful in JSPs. Of course, the application of a JavaBean is not restricted to JSP. JavaBeans are used in creating servlets or even standalone Java applications. Interactions between JSP and JavaBeans typically center around the use of JavaBean properties. Chapter 9, "JSP and JavaBeans," describes in detail the use of JavaBeans within JSPs.

A read/write property of a bean will allow both the get and set operations. The get operation obtains the current value of a JavaBean property. The set operation sets the value of a JavaBean property.

> In a production development shop, the development team members responsible for the business logic will typically supply you with JavaBeans that you can use within your JSPs. They should also provide you with a description of a bean's properties, and instructions on how to use it.

A JavaBean can be used to generate dynamic content for the portal home pages.

The JavaBean used for our example is a `NewsFeed` JavaBean. It simulates the action of a real newsfeed. *Newsfeeds* are electronic data connections that supply news information items.

To get a news item in a topic, you need to set the topic filter, and then read from the JavaBean. The following table describes the properties of this `NewsFeed` JavaBean.

Property	Read/Write	Description
topic	Write only	Set to "news," "weather," or "entertainment" to filter the newsfeed. This must be set before accessing the `value` or `values` property.
value	Read only	This property supplies a single information item once the `topic` property is set.
values	Read only	This property will supply a list of information items once the `topic` property is set. For our example, this property will have value only if "weather" is the `topic`.

According to the preceding table, to get the latest news item, it is necessary to:

1. Set the `topic` property to news.
2. Read the `value` property.

To get the latest entertainment information:

1. Set the `topic` to entertainment.
2. Read the `value` property.

To get the latest weather information:

1. Set the `topic` property to weather.
2. Read the `values` property.

This is exactly what happened within the `news.jsp` portal page; the responsible segment of JSP code is reproduced here:

```
<jsp:useBean id="newsfeed" class="com.wrox.begjsp.ch2.NewsFeed" scope="request" >
  <jsp:setProperty name="newsfeed" property="topic" value="news"/>
  <jsp:getProperty name="newsfeed" property="value"/>
</jsp:useBean>
```

The `<jsp:useBean>` tag is used to create an instance of a JavaBean, of Java class `com.wrox.begjsp.ch2.NewsFeed`. This instance is attached to the current request, ensuring that each request will have its own instance. If the JavaBean creation is successful, then the `<jsp:setProperty>` tag is used to set the bean's topic property to the value `"news"`. After setting the topic property, the `<jsp:getProperty>` tag is used to read and render (display) the value property of the bean.

The `<jsp:useBean>` tag is used to either locate an existing instance of a JavaBean or to create a new instance if one is not found. Chapter 8 provides details about this versatile standard action. Only the attributes used in this example are described in the following table.

Attribute	Description
id	The name of the created JavaBean instance. A scripting variable with the same name is also created.
class	The Java class (compiled code) of the JavaBean. The JSP container must be able to locate this class in order to instantiate it. This typically means that it must be located under the application's WEB-INF/classes directory or in one of the JAR files in the application's WEB-INF/lib directory.
scope	Can be page, request, session, or application. The request scope means the JavaBean instance created is unique to only this request. The other scopes are explained in Chapter 8.

Readers who are interested in the Java source code of the `NewsFeed` object can locate it in the `<Tomcat Installation Directory>\webapps\ch02\example2\WEB-INF\classes\com\wrox\begjsp\ch02` directory.

The `<jsp:useBean>` tag can optionally have a body. If a body is specified, as it is in the second example, the body will be executed only if the JavaBean is created successfully. This means that if the JavaBean creation is not successful, the JSP will not attempt to access its properties. No headline will be generated by `news.jsp` in this case.

Within the body of the `<jsp:useBean>` tag, this code line sets the topic property of the newly created bean to `"news"`. The syntax of this standard action is quite self-explanatory. Note the use of the name "newsfeed," corresponding to the ID given to the newly created JavaBean instance in the `<jsp:useBean>` tag:

```
<jsp:setProperty name="newsfeed"  property="topic" value="news"/>
```

Note that both the `<jsp:useBean>` and the `<jsp:setProperty>` standard actions do not generate any output if they are successful in their operations. This is not true with the `<jsp:getProperty>` tag. The output of this tag is the value of the JavaBean's property converted to a string. This output will be placed at the location of the tag. For example, the line that renders the headline in news.jsp is as follows:

```
<jsp:getProperty name="newsfeed" property="value"/>
```

Again, notice the name reference to the JavaBean instance created earlier: "newsfeed."

The portal page that displays the entertainment news works in the same way. entertain.jsp, located at <Tomcat Installation Directory>\webapps\ch02\example2\entertain.jsp, is reproduced here:

```
<head>
  <link rel=stylesheet type="text/css" href="portal.css">
  <title>Weather Portal</title>
</head>
<body>
  <table class="mainBox" width="600">
    <tr><td class="boxTitle" >
      Entertainment News Just for You!
    </td></tr>
    <tr><td>
      <span class="headLine">
        <jsp:useBean id="newsfeed" class="com.wrox.begjsp.ch2.NewsFeed"
scope="request" >
          <jsp:setProperty name="newsfeed"  property="topic"
value="entertainment"/>
          <jsp:getProperty name="newsfeed" property="value"/>
        </jsp:useBean>
      </span>
      <span class="newsText">
        <jsp:include page="dummytext.html" />
      </span>
    </td></tr>
  </table>
```

Compare the highlighted JSP lines with news.jsp and check it against the instructions on how to use the NewsFeed JavaBean. You will find that the code is the same as news.jsp, except that the topic property is set to "entertainment" before accessing the value property.

The situation is quite different, however, in the rendering of the weather portal page. This is because the values property of the NewsFeed JavaBean is used in this case, instead of the value property. Unlike the value property, the values property returns more than one value. In fact, it returns an entire table of cities and temperatures. It turns out that no standard JSP action can handle this type of property easily. This is one of the reasons why JSP 2.0 is designed to work with JSTL 1.1 — combining custom actions in JSTL 1.1 with the Expression Language in JSP 2.0, multivalued properties can be handled very easily.

Rendering a multivalued JavaBean property with JSTL/EL

The weather.jsp JSP, located at <Tomcat Installation Directory>\webapps\ch02\example2\weather.jsp, is reproduced here:

```
<%@ taglib prefix="c" uri="http://java.sun.com/jsp/jstl/core" %>
<head>
```

```
    <link rel=stylesheet type="text/css" href="portal.css">
    <title>Weather Portal</title>
  </head>
  <body>
    <table class="mainBox" width="600">
      <tr><td class="boxTitle" >
        You Get the Latest Weather!
      </td></tr>
      <tr><td>
      <jsp:useBean id="newsfeed" class="com.wrox.begjsp.ch2.NewsFeed" scope="request"
>
        <jsp:setProperty name="newsfeed"  property="topic" value="weather"/>
      </jsp:useBean>
      <table>
        <c:forEach items="${newsfeed.values}" var="row" >
          <tr><td class="tableCell" width="200">  ${row.city}  </td>
        <td> ${row.temp}</td>
          </tr>
        </c:forEach>
      </table>
      </td></tr>
    </table>
```

Referring back to Figure 2-7, you can see that the highlighted code is responsible for dynamically generating the table of cities and associated temperatures. Of course, this data is obtained from the NewsFeed JavaBean. Both the <jsp:useBean> and <jsp:setProperty> standard actions appear again. They are used to create the NewsFeed JavaBean instance and set the topic property to weather. However, the <jsp:getProperty> standard action is not used.

Instead, the JSTL iteration tag is used to create the table. In general, the JSTL iteration tag has the following form:

```
<c:forEach items=".. a collection of objects .." var=".. var name.." >
       ... code that executes once for each object in the collection...
</c:forEach>
```

The two attributes used are described in the following table.

Attribute	Description
items	An expression that results in a collection of objects. In Java programming terms, the object returned must support the java.util. Collection interface. For example, this can be a property of a JavaBean that returns a collection of objects.
var	During each repetition through the loop, an object is selected from the collection specified in items. The object is given this name and can be referred to within the body by this name.

Chapter 6 features more comprehensive coverage of JSTL in general, and the iteration tag in particular.

This `<c:forEach>` tag enables us to iterate through all the values of the `values` property on the `NewsFeed` JavaBean. It will generate one table row for each value returned. The code to generate the table is reproduced here:

```
<table>
  <c:forEach items="${newsfeed.values}" var="row" >
    <tr><td class="tableCell" width="200">  ${row.city}  </td>
      <td> ${row.temp}</td>
    </tr>
  </c:forEach>
</table>
```

In the description of `<jsp:useBean>`, you learned that a scripting variable is created that refers to the JavaBean specified by the tag. The name of this scripting variable is specified in the `id` attribute. In this case, the scripting variable is used in the EL expression `${newsfeed.values}`, referring to the values property of the `NewsFeed` JavaBean. This property is supplied for the `items` attribute of the JSTL iteration tag.

Each object returned by the `NewsFeed` JavaBean is assigned to the variable "row" set in the `var` attribute of the `<c:forEach>` tag. It is used within the body to obtain the city and temperature value. These values are obtained via the `${row.city}` and `${row.temp}` EL expressions. From a JSP perspective, `city` and `temp` are properties of the objects in the collection returned by the `values` property of the `NewsFeed` JavaBean.

For readers fluent with the Java programming language, the `values` *property of the* `NewsFeed` *JavaBean returns an* `ArrayList` *of* `HashMaps`. *This combination of data structures enable convenient access to tabular data from JSPs using JSTL 1.1 and EL.*

Web site personalization

JSP can be used to create personalized Web applications. A personalized Web application is aware of the user's identity. This is certainly useful, for example, to provide users with their own set of preferences while using your application. A more concrete scenario may be an online book seller customizing a home page to feature books that match a user's favorite topic in an attempt to increase sales. There are many aspects to creating a personalized Web site. The chapters in this book build upon each other, presenting to you features that enable you to use JSP in Web site personalization. Chapter 27, "Project I: Personalized Portal," demonstrates how such a personalized Web site can be built.

The last example in this chapter reveals how the portal selection system can be used to propagate (send) user information to the independent portal pages. This enables each of the portal pages to greet users by their first name, creating a personalized experience.

Try It Out   **Web Site Personalization**

To see the personalization of the portal application in action, make sure the `ch02` application is running on Tomcat and access the following URL:

```
http://localhost:8080/ch02/example3/index.jsp
```

The portal selection form is displayed. This time, the form also enables you to enter your first name for personalization purposes. This form is shown in Figure 2-11.

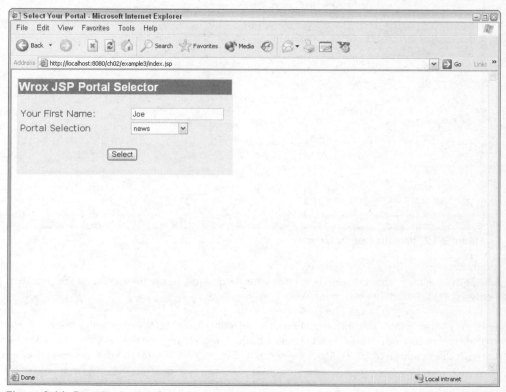

Figure 2-11: Portal selection form for personalization

Enter your first name, select the news portal, and then click the Select button. You should now see a personalized news portal, as shown in Figure 2-12.

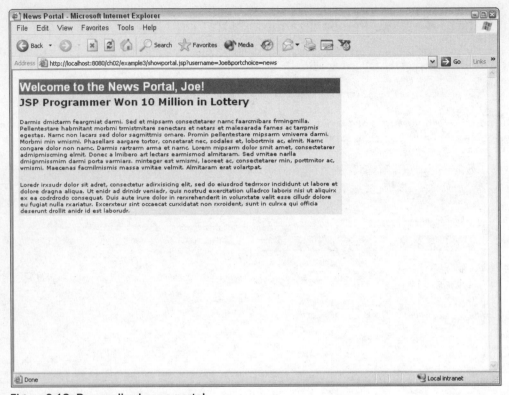

Figure 2-12: Personalized news portal

Note that the portal is now personalized with your own name. In the previous case, the name of Joe was entered.

Enter the URL again into your browser. Once the selection form is displayed, enter your first name and select the entertainment portal. Click the Select button. You should see the personalized entertainment portal with the headline obtained from the simulated newsfeed, similar to what is shown in Figure 2-13.

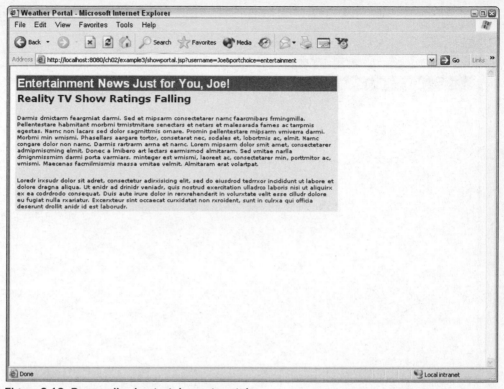

Figure 2-13: Personalized entertainment portal

Finally, enter the URL again into your browser. From the selection form, enter your first name and select the weather portal. Click the Select button to see the personalized weather portal page, as shown in Figure 2-14.

Although this example shows the name of the user being used only in a personalized greeting, a lot more can be done. For example, the username can be used to retrieve user-specific information from a database (using JavaBeans, perhaps) and customize the user's experience accordingly.

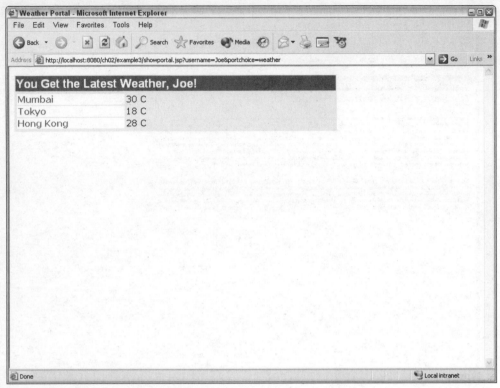

Figure 2-14: Personalized weather portal

Observing HTTP GET method URL encoding

Using this example, it is possible to observe the effect of parameter encoding when the form parameters are submitted using the HTTP GET method. To try this, enter the URL for the selection page on the browser. On the portal selection page, enter the following for a username:

```
J?o= e
```

Note that there is a space character after the equal sign and before the final e.

Select the news portal and click the Select button. You should now see the news portal greeting with this rather strange username, as shown in Figure 2-15.

The thing to note here is that the parameter username has been encoded by the browser. You should see the following URL:

```
http://localhost:8080/ch02/example3/showportal.jsp?username=J%3Fo%3D+e&portchoice=n
ews
```

The ?, =, and space have been encoded by the browser.

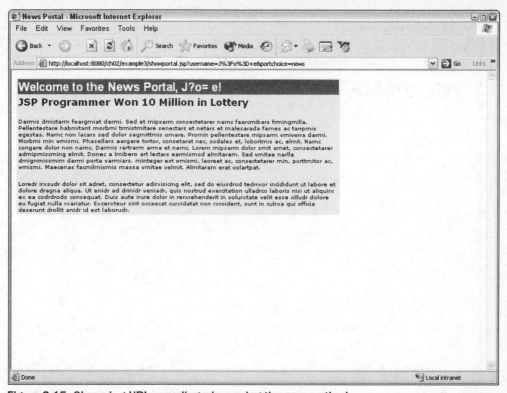

Figure 2-15: Observing URL encoding when using the GET method

Vulnerability of the HTTP GET method of form submission

This quick experiment will show that the GET method for form submission is very easy for malicious users to hack. After viewing the news portal, modify the URL at the browser by hand. For example, if you have just entered "Joe" as your name and accessed the news portal, the following URL should be displayed:

```
http://localhost:8080/ch02/example3/showportal.jsp?username=Joe&portchoice=news
```

Now, from the browser, simulate a malicious hacker and modify the URL to the following:

```
http://localhost:8080/ch02/example3/showportal.jsp?username=Joe&portchoice=news123
```

The portchoice parameter now has the value news123. Press Enter (or Return) in the browser. Because this is not an anticipated portal choice, showportal.jsp will generate a page similar to the one shown in Figure 2-16.

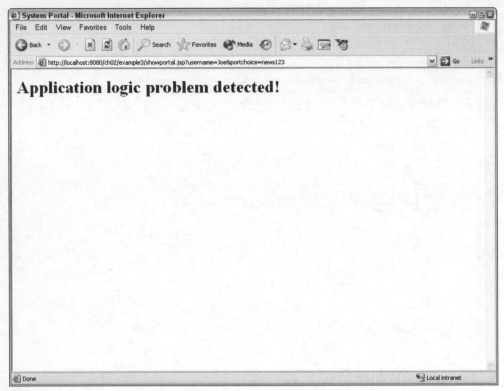

Figure 2-16: Resulting page from a hacked port selection URL

Recall from our discussion earlier that the HTTP POST method can also be used to submit form data. To see this, modify the <form> element in the index.jsp file to the following:

```
<form action="showportal.jsp" method="post">
```

Try the previous form submission again, and you should see that the URL used to access the portal no longer contains visible parameter values. In our case, the URL selecting a news portal looks as follows:

```
http://localhost:8080/ch02/example3/showportal.jsp
```

The parameters are still passed to the server, but this is done invisibly using HTTP message body. While this is still not an entirely secure way of sending form data, it does not invite hacking in the way that the GET method does (i.e., by plainly exposing the parameter values).

How It Works

The index.jsp file is modified to include the <input> HTML element for the input of the user's name. Note that the name given to the HTML element is username. This will become the parameter name when the form is submitted to Tomcat. index.jsp is reproduced below, with the new lines highlighted:

```
<html>
  <head>
    <link rel=stylesheet type="text/css" href="portal.css">
    <title>Select Your Portal</title>
  </head>
  <body>
    <table class="mainBox" width="400">
      <tr><td class="boxTitle" colspan="2">
        Wrox JSP Portal Selector
      </td></tr>
      <tr><td colspan="2"> </td></tr>
      <tr><td>
      <form  action="showportal.jsp" method="get">
        <table>
          <tr>
            <td width="200">
              Your First Name: </td>
            <td><input name="username" type="text" size="25"/></td>
          </tr>
          <tr>
            <td width="200">Portal Selection</td>
            <td>
              <select name="portchoice">
                <option>news</option>
                <option>weather</option>
                <option>entertainment</option>
              </select>
            </td>
          </tr>
          <tr><td colspan="2"> </td></tr>
          <tr><td colspan="2" align="center">
            <input type="submit" value="Select"/>
          </td></tr>
        </table>
      </form>
      </td></tr>
    </table>
  </body>
</html>
```

Passing parameters to included JSPs

Instead of submitting just the `portchoice` parameter as shown in example 2, the `index.jsp` form now submits two parameters: `protchoice` and `username`. On the server side, `showportal.jsp` is modified to pass the new `username` parameter to the selected portal JSP. `showportal.jsp` is reproduced here, with the new code to process the `username` parameter highlighted:

```
<%@ taglib prefix="c" uri="http://java.sun.com/jsp/jstl/core" %>
<html>
  <c:choose>
    <c:when test="${param.portchoice == 'news'}">
      <jsp:include page="news.jsp" >
        <jsp:param name="user" value="${param.username}"/>
      </jsp:include>
```

```
      </c:when>
      <c:when test="${param.portchoice =='weather'}">
        <jsp:include page="weather.jsp" >
          <jsp:param name="user" value="${param.username}"/>
        </jsp:include>
      </c:when>
      <c:when test="${param.portchoice == 'entertainment'}">
        <jsp:include page="entertain.jsp" >
          <jsp:param name="user" value="${param.username}"/>
        </jsp:include>
      </c:when>
      <c:otherwise>
        <head><title>System Portal</title></head>
        <body>
          <h1>Application logic problem detected!</h1>
        </body>
      </c:otherwise>
    </c:choose>
    </body>
</html>
```

The `<jsp:include>` standard action supports an optional body. Prior versions of this `showportal.jsp` page did not need this body. This time, the body is used. Within the body, a `<jsp:param>` standard action is used to specify a parameter for the included JSP. For example, the following line specifies a `user` parameter:

```
<jsp:include page="entertain.jsp" >
  <jsp:param name="user" value="${param.username}"/>
</jsp:include>
```

When executed, the included `entertain.jsp` file will have access to a parameter called `user`; and the parameter will have the value equal to the `username` parameter that is submitted from the form. Using the `<jsp:param>` tag is the best way to pass parameters to any included JSPs.

> Strictly speaking, the included JSP also has access to all the parameters available in the JSP page doing the inclusion. This means that an included `entertain.jsp` could have used the `user` parameter from the form instead of the `username` parameter from the `<jsp:param>` action. However, having the included JSP depend on a parameter of the main page is a bad programming practice. This is because the JSP being included will not be able to work with an including page that does not have a parameter with the required name—greatly reducing the reuse possibility of the included JSP.

Modifying the included JSP to use personalization data

The change required in the portal pages to support the simple personalization is minimal. The `news.jsp` portal page is reproduced here, with the changed code highlighted:

```
<head>
  <link rel=stylesheet type="text/css" href="portal.css">
  <title>News Portal</title>
```

```
  </head>
  <body>
    <table class="mainBox" width="600">
      <tr><td class="boxTitle" >
        Welcome to the News Portal, ${param.user}!
      </td></tr>
      <tr><td>
        <span class="headLine">
          <jsp:useBean id="newsfeed" class="com.wrox.begjsp.ch2.NewsFeed"
scope="request" >
            <jsp:setProperty name="newsfeed"  property="topic" value="news"/>
            <jsp:getProperty name="newsfeed" property="value"/>
          </jsp:useBean>
        </span>
        <span class="newsText">
          <jsp:include page="dummytext.html" />
        </span>
      </td></tr>
    </table>
```

The EL expression `${param.user}` is used to access the parameter passed by the `<jsp:include>` standard action. Like the original `showportal.jsp`, it uses the EL implicit object, `param`, to obtain and render the value of the `user` parameter.

The `entertain.jsp` file is modified to support the personalization as well. The single modified line is highlighted here:

```
<head>
  <link rel=stylesheet type="text/css" href="portal.css">
  <title>Weather Portal</title>
</head>
<body>
  <table class="mainBox" width="600">
  <tr><td class="boxTitle" >
    Entertainment News Just for You, ${param.user}!
  </td></tr>
  <tr><td>
    <span class="headLine">
      <jsp:useBean id="newsfeed" class="com.wrox.begjsp.ch2.NewsFeed"
scope="request" >
        <jsp:setProperty name="newsfeed"  property="topic" value="entertainment"/>
        <jsp:getProperty name="newsfeed" property="value"/>
      </jsp:useBean>
    </span>
    <span class="newsText">
      <jsp:include page="dummytext.html" />
    </span>
  </td></tr>
</table>
```

The only change to the `weather.jsp` file is highlighted in the following code:

```
<%@ taglib prefix="c" uri="http://java.sun.com/jsp/jstl/core" %>
<head>
  <link rel=stylesheet type="text/css" href="portal.css">
```

```
      <title>Weather Portal</title>
   </head>
   <body>
      <table class="mainBox" width="600">
        <tr><td class="boxTitle" >
          You Get the Latest Weather, ${param.user}!
        </td></tr>
        <tr><td>
          <jsp:useBean id="newsfeed" class="com.wrox.begjsp.ch2.NewsFeed"
scope="request" >
            <jsp:setProperty name="newsfeed"  property="topic" value="weather"/>
          </jsp:useBean>
          <table>
            <c:forEach items="${newsfeed.values}" var="row" >
              <tr><td class="tableCell" width="200">  ${row.city}  </td>
                <td> ${row.temp}</td>
              </tr>
            </c:forEach>
          </table>
        </td></tr>
      </table>
```

Again, the implicit EL object param is used to obtain the user parameter from the JSP container. The username parameter is used to personalize the title.

Summary

The main role of JSP in a Web-based application is to create a dynamic presentation of information or data. This chapter focused on the elements that enable these dynamic presentation capabilities.

All JSP pages are composed of the following elements:

❑   Directives

❑   Actions

❑   Template data

❑   Scripting elements

HTML form submission is managed on the client side by the browser. On the server side, a JSP container can greatly simplify the handling of form submission. Parameters are passed with the URL request from the browser to the server using either the HTTP GET or the HTTP POST method. The GET method attaches the parameters to the URL as trailing text, while the POST method uses the HTTP message body to carry the parameters. The EL implicit object, param, can be used on the JSP side to directly access the submitted form parameters.

The form-processing task involves accepting the submitted parameters and dynamically generating a response page.

JSTL 1.1 features many custom actions that can be useful in JSP programming. The <choose> ..<when>..<otherwise> JSTL tags construct can be used to selectively generate different content depending on an EL expression. EL expressions enable you to access objects — either implicit objects or ones created by Java or business logic developers.

The `<jsp:include>` standard action can be used to render the output of one JSP page (or HTML page) within another JSP page.

JavaBeans are reusable code components. They are often used by Java developer to supply data to JSP developers in the creation of the presentation layer. Their properties and usage must be documented. The standard actions, `<jsp:useBean>`, `<jsp:setProperty>`, and `<jsp:getProperty>`, work with JavaBeans. However, to access bean properties that return multivalued data, the use of JSTL and EL may be necessary. The `<forEach>` iteration tag of JSTL is very useful for rendering tabular data values from JavaBeans.

Because JSP has complete control on the dynamic generation of the response page to an incoming request, it can be also be used to create Web applications that feature a personalized user experience. The final example illustrates the basic principles involved in Web site personalization.

Exercises

1. Using the JSP code in the second Try It Out exercise as a base, write a JSP that will display the combined portals shown in Figure 2-17.

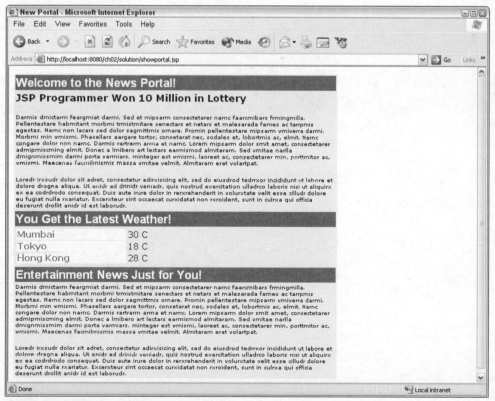

Figure 2-17: Exercise 1 output

2. You can use JSP to create highly flexible data presentation. Exercise 1 revealed that essentially the same JSP portal pages can be used in diversely different user presentations. This code reuse practice is highly encouraged. Using Exercise 1 as a base, modify `news.jsp`, `weather.jsp`, and `entertain.jsp` in a way such that they can also be used within the second Try It Out exercise. Test these new pages with the second Try It Out exercise. You are not allowed to change the `showportal.jsp` code for the second Try It Out.

JSP Basics 2: Generalized Templating and Server Scripting

The previous chapter presented JSP as a server-side mechanism used in the generation of dynamic HTML responses to an incoming request. It also demonstrated how static templated data (such as a fragment or a whole page of HTML) can be included and combined as part of the output. This chapter adds another dimension, showing how JSP generalized templating can be combined with scripting code written in the Java programming language.

The ability to include Java elements in a JSP page is the center of focus in this chapter. When working with JSP 2.0 and JSTL 1.1, there is very little reason to embed raw Java programming code into a JSP page. However, the Expression Language (EL) and JSTL features presented in the previous chapter are brand-new to most commercial JSP containers (compliant to the JSP 2.0 standard). Older, existing production code will typically not be using JSTL/EL, and will very likely have embedded Java code. This body of production code will need to maintained, and perhaps migrated. In this chapter, you will learn how to deal with legacy code that makes extensive use of embedded Java code via scripting elements in JSPs.

The primary mechanism of embedding Java code into a JSP page is called *scripting*. Scripting is typically done through scripting elements — declarations, expressions, and scriptlets — within a JSP. These elements are covered briefly in the previous chapter. This chapter fully explores the role of these elements within the composition of a JSP page.

The sample code within the chapter makes extensive use of scripting elements. This sample code features the design and creation of a simple Web-based storefront that displays different categories of products and allows users to add products to their shopping cart. Through three successively more complex examples, you will discover the fundamental coding techniques that are used on e-commerce sites.

Scoping is a very important concept for the JSP developer. This chapter explores global application scope, session scope, and request scope. Actual code from the e-commerce example will take advantage of all of these scopes. Exploring session scope requires an understanding of the *container-managed session*. This chapter introduces the concept of a session, reveals how it is implemented, and shows how it can be extremely useful in the JSP implementation of e-commerce applications. By the end of this chapter, you should

- ❑   Understand the interaction between a JSP and embedded Java code

- ❑   Be fluent in the use of scripting elements within JSP

- ❑   Be able to maintain, enhance, and migrate JSP code that contains scripting elements

- ❑   Be familiar with the design and operation of a basic electronic storefront

- ❑   Be able to implement a working shopping cart using JSP

- ❑   Understand the application, session, and request scopes in JSP

- ❑   Understand why sessions are necessary and how to work with them from within your JSP

Scripting Elements for Java Code Embedding

Historically, JSP and Java go hand-in-hand. In early versions of the JSP standard, Java code was used routinely as the glue for supplementing the standard JSP actions during content generation.

In fact, JSP 1.0 lacked a mechanism for implementing custom actions, and the standard actions that were included were extremely limited. This virtually guaranteed extensive embedding of Java coding in all but the simplest JSP 1.0 code.

The first version that supported a workable way of extending JSP standard actions was JSP 1.1. Even though JSP 1.1 started to support third-party tag libraries, the art of tag library creation and integration is not well documented. As a result, a standard set of available generalized tags was lacking. Not until JSP 1.2 did the use of custom tag libraries became popular.

JSP 2.0 is the first version of JSP to introduce an Expression Language (EL) designed to work in conjunction with a standard tag library (JSTL 1.1). It is also the first version of JSP to simplify the creation of custom tags, via support of *tagfiles* (creating new tags using JSP as the implementation language). In other words, JSP 2.0 is the first version of JSP that enables the creation of pure JSP coding right out of the box without the need to embed Java coding.

As a result, if you ever need to look at existing or legacy code, you are likely to see embedded Java within JSP pages. In this old JSP code, there was simply no other way to accomplish tasks that are not covered by standard JSP actions.

As a JSP developer, you should be aware that JSP is considered a *presentation layer* technology. In other words, it should be used in the creation of a dynamic presentation of data. In fact, JSP containers are designed and optimized specifically for this purpose. This also means that JSP should not be used as the primary way to process or manipulate data within an application. These activities are best left for developers at the business tier, using technology such as Enterprise JavaBeans (EJBs) or through the creation of custom Java classes. Allowing embedded Java code in JSP pages encourages the mixing of data processing functions, which JSP is not designed for and cannot do well. In fact, years of industry experience confirm that mixing JSP and Java coding can lead to code that is difficult to maintain. Therefore, given a choice, modern JSP developers should seek to reduce or completely eliminate the use of embedded Java code in their JSPs. Having said this, in some real-world situations, you may be asked to enhance or maintain legacy JSP code that is written using earlier versions of the JSP standard. In these cases, you will need to have a working knowledge of scripting elements within JSPs.

Scripting elements

To embed Java coding into a JSP page, you need to use scripting elements. There are three general ways to do this, as briefly mentioned in Chapter 2. Fully explored in this chapter are the following three types of scripting elements:

❑   Declarations

❑   Expressions

❑   Scriptlets

Declaration scripting elements

Declaration scripting elements are used to insert methods, constants, and variable declarations into JSP pages. Here is a declaration scripting element that declares three constants (EXAMPLE, SHOP_PAGE, and CART_PAGE), and a method called dispPrice ():

```
<%!
  private static String EXAMPLE = "/example2";
  private static String SHOP_PAGE = "/estore.jsp";
  private static String CART_PAGE = "/shopcart.jsp";
  private  String dispPrice( String price)
  {
      int len = price.length();
      if (len <= 2)
          return price;
      else
      return "$" + price.substring(0,len -2) + "."
        + price.substring(len-2);
  }
%>
```

The following properties are illustrated by the preceding declaration scripting element:

❑   Declaration scripting elements are enclosed by <%! ... %>.

❑   The content of scripting elements in general, and declaration scripting elements specifically, is actually code fragments written in Java.

❑   Constants, variables, and methods declared within declaration scripting elements are used within the JSP page, by other scripting elements, EL expressions, or JSP actions.

You can have multiple declaration scripting elements within a single JSP page. The JSP container will merge them into one when processing the page, so it isn't necessary to separate them.

In the preceding embedded Java code, note that the constant paths (EXAMPLE, SHOP_PAGE, and CART_PAGE) are hard-coded into the JSP. If these paths were to change in the future, all of the code containing them would have to be changed. Chapter 17, "Model View Controller," illustrates a more flexible approach whereby the application flow can be configured without changing any JSP or Java code.

Working with jspInit() and jspDestroy()

You can define two very special methods within a declaration scripting element. They are methods with the following signatures:

- ❏ `public void jspInit(void);`
- ❏ `public void jspDestory(void);`

These methods are special because the JSP container will call them at two well-defined points during the life of a JSP page. The following table describes when the container calls these methods.

Method Name	When It Is Called
`void jspInit()`	Called during the initialization of the JSP page, before the first request is processed by the page. This method can be used to acquire global resources that may be used by the page's request processing logic. This method is optional for a JSP page author. Most JSP pages have no need to declare this method.
`void jspDestroy()`	Called by the container just before destroying the JSP page. This method can be used to release the resources that it acquired in `jspInit()`. Most JSP pages have no need to declare this method.

To fully understand what these methods do, you must realize that a JSP container typically creates only one single instance (see the following note) of a JSP to service all incoming requests. The `jspInit()` method is called by the container during the initialization of this single instance. If the incoming request processing load is heavy, a JSP container may eliminate some initialized JSPs that have not been used for a while. If this happens, the container is obliged to call the `jspDestroy()` method before eliminating the JSP.

Some JSP containers may take advantage of multiple Java Virtual Machines (JVMs) on a Symmetric MultiProcessor (SMP), or a clustering system. These specialized containers may maintain one instance of a JSP per JVM to process incoming requests.

The following declaration scripting element declares the two special methods. In this case, the Java code attaches an object as an attribute to the `ServletContext` in the `jspInit()` method, and the `jspDestroy()` method removes this attribute.

For readers who are avid Java programmers, the following information will enable you to determine what code can go into these methods. Every JSP is actually a Java class. A JSP Java class implements the `javax.servlet.Servlet` interface. In other words, a JSP is always a servlet. It implements all of the methods of the Servlet interface. For example, the following code uses the `getServletContext()` of the Servlet interface. The servlet context of a JSP corresponds to its implicit `application` object. The `application` object is readily available for use in expression scripting elements and scriptlet scripting elements.

```
<%!
  public void jspInit()
  {
      getServletContext().setAttribute("cats", EShop.getCats());
  }

  public void jspDestroy()
  {
      getServletContext().removeAttribute("cats");
  }
%>
```

Expression scripting element

An expression scripting element is an embedded Java expression that is evaluated and converted to a text string. The resulting text string is placed in the JSP output, in the location at which the element appears. You will find expression scripting elements in a JSP in the following locations:

❑   Within certain attributes of JSP actions (standard or custom)

❑   Within templated data

For example, the following expression scripting elements are used to print out some data values within a row of a table:

```
<table>
  <tr>
    <td><%= curItem.getName() %></td>
    <td><%= dispPrice(String.valueOf(curItem.getPrice())) %></td>
  </tr>
</table>
```

From the example, note the following about expression scripting elements:

❑   They are bracketed by <%= .... %>.

❑   They contain expressions in the Java programming language — for example, a variable, a field, or the result of a method call.

❑   Their output is merged with the template data, HTML in the preceding example.

Expression scripting elements may also be used in attributes of JSP actions. The following example shows an expression scripting element used in the value attribute of the standard <jsp:param> action:

```
<jsp:include page="weather.jsp" >
  <jsp:param name="user"
        value="<%= request.getParameter("username")%>"/>
</jsp:include>
```

In this case, the expression scripting element will be evaluated first. The text string value of the request.getParameter() method call will be substituted before the <jsp:param> action is evaluated. The expression scripting element in this case is said to be a *request time expression* (because it is evaluated during request processing).

Scriptlet scripting element

Scriptlet scripting elements are used to include complete fragments of Java code in the body of the JSP. These elements differ from declarations and expressions in two ways:

❑ They are not limited to the declaration of methods, variables, and constants.

❑ They do not generate a string output directly, as expressions do.

If you need to generate output within a scriptlet scripting element, you can use the *out* implicit object. The *out* implicit object is of the `javax.servlet.jsp.JspWriter` type, which in turn is a subclass of `java.io.Writer`, and all of its methods are available. For example, the following scriptlet scripting element prints a total cost, conditionally with local tax added on:

```
<%
  if (state.isLocal())
      out.print(totalCost * localTax);
  else
      out.println(totalCost);
%>
```

The following is an example of several scriptlet scripting elements in the layout of a table with varying numbers of output rows. Note the free mix of template data and scriptlet scripting elements:

```
<table border="1">
  <tr><th align="left">Item</th><th align="left">Price</th></tr>
  <%
    String selectedCat = request.getParameter("catid");
    if (selectedCat == null)
        selectedCat = "1";
    ArrayList items = (ArrayList) EShop.getItems(selectedCat);
    for (int i=0; i< items.size(); i++)
    {
        Product curItem = (Product) items.get(i);
  %>
  <tr>
    <td><%= curItem.getName()    %></td>
    <td><%= dispPrice(String.valueOf(curItem.getPrice()))  %></td>
  </tr>
  <%
    }
  %>
</table>
```

An especially important technique to note is the use of scriptlet scripting elements in the control flow of the JSP. In the preceding case, the highlighted code implements a loop that prints a row for each element in the `items` `ArrayList` collection. The use of scriptlet scripting elements — expression scripting elements and template data (HTML) — is freely mixed. Note the following characteristics of scriptlet scripting elements:

❑ They are Java code fragments that are bracketed in `<% ... %>`.

❑ They can be placed anywhere within the JSP body, mixed among the template data.

❑ All the Java control flow structures (`if`, `for`, `while`, `switch`, and so on) may be used for control flow within a JSP page.

Java class syntax and scripting elements layout

If the placement of scripting elements within a JSP reminds you of the coding syntax of a Java class, you are very observant. In fact, the combined scripting elements on a JSP page match precisely certain elements in a Java class. In most JSP containers, the entire JSP page is translated to a Java class in source code before compilation. Figure 3-1 illustrates the correspondence between scripting elements in the layout and the syntax of a Java class.

Declaration scripting elements are placed as the first thing in the body of the Java class definition.

The JSP body, including any scriptlets scripting elements, is placed in the body of the Java class immediately after JSP generated code that defines the JSP implicit objects and sets up the page environment. This implies the following:

❑ Within declaration scripting elements, you do not have access to the implicit objects and page-specific elements.

❑ Within scriptlet and expression scripting elements, you have full access to the implicit objects and page-specific elements.

```
public final class estore_jsp extends org.apache.jasper.runtime.HttpJspBase {
```

Declaration scripting elements placed here

JSP generated code to set up implicit objects
and support environment

**A mix of scriptlet scripting elements, expression scripting
elements, code generated from template data,
and code generated from actions placed here**

```
}
```

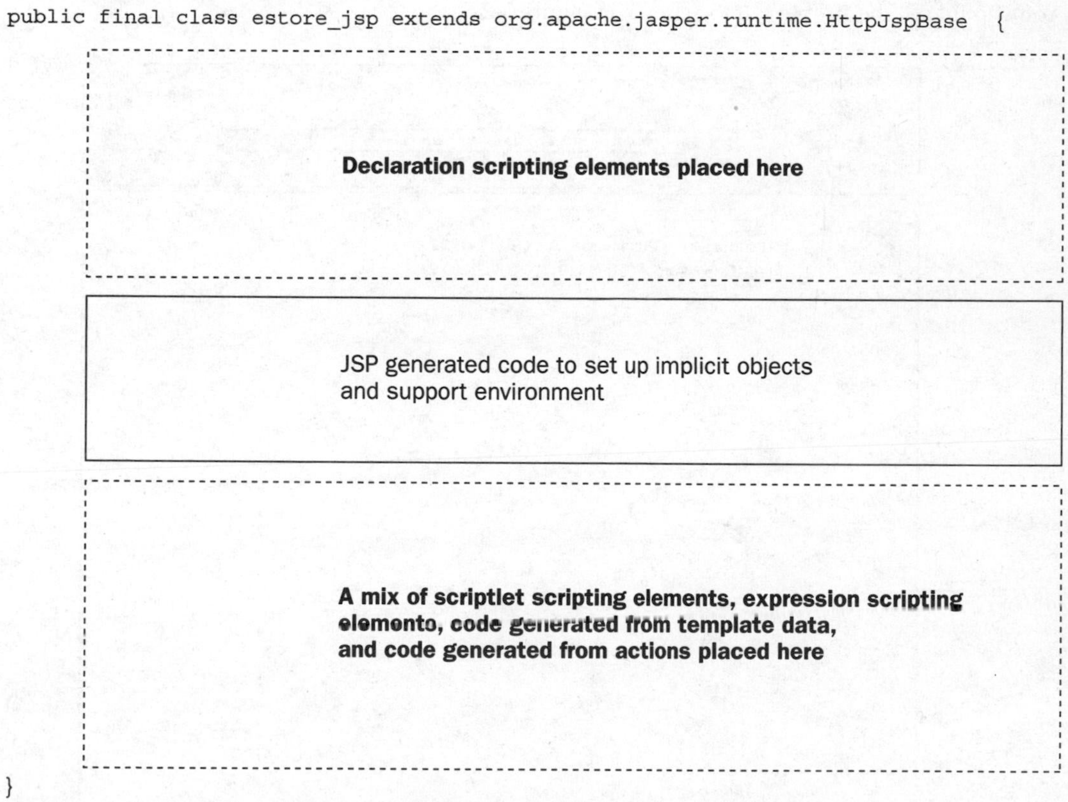

Figure 3-1: The scripting elements and their equivalent Java class placement

Creating a Simple Web Storefront

You are likely to have encountered many Web-based stores in your daily Internet surfing activities. The example in this chapter provides a glimpse into how these stores are built. More specifically, you will see how JSP can be used to implement navigation and presentation in the user interface of a Web-based store. The JSP in this example makes extensive use of embedded Java coding and provides you with hands-on experience working with scripting elements.

The first example implements a catalog of products. Within this catalog, shoppers may select a product category, and the products in that category will be displayed on the screen with their prices.

Try It Out   **Creating a Products Catalog**

To try out the first example, make sure Tomcat 5 is running and deploy the ch03.war file (see Chapter 1 for details if you do not remember how to use the Manager application to deploy a war file). Point your browser to the following URL:

```
http://localhost:8080/ch03/example1/estore.jsp
```

You should see the simple catalog shown in Figure 3-2.

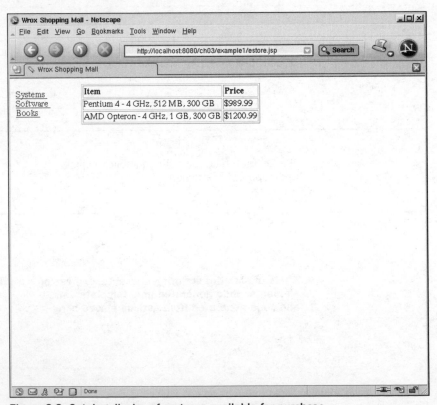

Figure 3-2: Catalog display of systems available for purchase

In Figure 3-2, the categories of products are displayed on the left side of the page. Each product category is represented by a hyperlink. If you click the product category hyperlink, a list of products and their prices are displayed on the right-hand side. Now try clicking the link for the Software product category. You should see the selection of software available, as shown in Figure 3-3.

The software selection shows two Tomcat servers available and their prices. Finally, click the Books product category. You should see the three books that are available, as shown in Figure 3-4.

This catalog application is simple and free of fancy HTML formatting so we can focus on the JSP and scripting code. It is always a good idea to test your code before adding formatting elements. This best practice is covered in Chapter 1.

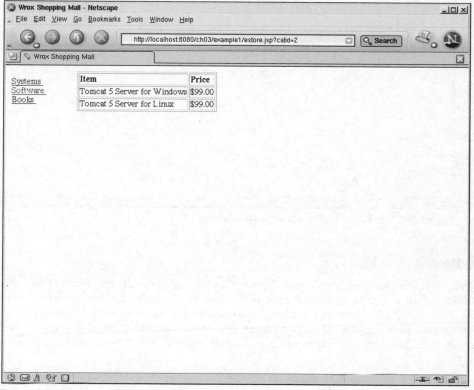

Figure 3-3: Display of software available for purchase

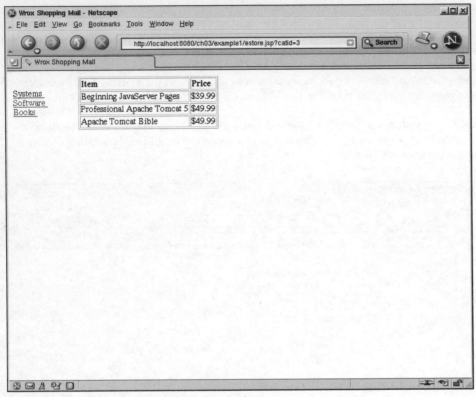

Figure 3-4: Display of books available for purchase

How It Works

This catalog makes use of only a single JSP page. This JSP page presents the information contained in a set of objects. These objects are already provided for us. Similar to the JavaBean used in Chapter 2, the objects are coded in Java. In most production environments, the description of the objects that you can use within your JSPs is provided for you. In a production environment, the objects are often called *business objects*. The following table describes the available objects.

Object Name	Description
EShop	An object containing static convenience methods. The `getCats()` method can be used to obtain the current catalog categories. The `getItems()` method can be used to obtain the products in a specific category.
Category	Represents a single category and has fields containing the name, description, and a unique category ID. This object can be accessed as a JavaBean.
Product	Represents a single product. It has a unique SKU identifier, a name, a description, and a price. This object can be accessed as a JavaBean.

The compiled code for these Java objects is located in a package called `com.wrox.begjsp.ch03`; you can find it under the `<Tomcat Installation Directory>/webapps/WEB-INF/classes` directory. Figure 3-5 illustrates how the Java objects are used within the catalog.

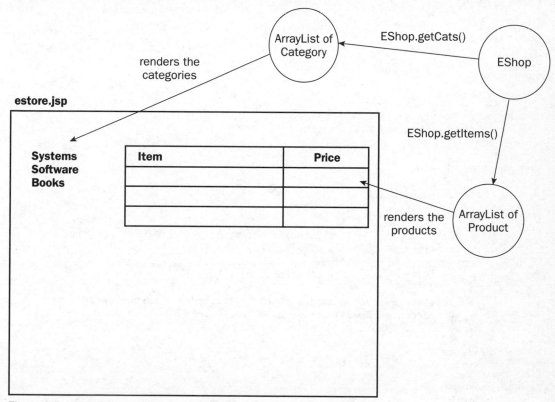

Figure 3-5: Using EShop, Category, and Product objects in the catalog

In Figure 3-5, Java coded scripting elements will be used to glue the object data to the JSP template, resulting in the generated HTML catalog page.

The code to this catalog can be located in the `estore.jsp` JSP page. The `estore.jsp` file is reproduced here, but you can find it in the `<Tomcat Installation Directory>/ch03/example1/estore.jsp` file:

```
<%@ page language="java"
  import = "com.wrox.begjsp.ch03.*,java.util.*" %>
```

```
<%!
  public void jspInit()
  {
      getServletContext().setAttribute("cats", EShop.getCats());
  }

  public void jspDestroy()
  {
      getServletContext().removeAttribute("cats");
```

```
    }
    private  String dispPrice( String price)
    {
        int len = price.length();
        if (len <= 2)
            return price;
        else
            return "$" + price.substring(0,len -2) + "." + price.substring(len-2);
    }
%>
```

```html
<html>
<head>
  <title>Wrox Shopping Mall</title>
</head>
<body>
  <table width="600">
    <tr>
      <td width="20%">
       <%

         ArrayList cats = (ArrayList) application.getAttribute("cats");
         for (int i=0; i< cats.size(); i++)
         {
             Category curCat = (Category) cats.get(i);
       %>
      <a href="<%= request.getRequestURL() + "?catid=" + curCat.getId() %>">
        <%=  curCat.getName()  %>
      </a>
      <br/>
       <%
         }
       %>
      </td>
      <td>
        <h1></h1>
        <table border="1">
          <tr><th align="left">Item</th><th align="left">Price</th></tr>
          <%
            String selectedCat = request.getParameter("catid");
            if (selectedCat == null)
                selectedCat = "1";
            ArrayList items = (ArrayList) EShop.getItems(selectedCat);
            for (int i=0; i< items.size(); i++)
            {
                Product curItem = (Product) items.get(i);
          %>
          <tr>
            <td><%= curItem.getName()    %></td>
            <td><%= dispPrice(String.valueOf(curItem.getPrice()))   %></td>
          </tr>

          <%
            }
          %>
```

```
            </table>
          </td>
        </tr>
      </table>
    </body>
  </html>
```

Lines containing scripting elements are highlighted in the preceding code. You can see plenty of examples of all three types of scripting elements (declarations, expressions, and scriptlets).

At the top of the JSP is a `<%@page>` directive. This is a directive that has not appeared before:

```
<%@ page language="java"
  import = "com.wrox.begjsp.ch03.*,java.util.*" %>
```

The `<%@page>` directive describes certain properties of the JSP, via its attributes, to the container. For example, this `<%@page>` directive is saying that the programming language used in scripting elements is "java", and that the classes in packages com.wrox.begjsp.ch03.* and java.util.* should be imported. The import attribute is equivalent to the following Java code:

```
import com.wrox.begjsp.ch03.*;
import java.util.*;
```

The next section in estore.jsp is a declaration scripting element. In this case, the special jspInit() and jspDestroy() methods are defined. Also note the declaration of a Java method called dispPrice() that takes a string representation of a number and displays it in the dollar price $???.?? format:

```
<%!
  public void jspInit()
  {
      getServletContext().setAttribute("cats", EShop.getCats());
  }

  public void jspDestroy()
  {
      getServletContext().removeAttribute("cats");
  }

  private  String dispPrice( String price)
  {
      int len = price.length();
      if (len <= 2)
         return price;
      else
         return "$" + price.substring(0,len -2) + "." + price.substring(len-2);
  }
%>
```

The jspInit() method attaches an attribute to the servlet context of the JSP. The servlet context of a JSP is completely equivalent to the application implicit object. However, remember from our earlier discussion that implicit objects are not yet set up and are therefore not available from within the jspInit() method. This is why it is necessary to call getServletContext() instead. getServletContext() is a method on the `javax.servlet.Servlet` interface, an interface that the underlying class of a JSP implements. Calling `EShop.getCats()` will return an `ArrayList` containing `Category` objects that describe the categories available in the catalog. Therefore, the following line will attach an attribute with the name `"cats"` to the application implicit object:

```
getServletContext().setAttribute("cats", EShop.getCats());
```

This means that the categories will be attached to the application implicit object when the JSP is first used by the container, even before the first request is processed. `jspInit()` will never be called again, unless the page is destroyed and recreated by the container. Should the page be destroyed to make more room for others, the container will call the `jspDestroy()` method, which will in turn remove the attribute.

Later within the JSP code, you can obtain the categories `ArrayList` using the following Java code:

```
ArrayList cats = (ArrayList) application.getAttribute("cats");
```

This is exactly what happens in the first scriptlet scripting element within the `estore.jsp` page. Note the use of the application implicit object instead of the equivalent but more cumbersome `getServletContext()` call.

You will frequently see this practice of attaching an attribute to an object, to be retrieved during processing by the JSP. This pattern occurs regularly in JSP programming.

Attaching attributes to implicit objects

Attaching attributes to implicit objects is the primary mechanism that enables the different elements of a JSP page to cooperate. It can also be used as a mechanism for passing information between a JSP page and any included JSP page, or even between JSP pages within the same application. Figure 3-6 illustrates the basic action of attaching attributes to JSP implicit objects for request processing.

In Figure 3-6, attributes attached by an element of a JSP page (for example, a declaration scripting element) are later used by another element within the JSP page (a scriptlet element, the `<jsp:UseBean>` standard action, a custom tag, and so on).

Attributes are any Java-based object that can be attached to certain implicit objects using a textual name. JSP or scripting code can then later retrieve an attribute as long as it knows the textual name. The primary implicit objects that you can attach attributes to are the scoping objects, including the following:

❑ `pageContext`

❑ `request`

❑ `session`

❑ `application`

Each of these objects implements an interface that has the `setAttribute()` and `getAttribute()` method, enabling you to attach Java objects as attributes.

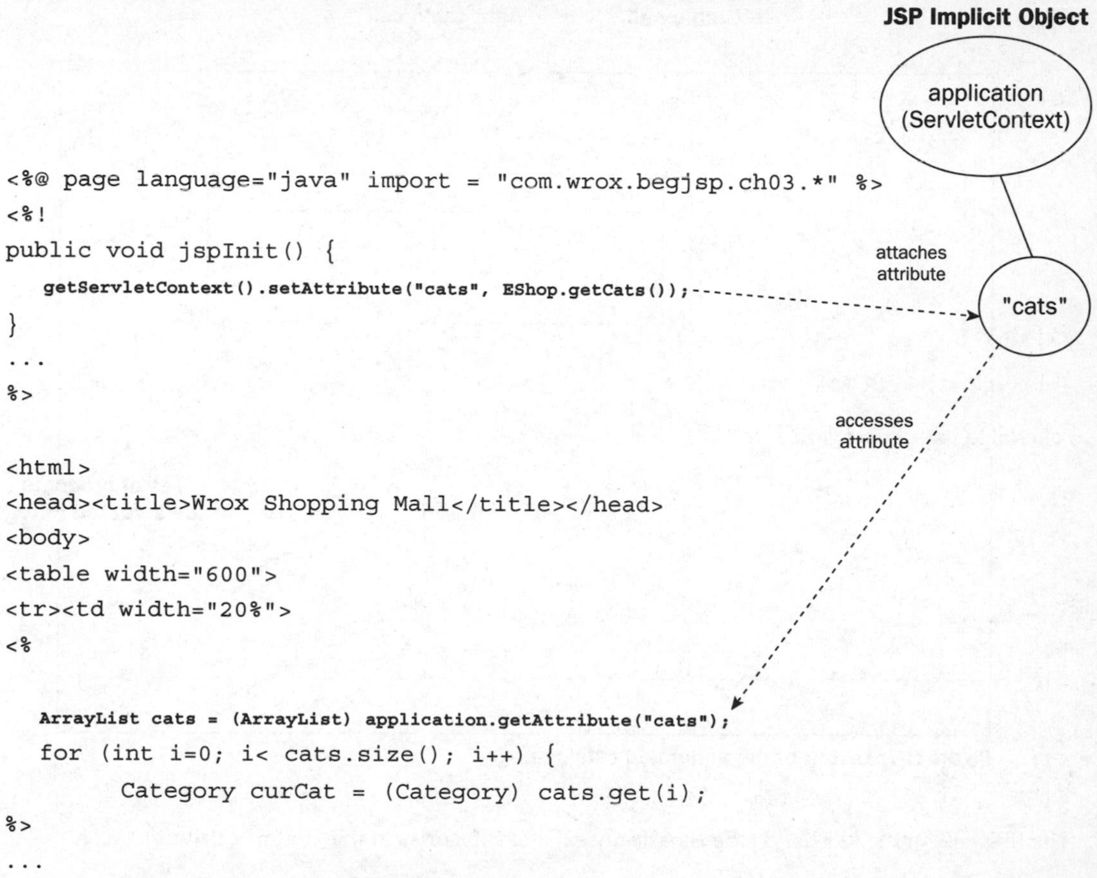

JSP Implicit Object

application
(ServletContext)

```
<%@ page language="java" import = "com.wrox.begjsp.ch03.*" %>
<%!
public void jspInit() {
    getServletContext().setAttribute("cats", EShop.getCats());
}
...
%>


<html>
<head><title>Wrox Shopping Mall</title></head>
<body>
<table width="600">
<tr><td width="20%">
<%


    ArrayList cats = (ArrayList) application.getAttribute("cats");
    for (int i=0; i< cats.size(); i++) {
        Category curCat = (Category) cats.get(i);
%>
...
```

attaches
attribute

"cats"

accesses
attribute

Figure 3-6: Attaching attributes to implicit objects

The following table shows the interfaces that enable attribute attachment for each of the implicit objects.

Implicit Object	Interface/Superclass Supporting Attributes
pageContext	javax.servlet.jsp.JspContext superclass
request	javax.servlet.ServletRequest interface
session	javax.servlet.http.HttpSession interface
application	javax.servlet.ServletContext interface

Each implicit object that supports the attachment of attributes has a unique scoping. Scoping determines how long and under what circumstances the attributes attached will be available. Scoping is explained in detail after the next example.

Let's turn our attention back to estore.jsp; the page is laid out into two table cells, as illustrated in Figure 3-7.

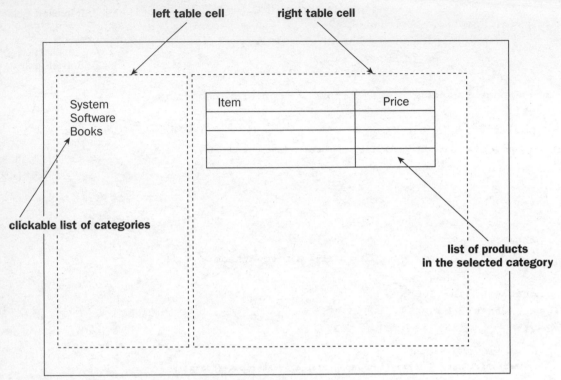

Figure 3-7: Layout of the generated catalog page

The first cell on the left-hand side is basically a list of categories in the "cats" attribute.

Rendering the list of categories

The code that performs the rendering of the list of categories on the left side of Figure 3-7 is reproduced here. The code involves several scriptlet scripting elements mixed among template data (HTML) and expression scripting elements:

```
<td width="20%">
  <%

    ArrayList cats = (ArrayList) application.getAttribute("cats");
    for (int i=0; i< cats.size(); i++)
    {
        Category curCat = (Category) cats.get(i);
  %>
  <a href="<%= request.getRequestURL() + "?catid=" + curCat.getId() %>">
    <%= curCat.getName()  %>
  </a>
  <br/>
  <%
    }
  %>
</td>
```

In the highlighted scriptlet scripting element, note that the `"cats"` attribute is retrieved from the `application` implicit object and placed into the `cats` `ArrayList`. Then the code iterates through all the categories in this list and assigns each category to the temporary `curCat` variable.

The `curCat` variable is then used to display the category name, using the expression scripting element:

```
<%=  curCat.getName()  %>
```

This name is made into a hyperlink using another expression scripting element within an HTML `<a>` element:

```
<a href="<%= request.getRequestURL() + "?catid=" + curCat.getId() %>">
  ...
</a>
```

The `getRequestURL()` method on the request implicit object obtains the URL that is used to access the current JSP. During runtime, this may be transformed to a URL such as the following:

```
http://localhost:8080/ch03/example1/estore.jsp?catid=3
```

You may recognize this as the form submission GET method that was used in Chapter 2 to attach parameters to a request URL. Indeed, this is a technique frequently used in JSP programming to send parameters to another JSP for processing.

While this method of creating a URL is simple and works under most circumstances, it can be problematic when user sessions are used. Sessions are explained later in this chapter. Chapter 6, "JSP Tag Libraries and JSTL," describes some tags that can be used to create URLs that will automatically maintain session information.

Rendering the list of products in a given category

In the right-hand cells of the table in Figure 3-7, the products in the currently selected category are displayed. This cell is rendered using the following code. Note that the structure of the code is very similar to the code presented for the categories list.

```
<table border="1">
  <tr><th align="left">Item</th><th align="left">Price</th></tr>
  <%
    String selectedCat = request.getParameter("catid");
    if (selectedCat == null)
        selectedCat = "1";
    ArrayList items = (ArrayList) EShop.getItems(selectedCat);
    for (int i=0; i< items.size(); i++)
    {
        Product curItem = (Product) items.get(i);
  %>
  <tr>
    <td><%= curItem.getName()   %></td>
    <td><%= dispPrice(String.valueOf(curItem.getPrice())) %></td>
  </tr>
```

```
<%
    }
%>
</table>
```

In the description of the previous section, you saw that clicking a category hyperlink within the left-hand cell generates a (GET method) submit to the estore.jsp with a catid parameter.

The first scriptlet scripting element obtains this catid parameter from the request implicit object. Note that the first time the page is displayed, there is no catid parameter included with the URL. In this case, the default is simply set to the value of "1".

Next, the EShop.getItems() static method call obtains all the products in a category. This is returned in an ArrayList and assigned to a variable called items by the code:

```
ArrayList items = (ArrayList) EShop.getItems(selectedCat);
```

The rest of the code iterates through the list of products in the items ArrayList. Each product's name and price are printed as a table cell. Each product in the items ArrayList will cause a row in the table to be rendered. Note the use of the dispPrice() method, defined in the declaration scripting element, to display the price in $???.?? format.

Adding a Shopping Cart to a Catalog

After finishing the interactive catalog to display categories and products, the next step in building an electronic storefront is adding a shopping cart. This Try It Out exercise reveals how you can add a simple shopping cart to the product catalog example described in the preceding section.

In this example, the user will be enabled to do the following:

1. Browse through the catalog
2. Click a Buy link to place an item into her or his shopping cart
3. Increase the quantity of the product placed into the shopping cart

Try It Out   Adding a Shopping Cart

Use the following URL to test the second example:

```
http://localhost:8080/ch03/example2/estore.jsp
```

You should see the new catalog page, as illustrated in Figure 3-8. It looks the same as the one in the previous Try It Out exercise except that every product displayed now has an associated Buy hyperlink.

Click the Books category on the left-hand side. The list of available books will be displayed, as shown in Figure 3-9.

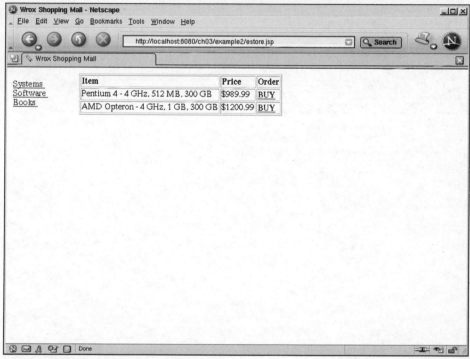

Figure 3-8: Catalog with Buy hyperlink

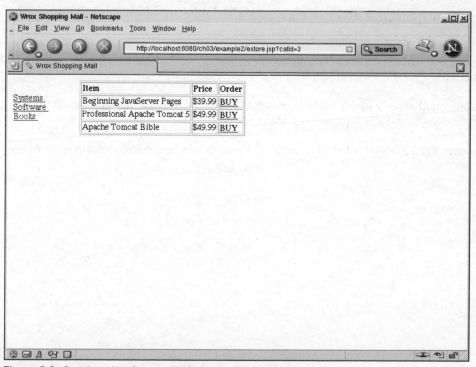

Figure 3-9: Catalog showing available books for purchase

To purchase the Beginning JavaServer Pages book, click the Buy hyperlink. At this point, your shopping cart is displayed, as shown in Figure 3-10.

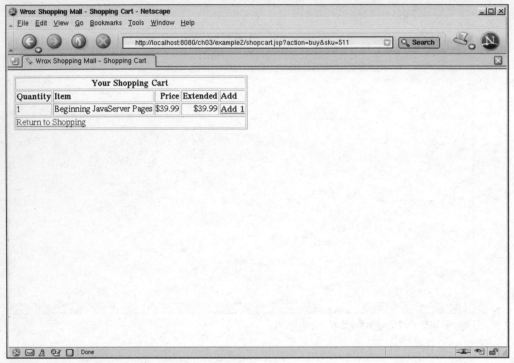

Figure 3-10: Shopping cart with selected book

One copy of the book has been placed into the shopping cart. In Figure 3-10, you can see that the extended price for this order is $39.99.

Now, buy another copy of this book. Do this by clicking the Add 1 hyperlink. You should see the quantity increase to 2, and a new extended price of $79.98, as shown in Figure 3-11.

If you click the Add 1 link a few more times, the quantity and price will increase accordingly.

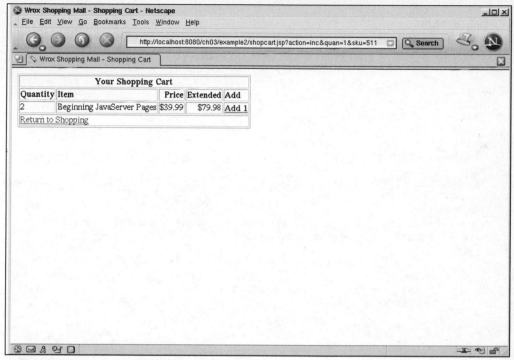

Figure 3-11: Shopping cart with two books

How It Works

To create the Add 1 hyperlink for each product, the estore.jsp file is modified. You can find the modified file at <Tomcat Installation Directory>/webapps/ch03/example2/estore.jsp. The content of this file is reproduced in the following code, with modifications highlighted:

```
<%@ page language="java"
  import = "com.wrox.begjsp.ch03.*,java.util.*" %>
<%!
  public void jspInit()
  {
      getServletContext().setAttribute("cats", EShop.getCats());
  }

  public void jspDestroy()
  {
      getServletContext().removeAttribute("cats");
  }

  private  String dispPrice( String price)
  {
      int len = price.length();
      if (len <= 2)
```

```
                return price;
        else
            return "$" + price.substring(0,len -2) + "." + price.substring(len-2);
  }
%>


<html>
<head>
  <title>Wrox Shopping Mall</title>
</head>
<body>
  <table width="600">
  <tr>
    <td width="20%">
      <%

        ArrayList cats = (ArrayList) application.getAttribute("cats");
        for (int i=0; i< cats.size(); i++)
        {
            Category curCat = (Category) cats.get(i);
      %>
      <a href="<%= request.getRequestURL() + "?catid=" + curCat.getId() %>">
        <%=  curCat.getName()  %>
      </a>
      <br/>
      <%
        }
      %>
    </td>
    <td>
      <h1></h1>
      <table border="1">
        <tr><th align="left">Item</th><th align="left">Price</th>
          <th align="left">Order</th></tr>
        <%
        String selectedCat = request.getParameter("catid");
        if (selectedCat == null)
            selectedCat = "1";
        ArrayList items = (ArrayList) EShop.getItems(selectedCat);
        for (int i=0; i< items.size(); i++)
        {
            Product curItem = (Product) items.get(i);
        %>
        <tr>
        <td><%= curItem.getName()   %></td>
        <td><%= dispPrice(String.valueOf(curItem.getPrice())) %></td>
        <td><a href="<%= request.getContextPath() +
"/example2/shopcart.jsp?action=buy&sku=" + curItem.getSku() %>">
          <b>BUY</b></a>
        </td>
        </tr>
        <%
          }
        %>
```

```
          </table>
        </td>
      </tr>
    </table>

  </body>
</html>
```

The highlighted code creates a hyperlink out of the word BUY. This is done via the generation of an `<a>` HTML element. The URL generated for the `href` attribute of the `<a>` elements is as follows:

```
http://localhost:8080/ch03/example2/shopcart.jsp?action=buy&sku=511
```

This URL will call up the `shopcart.jsp` page, with two parameters. The first parameter is `action`, with value `"buy"`. The second parameter is `sku`, and the value is the actual `sku` of the product that you have selected.

Creating the Shopping Cart

The shopping cart is implemented in the `shopcart.jsp` page. The `shopcart.jsp` page can be located at `<Tomcat Installation Directory>/webapps/ch03/example2/shopcart.jsp`. It is reproduced here with the scripting elements highlighted:

```
<%@ page language="java"
   import = "com.wrox.begjsp.ch03.*,java.util.*" %>

<%!
  private static String EXAMPLE = "/example2";
  private static String SHOP_PAGE = "/estore.jsp";
  private static String CART_PAGE = "/shopcart.jsp";

  private  String dispPrice( String price)
  {
      int len = price.length();
      if (len <= 2)
          return price;
      else
          return "$" + price.substring(0,len -2) + "." + price.substring(len-2);
  }
%>

<html>
<head>
  <title>Wrox Shopping Mall - Shopping Cart</title>
</head>
<body>

  <%
    int quan = 1;
    String action = request.getParameter("action");
    if (action.equals("inc"))
```

```
      {
           String oldQuan = request.getParameter("quan");
           quan = Integer.parseInt(oldQuan);
           quan++;
      }  // else - action=buy

%>
<table width="600">
    <tr>
      <td>
        <h1></h1>
        <table border="1">
          <tr><th colspan="5">Your Shopping Cart</th></tr>
          <tr><th align="left">Quantity</th><th align="left">Item</th>
            <th align="right">Price</th>
            <th align="right">Extended</th>
            <th align="left">Add</th>
          </tr>

          <%
            String sku = request.getParameter("sku");
            Product item = null;
            if (sku != null)
                item = EShop.getItem(sku);
          %>

          <tr>
            <td><%= quan %></td>
            <td><%= item.getName()    %></td>
            <td align="right"><%= dispPrice(String.valueOf(item.getPrice())))
%></td>
            <td align="right"><%= dispPrice(String.valueOf(item.getPrice() * quan))
%></td>
            <td>
              <a href="<%= request.getContextPath() + EXAMPLE + CART_PAGE +
"?action=inc&quan=" + quan + "&sku=" + sku %>">
                <b>Add 1</b></a>
            </td>
          </tr>

          <tr>
            <td colspan="5">
              <a href="<%= request.getContextPath() + EXAMPLE + SHOP_PAGE %>">
Return to Shopping</a>
            </td>
          </tr>

        </table>
      </td>
    </tr>
  </table>
</body>
</html>
```

The initial declaration scripting element contains the same `dispPrice()` method for formatting the product price. It also contains three constant declarations for `EXAMPLE`, `SHOP_PAGE`, and `CART_PAGE`.

Decoding incoming request parameters

The first scriptlet scripting element decodes the incoming URL parameters. This element is reproduced here for convenience:

```
<%
    int quan = 1;
    String action =  request.getParameter("action");
    if (action.equals("inc"))
    {
        String oldQuan = request.getParameter("quan");
        quan = Integer.parseInt(oldQuan);
        quan++;
    }  // else - action=buy

%>
```

The variable `quan` tracks the quantity of the item. It defaults to 1. The default is used when the Buy hyperlink on the `estore.jsp` page is clicked. In this case, the incoming URL is similar to the following:

```
http://localhost:8080/ch03/example2/shopcart.jsp?action=buy&sku=511
```

Note that there is no `quan` request parameter in the URL, resulting in the use of the default quantity of 1.

If the Add 1 link on the `shopcart.jsp` page is clicked, the incoming URL is similar to the following:

```
http://localhost:8080/ch03/example2/shopcart.jsp?action=inc&quan=3&sku=511
```

Note that in this case, the URL has a `quan` request parameter. The default will not be used in this case. The `quan` parameter contains the quantity displayed before the Add 1 link is clicked. The action in this case is `inc` instead of `buy`. The preceding code ensures that the quantity is increased by 1 when the Add 1 link is clicked.

The second scriptlet scripting element in `shopcart.jsp` decodes the `sku` request parameter. This element is reproduced here:

```
<%
    String sku = request.getParameter("sku");
    Product item = null;
    if (sku != null)
        item = EShop.getItem(sku);
%>
```

In this case, if an `sku` parameter is available, the method `EShop.getItem()` is called. This method will retrieve the product associated with `sku` parameter. The preceding code assigns the `item` variable with this product.

Rendering order information

The order information is rendered as a row of the HTML table, as shown by the following code:

```
<tr>
  <td><%= quan %></td>
  <td><%= item.getName()    %></td>
  <td align="right"><%= dispPrice(String.valueOf(item.getPrice()))  %></td>
  <td align="right"><%= dispPrice(String.valueOf(item.getPrice() * quan))  %></td>
  <td>
  <a href="<%= request.getContextPath() + EXAMPLE + CART_PAGE + "?action=inc&quan="
+ quan + "&sku=" + sku %>">
    <b>Add 1</b>
  </a>
  </td>
</tr>
```

The quan variable is used within an expression scripting element to render the current quantity ordered. It is also used within the expression scripting element that renders the extended price. The item variable is used to access the name and price of the product (associated with the incoming sku request parameter). The dispPrice() method is used for both the price and extended price cells to format the output. The URL within the href attribute of the <a> HTML element around the Add 1 hyperlink is rendered here. It is typically in a form similar to the following:

```
http://localhost:8080/ch03/example2/shopcart.jsp?action=inc&quan=3&sku=511
```

Rendering the Return to Shopping hyperlink

The final expression scripting element in shopcart.jsp renders an HTML row that has a hyperlink for returning to the estore.jsp page. The code is as follows:

```
<tr>
  <td colspan="5">
  <a href="<%= request.getContextPath() + EXAMPLE + SHOP_PAGE %>">
Return to Shopping</a>
  </td>
</tr>
```

This code makes use of the getContextPath() method of the request implicit object. This will return a portion of the URL used to access this page, up to the application name (ch03 in our case). The constants EXAMPLE and SHOP_PAGE are appended, resulting in a URL similar to the following:

```
http://localhost:8080/ch03/example2/estore.jsp
```

The highlighted portion of the URL represents the portion returned by the getContextPath() method.

This concludes the coverage of how the shopping cart works in example 2. This implementation has some major limitations, however, as described in the following section.

Shopping cart limitations

To observe the limitations of this shopping cart, first repeat the action of the previous Try It Out exercise. This will result in two books in the shopping cart, similar to what is shown in Figure 3-11.

At this point, click the Return to Shopping hyperlink. This results in the display of the catalog page (refer to Figure 3-8), showing the available systems.

Now click the Software category on the left side. The list of software products is now displayed, as shown in Figure 3-12.

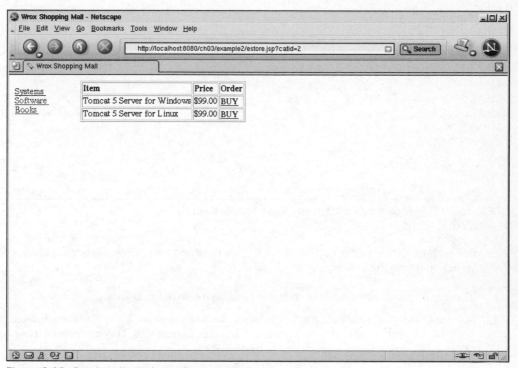

Figure 3-12: Catalog displaying software selection

Click the Buy link of the *Tomcat 5 Server for Windows* product. This will return you to the shopping cart, as shown in Figure 3-13.

The limitations of this shopping cart should be evident at this point:

❑   The shopping cart displays only the most recently purchased product.

❑   The previously purchased book has disappeared forever.

The next Try It Out exercise will eliminate these limitations. However, it is important to appreciate why these limitations exist.

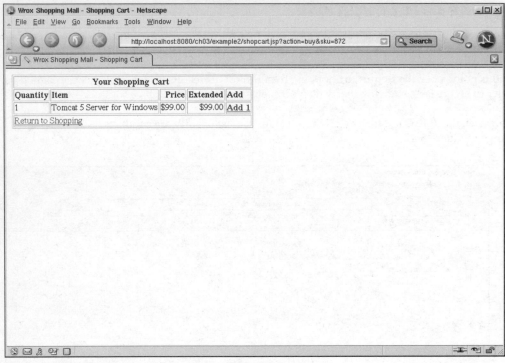

Figure 3-13: Shopping cart after purchase of Tomcat 5 server

If you consider how the shopping cart (shopcart.jsp) page and the catalog (estore.jsp) page work together, you will notice the following:

❑   There is no mechanism to remember what has been ordered previously.

❑   All communication and data passing between the two pages are limited to the parameters with the URL request; namely the action, sku, and quan parameters. This mechanism does not allow information for multiple items to be passed.

Overcoming the shopping cart limitations

Two steps are needed to overcome these limitations:

1.   Create a mechanism to remember what had been ordered.

2.   Use a communication mechanism that can pass an unlimited row of product and quantity information.

The following Try It Out exercise provides both. Try the example and see for yourself.

Try It Out   Overcoming the Shopping Cart Limitations

Access example 3 via the following URL:

```
http://localhost:8080/ch03/example3/estore.jsp
```

The catalog is displayed as shown in Figure 3-8 in the preceding Try It Out exercise.

The Systems category is displayed by default. The list of available systems are displayed on the right-hand side of the page. Click the Buy hyperlink of the first system (Pentium 4), adding it to your shopping cart. The improved shopping cart is now displayed as shown in Figure 3-14.

This new shopping cart calculates the total price of the order on a separate row of the table. It also has a link to clear the cart.

Now, click the Add 1 hyperlink to add another Pentium system. As shown in Figure 3-15, the cart shows two Pentium systems, and the total price is updated.

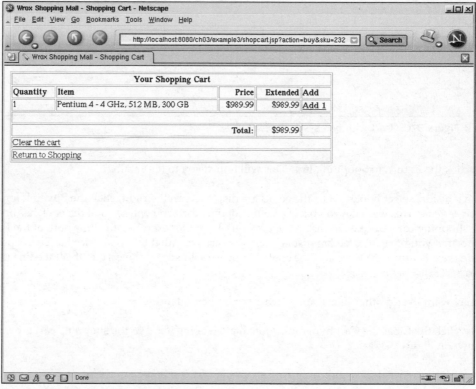

Figure 3-14: Example 3 shopping cart

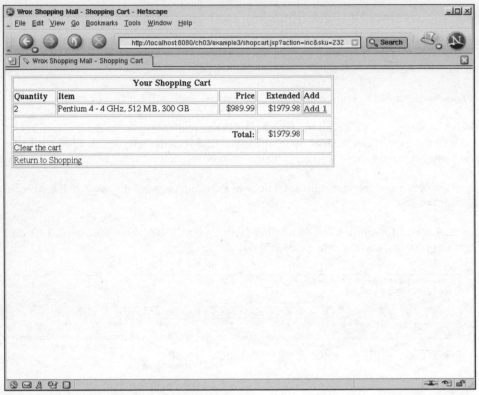

Figure 3-15: Cart with two systems ordered

Next, click the Return to Shopping link. This will return you to the catalog.

On the left side, select Books. Once the books are displayed on the right, click the Buy link for *Beginning JavaServer Pages*. This will take you back to your shopping cart. You will see that the book has been added to the shopping cart. Unlike the cart in the previous Try It Out exercise, this time both of the Pentium systems that you have ordered are displayed in the cart. Note that the total price has been updated to include the 2 Pentium systems and the book. Figure 3-16 illustrates the cart, with all the line items shown.

You may want to add other items, and try increasing their quantity.

Finally, click the Clear the Cart hyperlink. Note that all of the items in the shopping cart are now cleared, as shown in Figure 3-17.

The next section reveals how this improved shopping cart works behind the scenes.

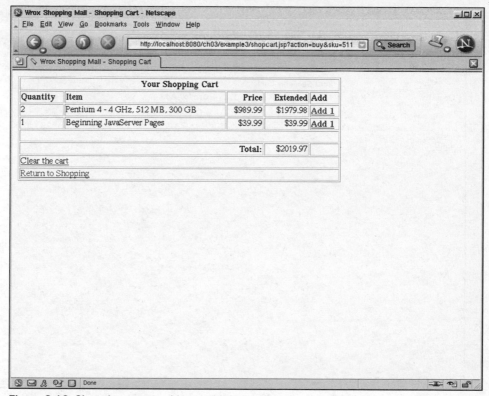

Figure 3-16: Shopping cart tracking multiple line items

How It Works

To implement this improved cart, the following new pieces are needed:

- ❑ A Java class that represents a single line item in the cart, called LineItem
- ❑ A new ArrayList of LineItems objects to track the objects ordered

The LineItem class has properties called quantity, sku, description, and price. The code for this Java class can be found in the com.wrox.begjsp.ch03 package. The source code for this package is located in the <Tomcat Installation Directory>/webapps/WEB-INF/classes directory. You may wish to study the source code for this class; this chapter focuses only on the JSP usage of this class.

The ArrayList to track products ordered is created within the shopping cart JSP code, presented next.

The estore.jsp for example 3, located at <Tomcat Installation Directory>/webapps/ch03/example3/estore.jsp, is identical to estore.jsp in the second Try It Out exercise, earlier in this chapter. This page is not presented again.

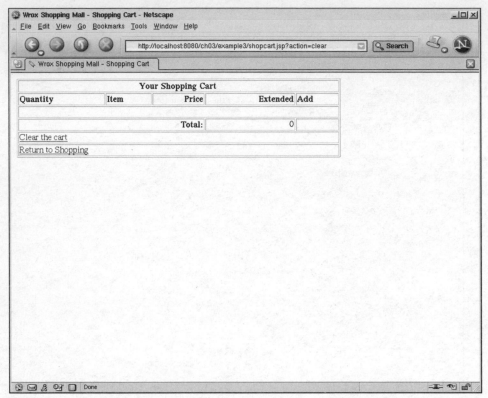

Figure 3-17: Shopping cart after clearing it of items

The shopcart.jsp for the current example is significantly different, and is located in
<Tomcat Installation Directory>/webapps/ch03/example3/shopcart.jsp. The code for this
shopcart.jsp is reproduced here, with major differences from the previous version highlighted:

```jsp
<%@ page language="java"
   import = "com.wrox.begjsp.ch03.*,java.util.*" session="true" %>

<%!
   private static String EXAMPLE = "/example3";
   private static String SHOP_PAGE = "/estore.jsp";
   private static String CART_PAGE = "/shopcart.jsp";

   private  String dispPrice( String price)
   {
       int len = price.length();
       if (len <= 2)
           return price;
       else
           return "$" + price.substring(0,len -2) + "." + price.substring(len-2);
   }
%>
```

```html
<html>
<head>
  <title>Wrox Shopping Mall - Shopping Cart</title>
</head>
<body>

  <%
    ArrayList items = (ArrayList) session.getAttribute("lineitems");
    String action =  request.getParameter("action");
    String sku = request.getParameter("sku");
    Product prod = null;
    if (sku != null)
        prod = EShop.getItem(sku);

    if (items == null)
    {  // add first item
        items = new ArrayList();
        items.add(new LineItem(1,sku,prod.getName(),
          prod.getPrice() ));
        session.setAttribute("lineitems", items);
    }
    else  if (action.equals("clear"))
        {
            items.clear();
        }
        else
        {
            boolean itemFound = false;
            // check to see if sku exists
            for (int i=0; i<items.size(); i++)
            {
                LineItem curItem = (LineItem) items.get(i);
                if (curItem.getSku().equals(sku))
                {
                    itemFound = true;
                    curItem.setQuantity(curItem.getQuantity() + 1);
                    break;
                }  // of if
            } //of for

            if (!itemFound)
                items.add(new LineItem(1,sku,prod.getName(),
                  prod.getPrice() ));

        } // of final else

    int total = 0;
  %>
  <table width="600">
    <tr>
      <td>
        <h1></h1>
        <table border="1" width="600">
          <tr><th colspan="5">Your Shopping Cart</th></tr>
          <tr><th align="left">Quantity</th><th align="left">Item</th><th
align="right">Price</th>
```

```
                <th align="right">Extended</th>
                <th align="left">Add</th></tr>

        <%
          for (int i=0; i< items.size(); i++)
          {
              LineItem curItem = (LineItem) items.get(i);
              int quan = curItem.getQuantity();
              long price = curItem.getPrice();
              long extended = quan * price;
              total += extended;
        %>

        <tr>
          <td><%= quan %></td>
          <td><%= curItem.getDesc()   %></td>
          <td align="right"><%= dispPrice(String.valueOf(price))   %></td>
          <td align="right"><%= dispPrice(String.valueOf(extended))  %></td>
          <td>
            <a href="<%= request.getContextPath() + EXAMPLE + CART_PAGE +
"?action=inc&sku=" + curItem.getSku() %>">
              <b>Add 1</b></a>
          </td>
        </tr>
        <%
          }
        %>
        <tr>
          <td colspan="5">  
          </td>
        </tr>
        <tr>
          <td colspan="3" align="right"><b>Total:</b></td>
          <td align="right"><%= dispPrice(String.valueOf(total)) %></td>
          <td> </td>
        </tr>
        <tr>
          <td colspan="5">
            <a href="<%= request.getContextPath() + EXAMPLE + CART_PAGE +
"?action=clear" %>">
              Clear the cart</a>
          </td>
        </tr>


        <tr>
          <td colspan="5">
            <a href="<%= request.getContextPath() + EXAMPLE + SHOP_PAGE %>">
Return to Shopping</a>
          </td>
        </tr>

      </table>
    </td>
```

```
    </tr>
  </table>
</body>
</html>
```

The first thing to note in this new `shopcart.jsp` is the new attribute, `session`, specified in the `<%@ page>` directive. The directive is reproduced here for reference:

```
<%@ page language="java"
import = "com.wrox.begjsp.ch03.*,java.util.*" session="true" %>
```

Specifying `session="true"` tells the JSP container explicitly that this page should participate in a session. While it is stated explicitly here for learning purposes, it is not necessary because the default value, when the attribute is not specified, is `true`. It is important to understand what a session is and how it is implemented.

Sessions and JSPs

A session is a managed object that resides on the server, within the JSP container. The main purpose of a session is to track incoming requests from the same user.

To understand the need for sessions, it is necessary to reexamine only the second Try It Out exercise. Observe the way that request URLs are marked up to include parameters (such as `action`, `sku`, `quan`), and think about what actually happens between the user's browser and the JSP container.

When the user clicks a Buy link on the `estore.jsp` in this example, the browser requests a URL similar to the following:

```
http://localhost:8080/ch03/example2/shopcart.jsp?action=buy&sku=511
```

From the perspective of the JSP container, an independent request (unrelated to the original request for `estore.jsp`) is asking for the `shopcart.jsp` page. The only things that link the two independent requests are the parameters encoded at the end of the URL.

From the perspective of the users, the two requests are absolutely related. When they click the Buy link, they expect to see the product in the shopping cart. This kind of perceived relationship between independent requests from the user perspective is the main motivation for establishing a session. A session binds these logically related requests together.

Therefore, it should be clear that you can encode GET method parameters to a URL within a generated page to create the illusion that two separate JSP pages belong to the same "session."

However, this method is clearly limited. There is no easy way to encode an entire shopping cart, full of items, to the same URL. Fortunately, this is a very common need, and the JSP container manages a session object specifically for this purpose. Figure 3-18 illustrates the JSP managed session.

In Figure 3-18a, encoding in the URL is used to tie together requests in the same session. All the data parameters are attached to the request by the JSPs in the application. In Figure 3-18b, the JSP container manages the session. The application only needs to attach data to the `session` implicit object as attributes. Any JSP element or JSP pages in the same session can then access these attributes for rendering.

(a) Using URL with encoded parameters

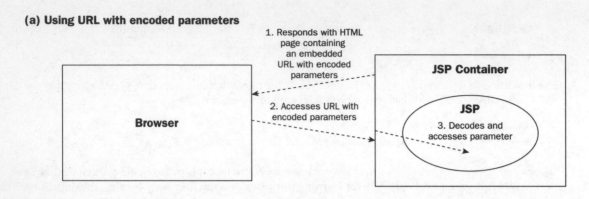

(b) Using container-managed session

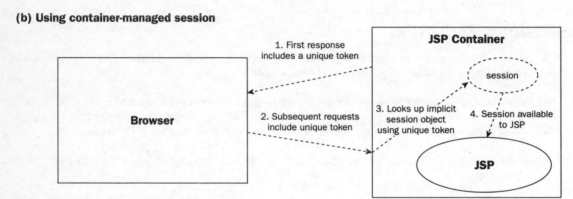

Figure 3-18: Session in JSP container

Session implementation

The JSP container cooperates with the browser to implement sessions using the standard HTTP protocol. A JSP developer never needs to implement sessions or work directly with the session implementation mechanism. JSP developers can take advantage of sessions in the following simple ways:

❑   By specifying in a `<@page>` directive that the page should have a session (or leaving it unspecified and using the `session="true"` default)

❑   By attaching attributes to the `session` implicit object, and writing rendering code that uses the attribute

In some cases, however, it is advantageous to have an appreciation for how sessions are actually implemented behind the scenes. The most common method for implementing a session is via *cookies*. Figure 3-19 illustrates this method of session implementation.

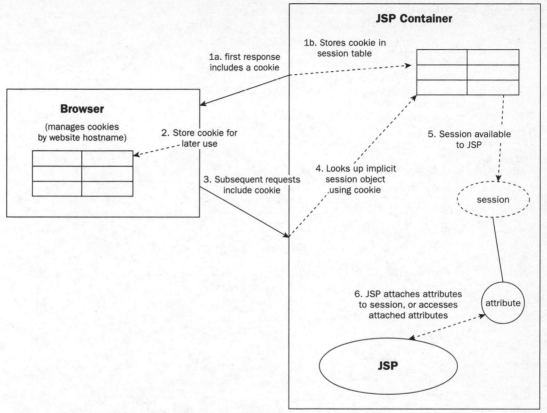

Figure 3-19: Session implementation using cookies

In Figure 3-19, the JSP container creates a unique token called a cookie and hands it to the browser on the first incoming request. The browser is programmed to hand this unique token back to the JSP container on subsequent requests (all modern browsers support cookies). Within the JSP container, a table maps the cookie's unique value to a session object. When a request comes into the JSP container, it is checked for a cookie. If a cookie is found, it is used to look up the session. Because the session object can have an unlimited number of attributes attached to it, the cookie (a very small token) can potentially be used to access a very large set of session-specific data (shopping cart information, user preferences, and so on).

Using a session to track line items in a shopping cart

Let's turn our attention back to the examination of the new shopcart.jsp; the code that maintains the line items in the current shopping cart is the first scriptlet scripting element, reproduced here for reference:

```
<%
    ArrayList items = (ArrayList) session.getAttribute("lineitems");
    String action =  request.getParameter("action");
    String sku = request.getParameter("sku");
    Product prod = null;
```

```
    if (sku != null)
        prod = EShop.getItem(sku);

    if (items == null)
    {  // add first item
        items = new ArrayList();
        items.add(new LineItem(1,sku,prod.getName(),
          prod.getPrice() ));
        session.setAttribute("lineitems", items);
    }
    else  if (action.equals("clear"))
          {
              items.clear();
          }
          else
          {
              boolean itemFound = false;
              // check to see if sku exists
              for (int i=0; i<items.size(); i++)
              {
                  LineItem curItem = (LineItem) items.get(i);
                  if (curItem.getSku().equals(sku))
                  {
                      itemFound = true;
                      curItem.setQuantity(curItem.getQuantity() + 1);
                      break;
                  }  // of if
              } //of for

              if (!itemFound)
                  items.add(new LineItem(1,sku,prod.getName(),
                    prod.getPrice() ));

          } // of final else

     int total = 0;
%>
```

This preceding Java code handles the decoding of three different types of requests:

❑ **When the user first clicks a Buy link in a session:** A session attribute called `lineitems` does not exist in this case. Create a new `ArrayList` of `LineItems` and attach it with the name `lineitems`. The product that the user wishes to purchase should be added to this initial `ArrayList` as a `LineItem`.

❑ **When the user clicks the Clear the Cart link:** The request carries an `action` parameter with the `clear` value; delete everything in the `lineitems` `ArrayList`.

❑ **When the user clicks the Add 1 link on the shopping cart for a specific line item:** The request carries an `action` parameter with the `inc` value. Go through the `lineitems` `ArrayList` and find the `LineItem` with the incoming `sku` and increase the quantity ordered.

Rendering the shopping cart using a session attribute

The table of line items is rendered by the following code:

```
<%
  for (int i=0; i< items.size(); i++)
  {
      LineItem curItem = (LineItem) items.get(i);
      int quan = curItem.getQuantity();
      long price = curItem.getPrice();
      long extended = quan * price;
      total += extended;
%>
```

```
<tr>
  <td><%= quan %></td>
  <td><%= curItem.getDesc()   %></td>
  <td align="right"><%= dispPrice(String.valueOf(price))  %></td>
  <td align="right"><%= dispPrice(String.valueOf(extended))  %></td>
  <td>
     <a href="<%= request.getContextPath() + EXAMPLE + CART_PAGE +
"?action=inc&sku=" + curItem.getSku() %>">
        <b>Add 1</b></a>
  </td>
</tr>
<%
  }
%>
```

The initial scriptlet scripting element contains the `for` loop that will render a table row for each `LineItem` in the `items` `ArrayList` (previously fetched from the session). The quantity is extracted from the `LineItem` to calculate the extended price. A variable called `total` is used to sum all the extended prices.

Rendering the total order price and the Clear the Cart hyperlink

The final segment of new code in `shopcart.jsp` renders the total price and the new Clear the Cart hyperlink, each in its own HTML table row:

```
<tr>
  <td colspan="3" align="right"><b>Total:</b></td>
  <td align="right"><%= dispPrice(String.valueOf(total)) %></td>
  <td> </td>
</tr>
```

```
<tr>
  <td colspan="5">
     <a href="<%= request.getContextPath() + EXAMPLE + CART_PAGE + "?action=clear"
%>">
     Clear the cart</a>
  </td>
</tr>
```

The Clear the Cart hyperlink has a URL with the value of the action parameter set to clear. This is a specific case handled by the first scriptlet scripting element on this page, and will clear everything within the lineitems session attribute.

Scoping of implicit objects in JSP

The final topic covered in this chapter is the scoping of implicit objects. Earlier in this chapter, you learned that typical JSP programming may involve the attachment of Java object attributes to one of the four JSP implicit objects:

❑ pageContext

❑ request

❑ session

❑ application

In Java programming terms, a reference to the attributes is maintained by one of these objects when an attribute is attached. Because destroying an implicit object will cause all attached attributes to disappear, the lifetime of the attributes depends on the lifetime of the object they are attached to.

The lifetime of an attribute and the accessibility of an attribute together make up the scope of the attribute. The following table summarizes the different scopes available when attributes are attached to the different implicit objects.

Implicit Object	Scope	Lifetime	Accessibility
pageContext	Page scope	Lasts only until all the output for the current request has been rendered, or when request processing is passed to another JSP page.	Accessible only within the current JSP page.
request	Request scope	Lasts until the end of the processing of the current request. This means that the object is still valid if the same request is being passed to another JSP page for processing.	Accessible from all the JSP pages that service the same request.
session	Session scope	Lasts until the end of the session. Note that a session can last over many independent requests. The precise lifetime of a session depends on the container.	Accessible from all the session-aware JSP pages (session attribute set to true with a <%@page> directive) that are accessed within the same session.

Implicit Object	Scope	Lifetime	Accessibility
application	Application scope	Lasts until the entire application is unloaded by the JSP container — for example, if the ch03 application is stopped or ch03.war undeployed.	Accessible within all the JSP pages within the application. This is the global scope.

In the third Try It Out exercise in this chapter, the lineitems attribute is attached to the request implicit object and therefore has a request scope. The cats attribute, however, is attached to the application scope within the jspInit() method in the estore.jsp page. This means that cats should be accessible from any JSP page within the same ch03 application. To convince yourself of this, try to access the following URL:

```
http://localhost:8080/ch03/examplex/showglob.jsp
```

You should see a list of the available categories, as shown in Figure 3-20.

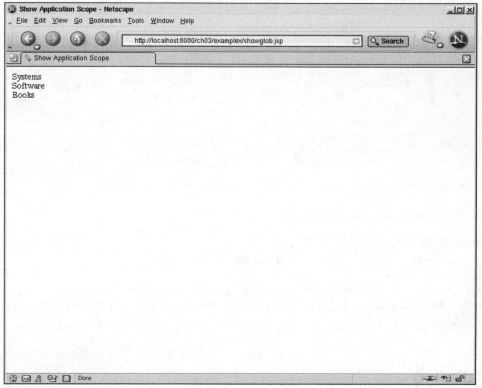

Figure 3-20: Accessing the cats application-scoped attribute

This shows that the `cats` attribute remains available, long after the earlier session testing. This global `cats` attribute is attached to the application scope, and accessed by the `showglob.jsp` page. The `showglob.jsp` file can be located at `<Tomcat Installation Directory>/webapps/ch03/examplex/showglob.jsp`. It is reproduced here, with scripting elements highlighted:

```
<%@ page language="java"
   import = "com.wrox.begjsp.ch03.*,java.util.*" %>
<html>
<head>
  <title>Show Application Scope</title>
</head>
<body>
  <table width="600">
    <tr>
      <td>
        <%
          ArrayList cats = (ArrayList) application.getAttribute("cats");
          for (int i=0; i< cats.size(); i++)
          {
              Category curCat = (Category) cats.get(i);
        %>

          <%= curCat.getName () %>

        <br/>
        <%
          }
        %>
      </td>
    </tr>
  </table>

</body>
</html>
```

The `cats` attribute is still available to `showglob.jsp` despite the following:

❑   `showglob.jsp` does not create the `cats` attribute.

❑   `estore.jsp` is executed before `showglob.jsp`.

❑   `showglob.jsp` is not even part of example 3.

Herein lie both the benefits and shortcomings of the application scope. The application scope is global to the entire application, allowing its attributes to be accessed by any JSP or other Web elements within the same application.

Summary

The JSP standard, prior to JSP 2.0, had shortcomings that necessitated the use of embedded Java programming code. In the earliest JSP incarnation, JSP 1.0, this was absolutely necessary.

Due to the existence of legacy code, the practicing JSP developer must be familiar with the mechanism and techniques used for embedding Java code within JSP. The primary mechanism for embedding Java code within JSP is through scripting elements.

Through three successive Try It Out exercises, you have thoroughly explored scripting elements in the form of declarations, expressions, and scriptlets.

Also presented in this chapter was an e-commerce example of an electronic storefront, which demonstrated the following concepts:

- How to implement an interactive catalog showing categories of products

- How to implement a working shopping cart

- How to use Java objects as attributes to pass information between JSP elements or multiple JSP pages

- How to use implicit JSP objects that support the attachment of attributes, and the lifetime of these implicit objects

- The importance of scoping in JSP, and how to take advantage of it in your applications

- The idea of a session, and how to make use of it in e-commerce applications

Exercises

1. Modify the `shopcart.jsp` in the third Try It Out exercise to calculate an 8 percent sales tax and print the grand total.

2. Modify `shopcart.jsp` in the third Try It Out exercise to include adding a link on each line item to subtract 1 from the displayed quantity.

CSS, JavaScript, VBScript, and JSP

You can use JSP as the vehicle to provide an interactive user experience over the Web. The previous chapter illustrated how this might be accomplished in an e-commerce environment. Creating a dynamic Web-based user interface is the primary way in which the JSP technology is used within Web-based applications.

Knowing that JSP can be used to generate the HTML-based user interface, readers who are Webmasters or Web site designers may have another question on their minds. If JSP is such a flexible dynamic presentation environment, maybe it can be used to generate some of the client-side user interface elements too. More specifically, it is very interesting to consider what can be achieved when JSP is used to generate client-side Web page elements, including the following:

- ❑ Cascading Stylesheet coding
- ❑ JavaScript coding
- ❑ VBScript coding

This chapter explores the exciting possibilities that are available when JSP is used in generating these elements. Unlike JSP logic, these elements have the unique property that they are interpreted and executed by the Web browser on the client side. Because it is possible to use JSP to generate code that will be executed on the client side, developers can enjoy features and capabilities beyond anything achievable via plain HTML and stylesheets.

In this chapter, two examples are presented. The first example shows how to implement a customizable user preference selector using JSP. Using this technique, you can enable your users to customize the style and look of their interactive experience. Behind the scenes, JSP is used to dynamically generate the Cascading Stylesheets (CSS) script that affects the look of the pages displayed by the browser.

The second example illustrates a technique to customize an interactive drop-down menu, enabling the user to control the selections on the menu. HTML designers will recognize this as a DHTML (Dynamic HTML) menu. Using JSP, a portion of the JavaScript code of the menu is generated on the fly, resulting in DHTML that is customized to the application's need or the user's preference.

After reading this chapter and going through these examples, you will:

❑ Understand how you can use JSP to gain fine-grain control over the look-and-feel of the interactive Web-based user interface

❑ Appreciate how JSP can be used to generate CSS and JavaScript/VBScript elements that will be executed on the client's browser

❑ Learn one way to customize user preferences for your own Web application using JSP

❑ Learn how to implement a JSP-based customizable DHTML menu for your Web applications

❑ Appreciate how JSP can be effective in generating user interface elements beyond simple HTML

Code Elements That Execute on the Client Side

The template data in the JSP pages within the examples thus far have been HTML. However, modern Web pages contain more that just HTML. In fact, most Web pages contain non-HTML elements that may include some of the following:

❑ CSS (Cascading Stylesheets)

❑ JavaScript or VBScript code

All of the elements listed are sent to the browser with the HTML page. These elements are then processed by the client's browser. Figure 4-1 illustrates this.

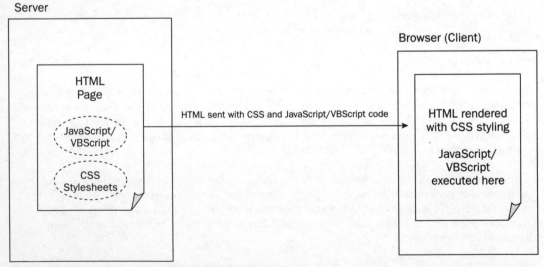

Figure 4-1: Elements that execute on the client side

In Figure 4-1, the CSS stylesheets are sent to the browser, and used by the browser's CSS processor to stylize the HTML rendering. The JavaScript or VBScript code is also sent to the browser. This code will be executed by the JavaScript or VBScript interpreter within the browser. Almost all modern browsers, including the most popular Internet Explorer 6.*x* and Netscape 7.*x* versions, support CSS and JavaScript. VBScript is unique to Microsoft's browsers.

The CSS, JavaScript, and VBScript elements originate from the server, and are often embedded as a part of the base HTML page. Because JSP is frequently used to generate HTML, these elements are also subjected to dynamic generation using JSP. Figure 4-2 shows JSP being used to generate these elements dynamically.

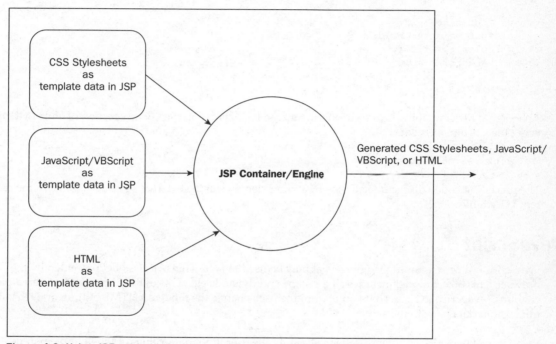

Figure 4-2: Using JSP to dynamically generate CSS, JavaScript, or VBScript

In Figure 4-2, CSS and JavaScript/VBScript coding are all template data within a JSP. Portions of the resulting JSP output are generated upon the receipt of an incoming request by the JSP container. This allows for the customization of the output depending on the incoming request. JSP scoping mechanisms, including sessions, may also be used to customize the generated output.

Cascading Stylesheets

A Cascading Stylesheet (CSS) is a set of style descriptions that can be used to affect how the browser displays (renders) specific HTML elements. Some versions of CSS may also be used to format XML data, rendering it as HTML formatted data.

119

Individual HTML elements can be associated with style elements in a CSS. The style elements describe how the associated HTML element should appear on the page. Note that any single CSS style element can be associated with many HTML elements. CSS enables a Web designer to separate the HTML structural layout from the formatting and styling. If the CSS element is changed, the corresponding HTML element will be rendered with the modified style, without affecting the HTML structure.

CSS elements can be included within an HTML page using the `<style>` element. For example, the following HTML segment embeds a CSS style class definition called `.boxTitle` into the page:

```
<style>
  .boxTitle
  {
     font-size : 22;
     font-weight : bold;
     color : #ffffff;
     background-color: blue;
  }
</style>
```

An external file containing CSS styling elements can be included in the `<head>` section of an HTML page using the `<link>` element:

```
<link rel=stylesheet type="text/css" href="portal.css">
```

The preceding code will include all the CSS styling elements in the external `portal.css` file in the current HTML file.

JavaScript

JavaScript is a programming language that may be used to access the object model presented by the browser. This object model includes all the static and dynamic elements of the displayed/rendered page, enabling JavaScript to access data input from the user, change the rendered HTML output, or even submit custom data back to the server.

Frequently, JavaScript coding is used in validating the user input data values or when implementing dynamic behavior on a displayed Web page.

JavaScript has a turbulent history. During the early years of the browser wars, competing browser vendors (Netscape, Microsoft, and so on) supported different dialects of JavaScript and browser object models that were basically incompatible. Fortunately, the emergence of an ECMA (European Computer Manufacturers Association) standard JavaScript subset, coupled with the reduced competition in the browser space, has resulted in more compatible JavaScript dialects in modern versions of browsers. Even today, it is not uncommon to see scripting code that will detect a specific version of a browser, and then branch to version-specific coding.

JavaScript code can be included in an HTML page via the `<script>` HTML element. For example, the following HTML fragment embeds some JavaScript declarations into the page:

```
<script language="JavaScript">
  var keepstatic=1
```

```
    var menucolor="green"
    var submenuwidth=150
</script>
```

In addition, a file consisting of JavaScript code can be included inline into an HTML page using the following variant of the `<script>` element:

```
<script language="JavaScript" src="menu.js"></script>
```

The preceding code will include the JavaScript code within the `menu.js` file at the location where the `<script>` element is placed.

VBScript

VBScript is a Microsoft-specific scripting language that may be used on Microsoft browsers, instead of JavaScript. Unlike JavaScript, VBScript has a syntax that is familiar to Microsoft's Visual Basic developers. Microsoft also provides extensive debugging and tool support for this dialect of scripting language. Unfortunately, using VBScript to write client-side code restricts one's choice of browser to only Microsoft Internet Explorer.

However, because all modern versions of Microsoft browsers also support JavaScript, most professional developers code to JavaScript and avoid maintaining multiple versions of the same client-side coding.

User Preference Implementation

Some Web sites enable users to customize their look and feel. For example, a user may choose the color or the font that will be used to display the pages in a portal. Of course, this customization applies only to the individual user. A Web site supports multiple users, and this means that each user will be viewing the same Web site with his/her customizations applied. Figure 4-3 depicts this customization.

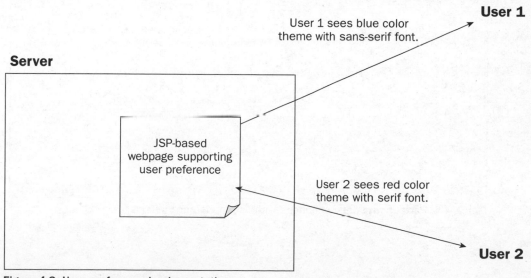

Figure 4-3: User preference implementation

In Figure 4-3, user 1 customized to a blue-colored theme and a sans serif font, whereas user 2 customized to a red-colored theme and a serif font. In this case, user 1 and user 2 can be simultaneously accessing the same data on the Web site, but each user will have a customized view of the site according to his or her preferences.

You can use JSP to implement this kind of customization. The first example in this chapter reveals how.

Try It Out   Customizing User Preferences

First, make sure your Tomcat 5 server is running. Next, deploy the ch04.war file on your Tomcat 5 server. If you do not remember how to deploy a Web application, revisit Chapter 1.

Now, try to access the following URL:

```
http://localhost:8080/ch04/example1/
```

This brings up the portal home page. You will recall this portal example from Chapter 2. Figure 4-4 illustrates this new portal home page.

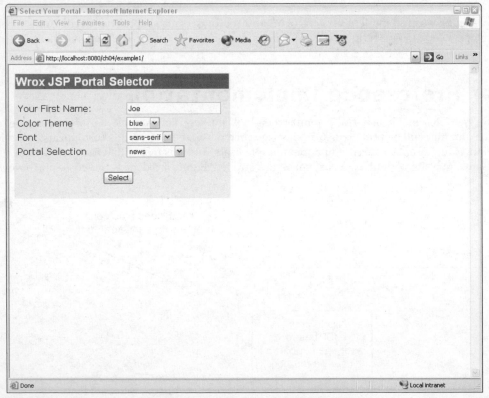

Figure 4-4: Portal home page enhanced with user preference options

This example is built on top of the Chapter 2 example to keep the additional details simple and familiar. Unlike the Chapter 2 example, however, there are two new selection boxes in Figure 4-4:

- ❑   One for color scheme selection
- ❑   One for font selection

These two selections enable users to customize the look of the portal on a per-user basis.

Key in the following values on the selection page:

- ❑   In the `Name` field, type **Joe**.
- ❑   In the `Color` field, select blue.
- ❑   In the `Font` field, select sans-serif
- ❑   In the `Portal` field, select news.

Now, click the Select button. You should see a customized portal, as shown in Figure 4-5.

In Figure 4-5, the page is now customized with the user's name, and is displayed in a blue color theme (not visible) with a sans-serif font face.

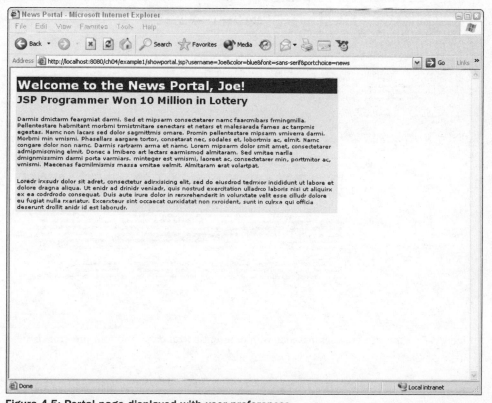

Figure 4-5: Portal page displayed with user preferences

To see how a different user of the portal may have a totally different visual experience, start another browser instance without closing the first one. Again, with the new browser instance, access the following URL:

```
http://localhost:8080/ch04/example1/
```

This time, enter the following values and selections:

- ❑ In the Name field, type **Mark**.
- ❑ In the Color list, select red.
- ❑ In the Font list, select serif.
- ❑ In the Portal list, select news.

This time, the news portal page is displayed with Mark's name, as shown in the bottom window of Figure 4-6.

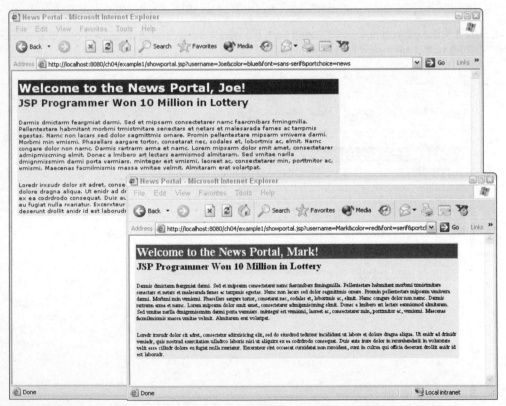

Figure 4-6: Separate browser instance with different portal color and font preference

In Figure 4-6, the same news portal page is now displayed in a red-colored theme, using a serif font. Using this technique, each user can set his or her own preferences, and view the portal pages according to the preferred look.

To show that the user preferences selected work on all the portal pages of the application, start yet another browser instance. Access the following portal URL:

```
http://localhost:8080/ch04/example1/
```

This time, enter the following values and data.

❑ In the Name field, type **John**.

❑ In the Color list, select green.

❑ In the Font list, select serif.

❑ In the Portal list, select weather.

Click Select; the resulting weather portal page should look like the one shown in Figure 4-7.

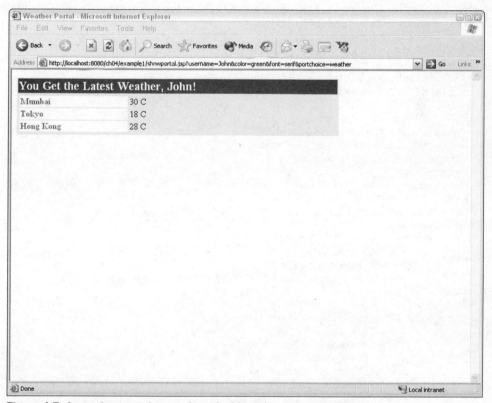

Figure 4-7: A weather portal page viewed with active user preferences

In Figure 4-7, the color scheme used is green, and a serif font is used as the per-user preference. As you can see, the customized user preferences worked across the news and weather portal pages (you can try the entertainment page on your own).

How It Works

The JSP pages in this application implement a simple user-preference selection mechanism. It enables the selection of only a color scheme and a font. The same mechanism, however, can readily be extended to support a larger set of user preferences.

In a nutshell, the user-specified color and font are passed as form submission parameters to a processing JSP. This JSP then modifies the content of a CSS on the fly, depending on the parameter values. The browser on the client then renders the HTML page according to this modified CSS, resulting in the customized look of the portal page.

Adding user preference form fields

The application's initial Web page contains an HTML form; the page is called index.jsp, and is located at <Tomcat Intallation Directory>/webapps/ch04/example1/index.jsp. Two new parameters are introduced: color and font. The color parameter contains the color selected by the user, and font contains the font type. The index.jsp page is reproduced in the following code, with modifications made to the original index.jsp highlighted:

```html
<html>
<head>
  <link rel=stylesheet type="text/css" href="portal.css">
  <title>Select Your Portal</title>
</head>
<body>
  <table class="mainBox" width="400">
    <tr><td class="boxTitle" colspan="2">
      Wrox JSP Portal Selector
    </td></tr>
    <tr><td colspan="2"> </td></tr>
    <tr><td>
      <form  action="showportal.jsp" method="get">
        <table>
          <tr>
            <td width="200">
              Your First Name: </td>
            <td><input name="username" type="text" size="25"/></td>
          </tr>
          <tr>
            <td width="200">Color Theme</td><td>
              <select name="color">
                <option>blue</option>
                <option>red</option>
                <option>green</option>
              </select>
            </td>
          </tr>

          <tr>
            <td width="200">Font</td><td>
```

```
          <select name="font">
            <option>sans-serif</option>
            <option>serif</option>
          </select>
        </td>
      </tr>

      <tr>
        <td width="200">Portal Selection</td><td>
          <select name="portchoice">
            <option>news</option>
            <option>weather</option>
            <option>entertainment</option>
          </select>
        </td>
      </tr>
      <tr><td colspan="2"> </td></tr>
      <tr><td colspan="2" align="center">
        <input type="submit" value="Select"/>
      </td></tr>
    </table>
  </form>
</td></tr>
</table>
</body>
</html>
```

The two new parameters, color and font, will be available to the form processing JSP when this form is submitted. The form processing JSP will be showportal.jsp, as specified in the action attribute of the <form> HTML element.

Dynamic generation of CSS stylesheet content

The look of the pages is predicated on a CSS, as was the case with the original Chapter 2 example. This stylesheet is called portal.css, and its content is reproduced here:

```
.tableCell
{
  font-family : Verdana, Geneva, Arial, Helvetica, sans-serif;
  font-size : 16;
  font-weight : bold;
  color : #0f7fcf;
  background-color: #ffffff;
}

.valueCell
{
  font-family : Verdana, Geneva, Arial, Helvetica, sans-serif;
  font-size : 16;
  color : #000000;
  background-color: #fefefe;
}
.headLine
```

```
{
  font-family : Verdana, Geneva, Arial, Helvetica, sans-serif;
  font-size : 18;
  font-weight : bold;
  color: #000000;
}

.newsText
{
  font-family : Verdana, Geneva, Arial, Helvetica, sans-serif;
  font-size : 10;
  color: #000000;
}
.boxTitle
{
  font-family : Arial, Helvetica, sans-serif;
  font-size : 22;
  font-weight : bold;
  color : #ffffff;
  background-color: #0F7ACA;
}
.mainBox
{
  font-family : Verdana, Geneva, Arial, Helvetica, sans-serif;
  font-size : 12;
  color : #ffffff;
  background-color: #eeeeee;
}
```

To see how the preceding stylesheet affects the news portal page, examine the HTML template data within the news.jsp portal page, which remains unchanged in this application. The news.jsp page is found in <Tomcat Installation Directory>/ch04/example1/news.jsp, and is reproduced here:

```
<%@ taglib prefix="c" uri="http://java.sun.com/jsp/jstl/core" %>
<title>News Portal</title>
</head>
<body>
  <table class="mainBox" width="600">
    <tr><td class="boxTitle" >
      Welcome to the News Portal, ${param.user}!
    </td></tr>
    <tr><td>
      <span class="headLine">
        <jsp:useBean id="newsfeed" class="com.wrox.begjsp.ch2.NewsFeed"
scope="request" >
          <jsp:setProperty name="newsfeed"  property="topic" value="news"/>
          <jsp:getProperty name="newsfeed" property="value"/>
        </jsp:useBean>
      </span>
      <span class="newsText">
        <jsp:include page="dummytext.html" />
      </span>
    </td></tr>
  </table>
```

The highlighted `class` attributes throughout the HTML template data control the way the final page is displayed. This includes both color and font used. For example, in the `.boxTitle` class, font is specified to be `Arial`, `Helvetica`, `sans-serif`, and the foreground color is specified as an RGB value of `#ffffff` (white), while background color is specified as an RGB value of `#0f7aca` (a shade of blue):

```
.boxTitle
{
    font-family : Arial, Helvetica, sans-serif;
    font-size : 22;
    font-weight : bold;
    color : #ffffff;
    background-color: #0F7ACA;
}
```

To change the appearance of the resulting HTML page, it is necessary to change the highlighted attributes in the preceding code. One way to do this within a JSP is to introduce some EL expressions:

```
.boxTitle
{
    font-family : ${selfont};
    font-size : 22;
    font-weight : bold;
    color : #ffffff;
    background-color: ${selcolor};
}
```

Now, the color and font that will be used in the style, and thus in the output HTML, will depend on the values of the `selfont` and `selcolor` variables. The only work remaining is to set the value of these variables according to the user-selected `font` and `color` parameters. This is done within the `showportal.jsp` page, the form processor in this application.

Decoding form parameters and setting style variables

The `showportal.jsp` file found in `<Tomcat Installation Directory>/webapps/ch04/example1/showportal.jsp` contains the code to set the `selfont` and `selcolor` variables. The entire `showportal.jsp` file is reproduced here, with the code for decoding the form parameters and setting the `selfont/selcolor` variables highlighted:

```
<%@ taglib prefix="c" uri="http://java.sun.com/jsp/jstl/core" %>
<html>
<head>
    <c:choose>
        <c:when test="${param.color == 'blue'}">
            <c:set var="selcolor" value="blue"/>
        </c:when>
        <c:when test="${param.color == 'red'}">
            <c:set var="selcolor" value="red" />
        </c:when>
        <c:when test="${param.color == 'green'}">
            <c:set var="selcolor" value="green" />
        </c:when>
    </c:choose>

    <c:choose>
```

```
      <c:when test="${param.font == 'sans-serif'}">
        <c:set var="selfont" value="Verdana, Geneva, Arial, Helvetica, sans-serif"/>
      </c:when>
      <c:when test="${param.font == 'serif'}">
        <c:set var="selfont" value="'Times New Roman',Times,serif" />
      </c:when>
  </c:choose>
<style>
.tableCell
{    font-family : ${selfont};
   font-size : 16;
   font-weight : bold;
   color : #0f7fcf;
   background-color: #ffffff;
}

.valueCell
{
   font-family : ${selfont};
   font-size : 16;
   color : #000000;
   background-color: #fefefe;
}
.headLine
{
   font-family : ${selfont};
   font-size : 18;
   font-weight : bold;
   color: #000000;
}

.newsText
{
 font-family : ${selfont};
 font-size : 10;
 color: #000000;
}
.boxTitle
{
 font-family : ${selfont};
 font-size : 22;
 font-weight : bold;
 color : #ffffff;
 background-color: ${selcolor};
 }
.mainBox
{
   font-family : ${selfont};
   font-size : 12;
   color : #ffffff;
   background-color: #eeeeee;
}
```

```
    </style>

    <c:choose>
      <c:when test="${param.portchoice == 'news'}">
        <jsp:include page="news.jsp" >
          <jsp:param name="user" value="${param.username}"/>
        </jsp:include>
      </c:when>
      <c:when test="${param.portchoice =='weather'}">
        <jsp:include page="weather.jsp" >
          <jsp:param name="user" value="${param.username}"/>
        </jsp:include>
      </c:when>
      <c:when test="${param.portchoice == 'entertainment'}">
        <jsp:include page="entertain.jsp" >
          <jsp:param name="user" value="${param.username}"/>
        </jsp:include>
      </c:when>
      <c:otherwise>
        <head><title>System Portal</title></head>
        <body>
          <h1>Application logic problem detected!</h1>
        </body>
      </c:otherwise>
    </c:choose>
  </body>
</html>
```

In the highlighted section of the preceding code, a JSTL <choose> construct is used to decode the incoming form parameters. The value of the `selcolor` variable is set according to the following table.

Incoming Color Parameter	Value of `selcolor`
red	red
blue	blue
green	green

It so happens that the color constants used in the CSS are exactly the same as the form selection values. Another JSTL <choose> construct is used to decode the incoming `font` parameter. The value of the `selfont` variable is set according to the following table.

Incoming Font Parameter	Value of `selfont`
serif	`'Times New Roman',Times,serif`
sans-serif	`Verdana, Geneva, Arial, Helvetica, sans-serif`

Note that in showportal.jsp, the entire portal.css stylesheet is included as a <style> HTML element. Embedding the CSS makes it possible to use EL expressions and other JSP facilities to dynamically modify the stylesheet content. For example, if the user selects serif as the font and green as the color, the following .boxTitle style will be generated:

```
.boxTitle
{
   font-family : 'Times New Roman',Times,serif;
   font-size : 22;
   font-weight : bold;
   color : #ffffff;
   background-color: green;
}
```

The content of the other JSPs within the application remains the same as the original Chapter 2 example. By using CSS to abstract the appearance of the portal pages, it is possible to customize the final appearance of your page without modifying the underlying pages themselves (by just modifying the CSS classes).

Creating a User-Customizable DHTML Menu

One of the most common applications of client-side scripting, using JavaScript or VBScript, is the creation of a DHTML menu. A DHTML menu provides a menu with a drop-down submenu via a highly familiar, non-Web-style, interactive interface. This interface is familiar because all standard Windows-based GUIs use a similar menu structure. Figure 4-8 illustrates one such menu.

Unlike regular HTML-based menus, the menu in DHTML is not constructed out of hyperlink or HTML form elements. Instead, HTML code is modified on the fly using style and positioning elements to create a highly interactive experience for the end user.

Combining JSP with DHTML enables user-specific customization that is otherwise unachievable with client-side scripting alone. For example, JSP can be used to generate the scripting code that sets up the individual menu and submenu items. This enables an application to present a different menu to each user, customized to their needs.

The example in the next Try It Out exercise builds on the first, and shows how to add a customized DHTML menu using JSP.

Try It Out   Adding a Customized DHTML Menu

Before you can try out this example, you will need to download the code for the DHTML menu. The URL for the download is as follows:

```
http://www.dynamicdrive.com/dynamicindex1/sm/index.htm
```

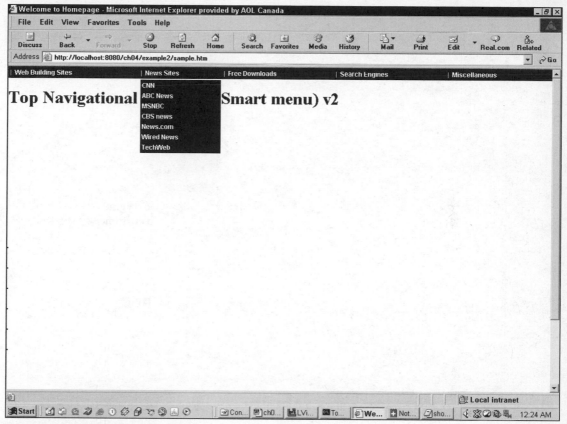

Figure 4-8: A DHTML menu in action

Make sure you download Top Nav Bar script version 2.1 or later. Dynamic drive is a resource center for client-side scripting programmers. You will find a wide selection of handy scripts that you can use on your own Web site.

This specific DHTML menu will self-adapt to work with all major browsers, including Internet Explorer 6 and Netscape 7.

The file that you will need is menu.js. Place this in the <Tomcat Installation Directory>/ webapps/ch04/example2 directory. Now, you are ready to try out the customized dynamic menu. Access the following URL:

```
http://localhost:8080/ch04/example2/
```

The familiar portal selection form is displayed (see Figure 4-9), but this time with an additional menu selection.

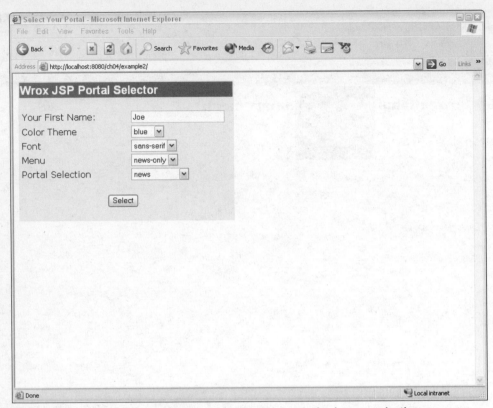

Figure 4-9: Portal selection form with an additional customized menu selection

In Figure 4-9, you can select either the news-only or all-menu option. First, try entering the following data into the form:

❑   In the Name field, type **Joe**.

❑   In the Color list, select blue.

❑   In the Font list, select sans-serif.

❑   In the Menu list, select news-only.

❑   In the Portal Selection list, select news.

Click Select. You should see the news portal screen with the DHTML menu, as shown in Figure 4-10.

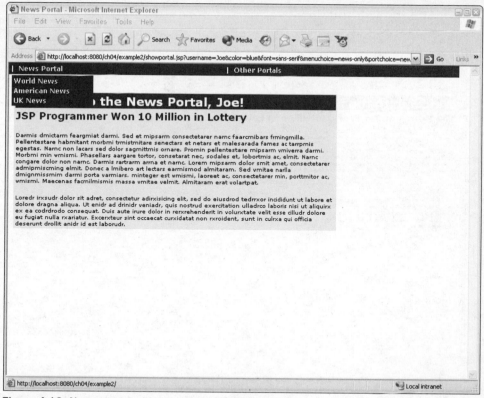

Figure 4-10: News portal with "news-only" DHTML menu

Although you can't see it in the black-and-white screenshot, the menu's color is consistent with the user-specified color — blue in this case. Note also that the font used in the menu is also consistent with the user preference — a sans-serif font.

Move your cursor over the DHTML menu and notice the selections that are available. They are all news-related sites. (The links do not actually work, of course; they will simply redirect you back to the example.) Figure 4-11 shows the same page with another menu selected.

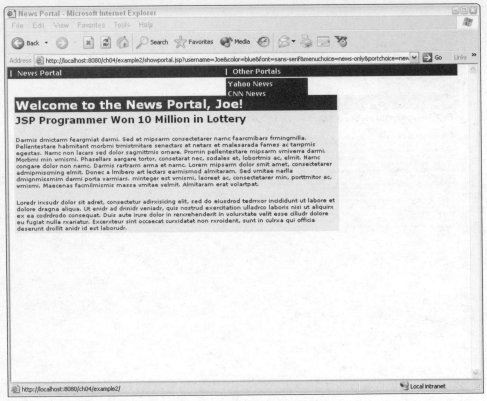

Figure 4-11: News portal page with alternative menu selection

Now, to test DHTML customization using JSP, start another instance of a Web browser without closing the first. With the new browser instance, access the following URL:

```
http://localhost:8080/ch04/example2/
```

Enter the following data into the portal selection form:

- ❏ In the Name field, type **Mark**.
- ❏ In the Color list, select green.
- ❏ In the Font list, select serif.
- ❏ In the Menu list, select all.
- ❏ In the Portal Selection list, select news.

Click Select. You should see the green news portal page with a different DHTML menu, similar to what is shown in Figure 4-12.

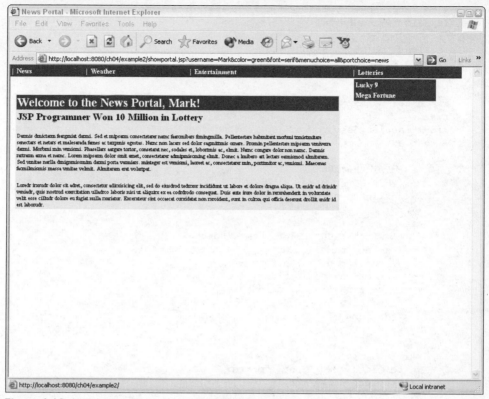

Figure 4-12: News portal with the "all" DHTML menu

Figure 4-12 shows how the same JSP page can be used to display different DHTML menus to different users. The menu color is now green, and the font used in the menu is a serif style, again consistent with the user's preferences. This is an example of how the menu's appearance can be controlled by a JSP-generated stylesheet.

Move the cursor over the different menu selections, and note how this menu is very different from the news-only selection.

To focus on the concepts and keep the code simple, the JSP code in this example is used to generate one of only two different DHTML menus. Using the same technique, it is possible to allow fine-grained user customization down to a single menu item, enabling users to completely customize their menus. This possibility is left as an area of further exploration for you.

How It Works

To support the additional form field, `index.jsp` is modified. The new `index.jsp` can be located at `<Tomcat Installation Directory>/webapps/ch04/example/index.jsp`. The modification is highlighted in the following `index.jsp` listing:

```
<html>
<head>
```

```
      <link rel=stylesheet type="text/css" href="portal.css">
      <title>Select Your Portal</title></head>
<body>
    <table class="mainBox" width="400">
      <tr><td class="boxTitle" colspan="2">
        Wrox JSP Portal Selector
      </td></tr>
      <tr><td colspan="2"> </td></tr>
      <tr><td>
        <form  action="showportal.jsp" method="get">
          <table>
            <tr>
              <td width="200">
                Your First Name: </td>
              <td><input name="username" type="text" size="25"/></td>
            </tr>
            <tr>
              <td width="200">Color Theme</td><td>
                <select name="color">
                  <option>blue</option>
                  <option>red</option>
                  <option>green</option>
                </select>
              </td>
            </tr>

            <tr>
              <td width="200">Font</td><td>
                <select name="font">
                  <option>sans-serif</option>
                  <option>serif</option>
                </select>
              </td>
            </tr>

            <tr>
              <td width="200">Menu</td><td>
                <select name="menuchoice">
                  <option>news-only</option>
                  <option>all</option>
                </select>
              </td>
            </tr>

            <tr>
              <td width="200">Portal Selection</td><td>
                <select name="portchoice">
                  <option>news</option>
                  <option>weather</option>
                  <option>entertainment</option>
                </select>
              </td>
            </tr>

            <tr><td colspan="2"> </td></tr>
            <tr><td colspan="2" align="center">
```

```
            <input type="submit" value="Select"/>
        </td></tr>
      </table>
    </form>
  </td></tr>
</table>
</body>
</html>
```

The new form parameter is called `menuchoice`. This form parameter is passed into `showportal.jsp`, the form processor JSP. `showportal.jsp` can be found in `<Tomcat Installation Directory>/webapps/ch04/showportal.jsp`.

`showportal.jsp` does not directly work with the `menuchoice` parameter. Instead, `news.jsp` is where the DHTML menu is generated, and the `menuchoice` parameter processed.

Customizing the DHTML menu with user color and font preferences

The `showportal.jsp` file, however, has several new stylesheet and script elements that affect the DHTML menu. This enables us to customize the color and font used in the DHTML menu. The following is a listing of the new `showportal.jsp`, with the DHTML's stylesheet and script elements highlighted:

```
<%@ taglib prefix="c" uri="http://java.sun.com/jsp/jstl/core" %>
<html>
<head>
  <c:choose>
    <c:when test="${param.color == 'blue'}">
      <c:set var="selcolor" value="blue"/>
    </c:when>
    <c:when test="${param.color == 'red'}">
      <c:set var="selcolor" value="red" />
    </c:when>
    <c:when test="${param.color == 'green'}">
      <c:set var="selcolor" value="green" />
    </c:when>
  </c:choose>

  <c:choose>
    <c:when test="${param.font == 'sans-serif'}">
      <c:set var="selfont" value="Verdana, Geneva, Arial, Helvetica, sans-serif"/>
    </c:when>
    <c:when test="${param.font == 'serif'}">
      <c:set var="selfont" value="'Times New Roman',Times,serif" />
    </c:when>
  </c:choose>

  <style>
  .tableCell
  {
    font-family : ${selfont};
    font-size : 16;
    font-weight : bold;
    color : #0f7fcf;
```

```
    background-color: #ffffff;
}

.valueCell
{
  font-family : ${selfont};
  font-size : 16;
  color : #000000;
  background-color: #fefefe;
}
.headLine
{
  font-family : ${selfont};
  font-size : 18;
  font-weight : bold;
  color: #000000;
}

.newsText
{
  font-family : ${selfont};
  font-size : 10;
  color: #000000;
}
.boxTitle
{
  font-family : ${selfont};
  font-size : 22;
  font-weight : bold;
  color : #ffffff;
  background-color: ${selcolor};

}
.mainBox
{
  font-family : ${selfont};
  font-size : 12;
  color : #ffffff;
  background-color: #eeeeee;
}
all.clsMenuItemNS, .clsMenuItemIE
{
  text-decoration: none;
  font: bold 12px;
  font-family: ${selfont};
  color: white;
  cursor: hand;
  z-index:100
}
</style>
<script language="JavaScript">
  var keepstatic=1
  var menucolor="${selcolor}"
  var submenuwidth=150
</script>
```

```
<c:choose>
  <c:when test="${param.portchoice == 'news'}">
    <jsp:include page="news.jsp" >
      <jsp:param name="user" value="${param.username}"/>
    </jsp:include>
  </c:when>
  <c:when test="${param.portchoice =='weather'}">
    <jsp:include page="weather.jsp" >
      <jsp:param name="user" value="${param.username}"/>
    </jsp:include>
  </c:when>
  <c:when test="${param.portchoice == 'entertainment'}">
    <jsp:include page="entertain.jsp" >
      <jsp:param name="user" value="${param.username}"/>
    </jsp:include>
  </c:when>
  <c:otherwise>
    <head><title>System Portal</title></head>
    <body>
      <h1>Application logic problem detected!</h1>
    </body>
  </c:otherwise>
</c:choose>
</body>
</html>
```

Generating JavaScript code with JSP for the DHTML menu

The news.jsp file has the embedded DHTML menu and the code that configures it. This file is located in <Tomcat Install Directory>/webapps/ch04/news.jsp and is reproduced as follows. The highlighted code is the JSP construct that generates the JavaScript code to configure the menu. Note that it will construct two very different menus depending on the value of the menuchoice form parameter.

```
<%@ taglib prefix="c" uri="http://java.sun.com/jsp/jstl/core" %>
  <title>News Portal</title>
</head>
<body>
  <script language="JavaScript" src="menu.js"></script>
  <script language="JavaScript">
    function showToolbar()
    {
     menu = new Menu();

        <c:choose>
          <c:when test="${param.menuchoice == 'news-only'}">
            menu.addItem("newsportalid", "News Portal", "News Portal", null, null);
            menu.addItem("otherportalid", "Other Portals", "Other Portals",
              null, null);
            menu.addSubItem("newsportalid", "World News", "World News",
              "http://localhost:8080/ch04/example2/","");
            menu.addSubItem("newsportalid", "American News", "American News",
              "http://localhost:8080/ch04/cxample2/","");
            menu.addSubItem("newsportalid", "UK News", "UK News",
```

```
                    "http://localhost:8080/ch04/example2/","");

            menu.addSubItem("otherportalid", "Yahoo News", "Yahoo News",
               "http://localhost:8080/ch04/example2/","");
            menu.addSubItem("otherportalid", "CNN News", "CNN News",
               "http://localhost:8080/ch04/example2/","");
        </c:when>
        <c:when test="${param.menuchoice == 'all'}">
          menu.addItem("newsid", "News", "News", null, null);
          menu.addItem("weatherid", "Weather", "Weather", null, null);
          menu.addItem("entid", "Entertainment", "Entertainment", null, null);
          menu.addItem("lotid", "Lotteries", "Lottories", null, null);
          menu.addSubItem("newsid", "World News", "World News",
             "http://localhost:8080/ch04/example2/","");
          menu.addSubItem("newsid", "American News", "American News",
             "http://localhost:8080/ch04/example2/","");
          menu.addSubItem("newsid", "UK News", "UK News",
             "http://localhost:8080/ch04/example2/","");

          menu.addSubItem("newsid", "Yahoo News", "Yahoo News",
             "http://localhost:8080/ch04/example2/","");
          menu.addSubItem("newsid", "CNN News", "CNN News",
             "http://localhost:8080/ch04/example2/","");

          menu.addSubItem("weatherid", "Accurate Weather", "Accurate Weather",
             "http://localhost:8080/ch04/example2/","");
          menu.addSubItem("weatherid", "Weather Central", "Weather Central",
             "http://localhost:8080/ch04/example2/","");

          menu.addSubItem("entid", "E Motion", "E Motion",
             "http://localhost:8080/ch04/example2/","");

          menu.addSubItem("entid", "Hollywood on the Run", "Hollywood on the Run",
             "http://localhost:8080/ch04/example2/","");


          menu.addSubItem("lotid", "Lucky 9", "Lucky 9",
             "http://localhost:8080/ch04/example2/","");

          menu.addSubItem("lotid", "Mega Fortune", "Mega Fortune",
             "http://localhost:8080/ch04/example2/","");

        </c:when>
      </c:choose>
   menu.showMenu();
 }

 showToolbar();

 function UpdateIt()
 {
   if (ie&&keepstatic&&!opr6)
     document.all["MainTable"].style.top = document.body.scrollTop;
     setTimeout("UpdateIt()", 200);
```

```
    }
    UpdateIt();
</script>
<br/>
<br/>

<table class="mainBox" width="600">
  <tr><td class="boxTitle" >
    Welcome to the News Portal, ${param.user}!
  </td></tr>
  <tr><td>
    <span class="headLine">
      <jsp:useBean id="newsfeed" class="com.wrox.begjsp.ch2.NewsFeed"
        scope="request" >
        <jsp:setProperty name="newsfeed"  property="topic" value="news"/>
        <jsp:getProperty name="newsfeed" property="value"/>
      </jsp:useBean>
    </span>
    <span class="newsText">
      <jsp:include page="dummytext.html" />
    </span>
  </td></tr>
</table>
```

Note that the code generated by the JSTL `<choose>` construct is not a complete JavaScript function. Rather, it is a code fragment within the `showToolBar()` function that is used to generate the DHTML menu.

Summary

You can use JSP to dynamically generate textual output within any template data. While previous examples have been focused on HTML template data, this chapter explores two alternatives:

❑   Cascading Stylesheets (CSS)

❑   Client-side scripting code (JavaScript)

JSP can be used to dynamically generate CSS code. With CSS, you can

❑   Affect how HTML elements are displayed by the browser

❑   Directly control the appearance of the page to the end user

By using JSP to dynamically generate CSS elements, it is possible to customize the look of the final page programmatically. One application area is customizing the look of Web pages according to specific user preferences.

In this chapter, the first Try It Out and How It Works sections reveal how user preferences may be implemented using JSP to generate request-dependent CSS code on-the-fly.

Another non-HTML template data that JSP can work with is client-side scripting code. Client-side scripting code is

❑ Typically JavaScript or VBScript code that is part of the HTML page served by the server

❑ Executed on the client side by the browser

A common use of client-side scripting code is the implementation of a DHTML menu. DHTML menus typically provide a familiar drop-down menu to the user of a Web application.

This chapter's second Try It Out and How It Works sections demonstrate how you can use JSP to generate JavaScript code on-the-fly, which can be used to customize a DHTML menu depending on application needs.

Creatively combining JSP's data-driven dynamic generation capability with non-HTML template data can result in exciting new application possibilities.

Exercises

1. Modify the code in the first Try It Out exercise to enable users to select the style of font used: either normal or italic.

2. Add customized DHTML menu support to the weather (weather.jsp) and entertainment (entertain.jsp) portal pages in the second Try It Out exercise.

5

JSP and EL

The previous chapters in this book demonstrated the breadth of JSP technology and introduced some basic techniques of JSP development. The aim thus far has been to provide you with some fast, hands-on experience with the JSP technology. The working examples in these earlier chapters enabled you to try out real JSP code, and see what JSP can be used for in the real world.

Unlike the earlier chapters, this chapter provides a more in-depth exploration of a cornerstone element of the JSP standard: JSP's *Expression Language,* or EL for short.

In this chapter, you will discover the following:

❑ Why EL is an indispensable part of JSP 2.0

❑ How to use EL named variables

❑ How to perform type conversion and coercion in EL

❑ How to handle null values in EL

❑ How to work with arithmetic, logical, comparison, and other operators in EL

❑ The different ways of accessing members of a collection in EL

❑ How to access properties of objects in EL

❑ How to access nested object properties in EL

❑ How to use implicit objects in EL

❑ How to define and access functions in EL

❑ How to use a namespace when referencing EL functions

This chapter covers a lot of ground, and includes five separate examples. By the end of the chapter, you should be very familiar with EL, and be comfortable using it in your own applications.

EL and Its Vital Role in JSP

EL was not part of the JSP standard prior to 2.0. One of the main reasons for creating EL was to ensure that presentation-level JSP pages could be created without relying on scripting elements. Chapter 3, "JSP Basics 2: Generalized Templating and Server Scripting," covered the use of scripting elements (typically code written in Java) that are embedded within a JSP page.

The need for scripting elements within JSP is typically driven by the requirements of an application. Major application requirements that demand the use of scripting elements include the following:

❑ To provide control-flow for JSP execution

❑ To set, and subsequently access, variables that are local to the JSP page

❑ To render a value from a complex expression that involves Java objects

❑ To access properties of an arbitrary Java object

❑ To call methods of JavaBeans or other Java objects

Unfortunately, experience has shown that the use of scripting elements in JSPs makes large projects difficult to maintain over the long term. It also encourages programming practices that may tightly couple the presentation (user interface) of an application to its business logic, reducing its flexibility and scalability. This is a highly undesirable practice in the creation of Web applications and services. Ideally, JSPs should be created free of scripting elements if at all possible.

In order to create a JSP version that can work completely free of scripting elements, it is essential that all five of the application requirements can be satisfied without the use of embedded Java coding. JSP 2.0 satisfies these requirements. The first two items are handled by JSTL (explored in detail in Chapter 6, "JSP Tag Libraries and JSTL"), while the last three requirements are handled by EL.

> *EL is independent of JSP 2.0. Despite the vital role of EL in JSP 2.0, the use of EL is not exclusive to JSP containers. The EL parser is also not tightly integrated into the JSP parser, but can be detached and reused for other purposes. In fact, EL is incorporated into both Java Server Faces (JSF, a server-side GUI construction kit technology; see Chapter 21, "JavaServer Faces," for more information), and JSTL. Therefore, becoming familiar with EL will save you time when exploring these other technologies.*

EL Named Variables

When working with EL (and JSTL), you will frequently work with named variables. Named variables in EL refer to attributes attached to JSP scoping objects. For example, the following EL expression will render the value of the named variable called `bearCount`:

```
<b>There are ${bearCount} bears in the cave.</b>
```

The EL parser will search for the attribute through the various JSP scoping objects in the following order:

1. Page
2. Request

3. Session (if currently valid)

4. Application

In practice, this is equivalent to a call to the Java `PageContext.findAttribute()` method. If you are maintaining legacy JSP code with embedded Java, you may see this call. You can consult the JSP Javadocs (API documentation) to see how this method works.

Figure 5-1 illustrates the search for an EL named variable.

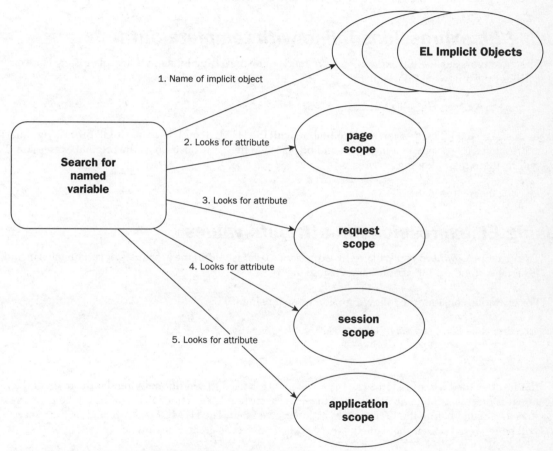

Figure 5-1: Order of search for an EL named variable

In Figure 5-1, you can see the search order for an EL named variable: First the set of EL implicit objects is searched for a matching name (EL implicit objects are covered later in this chapter), and then the four scopes. If the named variable is not found, some action may create it.

> *If the attribute with the specified name cannot be located in any scope, a null value is returned. The null value will render as a " " (empty string) in the output, and will not trigger any error.*

Applying EL

As the name implies, the Expression Language works with expressions. It is a programming language used in the construction of expressions. All EL expressions are enclosed in the ${ . . . } notation. The expression is evaluated before the rest of the JSP is evaluated. You can place EL expressions in two places within a JSP:

❑   Inline with template data

❑   Within attributes of JSP actions, standard or custom

Using EL expressions inline with template data

The most typical use of EL expressions is to render a textual string inline with template data. For example, consider the following JSP fragment:

```
<b>There are ${5 + 1} bears in the cave.</b>
```

In this case, the EL expression is placed inline with the HTML template data. At JSP processing time, the expression ${5+1} will evaluate to 6, and be placed at the same position as the original expression. This will result in the following HTML:

```
<b>There are 6 bears in the cave.</b>
```

Using EL expressions in attribute values

The other place where you will see EL expressions used is within the attributes of certain tags, including JSTL tags, standard JSP actions, and custom tags.

For example, consider the following JSP fragment using JSTL:

```
<c:if test="${salary > 100000}">
  <b>Rich cousin!</b><br/>
</c:if>
```

In this case, the EL expression ${salary > 100000} is used to conditionally render the body of the JSTL tag. It is placed in the test attribute of the <c:if> custom JSTL action. This will cause the EL expression to be evaluated before the JSTL custom action is evaluated. The HTML Rich cousin!
 will be rendered only if the named variable called salary is greater in value than 100,000.

For example, consider the following JSP fragment featuring the JSTL <c:set> tag:

```
<c:set var="datetime" val='${dateNow} - ${timeNow}'/>
```

If the dateNow named variable contains the string "May 1, 2005" and timeNow contains "11:00 AM", then the resulting datetime named variable will contain "May 1, 2005 - 11:00 AM".

As shown in the preceding section, an EL expression can be an arithmetic expression, or an expression featuring a comparison. The following Try It Out section explores some of these EL expressions.

Applying EL Expressions

To try out the first example, deploy ch05.war to your Tomcat 5 server. Review Chapter 1 if you do not remember how to deploy a WAR file.

Access the following URL using your browser to see the example's output:

    http://localhost:8080/ch05/example1/

You should see something similar to what is shown in Figure 5-2.

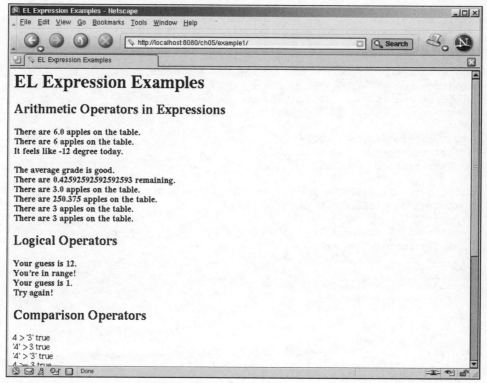

Figure 5-2: Output result of EL expressions

The output in Figure 5-2 is the result of a collection of different EL expressions. The following How It Works section examines the EL expressions used to generate this output.

How It Works

The JSP used to generate the output shown in Figure 5-2 is located at <Tomcat Installation Directory>/webapps/ch05/example1/index.jsp. The code in this index.jsp is reproduced here:

```
<%@ taglib prefix="c" uri="http://java.sun.com/jsp/jstl/core" %>
<%@ taglib prefix="fmt" uri="http://java.sun.com/jsp/jstl/fmt" %>

<html>
```

```
<head>
  <title>EL Expression Examples</title>
</head>
<body>
  <h1>EL Expression Examples</h1>

  <h2>Arithmetic Expressions</h2>
  <b>There are ${1 + 2 * 4 - 6 / 2} apples on the table.</b><br/>
  <b>There are
    <fmt:formatNumber pattern="#####"/>${1 + 2 * 4 - 6 / 2}</fmt:formatNumber>
    apples on the table.</b><br/>


  <b>It feels like ${-4 - 8} degrees today.</b><br/>
  <c:set var="myGrade" value="11"/><br/>
  <b>The average grade is ${(myGrade == 10) ? "perfect" : "good"}. </b><br/>
  <b>There are ${23/54} remaining. </b><br/>
  <b>There are ${6 div 2} apples on the table.</b><br/>
  <b>There are ${2003 div 8} apples on the table.</b><br/>
  <b>There are ${2003 mod 8} apples on the table.</b><br/>
  <b>There are ${2003 % 8} apples on the table.</b><br/>

  <h2>Logical Operators </h2>
  <c:set var="guess" value="12"/>
  <b>Your guess is ${guess}.</b><br/>

  <c:if test="${(guess >= 10)  && (guess <= 20)}">
    <b>You're in range!</b><br/>
  </c:if>
  <c:if test="${(guess < 10)  || (guess > 20)}">
    <b>Try again!</b><br/>
  </c:if>

  <c:set var="guess" value="1"/>
  <b>Your guess is ${guess}.</b><br/>

  <c:if test="${(guess >= 10)  and (guess <= 20)}">
    <b>You're in range!</b><br/>
  </c:if>
  <c:if test="${(guess < 10)  or (guess > 20)}">
    <b>Try again!</b><br/>
  </c:if>

  <h2>Comparison Operators </h2>

  4 > '3'     ${4 > '3'}<br/>
  '4' > 3     ${'4' > 3}<br/>
  '4' > '3'   ${'4' > '3'} <br/>
  4 >= 3      ${4 >= 3}<br/>
  4 <= 3      ${4 < 3}<br/>
  4 == '4'    ${4 == 4}<br/>
  <h2>empty Operator</h2>
  empty "" ${empty ""}<br/>
  empty "sometext" ${empty "sometext"}<br/>
```

```
empty Junk ${empty Junk}<br/>
empty guess ${empty guess}<br/>

<h2>Boolean and Null Values</h2>

<c:set var="StrVar" value="true"/>
<c:if test="${StrVar}">
  equal!
</c:if><br/>

null == null  ${null == null}<br/>
"null" == null ${"null" == null}<br/>

</body>
</html>
```

The page consists of many different EL expressions. The highlighted code shows the two major uses of EL expressions in JSP: inline with template data, and within attributes of tags.

The first highlighted line shows the EL expression ${1 + 2 * 4 - 6 / 2} used inline with the HTML template data:

```
<b>There are ${1 + 2 * 4 - 6 / 2} apples on the table.</b><br/>
```

The second highlighted line shows the same EL expression in the value attribute of the JSTL <fmt:formatNumber> tag:

```
<fmt:formatNumber pattern="#####"/>${1 + 2 * 4 - 6 / 2}</fmt:formatNumber>
```

Operators

The expressions in index.jsp are created using operators available within EL. These operators include the following:

❑   Arithmetic operators

❑   Logical operators

❑   Comparison operators

❑   The empty prefix operator

The preceding example contains expressions using every one of these operators. An explanation of these expressions used in the index.jsp file follows.

Arithmetic operators

All the basic arithmetic operators that you are familiar with are available within EL expressions. This includes addition, subtraction, multiplication, division, and modulus. For example, consider this line in index.jsp:

```
<b>There are ${1 + 2 * 4 - 6 / 2} apples on the table.</b>
```

This results in the following HTML:

```
<b>There are 6.0 apples on the table.</b>
```

Note that operator precedence has caused the multiplication and division to be executed first. Furthermore, the calculation has caused a decimal to appear in the output. You can use the numeric formatting tags in JSTL to eliminate this. For example, the following JSP fragment in `index.jsp` renders the same result without the decimal point:

```
<b>There are
<fmt:formatNumber value="${1 + 2 * 4 - 6 / 2}" pattern="#####"/>
apples on the table.</b><br/>
```

The `formatNumber` JSTL tag is used to format the numerical output, using a pattern that specifies no decimal point should be displayed. This results in the following output:

```
<b>There are 6 apples on the table.</b>
```

Note that the set of JSTL formatting tags must be included with the `<taglib>` directive at the top of `index.jsp`:

```
<%@ taglib prefix="fmt" uri="http://java.sun.com/jsp/jstl/fmt" %>
```

This `<taglib>` directive also associates the namespace `fmt` with these formatting tags. Formatting tags and JSTL are covered extensively in Chapter 6, "JSP Tag Libraries and JSTL."

The `div` operator is another way to specify the divide (/) operator, and may be used interchangeably. Therefore, the following two lines are completely equivalent:

```
<b>There are ${1 + 2 * 4 - 6 div 2} apples on the table.</b>
<b>There are ${1 + 2 * 4 - 6 / 2} apples on the table.</b>
```

The `mod` operator, sometimes expressed by using the symbol `%`, may be used to obtain the remainder after a division. For example, consider the following EL expressions in `index.jsp`:

```
<b>There are ${2003 div 8} apples on the table.</b>
<b>There are ${2003 mod 8} apples on the table.</b>
<b>There are ${2003 % 8} apples on the table.</b>
```

The following code shows the resulting HTML output:

```
<b>There are 250.375 apples on the table.</b>
<b>There are 3 apples on the table.</b>
<b>There are 3 apples on the table.</b>
```

You can also work with negative numbers, using the unary operator, as in the following fragment from `index.jsp`:

```
<b>It feels like ${-4 - 8} degrees today.</b>
```

This will result in the following HTML output:

```
<b>It feels like -12 degrees today.</b>
```

Floating-point numbers are also supported; the following calculation from index.jsp results in a fractional number:

```
<b>There are ${23/54} remaining. </b>
```

This renders the following HTML output:

```
<b>There are 0.42592592592592593 remaining. </b>
```

The conditional operator can also be used:

```
<c:set var="myGrade" value="10"/>
<b>The average grade is ${(myGrade == 10) ? "perfect" : "good"}. </b>
```

The JSTL <c:set> custom action is used to create a named variable. It is an attribute (by default, created in page scope) called myGrade with the integer value 10. The EL expression will render "perfect" if the grade is 10, or "good" otherwise. If myGrade is 10, as in the case of index.jsp, the following HTML is rendered:

```
<b>The average grade is perfect. </b>
```

Logical operators

Logical operators can be used to combine multiple Boolean expressions. The two logical operators supported by EL are && and ||. Alternatively, the textual form and and or may also be used. For example, consider the following JSP segment from index.jsp:

```
<h2>Logical Operators </h2>
<c:set var="guess" value="12"/>
<b>Your guess is ${guess}.</b><br/>

<c:if test="${(guess >= 10)  && (guess <= 20)}">
  <b>You're in range!</b><br/>
</c:if>
<c:if test="${(guess < 10)  || (guess > 20)}">
  <b>Try again!</b><br/>
</c:if>
```

The JSTL <c:if> custom action is used to implement a simple "guess the number" game. If the guess is between 10 and 20 inclusive, the message "You're in range!" is printed; otherwise, the player is asked to "Try again!" Because guess in this case is set to 12, the resulting output is as follows:

```
Your guess is 12.
You're in range!
```

The following is the same expression, using the textual form of the logical operators:

```
<c:set var="guess" value="1"/>
<b>Your guess is ${guess}.</b><br/>

<c:if test="${(guess >= 10) and (guess <= 20)}">
  <b>You're in range!</b><br/>
</c:if>
<c:if test="${(guess < 10) or (guess > 20)}">
  <b>Try again!</b><br/>
</c:if>
```

Comparison operators

EL supports the entire range of comparison operators found in most programming languages. Each of the operators has a symbolic form and an abbreviated textual form. The following table enumerates the available operators.

Operator	Alternate Form	Description
>	Gt	Greater than
>=	Ge	Greater than or equal to
<	Lt	Less than
<=	Le	Lesser than or equal to
==	Eq	Equal to
!=	Ne	Not equal to

The following fragment of index.jsp tests some of these comparison operators:

```
<h2>Comparison Operators </h2>

4 > '3'    ${4 > '3'}<br/>
'4' > 3    ${'4' > 3}<br/>
'4' > '3'  ${'4' > '3'} <br/>
4 >= 3     ${4 >= 3}<br/>
4 <= 3     ${4 < 3}<br/>
4 == '4'   $(4 == 4}<br/>
```

The resulting output is shown here:

```
4 > '3' true
'4' > 3 true
'4' > '3' true
4 >= 3 true
4 <= 3 false
4 == '4' true
```

Note that in the previous comparison EL always attempts to convert the type of the data being compared "in the right way." That is, the character data is converted to numeric value before being compared, except in the case where two characters are compared.

XML document validity

The >, >=, <, and <= operators contain the < and > special symbols. These symbols typically need to be escaped if the template text is an XML document. For example, consider the following expression:

```
<bucketLevel>
  <c:if  test="${appleCount >= 100}">
    full
  </c:if>
</bucketLevel>
```

The preceding JSP fragment is not valid XML due to the > character in the expression. Instead, you should use the alternate form, as follows:

```
<bucketLevel>
  <c:if  test="${appleCount ge 100}">
  full
  </c:if>
</bucketLevel>
```

Using this alternate form enables the gt, ge, lt, and le operators to be used without affecting the validity of the surrounding XML template text.

The empty operator

The empty operator is a prefix operator, meaning that it takes only one single operand on its right. It can be used to test for a null value. For example, consider the following JSP fragment from index.jsp in the previous Try It Out exercise:

```
<h2>empty Operator</h2>
empty "" ${empty ""}<br/>
empty "sometext" ${empty "sometext"}<br/>
empty Junk ${empty Junk}<br/>
empty guess ${empty guess}<br/>
```

The resulting output is as follows:

```
empty Operator
empty "" true
empty "sometext" false
empty Junk true
empty guess false
```

In the previous example, the empty string " " is considered empty while any other string value is not. A nonexistent variable, Junk, is given a null value in EL. This null value is considered empty when tested with the empty operator. On the other hand, the guess variable exists (used earlier) and therefore is not empty. In other words, depending on the data type of the operand, the empty operator can also be used to test for the conditions shown in the following table.

Operand Data Type	Empty Value
String	""
Any named variable	Null
Array	no elements
Map	no elements
List	no elements

An ambiguity exists if a named variable is tested to be empty, as it can either contain the null value or the empty string " ".

Boolean variables and nulls

The following JSP fragment from index.jsp of the previous Try It Out exercise illustrates some interesting conversion properties to Boolean types and working with null values.

```
<h2>Boolean and Null Values</h2>
<c:set var="StrVar" value="true"/>
<c:if test="${StrVar}">
  equal!
</c:if><br/>

null == null  ${null == null}<br/>
"null" == null ${"null" == null}<br/>
```

The resulting output is as follows:

```
equal!
null == null true
"null" == null false
```

The named variable StrVar is initially set to the string true. This is a variable of type String. However, because the test attribute of the JSTL <c:if> tag requires a Boolean expression, it is automatically converted to a Boolean by EL before use. This causes the printing of the "equal!" message.

Finally, the comparison operator is being used on the special null value. It is shown here that while a null value can be successfully compared to another null value, the string "null" is not considered equal to the null value.

This concludes the coverage of the first example in this chapter. The next section takes a more detailed look at automatic type conversion, encountered earlier.

Coercion: Automatic Type Conversion

Programming in JSP in general, and in EL in particular, tends to be rather *weakly typed*. It is not necessary to declare the type of a variable before using it. This is rather unlike the Java programming language, where the data type and name of each variable must be declared before use.

The advantage of a weakly typed language such as EL is the ease of programming with it. The JSP/EL developer does not have to worry about declaring every variable used and figuring out the most appropriate type for each variable. Further adding to the ease of programming, the developer usually does not need to call any type of data-type conversion functions. Instead, developers can completely rely on a set of built-in rules, EL's type coercion rules in this case, to take care of type coercion for them.

The disadvantage of a weakly typed approach is that in some programming situations, you may need finer control over the data type conversion outcome. In these cases, you will need to understand different built-in rules and how they may affect the output.

Boxing and unboxing

The basic type conversion is based on *boxing*. Boxing is simply the action of creating an associated Java object from a primitive type. The following table shows the common Java primitive types and their boxed form.

Primitive Type	Boxed Type
int	Integer
long	Long
double	Double
char	Character
boolean	Boolean

To box an `int` variable means to wrap it in an `Integer`. To box a `long`, wrap it up in a `Long` instance. The action of converting a wrapped value to its associated primitive value is called *unboxing*. For example, unboxing a `Boolean` means obtaining the primitive `boolean` value from a `Boolean` instance.

Coercion, or automatic type conversion, occurs when the required type does not match the type of the incoming value/variable. For example, the attribute of a tag may require an `Integer` value, but the input value is a `String`. Before this conversion can happen, EL will always box a primitive type. The following sections take a look at the most commonly used coercions to examine what goes on under the hood.

Coercion to a string

Variable values are coerced to a `String` type as follows:

1. Box the variable if it is primitive.
2. Use the `toString()` method of the wrapping object to obtain the String equivalent.

157

Note that null values are returned as a null string, "". This ensures that nothing is rendered in the output if the object value is null. An error will result if the call of toString() throws an exception.

Coercion to a number

Number types include short, int, float, double, and their boxed types.

Variables of any type are coerced to number types by first boxing them if necessary; then, follow these steps:

1. If the type is String, use the valueOf() method to get its value; "" (empty string) will return 0.

2. If the type is Character, use new Short((short) v.charValue()), assuming the Character variable is called v.

3. Unbox the variable if necessary.

Null values in this case are returned as 0. If the type is a Boolean, an error will result. Numbers can always be converted successfully among themselves (for example, Integer to Float). If the call to valueOf() throws an exception, it results in an error.

Coercion to a character

Variable values are coerced to Character type by the following rules:

1. If the type is a Number type, first it is coerced to the type Short; then a Character is returned that is numerically equivalent to the short value.

2. If the type is String, the method charAt(0) is used to obtain the Character. This is essentially the first character of the string.

A null value causes a result of (char) 0. A Boolean incoming type will cause an error.

Best attempt to "do the right thing" without error

It should be clear that the automatic type conversion rules are designed to "do the right thing" in most circumstances. They will always try directing conversion if possible — for example, converting directly between the numeric data types.

Null values will always be converted to trivial type-correct values. For example, a null value for a String type is converted to an empty string, "". Null is converted to 0 for Numeric type, and (char) 0 to Character type. This enables a JSP to render a null value in most cases, without resulting in an error.

The following Try It Out exercise shows this automatic type conversion in action.

Try It Out   **Automatic Type Conversion**

With ch05.war deployed, access the following URL with your browser:

```
http://localhost:8080/ch05/example2/
```

The output of this example is illustrated in Figure 5-3.

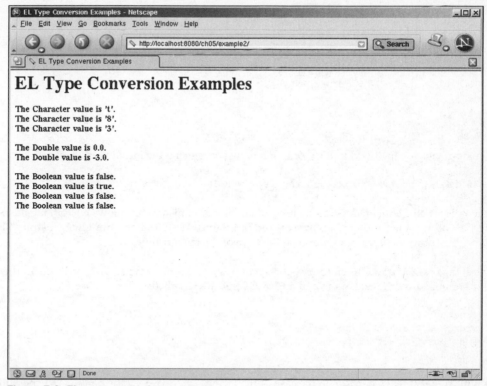

Figure 5-3: EL type conversion examples

In Figure 5-3, each line is the output of a custom tag from a custom tag library. These tags all have a `val` attribute that is a different data type. By supplying EL expressions of varying data types for the value of these attributes, the automatic type conversion feature of EL can be observed.

How It Works

You can find the JSP that produced the output in Figure 5-3 in `<Tomcat Installation Directory>/webapps/ch05/example2/index.jsp`. The content of this file is reproduced here:

```
<%@ taglib prefix="wroxtags" tagdir="/WEB-INF/tags" %>

<html>
<head>
  <title>EL Type Conversion Examples</title>
</head>
<body>
  <h1>EL Type Conversion Examples</h1>

  <wroxtags:CharacterType val="this is it"/>
  <wroxtags:CharacterType val="8"/>
```

```
<wroxtags:CharacterType val="3.0001"/>
<br/>
<wroxtags:DoubleType val=""/>
<wroxtags:DoubleType val="-3"/>
<br/>
<wroxtags:BooleanType val=""/>
<wroxtags:BooleanType val="true"/>
<wroxtags:BooleanType val="t"/>
<wroxtags:BooleanType val="3,1"/>

</body>
</html>
```

The custom tags are included in the `wroxtags` namespace using the initial `taglib` directive:

```
<%@ taglib prefix="wroxtags" tagdir="/WEB-INF/tags" %>
```

All the tags are implemented using the JSP 2.0 tag file mechanism. This allows custom tags to be created using JSP coding. Tags and tag files are covered in Chapter 11, "Building Your Own Custom JSP Tag Library." For now, focus your attention on the type of the tag attribute.

The first tag, `<wroxtags:CharacterType>`, requires a `Character` typed `val` attribute. In the `index.jsp` code, a `String`, an int, and a `float` value are supplied:

```
<wroxtags:CharacterType val="this is it"/>
<wroxtags:CharacterType val="8"/>
<wroxtags:CharacterType val="3.0001"/>
<br/>
```

This will trigger the EL coercion. In the case of the String "this is it", the `charAt(0)` method is used, resulting in a value of 't'. See the earlier section entitled "Coercion to a character" for details. The corresponding output from the tag is as follows:

```
The Character value is 't'.
```

In the case of the int 8, the number is boxed into an `Integer` object and coerced into a `Short`, and then a `Character` numerically equal to the `Short` is returned. The corresponding output from the tag follows:

```
The Character value is '8'.
```

In the case of the `float` 3.001, the number is boxed into a `Float` object and coerced into `Short`, and then a `Character` numerically equal to the `Short` is returned. The corresponding output from the tag follows:

```
The Character value is '3'.
```

The next tag is called `<wroxtags:DoubleType>` and requires a `Double` typed attribute. The following JSP code fragment from `index.jsp` tries to supply the value of various data types:

```
<wroxtags:DoubleType val=""/>
<wroxtags:DoubleType val="-3"/>
<br/>
```

The first line supplies an empty string as the value. According to the "Coercion to number" section earlier, an `" "` (empty string) will result in a numeric value of `0`. The resulting output is as follows:

```
The Double value is 0.0.
```

The second line supplies an integer value of `-3`. This `Numeric` type is boxed and converted to `Double`, resulting in the following output:

```
The Double value is -3.0.
```

The last tag is called `<wroxtags:BooleanType>` and requires a `Boolean` typed attribute. The code in `index.jsp` tries to assign the attribute with values of different data types:

```
<wroxtags:BooleanType val=""/>
<wroxtags:BooleanType val="true"/>
<wroxtags:BooleanType val="t"/>
<wroxtags:BooleanType val="3.1"/>
```

If you consult the JSP 2.0 specification, you will find that the coercion uses the `Boolean.valueOf()` method to obtain the value. The API documentation of this method basically says that only the text string `"true"` can be coerced into the Boolean value of `true`. Any other data type (except `boolean` or `Boolean`, of course) or value will result in `false`. Therefore, the following output results from the preceding JSP fragment:

```
The Boolean value is false.
The Boolean value is true.
The Boolean value is false.
The Boolean value is false.
```

For completeness, and the more curious readers, the rest of this section examines the tag's source code.

The source code to the tag files can be located at `<Tomcat Installation Directory>/webapps/ch05/WEB-INF/tags`. The `CharacterType.tag` file contains the following source code:

```
<%@attribute name="val" type="java.lang.Character" %>
<b>The Character value is '${val}'.</b><br/>
```

The `DoubleType.tag` file contains this source code:

```
<%@ attribute name="val" type="java.lang.Double" %>
<b>The Double value is ${val}.</b><br/>
```

The `BooleanType.tag` file contains this source code:

```
<%@ attribute name="val" type="java.lang.Boolean" %>
<b>The Boolean value is ${val}.</b><br/>
```

This concludes our examination of the second Try It Out exercise and EL's automatic type conversions.

The EL named variables refer to scoped attributes. Frequently, these attributes are Java objects or beans that have various properties. Occasionally, an attribute may be a Java collection that can be iterated through to obtain contained values. The following section examines how EL can be used to access properties of Java objects and collections.

Accessing Object Properties and Collections

When using EL to address the properties of a named variable, the "." or "[ ]" (square brackets) operators are used. For example, consider the following JSP fragment:

```
<b>You must earn ${member.minQual} points to maintain your membership.</b>
```

If the member named variable refers to a JavaBean, its minQual property is read and substituted. Of course, the property must exist and be readable. The getMinQual() method of the underlying JavaBean will be invoked to obtain the property value.

With EL, the preceding syntax is completely interchangeable with the following:

```
<b>You must earn ${member["minQual"]} points to maintain your membership.</b>
```

In addition to JavaBeans, the preceding syntax can also be used to address the following Java object types:

❏ Map

❏ List

❏ Array

For example, the expression ${pointsArray[8]} refers to the ninth element of the pointsArray array.

For a more complex data structure, consider a named variable (a JavaBean) called car that has a property called door, which is in turn a JavaBean that has a property called color that is a String type. The EL expression that accesses the color of the door will be ${car.door.color}. The "." operator can be used to access nested properties in this way.

For another example, consider a named variable (a JavaBean) called newsfeed. This named variable has a property (a Java HashMap) called temp containing world temperatures. This map consists of entries that map city names to their current temperatures. For example, {"Hong Kong" , "28 C"} may be an entry in this map, and {"Mumbai", "30 C"} may be another. Using EL, the temperature of Hong Kong can be referred to via ${newsfeed.temp ["Hong Kong"]}. The temperature of Mumbai can be accessed via the EL expression ${newsfeed.temp.Mumbai}.

Occasionally, you may need to work with an attribute attached to a JSP implicit scope object that may have a name containing the "." character, other special characters, or even characters from foreign character sets. In this case, the `[ ]` *notation is your only choice. For example, to obtain the value of an attribute named* `"javax.security.password"` *attached to the request scope, you must use the EL expression* `${requestScope["javax.security.password"]}`. *The EL implicit object,* `requestScope`, *will be covered shortly in this chapter.*

Time to see this in action. The next Try It Out example illustrates nested property access and the equivalence of the "`.`" and "`[ ]`" notations.

Try It Out   EL Access to Nested Properties

With `ch05.war` deployed, point your browser to the following URL:

```
http://localhost:8080/ch05/example3/
```

This example uses a `NewsFeed` Java object similar to the one used in the Chapter 2 portal example. EL is used to access the properties of this newsfeed object. The output of this page is shown in Figure 5-4.

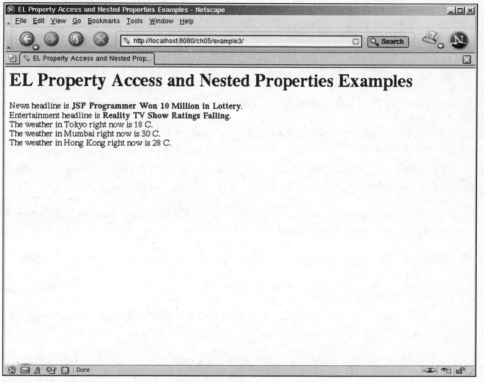

Figure 5-4: EL property access and nested properties examples

In Figure 5-4, the news headline and entertainment headline are shown, as well as the current temperature in three cities.

How It Works

The `index.jsp` that produced the output in Figure 5-4 is located at `<Tomcat Installation Directory>/webapps/ch05/example3/index.jsp`. The content of this file is reproduced here:

```
<%@ taglib prefix="c" uri="http://java.sun.com/jsp/jstl/core" %>
<jsp:useBean id="newsfeed" class="com.wrox.begjsp.ch5.NewsFeed" scope="page" />
<html>
<head>
  <title>EL Property Access and Nested Properties Examples</title>
</head>
<body>
  <h1>EL Property Access and Nested Properties Examples</h1>

  <jsp:setProperty name="newsfeed"  property="topic" value="news"/>
  News headline is <b>${newsfeed.value}</b>.<br/>

  <jsp:setProperty name="newsfeed"  property="topic" value="entertainment"/>
  Entertainment headline is <b>${newsfeed["value"]}</b>.<br/>
  <jsp:setProperty name="newsfeed"  property="topic" value="weather"/>
  The weather in Tokyo right now is ${newsfeed.values.Tokyo}.<br/>
  The weather in Mumbai right now is ${newsfeed["values"].Mumbai}.<br/>
  The weather in Hong Kong right now is ${newsfeed.values["Hong Kong"]}.<br/>
</body>
</html>
```

As a refresher, recall from Chapter 2 that the `NewsFeed` object can be used as follows:

❑　First set the `topic` property to either `news` or `entertainment`, and then read the `value` property for the headline of the news or entertainment section.

❑　First set the `topic` property to `weather`, and then read the `values` property for the temperature of various cities.

In this case, the `values` property for reading the weather information is actually a Java `Map`, with the name of the city as the key and the temperature of the city as the value.

First, an instance of the `NewsFeed` object is created by the standard `<jsp:useBean>` action:

```
<jsp:useBean id="newsfeed" class="com.wrox.begjsp.ch5.NewsFeed" scope="page" />
```

This action creates a `page` scoped attribute that is accessible as an EL named variable, via the name `newsfeed`. The `newsfeed` named variable can immediately be used in EL expressions.

To print out the news headline, first the `topic` property of `newsfeed` is set to `news`; then the `value` property is read to get the headline. This is done via the following JSP code, involving the `<jsp:setProperty>` standard action and an inline EL expression:

```
<jsp:setProperty name="newsfeed"  property="topic" value="news"/>
News headline is <b>${newsfeed.value}</b>.<br/>
```

Note that the `${newsfeed.value}` expression is used to access the `value` property of the `newsfeed` JavaBean. The resulting HTML output is as follows:

```
News headline is <b>JSP Programmer Won 10 Million in Lottery.</b><br/>
```

To print out the entertainment headline, the exact same approach is used. This time, the `topic` property is set to `entertainment` and the `value` property is read to get the headline. The following JSP code from `index.jsp` is responsible for this:

```
<jsp:setProperty name="newsfeed"  property="topic" value="entertainment"/>
Entertainment headline is <b>${newsfeed["value"]}</b>.<br/>
```

Note that the `${newsfeed["value"]}` EL expression is used to access the entertainment headline. As mentioned earlier, this is entirely equivalent to the expression `${newsfeed.value}` used to fetch the news headline. The resulting HTML output is as follows:

```
Entertainment headline is <b>Reality TV Show Ratings Falling.</b><br/>
```

To access the weather information, a more complex data structure needs to be accessed. This is the `values` property of the `newsfeed` object. Figure 5-5 shows this Java data structure.

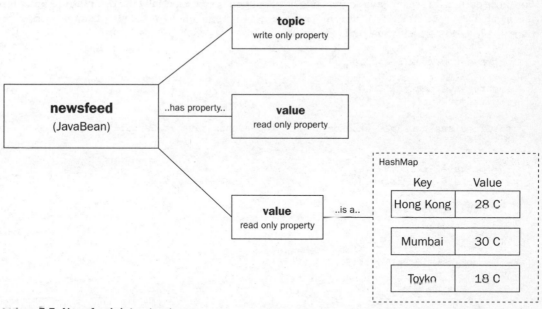

Figure 5-5: Newsfeed data structure

In Figure 5-5, the `values` property is a readable property of the `newsfeed` JavaBean. This property is accessible only after the topic is set to `weather`. The property itself is a `Map`. The key of the map is the name of the cities, and the associated value is the temperature.

The following code in the `index.jsp` file used in this example will access and print out the cities and their temperature:

```
<jsp:setProperty name="newsfeed"  property="topic" value="weather"/>
The weather in Tokyo right now is ${newsfeed.values.Tokyo}.<br/>
The weather in Mumbai right now is ${newsfeed["values"].Mumbai}.<br/>
The weather in Hong Kong right now is ${newsfeed.values["Hong Kong"]}.<br/>
```

The EL expression `${newsfeed.values.Tokyo}` is used to access the temperature in Tokyo; note the nested property access using the `.` operator. As a variation, the temperature of Mumbai is accessed using the EL expression `${newsfeed["values"].Mumbai}`; of course, this is entirely equivalent to the EL expression `${newsfeed.values.Mumbai}`. You may want to try changing it and see for yourself. Finally, the temperature in Hong Kong is displayed using the EL expression `${newsfeed.values["Hong Kong"]}`. Because there is a space character in the city name, this is the most convenient way of accessing the temperature value. Executing the previous JSP fragment will result in all the temperatures being displayed via the following HTML:

```
The weather in Tokyo right now is 18 C.<br/>
The weather in Mumbai right now is 30 C.<br/>
The weather in Hong Kong right now is 28 C.<br/>
```

For those curious to see the Java source code of `NewsFeed.java`, especially the complex `values` property, it is located at `<Tomcat Installation Directory>/webapps/ch05/WEB-INF/classes/com/wrox/begjsp/ch5/NewsFeed.java`, and is reproduced here:

```
package com.wrox.begjsp.ch5;

import java.beans.*;
import java.util.*;

public class NewsFeed extends Object implements java.io.Serializable
{
    private String topic;
    private String value;
    private HashMap values;

    public NewsFeed()
    {
    }

    public void setTopic(String topic)
    {
        value = "";
        values = null;
        if (topic.equals("news"))
        {
            value = "JSP Programmer Won 10 Million in Lottery";
        }
```

```
        if (topic.equals("entertainment"))
        {
            value = "Reality TV Show Ratings Falling";
        }
        if (topic.equals("weather"))
        {
            values = new HashMap();
            values.put("Mumbai", "30 C");
            values.put("Tokyo", "18 C");
            values.put("Hong Kong", "28 C");
        }
    }

    public String getValue()
    {
        return this.value;
    }

    public Map getValues()
    {
        return this.values;
    }
}
```

This concludes the coverage of this Try It Out example and EL-based property access.

When named variables were discussed earlier, you learned that EL will first try to match a name to EL implicit objects before attributes attached to scoping objects are checked. Now is a good time to take a look at the set of available EL implicit objects and how you can use them.

Implicit EL Objects in JSP 2.0

Implicit objects in EL are available to the JSP developer, within an EL expression, without any explicit coding or declarations. Implicit objects are designed to facilitate JSP programming and make the most common aspects of a JSP page immediately available to code written in EL.

There are a total of 11 implicit objects. These 11 implicit objects can be classified into five major categories:

❑   JSP implicit object

❑   Convenience scoping access implicit objects

❑   Convenience parameter access implicit objects

❑   Convenience header access implicit objects

❑   The convenience initialization parameter access implicit object

The only EL implicit object in the JSP implicit object category is the `pageContext` implicit object. This is the very same object as the JSP implicit object of the same name (JSP implicit objects and their use are covered later in Chapter 9, "JSP and JavaBeans"). The rest of the EL implicit objects are Java maps, and they simply provide easier means for accessing certain properties of the `pageContext` implicit object.

There are four convenience scoping access implicit objects, called `pageScope`, `requestScope`, `sessionScope`, and `applicationScope`. These are maps that enable easy access to scoped attributes. For example, an attribute called `username` attached to the `request` scope can be accessed directly via the EL expression `${requestScope.username}`.

There are two convenience parameter access implicit objects for accessing the HTTP request parameters (the form submission parameters): `param` and `paramValues`. The `param` is a map used to access single-valued parameters, and `paramValues` can be used to access parameters that may contain multiple values. The next Try It Out example shows how this is handled.

There are three convenience header access implicit objects for accessing the HTTP headers: `header`, `headerValues`, and `cookie`. These are maps that are useful in cases where you may need raw access to HTTP header and/or cookies.

There is one convenience initialization parameter access implicit object, `initParam`. This map can be used to access the value of initialization parameters, typically set in `web.xml`.

Any information obtainable using a convenience object may also be obtained via the `pageContext` implicit object, although the access may involve complex nested property access.

If you use one of the names mentioned in this section for any attributes that you attach to scoping objects, the attribute may become inaccessible. The names provided here always return the implicit object instead of any attributes. For example `${param}` always refers to the EL implicit object, and not a named attribute called `param`.

The next Try It Out example shows how to work with several of the EL convenience access implicit objects.

Try It Out EL Implicit Objects

With `ch05.war` deployed, access the following URL to try out example 4:

```
http://localhost:8080/ch05/example4/
```

This JSP page presents a Design a Cake form, as shown in Figure 5-6.

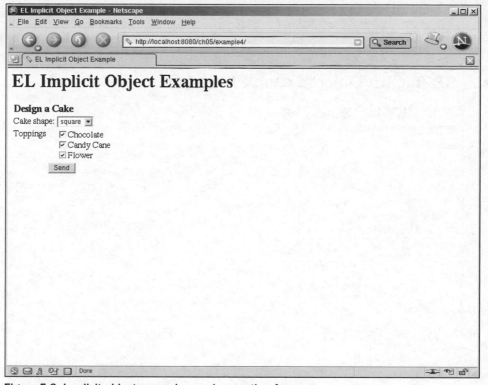

Figure 5-6: Implicit object example: a cake creation form

In Figure 5-6, you can select the shape of the cake that you want to make, and up to three toppings for the cake.

When you click the Send button, the form parameters are sent to another JSP called `formproc.jsp` for processing. The resulting page is displayed in Figure 5-7. In this case, the square cake is selected with all three of the toppings.

Note that in Figure 5-7, the incoming form parameters are printed out. This includes the shape, and the ingredients, which can have multiple values. In addition, the identifier of the user's browser is also displayed. This browser information is obtained from the HTTP header of the incoming request.

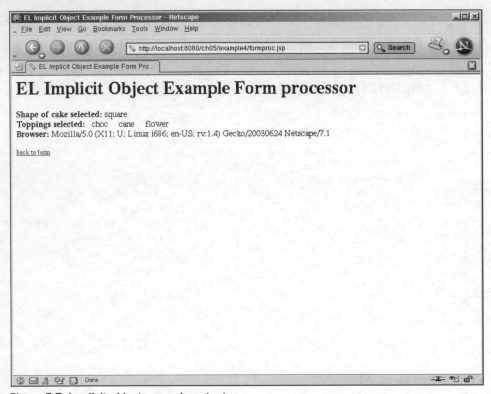

Figure 5-7: Implicit object example output

How It Works

The `index.jsp` that creates the cake creation form in Figure 5-6 is located at `<Tomcat Installation Directory>/webapps/ch05/example4/index.jsp`. The content of this JSP is reproduced here:

```
<%@ taglib prefix="c" uri="http://java.sun.com/jsp/jstl/core" %>

<html>
<head>
  <title>EL Implicit Object Example</title>
</head>
<body>
  <h1>EL Implicit Object Examples</h1>
  <form action="formproc.jsp" method="post">
    <table>
      <tr>
        <td colspan="2"><h3>Design a Cake</h3></td>
      </tr>
      <tr>
        <td>Cake shape:</td>
        <td>
          <select name="shape">
```

```
            <option>round</option>
            <option>square</option>
            <option>heart</option>
          </select>
        </td>
      </tr>
      <tr>
        <td valign="top">Toppings</td>
        <td>
          <input type="checkbox" name="topping" value="choc">Chocolate</input><br/>
          <input type="checkbox" name="topping" value="cane">Candy Cane</input><br/>
          <input type="checkbox" name="topping" value="flower">Flower</input><br/>
        </td>

      </tr>

      <tr>
        <td colspan="2">
        <center><input type="submit" value="Send"/></center>
        </td>
      </tr>
    </table>
  </form>
</body>
</html>
```

This JSP page has no active JSP code, just an HTML form. The shape selection is offered through a
`<select>` HTML tag. Upon form submission, this will result in an HTTP request parameter (form
submission) called shape, with a value of round, square, or heart:

```
<select name="shape">
  <option>round</option>
  <option>square</option>
  <option>heart</option>
 </select>
```

The selection of toppings is provided through a series of HTML check boxes. This allows for the selection of multiple values:

```
<input type="checkbox" name="topping" value="choc">Chocolate</input><br/>
<input type="checkbox" name="topping" value="cane">Candy Cane</input><br/>
<input type="checkbox" name="topping" value="flower">Flower</input><br/>
```

Upon form submission, this will result in an HTTP request parameter called topping that can contain
zero or more of choc, cane, and/or flower.

When the form is submitted, the POST method is used to send the request parameters via an HTTP
header back to the server. The attributes of the HTML `<form>` tag specified this:

```
<form action="formproc.jsp" method="post">
```

171

The form processing JSP is `formproc.jsp`, located at `<Tomcat Installation Directory>`/webapps/
`ch05/example4/formproc.jsp` and reproduced here:

```
<%@ taglib prefix="c" uri="http://java.sun.com/jsp/jstl/core" %>

<html>
<head>
  <title>EL Implicit Object Example Form Processor</title>
</head>
<body>
  <h1>EL Implicit Object Example Form processor</h1>

  <b>Shape of cake selected:</b> ${param.shape}<br/>
  <b>Toppings selected:</b>

  <c:forEach var="aTopping" items="${paramValues.topping}">
      ${aTopping}  
  </c:forEach>
  <br/>

  <b>Browser:</b> ${header["user-agent"]}<br/>

  <br/>
  <small><a href="index.jsp">back to form</a></small>
</body>
</html>
```

The convenience access implicit object, `param`, is used to render the value of the cake's shape. This is
done in `formproc.jsp` via the following code:

```
<b>Shape of cake selected:</b> ${param.shape}<br/>
```

Note how easy it is to access form submission parameters through the `param` implicit object. In this case,
this will result in the following output:

```
<b>Shape of cake selected:</b> square<br/>
```

Because the `topping` parameter may have multiple values, it is necessary to access it through the
`paramValues` implicit object. The following code in `formproc.jsp` renders all the selected toppings:

```
<b>Toppings selected:</b>
<c:forEach var="aTopping" items="${paramValues.topping}">
    ${aTopping}  
</c:forEach>
```

The JSTL `<c:forEach>` iterator tag is used to go through each value of the `paramValues.topping`
request parameter. Note that the `paramValues` implicit object has made the processing of multivalued
form parameters quite simple. In this case, all toppings are selected, with the resulting HTML:

```
<b>Toppings selected:</b>
  choc  
  cane  
  flower  
```

Last but not least, the final active line in `formproc.jsp` accesses the HTTP header called `user-agent`, which contains an identifier to the browser being used by the client. The following code renders this identifier:

```
<b>Browser:</b> ${header["user-agent"]}<br/>
```

Note the use of the EL implicit `header` object. The EL expression `${header["user-agent"]}` accesses the HTTP header called `user-agent` directly. When Internet Explorer 6 on Windows XP is used to access this Try It Out example, the following browser identifier is rendered:

```
<b>Browser:</b> Mozilla/4.0 (compatible; MSIE 6.0; Windows NT 5.1)<br/>
```

This concludes our coverage of the Try It Out example and EL implicit objects.

User-Supplied Functions within EL

When you are using JSP to create your application's Web user interface, you may need to transform, manipulate, or format the data that you are rendering. Typically, a custom tag library can be used to achieve this. However, you may occasionally have a need to do this at the EL expression level. Unfortunately, EL has no built-in function library for this purpose. Thankfully, EL does support the notion of user-supplied EL functions.

Namespace and EL functions

The EL syntax to access a user-supplied function includes the use of a namespace. This is a borrowed concept from tags. In fact, EL functions are described in the Tag Library Descriptors (TLD) file. Creating tags and TLDs is covered in detail in Chapter 11. The information provided here will enable you to create some EL-accessible functions.

For example, to use an EL function that returns the absolute value of a number, called `abs()`, you may use the following EL expression: `${wf:abs(num)}`.

This means that the `wf` namespace is defined in a `<taglib>` directive earlier — for example, a `<taglib>` directive similar to the following:

```
<%@ taglib prefix="wf" uri="http://www.wrox.com/begjsp/el-functions-taglib" %>
```

This syntax enables you to use functions with the same name, but with totally different implementations, using different namespace prefixes. For example, `wf:abs()` may have a completely different implementation than `wroxdp:abs()` has.

Static methods of a Java class

EL functions are static methods defined in Java code. They can return the value of any data type, although the `String` return type is most useful when rendering in EL expressions. These methods may also have any number of arguments. The TLD must describe the return data type and the arguments' data types of the methods. For example, the following TLD fragment describes a function that returns a `String` and takes a `String` and an `int` as arguments:

```
<function>
  <description>Repeat String Function</description>
  <name>rep</name>
  <function-class>com.wrox.begjsp.ch05.ElFuncs</function-class>
  <function-signature>String rep(String,  int )</function-signature>
</function>
```

The final Try It Out example in this chapter shows how to expose a couple of `java.lang.Math` methods for use in EL expressions.

Try It Out   Your Own EL Functions

With `ch05.war` deployed, point your browser to the following URL to try out example 5:

```
http://localhost:8080/ch05/example5/
```

This example utilizes two EL functions: One function takes the absolute value of an integer and the other function rounds a float number to an integer. The result is shown in Figure 5-8.

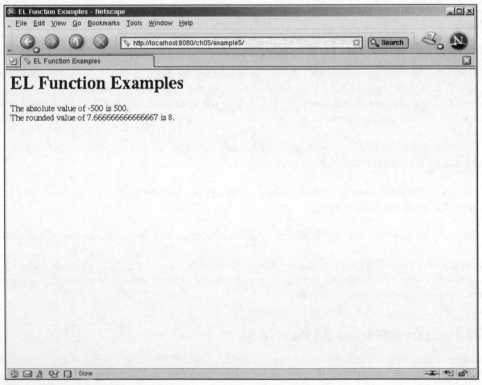

Figure 5-8: EL function examples

In Figure 5-8, the absolute value of –500 is obtained using the EL absolute value function, while a long float number is rounded up using the EL round function.

How It Works

Instead of coding our own static methods in our own Java classes, the code in this Try It Out example simply exposes the `abs()` and `round()` static methods from the `java.lang.Math` Java library package.

The `index.jsp` that exercises the two functions, as in Figure 5-8, can be located at `<Tomcat Installation Directory>/webapps/ch05/example5/index.jsp`. The content of this JSP is reproduced here:

```
<%@ taglib prefix="c" uri="http://java.sun.com/jsp/jstl/core" %>
<%@ taglib prefix="wf" uri="http://www.wrox.com/begjsp/el-functions-taglib" %>

<html>
<head>
  <title>EL Function Examples</title>
</head>
<body>
  <h1>EL Function Examples</h1>
  <c:set var="num" value="-500"/>
  The absolute value of ${num} is ${wf:abs(num)}.<br/>

  <c:set var="calc" value="${1 + 2 * 3 + 4 div 6}"/>
  The rounded value of ${calc} is ${wf:round(calc)}.<br/>

</body>
</html>
```

Note that the namespace used to map the functions is `wf`, and is defined by the `<taglib>` directive:

```
<%@ taglib prefix="wf" uri="http://www.wrox.com/begjsp/el-functions-taglib" %>
```

The `abs()` function is called in the following code from the `index.jsp`:

```
<c:set var="num" value="-500"/>
The absolute value of ${num} is ${wf:abs(num)}.<br/>
```

The function is invoked in the EL expression `${wf:abs(num)}`. The resulting output, after the `abs()` function is called, is as follows:

```
The absolute value of -500 is 500.
```

The `round()` function is called in the following code from the `index.jsp`:

```
<c:set var="calc" value="${1 + 2 * 3 + 4 div 6}"/>
The rounded value of ${calc} is ${wf:round(calc)}.<br/>
```

The round function is invoked in the EL expression `${wf:round(calc)}`. The resulting output is as follows:

```
The rounded value of 7.666666666666667 is 8.
```

The `<taglib>` directive in `index.jsp` uses a URI of `http://www.wrox.com/begjsp/el-functions-taglib` to select the TLD to use. The following section shows how this is mapped to the `java.lang.Math` methods.

Deployment descriptor entries

The first file to look at is the `ch05` application's `web.xml` file, its deployment descriptor. You can locate this file at `<Tomcat Installation Directory>/webapps/ch05/example5/WEB-INF/web.xml`. This file is reproduced here, with the tag library declaration entry highlighted:

```xml
<?xml version="1.0" encoding="ISO-8859-1"?>
<web-app xmlns="http://java.sun.com/xml/ns/j2ee"
    xmlns:xsi="http://www.w3.org/2001/XMLSchema-instance"
    xsi:schemaLocation="http://java.sun.com/xml/ns/j2ee
http://java.sun.com/xml/ns/j2ee/web-app_2_4.xsd"
    version="2.4">

  <description>
    Wrox Beginning JSP Examples - Chapter 5
  </description>
  <display-name>Chapter 5 Example (Wrox Beginning JSP)</display-name>

    <taglib>
     <taglib-uri>
       http://www.wrox.com/begjsp/el-functions-taglib
     </taglib-uri>
     <taglib-location>
       /WEB-INF/jsp/function-taglib.tld
     </taglib-location>
    </taglib>

</web-app>
```

The URI `http://www.wrox.com/begjsp/el-functions-taglib` is mapped to a TLD file, located at `WEB-INF/jsp/function-taglib.tld` as indicated by the `<taglib>` declaration in the preceding code.

TLD function definitions

The EL functions are declared within the `function-taglib.tld` file. This file is located at `<Tomcat Installation Directory>/webapps/ch05/example5/WEB-INF/jsp/function-taglib.tld`. This TLD file is reproduced here, with the function declarations highlighted:

```xml
<?xml version="1.0" encoding="UTF-8" ?>

<taglib xmlns="http://java.sun.com/xml/ns/j2ee"
    xmlns:xsi="http://www.w3.org/2001/XMLSchema-instance"
    xsi:schemaLocation="http://java.sun.com/xml/ns/j2ee web-jsptaglibrary_2_0.xsd"
    version="2.0">
  <description>A taglib to define some EL accessible functions.</description>
  <tlib-version>1.0</tlib-version>
  <short-name>ELFunctionTaglib</short-name>
  <uri>/ELFunctionTagLibrary</uri>
```

```
  <function>
    <description>Exposes the abs() function from java.lang.Math
package</description>
    <name>abs</name>
    <function-class>java.lang.Math</function-class>
    <function-signature>int abs( int )</function-signature>
  </function>

  <function>
    <description>Exposes the round() function from java.lang.Math
package</description>
    <name>round</name>
    <function-class>java.lang.Math</function-class>
    <function-signature>int round( double )</function-signature>
  </function>
</taglib>
```

Note how the class implementing the function is specified within the `<function-class>` sub-element, and the signature of the function is declared in the `<function-signature>` sub-element of the declaration.

This concludes our coverage of the final Try It out example and EL functions.

Summary

This chapter covered the JSP Expression Language (EL) in detail. EL is essential to JSP 2.0 because it enables the creation of scriptless JSP applications. Scriptless JSPs focus on the presentation of the data, do not contain embedded Java language elements, and are easier to maintain for the long term.

To summarize what we covered:

- ❏ EL expressions may be used inline with template data, or within certain attributes of standard or custom actions.

- ❏ EL provides a rich set of operators, including arithmetic operators, logical operators, the comparison operator, and the empty prefix operator.

- ❏ Working together with JSTL custom tags, EL expressions can be used in the flow control of JSP logic, eliminating the need for scriptlets.

- ❏ Named variables in EL are scoped attributes. The properties of any JavaBean-based object can be accessed via the " . " operator, and this can be applied in a nested fashion. The " . " operator is equivalent to the " [. .] " operator. Either notation can be used.

- ❏ EL features 11 implicit objects that can be used to access the `PageContext`, attributes attached to JSP scoping objects, HTTP headers, request parameters, JSP initialization parameters, and HTTP cookies.

- ❏ EL programming is weakly typed. The developer relies on the automatic type conversion provided by EL to coerce data into the required data type. The automatic type conversion provided by EL is well documented. It will attempt to do the right thing most of the time. However, understanding how this conversion takes place can be useful in certain uncommon programming situations.

❑ Whenever possible, null values are converted into the appropriate type (for example, null strings or zero value) to avoid errors during JSP processing.

❑ Static functions of Java classes can be mapped via a Tag Library Descriptor to functions that can be accessed through EL expressions. This can be used to extend EL's functionality.

Exercises

1. Create a JSP-based application that takes a number between 1 to 10 as input, and then prints a simple multiplication table. For example, if the number 5 is entered, the following should appear in the output page:

> 5 times 1 is 5.
>
> 5 times 2 is 10.
>
> 5 times 3 is 15.
>
> 5 times 4 is 20.
>
> 5 times 5 is 25.
>
> 5 times 6 is 30.
>
> 5 times 7 is 35.
>
> 5 times 8 is 40.
>
> 5 times 9 is 45.
>
> 5 times 10 is 50.

Use EL and EL expressions wherever possible in your solution.

2. Write code to expose the following additional functions from the `java.lang.Math` package to EL expressions:

> `min()`
>
> `max()`
>
> `sin()`
>
> `cos()`
>
> `sqrt()`

3. Create a JSP page to test the functions.

JSP Tag Libraries
and JSTL

During the detailed examination of JSP's expression language (EL) in the last chapter, you saw that it is almost impossible not to use JSTL in conjunction with EL. In fact, the JSP Standard Tag Library (JSTL) and EL are so highly integrated that they are almost always mentioned as one entity by developers.

JSP developers can readily extend the capability of their Web applications by making use of tag libraries. A tag library makes a set of new tags available to your JSP programs. JSTL is the most commonly used library by JSP developers. It adds essential features to JSP, such as conditional flow control and iteration, that enable JSP programming without the need for embedded Java code.

This chapter introduces the basics of the tag library extension mechanism in JSP. It also examines JSTL in detail. The chapter explains the following concepts:

- ❑ What a tag library is
- ❑ Why you need tag libraries
- ❑ How to use a tag library
- ❑ Tag library packaging
- ❑ The Tag Library Descriptor (TLD)
- ❑ JSTL named variables
- ❑ JSTL control flow
- ❑ JSTL iteration
- ❑ JSTL formatting tags
- ❑ JSTL custom functions

To provide some hands-on experience with JSTL, the chapter features a real-world example. The example involves the conversion of an e-commerce site originally programmed using extensive scripting (embedded Java code) to one that uses only JSTL. This is a very common activity in production JSP programming. Developers are frequently asked to maintain or migrate legacy JSP code to the new JSP 2.0 standard. Due to the complexity of this example, it is presented in two separate parts.

By the end of this chapter, you will understand the role of tag libraries, and appreciate their importance for JSP development. In addition to becoming very familiar with the most frequently used tags in JSTL, you will learn many techniques used by production developers when converting legacy scripting-based JSP pages to JSTL-based ones.

The Vital Role of JSP Tag Libraries

JSP tag libraries are collections of custom actions (tags) that can be made available in JSP pages. Once a tag library is added to a JSP page, all its tags are available for programming.

Tag libraries provide additional functionality above and beyond that provided by the standard actions and implicit objects of JSP. Tag libraries are typically created to be portable between different JSP containers. This portability ensures that JSP code created using the tag library can be deployed across all JSP containers.

The wide availability and standardization of tag libraries makes it possible to create JSP pages without the need for scripting elements (embedded Java language coding within a JSP). Before the availability of tag libraries, JSP programmers were forced to embed Java code within JSP to access additional functionality.

As you learned in Chapter 3, "JSP Basics 2: Generalized Templating and Server Scripting," using scripting elements (embedding Java programming language code) within JSP is now a practice that is highly discouraged. Included among the many reasons for this are the following:

❑   Using Java coding, the developer is exposed to the entire API set, and it is easy to create non-portable code that has dependencies on a specific machine and/or system configuration.

❑   Having the capability to access system elements via the Java programming language encourages the mixing of application business logic within the JSP, potentially polluting the presentation layer with it.

❑   Embedded Java code mixed with JSP is difficult to read and debug, and therefore difficult to maintain.

❑   In production projects, UI/visual layout of a Web page is usually created and modified by Web designers, who are generally not Java developers. Tag libraries, with their HTML-like syntax, are easier for them to handle than embedded Java scriptlets.

Without adequate basic tag library support, it is impossible not to use scripting elements in JSPs. The basic set of standard actions and implicit objects falls short of the capabilities of a general programming language. Among the missing features are the following:

- Capability to work with data of different types

- Capability to work with arithmetic and logical expressions

- Capability to work with properties of Java objects

- Capability to create variables that can be associated with different scopes

- Control flow constructs (if...then...else, and so on)

- Iterative constructs

- Functions to convert and work with strings

- Functions to format data of different types

- Capability to flexibly work with URLs

- Capability to access a database

All of these missing capabilities are frequently needed by JSP developers. They can be added by using a tag library. In fact, the demand for these features is so high that a standard tag library, eventually to be made a part of standard JSP, has been created to fulfill the void.

The JSP Standard Tag Library

JSTL is the most frequently used JSP tag library. The latest available version is JSTL 1.1. This tag library includes a set of useful tags that address the following programming areas:

- General tags to set scoped variables, display expressions and values, remove scoped variables, and catch exceptions

- Conditional flow control tags, including if and a switch...case-like construct

- An iteration tag for iteration through elements in a collection or counted iterations

- URL tags for working with URLs within your JSP, and for loading resources via a URL

- Tags to support the internationalization of your application

- Tags to format numbers and dates

- Tags to access a relational database

- A set of EL accessible functions for string manipulation

The syntax of these tags and functions is described in detail in Appendix C, "JSTL Reference." These descriptions are mentioned only briefly in this chapter. The focus of this chapter is on examples that demonstrate how the tags may be used in actual applications.

Anatomy of a Tag Library

Figure 6-1 illustrates the code and description files that make up a tag library.

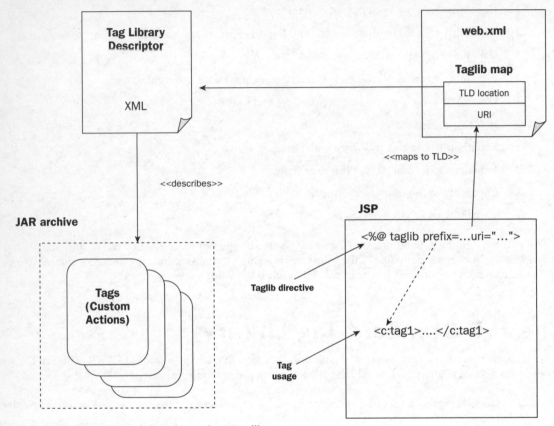

Figure 6-1: The code and descriptors in a tag library

Figure 6-1 shows that a Tag Library Descriptor file (TLD) is included with most tag libraries. The content of this file describes the tags and their parameterization to the container (or a development tool). TLD files are text files created in the XML format.

The Tag Library Descriptor

When tags are used in JSP, a TLD is always involved. However, it may not be necessary to explicitly create a TLD file under certain circumstances. For example, a development tool or IDE may generate the TLD automatically. Also, when creating tags using JSP — a feature of JSP 2.0 called *tag files* (covered in Chapter 11, "Building Your Own Custom JSP Tag Library") — the container can create a TLD internally.

Note also in Figure 6-1 that the actual implementation of the tags can reside in the <application directory>/WEB-INF/lib directory, the <application directory>/WEB-INF/classes directory, or in JSP-based tag files residing in a directory below <application directory>/WEB-INF.

A JSP page declares (to the JSP container) that it needs a specific tag library by using a `<taglib>` directive. The `<taglib>` directive refers to a URI that designates the tag library that will be used. In addition, the `<taglib>` directive also associates a prefix, called a *namespace,* with the tags in a tag library. For example, consider the following JSP fragment:

```
<%@ taglib prefix="wxshop" uri="http://www.wrox.com/begjsp/eshop-functions-taglib" %>
```

The preceding `<taglib>` directive declares the use of tags in the tag library associated with the URI `http://www.wrox.com/begjsp/eshop-functions-taglib`. It also declares that all tags in this tag library should be prefixed with `wxshop:`.

The URI can be any valid URL. It is never used directly to access the tag library over a network. Rather, it is a means for mapping a unique string to the actual TLD.

The taglib map in the web.xml deployment descriptor

Additional mapping information is required to locate the actual TLD file. The mapping is called the *taglib map.* The taglib map consists of a `<taglib>` element in the application's `web.xml` deployment descriptor file. For example, the following is a `<taglib>` element:

```
<taglib>
  <taglib-uri>
    http://www.wrox.com/begjsp/eshop-functions-taglib
  </taglib-uri>
  <taglib-location>
    /WEB-INF/jsp/eshop-taglib.tld
  </taglib-location>
</taglib>
```

The previous taglib map specifies that the URI `http://www.wrox.com/begjsp/eshop-functions-taglib` should map to the taglib described by the `/WEB-INF/jsp/eshop-taglib.tld` TLD file. The path specified in the `<taglib-location>` element is relative to the Web application's main directory (with Tomcat 5, this is the `<Tomcat Installation Directory>/webapps/<application name>` directory).

Through the taglib map in the `web.xml` file, the JSP container locates the actual TLD file. The container can then read the TLD file and determine the following:

- ❑ The location of the implementation code for the tags
- ❑ The name of the tags
- ❑ The attributes of each tag and their expected data type
- ❑ Whether the attribute can be dynamic (and take runtime expressions, such as an EL expression)
- ❑ Information interesting to the container, including how to load and run the tags, and whether certain tags work in collaboration with others

The content of the TLD, therefore, is interesting mostly to containers and development tools. Anyone who writes his or her own tags must also know the format intimately. Chapter 11 explores the format when you create your own custom tag library.

Locating JSTL and understanding tag library packaging

As with Tomcat, the reference JSTL implementation can be downloaded from the Jakarta project:

```
http://jakarta.apache.org/site/binindex.cgi
```

Finding the actual download is not quite straightforward. First, look for the `Taglibs` binaries on this page. You will then be directed to a directory with many different tag libraries. All of these libraries are maintained by the Jakarta folks. JSTL is in the `standard` directory. You should find the latest version of JSTL in this directory (JSTL 1.1 in this case).

When you extract the download, you will find two JAR files: `jstl.jar` and `standard.jar`. To use JSTL with your JSPs, you need only to place these two JAR files into your application's `WEB-INF/lib` directory. The container will load any JAR files placed into this directory and make their classes available to the JSPs.

You may wonder where the TLD files for the JSTL tags are and why you don't need to create a taglib map for JSTL in the application's `web.xml`. The TLD files are actually inside the JAR files. All JSP containers will check the JAR file (under the `META-INF` directory within the JAR, to be exact) for TLD files. Because the container can locate the JSTL TLD files without using a taglib map, there is no need to keep the location information in `web.xml`. The mapping URI information, however, still exists and is actually an element within the TLD file itself.

In summary, tag libraries can be packaged in many different ways, as described in the following table.

Tag Library Packaging	Description
In JAR archives	TLD expected under the `META-INF` directory; the URI used to map the taglib should be specified in the TLD; all implementations for the tags should be included.
Binaries under the `WEB-INF/classes` directory	The taglib maps in `web.xml` that specify the URI used to access the taglib, and specify the location of the TLD file.
Tag files under the `WEB-INF` subdirectories	The taglib directive inside the JSP page directly specifies the directory in which the tag files reside; no need for the TLD or taglib map in `web.xml`.

JSTL tags

There are many very useful tags in JSTL 1.1. These tags can be classified, according to their functions, into four groups that can be used when creating a JSP page:

❑   Core tags

❑   Formatting tags

❑   XML tags

❑   SQL tags

The following sections briefly describe some of the more frequently used tags in each of these groups. See Appendix C, "JSTL Reference," for a more complete description of JSTL tags and their syntax.

Core tags

The core group of tags are the most frequently used JSTL tags. Some useful core tags include the following:

❑   `<c:if>` for conditional flow

❑   `<c:forEach>` and `<c:forTokens>` for iteration

❑   `<c:choose>`...`<c:when>`....`<c:otherwise>` for selective flow between mutually exclusive code

❑   `<c:set>` and `<c:remove>` for working with scoped variables

❑   `<c:out>` for rendering the value of variables and expressions

❑   `<c:catch>` for working with Java exceptions

❑   `<c:url>` for creating and working with URLs

Formatting tags

The JSTL formatting tags are used to format and display text, the date, the time, and numbers. More specifically, they can be used to create internationalized Web applications. Internationalization is the ability to adapt an application for use in different part of the world — using different languages, character sets, input methods, date and time conventions, and so on. Internationalization is the subject of Chapter 13, "Internationalization and Localized Content."

Tags from this library that are frequently used in JSP include the following:

❑   **`<fmt:formatNumber>`:** To render numerical value with specific precision or format

❑   **`<fmt:formatDate>`:** To render date and time values in a specific format (and according to international locale-specific conventions)

❑   **`<fmt:message>`:** To display an internationalized message (for example, a message in a different language using a different character set)

See Appendix C for a more comprehensive reference to the tags in this group. Consult Chapter 13 to see how to use these tags to create internationalized applications.

XML tags and SQL tags

The JSTL XML tags are designed to process XML data. It includes tags that support XML data-parsing, transforming XML, plus data and flow control based on XPath expressions. These tags are used only when you need to work directly, within the JSP, with XML data.. See Appendix C for more information.

The JSTL SQL tags are designed to work directly with relational databases for rapid prototyping or proof-of-concept purposes. Chapter 23, "Access to Databases," shows many of these tags in action. While useful, these tags are not recommended for general production use. This is because accessing relational databases at the JSP presentation layer is not an encouraged programming practice. See Appendix C for more information on the detailed syntax of these tags.

The example in this chapter uses many of the JSTL tags from the core and formatting groups in very practical ways. There are two JSPs in the example application. The next section takes a look at only the first JSP page in the application.

Try It Out   Converting a Legacy Scripting Application to JSTL

To try out the example, first deploy `ch06.war` on your Tomcat 5 server. Review Chapter 1 if you do not remember how to deploy a WAR file.

Access the following URL with your browser to see the output of the example:

```
http://localhost:8080/ch06/example1/estore.jsp
```

You should see the welcome screen of the e-commerce application, similar to the window shown in Figure 6-2.

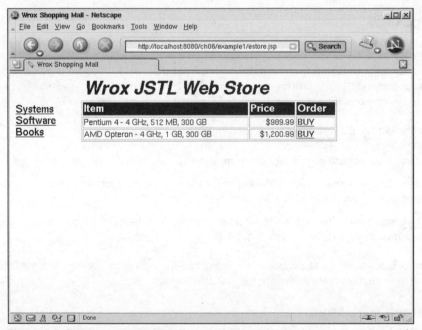

Figure 6-2: E-commerce application welcome screen

The Web store shown in Figure 6-2 looks just like the one in Chapter 3, "JSP Basics 2: Generalized Templating and Server Scripting." In fact, the logic is identical. However, this Web store is implemented completely script-free — without any embedded Java code. All of the logic is implemented using JSTL/EL and JSP standard actions. In addition, a stylesheet has been added to improve the appearance of the Web store.

Figure 6-2 shows the computer systems in the store available by default. Try clicking the Software category link on the left. You should end up with the software products being displayed, as shown in Figure 6-3.

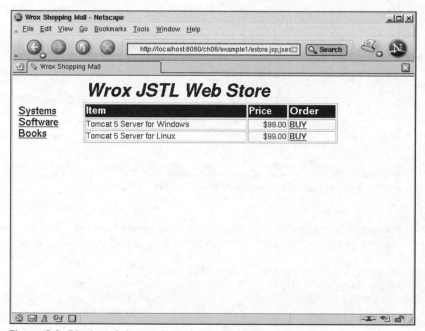

Figure 6-3: Display of the products in the Software category

Next, click the Books category link on the left. The page should display all the books available, as shown in Figure 6-4.

Do not click any Buy links for now.

How It Works

This application is converted from the e-store application from Chapter 3. The original JSP made extensive use of scripting elements. Several very interesting issues arise when conversion to JSTL is attempted. The following discussion contrasts the original code with the new JSTL-based code, section by section. It also provides a detailed discussion of the problems encountered, along with their solutions.

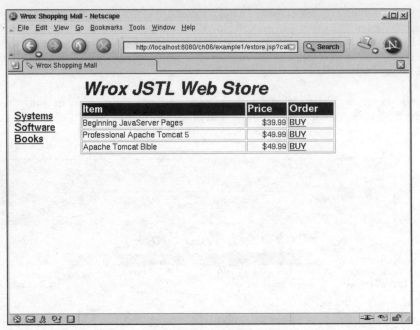

Figure 6-4: Display of the products in the Books category

The JSP used to create the e-store can be located at `<Tomcat Installation Directory>/webapps/ch06/example1/estore.jsp`. The code in this `estore.jsp` page is reproduced here:

```
<%@ taglib prefix="c" uri="http://java.sun.com/jsp/jstl/core" %>
<%@ taglib prefix="fmt" uri="http://java.sun.com/jsp/jstl/fmt" %>
<%@ taglib prefix="wxshop" uri="http://www.wrox.com/begjsp/eshop-functions-taglib" %>

<%@ page  session="true" %>
<c:if test="${empty cats}">
  <c:set var="cats" value="${wxshop:getCats()}" scope="application"/>
</c:if>

<html>
<head>
  <title>Wrox Shopping Mall</title>
  <link rel=stylesheet type="text/css" href="store.css">
</head>
<body>
  <table width="600">
    <tr><td colspan="2" class="mainHead">Wrox JSP Web Store</td></tr>

    <tr>
      <td width="20%">
        <c:forEach var="curCat" items="${cats}">
          <c:url value="/example1/estore.jsp" var="localURL">
            <c:param name="catid" value="${curCat.id}"/>
          </c:url>
```

```
        <a href="${localURL}" class="category">${curCat.name}</a>
        <br/>
      </c:forEach>
    </td>
    <td width="*">
      <h1></h1>
      <table border="1" width="100%">
        <tr><th align="left">Item</th><th align="left">Price</th><th
align="left">Order</th></tr>
        <c:set var="selectedCat"  value="${param.catid}"/>
        <c:if test="${empty selectedCat}">
          <c:set var="selectedCat"  value="1"/>
        </c:if>
        <c:forEach var="curItem" items="${wxshop:getItems(selectedCat)}">
          <tr>
            <td>${curItem.name}</td>
            <td align="right">
              <fmt:formatNumber value="${curItem.price / 100}" type="currency"/>
            </td>
            <td>
              <c:url value="/example1/shopcart.jsp" var="localURL">
                <c:param name="action" value="buy"/>
                <c:param name="sku" value="${curItem.sku}"/>
              </c:url>
              <a href="${localURL}"><b>BUY</b></a>
            </td>
          </tr>
        </c:forEach>
      </table>
    </td>
  </tr>
</table>
</body>
</html>
```

Eliminating scripting declarations

The original `estore.jsp`, located at `<Tomcat Installation Directory>/webapps/ch03/example3/` `estore.jsp`, starts with the following declarations and scripting elements:

```
<%@ page language="java"
import = "com.wrox.begjsp.ch03.*,java.util.*" session="true" %>

<%!
  public void jspInit()
  {
      getServletContext().setAttribute("cats", EShop.getCats());
  }

  public void jspDestroy()
  {
      getServletContext().removeAttribute("cats");
  }

  private  String dispPrice( String price)
  {
```

```
        int len = price.length();
        if (len <= 2)
            return price;
        else
            return "$" + price.substring(0,len -2) + "." + price.substring(len-2);
    }
%>
```

In the new `estore.jsp`, the code becomes the following:

```
<%@ taglib prefix="c" uri="http://java.sun.com/jsp/jstl/core" %>
<%@ taglib prefix="fmt" uri="http://java.sun.com/jsp/jstl/fmt" %>
<%@ taglib prefix="wxshop" uri="http://www.wrox.com/begjsp/eshop-functions-taglib" %>

<%@ page  session="true" %>
<c:if test="${empty cats}">
  <c:set var="cats" value="${wxshop:getCats()}" scope="application"/>
</c:if>
```

The next section explains this new code.

Declaring taglib usage

The `<%@page>` directive in the preceding new code is significantly simpler, and it no longer directly imports the Java classes because the new code has no scripting elements. The new `<%@ taglib>` directives declare the use of two JSTL sublibraries. The first one is the `core`, referenced by the URI `http://java.sun.com/jsp/jstl/core`. This library contains the general-purpose tag, control flow tags, and so on. The second tag library is referenced by the URI `http://java.sun.com/jsp/jstl/fmt`. This is the formatting library of JSTL. Note the `dispPrice()` Java method in the original `estore.jsp`. This method is used to format the price into dollars and cents. This is no longer necessary. The JSTL formatting library has tags that can be used to perform the same task.

The third `<%@taglib>` directive references the URI `wrox.com/begjsp/eshop-functions-taglib`, which is mapped via a taglib map in `web.xml` to a TLD file called `eshop-taglib.tld`. This file contains declarations for several EL-accessible functions. This TLD file is examined later.

Converting static method calls to EL accessible functions

The original `estore.jsp` hooks into the `jspInit()` method and calls the static `EShop.getCats()` method. This method returns an `ArrayList` of the category names. The old code then attaches this `ArrayList` as a named attribute called `cats` at the application scope.

The converted code uses an EL-accessible function, and JSTL's `<c:set>` tag, to accomplish the same thing:

```
<c:if test="${empty cats}">
  <c:set var="cats" value="${wxshop:getCats()}" scope="application"/>
</c:if>
```

> There is no simple way to get JSTL logic into the `jspInit()` and `jspDestroy()` methods. Instead, the approach used here is the same as the approach for obtaining the global category list.

Note the use of EL's `empty` operator to determine whether `cats` is `null` (or empty). The `EShop.getCats()` method is wrapped by the `wxshop:getCats()` function, enabling it to be accessed from an EL expression. The `scope` attribute of the JSTL `<c:set>` tag is used to create a scoped variable (at the `application` scope).

Scoped variables are objects that are attached as named attributes to the various scoping implicit objects. This needs to be differentiated from scripting variables. Scripting variables are not objects attached as attributes, but are actual Java source code variables. If a JSP is script-free, there is usually no need for scripting variables.

To call the `getCats()` static methods from JSTL code, it is necessary to map them to EL-accessible functions. No general mechanism exists in JSP or JSTL to directly invoke a method of a Java class. The `<%@ taglib>` directive maps the URI `wrox.com/begjsp/eshop-functions-taglib` to the tag library. The mapping is specified in the taglib map in the `web.xml` file. The `web.xml` file, located at `<Tomcat Installation Directory>/webapps/ch06/WEB-INF/web.xml`, is reproduced here with the taglib map highlighted:

```xml
    <?xml version="1.0" encoding="ISO-8859-1"?>
<web-app xmlns="http://java.sun.com/xml/ns/j2ee"
  xmlns:xsi="http://www.w3.org/2001/XMLSchema-instance"
  xsi:schemaLocation="http://java.sun.com/xml/ns/j2ee
  http://java.sun.com/xml/ns/j2ee/web-app_2_4.xsd"
  version="2.4">

<description>
  Wrox Beginning JavaServer Pages Examples - Chapter 6
</description>
<display-name>Chapter 6 Example (Wrox Beginning JavaSever Pages)</display-name>

<taglib>
  <taglib-uri>
    http://www.wrox.com/begjsp/eshop-functions-taglib
  </taglib-uri>
  <taglib-location>
    /WEB-INF/jsp/eshop-taglib.tld
  </taglib-location>
</taglib>
</web-app>
```

Note how the `<taglib-uri>` element is used to specify the associated URI, while `<taglib-location>` specifies where the TLD file is located. The EL function mapping to the static `EShop.getCats()` method is performed within the `eshop-taglib.tld` file. This file, located at `<Tomcat Installation Directory>/webapps/ch06/WEB-INF/jsp/eshop-taglib.tld`, is reproduced here, with the mapping of the `getCats()` method highlighted:

```
<?xml version="1.0" encoding="UTF-8" ?>

<taglib xmlns="http://java.sun.com/xml/ns/j2ee"
  xmlns:xsi="http://www.w3.org/2001/XMLSchema-instance"
  xsi:schemaLocation="http://java.sun.com/xml/ns/j2ee web-jsptaglibrary_2_0.xsd"
  version="2.0">
  <description>A taglib for eshop functions.</description>
  <tlib-version>1.0</tlib-version>
  <short-name>EShopunctionTaglib</short-name>
  <uri>/EShopFunctionTagLibrary</uri>
  <function>
    <description>Obtain the catalog categories</description>
    <name>getCats</name>
    <function-class>com.wrox.begjsp.ch03.EShop</function-class>
    <function-signature>java.util.ArrayList getCats()</function-signature>
  </function>



  <function>
    <description>Obtain the items in a category
    </description>
    <name>getItems</name>
    <function-class>com.wrox.begjsp.ch03.EShop</function-class>
    <function-signature>
      java.util.ArrayList getItems(java.lang.String)
    </function-signature>
  </function>



  <function>
    <description>Obtain an item given an sku
    </description>
    <name>getItem</name>
    <function-class>com.wrox.begjsp.ch03.EShop</function-class>
    <function-signature>
      com.wrox.begjsp.ch03.Product getItem(java.lang.String)
    </function-signature>
  </function>

  <function>
    <description>Clear a list</description>
    <name>clearList</name>
    <function-class>com.wrox.begjsp.ch03.EShop</function-class>
    <function-signature>
      void clearList(java.util.List)
    </function-signature>
  </function>

  <function>
    <description>Add an item to a list</description>
    <name>addList</name>
    <function-class>com.wrox.begjsp.ch03.EShop</function-class>
    <function-signature>
```

```
          void addList(java.util.List, java.lang.Object)
        </function-signature>
      </function>

  </taglib>
```

Many other EL-accessible functions are declared here. They are covered later in the chapter.

Replacing scripting iteration with the JSTL iteration tag

Back to the original `estore.jsp` file using scripting elements, the next section prints out the list of categories as hyperlinks:

```
<html>
<head>
  <title>Wrox Shopping Mall</title>
</head>
<body>
  <table width="600">
    <tr>
      <td width="20%">
      <%

        ArrayList cats = (ArrayList) application.getAttribute("cats");
        for (int i=0; i< cats.size(); i++)
        {
            Category curCat = (Category) cats.get(i);
      %>
        <a href="<%= request.getRequestURL() + "?catid=" + curCat.getId() %>">
          <%= curCat.getName() %>
        </a>
        <br/>
      <%
        }
      %>
      </td>
```

This section of code (highlighted in both the scripting elements and the JSTL listings) can be elegantly replaced with the JSTL iteration tag. Because `cats` is a `Collection` and the `<c:forEach>` tag works directly with any `Collection`, the conversion is very straightforward. The converted code is reproduced here:

```
<html>
<head>
  <title>Wrox Shopping Mall</title>
  <link rel=stylesheet type="text/css" href="store.css">
</head>
<body>
  <table width="600">
    <tr><td colspan="2" class="mainHead">Wrox JSTL Web Store</td></tr>

    <tr>
      <td width="20%">
```

```
        <c:forEach var="curCat" items="${cats}">
          <c:url value="/example1/estore.jsp" var="localURL">
            <c:param name="catid" value="${curCat.id}"/>
          </c:url>
          <a href="${localURL}" class="category">${curCat.name}</a>
          <br/>
        </c:forEach>
    </td>
```

JSTL's <c:url> tag is used to fabricate the hyperlinks, instead of manual concatenation. The use of this tag is explained next.

JSTL's versatile URL creation tag

It's better to use the <c:url> tag to create hyperlinks, rather than doing manual concatenation. This is because the tag will perform many tedious tasks for us. It knows about JSP sessions, and will ensure that the URL created will maintain the JSP session. This tag can also take specified parameters and encode them onto the URL for us. If necessary, this tag will also escape special characters in the URL or parameters passed. Furthermore, this tag automatically appends the required context path to the value attribute.

The final section of code in estore.jsp represents a table that prints out all the products in the selected category. The original estore.jsp contains the following:

```
<table border="1">
  <tr><th align="left">Item</th><th align="left">Price</th><th
align="left">Order</th></tr>
  <%
    String selectedCat = request.getParameter("catid");
    if (selectedCat == null)
        selectedCat = "1";
    ArrayList items = (ArrayList) EShop.getItems(selectedCat);
    for (int i=0; i< items.size(); i++)
    {
        Product curItem = (Product) items.get(i);
  %>
  <tr>
    <td><%= curItem.getName()    %></td>
    <td><%= dispPrice(String.valueOf(curItem.getPrice()))  %></td>
    <td><a href="<%= request.getContextPath() +
"/example3/shopcart.jsp?action=buy&sku=" + curItem.getSku() %>">
    <b>BUY</b></a>
    </td>
  </tr>
  <%
    }
  %>
</table>
```

The new code once again uses JSTL's <c:forEach> tag to replace the former iterative scripting element:

```
<table border="1" width="100%">
  <tr><th align="left">Item</th><th align="left">Price</th><th
align="left">Order</th></tr>
```

```
      <c:set var="selectedCat"  value="${param.catid}"/>
      <c:if test="${empty selectedCat}">
        <c:set var="selectedCat"  value="1"/>
      </c:if>
      <c:forEach var="curItem" items="${wxshop:getItems(selectedCat)}">
        <tr>
          <td>${curItem.name}</td>
          <td align="right">
            <fmt:formatNumber value="${curItem.price / 100}" type="currency"/>
          </td>
          <td>
            <c:url value="/example1/shopcart.jsp" var="localURL">
              <c:param name="action" value="buy"/>
              <c:param name="sku" value="${curItem.sku}"/>
            </c:url>
            <a href="${localURL}"><b>BUY</b></a>
          </td>
        </tr>
      </c:forEach>
    </table>
```

The `items` attribute of the `<c:forEach>` tag is actually a call to the static `EShop.getItems()` method. This EL-accessible method is mapped in the `eshop-taglib.tld` file. It returns all the items associated with a specified category.

Note the use of the JSTL number formatting tag to render the price in currency format. This tag is locale aware and will render the correct symbol for currency:

```
<fmt:formatNumber value="${curItem.price / 100}" type="currency"/>
```

This eliminates the need for the old `dispPrice()` method.

The code also takes advantage of EL's implicit `param` object, a map, to get at the incoming `catid` parameter value:

```
<c:set var="selectedCat"  value="${param.catid}"/>
```

The `<c:url>` tag is once again used to create the Buy hyperlink for each product:

```
<c:url value="/example1/shopcart.jsp" var="localURL">
  <c:param name="action" value="buy"/>
  <c:param name="sku" value="${curItem.sku}"/>
</c:url>
<a href="${localURL}"><b>BUY</b></a>
```

This concludes our coverage of the first JSP of the Web store application: `estore.jsp`. The next example examines the conversion of the second application JSP: the shopping cart page.

Try It Out   Creating a JSTL-Based Shopping Cart

With the Books category selected at the e-store, click the Buy link of the *Beginning JavaServer Pages* book. This will take you to the shopping cart page, with a copy of the book in the cart. Your cart should look like the one shown in Figure 6-5.

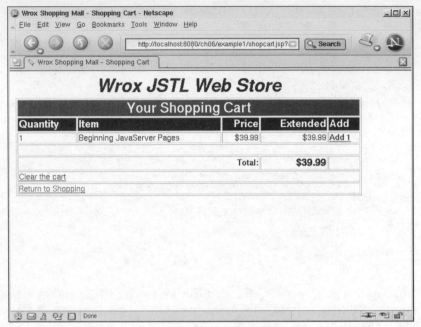

Figure 6-5: Shopping cart containing an ordered book

Click the Add 1 link of the book selected to order another one. The new shopping cart should look like the one displayed in Figure 6-6.

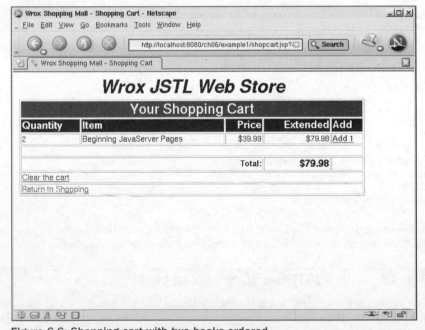

Figure 6-6: Shopping cart with two books ordered

Note that the shopping cart has multiplied the quantity by the unit price to obtain the extended price. The total for the entire order is also calculated.

Next, click the Return to Shopping hyperlink to return to the estore.jsp page. This time, select Systems and order a Pentium 4 system. You now have two books and one computer in the shopping cart, as shown in Figure 6-7.

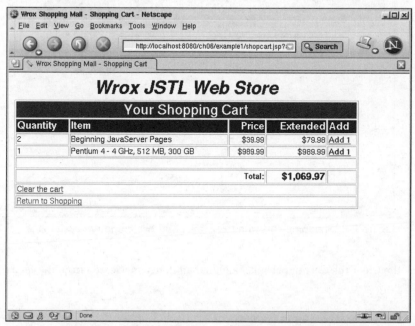

Figure 6-7: Shopping cart with two books and one computer system ordered

Again, the cart has calculated the extended price for each item, and added the amounts for the total. Click the Add 1 link of the Pentium 4 system and order another one. You now have two systems ordered with the books. The cart should look like the one shown in Figure 6-8.

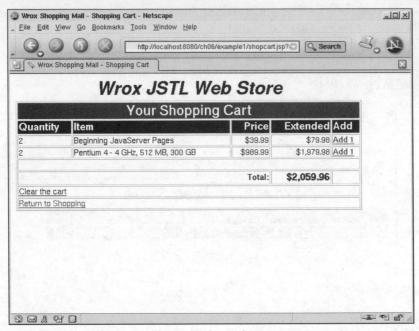

Figure 6-8: Shopping cart with two books and two computer systems

Finally, click the Clear the Cart hyperlink. Note that all items are cleared from the cart, as shown in Figure 6-9.

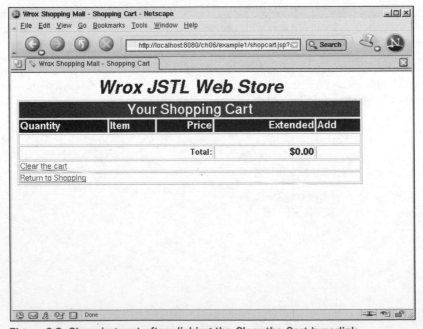

Figure 6-9: Shopping cart after clicking the Clear the Cart hyperlink

How It Works

Following the lead of the first Try It Out section, the original shopping cart JSP using scripting elements will be converted to a JSTL-only version.

The resulting shopping cart JSP is called shopcart.jsp, and is located at <Tomcat Installation Directory>/webapps/ch06/example1/shopcart.jsp. The code in this shopcart.jsp page is reproduced here in its entirety:

```
<%@ taglib prefix="c" uri="http://java.sun.com/jsp/jstl/core" %>
<%@ taglib prefix="fmt" uri="http://java.sun.com/jsp/jstl/fmt" %>
<%@ taglib prefix="wxshop" uri="http://www.wrox.com/begjsp/eshop-functions-taglib" %>

<%@ page session="true" %>

<c:set var="EXAMPLE" value="/example1"/>
<c:set var="SHOP_PAGE" value="/estore.jsp"/>
<c:set var="CART_PAGE" value="/shopcart.jsp"/>

<html>
<head>
  <title>Wrox Shopping Mall - Shopping Cart</title>
  <link rel=stylesheet type="text/css" href="store.css">
</head>
<body>
  <c:if test="${!(empty param.sku)}">
    <c:set var="prod" value="${wxshop:getItem(param.sku)}"/>
  </c:if>

  <jsp:useBean id="lineitems" class="java.util.ArrayList" scope="session"/>

  <c:choose>
    <c:when test="${param.action == 'clear'}">
      ${wxshop:clearList(lineitems)}
    </c:when>

    <c:when test="${param.action == 'inc' || param.action=='buy'}">
      <c:set var="found" value="false"/>

      <c:forEach var="curItem" items="${lineitems}">

        <c:if test="${(curItem.sku) == (prod.sku)}">
          <jsp:setProperty name="curItem" property="quantity"
value="${curItem.quantity + 1}"/>
          <c:set var="found" value="true" />
        </c:if>
      </c:forEach>
      <c:if test="${!found}">
        <c:remove var="tmpitem"/>
        <jsp:useBean id="tmpitem" class="com.wrox.begjsp.ch03.LineItem">
          <jsp:setProperty name="tmpitem" property="quantity" value="1"/>
          <jsp:setProperty name="tmpitem" property="sku" value="${prod.sku}"/>
          <jsp:setProperty name="tmpitem" property="desc" value="${prod.name}"/>
          <jsp:setProperty name="tmpitem" property="price" value="${prod.price}"/>
```

```
          </jsp:useBean>
          ${wxshop:addList(lineitems, tmpitem)}
       </c:if>
    </c:when>
  </c:choose>

  <c:set var="total" value="0"/>
  <table width="640">
    <tr><td class="mainHead">Wrox JSTL Web Store</td></tr>
    <tr>
      <td>
        <h1></h1>
        <table border="1" width="640">

          <tr><th colspan="5" class="shopCart">Your Shopping Cart</th></tr>
          <tr><th align="left">Quantity</th><th align="left">Item</th><th
align="right">Price</th>
          <th align="right">Extended</th>
          <th align="left">Add</th></tr>
          <c:forEach var="curItem" items="${lineitems}">
            <c:set var="extended" value="${curItem.quantity * curItem.price}"/>
            <c:set var="total" value="${total + extended}"/>
            <tr>
              <td>${curItem.quantity}</td>
              <td>${curItem.desc}</td>
              <td align="right">
               <fmt:formatNumber value="${curItem.price / 100}" type="currency"/>
              </td>
              <td align="right">
               <fmt:formatNumber value="${extended / 100}" type="currency"/>
              </td>
              <td>

                <c:url value="${EXAMPLE}${CART_PAGE}" var="localURL">
                  <c:param name="action" value="inc"/>
                  <c:param name="sku" value="${curItem.sku}"/>
                </c:url>
                <a href="${localURL}"><b>Add 1</b></a>
              </td>
            </tr>
          </c:forEach>
          <tr>
            <td colspan="5">  
            </td>
          </tr>
          <tr>
            <td colspan="3" align="right"><b>Total:</b></td>
            <td align="right" class="grandTotal">
              <fmt:formatNumber value="${total / 100}" type="currency"/>
            </td>
            <td> </td>
          </tr>

          <tr>
            <td colspan="5">
```

```
          <c:url value="${EXAMPLE}${CART_PAGE}" var="localURL">
            <c:param name="action" value="clear"/>
          </c:url>
          <a href="${localURL}">Clear the cart</a>
        </td>
      </tr>


      <tr>
        <td colspan="5">
          <c:url value="${EXAMPLE}${SHOP_PAGE}" var="localURL"/>
          <a href="${localURL}">Return to Shopping</a>
        </td>
      </tr>
    </table>
  </td>
 </tr>
</table>
</body>
</html>
```

In the following sections, the old shopcart.jsp page from Chapter 3, located at <Tomcat
Installation Directory>/webapps/ch03/example3/shopcart.jsp, is compared with the new
JSTL version.

Declaring constants with <c:set>

The first section of the old shopcart.jsp contains some constant declarations and the declaration of the
dispPrice() method:

```
<%@ page language="java"
  import = "com.wrox.begjsp.ch03.*,java.util.*" session="true" %>

<%!
  private static String EXAMPLE = "/example3";
  private static String SHOP_PAGE = "/estore.jsp";
  private static String CART_PAGE = "/shopcart.jsp";

  private  String dispPrice( String price)
  {
      int len = price.length();
      if (len <= 2)
          return price;
      else
          return "$" + price.substring(0,len -2) + "." + price.substring(len-2);
  }
%>

<html>
<head>
  <title>Wrox Shopping Mall - Shopping Cart</title>
</head>
```

The earlier example shows that the dispPrice() method can be replaced by JSTL's
<fmt:formatNumber> tag. The JSTL version of shopcart.jsp no longer needs its definition. The only
thing left is to declare the constants using JSTL's <c:set> tag:

```
<%@ taglib prefix="c" uri="http://java.sun.com/jsp/jstl/core" %>
<%@ taglib prefix="fmt" uri="http://java.sun.com/jsp/jstl/fmt" %>
<%@ taglib prefix="wxshop" uri="http://www.wrox.com/begjsp/eshop-functions-taglib"
%>

<%@ page session="true" %>

<c:set var="EXAMPLE" value="/example1"/>
<c:set var="SHOP_PAGE" value="/estore.jsp"/>
<c:set var="CART_PAGE" value="/shopcart.jsp"/>

<html>
<head>
  <title>Wrox Shopping Mall - Shopping Cart</title>
  <link rel=stylesheet type="text/css" href="store.css">
</head>
```

Replacing complex Java scripting logic

The next section in the old shopcart.jsp has a large section of embedded Java logic:

```
<body>
<%
  ArrayList items = (ArrayList) session.getAttribute("lineitems");
  String action =  request.getParameter("action");
  String sku = request.getParameter("sku");
  Product prod = null;
  if (sku != null)
      prod = EShop.getItem(sku);

  if (items == null)
  {   // add first item
      items = new ArrayList();
      items.add(new LineItem(1,sku,prod.getName(),
       prod.getPrice() ));
      session.setAttribute("lineitems", items);
  }
  else  if (action.equals("clear"))
        {
            items.clear();
        }
        else
        {
            boolean itemFound = false;
            // check to see if sku exists
            for (int i=0; i<items.size(); i++)
            {
                LineItem curItem = (LineItem) items.get(i);
                if (curItem.getSku().equals(sku))
                {
```

```
                        itemFound = true;
                        curItem.setQuantity(curItem.getQuantity() + 1);
                        break;
                }  // of if
            } //of for

        if (!itemFound)
            items.add(new LineItem(1,sku,prod.getName(),
                prod.getPrice() ));

        } // of final else

        int total = 0;
%>
```

The preceding code basically decodes the incoming parameters for the shopping cart. The action parameter is buy when the link is from the estore.jsp, and the sku refers to the item that the customer wants to buy. The action parameter is inc when the Add 1 hyperlink is clicked on the cart, and the sku is the associated product. The action can also be clear if the customer clicks the Clear the Cart hyperlink.

The new scriptless JSTL code that does the same thing is shown here:

```
<body>
<c:if test="${!(empty param.sku)}">
  <c:set var="prod" value="${wxshop:getItem(param.sku)}"/>
</c:if>

<jsp:useBean id="lineitems" class="java.util.ArrayList" scope="session"/>

<c:choose>
  <c:when test="${param.action == 'clear'}">
    ${wxshop:clearList(lineitems)}
  </c:when>

  <c:when test="${param.action == 'inc' || param.action=='buy'}">
    <c:set var="found" value="false"/>

    <c:forEach var="curItem" items="${lineitems}">

      <c:if test="${(curItem.sku) == (prod.sku)}">
        <jsp:setProperty name="curItem" property="quantity"
value="${curItem.quantity + 1}"/>
        <c:set var="found" value="true" />
      </c:if>
    </c:forEach>
    <c:if test="${!found}">
      <c:remove var="tmpitem"/>
      <jsp:useBean id="tmpitem" class="com.wrox.begjsp.ch03.LineItem">
        <jsp:setProperty name="tmpitem" property="quantity" value="1"/>
        <jsp:setProperty name="tmpitem" property="sku" value="${prod.sku}"/>
        <jsp:setProperty name="tmpitem" property="desc" value="${prod.name}"/>
        <jsp:setProperty name="tmpitem" property="price" value="${prod.price}"/>
      </jsp:useBean>
```

```
        ${wxshop:addList(lineitems, tmpitem)}
      </c:if>
    </c:when>
  </c:choose>

  <c:set var="total" value="0"/>
```

The items being displayed in the cart are stored in an `ArrayList`. This `ArrayList` is attached to the session scope as a scoped variable named `lineitems`. To create this scoped variable, the original embedded Java code was simply as follows:

```
ArrayList items = (ArrayList) session.getAttribute("lineitems");
...
if (items == null)
{   // add first item
    items = new ArrayList();
    ...
    session.setAttribute("lineitems", items);
```

To create the same effect without scripting elements, the `<jsp:useBean>` standard action is used:

```
<jsp:useBean id="lineitems" class="java.util.ArrayList" scope="session"/>
```

The `<jsp:useBean>` tag will create a new instance of `ArrayList` if the session scoped variable `lineitems` is not found. Otherwise, it will use the existing one. These are the exact semantics needed in our case.

To obtain the product description associated with the incoming `sku`, the `EShop.getItem()` static method must be called. The old code uses the following:

```
String sku = request.getParameter("sku");
Product prod = null;
if (sku != null)
    prod = EShop.getItem(sku);
```

The new code has to use an EL-accessible function. The `eshop-taglib.tld` file has mapped the `EShop.getItem()` static method to a `getItem()` function. The new code is as follows:

```
<c:if test="${!(empty param.sku)}">
  <c:set var="prod" value="${wxshop:getItem(param.sku)}"/>
</c:if>
```

Converting control flow

The complex Java control flow in the original code is replaced by a combination of JSTL's `<c:choose>` and `<c:if>` constructs. In general, `<c:choose>` can be used to replace the `if...then...else` and `switch...case` Java code constructs. The resulting JSTL control flow has the following general structure in the new `shopcart.jsp`:

```
<c:choose>
  <c:when test="${param.action == 'clear'}">
    ...
```

```
        </c:when>

        <c:when test="${param.action == 'inc' || param.action=='buy'}">
            ...
        </c:when>
    </c:choose>
```

The construct decodes the action parameter within shopcart.jsp.

Converting method calls

The original shopcart.jsp has code that does the following:

- ❑ Constructs a new LineItem instance, initializes it, and adds it to an ArrayList
- ❑ Clears the content of an ArrayList

The code in the old shopcart.jsp for the first action is:

```
items.add(new LineItem(1,sku,prod.getName(),
    prod.getPrice() ));
```

The code for second action in the old shopcart.jsp is:

```
items.clear();
```

While these actions can be accomplished by using one single line of code in Java, it is not so straightforward using JSTL. This is because no generalized way to invoke an arbitrary method of a scoped variable or Java object exists.

The only solution is to create EL-accessible functions using the JSTL 1.1 functions extension mechanism. Unfortunately, these mapped functions must be static methods. This means that they cannot be instance methods of objects.

To add an object to a list, an EL-accessible function called addList() is created. The code is placed as a static function in the EShop class. It is reproduced here:

```
public static void addList(java.util.List list, java.lang.Object item)
{
    list.add(item);
}
```

To clear a list, an EL-accessible function called clearList() is created. The code is in EShop as well:

```
public static void clearList(java.util.List list)
{
    list.clear();
}
```

These functions are mapped using `<function>` entries in the `eshop-taglib.tld` file:

```
<function>
  <description>Clear a list</description>
  <name>clearList</name>
  <function-class>com.wrox.begjsp.ch03.EShop</function-class>
  <function-signature>void clearList(java.util.List)</function-signature>
</function>


<function>
  <description>Add an item to a list</description>
  <name>addList</name>
  <function-class>com.wrox.begjsp.ch03.EShop</function-class>
  <function-signature>void addList(java.util.List, java.lang.Object)</function-
signature>
</function>
```

Note that the Java classes used to specify method return values and method parameters must include the full class name (fully qualified) to avoid errors.

Once these EL-accessible functions are created, the new `shopcart.jsp` uses the following code to clear the `lineitems` scoped variable (`ArrayList` type) when the user clicks the Clear the Cart hyperlink:

```
${wxshop:clearList(lineitems)}
```

The following code is used to construct a new `LineItem` instance, initialize it, and add it to the `lineitem` `ArrayList`. Note the verbose syntax required:

```
<c:remove var="tmpitem"/>
<jsp:useBean id="tmpitem" class="com.wrox.begjsp.ch03.LineItem">
  <jsp:setProperty name="tmpitem" property="quantity" value="1"/>
  <jsp:setProperty name="tmpitem" property="sku" value="${prod.sku}"/>
  <jsp:setProperty name="tmpitem" property="desc" value="${prod.name}"/>
  <jsp:setProperty name="tmpitem" property="price" value="${prod.price}"/>
</jsp:useBean>
${wxshop:addList(lineitems, tmpitem)}
```

Observe how the `<c:remove>` tag is used to remove a scoped variable created by `<jsp:useBean>` if it exists. This illustrates how standard JSP actions can work collaboratively (and interchangeably) with custom actions, including the JSTL tags.

Changing the lineitems table layout

The next section of code displays the content of `lineitems` and calculates the extended price and total cost. The old code is:

```
<table width="600">
  <tr>
    <td>
```

```
<h1></h1>
<table border="1" width="600">
  <tr><th colspan="5">Your Shopping Cart</th></tr>
  <tr><th align="left">Quantity</th><th align="left">Item</th><th
align="right">Price</th>
  <th align="right">Extended</th>
  <th align="left">Add</th></tr>

<%
  for (int i=0; i< items.size(); i++)
  {
      LineItem curItem = (LineItem) items.get(i);
      int quan = curItem.getQuantity();
      long price = curItem.getPrice();
      long extended = quan * price;
      total += extended;
%>

<tr>
  <td><%= quan %></td>
  <td><%= curItem.getDesc()    %></td>
  <td align="right"><%= dispPrice(String.valueOf(price))   %></td>
  <td align="right"><%= dispPrice(String.valueOf(extended))   %></td>
  <td>
    <a href="<%= request.getContextPath() + EXAMPLE + CART_PAGE +
"?action=inc&sku=" + curItem.getSku() %>">
      <b>Add 1</b></a>
  </td>
</tr>
<%
  }
%>
<tr>
  <td colspan="5">  
  </td>
</tr>
<tr>
  <td colspan="3" align="right"><b>Total:</b></td>
  <td align="right"><%= dispPrice(String.valueOf(total)) %></td>
  <td> </td>
</tr>

<tr>
  <td colspan="5">
    <a href="<%= request.getContextPath() + EXAMPLE + CART_PAGE +
"?action=clear" %>">
      Clear the cart
    </a>
  </td>
</tr>

<tr>
  <td colspan="5">
```

```
                <a href="<%= request.getContextPath() + EXAMPLE + SHOP_PAGE %>">
Return to Shopping</a>
            </td>
          </tr>
        </table>
      </td>
    </tr>
  </table>
```

The conversion is straightforward and very similar to the conversion performed previously with estore.jsp (the first example). The resulting code is presented here, with corresponding sections highlighted:

```
<table width="640">
  <tr><td class="mainHead">Wrox JSTL Web Store</td></tr>
  <tr>
    <td>
      <h1></h1>
      <table border="1" width="640">

        <tr><th colspan="5" class="shopCart">Your Shopping Cart</th></tr>
        <tr><th align="left">Quantity</th><th align="left">Item</th><th
align="right">Price</th>
        <th align="right">Extended</th>
        <th align="left">Add</th></tr>
        <c:forEach var="curItem" items="${lineitems}">
          <c:set var="extended" value="${curItem.quantity * curItem.price}"/>
          <c:set var="total" value="${total + extended}"/>
          <tr>
            <td>${curItem.quantity}</td>
            <td>${curItem.desc}</td>
            <td align="right">
              <fmt:formatNumber value="${curItem.price / 100}" type="currency"/>
            </td>
            <td align="right">
              <fmt:formatNumber value="${extended / 100}" type="currency"/>
            </td>
            <td>

              <c:url value="${EXAMPLE}${CART_PAGE}" var="localURL">
                <c:param name="action" value="inc"/>
                <c:param name="sku" value="${curItem.sku}"/>
              </c:url>
              <a href="${localURL}"><b>Add 1</b></a>
            </td>
          </tr>
        </c:forEach>
        <tr>
          <td colspan="5">  
          </td>
        </tr>
```

```
            <tr>
              <td colspan="3" align="right"><b>Total:</b></td>
              <td align="right" class="grandTotal">
                <fmt:formatNumber value="${total / 100}" type="currency"/>
              </td>
              <td> </td>
            </tr>

            <tr>
              <td colspan="5">
                <c:url value="${EXAMPLE}${CART_PAGE}" var="localURL">
                  <c:param name="action" value="clear"/>
                </c:url>
                <a href="${localURL}">Clear the cart</a>
              </td>
            </tr>

            <tr>
              <td colspan="5">
                <c:url value="${EXAMPLE}${SHOP_PAGE}" var="localURL"/>
                <a href="${localURL}">Return to Shopping</a>
              </td>
            </tr>
          </table>
        </td>
      </tr>
    </table>
```

The conversion uses a JSTL `<c:forEach>` tag to replace scripting iteration. It also uses the `<c:url>` tag to build the Add 1 hyperlinks. The `<fmt:formatNumber>` tag is once again used to convert the prices into currency format.

A common JSTL coding error

Before wrapping up this chapter, you should know about a very common error that is often made when coding JSTL. This error occurs when you specify the name of a scoped variable in error.

For example, see if you can identify the error in the following code segment:

```
<c:forEach var="curItem" items="lineitems">
  <c:set var="extended" value="${curItem.quantity * curItem.price}"/>
  ...
</c:forEach>
```

When the preceding JSP segment is executed, you will get an error similar to the following:

```
javax.servlet.ServletException: Unable to find a value for "quantity" in object of
class "java.lang.String" using operator "."
 org.apache.jasper.runtime.PageContextImpl.doHandlePageException(PageContextImpl.
java:825)
```

```
org.apache.jasper.runtime.PageContextImpl.handlePageException(PageContextImpl.
java:758)
org.apache.jsp.example1.shopcart_jsp._jspService(shopcart_jsp.java:199)
org.apache.jasper.runtime.HttpJspBase.service(HttpJspBase.java:94)
...
```

Note that the error is associated with the use of the quantity property. Its source is actually quite far away from the area identified as the cause of the problem.

The cause of the problem is actually the mistaken use of the string "lineitem" in place of the EL expression ${lineitems} for the items attribute of the <c:forEach> action. The correct form would be as follows:

```
<c:forEach var="curItem" items="${lineitems}">
```

If you encounter a similar error message, instead of looking at the code identified by the error, try examining all the attributes used in the enclosing tags and ask yourself whether you wanted an expression or a constant.

Summary

This chapter examined the role of tag libraries and JSTL. Some interesting discoveries about tag libraries include the following:

❑ A tag library is a collection of related custom actions. Tag libraries provide JSP developers with new functionality that is easily integrated into their applications.

❑ All tag libraries have tag implementation code and a Tag Library Descriptor (TLD). In some cases, the TLD can be automatically generated by the container or a tool.

❑ Tag libraries are typically distributed as JAR files that you placed into your application's WEB-INF/lib directory. The TLD should be included in the JAR file.

JSTL is one of the most important tag libraries to JSP developers and a standard part of JSP 2.0–compliant platforms. Some reasons for this include the following:

❑ JSTL provides tags that are essential to application programming using JSP.

❑ JSTL is tightly integrated with EL.

❑ Finally, JSTL (along with EL) enables the creation of script-free JSP pages, leading to more maintainable, portable, and scalable code.

Conversion from legacy scripting-based code to script-free JSTL/EL–based code is an art. The Web store example in this chapter illustrated several conversion and mapping techniques and pointed out common pitfalls.

Exercises

1. From the estore.jsp page, make each product description a hyperlink. The target of the hyperlink should be a product.jsp page. This page takes a sku as a parameter and displays the detail specification of a product. Make sure that you can order (and go to the shopcart.jsp page) from this page, and that you can go back to the estore.jsp from this page.

2. Modify the shopcart.jsp page to perform the following:

   a. Add 7 percent regional sales tax.

   b. Add 8 percent federal sales tax.

   c. Add a shipping charge of $10 for each item ordered.

JSP Directives

It is almost impossible to create a Web-based application using JSPs without the use of JSP directives. Yet, JSP directives do not generate code. They are not part of the logic within the JSP code. Rather, JSP directives provide directions and instructions to the container, telling it how to handle certain aspects of JSP processing.

JSP developers should have an intimate understanding of the following JSP directives and when they should be used:

- ❑ The `page` directive
- ❑ The `taglib` directive
- ❑ The `include` directive

This chapter presents the most common usage of each of the directives, together with other frequently used variations. Important attributes associated with each directive are also discussed. In some cases, the discussion leads to some more obscure uses of the directives.

Other topics relating to the use of JSP directives are also explored. These topics include the following:

- ❑ How a JSP is processed by the container
- ❑ JSP container processing and interactions with JSP directives
- ❑ How to use the XML representation of the directives
- ❑ Different ways of including JSP fragments

By the end of this chapter, you will have a thorough understanding of each JSP directive. You will be able to determine the situations under which a directive should be used. You will also be familiar with possible attribute values and their effect on JSP processing. Most important, you will be able to use the JSP directives productively in your daily JSP development.

Directive Basics

JSP directives can be found in almost every JSP page. Directives always appear as follows:

```
<%@ directive name [... one or more attributes...] %>
```

Directives, like actions, can have a number of attributes. The blanks between the @ symbol and the directive name, and between the last attribute and the closing %>, are optional.

You have already seen the <%@ page %> directive and the <%@ taglib %> directive used in many examples in previous chapters. These directives do not by themselves perform any action when a request is processed. Instead, they provide directions and instructions to the container.

Directives as instructions for the container

For example, consider the frequently seen taglib directive shown here:

```
<%@ taglib prefix="c" uri="http://java.sun.com/jsp/jstl/core" %>
```

This taglib directive does not perform any specific action during request processing. Rather, it tells the JSP container the following:

❑ This page will use the JSTL core tag library, associated with the URI http://java.sun.com/jsp/jstl/core.

❑ The tags from this JSTL core tag library will all be prefixed with the c: namespace within the JSP.

The container follows these instructions during the processing of the JSP page. Because JSP directives are specified per JSP page, each JSP page can have a different set of directives, and hence provide different instructions to the container.

Alternative XML syntax for directives

Because JSPs are frequently used to present XML data, especially in *Web services* (see Chapter 27, "JSP Project I: Personalized Portal," for an example), it is important that JSP pages can be created in the XML format. However, some elements of the standard JSP notation break XML compatibility, and a directive is one of them.

Directives are not XML elements, as their standard notation violates the XML syntax. However, JSP 2.0 has defined an XML-compatible format for all the directives. For example, the directive

```
<%@ page ....  %>
```

can be alternatively specified in the XML-compatible form as follows:

```
<jsp:directive.page ... />
```

Also, the directive

```
<%@ include .... %>
```

can alternatively be specified in the XML-compatible form as follows:

```
<jsp:directive.include .../>
```

Available JSP directives

As mentioned earlier, you can use three directives within a JSP page:

- ❑ The page directive
- ❑ The taglib directive
- ❑ The include directive

Each of these directives can have a number of attributes. Each attribute gives different directions to the container.

> There are additional directives that can be used only within tag files (tags written in JSP), but they are covered in Chapter 11, "Building Your Own Custom JSP Tag Library." Using these "tag files only" directives in standard JSP files will result in an error.

The following sections examine each of these directives, describe the most commonly used attributes, and demonstrate some examples. First, however, you should have a basic understanding of how a JSP container processes a JSP page.

Processing a JSP page: the container's perspective

The JSP directives give instructions to the container about how the JSP should be processed. The container is responsible for the processing of a JSP page. Figure 7-1 illustrates what happens under the hood.

In Figure 7-1, the processing performed by the container is divided into different stages, or phases.

In the first phase, the JSP page is actually first converted to Java source code. This is called the *translation phase*. In this phase, the JSP page is said to be *translated* into Java source code. The Java source code is generated in plain text format, and is human-readable. Anything that happens during this phase is said to have occurred during *translation time*.

During the second phase, the Java source code is compiled into executable byte code. This is called the *compilation phase*. The resulting executable byte code is in binary format and can be executed by any Java Virtual Machine (JVM). Anything that happens during this phase of the processing is said to have occurred during *compilation time*.

It is this compiled binary byte code that is actually executed when an incoming request arrives at the server. It is the container's responsibility to pass the request to the compiled binary code for execution. When the compiled JSP binary executes, it processes the incoming request. This phase is called the *request phase*. Anything that happens during this phase is said to have occurred *during request time*.

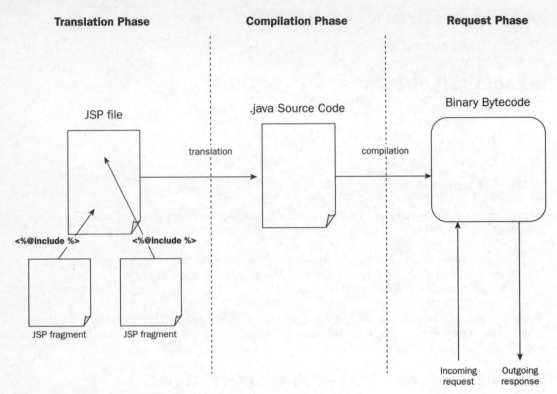

Figure 7-1: Processing of JSP directives

Once translated and compiled, the JSP binary is reused for every incoming request. This avoids the need for translation and compilation phases for each request. However, if the JSP is modified, the container must recognize the change and retranslate and recompile the page.

You will see these different phases mentioned throughout this book and in most JSP development text and documentation.

> *The container will automatically translate and compile JSP pages every time they are modified. There is a technique called JSP precompilation that can be used to optimize the performance of JSP in Web applications. This technique is covered in Chapter 25, "Performance."*

This brief description of the JSP processing phases is sufficient for our discussion of JSP directives. A more in-depth exploration of the different phases is presented in Chapter 25 when JSP performance enhancements are discussed.

Returning to the discussion of the available JSP directives, we first examine the page directive.

The page Directive

The page directive is used to provide instructions to the container that pertain to the current JSP page. From the perspective of the container, each JSP page (together with any included JSP fragments at translation time) is a separate *translation unit*. Each JSP page in the same application can have its own page directive, resulting in a different set of instructions for each translation unit.

The instructions are specified using the attributes of the page directive. Frequently used attributes of the page directive are described in the following sections. Attributes of the page directive are optional; the default values will be used if you do not specify them.

The language attribute

The language attribute specifies the scripting languages used when scripting elements are used within the JSP. For example, consider the following directive:

```
<%@ page language="java" %>
```

This specifies that the scripting language to be used on the page should be the Java programming language. This attribute is almost always java. While the JSP specification is written to enable other scripting languages, the only one implemented by today's containers is the Java programming language.

> The default value is "java" if the attribute is not specified. Therefore, it is not necessary to specify this attribute.

The extends attribute

In the translation phase, the container converts a JSP into a Java-language source program. In fact, each JSP page is translated into a Java class. The extends attribute enables you to specify the superclass that the container will use during this translation phase. For example, consider the following usage:

```
<%@ page language="java" extends="com.wrox.begjsp.ch07.EShop" %>
```

After translation by the container, this will result in a line of translated Java source code similar to the following:

```
...
public final class my_jsp extends com.wrox.begjsp.ch07.EShop implements
org.apache.jasper.runtime.JspSourceDependent
{
...
```

Because the JSP is inheriting from com.wrox.begjsp.ch07.Eshop, scripting elements within the page will have access to the protected and public members (both methods and fields) of the superclass.

> This technique, using the page directive's `extends` attribute to specify the super-class, should be used only if there are no other means of implementing the same functionality. Not only does using a superclass tie the JSP code to the Java code, it also encourages the use of scripting elements.

The import attribute

The `import` attribute is used to specify the library classes that will be used within the JSP page by the scripting elements. Each fully qualified library class name (i.e., the full name, starting with the package name) is separated by comma. When the container translates the JSP into Java source code, the value of this attribute is translated to one or more `import` declarations in the Java programming language. For example, consider the following example:

```
<%@ page language="java" import="com.wrox.begjsp.ch07.*,java.util.*" %>
```

This attribute tells the container to create `import` statements in the translation phase. After translation, the following Java source code statements will be created in the source code:

```
import com.wrox.begjsp.ch07.*;
import java.util.*;
```

Scripting elements within the JSP can then utilize any classes that are imported via this attribute.

The session attribute

Unlike the attributes seen thus far, this attribute gives the container directions that refer to *request-time* behavior. All the previously described attributes are instructions for translation-time behavior.

In the e-commerce example in Chapter 3, "JSP Basics 2: Generalized Templating and Server Scripting," a `lineitems` attribute attached to the session JSP implicit object is used to track the content of the shopping cart. The JSP container creates and maintains an HTTP session using cookies or other means (see Chapter 3 for more details).

The `session` attribute is a boolean-valued attribute. It can contain either a `true` or a `false` value. If `true`, the container will create and maintain an HTTP session:

```
<%@ page session="true" %>
```

The JSP code in the page with the preceding directive can then access the `session` implicit JSP scoping object. If this value is `false`, no session will be created by the container. Any access to the `session` object in JSP that has `session="false"` will result in an error.

> The default value for the session attribute is `true`. Therefore, it is not necessary to specify this attribute if you need session handling.

The info attribute

The `info` attribute can be used to specify information about the page. Any value you specify here is available to JSP developer tools. For example, a tool may use this information to display a list of pages, as shown by the following typical usage:

```
<%@ page info="Beginning JavaServer Pages - Chapter 7 Example" %>
```

The isELIgnored attribute

The `isELIgnored` attribute is a boolean attribute with either a `true` or a `false` value. If this attribute is set to `true`, as in

```
<%@ page  isELIgnored="true" %>
```

then any EL expression within the JSP page will be ignored. Any template text or attribute values with the `${...}` notation will not be considered an EL expression, and will be rendered as is.

This attribute provides a mean of maintaining backward compatibility for JSP pages. In almost all new JSP pages, you will want to set this attribute to `false`. On legacy JSP pages that do not use EL and may contain the `${...}` notation, you can set this attribute to `true`.

> For JSP 2.0, the default value of this attribute is `false`, and EL expressions are evaluated at request time.

The isErrorPage attribute

This is a boolean attribute that can have a `true` or `false` value. When handling JSP errors, you will be using this attribute as well as the `errorPage` attribute that is described next.

If this attribute is `true`, it tells the container that this JSP page is used by other JSP pages to handle errors. At request time, the container will make available a special implicit variable, called `exception`. This scoped variable is actually an attribute attached to the JSP request implicit object. The JSP code within this page can use the `exception` variable to access the information regarding the error that has occurred.

For example, consider the following directive:

```
<%@ page  isErrorPage="true" %>
```

A JSP page with the preceding directive will be used by the container to handle exceptions. The implicit `exception` variable will be made available within the page for access to exception information.

More information on JSP error handling is provided in Chapter 10, "Error Handling."

> The default for `isErrorPage` is `false`, as most JSP pages are not error-handling pages.

The errorPage attribute

This attribute is used in conjunction with the `isErrorPage` to handle errors in JSP. The value of the `errorPage` attribute is a URL to a JSP that will be executed when an error occurs that is not handled in the current page. For example, consider the following directive:

```
<%@ page errorPage="showerr.jsp" %>
```

This will tell the container that any unhandled errors in the current JSP should be handed to the `shower.jsp` page for handling. In practice, one single error-handling page can be used to handle errors for many JSP pages. This means that many JSPs will have the `errorPage` attribute set to the same URL value. You can find more details on how to handle errors in JSP in Chapter 10.

> There is no default value for `errorPage`. If not specified, the error not handled in this page will be reported by the container as an uncaught exception.

The contentType attribute

The `contentType` attribute tells the container what format the output of the JSP represents. This is very important for the container at request time. The container needs to generate the correct HTTP header, with a description of the content type, to the requesting browser for proper display. For example, consider this directive:

```
<%@ page contentType="text/html" %>
```

This directive tells the container that the response created by this JSP represents an HTML page. This information is used by the container to generate an HTTP header that tells the client browser to display the page as HTML.

The most common values for `contentType` are `text/html` for an HTML response, or `text/xml` for an XML response, although you can specify any MIME type and an optional character encoding for its value. MIME is an industry-standard way of describing Web content; see `http://www.iana.org/assignments/media-types/index.html` for a list of MIME types.

> By default, if you created your JSP in standard syntax, `contentType` has the default value `text/html`. If you have created your JSP in an XML-compatible syntax, then `contentType` will have the default value `text/xml`.

The example in the following Try It Out exercise uses the `contentType` attribute of the `<%@ page %>` directive to show how a directive gives request-time instructions to the container.

Try It Out   **The <%@ page %> Directive**

To try out the first example, make sure you have deployed ch07.war on your Tomcat 5 server. Review Chapter 1, "Getting Started with JavaServer Pages," if you do not remember how to deploy a WAR file.

Access the following URL using your browser to see the output of the first example:

```
http://localhost:8080/ch07/example1/index.jsp
```

The output of this page should be similar to Figure 7-2.

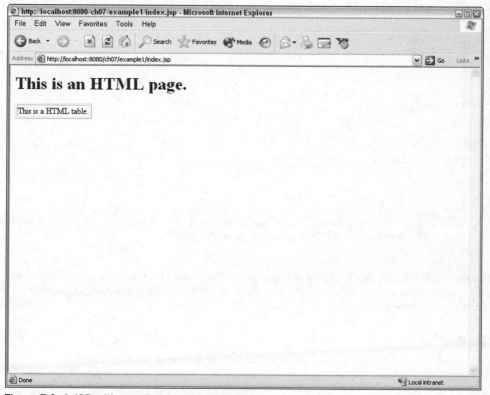

Figure 7-2: A JSP with text/html content type

Now, try accessing another URL using your browser. The second page in this example can be accessed through the following:

```
http://localhost:8080/ch07/example1/index2.jsp
```

Even though this page contains exactly the same HTML code as the first, it is displayed completely differently. This page has the content type set to text/xml. It is displayed as shown in Figure 7-3.

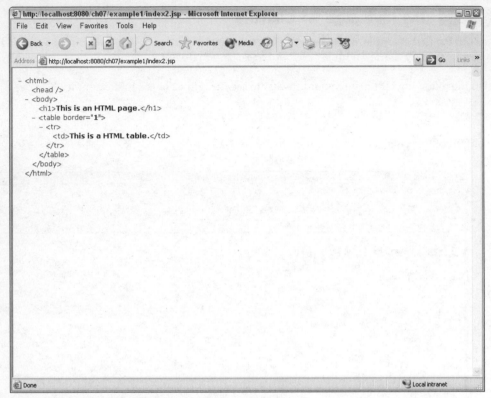

Figure 7-3: Display of a JSP with text/xml content type

In Figure 7-3, using Internet Explorer as the browser, the page is displayed as an XML document in a col-lapsible format. You can try expanding and collapsing the elements of the XML document by clicking the little icons on the page.

How It Works

The first page displayed in this example is called `index.jsp`, and can be located at `<Tomcat Installation Directory>/webapps/ch07/example1/index.jsp`. This page displays a line of HTML text and a simple HTML table. The code in this `index.jsp` page is reproduced here:

```
<%@ page language="java" contentType="text/html" %>
<html>
<head>
</head>
<body>
  <h1> This is an HTML page. </h1>
  <table border="1">
    <tr>
      <td>This is a HTML table.</td>
    </tr>
```

```
  </table>
</body>
</html>
```

The highlighted line in the preceding code is the `page` directive, giving instruction to the container. In this case, the container is told that the scripting language is Java (via the `language` attribute) and that the page contains HTML (via the `contentType` attribute).

Because both attributes specified in the `page` directive are set to their default value, it isn't necessary to use the `page` directive for this page. You can confirm this yourself by removing the `page` directive from the page, which will be rendered the same.

The effect of varying content type

When you access `index2.jsp`, the corresponding JSP file is located at `<Tomcat Installation Directory>/webapps/ch07/example1/index2.jsp`. This JSP contains the following code:

```
<%@ page language="java" contentType="text/xml" %>
<html>
<head>
</head>
<body>
  <h1> This is an HTML page. </h1>
  <table border="1">
    <tr>
      <td>This is a HTML table.</td>
    </tr>
  </table>
</body>
</html>
```

The difference between this page and `index.jsp` is highlighted above. The only change is in the value of the `contentType` attribute of the `page` directive. It has changed from "text/html" in `index.jsp` to "text/xml" in `index.jsp`.

Remember that the `contentType` attribute in the `page` directive actually tells the container that the response of the JSP should be considered an XML document. The container in turn sends an HTTP header to the browser indicating that the content of `text/xml` is MIME type. Internet Explorer has the capability to display an XML page using a specialized interactive collapsible stylesheet, which is why the second page is displayed differently.

The taglib Directive

The second directive to discuss here is the familiar `taglib` directive. This directive, as illustrated in many examples throughout earlier chapters, is used to tell the container which tag library a specific JSP requires. It is also used to assign a prefix that is used within the JSP page to identify tags from a specific tag library. After receiving this information, the container must locate the code for these tag libraries and get them ready for use by the JSP page.

Two general usage forms for the taglib directive

The `taglib` directive has two general usage forms. The first one specifies the `uri` and `prefix` attributes, and the second specifies the tag files.

Using a URI to map to the tag library

An example of this form is as follows:

```
<%@ taglib prefix="c" uri="http://java.sun.com/jsp/jstl/core" %>
```

This form is typically used for tag libraries that have a URI associated with them. In this case, it is the JSTL core tag library.

The `taglib` directive tells the container that the tag library associated with the URI `http://java.sun.com/jsp/jstl/core` will be used within this JSP. It also tells the container that all of the tags used from this tag library will be prefixed with the `c:` namespace within this JSP. Using this namespace prefix enables you to use tags from different tag libraries having the same name.

This URI can be associated with a tag library through a TLD file. The TLD can be mapped using a taglib map in the `web.xml` file, or via specific placement under the `META-INF` directory within a JAR archive. For more information on tag libraries and URI mapping, see Chapter 6, "JSP Tag Libraries and JSTL."

Specifying the directory of the tag files directly

The second usage form of the `<%@ taglib %>` directive is specific to tag files. Tag files are tag libraries that are implemented using JSP. Their usage is covered in Chapter 11, "Building Your Own Custom JSP Tag Library." This form specifies a `tagdir` attribute instead of the `uri` attribute (you may recall its usage in the very first example in Chapter 1):

```
<%@ taglib prefix="wroxtags" tagdir="/WEB-INF/tags" %>
```

Instead of using a URI to map to a specific tag library, the actual directory that contains the tag files is specified directly. This form is very handy for testing and for the rapid development of tag files.

The `taglib` directive in this case tells the container that this JSP uses tag files residing at the relative path `/WEB-INF/tags` (relative to the root directory of the application). It also tells the container that all tags used from this tag library will be prefixed with `wroxtags` within this JSP.

> In JSP 2.0, the `tagdir` attribute must contain a value that starts with `/WEB-INF/tags`. This means that all tag files should be placed in subdirectories under the `/WEB-INF/tags` directory.

Attributes of the taglib directive

The following table describes the three possible attributes for the `taglib` directive.

Attribute	Description
uri	This is a URI that will be used by the container to locate a TLD file that describes the tag library. The URI can be absolute, as in `http://java.sun.com/jsp/jstl/core`, or relative, as in `/tags/core`. The URI is just used as a unique identifier, and is not accessed directly.
tagdir	This attribute tells the container to look in the specified directory to find the tag files implementation for a tag library. This attribute must contain a path that begins with `/WEB-INF/tags`. This means that the tag files implementation specified with this attribute must reside under subdirectories of `WEB-INF/tags`.
prefix	This attribute tells the container that all tags of the associated tag library will be prefixed by the value of this attribute when used within the current JSP. For example, if the prefix specified is `c`, a tag from this tag library may appear as `<c:forEach>`.

The following Try It Out section illustrates how the `<%@ taglib %>` directive can affect JSP operations.

Try It Out   The <%@ taglib %> Directive

Make sure that you have `ch07.war` deployed. To see the output for this example, access the following URL using your browser:

    http://localhost:8080/ch07/example2/index.jsp

The output of this page should be similar to what is shown in Figure 7-4.

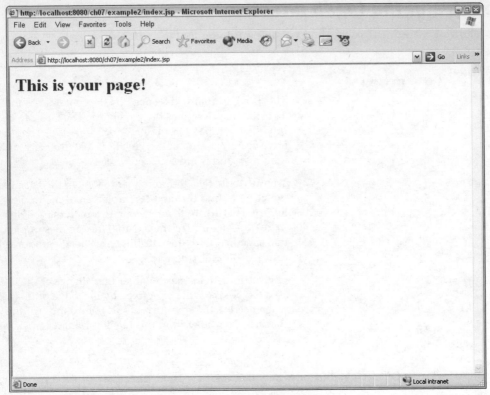

Figure 7-4: Example 2 JSP output with no request parameter

This JSP makes use of both forms of the `taglib` directive. It has a JSTL `<c:choose>` construct that will conditionally generate different output depending on the value of a `pg` request parameter. Try setting the parameter using the following URL:

```
http://localhost:8080/ch07/example2/index.jsp?pg=mines
```

The resulting output should be similar to what is shown in Figure 7-5.

In Figure 7-5, the output has changed because the `pg` request parameter is set to a value of `news`.

Next, try this URL:

```
http://localhost:8080/ch07/example2/index2.jsp
```

Satisfy yourself that `index2.jsp` works in exactly the same way as `index.jsp`. Try also supplying a `pg` parameter:

```
http://localhost:8080/ch07/example2/index2.jsp?pg=mine
```

It may come as a surprise to find out that `index.jsp` contains no `<%@ taglib %>` directive.

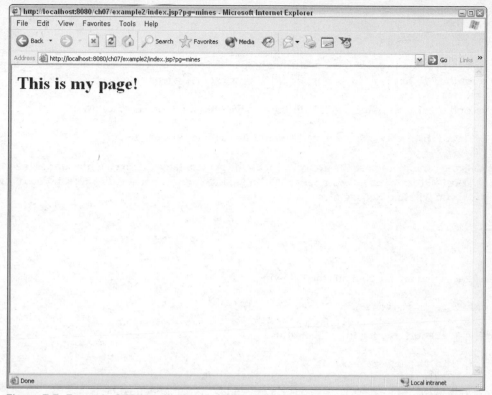

Figure 7-5: Example 2 JSP output with a pg request parameter

How It Works

The first page displayed in this example is called `index.jsp`, and can be located at `<Tomcat Installation Directory>/webapps/ch07/example2/index.jsp`.

This JSP page uses both forms of the `<%@ taglib %>` directive. The code in this `index.jsp` page is reproduced here:

```
<%@ taglib prefix="c" uri="http://java.sun.com/jsp/jstl/core" %>
<%@ taglib prefix="wt" tagdir="/WEB-INF/tags/wroxtags" %>

<html>
<head>
</head>
<body>
  <c:choose>
    <c:when test="${param.pg == 'mine'}">
      <wt:myPage/>
    </c:when>
    <c:otherwise>
      <wt:yourPage/>
    </c:otherwise>
```

```
      </c:choose>
    </body>
    </html>
```

The first form of the `taglib` directive, highlighted in the preceding code, tells the container to use the c prefix for the URI `http://java.sun.com/jsp/jstl/core`, referencing the JSTL core tags.

The second occurrence of the `taglib` directive in the preceding code is as follows:

```
<%@ taglib prefix="wt" tagdir="/WEB-INF/tags/wroxtags" %>
```

This tells the container to use the prefix wt for all the tags contained in the tag files under the `<Tomcat Installation Directory>/webapps/ch07/WEB-INF/tags/wroxtags` directory. If you browse to this directory, you will find two tag files:

❑   `myPage.tag`

❑   `yourPage.tag`

The `myPage.tag` tag file contains the following:

```
<h1>This is my page!</h1>
```

And the `yourPage.tag` tag file contains this:

```
<h1>This is your page!</h1>
```

Take a look at the JSTL `<c:choose>` construct in `index.jsp`, highlighted here:

```
<html>
<head>
</head>
<body>
  <c:choose>
    <c:when test="${param.pg == 'mine'}">
      <wt:myPage/>
    </c:when>
    <c:otherwise>
      <wt:yourPage/>
    </c:otherwise>
  </c:choose>
</body>
</html>
```

The two tag files are used to render the HTML output. If the pg parameter has the value mine, then the `<wt:myPage/>` tag is executed, resulting in This is my page! in the output; otherwise, the `<wt:yourPage/>` tag is executed, resulting in This is your page! in the output.

A JSP using tags without the taglib directive!

Now, open the `index2.jsp` file. Recall that this file performed identically to the `index.jsp` file. You can find this file at `<Tomcat Installation Directory>/webapps/ch07/example2/index2.jsp`. The content of this `index2.jsp` file is reproduced here:

```
<html>
<head>
</head>
<body>
  <c:choose>
    <c:when test="${param.pg == 'mine'}">
      <wt:myPage/>
    </c:when>
    <c:otherwise>
      <wt:yourPage/>
    </c:otherwise>
  </c:choose>
</body>
</html>
```

No, this is not a misprint. It really does not have any `<%@ taglib %>` directive. Otherwise, it is identical to the `index.jsp` file.

Without directives telling the container to use the tag libraries and associated prefix, how did the container know what to do?

The <include-prelude> and <include-coda> elements

The missing `taglib` directive, of course, is only an illusion. In fact, `index2.jsp` uses the exact same two `taglib` directives as `index.jsp` uses. The only difference is that they are specified somewhere else. They are specified in an `<include-prelude>` element, to be exact.

If you examine the `web.xml` deployment descriptor for the `ch07` application, located at `<Tomcat Installation Directory>/webapps/ch07/WEB-INF/web.xml`, you will find the `<include-prelude>` element:

```
<?xml version="1.0" encoding="ISO-8859-1"?>
<web-app xmlns="http://java.sun.com/xml/ns/j2ee"
  xmlns:xsi="http://www.w3.org/2001/XMLSchema-instance"
  xsi:schemaLocation="http://java.sun.com/xml/ns/j2ee
http://java.sun.com/xml/ns/j2ee/web-app_2_4.xsd"
  version="2.4">

  <description>
    Wrox Beginning JavaServer Pages Examples - Chapter 7
  </description>
  <display-name>Chapter 7 Example (Wrox Beginning JavaSever Pages)</display-name>

  <jsp-config>
```

```
    <jsp-property-group>
      <url-pattern>/example2/index2.jsp</url-pattern>
      <include-prelude>/WEB-INF/jspf/pre1.jspf</include-prelude>
    </jsp-property-group>
  </jsp-config>

</web-app>
```

The `<include-prelude>` element is a sub-element of the `<jsp-property-group>` element (specifying properties for a group of JSPs related to a URL pattern), which in turn is a sub-element of the `<jsp-config>` element (a configuration element for JSP) within the `web.xml` file. Therefore, to use the `<include-prelude>` element, you must make sure you have the other two elements enclosing it (as shown in the previous `web.xml` listing). See Chapter 16, "The Role of JSP in the Wider Context: Web Applications," for a description of the possible sub-elements of `<jsp-config>` and how they are used.

The typical use of the `<include-prelude>` element is to facilitate the implicit automatic inclusion of commonly used JSP lines in a project. For example, if you are in a project that uses ten different tag libraries on every JSP, specifying ten `taglib` directives at the top of every page can become tedious.

Instead, you can define an `<include-prelude>` element with an associated `<url-pattern>` element to apply the ten `taglib` directives to every JSP page.

The body of the `<include-prelude>` tag should be a jsp or jspf (JSP fragment) file that contains the lines to be included. If you take a look at the `<Tomcat Installation Directory>/webapps/ch07/WEB-INF/jspf/pre1.jspf` file, you will find the two missing `<%@ taglib %>` directives:

```
<%@ taglib prefix="c" uri="http://java.sun.com/jsp/jstl/core" %>
<%@ taglib prefix="wt" tagdir="/WEB-INF/tags/wroxtags" %>
```

If you take a look at the `<url-pattern>` associated with this `<include-prelude>` element, it is as follows:

```
<url-pattern>/example2/index2.jsp</url-pattern>
```

This pattern uniquely specifies one JSP, the `index2.jsp` file. In practice, since you will likely want to apply the directives to a set of JSPs, you may use a more general `<url-pattern>`, such as the following:

```
<url-pattern>*.jsp</url-pattern>
```

Using this `<url-pattern>` instead will add the content of `pre1.jspf` to every JSP.

Note that there is an `<include-coda>` element. The `<include-coda>` element works identically to the `<include-prelude>` element, except that it will place the specified JSP fragment at the end of the JSPs matching the `<url-pattern>`.

The action of `<include-prelude>` or `<include-coda>` is called *implicit include*. This is because these tags include extra content in the JSP implicitly. This is in contrast to the explicit include mechanism: the `<%@ include %>` directive, discussed next.

The include Directive

The last directive to cover is the `<%@ include %>` directive. The general usage form of this directive is as follows:

```
<%@ include file="news.jsp" %>
```

Here the `file` attribute is specified using a relative URL. For example, the `news.jsp` file is in the same directory as the JSP including it. This directive has only a single mandatory `file` attribute.

This directive tells the container to merge the content of other external files with the current JSP during the translation phase.

The include performed at translation time

It is very important to reiterate that the merging of the included files occurs at translation time, and not at request time. This means the following:

❑   None of the included JSP code is executed; it is not even compiled yet.

❑   The files are first merged and then the entire merged output is translated as a unit.

❑   If the included files are ever changed, there is no general way for the container to know and recompile the entire translation unit.

The standard `<jsp:include>` action occurs at request time and can overcome all of the preceding limitations. This action, along with others, is covered in detail in the next chapter.

Try It Out   The `<%@ include %>` Directive and XML Representation

The last example in this chapter works with the `<%@ include %>` directive. To try it out, first make sure you have `ch07.war` deployed.

With a browser, access the following URL:

```
http://localhost:8080/ch07/example3/index.jsp
```

The output of this page should be similar to Figure 7-6.

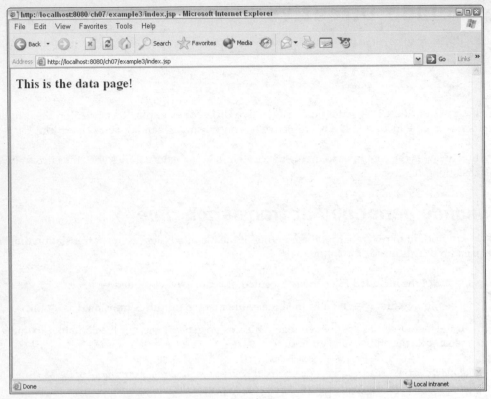

Figure 7-6: Testing the `<%@ include %>` **directive**

Try supplying a `pg` request parameter as in the previous Try It Out exercise. Try setting the parameter to `news` using the following URL:

```
http://localhost:8080/ch07/example3/index.jsp?pg=news
```

The resulting output should be similar to Figure 7-7.

Instead of a data page, a news page is now displayed. The logic of this page is very similar to the logic in the previous Try It Out exercise. Unlike that example, this example actually uses the `<%@ include %>` directive instead of custom tag files.

Finally, try to access this URL:

```
http://localhost:8080/ch07/example3/xindex.jsp
```

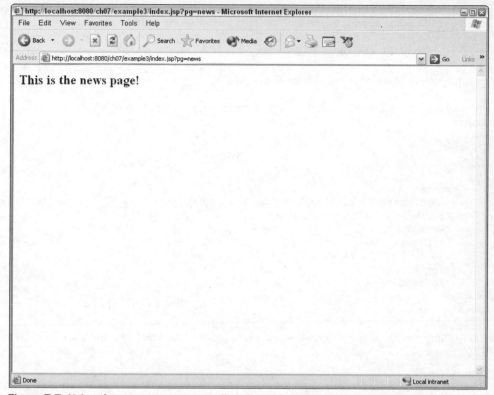

Figure 7-7: Using the `<%@ include %>` directive to include a news page

This is a JSP created as an XML document, using the alternative XML syntax. Note that the output is identical to `index.jsp`.

Now set the `pg` request parameter to `mines`, using the following URL:

```
http://localhost:8080/ch07/example3/xindex.jsp?pg=news
```

Again, even though it is using completely different notation, `xindex.jsp` works exactly the same way as `index.jsp`.

How It Works

The two JSP pages that are included by `index.jsp` and `xindex.jsp` are called `news.jsp` and `data.jsp`.

The `news.jsp` file, located at `<Tomcat Installation Directory>/webapps/ch07/example3/ news.jsp` contains the following code:

```
<h2>This is the news page!</h2>
```

The second included file, called `data.jsp`, is located at `<Tomcat Installation Directory>/webapps/ch07/example3/data.jsp` and contains the following code:

```
<h2>This is the data page!</h2>
```

The `index.jsp` file is coded in regular JSP syntax:

```
<%@ taglib prefix="c" uri="http://java.sun.com/jsp/jstl/core" %>
<html>
<head>
</head>
<body>

  <c:choose>
    <c:when test="${param.pg == 'news'}">
      <%@ include file="news.jsp" %>
    </c:when>
    <c:otherwise>
      <%@ include file="data.jsp" %>
    </c:otherwise>
  </c:choose>
</body>
</html>
```

There is nothing new or surprising on this `index.jsp` page. The first taglib directive's URI references the JSTL library:

```
<%@ taglib prefix="c" uri="http://java.sun.com/jsp/jstl/core" %>
```

Then the rendering of the HTML page starts, and a JSTL `<c:choose>` logical flow control construct is used to select one of two `<%@ include %>` directives. These directives are highlighted in the following code:

```
<c:choose>
    <c:when test="${param.pg == 'news'}">
      <%@ include file="news.jsp" %>
    </c:when>
    <c:otherwise>
      <%@ include file="data.jsp" %>
    </c:otherwise>
</c:choose>
```

The first `include` directive tells the container to insert the contents of the `news.jsp` file into the `index.jsp` file at translation time, and the second `include` directive does the same for the `data.jsp` file.

How the include directive and the <jsp:include> standard action differ

Note that unlike the `<jsp:include>` standard action, the `include` directive is evaluated at page translation time. This means that the preceding JSP fragment actually becomes the following JSP fragment for translation purposes:

```
<c:choose>
  <c:when test="${param.pg == 'news'}">
    <h2>This is the news page!</h2>
  </c:when>
  <c:otherwise>
    <h2>This is the data page!</h2>
  </c:otherwise>
</c:choose>
```

The content of both news.jsp and data.jsp is inserted into the JSP before the page is compiled by the container.

Figure 7-8 illustrates the translation-time operation of the include directive, as contrasted with the request-time execution of a <jsp:include> action.

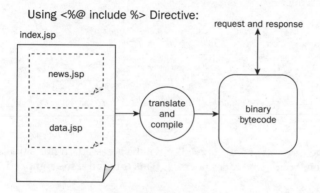

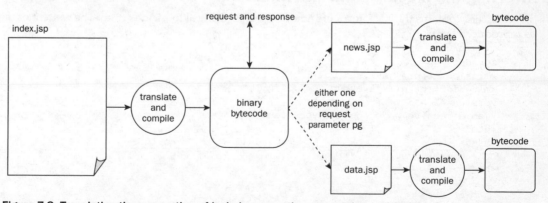

Figure 7-8: Translation-time operation of include versus the request-time execution of <jsp:include>

In Figure 7-8, the top flow shows what happens when the include directive is used. In this flow, both data.jsp and news.jsp are merged into the index.jsp before the entire JSP is translated into Java source code and then compiled into Java-executable code.

The bottom flow shows the sequence when the `<jsp:include>` standard action is used. In this case, both `data.jsp` and `news.jsp` are string attributes of the action that will not be evaluated during translation or compilation. This means that neither file will be accessed until the compiled code of `index.jsp` is executed at request time. When a request comes into the `index.jsp` binary, the `<c:choose>` control flow construct ensures that only one of the two alternatives will be included. At this time, either the `news.jsp` or `data.jsp` will be translated into Java source code, compiled into executable bytecode, and then executed.

Translation-time detection of errors versus request-time detection of errors

If the `data.jsp` and `news.jsp` files are missing, and the `<%@ include %>` directive is used, the error will be detected at translation time. If the `<jsp:include>` standard action is used, however, the error will not be detected until a request for service is received. In fact, if either `news.jsp` or `data.jsp` is missing and the branch is not taken, the use of the `<jsp:include>` action will not detect the missing JSP file at all. For example, consider the following JSP code:

```
<c:choose>
  <c:when test="${param.pg == 'news'}">
    <jsp:include page="news.jsp" />
  </c:when>
  <c:otherwise>
    <jsp:include page="data.jsp" />
  </c:otherwise>
</c:choose>
```

If the `pg` input parameter contains the value `news`, then only `news.jsp` will be accessed. In this situation, the code will not produce an error even if `data.jsp` does not exist. This is because the compiled code will not try to access `data.jsp`.

Converting the index.jsp file into XML form

`xindex.xml` contains the XML form of `index.jsp`. It is identical to `xindex.jsp`. The content of the file is reproduced here:

```
<jsp:root
  xmlns:c="http://java.sun.com/jsp/jstl/core"
  xmlns:jsp="http://java.sun.com/JSP/Page"
  version="2.0">
  <jsp:directive.page contentType="text/html"/>
  <html>
  <head>
  </head>
  <body>

    <c:choose>
      <c:when test="${param.pg == 'news'}">
        <jsp:directive.include file="news.jsp" />
      </c:when>
      <c:otherwise>
        <jsp:directive.include file="data.jsp" />
      </c:otherwise>
    </c:choose>
  </body>
```

```
    </html>
  </jsp:root>
```

Note the addition of a `<jsp:root>` element. This element is discussed in the next section.

The original `page` directive is now converted to its XML syntax:

```
<jsp:directive.page contentType="text/html"/>
```

Note the use of the `contentType` attribute here. If the container is not explicitly asked to render the response as `"text/html"` type via this directive, it will render it as an XML document by default.

The two `include` directives are also converted to their equivalent XML syntax:

```
        <jsp:directive.include file="news.jsp" />
...
        <jsp:directive.include file="data.jsp" />
```

You can use your browser to open this `xindex.xml` file directly. If you are using Internet Explorer, open the `xindex.xml` file directly by clicking File ➪ Open, and then selecting the file, as shown in Figure 7-9.

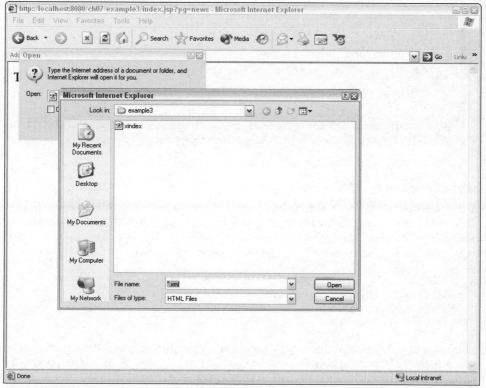

Figure 7-9: Opening `xindex.xml` for viewing

After you have loaded the XML file, Internet Explorer will display it in the collapsible format, as shown in Figure 7-10.

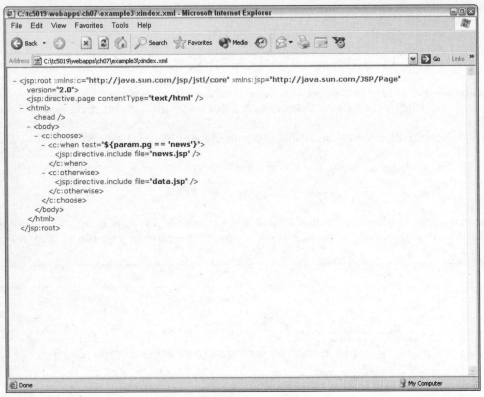

Figure 7-10: Display of `xindex.xml` using Internet Explorer

Converting directives to XML syntax

Unlike the page and include directives, the taglib directive has no associated `<jsp:directive.taglib />` directive. Instead, a tag library directive will convert to an XML namespace specification.

In the case of `xindex.xml`, a new `<jsp:root>` element is introduced:

```
<jsp:root
    xmlns:c="http://java.sun.com/jsp/jstl/core"
    xmlns:jsp="http://java.sun.com/JSP/Page"
    version="2.0">
```

This element wraps the content that is to be processed by the JSP container. It also serves as an enclosing tag to declare the XML namespaces that will be used. In this case, the prefix c is mapped to the namespace of the JSTL core library — via the URI `http://java.sun.com/jsp/jstl/core`.

The JSP standard actions are prefixed with `jsp:`. The second namespace is specified with this `jsp:` prefix and mapped via the URI `http://java.sun.com/JSP/Page`. Converting `<%@ taglib %>` to XML namespaces ensures that the resulting document is a well-formed XML document.

Summary

Directives are instructions for the container, embedded within a JSP page. This instruction can affect the container's behavior during any phase of JSP processing. This chapter covered these JSPs in detail. To summarize what we have covered:

❑ When a JSP is processed by the container, it goes through three separate phases. In the translation phase, the JSP is translated to Java source code. In the compilation phase, the Java source code is compiled to bytecode executable. The resulting binary is then used in the request processing phase to handle incoming requests.

❑ There are three major JSP directives: `page`, `taglib`, and `include`.

❑ The `page` directive has many attributes that give the container instructions and information specific to the JSP page.

❑ The `taglib` directive is used to declare the use of tag libraries.

❑ The `include` directive can be used to include external text files or JSP fragments during the translation phase of processing. This is unlike the `<jsp:include>` standard action, which operates during request time.

❑ Under some circumstances, it may be necessary to have JSPs that are well-formed XML documents. JSP 2.0 supports an alternative XML syntax. This syntax enables the creation of JSPs that are well-formed XML documents.

Exercises

1. Convert the `index.jsp` in example 1 to a JSP using XML syntax. Call this `xindex.jsp`. Test this resulting `xindex.jsp` on your Tomcat 5 server to make sure it works identically.

2. For the third Try It Out exercise, apply the `<include-prelude>` element in `web.xml` to eliminate the need to specify the `taglib` directive for `index.jsp`.

JSP Standard Actions

Standard actions are tags that are built right into every JSP implementation. These tags can be used without the addition of any additional tag libraries. These actions are very frequently used in JSP, and earlier examples have used them repeatedly. This chapter provides a more in-depth discussion of each of these standard actions, and reveals some subtlety in the usage and application of these workhorse tags.

The standard actions covered within this chapter include the following:

- ❑ `<jsp:useBean>`
- ❑ `<jsp:setProperty>`
- ❑ `<jsp:getProperty>`
- ❑ `<jsp:include>`
- ❑ `<jsp:forward>`
- ❑ `<jsp:param>`
- ❑ `<jsp:plugin>`
- ❑ `<jsp:params>`
- ❑ `<jsp:fallback>`

While there are other standard actions in JSP, they pertain to the creation of tag files, which are covered in more detail in Chapter 11, "Building Your Own Custom JSP Tag Library."

This chapter presents the syntax and most common usage of each of these standard actions. A series of four hands-on examples will guide you through their typical use.

JSP Standard Actions Are Built-in Tags

JSP standard actions are tags that are available in all JSP implementations. This set of available tags has not changed significantly between JSP 1.2 and JSP 2.0. Therefore, you can count on these standard actions to be supported by all JSP containers.

All standard actions are prefixed by `jsp:` and have the following general form:

```
<jsp:tagname   ... attributes ....  />
```

Some standard actions also have a body that can include other tags, typically parameters. For example:

```
<jsp:tagname   ... attributes ....  >
  <jsp:param ... attributes... />
  ... more parameters ....
</jsp:tagname>
```

The standard actions can be classified into six groups:

❑ **Actions that work with and manipulate JavaBean instances within JSPs:** This group includes the `<jsp:useBean>` action, the `<jsp:setProperty>` action, and the `<jsp:getProperty>` action.

❑ **Actions that include the output from additional JSP or Web resources at request time:** This group includes the `<jsp:include>` standard action.

❑ **Actions for forwarding the incoming request to another JSP or Web resource for further processing:** This group includes the `<jsp:forward>` standard action.

❑ **Actions for specifying parameters within the body of other standard actions:** This group includes the `<jsp:param>` standard action.

❑ **Actions for embedding Java objects such as applets and JavaBeans within a client's Web page:** This group includes the `<jsp:plugin>`, `<jsp:params>`, and `<jsp:fallback>` standard actions.

❑ **Actions used only within tag files:** This group includes the `<jsp:attribute>`, `<jsp:body>`, `<jsp:invoke>`, `<jsp:doBody>`, `<jsp:element>`, `<jsp:text>`, and `<jsp:output>` standard actions.

The following sections cover each of these groups in turn except for those actions used only within tag files. Those actions are covered later in Chapter 11, where they are put to use within custom tag files.

The first group presented here are the standard actions that work with JavaBeans.

Actions for Working with JavaBeans

Three standard actions are used in the creation and access of JavaBeans:

❑ `<jsp:useBean>` for creating a JavaBean instance or associating a name with an existing JavaBean instance

- ❑ `<jsp:setProperty>` to set the property of a JavaBean instance
- ❑ `<jsp:getProperty>` to render the value of a JavaBean property

JavaBeans are objects written in the Java programming language that follow a specific set of coding conventions. A full description of the JavaBean conventions is beyond the scope of this book. For our purpose, it is sufficient to know that JavaBeans are Java objects that have properties. These properties can be read via a `get` *operation, or changed via a* `set` *operation.*

Before a JavaBean instance can be accessed and manipulated within a JSP page, one must use the `<jsp:useBean>` standard action to make it available within the page.

The *<jsp:useBean>* standard action

The inconspicuous `<jsp:useBean>` standard action can easily be the most complex standard action in all of JSP.

The main purpose of `<jsp:useBean>` can be summarized as follows:

- ❑ Search for a JavaBean by the name specified if available.
- ❑ If the bean is found, make it available to this JSP page.
- ❑ If the bean cannot be found, then create an instance of it.

Once the JavaBean instance is created, it will be accessible within the page using the name specified.

The exact outcome of the action depends on the attributes that you specify. There are a variety of different ways to use this action, as shown next.

Using the <jsp:useBean> standard action

The basic usage syntax of this standard action is as follows:

```
<jsp:useBean id="......"  scope="...."  type="...." />
```

The attributes of `<jsp:useBean>` are tabulated in the following table.

Attribute Name	Description
id	The name of the JavaBean instance to look for. It is also the name used to refer to the new JavaBean instance if one is created. This attribute must be unique within a JSP (and any included content using the `<%@ include %>` directive). You cannot have two `<jsp:useBean>` standard actions using the same `id` attribute. This is a mandatory attribute.

Table continued on following page

243

Attribute Name	Description
class	This is the full Java class name of the JavaBean. It is used to create a new instance if the named bean cannot be found. This is an optional attribute, but either the class or type attribute (or both) must be specified.
type	This is a Java interface that the JavaBean instance implements, or a superclass that the JavaBean instance extends. This type is used in the generation of Java source code during the translation phase. The first Try it Out exercise will clarify the use of this attribute. This is an optional attribute, but either the class or type attribute (or both) must be specified.
scope	Specifies the scope in which the standard action will attempt to find a scoped attribute with the name corresponding to the id attribute. This is an optional attribute. The default value when not specified is the page scope.

Alternatively, this tag can have a body:

```
<jsp:useBean id="......"  scope="...."   type="....">

   ... content of body ....
</jsp:useBean>
```

When using this syntax, the body of the tag will be evaluated only if the `<jsp:useBean>` executes successfully and a JavaBean instance has been located or created.

> Because the id attribute is used to generate a Java variable, you must ensure that the attribute follows Java variable naming conventions. This includes the following restrictions: the id must begin with a letter, $, or "_", but not a number or other symbol, and the id must not be a Java keyword, Boolean literal (true or false), or null.

Using two `<jsp:useBean>` standard actions with the same id attribute within the same JSP is considered an error.

The following Try It Out example provides a chance to see how this standard action actually works.

Try It Out   The \<jsp:useBean> and \<jsp:setProperty> Standard Actions

The examples are bundled in the deployable ch08.war. First make sure that your Tomcat 5 server is running and then deploy ch08.war to the server. Review Chapter 1, "Getting Started with JavaServer Pages," if you do not remember how to deploy a WAR archive.

Open your browser, and access the following URL:

```
http://localhost:8080/ch08/example1/index.jsp
```

The page displays a simple table (see Figure 8-1) with two values from a `Product` JavaBean.

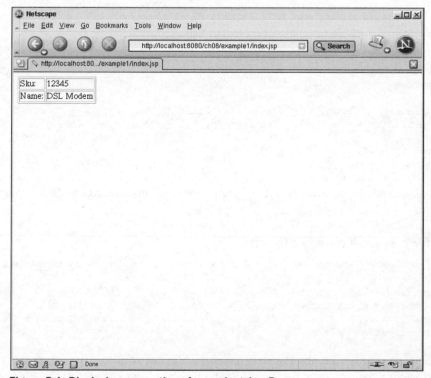

Figure 8-1: Displaying properties of a product JavaBean

The `Product` JavaBean instance is created using a `<jsp:useBean>` standard action. However, the `sku` property of this JavaBean instance is printed using embedded Java code within a scripting element; and the `name` of the product is printed using an EL expression.

How It Works

The only page displayed in this example is `index.jsp`, which is located at `<Tomcat Installation Directory>/webapps/ch08/example1/index.jsp`. This page uses the `<jsp:useBean>` standard action to create a JavaBean instance. The JavaBean instance created is an instance of the `com.wrox.begjsp.ch03.Product` class from the e-store example in Chapter 3, "JSP Basics 2: Generalized Templating and Server Scripting." This instance is then used by both scripting elements in the Java programming language, as well as the EL expression. The code in this `index.jsp` page is reproduced here:

```
<html>
<head>
</head>
```

```
<body>
  <jsp:useBean id="myProduct" class="com.wrox.begjsp.ch03.Product">
    <jsp:setProperty name="myProduct" property="sku" value="12345"/>
    <jsp:setProperty name="myProduct" property="name" value="DSL Modem"/>
  </jsp:useBean>
  <table border="1">
    <tr>
      <td>Sku:</td><td><%= myProduct.getSku() %></td>
    </tr>
    <tr>
      <td>Name:</td><td>${myProduct.name}</td>
    </tr>
  </table>

  <jsp:useBean id="myMap"  class="java.util.HashMap" />
  <jsp:useBean id="myMap2"  class="java.util.HashMap"  type="java.util.Map"/>

</body>
</html>
```

The highlighted code in the preceding listing shows the creation and usage of the Product JavaBean instance.

Searching for a scoped named attribute

The `<jsp:useBean>` standard action is used to create the Product instance with the following code:

```
<jsp:useBean id="myProduct" class="com.wrox.begjsp.ch03.Product">
  <jsp:setProperty name="myProduct" property="sku" value="12345"/>
  <jsp:setProperty name="myProduct" property="name" value="DSL Modem"/>
</jsp:useBean>
```

Note first that this tag has a body. The body has two `<jsp:setProperty>` standard actions (examined in the next section) that set the sku and name properties. sku is set to 12345, while the name property is set to "DSL Modem". This body will be executed only if the `<jsp:useBean>` can locate or create the myProduct instance successfully.

In the `<jsp:useBean>` standard action, only the id and class attributes are specified. The other two attributes, scope and type, are not specified. This will first cause a search for a named attribute called myProduct in the default page scope.

If an attribute named myProduct can be located in the page scope, it will be made available within the current JSP page. If the attribute cannot be found in any page scope, then an instance of the class com.wrox.begjsp.ch03.Product is created. This instance is then attached to the page scope as an attribute named myProduct.

Note that if the attribute with the name myProduct *is found, but it is not of the* com.wrox.begjsp. ch03.Product *class, an error will occur.*

In this particular case, myProduct cannot be found, and a new instance of the com.wrox.begjsp.ch03.Product JavaBean is created.

Container-generated Java source code

That's not all that this <jsp:useBean> standard action does. The complexity of this tag is evident when you consider the following:

❑ There is scriptlet code (i.e., embedded Java code) that needs to use the JavaBean.

❑ EL expressions also need to access the JavaBean.

The code that prints out the sku property of the Product is written in embedded Java code:

```
<td>Sku:</td><td><%= myProduct.getSku() %></td>
```

The code that prints the name property of the Product instance is coded as an EL expression:

```
<td>Name:</td><td>${myProduct.name}</td>
```

To make the JavaBean easy to access for both the embedded Java code writer and the EL expression user, the <jsp:useBean> standard action must do both of the following:

❑ Create a Java variable that references the JavaBean instance; this will enable any embedded Java code to access a property using the invocation of the myProduct.get<property name>() getter method

❑ Attach the JavaBean instance as an attribute named myProduct to the page scope; this will enable EL expressions to access a property of the bean using the simple myProduct.<property name> notation

If you specify the scope *attribute, it will change the scoping parameter passed into the* PageContext .getAttribute() *call, causing it to search for the attribute only in the specified scope.*

Figure 8-2 illustrates the operation of the <jsp:useBean> standard action in this example.

As shown in Figure 8-2, to create the Java language–accessible JavaBean reference called myProduct, it is necessary to generate custom code during the translation phase of JSP processing.

You can actually see this generated code in your installation of Tomcat 5. Locate the file called index_jsp.java at <Tomcat Installation Directory>/work/Catalina/localhost/ch08/org/apache/jsp/example1/index_jsp.java.

This is the result of the translation phase. When you first access your JSP after a change, the container will retranslate your JSP page into this Java source code file.

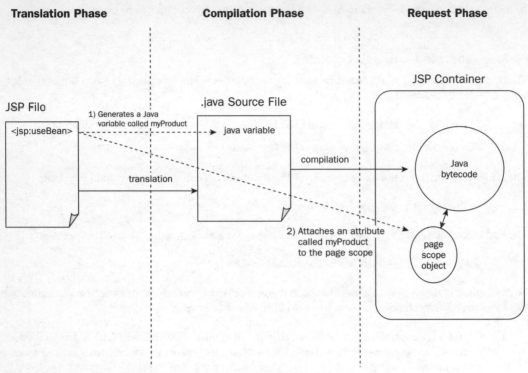

Figure 8-2: Operation of the `<java:useBean>` **standard action**

If you look inside this `index_jsp.java` file, the Java source code that the container will generate for the `<jsp:useBean>` standard action is similar to the following:

```
com.wrox.begjsp.ch03.Product myProduct = null;
synchronized (_jspx_page_context)
{
    myProduct = (com.wrox.begjsp.ch03.Product)
      jspx_page_context.getAttribute("myProduct", PageContext.PAGE_SCOPE);
    if (myProduct == null)
    {
        myProduct = new com.wrox.begjsp.ch03.Product();
        _jspx_page_context.setAttribute("myProduct", myProduct,
          PageContext.PAGE_SCOPE);
        out.write("\n");
        out.write("    ");
        org.apache.jasper.runtime.JspRuntimeLibrary.introspecthelper(

_jspx_page_context.findAttribute("myProduct"),
        "sku", "12345", null, null, false);
        out.write("\n");
        out.write("    ");
        org.apache.jasper.runtime.JspRuntimeLibrary.introspecthelper(_
```

```
                   _jspx_page_context.findAttribute("myProduct"), "name",
                     "DSL Modem", null, null, false);
               out.write('\n');
               out.write(' ');
               out.write(' ');
           }
       }
```

In the highlighted source code, a Java variable called `myProduct` of the `com.wrox.begjsp.ch03.Product` class is first declared. Next, a synchronized block is defined. This block contains the code that searches for a named attribute in the page scope by calling the `PageContext`'s `getAttribute()` method.

Synchronizing a Java reference with an attached attribute

If the `myProduct` attribute can be found in the page scope, it is assigned to the newly created `myProduct` Java variable. This enables the Java code generated to access this JavaBean instance through the `myProduct` variable. The page scope attribute is already accessible to EL expressions.

If the `PageContext`'s `getAttribute()` method returns `null`, an attribute named `myProduct` cannot be found in the page scope. In this case, a new `Product` instance is created and attached to the page scope as the `myProduct` attribute, via the `PageContext`'s `setAttribute()` method. The same instance is also assigned to the Java `myProduct` variable.

The value for the attribute named `"myProduct"` and the Java variable named `myProduct` are assigned within the same synchronized block. This is necessary to ensure that the two values act as one from the perspective of the JSP developer. The synchronized block ensures that no other concurrently executing JSP code can modify the values during the assignment.

Using a JavaBean in scripting elements

In `index.jsp`, the following JSP code renders the `sku` property value of `Product`:

```
        <td>Sku:</td><td><%= myProduct.getSku() %></td>
```

In `index_jsp.java`, it is translated into the following Java source code:

```
        out.write("      <td>Sku:</td><td>");
        out.print( myProduct.getSku() );
        out.write("</td>\n");
```

Because `myProduct` is a Java language variable that refers to the newly instantiated `Product` object (created by the `<jsp:useBean>` standard action), the call to `myProduct.getSku()` will yield the value of this property.

Using a JavaBean in an EL expression

In `index.jsp`, the following JSP code renders the `name` property value of `Product`:

```
        <td>Name:</td><td>${myProduct.name}</td>
```

In `index_jsp.java`, the corresponding Java source code generated during the translation phase is as follows:

```
out.write("    <td>Name:</td><td>");
out.write((java.lang.String)
org.apache.jasper.runtime.PageContextImpl.proprietaryEvaluate(
  "${myProduct.name}", java.lang.String.class,
  (PageContext)_jspx_page_context, null, false));
out.write("</td>\n");
```

The EL expression parser is called to evaluate `${myProduct.name}`. In Chapter 5, "JSP and EL," you saw that this will cause a search through the four scoping implicit objects to find an attribute with the name `myProduct`. This attribute will be found immediately at the page scope. The `<jsp:useBean>` standard action has attached it there previously. The "`.`" operator on the `myProduct` JavaBean will cause the `getName()` method of the bean to be invoked, rendering the value of the property.

Effect of the type attribute in <jsp:useBean>

The last two JSP code lines within the HTML `<body>` in the `index.jsp` page are as follows:

```
<jsp:useBean id="myMap"  class="java.util.HashMap" />
<jsp:useBean id="myMap2"  class="java.util.HashMap"  type="java.util.Map"/>
```

These two lines will each create an instance of a Java `HashMap`. Both instances are attached to page scope as named attributes. The first one will be named `"myMap"` and the second one will be named `"myMap2"`.

Two Java language variables will also be created when the JSP is translated to Java source code. These two JSP lines will translate to very different Java code.

The reason they are different is the use of the `type` attribute in the second line. The `type` attribute actually specifies the type of the Java language variable to create. In the case of `myMap2`, it is not the `java.util.HashMap` class, but the `java.util.Map` interface.

If you take a look at the generated code in `index_jsp.java`, you will see that the `useBean` tag without the `type` attribute generates:

```
java.util.HashMap myMap = null;
synchronized (_jspx_page_context)
{
    myMap = (java.util.HashMap) _jspx_page_context.getAttribute(

      "myMap", PageContext.PAGE_SCOPE);

    if (myMap == null)
    {
        myMap = new java.util.HashMap();
        _jspx_page_context.setAttribute(
            "myMap", myMap, PageContext.PAGE_SCOPE);
    }
}
```

The highlighted lines show that the `myMap` Java variable is declared to be of type `java.util.HashMap`.

The generated code for the second JSP line, the one that specifies a `type` attribute, is as follows:

```
java.util.Map myMap2 = null;
synchronized (_jspx_page_context)
{
    myMap2 = (java.util.Map) _jspx_page_context.getAttribute("myMap2",
      PageContext.PAGE_SCOPE);
    if (myMap2 == null)
    {
        myMap2 = new java.util.HashMap();
        _jspx_page_context.setAttribute("myMap2", myMap2,
          PageContext.PAGE_SCOPE);
    }
}
```

The highlighted lines in the preceding code show that the `myMap2` Java variable is declared to be of type `java.util.Map`. This is the type that is specified in the `type` attribute of the `<jsp:useBean>` custom action.

The `<jsp:setProperty>` standard action

In `index.jsp`, within the body of the `<jsp:useBean>` standard action, you can find two `<jsp:setProperty>` standard actions. These actions are used to set the properties of the newly created JavaBean instance; they will be executed only if the instance is created successfully.

The general usage form of this standard action is as follows:

```
<jsp:setProperty name=".. JavaBean name..." property=".. property name ..."   [
value="..value to set.." | param="... parameter name..."] />
```

This standard action does not support a body.

The following can be used to set the value(s) of a JavaBean via the `<jsp:setProperty>` standard action:

❑   A string constant

❑   A request parameter

❑   An expression (for example, an EL expression)

The attributes of this standard action are discussed in the following sections.

The name attribute

The specified `name` attribute is used to search through the scopes for an attached attribute, for a JavaBean instance with the same name. The scope search order is as follows:

1.   Page scope

2.   Request scope

3.   Session scope (if a session has been created by the container)

4.   Application scope

If an attribute with the specified name cannot be found in any of the scopes, an error will be issued during runtime.

The attribute found must have been previously made visible within the page by a `<jsp:useBean>` *standard action.*

The property attribute

The `property` attribute is used to set a property of the JavaBean that can be set (i.e., not a read-only property). The `property` attribute can also contain the special "*" notation. This will cause the container to match each request parameter against the properties of the JavaBean, and perform an assignment for each property with a corresponding request parameter name. The upcoming Try It Out example shows how this can be very useful for form processing.

The value or param attribute

Either the `value` or the `param` attribute need to be specified. If a `value` is specified, it is used to set the specified property directly. If a `param` attribute is specified, the request parameter with the corresponding name is used to set the value of the property.

Java code generated from <jsp:setProperty>

In `index.jsp`, within the body of the `<jsp:useBean>` standard action, are two `<jsp:setProperty>` standard actions:

```
<jsp:setProperty name="myProduct" property="sku" value="12345"/>
<jsp:setProperty name="myProduct" property="name" value="DSL Modem"/>
```

The corresponding generated Java source code, after translation to `index_jsp.java`, is as follows:

```
org.apache.jasper.runtime.JspRuntimeLibrary.introspecthelper(_
  _jspx_page_context.findAttribute("myProduct"), "sku", "12345", null, null, false);
out.write("\n");
out.write("    ");
org.apache.jasper.runtime.JspRuntimeLibrary.introspecthelper(

  jspx_page_context.findAttribute("myProduct"), "name", "DSL Modem", null,

  null, false);
```

The Java language's introspection feature is used here to set the actual property value. The `PageContest.findAttribute()` method is used to locate the JavaBean. As mentioned earlier, this method will search through the four different scopes — –page, request, session, and application — in an attempt to find the named attribute.

Try It Out   **The <jsp:setProperty> and <jsp:getProperty> Standard Actions**

This second example shows how the `<jsp:setProperty>` standard action can simplify form processing. To access this example, make sure that your Tomcat 5 server is running, with `ch08.war` deployed. Access the following URL with your browser:

```
http://localhost:8080/ch08/example2/index.jsp
```

This will display an HTML form (see Figure 8-3) for you to enter some product details.

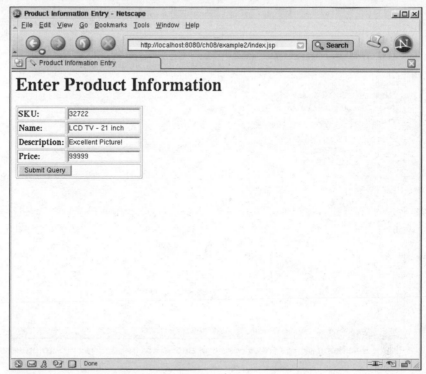

Figure 8-3: Product information entry form

Enter the following information for this product:

❑   For SKU, enter **32727.**

❑   For Name, enter **LCD TV - 21 inch.**

❑   For Description, enter **Excellent Picture!**

❑   For Price, enter **99999.**

Next, click the Submit Query button.

This will submit the form for processing. The JSP processing the form is called procprod.jsp. It uses the <jsp:setProperty> standard action to pass all the incoming request parameters to a JavaBean. In a production environment, this bean may be passed to a framework or back-end business logic for further processing. In this case, procprod.jsp simply uses the <jsp:getProperty> standard action to render the property values of the bean in a table. Figure 8-4 reveals the output of procprod.jsp.

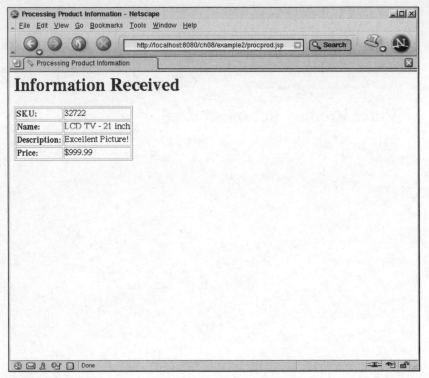

Figure 8-4: Using `<jsp:setProperty>` and `<jsp:getProperty>` to process requests

How It Works

The HTML form for data input is displayed by the `index.jsp` page. This page can be located at `<Tomcat Installation Directory>/webapps/ch08/example2/index.jsp`. Reproduced here, it is all HTML template text:

```html
<html>
<head>
  <title>Product Information Entry</title>
  <style>
    .label { font-weight: bold; }
  </style>
</head>
<body>
  <h1> Enter Product Information</h1>
  <form  action="procprod.jsp" method="post">
    <table border="1">
      <tr>
        <td class="label">SKU:</td> <td><input name="sku" type="text" width="40"/>
        </td>
      </tr>

      <tr>
```

```
            <td class="label">Name:</td> <td><input name="name" type="text"
              width="40"/>
            </td>
          </tr>
          <tr>
            <td class="label">Description:</td> <td><input name="desc" type="text"
              width="40"/>
            </td>
          </tr>
          <tr>
            <td class="label">Price:</td> <td> <input name="price" type="text"
              width="40"/>
            </td>
          </tr>

          <tr>
            <td colspan="2"> <input type="submit"/>
            </td>
          </tr>
        </table>
      </form>
  </body>
</html>
```

This index.jsp page contains a form with four request parameters: sku, name, desc, and price. When this form is submitted, it uses the HTTP POST method to submit the data to the procprod.jsp page. This is specified in the HTML <form> element:

```
<form  action="procprod.jsp" method="post">
```

Expediting form processing with <jsp:setProperty>

The procprod.jsp page processes the incoming form data. It can be located at <Tomcat Installation Directory>/webapps/ch08/example2/procprod.jsp. The content of procprod.jsp is reproduced here:

```
<%@ taglib prefix="fmt" uri="http://java.sun.com/jsp/jstl/fmt" %>
<html>
<head>
  <title>Processing Product Information</title>
  <style>
    .label { font-weight: bold; }
  </style>
</head>

<body>
  <jsp:useBean id="localProd" class="com.wrox.begjsp.ch03.Product" />
  <jsp:setProperty name="localProd" property="*" />
  <h1>Information Received</h1>
  <table border="1">
    <tr>
      <td class="label" >SKU:</td> <td><jsp:getProperty name="localProd"
        property="sku"/>
      </td>
    </tr>
```

```
    <tr>
      <td class="label">Name:</td> <td><jsp:getProperty name="localProd"
        property="name"/> </td>
    </tr>
    <tr>
      <td class="label">Description:</td> <td><jsp:getProperty name="localProd"
        property="desc"/> </td>
    </tr>
    <tr>
      <td class="label">Price:</td>
      <td>
        <fmt:formatNumber value="${localProd.price / 100}" type="currency"/>
      </td>
    </tr>

  </table>
</body>
</html>
```

The highlighted lines work with the JavaBean. A <jsp:useBean> standard action creates the JavaBean instance. There is one single <jsp:setProperty> standard action for the assignment of the incoming parameters to the JavaBean's properties. Finally, several <jsp:getProperty> standard actions render the bean's property.

Using the "*" special value for the <jsp:setProperty> standard action

If we look at the code of procprod.jsp, the <jsp:useBean> standard action is used to create an instance of a com.wrox.begjsp.ch03.Product JavaBean. This instance is associated with an attribute (and a Java variable) with the name "localProd":

```
<jsp:useBean id="localProd" class="com.wrox.begjsp.ch03.Product" />
```

Immediately after, all the incoming parameters are assigned to the properties of localProd with one single <jsp:setProperty> standard action:

```
<jsp:setProperty name="localProd" property="*" />
```

The use of the property="*" notation will cause the action to attempt to match incoming parameter names with bean property names and perform the assignment of values from each of the incoming parameters to its matching property.

In this case, the incoming request parameters are called sku, name, desc, and price, respectively. The com.wrox.begjsp.ch03.Product JavaBean has properties named sku, name, desc, and price. This is a one-to-one match, and the <jsp:setProperty> standard action will transfer all the request parameter values to the bean's property.

> In a production environment, the **property="x"** technique can be very handy when passing incoming form data to back-end business logic components for further processing.

The rest of the code for this JSP accesses the JavaBean instance and prints out the property values.

The <jsp:getProperty> standard action

The <jsp:getProperty> standard action is used to print out the property of a JavaBean. The general form is as follows:

```
<jsp:getProperty name="...javabean name..." property="...property name..." />
```

The two attributes of this tag are shown in the following table.

Attribute Name	Description
name	The name of the JavaBean whose property is to be rendered, typically made available by an earlier <jsp:useBean> standard action The name of the property to render
property	The name of the property to render

This standard action will first locate the named object. As with the <jsp:setProperty> standard action, it will search through all four scopes for the named attribute. Once the object is located, the specified property is read and converted to type String. This string is then output at the location of the tag itself.

In procprod.jsp, the values of the product's first three properties are rendered using the <jsp:setProperty> standard actions. The JSP code is as follows:

```
<tr>
  <td class="label" >SKU:</td> <td><jsp:getProperty name="localProd"
property="sku"/> </td>
</tr>

<tr>
  <td class="label">Name:</td> <td><jsp:getProperty name="localProd"
property="name"/> </td>
</tr>
<tr>
  <td class="label">Description:</td> <td><jsp:getProperty name="localProd"
property="desc"/> </td>
</tr>
```

Rendering property values using EL expressions

You are probably thinking about EL already. The more compact notation to render the value of a bean's property is the EL expression:

```
${attribute_name.property}
```

Because the EL interpreter will also look through the four scopes for a named attribute, and then the "." operator will result in a getXX() call, this notation is equivalent to the more verbose <jsp:getProperty> alternative.

In `procprod.jsp`, the very last property of the `localProd` instance is rendered using an EL expression. The JSP code is as follows:

```
<td class="label">Price:</td>
<td>
  <fmt:formatNumber value="${localProd.price / 100}" type="currency"/>
</td>
```

In fact, the JSTL formatting tag is used to render the property in proper currency format.

It is clear from the previous discussion that

❑   `<jsp:getProperty>` and `<jsp:setProperty>` standard actions do not depend on the generated Java variable

❑   EL expressions do not depend on the generated Java variable

In fact, only embedded Java code in JSP as scripting elements will ever depend on the generated Java variable.

The existence of the Java variable, and the maintenance of it, may create a tricky synchronization problem because there are two references to the same object.

If you follow our recommendation and write new JSP code without scripting elements, there will be no need for the container to create and maintain the Java variable, alleviating the burden. This is one reason why scriptless JSP code is preferred.

How `<jsp:useBean>` and JSTL `<c:set>` Differ

Before we leave the discussion of standard actions that work with JavaBean instances, the following table compares the `<jsp:useBean>` standard action with the JSTL's `<c:set>` action.

Their functionality actually overlaps for many programming scenarios. However, they each have some unique behaviors that make one or the other more appropriate for certain tasks. The following table will help with your decision when selecting between the two.

Feature	`<jsp:useBean>`	`<c:set>`
Searches for a named attribute in a specified scope (the default scope is `page`)	Yes	Yes
Creates a new object instance if the named attribute does not exist	Yes	No, unless the value contains an EL expression that creates a new object
Needs to know the specific class/type of the object instance	Yes	No, will work with any type
Creates a scripting variable by generating the Java language source code to declare the Java variable	Yes	No

Feature	<jsp:useBean>	<c:set>
Works with scripting elements written in the Java programming language	Yes	Not directly, but Java code can use the `findAttribute()` method of the `PageContext` to get the scoped variable
Has the special ability to work with a `java.util.Map`	No	Yes

Including JSP Output via <jsp:include>

The `<jsp:include>` standard action is a request-time action that will include the output of another JSP at the location of the tag within the calling JSP.

The general syntax for this standard action is as follows:

```
<jsp:include page="...url.." flush="true or false"/>
```

The tag can optionally contain a body:

```
<jsp:include page="...url..." flush="true or false">
  <jsp:param ..../>
</jsp:include>
```

In this usage, there are one or more `<jsp:param>` standard actions within the body of `<jsp:include>`. These `<jsp:param>` standard actions specify additional request parameters that will be available within the JSP whose output is being included.

This standard action has two attributes:

- ❑ **page:** A URL that is relative to the current JSP page at request time
- ❑ **flush:** Determines if the buffer for the output is flushed immediately, before the included page's output

> The page **attribute contains a URL, and not a file specification. URLs are subject to** <url-pattern> **mappings within the** web.xml **deployment descriptor.**

The following Try It Out example puts the `<jsp:include>` standard action to work.

Try It Out   The <jsp:include> Standard Action

This exercise shows the usage of the `<jsp:include>` standard action. It also contrasts its use with the `<%@ include %>` directive. To access this example, make sure that your Tomcat 5 server is running with ch08.war deployed.

Access the following URL with your browser:

```
http://localhost:8080/ch08/example3/index.jsp
```

The output will be several news headlines, as shown in Figure 8-5.

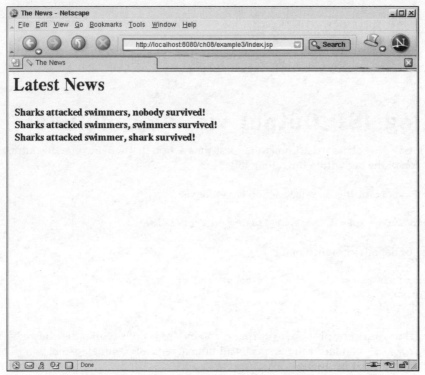

Figure 8-5: Example of the `<jsp:include>` **standard action vs. the**
`<%@ include %>` **directive**

While the output in Figure 8-5 may not seem immediately interesting, quite a bit is going on behind the scenes.

How It Works

Quite a few JSP pages are involved in the information displayed in Figure 8-5. Figure 8-6 illustrates these JSP pages.

In Figure 8-6, the main JSP page is called `index.jsp`. Within `index.jsp`, the `news1.jsp` page from the items subdirectory is included. Within the `news1.jsp` page, the `news2.jsp` page is included. Note that there are two different copies of `news2.jsp`, one residing in the same directory as `index.jsp`, the other one in the items subdirectory.

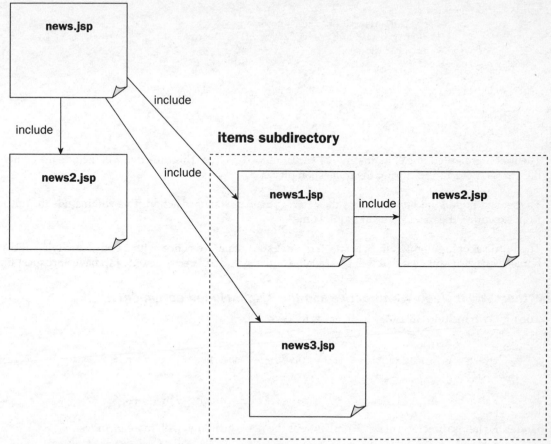

Figure 8-6: Operation of the `<jsp:include>` **example**

The main JSP, `index.jsp`, is located at `<Tomcat Installation Directory>/webapps/ch08/exam-ple3/index.jsp`. This page is reproduced here:

```
<html>
<head>
  <title>The News</title>
</head>
<body>
  <h1> Latest News</h1>
  <table>
    <tr>
      <td><h3><%@include file="items/news1.jsp" %></h3></td>
    </tr>
    <tr>
      <td><h3><jsp:include page="items/news1.jsp"/></h3></td>
    </tr>
    <tr>
```

```
        <td><h3>
              <jsp:include page="items/news3.jsp">
                <jsp:param name="survivor" value="shark"/>
              </jsp:include>
          </h3></td>
      </tr>
    </table>

  </body>
</html>
```

The first highlighted line contains an `<%@ include %>` directive. This directive will include the content of the `items/news1.jsp` during the translation phase.

The second highlighted line contains the `<jsp:include>` standard action. This will include the output from executing the `news1.jsp` at request time.

The third set of highlighted lines is an `<jsp:include>` standard action with a body, specifying additional request parameters that will be available to the included `items/news3.jsp` page at request time.

How the <%@ include %> directive and the <jsp:include> action differ

The first two includes in `index.jsp` are as follows:

```
<tr>
  <td><h3><%@include file="items/news1.jsp" %></h3></td>
</tr>
<tr>
  <td><h3><jsp:include page="items/news1.jsp"/></h3></td>
</tr>
```

Under the items directory, `news1.jsp` contains the news headline, with more includes:

```
Sharks attacked <%@ include file="news2.jsp" %>, <jsp:include page="news2.jsp"/>
survived!
```

There are two versions of `news2.jsp`, in different directories. At the top-level directory, the `news2.jsp` file contains the following:

```
nobody
```

In the `items` subdirectory, the `news2.jsp` file contains this:

```
swimmers
```

Within the `news1.jsp` page, the first occurrence of `news2.jsp` is included and uses a `<%@ include %>` directive, while the second occurrence uses the `<jsp:include>` standard action.

Note at this point that while both `index.jsp` and `news1.jsp` contain the same included files (using different mechanisms), the final output from these two lines in Figure 8-5 is different:

```
Sharks attacked swimmers, nobody survived!
Sharks attacked swimmers, swimmers survived!
```

Effects of nested includes

Here is what happened. Following is the first `<%@ include %>` directive within `index.jsp`:

```
<tr>
  <td><h3><%@include file="items/news1.jsp" %></h3></td>
</tr>
```

The entire content of `items/news1.jsp` is included at translation time. However, because the `news1.jsp` has another `<%@include %>` directive, that content must also be included at translation time. This will first result in `news2.jsp` being included within `news1.jsp`. At translation time, the line becomes the following:

```
<tr>
  <td><h3> Sharks attacked swimmers, <jsp:include page="news2.jsp"/> survived!
  </h3></td>
</tr>
```

Now, at request time, the `<jsp:include>` standard action will be executed at the top-level directory. This will include the request-time output of the `news2.jsp` in this directory, resulting in the following:

```
<tr>
  <td><h3> Sharks attacked swimmers, nobody survived!
  </h3></td>
</tr>
```

In the second case, in `index.jsp`, the `<jsp:include>` standard action is not triggered until an incoming request arrives:

```
<tr>
  <td><h3><jsp:include page="items/news1.jsp"/></h3></td>
</tr>
```

At request time, the output from `items/news1.jsp` is rendered. This forces the translation of `items/news1.jsp`. Then, `items/news1.jsp` will go through a translation phase, followed by compilation and execution. At translation time, the `<%@ include %>` directive merges with the content of `news2.jsp`, in the items directory. Following is the result after the translation phase, for `news1.jsp` in the items directory.

```
Sharks attacked swimmers, <jsp:include page="news2.jsp"/> survived!
```

Next, the page must be compiled and executed. At this point, the `<jsp:include>` standard action executes, still relative to the `items` directory. This will result in the inclusion of the following output from the execution of `items/news2.jsp`:

```
Sharks attacked swimmers, nobody survived!
```

Last but not least, the top-level `index.jsp` file will include this output via its `<jsp:include>` standard action, resulting in the following final output:

```
<tr>
  <td><h3> Sharks attacked swimmers, nobody survived!</h3></td>
</tr>
```

Adding parameters to a <jsp:include> action

One remaining set of lines in index.jsp uses the <jsp:include> action. This set of lines includes the output of items/news3.jsp at request time. This usage of the action also features a <jsp:param> standard action within the tag body:

```
<tr>
  <td><h3><jsp:include page="items/news3.jsp">
           <jsp:param name="survivor" value="shark"/>
         </jsp:include>
  </h3></td>
</tr>
```

The <jsp:param> standard action is used here to add a request parameter called survivor. This request parameter will be available within news3.jsp when it is executed during request time.

The content of items/news3.jsp is as follows:

```
Sharks attacked swimmer, ${param.survivor} survived!
```

This JSP prints the message and the value of the survivor parameter using an EL expression.

At request time, the <jsp:include> in index.jsp will cause the translation and execution of the items/news3.jsp. During its execution, it will have access to the survivor parameter. This will result in the following news3.jsp output:

```
Sharks attacked swimmer, shark survived!
```

This output is included at request time by the index.jsp <jsp:include> standard action, resulting in the following final output:

```
<tr>
  <td><h3> Sharks attacked swimmer, shark survived! </h3></td>
</tr>
```

Transferring Control Between JSPs

In the design of Web-based systems, there is often a need to transfer control between different JSPs. For example, a customer at an e-commerce site may want to place an order. But if the customer has not yet registered with the system, the shopping cart may need to transfer control to the JSP form that performs registration. The <jsp:forward> standard action is created specifically to satisfy this need.

The <jsp:forward> standard action

When the <jsp:forward> standard action is executed at request time, the current request is forwarded to another JSP page. The processing of the current JSP is terminated.

> Note that `<jsp:forward>` can actually be used to forward the incoming request to non-JSP resources. For example, the request may be forwarded to a servlet written in the Java programming language, or it may just be forwarded to a static HTML page. (See Chapter 15, "JSP and Servlets.")

Following is the basic form of the `<jsp:forward>` standard action:

```
<jsp:forward page="...url..." />
```

In yet another form, you might see a body consisting of `<jsp:param>` standard actions:

```
<jsp:forward page="..url...">
  <jsp:param ..../>
</jsp:forward>
```

This second form can be used to add parameters to the request. Then, they will be available within the JSP to which they are being forwarded.

The single attribute, `page`, is a request-time attribute. This attribute is interpreted relative to the URL to which the request will be forwarded. Like the `page` attribute in the `<jsp:include>` standard action, this URL may be mapped by entries in the `web.xml` file.

The JSP output buffer, if used, will be cleared prior to the forwarding. If the JSP uses a buffer, it must not be flushed prior to the forwarding. If the JSP does not use a buffer, it is illegal for the forwarding JSP to write any output before forwarding. Essentially, all output should be performed by the JSP being forwarded to.

The next Try It Out exercise in this chapter provides a hands-on example of using the `<jsp:forward>` standard action.

Specifying Parameters for Other Actions

Within the optional bodies of several standard actions (`<jsp:include>`, `<jsp:forward>`, `<jsp:params>`, and so on), parameters can be specified via the `<jsp:param>` standard action.

The *<jsp:param> standard action*

This action can appear in the body of the `<jsp:include>` and `<jsp:forward>` standard action. It can also be used within the `<jsp:params>` standard action (covered in the next section).

The general form of the `<jsp:param>` standard action is as follows:

```
<jsp:param name="...name..." value="...value..."/>
```

Each `<jsp:param>` standard action creates a parameter that has a name and a value. Exactly how these parameters will be used depends on the tag for which the parameters are specified.

For example, both the `<jsp:include>` and `<jsp:forward>` parameters are request parameters available for the JSP page being included (or being forwarded to).

Working with Plug-ins

Three standard actions are used to work with plug-ins. Plug-ins are embedded Java objects that are placed on a Web page. Figure 8-7 illustrates a plug-in.

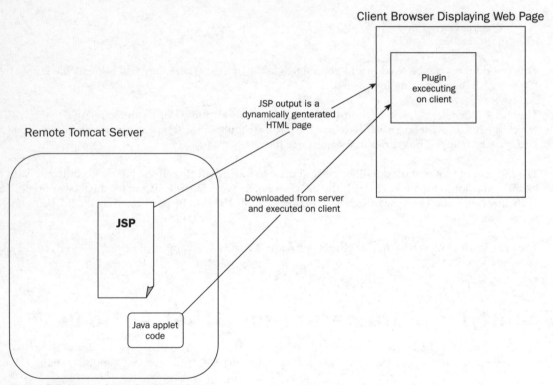

Figure 8-7: How a Java plug-in works

Note the following important points illustrated in Figure 8-7:

❑ The plug-in resides on the client, together with the browser.

❑ The plug-in requires a Java VM running on the client's PC.

❑ The Java code that is executing as the plug-in must be downloaded from the server (where JSP is executing) to the client.

The following standard actions work with plug-ins:

❏ `<jsp:plugin>` for specifying the attributes of the plug-in

❏ `<jsp:params>` for passing parameters to the plug-in on the HTML page

❏ `<jsp:fallback>` for specifying what happens if the client does not support Java plug-ins

The following sections describe each of these actions, followed by an example that uses them all together.

The *<jsp:plugin>* standard action

The `<jsp:plugin>` standard action will generate the HTML code to embed a Java object on the page. This is typically a Java applet (although it can also be an arbitrary JavaBean).

The general usage of the `<jsp:plugin>` standard action is as follows:

```
<jsp:plugin type="... applet or bean..."  code="..." codebase="..." archive="..."
....>
   ...
</jsp:plugin>
```

The `type` attribute is either an applet or bean, and specifies the type of Java object that will be embedded on the HTML page. Applets typically have a GUI or display on the page. The rest of the attributes are HTML attributes for the `<OBJECT>` or `<EMBED>` tag. See the *HTML, XHTML, and CSS Bible,* Third Edition, by Bryan Pfaffenberger, et al. (Wiley, ISBN: 0-7645-5739-4), for more information on these HTML attributes.

Some of the more commonly used HTML attributes for the `<OBJECT>` or `<EMBED>` tag are name, `code`, `codebase`, `archive`, `align`, `width`, `height`, `jreversion`, and `title`. These attributes can be specified with the `<jsp:plugin>` standard action, and will be passed on to the generated `<OBJECT>` or `<EMBED>` HTML tag.

The body of this standard action can contain `<jsp:params>` and `<jsp:fallback>` standard actions.

The *<jsp:params>* standard action

The `<jsp:params>` standard action can occur only within the body of the `<jsp:plugin>` tag. It is used to group `<jsp:param>` entries into a set. Its basic usage syntax is as follows:

```
<jsp:params>
  <jsp:param  ..../>
  <jsp:param  ..../>
    ...
</jsp:params>
```

There can be any number of `<jsp:param>` standard actions in the body of the `<jsp:params>` tag. Each of these will be translated to a parameter for the applet and/or bean embedded on the Web page.

The <jsp:fallback> standard action

The <jsp:fallback> standard action can be used only within the body of the <jsp:plugin> tag. This standard action is used to specify HTML that will be rendered (or JSP code that will be executed) if the browser does not support the plug-in.

Following is the basic syntax for <jsp:fallback>:

```
<jsp:fallback>
    ... HTML or JSP that will be rendered if the browser does not support plugin ...
</jsp:fallback>
```

The final Try It Out example shows how to use JSP to generate code that will dynamically change the appearance of a visual Java applet embedded within a Web page on the client's Web browser. It makes use of the <jsp:plugin> and associated actions.

Try It Out   **The <jsp:plugin> and Associated Standard Actions**

To access this example, make sure that your Tomcat 5 server is running with ch08.war deployed.

Access the following URL with your browser:

```
http://localhost:8080/ch08/example4/index.jsp
```

This page shows a red circle, as shown in Figure 8-8. The red color is not visible in the black-and-white figure, but you would be able to confirm it on your monitor.

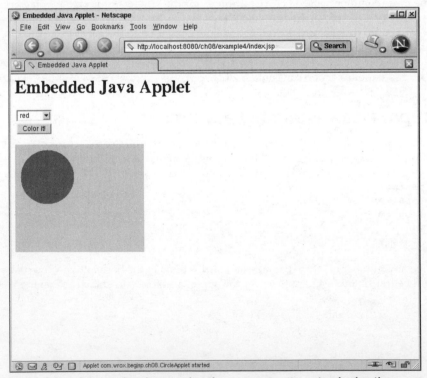

Figure 8-8: A Java applet shown using the <jsp:plugin> standard action

In Figure 8-8, the circle is actually created by an embedded applet on the Web page that draws circles of a specified size, in a specified color. There is also a drop-down list for selecting a color, and a Color It! button.

Try selecting the color blue, and then clicking the Color It! button. The circle immediately changes to a blue color, as shown in Figure 8-9.

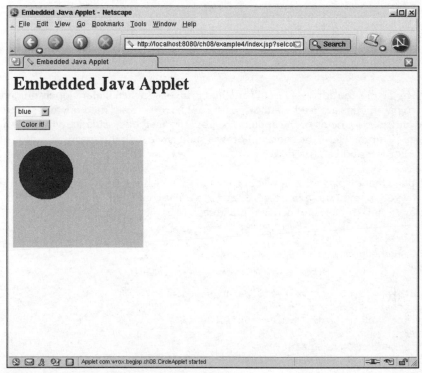

Figure 8-9: The applet changes color to blue

How It Works

The plug-in in this case is an applet that draws a circle on its display area. The color and radius are two properties that can be set on this applet. These two properties affect the appearance of the circle drawn by the applet.

The code of this applet is in com.wrox.begjsp.ch08.CircleApplet. It can be located at <Tomcat Installation Directory>/webapps/ch08/WEB-INF/classes/com/wrox.begjsp/ ch08/CircleApplet.java. The Java source code content of this class is reproduced here:

```
package com.wrox.begjsp.ch08;
import java.awt.*;
import java.applet.*;
public class CircleApplet extends java.applet.Applet
{

    private Color circColor = null;
```

269

```
    private int radius = 5;
    public void init()
    {
        circColor = Color.decode(this.getParameter("color"));
        radius = Integer.parseInt(this.getParameter("radius"));
    }
    public void paint(Graphics gr)
    {
        gr.setColor(circColor);
        gr.fillOval(10, 10, radius * 2, radius * 2);

    }
}
```

In the preceding code, the applet's `init()` method is invoked when it starts operating on the Web page. Here, the two parameters are read via the `Applet.getParameter()` method, and stored in the `circColor` and `radius` fields of the applet. The `paint()` method is called anytime the applet requires painting or re-painting. Here, the code will draw a solid circle with the specified radius using the values from the `circColor` and `radius` fields.

The HTML page that displays this applet is `index.jsp`, which is located at `<Tomcat Installation Directory>/webapps/ch08/example4/index.jsp`. The content of `index.jsp` is reproduced here, with the `<jsp:plugin>` standard action highlighted:

```
<head>
  <title>Embedded Java Applet </title>
</head>
<body>
  <c:set var="myColor" value="${param.selcolor}"/>
  <c:if test="${empty myColor}">
    <c:set var="myColor" value="0xff0000"/>
  </c:if>
  <h1> Embedded Java Applet</h1>
  <form action="index.jsp" method="get">
    <table width="500">
      <tr>
        <td>
          <select name="selcolor">
            <option value="0xff0000">red</option>
            <option value="0xffff00">yellow</option>
            <option value="0x00ff88">green</option>
            <option value="0x0000ff">blue</option>
          </select>
        </td>
      </tr>
      <tr>
        <td><input type="submit" value="Color it!"/></td>
      </tr>
    </table>
  </form>
  <jsp:plugin type="applet" code="com.wrox.begjsp.ch08.CircleApplet"
    archive="ch08obj.jar"    >
  <jsp:params>
```

```
      <jsp:param name="radius" value="50"/>
      <jsp:param name="color" value="${myColor}"/>
    </jsp:params>

    <jsp:fallback>
      <br/>
      This browser does not support the object.
    </jsp:fallback>
  </jsp:plugin>
```

```
  </body>
  </html>
```

In `<jsp:plugin>` in the preceding code, the type has been set to `applet`, and the `code` attribute is set to the class of the applet. The `archive` attribute is used to point to a JAR file that contains the required applet class. This JAR file must be created separately and placed into the same directory as the JSP page. In our case, the JAR archive is called `ch08obj.jar`. It is located at `<Tomcat Installation Directory>/webapps/ch08/example4/ch08obj.jar`. `ch08obj.jar` is created by making an archive of the `WEB-INF/classes` directory from the source code distribution. This JAR file will be downloaded from the Tomcat server to your browser during the testing. The applet is fetched from the downloaded JAR and executed on the client side by the browser.

Generating parameters for the applet

The `<jsp:params>` and `<jsp:param>` standard actions are used to generate parameters for the applet. In this example, they specify the color and radius of the circle being drawn. The code from `index.jsp` is as follows:

```
<jsp:params>
  <jsp:param name="radius" value="50"/>
  <jsp:param name="color" value="${myColor}"/></jsp:params>
```

While the radius is fixed at 50 pixels, the color parameter is set via an EL request-time expression, `${myColor}`. This parameter is the color selected by the user. The selection process is described in the following section.

Handling user color selection

The user selects a color by using a drop-down list on a form. This form is displayed within `index.jsp` using the following HTML/JSP code:

```
<form action="index.jsp" method-"get">
  <table width="500">
    <tr>
      <td>
        <select name="selcolor">
          <option value="0xff0000">red</option>
          <option value="0xffff00">yellow</option>
          <option value="0x00ff88">green</option>
          <option value="0x0000ff">blue</option>
        </select>
```

```
        </td>
      </tr>
      <tr>
        <td><input type="submit" value="Color it!"/></td>
      </tr>
    </table>
  </form>
```

The drop-down list is created by the `<select>` HTML element. The value of each color option is the corresponding RGB value in hexadecimal form. The user's selection is reflected in the `selcolor` parameter. Note that the form parameter is submitted using the `get` method, and the form is processed by `index.jsp` itself.

Processing the color parameter

The `index.jsp` uses a JSTL `<c:if>` action to set the value of the `selcolor` parameter to red if it doesn't exist. The `selcolor` parameter will have a value if `index.jsp` is currently processing the form, and will not exist if it is called up directly by a browser. The following code from `index.jsp` handles this processing:

```
<c:set var="myColor" value="${param.selcolor}"/>
<c:if test="${empty myColor}">
  <c:set var="myColor" value="0xff0000"/>
</c:if>
```

Rendering alternative output for browsers without applet support

The `<jsp:fallback>` standard action is used within the `<jsp:plugin>` to specify the HTML to render if the client's browser cannot display the applet. The code within `index.jsp` for this is as follows:

```
<jsp:fallback>
  <br/>
  This browser does not support Java applets.
</jsp:fallback>
```

In this case, a simple message is rendered to tell the user that her or his browser does not support the use of Java applets.

HTML generated by <jsp:plugin>

You can view the code that is generated by the entire `<jsp:plugin>` tag if you select View Source from your browser's menu. The generated code is an HTML `<embed>` or `<object>` tag. The generated HTML tag should be similar to the one shown here:

```
<OBJECT classid="clsid:8AD9C840-044E-11D1-B3E9-00805F499D93"
codebase="http://java.sun.com/products/plugin/1.2.2/jinstall-1_2_2-
win.cab#Version=1,2,2,0">
  <PARAM name="java_code" value="com.wrox.begjsp.ch08.CircleApplet">
  <PARAM name="java_archive" value="ch08obj.jar">
  <PARAM name="type" value="application/x-java-applet;">
  <PARAM name="radius" value="50">
  <PARAM name="color" value="0xff0000">
  <COMMENT>
```

```
<EMBED type="application/x-java-applet;"
pluginspage="http://java.sun.com/products/plugin/"
java_code="com.wrox.begjsp.ch08.CircleApplet"
java_archive="ch08obj.jar" radius="50" color="0xff0000"/>
<NOEMBED>
  <br/>
  This browser does not support Java applets.

</NOEMBED>
</COMMENT>
</OBJECT>
```

The `<jsp:plugin>` action has generated code for the HTML `<object>` tag and for its tedious and often browser-dependent syntax.

Practical real-world use of *<jsp:plugin>*

The `<jsp:plugin>`standard action is frequently used in production environments. While the example reveals a simplified scenario to facilitate understanding, consider the following real-world examples where `<jsp:plug-in>` may be applied:

❑ **The applet is a mapping applet.** After the user selects different areas of a region using a form, the JSP processes the form and fetches the coordinates from a large database and feeds them to the applet for map display.

❑ **The applet is a video viewer for movie playback.** The user logs in and selects different programs via the JSP forms, checking against database information and processing payment, and finally enabling the applet to show a certain video.

Standard Actions Specific to Tag Files

JSP 2 includes a set of standard actions that can be used only within tag files. Recall that tag files are a means of creating your own custom tag libraries using JSP as the programming language. This specialized set of standard actions includes the following:

❑ `<jsp:attribute>`

❑ `<jsp:body>`

❑ `<jsp:invoke>`

❑ `<jsp:doBody>`

❑ `<jsp:element>`

❑ `<jsp:text>`

❑ `<jsp:output>`

The syntax and use of these tag-file-only standard actions is covered in Chapter 11, "Building Your Own Custom JSP Tag Library," where you will be using these actions to build your very own tag library.

Summary

JSP standard actions are built-in tags that can be used within JSP code. They are all prefixed by `jsp:`. This chapter covered all of the JSP standard actions. Some interesting discoveries in the chapter include the following:

❑ The flexible syntax of the `<jsp:useBean>` standard action enables you to use it in many different ways.

❑ After the successful execution of `<jsp:useBean>`, a JavaBean instance will be associated with a name within the specified scope; a Java scripting variable is also generated at the translation phase.

❑ The `<jsp:setProperty>` action can be used to set the properties of the scoped instance.

❑ The `<jsp:getProperty>` tag can be used to render the value of a property on the JavaBean.

❑ The `property="*"` syntax of the `<jsp:setProperty>` standard action can be used to assign request parameters to the correspondingly named properties of a corresponding JavaBean. This can be handy for form processing.

❑ The `<jsp:param>` standard action is used to specify parameters for the `<jsp:include>`, `<jsp:forward>`, or `<jsp:params>` standard actions.

❑ The `<jsp:plugin>`, `<jsp:params>`, and `<jsp:fallback>` standard actions are used to embed Java applets or JavaBeans into the Web page displayed on the client's browser. These applets or JavaBean code is downloaded from the server to the client's machine for execution on the client.

❑ The `<jsp:plugin>` standard action will generate the required `<object>` or `<embed>` HTML tags to render the object.

Exercises

1. The Java classes from the e-store example in Chapter 3 are included within `ch08.war`. This means that the static `EShop.getCats()` method can be used to obtain a list of product categories. Modify `example1/index.jsp` to print out the categories by performing the following actions:

    a. Use a scripting element to attach the `categories` JavaBean to the page context as an attribute called `"myCats"`.

    b. Make this JavaBean instance available to the JSP page using a `<jsp:useBean>` standard action.

    c. Use JSTL and EL to print out the category values.

    d. Browse the generated source code after translation to show that a Java variable called `myCats` is created by the `<jsp:useBean>` standard action, and determine its type.

2. Modify the `example3/index.jsp` to accept an additional drop-down list that enables the user to select either HTML or XML. Modify `example3/procprod.jsp` to use the `<jsp:forward>` standard action and forward the request to either a `prodhtml.jsp` or `prodxml.jsp` page. The `prodhtml.jsp` page should render the product information in HTML format and the `prodxml.jsp` page should render the product information in XML format.

JSP and JavaBeans

JSP is a presentation technology. Unlike a programming language such as Java, JSP does not have any built-in capability to access features offered by the underlying operating system or environment. JSP's capabilities are focused mainly around the generation of dynamic Web content.

JavaBeans are software components written in the Java programming language. JSP has built-in capabilities to work with JavaBeans. These capabilities are provided by the JSP standard actions and EL expressions. Because of this, JavaBeans have become the main mechanism for passing data and custom behavior between the JSP logic and the rest of the system in large Web applications.

In this chapter, this intimate relationship between JSP and JavaBeans is explored fully. The key topics covered in the chapter include the following:

- ❏ Anatomy of a JavaBean
- ❏ Packaging JavaBeans
- ❏ JavaBean usage within JSPs
- ❏ Accessing JavaBeans with standard actions
- ❏ Accessing JavaBeans with EL
- ❏ Accessing JavaBeans from scriptlets
- ❏ Difference between a JavaBeans and an EJB

Two hands-on examples will clarify many of the concepts introduced. JavaBeans have already been used in the examples of previous chapters; most of the integration and application techniques are reviewed in this chapter.

Additional topics that are covered in the chapter include the following:

- ❏ The use of a front-end JSP page (often called a *front controller*) to handle common tasks such as data validation. A front controller is a common *design pattern* for Web presentation layers. These and other common design patterns are discussed in Chapter 26, "Best Practices and Tools."

❑ The typical flow of data, in a JSP Web application, using JavaBeans. The JavaBean used to collect and pass data across layers in your Web application is sometimes referred to as a *transfer object* or a *data transfer object*. This is another design pattern explained in more detail in Chapter 26.

By the end of this chapter, you will be familiar with JavaBeans as a software component, and their usage and application within JSPs. This will prepare you to work with the various JSP frameworks, where JavaBeans are used extensively to transport data between the business logic engine and the JSP-based presentation layer.

Anatomy of a JavaBean

A JavaBean is a specially constructed class written in the Java programming language. All JavaBeans are coded according to the JavaBeans API 1.0 Specifications for SUN (with a minor update to 1.01).

JavaBeans are reusable software components that can be wired together to create component-based applications. JavaBeans were originally designed for rapid application development environments. In these environments, visual JavaBeans can be dragged and dropped in the creation of user interfaces as well as application logic. All modern-day IDEs support the building of componentized applications using JavaBeans. The Swing API components are a good example of reusable JavaBean components.

Other than visual application design, JavaBeans are finding their way into many other uses, including the building of Web applications using JSP. In fact, even the earliest version of JSP had built-in standard actions that take advantage of JavaBeans.

The unique characteristics that distinguish a JavaBean from other Java classes include the following:

❑ It must have a default constructor (i.e., no argument).

❑ It may have a number of properties, the value of which can be read or written to.

❑ It may have a number of methods that can be invoked.

❑ Some JavaBeans are visual (i.e., AWT or Swing-based) and can be placed into an IDE during the design of a user interface.

❑ It is designed to be a self-contained component, used in assembling a components-based application.

> Every JavaBean should also be serializable (and implement the `Serializable` interface). This is necessary because the state of visual JavaBeans may be serialized by its container (i.e., an IDE during development, or a framework during runtime). However, many nonvisual JavaBeans (and even some visual JavaBeans) do not conform to this requirement.

Figure 9-1 illustrates these interesting characteristics of a JavaBean.

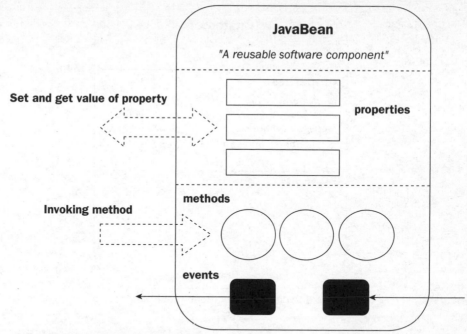

Figure 9-1: Characteristics of JavaBeans

Of the aforementioned unique characteristics of JavaBeans, the first three (constructor, properties, and methods) are the most important to JSP developers. The next two characteristics (events and visual design interface) are gaining relevance as sophisticated frameworks based on JavaBeans, such as JavaServer Faces (JSF), become available. JSF is covered in Chapter 21, "JavaServer Faces." The final characteristic is also important architecturally — a JavaBean adds incremental and reusable functionality to applications built using JSP, and thus enable the application to be built based on the assembly of software components.

JavaBean Properties

A JavaBean property is a named attribute that can be accessed by the user of the component. The attribute can be of any Java data type, including classes that you define. For example, the `firstName` property of a `Customer` JavaBean (for an auction Web site, for example) may be of type `String`, while the `lastOrder` property of the same JavaBean may be of a custom Java type called `Order`. Figure 9-2 shows such a `Customer` JavaBean with its properties.

The property of a JavaBean may be read/write, read only, or write only.

A read/write property is accessed through two methods in the JavaBean's implementation class:

- ❑   `get<PropertyName>()` method
- ❑   `set<PropertyName>()` method

277

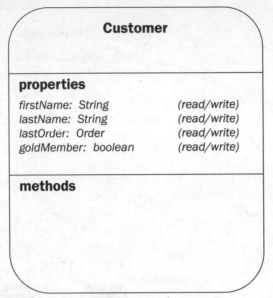

Figure 9-2: Customer JavaBean properties

For example, if the `firstName` property of the `Customer` JavaBean is read/write, then the `firstName` property can be accessed in one of the two following ways:

❑   `getFirstName()` method to obtain its value

❑   `setFirstName()` method to set its value

A read-only attribute will have only a `get<PropertyName>()` method, and a write-only attribute will have only a `set<PropertyName>()` method.

> **There is an exception to this rule: By JavaBean convention, a property of boolean primitive type is not obtained by a `get<PropertyName>()` method. The read access is implemented by a `is<PropertyName>()` method instead. For example, if the property called `goldMember` exists on the customer, then the boolean property can be tested with `Customer.isGoldMember()`.**

Coding JavaBean properties

The `Customer` JavaBean mentioned previously may have the following Java coding:

```
public class Customer
{
    private String firstName = null;
    private String lastName = null;
    private Order lastOrder = null;
```

```
        private boolean goldMember = false;

        public Customer()
        {
        }

        public long getFirstName()
        {
            return this.firstName;
        }


        public void setFirstName(String inName)
        {
            this.firstName = inName;
        }

        public long getLastName()
        {
            return this.lastName;
        }


        public void setLastName(String inName)
        {
            this.lastName - inName;
        }


        public Order getLastOrder()
        {
            return this.lastOrder;
        }

        public void setLastOrder(Order inOrder)
        {
            this.lastOrder = inOrder;
        }


        public boolean isGoldMember()
        {
            return this.goldMember;
        }

        public void setGoldMember(boolean inGoldMember)
        {
            this.goldMember = inGoldMember;
        }
    }
```

In the preceding code for the Customer JavaBean, all of the firstName, lastName, goldMember, and lastOrder properties have read/write access. As a result, there is a get<PropertyName>() method, and a set<PropertyName>() method associated with each property. For example, the firstName property has `getFirstName()` for reading and `setFirstName()` for writing. The only exception is the `goldMember` property. `goldMember` is a `boolean` typed property and its getter method is called `isGoldMember()` instead of `getGoldMember()`.

JavaBean methods

A method exported by a JavaBean is simply a public method within the Java class. For example, a `Shop` JavaBean may export a method called `CalculateShipping`. It may be coded as follows:

```
public class Shop
{
.....
    public long CalculateShipping(String sourceZIP, String destinationZIP, long
shipBy)
    {
...
    }
.....

}
```

Invoking JavaBean methods using scriptlets

Methods of JavaBeans may be invoked within a JSP page using scriptlets. Scriplets enable you to embed Java code within a JSP page. Chapter 3, "JSP Basics 2: Generalized Templating and Server Scripting," covers the use of scriptlets. For example, to invoke the preceding method on a JavaBean instance called `MyShop`, the following scriplet code may be used:

```
<%
    long shippingCharges = MyShop.CalculateShipping("32231", "32718", ShipBy.UPS);
%>
```

This code assumes that the result is stored in a Java variable called `shippingCharges`, to be used later in the JSP. It also assumes that the `ShipBy.UPS` constant is a long value that the `CalculateShipping()` method understands.

Scriptless JSP and EL functions

Scriplets and scripting elements are presented in Chapter 3. The main purpose of that coverage is to ensure that you will be able to maintain legacy code that contains embedded Java coding. Chapter 3 is explicit in its recommendation to not use scripting elements for any new JSP code if possible. The creation of scriptless JSP code leads to code that is easier to maintain in the long term.

Without scriplets, there is no direct way for a JSP to invoke methods of a JavaBean. This is a good feature if you consider the role of JSP within a Web application. JSP should be used for presentation only. This means that it should not be allowed to access any random method in an arbitrary Java class. Allowing such behavior can encourage the bundling of application logic within JSP coding. Bundling application logic with the JSP presentation layer leads to code that is hard to maintain, and applications that cannot scale to a large number of users.

> While scriptless JSP cannot invoke a JavaBean method directly, useful functions such as the `CalculateShipping()` shown earlier can be wrapped up as an EL function. EL functions are a feature of EL that enables you to extend its capability via the definition of pubic static functions in a Java class. See Chapter 5, "JSP and EL," for more information on EL and how to create EL functions.

Common JavaBean packaging

JavaBeans are compiled into Java classes and just like the other Java classes in your application, they can be packaged into a JAR file and placed into the `WEB-INF/lib` directory of your application.

During development, however, it is usually more convenient to place the individual class files, unarchived, under the `WEB-INF/classes` directory. If you are using an IDE, you can conveniently do this by setting your compilation target directory to the `WEB-INF/classes` directory. Doing this helps provide a faster modify-recompile cycle during development.

The following Try It Out example illustrates a technique for performing form input validation. It demonstrates one of the most typical uses of JavaBeans in JSPs: to carry data between pages (or between business logic and the presentation layer). This example presents the user interface of a very simple auction.

Try It Out   Using JavaBeans in JSP

This auction example is contained in `ch09.war`. First make sure that your Tomcat 5 server is running and then deploy `ch09.war` to the server. Review Chapter 1, "Getting Started with JavaServer Pages," if you do not remember how to deploy a WAR archive.

Open your browser and access the following URL:

```
http://localhost:8080/ch09/example1/index.jsp
```

You will be greeted by the Enter Your Bid screen, as shown in Figure 9-3.

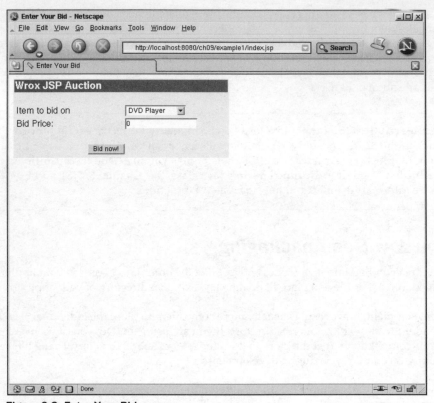

Figure 9-3: Enter Your Bid screen

Select one of the items to bid on. In Figure 9-3, the DVD Player is selected. Also enter an invalid bid amount, **0**, to show that the data validation code is working.

Click the Bid Now! button. At this point, the invalid input value will be detected, and you will be prompted to enter the bid again. You are returned to the Enter Your Bid page, which displays the invalid input message, as shown in Figure 9-4.

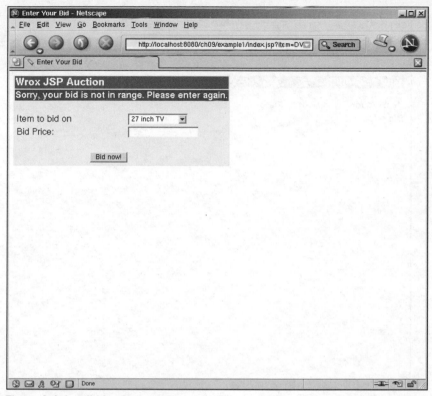

Figure 9-4: Invalid input message

Now, select the DVD Player again, but this time enter **199** for the bid price. Click the Bid Now! button again.

This time, the bid is within range, and the validation succeeds. The system will then display the item you bid on and the price that you have bid, as shown in Figure 9-5.

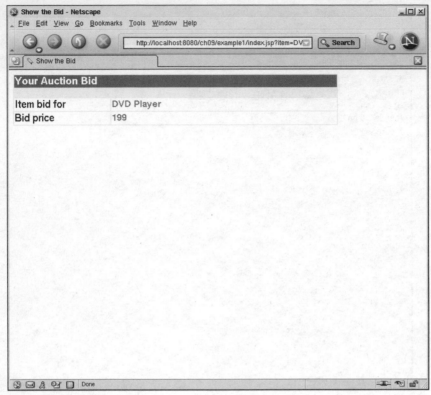

Figure 9-5: Successful bid

How It Works

During the experimentation in the previous section, you may have noticed one unusual browser behavior. Unlike the examples in previous chapters, all the screens in this example have the same URL:

```
http://localhost:8080/ch09/example1/index.jsp
```

If you look back at Figure 9-3, Figure 9-4, and Figure 9-5, you will notice that they all appear to be using the preceding URL, yet the screens being rendered and the functions being performed are definitely different.

Switching requests through a front controller

Indeed, every single request of this Try It Out application is first sent to the index.jsp page. The index.jsp page is then responsible for the following:

❑ Performing some common tasks such as input form data validation

❑ Redirecting the request to the appropriate JSP page

Figure 9-6 reveals this application's architecture.

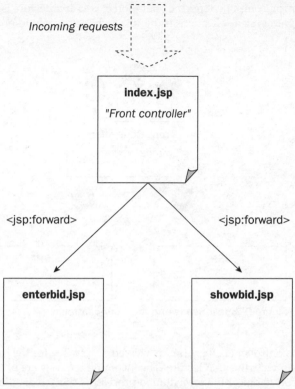

Incoming requests

index.jsp

"Front controller"

<jsp:forward>   <jsp:forward>

enterbid.jsp   **showbid.jsp**

Figure 9-6: Front controller architecture

In Figure 9-6, index.jsp forwards the requests to one of two different JSP pages:

❑   enterbid.jsp

❑   showbid.jsp

In production, index.jsp may actually forward requests to many different JSPs depending on application requirements. The major benefits delivered by this architecture include the following:

❑   **Application URL hiding:** The user sees only the index.jsp URL.

❑   **Factoring of reusable code/logic:** index.jsp does form data validation that may be required by many different forms within the application.

❑   **Elimination of hard-wired relationships between JSP pages:** This makes the application easier to maintain; the actual flow between pages in the application is determined by index.jsp, and not hard-coded in URL links within the JSP pages themselves.

In this capacity, the index.jsp page acts as controller (or front controller). It is easy to see how both the appearance and interactions of the entire application are controlled through the logic in index.jsp.

The key enabling technical component for the operation of this architecture is the JavaBean. Without the use of JavaBeans, designing JSP applications using this architecture would not be possible. To see why, consider Figure 9-7.

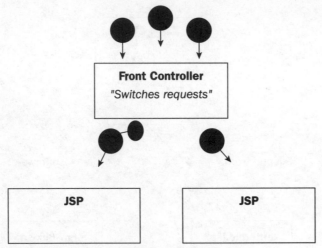

Figure 9-7: JavaBeans and the front controller

In Figure 9-7, the front controller (index.jsp) is viewed as a switch for the incoming requests. This is another common way to view the architecture. The incoming requests are processed by the front controller and then switched to one of the presentation processors (JSP) to display the output of the processed request. The only data element that is passed between the front controller and a JSP is the incoming request itself. To pass information between the front controller and the presentation JSPs, JavaBeans are attached as named attributes (attached data in Figure 9-7) to the request. The JavaBeans enable arbitrarily complex data elements to be passed between the front controller and the presentation JSPs — this is the vital role of JavaBeans in the architecture.

You will see this use of JavaBeans again and again in your daily JSP development. Almost all modern Web application frameworks deploy JavaBeans in this fashion.

The index.jsp front controller

Let's now examine the code that implements this. The index.jsp front controller can be located at <Tomcat Installation Directory>/webapps/ch09/example1/index.jsp. The entire index.jsp code is reproduced here:

```
<%@ taglib prefix="c" uri="http://java.sun.com/jsp/jstl/core" %>
<c:choose>
  <c:when test="${empty param.action}">
    <jsp:forward page="enterbid.jsp"/>
  </c:when>
  <c:when test="${param.action eq 'bid'}">
    <c:if test="${(param.price <= 0) || (param.price >= 999)}">
      <jsp:useBean id="biderror" class="com.wrox.begjsp.ch09.BidError"
scope="request">
```

```
            <jsp:setProperty name="biderror" property="msg" value="Sorry, your bid is
not in range. Please enter again."/>
        </jsp:useBean>
        <jsp:forward page="enterbid.jsp"/>
    </c:if>

    <jsp:useBean id="bidinfo" class="com.wrox.begjsp.ch09.Bid" scope="request">
        <jsp:setProperty name="bidinfo" property="*"/>
    </jsp:useBean>

    <jsp:forward page="showbid.jsp"/>
  </c:when>
</c:choose>
```

You can see that index.jsp consists of one JSTL <c:choose> construct. This construct is used to switch the incoming request to different presentation JSPs. In this case, it will be either enterbid.jsp or showbid.jsp. The incoming request parameter that the switching is dependent on is called action. The following code shows the <c:choose> construct used to switch the request based on the value of the action parameter:

```
<c:choose>
  <c:when test="${empty param.action}">
...
  </c:when>
  <c:when test="${param.action eq 'bid'}">
    ....
  </c:when>
</c:choose>
```

Initially, when the index.jsp page is called up, there will be no action parameter. In this case, the code in the first <c:when> tag is executed. When the bid form is submitted, the value of the action parameter will be set to 'bid', and the code in the second <c:when> will be executed. For any specific incoming request, only one of the <c:when> tags will be executed.

> The role of the action **parameter in this architecture is called the** forward. **The front controller switches requests to different targets (JSP pages) depending on the** forward **(different value of the** action **parameter).**

Forwarding to different targets

The code in the first <c:when> is quite straightforward. This code is executed when the index.jsp URL is first accessed:

```
<c:when test="${empty param.action}">
  <jsp:forward page="enterbid.jsp"/>
</c:when>
```

The EL empty operator is used determine that the action parameter is null (i.e., has not been defined). The action performed here is a forward of the request to the enterbid.jsp form for input of bid data.

The code in the second <c:when> is also quite straightforward. This code is executed when the enterbid.jsp form is submitted to the front controller (index.jsp). Within enterbid.jsp, a hidden parameter with the name action is set to the value of 'bid'. This signals index.jsp to perform data validation and then forward the request accordingly. Figure 9-8 shows the action performed by the code in this second <c:when> construct.

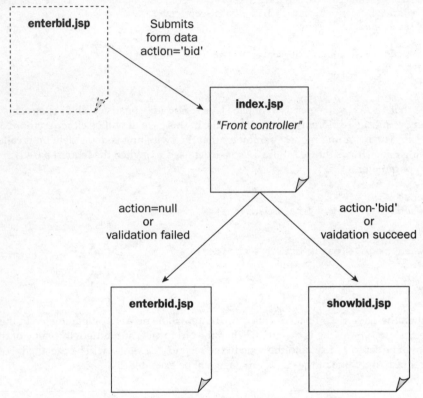

Figure 9-8: Front controller forwarding requests depending on the action parameter

In Figure 9-8, the request is forwarded to one of two targets:

❑   Back to enterbid.jsp if the bid is out of range (input data validation fails)

❑   To showbid.jsp if the bid is in the valid range (greater than 0 and less than 999)

JavaBean flow for validation error reporting

The code for this second <c:when> construct is as follows:

```
<c:when test="${param.action eq 'bid'}">
  <c:if test="${(param.price <= 0) || (param.price >= 999)}">
    <jsp:useBean id="biderror" class="com.wrox.begjsp.ch09.BidError"
scope="request">
```

```
    <jsp:setProperty name="biderror" property="msg"
value="Sorry, your bid is not in range. Please enter again."/>
    </jsp:useBean>
    <jsp:forward page="enterbid.jsp"/>
  </c:if>

  <jsp:useBean id="bidinfo" class="com.wrox.begjsp.ch09.Bid" scope="request">
    <jsp:setProperty name="bidinfo" property="*"/>
  </jsp:useBean>

  <jsp:forward page="showbid.jsp"/>
</c:when>
```

First, an EL expression is used to determine that the `action` parameter has the value `bid`:

```
<c:when test="${param.action eq 'bid'}">
```

Next, the incoming request parameter called `price` is validated to be within the allowed range:

```
<c:if test="${(param.price <= 0) ||  (param.price >= 999)}">
...
</c:if>
```

Accessing JavaBeans using standard actions

The code in this `<c:if>` tag will be executed only if the price is out of range. It is in this code that an error message JavaBean is created and sent back to the `enterbid.jsp` to be displayed to the user. The code in the `<c:if>` tag is reproduced here:

```
<jsp:useBean id="biderror" class="com.wrox.begjsp.ch09.BidError" scope="request">
  <jsp:setProperty name="biderror" property="msg"
value="Sorry, your bid is not in range. Please enter again."/>
  </jsp:useBean>
  <jsp:forward page="enterbid.jsp"/>
```

The `<jsp:useBean>` standard action is used to create an instance of the `BidError` JavaBean and attach it to the `request` scope. If you need a review of the `<jsp:useBean>` tag and how it creates new instances of JavaBeans, see Chapter 8, "JSP Standard Actions." This newly created instance of the JavaBean is attached to the `request` implicit object as an attribute named `biderror`. Because the request is passed during a `<jsp:forward>`, it will be available within the target `enterbid.jsp`.

Within the `<jsp:useBean>` tag, the `msg` property of the JavaBean is set to the required error message using the `<jsp:setProperty>` standard action. In this case, the error message is as follows:

```
Sorry, your bid is not in range. Please enter again.
```

The code within the `<jsp:useBean>` standard action will execute only if the named JavaBean is created successfully.

The validation error information JavaBean

The `BidError` JavaBean is created to carry error information between the front controller's form validation logic and the presentation JSPs. You can find the code at `<Tomcat Installation Directory>/`
`webapps/ch09/example1/WEB-INF/classes/com/wrox/begjsp/ch09/BidError.java`. The source
code of the `BidError.java` JavaBean is reproduced here:

```java
package com.wrox.begjsp.ch09;
public class BidError
{
    private String msg;
    public BidError()
    {
    }
    public String getMsg()
    {
        return this.msg;
    }


    public void setMsg(String msg)
    {
        this.msg = msg;
    }
}
```

This `BidError` JavaBean has only a single read/write property called `msg`. The `getMsg()` method is
implemented for the reading of this property, and the `setMsg()` method is implemented for writing this
property. Internally, the value of the property is kept in a `String` typed private field also called `msg`.

The enterbid.jsp target

The form that takes bids from the user is `enterbid.jsp`. It is located at `<Tomcat Installation`
`Directory>/webapps/ch09/example1/enterbid.jsp`. The content of `enterbid.jsp` is reproduced
here:

```jsp
<%@ taglib prefix="c" uri="http://java.sun.com/jsp/jstl/core" %>
<html>
<head>
  <link rel=stylesheet type="text/css" href="auction.css">
  <title>Enter Your Bid</title></head>
<body>
  <table class="mainBox" width="400">
    <tr><td class="boxTitle" colspan="2">
      Wrox JSP Auction
    </td></tr>
    <c:if test="${!(empty biderror)}">
    <tr>
      <td class="errorText" colspan="2">
        ${biderror.msg}
      </td>
    </tr>
    </c:if>
```

```
          <tr><td colspan="2"> </td></tr>
          <tr><td>
            <form  action="index.jsp" method="get">
              <table>
                <tr>
                  <td width="200">Item to bid on</td><td>
                    <select name="item">
                      <option>27 inch TV</option>
                      <option>DVD Player</option>
                      <option>Digital Camera</option>
                    </select>
                    <input type="hidden" name="action" value="bid"/>
                  </td>
                </tr>
                <tr>
                  <td>Bid Price:</td>
                  <td><input name="price" type="text" width="10"/>
                  </td>
                </tr>
                <tr><td colspan="2"> </td></tr>
                <tr><td colspan="2" align="center">
                  <input type="submit" value="Bid now!"/>
                </td></tr>
              </table>
            </form>
          </td></tr>
        </table>
      </body>
    </html>
```

It is an HTML form with a `<select>` form element and a `text` typed `<input>` form element. The high-lighted portion in the preceding code checks for and prints any validation error message if it exists. The `biderror` JavaBean from `index.jsp`, transported as an attribute attached to the request, is used to determine whether a validation has occurred. This JavaBean is accessed through the EL in this case.

Accessing JavaBeans through EL

The validation error message rendering code in the `enterbid.jsp` uses EL to access the `biderror` JavaBean. It adds an additional row to the table if an error occurred:

```
<c:if test="${!(empty biderror)}">
  <tr>
    <td class="errorText" colspan="2">
      ${biderror.msg}
    </td>
  </tr>
</c:if>
```

First, the empty EL operator determines whether the `biderror` attribute is available. The `biderror` attribute will not exist if `enterbid.jsp` is accessed for the first time because `index.jsp` forwards to the page without creating any JavaBean. Only if the `biderror` attribute is found will the extra row in the table be rendered. Note the very simple access to the `msg` property value of the `biderror` JavaBean using EL:

```
${biderror.msg}
```

Using EL to render a JavaBean property value is simple and concise.

Displaying bid information via a JavaBean

If the bid price entered by the user is within the allowable range, the front controller index.jsp will forward the request to the showbid.jsp target. The code to do this is in the second <c:when> tag within index.jsp, after the <c:if> check for bid price validity:

```
<jsp:useBean id="bidinfo" class="com.wrox.begjsp.ch09.Bid" scope="request">
  <jsp:setProperty name="bidinfo" property="*"/>
</jsp:useBean>
<jsp:forward page="showbid.jsp"/>
```

The preceding code creates a new Bid JavaBean instance and calls it bidinfo, using the <jsp:useBean> tag. Note that the special "*" value is used to assign the incoming input form data value to the properties of the bean.

Filling JavaBean properties with incoming request parameters

When the special "*" value for the property attribute is included in a standard <jsp:setProperty> action, the JSP runtime will match the name of the request parameter against the name of the properties of the JavaBean referenced. (For a discussion of this special value, see Chapter 8.) In this case, the JavaBean is called bidinfo and is an instance of the Bid JavaBean. This JavaBean has two properties:

❑ item
❑ price

This matches the incoming form parameters, filled out using enterbid.jsp, exactly. This will result in the assignment of the item parameter to the item property of bidinfo, and the assignment of the price parameter to the price property of bidinfo. Because the <jsp:useBean> created the bidinfo attribute in the request scope, the bidinfo JavaBean instance will travel with the forwarded request to showbid.jsp.

The Bid JavaBean

The code for the Bid JavaBean can be found at <Tomcat Installation Directory>/webapps/ch09/ WEB-INF/classes/com/wrox/begjsp/ch09/Bid.java. The Bid.java code is reproduced here:

```
package com.wrox.begjsp.ch09;
public class Bid
{
    private long price;
    private String item;

    public Bid()
    {
    }

    public long getPrice()
```

```
        {
            return this.price;
        }

        public void setPrice(long price)
        {
            this.price = price;
        }

        public String getItem()
        {
            return this.item;
        }

        public void setItem(String item)
        {
            this.item = item;
        }
    }
```

This JavaBean has two properties: price and item. They are both read/write properties. A get<PropertyName>() and a set<PropertyName>() method are created for each property.

The showbid.jsp target

Back in index.jsp, after creating the Bid JavaBean instance and setting its property values, the request is forwarded to the showbid.jsp target via a <jsp:forward> standard action:

```
<jsp:useBean id="bidinfo" class="com.wrox.begjsp.ch09.Bid" scope="request">
  <jsp:setProperty name="bidinfo" property="*"/>
</jsp:useBean>
<jsp:forward page="showbid.jsp"/>
```

The code for showbid.jsp can be located at <Tomcat Installation Directory>/webapps/ ch09/example1/showbid.jsp. The content of showbid.jsp is presented here:

```
<html>
<head>
  <link rel=stylesheet type="text/css" href="auction.css">
  <title>Show the Bid</title>
</head>
<body>
  <table class="mainBox" width="600">
    <tr><td class="boxTitle" colspan="2">
      Your Auction Bid
    </td></tr>
    <tr><td colspan="2"> </td></tr>
    <tr>
      <td class="tableLabel" width="30%">
        Item bid for
      </td>
```

```
      <td class="tableCell">
         ${bidinfo.item}
      </td>
   </tr>
   <tr>
     <td class="tableLabel">
       Bid price
     </td>
     <td class="tableCell">
        ${bidinfo.price}
     </td>
   </tr>
  </table>
 </body>
</html>
```

This JSP page renders the property values of the `bidinfo` JavaBean instance using EL. The two lines rendering the values are highlighted in the preceding code.

Formatting auction output pages with a CSS stylesheet

Both `enterbid.jsp` and `showbid.jsp` use a CSS stylesheet to format the HTML output. The stylesheet is called `auction.css` and can be located at `<Tomcat Installation Directory>/webapps/ch09/example1/auction.css`.

The content of this stylesheet is shown here:

```css
.tableCell
{
  font-family : Verdana, Geneva, Arial, Helvetica, sans-serif;
  font-size : 16;
  font-weight : bold;
  color : #0f7fcf;
  background-color: #ffffff;
}

.resultCell
{
  font-family : Verdana, Geneva, Arial, Helvetica, sans-serif;
  font-size : 16;
  font-style: italic;
  font-weight : bold;
  color : #000000;
  background-color: #ffffff;
}

.tableLabel
{
```

```
  font-family : Verdana, Geneva, Arial, Helvetica, sans-serif;
  font-size : 18;
  color : #000000;
  background-color: #ffffff;
}

.errorText
{
  font-family : Verdana, Geneva, Arial, Helvetica, sans-serif;
  font-size : 16;
  font-weight : bold;
  color : #ffffff;
  background-color: #ff0000;
}

.boxTitle
{
  font-family : Arial, Helvetica, sans-serif;
  font-size : 22;
  font-weight : bold;
  color : #ffffff;
  background-color: #0F7ACA;

}
.mainBox
{
  font-family : Verdana, Geneva, Arial, Helvetica, sans-serif;
  font-size : 12;
  color : #ffffff;
  background-color: #eeeeee;
}
```

This completes the coverage of the first example. The next Try It Out exercise is built on the first, and shows how you can use JavaBeans to carry information from custom application logic to the JSP pages.

Try It Out   Using JavaBeans to Display the Auction Result

First make sure that your Tomcat 5 server is running and then deploy ch09.war to the server.

Next, using your browser, access the following URL:

```
http://localhost:8080/ch09/example2/index.jsp
```

Enter the bid information shown in Figure 9-9.

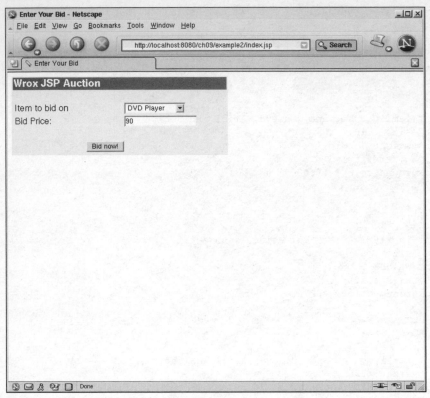

Figure 9-9: Bid Information for the DVD player

In Figure 9-9, you are bidding for the DVD Player, with a bid price of $90. Click the Bid Now! button. Because the input price is within range, the index.jsp routes the request to showbid.jsp. However, in this case, showbid.jsp also shows the bid result. Figure 9-10 displays the new showbid.jsp.

While the bid result here is simulated, the same technique can be used to display an actual bid result from a live production system.

How It Works

This example consists of the same three JSP pages as the first example:

❑ index.jsp

❑ enterbid.jsp

❑ showbid.jsp

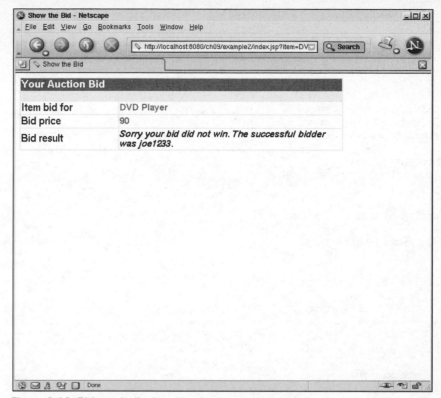

Figure 9-10: Bid result displayed by the new `showbid.jsp`

Only `enterbid.jsp` and `showbid.jsp` have been modified. The example also makes use of the JavaBeans shown in the following table.

JavaBean	Usage Description
Bid	Used to carry bid information from the front controller `index.jsp` to the `showbid.jsp` presentation page
BidError	Used to carry error information from the front controller `index.jsp` to the `enterbid.jsp` when a validation error occurs
Bidder	Used to simulate the action of bidding

The Bidder JavaBean

The new `Bidder` JavaBean is located at `<Tomcat Installation Directory>/webapps/ch09/WEB-INF/classes/com/wrox/begjsp/ch09/Bidder.java`.

The code is reproduced here:

```
package com.wrox.begjsp.ch09;

public class Bidder
{

    private String item;
    private long price;
    private String result;

    public Bidder()
    {
    }

    public String getItem()
    {
        return this.item;
    }

    public void setItem(String item)
    {
        this.item = item;
    }

    public long getPrice()
    {
        return this.price;
    }

    public void setPrice(long price)
    {
        this.price = price;
    }

    public String getResult()
    {
        /* simulate bid result */
        this.result = "Sorry your bid did not win. The successful bidder was
joe1233.";
        return this.result;
    }
}
```

This `Bidder` JavaBean simulates the bidding action. You need to do the following:

❑   Set the value of the `item` and `price` properties.

❑   Read the value of the `result` property.

The `result` property value contains a string that indicates the result of the bid.

In production, this method can access a back-end network to determine the actual result of the bid.

Modifying the controller to fetch bidding results

The `index.jsp` front controller page is modified to fetch the bidding result in an instance of the `Bidder` JavaBean before forwarding the request to the `showbid.jsp` page.

You can find the modified `index.jsp` at `<Tomcat Installation Directory>/webapps/ch09/example2/index.jsp`. The code of this modified page is presented here, with the modifications highlighted:

```
<%@ taglib prefix="c" uri="http://java.sun.com/jsp/jstl/core" %>
<c:choose>
  <c:when test="${empty param.action}">
    <jsp:forward page="enterbid.jsp"/>
  </c:when>
  <c:when test="${param.action eq 'bid'}">
    <!-- validation code -->
    <c:if test="${(param.price <= 0) || (param.price >= 999)}">
      <jsp:useBean id="biderror" class="com.wrox.begjsp.ch09.BidError"
scope="request">
        <jsp:setProperty name="biderror" property="msg" value="Sorry, your bid is
not in range. Please enter again."/>
      </jsp:useBean>
      <jsp:forward page="enterbid.jsp"/>
    </c:if>
    <!-- data validated -->
    <jsp:useBean id="bidinfo" class="com.wrox.begjsp.ch09.Bid" scope="request">
      <jsp:setProperty name="bidinfo" property="*"/>
    </jsp:useBean>

    <!-- perform bidding -->
    <jsp:useBean id="bidder" class="com.wrox.begjsp.ch09.Bidder" scope="request">
      <jsp:setProperty name="bidder" property="item"/>
      <jsp:setProperty name="bidder" property="price"/>
    </jsp:useBean>
    <c:set var="bidresult" value="${bidder.result}" scope="request"/>
    <jsp:forward page="showbid.jsp"/>
  </c:when>
</c:choose>
```

The `<jsp:useBean>` standard action is used here to create an instance of the `Bidder` JavaBean, attaching it as a `request` scoped attribute called `bidder`. The `<jsp:setProperty>` standard action is used to set the `item` and `price` property of the `bidder` JavaBean instance. Note that this could also have been done using the single `<jsp:setProperty>` action and the special "*" value:

```
<jsp:setProperty name="bidder" property="*"/>
```

Using JSTL to access a JavaBean

The last lines highlighted in the new `index.jsp` controller are as follows:

```
<c:set var="bidresult" value="${bidder.result}" scope="request"/>
<jsp:forward page="showbid.jsp"/>
```

Here, the JSTL `<c:set>` custom action is used to retrieve a JavaBean's property value. The value obtained is the value of the `result` property; it is of type `String`. This value is then attached to the request scope as a scoped variable called `bidresult`. This technique can be used to access an attribute of a JavaBean regardless of its data type. The resulting `bidresult` request scope variable will be available within the `showbid.jsp` target, together with the `bidinfo` JavaBean instance.

> One of the main purposes of a front controller in a system is to manage communications with back-end application logic. This communication can result in multiple JavaBeans attached to the requests, forwarded to the presentation JSP for rendering. In the preceding Try It Out exercise, this is exemplified by the data carrying both `bidinfo` and `bidresult` JavaBeans.

Presenting bid results in showbid.jsp

One other element changed from the `showbid.jsp` page of the last Try It Out exercise. This page has been modified to show the bid results. The new `showbid.jsp` is located at `<Tomcat Installation Directory>/webapps/ch09/example2/showbid.jsp`. The page is shown here, with modifications highlighted:

```
<html>
<head>
  <link rel=stylesheet type="text/css" href="auction.css">
  <title>Show the Bid</title></head>
<body>
  <table class="mainBox" width="600">
    <tr><td class="boxTitle" colspan="2">
      Your Auction Bid
    </td></tr>
    <tr><td colspan="2"> </td></tr>
    <tr><td class="tableLabel" width="30%">
        Item bid for
      </td>
      <td class="tableCell">
        ${bidinfo.item}</td>
    </tr>
    <tr>
      <td class="tableLabel">
        Bid price
      </td>
      <td class="tableCell">
        ${bidinfo.price}
      </td>
    </tr>
    <tr>
      <td class="tableLabel">
        Bid result
      </td>
      <td class="resultCell">
        ${bidresult}
      </td>
    </tr>

  </table>
</body>
</html>
```

Because the `bidresult` attribute is already of `String` data type, it is simply rendered within a new table row using the EL expression:

```
${bidresult}
```

This concludes the coverage of using JavaBeans to carry information between custom application logic and the JSP presentation layer.

How JavaBeans and EJBs Differ

The JavaBeans covered in this chapter are Java classes coded according to the JavaBeans API specification. They are reusable software components that expose properties, methods, and events for external access. The JSP usage of these JavaBeans is focused around the transfer of data between different JSP pages. In this chapter, JavaBeans are used to transfer data between a single front controller and many different presentation JSPs.

JSP is a technology residing exclusively in the presentation layer (of the Web tier) within the J2EE (Java 2 Enterprise Edition) architecture. J2EE is a large specification that encompasses many aspects of enterprise application building using Java as the programming language.

Enterprise JavaBeans, or EJBs for short, reside within the business logic tier of an enterprise system. This tier is completely separate and independent from the Web tier in which the JSP resides. In fact, it is entirely possible to create JSP-based applications without the use of EJB.

Unlike the JavaBeans presented here, EJBs execute within their own highly specialized container. The container will have access to an enterprise's database, communications, and security resources.

The J2EE architecture is covered in Chapter 22, "JSP in J2EE," and you will learn a little about EJB in that chapter. A thorough coverage of J2EE and/or EJB is beyond the scope of this book. The important thing to realize at this point is that the JavaBeans used in this chapter are not EJBs, and that EJBs are not essential to creating applications using JSPs. In fact, even within enterprise Java applications, JSP as a presentation technology seldom has access to EJBs. Instead, EJBs are usually accessed via code written in the Java programming language called a *servlet*. Servlets are covered in Chapter 15, "JSP and Servlets."

Summary

JavaBeans are software components created using the Java programming language that expose properties, methods, and events. JavaBeans . . .

❑ Play a vital role in the creation of applications using JSP.

❑ Are used to transfer complex data with the incoming request.

❑ Can be used in JSP via the built-in standard actions `<jsp:useBean>`, `<jsp:setProperty>`, and `<jsp:getProperty>`.

❑ Can be accessed using raw Java language code in the form of embedded scriplets scripting elements. This practice is now discouraged, although you might come across such JSPs while maintaining legacy code.

❑ Can be packaged into JAR files and placed into the application's `lib` directory.

❑ Can be placed under the `WEB-INF/classes` directory for a faster modify-recompile cycle during development.

❑ Can be manipulated readily using JSTL/EL, especially when used as scoped variables. The JSTL `<c:set>` tag can be used to attach a JavaBean-based attribute to the request implicit object. EL expressions can be used to render JavaBean property values.

JavaBeans are not the same as, and should not be confused with, Enterprise JavaBeans (EJBs). EJBs run in their own special container, and are in a different architectural tier than JSPs.

The chapter also explored the front controller design pattern. Having a front controller in a JSP application, you learned the following:

❑ By using a front controller to forward incoming requests to different JSPs, you can isolate common functions such as form data validation in one place.

❑ Using such a front controller enables you to write JSP applications in which the pages are not hard-wired to one another, leading to better maintainability.

Exercises

1. Modify the first Try It Out exercise to do the following:

    a. Remember the selected bid item when the `enterbid.jsp` is re-displayed during a validation error

    b. Remember the bid price entered when the `enterbid.jsp` is re-displayed

    c. Highlight the bid price label in red, emphasizing that the value is invalid

2. Modify the second Try It Out exercise to

    a. Include a new `winner.jsp` page

    b. Remove the upper bid limit of $999

    c. Forward to this new `winner.jsp` page if the incoming bid price is over $1,000

Error Handling

In an ideal world, you would be able to design a JSP-based application, code the pages, and have the system up and running in one single try. In the real world, however, there are many opportunities to make mistakes. Design and coding mistakes will result in errors. This chapter focuses on the different types of errors that you may encounter, and how to handle them using JSP.

The JSP error-handling mechanism is intimately tied to the exception handling mechanism of the Java programming language. This chapter explains this relationship, and also shows how you can use JSP to handle exceptions originating from Java code within the application.

This chapter covers the following topics:

❑   Coding and syntax errors in the Java programming language

❑   JSP coding errors

❑   Logical errors

❑   User data-entry errors

❑   Translation-time errors

❑   Request-time errors

❑   Handling errors using the JSTL <c:catch> action

❑   Handling errors using the JSP error page mechanism

Understanding the Origin of Errors

Developers often talk about error handling as if it were a very simple matter, and assume that code can be easily added to handle errors after the completion of a project. This is far from the truth. A usable and robust application relies on an *a priori* design, and the thought given to the source and handling of possible error conditions.

It is very important to appreciate that there are different sources of error. Each source can also emit errors at different times during the development and deployment cycle.

When you are writing JSP code, coding errors can occur at different parts of your code. Because a JSP page is made up of so many separate elements, errors can be introduced by any of these components.

Some of the possible sources of errors include the following:

❑ In the coding of your JavaBeans or Java classes

❑ Within scripting elements

❑ In JSP directives and actions

❑ In JSTL and EL coding

❑ Within template data

The sections in this chapter examine these possibilities one by one, and discuss how the errors may be handled in each case.

> **Custom tag libraries are constructed out of the same five types of elements listed in this section. Older tag libraries tend to use a lot of custom Java language coding, whereas newer tag libraries tend to make more use of JSP-based tag files.**

Errors in Java language coding

JSP uses custom JavaBeans to transport data between JSP pages and back-end elements such as business-logic Java code or servlets. The JavaBeans and custom Java classes are coded and tested separately from the JSP pages.

JavaBeans and/or classes are code written in the Java programming language. Java code is compiled before the beans or classes are executed. For this code, errors may be caught when you compile the code or when you run and test the code.

Syntax errors in coding will be caught by the compiler when the code is compiled. For example, the following code to add up 50 numbers will result in a compilation error:

```
int sum = 0;
for {int i=0; i< 50;  i++}
    sum = sum + i;
```

When the code is compiled with a Java compiler, you will get an error message similar to the following:

```
classname.java:4: '(' expected
    for {int i=0; i< 50;  i++}
       ^
classname.java:6: illegal start of expression
```

This is a syntax error, and you must correct the code and recompile until there are no more syntax errors. Once the compiler successfully compiles the source code into bytecode, the code is free of syntax errors. However, logic errors may still remain in the compiled code.

Errors in logic within JavaBeans/Java classes should be detected and corrected during the unit testing and debugging of the component. Coverage of testing and debugging techniques for Java programs is beyond the scope of this book.

> The execution of compiled code (JavaBeans/Java classes) is orchestrated by the JSP that uses them (for example, by a `<jsp:useBean>` action). During the execution phase, runtime errors can still occur. These runtime errors result in Java exceptions being thrown. A later section in this chapter will show how JSP can handle these Java language runtime exceptions.

Errors in scripting elements

Like JavaBeans and custom Java classes, scripting elements are also code written in the Java programming language. Unlike their cousins, however, the developer need not compile, test, and debug these embedded Java language fragments separate from the JSP pages.

Instead, the Java code embedded within scripting elements is compiled and executed together with the rest of the JSP page. This typically occurs when the JSP page is first accessed by a request. Figure 10-1 illustrates the compilation and execution of scripting element Java coding.

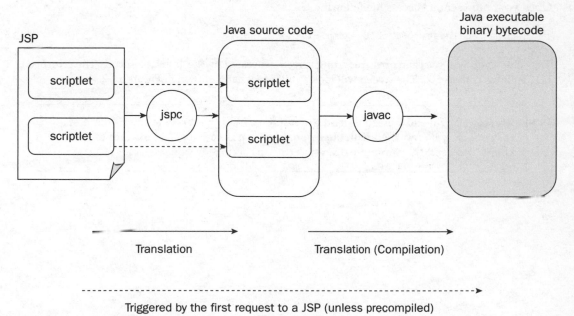

Figure 10-1: Compilation and execution of scripting elements

Because the Java code in scripting elements is not compiled and tested separately, any syntax error in the coding will show up only after compilation — at request time (unless the JSPs are precompiled; see Chapter 25, "Performance," for more information on precompilation). In practice, you will be debugging both the JSP program logic and the embedded Java code at the same time. This increased complexity in debugging (and maintenance) is one reason why the use of scripting elements is discouraged in new JSP code.

The following Try It Out exercise shows a coding error within a scripting element.

> Other than returning an HTTP 500 status code, the JSP specification does not specify how errors from scripting elements should be displayed or handled. The behavior will be container-specific. If you are not using Tomcat as your server, the diagnosis and debugging process for scripting elements may be different from the one in the Try It Out exercise.

Try It Out   Catching Errors in Scripting Elements

This first example shows how the Tomcat 5 server displays a Java syntax error within a scripting element.

The example is contained in ch10.war. First make sure that your Tomcat 5 server is running and then deploy ch10.war to the server. Review Chapter 1 if you do not remember how to deploy a WAR archive.

Open your browser and access the following URL:

```
http://localhost:8080/ch10/example1/index.jsp
```

The screen you will see is an error-reporting screen generated by the Tomcat 5 server. The returned HTTP status code is 500. The screen will look similar to what is shown in Figure 10-2.

> The HTTP protocol is used to send the response from the server to the client. A status code may be returned with the response. A status code of 500 indicates to the client (browser) that an internal server error has occurred.

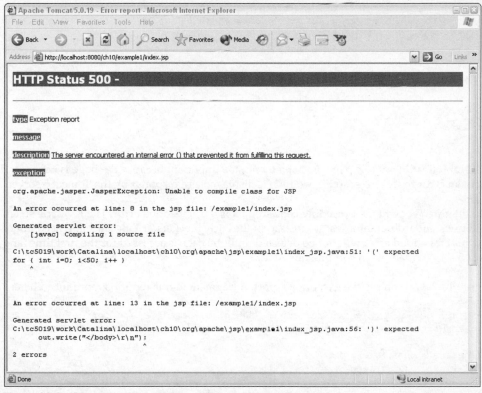

Figure 10-2: JSP page with a syntax error in a scripting element

How It Works

The `index.jsp` page in this example is coded to include a syntax error in the Java coding embedded within a scripting element. The JSP page is located at `<Tomcat Installation Directory>/webapps/ch10/example1/index.jsp`. The `index.jsp` code is reproduced here:

```
<html>
<head>
  <title>Error in Scripting Element</title>
</head>
```

```
<body>
  <h1>Page with error in scripting element</h1>

  <%
  int sum= 0;
  for { int i=0; i<50; i++ }
      sum = sum + i;

  %>
</body>
</html>
```

The title and heading of this page are actually not too important because the page is never rendered. Instead, an error report (refer to Figure 10-2) is displayed as a response by the Tomcat 5 server.

The highlighted code in the preceding code snippet is the embedded error. The Java for statement should use standard parentheses " (" instead of the curly brackets "{." Because JSP need not be precompiled, this embedded error will not be detected until the page is accessed for the first time (and the Tomcat 5 server attempts to compile this code).

In Figure 10-2, you can see the exception report. A fragment of this report is reproduced here:

```
org.apache.jasper.JasperException: Unable to compile class for JSP
An error occurred at line: 8 in the jsp file: /example1/index.jsp

Generated servlet error:
    [javac] Compiling 1 source file

C:\jdk1.3\tc5025\work\Catalina\localhost\ch10\org\apache\jsp\example1\index_jsp.
java:51: '(' expected
for { int i=0; i<50; i++ }
    ^
```

The highlighted lines in the preceding report pinpoint the Java syntax error. First, note that the error is reported as follows:

```
org.apache.jasper.JasperException: Unable to compile class for JSP
```

This clearly states that something has gone wrong while trying to compile the code generated for the JSP. Next, this is confirmed by the compiler's status message:

```
[javac] Compiling 1 source file
```

Finally, the exact offending line and syntax error are pointed out. The wrong use of a curly bracket is pinpointed by the compiler. It even indicates that the round bracket " (" is expected.

```
C:\jdk1.3\tc5025\work\Catalina\localhost\ch10\org\apache\jsp\example1\index_jsp.
java:51: '(' expected
for { int i=0; i<50; i++ }
    ^
```

In general, Java syntax errors within embedded scripting elements are caught and displayed as an exception report in the translation phase by the Tomcat server. The diagnostic message provided by the `javac` compiler is typically very helpful in isolating the cause of the syntax error.

These syntax errors, of course, should be corrected in the testing and debugging phase of a typical JSP application.

> **Coding syntax errors must be corrected before the application can be deployed. These errors are corrected in the debugging phase of the development cycle. Chapter 14, "JSP Debugging Techniques," describes in detail how to track down development-time errors and correct them.**

Errors in JSP directives and actions

Another source of common errors is syntax or typographical mistakes in standard JSP directives and actions.

For example, consider the following JSP directive:

```
<%@page lang="java" %>
```

The `page` directive gives instructions to the container. In this case, the developer wanted to tell the container that the page uses Java as the scripting language. However, an error is made because the attribute used to specify the scripting language is `language`, not `lang`.

The container should catch this error at the JSP page's translation time and issue an error report.

For another example, consider the following JSP standard action:

```
<jsp:include bad="abc" page="nosuch.jsp" />
```

This action contains two errors:

- ❑ The attribute `bad` is not a valid attribute for the `<jsp:include>` standard action.
- ❑ The page `nosuch.jsp` does not exist.

While a container is expected to catch the first error during the translation phase of processing (when the JSP code is translated to Java code), the second error cannot be detected until request processing time. In fact, the semantics of the `<jsp:include>` tag states that no error should be generated if the page to be included is not found.

The next Try It Out exercise shows the output of Tomcat when errors are detected in JSP directives and standard actions.

Try It Out   Catching Errors in JSP Directives and Actions

This example reveals how the Tomcat 5 server deals with common JSP coding errors in directives and standard actions.

Make sure ch10.war is deployed on your Tomcat 5 server. Then, open your browser and access the following URL:

```
http://localhost:8080/ch10/example2/index.jsp
```

This will cause an error-reporting screen to be displayed, similar to Figure 10-3. The error being reported to the browser is again HTTP status 500, an internal server error.

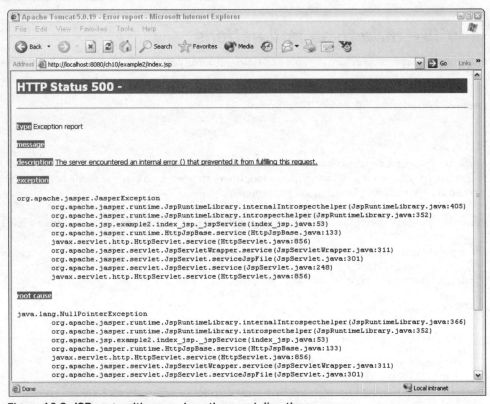

Figure 10-3: JSP page with errors in actions and directives

In Figure 10-3, the error report is specifying an invalid attribute called lang.

How It Works

The `index.jsp` page in this example has multiple coding errors in JSP directives and standard actions. The `index.jsp` page is located at `<Tomcat Installation Directory>/webapps/ch10/example2/index.jsp`. The code of `index.jsp` is reproduced here:

```
<%@page lang="java" %>
<html>
<head>
  <title>Error in JSP directives and actions</title>
</head>
<body>
  <h1>Page with error in JSP directive and actions</h1>

  <jsp:include page="nosuch.jsp" bad="abc" />
  <jsp:setProperty name="errobj" property="nosuch" value="This is invalid" />
</body>
</html>
```

The first highlighted line is the `page` directive. The `lang` attribute is a valid attribute for the `<%@ page %>` directive:

```
<%@page lang="java" %>
```

The second highlighted line is a `<jsp:include>` standard action. The `bad` attribute is an invalid attribute. In addition, `nosuch.jsp` does not exist, although that is not considered an error:

```
<jsp:include page="nosuch.jsp" bad="abc" />
```

The last highlighted line is a `<jsp:setProperty>` standard action that does not contain a syntax error. This means that it should translate to proper Java code. However, there will still be an error when the code is executed because the JavaBean called `errobj` does not exist:

```
<jsp:setProperty name="errobj" property="nosuch" value="This is invalid" />
```

Errors in the <%@page %> directive

When the page is first accessed, the error report in Figure 10-3 is displayed. Note that even though the page contains multiple errors, only the first one is caught and displayed by the error report. This behavior enables you to fix coding errors one by one.

This initial error report clearly identifies the culprit — the invalid `lang` attribute of the page directive.

```
org.apache.jasper.JasperException: /example2/index.jsp(1,1) Page directive has
invalid attribute: lang
org.apache.jasper.compiler.DefaultErrorHandler.jspError(DefaultErrorHandler.java:39)
  org.apache.jasper.compiler.ErrorDispatcher.dispatch(ErrorDispatcher.java:376)
  org.apache.jasper.compiler.ErrorDispatcher.jspError(ErrorDispatcher.java:200)
  org.apache.jasper.compiler.JspUtil.checkAttributes(JspUtil.java:304)


org.apache.jasper.compiler.Validator$DirectiveVisitor.visit(Validator.java:100)
```

To fix the problem, edit the index.jsp file — located at <Tomcat Installation Directory>/ webapps/ch10/example2/index.jsp — by changing the lang attribute of the <%@page %> directive to language. This eliminates the first error:

```
<%@page language="java" %>
```

Next, access the following URL again using your browser:

```
http://localhost:8080/ch10/example2/index.jsp
```

Make sure you force a reload of the page on your browser if you already have it displayed.

Errors in the <jsp:include> action

The new error report, generated by Tomcat 5, now points to the invalid attribute called bad in the <jsp:include> action:

```
org.apache.jasper.JasperException: /example2/index.jsp(9,0) Include action has
invalid attribute: bad

org.apache.jasper.compiler.DefaultErrorHandler.jspError(DefaultErrorHandler.java:39)
 org.apache.jasper.compiler.ErrorDispatcher.dispatch(ErrorDispatcher.java:376)
 org.apache.jasper.compiler.ErrorDispatcher.jspError(ErrorDispatcher.java:200)
 org.apache.jasper.compiler.JspUtil.checkAttributes(JspUtil.java:304)
```

Now, again modify index.jsp, located at <Tomcat Installation Directory>/webapps/ch10/ example2/index.jsp, to correct this second error.

Remove the bad attribute from the <jsp:include> directive:

```
<jsp:include page="nosuch.jsp"  />
```

Try accessing the following URL again using your browser:

```
http://localhost:8080/ch10/example2/index.jsp
```

Translation-time errors versus request-time errors

Unlike the previous error report, the resulting error report this time is quite cryptic. It is partially reproduced here:

```
org.apache.jasper.JasperException
org.apache.jasper.runtime.JspRuntimeLibrary.internalIntrospecthelper(JspRuntimeLibr
ary.java:359)
 org.apache.jasper.runtime.JspRuntimeLibrary.introspecthelper(JspRuntimeLibrary.
java:306)
 org.apache.jsp.example2.index_jsp._jspService(index_jsp.java:53)
 org.apache.jasper.runtime.HttpJspBase.service(HttpJspBase.java:94)
 javax.servlet.http.HttpServlet.service(HttpServlet.java:810)
 org.apache.jasper.servlet.JspServletWrapper.service(JspServletWrapper.java:298)
 org.apache.jasper.servlet.JspServlet.serviceJspFile(JspServlet.java:292)
```

```
org.apache.jasper.servlet.JspServlet.service(JspServlet.java:236)
javax.servlet.http.HttpServlet.service(HttpServlet.java:810)

root cause
java.lang.NullPointerException
 org.apache.jasper.runtime.JspRuntimeLibrary.internalIntrospecthelper(JspRuntime
Library.java:320)
 org.apache.jasper.runtime.JspRuntimeLibrary.introspecthelper(JspRuntimeLibrary.
java:306)
 org.apache.jsp.example2.index_jsp._jspService(index_jsp.java:53)
 org.apache.jasper.runtime.HttpJspBase.service(HttpJspBase.java:94)
 javax.servlet.http.HttpServlet.service(HttpServlet.java:810)
 org.apache.jasper.servlet.JspServletWrapper.service(JspServletWrapper
```

The main differences to note in this error report are as follows:

❑   This error is a runtime error.

❑   It has a root cause of `NullPointerException`.

The fact that this is a runtime error indicates that the translation and compilation phases have completed successfully.

> While *runtime error* is Java programming terminology, JSP developers call these
> errors *request-time errors* because they occur while JSP is processing a request.

The main thing to keep in mind is that a translation-time error occurs while the container is translating the JSP code to Java source code. A request-time error occurs when the compiled Java bytecode is executed to process an incoming request.

This request-time error is caused by the `<jsp:setProperty>` standard action:

```
<jsp:setProperty name="errobj" property="nosuch" value="This is invalid" />
```

This is a request-time error because the specified `errobj` JavaBean instance does not exist on the JSP page. The generated JSP code will search for this scoped variable during request time.

If you examine the Java code generated during the translation phase, located at `<Tomcat Installation Directory>/work/Catalina/localhost/ch10/org/apache/jsp/example2/index_jsp.java`, you can find the corresponding generated Java code:

```
out.write('\n');

org.apache.jasper.runtime.JspRuntimeLibrary.introspecthelper(_jspx_page_context.fin
dAttribute("errobj"), "nosuch", "This is invalid", null, null, false);
out.write("\r\n");
```

The highlighted code indicates where the exception occurred. Setting a property for a non-existent bean has caused the request-time error.

Handling request-time errors in JSP

While the JSP specification does not specify what a container must do for translation-time errors, it specifies two mechanisms to deal with request-time errors:

❏   Through JSTL, the `<c:catch>` action for dealing with errors to be handled within a JSP page

❏   Through an error page forwarding mechanism

Both of these mechanisms are very useful in the implementation of your own error-handling code. Writing your own error-handling code in JSP, you can detect errors and provide graceful recovery or display useful information to the end user.

Handling errors locally using the JSTL <c:catch> action

The JSTL `<c:catch>` action has the following general form:

```
<c:catch [var="...var name..."]>
  ... other JSP code that may cause request time error ...
</c:catch>
```

The only allowed attribute, if specified, is the `var` attribute.

This `<c:catch>` action will catch any errors that occur in the JSP code residing within its body. For example, consider the following JSP fragment:

```
<c:catch>
  <jsp:setProperty name="errobj" property="nosuch" value="This is invalid" />
</c:catch>
```

In this case, if the `errobj` JavaBean instance cannot be found, the `<jsp:setProperty>` will cause a request-time error to occur. This error will be caught by the `<c:catch>` action. However, the action does not do anything with the error information. When the optional `var` attribute for `<c:catch>` is not specified, the `<c:catch>` action will simply ignore the error.

If you specify the `var` attribute, it will be assigned with an object that contains information on the error that has occurred. You can then use EL to query or render properties of this object. This object is always of a type derived from `java.lang.Throwable`. You can check the Javadocs for `java.lang.Throwable` to find the properties that can be accessed. The following examples involve some of the most frequently used properties. Assuming that the `var` attribute in the `<c:catch>` phase is set to `localerr`, and that an error has occurred, consider the following EL expression:

```
${localerr}
```

This expression will display the error being caught. An error output rendered by this expression may be similar to the following:

```
org.apache.jasper.JasperException org.apache.jasper.runtime.JspRuntimeLibrary.
internalIntrospecthelper(JspRuntimeLibrary.java:359)
```

The `stackTrace` property of the object can be accessed to obtain an array of trace elements. Each element contains information on a nested call within the Java Virtual Machine stack at the time the error is detected. This trace information may be useful for automated error interpretation and recovery, or general debugging. This array can be easily handled using JSTL. For example, the following code will print out each element in the stack trace (assuming again that `localerr` contains the error object):

```
<c:forEach var="trace" items="${localerr.stackTrace}">
  <p> ${trace} </p>
</c:forEach>
```

A sample of output from this code is a detailed trace of the stack:

```
org.apache.jasper.runtime.JspRuntimeLibrary.internalIntrospecthelper(JspRuntime
Library.java:359)
org.apache.jasper.runtime.JspRuntimeLibrary.introspecthelper(JspRuntimeLibrary.
java:306)
org.apache.jsp.example3.index_jsp._jspx_meth_c_catch_0(index_jsp.java:108)
org.apache.jsp.example3.index_jsp._jspService(index_jsp.java:63)
org.apache.jasper.runtime.HttpJspBase.service(HttpJspBase.java:94)
...
```

Last but not least, you can use the `class` property of the object to determine the exact Java type of the error. This will enable you to handle each type of request-time error using different code. For example, the following JSP fragment will render the phrase bad code in HTML if a request-time error has the type `org.apache.jasper.JasperException`:

```
<c:if test="${localerr.class eq 'class org.apache.jasper.JasperException'}">
  <h2>bad code!</h2>
</c:if>
```

The `<c:catch>` action is ideal for handling errors that occur within a page when using a page-specific error treatment strategy. Using `<c:catch>`, you can provide a different way of handling errors for each page. Another error-handling mechanism that will be covered in the "Handling errors using JSP error page forwarding" section will show you how to use the same error-handling scheme for a large set of pages.

The following Try It Out exercise demonstrates how to use the `<c:catch>` JSTL action to catch and handle local errors within a JSP page.

Try It Out   **Handling Request-Time Errors Using the JSTL <c:catch> Action**

This example is contained in `ch10.war`. Make sure that your Tomcat 5 server is running and then deploy `ch10.war` to the server.

Open your browser and access the following URL:

```
http://localhost:8080/ch10/example3/index.jsp
```

The initial `index.jsp` contains a `<jsp:setProperty>` standard action that refers to a non-existent JavaBean instance. This should generate a request-time error. However, no error is reported by `index.jsp`. The screen looks similar to the one shown in Figure 10-4.

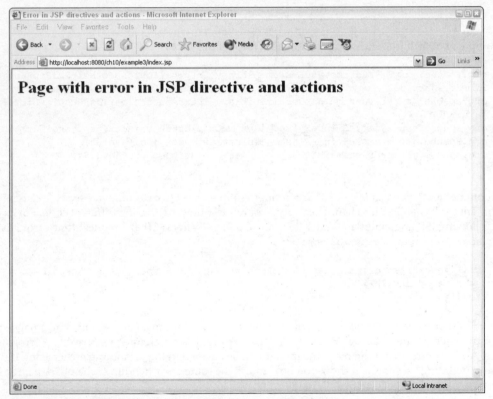

Figure 10-4: Handling errors with the JSTL `<c:catch>` action

How It Works

The `index.jsp` page in this example is coded using the JSTL `<c:catch>` action. The initial version catches the error but does not perform additional handling or processing. This has the effect of ignoring the error and stopping it from propagating beyond this page.

This `index.jsp` page is located at `<Tomcat Installation Directory>/webapps/ch10/example3/index.jsp`. The code is the same as the last modified version of the `index.jsp` from the previous Try It Out exercise. The `index.jsp` code is reproduced here with additional lines highlighted:

```
<%@ taglib prefix="c" uri="http://java.sun.com/jsp/jstl/core" %>
<%@page language="java" %>
<html>
<head>
  <title>Error in JSP directives and actions</title>
</head>
<body>
  <h1>Page with error in JSP directive and actions</h1>
  <c:catch>
    <jsp:include page="nosuch.jsp"  />
    <jsp:setProperty name="errobj" property="nosuch" value="This is invalid" />
  </c:catch>
</body>
</html>
```

Because the `<c:catch>` action is used without a `var` attribute, the error is caught but not available for further processing. As a result, no further error processing or handling is possible.

To make this code a little more useful, a `var` attribute can be added and the error information printed out. To try this, modify the `index.jsp` file (`<Tomcat Installation Directory>/webapps/ch10/example3/index.jsp`) to contain the following:

```
<c:catch var="localerr">
  <jsp:include page="nosuch.jsp"  />
  <jsp:setProperty name="errobj" property="nosuch" value="This is invalid" />
</c:catch>
${localerr}
```

Save the modified file. Try accessing the example URL again:

```
http://localhost:8080/ch10/example3/index.jsp
```

The output this time should be similar to Figure 10-5.

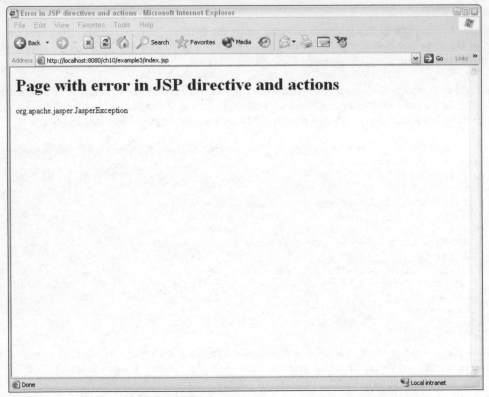

Figure 10-5: Reporting the source exception

In this case, the cause of the request-time error is rendered using the following EL expression:

```
${localerr}
```

Using the stackTrace property of the localerr object, a Java VM stack trace at the time of the error can be obtained. The EL <c:forEach> iterative action can be used to access this trace information programmatically. Modify the example to show this stack of nested method calls. Edit the index.jsp file (<Tomcat Installation Directory>/webapps/ch10/example3/index.jsp) to contain the following:

```
<c:catch var="localerr">
  <jsp:include page="nosuch.jsp"  />
  <jsp:setProperty name="errobj" property="nosuch" value="This is invalid" />
</c:catch>
<c:forEach var="trace" items="${localerr.stackTrace}">
  <p>${trace}</p>
</c:forEach>
```

Save the modified file. Try accessing the example URL again:

```
http://localhost:8080/ch10/example3/index.jsp
```

The output is similar to Figure 10-6.

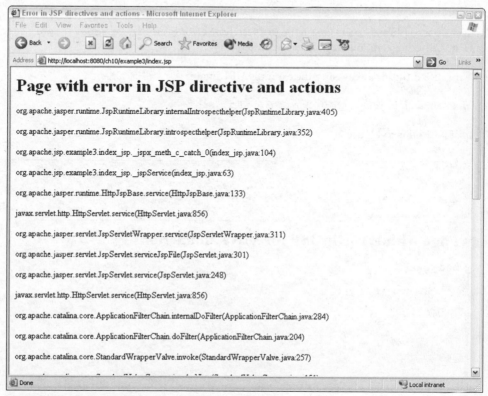

Figure 10-6: Reporting error with a trace of the stack

In Figure 10-6, the stack trace elements are iterated through using JSTL, and each element is rendered using an EL expression:

```
<c:forEach var="trace" items="${localerr.stackTrace}">
  <p>${trace}</p>
</c:forEach>
```

Finally, modify the example code to test for the type of error. Change index.jsp (<Tomcat Installation Directory>/webapps/ch10/example3/index.jsp) to contain the following:

```
<c:catch var="localerr">
  <jsp:include page="nosuch.jsp"  />
  <jsp:setProperty name="errobj" property="nosuch" value="This is invalid" />
</c:catch>
<c:if test="${localerr.class eq 'class org.apache.jasper.JasperException'}">
  <h2>bad code!</h2>
</c:if>
```

This will cause the phrase bad code! to be printed if the error is an org.apache.jasper.Jasper Exception. Otherwise, no message will be printed.

Save the modified file. Try accessing the example URL again:

```
http://localhost:8080/ch10/example3/index.jsp
```

The output is similar to Figure 10-7.

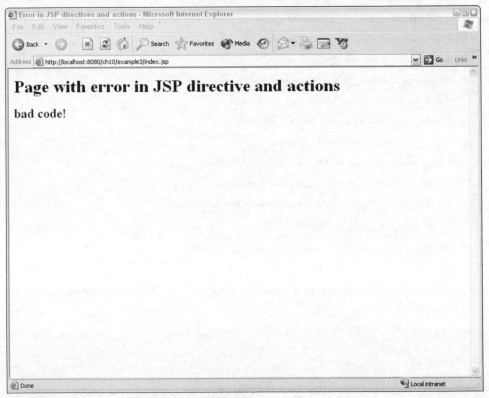

Figure 10-7: Error reporting with custom diagnosis

In Figure 10-7, the phrase bad code! is printed because the error is of type org.apache.jasper .JasperException. This technique can be used to write error-handling code that depends on a specific aspect of the detected error.

Handling errors using JSP error page forwarding

The JSP error page forwarding mechanism enables you to use a specific JSP page to handle or display errors. This provides for a more global error-handling mechanism than the JSTL `<c:catch>` action presented earlier. It also enables a large set of JSP pages to use the same JSP error page for handling the error.

Figure 10-8 illustrates the flow of the error page forwarding mechanism.

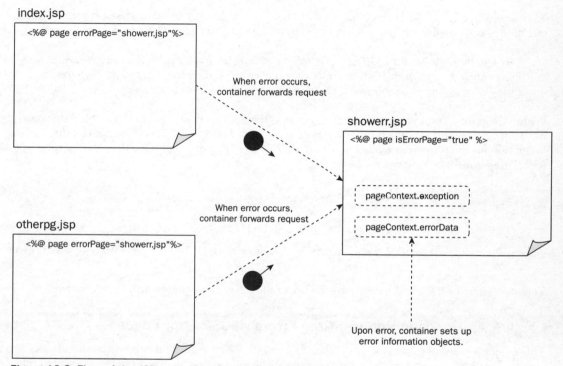

index.jsp

```
<%@ page errorPage="showerr.jsp"%>
```

When error occurs, container forwards request

showerr.jsp

```
<%@ page isErrorPage="true" %>
```

pageContext.exception

pageContext.errorData

otherpg.jsp

```
<%@ page errorPage="showerr.jsp"%>
```

When error occurs, container forwards request

Upon error, container sets up error information objects.

Figure 10-8: Flow of the JSP error page forwarding mechanism

In Figure 10-8, a JSP page can be associated with an error-handling page by specifying an `errorPage` attribute within a `<%@ page %>` directive. For example, to specify that the `showerr.jsp` page will be used for error handling, use the following code:

```
<%@page errorPage="showerr.jsp" %>
```

It is possible to create an error-handling JSP page that services many JSP pages. A JSP page is designated as an error-handling page by specifying an `isErrorPage` attribute in its `<%@page %>` directive. For example, the `showerr.jsp` error-handling page may have the following directive:

```
<%@page isErrorPage="true" %>
```

321

Also in Figure 10-8, the incoming request is forwarded from the page causing the error to the error-handling page. The container will also make information regarding the request-time error available to the error-handling page. The `pagecontext.exception` object will be available in the page for this purpose.

For example, use the following EL expression to render the error message:

```
${pagecontext.exception}
```

The `pagecontext.exception` object is a subclass of `java.lang.Throwable`. As a result, the same techniques used earlier for the `<c:catch>` JSTL coding can also be used here to decode the error.

> *Note that the error-handling JSP page will have a usable instance of the* `pagecontext.exception` *object only if it is executed (forwarded to as a result of an error on another page) by the container during error handling. If you load the page directly, this object will not be available.*

Within the error-handling page, you can also access the `pagecontext.errorData` object during error handling. This object is of the type `javax.servlet.jsp.ErrorData`. Check the JSP Javadoc API documentation for the properties available with this class. The following table describes the useful properties for writing error-handling code.

EL Expression	Description
`pageContext.errorData.status`	The HTTP status code returned by the error
`pageContext.errorData.requestURI`	The original URL of the page that caused the error

The following Try It Out exercise shows the use of the JSP error page forwarding mechanism.

Try It Out   Handling Request-Time Errors via JSP Error Pages

This example consists of two JSP pages (one to generate the error, and the other to handle it), as well as a custom JavaBean for on-demand error generation. The following table describes the associated files.

File	Description
`index.jsp`	The page that will cause an error to occur
`showerr.jsp`	The error-handling page for `index.jsp`
`ErrorGenerator.java`	The JavaBean used to generate the error at any time

This example is contained in `ch10.war`. Make sure that your Tomcat 5 server is running and that `ch10.war` is deployed.

Open your browser and access the following URL:

```
http://localhost:8080/ch10/example4/index.jsp
```

The `index.jsp` page actually has an error in it. This error is generated by an `ErrorGenerator` JavaBean. This request-time error will cause the container to forward the page to an error-handling JSP. The result is displayed as shown in Figure 10-9.

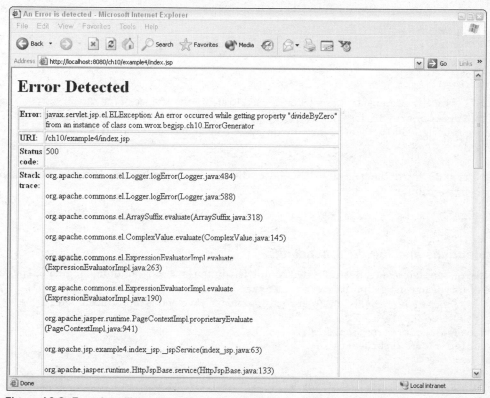

Figure 10-9: Error handling using a designated error-handling JSP page

How It Works

The `index.jsp` page in this example is code that uses `showerr.jsp` as its error page. The `showerr.jsp` error-handling page will use the `pagecontext.exception` object to print some information about the error.

This `index.jsp` is located at `<Tomcat Installation Directory>/webapps/ch10/example4/index.jsp`, and is reproduced here:

```
<%@ taglib prefix="c" uri="http://java.sun.com/jsp/jstl/core" %>
<%@page errorPage="showerr.jsp" %>
<html>
<head>
  <jsp:useBean id="errgen" class="com.wrox.begjsp.ch10.ErrorGenerator" />

  <title>Error Generating page</title>
</head>
```

```
<body>
  <h1>Page to Generate Error</h1>
  <table>
    <tr>
      <td><h3>${errgen.divideByZero}</h3></td>
    </tr>
  </table>

</body>
</html>
```

The JSTL <jsp:useBean> standard action is used to create an instance of the com.wrox.begjsp .ch10.ErrorGenerator class. The divideByZero property of this instance is then accessed. This instance is designed to generate a Java divide-by-zero arithmetic exception when the property is accessed.

Note that at the top of the page, the <%@page %> directive specifies the error-handling page using the errorPage attribute:

```
<%@page errorPage="showerr.jsp" %>
```

Java exceptions and JSP error handling

The ErrorGenerator JavaBean is coded completely in the Java programming language. The source code of this bean can be found at <Tomcat Installation Directory>/webapps/ch10/WEB-INF/ classes/com/wrox/begjsp/ch10/ErrorGenerator.java and is reproduced here:

```
package com.wrox.begjsp.ch10;
public class ErrorGenerator
{

    private Integer[] tpArray = new Integer[3];

    public ErrorGenerator()
    {
    }

    public String getOutOfRange()
    {
        tpArray[3] = tpArray[2];
        return "";
    }
    public String getDivideByZero()
    {
        tpArray[3] = new Integer(1/0);
        return "";
    }
}
```

Both the getOutOfRange() and getDivideByZero() method return an empty string, "". In addition, they will cause a runtime error to occur in the Java code. The getOutOfrange() method will generate a common "array index out of range" runtime exception. The getDivideByZero() method will generate a divide-by-zero arithmetic exception at runtime. These methods are designed to be accessed as properties of the bean, facilitating their usage from JSP and EL.

Note that the errors generated here are Java runtime exceptions. One is java.lang.ArrayIndexOutOfBoundsException, and the other one is java.lang.ArithmeticException. Because these exceptions are not caught within the JavaBean itself, they are propagated to the JSP execution environment provided by the container. The container ensures that the JSP error-handling mechanism will see these exceptions.

Therefore, at request time, any unhandled exceptions from JavaBeans, custom Java coding, or scriptlets are propagated to the enclosing JSP for error handling. This very intimate relationship ties the compiled Java code with the JSP code.

Accessing error information in an error-handling page

The showerr.jsp page is located at <Tomcat Installation Directory>/webapps/ch10/example4/showerr.jsp.

This page is used for error handling. The container will make a pagecontext.exception object and a pagecontext.errorData object available. The incoming request is also routed to this error-handling JSP, enabling it to access properties and attributes of the incoming requests. The code of showerr.jsp is reproduced here:

```
<%@ taglib prefix="c" uri="http://java.sun.com/jsp/jstl/core" %>
<%@page isErrorPage="true" %>

<html>
<head>
  <title>An Error is detected</title>
</head>
<body>
  <h1>Error Detected</h1>
  <table width="600" border="1">

    <tr valign="top">
      <td width="250"><b>Error:</b></td>
      <td>${pageContext.exception}</td>
    </tr>

    <tr valign="top">
      <td><b>URI:</b></td>
      <td>${pageContext.errorData.requestURI}</td>
    </tr>

    <tr valign="top">
      <td><b>Status code:</b></td>
      <td>${pageContext.errorData.statusCode}</td>
    </tr>
```

```
    <tr valign="top">
      <td><b>Stack trace:</b></td>

      <td>
        <c:forEach var="trace" items="${pageContext.exception.stackTrace}">
          <p>${trace}</p>
        </c:forEach>
      </td>
    </tr>
  </table>
</body>
</html>
```

In the preceding code, the error itself is rendered using the following EL expression:

```
<td>${pageContext.exception}</td>
```

The other object that is available is `pageContext.errorData`, and it can be used to obtain the incoming URI that contains the error:

```
<td>${pageContext.errorData.requestURI}</td>
```

The `pageContext.errorData` object is also used to render the HTTP status code that is returned to the browser:

```
<td>${pageContext.errorData.statusCode}</td>
```

The stack trace is accessed via the `stackTrace` property of the `pageContext.exception` object. This object is a subclass of `java.lang.Throwable`. This is the same technique used in the third Try It Out exercise in this chapter:

```
<c:forEach var="trace" items="${pageContext.exception.stackTrace}">
    <p>${trace}</p>
</c:forEach>
```

Continuing the exploration of the different types of errors that can occur with JSP programming, the following section briefly examines JSTL errors and EL errors.

JSTL errors and EL errors

JSTL tags are custom actions and will generate code during the translation phase. This means that JSTL coding syntax errors will be detected at translation time. Like JSP standard actions, JSTL actions work with dynamic parameters and attribute values. This means JSTL actions are also subjected to request-time errors. Any request-time error from JSTL can also be caught and handled using the JSP error-handling mechanism described in the preceding sections.

EL expressions are code that is evaluated only at request time. This means that any EL-originated error is request-time in nature. These errors can also be caught and handled using the JSP error-handling mechanisms described in the preceding sections.

Note that when an error occurs within an EL expression, the type of error object is always `javax.servlet.jsp.el.ELException`. To get the underlying cause, you should access the `rootCause` property of this object. The property can be accessed using the following EL expression: `pageContext.exception.rootCause`.

User data-input errors

Data-input errors cannot be detected by the JSP container. In most cases, they are dependent on the logic of the application itself. For example, a user being asked to enter a bid for an auction may only be allowed to enter a numeric value between 1 and 100.

To enforce this range of input values, the code to check the input must be implemented as part of the JSP logic. This checking is called *input validation*.

In Chapter 9, "JSP and JavaBeans," the bidding example implements data validation for the bid input. Instead of using the JSP error-handling mechanism, the application logic sends the bid information to the data entry screen, informing the user that his or her input is out of the allowable range.

Errors found in JSP template data

The most typical template data within JSP pages is HTML. Errors in HTML, or any other template data, are not detected by the container. Because the container cannot detect the errors, JSP-based error-handling mechanisms cannot be used for these errors.

In fact, these errors will be evident only during the rendering phase on the client. However, any error in the rendered template data can adversely affect the user experience. For example, if badly formed, the HTML page may be completely unusable when rendered on a browser.

This again reinforces the importance of testing when developing JSP-based applications.

In all of the examples in this chapter, application error details and stack traces are displayed using the error-handling page(s). This is very useful in the development and debugging phase of a project. When a well-designed project goes into production, request-time errors should not occur. In the unlikely case that they do occur, the error should be handled gracefully. For example, provide more information and ask the user to retry at a later time, or show a page with a support phone number for the user to call. In either case, the Web application should log enough information about the error to enable developers to debug and fix the problem. More on debugging and logging from Web applications is covered in Chapter 14, "JSP Debugging Techniques."

This completes the discussion of the final Try It Out exercise and error-handling in general using JSP.

Summary

Errors can occur at any time during application development. With JSP development, they can also be caused by coding mistakes in any of its components. The iterative act of coding, testing, and debugging in application development should eliminate all syntax errors before deployment. Other errors include the following:

❑ Translation-time errors occur when the JSP code is translated to Java by the container, or when the generated code is compiled into executable bytecode.

❑ Request-time errors occur during the processing of the request when the compiled JSP code is executed.

❑ User data-input errors are logical errors specific to the requirements of an application. These errors are detected and presented to the user for correction using application logic code.

❑ Errors in template data cannot be detected by the container, and can only be corrected through vigorous testing.

The following points concerning handling errors in JSP were discussed:

❑ Translation-error presentation and handling is container-dependent. The Tomcat 5 server typically reports an HTTP 500 – internal server error, and provides an error report that can help track down the source of the error.

❑ JSTL's `<c:catch>` action can be used to handle request-time errors, and it is possible to catch errors within a JSP page and process them locally.

❑ The `errorPage` and `isErrorPage` attributes of the `<%@page %>` directive can also handle request-time errors. They can be used to specify JSP pages for handling errors. An error occurring within a JSP will cause the request to be forwarded to the associated error page.

❑ The exception mechanism in the Java programming language is intimately tied to JSP error handling. Exceptions that are thrown in Java coding, such as JavaBeans and scriptlets, are passed to the JSP error-handling mechanism by the container.

Exercises

1. The `ErrorGenerator` JavaBean in the fourth Try It Out exercise can be used to generate two different types of Java runtime exceptions. These exceptions are propagated by the container and can be handled using the JSP error-handling mechanism.

Modify `index.jsp` from this example to use the JSTL `<c:catch>` mechanism instead of error pages. Add code to check for the type of error. If it is an "array out of range" error, print the message "Fix array index!" If it is a divide-by-zero error, print the message "Do not divide by zero!"

Test your code against both types of errors.

2. Modify the `index.jsp` in example 3 to use an error-handling JSP page instead of the JSTL `<c:catch>` action. Name the error-handling page `disperr.jsp`. Within `disperr.jsp`, make sure you print out the error (the actual root cause), the status code, and the URI of the original request.

Building Your Own Custom JSP Tag Library

JSP tag libraries were introduced in JSP 2.0. Before that, custom tag development was the domain of experienced Java developers. Custom JSP tags can now be developed to encapsulate pieces of repeatable JSP code without the need to program in Java.

This chapter introduces custom tags (also referred to as *custom actions*) developed as text files, explains their semantics, and provides some examples along the way that illustrate what an extremely powerful addition they are to the J2EE architecture. The chapter concludes with a short discussion about how you decide when to use Java custom tags and JSP custom tags.

Specifically, this chapter covers the following areas:

- ❏ Creating a simple JSP tag file
- ❏ Understanding the advantages of tag files
- ❏ Developing tag files
- ❏ Packaging tag files

What Is a Tag File?

A tag file is a special kind of custom action that is developed much like a JSP page. Unlike JSP pages, tag files can be invoked from within JSP pages in the same way Java Standard Tag Library (JSTL) tags are used. Tag files, for instance, can be passed parameters to use, and they can expose values to the calling JSP page, and invoke fragments of JSP code.

A developer implements a tag file using a text file and places it within a special directory of the Web application. From there, its invocation and usages are much like any other custom tag an application may use.

In contrast, custom tags have usually been developed using Java classes that comply with a set of interfaces that the servlet container recognizes. Java custom tags are also accompanied by a Tag Library Descriptor (TLD) file that informs the container of how the tag behaves and should be invoked. This form of custom tag caters to complex scenarios, as its internal logic can be implemented using Java. For instance, a Java custom tag might be used to produce a paged and formatted table using a collection of objects. More simple tasks can be undertaken with tags developed as tag files, the subject of this chapter.

A Simple Tag File: Displaying Today's Date

To give you some context for understanding this chapter, we are going to begin with a simple demonstration of how a tag file is created and invoked in a JSP page; call it the "Hello World" of tag files.

The tag demonstrated here will display a message and the current date in the format day/month/year. Its output will look something like the following:

```
Today's date is: 9 / 5 / 2005
```

The JSP page that invokes the tag file will appear as follows:

```
<%@ taglib prefix="beginjsp" tagdir="/WEB-INF/tags" %>

<beginjsp:todaysdate/>
```

First, the taglib JSP directive is used to define the tags that will be used on this page. In this case, the prefix used is beginjsp. The taglib directive also identifies the folder in which the tag files can be found: /WEB-ING/tags, using the tagdir attribute. For instance, if your application were on your computer as C:\mywebsite\, the tagdir attribute used above would be the directory located at C:\mywebsite\WEB-INF\tags.

The invocation of the tag is like any other custom tag invocation you have seen throughout this book: <beginjsp:todaysdate/>.

To create the tag itself, a file called todaysdate.tag is placed in the /WEB-INF/tags folder of the Web application. All tag files must be placed in this directory or a directory below it. The content of todaysdate.tag is as follows:

```
<%@ tag body-content="empty" %>
<jsp:useBean id="today" scope="page" class="java.util.Date"/>
Today's date is: ${today.date} / ${today.month} / ${today.year + 1900}
```

As you can see, the content of the tag file is very simple. The tag directive is first defined in order to declare some properties of the tag. Various attributes can be used in this directive, but for this example only the body-content attribute is required. This and other attributes are defined later in this chapter.

After the tag directive, the logic of the tag itself begins. jsp:useBean is used to define a new instance of the java.util.Date object. By default, this native Java object is instantiated with the current system date. Perfect for our purposes!

The output is then prepared in the tag file to display the properties of the Date object. For this we have used Expression Language (EL) to access the getDate() (today.date), getMonth() (today.month), and getYear() (today.year) methods. You saw examples of this in Chapter 9. The todaysdate action can now be used throughout the application wherever the output of the current date is needed. This example shows the simplicity with which tag files can be created and invoked.

Behind the scenes, the tag file is converted by the servlet container (for instance, Tomcat) into a more useable form. Tomcat converts the tag file into a Java source file, and then compiles it, much as it would a normal JSP page.

Advantages of Tag Files

The advantages of using tags, in general, over alternative methods are obvious. Generally, these advantages apply as much for normal Java-developed custom tags as they do for tag files. Briefly, the advantages are as follows:

- ❑ Code reuse
- ❑ Hiding complexity
- ❑ Separation of concerns
- ❑ Simplicity
- ❑ Flexible packaging

Code reuse

The example in the preceding section illustrated the simplicity with which JSP code can be encapsulated and used in many parts of an application. This is code reuse. However, sometimes it is not that easy to ensure that a piece of code is reusable. Simple scenarios, like printing content or individual values, are easy to achieve, but it may be more difficult to make a complicated tag generic enough for the entire application to use. A good rule of thumb might be that if what you are trying to encapsulate is very complicated, perhaps a tag file is not an ideal solution. Nevertheless, tag files can be designed to cater to generalized situations that occur more than once in a Web application. For instance, formatting output is an excellent example of the type of code reuse provided by tag files.

Hiding complexity

Custom tags, of all types, are excellent tools to hide complexity away from the view components of an application. Mixing Java scriptlets with HTML can result in some fairly ugly and highly complicated pages. If properly designed, such HTML generation can be moved to a tag file, to hide the complexity and make the application more modular.

Separation of concerns

Separation of concerns is a principle of application design that states that structures should be as independent of other structures in an application as possible. This ensures that they are *decoupled* from other things. Decoupling ensures that a change in one part of an application has little or no effect on other parts of the application.

In the context of tag files, this principle is especially applicable. If a tag file deals with an individual function such as formatting text or generating an HTML table given a generic set of attributes, it is far less likely to require changes should the invoking JSP files change. In this way, the tag file "does one thing and does it well."

Simplicity

The implementation of custom tag files is generally a simple process, depending on how complicated the file needs to be. This simplicity means that non-Java programmers can implement reusable functionality within an application. This sophisticated concept is now accessible by more and more people involved in making Web applications.

The importance of the addition of tag files to the JSP specification cannot be understated. They effectively place within the grasp of non-Java programmers a powerful tool that does not compromise the relatively simple implementation that should accompany display-level development. Introducing this further level of separation within the display layer of J2EE applications will hopefully enhance their maintainability and provide more robust applications as a result.

Flexible packaging

Custom actions developed as tag files are simple to deploy either within the file system or as a packaged JAR file, much like custom actions developed in Java. This makes the transition from one method to the other less of a headache, as its effect on other parts of an application is minimal, if present at all.

Developing Tag Files

Now that you understand the importance of tag files and have seen a simple example showing the place they take within JSP development, this chapter will discuss the semantics of implementing custom actions using tag files.

Scope and implicit objects

It is important to have an understanding of the scope that tag files, and the values used by them, have within the application.

JSP files and the tag files they invoke share the `application`, `session`, and `request` scopes, while each has their own `page` scope. In an encapsulation sense, `application`, `session`, and `request` scopes provide global variables, common to both the tag and the JSP file, and the `page` scope provides only local variables to each. The `page` scope variables of the JSP page cannot be used inside the tag file, and vice versa.

To illustrate this important point, the following example uses a JSP page to set some variables in all four scopes. These variables will be displayed from the JSP page. Then a simple tag will create a `page` scope variable of the same name as the JSP `page` scope variable and display it and the variables in the other scopes. The `session` scoped variable will then be changed from within the tag. The JSP page will then display all four variables again showing that the `page` scope variable contains the same value it contained before the tag was invoked, and that the `session` scope variable changed.

Therefore, the JSP page to construct this chain of events is as follows:

```
<%@ taglib prefix="beginjsp" tagdir="/WEB-INF/tags" %>
<%@ taglib prefix="c" uri="http://java.sun.com/jsp/jstl/core" %>

<c:set var="appVar" value="this is an application variable" scope="application"/>
<c:set var="sessVar" value="this is a session variable" scope="session"/>
<c:set var="rVar" value="this is a request variable" scope="request"/>
<c:set var="pVar" value="this is a page variable set in the JSP" scope="page"/>

<b>Calling in the JSP page:</b>
<p>
Application: ${applicationScope.appVar}<br>
Session: ${sessionScope.sessVar}<br>
Request: ${requestScope.rVar}<br>
Page: ${pageScope.pVar}
<p>

<beginjsp:scope/>

<p>
<b>Calling in the JSP page after the tag:</b>
<p>
Application: ${applicationScope.appVar}<br>
Session: ${sessionScope.sessVar}<br>
Request: ${requestScope.rVar}<br>
Page: ${pageScope.pVar}
```

The `scope.tag` file contains code to create its own `page` scope variable (`pVar`) and display all variables. It will then change the `session` scope variable `sessVar`:

```
<%@ tag body-content="empty" %>

<%@ taglib prefix="c" uri="http://java.sun.com/jsp/jstl/core" %>

<c:set var="pVar" value="this is a page variable set in the Tag File"
       scope="page"/>

<b>Calling in the Tag File:</b>
<p>
Application: ${applicationScope.appVar}<br>
Session: ${sessionScope.sessVar}<br>
Request: ${requestScope.rVar}<br>
Page: ${pageScope.pVar}

<c:set var="sessVar" value="this is a changed session variable" scope="session"/>
```

The effect of this example is to show the `page` scope variable in the JSP page *not* changing as a result of the tag file implementing a variable of the same name and scope, whereas the `session` scope variable has changed. Figure 11-1 shows the output in a browser.

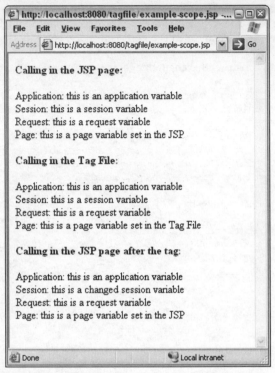

Figure 11-1: Scope changes between JSP and custom actions

Note the inherent danger in using global variables (`application`, `session`, `request`) inside the tag file. Doing so tightly couples the tag file with the application and the existence of that variable. As you will see later in the chapter, certain tag file directives can be used to pass values to and from the tag file and the JSP page.

Within a tag file, as in a JSP page, certain objects are implicitly available for use. The most commonly used objects are defined in the following table.

Implicit Object	Description
request	Represents the request from the client invoking the JSP page in its browser (`javax.servlet.http.HttpServletRequest`)
response	Represents the response being prepared for the user's browser (`javax.servlet.http.HttpServletResponse`)
session	Represents the user session that invoked the request for this JSP page (`javax.servlet.http.HttpSession`)
out	An instance of `JspWriter` allowing output to be written to the response
jspContext	An object representing the `JspContext` of the calling JSP page

Therefore, within a tag file, the `out` implicit object can be invoked as follows:

```
<%@ tag body-content="empty" %>
<jsp:useBean id="today" scope="page" class="java.util.Date"/>
<%
    out.println("Today's date is: "
        + today.getDate() + "/"
        + today.getMonth() + "/"
        + (today.getYear() + 1900));
%>
```

Other implicit objects include `config` and `application`.

Using directives in tag files

A number of directives can be used within JSP tag files, such as `tag`, `taglib`, `include`, `attribute`, and `variable`.

As in normal JSP files, directives are included to affect the overall processing of the page being constructed. You have already seen the `tag` directive being used in a preceding example. You will notice that some of the directives explained here are used in standard JSP pages; others, such as `attribute` and `variable`, can only be used within tag file custom actions. The following sections describe the directives for tag files, with appropriate examples for each.

tag

The `tag` directive plays a similar role to the `page` directive used in normal JSP pages. It handles a number of useful attributes that affect the processing and presentation of the tag file generally, and how it is used in a JSP file. Its usage is shown here:

```
<%@ tag body-content="empty" import="java.util.ArrayList" %>
```

The attributes in the following table apply to the `tag` directive.

Attribute	Description
body-content	Indicates the nature of the body of the tag when it is invoked. Values here can be `empty`, `tagdependent`, or `scriptless`. This attribute is optional. The default is `scriptless`.
description	An optional description for the tag.
display-name	An optional simple name for the tag. May be used by IDE or XML tools. The default value is the name of the file without the `.tag` extension.
example	A simple illustration of how the tag functions.
import	An optional attribute used to import packages or classes into the scope of the tag.

Table continued on following page

Attribute	Description
isElIgnored	Indicates that Expression Language (EL) expressions will be ignored. The default is false.
language	The scripting language used in the tag. The default is the only available option: Java.
large-icon	Optional attribute that can be used to relate an image file with the tag.
pageEncoding	The character encoding for this file. IANA encoding names must be used.
small-icon	Optional attribute used to relate an image file with the tag.
dynamic-attributes	Indicates that dynamic attributes can be passed to this tag, and the value of this attribute names a page scope Map object where their name and value pairs are stored. This attribute is explained in more detail later in the chapter.

The body-content attribute indicates if the tag, when invoked, will contain body content, and if so, what type. This attribute can be used to enforce a certain usage in this sense. For instance, empty means that the tag must not have a body, and would therefore be of the following form:

```
<beginjsp:sometagname />
```

and not:

```
<beginjsp:sometagname>
</beginjsp:sometagname>
```

The preceding code would cause an exception. A value of scriptless indicates that the tag should not contain any Java code, but you can use standard and custom actions within the body. With a value of tagdependent, the body content is treated as plain text.

taglib

A tag file can also make use of the taglib directive in order to make use of other custom actions. This is extremely useful where you need to use JSTL custom tags within a tag file. You can see the taglib directive used in many places throughout this book where JSTL tags are used.

The use here is no different. To illustrate, the following tag file makes use of a tag file developed earlier in this chapter to display today's date: todaysdate.tag.

This new tag file is called taglibuser.tag and has the following content:

```
<%@ tag body-content="empty" %>
<%@ taglib prefix="beginjsp" tagdir="/WEB-INF/tags" %>

<beginjsp:todaysdate/>
```

As you can see, the `taglib` directive is used to give a `prefix` to the collection of tags within the `/WEB-INF/tags` directory, specifically for the `todaysdate` tag. The JSP page to invoke `taglibuser.tag` is as follows:

```
<%@ taglib prefix="beginjsp" tagdir="/WEB-INF/tags" %>
<beginjsp:taglibuser/>
```

The result of this is to simply display the current date in the browser, as shown in Figure 11-2.

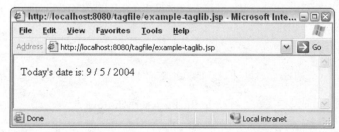

Figure 11-2: Using a custom action within a custom action using the `taglib` directive

include

The `include` directive works in much the same way as the `include` directive in a normal JSP file. It is used to include static and dynamic content. For instance, within a tag file, the `include` directive could be used to include the content from an HTML file, or the dynamic result of a tag file fragment.

For example, if a tag file (`includeresources.tag`) were to include the result of an HTML page (`includeme.html`) and a tag file fragment (`includedmetoo.tagf` — note the recommended `.tagf` extension for tag fragments), it would appear as follows:

```
<%@ tag body-content="empty" %>

<%@ include file="/includeme.html" %>
<P>
<%@ include file="/WEB-INF/tagf/includedmetoo.tagf" %>
```

Each of these files would be included in turn and represent the output of the tag file. The tag file fragment, `includedresource.tagf`, is treated as a segment of the tag file; it can therefore include any part of the tag file as long as the result of the tag file itself and its fragments make up a legitimate tag file. For instance, tag file fragments can also use the `include` directive to include other fragments, and so on.

attribute

The `attribute` directive allows tag files to be passed values from the invoking JSP page. This gives real power to the use of tag files, as it does to other custom actions. When a tag file uses the `attribute` directive, JSP pages can pass values through to the tag file for processing. A simple "hello, world" example here can illustrate the basic use of the `attribute` directive.

The following code represents the content of a new tag file called `printstring.tag`. As the name suggests, this tag file will simply print the value of the attribute it has been passed:

```
<%@ tag body-content="empty" %>
<%@ taglib prefix="c" uri="http://java.sun.com/jsp/jstl/core" %>

<%@ attribute name="value" required="true"%>
<c:out value="${value}"/>
```

The third line of this tag file makes use of the `attribute` directive to force invoking JSP files to pass a value in an attribute named `value`. An invoking JSP file may appear as follows:

```
<%@ taglib prefix="beginjsp" tagdir="/WEB-INF/tags" %>

<beginjsp:printstring value="hi there"/>
```

This will output the message `"hi there"` in the browser window.

The `attribute` directive can use several attributes. For instance, in the preceding example the `required` attribute was used to enforce the use of the `value` attribute in the invoking JSP page; therefore, if the `printstring` tag was invoked with just `<beginjsp:printstring/>`, an exception would be thrown, informing the developer that the `value` attribute is required. The default for the `required` attribute is `false`.

The following table explains the other attributes that can be used with the `attribute` directive.

Attribute	Description
description	A description of the attribute for this tag file. This attribute is optional.
fragment	This attribute indicates whether the attribute being passed is a fragment attribute (`true`). Fragment attributes are explained later in the chapter. The default value of this optional attribute is `false`.
name	The name that the value this attribute represents will take within the tag file's scope. Within the tag file, the value of this attribute is referred to by this name. It must be unique. This value also forms the name of the tag attribute that will provide the value to the tag file when it is called in the JSP page. This attribute is required.
required	Indicates that the attribute is required (`true`) when the custom action is being invoked in the JSP page. The default value of this optional attribute is `false`.
rtexprvalue	Whether real-time expressions are available for this attribute, the default is `true`. This attribute is optional.
type	The type of the attribute that is being passed. The value of this attribute is a fully qualified class name. The default is `java.lang.String`. This attribute is optional.

variable

The `variable` directive is used to expose values of the tag file to the calling JSP page. This of course becomes extremely useful when the result of a tag file is not to be simply displayed, as it might be in a simple formatting tag. Think of the `variable` directive as similar to a value being returned from the tag file, much like a value is returned from a normal Java method. The attributes for this directive are described in the following table.

Attribute	Description
description	A simple description of the variable. This attribute is optional.
name-given or name-from-attribute	One of these tags must be used in the variable directive, but they cannot be used together. The `name-given` attribute gives the returning value a name that the calling JSP page can use when referencing it. The `name-from-attribute` attribute also gives the returning value a name the calling JSP page can use when referencing it, but the name is that of an attribute for this custom action.
alias	Used in conjunction with the `name-from-attribute` attribute to synchronize names used between a tag file and a JSP page. The alias forms the tag's name for the variable, as opposed to the name provided by the attribute in `name-from-attribute`. This attribute is required when `name-from-attribute` is used.
variable-class	The class name of the variable being returned. This attribute is optional and its default value is `java.lang.String`.
declare	A message to the container to declare the returning value in the JSP page. The default is `true`. This attribute is optional.
scope	The scope of the returning variable, with respect to the tag itself. Values here are `AT_BEGIN`, `NESTED`, and `AT_END`. The default is `NESTED`. This attribute is optional.

To illustrate the simplest example of this directive in action, a String will be created in a tag file and displayed on the calling JSP page. The calling JSP page will use the variable name given by the tag file to display its value.

The tag file `returnvalue.tag` contains the following:

```
<%@ tag body-content="empty" %>
<%@ taglib prefix="c" uri="http://java.sun.com/jsp/jstl/core" %>
<%@ variable name-given="foo" scope="AT_END"%>

<c:set var="foo" value="this is from the tag"/>
```

The `variable` directive here defines the variable that will be provided to the calling JSP page. This variable, `foo`, will be available to the JSP page after the tag has been executed due to the `scope` attribute value of `AT_END`. This is not scope in the sense that you are probably used to (`application`, `session`, `request`, and `page`). The scope value here refers to the scope of the variable with respect to the tag itself and its invocation on the calling JSP page. This is explained at the end of this section.

The variable `foo` is then declared and assigned a value using the JSTL `c:set` tag. By default, variables created with the `c:set` tag are placed in the `page` scope. As the `variable` directive has been used here, and the `declare` attribute has been left as `true` (the default), the container has declared a variable named `foo` in the `page` scope of the JSP page, *returning it*, so to speak. It would perhaps be more accurate to say that the tag file has in fact *exported* the variable to the scope of the JSP page. The JSP page can then print out this value using the following:

```
<%@ taglib prefix="beginjsp" tagdir="/WEB-INF/tags" %>

<beginjsp:returnvalue/>

This is the value of foo:${pageScope.foo}
```

This would output the following message in the browser:

```
This is the value of foo: this is from the tag
```

Variable scope

As mentioned earlier, the `scope` attribute of the `variable` directive denotes the scope of the variable value with respect to the invocation of the tag file on the calling JSP page. This is sometimes referred to as the *synchronization* of variables between the tag file and its calling JSP page.

Its potential values are as follows:

❑ **AT_BEGIN:** The variable is available as soon as the tag has been invoked; therefore, for a tag with a body, this could mean within the body of the tag. The variable will also be available after the tag invocation.

❑ **NESTED:** The variable is available only between the opening and closing lines of the tag invocation, not after the tag has been invoked.

❑ **AT_END:** The variable is available only after the tag has been invoked.

As an example, consider a random-number generator tag. This tag returns a variable named `randomNumber` and will be used to illustrate different values of the `scope` attribute and their effect on where this variable can be referenced.

The variable is declared in the `randomnumber` tag with a scope of `AT_BEGIN`:

```
<%@ variable name-given="randomNumber" variable-class="java.lang.Integer"
            scope="AT_BEGIN"%>
```

The value of `randomNumber` can be referenced as soon as the first line of the tag has been called, within the body of the tag and after the tag has been completed:

```
<beginjsp:randomnumber>
    AT_BEGIN:${randomNumber}
</beginjsp:randomnumber>
 after tag:{$randomNumber}
```

Here, the variable is declared in the `randomnumber` tag with a scope of `NESTED`:

```
<%@ variable name-given="randomNumber" variable-class="java.lang.Integer"
             scope="NESTED"%>
```

The value of `randomNumber` can be referenced only within the opening and closing lines of the tag:

```
<beginjsp:randomnumber>
    NESTED:${randomNumber}
</beginjsp:randomnumber>
```

Next, the variable is declared in the `randomnumber` tag with a scope of `AT_END`:

```
<%@ variable name-given="randomNumber" variable-class="java.lang.Integer"
             scope="AT END"%>
```

The value of `randomNumber` can be referenced only after the tag has been invoked:

```
<beginjsp:randomnumber/>
AT_END: ${randomNumber}
```

Which scope you decide to use will depend largely on how you intend the tag to be used.

Body processing

In most of the examples in this chapter so far, the `tag` directive has forbidden tag body content (by using a value of `empty`). For instance, given the `returnvalue` tag file in the previous section, with a body-content value of `empty`, we could not do the following:

```
<beginjsp:returnvalue>
    there is no spoon.
</beginjsp:returnvalue>
```

Doing so would cause an exception to be thrown when the servlet container attempts to process the JSP page because the tag invocation contains a body. This section illustrates how content that is placed in the body of a tag can be processed.

Conveniently, a handy action is available that can be used only inside a tag file. This action allows the body content of the tag's invocation to be accessed. Therefore, we could get the value `there is no spoon` from the preceding example and process it in some way inside the tag. We can do this using the `jsp:doBody` action.

jsp:doBody

The `jsp:doBody` action evaluates the body of a tag for all values of the `body-content` attribute in the tag directive. Therefore, a value of `empty` wouldn't evaluate much, whereas a value of `scriptless` (the default) would process the standard, custom actions and plain text that was found.

The output of this processing can be simply output to the calling page or assigned to a variable using the `var` or `varReader` attributes of the `jsp:doBody` action. The `var` and `varReader` attributes merely create a different type of object when assigning the variable to the tag body's output. `var` creates a `java.lang.String` object, whereas `varReader` creates a `java.io.Reader` object for processing results that are generally considered large. `var` will suffice in almost all cases.

In the following Try It Out example, we will develop a custom tag to make use of the `jsp:doBody` standard action in processing the body of a tag.

Try It Out   Developing a Custom Tag with the jsp:doBody Standard Action

This exercise creates a tag that searches through the text placed in the body of the tag and allows only certain known HTML elements to be rendered correctly. We will allow only bold (`<b></b>`) and italic (`<i></i>`) HTML elements to be rendered; everything else will be disabled and just rendered as it appears. Therefore, if the tag invocation contains

```
<beginjsp:cleanhtml>
    <img src="/images/someimage.gif">
</beginjsp:cleanhtml>
```

it will display:

<img src="/images/someimage.gif">

rather than rendering the image at that location. But

```
<b>This is in bold</b>
```

would display as

This is in bold

We achieve this by replacing every < character with `&lt;`, the character code for that character. When a browser comes across this, it will simply display the < character instead of performing whatever the HTML tag would do. The same will apply for > characters, which will be replaced with `&gt;` characters. The JSTL function `escapeXML` performs all this for us.

We will then replace all instances of `&lt;b&gt;` with `<b>` and all instances of `&lt;i&gt;` with `<i>`. To close these tags, instances of `&lt;/b&gt;` will be replaced with `</b>`, and instances of `&lt;/i&gt;` will be replaced with `</i>`. All this logic will be implemented in the tag file.

We start off the tag by creating a `cleanhtml.tag` file in the `/WEB-INF/tags` directory of the Web application. We don't need any attributes or variable directives for this tag, as the only input will be the body of the tag itself. Therefore, the tag will begin with the `tag` directive, indicating that the body content is to be `scriptless`, and two `taglib` directives to provide the required standard tag libraries:

```
<%@ tag body-content="scriptless" %>
<%@ taglib prefix="c" uri="http://java.sun.com/jsp/jstl/core" %>
<%@ taglib prefix="fn" uri="http://java.sun.com/jsp/jstl/functions" %>
```

We now need to assign the body of the tag to a `page` scope variable (only to the `page` scope of the tag, though), so enter the following code:

```
<jsp:doBody var="content" scope="page"/>
```

The `page` scope variable `content` now contains the body that has been placed in the body of the tag invocation. Standard JSTL actions will now be used to parse this variable and produce a String that has had all HTML disabled, except the bold and italic HTML tags:

```
<c:set var="content" value="${fn:escapeXml(content)}"/>

<c:set var="enabledSomeHTML"
       value="${fn:replace(content, '&lt;b&gt;','<b>')}"/>
<c:set var="enabledSomeHTML"
       value="${fn:replace(enabledSomeHTML, '&lt;/b&gt;','</b>')}"/>

<c:set var="enabledSomeHTML"
       value="${fn:replace(enabledSomeHTML, '&lt;i&gt;','<i>')}"/>
<c:set var="enabledSomeHTML"
       value="${fn:replace(enabledSomeHTML, '&lt;/i&gt;','</i>')}"/>
```

The result of this processing is a variable named `enabledSomeHTML` that can be simply output to the screen with the following:

```
${enabledSomeHTML}
```

To illustrate the use of this tag, the following JSP page will display the result of this tag's processing:

```
<%@ page contentType="text/html" %>
<%@ taglib prefix="beginjsp" tagdir="/WEB-INF/tags" %>

<html>
<head>
<title>beginjsp:cleanhtml example</title>
</head>
<body>

<beginjsp:cleanhtml>
    <b>This is bold</b>
</beginjsp:cleanhtml>
<p>
<beginjsp:cleanhtml>
```

```
        <i>This is italic</i>
</beginjsp:cleanhtml>
<p>
<beginjsp:cleanhtml>
    <img src="/images/someimage.gif">
</beginjsp:cleanhtml>

</body>
</html>
```

The output of this JSP page in the browser would therefore be displayed as desired, as shown in Figure 11-3.

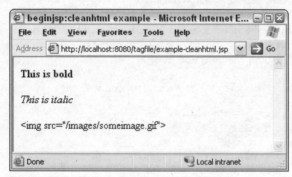

Figure 11-3: Output of the `cleanhtml` **tag**

As we told the `tag` directive in the tag that the body content was to be `scriptless`, the tag could also be invoked with the following, using EL in the body:

```
<c:set var="unclean"
       value="<font face=verdana>This is in verdana</font>"
       scope="page"/>

<beginjsp:cleanhtml>
    ${unclean}
</beginjsp:cleanhtml>
```

How It Works

The example described in the preceding section shows how a tag file can be used to format content to suit the requirements of the view layer of the application. The tag that was created receives some text and disables the HTML content it may contain. Certain HTML tags are then enabled in the text — specifically, the bold tag and the italic tag. This simple yet effective task was achieved using the `fn:escapeXML` and `fn:replace` JSTL functions.

What results from the processing within the custom tag file is specially formatted output to the browser. All HTML tags, except the bold and italic tags, are rendered as their source code, rather than the Web site visitor's browser interpreting them and producing formatted output.

Attributes

Attributes enable values to be passed to custom actions to be used in processing. A simple example earlier in the chapter printed a message to the screen through a tag file. That example used a simple `String` object to illustrate this concept. This section will build on that example, providing more complex examples using some of the more advanced features of attributes with custom tag files.

Simple attributes revisited

To illustrate the use of more complex objects used as attributes to custom actions, the following Try It Out exercise illustrates a custom tag generating a table from any `java.util.Map` object it is passed. In simple terms, a `Map` object is a list of unique key/value pairs that are based on the value of the key. For instance, a `Map` object may contain the entries shown in the following table.

Key	Value
Australia	Canberra
United States	Washington DC
France	Paris
Germany	Berlin

The tag developed in this example will display something similar to the preceding table, listing the contents of a `java.util.Map` object.

Try It Out   Generating a Table Using Custom Tags

We start off by creating a new tag file in the `/WEB-INF/tags` directory called `simpletable.tag`.

This new tag will accept four attributes:

❑ A `java.util.Map` object representing the data to be displayed. This attribute is required.

❑ A `String` object representing the title of the table. This attribute is optional.

❑ A `String` object representing the title of the first column (the keys). This attribute is optional.

❑ A `String` object representing the title of the second column (the values). This attribute is optional.

In developing this tag, our first step is to deal with the required directives. In addition to the compulsory tag directive and access to the core standard tag library, each attribute will require its own directive, so enter the following code at the top of the `simpletable.tag` file that was just created:

```
<%@ tag body-content="empty" %>
<%@ taglib prefix="c" uri="http://java.sun.com/jsp/jstl/core" %>

<%@ attribute name="data" required="true" type="java.util.Map" %>
<%@ attribute name="title" required="false" %>
<%@ attribute name="columnOne" required="false" %>
<%@ attribute name="columnTwo" required="false" %>
```

The name attribute to the attribute directive forms the name of the attribute when invoking the tag from the JSP page, as shown here:

```
<beginjsp:simpletable data="someData" title="My Data"/>
```

As we have indicated that the columnOne and columnTwo attributes are optional, enter the following code to provide some default values should they be empty:

```
<c:if test="${empty columnOne}">
    <c:set var="columnOne" value="Key"/>
</c:if>

<c:if test="${empty columnTwo}">
    <c:set var="columnTwo" value="Value"/>
</c:if>
```

This will ensure that if the first column attribute value is empty, then the table will display Key in its place, and Value for the second column.

The tag can now set about generating the table itself, using the data provided. The following code is now entered in the simpletable.tag:

```
<table cellspacing=0 cellpadding=0 border=1>
<c:if test="${not empty title}">
<tr>
    <td colspan="3"><h1>${title}</h1></td>
</tr>
</c:if>
<tr>
    <th>Count</th>
    <th>${columnOne}</th>
    <th>${columnTwo}</th>
</tr>
<c:forEach items="${data}" var="thisElement" varStatus="status">
    <tr>
    <td>${status.count}</td>
    <td>${thisElement.key}</td>
    <td>${thisElement.value}</td>
    </tr>
</c:forEach>
</table>
```

As the title attribute is optional, the tag conditionally displays it along the top row of the table. Each column is then defined with the appropriate value. A Count column has been added to provide an index against each element that is displayed. Finally, the data Map object is iterated over, using the core forEach tag. You have seen this tag in Chapter 6, "JSP Tag Libraries and JSTL."

The `simpletable` tag was created with flexibility in mind. Given any `java.util.Map` object (Map is in fact an interface, so any object that implements this interface can be used), this tag will display each element, as well as a descriptive title and column information, these being optional.

Therefore, the following JSP page will execute this tag in two ways: first to display a list of countries and capitals, and second to display the list of `request` parameters passed to the page. The following code could be entered into a JSP page to use the `simpletable.tag` file we have just created:

```
<%@ page import="java.util.HashMap" %>
<%@ page import="java.util.Map" %>
<%@ taglib prefix="beginjsp" tagdir="/WEB-INF/tags" %>

<%
  HashMap values = new HashMap();
  values.put("Australia","Canberra");
  values.put("United States","Washington DC");
  values.put("France","Paris");
  values.put("Germany","Berlin");
  values.put("Russia","Moscow");
  values.put("Egypt","Cairo");

  pageContext.setAttribute("values", values);
%>

<beginjsp:simpletable title="Countries and their capitals"
                      columnOne="Country"
                      columnTwo="Capital"
                      data="${pageScope.values}"/>
<P>
<beginjsp:simpletable title="Request Parameters" data="${param}"/>
```

How It Works

The first invocation of the custom action `simpletable` uses a Map object with Country/Capital pairs. This invocation uses all the attributes available to the `simpletable` tag. The second invocation uses a Map object that is implicit in any JSP page: `param`. This Map object lists the GET `request` parameters (i.e., from the query string). For instance, if you were to request `http://localhost:8080/tagfile/example-simpletable.jsp?color=red&size=large`, the `param` object would contain two entries:

Key	Value
Color	red
Size	large

You can see the result of this JSP page using the `simpletable` tag in Figure 11-4.

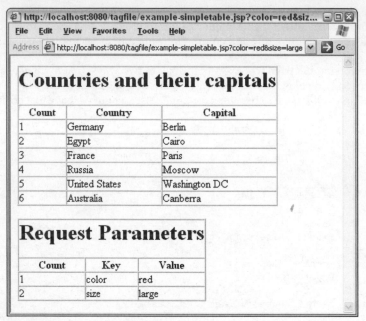

Figure 11-4: `simpletable` **tag results**

You can see that this simple tag provides a reusable component to display the contents of a Map object.

Fragment attributes

Fragment attributes passed to custom actions effectively enable the developer to pass a fragment of JSP to a tag file. This fragment can then be invoked within the custom action using a special standard action called `jsp:invoke`. `jsp:invoke` can only be used inside a tag file. Like all standard actions, certain attributes can be used with it. The following table describes the attributes for the `jsp:invoke` action.

Attribute	Description
fragment	Name of the fragment of JSP code that is being invoked.
Var	Similar to the var attribute used in the jsp:doBody action described earlier. When used, the result of the invocation can be stored as a String object under the name provided by this attribute.
varReader	Similar to the varReader attribute used in the jsp:doBody action described earlier. When used, the result of the invocation is stored as a java.io.Reader object under the name provided by this attribute.
Scope	Used in conjunction with the var or varReader attributes. Defines the scope where those variables will be placed: application, session, request or page. This attribute is optional, and the default is page.

jsp:invoke is used much like jsp:doBody; however, jsp:invoke is specifically targeted at a named segment of JSP code that is passed to the custom action as an attribute, rather than the body of the tag itself.

The following Try It Out example builds on the `simpletable` tag developed earlier to illustrate the power of `jsp:invoke` and fragment attributes.

Try It Out   Highlighting a Search Result

The `simpletable` tag displayed the contents of a `java.util.Map` object. To enhance this tag, this example will send a search String to the tag and highlight elements of the `Map` that match the search. Elements of the `Map` that match the search String will be displayed in a different color. The color to highlight a hit against an element of the `Map` will be passed as a `jsp:attribute` within the body of the tag invocation. An example of an invocation of this new tag is as follows:

```
<beginjsp:highlighttable title="Countries and their capitals"
                         search="ia"
                         columnOne="Country"
                         columnTwo="Capital"
                         data="${pageScope.values}">


    <jsp:attribute name="highlight">
        orange
    </jsp:attribute>

    <jsp:attribute name="lolight">
        white
    </jsp:attribute>

</beginjsp:highlighttable>
```

This example will create a new tag based on the `simpletable` tag created earlier. This new tag is called `highlighttable`. This tag is simply a copy of the `simpletable` tag with some additional changes to implement the new functionality. The preceding JSP code shows that this new tag has a `search` attribute that is used to specify the search string that it is passed. `jsp:attribute` elements are then used to specify the colors that the highlighting will use.

To make things simpler, we're going to create a copy of the `simpletable` tag file and call it the `highlighttable` tag (`highlighttable.tag`). As usual, you place this file in the `/WEB-INF/tags` directory of the Web application directory structure. The following explanation highlights the important changes from the `simpletable` tag.

This new tag will require three extra `attribute` directive entries: one for the search String, and two more — the `highlight` and `lolight` [sic] fragments that the tag will be passed:

```
<%@ tag body-content="empty" %>
<%@ taglib prefix="c" uri="http://java.sun.com/jsp/jstl/core" %>
<%@ taglib prefix="fn" uri="http://java.sun.com/jsp/jstl/functions" %>

<%@ attribute name="data" required="true" type="java.util.Map" %>
<%@ attribute name="search" required="true" %>
<%@ attribute name="highlight" fragment="true" required="true" %>
<%@ attribute name="lolight" fragment="true" required="true" %>
<%@ attribute name="title" required="false" %>
<%@ attribute name="columnOne" required="false" %>
<%@ attribute name="columnTwo" required="false" %>
```

You'll notice that another `taglib` directive has been added so that JSTL functions can be used. The `search` attribute is much like the other attributes you have already seen for custom tag files. The big change is in the addition of the `highlight` and `lolight` attributes. Notice that the `fragment` attribute for these attributes is set to `true`. This indicates that these items can be used in `jsp:invoke` invocations within the tag file. The `required` attribute has been set to `true` for these attributes, as they are required for the tag to function properly.

The rest of the tag appears as follows. The changes are highlighted to show the differences between this new tag and the `simpletable` tag presented earlier. If you are creating this new tag, these are the changes you should make to the `highlighttable` copy of the `simpletable` tag:

```
<c:if test="${empty columnOne}">
    <c:set var="columnOne" value="Key"/>
</c:if>

<c:if test="${empty columnTwo}">
    <c:set var="columnTwo" value="Value"/>
</c:if>

<table cellspacing=0 cellpadding=0 border=1>
<c:if test="${not empty title}">
<tr>
    <td colspan="3"><h1>${title}</h1></td>
</tr>
</c:if>
<tr>
    <th>Count</th>
    <th>${columnOne}</th>
    <th>${columnTwo}</th>
</tr>
<c:forEach items="${data}" var="thisElement" varStatus="status">
    <c:choose>
        <c:when test="${fn:containsIgnoreCase(thisElement.key, search) or
                        fn:containsIgnoreCase(thisElement.value, search)}">
            <tr bgcolor="<jsp:invoke fragment="highlight"/>">
        </c:when>
        <c:otherwise>
            <tr bgcolor="<jsp:invoke fragment="lolight"/>">
        </c:otherwise>
    </c:choose>
    <td>${status.count}</td>
    <td>${thisElement.key}</td>
    <td>${thisElement.value}</td>
    </tr>
</c:forEach>
</table>
```

How It Works

As you can see, the new tag is not very different from the original `simpletable` tag, with the exception of the `c:choose` added within the `forEach` loop. The logic here tests the value of the `search` attribute against both the key and value of each entry in the `data` object using the JSTL function containsIgnoreCase. If either the key or the value of the entry contains the value of the search attribute, the row will be built using the highlight fragment:

```
<tr bgcolor="<jsp:invoke fragment="highlight"/>">
```

This effectively places the resulting JSP contained in the fragment as the background color on the row. If neither the key nor the value is matched to the search attribute, the lolight attribute is used in the same way instead. Figure 11-5 shows you how this tag invocation would be displayed on the screen with a search attribute of ia (so that we get a couple of hits).

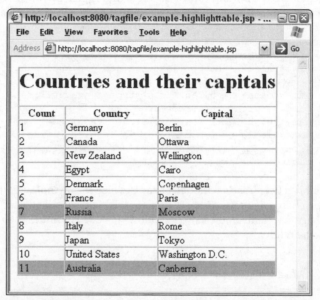

Figure 11-5: Results from the highlighttable tag

This is a very simple example; the fragments invoked within the tag contained only plain text. It is possible to include dynamic content within each fragment, to be evaluated as part of its processing. The next example illustrates this.

The following Try It Out example enhances the highlighttable tag to display the number of hits that the search has resulted in. It highlights two features of tag files:

❑   The ability to specify the name of a variable exported by a tag file

❑   The ability to use EL in JSP fragment attributes

The output of these enhancements will be a new tag called highlighttableext.

Try It Out   Search Results Counter

The enhancements we make here will enable the JSP developer to access a variable that contains the number of hits that have resulted from the tag invocation, and to use this variable to display a hit result row at the bottom of the table. It also enables the developer to specify the name of the variable accessible in the JSP page.

The example discussed here is an extension of the `highlighttable` tag explained in the preceding section. This new tag would be a copy of the `highlighttable.tag` file called `highlighttableext.tag`. This section explains the changes that need to be made to this copy in order to fulfill the functionality described.

The first change to be made is the addition of another fragment attribute to the tag's directive list. This optional fragment will form the bottom row of the table that is generated, with the intention that it will contain the result of the search. The new attribute is shown highlighted:

```
<%@ tag body-content="empty" %>
<%@ taglib prefix="c" uri="http://java.sun.com/jsp/jstl/core" %>
<%@ taglib prefix="fn" uri="http://java.sun.com/jsp/jstl/functions" %>

<%@ attribute name="data" required="true" type="java.util.Map" %>
<%@ attribute name="search" required="true" %>
<%@ attribute name="highlight" fragment="true" required="true" %>
<%@ attribute name="lolight" fragment="true" required="true" %>
<%@ attribute name="result" fragment="true" required="false" %>
<%@ attribute name="title" required="false" %>
```

The `result` fragment has been made optional, as the developer may not want to display the result row on the table. The next change is required to set up the variable that will be used to hold the number of hits that is recorded against items in the list. The following code continues the new tag, highlighting the changes that need to be made:

```
<%@ attribute name="columnOne" required="false" %>
<%@ attribute name="columnTwo" required="false" %>
<%@ attribute name="countVar" required="true" rtexprvalue="false" %>
<%@ variable name-from-attribute="countVar"
             alias="counter"
             variable-class="java.lang.Integer" scope="NESTED"%>
<c:set var="counter" value="0"/>
...
```

The `countVar` attribute will contain the name of the variable the developer wishes to use in the JSP page. This attribute must be `required` and have a `false` value for the `rtexprvalue` attribute so that it can be referenced in the `variable` directive. The `variable` directive sets up this variable for the tag. It uses the `name-from-attribute` attribute in order to assign itself to the name specified by the developer in the `countVar` attribute. The `alias` attribute is used to give this value an internally scoped variable name (`counter`) that can be used as the tag is processed. The `counter` variable is then initialized to 0.

The final modification to the tag is to increment the `counter` variable when a record is matched with the search criteria and to display the result row at the bottom of the table. The following code listing completes the changes that need to be made to this new tag:

```
<table cellspacing=0 cellpadding=0 border=1>
<c:if test="${not empty title}">
<tr>
```

```
        <td colspan="3"><h1>${title}</h1></td>
    </tr>
    </c:if>
    <tr>
        <th>Count</th>
        <th>${columnOne}</th>
        <th>${columnTwo}</th>
    </tr>
    <c:forEach items="${data}" var="thisElement" varStatus="status">
        <c:choose>
            <c:when test="${fn:containsIgnoreCase(thisElement.key, search) or
                            fn:containsIgnoreCase(thisElement.value, search)}">
                <tr bgcolor="<jsp:invoke fragment="highlight"/>">
                    <c:set var="counter" value="${counter + 1}"/>
            </c:when>
            <c:otherwise>
                <tr bgcolor="<jsp:invoke fragment="lolight"/>">
            </c:otherwise>
        </c:choose>
        <td>${status.count}</td>
        <td>${thisElement.key}</td>
        <td>${thisElement.value}</td>
        </tr>
    </c:forEach>
    <tr>
        <td colspan="3"><jsp:invoke fragment="result"/></td>
    </tr>
    </table>
```

The JSP page to invoke this new tag is much like the invocation of the `highlighttable` tag:

```
<beginjsp:highlighttableext title="Countries and their capitals"
                            search="ia"
                            columnOne="Country"
                            columnTwo="Capital"
                            data="${pageScope.values}"
                            countVar="foo">
    <jsp:attribute name="highlight">
        orange
    </jsp:attribute>
    <jsp:attribute name="lolight">
        white
    </jsp:attribute>
    <jsp:attribute name="result">
        Total hits found: ${foo}
    </jsp:attribute>
</beginjsp:highlighttableext>
```

How It Works

The `countVar` attribute specifies that a variable called `foo` will have NESTED scope within this tag and can therefore be used, as `foo`, in the `result` attribute that has also been added. The result is a single row at the bottom of the generated table that contains the number of hits recorded, as displayed in Figure 11-6.

Figure 11-6: Final modification of the `highlighttableext` tag

The use of the `name-from-attribute` attribute in the variable directive can be a little confusing. Using the `variable` directive in this way is simply a way for the JSP developer to name the variable the tag returns, rather than it being given an explicit name inside the tag with `name-given`.

Dynamic attributes

Tag files also enable developers to pass unspecified attributes to a tag in its invocation. This is handy where a large number of attributes are required or where the attributes themselves may change or are unknown and need to be dynamic. These ad-hoc attributes added to a tag's invocation deliver a `Map` of name-value pairs to the tag's `page` scope. Take the following tag invocation:

```
<beginjsp:dynalist favColor="blue" name="Rupert" address="123 Foo Avenue"/>
```

The attributes here have not been specifically declared with `attribute` directives within the tag file; rather, these names and values are available within the tag via a `Map` object that can be queried, looped over, or whatever else a `Map` object allows you to do.

Tag files won't allow such dynamic attributes by default; the `tag` directive must specify that such attributes be allowed using the `dynamic-attributes` attribute to the `tag` directive. The `tag` directive within this tag is as follows:

```
<%@ tag body-content="empty" dynamic-attributes="mapData" %>
```

If you don't declare the `dynamic-attributes` attribute, the server will throw an exception when unspecified attributes are used. With this attribute added to the `tag` directive, a variable named `mapData` is now available within the `page` scope of the tag. This `Map` object can now be accessed to retrieve the name-value pairs that were entered as dynamic attributes. Given the preceding example, `mapData` would contain the entries shown in the following table.

Name	Value
favColor	Blue
name	Rupert
address	123 Foo Avenue

The content of the tag file that iterates over this `Map` of dynamic attributes is as follows:

```
<%@ tag body-content="empty" dynamic-attributes="mapData" %>
<%@ taglib prefix="c" uri="http://java.sun.com/jsp/jstl/core" %>

<c:forEach items="${mapData}" var="thisElement">
    ${thisElement.key} = ${thisElement.value}<br>
</c:forEach>
```

Of course, this is no different from providing a single `Map` attribute to the tag as a normal attribute to perform the same function. Dynamic attributes make a key difference when the name of the attribute is also dynamic and has meaning in itself. An excellent example of where this can be beneficial is in the formatting of HTML elements that have many optional formatting attributes as part of their syntax.

This concludes the description and illustration of attributes and tag files. The Try It Out examples provided in this section were deliberately designed to provide basic illustrations of the many flavors of attribute usage that tag files support.

Packaging Tag Files

You've just developed a large collection of highly useful tag files that developers of all skill levels can use their current projects. Each tag was created with a `*.tag` file in the `/WEB-INF/tags` directory of your Web application.

This section explains how to take these tag files and package them into a single JAR file that can be included in the `/WEB-INF/lib` directory just like other resources an application may use. You may be asking why such packaging may be necessary. Sure, the `tags` directory is a simple and accessible place for them to be stored, but when your project is completed and you wish to deploy all these tags with your application, handling as few files as possible is optimal. Packaging files in this way also reduces the complexity of the environment and makes the files less accessible; it is hoped that the temptation to manipulate them outside of your development environment will be reduced. And as we shall see, packaging tag files in this way can reduce application-wide changes if any of the tags are redeveloped as Java custom actions.

But first, let's review some context that is important for this discussion. When custom tags are developed using Java, a Tag Library Descriptor (TLD) file is created that defines the tag (or tags) and their usage for the container. The TLD file is simply an XML file that conforms to a predefined schema (structure) and is referenced in the `uri` attribute of the `taglib` directive used in JSP files. Doing so identifies the set of tags defined in the TLD under a common name, or prefix.

So far, we have not had to create a TLD file for custom tags in this chapter; however, when packaging them into a single JAR file, a TLD file must be created. Once this file is created, the JAR file can be generated containing the TLD file and each `*.tag` file. These files must conform to a certain directory structure inside the JAR file:

```
/META-INF/*.tld
```

```
/META-INF/tags/*.tag
```

The TLD file is placed in the `/META-INF` directory, and the associated tag files are placed in the `/META-INF/tags/` directory (or a subdirectory). Once this structure has been set up, the JAR file can be created at the command line, or with a build tool such as Ant, and placed in the `/WEB-INF/lib` directory of the application, where it can be used by the application. In order for JSP files to reference the tags contained in the JAR file, the associated `taglib` directives must be changed to use the `uri` attribute, rather than `tagdir`.

The following Try It Out exercise walks you through these steps in detail, packaging three tag files created during this chapter, and then illustrates a JSP page invoking one of them. If you haven't created tag files during the course of the chapter but want to follow along with this example, just use the example code available from the Wrox Web site at www.wrox.com/.

Try It Out   Packaging Tag Files

Create a file called `beginjsptags.tld` in the `/META-INF` directory discussed earlier. As mentioned, this file defines the tags that the JAR file will contain. For our purposes, it has a fairly straightforward structure, but it can get decidedly more complex when defining custom actions developed in Java.

The JAR file will contain the `cleanhtml`, `simpletable`, and `highlighttable` tags, and the TLD file must have entries for each. Add the following content to the `beginjsptags.tld` file:

```xml
<?xml version="1.0" encoding="UTF-8" ?>

<taglib xmlns="http://java.sun.com/xml/ns/j2ee"
        xmlns:xsi="http://www.w3.org/2001/XMLSchema-instance"
        xsi:schemaLocation="http://java.sun.com/xml/ns/j2ee web-
jsptaglibrary_2_0.xsd"
        version="2.0">

        <description>Beginning JSP Tag Files</description>
        <tlib-version>1.0</tlib-version>
        <short-name>beginjsp</short-name>
        <uri>beginjsptags</uri>

        <tag-file>
            <name>cleanhtml</name>
            <path>/META-INF/tags/cleanhtml.tag</path>
```

```
            </tag-file>

            <tag-file>
                <name>simpletable</name>
                <path>/META-INF/tags/simpletable.tag</path>
            </tag-file>

            <tag-file>
                <name>highlighttable</name>
                <path>/META-INF/tags/highlighttable.tag</path>
            </tag-file>
    </taglib>
```

As you can see, the TLD file conforms to a fairly simple structure. The important content here is within the `taglib` element. First, some descriptive elements are defined, as shown in the following table.

Element	Description
description	Brief description of the tag library.
tlib-version	Version of the tag library.
short-name	Prefix used for this tag library. The value here is merely a suggested prefix; the developer can define a prefix to use in the `prefix` attribute of the `taglib` directive in the JSP that uses this tag library.
uri	The URI (Universal Resource Identifier) for this tag library. Used in the `uri` attribute of the `taglib` directive on a JSP page that will use this library.

Below these are `tag-file` elements for each of the tags being added to this package. The `name` attribute merely provides an alias to be used when invoking the tag. Although the convention is to assign a `name` value in accordance with the tag file's actual filename (less the `.tag` extension), the `name` value could be anything you like; it will, however, identify the name of the tag when used within the JSP page, so it should at least be somewhat appropriate. The `path` attribute points to the path of the tag file itself within the JAR file. Note that the path to each tag file uses the directory structure defined earlier, i.e., using `META-INF`, not `WEB-INF`.

Once you have copied the appropriate tag files into the `/META-INF/tags` directory, the JAR file can be generated. The following instructions apply to a Microsoft Windows environment.

Start up a command-line prompt by clicking the Start button and then clicking Run. Type **cmd** in the Open input field. A command-line prompt should open. Change to the directory above the `META-INF` directory created for this example and type the following command at the prompt:

```
    jar -cvf beginjsptags.jar META-INF
```

A JAR file named `beginjsptags.jar` should have been generated in the current directory. Place this JAR file in the `/WEB-INF/lib` directory of your Web application.

How It Works

Once you have restarted your servlet container, you should be able to use the tags contained in this JAR file from your JSP pages.

The `taglib` directive used in JSP pages will now use a `uri` attribute when using tag files packaged in a JAR file, instead of the `tagdir` attribute used throughout this chapter. The `uri` attribute should match the `uri` value placed in the `beginjsptags.tld` file created earlier:

```
<%@ taglib prefix="beginjsp" uri="beginjsptags"%>

<beginjsp:simpletable title="Request Parameters" data="${param}"/>
```

The preceding code would invoke the `simpletable` tag file packaged in the JAR file. Of course, we had to make a change to the JSP files that reference the tag files formerly placed directly in the file system. In a large application, this could become quite hazardous, as it may not be feasible to ensure that every page is configured correctly once the change has been made.

A safer method of transition from file system–based tag files to JAR file–based tag files would have been to use the `uri` attribute in the JSP files all along, rather than the `tagdir` attribute. In order to achieve this central referencing of the tag files, a TLD file would be created in the `/WEB-INF/` directory (or a subdirectory) of the Web application, with each tag's `path` attribute pointed to the tag files in the `/WEB-INF/tags` directory. JSP pages would then be free to use the value of the `uri` element in the TLD file as their `uri` value. No change to JSP files would be necessary when moving from one method to another. If the custom actions were then redeveloped in Java, as long as their usage was the same, the JSP files that referenced them would require no changes at all.

Java custom actions versus tag file custom actions

Should you develop your custom actions as simple tag files or as Java class files? As with many technical decisions, the answer depends on a consideration of several factors. The following sections examine these factors.

Complexity of the problem

Most of the examples presented in this chapter have been deliberately simple in order to convey basic syntax and patterns of usage. The use of tag files for each of them is entirely appropriate. However, real-life applications often involve situations where a tag has a very complex task to perform, usually in order to display some formatted output from the system. Developers should consider moving these tags to Java as soon as the complexity of the logic they contain gets unwieldy and difficult to maintain. Tags developed in Java can take advantage of Java's object-oriented nature, with a capability to solve complex problems in a more structured way.

Team skills and alien artifacts

The skills available in a software development team should, to a certain extent, dictate the technology and techniques being used in development. Sometimes specialist "niche" software developers are temporarily hired to solve a particular problem, using a technology that no one else on the team has any experience with. The contractor is then sent on his or her way when the project comes to an end. The remaining staff is left to maintain a system they may not understand, at least not without some training, and even then, it may not be enough to provide commercially viable support.

Elements of systems that are developed in this way are sometimes referred to as *alien artifacts*. The mysterious, magical thing that the specialist contractor created cannot be touched or managed in any reasonable way for fear of it breaking. Custom tags developed in Java run the risk of becoming alien artifacts should the skills of the team be unable to support them. A software team should have the skills available to develop, manage, and maintain all aspects of the system.

In short, there is no definitive answer regarding which method should be used. An "as required" approach should be taken, moving tags that require the sophistication of Java to Java-developed tags and, conversely, moving tags from Java-developed code to tag files if it is appropriate given the level of complexity involved and team-related factors.

Summary

This chapter has covered the syntax and basic usage patterns of custom actions developed as tag files. This powerful mechanism included in the JSP 2.0 specification provides more power in the hands of JSP developers, who are now better able to modularize components of their applications. Tag files also benefit Java developers, who can now rapidly implement simple tags if Java-developed tags are inappropriate or considered overkill.

The first part of the chapter provided a simple example and looked at the advantages that tag files specifically provide for developers:

- ❑ Code reuse
- ❑ Hiding complexity
- ❑ Separation of concerns
- ❑ Simplicity
- ❑ Flexible packaging

Developing tag files was then discussed at length; we first investigated each of the important directives available in tag files and then looked in more detail at tag body processing and the various attributes that can be used. In the closing sections, we looked at tag file packaging, and briefly discussed the choice between custom actions developed in Java or as tag files.

Exercises

1. Create a tag to generate a random number. Ensure that the random number result is available from the JSP page. Add an attribute to the tag to specify the maximum value of the random number, i.e., between 0 and *n*.

2. Create a tag that formats the display of a Calendar object using two attributes. One is the Calendar instance; the other is the pattern with which to display the date. The output on the page should just be the result of the formatting. Output the current date in the following format:

```
Tuesday 3 June 2005 AD
```

You will find valid patterns to use in the Javadocs for the SimpleDateFormat class. See http://java.sun.com/j2se/1.4.2/docs/api/index.html.

Advanced Dynamic Web Content Generation

At this point in the book, you have examined and worked with every single aspect of JavaServer Pages. The knowledge that you have gained thus far can be put immediately to use in creating new Web applications using JSP technology, or in the maintenance of existing JSP projects. Although most of the projects in this book work mainly with the dynamic generation of HTML template data, creating interactive Web-based interfaces, this chapter focuses on the dynamic generation of content that is not HTML. While using exactly the same set of JSP techniques, the dynamic content generated will be client-side scripting elements and XML documents.

Client-side scripting elements, typically coded in the JavaScript programming language, can be used to enhance the user's interactive experience. One very practical application of JavaScript on the client side is for the validation of data entered within forms. The examples in this chapter show how JSP-generated client-side scripting elements can be used to perform client-side data validation.

Many concepts and techniques introduced in the previous chapters are put to work in this chapter. Concepts and techniques reviewed in this chapter include the following:

❑ Standard JSP actions

❑ JSP directives

❑ JSP actions

❑ JavaBeans

❑ Custom actions in JSTL

❑ EL

❑ Use of implicit objects

❑ Alternate XML syntax for JSP

❑ Using a front controller to forward requests

❑ Processing request parameters using JSP

❑ Creating a custom tag library using JSP tagfiles

There are three hands-on examples in the chapter, providing step-by-step illustrations of how to use JSP in generating non-HTML Web application elements.

By the end of the chapter, you will know how to generate client-side validation code from your JSP applications. In addition, you will be familiar with the techniques used in generating XML-based content.

Data Validation in Web Applications

You already examined data validation in the first auction bidding example of Chapter 9, "JSP and JavaBeans." The example presents a form for users to input their bids for items. The following is a brief review. The range of the incoming bid is checked to ensure that it is between 0 and 999, inclusive. This check is coded in JSP. The data validation is performed by the following highlighted JSP highlighted code in the Chapter 9 index.jsp file (the first Try It Out exercise):

```
<%@ taglib prefix="c" uri="http://java.sun.com/jsp/jstl/core" %>
<c:choose>
   <c:when test="${empty param.action}">
    <jsp:forward page="enterbid.jsp"/>
   </c:when>
   <c:when test="${param.action eq 'bid'}">
    <c:if test="${(param.price <= 0) || (param.price >= 999)}">
      <jsp:useBean id="biderror" class="com.wrox.begjsp.ch09.BidError"
        scope="request">
       <jsp:setProperty name="biderror" property="msg"
        value="Sorry, your bid is not in range. Please enter again."/>
      </jsp:useBean>
      <jsp:forward page="enterbid.jsp"/>
    </c:if>
    <jsp:useBean id="bidinfo" class="com.wrox.begjsp.ch09.Bid" scope="request">
      <jsp:setProperty name="bidinfo" property="*"/>
    </jsp:useBean>

    <jsp:forward page="showbid.jsp"/>
   </c:when>
</c:choose>
```

The validation is performed using the JSTL `<c:if>` flow control action. The `test` attribute is specified as an EL expression:

```
${(param.price <= 0) || (param.price >= 999)}
```

The user will be asked to reenter his or her bid if the incoming bid is out of this range. The form input is handled by the enterbid.jsp page.

While this solution works reasonably well, it is not the preferred way of performing data validation. It is not preferred because it is inefficient, as you will see in the following section.

Server-side validation and efficient usage of resources

Figure 12-1 illustrates why data validation using JSP is rather inefficient.

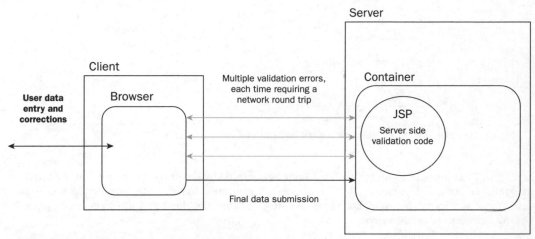

Figure 12-1: JSP-based server-side data validation

In Figure 12-1, the user input data must be transmitted between a user's browser and the server before the data can be validated. If the data is in error, it must be reentered and retransmitted to the server for validation. Because the JSP logic is executed in the container on the server, data validation code implemented in JSP always occurs on the server side.

> **Data validation implemented using JSP logic occurs on the server side.**

Server-side validation is generally inefficient for the following reasons:

❑ Each validation and retry sequence requires a separate network call.

❑ The bandwidth and processing power of the server may be burdened by the validation task.

❑ The user may have to wait a significant amount of time before the data can be validated, especially if the server is clogged with validation requests from other users.

There is a lot of computing power on modern client computers. Current versions of popular browsers (such as Microsoft Internet Explorer 6.x and Netscape 7.x) are feature-rich and support powerful scripting languages that can be used to write client-side programs. You can exploit this combination of computing power and browser scripting capability to perform data validation on the client side. Figure 12-2 illustrates client-side validation.

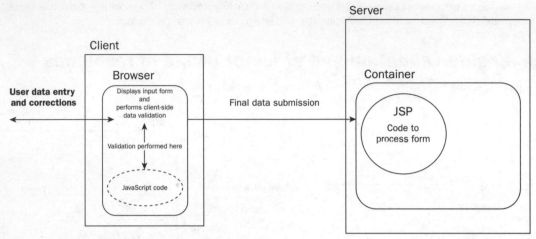

Figure 12-2: Operation of client-side data validation

In Figure 12-2, the user input is validated on the client side by script code executed on the browser. If a validation error is detected, the user is immediately prompted to correct the input. There is no network access during this entire phase. Data is transmitted between the client and the server only when it is validated successfully on the client.

Client-side data validation

Performing data validation on the client side has the following advantages:

❑   The server does not have the burden of low-level data validation.

❑   Bandwidth between client and server is conserved by eliminating the need to transmit potentially invalid input to the server.

❑   The user always experiences a fast response because the validation code executes on the powerful client hardware.

Because client-side validation is generally more efficient than server-side validation, one might imagine that all data validation should be performed on the client side. This is not possible in practice, and you will learn the reason why in the next section.

> **Client-side data validation is generally more resource-efficient than server-side validation.**

The need for server-side validation

It is not possible to perform all data validation on the client side because some validation work requires access to server resources. For example, an application may need to verify that an item is in stock before an order can be placed. The client's browser cannot determine this information alone.

Another less common reason why server-side validation is necessary occurs in networks where a user's legacy browser may not support the execution of scripting code. In these cases, the implementation of client-side data validation is not possible.

> **Not all validation tasks can be performed on the client side.**

Common client-side validation scenarios

Certain types of data validation tasks can be, and should be, performed on the client. They include the following:

❑ Verifying that numerical values are valid numbers

❑ Verifying the length of textual input data

❑ Verifying that input data is in particular textual formats (for example, an all-numeric serial number, a telephone number, a credit card number, an e-mail address, or a postal code)

❑ Checking the value range of numeric data (if the range is fixed and does not depend on server information)

The common characteristic of all the items in the preceding list is that they can all be accomplished independently, without accessing server-side data or information.

Therefore, in a typical Web application, data validation is separated into two stages. The client-side validation checks input for allowable range, data format, and type validity. The server-side validation, if it exists, performs checks that require access to server side resources, such as databases.

> **In most real-world applications, data validation is performed both on the client and on the server.**

Operation of client-side validation

Figure 12-3 shows the components that are involved in client-side validation.

In Figure 12-3, the client-side validation code is embedded in the HTML page. This code is transmitted from the server to the client when the HTML page is fetched. The user then enters data into the form presented by the HTML. When the user clicks a button to submit the form, the client-side validation script code is executed. If errors are detected, the data is not submitted to the server.

The user is requested to correct any error and resubmit the form. The data is transmitted to the server only when all the client-side validation is performed successfully.

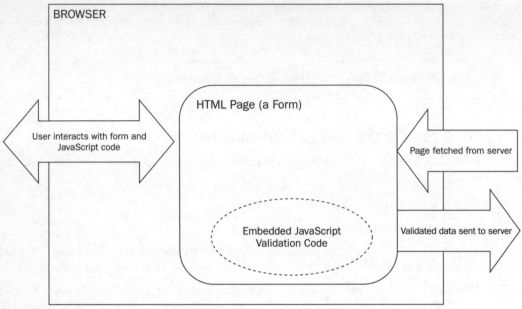

Figure 12-3: Components of client-side validation

The client-side scripting language

The client-side validation code is written in an interpreted script language. The interpreter for this scripting language is embedded in the browser. There are two very popular scripting languages:

❑ JavaScript (sometimes referred to as ECMAScript)

❑ VBScript

ECMAScript is a standard scripting language that is actually a subset of JavaScript. Scripting code written in the ECMAScript subset is most portable across different browsers.

VBScript has a syntax that is similar to Microsoft's Visual Basic programming language. VBScript is supported only by the Microsoft Internet Explorer browser. JavaScript is supported by both Netscape and Microsoft browsers. In order to write client-side validation code that will work on both Internet Explorer and Netscape, JavaScript should be used.

The following Try It Out exercise shows how JavaScript can be used for client-side data validation.

Try It Out   Client-Side Validation

This first example enables a user to enter information for a product offered by an e-commerce store. The form is generated and processed by JSPs. The form uses client-side JavaScript code to perform client-side data validation for the form. To try out this example, you will need the `ch12.war` archive.

Make sure that your Tomcat 5 server is running and then deploy ch12.war to the server. Review Chapter 1 if you do not remember how to deploy a WAR archive.

Open your browser and access the following URL:

```
http://localhost:8080/ch12/example1/index.jsp
```

A form similar to the one shown in Figure 12-4 will be displayed, enabling you to enter the product information.

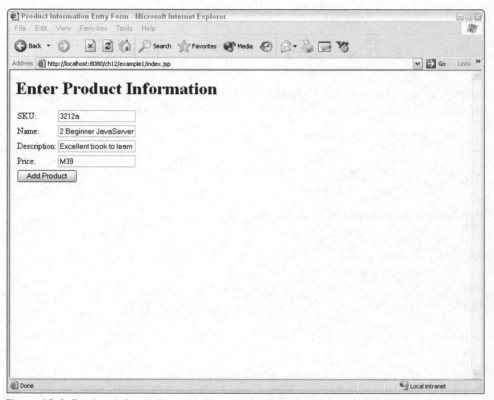

Figure 12-4: Product information entry form with client-side data validation

Enter the following values into the form:

❑   For the sku field, enter **3212a**.

❑   For the name field, enter **2 Beginning JavaServer Pages**.

❑   For the desc field, enter **Excellent book to learn JSP with**.

❑   For the price field, enter **M39**.

By design, the previous input values contain several errors. These errors should be caught by the validation code.

Click the Add Product button. This will start the client-side validation code. The errors are detected and you should see a pop-up dialog box, as shown in Figure 12-5.

Figure 12-5: Pop-up box announcing data entry errors

Click the OK button to dismiss the dialog box. The errors are now highlighted in the form. No data has been sent to the server yet at this point. Your form now looks similar to Figure 12-6.

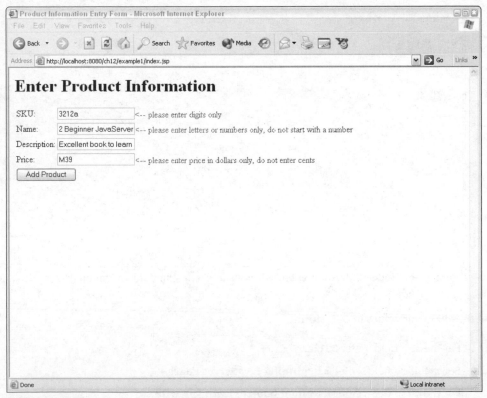

Figure 12-6: Data entry errors detected by client-side data validation

Figure 12-6 shows that three errors were detected. The first one is in the value entered for sku. The sku format should contain all numeric digits, and does not allow any characters. To fix this, delete the trailing a character. Click the Add Product button again. The resulting screen is shown in Figure 12-7.

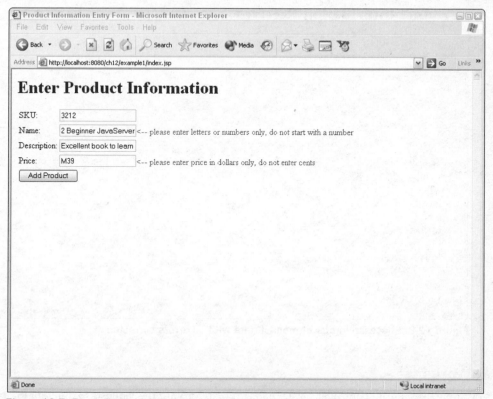

Figure 12-7: Form display after one entry error has been corrected

Note in Figure 12-7 that the sku is now valid, and only two errors remain. To correct these errors:

1. Remove the leading 2 in the name field, as this field must begin with an alpha character.

2. Remove the leading M in the price field, as this field must contain the numeric dollar value only.

Click the Add Product button again.

This time, all the values pass validation, and the form data is finally submitted to the server. The form data is processed by a server-side JSP. This JSP simply displays the values of the form fields. The resulting display should be similar to Figure 12-8.

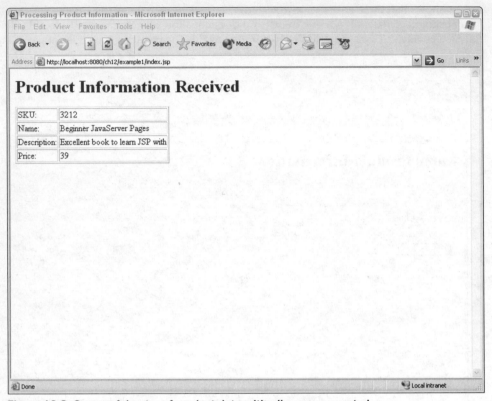

Figure 12-8: Successful entry of product data with all errors corrected

How It Works

This example uses a front controller page, index.jsp, to forward the requests to different JSP pages. Figure 12-9 shows the architecture.

In Figure 12-9, the request attribute called action is used to determine where to forward the request. When index.jsp is first accessed, the action attribute will have no value. In this case, the request is forwarded to the prodform.jsp page. The prodform.jsp page prompts for the entry of product information. The prodform.jsp page also has client-side validation built in. When the data from prodform.jsp is submitted, the action attribute has the value prodsubmit. When the action attribute has the value of prodsubmit, index.jsp forwards the request to procprod.jsp. The procprod.jsp page renders the values entered for the product.

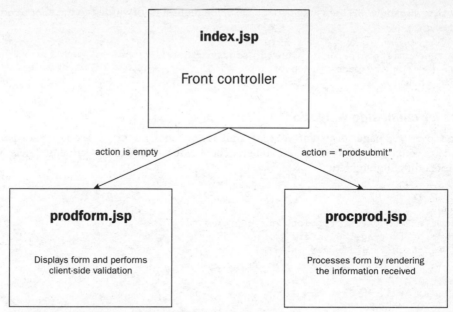

Figure 12-9: Application flow with front controller

Using a front controller to forward requests

The front controller in this example is the index.jsp page. The index.jsp page is located at
`<Tomcat Installation Directory>/webapps/ch12/example1/index.jsp`. It is reproduced
here:

```
<%@ taglib prefix="c" uri="http://java.sun.com/jsp/jstl/core" %>
<c:choose>
  <c:when test="${empty param.action}">
    <jsp:forward page="prodform.jsp"/>
  </c:when>

  <c:when test="${param.action eq 'prodsubmit'}">
    <jsp:forward page="procprod.jsp"/>
  </c:when>
</c:choose>
```

A JSTL `<c:choose>` construct is used to forward incoming requests depending on the action
request attribute. If the `action` attribute does not exist, the request is forwarded to the `prodform.
jsp` page by the following code:

```
<c:when test="${empty param.action}">
  <jsp:forward page="prodform.jsp"/>
</c:when>
```

If the `action` attribute has the value `prodsubmit`, the request is forwarded to the `procprod.jsp` page for processing:

```
<c:when test="${param.action eq 'prodsubmit'}">
  <jsp:forward page="procprod.jsp"/>
</c:when>
```

JavaScript for client-side validation

The `prodform.jsp` page, located at `<Tomcat Installation Directory>/webapps/ch12/example1/prodform.jsp`, contains the code for client-side validation. It is presented here, with JavaScript coding highlighted:

```html
<html>
<head>
  <title>Product Information Entry Form</title>
  <script language="JavaScript">
    function isDigitsOnly(inParam)
    {
        var chkExp = /^\d+$/;
        return (chkExp.test(inParam));
    }
    function isTextOnly(inParam)
    {
        var chkExp = /^[a-z][a-z\d ]+$/i;
        return (chkExp.test(inParam));
    }
    function validateForm()
    {
        var formValid = true;
        if (!isDigitsOnly(document.prodform.sku.value))
        {
            document.getElementById("skuError").style.visibility = "visible";
            formValid = false;
        }
        else
            document.getElementById("skuError").style.visibility = "hidden";

        if (!isTextOnly(document.prodform.name.value))
        {
            document.getElementById("nameError").style.visibility = "visible";
            formValid = false;
        }
        else
            document.getElementById("nameError").style.visibility = "hidden";

        if (!isTextOnly(document.prodform.desc.value))
        {
            document.getElementById("descError").style.visibility = "visible";
            formValid = false;
```

```
        }
        else
            document.getElementById("descError").style.visibility = "hidden";

        if (!isDigitsOnly(document.prodform.price.value))
        {
            document.getElementById("priceError").style.visibility = "visible";
            formValid = false;
        }
        else
            document.getElementById("priceError").style.visibility = "hidden";

        if (!formValid)
            alert("Some values you entered are invalid, please correct the entries
marked in red." );

        return formValid;
    }
  </script>
```

```
  <style>
    span.validateError
    {
      color: red;
      visibility: hidden;
    }
  </style>
</head>
<body>
  <h1>Enter Product Information</h1>
  <form  name="prodform" action="index.jsp" method="post"
    onsubmit="return validateForm()">
    <table border="0" >
      <tr>
        <td>SKU:</td>
        <td>
          <input name="sku" type="text" width="40"/>
          <span id="skuError" class="validateError">
            <-- please enter digits only
          </span>
        </td>
      </tr>

      <tr>
        <td>Name:</td>
        <td>
          <input name="name" type="text" width="40"/>
          <span id="nameError" class="validateError">
            <-- please enter letters or numbers only, do not start with a number
          </span>
        </td>
```

```
        </tr>
        <tr>
          <td>Description:</td>
          <td>
            <input name="desc" type="text" width="40"/>
            <span id="descError" class="validateError">
              <-- please enter letters or numbers only, do not start with a number
            </span>
          </td>
        </tr>
        <tr>
          <td>Price:</td>
          <td>
            <input name="price" type="text" width="40"/>
            <span id="priceError" class="validateError">
              <-- please enter price in dollars only, do not enter cents
            </span>
          </td>
        </tr>

        <tr>
          <td colspan="2">
            <input type="submit" value="Add Product" />
            <input type="hidden" name="action" value="prodsubmit"/>
          </td>
        </tr>
      </table>
    </form>
  </body>
</html>
```

The following paragraphs provide an analysis of the client-side validation coding.

JavaScript coding is embedded in an HTML page using the <script> tag. Because browsers such as Microsoft Internet Explorer also support VBScript, the language attribute of the <script> tag is used to specify JavaScript as the scripting language:

```
<script language="JavaScript">
```

Only two validation functions are necessary in this example. The first utility validation function, isDigitsOnly(), verifies that an incoming parameter consists of all numeric digits. Embedded character or blanks are not allowed in this case. The isDigitsOnly() function is implemented as follows:

```
function isDigitsOnly(inParam)
{
    var chkExp = /^\d+$/;
    return (chkExp.test(inParam));
}
```

In the isDigitsOnly() function, a JavaScript regular expression object called chkExp is used to perform the validation. The test() method of a JavaScript regular expression is used to determine if the inParam parameter matches the specified expression. The test() method will return a Boolean true value if a match is determined, or false if no match is found. This expression matches only runs of numeric digits.

> *A detailed description of the JavaScript programming language, and the associated regular expression engine, is beyond the scope of this book. Interested readers are encouraged to consult Beginning JavaScript, 2nd Edition (ISBN 0-7645-5587-1).*

A JavaScript regular expression is framed by the slash (/) character. The following table describes the symbols used in this expression.

Symbol	Matches
^	The beginning of the string to match
\d	Matches a single numeric digit
$	The end of the string to match
+	One or more occurrences of the matched character immediately before

The second and last utility validation function, isTextOnly(), checks to see if the incoming parameter contains alphanumeric characters or blanks. The incoming parameter must start with a letter and not a numeric character or a blank:

```
function isTextOnly(inParam)
{
    var chkExp = /^[a-z][a-z\d ]+$/i;
    return (chkExp.test(inParam));
}
```

In isTextOnly(), a JavaScript regular expression object is also used. The trailing i at the end of the expression indicates that the expression match should be performed without consideration to uppercase or lowercase. The i stands for insensitive, as in case-*insensitive*. The following table describes two other new matching symbols in the expression.

Symbol	Matches
[a-z]	A single alphabet letter
[a-z\d]	A single alphabet letter, a numeric digit, or a blank

chkExp.test() will attempt a match of the regular expression against the incoming parameters, and return a Boolean true if a match is found (or false otherwise).

Following the isTextOnly() utility function, the next function is the actual function used to validate the form. This function is called validateForm(). The first thing that it does is to set a Boolean JavaScript variable called formValid to the true value. This variable will be returned to the caller. It is set to false if any validation error is detected.

```
function validateForm()
{
    var formValid = true;
```

Next in the validateForm() function is a series of checks that access the value of the form fields. When using JavaScript, the form fields can be accessed through the *object model* provided by the browser. Roughly speaking, each HTML or form element can be given an ID. The element can then be accessed in the scripting language to modify its properties or attributes. For example, in the first set of validation codes, the value of the sku field can be accessed via the JavaScript expression document.prodform. sku.value. This expression will access the sku value just entered by the user. In this case, the value is passed to isDigitsOnly() to ensure that the sku consists of all numeric digits:

```
if (!isDigitsOnly(document.prodform.sku.value))
{
    document.getElementById("skuError").style.visibility = "visible";
    formValid = false;
}
else
    document.getElementById("skuError").style.visibility = "hidden";
```

Note that the document.getElementById() method (a method provided by the Document Object Model, or DOM, and supported by the browser) is used to modify the CSS style of an element called skuError. This element is used to render the validation error.

Using the hidden <span> tag to reveal multiple validation errors

When a validation error is detected, it is possible to

❑   Immediately ask the user to correct it

❑   Remember it and continue with validation

The first Try It Out example uses the second alternative, which provides a less cumbersome user experience because multiple errors will be detected at one time. This enables the user to correct multiple errors without being repeatedly bothered by the notification pop-up window.

The validation error message appears right next to the field in which the error occurs. Refer to Figure 12-6 to see where the error messages are displayed.

These error messages are actually rendered as part of the table, but they are made invisible using CSS properties within a <span> tag. The style under which each error message is created is defined in the validateError CSS class. This is embedded as a <style> element within index.jsp:

```
...
<style>
  span.validateError
  {
    color: red;
    visibility: hidden;
  }
</style>
</head>
<body>
```

Note that the `visibility` attribute is set to `hidden`, which makes the error messages invisible initially.

For example, the row containing the validation error for the `sku` field is pre-rendered as follows:

```
<tr>
  <td>SKU:</td>
  <td>
    <input name="sku" type="text" width="40"/>
    <span id="skuError" class="validateError">
      <-- please enter digits only</span>
  </td>
</tr>
```

Because the error message is specified to have the `validateError` style class, it is initially invisible.

Upon validation, the visibility of this `<span>` tag is toggled to visible if an error occurs. During the validation process, the following highlighted code is responsible for turning the visibility of this tag on and off:

```
if (!isDigitsOnly(document.prodform.sku.value))
{
    document.getElementById("skuError").style.visibility = "visible";
    formValid = false;
}
else
    document.getElementById("skuError").style.visibility = "hidden";
```

Note that it is necessary to turn the visibility off for the fields that have valid data. This is because a user may not have corrected all the errors before attempting to submit the form again.

Client-side validation prior to form submission

When the user submits the form, the browser will send the data to the server. However, if a JavaScript `onsubmit` handler is specified, it will be called before the actual submission. This allows for hooking in the data validation code as a handler. The following form element, from `index.jsp`, calls this handler:

```
<form  name="prodform" action="index.jsp" method="post"
  onsubmit="return validateForm()">
```

The action *attribute of the form specifies that* index.jsp *should be used to process the form. Recall that* index.jsp *is actually a front controller. It will forward the request to* procprod.jsp *for processing because a request attribute called* action *is set to the value* prodsubmit *within the form.*

Note the use of a JavaScript code segment in the onsubmit attribute:

```
return validateForm()
```

If the onsubmit handler returns true, the form data is sent to the server for further processing. If the onsubmit handler returns false, the original form is displayed and no data will be sent to the server.

The validateForm() method uses its own formValid Boolean variable to determine whether any validation error occurred. This variable is returned to the caller, which means that the form will not submit any data to the server until all validation errors are corrected.

Displaying product data

The form data is finally submitted back to index.jsp and the request is forwarded to procprod.jsp for processing. procprod.jsp is located at <Tomcat Installation Directory>/webapps/ch12/example1/procprod.jsp. The content of procprod.jsp is reproduced here:

```jsp
<%@ taglib prefix="c" uri="http://java.sun.com/jsp/jstl/core" %>
<html>
<head>
  <title>Processing Product Information</title>
</head>
<body>
  <jsp:useBean id="localProd" class="com.wrox.begjsp.ch03.Product" />
  <jsp:setProperty name="localProd" property="*" />
  <h1>Product Information Received</h1>
  <table border="1">
    <tr>
      <td>SKU:</td> <td><jsp:getProperty name="localProd" property="sku"/> </td>
    </tr>

    <tr>
      <td>Name:</td> <td><jsp:getProperty name="localProd" property="name"/> </td>
    </tr>
    <tr>
      <td>Description:</td>
      <td><jsp:getProperty name="localProd" property="desc"/>
      </td>
    </tr>
    <tr>
      <td>Price:</td> <td> ${localProd.price}</td>
    </tr>

  </table>
</body>
</html>
```

This code is taken directly from the first example in Chapter 9. It creates an instance of the `com.wrox.begjsp.ch03.Product` JavaBean. The properties of this JavaBean are set with the values entered by the user. These property values are subsequently rendered using a mixture of `<jsp:getProperty>` standard actions and EL expressions.

This concludes the coverage of the Try It Out exercise. While the `index.jsp` in this first example implemented client-side data validation JavaScript code, the code was not generated dynamically using JSP. Instead, the entire JSP acted more like a static HTML page.

Dynamic generation of client-side JavaScript code

Instead of placing the client-side validation code in the JSP file as static template text, it is possible to create a JSP tag library that generates this code.

Using JSP to generate the client-side validation code has the following advantages:

❏ It reduces the amount of complex coding required in the main JSP page, simplifying long-term maintenance.

❏ It enables easy reuse of the JavaScript code and validation mechanism.

❏ It enables developers who are not fluent in JavaScript coding to implement client-side validation, by simply using the JSP tag library.

The last advantage is very important indeed. In fact, modern JSP-based frameworks, such as JSF (JavaServer Faces, covered in Chapter 21, "JavaServer Faces"), makes extensive use of this capability to create highly interactive user interface components.

The next Try It Out exercise performs exactly the same function as the first one. However, a custom tag library is used to dynamically generate the client validation code.

Try It Out   Dynamic Generation of Client Data Validation Code

The important thing to realize about this example is that it works identically to the first example.

The flow of code is identical: `index.jsp` acts as a front controller, the action forward is used to direct requests to either `prodform.jsp` for entry of product data or to `procprod.jsp` for display of the form entry data. The main difference lies in how `prodform.jsp` is created, which is examined in detail after this example.

First ensure that the `ch12.war` archive is deployed on your Tomcat 5 server. Of course, make sure that the server is up and running as well.

Point your browser to the following URL:

```
http://localhost:8080/ch12/example2/index.jsp
```

The form displayed should be identical to the one shown in Figure 12-4.

Enter the following values into the form:

❑   For the sku field, enter **3212a.**

❑   For the name field, enter **2 Beginning JavaServer Pages.**

❑   For the desc field, enter **Excellent book to learn JSP with.**

❑   For the price field, enter **M39.**

These input values contain several errors that will be caught by the validation code.

Click the Add Product button. This will start the client-side validation code. The errors are detected and you should see a pop-up dialog box, as shown in Figure 12-5.

Click the OK button to dismiss the dialog box. The errors are now highlighted in the form. No data has been sent to the server yet at this point. Your form now looks similar to Figure 12-6.

In Figure 12-6, three errors are detected. The first one is in the value entered for sku. The sku format should contain all numeric digits, and does not allow any characters. To fix this, delete the trailing a character. Click the Add Product button again. The resulting screen is shown in Figure 12-7.

Note in Figure 12-7 that the sku is now valid, and only two errors remain. To correct these errors:

1.   Remove the leading 2 in the name field, as this field must begin with an alpha character.

2.   Remove the leading M in the price field, as this field must contain the numeric dollar value only.

Click the Add Product button again.

This time, all the values pass validation, and the form data is finally submitted to the server. The form data is processed by a server-side JSP. This JSP simply displays the values of the form fields. The resulting display should be similar to Figure 12-8.

Notice that the client-side data validation code worked identically to the code in the first example. Any validation error is flagged with a red highlighted message next to the error. The client-side validation code will allow submission of form data only if there is no further validation error.

Despite the fact that this new prodform.jsp is created using a custom tag library, and not raw JavaScript coding, there is no observable difference in its behavior when compared to the raw JavaScript version.

How It Works

Because the index.jsp and procprod.jsp pages in this example remain unchanged from those in the previous example, they are not revisited here.

The major difference between the two examples is in the prodform.jsp page, located at <Tomcat Installation Directory>/webapps/ch12/example2/prodform.jsp. It is reproduced here:

```
<%@ taglib prefix="my" tagdir="/WEB-INF/tags/wroxtags" %>
<html>
<head>
  <title>Product Information Entry Form</title>
  <my:validateFunctions>
    <my:checkField name="sku" type="digits"/>
    <my:checkField name="name" type="alphanum"/>
    <my:checkField name="desc" type="alphanum"/>
    <my:checkField name="price" type="digits"/>
  </my:validateFunctions>
</head>
<body>
  <h1>Enter Product Information</h1>
  <form  name="prodform" action="index.jsp" method="post"
    onsubmit="return validateForm()">
  <table border="0" >
    <tr>
      <td>SKU:</td>
      <td>
        <input name="sku" type="text" width="40"/>
        <my:validateErrMsg name="sku"
          msg="<-- please enter digits only"/>
      </td>
    </tr>

    <tr>
      <td>Name:</td>
      <td>
      <input name="name" type="text" width="40"/>
      <my:validateErrMsg name="name"
        msg="<-- please enter letters or numbers only, do not start with a
number"/>
      </td>
    </tr>
    <tr>
      <td>Description:</td>
      <td>
        <input name="desc" type="text" width="40"/>
        <my:validateErrMsg name="desc"
          msg="<-- please enter letters or numbers only, do not start with a
number"/>
      </td>
    </tr>
    <tr>
      <td>Price:</td>
      <td>
        <input name="price" type="text" width="40"/>
        <my:validateErrMsg name="price"
          msg="<-- please enter price in dollars only, do not enter cents"/>
      </td>
    </tr>
```

```
    <tr>
      <td colspan="2">
        <input type="submit" value="Add Product" />
        <input type="hidden" name="action" value="prodsubmit"/>
      </td>
    </tr>


  </table>
  </form>
</body>
</html>
```

Compare this to the prodform.jsp from the first example. You will notice the improvements.

Using a custom tag library for client-side data validation

Instead of the embedded JavaScript code, this new prodform.jsp page contains the following set of tags:

```
<my:validateFunctions>
  <my:checkField name="sku" type="digits"/>
  <my:checkField name="name" type="alphanum"/>
  <my:checkField name="desc" type="alphanum"/>
  <my:checkField name="price" type="digits"/>
</my:validateFunctions>
```

The my prefix is used to address a custom tag library. This custom tag library is included using the <%@ taglib %> directive:

```
<%@ taglib prefix="my" tagdir="/WEB-INF/tags/wroxtags" %>
```

This usage of the <%@ taglib %> directive specifies that the tag files making up the tag library can be found in the <Tomcat Installation Directory>/webapps/ch12/WEB-INF/tags/wroxtags directory.

There are three custom tags in this tag library. The following table describes the usage of each tag.

Tag	Description
validateFunctions	Used to wrap a set of checkField tags.
checkField	Each checkField tag has a name attribute, which should be the name of the <input> element that contains the user input. It also has a type attribute. This attribute can contain either alphanum to validate against alphanumeric input (with a leading letter), or digits to validate against only numeric digits input.
validateErrMsg	Used to render an error message that will be visible only when the associated field validation fails. The name attribute should be the name of the <input> element that contains the user input to be validated. The msg attribute should contain the error message to display when validation fails.

Using these tags, a JSP developer can

❑ Provide client-side data validation, without knowing anything about the coding of JavaScript functions

❑ Easily add new validated fields to the form

To render a validation error, the `<my:validateErrMsg>` tag is used. For example, the following code renders the validation error for the sku field:

```
<tr>
  <td>SKU:</td>
  <td>
    <input name="sku" type="text" width="40"/>
    <my:validateErrMsg name="sku"
      msg="<-- please enter digits only"/>
  </td>
</tr>
```

The highlighted code is the `<my:validateErrMsg>` tag that renders the validation error message.

Tag library implementation details

If we look inside the tag files that implement this library, it is evident that the very same JavaScript code used in the first example is at work.

The `<my:validateFunctions>` custom tag

First, the `<my:validateFunctions>` tag, contained in the `<Tomcat Installation Directory>/webapps/ch12/WEB-INF/tags/wroxtags/validateFunctions.tag` file, is reproduced here:

```
<script language="JavaScript">
function isDigitsOnly(inParam)
{
    var chkExp = /^\d+$/;
    return (chkExp.test(inParam));
}
function isTextOnly(inParam)
{
    var chkExp = /^[a-z][a-z\d ]+$/i;
    return (chkExp.test(inParam));
}
function validateForm()
{
    var formValid = true;
    <jsp:doBody/>
    return formValid;
}
</script>
```

```
<style>
  span.validateError
  {
    color: red;
    visibility: hidden;
  }
</style>
```

This tag contains the embedded JavaScript code, with an embedded `<jsp:doBody>` standard action. The body content of this `<my:validateFunctions>` tag will be rendered at the location of this tag.

First, this tag defines the utility JavaScript functions:

```
<script language="JavaScript">
function isDigitsOnly(inParam)
{
    var chkExp = /^\d+$/;
    return (chkExp.test(inParam));
}
function isTextOnly(inParam)
{
    var chkExp = /^[a-z][a-z\d ]+$/i;
    return (chkExp.test(inParam));
}
```

Next, the tag defines the `validateForm()` function, but without the actual code to do the validation. This is because that code will be generated by a separate `<my:checkField>` tag for each field on the form. The output from these `<my:checkField>` tags will be rendered at the location of the `<jsp:dobody/>` tag:

```
function validateForm()
{
    var formValid = true;
    <jsp:doBody/>
    return formValid;
}
</script>
```

Last but not least, this tag also uses the `<style>` element to define the CSS style for the validation error message:

```
<style>
  span.validateError
  {
    color: red;
    visibility: hidden;
  }
</style>
```

The <my:checkField> custom tag

The second tag, <my:checkField>, is used to generate the code that performs the validation using the utility JavaScript functions; it takes two attributes as parameters. This tag, contained in the <Tomcat Installation Directory>/webapps/ch12/WEB-INF/tags/wroxtags/checkField.tag file, is reproduced here:

```
<%@ taglib prefix="c" uri="http://java.sun.com/jsp/jstl/core" %>
<%@attribute name="name" type="java.lang.String" %>
<%@attribute name="type" type="java.lang.String" %>

<c:choose>
  <c:when test="${type eq 'alphanum'}">
    if (!isTextOnly(document.prodform.${name}.value))
    {
  </c:when>

  <c:when test="${type eq 'digits'}">
    if (!isDigitsOnly(document.prodform.${name}.value))
    {
  </c:when>
</c:choose>
document.getElementById("${name}Error").style.visibility = "visible";
formValid = false;
    }
  else
    document.getElementById("${name}Error").style.visibility = "hidden";
```

This tag uses the JSTL library. The two attributes, name and type, are both declared as of type String using the <jsp:attribute> directive:

```
<%@ taglib prefix="c" uri="http://java.sun.com/jsp/jstl/core" %>
<%@ attribute name="name" type="java.lang.String" %>
<%@ attribute name="type" type="java.lang.String" %>
```

A JSTL <c:choose> construct is used to generate either a call to isTextOnly() or the isDigitsOnly() utility validation function. The decision is made based on the value of the type attribute of this <my:checkField> tag. Note the use of the EL expression, ${name}, in rendering the value of the name parameter:

```
<c:choose>
  <c:when test="${type eq 'alphanum'}">
    if (!isTextOnly(document.prodform.${name}.value))
    {
  </c:when>

  <c:when test="${type eq 'digits'}">
    if (!isDigitsOnly(document.prodform.${name}.value))
    {
  </c:when>
</c:choose>
```

The last part of this tag file contains the rest of the validation logic, setting the visibility of the hidden error message <span> element, and the value of the formValid Boolean variable:

```
        document.getElementById("${name}Error").style.visibility = "visible";
        formValid = false;
    }
    else
        document.getElementById("${name}Error").style.visibility = "hidden";
```

In the preceding code, again note the use of the EL expression, ${name}, to render the actual name of the field to be validated.

The <my:validateErrMsg> custom tag

The last tag in the library, the <my:validateErrMsg> tag, is used to render the <span> that contains the validation error message. This <my:validateErrMsg> tag, contained in the <Tomcat Installation Directory>/webapps/ch12/WEB-INF/tags/wroxtags/validateErrMsg.tag file, is reproduced here:

```
<%@attribute name="name" type="java.lang.String" %>
<%@attribute name="msg" type="java.lang.String" %>
<span id="${name}Error" class="validateError">${msg}</span>
```

This tag is very straightforward. The two attributes are both of type String. They are rendered into the HTML code fragment using EL expressions. The resulting <span> tag is initially invisible, but will be made visible if a validation error occurs with the associated field.

This concludes our coverage of the second example, and of dynamically generating client-side JavaScript code.

Another interesting non-HTML content type that JSP often generates is XML. The last example of this chapter works with the generation of XML data.

Dynamic generation of XML using JSP

The examples in Chapter 7, "JSP Directives," explored the generation of XML documents using JSP. This section reviews some of the techniques and concepts, and continues the exploration.

Remember the following points when using JSP to generate XML:

❑   JSP can be used to generate any textual data; XML is just another textual data type.

❑   Use the contentType attribute of the <%@page %> directive and set it to text/xml for maximal browser/application compatibility.

❑   All JSP 2.x pages can also be expressed in an XML view, where the entire unprocessed JSP page is in a well-formed XML document.

The last point is less important for most developers, but important for vendors who create tools. Having a JSP in a pure XML format enables development tools to easily parse and work with the page.

The last Try It Out exercise in this chapter examines a very common problem with the generation of XML documents using JSP.

Try It Out   Generating XML

This chapter's last Try It Out example is a JSP that generates an XML document. This XML document displays a programming tip of the day for the user, presumably retrieved from a database, although in the example, a custom tag is used to generate the data for display.

To view the generated XML document, you can use your browser. If you are using the Microsoft Internet Explorer browser, it can display a well-formed XML file in a collapsible view.

To try out this example, make sure that the `ch12.war` archive is deployed on your running Tomcat 5 server, and then access the following URL:

```
http://localhost:8080/ch12/example3/index.jsp
```

If you are using Internet Explorer as a browser, you will see that the resulting XML file has an error. Figure 12-10 illustrates what you will see.

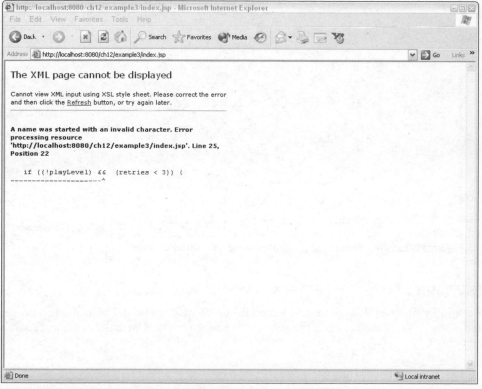

Figure 12-10: Error encountered during XML document generation

The resulting XML document is not valid because certain XML reserved characters conflict with the characters in the printed code. For example, the characters & and < are reserved in XML.

To see a properly working JSP without this problem, try the following URL:

```
http://localhost:8080/ch12/example3/index1.jsp
```

This time, the JSP generates a well-formed XML and the browser displays it in a collapsible view (if you are using Microsoft Internet Explorer). Figure 12-11 illustrates the well-formed document.

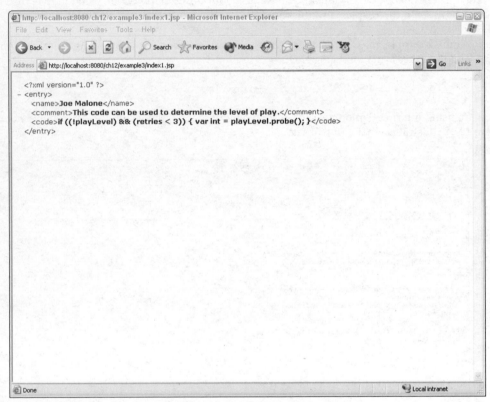

Figure 12-11: XML document generated after correction of error

How It Works

First, take a look at the JSP page that generated the bad XML document. This is the index.jsp page, located at <Tomcat Installation Directory>/webapps/ch12/example3/index.jsp. It is reproduced here:

```
<%@ taglib prefix="my" tagdir="/WEB-INF/tags/wroxtags" %>
<%@page contentType="text/xml" %>
<?xml version="1.0"?>
<entry>
  <my:getInfo/>
  <name>
    ${name}
  </name>
  <comment>
    ${comment}
  </comment>
  <code>
    ${code}
  </code>
</entry>
```

First, the `<%@ taglib %>` directive associates the my prefix with the tag files in the `<Tomcat Installation Directory>`/webapps/ch12/WEB-INF/tags/wroxtags directory:

```
<%@ taglib prefix="my" tagdir="/WEB-INF/tags/wroxtags" %>
```

Next, the `<%@ page %>` directive is used to set the generated content type to XML. This directive is followed immediately by the obligatory XML declaration:

```
<%@page contentType="text/xml" %>
<?xml version="1.0"?>
```

After the XML declaration, the root element `<entry>` starts. One of the tags in the tag library is called. This tag is named `<my:getInfo>`. This tag retrieves the details of the "programming tip of the day." When invoked, this tag simply sets three scoped variables called name, comment, and code, respectively.

The values of these variables are rendered using EL expressions within the XML template data. The EL expressions that render the variables are highlighted here:

```
<entry>
  <my:getInfo/>
  <name>
    ${name}
  </name>
  <comment>
    ${comment}
  </comment>
  <code>
    ${code}
  </code>
</entry>
```

While everything looks okay, it was observed earlier that this JSP will produce a bad XML document.

Escaping reserved characters when generating XML

The culprit is within the code variable. This variable contains the following code fragment:

```
if ((!playLevel) && (retries < 3))
{
    var int = playLevel.probe();
}
```

Both the & character and the < character are reserved, and have special meanings in XML documents. To use them in other parts of the XML document, they must be escaped. The following table shows the corresponding escaped characters.

Character	XML Escape
&	&amp;
<	&lt;

Therefore, for a well-formed XML document, the code fragment must be expressed as follows:

```
if ((!playLevel) &amp;&amp; (retries &lt; 3))
{
    var int = playLevel.probe();
}
```

Unfortunately, simply using EL expressions is not sufficient. Thankfully, however, the JSTL output tag, `<c:out>`, will escape XML by default.

Therefore, it is a simple matter of replacing the EL expressions with the `<c:out>` JSTL action. This is exactly what happened in `index1.jsp`, located at `<Tomcat Installation Directory>/webapps/ch12/example3/index1.jsp`. The content of this XML file is reproduced here, with the new `<c:out>` tags highlighted:

```
<%@ taglib prefix="c" uri="http://java.sun.com/jsp/jstl/core" %>
<%@ taglib prefix="my" tagdir="/WEB-INF/tags/wroxtags" %>
<%@page contentType="text/xml" %>
<?xml version="1.0"?>
<entry>
  <my:getInfo/>
  <name>
    <c:out value="${name}"/>
  </name>
  <comment>
    <c:out value="${comment}"/>
  </comment>
  <code>
    <c:out value="${code}"/>
  </code>
</entry>
```

An EL function called `escapeXml()` can also be used instead of JSTL `<c:out>`. For example, you can use `${fn:escapeXml(name)}` to achieve the same effect.

When working with XML data, it is very important to know if the dynamically generated data is escaped for the XML special characters, and to perform the required escape if necessary. This awareness will help you avoid common programming mistakes such as the following:

❑ Using un-escaped text in XML document, as shown in the preceding example

❑ Showing escaped text when displaying a non-XML document

The *<my:getInfo>* custom tag

The `<my:getInfo>` custom tag is the only thing remaining in this example that has not been discussed. This tag generating the data for the XML file is called `<my:getInfo>`. The code for this tag can be found in the `<Tomcat Installation Directory>/webapps/ch12/WEB-INF/wroxtags/getInfo.tag` file. The content of this file is shown here:

```
<%@ tag body-content="empty" %>
<%@ taglib prefix="c" uri="http://java.sun.com/jsp/jstl/core" %>
<%@ variable name-given="code" variable-class="java.lang.String" scope="AT_END" %>
<%@ variable name-given="name" variable-class="java.lang.String" scope="AT_END" %>
<%@ variable name-given="comment" variable-class="java.lang.String"
scope="AT_END" %>
<c:set var="code">
  if ((!playLevel) &&  (retries < 3))
  {
      var int = playLevel.probe();
  }
</c:set>
<c:set var="name">
  Joe Malone
</c:set>
<c:set var="comment">
  This code can be used to determine the level of play.
</c:set>
```

First, the `<%@ tag %>` directive is used to specify that the tag cannot have a body:

```
<%@ taglib prefix="c" uri="http://java.sun.com/jsp/jstl/core" %>
```

Next, the JSTL tag library is included and the three variables are defined using the `<%@ variable %>` directive. All of them are of type `String`, and they are synchronized at the end, making them available to the calling JSP page at the end of the tag's appearance:

```
<%@ taglib prefix="c" uri="http://java.sun.com/jsp/jstl/core" %>
<%@ variable name-given="code" variable-class="java.lang.String" scope="AT_END" %>
<%@ variable name-given="name" variable-class="java.lang.String" scope="AT_END" %>
<%@ variable name-given="comment" variable-class="java.lang.String"
scope="AT_END" %>
```

The value for the code variable is set to the following code fragment:

```
<c:set var="code">
  if ((!playLevel) &&  (retries < 3))
  {
      var int = playLevel.probe();
  }
</c:set>
```

Finally, the value of the name and comment variables is also set:

```
<c:set var="name">
  Joe Malone
</c:set>
<c:set var="comment">
  This code can be used to determine the level of play.
</c:set>
```

Upon the execution of this tag, the three variables will be available within the calling page, containing the desired data.

Summary

JSP, as a presentation technology, is not restricted to the dynamic generation of HTML content. It can be used to generate any type of dynamic textual content. One common alternative content type is XML. When generating XML, be careful of the need to escape certain reserved special characters. Careful use of the JSTL <c:out> tag in generating dynamic XML output can help alleviate any problems.

This chapter used JSP to generate validation code for execution on the user's browser. This code is created in the JavaScript programming language. Also explored was the possibility for JSP to dynamically generate executable code. The process of client-side data validation is simplified when JSP is used to generate the code. The following validation topics are covered:

❑   Form data validation can be performed on the server-side (i.e., via JSP) or on the client-side (using JavaScript code).

❑   Server-side data validation is generally inefficient, requiring network access and server-side CPU time. However, it is absolutely necessary for certain validation tasks.

❑   A well-designed Web application will take advantage of client-side validation wherever possible but may still have server-side data validation logic.

❑   By encapsulating the dynamic generation of client-side executable JavaScript code in a custom tag library, it is possible to reuse the logic. This enables even developers with no knowledge of JavaScript coding to create JSP code that takes advantage of client-side validation.

Exercises

1. Using the custom tag library in the second Try It Out exercise, create a form that will accept the following user input for an auction:

   Name: The name of the bidder; should be an alphanumeric input

   Item Number: The number of the item to bid on; should be a numeric value

   Bid Price: The bid in dollars; should be a numeric value

   Test the client-side data validation using this new form thoroughly.

2. Modify index1.jsp from the third Try It Out exercise to use the EL function escapeXml() to render a well-formed XML document.

Internationalization and Localized Content

In popular media, it is often said that the Internet has created a "global village." For the first time in history, anyone with Internet access is connected to everyone else. Interestingly enough, after everyone was connected, it became apparent that the "global village" concept isn't entirely accurate unless everyone speaks the same language. The fact is, they don't.

Even before the Internet phenomenon, creators of software products discovered the need to create software that can be sold and used internationally. When creating such applications, care must be taken not to assume or hard-code certain user interface conventions (such as English as the only language). The act of readying a software product for adaptation internationally is called *internationalization*. Because internationalization is such a long word, it is often just called *i18n* for short (there are 18 characters between the beginning *i* and the final *n*).

I18n is the main topic of this chapter. You will learn how to i18n-enable your JSP applications so that they can be used by people whose native language may not be English. More specifically, you will discover the following:

❑   Two main methods of internationalizing any text within your application

❑   Why and when one method is preferred over the other

❑   How to use internationalized resource bundles in JSP

❑   How a family of JSTL tags greatly simplifies i18n in your JSP programs

❑   Some of the quirks that you will encounter when attempting to internationalize your JSP application

About Internationalization-Ready Applications

Before an i18n-ready application can be sold to, and used in, a different region of the world, it must be localized. *Localization* is the act of adapting an i18n-ready application for use in a specific region. Localization is sometimes called *l10n* (10 characters between the first l and the final n). The act of localization may involve the following:

1. Translating the text to the local language.

2. Changing numeric formatting to the local convention—for example, the separator for thousands.

3. Changing currency symbols used—for example, using the euro symbol versus the dollar symbol as per the local convention.

4. Changing the date formatting to the local convention.

5. Other changes in the application to make it usable locally, such as adaptation to local input method editors (a system software utility used to enter the symbols of the local language).

This chapter includes four complete examples that describe in detail how you can perform actions 1 to 4 using JSP, while action 5 will depend on the region involved and cannot be easily generalized.

The client-server nature of JSP and Web application operation has created i18n and l10n requirements that are different from standard Java requirements. For example, a standalone application can always depend on the local Java VM that it is running on to tell it what region the user is operating in (usually via the underlying operating system settings). A Web application running on a server, on the other hand, may have one request coming in from an English-speaking user, and immediately service any user from the Far East, requiring completely different localization.

This chapter fully explores the set of unique i18n and l10n requirements of Web/JSP applications, clarifying how they differ from standalone applications.

While not every JSP developer will need to code and create new i18n-ready code, it is a valuable asset to understand how these very important concepts work. In fact, if you ever need to modify or maintain commercial or open-source software, you will very likely need to have i18n and l10n knowledge in order to understand the coding style of i18n-ready applications.

Internationalization and Localization

Internationalization is the act of creating code, applications, or systems that can be customized for use in different countries and regions. Back in the days when applications ran only on a client PC, this meant that software vendors would have to create a master copy of a software project that could be customized by their branch offices around the world for local use. This typically required that all text strings used in the program be isolated, and that the date, number, and currency format be customizable for each local market. Figure 13-1 illustrates this.

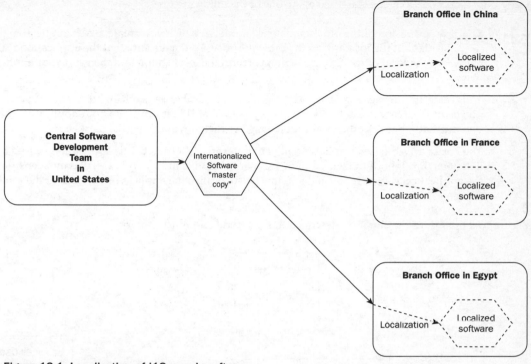

Figure 13-1: Localization of i18n-ready software

The branch offices, in turn, must perform localization on the master software. The act of localization is to take an i18n-ready piece of software and customize it for the local market. This typically means translating and replacing all textual strings, and making sure that formats such as date, number, and currency are consistent with the locally accepted convention. In practice, localization may involve intricate and specific customization aspects other than those described here.

> *I18n deals with the preparation of an application for international distribution. L10n is the actual work that needs to be performed in adapting an i18n-ready application for a particular local market.*

The unique i18n requirements of a Web-based JSP application

In a client/server environment, the picture shown in Figure 13-1 is slightly different. The line between i18n and l10n may also blur in some scenarios involving a server and many clients.

Generally, the scenario can be classified along one of the following lines:

1. This is an extension of the old "standalone" model in which you create a Web application that is used throughout the local offices in your enterprise. You make sure that the application is i18n-ready, but the local offices in each region perform the localization and then run your application over their own intranets.

2. You create an Internet-based service, which must be usable by users in their own native language. In this scenario, not only must you ensure that i18n is built into your application, but you must also perform the localization work for each of your potential markets.

3. You create a Web-based application in your enterprise's intranet. This application is used by divisions throughout the world. In this scenario, just like the second case, you must ensure that the application is i18n-ready and you must also localize the application for each of the foreign divisions.

Figure 13-2 illustrates the situation described in the second and third scenario.

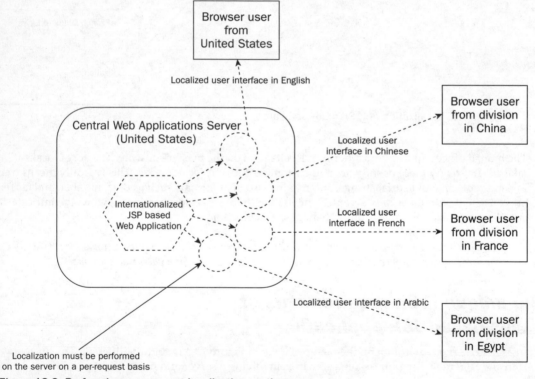

Figure 13-2: Performing per-request localization on the server

In Figure 13-2, each incoming request may have different l10n requirements, as every incoming request may be from a different region. However, if the server is keeping track of user sessions, each session will represent the request for one single user. All the requests in the same user session should have the same l10n requirement because they would be from the same location. This sort of i18n and l10n requirement is unique to Web-based applications. Essentially, even though the application is located at one centralized server, it must present a different user interface to each user depending on where they are located.

Building on the Java Platform's i18n Capabilities

The Java 2 platform's i18n features form the foundation of the i18n capabilities of a Web application. However, this is not to say that the i18n requirements of a standalone Java application running on a client's PC are the same as those of a Web application. Common elements between them exist, including the following:

❑ The existence and determination of locales

❑ The use of different character encoding depending on the requirements

❑ The use of i18n resource bundles

The concept of a locale

The Java 2 platform uses the concept of a *locale* to represent a specific set of localization requirements. A locale is specified using a string in the following format:

    xx_YY

where

❑ xx is a language code. It is specified as an ISO-639 code; see `http://ftp.ics.uci.edu/pub/ietf/http/related/iso639.txt` for a list. This language code is always two characters and in lowercase.

❑ YY is a code for the country that uses the language. It is specified as ISO-3166 code, and a list can be located at `www.iso.ch/iso/en/prods-services/iso3166ma/02iso-3166-code-lists/list-en1.html`. This country code is always two characters and in uppercase.

For example, for the en_US locale, American-English is the language used, while currency is USD (U.S. dollar) and date is displayed in the American-style date format. However, even though the United Kingdom also uses English for the language, the currency convention (British Pounds) is completely different.

Of course, the set of localization requirements will be completely different for international locales such as zh_CN, where Chinese is the language used, currency is RMB (Chinese yuan), and the date format is displayed in Chinese.

The following table describes some typical locales.

Locale	Description
en_US	The English language, with localization for the United States
en_GB	The English language, with localization for the United Kingdom
es_MX	The Spanish language, with localization for Mexico
es_ES	The Spanish language, with localization for Spain
fr_FR	The French language, with localization for France
zh_CN	The Chinese language, with localization for China
zh_TW	The Chinese language, with localization for Taiwan

You may note elsewhere that the language and country code of the locale are sometimes separated by a hyphen (-), instead of the underscore (_). For example: en-US. *Both formats are equivalent. However, this chapter uses only the underscore separator.*

Maintaining locale information

On a standalone Java application running on a single system, the locale can be set by the underlying operating system. This system locale information can be passed into the Java VM that is running the application, and this locale will never change in the execution lifetime of the standalone application.

When operating a server such as Tomcat 5, running Web applications and JSP pages, the locale of the server's JVM is of no interest to the application. Each and every incoming request can be from a different locale. This means that localization must be reflected on a per-request basis.

The Java 2 locale mechanism is used for localization of JSP applications. Unlike a standalone application, where the locale of the JVM is always the locale of the application and does not change, the locale of a JSP application must be determined and handled on a per-request basis.

Still unanswered are the questions regarding how one goes about determining the locale of a request and how one may maintain this information. The first Try It Out exercise demonstrates one method that can be used to determine the locale and handle l10n.

Try It Out   Explicit Locale Determination and l10n for JSPs

This first example presents a form to the user for data input. The data the user entered is then displayed. Unlike earlier similar examples, this one will handle two extremely different `locales`:

❏　English for the U.S.

❏　Chinese for Hong Kong SAR

To try out this example, you need the ch13.war archive. Make sure that your Tomcat 5 server is running and then deploy ch13.war to the server. Review Chapter 1 if you do not remember how to deploy a WAR archive.

Working with the English localization

Open your browser and access the following URL:

```
http://localhost:8080/ch13/example1/index.jsp
```

The main screen will present a selection of two languages to use for the application, either English or Chinese. Each selection is presented in its own language. The display for this main screen is similar to Figure 13-3.

Figure 13-3: Selecting English or Chinese for the localized user interface

Click the English selection. This will display an HTML form (the Application Form) in English, as shown in Figure 13-4.

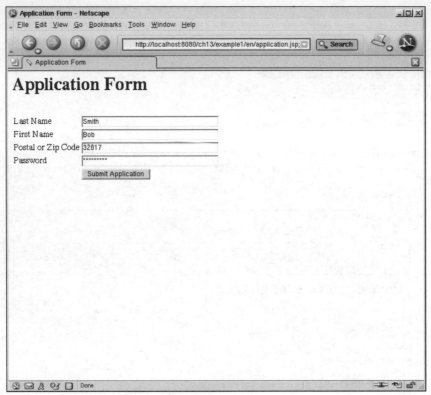

Figure 13-4: An English Application Form

Enter the following data into this form, and then click the Submit Application button.

Data Field	Value
Last Name	Smith
First Name	Bob
Postal or Zip Code	32817
Password	basepass1

After the Submit Application button is clicked, the data is submitted to the processor, which simply prints it out within an HTML table in this case. The resulting output is similar to what is shown in Figure 13-5.

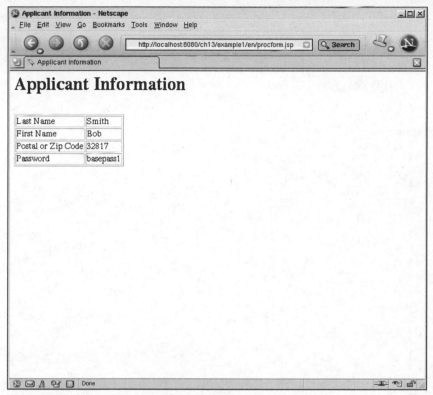

Figure 13-5: Successful submission of English form

The table in Figure 13-5 is simply a direct display of the data entered. This first portion shows the English localization for the application. The next section presents the localized Chinese user interface.

Working with the Chinese localization

Select the same URL with the browser again:

```
http://localhost:8080/ch13/example1/index.jsp
```

You will again see the language selection screen (refer to Figure 13-3). This time, click the Chinese character (the selection on the bottom). You will see the application form presented in Chinese characters. There are over 30,000 uniquely different characters, based on ideograms, in the Chinese character set. The form you will see is shown in Figure 13-6.

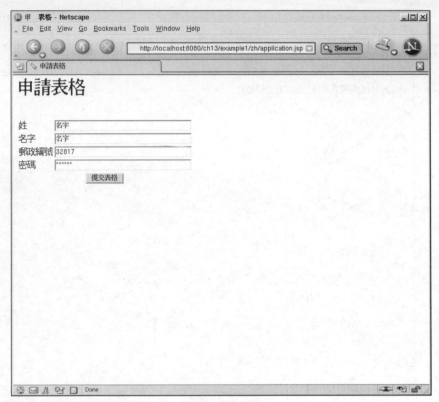

Figure 13-6: A localized Chinese application form

You should be able to figure out what the various fields in Figure 13-6 represent by comparing them to the English form (unless you can read Chinese, of course!).

Unless you are on a computer system that is Chinese-enabled (the most popular input method editor uses a pen and a writing tablet), you will not be able to enter Chinese characters into the fields. However, it is possible to cut and paste to take some text from the label and enter it into the fields.

To test Chinese character submission, using the browser's cut-and-paste feature, cut the label for Last Name and paste it into the first two fields. You should also use the symbols as a part of the password, as detailed in the following table.

Data Field	Value
姓	名字
名字	名字
郵政編號	32817
密碼	12名字34

Of course, if you know Chinese and have the input mechanism, you can enter actual Chinese data for this test.

Now, click the Submit Application button. This button is also labeled in Chinese. The Chinese data is submitted to a form processor. This form processor simply prints the submitted data values — in Chinese, of course. The final screen you should see is similar to Figure 13-7.

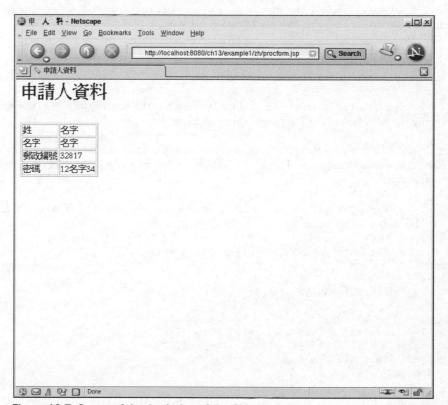

Figure 13-7: Successful submission of the Chinese form

In Figure 13-7, notice that all the information that has been submitted is received by the form processor as Chinese characters.

This JSP-based form application is i18n-ready; it currently supports English and Chinese, but can readily be expanded to support many more languages. The next section explores how the application is made i18n-ready, and how user interface language localization for both English and Chinese is performed.

How It Works

This first example uses a very direct and reliable way to determine the locale of the user: It simply asks the users which locale they wish to use.

Explicit user selection of locale

The first page, index.jsp, presents two languages for the user to select from. Each language selection is in turn written in the respective language. The English selection is in English, and the Chinese selection is in Chinese.

Because it is not possible to know whether the user has the capability to display any special language at this point, it is not possible to assume that the user's browser can display Chinese characters correctly. Therefore, the selection actually makes use of two graphical GIF files:

❑ english.gif with the text English

❑ chinese.gif with the Chinese characters representing "Chinese"

This method of selection can be used to enable the user the select a specific locale. In this first example, however, only the selection of the language will be offered.

> *When presenting a user with the initial locale selection, you should not assume that the user can display text in any other language. The use of a graphical image, such as the flag of the country, is recommended.*

This index.jsp file is located at <Tomcat Installation Directory>/webapps/ch13/example1/ index.jsp. It is reproduced here:

```
<%@ taglib prefix="c" uri="http://java.sun.com/jsp/jstl/core" %>
<html>
<head>
  <title>Select a language</title>
</head>
<body>
  <h1>Please select a language:</h1>
  <c:url value="en/application.jsp" var="engURL"/>
  <a href="${engURL}">
    <img src="english.gif"/>
  </a>
  <br/>
  <br/>
  <c:url value="zh/application.jsp" var="chineseURL"/>
  <a href="${chineseURL}">
    <img src="chinese.gif"/>
  </a>
</body>
</html>
```

Linking to the English form

Examining the code, you can see that the JSTL <c:url> tag is being used to generate a URL variable. For the English application form, the code is as follows:

```
<c:url value="en/application.jsp" var="engURL"/>
<a href="${engURL}">
  <img src="english.gif"/>
</a>
```

The <c:url> tag is used to ensure that special URL characters are escaped and that sessions are maintained in all cases. You may want to revisit Chapter 6, "JSP Tag Libraries and JSTL," if you want more information on the <c:url> action.

The link generated in ${engURL} is essentially as follows:

```
http://localhost:8080/ch13/example1/en/application.jsp
```

Linking to the Chinese form

Similar to the English application form, a JSTL <c:url> tag is being used to generate the link, as shown by the following code:

```
<c:url value="zh/application.jsp" var="chineseURL"/>
<a href="${chineseURL}">
  <img src="chinese.gif"/>
</a>
```

The link generated when you click the Chinese selection is essentially as follows:

```
http://localhost:8080/ch13/example1/zh/application.jsp
```

When you compare this to the English example, you can see that the English and Chinese forms are actually stored under different directories in the Web application. For many production scenarios, maintaining duplicate sets of translated JSP and HTML pages (one for each language supported) is a practical way of managing i18n-ready content.

Handling i18n using duplicated sets of translated pages

Figure 13-8 shows the JSP pages that are involved within this i18n-ready application.

Two sets of JSP application pages are shown in Figure 13-8. The application.jsp and procform.jsp pages exist under both the en directory and the zh directory.

The set of JSP pages in the en directory is in English, and the set under the zh directory is pre-translated into Chinese. This scheme can obviously be extended. For example, Spanish support can be added by creating an es directory, and pre-translating the JSP pages to Spanish.

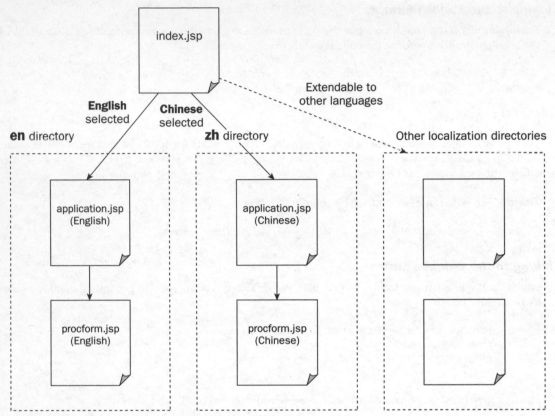

Figure 13-8: Supporting i18n using duplicated JSP pages

The main advantages of this approach are as follows:

❑   If there is only a small probability that the application will require internationalization in the future, this approach requires the least amount of additional work.

❑   If the JSP pages have heavily stylized layouts and have complex client-side scripting elements, this approach enables the pages to be localized and customized for the best look in every language that is supported.

Following are the main disadvantages of this approach:

❑   All the JSP pages need to be duplicated for each supported language/locale, increasing the number of files that needs to be managed.

❑   Any code change must be made identically to each set of language/locale-specific pages.

❑   For JSP pages that are code-heavy, this approach is not practical.

You can create an i18n-ready application by simply creating a separate set of JSP pages for each locale that is supported. Each localized set of pages should be pre-translated into the associated language.

The localized English pages

For the English pages, the form resides in the en directory as `application.jsp`. It is located at `<Tomcat Installation Directory>/webapps/ch13/example1/en/application.jsp` and is reproduced here:

```
<%@ taglib prefix="c" uri="http://java.sun.com/jsp/jstl/core" %>
<html>
<head>
  <title>Application Form</title>
</head>
<body>
  <h1>Application Form</h1>
  <br/>
  <c:url value="procform.jsp" var="actionURL"/>
  <form action="${actionURL}" method="post">
    <table>
      <tr>
        <td>Last Name</td>
        <td><input type="text" name="lastname" size="40"/></td>
      </tr>
      <tr>
        <td>First Name</td>
        <td><input type="text" name="firstname" size="40"/></td>
      </tr>
      <tr>
        <td>Postal or Zip Code</td>
        <td><input type="text" name="postcode" size="40"/></td>
      </tr>
      <tr>
        <td>Password</td>
        <td><input type="password" name="pass" size="40"/></td>
      </tr>
      <tr>
        <td colspan="2" align="center">
          <input type="submit" value="Submit Application"/>
        </td>
      </tr>
    </table>

  </form>

</body>
</html>
```

This page simply presents the HTML form. The JSTL `<c:url>` tag is once again used to generate the URL that is used for the HTML `<form>` tag's `action` attribute. This is the JSP page that will be used to process the form, as shown in the following code:

```
<c:url value="procform.jsp" var="actionURL"/>
<form action="${actionURL}" method="post">
```

The `${actionURL}` request scoped variable is used to temporarily hold the form processor's URL. Essentially it will contain the following:

```
http://localhost:8080/ch13/example1/en/procform.jsp
```

Because this is under the en directory, it is a version of the form processor that is localized for the English `locale`.

The English form processor

The localized English form processor page resides in the en directory and is called `procform.jsp`. It is located at `<Tomcat Installation Directory>/webapps/ch13/example1/en/procform.jsp` and is reproduced here:

```
<html>
<head>
  <title>Applicant Information</title>
</head>
<body>
  <h1>Applicant Information</h1>
  <br/>

  <table border="1">
    <tr>
      <td>Last Name</td>
      <td>${param.lastname}</td>
    </tr>

    <tr>
      <td>First Name</td>
      <td>${param.firstname}</td>
    </tr>


    <tr>
      <td>Postal or Zip Code</td>
      <td>${param.postcode}</td>
    </tr>

    <tr>
      <td>Password</td>
      <td>${param.pass}</td>
    </tr>

  </table>
</body>
</html>
```

This is basically an HTML table that prints out the submitted request parameters for the form. The values of the request parameters are obtained via EL expressions highlighted in the preceding listing. Note that all the EL expressions use the `param` implicit object in EL to directly access the request parameters. If you need a refresher on EL expressions and EL implicit objects, see Chapter 5, "JSP and EL."

The localized Chinese pages

The Chinese application form page resides in the `zh` directory as `application.jsp`. `zh` is the ISO-639 two-letter code for the Chinese language. Although you can use any directory name, using the ISO-639 letter code is recommended to facilitate long-term maintenance of your application.

The localized `application.jsp` is located at `<Tomcat Installation Directory>/webapps/ch13/example1/zh/application.jsp` and is reproduced here, with the translated localized code highlighted:

```
<%@ taglib prefix="c" uri="http://java.sun.com/jsp/jstl/core" %>
<html>
<head>
  <meta http-equiv="Content-Type" content="text/html;charset=utf-8" >
  <title>申請表格</title>
</head>
<body>
  <h1>申請表格</h1>
  <br/>
  <c:url value="procform.jsp" var="actionURL"/>
  <form action="${actionURL}" method="post">
    <table>
      <tr>
        <td>姓</td>
        <td><input type="text" name="lastname" size="40"/></td>
      </tr>

      <tr>
        <td>名字</td>
        <td><input type="text" name="firstname" size="40"/></td>
      </tr>


      <tr>
        <td>郵政編號</td>
        <td><input type="text" name="postcode" size="40"/></td>
      </tr>


      <tr>
        <td>密碼</td>
        <td><input type="password" name="pass" size="40"/></td>
      </tr>

      <tr>
        <td colspan="2" align="center">
          <input type="submit" value="提交表格"/>
        </td>
      </tr>

    </table>
  </form>
</body>
</html>
```

411

The thing to notice in the preceding code is that all the contained text has been translated to Chinese. However, to ensure that the Chinese characters are displayed and stored properly, you must ensure the following:

❑ That your system has the appropriate font installed; on Win32 systems this will require the installation of an update.

❑ That you create and edit this file using only a Unicode-capable editor. The Notepad editor on most Win32 systems is Unicode-capable, as are many editors on Linux systems. When in doubt, check the documentation of the text editor to make sure.

❑ That when you save these files, you save them as UTF-8 files (UTF-8 being the Unicode format that has the widest and most robust Web support at this time).

To represent the 30,000 characters in the Chinese language, the character encoding used for the text file must be able to handle and represent them. The Unicode character set is a single character set that can be used to represent most written languages in the world. The use of Unicode is highly recommended in any new projects. Unicode is supported by all Win32-based operating systems, as well as UNIX operating systems. Unicode is also well supported by the latest version of all major browsers.

Many different character encodings are available. Very old legacy browsers running on 16-bit operating systems used restrictive code pages-based character sets to support foreign languages. There existed a large number of these character sets, each accommodating only a few languages (English is a common factor of every character set).

With the availability of 32-bit microprocessors, the Unicode character encodings have become the most popular because the Unicode character set can represent most languages in the world without the need to switch character sets.

Unicode itself can be encoded in either an 8-bit or 16-bit format. The most common and widely supported Unicode encoding format at this time is UTF-8, which is an 8-bit encoding of the Unicode characters. UTF-8 uses multiple 8-bit characters to encode a single character, if necessary.

For this Chinese application.jsp page, the encoding is specified to be UTF-8 for the browser using a <meta> header tag:

```
<meta http-equiv="Content-Type" content="text/html;charset=utf-8" >
```

Browsers that support UTF-8 will honor this header, ensuring that the characters being sent are decoded properly and displayed properly using the appropriate Unicode font. All major browsers support UTF-8 encoding on Win32 or UNIX systems.

To save runtime memory, and disk storage space, many operating systems do not pre-install the fonts necessary to display foreign character sets. This is especially true with the very large Far Eastern character sets. The browsers on most operating systems do not manage their own fonts and rely on the operating system to supply the font. This means that while most browsers support Unicode, they may not display the correct character if the necessary font is not available. You will need to make sure that you have installed the Chinese Big5 font support update to see this example properly. On Win32 systems with Internet Explorer, this update can be automatically performed online when the page using the characters is first accessed.

The Chinese form processor

The JSP page used to process the form data, and display the input data, has also been localized to the Chinese language. The page resides in the zh directory, and is called procform.jsp. It is located at `<Tomcat Installation Directory>/webapps/ch13/example1/zh/procform.jsp` and is reproduced here (the localized, translated, text lines are highlighted):

```
<html>
<head>
  <meta http-equiv="Content-Type" content="text/html;charset=utf-8" >
  <title>申請人資料</title>
</head>
<body>
  <h1>申請人資料</h1>
  <br/>

  <table border="1">
    <tr>
      <td>姓</td>
      <td>${param.lastname}</td>
    </tr>

    <tr>
      <td>名字</td>
      <td>${param.firstname}</td>
    </tr>

    <tr>
      <td>郵政編號</td>
      <td>${param.postcode}</td>
    </tr>

    <tr>
      <td>密碼</td>
      <td>${param.pass}</td>
    </tr>

  </table>

</body>
</html>
```

Once again, notice the use of the `<meta>` tag in the `<head>` section to specify UTF-8 as the character set encoding for this page. As with the Chinese application.jsp page, this file must be created and edited with an editor that supports Unicode. Most modern IDEs include built-in editors that work well with Unicode files.

This concludes our coverage of the first example. The next example shows another way to make your JSP application i18n-ready without the need to replicate all of the JSP pages in the application.

Try It Out   **L10n Using Java 2's Resource Bundles**

This example provides the same dual-locale form submission function as the first example. However, instead of replicating the set of JSP pages for each supported language, this example uses only one set of JSP pages.

To try out this example, make sure that your Tomcat 5 server is running and that ch13.war is currently deployed. Access the following URL with a browser:

```
http://localhost:8080/ch13/example2/index.jsp
```

Trying out the English pages

The initial welcome screen that you see at this point should be identical to the one from the first example (refer to Figure 13-3).

Select the English pages by clicking the English selection. Verify that you have the English form displayed, similar to the one shown in Figure 13-4. One thing that you may notice, however, is that the base URL accessing the form is no longer under the en subdirectory as it was in example 1, but simply:

```
http:// localhost:8080/ch13/example2/application.jsp
```

Now, enter the data that you see in the following table into the form.

Data Field	Value
Last Name	Smith
First Name	Bob
Postal or Zip Code	32817
Password	basepass1

Click the Submit Application button, and the procform.jsp page will be called to process the form. This page, exactly like that in the previous example, will print out the submitted information. This will result in a final display similar to what is shown in Figure 13-5 earlier. Again, note that the base URL to access this final page is no longer in an en subdirectory.

Trying out the Chinese localization

Now, to try out the Chinese pages, access this URL again:

```
http://localhost:8080/ch13/example2/index.jsp
```

This time, click the Chinese selection. You should see the localized, translated, Chinese welcome screen, as shown in Figure 13-6. Note that for this page, the base URL is no longer in the zh directory. In fact, it is the same base URL that displayed an English form just a little earlier:

```
http:// localhost:8080/ch13/example2/application.jsp
```

Using the cut-and-paste feature of your browser, cut out the text of the Chinese label for Last Name and paste it into the form as input values. Use the following table as a guide.

Data Field	Value
姓	名字
名字	名字
郵政編號	32817
密碼	12名字34

To submit the form's data, click the Submit Application button. This button is localized to Chinese. Upon clicking, the Chinese data is submitted to the form processor. The form processor is localized to Chinese and displays the data as shown in Figure 13-7 (from the first example).

Overall, the operation of this second example is indistinguishable from that of the first example. However, the actual i18n preparation is quite different.

How It Works

This example uses the Java 2 platform's ability to support i18n resource bundles.

Java 2 resource bundles

A resource bundle is an i18n mechanism that is delivered as part of the Java 2 platform. Resource bundles enable Java applications to use locale-sensitive text string resources. Figure 13-9 shows how resource bundles work.

In Figure 13-9, the application does not contain any text strings that may need to be translated. Instead, specific names are given to each of these strings, and a resource bundle can be created. The bundle can contain multiple sets of translated strings for each name, one set for each language that is supported by the application. The name for a string can be used to fetch the corresponding internationalized text from a resource bundle. To illustrate how this works, a hypothetical function called getLocalizedText() is used. The actual text retrieved from the resource bundle will be sensitive to the locale that is in effect. The Java 2 platform provides an actual API to set the current locale, and to retrieve locale-sensitive strings from the resource bundle.

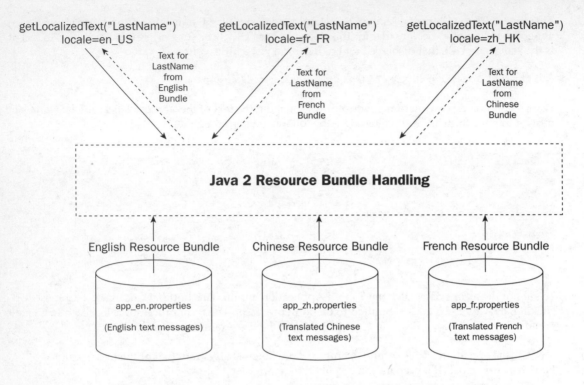

Figure 13-9: Using Java 2 resource bundles for i18n

For example, in Figure 13-9, if the current locale is en_US, then calling getLocalizedText ("LastName") will obtain the English text string "Last Name". However, if the locale is zh_HK, then calling getLocalizedText("LastName") will obtain the Chinese text string.

Creating a resource bundle

Java 2 resource bundles can be implemented either as properties files or Java classes. The easiest way to include i18n strings is via the use of properties files. Each line of a property file for Java 2 has the following general format:

```
<property name>=<property value>
```

For example, the property file that contains the English i18n text strings is the app.properties file (located at <Tomcat Installation Directory>/webapps/ch13/example2/WEB-INF/classes/app. properties). It has the following content:

```
newTitle=Application Form
lastName=Last Name
firstName=First Name
postalCode=Postal or Zip Code
password=Password
submitForm=Submit Form
appInfo=Applicant Information
```

In order for resource bundles to be available to the application, the server must be able to locate the property files and load them. For Web applications running on Tomcat 5 servers, this means that they must be found in the Web application's `classpath`. Each Web application running on a Tomcat 5 server can have its own independent `classpath`. One beneficial side-effect of this per-application partitioning is the ability to keep the internationalized strings of one application separate from those of another.

Because the resource bundle must be in the `classpath`, the i18n properties files are typically

❑ Placed under the `WEB-INF/classes` directory during development, which enables them to be quickly modified during testing

❑ Archived into JAR files and placed into the `WEB-INF/lib` directory of the application during production deployment

In order to make the properties files easy to access and modify, they are placed under the application's `WEB-INF/classes` directory for this example. That is why the `app.properties` file shown earlier is placed in the `<Tomcat Installation Directory>/webapps/ch13/example2/WEB-INF/classes` directory.

How Java 2 selects i18n strings

Each set of locale-specific strings is stored in a separate properties file. The Java 2 runtime will select the string to use based on the current locale. For example, the properties file containing the localized Chinese string is called `app_zh.properties`. This file is located in the same `<Tomcat Installation Directory>/webapps/ch13/example2/WEB-INF/classes` directory, and its contents are reproduced here:

```
newTitle=\u7533\u8acb\u8868\u683c
lastName=\u59d3
firstName=\u540d\u5b57
postalCode=\u90f5\u653f\u7de8\u865f
password=\u5bc6\u78bc
submitForm=\u63d0\u4ea4\u8868\u683c
appInfo=\u7533\u8acb\u4eba\u8cc7\u6599
```

You will immediately note the following:

❑ The names of the properties are exactly the same as the properties in the English `app.properties` file.

❑ There are no UTF-8 Chinese characters in this file.

The first point comes as no surprise. When the `locale` is set to `zh_HK` or another locale with `zh` Chinese language, then the string from `app_zh.properties` will be used. If the `locale` is set to anything else, then the default `app.properties` file will be used. If the application were to be modified to support another language, say French, you'd need to create a new `app_fr.properties` file containing the translated strings.

The second point, however, is quite surprising. Why is the property file not a UTF-8 file with all the Chinese characters in it? On the Java 2 platform, a restriction on properties files specifies that they must contain only ASCII characters.

Creating the Chinese l10n properties file

Because Java 2 can work only with ASCII-based properties files, any Unicode-encoded file will need to be converted to use ASCII escape codes.

If you are working with an IDE or specialized resource editor, you may be able to generate these files directly using those tools.

If you do not have a resource editor that will produce ASCII properties directly, you can use a Unicode editor together with a utility called `native2ascii`—supplied in the `bin` directory of the Java 2 SDK.

For example, consider the following Unicode properties file, called `app_zh.ucd`. You can find this file at `<Tomcat Installation Directory>/webapps/ch13/example2/WEB-INF/classes/app_zh.ucd`. The content is reproduced here:

```
newTitle=申請表格
lastName= 姓
firstName= 密碼
postalCode= 郵政編號
password= 密碼
submitForm= 提交表格
appInfo= 申請人資料
```

This file can be created and modified using the Notepad editor on Windows XP or Windows 2000 (or any Unicode editor on UNIX/Linux). The file is then saved as type "Unicode Big Endian."

Next, using the `native2ascii` utility from JDK 1.4 SDK, you can use the following command to convert this file to an ASCII file:

```
native2ascii -encoding UnicodeBig app_zh.ucd app_zh.properties
```

The resulting output `app_zh.properties` file will contain the required escape code, shown previously as `app_zh.properties`.

When using Java 2 properties-based resource bundles for i18n, any properties files that contain non-ASCII Unicode characters must first be converted to escape notation in an ASCII file.

The Locale selection page

Looking back at the example, the first JSP page of the application is again `index.jsp`, located at `<Tomcat Installation Directory>/webapps/ch13/example2/index.jsp`. The content is reproduced here, with differences from the first example highlighted:

```
<%@ taglib prefix="c" uri="http://java.sun.com/jsp/jstl/core" %>
<html>
<head>
  <title>Select Language</title>
</head>
```

```
<body>
  <h1>Please select language:</h1>
  <c:url value="application.jsp" var="engURL">
    <c:param name="locale" value="en_US"/>
  </c:url>

  <a href="${engURL}">
    <img src="english.gif"/>
  </a>
  <br/>
  <br/>
  <c:url value="application.jsp" var="chineseURL">
    <c:param name="locale" value="zh_HK"/>
  </c:url>

  <a href="${chineseURL}">
    <img src="chinese.gif"/>
  </a>
</body>
</html>
```

If you select the English language, the `<c:url>` tag will create a hyperlink to the `application.jsp` form. However, it will also add a request parameter called `locale`, with the value `en_US`. This will be used to set the `locale` of the user to use the English language. The actual URL produced will be as follows:

```
http://localhost:8080/ch13/example2/application.jsp?locale=en_US
```

If you select the Chinese language, the `<c:url>` tag will assign the value `zh_HK` to the locale request parameter. The resulting URL will be as follows:

```
http://localhost:8080/ch13/example2/application.jsp?locale=zh_HK
```

Generating a localized form using JSP

The `application.jsp` page is used to display the input form. The `application.jsp` page must generate a form in a different language depending on the value of the incoming `locale` request parameter. The page is located at `<Tomcat Installation Directory>/webapps/ch13/example2/application.jsp`.

Here is the content of `application.jsp`, with the i18n coding highlighted:

```
<%@ page pageEncoding="UTF-8" %>
<%@ taglib prefix="c" uri="http://java.sun.com/jsp/jstl/core" %>
<%@ taglib prefix="fmt" uri="http://java.sun.com/jsp/jstl/fmt" %>
<html>
<c:set var="loc" value="en_US"/>
<c:if test="${!(empty param.locale)}">
  <c:set var="loc" value="${param.locale}"/>
</c:if>
```

```
<fmt:setLocale value="${loc}" />


<fmt:bundle basename="app">
<head>
  <title><fmt:message key="newTitle"/></title>
</head>
<body>
  <h1><fmt:message key="newTitle"/></h1>
  <br/>
  <c:url value="procform.jsp" var="formActionURL" />

  <form action="${formActionURL}" method="post">
    <table>
      <tr>
        <td><fmt:message key="lastName"/></td>
        <td>

          <input type="hidden" name="locale" value="${loc}"/>
          <input type="text" name="lastname" size="40"/></td>
      </tr>

      <tr>
        <td><fmt:message key="firstName"/></td>
        <td><input type="text" name="firstname" size="40"/></td>
      </tr>

      <tr>
        <td><fmt:message key="postalCode"/></td>
        <td><input type="text" name="postcode" size="40"/></td>
      </tr>

      <tr>
        <td><fmt:message key="password"/></td>
        <td><input type="password" name="pass" size="40"/></td>
      </tr>

      <tr>
        <td colspan="2" align="center">
          <input type="submit" value="<fmt:message key='submitForm'/>"/></td>
      </tr>

    </table>
  </form>
</body>
</fmt:bundle>
</html>
```

Note that there is absolutely no locale-specific text in the application.jsp file. Instead, <fmt:setLocale>, <fmt:bundle>, and <fmt:message> are used to access the i18n resource bundle.

JSTL tags that support i18n

The JSTL tags that support i18n are contained in the `fmt` subset of the tag library. This subset can be included via the following `<%@ taglib %>` directive. This directive also specifies that the prefix to use for these tags is `fmt`:

```
<%@ taglib prefix="fmt" uri="http://java.sun.com/jsp/jstl/fmt" %>
```

The `<fmt:setLocale>` tag is used to set the current locale, which is a configuration variable called `javax.servlet.jsp.jstl.fmt.locale`. This variable is maintained by the JSP runtime, and is used to determine the locale to use for various JSTL tags.

The syntax of the `<fmt:setLocale>` tag is as follows:

```
<fmt:setLocale value="...locale value..." [variant="...variant value..."]
[scope="...scope of var..."] />
```

The attributes are described in the following table.

Attribute Name	Mandatory/Optional	Description
value	Mandatory	The `value` attribute is typically set with the locale name — for example, `en_US` or `zh_HK`.
variant	Optional	The `variant` attribute is optional and only rarely used for specialized locales that have a browser-specific variant value in addition to the language and country components.
scope	Optional	The `scope` attribute, if specified, determines the scope of the application-based locale variable. By default, this is assumed to be `page` scoped. Some applications may want to set scope to `session`, for all the requests from the same user to track the locale.

Once the application locale is set, the `<fmt:bundle>` tag can be used to frame a set of `<fmt:message>` tags that will display localized text. The `<fmt:bundle>` tag has the following syntax:

```
<fmt:bundle basename="...the bundle's base name" [prefix="...prefix name..."]/>
```

This tag sets the resource bundle to be used for all the `<fmt:message>` tags within its body (unless specifically overridden). Its attributes are described in the following table.

Attribute Name	Mandatory/Optional	Description
basename	Mandatory	The base name of the resource bundle. For our example, the base name is app. The Chinese localized bundle can be accessed as app_zh. properties.
prefix	Optional	If specified, a prefix that is prepended to nested <fmt:message> tags within the body.

Within the <fmt:bundle> tag, you can have several <fmt:message> tags. Each <ftm:message> tag will render a local specific string. The most common syntax of <fmt:message> is as follows:

```
<fmt:message key="...name of property..." [bundle="...resourceBundle...."] [var="..
variable name.."] [scope="... scope of var..."]/>
```

This tag renders a localized text string by extracting a property from the properties file. The current locale is used, along with the key attribute (reflecting the name of the property), to find the string to use. The attributes for this tag are shown in the following table.

Attribute Name	Mandatory/Optional	Description
key	Mandatory	The name of the key used to find a string in the l10n properties file.
bundle	Optional	If specified, the resource bundle used to extract the localized string. If not specified, but if the tag is within a <fmt:bundle> tag, the resource bundle specified by the <fmt:bundle> tag will be used.
var	Optional	If specified, creates a String variable with the specified name to contain the localized string.
scope	Optional	If specified, determines the scope of the variable created by the var attribute. The default is page scope.

Applying the JSTL i18n tags

In applicaton.jsp, the first few lines declare the use of both the core and the i18n JSTL tag libraries. These lines are highlighted here:

```
<%@ page pageEncoding="UTF-8" %>
<%@ taglib prefix="c" uri="http://java.sun.com/jsp/jstl/core" %>
<%@ taglib prefix="fmt" uri="http://java.sun.com/jsp/jstl/fmt" %>
```

Note the use of the pageEncoding attribute of the <%@ page %> directive to specify that the response generated by this JSP page is encoded as UTF-8. This ensures that both the container and the user's browser expect to work with a UTF-8-encoded Unicode page.

To set the application locale, the incoming request parameter called `locale` is used. This parameter is set as a result of the user's selection from the `index.jsp` page. The code in `application.jsp` ensures that the default `locale` is set to en_US even if the `locale` parameter is not set:

```
<c:set var="loc" value="en_US"/>
<c:if test="${!(empty param.locale)}">
  <c:set var="loc" value="${param.locale}"/>
</c:if>
<fmt:setLocale value="${loc}" />
```

The application `locale` is now set to the same value of the incoming `locale` parameter.

In the next statement, the `<fmt:bundle>` tag will select the resource bundle to use depending on the application locale. This `<fmt:bundle>` tag specifies that the resource bundle has a `basename` of `"app"`. The server will look for `app.properties` and `app_zh.properties` for localized strings. Because the `<fmt:bundle>` tag is not closed until the end of the JSP page, all of the `<fmt:message>` actions will use the selected resource bundle:

```
<fmt:bundle basename="app">
```

For example, in the `<title>` tag shown next, the `<fmt:message>` tag is used to obtain the locale-specific `"myTitle"` string. If the locale selected by the user is `"en_US"`, then the string `"Application Form"` will be used. If the locale selected by the user is `"zh_HK"`, then the Chinese Unicode string will be used.

```
<head>
  <title><fmt:message key="newTitle"/></title>
</head>
```

The rest of the JSP page contains other `<fmt:message>` tag instances that are processed in a similar fashion.

A hidden field is used to pass the `locale` information on to the form processing JSP. It is specified by using the value of the incoming `locale` parameter (value assigned earlier to the `loc` variable):

```
<input type="hidden" name="locale" value="${loc}"/>
```

Creating an i18n-ready form processing JSP

The `procform.jsp` in this example will display in different languages, depending on the incoming request parameter: `locale`. This page is located at `<Tomcat Installation Directory>/webapps/ch13/example2/procform.jsp`.

The listing of `procform.jsp` is shown here, with the i18n coding highlighted:

```
<%@ page pageEncoding="UTF-8" %>
<%@ taglib prefix="fmt" uri="http://java.sun.com/jsp/jstl/fmt" %>
<fmt:requestEncoding value="UTF-8" />
<html>
<fmt:setLocale value="${param.locale}"  />
<head>
  <fmt:bundle basename="app">
  <title><fmt:message key="appInfo"/></title>
```

```
    </head>
    <body>
      <h1><fmt:message key="appInfo"/></h1>
      <br/>

      <table border="1">
        <tr>
          <td><fmt:message key="lastName"/></td>
          <td>${param.lastname}</td>
        </tr>

        <tr>
          <td><fmt:message key="firstName"/></td>
          <td>${param.firstname}</td>
        </tr>

        <tr>
          <td><fmt:message key="postalCode"/></td>
          <td>${param.postcode}</td>
        </tr>

        <tr>
          <td><fmt:message key="password"/></td>
          <td>${param.pass}</td>
        </tr>

      </table>

    </body>
    </fmt:bundle>

  </html>
```

Some of the preceding code is very similar to application.jsp shown earlier. The application's locale is set via the hidden form request parameter in the application.jsp called locale:

```
    <fmt:setLocale value="${param.locale}"  />
```

A <fmt:bundle> action is used to set the resource bundle that is used by all the enclosed <fmt:message> actions:

```
    <fmt:bundle basename="app">
    <title><fmt:message key="appInfo"/></title>
    </head>
    <body>
      <h1><fmt:message key="appInfo"/></h1>
      <br/>
    ...
    </body>
      </fmt:bundle>
    </html>
```

One new JSTL tag used in this JSP is the <fmt:requestEncoding> action. This tag is essential for submitting form data that may be Unicode-encoded.

Setting request parameter encoding

Incoming request parameters to a JSP form processor cannot be decoded correctly if the JSP container does not know what type of encoding is used on the parameters.

In the case of our example, the browser submits the parameter using the same encoding as the application.jsp page. This means that the parameters are submitted using UTF-8 encoding but the server/container will have no way of knowing this unless explicitly told. Therefore, it is necessary to specify to the container that the request encoding is UTF-8 in the procform.jsp page:

```
<fmt:requestEncoding value="UTF-8" />
```

According to the HTTP protocol specification, the browser is supposed to have set an HTTP header, called Content-Type, *that will describe the encoding. Unfortunately, even the latest browsers do not seem to do this. That is why the* <fmt:requestEncoding> *tag is used frequently.*

To see the vital role that the <fmt:requestEncoding> tag plays, you may want to try removing it from the procform.jsp page and submit the form data again. When you submit Chinese characters again, you will see that the request parameters are decoded incorrectly. Your window may look similar to the one displayed in Figure 13-10.

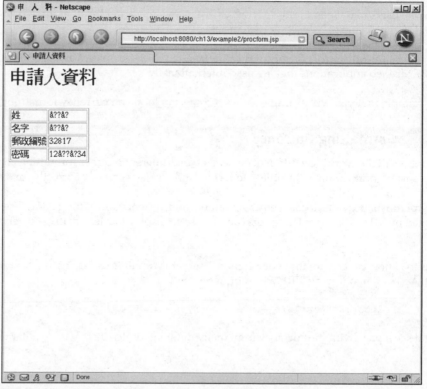

Figure 13-10: Result of incorrect request parameter encoding

In Figure 13-10, the incoming request parameters are decoded incorrectly because the JSP container does not know that they are encoded in Unicode.

The first two Try It Out exercises ask the user explicitly for the locale that they want to use for the session, but there is another way that an application can determine the user `locale`.

Determining a user's locale automatically (almost!)

When an HTML request comes into the server, the HTTP headers supplied by the browser can indicate a set of preferred locales that the user wants to use. This list is carried in the Accept-Language HTTP header. The JSP container has access to this header information, and the JSTL tags will use the preferred locale on this list if the application locale is not explicitly specified using the `<c:setLocale>` action.

Unfortunately, this is a highly unreliable approach to determine the locale that a user wants to use, for the following reasons:

❑ Different browsers configure this list of preferred locales differently.

❑ Most users never configure their browser's preferred locales.

❑ Some users may want to access pages using a different locale than the configured preferred locales.

❑ Some users may open multiple browser instances (supported by all modern browsers) but want a different locale to be used in each instance.

Because of these uncontrollable factors, it is recommended that you always ask users for the locale they want to use for Web applications that are used internationally.

The next example that you will examine shows the effect of locale on currency formatting.

Try It Out   Formatting Currency

Many countries in the world use different currencies and different number formatting conventions. An important part of localization is the ability to format and display currency correctly for a specific locale.

The Java 2 platform provides locale-sensitive number and currency formatting APIs. These APIs are encapsulated by JSTL i18n tags. These tags can be used to display locale-sensitive currencies and numbers.

To see this in action, make sure that your Tomcat 5 server is running and that `ch13.war` is currently deployed. Access the following URL with a browser:

```
http://localhost:8080/ch13/example3/index.jsp
```

You should see a page with the currency from many different locales displayed, similar to Figure 13-11.

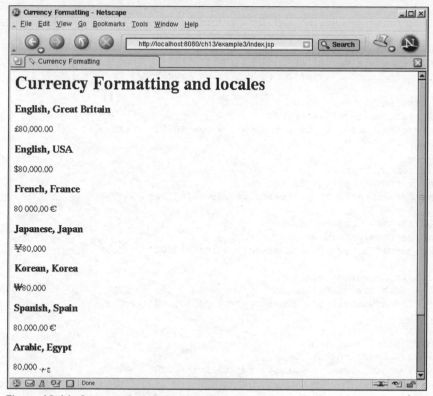

Figure 13-11: Currency formatting for different locales

In Figure 13-11, the current `locale` is set to a different value while a currency amount is printed. This shows how JSTL tags can be used to control the currency symbol and numeric format that is used during localization activities.

How It Works

This example uses the JSTL's `<fmt:formatNumber>` tag to display currency values and shows how the resulting format is affected by the current application locale.

The code is in the `index.jsp` file. You can find it at `<Tomcat Installation Directory>/webapps/ch13/example3/index.jsp`. The code is listed here:

```
<%@ page pageEncoding="UTF-8" %>
<%@ taglib prefix="c" uri="http://java.sun.com/jsp/jstl/core" %>
<%@ taglib prefix="fmt" uri="http://java.sun.com/jsp/jstl/fmt" %>
<html>
<head>
  <title>Currency Formatting</title>
</head>
```

```
<body>
  <h1>Currency Formatting and locale</h1>

  <h3>English, Great Britain</h3>
  <fmt:setLocale value="en_GB" />
  <fmt:formatNumber type="currency" value="80000" /><br/>

  <h3>English, USA</h3>
  <fmt:setLocale value="en_US" />
  <fmt:formatNumber type="currency" value="80000" /><br/>


  <h3>French, France</h3>
  <fmt:setLocale value="fr_FR" />
  <fmt:formatNumber type="currency" value="80000" /><br/>

  <h3>Japanese, Japan</h3>
  <fmt:setLocale value="ja_JP" />
  <fmt:formatNumber type="currency" value="80000" /><br/>

  <h3>Korean, Korea</h3>
  <fmt:setLocale value="ko_KR" />
  <fmt:formatNumber type="currency" value="80000" /><br/>


  <h3>Spanish, Spain</h3>
  <fmt:setLocale value="es_ES" />
  <fmt:formatNumber type="currency" value="80000" /><br/>

  <h3>Arabic, Egypt</h3>
  <fmt:setLocale value="ar_EG" />
  <fmt:formatNumber type="currency" value="80000" /><br/>

  <h3>Using Local Numeric Formatting for Different Currency</h3>
  <h4>English, Great Britain</h4>
  <fmt:setLocale value="en_GB" />

  <fmt:formatNumber type="currency" value="80000" /><br/>
  <fmt:formatNumber type="currency" value="80000" currencyCode="EUR"/><br/>

</body>
</html>
```

In the preceding code, first the container is told to generate UTF-8 encoded output using the
<%@ page %> directive. This ensures that foreign characters will show up properly. The JSTL core
and fmt tags are then included using <%@ taglib %> directives:

```
<%@ page pageEncoding="UTF-8" %>
<%@ taglib prefix="c" uri="http://java.sun.com/jsp/jstl/core" %>
<%@ taglib prefix="fmt" uri="http://java.sun.com/jsp/jstl/fmt" %>
```

To render the $80,000 currency using conventions in different locales, code similar to the following is used throughout the JSP:

```
<h3>English, Great Britain</h3>
<fmt:setLocale value="en_GB" />
<fmt:formatNumber type="currency" value="80000" /><br/>
```

The `<fmt:setLocale>` action is first used to set the locale. In the preceding case, the locale is set to `"en_GB"`. The JSTL `<fmt:formatNumber>` action is used to print the number 80,000 as currency. This tag will render the number as a local currency value with the proper currency symbol, decimal, and thousand separators. For the preceding code, this results in currency formatted with the British pound symbol:

```
£ 80,000.00
```

Later in the JSP, `<fmt:setLocale>` is used to set the application `locale` to `"fr_FR"`:

```
<h3>French, France</h3>
<fmt:setLocale value="fr_FR" />
<fmt:formatNumber type="currency" value="80000" /><br/>
```

In this case, the currency symbol is the euro, and the numeric format displayed is quite differently:

```
80 000,00 €
```

The last `<fmt:formatNumber>` tag is of special interest. In this case, the locale is `"en_GB"`, English in Great Britain (United Kingdom). The currency used in the UK at this time is the pound. However, the euro is commonly used throughout Europe, and occasions often arise when an amount in euros must be displayed. It is preferable that the number format remain the same (thousand separator, decimal separator, and so on) while only the currency symbol is changed.

In order to achieve this, the `currencyCode` attribute of the `<fmt:formatNumber>` action is used to specify the euro, `"EUR"`, without any change to the locale. Because the locale stays the same, the number formatting will remain the same:

```
<h3>Using Local Numeric Formatting for Different Currency</h3>
<h4>English, Great Britain</h4>
<fmt:setLocale value="en_GB" />

<fmt:formatNumber type="currency" value="80000" /><br/>
<fmt:formatNumber type="currency" value="80000" currencyCode="EUR"/><br/>
```

The value of the `currencyCode` attribute must be an ISO-4217 currency code. A table of these three-letter (all uppercase) currency codes can be found at `unece.org/cefact/rec/cocucod.htm`. However, not all codes are supported in all locales. The support is highly dependent on the Java 2 platform implementation that you are using.

The next example in this chapter shows how locales can affect the way date and time information is formatted.

Try It Out   **Formatting Dates**

Like numeric and currency formatting, the `locale` used also affects the way date and time are rendered. Different regions in the world have different time-telling conventions and may use different languages in describing time.

To see locale-sensitive date formatting in action, make sure that your Tomcat 5 server is running and that `ch13.war` is currently deployed. Access the following URL with a browser:

    http://localhost:8080/ch13/example4/index.jsp

You should see a Web page displaying the date formatted in accordance to the convention of several different locales, as shown in Figure 13-12.

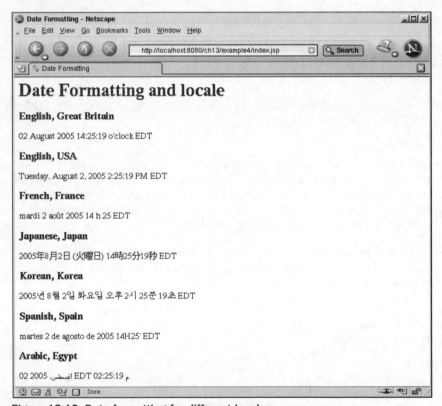

Figure 13-12: Date formatting for different locales

In Figure 13-12, the locale is set to a different value while the current date is printed. This shows how JSTL tags can be used to control the date format being rendered with a JSP page.

How It Works

The code for this page is in the `index.jsp` file. You can find it at `<Tomcat Installation Directory>/webapps/ch13/example4/index.jsp`. The code is listed here, with the date formatting code highlighted:

```jsp
<%@ page pageEncoding="UTF-8" %>
<%@ taglib prefix="c" uri="http://java.sun.com/jsp/jstl/core" %>
<%@ taglib prefix="fmt" uri="http://java.sun.com/jsp/jstl/fmt" %>

<html>
<head>
  <title>Date Formatting</title>
</head>
<body>
  <h1>Date Formatting and locale</h1>
  <fmt:timeZone value="EST">
    <jsp:useBean id="currentTime" class="java.util.Date"/>

    <h3>English, Great Britain</h3>
    <fmt:setLocale value="en_GB" />
    <fmt:formatDate type="both" dateStyle="full"
      timeStyle="full" value="${currentTime}" /><br/>

    <h3>English, USA</h3>
    <fmt:setLocale value="en_US" />
    <fmt:formatDate type="both" dateStyle="full"
      timeStyle="full" value="${currentTime}" /><br/>

    <h3>French, France</h3>
    <fmt:setLocale value="fr_FR" />
    <fmt:formatDate type="both" dateStyle="full" timeStyle="full"
      value="${currentTime}" /><br/>

    <h3>Japanese, Japan</h3>
    <fmt:setLocale value="ja_JP" />
    <fmt:formatDate type="both" dateStyle="full" timeStyle="full"
      value="${currentTime}" /><br/>

    <h3>Korean, Korea</h3>
    <fmt:setLocale value="ko_KR" />
    <fmt:formatDate type="both" dateStyle="full" timeStyle="full"
      value="${currentTime}" /><br/>


    <h3>Spanish, Spain</h3>
    <fmt:setLocale value="es_ES" />
    <fmt:formatDate type="both" dateStyle="full" timeStyle="full"
      value="${currentTime}" /><br/>


    <h3>Arabic, Egypt</h3>
    <fmt:setLocale value="ar_EG" />
    <fmt:formatDate type="both" dateStyle="full" timeStyle="full"
      value="${currentTime}" /><br/>
```

```
      </fmt:timeZone>
  </body>
  </html>
```

In addition to setting a locale, it is also important to set a time zone for the user before printing the time. Just rendering the time in the server's time zone is usually meaningless for applications that may be accessed internationally. Ideally, the time zone should also be selected by the user, in a manner similar to that used to select the locale.

In this example, the time zone is set to Easter Standard Time. It is performed using the JSTL `<fmt:timeZone>` tag:

```
<fmt:timeZone value="EST">

  ...
</fmt:timeZone>
```

The `value` attribute is set with a time zone ID. The `<fmt:timeZone>` tag makes use of the `java.util.TimeZone` API to work with time zones. You can consult the Javadoc for this API to find out the values that you may specify.

In this example, the time zone will be set to EST within the body of the `<fmt:timeZone>` tag. It is within this body that the `<fmt:setLocale>` calls are made to change the application locale.

An instance of the `java.util.Date` class is created as a JavaBean, using the standard `<jsp:useBean>` action, in order to access the current time (on the server). Note that the `Date` JavaBean instance is assigned to a `page` scoped variable called `currentTime`:

```
<jsp:useBean id="currentTime" class="java.util.Date"/>
```

To render the date in a specific locale and time zone format, the `<fmt:formatDate>` action is used. Here is the first set of `<fmt:setLocale>` and `<fmt:formatData>` tags:

```
<h3>English, Great Britain</h3>
<fmt:setLocale value="en_GB" />
<fmt:formatDate type="both" dateStyle="full" timeStyle="both"
value="${currentDate}" /><br/>
```

The attributes that are used in this example are described in the following table.

Attributes	Description
type	Can be time, date, or both. Controls if only the time is rendered, only the date, or both the time and date. In this example, both will be rendered.
dateStyle	Can be short, medium, long, or full (or default). Controls the actual format used to print the date.
timeStyle	Can be short, medium, long, or full (or default). Controls the actual format used to print the time.
value	A java.util.Date typed value that will be used to render the date and time.

The resulting time and date rendered for the `English, Great Britain` locale is as follows:

```
02 August 2005 11:32:28 o'clock EDT
```

The other `<fmt:setLocale>` and `<fmt:formatDate>` action pairs work similarly. For example, the date and time are rendered in Japanese for the `Japanese, Japan` locale using the following:

```
<h3>Japanese, Japan</h3>
<fmt:setLocale value="ja_JP" />
<fmt:formatDate type="both" dateStyle="full" timeStyle="full"
value="${currentTime}" /><br/>
```

The resulting localized Japanese date and time rendered are:

```
2005年8月2日 (火曜日) 11時32分28秒 EDT
```

Summary

Internationalization, or i18n for short, deals with the actions necessary to prepare an application for world-wide distribution. The application must be able to work with different languages, date formats, number and currency formats, and other local idiosyncrasies.

Localization, or l10n, is the act of adapting an i18n-ready application for use in a specific locality or region. This will inevitably include translating all text messages, customizing date, number and currency formats, as well as any other required customizations.

The i18n and l10n requirements of Web-based applications vary greatly and depend on your specific application distribution and deployment scenario:

- ❑ If you are creating a Web application for use at one single location, such as a departmental computer, there may be no i18n requirements at all.

- ❑ If the same application may be accessed by users from different regions across the world, you may need to perform l10n on every incoming request.

The Java 2 platform supports an i18n concept known as a *locale,* which represents a language and a country/region where a specific set of l10n features will apply. It includes the following points:

- ❑ The most reliable way of establishing locales is to explicitly ask users what locale they want to use.

- ❑ While it is also possible to determine the user's locale by using the preferred locales specified by the HTTP Accept-Languages header in a browser's request, this method is not robust because it depends on the user's specific browser and operating system settings.

- ❑ The locale can be stored with the user's session or passed from one request to another using hidden form fields.

To localize an application, any text in the user interface must be translated to the locale's language. It is possible to do the following:

❑   Keep multiple translated sets of JSP pages, and select between them as the user selects different locales. This results in a duplicate set of pages for each language supported.

❑   Take advantage of the Java 2 platform's resource bundles and retrieve different text strings according to the current locale selected. The JSTL tags `<fmt:setLocale>`, `<fmt:message>`, and `<fmt:bundle>` can be used for this technique.

Choosing a specific locale also influences how date, number, and currency are displayed by the Java runtime. Using the JSTL formatting actions such as `<fmt:timeZone>`, `<fmt:formatNumber>`, and `<fmt:formatDate>`, you can control on a fine-grained level the different formats that are displayed in a JSP application.

In addition to the JSTL tag library, other mechanisms support internationalization in Web applications. In Chapter 19 and in the two project chapters (Chapter 27 and Chapter 28), you will see examples of how Struts handles internationalization.

Exercises

1.   The first Try It Out exercise used duplicated sets of JSP pages in separate directories to make the application i18n-ready. Using the same approach, extend the example to support French. The following translation table is provided to assist you in the implementation.

Text	Translated Text in French
Application Form	Formulaire de Demande
Last Name	Prénom
First Name	Nom
Postal Code	Code postal
Password	Mot de passé
Submit Form	Valider
Applicant Information	L'information de demadeur

2.   The second Try It Out exercise used the Java 2 platform's support for i18n resource bundles to make the application i18n-ready. Using the same approach, extend this example to support French.

JSP Debugging Techniques

Once a programmer I knew was asked how he approached the problem of debugging his software. He responded, "I try not to put the bugs in in the first place." This is wise and sage advice. Good design and careful review of your code can minimize the need for debugging. However, even the most experienced developer makes coding mistakes. Furthermore, what happens when you are called upon to repair code written by someone else? Some mistakes are obvious and easy to find; others can be much more subtle and offer a real challenge. Many real-world projects miss their deadlines because problems are encountered that are difficult to find and fix. In this chapter, we cover methods and techniques that you can use to find and fix problems in your JSP code.

Problems in code are referred to as *bugs*. The story behind this term is that in 1945, Grace Hopper, a pioneer computer scientist, found a moth trapped in the relays of one of the earliest computers. She removed the moth and fixed the computer. Thus, the term *debugging* was coined and has been used to describe fixing computer problems ever since.

Debugging an application involving JSP can be quite a challenge. Developers often need to have an understanding of the various layers that make up the JSP application they are working on, and they need to understand how multiple languages, HTML, Java, JavaScript, and JSP combine to create the page on the browser.

Many people consider debugging to be an art, but as you shall see, it is really a science.

This chapter explores the science of debugging as it specifically applies to JavaServer Pages. Some of the key topics covered include the following:

- ❑ Catching bugs at compile time
- ❑ Instrumenting code
- ❑ Using logging systems
- ❑ Using debugging tools
- ❑ Debugging code in production environments
- ❑ Finding intermittent problems

The Science of Debugging

The scientific method provides us with a solid process that can be used for debugging. The scientific method consists of the following steps:

1. **Observation:** An observation is made that the program does not work as expected.

2. **Hypothesis:** A guess is made about what causes the unexpected behavior.

3. **Prediction:** A prediction is made about how a change in the code or the data will affect the observation.

4. **Test:** The prediction is tested by making the change and observing the results.

This process is then repeated until the problem has been fixed. Let's try this out on a simple example.

Try It Out   **Debugging with the Scientific Method**

For this example, the following JSP code is supposed to print the numbers from –5 to +5, incrementing by 1:

```
<%@page contentType="text/html"%>
<%@page pageEncoding="UTF-8"%>
<%@taglib prefix="c" uri="http://java.sun.com/jsp/jstl/core" %>
<html>
<head><title>JSP Page</title></head>
<body>
<c:forEach var="counter" begin="1" end="10" step="1" >
    <c:out value="${counter-5}"/><br/>
</c:forEach>
</body>
</html>
```

For this chapter, we assume that you have a basic standard Web application directory structure established for these examples and that the JSP files will be stored in the root directory of the Web application or WAR file. If you are unsure about how to set this up, then see Chapter 16, "Role of JSP in the Wider Context: Web Applications," to create the directory structure.

You will also need to have the jstl jar *and* standard.jar *files installed in the* WEB-INF/lib *directory along with the supporting* tld *files in the* WEB-INF/tld *directory. The* web.xml *file should be configured to find the tag library descriptors. Configuring a Web application to use JSTL is covered in Chapter 6, "JSP Tag Libraries and JSTL."*

You can also just copy the directory structure and its contents from the source code file that can be downloaded for the book.

If you are running Tomcat with this setup, then you should be able to edit the examples in place inside this directory. If you are using an IDE, then you should be able to execute the files from within the IDE.

Name this `Example1.jsp`. When you execute the JSP, you get the following output:

```
-4
-3
-2
-1
0
1
2
3
4
5
```

It is hoped that you have observed that something is wrong. The output begins at –4 and not at –5 as required. Our guess or hypothesis about why this does not work correctly is that there is something wrong with the `forEach` loop, or something wrong with the math in the `c:out` statement. By examining the code, you can see that when `counter=1`, then `counter-5 = -4`. So the next step is to create an experiment to see what happens when the beginning value is set to `0` instead of `1`.

Change the following line:

```
<c:forEach var="counter" begin="1" end="10" step="1" >
```

to

```
<c:forEach var="counter" begin="0" end="10" step="1" >
```

Now when the code is executed you should get the desired result.

How It Works

While this was a simple example, all debugging basically follows this same process. As problems become more complex, the ability to observe the problem or predict correctly the causes becomes more difficult. The challenge becomes one of getting more information or a better understanding about what is happening within the code being tested.

Catching Bugs at Compile Time

The previous example is what we call a *runtime bug*. A runtime bug is apparent only when the program executes. Java programs are compiled before they are executed. The compiler provides messages describing mistakes in the code that prevent it from compiling and being executed. The programmer must fix these mistakes before the program will compile and execute. A JSP, however, is often compiled for the first time when it is being executed. If the JSP fails to compile, the servlet container often returns a message to the browser explaining the problem. Let's look at an example in the next Try It Out exercise.

Try It Out   Debugging at Compile Time

First we modify the preceding example to introduce an error that will prevent it from compiling:

```
<%@page contentType="text/html"%>
<%@page pageEncoding="UTF-8"%>
<%@taglib prefix="c" uri="http://java.sun.com/jsp/jstl/bore" %>
<html>
<head><title>JSP Page</title></head>
<body>
<c:forEach var="counter" begin="0" end="10" step="1" >
    <c:out value="${counter-5}"/><br/>
</c:forEach>
</body>
</html>
```

In the preceding example code, we have changed core so that it now reads bore on the shaded line. If we deploy and try to run this JSP, we get the response shown in Figure 14-1.

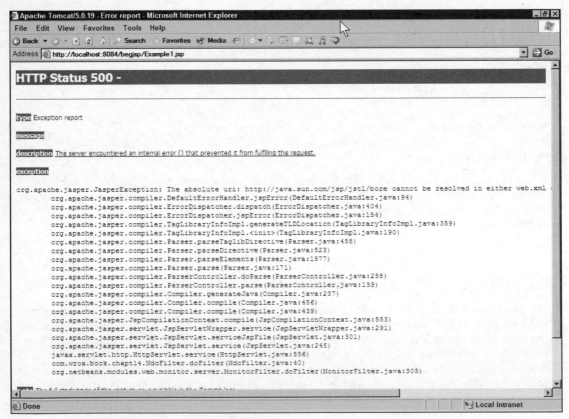

Figure 14-1: Response for JSP that failed to compile

The problem is marked on the following line, which was wrapped to fit the page, but is a single line in the browser window:

```
org.apache.jasper.JasperException: The absolute uri: http://java.sun.com/jsp/jstl/
bore cannot be resolved in either web.xml or the jar files deployed with this
application
```

How It Works

Tomcat is telling us it can't find whatever is referenced by `http://java.sun.com/jsp/jstl/bore`. Think of this as an observation in our scientific method. Now examine the code and find the line that matches what Tomcat is complaining about. This is of course the highlighted line from the example. The hypothesis is that `bore` should be `core`. Now you can create an experiment by changing the line so that `bore` is replaced by `core`. When you run the experiment, you'll notice that the problem has been repaired.

Let's look at another example that illustrates a common error when using scriptlets with a JSP.

<hr>

Try It Out   **Debugging When Using Scriptlets in a JSP**

The following JSP is supposed to print a single random integer from 1 to 6. Call this `Example2.jsp`.

```
<%@page contentType="text/html"%>
<%@page pageEncoding="UTF-8"%>
<html>
<head><title>JSP Page</title></head>
<body>
  <% Random r = new Random();
     int i = r.nextInt(6)+1;
     out.println("value="+i);
  %>
</body>
</html>
```

When the JSP is executed, we get a page that returns the following errors:

```
org.apache.jasper.JasperException: Unable to compile class for JSP

An error occurred at line: 6 in the jsp file: /Sample2p1.jsp

Generated servlet error:
    [javac] Compiling 1 source file

C:\Documents and Settings\jtbell\.netbeans\3.6\jakarta-tomcat-
5.0.19_base\work\Catalina\localhost\begjsp\org\apache\jsp\Sample2p1_jsp.java:48:
cannot resolve symbol
symbol  : class Random
location: class org.apache.jsp.Sample2p1_jsp
 Random r = new Random();
 ^
```

```
An error occurred at line: 6 in the jsp file: /Sample2p1.jsp

Generated servlet error:
C:\Documents and Settings\jtbell\.netbeans\3.6\jakarta-tomcat-5.0.19_base\work\
Catalina\localhost\begjsp\org\apache\jsp\Sample2p1_jsp.java:48: cannot resolve
symbol
symbol  : class Random
location: class org.apache.jsp.Sample2p1_jsp
 Random r = new Random();
              ^

An error occurred at line: 6 in the jsp file: /Sample2p1.jsp

Generated servlet error:
C:\Documents and Settings\jtbell\.netbeans\3.6\jakarta-tomcat-5.0.19_base\work\
Catalina\localhost\begjsp\org\apache\jsp\Sample2p1_jsp.java:49: incompatible types
found   : java.lang.String
required: int
     int i = r.nextInt(6)+1;
                    ^

3 errors
```

The response has been edited and reformatted to fit the page.

How It Works

Again, the program did not compile, but this time it is because we have a Java error in the servlet code that was generated by the JSP. Remember that the JSP is compiled into a Java servlet, and that servlet is then compiled into Java bytecode. The first few lines, repeated here, tell us that something went wrong:

```
org.apache.jasper.JasperException: Unable to compile class for JSP

An error occurred at line: 6 in the jsp file: /Sample2p1.jsp

Generated servlet error:
    [javac] Compiling 1 source file
```

The JSP compiler (named Jasper) was unable to compile the JSP; the error occurred on line 6 of the JSP, and it is an error with the generated servlet.

The next lines provide specific information about the error. The line that follows tells us that the problem was found on line 48 of the generated servlet and that the Java compiler cannot resolve a symbol:

```
C:\Documents and Settings\jtbell\.netbeans\3.6\jakarta-tomcat-
5.0.19_base\work\Catalina\localhost\begjsp\org\apache\jsp\Sample2p1_jsp.java:48:
cannot resolve symbol
```

The next lines tell us that the symbol that cannot be resolved is class Random:

```
symbol  : class Random
location: class org.apache.jsp.Sample2p1_jsp
 Random r = new Random();
 ^
```

The caret (^) shown on the last line points to the place in the code that caused the error. In this case, it points to the first time `Random` is used.

This sequence is repeated three times because the Java compiler is reporting what it recognizes as three separate errors. Often when multiple errors are reported it is because of a single root error, so the best approach is to tackle the first error and then test the code again to determine whether the other errors are cleared up. In this case, the error in the second stanza points to the second use of `Random` on the same line. The third error does at first glance seem to be related, so we will address it later.

Our observation now is that we have an error on line 6 of the JSP. We need to make an educated guess about how to fix the problem. If the compiler does not recognize a class, that normally means that we either omitted an `import` statement or the `import` statement or class was misspelled. A quick review of the code shows that we did indeed forget any `import` statements. Our experiment is to add the appropriate `import` statement and retry the code. Modify the code by adding the shaded line as shown:

```
<%@page contentType="text/html" %>
<%@page pageEncoding="UTF-8" %>
<%@page import="java.util.Random" %>
<html>
<head><title>JSP Page</title></head>
<body>
  <% Random r = new Random();
     int i = r.nextInt(6)+1;
     out.println("value="+i);
  %>
</body>
</html>
```

This time the code should compile and execute as expected. We didn't have to deal with the third error because it was really just an artifact of the previous errors.

It would be nice if we could precompile our JSP so that we could find errors before the JSP were compiled by the container. Another advantage of precompiling JSPs is better performance. Chapter 26, "Best Practices and Tools," illustrates how this can be done.

Using a Debugging System versus a Production System

It would be nice if every bug could be caught at compile time. Unfortunately, bugs are often discovered only after the software is already deployed onto a production system. The *production system* is where the software is published or installed so that the *end users*, the people who use the software, can access and use it. Normally, production systems can be used to observe the problem, but they can't be used to fix the problem. This is because finding and fixing a bug usually requires the developers to run experiments to test their guesses about the problems, and a production system is normally busy serving users, and therefore not normally available for running experiments. For this reason, debugging most often occurs on a system other than the one on which the bug was observed.

Using a different system for debugging purposes has a number of advantages:

❑ Debugging won't affect the performance of the production system.

❑ A wider variety of tools may be available on the debugging system to help find the problem.

❑ Experiments can be conducted more quickly because they don't require coordination with the production system and its users.

❑ Variables that might affect the outcome of the experiment are easier to control.

There are, however, some disadvantages that must be overcome. The most important of these is that it can be difficult to replicate a problem observed in production on a debugging system. To overcome this limitation, it is often necessary to collect additional information from the production system in order to improve our observations and create a better laboratory.

Even when working on a debugging system, we will often want to collect more information than is returned directly by the JSP. To do this, we *instrument* our code. An instrument is something that logs or measures. In this case, you will be adding code to report on or log the state of the system as it goes through its various steps and processes.

Using System.out.println() to Instrument Code

Java programmers since the earliest days of the language have used a built-in feature of Java to print messages relating to the status of their programs. The System object in Java provides two separate PrintStreams, out and err, that can be used to print messages on the console. Out is normally mapped to standard out and err is mapped to standard err. If an application is being run from the command line, both standard err and out are normally sent to the console. The *console* is a text window like the example Tomcat 4.1 console output shown in Figure 14-2. Instead of displaying these messages in the console window, many Web containers capture these streams and send the output to log files. This is the default behavior in Tomcat 5. If you are running in an Integrated Development Environment (IDE), then normally the IDE provides a window to display the console streams. We can use this feature to instrument our JSP code.

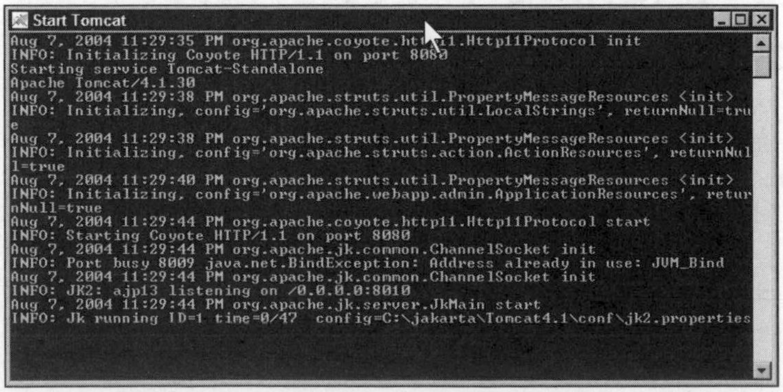

Figure 14-2: Tomcat 4.1 output in the console window

In the following Try It Out exercise, we will use the example of printing the numbers from –5 to 5.

Try It Out   Instrumenting Code with System.out.println()

This time, add a `println` statement inside the `forEach` loop to expose what is going on with the value we care about:

```
<%@page contentType="text/html"%>
<%@page pageEncoding="UTF-8"%>
<%@taglib prefix="c" uri="http://java.sun.com/jsp/jstl/core" %>
<html>
<head><title>JSP Page</title></head>
<body>
<c:forEach var="counter" begin="1" end="10" step="1" >
    <c:out value="${counter-5}"/></br>
    <% System.out.println( "counter="+pageContext.findAttribute("counter") ); %>
</c:forEach>
</body>
</html>
```

Call this `Example3.jsp` and note the added line (shown shaded) in the listing. This line is a scriptlet that sends the value of the counter to `standard out` each time the loop is repeated. The counter is stored as an attribute within the `pageContext` of the JSP, so we have to use the call to `pageContext.findAttribute()` to print the value.

While the output displayed in the Web browser still shows the numbers from –4 to 5, the console now shows the following:

```
counter=1
counter=2
counter=3
counter=4
counter=5
counter=6
counter=7
counter=8
counter=9
counter=10
```

If you are using Tomcat, you will also find these lines appended to the end of `stdout.log` in the `logs` directory.

Make the following changes to your code to get a better view of exactly what is happening:

```
<%@page contentType="text/html"%>
<%@page pageEncoding="UTF-8"%>
<%@taglib prefix="c" uri="http://java.sun.com/jsp/jstl/core" %>
<html>
<head><title>JSP Page</title></head>
<body>
```

```
<c:forEach var="loopCount" begin="1" end="10" step="1" >
    <c:set var="myCount" value="${loopCount-5}" />
    <c:out value="${myCount}"/></br>
    <%
      System.out.println(
          "loopCount="
        + pageContext.findAttribute("loopCount")
        + " myCount="
        + pageContext.findAttribute("myCount")
      );
    %>
</c:forEach>
</body>
</html>
```

How It Works

Call this new version `Example4.jsp`. This time, you made a number of changes. Some of these will help with the debugging and readability of your code. You first added the following line:

```
<c:set var="myCount" value="${loopCount-5}" />
```

This stores the value of `loopCount-5` into a variable so that you can easily log it. It is often a good idea to store intermediate calculations in variables that can be examined when needed. To make it easier to distinguish between variable names, you changed the loop variable from `count` to `loopCount` and then used `myCount` for the value that should range from –5 to 5. Finally, you enhanced the `println` statement so that it prints both the loop counter and the `myCount` value of interest. When you run the program this time, the console output looks like this:

```
loopCount=1 myCount=-4
loopCount=2 myCount=-3
loopCount=3 myCount=-2
loopCount=4 myCount=-1
loopCount=5 myCount=0
loopCount=6 myCount=1
loopCount=7 myCount=2
loopCount=8 myCount=3
loopCount=9 myCount=4
loopCount=10 myCount=5
```

Now it should be obvious that `loopCount` needs to start at 0 and not 1 if we need to go from –5 to 5.

You may wonder why the subtraction wasn't done in the scriptlet. The value returned by `pageContext` `.findAttribute()` is of type `Object`. These objects would have to be converted into numeric types before they could be used in arithmetic operations. It is easier to perform the operations using the built-in expression language and JSTL than it is to do them in the Java scriptlet.

The tags `c:out` *and* `c:set` *are a standard part of the core JSTL tags covered in Chapter 6. By using these tags and limiting our EL expressions (covered in Chapter 5, "JSP and EL") to attributes of the tags, we can make this example compatible with both the JSP 1.1 and JSP 2 specifications.*

Println is a way to instrument the code to make better observations about what is occurring as the code executes. It is hoped that by this point you can see some of the value in using `println` statements to help debug your code. However, `println` is a very primitive feature. There are better ways to instrument a JSP and log actions as they occur.

Using a Logging System

While `System.out.println` provides a basic capability to output information, it is often not the best choice to use for this purpose. To use `println`, you must create all of the information that will be logged, including timestamps, filenames, and other things that you might want to standardize for all messages. Nor do you have an easy to way to enable the messages when you need them and disable them when you don't need them. In general, you don't want to leave `println` statements in the code when you put it into production. This makes them useful mostly for rapid turnaround types of experiments and not something that can be used to enhance the long-term ability to observe what is going on within the code. A *logging system* addresses these issues.

Logs are regularly recorded information. For centuries, ship captains kept logs recording the events that occurred on the ship, recording the ships location, temperature, and weather at regular intervals, and special events as they happened. Logs serve a similar function for computers. A log is used to record the state of the program and the events that occur as the program executes. *Logging* is the process of creating and writing to the logs.

Logging through the servlet container

`System.out.println` provides a very primitive logging capability. However, every servlet container is required to provide a standard logging service that can be used to log messages. This logging service is available from a servlet simply by calling the `log()` method on the servlet, as you will see in the next Try It Out.

Try It Out   Calling the log Method

Because a JSP is compiled into a servlet, you can send messages to the container-provided logging facility, as illustrated in the following JSP:

```
<%@page pageEncoding="UTF-8"%>
<%@taglib prefix="c" uri="http://java.sun.com/jsp/jstl/core" %>
<html>
<head><title>JSP Page</title></head>
<body>
<c:forEach var="loopCount" begin="1" end="10" step="1" >
    <c:set var="myCount" value="${loopCount-5}" />
    <c:out value="${myCount}"/></br>
    <% String message = "loopCount="
          + pageContext.findAttribute("loopCount")
          + " myCount="
          + pageContext.findAttribute("myCount");
       this.log( message );
    %>
```

```
    </c:forEach>
    </body>
    </html>
```

Enter the code and name it `Example5.jsp`. This is basically the same code used previously with `System.out.println`, but instead of sending the messages to `standard out`, they are sent to the containers log file. You use the following line to do this:

```
        this.log(message);
```

The example output from the Tomcat 5 log file is shown here:

```
2004-07-12 21:51:17 StandardContext[/BegJsp]jsp: loopCount=1 myCount=-4
2004-07-12 21:51:17 StandardContext[/BegJsp]jsp: loopCount=2 myCount=-3
2004-07-12 21:51:17 StandardContext[/BegJsp]jsp: loopCount=3 myCount=-2
2004-07-12 21:51:17 StandardContext[/BegJsp]jsp: loopCount=4 myCount=-1
2004-07-12 21:51:17 StandardContext[/BegJsp]jsp: loopCount=5 myCount=0
2004-07-12 21:51:17 StandardContext[/BegJsp]jsp: loopCount=6 myCount=1
2004-07-12 21:51:17 StandardContext[/BegJsp]jsp: loopCount=7 myCount=2
2004-07-12 21:51:17 StandardContext[/BegJsp]jsp: loopCount=8 myCount=3
2004-07-12 21:51:17 StandardContext[/BegJsp]jsp: loopCount=9 myCount=4
2004-07-12 21:51:17 StandardContext[/BegJsp]jsp: loopCount=10 myCount=5
```

The Tomcat log file can be found in the `logs` directory of your Tomcat installation and will normally be named `localhost_log.<<date_string>>.txt`. Now you have date and timestamp information, as well as context information that was prepended to each log entry by Tomcat's logging system.

How It Works

Calling the log method inside a JSP works because a Web-based JSP is compiled into a servlet that implements (or extends) the same contract as an `HttpServlet`. `HttpServlet` extends `GenericServlet`, which exposes a set of log functions provided by the container. The log functions are also accessible using the `ServletContext`.

Two log methods are available from the container. The method signatures are as follows:

❑   `void ServletContext.log( String msg )`

❑   `void ServletContext log( String msg, Throwable throwable )`

You have already seen the first method. The second method provides a way to log exceptions when they occur. As a general rule, exceptions should be logged only if they are being handled and not re-thrown.

Using the logging system provided by the container offers some improvement over using `println` statements. The container-based logging system is limited. For example, it does not give us much control over determining when messages should be logged. To get that kind of control, we need a logging framework.

Logging with the JDK logger

In the J2SE 1.4 release, a logging framework was introduced as a standard part of the Java language. This logging framework is designed to provide logging services for any class running in the JVM. This means that it is available for use by servlets and JSPs as well.

Try It Out   Using the JDK Logger

Let's start by reviewing a code sample that uses the logging framework:

```jsp
<%@page pageEncoding="UTF-8"%>
<%@page import="java.util.logging.Logger" %>
<%@taglib prefix="c" uri="http://java.sun.com/jsp/jstl/core" %>
<html>
<head><title>JSP Page</title></head>
<body>
<%     Logger logger = Logger.getLogger(this.getClass().getName()); %>
<c:forEach var="loopCount" begin="1" end="10" step="1" >
    <c:set var="myCount" value="${loopCount-5}" />
    <c:out value="${myCount}"/></br>
    <% String message = "loopCount="
            + pageContext.findAttribute("loopCount")
            + " myCount="
            + pageContext.findAttribute("myCount");
        logger.info( message );
    %>

</c:forEach>
</body>
</html>
```

Name this example `Example6.jsp`.

How It Works

This example is similar to the preceding example except for the highlighted lines. The `import` statement imports the class we need to use the JDK logging system:

```jsp
<%@page import="java.util.logging.Logger" %>
```

The next line gets an instance of the `logger` class for us to use:

```jsp
<%     Logger logger = Logger.getLogger(this.getClass().getName()); %>
```

When you get the logger, you also pass in the name of the class that will be generating the log messages by calling `this.getClass().getname()`. This name is used to name the logger. After a logger has been created with that name, later calls to `getLogger()` with the same name will return the same logger instance.

Using the LogManager class

The class name does not have to be used to name the logger, but often it is a good idea. The logger is managed by a class called the LogManager, which controls a hierarchy of loggers. This class does not show up in our code, but it is working behind the scenes. The LogManager uses dot-separated names to control and structure the hierarchy. In other words, the hierarchy is based on dot-separated names. A logger inherits it properties from its parent logger in the hierarchy, as shown in Figure 14-3. A logger named examples.webapps.HelloJsp inherits its properties first from examples.webapps, then from examples, and finally from the root logger, as shown in the highlighted path in the figure.

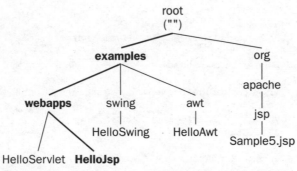

Figure 14-3: Example logger hierarchy and inheritance

Loggers and logging levels

Each logger has a level associated with it. The level controls what messages the logger will log. Loggers only log messages sent at or above the associated logging level. If the logging level is not set for a logger, then the level is inherited from its parent logger in the logger hierarchy. The level is set by calling the logger.setLevel() method.

The supported logging levels for JDK loggers are shown in the following table.

Logging Level	Description
SEVERE	The highest value, used for the most important messages, such as fatal program errors.
WARNING	Used for sending warning messages.
INFO	Default level, unless properties have been changed. Used for informational messages.
CONFIG	Used to report configuration settings as they are set or changed.
FINE	Used to provide more detail. Normally used when diagnosing or debugging problems.

Logging Level	Description
FINER	Provides even greater detail than FINE.
FINEST	The lowest level for the most detailed messages.

There are two other levels: ALL, which enables all logging levels, and OFF, which disables all logging levels. These are provided as utility levels to control logging output and can't be used to send messages.

If a message is sent at a level below the level set for the logger, then the message is not sent to the handler (which we will discuss shortly in this section) and is not written to the console, a file, or any other output device.

Messages can be sent at various levels by using the convenience functions severe(), warning(), info(), config(), fine(), finer(), and finest(), or by using the method log(Level, message). Functions are also provided to aid in logging exceptions and using resource bundles.

The line of code in our example that sends the log message is shown here:

```
logger.info( message );
```

This line logs a message at the INFO level. If we had used

```
logger.fine( message );
```

instead, the message would have been logged at the FINE level.

In the example JSP, the message is sent at the INFO level. This was done because INFO is the default level configured for the root logger when the JVM is installed as part of the SDK. The intention was to make the example simple so it would work without changing the properties of the logger and without making any configuration changes. In the absence of any set properties, the logger inherits the properties of its parents. If the properties are not set on the parents, then this inheritance continues through the hierarchy until ultimately the properties are set to the values of the root logger.

As stated earlier, the logger is configured to accept messages at or above a certain level. By default, the logger is configured to accept messages logged at the INFO level or above. If we don't change the defaults but use logger.fine() to log our messages, then the logged messages will not appear in the logs because they were sent at a level below the level currently associated with the logger instance. Therefore, using the default settings, a message logged at the FINE level will not appear in the logs. This feature provides the capability to control the level of output we desire from the logging system without requiring the code to be changed.

In general, debugging messages should be printed at one of the FINE levels. When the code is being executed during testing and debugging, the loggers would be configured to accept messages logged at the FINE levels or above. When the code is placed into production, the loggers would be reconfigured to ignore anything below the INFO level. The levels FINE, FINER, and FINEST provide three different levels of detail that we can use for debugging purposes. Often, only one of these levels is required.

Handlers

We have now looked at two of the three primary classes that need to be understood in order to grasp how the JDK logging system works. Recall the three classes:

❏ `java.util.logging.Logger`

❏ `java.util.logging.LogManager`

❏ `java.util.logging.Handler`

Loggers provide methods for logging messages at various levels of detail. The `LogManager` manages loggers based on a hierarchy of names. Loggers are created with a name to place them within the hierarchy managed by the `LogManager`. This allows them to inherit properties from their parents and other ancestor loggers in the path within the hierarchy.

The third class we have hinted at but now needs to be discussed in more detail. This piece, the handler, determines how a log message is sent to an output device. When a logger gets a message, it calls one or more handlers. Each handler sends the message to an output device. The output device may be the console, a file, or even a database, but the output device is determined by the handler. Each logger may have many handlers allowing each message to be logged into multiple places with a single call to the logger. Loggers inherit handlers from their parent loggers just as they inherit level settings from their parents. Each handler can be configured to accept or ignore messages logged at or below a set logging level, just as the loggers can. The settings for the handlers are independent of the settings for the loggers.

The consequence of these characteristics is that if we were to set the logger at the `FINE` level instead of the `INFO` level and then log the messages using `logger.fine()`, the messages would still not be logged unless a handler was also configured to accept messages at the `FINE` level or above. For a message to be logged, both a logger and a handler used by that logger must have the level set at or below the level of the logged message.

> *The logging level on both the logger and a handler must be set to a level that is the same or lower than the level of the desired messages if those messages are to appear in the log output.*

This means that you can have one handler that sends all messages at or above the `WARNING` level to a file, but also have a different handler connected to the same logger that sends messages logged at or above the `FINE` level to the console.

Three handler classes are commonly used:

❏ **ConsoleHandler:** Sends output to `System.err`

❏ **FileHandler:** Sends output to a file

❏ **SocketHandler:** Sends output to a network stream connection

`ConsoleHandler` is configured as the default handler when the SDK is installed.

Configuring the SDK logging framework

By default, the SDK logging framework is configured by reading a properties file. The default file is found in the `<JAVA_HOME>/jre/lib` directory and is called `logging.properties`. Changes to this file affect every program that runs using that JVM; therefore, it is recommended that you make a backup copy of this file before you edit it. The properties file used to configure the logger can be changed from the default by adding a command-line parameter when starting the JVM, as shown in the following example:

```
java -Djava.util.logging.config.file=mylog.properties MyClass
```

A simple example configuration file follows:

```
############################################################
#       Global properties
############################################################
handlers= java.util.logging.ConsoleHandler
.level= INFO

# Sends all log messages to the console
java.util.logging.ConsoleHandler.level = ALL
java.util.logging.ConsoleHandler.formatter = java.util.logging.SimpleFormatter

############################################################
#       Logger Specific properties
############################################################
org.apache.jsp.level = FINE
```

This is in the format of a normal Java properties file. Lines starting with # are comments. The line

```
handlers= java.util.logging.ConsoleHandler
```

is a comma-separated list of handler classes that will be used. In this case, only the `Consolehandler` is being used.

`.level= INFO` sets the default logging level for loggers (the root of the `LogManager` hierarchy to `INFO`. Do not forget the leading dot.

The following line configures the `ConsoleHandler` to accept messages from `ALL` logging levels:

```
java.util.logging.ConsoleHandler.level = ALL
```

Formatters have not been discussed and are beyond the scope of this chapter. By default, a `SimpleFormatter` is associated with the `ConsoleHandler`. We explicitly set it here using the following line (shown primarily for documentation purposes):

```
java.util.logging.ConsoleHandler.formatter = java.util.logging.SimpleFormatter
```

There are a number of other formatters that are available, too, such as the XMLFormater that formats log messages in an XML format:

The last line, which follows, specifically configures the sample JSP and all other JSP files that use loggers in the org.apache.jsp hierarchy (the default for JSP files in Tomcat) to log at the FINE level:

```
org.apache.jsp.level = FINE
```

This setting overrides the default setting of INFO set for the root logger.

In the next Try It Out exercise, you will need to make several changes to existing files.

Try It Out   Logging with the SDK Logging Framework

First, make a copy of the logging.properties file and replace the original with the file listed previously. You will have to stop and restart Tomcat so the new logging.properties file can be read. Next, you will change the JSP file named example6.jsp that we used previously. Change the line that reads

```
logger.info( message );
```

so that it now reads

```
logger.fine( message );
```

and save the JSP file.

When you run the JSP file this time, you should see the following lines in the console output or in the Tomcat stderr.log file:

```
Jul 16, 2004 12:33:26 AM org.apache.jsp.Sample5_jsp _jspService
FINE: loopCount=1 myCount=-4
Jul 16, 2004 12:33:26 AM org.apache.jsp.Sample5_jsp _jspService
FINE: loopCount=2 myCount=-3
Jul 16, 2004 12:33:26 AM org.apache.jsp.Sample5_jsp _jspService
FINE: loopCount=3 myCount=-2
Jul 16, 2004 12:33:26 AM org.apache.jsp.Sample5_jsp _jspService
FINE: loopCount=4 myCount=-1
Jul 16, 2004 12:33:26 AM org.apache.jsp.Sample5_jsp _jspService
FINE: loopCount=5 myCount=0
Jul 16, 2004 12:33:26 AM org.apache.jsp.Sample5_jsp _jspService
FINE: loopCount=6 myCount=1
Jul 16, 2004 12:33:26 AM org.apache.jsp.Sample5_jsp _jspService
FINE: loopCount=7 myCount=2
Jul 16, 2004 12:33:26 AM org.apache.jsp.Sample5_jsp _jspService
FINE: loopCount=8 myCount=3
Jul 16, 2004 12:33:26 AM org.apache.jsp.Sample5_jsp _jspService
FINE: loopCount=9 myCount=4
Jul 16, 2004 12:33:26 AM org.apache.jsp.Sample5_jsp _jspService
FINE: loopCount=10 myCount=5
```

How It Works

The replacement `logging.properties` file directed the log messages to be sent to the console. Tomcat displays these messages on the console and logs them to its logging files. The logging level is set to `FINE` so that all of the messages generated by the JSP are logged. To try this out, you will need to make several changes to existing files. To disable the output, change the last line in `logging.properties` from

```
org.apache.jsp.level = FINE
```

to

```
org.apache.jsp.level = INFO
```

and restart your servlet container.

Stopping and restarting the servlet container each time you want to make a change to the logging configuration can be inconvenient. In the Next Try It Out exercise, you learn to change the log settings without restarting the container.

Try It Out   Changing the Log Settings without Restarting the Container

The following script demonstrates one way to force the configuration file to be reread without restarting the JVM. Enter this code:

```
<%@page pageEncoding="UTF-8"%>
<%@page import="java.util.logging.LogManager" %>
<%@page import="java.util.logging.Logger" %>
<%@taglib prefix="c" uri="http://java.sun.com/jsp/jstl/core" %>
<html>
<head><title>Log Reset</title></head>
<body>
  <%
    LogManager lm = LogManager.getLogManager();
    lm.readConfiguration();
    Logger logger = Logger.getLogger("org.apache.jsp");
    out.println("Logger("+logger.getName()+") is now set to "+logger.getLevel());
  %>
</body>
</html>
```

Save this file as `ResetLogger.jsp`. To enable the output again, change the last line in `logging.properties` from

```
org.apache.jsp.level = INFO
```

to

```
org.apache.jsp.level = FINE
```

Now, instead of restarting the container, execute the `ResetLogger.jsp` to start logging messages again.

How It Works

The lines

```
LogManager lm = LogManager.getLogManager();
lm.readConfiguration();
```

retrieve the instance of the `LogManager` and tell it to reread the configuration file. The lines

```
Logger logger = Logger.getLogger("org.apache.jsp");
out.println("Logger("+logger.getName()+") is now set to "+logger.getLevel());
```

get the `org.apache.jsp` logger instance and report the current setting for the logger level. If the level is null, then the settings are being inherited from the parent logger. Try this out by leaving the last line of the `logging.properties` file set to:

```
org.apache.jsp.level = INFO
```

and executing the `sample.jsp`. No log messages should appear on the console. Next, edit this line in `logging.properties` so it now reads as follows:

```
org.apache.jsp.level = FINE
```

Now execute the `ResetLogger.jsp`. The output should look like this:

```
Logger(org.apache.jsp) is now set to FINE
```

If you rerun the original JSP, the logger output should now appear on the console (and/or in `stderr.log`).

Logging with Log4j

Log4j is an open-source logging framework. It has been around for several years, and until the SDK logging framework came along it was considered by many to be the standard logging framework for Java applications. Most developers still prefer using Log4j over the built-in SDK Logger system because Log4j is extremely flexible and powerful. Log4j provides at least one major advantage for Web applications over the built-in SDK logging system. The Log4j JAR file can be deployed and configured as part of the Web application and does not have to be globally configured like the SDK Logger.

The following code for `Eample7.jsp` shows our sample file modified to use Log4j:

```
<%@page pageEncoding="UTF-8"%>
<%@page import="org.apache.log4j.Logger" %>
<%@taglib prefix="c" uri="http://java.sun.com/jsp/jstl/core" %>
<html>
<head><title>JSP Page</title></head>
<body>
<%
```

```
       Logger logger = Logger.getLogger(this.getClass().getName());
%>
<c:forEach var="loopCount" begin="1" end="10" step="1" >
    <c:set var="myCount" value="${loopCount-5}" />
    <c:out value="${myCount}"/></br>
    <% String message = "loopCount="
         + pageContext.findAttribute("loopCount")
         + " myCount="
         + pageContext.findAttribute("myCount");
       logger.info( message );
    %>

</c:forEach>
</body>
</html>
```

You will need to copy the Log4j JAR file into the WEB-INF/lib *directory of the Web application and a* log4j.properties *file in the* WEB-INF/classes *directory to run this JSP. The* log4j *.properties file settings are covered later in this section.*

The shaded line is the only line that has changed from our previous example. Like the SDK Logger discussed in the previous section, Log4j maintains a hierarchy of loggers. The hierarchy is represented as dot-separated lists of logging category names. Loggers inherit configuration information from their ancestors within the tree. When a logger is retrieved, a category name is used to retrieve it. In the following line of code, the string passed to the getLogger method represents the category:

```
       Logger logger = Logger.getLogger("org.apache.jsp.TryLog4j.jsp");
```

The same instance of the logger is always returned for the same category name. The ancestors of the category used to retrieve the logger in this example are as follows:

❑   org.apache.jsp

❑   org.apache

❑   org.apache

❑   org

❑   root (nameless)

These are shown in the order of inheritance. The root of the tree does not have a name, but can be retrieved by calling Logger.getRootLogger().

Each logger may have a logging level associated with it. If there is no logging level, then the logger inherits the logging level of the nearest ancestor that does have a logging level. The root logger is guaranteed to have a logging level that can be inherited by loggers in the hierarchy.

The logging level is used to prevent messages from being logged. The default logging levels are shown in the following table.

Logging Levels	Description
FATAL	The highest value, used when the program is likely to abort.
ERROR	Severe error, but the program may be able to continue running.
WARN	Used for sending warning messages.
INFO	Used for informational messages.
DEBUG	The lowest level, used for debugging.

Two additional levels, ALL for enabling all log messages and OFF for disabling all messages, are also provided for configuring loggers. Messages logged at or above the effective level for the current message will be sent to Appenders (described in the following section). Messages logged at a level below the set level for the logger will be dropped.

Appenders and Layouts

There are three primary components to the Log4j framework: loggers, Appenders, and Layouts. Loggers were discussed earlier. Log4j also defines Appenders and Layouts. Appenders determine the output destinations of the log entries. They are similar to handlers in the SDK Logger. Each logger may have many Appenders attached to the logger. The logger will send messages to all of the Appenders attached to that logger and to all of the Appenders attached to its ancestor loggers. Appenders do not have level settings like the handlers of the SDK logging system. Once a message is sent to the Appender, the Appender will send it to the output device.

Log4j provides a much wider selection of pre-created Appenders than the SDK provides for handlers. In addition to file, console, and socket Appenders, Log4j provides Appenders that log records to databases, to JMS-based messaging systems, to GUI-based console systems, to NT event logs, and to UNIX syslogs. There are also several different types of file-based loggers that can handle file rollover and other common log file issues.

Each Appender is associated with a Layout. A Layout object determines the format of the message records that will be logged. While this is the same role as a formatter in the SDK Logger, Log4j provides a much richer set of layouts. The SimpleLayout class provides the same basic logging features as the SimpleFormatter in the SDK Logger. It is more common for the PatternLayout to be used. PatternLayout accepts a pattern or template that is used to format the log messages. Patterns are built using a series of tokens, each preceded by a percent sign (%). Many tokens can be followed by an optional *precision specifier* inside of curly braces. The tokens available to create the patterns are described in the following table.

Token	Effect
`%c{1}`	Outputs the category of the logger. Precision specifier is a constant integer. If the precision specifier is given, then only the rightmost category names will be printed. For example, given the category `"a.b.c"`, `%c{2}` would print `"b.c"`.
`%C{1}`	Outputs the fully qualified class name of the caller issuing the logging request. If the precision specifier is given, then only the rightmost portion of the class name will be printed. For example, given the class `"com.wrox.jsp.MyServlet"`, `%C{1}` would print `"MyServlet"`.
`%d{ISO8601}`	Used to output the date. The date conversion specifier may be followed by a date format specifier enclosed between braces. For example, `%d{HH:mm:ss,SSS}` or `%d{dd MMM yyyy HH:mm:ss,SSS}`. If no date format specifier is given, then ISO8601 format is assumed.
`%f`	Outputs the filename from which the logging request was issued.
`%l`	Used to output the location information of the caller that generated the logging event. Location normally includes filename, method, and line number. This operation can be extremely slow.
`%L`	Outputs the line number from which the logging request was issued. This operation can be extremely slow.
`%m`	Outputs the message sent to the logger.
`%M`	Outputs the method name that the message was logged from. This can be a slow operation.
`%n`	Outputs the platform-dependent line-separator character (newline or end of line sequence).
`%p`	Outputs the priority of the logging event. Priority is the level at which the event was logged: FATAL, ERROR, WARN, and so on.
`%r`	Outputs milliseconds elapsed since the start of the application until the logging event.
`%t`	Outputs the name of the thread that generated the event.
`%x`	Outputs a nested diagnostic context (NDC) associated with the thread that created the event.
`%X{mapkey}`	Outputs a mapped diagnostic context (MDC) associated with the thread that created the event. The key for the map must be in the braces following the token.
`%%`	Outputs a single percent sign.

More detail about these tokens is available in the Javadocs for the PatternLayout class. The concepts of nested and mapped diagnostic contexts are discussed later in this chapter. There are also *format specifiers* that can be included between the percent sign and the token. These control padding, truncation, and justification for the value output by the tokens. A minus sign, for example, will left-justify the field.

Configuring Log4j

Log4j will try to automatically configure itself by looking for a file called log4j.properties in its classpath. For a Web application, you can place the log4j.properties file in the WEB-INF/classes directory of the Web application. Here is a sample configuration file:

```
# Set root logger level to INFO and its only Appender to ConsoleOut.
log4j.rootLogger=INFO, ConsoleOut

# ConsoleOut is set to be a ConsoleAppender.
log4j.appender.ConsoleOut=org.apache.log4j.ConsoleAppender

# ConsoleOut is set to use PatternLayout.
log4j.appender.ConsoleOut.layout=org.apache.log4j.PatternLayout
log4j.appender.ConsoleOut.layout.ConversionPattern=%-5p: %d [%t] %c{1} - %m%n
```

The comments explain most of what this configuration file does. First the rootLogger is set to default at the INFO level and has a single Appender, named ConsoleOut, associated with it. Appenders form a comma-separated list after the logger's level has been set. If additional Appenders are needed they can be added after the ConsoleOut Appender.

The class used to implement the ConsoleOut Appender is ConsoleAppender. The ConsoleOut Appender is assigned the PatternLayout to use as its layout class. The instance of PatternLayout is provided with a pattern to use in the following line:

```
log4j.appender.ConsoleOut.layout.ConversionPattern=%-5p: [%d] %c{1} - %m%n
```

This pattern will print the priority of the logged message, left-justified in a field five characters wide. It then prints a colon and the date and time inside square brackets and formatted in ISO8601 format. This is followed by the last element of the logging category. If the class name is used to establish the logging category, then this will be the class name. This is followed by a dash and then the logged message is printed, followed by a line termination character.

Try It Out   Logging with Log4j

Assuming that you have created the Example7.jsp file and provided the Log4j configuration file previously described, then you are ready to run the example and observe the logging. Running the example JSP with this configuration provides log entries like the following:

```
INFO : [2004-07-16 23:00:35,828] TryLog4j_jsp - loopCount=1 myCount=-4
INFO : [2004-07-16 23:00:35,828] TryLog4j_jsp - loopCount=2 myCount=-3
INFO : [2004-07-16 23:00:35,828] TryLog4j_jsp - loopCount=3 myCount=-2
INFO : [2004-07-16 23:00:35,828] TryLog4j_jsp - loopCount=4 myCount=-1
INFO : [2004-07-16 23:00:35,828] TryLog4j_jsp - loopCount=5 myCount=0
```

```
INFO : [2004-07-16 23:00:35,828] TryLog4j_jsp - loopCount=6 myCount=1
INFO : [2004-07-16 23:00:35,828] TryLog4j_jsp - loopCount=7 myCount=2
INFO : [2004-07-16 23:00:35,828] TryLog4j_jsp - loopCount=8 myCount=3
INFO : [2004-07-16 23:00:35,921] TryLog4j_jsp - loopCount=9 myCount=4
INFO : [2004-07-16 23:00:35,921] TryLog4j_jsp - loopCount=10 myCount=5
```

You can change the logging level for the JSP you are testing by adding a line to the configuration file. Because you are logging at the INFO level, you should also change the example to log at the DEBUG level. Change the original line in the same JSP that reads

```
logger.info( message );
```

so that it now reads

```
logger.debug( message );
```

This change will send the messages out at the DEBUG level. Next add the following line to the end of the log4j.properties configuration file and restart your container:

```
log4j.logger.org.apache.jsp=DEBUG
```

Now re-execute the example JSP. The JSP-generated log entries should now be logged at the DEBUG level. But log entries for classes that are not created by the JSP compiler will still be logged at the INFO level.

How It Works

The logger methods info() and debug() send the messages to the logger at the corresponding priority levels. The Logger.getLogger() line in the JSP established that the messages would be sent through a category below org.apache.jsp. The final change made to the configuration file instructed the logger to log messages in all categories at or below the org.apache.jsp category at the DEBUG priority level. Messages for other classes are logged at the root logger configuration, which is set to the INFO level.

Changing the Log4j configuration without restarting the container

Again, it would be nice to be able to change the Log4j configuration settings without restarting the container. The following JSP named ResetLog4j.jsp rereads the log4j.properties file and then displays the new settings:

```
<%@page contentType="text/html"%>
<%@page pageEncoding="UTF-8"%>
<%@page import="java.net.URL" %>
<%@page import="java.io.PrintWriter" %>
<%@page import="org.apache.log4j.*" %>
<%@page import="org.apache.log4j.config.PropertyPrinter" %>
<%@taglib prefix="c" uri="http://java.sun.com/jsp/jstl/core" %>
<html>
<head><title>Log Reset</title></head>
<body>
<pre>
<%
```

```
        LogManager.resetConfiguration();
        ClassLoader cl = this.getClass().getClassLoader();
        URL log4jprops = cl.getResource("log4j.properties");
        if (log4jprops != null)
        {
            PropertyConfigurator l4jconfig = new PropertyConfigurator();
            l4jconfig.configure(log4jprops);
        }
        out.println("#Log4j configuration");
        PrintWriter pw = new PrintWriter( out );
        PropertyPrinter pp = new PropertyPrinter(pw);
        pp.print(pw);
        out.println("#End of Config");
%>
</pre>
</body>
</html>
```

The line

```
        LogManager.resetConfiguration();
        URL log4jprops = cl.getResource("log4j.properties");
```

resets the Log4j configuration and then looks for the configuration file along the classpath. The following lines then reconfigure Log4j using the properties file:

```
            PropertyConfigurator l4jconfig = new PropertyConfigurator();
            l4jconfig.configure(log4jprops);
```

Finally, these lines use a Log4j-provided utility to print the current configuration:

```
        PrintWriter pw = new PrintWriter( out );
        PropertyPrinter pp = new PropertyPrinter(pw);
        pp.print(pw);
```

We have to create a `PrintWriter` to pass to the `PropertyPrinter` constructor and to the `PropertyPrinter.print` method because the `out` object in a JSP is not really a `PrintWriter`. It is instead a `JspWriter`, which does not extend the `PrintWriter` class, and the methods expect a `PrintWriter`. The output is enclosed within a `<pre>` element because it is not formatted as HTML text.

Logging with tag libraries

All of the logging examples up to this point have required the use of scriptlets. Many development shops do not like or allow the use of scriptlets in new code. The preference is to use tag libraries, so that there is no mixing of business logic with presentation logic and markup. Fortunately, the Jakarta taglibs project provides a tag library specifically designed to enable logging from with JSP pages. The project can be found at `http://jakarta.apache.org/taglibs/doc/log-doc/intro.html`. The tag library supports the Log4j logging framework, so configuration of the logging framework is the same as that for Log4j.

To set up the tag library so it can be used in your application, you need to copy the JAR file into the WEB-INF/lib directory of the Web application. You will also need to have the log4j.jar file in the WEB-INF/lib directory or in a common library directory shared by all of the Web applications. Next, you copy the tag library descriptor (.tld file) into the WEB-INF/tld directory. Finally, you add the following lines to the <jsp-config> section of the web.xml file:

```
<taglib>
    <taglib-uri>http://jakarta.apache.org/taglibs/log-1.0</taglib-uri>
    <taglib-location>/WEB-INF/tld/log.tld</taglib-location>
</taglib>
```

The log tag library provides six tags that can be used to log from within a JSP:

- ❏ fatal
- ❏ error
- ❏ warn
- ❏ info
- ❏ debug
- ❏ dump

Most of these tags correspond to Log4j logging levels. All but the dump tag support the attributes described in following table.

Attribute Name	Required	Runtime Expression Evaluation
category: The Log4j category name used for logging this message. If not specified, the default Log4j category is used.	No	Yes
message: The message to log. If this is not specified, the body of the tag is used instead.	No	Yes

Dump is a special tag. It has a single required attribute, scope. The scope attribute can be set to one of the following values:

- ❏ page
- ❏ request
- ❏ session
- ❏ application

The dump tag sends all of the objects in the specified scope to its output.

Try It Out   Coding with Log Tags

The following code demonstrates the use of these tags:

```
<%@page contentType="text/html"%>
<%@page pageEncoding="UTF-8"%>
<%@taglib prefix="c" uri="http://java.sun.com/jsp/jstl/core" %>
<%@taglib prefix="log" uri="http://jakarta.apache.org/taglibs/log-1.0" %>
<html>
<head><title>JSP Log Tags Page</title></head>
<body>
    <c:set var="myvar" value="Message comes from an EL expression" scope="page" />
    <c:set var="logCat" value="${pageContext.page.class.name}" scope="page" />
    <log:debug>It is bad practice to log messages without a category</log:debug>
    <log:debug category="${logCat}" >
        This should appear in the logs if DEBUG is enabled.
    </log:debug>
    <log:info category="${logCat}" message="${myvar}" />
    <log:warn
        category="${logCat}"
        message="URI is ${pageContext.request.requestURI}"
    />
    <log:error category="${logCat}">
        This is logging body content as the  message
    </log:error>
    <log:fatal category="${logCat}" message="fatal message" />

    You should see output in the info logs now.
    <log:dump scope="application" />
</body>
</html>
```

When we run the JSP with the `log4j.properties` file previously configured, we should see something like what follows in the logs:

```
DEBUG: [2004-08-07 23:18:26,140] LogTags_jsp - This should appear in the logs if
DEBUG is enabled.
INFO : [2004-08-07 23:18:26,140] LogTags_jsp - Message comes from an EL expression
WARN : [2004-08-07 23:18:26,140] LogTags_jsp - URI is /begjsp/LogTags.jsp
ERROR: [2004-08-07 23:18:26,140] LogTags_jsp - This is logging body content as the
message
FATAL: [2004-08-07 23:18:26,140] LogTags_jsp - fatal message
```

The browser should display something like the following:

```
You should see output in the info logs now.
org.apache.catalina.jsp_classpath
/C:/mysrc/BegJsp/WEB-INF/classes/;/C:/mysrc/BegJsp/WEB-INF/lib/jstl.jar;/C:/mysrc/
BegJsp/WEB-INF/lib/log4j-1.2.8.jar;/C:/mysrc/BegJsp/WEB-INF/lib/standard.jar;/C:/
mysrc/BegJsp/WEB-INF/lib/taglibs-log.jar;C:/openjava/NetBeans3.6/jakarta-tomcat-
5.0.19/common/classes/;C:/openjava/NetBeans3.6/jakarta-tomcat-5.0.19/common/endorse
d/xercesImpl.jar;C:/openjava/NetBeans3.6/jakarta-tomcat-5.0.19/common/endorsed/
xmlParserAPIs.jar;C:/openjava/NetBeans3.6/jakarta-tomcat-5.0.19/common/lib/ant.jar;
```

```
C:/openjava/NetBeans3.6/jakarta-tomcat-5.0.19/common/lib/commons-collections.jar;
C:/openjava/NetBeans3.6/jakarta-tomcat-5.0.19/common/lib/commons-dbcp-1.1.jar;C:/
openjava/NetBeans3.6/jakarta-tomcat-5.0.19/common/lib/commons-el.jar;C:/openjava/
NetBeans3.6/jakarta-tomcat-5.0.19/common/lib/commons-pool-1.1.jar;C:/openjava/
NetBeans3.6/jakarta-tomcat-5.0.19/common/lib/httpmonitor.jar;C:/openjava/
NetBeans3.6/jakarta-tomcat-5.0.19/common/lib/jasper-compiler.jar;C:/openjava/
NetBeans3.6/jakarta-tomcat-5.0.19/common/lib/jasper-runtime.jar;C:/openjava/
NetBeans3.6/jakarta-tomcat-5.0.19/common/lib/jmx.jar;C:/openjava/NetBeans3.6/
jakarta-tomcat-5.0.19/common/lib/jsp-api.jar;C:/openjava/NetBeans3.6/jakarta-
tomcat-5.0.19/common/lib/naming-common.jar;C:/openjava/NetBeans3.6/jakarta-tomcat-5
.0.19/common/lib/naming-factory.jar;C:/openjava/NetBeans3.6/jakarta-tomcat-
5.0.19/common/lib/naming-java.jar;C:/openjava/NetBeans3.6/jakarta-tomcat-5.0.19/com
mon/lib/naming-resources.jar;C:/openjava/NetBeans3.6/jakarta-tomcat-5.0.19/
common/lib/schema2beans.jar;C:/openjava/NetBeans3.6/jakarta-tomcat-5.0.19/common/
lib/servlet-api.jar;/C:/j2sdk1.4.2_04/lib/tools.jar;/C:/openjava/NetBeans3.6/
jakarta-tomcat-5.0.19/bin/bootstrap.jar;/C:/j2sdk1.4.2_04/jre/lib/ext/dnsns.jar;
/C:/j2sdk1.4.2_04/jre/lib/ext/ldapsec.jar;/C:/j2sdk1.4.2_04/jre/lib/ext/localedata.
jar;/C:/j2sdk1.4.2_04/jre/lib/ext/sunjce_provider.jar
javax.servlet.context.tempdir
C:\Documents and Settings\jtbell\.netbeans\3.6\jakarta-tomcat-5.0.19_base\work\
Catalina\localhost\begjsp
org.apache.catalina.resources
org.apache.naming.resources.ProxyDirContext@6c5356
org.apache.catalina.WELCOME_FILES
[Ljava.lang.String;@1d349e2
```

How It Works

If we examine the JSP to understand what is happening, we see the following first line of interest enables access to the tag library by using the prefix log:

```
<%@taglib prefix="log" uri="http://jakarta.apache.org/taglibs/log-1.0" %>
```

A page variable is then set with the class name to use as a logging category:

```
<c:set var="logCat" value="${pageContext.page.class.name}" scope="page" />
```

We didn't have to do this, but it makes the code easier to read when we use the expression ${logCat} in the tags instead of ${pageContext.page.class.name}. The following line demonstrates that it is possible to use the tags without a logging category. In this case, the messages will be logged using the settings of the root logger:

```
<log:debug>It is bad practice to log messages without a category</log:debug>
```

The next lines of interest demonstrate using EL expressions for the log message. When using JSP 2.0, the EL expressions can appear as part of the body content of the tag as well:

```
<log:info category="${logCat}" message="${myvar}" />
<log:warn
    category="${logCat}"
    message="URI is ${pageContext.request.requestURI}"
/>
```

Finally, we send some text back to the browser and dump the application context using the dump tag and send it to the browser:

```
You should see output in the info logs now.
<log:dump scope="application" />
```

This example has demonstrated how the log tag library provides convenient access to Log4j logging functions from within the JSP page simply by using JSP tags.

Debugging with Tools

Logging provides a good way to improve the quality of the observations we make about the code. As you will see later in the chapter, effective use of logging is the best way to identify bugs when working within a production environment. However, it would also be nice to watch a JSP as it works and be able to step through each action, as is commonly done when debugging Java programs. Fortunately, most development environments that support JSP development also support a JSP debugger. A debugger is a tool that enables code to be monitored as it executes.

All of the code for this chapter has been created with the NetBeans IDE (version 3.6). NetBeans is a free and open-source Java Integrated Development Environment that supports the development of stand-alone Java applications and Web applications supporting the JSP and servlet specifications. NetBeans includes a JSP debugger. The concepts covered in this section, however, apply to all of the development environments that support J2EE development. These include IntelliJ, JBuilder, and WebSphere Application Developer, for example. It may also be possible to use Eclipse with appropriate plug-ins.

This section covers three primary concepts:

❑   Breakpoints

❑   Stepping through code

❑   Watchpoints

These are common concepts for all debuggers.

Setting breakpoints

A breakpoint marks a location within the code where you want execution of the code to pause or stop. By pausing the execution of the code, you can gain control over the code to start single-stepping through it or to examine the state of the system. In most environments, breakpoints are set by placing the cursor on a line of code and selecting an item from a menu to toggle or set a breakpoint. With NetBeans, for example, you set a breakpoint by double-clicking the line of code or by right-clicking and selecting Toggle Breakpoint from the context menu. Figure 14-4 shows source code in NetBeans with two breakpoints set.

> *When the program is paused at a breakpoint, it is not sending a response to the browser. The browser may time out, which can affect the behavior of the program you are testing. This is one of the known limitations of using debuggers in a Web application environment.*

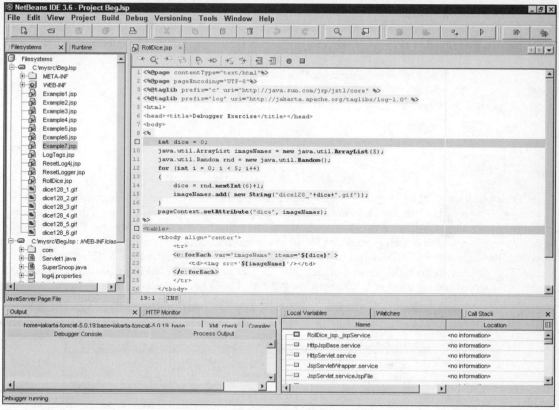

Figure 14-4: NetBeans with breakpoints set in JSP

Try It Out   Using the Debugger

The following code example demonstrates the use of the debugger:

```
<%@page contentType="text/html"%>
<%@page pageEncoding="UTF-8"%>
<%@taglib prefix="c" uri="http://java.sun.com/jsp/jstl/core" %>
<%@taglib prefix="log" uri="http://jakarta.apache.org/taglibs/log-1.0" %>
<html>
<head><title>Debugger Exercise</title></head>
<body>
<%
    int dice = 0;
    java.util.ArrayList imageNames = new java.util.ArrayList(5);
    java.util.Random rnd = new java.util.Random();
    for (int i = 0; i < 5; i++)
    {
        dice = rnd.nextInt(6)+1;
        imageNames.add( new String("dice128_"+dice+".gif"));
    }
```

```
        pageContext.setAttribute("dice", imageNames);
%>
<table>
    <tbody align="center">
        <tr>
        <c:forEach var="imageName" items="${dice}" >
            <td><img src='${imageName}'/></td>
        </c:forEach>
        </tr>
    </tbody>
    </table>
</body>
</html>
```

Call this program `RollDice.jsp`. This JSP rolls five dice and then displays them graphically in the browser. The scriptlet handles randomly generating the values for the dice and creating an array mapping the rolls to image files in the Web application. The names of the selected images files are placed in an array list, which is then placed into the page context. In a Model-, View-, or Controller-based application, the scriptlet could be moved to the Controller. The rest of the JSP creates a table, loading the appropriate image into each element of the table. The images are included in the source code file that can be downloaded for this book. You may use your own images as long as you name them `dice128_1.gif` through `dice128_6.gif`. When the JSP is executed, the output resembles what is shown in Figure 14-5.

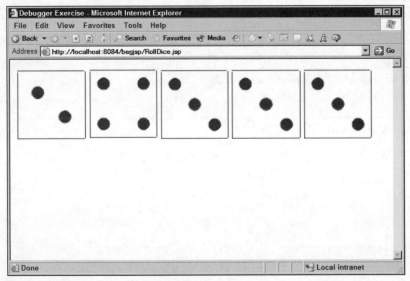

Figure 14-5: Result of running `RollDice.jsp`

Each time the JSP is run, a different set of dice will be shown. Set a breakpoint at the line that reads as follows:

```
<table>
```

After the breakpoint is set, start running the application in the debugger. Look for a menu item in the Debug or Run menu that enables you to run the application in the debugger. For NetBeans, select Debug ⇨ Start Session ⇨ Run in Debugger, which can also be accessed using Alt+F5. If your environment doesn't automatically open a browser, then open a browser window and provide it with the URL of the `RollDice.jsp` file within the application. On my system, this is `http://localhost:8084/chapt14/RollDice.jsp`.

When the container in the IDE encounters the breakpoint, it will pause the execution. Your browser may appear to be hung. This is normal. Now we are ready to move on to the next topic, examining variables and setting watchpoints.

Examining variables and setting watchpoints

Once the code has been paused, you can examine the state of the system. Mostly this means looking at variables and their values. In our example, we can see the current values for dice and `imageNames`. The variables that are created as a part of the servlet generated by the JSP are also visible. Remember that variables accessed through EL expressions are really contained within the page, request, session, or application contexts. These are all available to browse. Figure 14-6 shows the object browser window of NetBeans. To see the dice attribute in the `pageContext`, we need to open `pageContext`, examine the HashMap for an entry with the key `"dice"`, and then finally open the value for that entry.

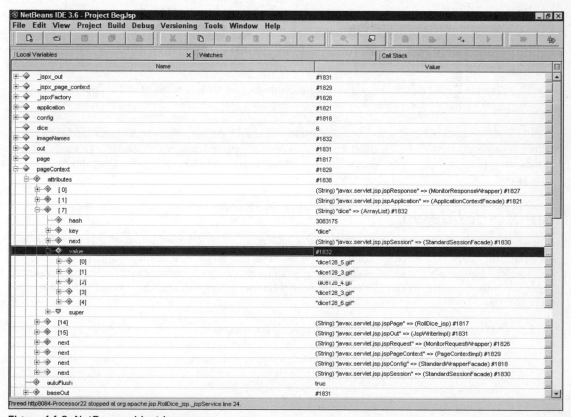

Figure 14-6: NetBeans object browser

Watchpoints provide an easier way to monitor the variables that are important to us. A *watchpoint* is a variable that the debugger has been asked to watch. Normally, these variables are tracked in a different window so they can be monitored and viewed as needed. In the case of NetBeans, when you have browsed to the expression you are interested in, you can right-click to make it a watchpoint. As you are stepping through the code, the watchpoints update as the values of the variables that are watching are changed by the code.

One final note: Many debuggers will not only allow you to examine the variables, but also to change their values. This can be a very useful way to create a quick experiment to check a hypothesis.

Stepping through code

After we have paused at a breakpoint we can step through the code one line at a time. Most debuggers provide at least the following functions for stepping through code:

- ❑ **Step Over:** Executes the next single line of code without stepping into other methods or functions that might be called on the current line, and then pauses again.

- ❑ **Step Into:** Executes the next single line of code but steps into each function or method called on the line of code and pauses at the first executable line within the method. From this pause you can continue to single-step inside the stepped-into function.

- ❑ **Step Out:** Continues running the current function until the function or method returns. This is useful if you stepped into an uninteresting function.

- ❑ **Continue:** Continues running the program at full speed until the next breakpoint is encountered.

- ❑ **Terminate:** Ends the program without completing it. This is often useful if you know the program will not complete successfully because of a bug.

With each step command, the watchpoints are updated and the variables can be examined. The result of these commands is to allow the programmer to watch the program execute one line at a time. When the interesting portion of the code has executed, the programmer can then allow the program to continue at full speed.

Remote debugging

Tomcat can be started in a way that supports remote debugging of Web applications. If your IDE does not have an integrated Web development environment, this might be a useful option. Debugging remotely is essentially the same as debugging in an integrated environment except that the server can be on a separate machine. To start Tomcat and prepare it for remote debugging on Windows, follow the these steps:

1. Make sure that Tomcat starting as a service is disabled. On Windows, this is done by using the service applet from the Control Panel. Find the Apache Tomcat service (if it isn't there you can skip this step) and double-click to get to the properties screen. From properties, select Stop and then set the startup type to Manual. This will prevent Tomcat from starting each time the machine restarts.

2. Open a command-line window and navigate to the directory `\bin` below where Tomcat is installed. The default installation directory for Tomcat 5 on Windows is `C:\Program Files\Apache Software Foundation\Tomcat 5.0`.

3. Enter the following commands to start Tomcat:

```
SET JPDA_TRANSPORT=dt_socket
SET JPDA_ADDRESS=8000
Catalina jpda start
```

These lines will configure Tomcat to listen for a debugger on port 8000 and start Tomcat in debugging mode.

4. To attach a remote debugger, provide it with the machine name and the debugging port for the Tomcat instance. For example, using NetBeans, select Debug ➪ Start Session ➪ Attach and fill in the Attach dialog as shown in Figure 14-7.

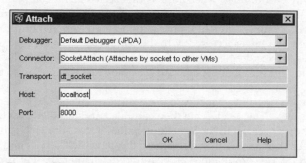

Figure 14-7: NetBeans remote debugging Attach dialog box

The settings should be as follows:

❑ **Debugger:** Default Debugger (JPDA)

❑ **Connector:** SocketAttach (Attaches by Socket to other VMs)

❑ **Transport:** `dt_socket`

❑ **Host:** localhost or host name of your remote machine

❑ **Port:** 8000

After this is done, you can start debugging the program just as if it were running in the IDE.

Debugging Code in Production Environments

Normally, it is not possible to use debuggers in production environments. If the site gets a lot of traffic, it is often not possible to store all of the log messages that can be generated. The next few paragraphs discuss issues with debugging in production, and techniques that you can use to help find and fix problems discovered in a production environment. The first production issue we will examine is precompiled JSPs.

The best tool for debugging production systems is often a good logging environment and good logging messages generated by the code. Of the logging solutions examined, Log4j combined with the log tag library provides the most flexibility and is the most useful in production. The other logging solutions are useful, but are better in those cases where quick experiments need to be conducted, such as when code is first being developed. The rest of this discussion assumes that you will be using Log4j or a logger with similar capabilities.

Debugging when the JSP is precompiled

It is common to precompile each JSP before it is deployed in a production environment. Precompiling prevents the long delay encountered when a JSP is first accessed. Precompilation, however, can take on several forms. Some Web servers, such as WebSphere, provide an option to precompile pages as they are deployed. The JSP spec requires that a container support a precompiler hint to indicate that the page should be precompiled. If a JSP is accessed with the parameter `?jsp_precompile=true`, then the container is not supposed to execute the JSP but instead may compile the JSP. The servlet container is free to ignore the request and not compile the page, but it cannot pass the request to the JSP for processing.

Another approach to precompiling pages is to use an Ant script and the Jasper JSP compiler task to compile the pages into servlets. The servlets are then compiled and installed into the `web.xml` file and are handled just like any other servlet in the Web application. If this approach is used, you must remember that when using a debugger, you will be debugging the generated servlet and not looking at the JSP file itself. More details on JSP precompilation can be found in Chapter 25, "Performance."

As far as log messages are concerned, they are always generated from the compiled servlet and not the JSP. When using the logging tag library, the category name should be set to something that is recognizable. The sample code demonstrated how to use an EL expression to get the fully qualified name of the class to use as the category name. That sample code is repeated here:

```
<c:set var="logCat" value="${pageContext.page.class.name}" scope="page" />
<log:info category="${logCat}" message="informational log message" />
```

The expression `${pageContext.page.class.name}` will uniquely identify each JSP in the logs and allow the logs to be configured separately for individual JSPs if needed. If the name of the JSP changes, the catalog name will change automatically. Another approach might be to use the request URL for the category name, but this requires a function to replace the / characters with dots.

Debugging under load

In general, you don't want to debug in a production environment, but you must often have a laboratory environment that is as close to the production system as possible. The goal in the production environment to is gather enough information and make enough observations so that you can reproduce the problem in a debugging or laboratory environment. But what happens if the problem is only observed when a certain number of users are accessing the system?

The amount of use a system gets is often called the *load*. There are many ways to express this value, but often it is expressed as a number of concurrent users. Concurrent users are users that are accessing the system simultaneously. When looking for problems that are load-related, it is important to be able to apply to the debug system (scaled if needed) the same load that is represented on the actual production system.

The debugging system does not have to be the same as the production system but you need to consider the differences when accounting for the load. For example, if the production system is made up of a cluster of 8 machines and handles 6,000 concurrent users, then a debug system of 2 machines should handle at least 1,500 users.

Normally, a load generator is used to simulate large numbers of users. Several free and commercial products are available for load generation. Examples include Load Runner from Mercury Interactive, Jakarta JMeter, and Apache Flood.

It is easy to see that the log files are likely to become very large when a system has the type of load we are discussing. Even if the files can be stored on the system, there is still the problem of finding the information you need within millions of lines of log files.

Adding contextual information to log files

You can use several techniques to help isolate the specific log messages you are interested in. Most of these are based on adding specific information to each log entry. We have already seen time stamps added to log entries. A timestamp can be used to maintain the order of entries as they are examined and to limit the entries examined to those that occurred near the event of interest.

Now let's examine some other common use cases:

- ❑ Find all log entries related to a specific application
- ❑ Find all log entries related to a specific user
- ❑ Find all log entries from a specific IP address
- ❑ Find all log entries related to a specific session

The first case would seem to be pretty easy based on what we already know about the logging framework. We just need to enable logging for those classes that make up the application. But what happens for classes that are shared between multiple applications? Do we want those instances to log their message, too? The other cases are a little more difficult. How can a logger in a class that doesn't even know that it is part of a Web application log user and session information?

The solution for all of these problems is the *Nested Diagnostic Context*, or *NDC*. An NDC is a mechanism that helps you to distinguish interleaved log messages from different sources. Log4j provides a class called NDC that supports adding and removing thread-specific information that can be logged as a part of the logging record. For a Web application, the best way to use this is to add the NDC information in a filter and then remove the information using the same filter. A sample filter that adds the session ID to each log message is as follows:

```
package com.wrox.book.chapt14;

import java.io.IOException;
import javax.servlet.*;
import javax.servlet.http.HttpServletRequest;
import javax.servlet.http.HttpSession;
import org.apache.log4j.NDC;


public class NdcFilter implements Filter
{
    private FilterConfig filterConfig = null;

    public NdcFilter()
    {
    }

    public void init(FilterConfig fc)
    {
        filterConfig = fc;
    }


    public void doFilter(ServletRequest request,
        ServletResponse response, FilterChain chain)
    throws IOException, ServletException
    {
        // adds the session ID to the NDC
        HttpServletRequest hreq = null;
        if( request instanceof HttpServletRequest )
        {
            hreq = (HttpServletRequest)request;
            HttpSession session = hreq.getSession();
            if( session != null )
                NDC.push(session.getId());
            else
                NDC.push("No session present");
        }
        else
            NDC.push( "Not an HttpServlet request!" );
        chain.doFilter(request, response);
        NDC.pop();
    }

    public void destroy()
    {
    }
}
```

The line

```
if( request instanceof HttpServletRequest )
```

ensures that the request is an `HttpServletRequest` before we cast it to one. We need an `HttpServletRequest` in order to get the session. In this case, we always want a session ID so we allow `hreq.getSession()` to create a session if one does not exist. We can change this behavior by replacing

```
HttpSession session = hreq.getSession();
```

with

```
HttpSession session = hreq.getSession(false);
```

Once we have the session, we push the session ID onto the NDC stack. Now this value is available to every logger called in this thread of execution. The line

```
chain.doFilter(request, response);
```

allows the filter chain to continue processing if needed and will eventually lead to our Web application being called. When we again get control after the servlets and JSP and other filters have processed the request and response, the context is popped off the NDC stack with this line:

```
NDC.pop();
```

We need to configure the filter in the `web.xml` file by adding the following lines below the `<web-app>` element:

```
<filter>
  <filter-name>NdcFilter</filter-name>
  <filter-class>com.wrox.book.chapt14.NdcFilter</filter-class>
</filter>
<filter-mapping>
  <filter-name>NdcFilter</filter-name>
  <url-pattern>/*</url-pattern>
</filter-mapping>
```

The `url-pattern` element in the previous XML matches all URLs for this Web application. If we want to do this only for a subset of the URLs, then we can change the pattern accordingly.

We also need to make a configuration change to the `log4j.properties` file to see the NDC context. Replace the following line from the sample `log4j.properties` file earlier in this chapter:

```
log4j.appender.ConsoleOut.layout.ConversionPattern=%-5p: [%d] %c{1} - %m%n
```

with the following:

```
log4j.appender.ConsoleOut.layout.ConversionPattern=%-5p: [%d] %x %c{1} - %m%n
```

The `%x` will print the current NDC context on each log line. Once this has been done, every method that logs a message will also log the session ID, even if the method is unaware that it is running as a part of a Web application and knows nothing about sessions.

We hope you can see how this feature can be used to track an individual user or to track other application-specific information. Once this information is in the logs, it is easy to extract it using a command-line tool such as `grep`.

Adding log filters

The previous discussion assumes that we will capture all of the log entries and then filter them as part of the analysis. It has also been pointed out that it might not be viable to collect all of the log entries generated due to the volume in a high load environment. There are a couple of potential solutions to this problem, but the most common one is to use log filtering. We have already seen how both Log4j and the SDK Logger provide the capability to limit the number of log messages that are generated by using logging levels or priorities combined with the practice of naming the loggers with the fully qualified class names. Both frameworks also provide a filter capability to further restrict log messages from being logged. The SDK Logger supports the creation of filters for both the logger and the handler, whereas Log4j supports filters on the Appenders. The SDK does not provide any filters. If you need one, you must provide it. Log4j provides four filters:

- ❑ **DenyAll:** Blocks all log messages
- ❑ **LevelMatch:** Logs or blocks only messages logged at a specific level
- ❑ **LevelRange:** Logs or blocks messages logged within a defined range of levels
- ❑ **StringMatch:** Logs or blocks messages based on matching strings in the message text

Log4j filters are extended from the abstract `org.apache.log4j.spi.Filter` class and must implement a single method, called `decide()`.

Finding the Intermittent Problem

Intermittent problems are problems that seem to come and go and are difficult to pinpoint and reproduce. Finding an intermittent problem is really similar to any other debugging task: Apply the scientific method. It is critical, however, to make as many observations and collect as many data points as possible. The following sections describe a few techniques that help add critical information that may be helpful in finding the problem.

Adding information as response comments

Because most intermittent problems are difficult to reproduce until you understand them, one technique that is often useful is to add information as comments into the HTML document created as a part of the HTTP response. These comments can be used as clues to help find the problem. One approach to doing this is to create an `ArrayList` of strings and place them into the request. When the JSP renders the page, it appends the list of strings to the end of the resulting HTML document as comments. When the problem is encountered by a user, ask the user to click View ➪ Source in the browser and read the comments back to you or cut and paste them into an e-mail message. Be careful that no sensitive information is placed in these comment blocks.

Snoop application

Another technique is to have the user access a *snoop application*. There are many variations on snoop applications; Tomcat even comes with a very lightweight snoop.jsp. The basic premise is that the application echoes back to the user what the application knows about the current contexts. This information is then copied from the browser and sent back to the developer to help with debugging.

The following code illustrates a servlet called SuperSnoop that prints all of the information in the request, session, and application scopes. This servlet is more comprehensive than most of the other snoop applications available. In some cases, you may want to customize this application to make sure sensitive information is not revealed.

```java
import java.io.*;
import java.net.*;
import java.text.DateFormat;
import java.util.Date;
import java.util.Enumeration;
import java.util.Properties;

import javax.servlet.*;
import javax.servlet.http.*;

public class SuperSnoop extends HttpServlet {

    private String makeTitle( String title )
    {
        return new String("<H2>"+title+"</H2>\n");
    }

    private String makeRow( String left, String right ) {
        StringBuffer sb = new StringBuffer(128);
        sb.append( "<tr>\n" );
        sb.append( "\t<td>"+left+"</td>\n");
        sb.append( "\t<td>"+right+"</td>\n");
        sb.append( "</tr>\n" );
        return sb.toString();
    }

    private String today()
    {
        Date now = new Date();
        DateFormat dateFormatter = DateFormat.getDateTimeInstance();
        return dateFormatter.format( now );
    }

    private String showHeaders( HttpServletRequest request ) {
        StringBuffer sb = new StringBuffer(512);
        Enumeration e = request.getHeaderNames();
        String key = null;
        String value = null;
        sb.append( makeTitle("Request Headers"));
        sb.append("<table>");
        while( e.hasMoreElements() ){
```

```
                key = (String)e.nextElement();
                value = request.getHeader(key);
                sb.append( makeRow( key, value ));
            }
            sb.append("</table>");
            return sb.toString();
        }

    private String showRequestInfo(HttpServletRequest request) {
        StringBuffer sb = new StringBuffer(512);
        sb.append(makeTitle( "Request Info"));
        sb.append("<table>\n");
        sb.append( makeRow( "ContextPath", request.getContextPath() ));
        sb.append( makeRow( "Method", request.getMethod() ));
        sb.append( makeRow( "RequestURL", request.getRequestURL().toString()));
        sb.append( makeRow( "ServletPath", request.getServletPath() ));
        sb.append( makeRow( "CharacterEncoding", request.getCharacterEncoding() ));
        sb.append( makeRow( "ContentType", request.getContentType() ));
        sb.append( makeRow( "RemoteAddress", request.getRemoteAddr() ));
        sb.append( makeRow( "RemoteHost", request.getRemoteHost() ));
        sb.append( makeRow( "Scheme", request.getScheme() ));
        sb.append( makeRow( "ServerName", request.getServerName() ));
        sb.append( makeRow( "ServerPort", Integer.toString(request.getServerPort())
));
        sb.append("</table>\n");
        return sb.toString();
    }


    private String showRequestParams( HttpServletRequest request )
    {
        StringBuffer sb = new StringBuffer(512);
        Enumeration e = request.getParameterNames();
        String key = null;
        String value = null;
        sb.append(makeTitle("Request Parameters"));
        sb.append("<table>");
        while( e.hasMoreElements() ){
            key = (String)e.nextElement();
            value = request.getParameter(key);
            sb.append( makeRow( key, value ));
        }
        sb.append("</table>");
        return sb.toString();
    }

    private String showSysProps() {
        StringBuffer sb = new StringBuffer(512);
        Properties p = System.getProperties();
        Enumeration e = p.propertyNames();
        String key = null;
        String value = null;
        sb.append(makeTitle("System Properties"));
        sb.append("<table>");
        sb.append(makeRow("System Time", today() ));
```

```
        while( e.hasMoreElements() ){
            key = (String)e.nextElement();
            value = p.getProperty( key );
            sb.append( makeRow( key, value ));
        }
        sb.append("</table>");
        return sb.toString();
    }

    private String showInitParams() {
        StringBuffer sb = new StringBuffer(512);
        ServletContext context = getServletContext();
        Enumeration e = context.getInitParameterNames();
        String key = null;
        String value = null;
        sb.append(makeTitle("Initialization Parameters"));
        sb.append("<table>");
        while( e.hasMoreElements() ){
            key = (String)e.nextElement();
            value = context.getInitParameter(key);
            sb.append( makeRow( key, value ));
        }
        sb.append("</table>");
        return sb.toString();
    }

    private String showServletContextInfo()
    {
        StringBuffer sb = new StringBuffer(512);
        ServletContext context = getServletContext();
        sb.append(makeTitle("Servlet Context"));
        sb.append("<table>");
        sb.append( makeRow( "Server Info", context.getServerInfo()));
        sb.append( makeRow( "Servlet Context Name",
context.getServletContextName()));
        sb.append( makeRow( "Real Path", context.getRealPath("/")));
        sb.append("</table>");
        return sb.toString();
    }

    private String showContextAttributes() {
        StringBuffer sb = new StringBuffer(512);
        ServletContext context = getServletContext();
        Enumeration e = context.getAttributeNames();
        String key = null;
        String value = null;
        sb.append(makeTitle("Servlet Context Attributes"));
        sb.append("<table>");
        while( e.hasMoreElements() ){
            key = (String)e.nextElement();
            value = context.getAttribute(key).toString();
            sb.append( makeRow( key, value ));
        }
        sb.append("</table>");
```

```java
            return sb.toString();
    }

    public void doGet(HttpServletRequest request, HttpServletResponse response)
    throws ServletException, IOException {
        response.setContentType("text/html");
        PrintWriter out = response.getWriter();

        out.println("<html>");
        out.println("<head>");
        out.println("<title>SysProps Servlet</title>");
        out.println("</head>");
        out.println("<body>");

        out.println( today() );
        out.println( showHeaders(request) );
        out.println( showRequestInfo(request) );
        out.println( showRequestParams(request) );
        out.println( showServletContextInfo() );
        out.println( showContextAttributes() );
        out.println( showInitParams() );
        out.println( showSysProps() );

        out.println("</table>");
        out.println("</body>");
        out.println("</html>");

        out.close();
    }

    public void doPost(HttpServletRequest request, HttpServletResponse response)
    throws ServletException, IOException
    {
        doGet(request, response);
    }

    public String getServletInfo() {
        return "Prints Java System Properties";
    }
}
```

The servlet code is pretty straightforward and shouldn't require any explanation. When the user experiencing the problem executes the servlet, the result can be cut and pasted into an e-mail message. The session ID information is included, so if the NdcFilter is in place, any logged information about the user's session can be easily found.

Once key information has been collected from the user, the logging system can be dynamically reconfigured as demonstrated earlier, to capture the specific detailed information required on the server side as the user reproduces the bug.

Avoiding Concurrency Issues

A JSP is compiled into a servlet. The service method of a servlet or a JSP may be called many times simultaneously by the container, but there may be only a single instance of the servlet. Each of these calls represents a separate thread of execution, but within a single servlet instance. This means that class variables in a servlet are actually shared by all of the users accessing that servlet at the same time. Servlets, and therefore JavaServer Pages, should rarely have class writable variables. On those rare occasions when a writable class variable is warranted, access to that variable needs to be handled through synchronization. Synchronization limits an object to one user at a time. Other threads that need to access a synchronized object must wait until the previous thread has completed its access. This slows the application down and limits the load that it can handle.

In general, if you need to do synchronization, it shouldn't be done in a JSP. While this may seem obvious, I once spent significant time trying to figure out why a Web application that I was asked to fix would show one user's private registration information to other users at random. It turned out that the programmer had placed a copy of the user's `profile` object into a `servlet` class variable instead of into a `session` or `request` variable. If a second user came along and completed his or her task before the first user, then the first user would suddenly see the second user's data.

Summary

This chapter has demonstrated that debugging is a science. Every science, however, is part art. The art of all science is in making good hypotheses or guesses and designing the right experiments. The best way to improve the guesses is to improve the observations. Observations are made by using tools such as debuggers and loggers. Loggers send output that should describe what is occurring in the process to log files, consoles, or other places where the logs can be examined. The logs provide more points of information for the observations. In many cases, the amount of information in the logs can be overwhelming, so you also learned techniques that you can use to better focus the information that is gathered or examined so that it is more useful for solving the problem at hand. One final thought: It is not enough to just fix a bug. You must understand the bug in order to make sure that the bug was really fixed and is not just masked and hiding, waiting to return at some inopportune moment. If you do not understand the bug and it disappears, it will reappear someday to haunt you.

Exercises

1. Create a Log4j `Filter` class to accept or deny messages based on the NDC for the message.

2. Create a servlet filter that pushes the requesting IP address onto the NDC stack.

3. Use `RollDice.jsp` and insert statements to create log messages using Log4j that show the file names of the images file that will be used. Instrument both the loop in the scriptlet and the JSTL `forEach` loop, but do not add a scriptlet to the `forEach` loop. Log the messages at the `DEBUG` priority level in the scriptlet and at the `INFO` priority level in the `forEach` loop.

Part II: JSP and Modern Web Server Software Development

15

JSPs and Servlets

JSPs are intimately tied with servlets. In Chapter 1, it was shown that servlets provide a componentized, efficient, Java-specific way of performing server-side operations. Servlets are essentially server-side software components. JSPs, working under the auspices of the servlet mechanism, actually make these components easier to create, modify, and maintain.

In Chapter 3, you were shown how the `getServletContext()` method can be used within the `jspInit()` and `jspDestroy()` methods to access the servlet context object. Then, in Chapter 7, you learned how the Web container actually translates all JSP code into servlets during processing. It is this servlet code that is finally compiled and executed.

Up until this point in the book, there has been no detailed coverage of servlets. However, it is certainly very important to have an understanding of servlets as you head toward the more advanced application of JSPs. As a developer of Web-based applications and services using JSP, it is vital to be familiar with servlets, as many nonpresentation tasks are better implemented using servlets than with JSP. This difference will be highly evident in this and later chapters of the book, when larger and more complex Web applications and frameworks are presented.

This chapter presents Java servlets in their own right. Specifically, it describes the following:

- ❏ How the Tomcat server treats servlets
- ❏ The lifecycle of a servlet
- ❏ Configuration of a servlet
- ❏ How servlets can collaborate with JSPs within a Web-based application
- ❏ The role of servlets as a Controller (as in a typical MVC framework)

Two hands-on examples provide you with an opportunity to work with servlets, creating and deploying them. Specifically, the examples show the following:

❑   How to create servlet mappings in the Web deployment descriptor. Servlet mapping can be used to control how a server process servlets or JSPs.

❑   How to provide initialization parameters to a servlet. The same mechanism can be also be used to provide initial parameters to a JSP.

By the end of this chapter, you will have a working knowledge of servlets and how they operate. You will also be familiar with servlet configuration and how to productively combine the use of servlets and JSPs within your application design. You will also understand the more advanced application of JSPs within large Web applications and/or Web application frameworks.

A JSP Is a Servlet

Chapter 7 showed how the Tomcat server translates JSP page code to Java source code. In fact, the translated code is actually a servlet. This means that every single JSP page is, in fact, a servlet. Figure 15-1 illustrates this.

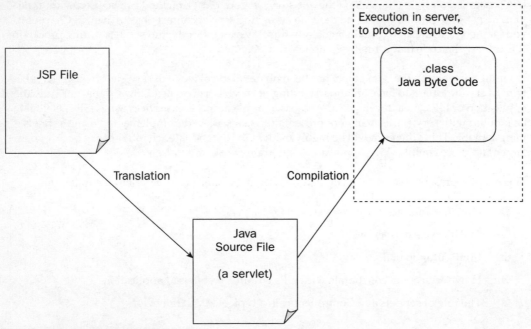

Figure 15-1: A JSP is actually a servlet

In Figure 15-1, a JSP page is translated into a Java source file by the JSP compiler (code-named Jasper for the Tomcat 5 server). This Java source file actually contains a class that is a servlet. The JSP container then compiles this servlet into a `.class` file. The `.class` file is executable Java bytecode, and is used by the container to process incoming requests.

Because every JSP is a servlet, it would be very useful to learn a little more about servlets and how the server handles them. This will shed some light on additional techniques that may also apply to JSP.

A JSP is a servlet. A servlet is a Java class representing a server-side component. The container (application server) creates and manages instance(s) of a servlet to handle incoming requests.

The first Try It Out exercise illustrates that a JSP is just a servlet. It also shows the lifecycle of a servlet, and some servlet configuration details

Try It Out   Servlets and JSP

To try out the first example, make sure you have deployed `ch15.war` on your Tomcat 5 server. Review Chapter 1 if you do not remember how to deploy a WAR file.

Access the following URL using your browser to see the output of the first example:

```
http://localhost:8080/ch15/
```

The output of this page should be similar to Figure 15-2.

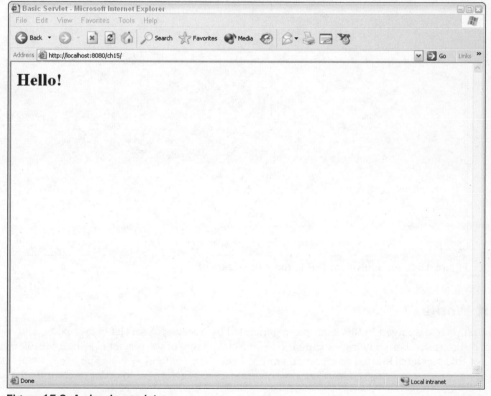

Figure 15-2: A simple servlet

Not surprisingly, the page just prints out the word "Hello!" However, unlike examples shown earlier in the book, this display is generated by a servlet and not a JSP.

However, because a JSP is a servlet, a JSP can trivially generate the same display. To try out the JSP version, access the following URL:

```
http://localhost:8080/ch15/example1/index.jsp
```

This is a more familiar URL, and points to a JSP page that does exactly the same thing as the servlet in Figure 15-2, as you can see in Figure 15-3.

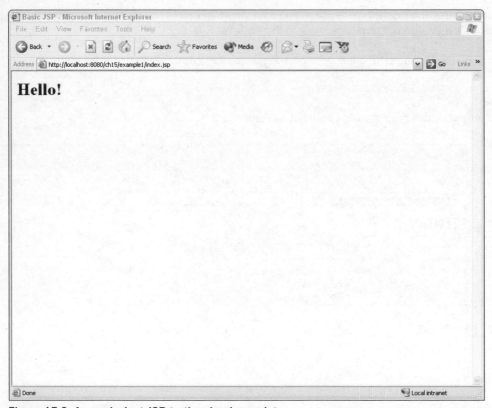

Figure 15-3: An equivalent JSP to the simple servlet

How It Works

The first page displayed in this example is generated by a servlet. A servlet is Java code, and as such must be compiled before being executed. The Java class name of the servlet is `BasicServlet`, and the code of this servlet is located at `<Tomcat Installation Directory>/webapps/ch15/WEB-INF/classes/com/wrox/begjsp/ch15/servlet/BasicServlet.java`. In order to compile the servlet, you will need the `<Tomcat Installation Directory>/common/lib/servlet-api.jar` JAR file in your classpath. The following command shows this being done:

```
javac -classpath %TOMCAT_HOME%\common\lib\servlet-api.jar
com\wrox\begjsp\ch15\servlet\*.java
```

If you download the code for this chapter from the Wrox Web site, it comes with the servlet already compiled and packaged as a WAR file, so you don't have to do this step.

The `BasicServlet` servlet is a simple servlet that prints out the word "Hello." However, it is a complete servlet and reveals many servlet programming details. The code for this `BasicServlet.java` page is reproduced here:

```
package com.wrox.begjsp.ch15.servlet;
import javax.servlet.*;
import javax.servlet.http.*;

public class BasicServlet extends HttpServlet
{

    public void init(ServletConfig config) throws ServletException
    {
        super.init(config);
    }

    public void destroy()
    {
    }

    protected void processRequest(HttpServletRequest request,
      HttpServletResponse response)
      throws ServletException, java.io.IOException
    {

        try
        {
        response.setContentType("text/html");
        java.io.PrintWriter out = response.getWriter();
        out.write("<html>\n");
        out.write("<head>\n");
        out.write("<title>Basic Servlet</title>\n");
        out.write("</head>\n");
        out.write("<body>\n");
        out.write("<h1>Hello!</h1>\n");
        out.write("</body>\n");
        out.write("</html>");
        out.close();
        }
        catch(Exception e)
        {
```

```
        throw new ServletException(e);
    }
}

protected void doGet(HttpServletRequest request,
  HttpServletResponse response)
  throws ServletException, java.io.IOException
{
    processRequest(request, response);
}

protected void doPost(HttpServletRequest request,
  HttpServletResponse response)
  throws ServletException, java.io.IOException
{
    processRequest(request, response);
}

}
```

Anatomy of a servlet

Unlike its JSP cousin, `BasicServlet.java` is quite a bit of code. Taking a look at `BasicServlet.java`, you can observe the following:

❑   It extends a class called `HttpServlet`.

❑   It implements four methods: `init()`, `destroy()`, `doGet()`, and `doPost()`.

❑   It also implements a helper method named `processRequest()`.

The mark of a servlet: the javax.servlet.Servlet interface

According to the Servlet 2.4 (or 2.3) specifications, the distinguishing feature that makes a Java class a servlet is the fact that all servlets must implement the `javax.servlet.Servlet` interface. This interface is the contract between the container (application server) and the servlet. All containers conforming to the Servlet 2.4 (or 2.3) specification will use this interface to access the features provided by a servlet. The following table describes the methods of the `javax.servlet.Servlet` interface that all servlets must implement.

Method Name	Description
init()	Called by the container to initialize the servlet; any initialization parameters should be processed here. The section "The lifecycle of a servlet," later in this chapter, provides more details about this very important method.
destroy()	Called by the container to indicate to the servlet that the servlet is being put out of commission. For more information, see "The lifecycle of a servlet," later in this chapter.

Method Name	Description
getServletInfo()	Called by a container or a tool to get information on the servlet. The return value is a string that may contain vendor name, copyright notice, and so on.
getServletConfig()	Called by a container to obtain the javax.servlet.ServletConfig object associated with this servlet instance. This object is passed into the servlet when init() is called by the container.
service()	This is the core servlet method. It is called by a container to pass a request for a servlet to process. The servlet must process the request and supply a response.

Implementing the Servlet interface through the helper HttpServlet class

BasicServlet.java, like most servlets, does not implement the javax.servlet.Servlet interface directly. Instead, it extends a helper class that implements this interface. Figure 15-4 reveals the class hierarchy.

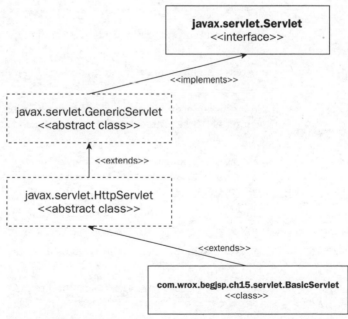

Figure 15-4: Using the HttpServlet helper class to implement the servlet interface

In Figure 15-4, `BasicServlet.java` implements the `javax.servlet.Servlet` interface through the abstract `javax.servlet.http.HttpServlet` helper class (see the following highlighted code):

```
package com.wrox.begjsp.ch15.servlet;
import javax.servlet.*;
import javax.servlet.http.*;

public class BasicServlet extends HttpServlet
{
```

The `javax.servlet.http.HttpServlet` helper class provides the implementation to any of the required methods for you. You need only to override the method that you need to change. The `javax.servlet.http.HttpServlet` is an abstract Java class (i.e., you cannot create an instance of this class directly, but you can extend it) whose sole purpose is to simplify the coding of a servlet based on the `HTTP` protocol. Because almost all Web applications use servlets that process `HTTP` protocol requests (i.e., the client is a Web browser), this abstract class is frequently used as the base class for servlets.

The `javax.servlet.http.HttpServlet` abstract base class transparently decodes the `HTTP` protocol details, leaving you to focus on the core functionality of your servlet. As a subclass of the `javax.servlet.http.HttpServlet` abstract class, you can override any of the methods in the following table.

Method Name	Description
doGet()	Processes an incoming request that is sending data via the `HTTP GET` action
doPost()	Processes an incoming request that is sending data via the `HTTP POST` action
doPut()	Processes an incoming request that is sending data via the `HTTP PUT` action (this `HTTP` protocol action is seldom used and outside the scope of this book)
doDelete()	Processes incoming request to delete server content via the `HTTP DELETE` action (this `HTTP` protocol action is seldom used and outside the scope of this book)
init()	Same as the `init()` method of the `javax.servlet.Servlet` interface
destroy()	Same as the `destroy()` method of the `javax.servlet.Servlet` interface
getServletInfo()	Same as the `getServletInfo()` method of the `javax.servlet.Servlet` interface

Overriding methods that you want to implement

Remember that any of the methods shown in the preceding table that you do not override will have default implementation in the `javax.servlet.http.HttpServlet` class. Because almost all incoming client requests in a Web application are performed using the HTTP GET method, the doGet() method is usually overridden. The HTTP POST action is occasionally used for form data submission, and the doPost() method will be overridden in this case. Referring back to our BasicServlet.java class, you see that both the doGet() and doPost() methods are overridden. The overriding code is shown here:

```java
protected void doGet(HttpServletRequest request,
   HttpServletResponse response)
   throws ServletException, java.io.IOException
{
    processRequest(request, response);
}

protected void doPost(HttpServletRequest request,
   HttpServletResponse response)
   throws ServletException, java.io.IOException
{
    processRequest(request, response);
}
```

Delegating processing to a common helper method

Both doGet() and doPost() delegate the processing to a processRequest() method. Because most servlets will perform the same request processing logic regardless of whether the incoming HTTP request is using a POST or GET method, the delegation of the logic to a helper method is quite a common practice. The processRequest() method in this case creates the response, which is an HTML page with the word "Hello." The code to processRequest() is shown here:

```java
protected void processRequest(HttpServletRequest request,
   HttpServletResponse response)
   throws ServletException, java.io.IOException
{

    try
    {
        response.setContentType("text/html");
        java.io.PrintWriter out = response.getWriter();
        out.write("<html>\n");
        out.write("<head>\n");
        out.write("<title>Basic Servlet</title>\n");
        out.write("</head>\n");
        out.write("<body>\n");
        out.write("<h1>Hello!</h1>\n");
        out.write("</body>\n");
        out.write("</html>");
        out.close();
    }
    catch(Exception e)
    {
        throw new ServletException(e);
    }
}
```

The incoming `HttpServletResponse` object implements the `javax.servlet.ServletResponse` interface. Calling the `getWriter()` method of this interface will obtain a `PrintWriter` object that you can use to write out the HTML document. This is how a servlet generates the response output. Of course, a servlet is just Java code, so you can use Java language techniques and mechanisms to obtain or transform information during the creation of the response page.

The init() and destroy() methods

The `init()` and `destroy()` methods of `BasicServlet.java` are shown here:

```
public void init(ServletConfig config) throws ServletException
{
    super.init(config);
}

public void destroy()
{
}
```

In our example, these methods have no implementation, so they really don't need to be overridden. However, they are explicitly overridden to show the existence of these very important methods. In addition, they also provide a context for the following discussion of the concept of a servlet lifecycle.

The lifecycle of a servlet

A container can create an instance of a servlet for each incoming request, but this is certainly not efficient. Today's modern servers can handle thousands of requests per second. Every instance of a Java class takes significant time to create and consumes significant memory on the server. Using this primitive approach of instantiating servlets will exhaust a server's memory and processing resources very quickly.

To handle incoming requests in an efficient manner, the container must optimize the creation of servlet instances. Every Servlet 2.4 (2.3) container optimizes by doing the following:

❑   Creating as few instances of the same servlet as possible (often only one instance) and reusing it to handle all incoming requests

❑   Managing the instances of servlets created, destroying older unused ones if the server runs low on memory

This means that every single servlet, or server-side software component, has a lifetime. It starts life when the container creates an instance. Its life terminates when the container removes it from service and destroys it. To describe when these very important events happen, the term *servlet lifecycle* is used.

A servlet lifecycle consists of the creation, initialization, and destruction of a servlet instance. It describes precisely the manner in which the container is expected to interact with the servlet during these important life events.

This lifecycle describes how the container manages instances of Java objects that represent servlets, and can be summarized in the following steps:

1. Create an instance of a servlet the first time it is accessed.

2. Initialize the instance if necessary.

3. Keep this instance around to process future requests.

4. Destroy the instance if it is necessary to make room for new servlet instances.

Figure 15-5 shows the lifecycle of a servlet.

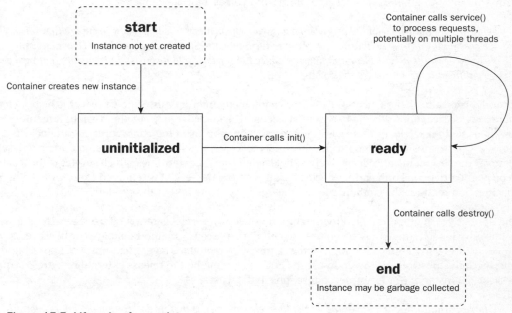

Figure 15-5: Lifecycle of a servlet

In Figure 15-5, a servlet instance is created by the container when the first incoming request asks for it. After the creation of the instance, and before passing the first request to the servlet for processing, the container initializes the servlet. The initialization should be performed only once per created servlet instance, and is performed by calling the init() method of the servlet.

> *This is the most typical situation. However, this timing is not mandated by the Servlet 2.4 or 2.3 specifications, and a container may choose to instantiate certain servlets well before the arrival of the first request (to enhance system performance, for example). However, the Servlet specifications do mandate that the servlet be initialized before the first incoming request is passed into it.*

Once a servlet is initialized by the server (its `init()` method has been called, etc.), the servlet is in a ready state. In this state, the servlet may be called on to process incoming requests at any time. The container will call the servlet's `service()` method any number of times during this phase of a servlet's lifecycle. In particular, the container may call the `service()` method of a single servlet many times, and maybe even simultaneously through multiple Java threads. This is very important. The request processing logic in a servlet should always be written in a thread-safe manner. This typically means that if you are accessing any global variables and/or resources, they must be synchronized.

The requirement to ensure that servlets are thread-safe can often make the writing of servlet code quite tricky. Fortunately, when creating JSPs that are free of scripting elements, this is almost automatic. The EL expression parser, and the most common tag libraries, such as JSTL, are all coded to be thread-safe, which alleviates a great deal of responsibility from you as a JSP developer.

> *While all tag libraries should be written in a thread-safe manner, it is important to ensure that this is the case with third-party libraries before using them in your JSP applications. Using code that is not thread-safe in the JSP/servlet environment can lead to unstable and inconsistent behaviors that may be very difficult to isolate or troubleshoot.*

A servlet typically spends most of its life servicing incoming requests. When a server is heavily loaded, there may be situations when a new servlet needs to be loaded, but there aren't enough memory resources to do it safely. In these cases, the resource management logic in a container may elect to remove a servlet instance from service. In almost all cases, this resource management logic will select for removal the servlet instance least likely to be needed (how it determines which servlet is the least likely to be needed depends on vendor-specific design). Before the servlet is removed from service, the Servlet specification requires the container to call the `destroy()` method of the servlet.

The `destroy()` method is called by the container before a servlet is removed from service. If a server is not heavily loaded, there may be no need to call the `destroy()` method instance (until server shutdown). Putting any application logic in the `destroy()` method is a very bad practice and is highly discouraged. It is possible, however, to use the `destroy()` method to release external resources acquired by a servlet instance (for example, connections to databases).

> *One important thing to note in the servlet lifecycle, however, is that its description does not constrain innovative server design. The specification only deals with how the container must interact with the servlet. The exact strategy used in the creation, management, and destruction of a servlet is not specified. The strategy used is a highly contested area among competitive rival application server products, as it can have a substantial impact on the overall performance of a server.*

The `BasicServlet.java` servlet has the typical structure of a servlet. Its logic has been kept trivial in order to focus attention on the servlet mechanism. A point that is not immediately clear is how a server/container knows about the existence of this servlet. In addition, how did the container determine that the URL `http://localhost:8080/ch15/` corresponds to this servlet?

The answer to both of these questions lies in a Web application configuration file called the *deployment descriptor*.

Describing servlets to containers in the deployment descriptor

In every chapter thus far, a WAR archive file is used to deploy the examples. Inside this WAR file is a configuration file called the deployment descriptor. The deployment descriptor is a file named web.xml under the WEB-INF directory. The content of this file is described by the J2EE (Java 2 Enterprise Edition) specification. This file is required for every Web application. The main purpose of this file is to describe to the container how to deploy the Web application.

> *The deployment descriptor, web.xml, contains a description of the components in a Web application (such as a servlet) and tells the container how to deploy the application.*

Because the format of this web.xml file follows the J2EE specification, it is actually independent of the container (application server) used. This means that the same web.xml file can work across containers from different vendors. For example, the same web.xml can work on Tomcat 5, WebSphere, or BEA WebLogic servers.

> *This is actually not entirely accurate. The J2EE specification does not prohibit server-specific extensions for the deployment descriptor. This means that you can create web.xml files using server-specific extensions that will run only within a specific container.*

There are many possible descriptor elements, and this chapter discusses only frequently used elements relating directly to the deployment of servlets (and JSPs). Further details on the deployment descriptor are covered in Chapter 16, "Role of JSP in the Wider Context: Web Applications."

The deployment descriptor for BasicServlet.java can be found in <Tomcat Installation Directory>/webapps/ch15/WEB-INF/web.xml. This web.xml file has descriptor elements for both Try It Out exercises used in this chapter. In order to focus our attention only on the elements that relate to this example, there is another file called <Tomcat Installation Directory>/webapps/ch15/WEB-INF/web.ex1. This file has isolated all the elements that relate to this example only. The content of this file is reproduced here:

```xml
<?xml version="1.0" encoding="ISO-8859-1"?>

<web-app xmlns="http://java.sun.com/xml/ns/j2ee"
  xmlns:xsi="http://www.w3.org/2001/XMLSchema-instance"
  xsi:schemaLocation="http://java.sun.com/xml/ns/j2ee
http://java.sun.com/xml/ns/j2ee/web-app_2_4.xsd"
  version="2.4">

  <description>
    Wrox Beginning JavaServer Pages Examples - Chapter 15
  </description>
  <display-name>Chapter 15 Example (Wrox Beginning JavaServer Pages)</display-name>
```

```
<servlet>
  <servlet-name>BasicServlet</servlet-name>
  <servlet-class>com.wrox.begjsp.ch15.servlet.BasicServlet</servlet-class>
</servlet>


<servlet-mapping>
  <servlet-name>BasicServlet</servlet-name>
  <url-pattern>/</url-pattern>
</servlet-mapping>

</web-app>
```

As you can see, the deployment descriptor is an XML document. Its root element must be `<web-app>`. Because of this, the following lines are found at the top of every compliant deployment descriptor:

```
<?xml version="1.0" encoding="ISO-8859-1"?>
<web-app xmlns="http://java.sun.com/xml/ns/j2ee"
  xmlns:xsi="http://www.w3.org/2001/XMLSchema-instance"
  xsi:schemaLocation="http://java.sun.com/xml/ns/j2ee
http://java.sun.com/xml/ns/j2ee/web-app_2_4.xsd"
  version="2.4">
```

If you are working with an older version of Tomcat, or other application servers that support only the Servlet 2.3 specification, you will not see the namespace and schema declaration. Servlet 2.3–compliant servers support a deployment descriptor with an XML DTD. A typical Servlet 2.3 web.xml looks like the following:

```
<?xml version="1.0" encoding="UTF-8"?>
<!DOCTYPE web-app PUBLIC "-//Sun Microsystems, Inc.//DTD Web Application 2.3//EN"
"http://java.sun.com/dtd/web-app_2_3.dtd">
<web-app>
```

If you are not familiar with XML DTDs and schemas, do not be concerned. This will be the only mention of them. Basically, they enforce both the structure and format of the XML document. However, XML schemas are a newer standard and can support more complex enforcement rules.

The `<description>` and `<display-name>` elements provide tools and the server with information about the servlet:.

```
<description>
  Wrox Beginning JavaServer Pages Examples - Chapter 15
</description>
<display-name>Chapter 15 Example (Wrox Beginning JavaServer Pages)</display-name>
```

For example, when you are using the Tomcat 5 Manager Web application to deploy the application, you will see the application's `<display-name>` element, as shown in Figure 15-6.

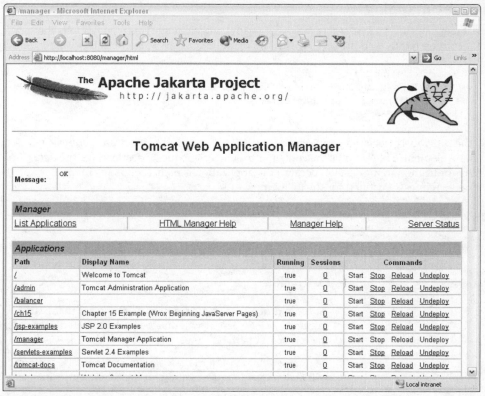

Figure 15-6: The <display-name> element in Tomcat's Manager Application list

The servlet declaration

To notify the container about the existence of the servlet, you must create a *servlet declaration entry*. This maps a human-readable name to the associated Java class. For BasicServlet, the entry is as follows:

```
<servlet>
  <servlet-name>BasicServlet</servlet-name>
  <servlet-class>com.wrox.begjsp.ch15.servlet.BasicServlet</servlet-class>
</servlet>
```

The name BasicServlet is certainly a lot more convenient than the fully qualified class name. More important, this name will be used within other elements in the deployment descriptor.

The servlet mapping

The last element in `web.xml` is the `<servlet-mapping>` element. This element tells the server how to route incoming requests to the servlet. The `<servlet-mapping>` element in this case is as follows:

```
<servlet-mapping>
  <servlet-name>BasicServlet</servlet-name>
  <url-pattern>/</url-pattern>
</servlet-mapping>
```

Here, the previously declared servlet name is used. It is mapped to incoming requests via a `<url-pattern>` element. The "/" tells the container to send any requests destined for the default path of the Web application to the servlet. Because the application is named `ch15` (as in `ch15.war`), the servlet will receive requests destined for the following:

`http://localhost:8080/ch15/`

Other URL patterns that can be used are described in the following table.

Pattern	Description
`/*`	At the end of a path; matches everything under that path; for example, `/example1/*` will match every request destined for the `example1` path.
`*.`	Beginning a URL; pattern matches extensions; for example, `*.do` will match every request asking for a URL ending with `.do`.
Any other exact URL	Matches the exact URL specified.

The equivalent JSP to `BasicSerlvet` is `index.jsp` and can be found at `<Tomcat Installation Directory>/webapps/ch15/index.jsp`. The code of this JSP is shown here.

```
<html>
<head>
  <title>Basic JSP</title>
</head>
<body>
  <h1>Hello!</h1>
</body>
</html>
```

This is basically a static HTML page within a JSP page, and not too interesting by itself.

What is really interesting is the Java servlet that is generated when this JSP page is processed by the JSP compiler. For the Tomcat server, you can find this translated Java source code at `<Tomcat Installation Directory>/work/Catalina/localhost/ch15/or/apache/jsp/example1/index_jsp.java`. The code is reproduced here:

```
package org.apache.jsp.example1;

import javax.servlet.*;
import javax.servlet.http.*;
import javax.servlet.jsp.*;

public final class index_jsp extends org.apache.jasper.runtime.HttpJspBase
  implements org.apache.jasper.runtime.JspSourceDependent
{

    private static java.util.Vector _jspx_dependants;

    public java.util.List getDependants()
    {
        return _jspx_dependants;
    }

    public void _jspService(HttpServletRequest request,
      HttpServletResponse response)
      throws java.io.IOException, ServletException
    {

        JspFactory _jspxFactory = null;
        PageContext pageContext = null;
        HttpSession session = null;
        ServletContext application = null;
        ServletConfig config = null;
        JspWriter out = null;
        Object page = this;
        JspWriter _jspx_out = null;
        PageContext _jspx_page_context = null;


        try
        {
            _jspxFactory = JspFactory.getDefaultFactory();
            response.setContentType("text/html");
            pageContext = _jspxFactory.getPageContext(this, request,
              response, null, true, 8192, true);
            _jspx_page_context = pageContext;
            application = pageContext.getServletContext();
            config = pageContext.getServletConfig();
            session = pageContext.getSession();
            out = pageContext.getOut();
            _jspx_out = out;

            out.write("<html>\r\n");
            out.write("<head>\r\n");
            out.write("<title>Basic JSP</title>\r\n");
            out.write("</head>\r\n");
            out.write("<body>\r\n");
            out.write("<h1>Hello!</h1>\r\n");
            out.write("</body>\r\n");
            out.write("</html>");
```

```
        }
        catch (Throwable t)
        {
            if (!(t instanceof SkipPageException))
            {
                out = _jspx_out;
                if (out != null && out.getBufferSize() != 0)
                    out.clearBuffer();
                if (_jspx_page_context != null)
                    jspx_page_context.handlePageException(t);
            }
        }
        finally
        {
            if (_jspxFactory != null)
                jspxFactory.releasePageContext(_jspx_page_context);
        }
    }
}
```

While most of the generated code is specific to the JSP runtime, note the following:

❑   The resulting code is a servlet because it extends the abstract `org.apache.jasper.runtime.`
    `HttpJspBase` class, which in turn implements the `javax.servlet.Serlvet` interface. This
    pattern is similar to the case of the `javax.servlet.http.HttpServlet` helper class discussed
    earlier.

❑   The servlet's `service()` method is implemented here by `jspService()` (instead of `doGet()`
    and `doPost()` in the `HttpServlet` case). But the internal logic, in the highlighted code, is
    almost exactly identical to our `BasicServlet`.

This should absolutely establish the equivalence of JSP and servlets for you. At this point, you may be
wondering if it is possible to pre-translate JSP pages into servlets Java code and then use servlet declarations and mappings in the deployment descriptor to deploy these generated servlets.

The answer is yes, absolutely. In fact, this is a commonly practiced technique to enhance the startup performance of JSP pages, called *precompilation*. More details about this performance enhancement technique are provided in Chapter 25, "Performance."

Because JSP is equivalent to a servlet, and is considerably easier to write and maintain, you may
question why servlets would be needed at all. The next Try It Out example will answer this puzzling
question.

Try It Out   A Controller Servlet

Before trying this second example, confirm that you have `ch15.war` deployed on your Tomcat 5 server.
If you need assistance in deploying WAR files, refer to Chapter 1.

This example shows the construction of a Controller servlet. Please review Chapter 9, "JSP and
JavaBeans," if you need some background on what a Controller is. Basically, a Controller is a front-end

to an application that routes incoming requests to different resources depending on application require-ments. A Controller "controls" the general flow of a Web application. Chapter 17, "Model View Controller," is completely devoted to the Model-View-Controller model and has a lot more to say about Controllers in general.

Access the following URL using your browser to see the output of this second example:

```
http://localhost:8080/ch15/example2/hot.do
```

Note that the URL does not request a JSP or servlet, but a .do action. You will see a completely red HTML page displayed in your browser. The output of this page is similar to Figure 15-7, although you can't see the color in this image.

Figure 15-7: Output from the hot.do action

Next, try the following URL:

```
http://localhost:8080/ch15/example2/cool.do
```

This time, the displayed Web page in your browser should be completely blue (see Figure 15-8).

Figure 15-8: Output from the cool.do action

This application shows the power of request mapping. The action `hot.do` maps to a red HTML page, whereas the `cool.do` maps to a blue HTML page. However, this mapping is not necessarily hard-coded within the application. This allows for flexible modification of the "flow" of a Web application, without having to rewrite the source code.

How It Works

Figure 15-9 illustrates the operation of this example.

In Figure 15-9, the container will send all incoming requests for a `.do` action to the `Controller Servlet`. From the first example, you should recognize this as the work of a `<servlet-mapping>` element in the deployment descriptor.

Once the `ControllerServlet` receives the incoming request, it will determine how to route it. It determines the routing by consulting a mapping that is loaded during servlet initialization. This mapping specifies that `hot` should be routed to `/example2/red.jsp`, while `cool` should be routed to `/example2/blue.jsp`.

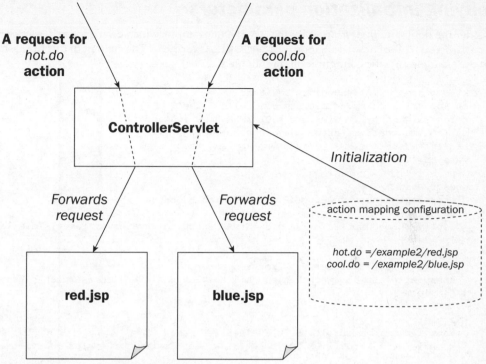

Figure 15-9: Action mapping via the ControllerServlet

Using servlets when JSP is available

There is one vital reason why servlets are still needed when JSPs are available, and it is a main thesis of this book. Even though JSPs can be created, modified, and maintained easily, the following reason explains why servlets are necessary:

❑   JSP is designed for, and should only be used in, the implementation of presentation elements in your Web applications.

You may remember from Chapters 2, 3, 5, and 6 that JSP should be used for presentation. Any business logic, application flow, or system access code should be relegated to other non-JSP mechanisms. Servlets are the preferred choice in these cases.

In the second Try It Out example, a front-end component is required to flexibly route incoming requests according to application-specific mapping. Because this is not presentation-layer functionality, a Controller servlet is the best choice for its implementation.

Specifying initialization parameters

Consider the deployment descriptor for this Try It Out example, which can be located at `<Tomcat Installation Directory>/webapps/ch15/WEB-INF/web.xml`. The content of this file is shown here, with the example-specific configurations highlighted:

```xml
<?xml version="1.0" encoding="ISO-8859-1"?>
<web-app xmlns="http://java.sun.com/xml/ns/j2ee"
  xmlns:xsi="http://www.w3.org/2001/XMLSchema-instance"
  xsi:schemaLocation="http://java.sun.com/xml/ns/j2ee
http://java.sun.com/xml/ns/j2ee/web-app_2_4.xsd"
  version="2.4">

<description>
  Wrox Beginning JavaServer Pages Examples - Chapter 15
</description>
<display-name>Chapter 15 Example (Wrox Beginning JavaServer Pages)</display-name>

<servlet>
  <servlet-name>BasicServlet</servlet-name>
  <servlet-class>com.wrox.begjsp.ch15.servlet.BasicServlet</servlet-class>
</servlet>

<servlet>
  <servlet-name>ControllerServlet</servlet-name>
  <servlet-class>com.wrox.begjsp.ch15.servlet.ControllerServlet</servlet-class>

  <init-param>
    <param-name>hot</param-name>
    <param-value>/example2/red.jsp</param-value>
  </init-param>
  <init-param>
    <param-name>cool</param-name>
    <param-value>/example2/blue.jsp</param-value>
  </init-param>
</servlet>

<servlet-mapping>
  <servlet-name>BasicServlet</servlet-name>
  <url-pattern>/</url-pattern>
</servlet-mapping>

<servlet-mapping>
  <servlet-name>ControllerServlet</servlet-name>
  <url-pattern>*.do</url-pattern>
</servlet-mapping>
</web-app>
```

In this deployment descriptor, the servlet declaration for `ControllerServlet` is specified as follows:

```
<servlet>
  <servlet-name>ControllerServlet</servlet-name>
  <servlet-class>com.wrox.begjsp.ch15.servlet.ControllerServlet</servlet-class>

  <init-param>
    <param-name>hot</param-name>
    <param-value>/example2/red.jsp</param-value>
  </init-param>
  <init-param>
    <param-name>cool</param-name>
    <param-value>/example2/blue.jsp</param-value>
  </init-param>
</servlet>
```

Other than associating the `ControllerServlet` name with the Java class, this `<servlet>` element also specifies some initialization parameters. These initialization parameters are specified in `web.xml` through the use of nested `<param-name>` and `<param-value>` sub-elements inside a `<init-param>` element. You can supply as many initialization parameters here as you need.

Typically, initialization parameters are used to specify the location and name of configuration files and resources. They may also be used to specify the configuration details of external resources, such as an external database.

Recall from our discussion of the servlet cycle that these parameters are typically accessed only once by each servlet instance: when the `init()` method of the servlet is called. The `init()` method is always called by the container prior to the processing of the very first incoming request by the servlet. Here, the parameter called `hot` is associated with the JSP page `/example2/red.jsp`; while the parameter called `cool` is associated with `/example2/blue.jsp`.

The `<servlet-mapping>` element tells the container when to send incoming requests to a servlet. In the case of `ControllerServlet`, the servlet mapping is as follows:

```
<servlet-mapping>
  <servlet-name>ControllerServlet</servlet-name>
  <url-pattern>*.do</url-pattern>
</servlet-mapping>
```

This tells the container that any request for the `.do` action should be passed to the `ControllerServlet`.

The `ControllerServlet` is then responsible for fetching the forwarding mapping from the initialization parameters and actually forwarding the incoming request.

Accessing initialization parameters within the ControllerServlet

The Java code for the `ControllerServlet` is located at `<Tomcat Installation Directory>/webapps/ch15/WEB-INF/classes/com/wrox/begjsp/ch15/servlet/ControllerServlet.java`. The code of `ControllerServlet` is reproduced here, with the code to access initialization parameters highlighted:

```java
package com.wrox.begjsp.ch15.servlet;
import javax.servlet.*;
import javax.servlet.http.*;
import java.util.HashMap;

public class ControllerServlet extends HttpServlet
{
    private HashMap forwards;
    private final static String HOT="hot";
    private final static String COOL="cool";

    public void init(ServletConfig config) throws
      ServletException
    {
        super.init(config);
        forwards = new HashMap();
        forwards.put(HOT, config.getInitParameter(HOT));
        forwards.put(COOL, config.getInitParameter(COOL));
    }

    public void destroy()
    {
    }

    protected void processRequest(HttpServletRequest request,
      HttpServletResponse response)
      throws ServletException, java.io.IOException
    {
        try
        {
            //forward request to the associated page
            ServletContext context = getServletContext();
            String logicalName = request.getServletPath();
            String physicalURL = "/";
            logicalName= logicalName.substring(logicalName.lastIndexOf('/') + 1,
             logicalName.indexOf('.'));

            if (logicalName.equals(HOT))
                physicalURL= (String) forwards.get(HOT);

            if (logicalName.equals(COOL))
                physicalURL= (String) forwards.get(COOL);
```

```
            RequestDispatcher dispatcher =
              context.getRequestDispatcher(physicalURL);
            dispatcher.forward(request, response);
        }
        catch(Exception e)
        {
            throw new ServletException(e);
        }
    }


    protected void doGet(HttpServletRequest request,
      HttpServletResponse response)
      throws ServletException, java.io.IOException
    {
        processRequest(request, response);
    }

    protected void doPost(HttpServletRequest request,
      HttpServletResponse response)
      throws ServletException, java.io.IOException
    {
        processRequest(request, response);
    }
}
```

In `ControllerServlet`, the forward mapping is maintained in `HashMap` for easy access. This is shown in the following code with definitions for the two constants, the name of the parameters:

```
private HashMap forwards;
private final static String HOT="hot";
private final static String COOL="cool";
```

The actual access to the initialization parameters is performed within the `init()` method, shown in the following code:

```
public void init(ServletConfig config) throws
  ServletException
{
    super.init(config);
    forwards = new HashMap();
    forwards.put(HOT, config.getInitParameter(HOT));
    forwards.put(COOL, config.getInitParameter(COOL));
}
```

When the `init()` method is called, the container will pass in a `ServletConfig` object. The `getInitParameter()` method of this object can be used to access the value of any initialization parameter by name. If you don't know the name of the parameters, they can also be retrieved using the `getInitParameterNames()` method of the `ServletConfig` object. See the Javadoc for the Servlet API for more information. The code in the `init()` method of `ControllerServlet` reads the forwarding values for the `hot` and `cool` parameters and builds a `HashMap` based on it. The `HashMap` is called `forwards`. This `HashMap` will be used during request processing to determine the forwarding target page.

Custom forwarding of incoming requests via the controller servlet

Like the `BasicServlet` in the first Try It Out example, `ControllerServlet` also delegates to `processRequest()` from the `doGet()` and `doPost()` methods. This delegation is shown in the following code fragment:

```
protected void doGet(HttpServletRequest request,
    HttpServletResponse response)
    throws ServletException, java.io.IOException
{
    processRequest(request, response);
}

protected void doPost(HttpServletRequest request,
    HttpServletResponse response)
    throws ServletException, java.io.IOException
{
    processRequest(request, response);
}
```

The `processRequest()` method must first decode the incoming request to determine if hot or cool is requested. The first portion of the `processRequest()` method, shown in the following code, accomplishes this:

```
protected void processRequest(HttpServletRequest request,
    HttpServletResponse response)
    throws ServletException, java.io.IOException
{
    try
    {
        //forward request to the associated page
        ServletContext context = getServletContext();
        String logicalName = request.getServletPath();
        String physicalURL = "/";
        logicalName= logicalName.substring(logicalName.lastIndexOf('/') + 1,
            logicalName.indexOf('.'));
```

In the preceding code, first the `ServletContext` is obtained. Then the `getServletPath()` method is called. Because it is known ahead of time that the container will send only requests matching the `*.do` URL pattern to the `ContollerServlet` (specified by the `<servlet-mapping>` element in the deployment descriptor), this code extracts the string between the last "/" and the "." in the servlet path. This will result in either hot or cold in our tests.

The rest of the code in `processRequest()`, shown next, retrieves the forwarding target (assigned to `physicalURL`) from the `forwards` HashMap. It then obtains the `RequestDispatcher` object from the

ServletContext. This object can be used to tell the container to forward a request for further processing. In this case, the RequestDispatcher object is used to forward the request to the selected target.

```
if (logicalName.equals(HOT))
    physicalURL= (String) forwards.get(HOT);

if (logicalName.equals(COOL))
    physicalURL= (String) forwards.get(COOL);

RequestDispatcher dispatcher = context.getRequestDispatcher(physicalURL);
dispatcher.forward(request, response);
}
catch(Exception e)
{
    throw new ServletException(e);
}
}
```

The forwarding targets

In ControllerServlet, requests are forwarded to either /example2/red.jsp or /example2/blue.jsp.

The red.jsp page is located at <Tomcat Installation Directory>/webapps/ch15/example2/red.jsp and contains the following:

```
<html>
<head>
  <title>Red Page</title>
</head>
<body bgcolor="red">
  <h1>Red page!</h1>
</body>
</html>
```

The blue.jsp page is located at <Tomcat Installation Directory>/webapps/ch15/example2/blue.jsp and contains the code shown here:

```
<html>
<head>
  <title>Blue Page</title>
</head>
<body bgcolor="blue">
  <h1>Blue page!</h1>
</body>
</html>
```

Summary

This chapter demonstrated the following points:

❑ Servlets are essential, non-JSP components in Web applications.

❑ All servlets implement the `javax.servlet.Servlet` interface.

❑ An abstract helper class called `javax.servlet.http.HttpServlet` from the Servlet API library is typically used to simplify the coding of Web application servlets.

❑ The servlet container is responsible for instantiating, initializing, and managing servlets.

❑ A servlet's `init()` method is called before the first request is sent to its `service()` method.

❑ The `destroy()` method will be called before a servlet instance is put out of commission.

❑ The `service()` method of a servlet may be concurrently called by many threads.

❑ In a servlet's `init()` method, the container passes in a `ServletConfig` object that can be used to fetch initialization parameters. These parameters can be specified in the deployment descriptor, `web.xml`, within the servlet declaration element.

❑ The deployment descriptor, or `web.xml` file, tells the container about the servlets that are in the application. The `<servlet>` element associates a name with the Java class that implements the servlet. The `<servlet-mapping>` element tells the container when to send incoming requests to the servlet for processing.

JSPs are closely related to servlets:

❑ Before a JSP can be used to process requests, the container actually translates the JSP code into Java code. This translated Java code is in the form of a servlet.

❑ From the perspective of the container, both JSP and servlets are really the same type of server-side software component.

❑ JSPs are best used in creating the user interface and presentation elements of an application, whereas servlets are best suited for the nonpresentation aspects.

❑ Most available Web application frameworks make extensive use of both servlets and JSPs.

Exercises

1. Write and test a servlet called `MessageServlet` that prints out a message obtained from an initialization parameter. This initialization parameter should be called `message` and have a value of "Hello, world!" The servlet should be executed when the user accesses the following URL:

    http://localhost:8080/ch15/talktomeplease

2. Modify the second Try It Out example as follows:

    a. Route requests for the target `warm.do` to a new JSP called `example2/message.jsp`.

    b. Have `message.jsp` print a message specified in an initialization parameter named "message" (Use "Hello, world!" for the value of this parameter).

The Role of JSP in the Wider Context: Web Applications

This chapter will start to explore how the JSP fits within the server-side Java programming environment. All of the previous chapters have provided a thorough background on developing and using JSP, and this chapter takes the next step toward enlightenment, showing how the JSP components are packaged along with other resources to form a Web archive (WAR), the standard deployment unit for J2EE Web applications.

This chapter examines the composition of a Web archive and describes many of the likely configuration options needed for JSP developers creating a Web application. This chapter also covers a number of options available when deploying a Web archive, highlighting the differences between development and production system requirements. Finally, the chapter provides some examples of how to package and deploy a Web archive for the Tomcat server.

Also included in this chapter is a lot of background information about Web applications and how they fit into the overall scheme of development. While it is not essential to read and understand everything in this chapter, the contents provide another foundation stone in learning about JSP development. It is highly recommended that readers new to JSP and Java development work through the examples at the end of the chapter.

In particular, this chapter does the following:

❑   Examines the structure of a Web application

❑   Describes the important elements of the Web application deployment descriptor (web.xml)

❑   Provides some examples of developing and deploying a Web application

What Is a Web Application?

A Web application is a collection of resources bundled together in a specific structure defined by the servlet specification. A Web application contains the JSP files, servlets, HTML pages, tag libraries, and images that, as a group, comprise a complete application to be deployed and run by a servlet container.

That might all sound a little confusing, but in reality, it's very simple: A Web application provides a standard means of packaging all the JSP files and other application resources in a manner that all J2EE-compliant Web application servers can understand.

The servlet specification (at this stage, up to version 2.4) is the document that defines all the rules and regulations regarding how servlet containers should operate and what functionality should be provided for servlet developers in the way of API functionality. The JSP specification works closely with the servlet specification to define the functionality for JSP development.

Part of the servlet specification is the definition of the directory structure required for a Web application, a topic explored in the next section.

Directory Structure for a Web Application

The following listing shows the directory and file structure for a Web application as defined by the servlet specification:

```
webapp/
    WEB-INF/web.xml
    WEB-INF/classes
    WEB-INF/lib
```

In addition, the JSP 2.0 specification recommends the use of a `WEB-INF/tags` directory for packaging tag files. More information on creating tag libraries and using tag files can be found in Chapter 6, "JSP Tag Libraries and JSTL."

The `webapp` directory (also known as the root of the Web application) normally contains the JSP files, images, and HTML files. The `webapp` directory can also contain subdirectories such as `images` or `html` or can be organized by function, such as `public` or `private`.

The `WEB-INF/web.xml` file is called the *deployment descriptor* for the Web application. This file contains configuration information specifying how the Web application is constructed, including the mappings of URLs to servlets and filters. The `web.xml` file also contains configuration information for security, MIME type mapping, error pages, and locale settings.

The `web.xml` deployment descriptor has changed for version 2.0 of the JSP specification, and is now validated by a schema rather than the DTD that was used previously. A major source of confusion for developers in previous versions of `web.xml` was the very strict ordering required within the elements of the file. In version 2.0, this strict ordering has been relaxed for the top-level configuration items. However, within each of the configuration elements, ordering is still important.

The `WEB-INF/classes` directory contains the class files for the servlets, JSP files, tag libraries, and any other utility classes that are used in the Web application.

The `WEB-INF/lib` directory contains JAR files for libraries that are used by the Web application. These are generally third-party libraries or classes for any tag libraries used by the Web application.

When a Web application is loaded by the server, classes are loaded from the `WEB-INF/classes` directory first, and then from the `WEB-INF/lib` directory.

In general, the Web application directory structure also defines the URL of the JSP pages and other resources.

The Deployment Descriptor

This section describes many of the deployment descriptor elements that a JSP developer is likely to need to understand, or change. The number of elements in the deployment descriptor is quite large, and in many cases not all of them are needed for the development of Web applications.

The following elements are the ones most relevant for JSP developers, and while they might not appear to be relevant in many situations, some of them are new in JSP 2.0 and provide great alternatives to other programming techniques that have been used previously. It will be valuable for you to become familiar with the elements outlined in the following sections, as many of them can make a hard or time-consuming task much easier.

Deployment descriptor elements for a JSP developer

This section does not contain an exhaustive list of the elements contained in the deployment descriptor; nor does it contain all the elements that a JSP developer might need to use. This section contains the elements that are most likely to be used when developing JSP applications.

This section is divided into two parts:

❑   Common JSP

❑   Enterprise JSP

Common JSP contains the elements that most JSP developers are likely to work with, or need to configure at some stage. Enterprise JSP contains the elements needed by JSP developers who are working with more complex systems and interacting with databases, implementing security and working with servlets.

Keep in mind that not every element in the deployment descriptor is covered in this section, or in this book. The detailed information provided here covers the most common cases, both for general and enterprise JSP development. For further information on the elements not covered, see the JavaServer Pages Specification Version 2.0 and the Java Servlet Specification Version 2.4. Alternatively, the Wrox title *Professional Apache Tomcat 5* (ISBN 0-7645-5902-8) provides extended coverage of this topic.

Common JSP

JSP developers are most likely to work with the following four elements:

❑ `jsp-config`

❑ `context-param`

❑ `welcome-file-list`

❑ `error-page`

These elements are used and modified by JSP developers in nearly every Web application.

jsp-config

The `jsp-config` element is a global definition for the JSP files that form part of the Web application. This element is comprised of two sub-elements:

❑ `taglib`

❑ `jsp-property-group`

taglib

The `taglib` element defines the mapping for a human-understandable name of a tag library with the actual location of the Tag Library Descriptor (TLD). This location may be an actual file or the name of the JAR file that contains the TLD. For example:

```
<taglib>
  <taglib-uri>mytaglib</taglib-uri>
  <taglib-location>WEB-INF/lib/mytaglib-v1.jar</taglib-location>
</taglib>
```

The `taglib-uri` is the name that is used in the JSP page `taglib` directive.

```
<%@ taglib prefix="my" uri="mytaglib" %>
```

However, with the new auto-discovery of tag library features in the JSP 2.0 specification, the need to declare tag libraries in this way has somewhat diminished.

jsp-property-group

The `jsp-property-group` element provides a grouping for a set of JSP files. The grouping is defined in a similar way to `servlet-mapping` elements. Groups are defined by a URL pattern, which is shown in more detail later in this section.

Any number of property-group elements may be created in the `jsp-config` element. A `jsp-property-group` is created to provide specific configuration information about that group of JSP files.

Within a `jsp-property-group` element are a number of elements that control the configuration for the group of JSP files specified. Unfortunately, the actual specifications have muddled the definitions somewhat, and while it may seem sensible that the configuration within a `jsp-property-group` apply only to that grouping of JSP files, that is not always the case. Where these inconsistencies occur, they are highlighted in the text.

The elements that exist within the `property-group` are as follows:

- ❑   `url-pattern`
- ❑   `el-ignored`
- ❑   `page-encoding`
- ❑   `scripting-invalid`
- ❑   `is-xml`
- ❑   `include-prelude`
- ❑   `include-coda`

The `url-pattern` element defines the group of files that are configured by this `property-group`. The `url-pattern` follows these rules:

- ❑   A pattern starting with a `/` and terminating with a `/*` is used for matching a path.
- ❑   A pattern starting with `*.` is used as extension mapping.
- ❑   A pattern that consists of only a `/` matches the default servlet.
- ❑   All other patterns are exact matches.

These patterns are matched against the resources in the Web application in the following order, and if a match is found the searching ceases:

- ❑   **Exact match:** The container attempts to find an exact match.
- ❑   **Longest path-prefix:** The container attempts to find the `url-pattern` that matches the largest number of common directories in the path, starting at the highest directory.
- ❑   **Extension match:** The container attempts a match using the extension.

A matched URL is then part of that `jsp-property-group`, and the other elements provide the configuration that is applied to those URLs.

The `el-ignored` element controls whether the expression language should be evaluated in the JSP page. This setting is useful when transitioning older JSP pages to run on newer JSP containers, as the expression language (EL) evaluation may conflict with patterns that look like `${expression}` already in the JSP pages. This occurs because these patterns were not designated as "reserved words" in previous versions of the JSP specification. Therefore, the developers of the JSP standard have provided an appropriate mechanism for moving forward, rather than making everything developed previously break.

These patterns may have just been text that was expected to be displayed, or passed to other components as literals. The valid values for el-ignored are true and false.

The following configuration will ignore, and therefore not evaluate, any requested EL expressions or files that end in jsp:

```
<jsp-property-group>
  <url-pattern>*.jsp</url-pattern>
  <el-ignored>true</el-ignored>
</jsp-property-group>
```

The page-encoding element declares the pageEncoding property for the set of JSP files in the jsp-property-group. This element and property are used to describe the output character set produced by the JSP page. This is an important consideration when developing pages that will be viewed by people speaking and reading languages other than English — for example, the multibyte character sets found in Japanese.

```
<jsp-property-group>
  <url-pattern>/ja/*</url-pattern>
  <page-encoding>Shift_JIS</page-encoding>
</jsp-property-group>
```

The scripting-invalid element controls the use of JSP scripting tags within the set of JSP pages. If the scripting-invalid element is set to true, then using <% and %> will generate an error while processing the JSP page. The value of the scripting-invalid element defaults to false, allowing scripting within the JSP pages. The following jsp-property-group disallows scripting in JSP pages that end in jsp:

```
<jsp-property-group>
  <url-pattern>*.jsp</url-pattern>
  <scripting-invalid>true</scripting-invalid>
</jsp-property-group>
```

When set to true, the is-xml element declares that the group of files is defined by the url-pattern JSP documents, and must be interpreted as XML documents. The following configuration declares that files ending in xhtml should be treated as JSP documents, and translated accordingly:

```
<jsp-property-group>
  <url-pattern>*.xhtml</url-pattern>
  <is-xml>true</is-xml>
</jsp-property-group>
```

The include-prelude element is used to define a path to a JSP fragment that is included as a header on all JSP pages that match the url-pattern for the jsp-property-group. Likewise, the include-coda element defines a footer JSP fragment. The common naming convention for the JSP fragments is to include the file extension .jspf, These fragment files must follow the same rules as those used for standard JSP include files: start and end tags must be in the same file.

The include-prelude and include-coda elements work slightly differently than the other jsp-property-group elements do. The other jsp-property-group elements are selected by the url-pattern according to the matching criteria described previously. These will select only one of the jsp-property-group elements. However, for the include-prelude and include-coda elements, each matching jsp-property-group will be applied in the order it is defined in the web.xml. The following is an example of the jsp-property-group element, showing the use of include-prelude and include-coda elements:

```
<jsp-property-group>
  <url-pattern>/admin/*</url-pattern>
  <include-prelude>/WEB-INF/include/admin-header.jspf</include-prelude>
  <include-coda>/WEB-INF/include/admin-footer.jspf</include-coda>
</jsp-property-group>
```

Note that these includes are done during translation of the JSP pages. This means that they occur when the JSP pages are being parsed and compiled into servlets. Note a common trap in using the includes: The servlet containers look for changes to the JSP files to recompile (or retranslate) the JSP page. Adding the include-prelude and include-coda to the web.xml will not change the output for JSP pages that have already been translated.

During development, the easiest path to take is to delete the work directory, which will cause the JSP files to be recompiled.

context-param

The context-param element is used to provide initialization information to the Web application. The Web application can retrieve these parameters by using the getInitParameter() and getInit ParameterNames() methods on the ServletContext object. There can be many context-param elements in the web.xml and they are generally used for configuring items that do not change. These might be items such as the e-mail address of the administrator of the Web server, the name of the Web application, or the version of the Web application:

```
<web-app>
  <context-param>
    <param-name>adminEmailAddress</param-name>
    <param-value>admin@mycompany.com</param-value>
  </context-param>
  <context-param>
    <param-name>applicationName</param-name>
    <param-value>My Web Application</param-value>
  </context-param>
  <context-param>
    <param-name>applicationVersion</param-name>
    <param-value>1.0.2</param-value>
  </context-param>
</web-app>
```

The following code shows how to obtain and use these values within a JSP page:

```
<%@ taglib prefix="c" uri="http://java.sun.com/jsp/jstl/core" %>

<html>
  <head><title>Parameter Listing</title></head>
  <body>
    <h1> Parameter Listing <h1>

    <table border=1>
      <tr><th>Parameter Name</th><th>Parameter Value</th></tr>
      <c:forEach items="${initParam}" var="current" >
        <tr><td>${current.key}</td><td>${current.value}</td></tr>
      </c:forEach>
    </table>
  </body>
</html>
```

welcome-file-list

The `welcome-file-list` element is an ordered list of files that will be searched when a directory is requested. The files are described as "partial URIs" by the servlet specification, and are really just the last section of the URL. A request for a directory entry in the Web application using the example `welcome-file-list` will search for an `index.html` first, a `hello.jsp` second, and the `processor` servlet third:

```
<web-app>
  <welcome-file-list>
    <welcome-file>index.html</welcome-file>
    <welcome-file>hello.jsp</welcome-file>
    <welcome-file>processor</welcome-file>
  </welcome-file-list>
</web-app>
```

If none of these partial URIs combined with the directory URL match a valid resource in the Web application, then the results are unpredictable. For example, the Tomcat server will return a directory listing, but this is not guaranteed behavior for all servers.

error-page

The `error-page` element declares a mapping between an error and a resource in the Web application that is called when that error occurs. The errors can be caused by HTTP errors (such as 404 Not Found) and Web application exceptions (like a `ServletException`). The errors can be mapped to any valid resource in the Web application, so it may be handled by a static HTML page, a JSP page, or a servlet.

The `error-page` element is useful for defining error pages that are customized for the particular Web application. The advantage of using the JSP pages and servlets is that additional information about the error can be presented to the user for reporting the error:

```
<web-app>
  <error-page>
    <error-code>404</error-code>
    <location>/file-not-found.html</location>
  </error-page>
  <error-page>
    <exception-type>javax.servlet.ServletException</exception-type>
    <location>/oopsy.jsp</location>
  </error-page>
</web-app>
```

Enterprise JSP

The additional elements needed in more complex applications are as follows:

- ❏ login-config
- ❏ security-constraint
- ❏ security-role
- ❏ env-entry
- ❏ resource-ref
- ❏ servlet
- ❏ servlet-mapping

Other elements, such as ejb-ref, service-ref, and message-destination-ref, are used to interoperate with Enterprise Java Beans (EJB) systems or Web services; however, these advanced topics are not covered in this book.

login-config

login-config declares the authentication mechanism to be used, the realm name of the Web application, and, if required, the configuration to be used by the specific authentication mechanism.

login-config is not enough to secure a Web application; security-constraint is required to identify the resources that are secured, and login-config defines the way the resources are secured.

There is only one login-config for a Web application, so all resources identified by the security-constraint elements will authenticate the user in the same way.

The login-config element consists of the following child elements:

- ❏ **auth-method:** This element is used to define the mechanism for the authentication scheme. The authentication scheme can be BASIC, DIGEST, or FORM.

- ❏ **realm-name:** If the auth-method is BASIC or DIGEST, then the realm-name defines the name of the authentication realm.

- ❏ **form-login-config:** If the auth-method is FORM, then the form-login-config defines the parameters needed for form login configuration.

The `login-config` element is explored in more detail in Chapter 24, "Security."

An example of a `login-config` for basic authentication follows:

```
<web-app>
  <login-config>
    <auth-method>BASIC</auth-method>
    <realm-name>My Web Application</realm-name>
  </login-config>
</web-app>
```

An example of a `login-config` for form authentication follows:

```
<web-app>
  <login-config>
    <auth-method>FORM</auth-method>
    <form-login-config>
      <form-login-page>/login.jsp</form-login-page>
      <form-error-page>/fail.jsp</form-error-page>
    </form-login-config>
  </login-config>
</web-app>
```

security-constraint

The `security-constraint` element defines the security constraints that are applied to a group of resources in the Web application. The resources are defined by the `web-resource-collection` using a `url-pattern` to specify the matching pattern.

There can be many `security-constraint` elements in the `web.xml` and each can refer to a different role, or group of roles, that may access the resources.

The `security-constraint` contains the following elements:

❑ **web-resource-collection:** Defines a subset of resources in the web application.

❑ **auth-constraint:** Defines the user roles that are permitted to access the resources, provided they authenticate successfully.

❑ **user-data-constraint:** Defines the protection (if any) on the transmission of the resources from the server to the client. Normally, this element is used to force the server to use SSL to transfer the data securely.

The `security-constraint` element is explored in more detail in Chapter 24, "Security."

An example of `security-constraint` follows:

```
<web-app>
  <security-constraint>
    <web-resource-collection>
      <web-resource-name>Administration</web-resource-name>
      <url-pattern>/administration/*</url-pattern>
```

```
      <http-method>GET</http-method>
      <http-method>POST</http-method>
    </web-resource-collection>
    <auth-constraint>
      <role-name>admin</role-name>
      <role-name>manager</role-name>
    </auth-constraint>
    <user-data-constraint>
      <transport-guarantee>CONFIDENTIAL</transport-guarantee>
    </user-data-constraint>
  </security-constraint>
</web-app>
```

security-role

The `security-role` element defines a security role for a Web application. A security role is a name that may be used within the `role-name` element of the `security-constraint` element, and defines a group of users that are configured in a container-specific manner. The group identity defined by the server and the `role-name` must match so that users can be associated with the correct security role.

In the basic install of the Tomcat server, `conf/tomcat-users.xml` is the configuration file for the roles and users, and the roles defined in this file need to match the `role-name` of the `security-role` for the Web application in order to authenticate the users.

Following is an example of the `security-role` element:

```
<web-app>
  <security-role>
    <role-name>admin</role-name>
  </security-role>
  <security-role>
    <role-name>manager</role-name>
  </security-role>
</web-app>
```

env-entry

The `env-entry` element declares an environment entry for a Web application. Like `context-param`, `env-entry` provides a means to configure the Web application from values not in the Web application. However, in various servers, `env-entry` can be changed during runtime using server-specific tools, potentially changing the behavior of the Web application during runtime.

Following is an example of the `env-entry` element:

```
<web-app>
  <env-entry>
    <env-entry-name>debug</env-entry-name>
    <env-entry-type>java.lang.Boolean</env-entry-type>
    <env-entry-value>false</env-entry-value>
  </env-entry>
  <env-entry>
    <env-entry-name>debugLevel</env-entry-name>
```

```
      <env-entry-type>java.lang.Integer</env-entry-type>
      <env-entry-value>99</env-entry-value>
    </env-entry>
</web-app>
```

resource-ref

The `resource-ref` element declares an access point to a JNDI-accessible object factory. This provides the Web application with a means of accessing external resources that can be defined during deployment. These elements are normally resources like database connections.

This element is discussed in more detail in Chapter 23, "Access to Databases." Following is an example of the `resource-ref` element:

```
<web-app>
  <resource-ref>
    <description>Asset Database</description>
    <res-ref-name>jdbc/AssetDatabase</res-ref-name>
    <res-type>javax.sql.DataSource</res-type>
    <res-auth>Container</res-auth>
  </resource-ref>
</web-app>
```

servlet and servlet-mapping

The `servlet` and `servlet-mapping` elements are used to declare the servlets in a Web application, and the mapping of servlets to a URL pattern, respectively.

The `servlet` element declares a `servlet-name` that is used as the link to the `servlet-mapping` element and the `servlet-class` that is the fully qualified class name of the servlet.

The most common use of the `servlet` and `servlet-mapping` elements with JSP development is when JSP pages are precompiled before deployment to a server. In these cases, the JSP developer needs to declare the compiled JSP pages as servlets, and provide mappings for the original JSP name. This technique is shown in more detail in Chapter 25, "Performance."

An example of `servlet` and `servlet-mapping` for a precompiled JSP page follows:

```
<web-app>
  <servlet>
    <servlet-name>ViewJSP</servlet-name>
    <servlet-class>org.apache.jsp.View_jsp</servlet-class>
  </servlet>
  <servlet-mapping>
    <servlet-name>ViewJSP</servlet-name>
    <url-pattern>View.jsp</url-pattern>
  </servlet-mapping>
</web-app>
```

This concludes the group of elements that is covered in this chapter. The information presented here should provide a sufficient introduction for most JSP projects, with more detail to be found in other chapters. You should explore the servlet and JSP specifications for more information on other elements.

Using a Web Archive

The most common deployment format for a Web application is called a Web archive, or WAR. A WAR is a Java archive (JAR) file (which in turn is a ZIP file) that contains all the directories and files described previously. The servlet specification requires that a Web application server can work with WAR files, but many of the common servers also work with Web applications in an unpacked or open format.

The unpacked or open format of a Web application is extremely important for JSP developers. Without it, any change to a JSP page would require the WAR file to be recreated before deploying it to a Web application server. Even considering the increased capabilities of modern servlet and JSP containers, needing to recreate and redeploy for each change would make development far too slow.

During development, it is most convenient to use an unpacked Web application; and during deployment to a production system, it is best to use a WAR file. This is discussed further in the next section.

Development and Deployment Strategies

To get the most out of developing a JSP application, it is worth separating the development and deployment cycles. This is normally a very important aspect of all software development, but it has additional benefits with Web application development.

First what is needed is a brief definition of the two terms:

❑ **Development:** The development process represents what occurs when the Web application is being created. This includes the editing and debugging of JSP pages, and unit testing and configuration of the Web application to ensure that all user functionality is being met. The development stage is completed with a fully working Web application.

❑ **Deployment:** The deployment process occurs after completing the Web application, and represents the installation of the Web application in a production environment. The production environment might be a test server or the production server. This process involves the configuration and creation of a WAR file for the target environment, and the installation of the WAR file.

Although these activities as described might appear to be completely separate and linear, this is far from the case. In reality, development occurs for a period of time, deployment occurs for more formal testing, defects are found or enhancements are identified, and the cycle starts again.

It is useful to understand, from the descriptions, that development cycles occur very frequently; and the "write code and then test" cycle needs to happen quickly for productivity not to suffer. If a WAR file were created after every line of code was changed, development activities would grind to a halt.

The good news is that during development, the Web application can be left in an open, or unpacked, format (just the directories on disk); and during deployment, the Web application can be bundled up into a WAR file for more formal treatment of release activities.

Packaging and Deploying for Tomcat

This section contains a number of practical exercises for developing and deploying simple Web applications using the Tomcat server.

Before attempting these exercises, ensure that Tomcat is installed and configured properly. As these JSP pages use the JSTL tags, the JSTL libraries will need to be copied in the Web application `lib` directory for the Web application. This is described in more detail during the exercises, but requires a JSTL-compatible set of tag libraries, which can be downloaded from `http://jakarta.apache.org/taglibs`.

Try It Out   **Setting Up the Web Application Environment**

Create a directory structure as follows:

```
/chapter16
    /web
        /WEB-INF
        /lib
```

Copy `standard.jar` and `jstl.jar` from the taglibs distribution into the `lib` directory.

Create a skeleton `web.xml` in the `WEB-INF` directory containing the following:

```
<?xml version="1.0" encoding="ISO-8859-1"?>
<web-app version="2.4" uri="http://java.sun.com/xml/ns/j2ee" >

</web-app>
```

Create an `index.html` in the `web` directory containing the following:

```
<html>
  <head>
    <title> Chapter 16 Exercises </title>
  </head>
  <body>
  <h1> Chapter 16 Exercises </h1>
    <ol>
      <li> Exercise 1 - Creating and deploying the simplest web application
      <li> Exercise 2 - Adding a JSP page
      <li> Exercise 3 - Securing the JSP page
      <li> Exercise 4 - Adding headers and footers
    </ol>
  </body>
<html>
```

As this is possibly the simplest Web application that can be built, it's a good time to install it as a Web application in the Tomcat server.

You have several options for installing the Web application in Tomcat; for these examples, we will create a file called `chapter16.xml` containing the following:

```
<?xml version='1.0' encoding='utf-8'?>
<Context
    docBase="/path/to/myprojects/chapter16/web"
    path="/chapter16"
    reloadable="true"
    workDir="/path/to/myprojects/chapter16/work">
</Context>
```

In the preceding code, `/path/to/myprojects` is the actual path to where the `chapter16` directory has been created.

For JSP developers using Windows, the `chapter16.xml` may look like the following:

```
<?xml version='1.0' encoding='utf-8'?>
<Context
    docBase="c:/myprojects/chapter16/web"
    path="/chapter16"
    reloadable="true"
    workDir="c:\myprojects\chapter16\work">
</Context>
```

Copy this file to `<Tomcat Installation Directory>/conf/Catalina/localhost`, where it will be picked up by the Tomcat server. Start the Tomcat server and browse to the following URL:

```
http://localhost:8080/chapter16/
```

This should result in a screen like the one shown in Figure 16-1.

To see how easy it is to change the Web application while it is installed, edit the `index.html` file and include the following list item:

```
<ol>
  <li> Exercise 1 - Creating and deploying the simplest web application
  <li> Exercise 2 - Adding a JSP page
  <li> Exercise 3 - Securing the JSP page
  <li> Exercise 4 - Adding headers and footers
  <li> Exercise 5 - Dynamic HTML pages
</ol>
```

Refresh the browser. The resulting screen should look like the one shown in Figure 16-1, but with the addition of the extra text that has been added.

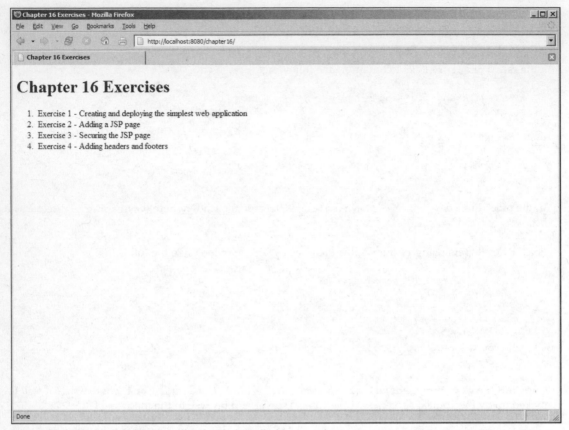

Figure 16-1: The simple Web application is installed

How It Works

This very simple Web application shows how to deploy during development using Tomcat. Many servlet and JSP containers will provide similar means to allow for development in a local directory and have the servlet container look outside the normal webapps directory for applications to be deployed.

The other interesting point is that the servlet/JSP container can act as a normal Web server and just serve static content as the index.html page shows, reflecting changes in the content as it is modified by the developer.

Try It Out   Adding JSP Pages to a Web Application

The exercise adds a JSP to the Web application, yet another step forward to world domination and Web application development mastery.

Create a file called showDate.jsp in the web directory with the following contents:

```
<%@ taglib prefix="fmt" uri="http://java.sun.com/jsp/jstl/fmt" %>
<jsp:useBean id="now" class="java.util.Date" />
```

```
<html>
 <head><title>Current Date and Time</title></head>
 <body>
   <h1> Date and Time </h1>

   The date and time is : <fmt:formatDate value="${now}" type="both" />
 </body>
</html>
```

Make a small edit to `index.html` so that the JSP page can be linked from the front page. It's not a necessity, as a direct URL would work, but this makes the Web application hang together as a whole.

```
<ol>
   <li> Exercise 1 - Creating and deploying the simplest web application
   <li> Exercise 2 - <a href="showDate.jsp">Adding a JSP page</a>
   <li> Exercise 3 - Securing the JSP page
   <li> Exercise 4 - Adding headers and footers
</ol>
```

Now refresh the front page and click the link for Exercise 2. This should display a screen that looks like the one shown in Figure 16-2.

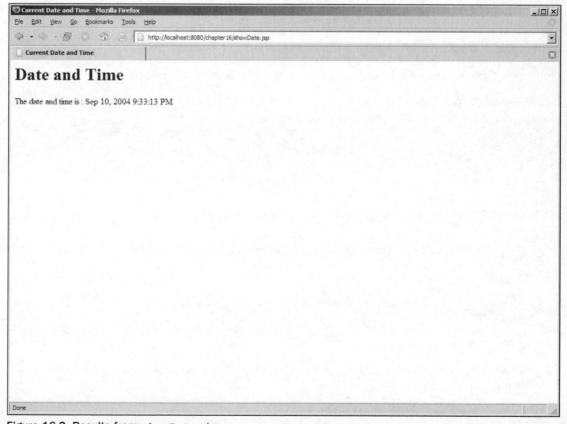

Figure 16-2: Results from `showDate.jsp`

How It Works

In addition to simple HTML, Web applications can contain pages with dynamic content, JSP. The JSP pages are placed in the Web application root, or in subdirectories where they are served by the servlet container.

Introduction to Web application security

Ensuring the security of Web applications is covered in much greater detail in Chapter 24, but this short example shows how simple it is to secure a Web application. For this exercise, the web.xml and some Tomcat configuration files will need to be modified.

The goal of this Try It Out exercise is to prevent unauthorized users from accessing the showDate.jsp page. The first step is to add the required authentication information to the Tomcat server.

Try It Out   Preventing Unauthorized Access to showDate.jsp

Edit the `<Tomcat Installation Directory>/conf/tomcat-users.xml` file to add the following entries:

```
<role rolename="chapter16role" />
<user username="chapter16" password="chapter16" roles="chapter16role"/>
```

In the web.xml file, add the following security configuration:

```
<?xml version="1.0" encoding="ISO-8859-1"?>

<web-app version="2.4" uri="http://java.sun.com/xml/ns/j2ee" >

<security-role>
  <role-name>chapter16role</role-name>
</security-role>

<security-constraint>
  <web-resource-collection>
    <url-pattern>showDate.jsp</url-pattern>
  </web-resource-collection>
  <auth-constraint>
    <role-name>chapter16role</role-name>
  </auth-constraint>
</security-constraint>

<login-config>
  <auth-method>BASIC</auth-method>
  <realm-name>Chapter 16 Realm</realm-name>
</login-config>

</web-app>
```

Now restart the Tomcat server to reload the user configuration information and browse to the following URL:

```
http://localhost:8080/chapter16/
```

Click the exercise 2 link, and the results should be the same as those shown in Figure 16-3. This is a basic security login. Enter the username (chapter16) and password (chapter16) that were entered into the `tomcat-users.xml`, as shown in Figure 16-2, and click the OK button. This will display the date screen.

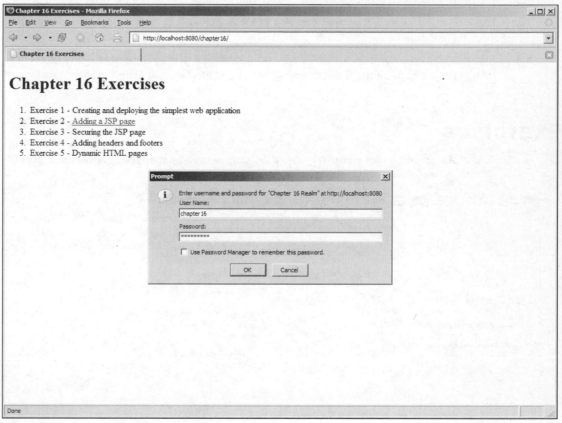

Figure 16-3: BASIC authentication dialog

How It Works

The `security-constraint` defines the resources that are protected and the credentials required to access the resources. The `login-config` defines the manner in which the user will authenticate. In this case, the standard HTTP `BASIC` authentication scheme is selected. For many Web applications this is sufficient protection of resources; however, Chapter 24 shows a number of additional mechanisms to work with container-provided security.

Summary

This chapter has covered a broad range of topics regarding Web applications, including their structure, configuration, development, and deployment.

To conclude this chapter, let's review some of its key points:

❑ Web applications conform to a standard directory structure.

❑ Web applications can contain static and dynamic resources as part of the directory structure.

❑ The Web application can be deployed as a WAR, or installed as an open directory structure in most JSP containers.

❑ The web.xml deployment descriptor can be used to change the behavior of many facets of a Web application, including implementing security, control scripting, and modifying the output.

Exercises

1. Add a header and footer element to every JSP page served by the Web application. Figure 16-4 shows a sample header and footer.

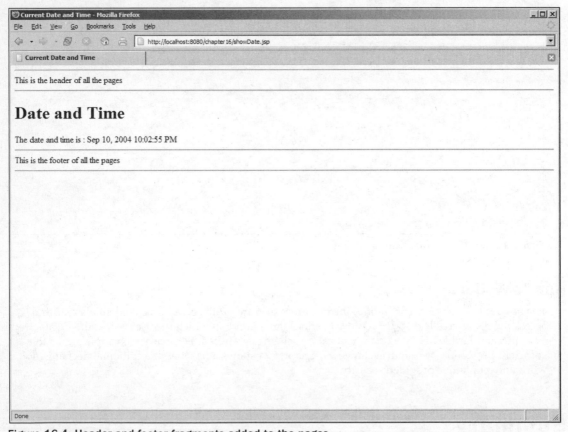

Figure 16-4: Header and footer fragments added to the pages

2. Implement a counter that increases each time the `index.html` page is viewed since the Web application has been started. An example of such a Web page is shown in Figure 16-5.

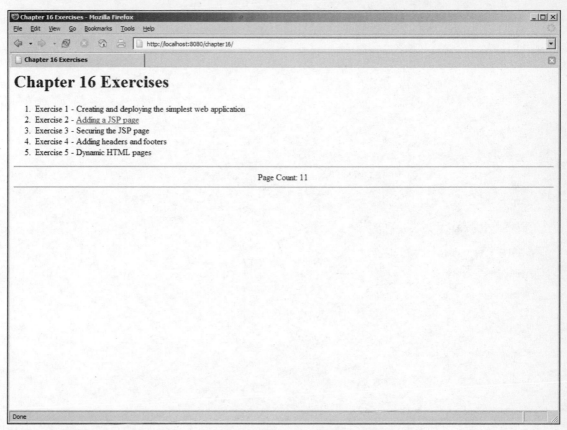

Figure 16-5: JSP page with an .html extension displaying a page counter

3. Modify exercise 2 to have a different counter for each user session.

Model View Controller

While the understanding and knowledge of syntax, libraries, and configurations are very useful, the place that effective application design takes in your arsenal of skills is many orders of magnitude more important. Developers who can build scalable, changeable applications that meet their requirements are highly regarded. Developers who don't have these skills, or simply don't apply them, and punch out the easiest, quickest solution are deemed to be *hacks*, in the derogatory sense of the word.

This chapter introduces one of many important architectural concepts that assist in the development of applications that have to display an interface to a user of a system. This is the *Model View Controller* architecture (or MVC). MVC's structure offers significant benefits for Web applications, and being familiar with it will enhance your understanding of a far wider range of concepts, some of which use or have borrowed ideas from MVC.

Specifically, this chapter covers the following:

❑ A definition of MVC

❑ An example of an MVC Model 2 implementation

❑ An explanation of the components of MVC with respect to the example

As mentioned earlier, this chapter covers the MVC architectural concepts and not specific MVC frameworks. These frameworks are covered in Chapter 18, "Web Frameworks" (Spring and WebWork) and Chapter 19, "Struts Framework."

What Is MVC?

MVC is a design concept that attempts to separate an application into three distinct parts. One part is concerned with the actual work the application conducts, another part is concerned with displaying the data or information of an application, and another part coordinates the former two in order to display the correct interface or execute some work that the application needs to complete. These parts are respectively:

- ❏ **Model:** The Model represents the part of an application that actually does the work and models the real-world problem that the application attempts to solve. For example, a customer may be modeled in an application, and there may be various ways to create new customers or change information relating to a customer.

- ❏ **View:** The View is the representation of the Model that the user can see and interact with. For example, a View might be a list of customers that have registered in an application.

- ❏ **Controller:** The Controller is the part of the application that responds to commands from the user, deciding how the Model should be changed or retrieved and which View should be displayed. For example, the Controller would receive a request to display a list of customers by interacting with the Model and delivering a View where this list could be displayed.

The logical separation of the application into these parts ensures that the Model layer knows nothing about how it is displayed; it is restricted to just representing the component parts of the problem being solved by the application. Likewise, the View layer is concerned only with displaying data and not with implementing business logic, which is handled by the Model layer. The Controller, much like a traffic officer, directs the views to be displayed and fires off data changes and retrievals from the Model layer.

The MVC approach is largely based on an event-driven environment in which the user drives the flow of the application by using the interface. It is not surprising, therefore, to find its roots in the earliest graphical user interface (GUI) developments.

Xerox PARC (Palo Alto Research Center), a highly influential research and development lab, developed the purely object-oriented (OO) language Smalltalk in 1972. Smalltalk was the first OO language to integrate a GUI, and its creation introduced the MVC design approach for implementations. The mouse-driven, point-and-click interface we take for granted today was born with Smalltalk, which went on to heavily influence other object-oriented languages such as C++ and Java.

MVC and Web Applications

MVC lends itself particularly well to Web-based applications, which, like traditional GUI applications, are almost entirely user-driven and have to present some sort of interface for that to occur.

When Web applications were first being developed using CGI or servlets, there was a tendency to embed the display logic (HTML) within the business logic of the application. Conversely, using server-side scripting languages such as ASP, PHP, and Perl, developers embedded business logic within the display. When JSP was first released, this pattern continued, with developers using a series of JSP pages to implement the business logic of the application as well as to display the interface to the user. This is referred to as a *Model 1 architecture*. Figure 17-1 illustrates how a Model 1 architecture may be structured.

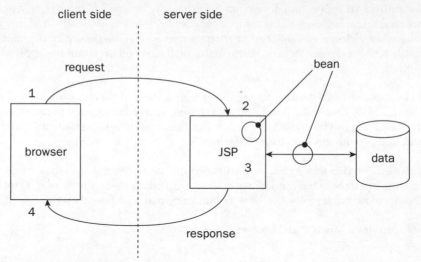

Figure 17-1: Model 1 architecture

The sequence of events explained in this example is simple if you've done any sort of Web application development. You can probably relate it to some of your own projects:

1. The user requests a Web page — for example, `home.jsp`.

2. The servlet container executes the logic contained in `home.jsp` as well as any include pages it may point to. This execution may include retrieving data from a database or other functions to satisfy the business logic. Beans provide representations of data within the JSP page.

3. Entwined within the business logic of the page are the makings of the HTML that will be presented to the user.

4. As a result of the processing, the final HTML is constructed and displayed to the user.

For a small application with limited amounts of business logic, this architecture may be more than adequate. It is simple and effective. However, in a more complicated application where the business logic is not only more in-depth but the display logic required is also significant, a Model 1 approach can lead to an unmaintainable mess. Much of the JSP page would be fragments of Java (scriptlets) generating HTML.

The classic example of this is an application that uses only one or two pages to cover all of its functionality. A massive `if`, `else if`, `else` construct typically surrounds the processing and display logic. You can see the disadvantages of this and other Model 1–type approaches in the following areas:

❑ **Code repetition:** Code to perform certain business rules or to affect what is displayed is often repeated. Changing multiple instances of this logic can be haphazard at best.

❑ **Maintainability:** If the business logic is entwined within display logic, making simple changes can be dangerous and difficult. In addition, the person making the changes has to have experience in both the programming language used and HTML.

❑ **Extensibility:** A change in the business rules of the application can force major restructuring; simple changes become expensive in a commercial environment.

❑ **Testability:** An application developed in such a way is very difficult to test. Applications are most testable when each of the components can be tested individually. A highly testable application makes maintenance much more manageable. Small changes can be evaluated quickly and simply and the developer is not left wondering if some other part of the application has been affected.

Challenged by these obvious disadvantages, developers identified a more sophisticated architecture using servlets and JSP. This *Model 2* architecture is based on an adaptation of the MVC architecture. In this implementation, a servlet is used as a Controller, fielding requests from the user, effecting changes in the Model, and providing views back to the user.

The views implemented in this architecture still used JSP pages, but the logic they contained related only to displaying the interface to the user, rather than implementing the business logic as well. The Model layer was encapsulated in Java objects that were unconcerned with how they were displayed.

Figure 17-2 illustrates a Model 2 architecture.

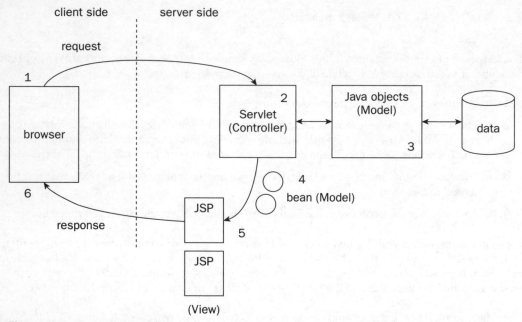

Figure 17-2: Model 2 architecture

The flow of events here is a little more complex:

1. The user requests the URL of a servlet. In the request would be some indication of the work that is required. For example, the URL might be something like /home?action=listCustomers, where action represents the work that the Controller should undertake.

2. The Controller receives the request and determines the work to complete based on the request. The Controller executes calls on the Model to undertake the required business logic.

3. The Model layer is instructed to provide a list of `Customer` objects by the Controller. It may access some sort of persistence layer such as a database to provide this.

4. The Controller is provided with the list of `Customer` objects to display in the View. The Controller also determines the appropriate View to provide for the user. Using the request dispatcher, the servlet can provide the list of `Customer` objects to the View selected (JSP page).

5. The View now has a reference to the data provided and renders the display of the list in accordance with its display logic.

6. The generated HTML as a result of this process is provided back to the user in the response.

The Model, or business logic layer, of the application is completely unconcerned with how it is displayed in the View; it merely responds to events triggered by the Controller. Additionally, the method of providing data is "hidden" away from other components. The method of accessing data and preparing it can be transparently changed without affecting the rest of the application.

Conversely, the View layer is devoid of all business logic. Its only responsibility is to render the information it is given according to a layout, and to provide forms, links, and buttons to enable further functionality.

Try It Out   Example Model 2 Application

This section walks you through a simple application. While building the application, it illustrates the importance of the separate components of MVC. You can download the application from the Wrox Web site at www.wrox.com.

This application has two primary functional tasks: to list a series of `Customer` objects and to enable the user to select one of these values and display it.

The following explanation examines how to implement the first piece of functionality using each of the MVC components. The discussion concludes by adding on the second piece of functionality: selecting an individual `Customer` object to display from the list.

Controller: SimpleController

As mentioned previously, the role of a Controller is to direct requests to the appropriate View and provide the required data along the way. `SimpleController` is a servlet that has been developed to accomplish this. When `SimpleController` is executed, it expects a parameter to identify the work that should be completed. In Web applications, such concepts are often referred to as *actions*. In GUI programming, this concept of an action may be referred to as an *event*. In this discussion, `SimpleController` has been mapped in the servlet container as `controller`. It will therefore be invoked as `http://localhost: 8080/mvc/controller`.

`SimpleController` tests the value of the `action` parameter and performs the required work accordingly. Figure 17-3 broadly illustrates this flow.

In the figure, a request to the servlet has specified that the `displaylist` action should be executed. A request of this sort might be as follows:

```
http://localhost:8080/mvc/controller?action=displaylist
```

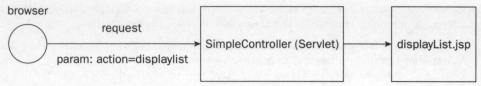

Figure 17-3: Controller using the `action` **parameter**

The `SimpleController` then has the task of executing the required functions appropriate to this action. If you look at the servlet code that does this, you can see that the evaluation of the `action` parameter determines the functionality that is executed. The following is a listing of the `SimpleController` servlet. The `displaylist` action is highlighted.

```java
package com.wrox.begjsp.ch17.mvc;

import java.io.IOException;

import java.util.List;

import javax.servlet.RequestDispatcher;
import javax.servlet.ServletException;
import javax.servlet.http.HttpServlet;
import javax.servlet.http.HttpServletRequest;
import javax.servlet.http.HttpServletResponse;

public class SimpleController extends HttpServlet
{
    protected void doPost(HttpServletRequest request,
        HttpServletResponse response) throws ServletException, IOException
    {
        String action = request.getParameter("action");
        String jspPage = "/index.jsp";

        if ((action == null) || (action.length() < 1))
        {
            action = "default";
        }

        if ("default".equals(action))
        {
            jspPage = "/index.jsp";
        }
        else if ("displaylist".equals(action))
        {
            CustomerManager manager = new CustomerManager();
            List customers = manager.getCustomers();
            request.setAttribute("customers", customers);

            jspPage = "/displayList.jsp";
        }
        else if ("displaycustomer".equals(action))
        {
```

```
            String id = request.getParameter("id");
            CustomerManager manager = new CustomerManager();
            Customer customer = manager.getCustomer(id);
            request.setAttribute("customer", customer);

            jspPage = "/displayCustomer.jsp";
        }

        dispatch(jspPage, request, response);
    }

    protected void dispatch(String jsp, HttpServletRequest request,
        HttpServletResponse response) throws ServletException, IOException
    {
        if (jsp != null)
        {
            RequestDispatcher rd = request.getRequestDispatcher(jsp);
            rd.forward(request, response);
        }
    }

    protected void doGet(HttpServletRequest request,
        HttpServletResponse response) throws ServletException, IOException
    {
        doPost(request, response);
    }
}
```

The `displaylist` action is just one of three separate actions implemented in `SimpleController`. The `displaylist` action first instantiates a `CustomerManager` object in order to get the required data for this action. From the `CustomerManager`, a list of `Customer` objects is obtained and then added to the request. Finally, the action assigns an appropriate path to a JSP file (the View) to be displayed: `/displayList.jsp`.

Model: Customer

The application needs to represent the concept of a customer for various areas of functionality that may be required. For our purposes in this example, it is important to understand how a simple JavaBean (`Customer`) is accessed by the Controller layer and displayed on the View layer.

The `Customer` class implemented here is nothing too exciting; it has four properties representing an identifier, the customer's first name, the customer's last name, and an address. Each has associated GET and SET methods. The code for this class is listed here:

```
package com.wrox.begjsp.ch17.mvc;

public class Customer
{
    private String _id;
    private String _firstName;
    private String _lastName;
    private String _address;
```

```
    public Customer(String id, String firstName, String lastName, String address)
    {
        _id = id;
        _firstName = firstName;
        _lastName = lastName;
        _address = address;
    }

    public String getAddress()
    {
        return _address;
    }

    public void setAddress(String address)
    {
        _address = address;
    }

    public String getFirstName()
    {
        return _firstName;
    }

    public void setFirstName(String firstName)
    {
        _firstName = firstName;
    }

    public String getLastName()
    {
        return _lastName;
    }

    public void setLastName(String lastName)
    {
        _lastName = lastName;
    }

    public String getId()
    {
        return _id;
    }

    public void setId(String id)
    {
        _id = id;
    }
}
```

This class models the real-world concept of a customer. The system will display a list of these Customer objects on one of its pages.

Web applications store their information in various ways. The most common method is in a database. Although this simple example doesn't use a database, we need to implement something that retrieves a List of Customer objects from somewhere. That somewhere is not really important here, but the simulation of that access is. We can therefore extend the Model layer to include a class whose job it is to retrieve Customer objects and provide them to whomever calls for them—notably, the SimpleController class.

In the SimpleController code listed previously, a CustomerManager object was instantiated and a List of Customer objects was retrieved from it (see Figure 17-4). The CustomerManager is basically a simulation of something that accesses a persistence service such as a database.

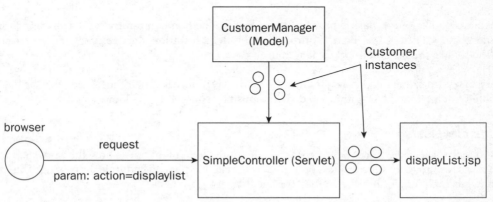

Figure 17-4: The SimpleController **retrieves** Customer **objects from** CustomerManager

Figure 17-3 has been enhanced in Figure 17-4 to show the interaction of the Controller with the CustomerManager. Customer objects are obtained from this class and passed onto the JSP page within a List object. For our purposes, the CustomerManager class is very simple:

```
package com.wrox.begjsp.ch17.mvc;

import java.util.ArrayList;
import java.util.List;


public class CustomerManager
{
    public List getCustomers()
    {
        return generateCustomers();
    }

    private List generateCustomers()
    {
        List rv = new ArrayList();

        for (int i = 0; i < 10; i++)
        {
```

```
            rv.add(getCustomer(String.valueOf(i)));
        }

        return rv;
    }

    public Customer getCustomer(String id)
    {
        return new Customer(id, id + "First", "Last" + id,
            "123 Caroline Road Fooville");
    }
}
```

The `CustomerManager` class exposes a `getCustomers` method that returns a `List` of `Customer` objects to the `SimpleController`. For the purposes of this demonstration, the `Customer` objects are created on-the-fly to simulate some sort of data store access.

You can see from these code samples that the Model layer is very much concerned with the business problems at hand and has nothing to do with how it is rendered in the View.

View: displayList.jsp

If you look back at the `SimpleController` code listing, you might notice how the `SimpleController` forwards resources and the request onto an appropriate JSP page to continue processing. The following listing has highlighted this within the `SimpleController`:

```
...
    else if ("displaylist".equals(action))
    {
        CustomerManager manager = new CustomerManager();
        List customers = manager.getCustomers();
        request.setAttribute("customers", customers);

        jspPage = "/displayList.jsp";
    }
...
    dispatch(jspPage, request, response);
}

protected void dispatch(String jsp, HttpServletRequest request,
    HttpServletResponse response) throws ServletException, IOException
{
    if (jsp != null)
    {
        RequestDispatcher rd = request.getRequestDispatcher(jsp);
        rd.forward(request, response);
    }
}
...
```

The logic to achieve this is found in the `dispatch` method that is called at the end of the `doPost` method of the `SimpleController` servlet. The `dispatch` method uses an object called `RequestDispatcher` to forward the `HttpServletRequest` and `HttpServletResponse` objects onto an appropriate resource—in this case, as a JSP file.

In the action code, the `Customer` object `List` retrieved from the `CustomerManager` was added to the request as an attribute called `customers`. The code then identified the path to the appropriate JSP file to use: `/displayList.jsp`. The `dispatch` method was then called in turn.

The code to implement in the View now becomes very simple. Its only job is to render the list of `Customer` objects that it has been provided by the `SimpleController`. The contents of `displayList.jsp` are as follows (the code to render the table of `Customer` objects is shaded):

```jsp
<%@ taglib prefix="c" uri="http://java.sun.com/jsp/jstl/core" %>

<html>
<head>
    <title>Display Customer List</title>
</head>
<body>

<table cellspacing="3" cellpadding="3" border="1" width="500">
<tr>
    <td colspan="4"><b>Customer List</b></td>
</tr>
<tr>
    <td><b>Id</b></td>
    <td><b>First Name</b></td>
    <td><b>Last Name</b></td>
    <td><b>Address</b></td>
</tr>
<c:forEach var="customer" items="${requestScope.customers}">
<tr>
    <td>
        <a href="controller?action=displaycustomer&id=${customer.id}">
            ${customer.id}
        </a>
    </td>
    <td>${customer.firstName}</td>
    <td>${customer.lastName}</td>
    <td>${customer.address}</td>
</tr>
</c:forEach>
</table>
</body>
</html>
```

You can see that the `c:forEach` JSTL tag has been used. The `customers` `List` was added to the request in the `SimpleController`. Accordingly, the tag to iterate over this `Collection` has referenced this `List` from the `requestScope` in its `items` attribute. The list displayed might look something like what is shown in Figure 17-5.

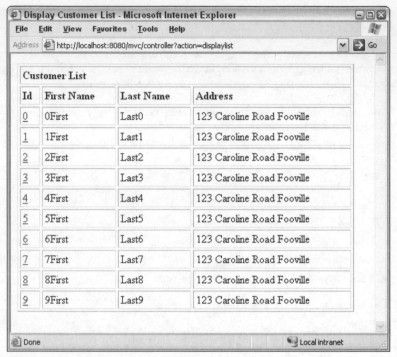

Figure 17-5: List of customers displayed

Each customer object represented in the list has an identifier (the `id` property) that uniquely identifies it. Displaying this property in the list helps to form an HTML link to the `controller` servlet with an appropriate `action` parameter to tell the `SimpleController` that the `displaycustomer` action should be executed. Additionally, the unique identity of the `Customer` object has been added as a parameter in this link called `id`. This parameter will be used in `SimpleController`'s `displaycustomer` action to get the correct `Customer` from the Model layer.

Selecting a single customer for display

The functionality to display a single customer record for the user in response to a selection in the customer list follows the same pattern.

`SimpleController` has an appropriate action for this functionality: `displaycustomer`. This segment of the `SimpleController` is relisted here:

```
...
else if ("displaycustomer".equals(action))
{
    String id = request.getParameter("id");
    CustomerManager manager = new CustomerManager();
    Customer customer = manager.getCustomer(id);
    request.setAttribute("customer", customer);
```

```
        jspPage = "/displayCustomer.jsp";
    }
    ...
```

First, the `id` parameter is retrieved from the request and used in the `getCustomer(id)` call to `CustomerManager` to retrieve the appropriate `Customer` object. The retrieved value is then added to the request as an attribute called `customer`. Finally, the action assigns the path to an appropriate JSP file in order for the View to be displayed: `/displayCustomer.jsp`.

The `displayCustomer.jsp` page is listed here:

```
<%@ taglib prefix="c" uri="http://java.sun.com/jsp/jstl/core" %>

<c:set var="customer" value="${requestScope.customer}"/>
<html>
<head>
    <title>Display Customer</title>
</head>
<body>

<table cellspacing="3" cellpadding="3" border="1" width="60%">
<tr>
    <td colspan="2"><b>Customer:</b>
     ${customer.firstName} ${customer.lastName}
    </td>
</tr>
<tr>
    <td><b>Id</b></td>
    <td>${customer.id}</td>
</tr>
<tr>
    <td><b>First Name</b></td>
    <td>${customer.firstName}</td>
</tr>
<tr>
    <td><b>Last Name</b></td>
    <td>${customer.lastName}</td>
</tr>
<tr>
    <td><b>Address</b></td>
    <td>${customer.address}"</td>
</tr>
</table>
</body>
</html>
```

`displayCustomer.jsp` is a simple JSP page along the same lines as `displayList.jsp` described earlier. However, the single `customer` attribute is copied from the `requestScope` to the `page` scope to make its accesses a little less verbose. Each of the values is then printed out in a tabular format. This JSP page will render something similar to what is shown in Figure 17-6.

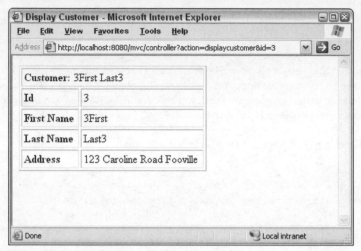

Figure 17-6: The Display customer details JSP

This completes a simple example of an MVC architecture using servlets and JSP. This example has illustrated in a somewhat contrived manner the clean separation of concerns that MVC provides:

❑ **Model:** The `Customer` and `CustomerManager` concerned themselves with modeling the business logic of the application.

❑ **View:** The two JSP pages simply displayed the Model information they were provided. The JSP pages are simple and easy to understand.

❑ **Controller:** The `SimpleController` acted as a traffic cop, fielding requests from the user, retrieving data from the Model, and directing traffic to the appropriate action for execution.

Summary

When learning a new language (or a new anything for that matter) developers conquer the ground-level syntax and techniques for solving problems. Learning design techniques such as MVC is equally (if not more) important, as developers gain a greater understanding of the implications of their decisions in development. As developers mature, the importance of these techniques increases, as does the quality of their applications.

MVC is just one of countless design techniques that are extremely important in Web application development. These design techniques are often referred to as *patterns*. Patterns are generalized approaches to solving design problems on a micro and macro scale.

This chapter has presented the following:

❑ An introduction to the MVC architecture, with a focus on Web applications

❑ Descriptions of the individual components (Model, View, and Controller) of MVC.

❑ A comparison of earlier approaches to developing Web applications with MVC approaches. The Model 1 architecture was compared to the Model 2 implementation of MVC to illustrate the significant advantages this approach provides.

❑ The benefits of using MVC were illustrated using a simple example application that showed the individual components interacting to satisfy some simple functionality.

MVC is an important concept to keep in mind when embarking on the next few chapters in this book. Chapter 18, "Web Frameworks," introduces other tools that can be used to help develop an application by providing important infrastructure and promoting a particular design. As you shall see, many such frameworks promote or even enforce the use of MVC.

Exercise

1. Add a new action to the Model 2 example to present the properties of a customer ready for editing in a form. Add a link to this new action at the base of the JSP that displays customer details (`displayCustomer.jsp`).

Web Frameworks

This chapter introduces you to the world of frameworks. It first defines what a framework is and explains why they are desirable in your application development.

The chapter then introduces some available frameworks that you can use and explains their basic structure. This chapter will prepare you for the next chapter, which explains a Web framework in significantly more detail. Of course, this chapter assumes you have followed the steps outlined in Chapter 1, "Getting Started with JavaServer Pages," about setting up Tomcat and your development environment.

This chapter covers the following topics:

- ❏ A general definition of frameworks
- ❏ Why frameworks are generally considered a good practice
- ❏ Different types of Web frameworks
- ❏ An example using the WebWork framework
- ❏ An example using the MVC components of the Spring framework

This chapter will prepare you for Chapter 19 on the Struts framework and Chapter 20 on the Tiles framework.

What Is a Framework?

As programmers, we can generally define what we do as solving problems. Every problem has one or many solutions that we might implement to achieve our goals. (Few problems have no solution!) These solutions can vary in any number of ways—from their complexity to their general architecture.

Problems to be solved exist at all levels of software development, from figuring out how to structure an application to choosing between a for-loop and a while-loop. Different programmers will typically solve a problem differently. Give ten programmers the same problem, and you will more than likely get ten different solutions.

Most problems encountered by programmers have been solved before. There are characteristics of problems that generally enable them to be categorized. Sure, there may be slight differences between any two problems in the same category, but they are generally the same, and therefore will have similar solutions.

When someone develops a way of solving a particular type of problem that can generally be repeated when that problem (or something like it) next appears, then we say they are using a *pattern* to provide a solution to that problem. Patterns are ways of solving *types* of problems. Patterns can provide solutions to problems at all levels of application development, from architectural issues to defining the relationships between two classes. The use of widely accepted patterns in solving common problems is good practice. The Model View Controller (MVC) architecture introduced in Chapter 17 is an example of a very common pattern.

A great J2EE Web site that has a huge repository of useful patterns submitted by readers is The Server Side (www.theserverside.com). A lot of the patterns listed in this site are extensions or variations of some crucial cornerstone patterns that experienced developers are familiar with.

So where do frameworks fit in? Like patterns, frameworks are repeatable ways of solving a particular problem. Frameworks are a prescriptive set of building blocks and services the developer can use to achieve some goal; this may include developing an entire application, building part of an application, testing an application, and so on. Basically, a framework provides the infrastructure to solve a type of problem. A framework is not the solution to a problem; it is simply the tool with which we structure a solution.

In terms of helping you design the solution to your problem, frameworks vary in their degree of intrusiveness. Some frameworks dictate certain ways of structuring a solution, whereas others provide a generic infrastructure and leave many decisions to the developer.

In providing this structure, a framework will typically use proven patterns in its architecture. For instance, the MVC pattern is used in many Web application frameworks available today. Most MVC-based Web frameworks have a central representation of the Controller component. Sometimes this Controller is configurable so that requests are passed to other classes as part of the different actions it might execute. Web frameworks may also handle the translation of HTML form parameters into fully defined objects available for the developer to access and process data as appropriate. Validation, centrally defined, may also feature in this translation. All this integration with the application means the developer can spend more time solving business problems.

Why Frameworks Are Good

Frameworks are good for a number of reasons. First, frameworks provide a structure for our solution. This invariably saves us time, enabling us to concentrate on solving the business problem at hand. Using a popular framework usually means applying a structure or tools that many other developers have analyzed and improved over a period of time. Developers can rest assured that many experienced people have developed and used the framework to provide a structure for their applications.

For instance, the MVC pattern has probably been applied in a hundred billion different ways for a Web site. Yet using a strong, popular, and flexible framework to provide the structure for your MVC solution ensures that your time isn't spent adding yet another MVC approach to the ever-growing pile.

This is not to say that new ways of structuring an implementation of the MVC pattern are not welcome, but when a particular framework has withstood scrutiny from developers around the world, chances are that your application problems can be solved by it as well. As a rule of thumb, if it's not your intention to design a framework of your own, one of the many popular frameworks available on the Internet will almost certainly provide 95 percent of the functionality you require, and the remaining 5 percent can be added on by your own brilliance.

Frameworks also promote a kind of quasi-standard approach to resolving a particular problem, depending on its ubiquity within the development community. For instance, the Struts framework is a very popular application framework, so many developers are familiar with the Struts method of structuring an application. This has benefits in the workplace, where developers can immediately understand a part of an application that has been developed using Struts, rather than some proprietary method that they would have to be taught.

Types of Frameworks

As mentioned earlier, frameworks provide a structure for many types of problems, from developing part of an application to managing a project's documentation. Because frameworks are becoming ubiquitous with Java development, the following sections categorize them and put them into a context that will help you choose from the many that are now available.

Application frameworks

An application framework is a framework that provides some type of structure to an aspect of application development. Most frameworks will provide the developer with a set of tools to use, including, but not limited to the following:

- ❑ Architectural patterns
- ❑ Validation mechanisms
- ❑ Internationalization
- ❑ Templating

Architectural patterns

Many frameworks subscribe to an architectural pattern. Most Web application frameworks use an MVC Model 2 architecture on which an application can be based. As discussed in Chapter 17, this allows for a clear separation of concerns between the business and presentation layers of the application.

Validation mechanisms

Validating business rules and user input is one of the more cumbersome areas of Web application development. Most Web application frameworks, therefore, have at least one strategy for defining validation rules and displaying appropriate messages when those rules are broken. For instance, the Struts framework uses an XML file to define validation rules. Struts also enables the developer to define validation rules in the objects that define the form or user input interface being invoked. This type of flexibility is invaluable.

Internationalization

A growing number of Web applications need to be multilingual; after all, the Internet is a global place. As a result, many Web frameworks provide the infrastructure to handle this. This is commonly referred to as internationalization, or i18n for short. Many frameworks include support for internationalized images and messages to be presented to the user.

Templating

The visual presentation of a Web page often can be organized into a number of elements that are repeated throughout the site. A prime example of this is a menu. Templating utilities within a framework enable the placement of these common elements on various pages without repeating code.

The Struts framework is packaged (as of Struts 1.1) with a templating utility called *Tiles*. Tiles enables developers to segment the visual presentation of a Web page into a set of components, such as a login form, a menu, a stock ticker, and so on. A Web page, therefore, becomes a collection of predefined "tiles," laid out in the manner desired. Chapter 19, "Struts Framework," has an in-depth introduction to the use of Struts, and Chapter 20, "Layout Management with Tiles," focuses on Tiles.

Persistence frameworks

Other frameworks provide a structure for the interaction between an application and some sort of data store, such as a database. This is commonly referred to as *persistence*. Persistence frameworks are very popular because they attempt to abstract the relationship between an application and its data storage medium. This means the application is less dependant on the storage medium itself. In theory, it is therefore possible for an application to switch between one database and another, without having to worry about the peculiarities of any dependencies that the application may have for a particular database provider.

Persistence frameworks also enable the developer to focus on an object-oriented view of business problems, as the framework handles the translation between the "relational" world of the database and the object-oriented world of the application. Some persistence frameworks also provide for other conveniences such as query caching, connection handling, and transactions.

Many persistence-type frameworks provide some or all of the above. Probably the most common is EJB, or Enterprise JavaBeans (EJB). EJB is a specification for a component architecture issued by Sun Microsystems as part of the J2EE. Many implementations of the EJB specification are commonly found in Java application servers, such as BEA Weblogic, IBM Websphere, and JBOSS.

Other persistence frameworks that are of varying popularity are Hibernate, JDO (provided by the Java Community Process (JCP)), TopLink, and Coco Base.

EJB is covered briefly in Chapter 22, "JSP in J2EE," and Hibernate in Chapter 23, "Access to Databases."

Utility frameworks

Utility frameworks fill a variety of requirements for application development. JUnit, for instance, is a very popular testing framework. It provides developers with an excellent framework for developing tests of an application during development. BSF (Bean Scripting Framework) is an API that enables an application to access Java objects within scripting languages, and enables other scripting languages to be accessed from within Java applications.

Other frameworks, such as Forrest, are used to generate documentation based on XML (Extensible Markup Language) and XSLT (Extensible Stylesheet Language Extensions).

As you can see, a wide variety of frameworks are available to the developer. The following table provides a list of frameworks and their associated URLs, where you can find more information. The next section of this chapter goes into a little more depth about two of the frameworks mentioned, WebWork and Spring, both of which are application frameworks. As mentioned earlier, Chapter 19 provides detailed information about one of the more popular frameworks, Struts. Chapter 20 explains Tiles, a templating framework that accompanies Struts.

Framework	URL	Type	Description
Action Servlet	http://actionframework.org/	Application	An MVC framework for building Web applications
Barracuda	http://barracudamvc.org/Barracuda/	Application	Web presentation framework
BSF	http://jakarta.apache.org/bsf/	Utility	A bean scripting framework
Coco Base	http://thoughtinc.com/cber_index.html	Persistence	An OR Mapping persistence framework
Forrest	http://xml.apache.org/forrest/	Utility	A project documentation framework
Hibernate	http://hibernate.org/	Persistence	An object persistence framework
Jakarta Struts	http://jakarta.apache.org/struts	Application	A very popular MVC framework
JUnit	http://junit.source forge.net/	Utility	A popular unit-testing framework
OracleAS TopLink	http://otn.oracle.com/products/ias/toplink/	Persistence	A persistence framework
Tapestry	http://jakarta.apache.org/tapestry/	Application	A Web application framework
TeaServlet	http://teatrove.source forge.net/	Application	A templating framework for developing Web applications

Table continued on following page

Framework	URL	Type	Description
Turbine	`http://jakarta.apache.org/turbine/`	Application	A servlet-based application framework
Webwork	`http://opensymphony.com/webwork/`	Application	A Web application development framework
Spring	`http://springframework.org/`	Application	A framework covering many aspects of application development

WebWork

WebWork is an open-source application framework provided by Open Symphony, which contends that using it keeps things simple while adhering to best-practice design patterns and techniques. You can download WebWork from the Open Symphony Web site at `http://opensymphony.com/webwork/`. This chapter uses the latest version at the time of writing, 1.4.

Developers who choose to use WebWork in their application are provided with the following tools:

❑ A set of Dispatchers that act as entry points to the application. A variety of Dispatchers are provided for different requirements.

❑ A set of specific WebWork custom tags

❑ Support for different types of view technologies, such as JSP, Velocity, and Jasper reports

❑ Validation mechanisms

❑ Logging using Commons logging (`http://jakarta.apache.org/commons/logging/`), which provides a wrapper over logging mechanisms such as native Java Logging or Log4J from Jakarta

❑ A Pull HMVC (Hierarchical Model View Controller) architecture

The following section describes the items in the preceding list in the context of an application you may build using WebWork. Although WebWork boasts an architecture that could be used in many types of applications, we will be focusing on their use in the capacity of building an application for the Internet.

Components of WebWork

WebWork comprises two central components fulfilling the View and Controller aspects of the MVC model: Dispatchers and Views.

Dispatchers

As described in Chapter 17, the Controller aspect of an MVC application can use servlets to define and implement the glue between the Model layer and the View layer. Controllers act as a conduit, fielding requests from somewhere (in our case, the Internet), triggering some business logic, and forwarding resources on to other Controllers or a View technology to display to a user.

These controllers usually fulfill one or more actions in the application. For instance, a form may be submitted to an action, or a list from the database will be displayed once a particular action has been invoked. Actions, in turn, generally forward resources to display technologies such as JSP files. They can even forward control to other actions.

In WebWork, Dispatchers act as facades through which all requests must pass before these action servlets are invoked. WebWork supports three Dispatchers, developed with different scenarios in mind.

ServletDispatcher

The ServletDispatcher is a central point of invocation provided by WebWork. Requests, based on the URL requested, are mapped to this servlet. Based on the configuration defined by the application developer, these requests are then passed on to actions that perform various tasks for the application. Actions will typically then forward resources to a View technology for display. As you can see, this Dispatcher is specifically designed for use in a Web application. The action described here is merely a servlet defined and inherited from the framework.

The diagram in Figure 18-1 illustrates the interactions of the `ServletDispatcher` within the context of the WebWork framework.

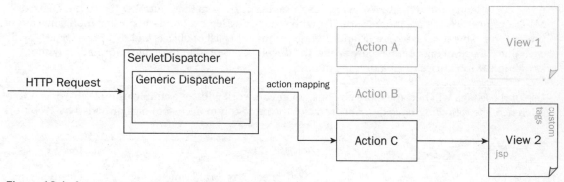

Figure 18-1: A request mapped through the framework to a view

As shown in Figure 18-1, the `ServletDispatcher` is merely a `GenericDispatcher` wrapped to provide a Web context. We will be concentrating only on the `ServletDispatcher` in this section. The other Dispatchers provided by Web Work are described briefly in the following sections.

The mapping to the appropriate action classes is achieved by entries in the application's `view. properties` file.

GenericDispatcher

`GenericDispatcher`, as the name suggests, is a more generalized dispatcher that does not assume the nature of the invocation is receives. It is invoked via a Java method call. In an architectural sense, it plays a role similar to that of `ServletDispatcher`.

ClientDispatcher

ClientDispatcher is used for the remote invocation of ClientServletDispatchers. Using a serialized request, ClientDispatcher can communicate with remote clients. These remote clients can then map requests locally to actions, and perform them appropriately.

Views

WebWork supports a number of view technologies for the presentation of information. By *view technology*, we mean a mechanism for organizing and displaying visual information to the user; that's right, we're referring to the presentation tier.

JSP

At this point, you know all about JSP and its benefits in providing an extremely powerful presentation layer to your application. What is important in the context of WebWork is the large number of custom tags that are provided to help generate, present, and manipulate this dynamic content.

The WebWork Custom Tag Library can be broadly divided into two groups: user-interface-related and logic-related. The user interface tags assist in the presentation of information while integrating with the rest of the framework, providing a link between the data set up for presentation in an action and the page on which it will be presented. More often than not, this capability is used for the presentation of forms and validating the inputs that your users may enter into them.

Logic custom tags provided by WebWork also use resources from the Controller tier of the WebWork MVC architecture, but are more concerned with structuring logic around the presentation, such as "only present this table if <some rule>," and "iterate through this list of objects and do <something> with each one." Custom tags in this sense enable the developer to present dynamic information without knowing the intricacies of Java programming.

Use of these tags will become more obvious when you work with an example using WebWork. As a brief reference, the following table describes some of the more common custom tags provided by WebWork.

Tag Name	Description	Used In
checkbox: <ui:checkbox.../>	HTML check box form element.	Forms
combobox: <ui:combobox../>	HTML input form element and select box working together to present selected items.	Forms
label: <ui:label../>	HTML label tag to present information in the same format as other elements used.	User interface
password: <ui:password../>	HTML input form element for password input.	Forms
radio: <ui:radio../>	HTML radio button form element.	Forms
select: <ui:select../>	HTML select list form element.	Forms
tabbedpane: <ui:tabbedpane../>	Handy element to present a pane presentation of different views.	User interface

Tag Name	Description	Used In
table: `<ui:table../>`	Tag to output an HTML table.	User interface
textarea: `<ui:textarea../>`	HTML `textarea` form element.	Forms
action: `<webwork:action../>`	Tag to invoke another action defined within WebWork.	Logic
append: `<iterator:append../>`	Tag to append a series of iterations together and be treated as one.	Logic
bean: `<webwork:bean../>`	Tag to set up a bean within the context of the JSP page. Nested `param` tags set the various properties of the bean.	Logic
if, else, elseif: `<webwork:if../>`, `<webwork:elseif../>`, `<webwork:else../>`	Tags to provide conditional logic.	Logic
Include: `<webwork:include../>`	Tag to include the results of another pageor action.	Logic
iterator: `<webwork:iterator../>`	Tag to loop over a value, such as a Collection, etc.	Logic
Sort: `<webwork:sort../>`	Tag to sort a value in an iterator tag.	Logic
Text: `<webwork:text../>`	Tag to print out a text value defined in a properties file.	Logic

Those who have read Chapter 6, "JSP Tag Libraries and JSTL," will note a common thread of functionality running through this list of custom tags and, for example, those provided by JSTL and the Custom Tag Lib implementations from Jakarta. However, these tags are designed to integrate primarily with the resources provided by other WebWork components such as actions, as well as others.

Velocity

Velocity is a templating engine that can be integrated with WebWork actions to provide for the visual requirements of a Web application. Velocity specifics are not described here. What is important in the context of our discussion is that actions invoked in WebWork can pass control and resources to Velocity templates.

XSLT

WebWork can also convert some of the data produced by actions into XML, which, in turn can be presented to the user with the help of XSLT stylesheets. In this sense, the logic capabilities of XSLT are used to determine which data to present and how it is presented.

Jasper Reports

Jasper Reports is a tool used to generate reports based on data sources provided to it. WebWork actions can be integrated as these data sources, thereby providing the logic to determine which data will be included in the report. The support for the generation of Jasper Reports is fairly comprehensive but out of the scope of this book.

WebWork example

It's time now to actually have a go at creating something with WebWork. This section will lead you through the steps necessary to get the example application working with the latest version of Tomcat. The team at WebWork has kindly included with its distribution a skeleton application that serves as an excellent starting point for enhancement and working with some of the tools that this framework provides.

Installation

Once you have downloaded the latest version of WebWork from http://opensymphony.com/webwork/, the first step is to extract the zip file contents into a directory of your choice. Extracting the contents will create a directory called webwork-1.4 (lets assume it's C:\webwork-1.4). Inside this directory, you will find the following subdirectories.

- ❑ **docs:** WebWork documentation is found in this directory.

- ❑ **lib:** The lib directory contains some the core JAR and WAR files we will use when utilizing WebWork in an application.

- ❑ **etc:** Here you will find some extra files for special purposes. A zip file is included in this directory containing the skeleton application. We will get to this later.

- ❑ **src:** The kind people at WebWork have packaged up the source code for us to peruse if we feel so inclined. You will find it in this directory.

We're now ready to start exploring this framework by installing the example application that comes with WebWork.

Example applications

The examples that are packaged with WebWork are quite comprehensive and will give you an insight into the possibilities now available to you when using this framework. In the C:\webwork-1.4\lib directory, you will find a file called webwork.war. This WAR file contains an application that you can install on your Tomcat server. Install the WAR file by following these steps:

1. Stop the Tomcat server.

2. Copy the webwork-examples.war file into the C:\Tomcat\webapps directory.

3. Start the Tomcat server.

Once Tomcat has gone through its start-up sequence, you should have a new application context available. Start your favorite browser and navigate to http://localhost:8080/webwork/.

The first section of the page presents a list of tests you can invoke to ensure that you have the application installed correctly. However, if you scroll down a bit you will find the examples. They show some basic, typical Web site application effects such as form validation, shopping carts, and so on. Remember that you can look at the code for all these applications in the C:\webwork-1.4\src directory. These examples are invaluable in confirming your understanding of WebWork when the time comes.

Skeleton application

Sure, the examples are great, but we assume you want to do more than just look at the results of some-one else's code, right? Good to hear. You can now get the skeleton application working with Tomcat. The following steps will guide you through to this goal. These instructions assume you have set up the Ant build tool described in Chapter 26, "Best Practices and Tools."

1. In the `C:\webwork-1.4\etc` directory, locate `webwork-skeleton.zip`. Unzip this file into a directory of your choice. For our purposes, we will assume this is `C:\webwork-skeleton`.

2. Within the directory you just created, you should now have the contents of the zip file. Among these contents is a file called `build.xml`. This is an Ant build file we are going to use to build the skeleton application to get things going. After we have made some changes to the skeleton application, we will use the `build.xml` file to make them available to Tomcat.

3. Select Start ⇨ Run and type **cmd** at the prompt. A command console will open.

   Issue the following command to get to the skeleton application's directory:

   ```
   cd c:\
   cd webwork-skeleton
   ```

4. From the command console, type **ant compile**.

   Your command console should now appear something like what you see in Figure 18-2.

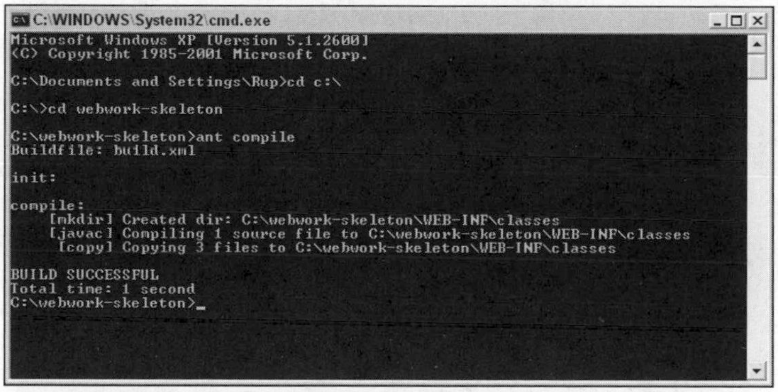

Figure 18-2: Console after building WebWork skeleton application

The source for the skeleton application has now been compiled and moved to an appropriate directory for Tomcat to look at.

5. Create a new context in Tomcat by logging into the administration application. First, ensure Tomcat is running and browse to `http://localhost:8080/admin`. Enter the username and password you chose when you installed Tomcat.

6. Once logged in, make a new context for the skeleton application. Open the following nodes in the tree on the left-hand panel: Service (Catalina) ⇨ Host (localhost). Select the Host (localhost) node. The right-hand panel should change to reflect the properties of the default host.

7. In the Available Actions box on the right side of the page, select Create New Context. Enter the following details in the corresponding fields for the context properties:

Field	Value
Document Base	C:\webwork-skeleton
Reloadable	True
Path	/skeleton

8. All other settings can be left at their default values. Now click the Save button. With any luck, the new context will be created for the skeleton application.

9. To make sure everything is okay, browse to http://localhost:8080/skeleton/. You should be presented with a simple link to "Form test." Click this link and a simple form will be displayed.

Before we get started, let's explore how this example has been set up.

The example consists of the following:

❑ A basic Action class called FormTest. FormTest is executed when the form page is first loaded, and then when the form is submitted.

❑ A simple JSP page called formtest.jsp, which displays the form before and after it is submitted.

❑ Entries in web.xml to define the ServletDispatcher and map it to a URL pattern, in this case *.action.

❑ webwork.jar in the WEB-INF/lib directory.

❑ Entries in a properties file for WebWork called webwork.properties. This file defines properties that enable WebWork to function.

❑ Entries in another properties file called views.properties. These entries define the Action class to be invoked for the URL, as well as the JSP files to which different eventualities of the action can pass control.

FormTest class

The FormTest class plays the action part in the application. If you look at the source code (located in C:\webwork-skeleton\WEB-INF\src\skeleton\action), you will notice this class extends a WebWork class called ActionSupport. This inheritance provides the very simplistic FormTest class with methods to pass errors onto the View layer, validate user entry, and perform *custom* processing that the developer may want to invoke. An important method in this class is the doExecute() method. The return value of this method determines the next resource to which this action will pass control, usually a JSP file. We will have a closer look at this class when we add some functionality.

formtest.jsp

formtest.jsp displays the form we see when the page loads. You will see the elements of this form represented in the FormTest class described earlier. The form in formtest.jsp submits to an action defined in the view.properties file.

web.xml

The web.xml file for this application contains some entries in order to set up WebWork's Dispatcher Servlet and provide an appropriate URL mapping. It also includes an entry for the WebWork tag library.

webwork.properties

This properties file includes settings that define how WebWork will function. Most important for us in this example is the property webwork.action.packages, which defines the package in which Action classes are found, i.e., webwork.action.packages=skeleton.action.

views.properties

views.properties contains property entries that map an action class to a URL and map different results of those actions to various JSP files. Remember the doExecute() method in the FormTest class? The result of that method maps to entries in this file for each action. Therefore, the property formtest.success=formtest.jsp means that the formtest.jsp file is to be used when the FormTest class results in success.

Enhancements

If you play with the form in the skeleton application, you will quickly discover that it does little more than validate that something is typed into the top input box when the form is submitted. We're going to add the following features to this example:

❑ Show the details entered in the form on a new page that is displayed after the form is successfully submitted.

❑ Add a new field to the form.

❑ Add validation to ensure that the user enters something in the text box.

❑ Present a list of information on the following page. We will form the list in the action and display its contents in the JSP page using the WebWork custom tags. The values in the list should depend on the values of another property of the form.

Try It Out   Displaying Form Details on a New Page

We want a new page to be displayed when the form is successfully submitted. This mechanism is controlled by the entries in the views.properties file.

In the views.properties file, change the value for the formtest.success property from formtest.jsp to formdisplay.jsp. formdisplay.jsp is a new JSP page that will be displayed when the form is successfully submitted. If a validation error occurs, the existing JSP page will continue to be displayed. Now that we have defined that the formdisplay.jsp file will be used when the FormTest doExecute() method returns success, so we had better create this file.

Create a file called formdisplay.jsp in the same directory as the formtest.jsp file. When you create this file, add some text such as **form has been submitted**. Now you can issue an ant compile command in the console, which you should still have open. Restart Tomcat, browse to the form, enter a value in the top form element, and submit it. You should see the message you placed in the new JSP file. Easy, wasn't it?

However, our task isn't quite complete here. We need to display the values entered in the form on the new page. Again, this is simple.

If you look closely at the `FormTest` class source code, you will notice that it contains member properties matching the elements of the form we are dealing with. For instance, the form has an input box called User. The `FormTest` class has a `String` property called `user` as well. There are also associated accessor methods for this property in `getUser` and `setUser`. When the form is submitted, the `setUser` method is invoked by the framework in order to set the value of the property in the `FormTest` class with the value that was entered in the form.

Once the properties of the form have been populated in the `FormTest` class, the `doValidation()` method is invoked. If any errors are found during the `doValidation()` method, the `doExecute()` method is not called. When this occurs, the view mapping executed is called `formtest.error`. You will see a corresponding property in the `views.properties` file: `formtest.error=formtest.jsp`. The `formtest.jsp` page is then redisplayed showing an appropriate error message next to the offending field(s).

Therefore, in order to print out the values of the form on the `formdisplay.jsp` page, we need to somehow access these accessor methods in the `FormTest` class. WebWork's custom tags to the rescue!

We can use the `<webwork:property../>` tag to print out these values for us. In the JSP file you created, add the following code:

```jsp
<%@ taglib uri="webwork" prefix="webwork" %>

<html>
<head>
<title>Form Results</title>
</head>
<body>
    <p>
    <b>User:</b> <webwork:property value="user"/><br>
    <b>Age:</b><webwork:property value="age"/><br>
    <b>Comments:</b><br>
    <webwork:property value="comments"/>
</body>
</html>
```

Notice that the `value` property of this tag uses the same name as the property in the `FormTest` class. This is deliberate. From this, the framework knows to call the `getUser()` method when this tag is encountered. When you have made the preceding change, save the `formdisplay.jsp` file and reload your browser. The result of this change is that now when the form is successfully submitted, the contents are immediately displayed on the next page.

Try It Out   Adding a New Field to the Form

Right now, our form is fairly dull, just a name and some comments. Let's add a new form element to collect the user's age. The new form element will be a list of numbers from 0 to 100. We will first modify the `formtest.jsp` page to display the new element. Open the file `formtest.jsp` and add the following highlighted code to this file:

```
<ui:textfield label="'User'" name="'user'"/>
<webwork:bean name="'webwork.util.Counter'" id="ages">
  <webwork:param name="'first'" value="0"/>
  <webwork:param name="'last'" value="100"/>
  <ui:combobox label="'Age'" size="3" maxlength="3" name="'age'" list="@ages"/>
</webwork:bean>

<ui:textarea label="'Comments'" name="'comments'" cols="30" rows="8"/>
```

The WebWork utility class `Counter` is used as a bean in this case to build our select list of user age values. We then added a WebWork combo box element in order to capture the user's selection. When you have saved the JSP page, your form should look like the one shown in Figure 18-3:

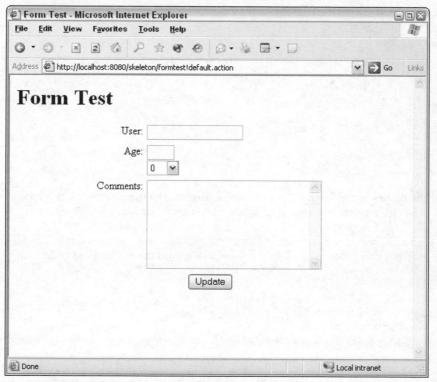

Figure 18-3: Form Test screen with a new field

Now that the form element has been added, we need to bind it to a value in the `FormTest` class. This will enable us to display the selected value on the next page and provide for any validation we may need. Therefore, we need to edit `FormTest.java`, located in the `C:\webwork-skeleton\WEB-INF\src\skeleton\action` directory.

First, we need to add a new property to this class:

```
...
String user = "";
String comments = "";
int age = 0;
...
```

We also need to add appropriate accessor methods to this class so that the framework has access to this new property. The new methods are shown highlighted:

```
...
public String getComments()
{
    return comments;
}

public int getAge()
{
    return age;
}

public void setAge(int age)
{
    this.age = age;
}
```

Note that the names of the methods here follow a pattern. The framework relies on the accessor of a property to have a particular name, with appropriate uppercase and lowercase letters.

Before we go any further, you should add an appropriate `<webwork:property../>` tag to the form display.jsp page in order to print out our new value. Add the highlighted code to the following JSP page:

```
<b>User:</b> <webwork:property value="user"/><br>
<b>Age:</b><webwork:property value="age"/><br>
<b>Comments:</b><br>
<webwork:property value="comments"/>
```

Save the files you have changed and issue an `ant compile` command using the Ant build tool, and then restart Tomcat. Submit the form page when you have entered a name and selected an age. The following page will display the value for the new field below the name you entered. Note that we can pretty much enter any numeric value we want in the age field. Try entering a letter in the input box for age, and click Submit. That's right, WebWork is smart enough to know that the value you enter should be a number. Pretty nifty, eh?

Note that when you change a class file, you will have to either reload the Tomcat/skeleton context or restart Tomcat entirely for your changes to appear.

However, we want to add some more validation to this field so that users can't submit the form with an inappropriate value. We'll need to add some validation code to the `FormTest` class. If you open the source code for this class again, you will notice a method called `doValidation();`.This method is called by the framework when you submit the form to perform any validation we need on the user's entry. For our simple example, we will assume that the user should not be able to select any value under 18 for age. Add the highlighted code to the `doValidation()` method of `FormTest` class:

```
...
if (user.equals(""))
{
    addError("user", "Missing name");
}

if (age < 18)
{
    addError("age", "Age cannot be less than 18");
}
...
```

You can see that we have added code to this method that tests the value of the `age` property of the object. If the property has a value less than 18, we want to add an error. The `addError` method is then called in order to advise WebWork that something has gone wrong and that we need to display a message to the user to inform them of it. The first parameter passed to this method is the field that has the associated error, and the second is the message we wish to display to the user. If you now save the changes you have made, and deploy and re-run the application, you will notice the error message appears just above the Age field when a value less than 18 is entered. This positioning of the message is conveniently provided to us when we identified the erroneous field in the call to the `addError` method.

Try It Out   Presenting a List of Things on the Page

One final requirement remains: We need to display a list of values on the `formdisplay.jsp` page. In addition, the list of things we display should depend on another value selected in the form. Hmm . . . Age looks convenient for this purpose. We start by adding the appropriate code to the `FormTest` class. First create a new property called `things`. This property should be of type `ArrayList`:

```
int age = 0;
ArrayList things = new ArrayList();
...
```

We will also need an accessor method to retrieve this value to display on the page:

```
...
public ArrayList getThings()
{
    return things;
}
```

Our `things` property is ready, but it doesn't have anything in it; let's add some values to it depending on the value of the `age` property. Modify the `getThings()` method to appear as follows:

```
...
public ArrayList getThings()
{
    if (age < 25)
    {
        things.add("Go to College");
        things.add("Buy a car");
        things.add("Travel overseas");
    }
    else if (age < 35)
    {
        things.add("Get a job");
        things.add("Buy a house");
        things.add("Get married");
    }
    else
    {
        things.add("Do whatever you want!");
    }

    return things;
}
...
```

Much better. We have added items to the list dependent on the value of the age property. We now need to ensure that the ArrayList things is listed on the displayform.jsp page, along with the results of the form:

Now we get a chance to use the <webwork:iterator../> custom tag in order to print out the value of the things property. Add the following highlighted code to the formdisplay.jsp page:

```
<webwork:property value="comments"/>
```

```
Advice<br>

<ul>
<webwork:iterator value="things">
    <li><webwork:property value="toString"/></li>
</webwork:iterator>
</ul>
...
```

Confused by the toString value in the property tag? Don't be, we haven't done anything magical. Remember that we added String objects to the things ArrayList. Every String has a method called toString; adding this value to the value attribute of the property tag just tells the framework to issue a call to toString for every object in the ArrayList. What results is a list of items on the page that varies depending on the value of age you selected.

You can see how the action path of this application, as well as the business logic, such as validation and determination of data, is separated from the display or view areas. We are using only the JSP pages to display and collect information, nothing more.

This section has been a very brief introduction to WebWork. Rather than showcase WebWork, it illustrates the position that many application frameworks occupy in an application. In the next chapter, we will investigate another framework in significantly more detail, the Apache Struts framework.

The Spring Framework

Spring is an open-source J2EE application framework released as version 1.0 in March 2004. Spring is really a collection of frameworks to be utilized in conjunction with each other or separately. It was designed to assist in easing J2EE development while promoting good programming practices. Spring also strives to make use of existing technologies, rather than reinventing the wheel. For instance, it doesn't provide much in the way of custom tag libraries (like WebWork or Struts); instead, it provides a discrete set of its own tags, but promotes the use of the Standard Tag Library for most other things. This pragmatic approach makes Spring an attractive framework to consider.

Spring covers more areas of the application pie than WebWork does. Whereas WebWork focuses on providing an MVC structure to applications, this is just a part of the Spring framework. The main areas within Spring are as follows:

❑ **Object Relational Mapping:** Spring provides built-in support and further abstraction for other technologies such as Hibernate and JDO.

❑ **Data Access Objects:** JDBC interface and transactional support.

❑ **Aspect Oriented Programming (AOP):** A programming approach to separate concepts into *aspects*.

❑ **Spring Context and Web:** Support for the business layer requirements of an application, such as JNDI and EJB.

❑ **Spring MVC:** Model View Controller facilities to abstract business rules away from the display layer.

Of course, we are most interested in the last area, Spring MVC. The others are beyond the scope of this book, but all are very important concepts for you to become familiar with.

Main components of the Spring MVC

The MVC section of Spring features a rich infrastructure that your application can use. The components identified in the following sections are configured within an XML file particular to the application. This is fine for our purposes, but a more sophisticated use of Spring will extend configuration to a number of `applicationContext.xml` files.

As you will see, the configuration file contains a list of beans that define the different components your application may use.

After looking at WebWork, the broad structure of Spring's MVC framework will be familiar to you.

Controllers and commands

Spring MVC centers around a hierarchy of Controllers that allow for differences in application requirements, such as wizards and Controllers than can handle more than one action (a *supercontroller*, if you like). The hierarchy enables the Controllers that we create to implement or use various methods that enhance the application's behavior.

In terms of the application's configuration of Controllers, the developer defines a central servlet dispatcher in the `web.xml` file in the usual manner. Controllers, via handler mappings, take responsibility for certain URL mappings defined in a file called `<centralservletname>-servlet.xml`. This file has other responsibilities for the Spring framework, but URL (handler) mapping is central to our discussion. The sequence that arises is much like the one outlined in Figure 18-1, which describes the flow of control from an HTTP request to an action. In a Spring context, the Controller fulfills the notion of an action.

The data we collected in forms and submitted to an application is referred to as a *Command* in Spring language. A Command represents a bean that is pieced together from a request. Command objects you implement do not extend an object or even implement an interface provided by Spring. You are free to adopt any inheritance structure your application requires. This is a key difference from the Struts framework, which enforces an inheritance relationship for form objects of this type.

Validators

Spring enables you to define objects that encapsulate validation requirements for your application. These objects are defined by the developer and registered in the application configuration against the Controller for which it will provide validation.

There is a significant advantage in having validation mechanisms separated from data objects (Commands) and architecturally able to make reference to other objects that define business logic. Validator objects in the Spring framework provide for this. You will see an example of a Validator in the Spring framework example that follows.

Views

Views are typically defined in a simple Web application as a path to a JSP file. In addition, however, Views can include specialist objects for such purposes as viewing a PDF or Microsoft Excel file created at runtime. A developer would implement the View interface when creating a class to handle this. This View can then be configured with other beans in the context of Spring.

JSP views are configured in Spring and can be referenced, by token, by the Controller, as part of its execution. This serves to decouple the name of the JSP file from the Java code in the Controller.

Unlike WebWork and Struts, Spring doesn't provide a long list of custom tags that the developer must use in order to satisfy the functionality of the framework. Rather, Spring provides only a modest list of tags and relies on the Standard Tag Library for everything else.

The tags Spring provides are described in the following table.

Tag Name	Description
`<spring:hasBindErrors../>`	Support for determining whether binding errors are associated with a bean, such as validation of a command object.
`<spring:bind path="somebean"../>`	Support for binding to a bean and evaluating its value and any associated errors. The `Status` variable, which this gives scope to, is bound to the bean defined in `path`. Useful when binding validation messages and existing values to form elements.
`<spring:transform../>`	Used to transform an object for display purposes.
`<spring:message../>`	Provides support for accessing a Message Source configured for the application, such as `messages.properties`. Useful for internationalization.
`<spring:theme../>`	Looks up a message defined for a theme.
`<spring:htmlEscape../>`	Sets the default HTML escape value for the current page.

While our main focus is on JSP providing a view for an application, it is important to note that Spring is view technology neutral. Developers are not forced to use a particular view technology, such as only JSP or only Velocity. The JSP tags listed in the preceding table are provided so that JSP can be used with this framework.

Internationalization

Spring MVC supports mechanisms that provide for the display of information in other languages, based on the language setting of the user's browser. This concept is extremely powerful and simple to implement. Many frameworks support this mechanism. Spring enables the developer to define a set of messages based on language preferences of the user. The JSP view can then access these messages via the `<spring:message../>` tag described earlier.

In addition to this is the concept of internationalized views, which enables the developer to provide for different view mappings based on language preferences.

An example using Spring

Much like the WebWork example discussed earlier, we are going to get a basic application up and running, have a look at the parts, and then make some enhancements. This section assumes you have set up Tomcat and Ant as described in Chapters 1 and 26. Unlike WebWork, there is no small simple application that comes packaged with Spring. We have prepared an application almost identical to the WebWork skeleton application as a starting point for this example. You can download this from the Wrox Web site at www.wrox.com.

Installation

You can download the latest version of Spring from `springframework.org` (this book uses version 1.0).

Download the `spring-base` application for Spring from the Wrox Web site and unzip the contents into a directory of your choosing; let's assume `c:\spring-base`. You will notice the following directories:

❑ **src:** This contains all source code as well as some configuration files such as `views.properties` and `messages.properties`.

❑ **web:** This contains all Web-related items.

❑ **web/WEB-INF:** This houses application configuration files such as `web.xml` and the Spring configuration file, `servlet-spring.xml`.

❑ **web/WEB-INF/jsp:** This contains the JSP files we will be using in the application.

In the root of the `spring-base` directory is an Ant build file, `build.xml`. This file is used to build and deploy the `spring-base` application. In order for you to be able to use the `spring-base` application, you must have followed the steps for getting Ant installed and working on your computer.

The following instructions will enable you to build and run the `spring-base` application using Ant and Tomcat.

1. Open the `build.xml` file and change the properties entries to reflect their correct values for your environment. The following highlighted properties in this listing will need to be changed:

```
...
<property name="app.name"        value="spring-base"/>
<property name="app.path"        value="/${app.name}"/>
<property name="app.version"     value="0.1-dev"/>
<property name="build.home"      value="${basedir}/build"/>
<property name="catalina.home"   value="c:/Tomcat"/>
<property name="dist.home"       value="${basedir}/dist"/>
<property name="docs.home"       value="${basedir}/docs"/>
<property name="manager.url"     value="http://localhost:8080/manager"/>
<property name="manager.username" value="admin"/>
<property name="manager.password" value="password"/>
<property name="src.home"        value="${basedir}/src"/>
<property name="web.home"        value="${basedir}/web"/>

<property name="spring.home" value="c:/spring-framework-1.0"/>
<property name="jstl.home"   value="c:/jakarta-taglibs"/>
...
```

The values you should change in this listing are as follows:

Property	Description
catalina.home	The directory in which you installed Tomcat
manager.url	The URL of the Tomcat Manager application
manager.username	The username for the Tomcat Manager application
manager.password	The password for the Tomcat Manager application
spring.home	The location at which you installed Spring
jstl.home	The location at which you installed the Jakarta JSTL implementation

This build file assumes you are using the Jakarta JSTL implementation with the appropriate `jstl.jar` and `standard.jar` files found in the `c:/jakarta-taglibs/standard/lib` directory.

2. In order for Ant to communicate with your Tomcat server, locate the file `<Tomcat Installation Directory>/server/lib/catalina-ant.jar` in your Tomcat server installation and copy it to your `ANT_HOME/lib` directory.

3. Ensure that Tomcat is running.

Open a command prompt to the directory in which you expanded the `spring-base` application. This directory should contain the `build.xml` file.

4. Issue the following command in the command console: **ant install**. This command will perform the following tasks for you:

   a. Compile the Java source files and place them in the `c:\spring-base\build\WEB-INF\classes` directory.

   b. Copy the `views.properties` and `messages.properties` files to the `c:\spring-base\build\WEB-INF\classes` directory.

   c. Copy the following files from where you installed them to the `c:\spring-base\build\WEB-INF\lib` directory:

      ❑ spring.jar

      ❑ jstl.jar

      ❑ standard.jar

   d. Copy the `spring.tld` file from the Spring installation directory to the `c:\spring-base\build\WEB-INF\` directory.

   e. Copy the `web.xml` and `spring-servlet.xml` files from the `c:\spring-base\web\WEB-INF` directory to the `c:\spring-base\build\WEB-INF\` directory.

f. Copy the JSP files from the `c:\spring-base\web\WEB-INF\jsp` directory to the `c:\spring-base\build\WEB-INF\jsp` directory.

g. Install the application in Tomcat with the context `spring-base`. This context is based in the `c:\spring-base\build` directory.

5. If you now browse to `http://localhost:8080/spring-base`, you should be presented with a rather plain form like the WebWork example presented earlier.

If you submit the form, you will see some validation occurring, and if you enter a name, a plain page is displayed. Nothing special, but underlying this rather simple interface are some key concepts that will help you grasp development with Spring.

Base application description

To help you understand this application so far, let's look at the components of the base application and how they piece together. This description simply walks through the components as they are, enhancements will be made in the next section.

Our application so far consists of a simple form, which is displayed at `/form.htm`. The `TestFormController` has been invoked by this URL, and in so doing has set up an initial value for the data collected in the form, represented by the `TestForm` object. The Controller causes the appropriate view to be rendered, `/WEB-INF/jsp/form.jsp`. When the form is submitted, the user's data input is validated by the `TestFormValidator` class; and if there are no validation errors, then another view is rendered. If there are validation errors, the form is again displayed along with any validation errors. The following sections look at each of these components in turn.

Controller: TestFormController

As discussed previously, a central servlet Dispatcher is registered with Tomcat and assigned to a URL pattern so that various requests will be assigned to it. If you look at the `WEB-INF/web.xml` file for the base application, you can see this entry:

```
<servlet>
  <servlet-name>spring</servlet-name>
  <servlet-class>org.springframework.web.servlet.DispatcherServlet</servlet-class>
  <load-on-startup>1</load-on-startup>
</servlet>

<servlet-mapping>
  <servlet-name>spring</servlet-name>
  <url-pattern>*.htm</url-pattern>
</servlet-mapping>
```

Spring's `DispatcherServlet` is registered with Tomcat and assigned a URL mapping of `*.htm`; therefore, all requests pointing to `http://localhost:8080/spring-base/*.htm` will be processed by this `DispatcherServlet`. The `DispatcherServlet` routes requests through to a handler registered in the application. Notice that the servlet has been given the name `spring` with the `servlet-mapping` entry. This name is used to specify the Spring configuration file: `spring-servlet.xml`. This file is located in the `/WEB-INF/` directory.

In the `spring-servlet.xml` file, two entries map requests to our `TestFormController`. This is a class that will perform the Controller role in this application. The first entry establishes our Controller in the framework:

```
<bean id="testFormController"
      class="com.wrox.begjsp.ch18.spring.TestFormController">
  <property name="sessionForm"><value>false</value></property>
  <property name="validateOnBinding"><value>true</value></property>
  <property name="bindOnNewForm"><value>false</value></property>
  <property name="commandName"><value>testForm</value></property>
  <property name="commandClass">
   <value>com.wrox.begjsp.ch18.spring.TestForm</value>
  </property>
  <property name="validator"><ref bean="testFormValidator"/></property>
  <property name="formView"><value>form</value></property>
</bean>
```

In addition to establishing the Controller as a bean in Spring, certain properties have been set so that the application will behave as required. You will see the effect of these in subsequent sections.

The second entry in the `spring-servlet.xml` file establishes a handler bean so that requests can be mapped to our Controller:

```
<bean id="urlMapping"
      class="org.springframework.web.servlet.handler.SimpleUrlHandlerMapping">
<property name="mappings">
  <props>
    <prop key="/form.htm">testFormController</prop>
  </props>
</property>
</bean>
```

The `SimpleUrlHandlerMapping` object configured here is a class provided by Spring. The mapping's property within this definition sets up a URL mapping to our Controller. Here we are saying that URL `/form.htm` should be dealt with by the `testFormController` bean defined earlier.

The `formView` property used to configure the `testFormController` bean tells the Controller which view should be used to display the form — in this case, the `form` view.

The `TestFormController` class itself extends `SimpleFormController` provided by Spring for the scenario our application fulfills. In `TestFormController` we override one method: `onSubmit`, which is invoked by the framework when no validation errors have been found by the `Validator` class. `onSubmit` receives an `Object` as its only parameter. This is the command object created by the form submission. This method returns a `ModelAndView` object that defines the View we want to render next. It also has the option to provide resources to be used by the view. In this implementation so far, we are using a `ModelAndView` constructor that takes a single parameter, which is the name of the View that we intend to display:

```
...
public class TestFormController extends SimpleFormController
{
    public ModelAndView onSubmit(Object object)
    {
        return new ModelAndView("success");
    }
}
```

Model: TestForm

The Model portion of this application appeared here and there in the previous section; it appeared in two of the parameters with which the testFormController was configured in spring-servlet.xml as commandClass and commandName. It also appeared as the object parameter received by the onSubmit method of TestFormController.

The Command object here represents the data collected in the form. The class TestForm has been developed to represent this information. This Command object is a simple Java bean, with a property for each field in the form and associated setter and getter methods for each:

```
package com.wrox.begjsp.ch18.spring;

public class TestForm
{
    private String _name = "";
    private String _comments = "";

    public String getComments()
    {
        return _comments;
    }

    public void setComments(String comments)
    {
        _comments = comments;
    }

    public String getName()
    {
        return _name;
    }

    public void setName(String name)
    {
        _name = name;
    }
}
```

The naming convention used for each of the methods is very important, as these methods are invoked by the framework when an instance of this class is being formed by a form submission. The rule here is that if the HTML form has an element named foo, then the GET and SET methods that will be invoked on the command object when the framework creates one will be setFoo and getFoo, with exact capitalization.

Note that Spring has not forced the developer to extend any framework class when implementing TestForm. Having such data objects decoupled from the framework itself is a good thing, as we are free to impose our own inheritance structure on this object.

Validator: TestFormValidator

In order to provide for the validation of the input the user enters in the form, a Validator class is implemented. Validator is an interface provided by Spring that enforces the implementation of two methods in our TestFormValidator class: validate and supports. validate() actually performs the validation logic for the TestForm, whereas supports() is used by the framework to determine whether the class being validated is appropriate for this Validator. The source code for the TestFormValidator in the base application is as follows:

```
package com.wrox.begjsp.ch18.spring;

import org.springframework.validation.Errors;
import org.springframework.validation.Validator;


public class TestFormValidator implements Validator
{
    public boolean supports(Class checkMe)
    {
        return checkMe.equals(TestForm.class);
    }

    public void validate(Object object, Errors errors)
    {
        TestForm form = (TestForm) object;

        if (form == null)
        {
            errors.rejectValue("testForm", "form.error.novalue",
                               "Value required.");
        }

        String testName = form.getName();

        if ((testName == null) || (testName.length() < 1))
        {
            errors.rejectValue("name", "form.error.name.missing",
                               "Name is missing.");
        }
    }
}
```

You can see the test on the name property of the TestForm object in the validate method. When a validation rule has been violated, an error is created with the call to errors.rejectValue(..). This method adds a new error to the Errors object provided by Spring. The first parameter is the name of the property in TestForm that has caused the error, the second is the name of the message that should be presented to the user, and the last acts as a backup message if the second parameter cannot be found.

The `TestFormValidator` class is registered with Spring in the `spring-servlet.xml` file discussed earlier, with the following bean definition:

```
<bean id="testFormValidator"
      class="com.wrox.begjsp.ch18.spring.TestFormValidator"/>
```

This bean was assigned to `TestFormController` in its bean definition:

```
...
<bean id="testFormController"
      class="com.wrox.begjsp.ch18.spring.TestFormController">
...
    <property name="validator"><ref bean="testFormValidator"/></property>
</bean>
...
```

Resources: messages.properties

One way in which frameworks support internationalization of their applications is by providing a mechanism to render text on an interface in different languages. This enables the developer to point to a common token or pointer of the text message to be displayed. These text message definitions are defined in a series of properties files within the classpath of the application (`/WEB-INF/classes/`), one for each of the languages supported. In order to register this resource with Spring, the following definition has been added the `spring-servlet.xml` file:

```
<bean id="messageSource"
      class="org.springframework.context.support.ResourceBundleMessageSource">
  <property name="basename"><value>messages</value></property>
</bean>
```

The `basename` property tells Spring the pattern of names for the internationalized message properties files this application will support. In this case, we have defined this as `messages`. Examples of the filenames Spring will use based on this basename for different languages include the following:

❏   `messages.properties` for the default set of messages; ours are in English.

❏   `messages_fr.properties` for messages in the French language.

❏   `messages_de.properties` for messages in the German language.

The `messages` file located in the `/WEB-INF/src` directory of the `spring-base` application contains message entries for all the labels displayed on the form:

```
form.title=Test Form

form.error.heading=Please fix all the errors!
form.error.name.missing=The name field is missing
form.error.novalue=Value required

form.name.title=Name
form.comments.title=Comments
```

The property `form.error.name.missing` was used in the `TestFormValidator` class.

Views: form.jsp and success.jsp

The application presents two views to the user that we have seen referenced in the classes and configuration file mentioned so far, `form` and `success`. In order to define these views to Spring, the `spring-servlet.xml` file contains the following entry:

```
<bean id="viewResolver"
      class="org.springframework.web.servlet.view.ResourceBundleViewResolver">
        <property name="basename"><value>views</value></property>
</bean>
```

The `viewResolver` bean defined here tells Spring that the views for this `DispatcherServlet` are defined in a file called `views[_language code].properties` within the classpath. The `views.properties` file can be found in the `/WEB-INF/classes/` directory.

The `views.properties` file contains two entries for the views discussed:

```
form.class=org.springframework.web.servlet.view.JstlView
form.url=/WEB-INF/jsp/form.jsp

success.class=org.springframework.web.servlet.view.JstlView
success.url=/WEB-INF/jsp/success.jsp
```

These views are JSP pages that will use JSTL tags, and they need the `messages.properties` file's resources exposed by Spring to be available. Therefore, the `JstlView` class has been used to tell Spring what kind of views can be expected from these definitions (`form.class` and `success.class`). The `form.url` and `success.url` properties define the location of the JSP files for these views.

The `form.jsp` file displays the form to the user. It also uses values from the Command object associated with this view `TestForm`. The properties of this object have been associated with the form elements in the HTML form via the Spring series of tags discussed earlier. The source code for the `form.jsp` file is as follows:

```
<%@ taglib prefix="spring" uri="/spring" %>
<%@ taglib prefix="fmt" uri="http://java.sun.com/jsp/jstl/fmt" %>

<html>
<head>
    <title><fmt:message key="form.title"/></title>
</head>
<body>

<h1><fmt:message key="form.title"/></h1>

<center>
<form method="POST">

<table width="350" border="0" cellpadding="3" cellspacing="0">
<spring:hasBindErrors name="testForm">
<tr>
    <td colspan=2><b><fmt:message key="form.error.heading"/></b></td>
</tr>
</spring:hasBindErrors>
```

```
<spring:bind path="testForm.name">
<tr>
    <td colspan=2><font color="red">${status.errorMessage}</font></td>
</tr>
<tr>
    <td><fmt:message key="form.name.title"/></td>
    <td><input type="text" name="name" value="${status.value}" size="30"></td>
</tr>
</spring:bind>
<spring:bind path="testForm.comments">
<tr>
    <td colspan=2><font color="red">${status.errorMessage}</font></td>
</tr>
<tr>

    <td valign="top"><fmt:message key="form.comments.title"/></td>
    <td>
        <textarea name="comments" cols="30" rows="8">${status.value}</textarea>
    </td>
</tr>
</spring:bind>
<tr>
    <td> </td>
    <td align="center"><input type=submit value="submit"></td>
</tr>
</table>
</form>
</center>
</body>
</html>
```

The first two lines of the form.jsp file are directives for the tag libraries this file requires: format, from the JSTL and spring, from the Spring framework.

The spring tags described earlier are used in this file to bind properties from the TestForm object to HTML form elements defined in the page. For instance, the name property of the form appears as follows:

```
<spring:bind path="testForm.name">
<tr>
 <td colspan=2><font color="red">${status.errorMessage}</font></td>
</tr>
<tr>
 <td><fmt:message key="form.name.title"/></td>
 <td><input type="text" name="name" value="${status.value}"
            size="30">
   </td>
</tr>
</spring:bind>
```

The <spring:bind../> tag has brought into scope the name value of the testForm object by using status.value, as well as any validation messages with status.errorMessage. Notice that we are using JSTL tags to output the messages.properties values (<fmt:message../>) and using EL for the values of the `TestForm` object within scope. Using the EL representation as the value of the HTML form element ensures that the field will be filled in with the current value of the object. Therefore, when validation errors occur, the form will be filled in as it was before being submitted. We can see this behavior when we submit the form after entering only a comment. Notice that when the validation error message appears, the content of the Comments field is still populated, as shown in Figure 18-4.

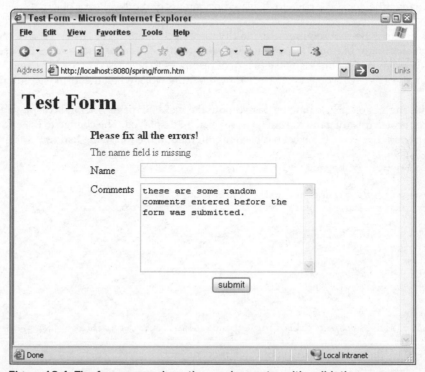

Figure 18-4: The form remembers the previous entry with validation errors.

Enhancements

Now that the base application has been installed and investigated, we can start introducing some enhancements. Much like the WebWork example, the enhancements will be as follows:

1. Show the details entered in the form on the success page that is displayed after the form is successfully submitted.

2. Add a new field to the form and provide some validation for it. Also ensure that the user enters something in the Comments field.

3. Provide for French-speaking visitors to the page.

The list of things required from the Web Work example has been removed and replaced with the capability to display the form and the success pages in another language, illustrating the effects of internationalization.

Try It Out   Displaying Form Details on the Success Page

This enhancement involves two changes to the current application:

1. Change the Controller to pass the resulting `TestForm` object onto the rendered view, `success`.

2. Change the `success` page to display the contents of the `TestForm` object.

In order to achieve the first requirement, modify the `TestFormController` `onSubmit` method to invoke a different constructor of `ModelAndView` as its return value. This constructor takes the expectant view alias (`success`) as before, but also takes a `Map` of resources to be passed to the JSP page. This new `Map` will contain the `TestForm` object constructed by the framework when the form was submitted.

This enables the `TestForm` bean to be passed onto the view JSP page when it is displayed. From there, its new properties, freshly gained from the form, can be displayed. The change to the `onSubmit` method of the `TestFormController` object has been highlighted in the following listing:

```
package com.wrox.begjsp.ch18.spring;

import org.springframework.web.servlet.ModelAndView;
import org.springframework.web.servlet.mvc.SimpleFormController;

import java.util.HashMap;
import java.util.Map;

import javax.servlet.ServletException;
import javax.servlet.http.HttpServletRequest;


public class TestFormController extends SimpleFormController
{
    public ModelAndView onSubmit(Object object)
    {
        TestForm form = (TestForm) object;
        Map items = new HashMap();
        items.put("testForm", form);

        return new ModelAndView("success", items);
    }
}
```

Now that the `TestForm` bean is within the scope of the view JSP page, `success.jsp`, we can modify this page to display the details of the form. The following listing shows the new content of the `success.jsp` file:

```
<%@ taglib prefix="fmt" uri="http://java.sun.com/jsp/jstl/fmt" %>

<html>
<head>
    <title><fmt:message key="success.title"/></title>
</head>
<body>
```

```
<h1><fmt:message key="success.title"/></h1>

<b><fmt:message key="form.name.title"/></b>:${testForm.name}<br>
<b><fmt:message key="form.comments.title"/></b><br>
${testForm.comments}

</body>
</html>
```

You can see that the JSP page can access the properties of the `TestForm` object (`testForm`) via EL. In order for the preceding page to render correctly, we also need to add a new property (`success.title`) to the `messages.properties` file for the page title. Open this file and add the property as per the highlighted addition in the following listing:

```
form.title=Test Form

form.error.heading=Please fix all the errors!
form.error.name.missing=The name field is missing
form.error.novalue=Value required

form.name.title=Name
form.comments.title=Comments

success.title=Success Page
```

You can now save these files and view the effect of the changes you have made. To do this, first ensure that Tomcat is still running and issue the following command via Ant: `ant reload`. This will compile and copy the changed files into the `build` directory and then reload the Tomcat context. If you now browse to the application and successfully submit the form, the contents you entered should appear on the following page.

Try It Out   Adding a New Field and Providing Validation

Adding the Age field in the WebWork example seemed to work pretty well, so we'll do that here, too. We need to make the following changes in order to meet this requirement:

1. Add a new property, `age`, to the `TestForm` class, along with associated `get` and `set` methods.

2. Provide a list of possible ages as reference data to the form view.

3. Change the `form.jsp` page to display the new field, along with possible values.

4. Add validation for the Age and Comments fields to the `TestFormValidator` class.

5. Change the `success.jsp` page to display the age selected when the form is successfully submitted.

Adding the new field to the `TestForm` class is a simple matter. We need to add the new property for age as an `int`, as well as associated GET and SET methods so that the value can be manipulated. Open the `TestForm.java` file and modify the class to look like the following listing (specific changes have been highlighted):

```
package com.wrox.begjsp.ch18.spring;

public class TestForm
{
    private String _name = "";
    private String _comments = "";
    private int _age = 0;

    public String getComments()
    {
        return _comments;
    }

    public void setComments(String comments)
    {
        _comments = comments;
    }

    public String getName()
    {
        return _name;
    }

    public void setName(String name)
    {
        _name = name;
    }

    public int getAge()
    {
        return _age;
    }

    public void setAge(int age)
    {
        _age = age;
    }
}
```

We now need to make a list of `Integer` objects available to the `form.jsp` page. This list will enable the user of the form to select an appropriate age from a select list form element. Data such as this list of numbers is what is called *reference data*. Reference data is not intended to change as part of the normal use of the application. For example, other reference data values might be tax rates in a shopping cart application, or even ZIP codes.

Fortunately, the `SimpleFormController` from Spring that was extended to create the `TestForm Controller` provides a convenient method to be overridden by the subclass that can provide the form view with this new data. We can implement the `referenceData(...)` method in our `TestForm Controller` object so that the framework provides the appropriate reference data to the view layer.

Open the `TestFormController.java` file and add the highlighted code in the following listing:

```java
package com.wrox.begjsp.ch18.spring;

import org.springframework.web.servlet.ModelAndView;
import org.springframework.web.servlet.mvc.SimpleFormController;

import java.util.ArrayList;
import java.util.HashMap;
import java.util.List;
import java.util.Map;

import javax.servlet.ServletException;
import javax.servlet.http.HttpServletRequest;

public class TestFormController extends SimpleFormController
{
    public ModelAndView onSubmit(Object object)
    {
        TestForm form = (TestForm) object;
        Map items = new HashMap();
        items.put("testForm", form);

        return new ModelAndView("success", items);
    }

    protected Map referenceData(HttpServletRequest request)
                        throws ServletException
    {
        Map refData = new HashMap();
        List ages = new ArrayList();

        for (int i = 0; i <= 100; i++)
        {
            ages.add(new Integer(i));
        }

        refData.put("ages", ages);

        return refData;
    }
}
```

The framework calls this method behind the scenes. This means that the Map ages will now be available to the JSP page under the alias ages

Now that the `TestForm` has been changed to support the new form value, and a list of appropriate select options has been provided to the view, we can set about modifying the JSP page to reflect this new functionality. Open the `form.jsp` file and add the following highlighted code:

```
<%@ taglib prefix="spring" uri="/spring" %>
<%@ taglib prefix="fmt" uri="http://java.sun.com/jsp/jstl/fmt" %>
<%@ taglib prefix="c" uri="http://java.sun.com/jsp/jstl/core" %>
...
<tr>
    <td><fmt:message key="form.name.title"/></td>
    <td><input type="text" name="name" value="${status.value}" size="30"></td>
</tr>
</spring:bind>
<spring:bind path="testForm.age">
<tr>
    <td colspan=2><font color="red">${status.errorMessage}</font></td>
</tr>
<tr>
    <td><fmt:message key="form.age.title"/></td>
    <td>
    <select name="age">
    <c:forEach var="age" items="${ages}">
        <c:if test="${status.value eq age}">
            <option value="${age}" selected>${age}</option>
        </c:if>
        <c:if test="${status.value ne age}">
            <option value="${age}">${age}</option>
        </c:if>
    </c:forEach>
    </select>
    </td>
</tr>
</spring:bind>
<spring:bind path="testForm.comments">
<tr>
...
```

The `<c:forEach../>` tag has been used to iterate over the `ages` Map provided by the `TestForm`
`Controller`. The `<c:if../>` tags allow the appropriate value to be selected on the form if validation
errors arise when the form is submitted. A new message property has also been added (`form.age.title`)
to show the name of the new field to the user. You should open the `messages.properties` file and add
this new message, as per the following listing:

```
form.title=Test Form

form.error.heading=Please fix all the errors!
form.error.name.missing-The name field is missing
form.error.novalue=Value required

form.name.title=Name
form.comments.title=Comments
form.age.title=Age

success.title=Success Page
```

Now that the new form element has been added, we can modify the success.jsp page so that the age value can be displayed to the user when the form is successfully submitted. Open the success.jsp page and modify it to match the following listing (changes are in bold):

```
<%@ taglib prefix="fmt" uri="http://java.sun.com/jsp/jstl/fmt" %>

<html>
<head>
    <title><fmt:message key="success.title"/></title>
</head>
<body>

<h1><fmt:message key="success.title"/></h1>

<b><fmt:message key="form.name.title"/></b>:${testForm.name}<br>
<b><fmt:message key="form.age.title"/></b>:${testForm.age}<br>
<b><fmt:message key="form.comments.title"/></b><br>
${testForm.comments}

</body>
</html>
```

Before the user gets to this page, however, we have to ensure that valid values for the Age and Comments fields have been entered. A small change is required in the TestFormValidator class. Open the TestFormValidator.java file and make the following changes, shown in bold, to the validate method:

```
...
public void validate(Object object, Errors errors)
{
    TestForm form = (TestForm) object;

    if (form == null)
    {
        errors.rejectValue("testForm", "form.error.novalue",
                           "Value required.");
    }

    String testName = form.getName();
    String testComments = form.getComments();
    int testAge = form.getAge();

    if ((testName == null) || (testName.length() < 1))
    {
        errors.rejectValue("name", "form.error.name.missing",
                           "Name is missing.");
    }

    if ((testComments == null) || (testComments.length() < 1))
    {
        errors.rejectValue("comments", "form.error.comments.missing",
                "Comments is missing.");
    }
```

```
        if (testAge < 18)
        {
            errors.rejectValue("age", "form.error.age.value",
                              "Age cannot be less than 18.");
        }
    }
    ...
```

The validation change ensures that the user cannot select a value less than 18 for the Age field and that the Comments field cannot be left empty. You can also see that various messages have been referenced when the errors are passed to the `errors` object. These and other new properties need to be added to the `messages.properties` file. Open the `messages.properties` file and add the following values, shown in bold:

```
form.title=Test Form

form.error.heading=Please fix all the errors!
form.error.name.missing=The name field is missing
form.error.comments.missing=The comments field is missing
form.error.age.value=Age cannot be less than 18
form.error.novalue=Value required

form.name.title=Name
form.comments.title=Comments
form.age.title=Age

success.title=Success Page
```

All that is left to do now is display the new property in the `success.jsp` page when the user successfully submits the form.

Once these changes have been saved, with Tomcat still running, execute the following command in Ant: `ant reload`.

The result of this enhancement is a new form element with appropriate validation, with the submitted value appearing on the `success` view once the form has been successfully submitted.

How It Works

This section added a new field to the form interface and added validation to the Comments field. This involved some simple adjustments to various components. First, the `TestForm` object was modified to include the new property representing the age of the user. Associated `get` and `set` methods ensure that the framework can modify this value when the form is submitted.

We then modified the `TestFormController` so that a list of potential ages was passed to the JSP view. This allowed the new select list on that page to provide various (make it 100) options to the user. This data was provided by the `referenceData(...)` method used by the framework. If additional reference data were required, another addition to this method would be required.

With the reference data and new property of the `TestForm` object, we set about modifying the `form.jsp` page so that the HTML form could display the new field with the appropriate data. This involved using the `spring:bind` tag to inform the framework that the form element being defined should in fact be mapped to the `TestForm` object. With the object now recording this response from the user, we were also able to present the new value when the form was successfully submitted. This involved simply referencing the `age` property in the `success.jsp` page.

To fulfill the validation requirements required here, we made a simple addition to the `TestFormValidator` object to ensure that the `comments` and `age` properties contained valid values. When invalid values were detected, errors were created via the `Errors` object provided by the framework. The framework knows to redisplay the form page when this `Errors` object contains values. The parameters of the `rejectValue` method identified the field that was in error and provided a key to the message to be displayed to the user.

The messages for errors and the new field were then added to the `messages.properties` file. The result of these changes is a far more intelligent form that can validate the values of all the fields accordingly. Figure 18-5 shows the form after it was submitted with empty values.

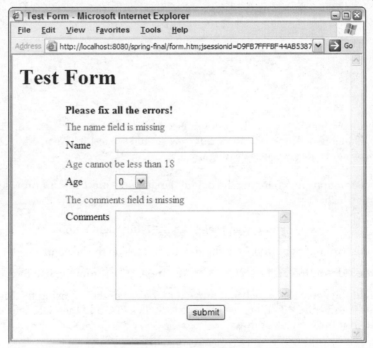

Figure 18-5: Test form with a new Age field and full validation

The final requirement is to present the form and result page in another language. For no particular reason whatsoever, French was chosen, and with a little help from one of the language translation tools available on the Internet, this requirement is easily achieved. We apologize in advance to any French-speaking readers.

The application so far has strictly adhered to using the `messages.properties` file for all form labels and messages for the user's interaction with the form. This is a real advantage. In order for the form to be presented in another language, a new `messages_fr.properties` file is created with entries in French. Create this new file in the `c:/spring-base/src` directory, alongside the existing `messages.properties` file, with the following content:

```
form.title=Examinez La Forme

form.error.heading=Veuillez fixer toutes les erreurs!
form.error.name.missing=La zone d'identification est absente
form.error.comments.missing=Le champ de commentaires est absent
form.error.age.value=Le champ d'âge ne peut pas être moins de 18
form.error.novalue=La valeur a exigé

form.name.title=Nom
form.comments.title=Commentaires
form.age.title=Âge

success.title=Page De Succès
```

Once this has been changed, execute the following command in Ant: `ant reload`. The new language should now be available on the application, but how should we test it? We need to change the default language our browser requests when visiting the site.

The following instructions for changing the default language request of your browser apply to Microsoft Internet Explorer 6.0.28:

1. Open a new browser window and select Tools ➪ Internet Options.

2. Select the Languages button from the row of buttons on the bottom.

3. Click the Add button and select `French (France) [fr]` from the list; then click OK.

4. Highlight the entry for French and move it to the top of the list using the Move Up button on the right-hand side. When French is at the top, click OK, and then OK again. You should now be back at your browser's window.

Once you have followed these steps, browse to the `spring-base` application. You should be presented with the form with the French language entries in all the appropriate places. If you attempt to submit the blank form, the validation messages should also be in French, as shown in Figure 18-6.

You can see how easy and effective this simple technique is. If you have finished testing, make sure you change the default language on your browser back to its previous settings by retracing the same steps.

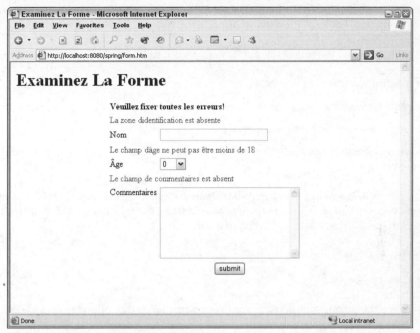

Figure 18-6: Form displayed in French

This is the end of our Spring framework example. Of course, we have only scratched the surface of this powerful framework, but a more in-depth discussion is beyond the scope and depth of this chapter. If you are interested in learning more about Spring, you are encouraged to visit their Web site at www .springframework.org/ and join their growing mailing list.

Summary

This chapter has introduced you to Web frameworks. Web frameworks form a particularly important part of Web application development, as demonstrated by the recent explosion of framework solutions available to the developer. The large number of available MVC frameworks has sometimes made implementation decisions difficult. Developers facing challenging decisions about how to architect and develop Web sites need to consider several factors before choosing an appropriate Web framework to use, including the following:

❑ Does the development team have the skills needed to manage and develop with the chosen framework?

❑ Will using the framework now make replacing it with other frameworks later on more difficult?

❑ Is the framework widely recognized and used by other developers?

❑ Will the framework enable the application to scale accordingly?

This chapter cannot answer these questions, but we hope that it has provided you with sufficient information to understand the place these questions hold in Web application development.

This chapter has covered the following points with regard to Web frameworks:

❑ The definition of a framework

❑ Why using frameworks is generally considered good practice

❑ An overview of the different types of frameworks that are available

❑ Working explanations and examples of two popular frameworks available today: WebWork and Spring

The next chapter will introduce another Web framework called Struts. Struts is one of the most popular frameworks available today. After the chapter about Struts, the following chapter introduces Tiles, a templating framework that has now become part of Struts.

Exercises

1. Enhance the Spring simple form application further in the following ways:

❑ When the form is submitted, add the `TestForm` object to a `List` of `TestForm`'s in the session.

❑ Add a new Controller and View to display the contents of the `List` of `TestForm` objects.

Struts Framework

This chapter builds on the experience you gained in Chapter 18, "Web Frameworks," by looking at a framework that has become very popular in the J2EE development community. Apache Struts gained prominence in the J2EE community through its evolution as a Jakarta Project, and as of early 2004 has become an official Apache Project.

This chapter will introduce Struts to you by first outlining how it fulfills the MVC Model 2 architecture for applications. As this is a JSP book, we will then look at some of the custom tags that come with the framework.

Finally, this chapter will show you how to develop a small application along the same lines as those in Chapter 18. Like any rapidly maturing technology, various methods become available to solve common problems such as validation and form bean implementation. This chapter covers these variances where space permits.

Following are the main topics of this chapter:

❑ A brief walk through the Struts framework.

❑ An explanation of Struts Actions, Forms and View components

❑ An example application using Struts

Introducing Struts

Apache Struts assists application developers in implementing an MVC Model 2 architecture in their J2EE applications. It provides them with a Controller-centric infrastructure that offers the usual lineup of MVC framework features:

❑ Internationalization

❑ Various validation techniques

❑ Flexibility to interact with the model layer

❑ Templating (Tiles)

❑ Configuration infrastructure for everything from the Controller to database connections

❑ JSP custom tags to integrate with the framework

❑ Application flow control

❑ Resource bundles

What differentiates Struts from the gamut of other MVC frameworks available today are the following important factors:

❑ A large volume of documentation available both on the Internet and in printed publications.

❑ An extremely active community. An indication of this is the amount of activity on the Struts User and Developer mailing lists.

❑ Simple, easy-to-use (and understand) components.

❑ Its frequent use in real-world application implementations. Struts is now a common item on many J2EE developers' resumes.

The popularity of Struts seems self-perpetuating; the more popular it gets, the more popular it gets, and so on. This is not to say that Struts doesn't have its drawbacks; many developers have run into weaknesses and problems with the Struts implementation. These are sometimes addressed specifically in other frameworks.

This chapter uses Struts 1.2.4, the latest production release at the time of writing. You can download Struts from `http://struts.apache.org`.

The example application discussed at the end of this chapter utilizes a basic starting point that can be downloaded from the Web site for this book. This download includes the necessary files to get this application running, but it does not include the entire Struts installation.

A Struts walkthrough

After reading Chapter 18, the general plan of attack used by Struts will be somewhat familiar to you.

In simple terms, a single servlet is configured (referred to as the Struts servlet) in the container. This servlet is configured for a certain pattern of URL that the application receives in a request from a browser. This Struts servlet is defined in the web.xml file in the same way that other servlets of an application are defined.

The Struts servlet is further configured via a Struts configuration file to pass control to an action. An *action* represents some business functionality that the application undertakes in response to the request from the user. Actions are implemented by the developer to respond to the request of the user and usually determine the appropriate View (usually a JSP page) or further action that will be invoked to fulfill the business purpose.

Actions can receive input from the request in a structured format. Think of a form that is filled out on a Web page and then submitted. A single object (usually created by the application developer) represents the different properties of the submitted form. Each property of the HTML form is associated with a property of this object. Struts handles the binding of the elements in the HTML form with the properties in the object.

Depending on the logic implemented in the receiving action, a view may be displayed to complete the response back to the client. This view may be provided by the action with resources to assist in display, such as data. The view, in turn, makes use of the many available Struts custom tags that provide for the following:

- ❑ Logic such as iteration and conditional processing.

- ❑ HTML elements such as forms. HTML custom tags are used by Struts to bind form elements with properties of the aforementioned Form objects. Other HTML elements are also catered to, such as images and links.

- ❑ Bean processing.

The view is then presented to the user as a result of all the processing that has occurred, providing the response.

Validation can be invoked at different stages of the preceding process, configurable by the developer. One strength of Struts is the various methods it provides to fulfill the validation requirements of the application.

The diagram shown in Figure 19-1 offers a simplistic representation of this chain of events.

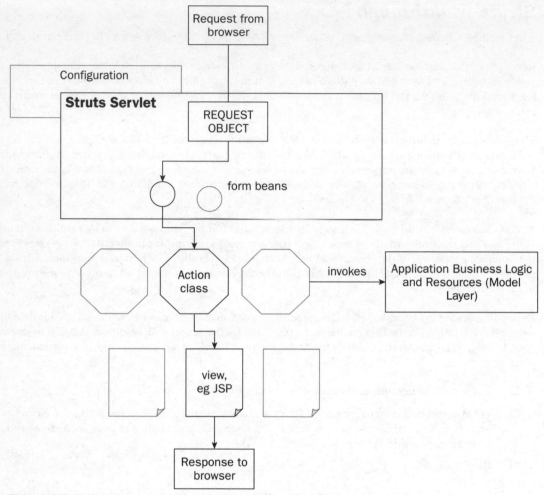

Figure 19-1: Tracing a request through an application using Struts

The Struts components are configured in a specific Struts configuration file called `struts-config.xml` located alongside the `web.xml` file in the `WEB-INF` directory of the Web application. You can refer to this diagram as you continue through the chapter. It will help you to develop an understanding of how the different pieces fit together.

Controller: actions and forms

The Struts servlet is the basis of the Controller component of the MVC framework provided by Struts. The Struts servlet is actually an `ActionServlet` class provided by Struts that is configured for the application by the developer when the application is set up. The `ActionServlet` is defined in the `web.xml` file located in the `WEB-INF` directory of the application. The following code illustrates such an entry:

```
...
  <servlet>
    <servlet-name>action</servlet-name>
    <servlet-class>org.apache.struts.action.ActionServlet</servlet-class>
    <init-param>
      <param-name>config</param-name>
      <param-value>/WEB-INF/struts-config.xml</param-value>
    </init-param>
    <load-on-startup>1</load-on-startup>
  </servlet>
...
  <servlet-mapping>
    <servlet-name>action</servlet-name>
    <url-pattern>*.do</url-pattern>
  </servlet-mapping>
...
```

In this example, you can see that the `<servlet-mapping>` entry has provided a URL pattern to associate with the `action` servlet. When a request is received that matches this URL pattern, the `Action Servlet` is put to work performing or delegating much of the setup work required for the application to function correctly. In the preceding example, the `action` servlet is configured to respond to requests that match the pattern: `*.do`; therefore, the following URL will invoke the `ActionServlet` configured in this way:

```
http://localhost:8080/yourapplication/login.do
```

When this URL is received, `ActionServlet` will initiate the following series of steps:

1. Establish some basic information, such as the path that has been invoked, the content type, and other request-specific information such as cache settings.

2. Determine any mappings to actions (`ActionMapping`) that are associated with the request that has been received. For instance, our previous example requested a resource called `login`. This is an alias to an `ActionMapping` that has been defined for this `ActionServlet` to recognize.

3. Create, populate, and validate any `ActionForm` objects that have been associated with the `ActionMapping`, according to the Struts configuration.

4. If necessary, forward the request to a resource if this has been configured.

5. Invoke the Action class created by the application developer. The specific functionality defined by the developer is executed here.

The following section describes actions in more detail.

Actions

Actions form the application-specific tasks that the application performs in response to requests. Action classes are developed by the application developer. Typically, an action will be created for tasks that represent some piece of work the application must undertake in response to the request. For instance, when the user clicks a link on a Web page to log in, pointing to `login.do`, a `LoginAction` class will be invoked. When the user uses some sort of search facility in an application, a `DoSearchAction` class may be used, and so on. How does the framework know which class to use? The answer lies in the ActionMappings we define in the Struts configuration. Each action is defined within a list of action mappings. An *action mapping* is a definition of an action within the application. Each configured action can have certain properties that are defined with the action element of the struts-config.xml file.

The following listing shows the definition for our LoginAction in the struts-config.xml file:

```
<struts-config>
...
<action-mappings>
    <action path="/login"
        type="com.wrox.begjsp.ch19.struts.LoginAction"
        name="loginForm"
        input="/login.jsp"
        scope="request">
        <forward name="success" path="/welcome.jsp"/>
    </action>
...
</action-mappings>
...
</struts-config>
```

The order of the items added to the struts-config.xml *file is very important. Placing form beans, action mappings, and other elements in this file in an incorrect order can result in some strange errors. The order of items must be as follows:*

1.   *data sources*

2.   *form beans*

3.   *global forwards*

4.   *action mappings*

5   *controller*

6.   *message resources*

7.   *plug-in*

Nested within the Action mapping is a forward element that defines a possible result of the action. This forward is named success and will be used in the action when determining which page to display next.

The key parameters to the action definition are as follows:

❑   **path:** The relative path to the action, in the context of the application; therefore, the previous action would be invoked with the following: http://localhost:8080/yourapplication/login.do.

❑   **type:** The package and class name of the action class created for this action.

❑   **name:** The mapping name of the form bean used for this action.

❑   **validate:** Whether validation is to be invoked when this action is requested.

❑ **input:** The action mapping or JSP file that provided input for this action.

❑ **scope:** The scope of this action, i.e., request or session scope.

❑ **forward:** The path to the JSP file or action that this action should forward to after processing has completed.

Action mappings can be simple, as illustrated previously, or very sophisticated, to cater to the wide variety of possible scenarios that developers may need when defining the workflow of the application and its interaction with the user.

These actions developed for an application are subclasses of a class provided by Struts that forms the basis of all actions in the framework. This class is called Action (not surprisingly).

When a developer creates an action for an application, this new class extends the Action class provided by Struts and must implement a specific method for the framework to execute. The signature of this method is listed here:

```
...
    public ActionForward execute(ActionMapping mapping, ActionForm form,
        HttpServletRequest request, HttpServletResponse response)
        throws Exception
...
```

The execute method receives the following parameters:

❑ **ActionMapping:** This represents the mapping configuration that led to this request finding its way to this Action class.

❑ **ActionForm:** This represents a form bean that may have been configured to be received by this Action.

❑ **HttpServletRequest:** This is an important native J2EE object that represents the HTTP request received by the application.

❑ **HttpServletResponse:** This is another important native J2EE object that represents the response to the client when all processing has been completed.

Within the execute method, the developer performs the logic required for this particular action. The execute method then returns an ActionForward object. An ActionForward object represents another resource configured in Struts. This usually points to a JSP file or even another Action class. For instance, in a login scenario, there may be one ActionForward returned if the login was successful, and another if not. The following code snippet shows a LoginAction class that might fulfill this scenario:

```
package com.wrox.begjsp.ch19.struts.simpleform;

import org.apache.struts.action.Action;

import org.apache.struts.action.ActionForm;
import org.apache.struts.action.ActionForward;
import org.apache.struts.action.ActionMapping;
import org.apache.struts.action.ActionMessage;
import org.apache.struts.action.ActionMessages;
```

```
import javax.servlet.http.HttpServletRequest;
import javax.servlet.http.HttpServletResponse;


public class LoginAction extends Action
{
    public ActionForward execute(ActionMapping mapping, ActionForm form,
        HttpServletRequest request, HttpServletResponse response)
        throws Exception
    {
        ActionMessages errors = new ActionMessages();
        LoginForm loginForm = (LoginForm) form;
        String userName = (String) loginForm.getUsername();
        String password = (String) loginForm.getPassword();

        ActionForward returnForward = null;

        if ("admin".equals(userName) && "opensesame".equals(password))
        {
            returnForward = mapping.findForward("success");
        }
        else
        {
            returnForward = mapping.getInputForward();
            errors.add(ActionMessages.GLOBAL_MESSAGE,
                new ActionMessage("error.login.invalid"));
        }

        if (!errors.isEmpty())
        {
            saveErrors(request, errors);
        }

        return returnForward;
    }
}
```

You can see in this simple example that we are conditionally returning one of two possible Action
Forward objects based on the success of the login (highlighted in the code example). The success
String points to an ActionForward configured by the developer in the Struts configuration file
(remember that this action was defined in the struts-config.xml file). The unsuccessful Action
Forward is found by making a call to the ActionMapping object that this method received. This is
an ActionForward configured as the input for this particular action.

It is important to note that the ActionForwards used represent other resources configured for the application. In the preceding scenario, the success forward would point to a JSP file (using the configuration
file action mapping entry illustrated, this JSP file would be welcome.jsp) or another action, and could
be the first screen the user sees after login.

The forward used in this example is available only to the login action. There are also other types
of forwards called *global forwards* that are available from all actions. A typical example of one of these
is a global forward pointing to an error.jsp page. Here is the struts-config.xml mapping for
this entry:

```
<global-forwards>
    <forward name="error" path="/error.jsp"/>
</global-forwards>
```

This new error global forward can now be referenced from all actions in the application. Naming these forwards and not just using the resource name directly is an important feature of many Web frameworks. The benefit is immediately apparent if you have ever had to change the name of a JSP page in a large application where such abstractions are not used. For example, if error.jsp were to change its name to, say, errorPage.jsp, only a single change would be required.

Getting back to the preceding action example, notice that there is also some validation added. When the login is not successful, an ActionMessage is added to an ActionMessages object called errors, instantiated at the beginning of the method. ActionMessages is simply a collection of messages that are appropriate to the results of this action. When the next resource is displayed, the ActionMessage objects provided for it can be displayed appropriately. The message to be displayed is a message resource (error.login.invalid); it would be defined in a messages.properties file. Notice in the action that the ActionMessages object is saved with a call to the saveErrors method provided by Struts. There is a similar method called saveMessages, where normal information messages can be saved. These methods modify a list of messages maintained by Struts that can be displayed in the view. You will see examples of this when Struts tags are explained later on.

Other data that is not represented in the form object can also be placed within the request scope of the JSP page referred to by this action. Providing the JSP file access to this data is simply a matter of adding an object to the HttpServletRequest object using the setAttribute method. For instance, within the LoginAction, a String object can be passed to the JSP page in the request scope using the following syntax:

```
String exampleObject = new String("this is my String");
request.setAttribute("testObject", exampleObject);
```

This object could then be accessed inside the JSP page as a bean via the alias it has been given, testObject. Similarly, the object could also be added to the session scope using the following:

```
HttpSession session = request.getSession();
session.setAttribute("user", user);
```

Note how Action classes enable the developer to trigger and implement business and control logic, away from the view layer of the application. Decisions about what should happen next, which data should be available, and whether the user has access to the application at all can all be made at this level.

Forms

HTML forms in an application can be represented by *form beans*. Form beans are classes implemented or defined by the developer to represent the particular forms in the application. All such beans extend a Struts-provided class such as ActionForm, ValidatorForm, or ValidatorActionForm, among others.

Form beans are typically a simple class with a number of properties, with each property being accessed via a *getter* and *setter* method. Each property represents an element of the HTML form. For instance, to continue our login example from before, a LoginForm class was used to represent the input from users when they logged in.

The HTML form submitted contained a username field and a password field. These fields would be represented by equivalent properties in the `LoginForm` object. The translation between the HTML form and the `LoginForm` object is handled by Struts. Struts matches the field names used in the HTML form with the setter and getter methods for their equivalent properties used in the form bean class that has been implemented.

The result of this translation is illustrated by the preceding code sample of the `LoginAction`. The `execute` method received an `ActionForm` object as one of its parameters, and this was simply cast to a `LoginForm` object. Getter and setter methods of this object were then used to obtain the content the user entered when the HTML form was submitted. The diagram in Figure 19-2 illustrates this transition for you.

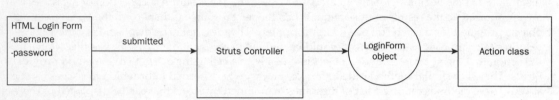

Figure 19-2: Transition from an HTML form to a Struts form object

The correct object (`LoginForm`) was instantiated by the Struts framework because of the particular configuration settings established for that action.

Like actions, form beans developed for the application must also be configured in the `struts-config.xml` file. An entry for the form bean illustrated here would look like the following:

```
<struts-config>
...
<form-beans>
    <form-bean name="loginForm"
                type="com.wrox.begjsp.ch19.struts.LoginForm"/>
...
</form-beans>
...
</struts-config>
```

Note that the name given to this form bean is `loginForm`, which (not coincidentally) maps to the `name` attribute configured for the `login` action defined earlier.

Notice, in an architectural sense, the place that form beans take in an application. It is better to think of them as simply a vehicle to move data input from the HTML form to the brains of your application. They do not represent business objects of your application, and hence they do not fit in the Model layer; they are simply a convenient Controller layer data vehicle.

Certain JavaBean conventions must be adhered to in order for `ActionForm` subclasses to work consistently with a Struts application. When a tag or some part of a configuration file references a property of a form bean, it will use a name such as `username`. The framework then relies on this exact case-sensitive spelling to access this property via a setter method named `setUsername` and a getter method called getUsername. The internal name of the property is not important, only that the reference and associated getter and setter methods are synchronized with this pattern in mind. The framework relies on this convention throughout.

Our LoginForm object would appear as follows:

```
package com.wrox.begjsp.ch19.struts.simpleform;

import org.apache.struts.action.ActionErrors;
import org.apache.struts.action.ActionForm;
import org.apache.struts.action.ActionMapping;
import org.apache.struts.action.ActionMessage;

import javax.servlet.http.HttpServletRequest;


public class LoginForm extends ActionForm
{
    private String _username;
    private String _password;

    public LoginForm()
    {
    }

    public String getPassword()
    {
        return _password;
    }

    public void setPassword(String password)
    {
        _password = password;
    }

    public String getUsername()
    {
        return _username;
    }

    public void setUsername(String username)
    {
        _username = username;
    }
]
```

Extending ActionForm allows the Struts framework to utilize the LoginForm class appropriately. Contrast this with the Command objects implemented in the Spring framework in Chapter 18. Command objects in Spring do not have to extend any framework class in order to function correctly. This has been a criticism of Struts. It is, however, a small price to pay, and in retrospect, probably forces the developer to structure the application in a more adept fashion. Forcing the extension of the ActionForm class (or ValidatorForm or ValidatorActionForm) encourages developers to define their own classes to represent business objects in the application, and leaves the form beans as merely transports for data from the HTML form to the form bean, and no more.

Besides being a convenient representation of the data entered into an HTML form, ActionForm subclasses can also be extended to perform simple validation. You will see an example of this in the "Validation" section of this chapter.

DynaActionForm

Implementing form beans with a concrete class for every form in an application, as just described, could become quite cumbersome. Struts has provided a way to represent these structures for the application at runtime by using definitions entered in the Struts configuration file. This is convenient when the classes you would otherwise implement are only providing getter and setter methods for your form properties.

If the LoginForm discussed previously were to be implemented as a DynaActionForm, the appropriate entry in the struts-config.xml file for this instance would be as follows:

```
<form-bean name="loginForm"
           type="org.apache.struts.validator.DynaActionForm">
  <form-property name="username" type="java.lang.String"/>
  <form-property name="password" type="java.lang.String"/>
</form-bean>
```

The form bean definition here has two major differences from the form bean definition for the custom-made ActionForm class LoginForm. First, note that the type property now points to a Struts class DynaActionForm, and not LoginForm. Second, note the specification of two form properties listed within the form bean definition. These properties correspond to the elements of the HTML form this form bean represents. Note also in the property definitions that the type of the property has been specified (java.lang.String). DynaActionForms support a range of different types in the type attribute for properties, such as Boolean, Integer, Double, Long, Short, Byte, Character, java.util.Date, and java.sql.Timestamp, among others. You can also place primitive types in this field, such as int, double, long, short, and boolean.

This definition of type is very convenient for retrieving values from the object when the form it represents is submitted. Typically in Web applications, all values from the HTTP request are provided as a string, and the developer must provide the appropriate translation into the correct type; here, Struts has done the hard work. This is obviously also an advantage when using form beans normally.

Another difference that occurs when using DynaActionForms in an application is the technique for accessing form properties within the action class that receives the form bean. In the LoginAction example illustrated earlier, the properties of the LoginForm class were accessed like normal Java object method calls:

```
    ...
    public class LoginAction extends Action
    {
        public ActionForward execute(ActionMapping mapping, ActionForm form,
            HttpServletRequest request, HttpServletResponse response)
            throws Exception
        {
            ActionMessages errors = new ActionMessages();
```

```
            LoginForm loginForm = (LoginForm) form;
            String userName = loginForm.getUsername();
            String password = loginForm.getPassword();
    ...
```

When a `DynaActionForm` is used, the properties entered must be accessed via a common `get(String)` method. This method call retrieves an `Object` from an internal collection of the values defined for this form. The preceding example would be rewritten with a `DynaActionForm` as follows:

```
    ...
    public class DynaLoginAction extends Action
    {
        public ActionForward execute(ActionMapping mapping, ActionForm form,
            HttpServletRequest request, HttpServletResponse response)
            throws Exception
        {
            ActionMessages errors = new ActionMessages();
            DynaActionForm loginForm = (DynaActionForm) form;
            String userName = (String) loginForm.get("username");
            String password = (String) loginForm.get("password");
    ...
```

You can see there is not much of a change. The internal collection of properties retained by the `DynaActionForm` enables the retrieval of property values via a key, the name designated for that property in the `struts-config.xml` file discussed earlier.

Model

The Model layer of an application should be notionally separated from the Controller and View aspects of a Struts application. As you learned in Chapter 18, "Web Frameworks," the Model layer of an application is deliberately unaware of any of the Controller or View components that are implemented. This provides for a simpler design with fewer couplings (dependencies) between different layers.

The View and Controller layers utilize certain resources and logic provided by the Model layer of an application via whatever accessibility has been deemed appropriate. For instance, various Model layer services (objects) may provide for the retrieval of data from a database. They will return Model layer representations of the data (as objects) to the Controller and View layers; however, these layers will be completely unaware of how they were retrieved or even where they came from.

Once a Model layer object — for instance, a `Customer` object — has found its way to the Controller and View layers of the application, it may be accessed, manipulated, and displayed as the application sees fit. The business decisions concerning the `Customer` object, however, are left in the hands of the Model layer.

The Model layer represents the business state and business activities of the system, and as such it is decoupled from the View and Controller layers. Smaller, simple applications may integrate Model layer functions within action classes, but generally it is safer to encourage a decoupled Model layer and leave the Controller and View layers to interpret what the Model layer provides.

Struts provides a flexible infrastructure that leaves the implementation of the Model layer as a separate concern.

View

JSP pages form the basis of the View layer discussed in this section. Struts provides the developer with a rich set of tools to develop the View layer of an application:

❑ Form bean interaction

❑ Internationalization

❑ Struts Tag Library

❑ Validation

Form bean interaction

A Struts application requires some degree of structured communication between the View layer (JSP files, etc.) and the Controller layer (actions and form beans). An HTML form designed to interact with a form bean configured in a Struts application must use the `html` series of custom tags provided by Struts. These tags enable Struts to transform the properties defined in form beans as values of the HTML form defined in the View layer, and vice versa.

Struts provides a collection of tags designed to provide this interaction. For instance, when creating a new form in a JSP page (such as `login.jsp` from the login example being used) using Struts, the `html:form` tag would be used:

```
<html:form action="/login" method="POST">
...
</html:form>
```

Note that the value assigned to the `action` attribute is the name of the action defined for our `LoginAction` in the `struts-config.xml` file.

Struts uses the `property` attribute of HTML form tags to identify the property of the form bean to retrieve and populate where appropriate. Without Struts doing this interaction for us, as well as validation that will be explained later, JSP pages would become quite complicated.

The form elements of a page are therefore displayed using a series of HTML tags provided by Struts. The elements of the login form discussed in this chapter would be defined within `login.jsp` as follows:

```
<html:text property="username"/>
<html:password property="password"/>
```

Note that the `property` attribute corresponds directly to the name of the setter and getter methods defined in the `LoginForm` bean. When these form elements are populated, the values contained in those properties of the form bean will be displayed. Without Struts, these form elements might appear as follows:

```
<input type="text" name="username" value="<%=loginForm.getUsername()%>">
<input type="password" name="password" value="<%=loginForm.getPassword()%>">
```

Of course, when these form elements are provided to the user's browser in the response they are rendered as standard HTML; there is no Struts magic occurring over there.

On the return trip, when the form is submitted, the names of the properties in the form are used to repopulate the form bean defined for the action, and so on. In the case illustrated here, the form is submitting to the action /login.do. This action has been defined as using a form bean, loginForm. Therefore, when the action is invoked, it will attempt to create a new LoginForm object with the appropriate properties contained in the request, such as username=admin and password=opensalami.

If you remember the code defined earlier for the LoginAction, the properties used in the form were tested to determine whether a successful login occurred. If you look at the code, you can see the password opensalami is incorrect:

```
...
public ActionForward execute(ActionMapping mapping, ActionForm form,
    HttpServletRequest request, HttpServletResponse response)
    throws Exception
{
    ActionMessages errors = new ActionMessages();
    LoginForm loginForm = (LoginForm) form;
    String userName = loginForm.getUsername();
    String password = loginForm.getPassword();

    ActionForward returnForward = null;

    if ("admin".equals(userName) && "opensesame".equals(password))
    {
        returnForward = mapping.findForward("success");
    }
    else
    {
        returnForward = mapping.getInputForward();
        errors.add(ActionMessages.GLOBAL_MESSAGE,
            new ActionMessage("error.login.invalid"));
    }

    if (!errors.isEmpty())
    {
        saveErrors(request, errors);
    }

    return returnForward;
}
...
```

Where the password is incorrect, the ActionForward to be displayed next is in fact the input attribute for this action — in this case, the JSP page that has just been submitted, login.jsp. This means that the login form will be redisplayed to the user.

Upon the second loading of this page, the LoginForm object has the values that were typed in by the user originally, before the form was submitted. The HTML form defined for this page knows to populate itself with values for this form bean. It will also display any errors that have been saved as a result of the action being executed. In the preceding case, a new ActionMessage was added to an ActionMessages collection. The error defined to display is shown as error.login.invalid. This key points to a value in the messages.properties file associated with this application. This ActionMessages collection can be displayed, as errors, on the JSP page using a Struts tag designed specifically for this purpose: html:errors.

If this description of events seems complicated, the diagram in Figure 19-3 may help.

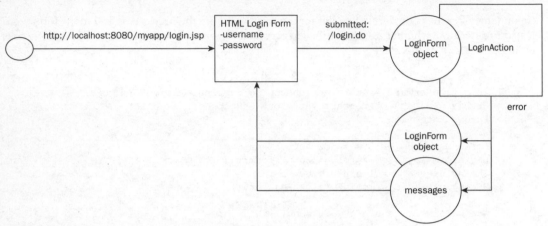

Figure 19-3: Login form submission and return via the LoginAction

This section has provided a brief introduction to the interaction between the form beans defined for an application and the HTML forms they represent. You will examine a more complete example later in the chapter.

Internationalization

Like many Web application frameworks, Struts provides for the internationalization of messages within an application. By configuring the application to be aware of message resource files, the application is able to request the value of messages to be displayed in a language appropriate for the user viewing the site, based on their browser settings. You saw an example of this in the previous chapter, where a simple form interface was displayed in French (probably bad French, but you get the idea!).

Besides the internationalization benefits this system provides, storing common labels, error messages, and so on in central file(s) is convenient should these messages ever need to be changed. For instance, in the action described earlier, an error message was sent to the JSP page via a Struts ActionMessage object:

```
errors.add(ActionMessages.GLOBAL_MESSAGE,

          new ActionMessage("error.login.invalid"));
```

The key used in this example is error.login.invalid, which corresponds to an entry in a properties file defined for the application as follows:

```
error.login.invalid=Login invalid
```

When this `ActionMessage` is displayed on the JSP page, the text `Login invalid` is displayed. If we were to simply pass the text `Login invalid` as a string in the action instead of referencing the messages resource, and a change was required for this message, the class would have to be changed and then recompiled. The class would then have to be redeployed to the live environment. In a large, important application, the downtime associated with this interruption may be unacceptable.

Messages for internationalization are stored in properties files that are located in the classpath, much like the class files of the application. The framework is then configured to know where these resources are located via an entry in the `struts-config.xml` file:

```
<struts-config>
...
<message-resources  parameter="messages"/>
...
</struts-config>
```

This would tell the framework that the properties resource (`messages.properties`) is located at the root of the classpath (the default package). The parameter value could also be `com.wrox.begjsp.ch19.Messages`, which would denote the file's location within that package. Other properties files could be added for the various languages the application should support, using a standard file-naming structure that indicates the language for which the file is responsible. Some examples might be `messages_fr.properties` for French, `messages_de.properties` for German, and so on.

Struts Tag Library

Some of the Struts custom tags have been explained already in form bean interactions. In that section, you saw some of the Struts specific custom tags in action. This section examines the most commonly used tags provided by Struts, and provides a brief explanation of their syntax and usage.

The tag libraries provided by Struts are, to say the least, extensive. They cover the following areas:

- ❑ **html:** A set of tags to render HTML elements, including HTML form elements that enable form bean interaction and other conveniences. The explanation of these tags later in this chapter has been separated into form tags and other tags.

- ❑ **logic:** A set of tags to provide conditional, iterative, and workflow-related tools for JSP pages. Much of the functionality provided by this set of tags is also covered by the JSTL.

- ❑ **bean:** A set of tags to provide for the declaration and accessing of beans in various scopes. Much of the functionality provided by this set of tags is also covered by the JSTL.

- ❑ **tiles:** Tiles is a templating tool that accompanies Struts (as of version 1.1). A set of Tiles tags is therefore provided. These tags are not included in this discussion; please refer to Chapter 20, "Layout Management with Tiles," for a full discussion of Tiles.

It is worth noting that many of the attributes available to Struts tags can take runtime expressions as their value. Consult the Struts documentation for specifics. For the examples included here, runtime expressions are not used.

HTML form tags

As already noted, there are Struts tags corresponding to most if not all of the traditional HTML form elements, as well as some other HTML fragments. Listed in the following table are some of the more commonly used HTML form tags and their common usage. For a complete list of the many tags provided by Struts, as well as the list of possible attributes, refer to the online documentation at http://struts. apache.org/userGuide/index.html.

It is important to note that many of the tags included in the Struts HTML tag library have many attributes to allow the developer full control over the functional and presentation capabilities of a JSP page employing these tags. For instance, many of the HTML tags allow the following attributes to be used:

Attribute(s)	Description
onsubmit, onclick, ondblclick, onchange, onkeypress, onkeyup, onmousedown, onmousemove, onmouseup, onblur	For the execution of JavaScript routines as a result of one of these events.
style, styleClass	For association of CSS classes with the element.
tabIndex	For assigning a tag key index with the element.
titleKey, title	Value of a mouse-over label for this element. Can be either the key of a value in messages.properties or a free-hand value.
disabled	Attribute to disable a form element from user input.

All the items listed in this section must be used within the confines of an html:form element. Generally, with HTML form tags, a property attribute denotes the associated form bean property that this element represents.

html:form

The html:form tag, shown in the following code, defines a Struts-powered form in a JSP page and indicates to the framework that this entry and its corresponding closing tag contain form elements that will be populated by a Struts form bean object. Once processed, the tag will render a typical <form..> HTML tag to be used appropriately by the browser. The value of the action attribute must correspond to a defined action in struts.

```
<html:form action="/login" method="POST">
...
</html:form>
```

html:text

This tag renders an input type text form element.

```
<html:text property="firstName"/>
```

html:password

This tag renders an input type password form element. This tag is basically the same as the `html:text` tag except that the value is not readable to the user. This element can also be set to be blanked out if the form is redisplayed because of some validation error with the `redisplay` attribute.

```
<html:password property="password" redisplay="true"/>
```

html:textarea

This tag is used to render a text area HTML element based on the property specified.

```
<html:textarea property="comments"></html:textarea>
```

html:hidden

This tag renders a hidden HTML form element for the specified property.

```
<html:hidden property="id"/>
```

html:checkbox

This tag renders an HTML check box form element, with its state appropriate to the form bean property specified. The form bean should use a `boolean` type property to denote such values.

An interesting problem often associated with a check box is that were it to be deselected by the user and submitted, there would be no corresponding request attribute associated with this form element. Struts handles this problem by advising that the property should be set to `false` in the form bean's `reset()` method. This enables the property to reflect the desired value when the form is submitted.

```
<html:checkbox property="approved"/>
```

html:radio

This tag renders an HTML radio button element based on the property specified.

```
<html:radio property="sex" value="M"/>
<html:radio property="sex" value="F"/>
```

html:select and html:options

```
<html:select property="name">
    <html:options collection="myList" property="value" labelProperty="label"/>
</html:select>
```

This extremely convenient tag combination renders a select list of the objects stored in the `Collection` object nominated under the `collection` attribute. In the preceding example, the name `myList` refers to an `ArrayList` of `LabelValueBean` objects that has been added to the scope of the JSP page. The `property` attribute in the `html:select` tag refers to the property of the form bean this select list represents, while the `property` and `labelProperty` attributes of the `html:options` tag represent values of each object rendered *within* the select list. Therefore, you can surmise from this that each `LabelValueBean` has at least two getter methods, `getValue()` and `getLabel()`. Using this tag enables the developer to select the current value in the provided list, corresponding to the current value in the form.

`LabelValueBean` is a convenience class provided by Struts for just this purpose, but an `html:select` tag could iterate over a collection of any object you nominate, as long as the `property` and `label` `Property` attributes correspond to getter methods of that object. You will see an example of this tag in the "Example application" section toward the end of this chapter.

html:submit

This tag renders an HTML Submit button for the form.

```
<html:submit value="Save"/>
```

Other HTML tags

As well as the form elements of the HTML set of tags, Struts provides another set of tags that help render HTML elements. These tags are described in the following sections.

html:link

This is a useful tag for rendering a link to the specified URL:

```
<html:link page="/somepage.jsp" name="myMap">my link</html:link>
```

Developers can dynamically provide a list of parameter name-value pairs in order to append to the link, so the preceding example might render the following in plain HTML:

```
<a href="/somepage.jsp?param1=value1&param2=value2">my link</a>
```

where the parameter names and values are stored in a `Map` object added to the scope of this page, in this case represented by the bean `myMap`.

html:errors

This very useful tag renders either a collection of error messages placed within the scope of the page or an individual error message from that collection. The `property` attribute denotes the name of the error to be displayed. Not using the `property` attribute will result in all errors being displayed. An example of an `ActionMessages` collection of `ActionMessage` objects being placed within the scope of a JSP page using the `saveErrors` method was illustrated earlier in the login form example.

```
<html:errors property="name"/>
```

The display of this tag can be enhanced by placing some specifically named properties within the `messages.properties` file for this application. Including the following properties and their example values will mean that each error message displayed will be contained within an HTML unordered list, and that each element of the list will be red:

```
errors.header=<ul>
errors.prefix=<li><font color=red>
errors.suffix=</font></li>
errors.footer=</ul>
```

html:messages

There are two basic examples of this:

Example A:

```
<html:messages id="message">
    <bean:write name="message"/>
</html:messages>
```

Example B:

```
<html:messages id="message" property="welcomeNote">
    <bean:write name="message"/>
</html:messages>
```

This is similar to the `html:errors` tag but is used to reference `ActionMessages` added to a scope of the JSP page as an iterable collection (example A), or to access a specific message, as in example B, where the `ActionMessage "welcomeNote"` is printed out. These messages may have been saved in a Struts action using the `saveMessages` method.

html:javascript

Use this tag to render dynamic validation configured for the form bean nominated in the `formName` attribute. An example of how this is configured will be introduced in the next section. The `staticJavascript` attribute alerts the tag to allow the developer to include custom JavaScript entries, in addition to the dynamic scripts generated by the framework.

```
<html:javascript
        formName="loginForm"
        dynamicJavascript="true"
        staticJavascript="false"/>
```

Logic tags

The logic tags provided by Struts offer much of the functionality provided within the JSTL. Indeed, the Struts documentation recommends that the JSTL be used wherever possible in preference to the Struts tags.

The logic tags provided by Struts deal with conditional and iterative operations, such as looping over a collection of objects and testing the value of bean properties.

logic:equal

The `logic:equal` tags allow for the test of a property of a bean within a certain scope. In the following example, the `LoginForm` bean's `username` property is being tested. If the value results in `"Nicholas"`, then the special message is displayed. All the attributes for this tag can utilize real-time expressions as values. This tag is equivalent to the `c:if` tag in JSTL.

```
<logic:equal name="loginForm"
             property="username"
             scope="request"
```

```
             value="Nicholas">

      This is a special message for Nicholas.

   </logic:equal>
```

logic:notEqual

This tag is the opposite of the `logic:equal` tag.

```
<logic:notEqual name="loginForm" property="username" value="Rupert">
```

This is a message for people who don't have Rupert as their username:

```
</logic:notEqual>
```

logic:match

This tag is used to test whether a property of a bean contains a substring, in this case `uper`. Other attributes such as `location` enable a substring match to be tested at a certain point in the property.

```
<logic:match name="loginForm" property="username" value="uper">
    This is special message for usernames with 'uper' in them
</logic:match>
```

logic:notMatch

This tag is basically the reverse of `logic:match`. The content is evaluated if the value being tested (in the `property` attribute) does not include as a substring the value of the `value` attribute.

```
<logic:notMatch name="loginForm" property="username" value="Jon">
    This is a special message for people without 'Jon' in their login name
</logic:notMatch>
```

logic:forward

This tag redirects the request to the global action forward nominated in the `name` attribute. The `name` attribute must refer to a configured global `ActionForward` entry.

```
<logic:forward name="error"/>
```

logic:redirect

This tag performs a redirect to a location it specifies. The three key attributes that specify that location are `forward`, `href`, and `page`. At least one of these must be specified. Parameters can be appended to the resulting URLs of these attributes by including a reference to a `Map` object of name-value pairs in the `name` attribute, similar to the `html:link` tag described earlier.

Alternatively, a single parameter can be added by specifying the name of the parameter in the `paramId` attribute and the corresponding value of the bean specified in the `paramName` attribute, as in the following example. Here, `favouriteColor` is a `String` bean whose value may resolve to `red` or `blue` and so on. The resulting URL would be `/login.do?color=red`.

```
<logic:redirect forward="error"/>
<logic:redirect name="myParameterMap" href="http://jakarta.apache.org/index.html"/>
<logic:redirect paramId="color" paramName="favouriteColor" page="/login.do"/>
```

logic:iterate

As the name suggests, the `logic:iterate` tag is used to iterate over its content for each item contained in the collection specified. The collection specified must be one of the following:

- An object that implements the interface `java.util.Collection`, such as `java.util.ArrayList`

- An object that implements the interface `java.util.Enumeration`, such as `java.util.StringTokenizer`

- An object that implements the interface `java.util.Iterator` (which can be retrieved from a `Collection` object)

- An object that implements the interface `java.util.Map`, such as `java.util.HashMap`

In the following example, the `ArrayList` used in the `html:select` example from earlier is used. The name of the bean referring to this collection is specified in the `name` attribute. The `id` element gives each member of the collection a name to refer to, scoped only within the boundaries of the tag. The `type` parameter tells the `logic:iterate` tag the class of the objects the collection contains. Each object is then accessed within the body of the tag by using the `bean:write` tag, which is explained in the next section. (For now, it just means "print this.")

```
<logic:iterate name="myList"
               id="thisElement"
               type="org.apache.struts.util.LabelValueBean">

   <bean:write name="thisElement" property="label"/> -
   <bean:write name="thisElement" property="value"/><br>

</logic:iterate>
```

This tag also supports various other convenient functions, such as starting the iteration at a certain index in the collection (`offset` attribute) and setting a maximum for the number of items that will be iterated over (`length` attribute).

logic:messagesPresent and logic:messagesNotPresent

There are two examples for this tag.

Example A:

```
<logic:messagesPresent property="name" message="false">
   <tr>
        <td><html:errors property="name"/></td>
   </tr>
</logic:messagesPresent>
```

613

Example B:

```
<logic:messagesNotPresent message="false">
    <tr>
        <td>So far, there have been no errors</td>
    </tr>
</logic:messagesNotPresent>
```

When messages are introduced to the scope of a JSP page, either as errors or as informational messages to the user, their presence, or absence, can be tested with these two complementary tags. In example A, the code is testing for the presence of an `ActionMessage` (assigned as an error — `saveErrors`) given the name `"name"`. In example B, the code is testing for the absence of *any* message assigned as an error within the scope of the page.

These two examples relate specifically to errors added to the scope of the JSP page. What if the presence of normal informational messages (`saveMessages`) needs to be tested? By changing the `message` attribute to `true`, the test would restrict itself to just these messages.

Bean tags

An additional set of tags provided by Struts relates to the manipulation of bean objects within the JSP page. Much of the functionality provided here is also available via the JSTL tags. The Struts documentation recommends using the JSTL tags over the Struts tags wherever possible.

Strut's bean tags provide the capability to create and access objects or beans within a JSP page. The tags are designed to allow this interaction across the multiple scopes that are available: `page`, `request`, `session`, or `application`. The beans these tags provide for could come from within the JSP page or as objects made available by an action class.

bean:define

The `bean:define` tag is used to define and manipulate beans from or in any scope. This tag can be used in many capacities, three of which are illustrated by the following examples.

Example A:

```
<bean:define id="testVariable" value="This is a new String"/>
<bean:write name="testVariable" scope="page"/>
```

Example B:

```
<bean:define id="newSessionBean"
             name="testVariable"
             scope="page"
             toScope="session"/>

<bean:write name="newSessionBean" scope="session"/>
```

Example C:

```
<bean:define id="customerName" name="myCustomer" property="name" scope="request"/>
```

In the first example, a new String bean has been defined in the JSP page, and then its value has been rendered for display to the browser in the response using the bean:write tag.

In the second example, the bean created in example A has been copied as a new bean into the session scope, available via the id newSessionBean. It has been printed out using the bean:write tag as well, but this time telling the tag that the bean it is looking for is in the session scope.

In the final example, a Customer object has been added to the request scope of this JSP page. A property from this object has been defined as a new bean within the JSP page, called customerName. The use of the property attribute tells us that there must be a getName method in the customer object for this value to be accessed.

The bean:define tag is similar in some ways to the jsp:useBean tag.

bean:write

You saw some examples of bean:write tags in the previous set of examples. As is obvious by now, the bean:write tag is used to render values to the browser in the response. In addition to rendering text, this tag can also be used to format its output as desired. This is illustrated in the following example:

```
<bean:write name="customerName" scope="page"/>
<bean:write name="money" format="$###,###.00" ignore="true"/>
```

The bean:write tag has made use of its format attribute to determine how the value of a Float object should be displayed. If the Float object represented 100.2, then this tag would print out $100.20. The values to place in the format attribute use a formatting syntax common to some of the formatting objects available in the Java language. For more details on this syntax, have a look at the Java API documentation for the DecimalFormat or SimpleDateFormat classes.

This example also uses the ignore attribute. This indicates to the JSP compiler that should the money bean not be found in the designated scope, nothing should be printed. If this were left as the default false, a JSP compile error would result when this page first loaded and no money bean was found.

bean:include

The bean:include tag enables the response from a request to another Web resource to be the value of a new bean; in the following example this is called theAge. The external resource can be referenced using one of three attributes:

❑ **href:** A fully qualified URL, as in the preceding example

❑ **forward:** The response generated from a global forward ActionForward defined in the application, such as error

❑ **page:** A resource located within the context of the current application, such as /error.jsp

```
<bean:include id="theAge" href="http://www.theage.com.au"/>
<bean:write name="theAge"/>
```

bean:message

This is another tag that provides the capability to display internationalized messages from the resources provided by the application.

```
<bean:message key="application.name"/>
```

```
<bean:message key="application.welcome" arg0="Peter"/>
```

The first example has simply rendered a value from the `messages.properties` file for this application called `application.name`. The entry in `messages.properties` would be something like the following:

```
application.name=My Application
```

The second example shown also renders an entry in the `messages.properties` file but it adds a parameter to the message. This way, the JSP page can display messages from the `messages.properties` file with runtime data intermingled into the message. In this example, the `application.welcome` message is being displayed and the parameter `"Peter"` is being added using the attribute `arg0`. The definition of the `application.welcome` message in the `messages.properties` file would be as follows:

```
application.welcome=Welcome {0} to My Application
```

This would render on the browser as `Welcome Peter to My Application`. Very handy. Up to four arguments can be specified using the attributes `arg0` through to `arg4`; these are replaced in the property using the `{0}..{3}` syntax to denote each parameter.

This section has introduced you to some of the more commonly used custom tags provided by Struts. It is by no means an exhaustive list; readers should consult the Struts documentation for that. What the documentation doesn't provide are clear concrete examples to solidify understanding. We hope that this discussion has achieved that for you.

Our tour through the Struts View layer is not yet over. The next section introduces some of the validation mechanisms available to application developers.

Validation

Validation of user input is a key requirement for many Web applications and presents the developer with many challenges. Struts provides a number of strategies to help you overcome these challenges while keeping the implementation clear and simple. Often, hand-crafted validation techniques leave the validation logic littered all over the application. Using a validation framework avoids this.

Validation can be divided into two areas:

❑ Validating the input from the user in the context of the form only. Examples might include verifying the following:

   ❑ That the data was entered in the correct format (date, numeric, alphabetic, e-mail addresses, passwords, and so on).

   ❑ That data was entered at all.

   ❑ That a certain combination of data was entered correctly. For example, if the user entered a value in form element A, then form element B should be empty, and so on.

❑ Validating that the input from the user does not violate any business rules defined in the system:

   ❑ If a new user is registering on a Web site, has the login name entered been used before?

   ❑ Does the username and password entered match a valid user record in the database?

   ❑ Was the credit card transaction approved?

The second category could be filled with endless business logic scenarios for which the answer lies not only in the form the user has just filled out and submitted but also in the state of the application and its underlying data at that time. Struts concentrates predominantly on the first category of validation, and provides two methods for this. These methods are described in this section. This validation discussion ends with a suggestion for how to handle business logic validation.

Generally, the goal of validation is to check the input from the user and, if a rule has been violated, display a message and redisplay the form page once again. This flow was described in the `LoginAction` discussion, where the login of the user was checked and if it was found to be incorrect, the previous page was redisplayed with an appropriate error message. Although this is an example of business logic validation, it illustrates the flow of events that is often desirable in a Web application.

The following sections describe the strategies Struts provides to validate input from the user.

Form bean validation

Form bean validation places the validation rules within the form bean class itself (`LoginForm` from the previous example). More specifically, it places it within a special method of the form bean that the Struts framework knows to call before the `execute` method of the `Action` class. The appropriate form bean and whether to call this special method are determined in the `struts-config.xml` file. Of course, this method does not apply to `DynaActionBeans`.

Here we build on the `LoginForm` example described earlier, the validation rules we may want to implement extend only to checking that the two fields, username and password, are not empty. With this knowledge, we can implement a `validate` method in the `LoginForm` class as follows:

```
...
public class LoginForm extends ActionForm
{
    private String _username;
    private String _password;

    public LoginForm()
    {
    }
...
    public ActionErrors validate(ActionMapping mapping,
        HttpServletRequest request)
    {
        ActionErrors errors = new ActionErrors();

        if ((_username == null) || (_username.length() < 1))
        {
            errors.add("username",
                new ActionMessage("error.login.username.missing"));
        }

        if ((_password == null) || (_password.length() < 1))
        {
            errors.add("password",
                new ActionMessage("error.login.password.missing"));
        }

        return errors;
    }
}
```

This new method is executed after the form is submitted but before the execute method of the LoginAction is invoked by the framework. If the ActionErrors object this class returns is null or empty, then processing continues on the LoginAction class as normal. If the ActionErrors object this method returns contains errors, then the input page that submitted the form is redisplayed and the values of the form are populated with what was originally entered. We should point out here the use of the ActionErrors object to house ActionMessages. ActionErrors is a subclass of ActionMessages. Some of the areas where ActionErrors have usually been used, such as in an Action class, have been deprecated in favor of the ActionMessages collection. For the time being, though, the validate method used here will need to return an ActionErrors collection. If you're using an older or a future version of Struts, make sure that you check the usage of these objects; otherwise, you may encounter problems. The Struts documentation alludes to a general theme of not using the ActionErrors object where possible, in favor of the ActionMessages object.

In the validate method in the previous code, the two fields _username and _password are checked to ensure they are not null and not empty, meaning that at least something has been typed in by the user. If either of the fields is found to be empty, a new error is added to the ActionErrors object. When adding the error to the ActionErrors object, the add method is used. This method, in this instance, takes two parameters. The first indicates the property for which this error applies. The second is the ActionMessage itself. The ActionMessage object is constructed with the name of an appropriate message property key available within the application. When the validate method returns a populated

`ActionErrors` object to the input page, these messages are available to inform the user of what happened. To show these messages to the user, the `html:errors` custom tag is used:

```
...
<html:errors property="username"/><br>
Username: <html:text property="username"/><br>
<P>
<html:errors property="password"/><br>
Password: <html:password property="password"/><br>
...
```

In the preceding example, the code to display the appropriate error messages above the associated form element has been highlighted.

So how does the framework know which bean's `validate` method to invoke? And where is this input page thing? Let's recall the `action-mapping` in `struts-config.xml` for the `LoginAction`:

```
...
<action-mappings>
  <action path="/login"
          type="com.wrox.begjsp.ch19.struts.simpleform.LoginAction"
          name="loginForm"
          input="/login.jsp"
          validate="true"
          scope="request">
    <forward name="success" path="/welcome.jsp"/>
  </action>
</action-mappings>
...
```

The three attributes responsible for making this validation flow work have been highlighted. The `name` attribute indicates which `form-bean` entry maps to this action. The `input` attribute indicates the path that invoked this action (and where to go if an error occurs), and the `validate` attribute being set to `true` tells the framework that when this action is invoked, the `validate` method of the `form-bean` should be used.

As you can see, setting up basic form validation in this way is very simple and straightforward. It also ensures that the logic to do this for each interface is in one place and that the workflow from form submission to form error is clear and concise when reading the code. Of course, this is not the only way to implement framework-sponsored validation using Struts.

Struts Validator

Using the form bean validation method means that all the validation logic, and in a big application it can be a lot of such logic, is localized in the `ActionForm` classes. Logic in this location is very difficult to change in a live application, and the person changing it must be a Java programmer. In response to these constraints, a more configurable validation mechanism has evolved.

The Struts Validator has evolved from a set of validation classes available under the Jakarta Commons project, and it has since been adopted into Struts 1.1 with some enhancements. Struts Validator places the validation rules for form beans inside an XML file, `validation.xml`. The rules defined in this XML file utilize a set of predefined validation mechanisms defined in a file provided by Struts, called `validator-rules.xml`. Put another way, the `validation.xml` file defines which rules will govern validation for forms and how they should behave, whereas `validator-rules.xml` defines these rules and references appropriate Struts objects to encapsulate the logic.

The validation provided by the Struts Validator can be called in two ways: on the client side or on the server side. Client-side validation is made possible by the fact that the validation rules provided by default with Struts also define equivalent JavaScript functions that can be placed on the page if required. This JavaScript is placed on the JSP page by using the Struts `html:javascript` tag:

```
<html:javascript dynamicJavascript="true"
                 formName="loginForm"/>
```

You can see from the preceding example that the `dyanamicJavascript` attribute of `true` indicates to the framework that the Validator-generated JavaScript should be placed here (you would put the tag above the HTML `<body>` tag). The `formName` attribute identifies the form bean to which the rules apply.

Leaving the preceding tag out of the JSP page leaves the validation to occur on the server side. In simple terms, each validation rule provided by Struts references an object that performs the validation based on the parameters it has been provided by the `validation.xml` file, and in so doing behaves almost exactly like the `LoginForm` validation that was implemented earlier.

The Struts Validator expects the form bean being validated to be of a certain type; therefore, the form bean used to represent the HTML form must now extend the `org.apache.struts.validator.ValidatorForm` (or `org.apache.struts.validator.ValidatorActionForm`) class instead of the `ActionForm` class.

If a `DynaActionForm` is currently being used, the `org.apache.struts.validator.DynaValidatorForm` (or `org.apache.struts.validator.DynaValidatorActionForm`) class must now be specified as the `type` attribute for the `form-bean` entry in the `struts-config.xml` file instead of the `DynaActionForm` class.

Defining the validation rules

So how do we actually define the validation rules? First, the Struts Validator is a plug-in to Struts, so it must have a corresponding entry in the `struts-config.xml` file:

```
<plug-in className="org.apache.struts.validator.ValidatorPlugIn">
    <set-property property="pathnames"
                  value="/WEB-INF/validator-rules.xml,
                         /WEB-INF/validation.xml"/>
</plug-in>
```

This entry tells the framework where these two all-important files are located. The preceding entry places them in the `/WEB-INF/` directory of the application.

As described, the `validation.xml` file tells the framework the rules that apply to each of the fields in each of the forms that the application uses. Let's look at the contents of this file for our login example. The validation rules implemented here specify that both of the fields, username and password, cannot be empty, i.e., that they are *required*:

```
<form-validation>
    <formset>
        <form name="loginForm">
          <field property="username" depends="required">
            <msg name="required" key="error.login.username.missing"/>
          </field>

          <field property="password" depends="required">
            <msg name="required" key="error.login.password.missing"/>
          </field>
        </form>
    </formset>
</form-validation>
```

The simple XML structure here is quite easy to read. The entry first defines a `formset`, the set of forms that this file defines validation for, and within this structure is a corresponding entry for each form. Within the `form` definition is an entry for each field of the form, and it is this entry that defines the validation rules and corresponding error messages for each of the form elements. Note the use of the `depends` attribute in the `form` element. In plain English, this would mean that this field *depends* on this rule. The `depends` attribute can also take a comma-separated list of rules that the field must satisfy. The nested `msg` element within the field entry nominates messages to be displayed for each of the rules specified in the `depends` attribute. Where no message is specified for a rule, the Struts Validator will search for a default message key in the `messages.properties` file. A list of these keys can be found in the `validator-rules.xml` file.

The `required` rule is a very simple one: The field is either empty or not. Other rules need variables to define their behavior, such as `minlength`. This rule ensures that the length of data placed in a field must be at least a certain length.

So what is the minimum length and how is this specified? Let's look at an example to explain this. If the login form needed the password to not only be required but also to be, for example, at least six characters long, the field entry would appear as follows:

```
<field property="password"
        depends="required,minlength">
 <msg name="required" key="error.login.password.missing"/>
 <msg name="minlength" key="error.login.password.length"/>
 <arg0 name="minlength" key="${var:minlength}" resource="false"/>
 <var>
        <var-name>minlength</var-name>
        <var-value>6</var-value>
 </var>
</field>
```

Whoa! Our simple validation entry just got a lot more complicated. Let's walk through this bit by bit. The field entry now depends on two rules: `required` and `minlength`:

```
<field property="password" depends="required,minlength">
```

A new error message has been added for cases when the `minlength` rule is broken:

```
<msg name="required" key="error.login.password.missing"/>
<msg name="minlength" key="error.login.password.length"/>
```

This is defined in the `messages.properties` file as follows:

```
error.login.password.length=The password must be {0} characters long
```

Note the parameter placeholder in the message. This is filled in by the next entry, an argument for the `minlength` msg entry:

```
<arg0 name="minlength" key="${var:minlength}" resource="false"/>
```

This passes a value to the error message for the `minlength` rule. The parameter passed to the message is represented by the value specified in the `key` attribute. And as with parameters passed in the `html:message` tag described earlier, up to four `arg` parameters (`arg0 . . . arg3`) can be used. In this case, the value is actually a reference to the next entry, where the `minlength` rule variable is specified:

```
<var>
    <var-name>minlength</var-name>
    <var-value>6</var-value>
</var>
```

One of the strengths of the Struts Validator is that it allows for some very sophisticated validation logic to be implemented, even when just using the default set of validation rules provided by Struts. Following is a list of the other rules that can be used with the default `validator-rules.xml`:

❑ **maxlength:** Similar to `minlength`. It takes only one variable, the maximum length for the field.

❑ **mask:** Allows a validation rule to be specified with regular expressions. Regular expressions are patterns designed to match strings of text. Regular expressions are an extremely powerful method for identifying a particular pattern of text. For instance, the following mask example requires that the field in question must contain only numbers and alphabetic characters, but nothing else:

```
<field property="username" depends="mask">
  <msg name="mask" key="errors.login.username.mask"/>
  <var>
    <var-name>mask</var-name>
    <var-value>^[0-9A-Za-z]*$</var-value>
  </var>
</field>
```

The mask rule takes one variable, the mask regular expression to be tested.

❑ **byte, short, integer, float, double, long:** All these rules ensure that the value entered in a field can be converted to the specified type. None of these rules require variables.

❑ **date:** Date validation is challenging on many levels. This rule ensures that at least what has been entered can be converted to a `java.util.Date` object. The date rule uses the

SimpleDateFormat class to confirm that the text entered can become a Date object. It also allows two variables to be optionally specified:

- ❑ **dateFormat:** The format in which the date should be entered
- ❑ **datePatternStrict:** This specifies whether the rule should be strictly applied, such as cases where the dateFormat dictates that the day field in the pattern dd/MM/yyyy should be two characters but the user enters 3/11/2005, i.e., only one character for the day. true or false are valid values here.

❑ **intRange, floatRange, and doubleRange:** Tests that the field is within a specified range of values defined by two variables. Fields that use these rules must also depend on the integer, float and double rules, respectively. The two variables required for these rules are as follows:

- ❑ **min:** The minimum value for the field
- ❑ **max:** The maximum value for the field

❑ **creditCard:** Validates the format of a credit card. The Struts Validator uses the *Luhn Formula* to determine whether the information is correct. The Luhn Formula is a credit card number validation technique supported by most major credit card companies.

❑ **email:** Validates that the field is a properly structured e-mail address. There are no guarantees, however, that the address actually exists!

❑ **requiredif:** This rule enables the developer to conditionally provide validation for a field based on conditions concerning the values of other fields. Note that this rule will be deprecated in the first Struts release after 1.1 in favor of a new rule called validwhen, and therefore may be removed in any future release after that.

As you can see, the validation rules provided by the Struts Validator can be very sophisticated and cover many common scenarios required by applications. If you find that the default set of rules does not satisfy your scenario, then you might consider adding your own Validator. The Struts documentation provides some brief instructions on doing this. Unfortunately, this topic is out of the scope of this book.

Business logic validation

Struts doesn't provide a mechanism to validate the business rules of an application simply because it shouldn't or can't. Rather, the breadth of validation required to ensure that the business rules of an application are kept in check is beyond the scope of an application framework like Struts. All the framework can do, and Struts does this admirably, is to provide a structure and infrastructure within which such rules can be tested, and if broken, dealt with.

One common strategy used in Struts applications is to perform the form element validation in the ways just described and to perform, or call on, business logic validation within the actions themselves.

Suppose you have a system dealing with new customer registration. The validation you need to implement falls into the two categories identified: The general form validation would cover problems such as empty fields, passwords that are not complicated enough, or invalid e-mail addresses. The business logic validation would cover more involved problems such as a login name that is already taken by another customer, or an invalid ZIP code

The register customer form would submit to an appropriate action, maybe `saveNewCustomer.do` (`SaveNewCustomerAction` class). Within the `execute` method of this class, other objects developed for the application could be called to do the appropriate checks and then return a `List` of error message keys back to the `Action` class. These error message keys would then be added to an `ActionMessages` object in the way you have already seen.

The key objectives you want to achieve in structuring business logic validation in this way are as follows:

❏ **Encapsulating the business logic (away from the concerns of the front end):** This helps for reuse elsewhere in the application. Imagine if the business logic rules for what constituted a valid new customer were locked away in the front end of an application and another mechanism other than the Web site needs to create a new customer. The logic isn't very reusable in the `Action` class.

❏ **Separation of concerns:** You don't want the business logic of the application to know or care about the front end. If it is not dependent on the front end, it can be utilized from other sources, or even separated and implemented elsewhere. This objective also promotes a clean and clearly structured implementation of the application.

The preceding example is just one suggestion for how such validation could be dealt with; there would literally be millions out there. It is a testament to the flexibility of Struts that it enables applications to be implemented in many different ways.

This concludes the discussion about the different layers of an MVC application developed using the Struts framework. A lot has been covered in this section, so it may be helpful to briefly recap the main points before moving on to the examples.

In the Controller layer, you saw the role that the `ActionServlet` and `Action` classes play in defining the flow of an application. You also learned how Struts encapsulates HTML forms with `ActionForm` and `DynaActionForm` beans. The Model layer was defined within the structure of an application, and it was ascertained that Struts doesn't play a big part in defining its use and architecture.

In the View layer, many points were covered. You first saw how the `ActionForm` and `DynaActionForm` beans can interact with the elements of an HTML form. Internationalization was then discussed, with reference to messages provided to the user. You also took a look at the Struts Tag Library, and saw how some of the more commonly used tags were applied. The View discussion was rounded off with validation techniques using Struts and a suggestion for how business logic may be implemented.

Example application

Our attention now turns to providing a simple example of a Struts application and its development. Chapter 18 introduced a simple form submission application to illustrate WebWork and Spring. We will continue using this example application in this section.

The following discussion details the steps involved in setting up a base version of this small application. If you missed the discussion in Chapter 18, this application is a simple form inviting users to enter their name and some comments into a form. The form can then be submitted. If the user has not entered a name, the application informs the user of the error and redisplays the form.

Once you have established that this base application is working with Tomcat and that you can deploy the application using Ant, you can begin to implement some enhancements.

Try It Out   Setting Up the Base Application

Download the files for this chapter from the Wrox Web site at www.wrox.com. Unzip the file titled struts-base.zip into an area on your hard drive. Let's assume this directory is c:\struts-base. You will notice the following directory structure within this directory:

- ❑ Within the root of the struts-base directory is the build.xml file. This Ant file will be used to build the application.

- ❑ src holds the source files for the application, which are stored in this directory in a package structure. There are two files within this directory:

    - ❑ **\com\wrox\begjsp\ch19\struts\TestAction.java:** The action invoked when the form is submitted

    - ❑ **\messages.properties:** An internationalization file for the application

- ❑ web includes the JSP files for the application that have been stored in this directory. This directory will contain the following:

    - ❑ **\index.jsp:** The page that displays the form

    - ❑ **\details.jsp:** The page displayed once the form is submitted

- ❑ **web\WEB-INF:** The configuration for the application is located in this directory. It contains the following files:

    - ❑ **web.xml:** The configuration file for the application within the Servlet container (Tomcat)

    - ❑ **struts-config.xml:** The configuration file for Struts

- ❑ **validation.xml and validator-rules.xml:** These are files to configure the validation requirements of the application.

Once this directory structure is in place, we can set about configuring the Ant build file to build and deploy the application appropriately. These instructions assume you have set up Ant and Tomcat already.

1. Download the latest binary version of Struts from http://struts.jakarta.org/. This chapter uses the latest version at the time of writing, version 1.2.4.

2. Unzip (or untar) the binary file you downloaded into an appropriate directory on your computer. For this illustration we will assume this is: c:\jakarta-struts-1.2.4.

3. Copy the catalina-ant.jar file from the c:\<tomcat home>\server\lib directory and place it in the Ant lib directory, which will be something like c:\apache-ant-1.6.2\lib. This JAR file enables the build.xml Ant script to communicate with Tomcat.

4. Open the build.xml file and change the following highlighted properties to reflect the correct values for your environment:

```
<property name="app.name"        value="struts-base"/>
<property name="app.path"        value="/${app.name}"/>
<property name="app.version"     value="0.1-dev"/>
<property name="build.home"      value="${basedir}/build"/>
<property name="catalina.home"   value="c:/Tomcat5.0.27"/>
<property name="dist.home"       value="${basedir}/dist"/>
<property name="docs.home"       value="${basedir}/docs"/>
<property name="manager.url"     value="http://localhost:8080/manager"/>
<property name="manager.username" value="admin"/>
<property name="manager.password" value="password"/>
<property name="src.home"        value="${basedir}/src"/>
<property name="web.home"        value="${basedir}/web"/>
<property name="struts.home"     value="c:/jakarta-struts-1.2.4"/>
```

These properties are explained in the following table.

Property	Description
catalina.home	The directory in which Tomcat was installed
manager.url	The URL of the Manager application for Tomcat
manager.username	The username specified for the administration user when Tomcat was set up
manager.password	The password specified for the administration user when Tomcat was set up
Struts.home	The directory in which Struts was installed (step 2)

The build.xml script we are using here is provided with Tomcat and is perfect for our purposes. It will automate the interaction required to control the server while changing the application. Once you have made these property changes, you are now in a position to deploy the application using the build.xml file.

5. Start up a command prompt and change to the directory in which the struts-base application was installed. The directory you are now in should contain the build.xml file.

6. Start up the Tomcat server.

7. Issue the following command at the command prompt: ant install. This command will perform a number of important tasks that we should step through:

    a. Create a new directory called c:\struts-base\build in which the application will be compiled and copied.

    b. Compile the Java source file in the application to c:\struts-base\build\WEB-INF\classes.

    c. Copy the contents of c:\struts-base\web to c:\struts-base\build.

d. Copy the following JAR files from the `c:\jakarta-struts-1.2.4\lib` directory to the `c:\struts-base\build\WEB-INF\lib` directory:

- ❑ `struts.jar`
- ❑ `commons-beanutils.jar`
- ❑ `commons-digester.jar`
- ❑ `commons-validator.jar`
- ❑ `jakarta-oro.jar`

e. Copy all `*.tld` files from the `c:\jakarta-struts-1.2.4\lib` directory to the `c:\struts-base\build\WEB-INF` directory.

f. Copy the `validator-rules.xml` file from the `c:\jakarta-struts-1.2.4\lib` directory to the `c:\struts-base\build\WEB-INF` directory.

g. Install a new context in the Tomcat server using the `c:\struts-base\build` directory as the document base.

You should now be able to point your browser at `http://localhost:8080/struts-base/index.jsp` and be presented with the screen shown in Figure 19-4.

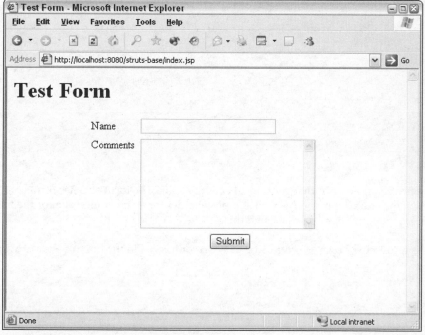

Figure 19-4: Struts base application

A plug-in entry has also been added to the `struts-config.xml` file for validation rules:

```
<plug-in className="org.apache.struts.validator.ValidatorPlugIn">
    <set-property property="pathnames"
             value="/WEB-INF/validator-rules.xml,
                    /WEB-INF/validation.xml"/>
</plug-in>
```

A messages resource has also been added:

```
<message-resources parameter="messages" null="false"/>
```

This denotes that a file called `messages.properties` will be located in the root package of the class-path. If you open the file located at `c:\struts-base\src\messages.properties` you will see the messages presented on the page, labels, the page title, and so on, as well as the error message that was displayed.

In the `validation.xml` file, also located in the `c:\struts-base\web\WEB-INF\` directory, rules for the form have been added. They currently ensure only that a value is entered in the Name field:

```
<?xml version="1.0" encoding="iso-8859-1"?>
<!DOCTYPE form-validation PUBLIC
    "-//Apache Software Foundation//DTD Commons Validator Rules Configuration
    1.1.3//EN"
    "http://jakarta.apache.org/commons/dtds/validator_1_1_3.dtd">
<form-validation>
    <formset>
        <form name="testForm">
                <field property="name" depends="required">
                  <msg name="required" key="form.error.name.missing"/>
                </field>
        </form>
    </formset>
</form-validation>
```

The `TestAction` that has been implemented is about as basic as it gets; the entire class listing is as follows:

```
package com.wrox.begjsp.ch19.struts;

import org.apache.struts.action.Action;
import org.apache.struts.action.ActionForm;
import org.apache.struts.action.ActionForward;
import org.apache.struts.action.ActionMapping;

import javax.servlet.http.HttpServletRequest;
import javax.servlet.http.HttpServletResponse;

public class TestAction extends Action
{
```

```
    public ActionForward execute(ActionMapping mapping, ActionForm form,
        HttpServletRequest request, HttpServletResponse response)
        throws Exception
    {
        return mapping.findForward("success");
    }
}
```

This action as well as the `success` forward, is configured in the `struts-config.xml` as follows:

```
...
<action-mappings>
  <action path="/test"
              type="com.wrox.begjsp.ch19.struts.TestAction"
              name="testForm"
              validate="true"
              input="/index.jsp"
              scope="request">
        <forward name="success" path="/details.jsp"/>
  </action>
</action-mappings>
...
```

You can see that the `testForm` form bean is referenced along with the `validate=true` setting, ensuring that this action validates the input as soon as it is invoked.

Adding enhancements

The discussion from here on will focus on adding some features to this simple application in order to use some of the Struts skills you have learned in this chapter. A modest list of enhancements to implement is as follows:

❑ Add validation for the Comments field, making sure it has a value when the form is submitted.

❑ Add validation for the Name field, making sure the name is only alphabetic characters when the form is submitted.

❑ Add a new field to the form for the user's e-mail address. Add validation to this field to ensure that only a properly structured e-mail address can be entered.

❑ Add another field to the form from which users select their favorite sport from a list of possible sports. Add validation to ensure that a sport is selected.

❑ Display all the information in the form on the following page after the form has been submitted.

The following example will lead you through making these changes to the `struts-base` application. If you'd like to skip ahead, you could download the completed application in the `struts-enhanced.zip` file from the Web site for this book. Simply follow the same steps as outlined previously to get it going.

Adding Validation: Comments Field Required

This is a very easy enhancement to add, especially given that the Struts Validator is being used.

First open the `validation.xml` file located in the `WEB-INF/` directory of the `struts-base` application. Add a new field entry beneath the existing entry indicating that the Comments field is also required. Allocate an appropriate comment message key:

```
...
<field property="name" depends="required,mask">
  <msg name="required" key="form.error.name.missing"/>
</field>
<field property="comments" depends="required">
  <msg name="required" key="form.error.comments.missing"/>
</field>
...
```

This addition has been highlighted. Make sure you add an appropriate message in the `messages .properties` file for the error this creates called `form.error.comments.missing`.

Now we need to add a place for this message to appear on the form when a user doesn't enter anything in the Comments field. Open the `index.jsp` file and locate the Comments field. Place a new messages row above the field, as shown in the following highlighted entry:

```
...
<logic:messagesPresent property="comments">
<tr>
     <td colspan=2><html:errors property="comments"/></td>
</tr>
</logic:messagesPresent>
<tr>
    <td valign="top"><bean:message key="form.comments.title"/></td>
    <td>
        <html:textarea property="comments" cols="30" rows="8"></html:textarea>
    </td>
</tr>
...
```

Save the changes and, with Tomcat running, issue an `ant reload` command in the command console, which you should still have open. The changes will be copied into the `c:\struts-base\build` directory and then the context will be reloaded within Tomcat. If you browse to the application now and try to submit the form without entering a comment, a new validation message will appear. Job complete!

How It Works

This change simply configures the Validator to ensure that the Comments field is submitted with a value. The JSP page was modified to ensure that an error message appears when an error for the Comments field is detected.

Try It Out   **Adding Validation: Name Field to Be Alphabetic Only**

To complete this requirement, a new rule needs to be added to the existing validation rule for the Name field. If you remember the Struts Validator discussion, a mask rule is appropriate here. Open the `validation.xml` file in the `c:\struts-base\web\WEB-INF\` directory and add the highlighted items in the following listing to the Name field's entry:

```
<field property="name" depends="required,mask">
  <msg name="required" key="form.error.name.missing"/>
  <msg name="mask" key="form.error.name.invalid"/>
  <var>
    <var-name>mask</var-name>
    <var-value>^[a-zA-Z]*$</var-value>
  </var>
</field>
```

Add an appropriate message to the `messages.properties` file for this new error (`form.error.name.invalid`). Once you have saved the changed files, issue another `ant reload` command. If you now browse to the form again and enter a non-alphabetic character into the Name field and click Submit, the new error message will appear.

How It Works

In order to enforce the requirement for the name field we have used a mask validation entry to the `validation.xml` file. This validation entry specifies that an error should be raised if the name field's value is something other than an upper- or lowercase alphabetic character. The ^ character tells the validation mechanism that errors are raised for characters not in the trailing expression `[a-zA-Z]`. This new validation rule is associated with the `mask` msg specified in the third line of the last listing.

Try It Out   **Adding a Field and Validation: E-mail Address**

In order to add a new e-mail address field to the form, another modification is required to the `struts-config.xml` file. Modify the `testForm` form bean in this file as follows:

```
...
<form-beans>

  <form-bean name="testForm"
             type="org.apache.struts.validator.DynaValidatorForm">
    <form-property name="name" type="java.lang.String"/>
    <form-property name="emailAddress" type="java.lang.String"/>
    <form-property name="comments" type="java.lang.String"/>
  </form-bean>

</form-beans>
...
```

To reflect this addition, changes are also required in the `index.jsp` file to add the input field and a space for its validation messages. Add these to the JSP page with the following (additions have been highlighted):

```
...
<tr>
    <td><bean:message key="form.name.title"/></td>
    <td><html:text altKey="form.name.title" property="name" size="30"/></td>
</tr>
<logic:messagesPresent property="emailAddress">
<tr>
    <td colspan=2><html:errors property="emailAddress"/></td>
</tr>
</logic:messagesPresent>
<tr>
    <td><bean:message key="form.emailaddress.title"/></td>
    <td><html:text altKey="form.emailaddress.title" property="emailAddress"
            size="30"/></td>
</tr>
...
```

In addition to this change, you should add a new message for the `form.emailaddress.title` key in the `messages.properties` file.

So far, the new form element has been defined and the JSP page has been updated to reflect the new input required of the user. The requirement also specified that validation should ensure that the e-mail address has been entered and that when it is entered it should be a properly structured e-mail address. The Struts Validator provides a simple mechanism for this to occur. Open the `validation.xml` file and add the following form entry to the `testForm` (again, the changes required have been highlighted):

```
...
<field property="name" depends="required,mask">
  <msg name="required" key="form.error.name.missing"/>
  <msg name="mask" key="form.error.name.invalid"/>
  <var>
    <var-name>mask</var-name>
    <var-value>^[a-zA-Z]*$</var-value>
  </var>
</field>
<field property="emailAddress" depends="required,email">
  <msg name="required" key="form.error.emailaddress.missing"/>
  <msg name="email" key="form.error.emailaddress.invalid"/>
</field>
...
```

The new field entry tells the framework that the `emailAddress` field is both required and should reflect a properly structured e-mail address using the `depends` attribute. The appropriate error messages are referenced within this element. Make sure you add a new entry to `messages.properties` for the two e-mail address errors, `form.error.emailaddress.missing` and `form.error.emailaddress.invalid`.

Save the changed files and issue another `ant reload` command. If you now browse to the application you will notice the new e-mail address input box. If you enter something obviously incorrect in the e-mail field and click the Submit button, an appropriate error message will be displayed, as shown in Figure 19-5.

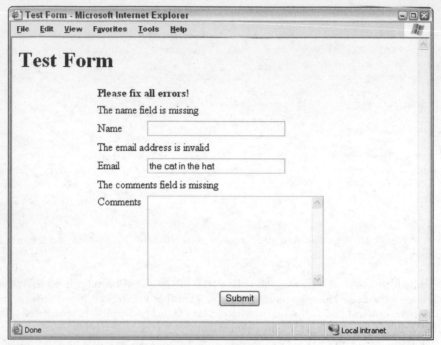

Figure 19-5: New e-mail address field with validation

Requirement three is complete.

How It Works

The new field was added to the definition of the form in the struts-config.xml file. With this new field available, we were able to add appropriate validation to the validation.xml file. In order to ensure that a properly formed e-mail address is entered by the user, the e-mail validation setting was used in the depends attribute for this field. The new field was also added to the index.jsp file so that the user has somewhere to enter the value. Messages were added to the messages.properties file so that validation and labels used in this change could be displayed where appropriate.

Try It Out   Adding a Field and Validation: Favorite Sport

Our imaginary client now needs users to be able to select their favorite sport from the form. For this we need a list of sports to display in a select list. We could simply define this list in the JSP page, but it would be more architecturally correct to pass the JSP page a list of sports and let it deal with only the display aspects, rather than the data as well. In order to achieve this, a new action will be required to display the form page. Instead of browsing to the form page (index.jsp) directly, the display of the form will become a successful ActionForward mapping from the new action. To achieve this, a series of changes will be required.

Because a file called index.jsp is generally the entry page for any application, this page should now become simply a redirection page to the new action that will be created. Create a new file called form.jsp in the c:\struts-base\web directory. Move all the content of index.jsp to this new file.

In the index.jsp file, enter the following:

```
<%@ taglib uri="/WEB-INF/struts-logic.tld" prefix="logic" %>
<logic:redirect page="/form.do"/>
```

This will redirect all requests directed at index.jsp to our new action, which will be called form.

The new action class must be created. Create a new file in the c:\struts-base\src\com\wrox\ begjsp\ch19\struts directory called FormAction.java. This new action will represent the class that actually presents the form.jsp page to the user. In this new file, enter the following code to represent the new class (you can pretty much just copy the content of the TestAction.java file and change the class name):

```
package com.wrox.begjsp.ch19.struts;

import org.apache.struts.action.Action;
import org.apache.struts.action.ActionForm;
import org.apache.struts.action.ActionForward;
import org.apache.struts.action.ActionMapping;
import org.apache.struts.util.LabelValueBean;

import java.util.ArrayList;
import java.util.List;

import javax.servlet.http.HttpServletRequest;
import javax.servlet.http.HttpServletResponse;


public class FormAction extends Action
{
    public ActionForward execute(ActionMapping mapping, ActionForm form,
        HttpServletRequest request, HttpServletResponse response)
        throws Exception
    {
        return mapping.findForward("success");
    }
}
```

This action is going to have to send a list of sports to the form.jsp page so that the user can select one from a list. This is easily done. Create a new method in the FormAction class called getSports(). This new method will return a List that will be added to the request in the execute method. An example of this new method is as follows:

```
...
private List getSports()
{
    List sports = new ArrayList();

    sports.add(new LabelValueBean("Tennis", "Tennis"));
    sports.add(new LabelValueBean("Hockey", "Hockey"));
    sports.add(new LabelValueBean("Football", "Football"));
    sports.add(new LabelValueBean("Baseball", "Baseball"));
    sports.add(new LabelValueBean("Soccer", "Soccer"));
```

```
        return sports;
    }
    ...
```

Struts provides a convenient object called `LabelValueBean` that enables name-value pairs of strings to be joined together. This is perfect for select lists for which the only data required is a label to be displayed to the user, and a value is the value of each element. For our purposes though, these are the same thing.

This new method should now be called from the `execute` method of the `FormAction` class. Add the following highlighted code:

```
...
public class FormAction extends Action
{
    public ActionForward execute(ActionMapping mapping, ActionForm form,
        HttpServletRequest request, HttpServletResponse response)
        throws Exception
    {
        request.setAttribute("sports", getSports());
        return mapping.findForward("success");
    }
...
}
```

With this change, the result of the `getSports` method is added to the `request` object. This places the `List` in the `request` scope of the `form.jsp` page under the alias `sports`.

So what's left to do? The mappings in the `struts-config.xml` file haven't been changed yet, the new field needs to be added to the `form.jsp` page, and we also need to add the associated validation entry.

Open the `struts-config.xml` file. Change the `/test` action mapping to appear as follows (the change has been highlighted):

```
...
<action path="/test"
        type="com.wrox.begjsp.ch19.struts.TestAction"
        name="testForm"
        validate="true"
        input="/form.do"
        scope="request">
    <forward name="success" path="/details.jsp"/>
</action>
...
```

With the `struts-config.xml` file still open, add a new action mapping to reflect the `FormAction` action that has been added. Remember that this action will provide the user with a view of the form page:

```
...
<action path="/form"
        type="com.wrox.begjsp.ch19.struts.FormAction"
        scope="request">
    <forward name="success" path="/form.jsp"/>
</action>
...
```

The action mappings have now been modified to reflect the new functionality required. Now the new field can be added to the form. Modify the form bean `testForm` to reflect the following (the changes have been highlighted):

```
...
<form-beans>

    <form-bean         name="testForm"
                       type="org.apache.struts.validator.DynaValidatorForm">
      <form-property name="name" type="java.lang.String"/>
      <form-property name="emailAddress" type="java.lang.String"/>
      <form-property name="favSport" type="java.lang.String"/>
      <form-property name="comments" type="java.lang.String"/>
    </form-bean>

</form-beans>
...
```

Save the `struts-config.xml` file. The validation for this new field involves a simple addition to the `validation.xml` file. Open this file and add the validation as follows:

```
...
<field property="emailAddress" depends="required,email">
  <msg name="required" key="form.error.emailaddress.missing"/>
  <msg name="email" key="form.error.emailaddress.invalid"/>
</field>
<field property="favSport" depends="required">
  <msg name="required" key="form.error.favsport.missing"/>
</field>
<field property="comments" depends="required">
  <msg name="required" key="form.error.comments.missing"/>
</field>
...
```

Save the `validation.xml` file. Now that all the prep work has been done, the new form element can be added to the `form.jsp` file.

The `form.jsp` page now has a `List` object within its `request` scope called `sports`. The `html:select` tag will be used to iterate through this `List` and render a select list with the desired values. However, a default value should be specified for the form as well, one that doesn't contain a sport and instructs the user to choose a value. This is achieved by adding a manual `html:option` entry to the select list.

Open the `form.jsp` page and make the following addition (the changes have been highlighted):

```
...
<logic:messagesPresent property="favSport">
<tr>
      <td colspan=2><html:errors property="favSport"/></td>
</tr>
</logic:messagesPresent>
<tr>
    <td valign="top"><bean:message key="form.favsport.title"/></td>
    <td>
        <html:select property="favSport">
            <html:option value="">Please choose</html:option>
            <html:options collection="sports" property="value"
                         labelProperty="label"/>
        </html:select>
    </td>
</tr>
<logic:messagesPresent property="comments">
<tr>
      <td colspan=2><html:errors property="comments"/></td>
</tr>
</logic:messagesPresent>
<tr>
...
```

Save this file and then make the appropriate additions to the `messages.properties` file for the messages used in this change and the error added in the validation change.

Once all these changes have been made, issue another `ant reload` command using Ant and point your browser to `http://localhost:8080/struts-base/`. The `index.jsp` page should be invoked, which will redirect you to `/form.do` where the form will be presented. The form should now have a new select list populated with the sports added in the `FormAction`. Submit the form and the validation will detect that no sport has yet been selected and display the appropriate message. This should look something like Figure 19-6.

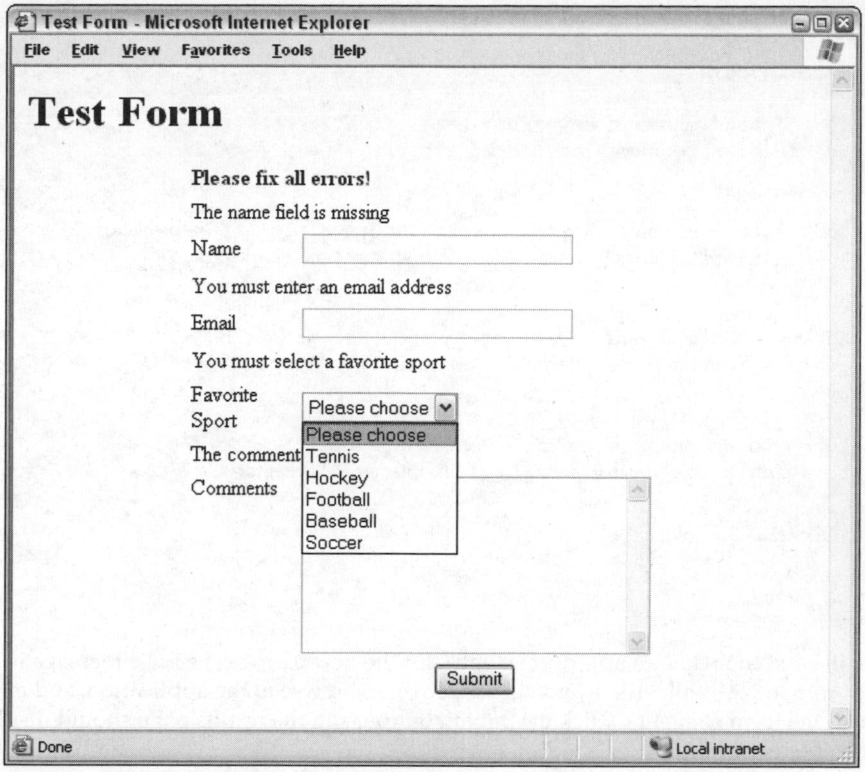

Figure 19-6: Favorite sport field with validation

Displaying All Information Submitted on the Next Page

These changes are all very well, but once the form is successfully submitted, the user is still presented with a mostly blank page.

In order to display the content of the form on the next page, the values of the form bean need to be output using the Struts `bean:write` tag. Open the `details.jsp` file and enter the following to display the contents of the form:

```
<%@ taglib uri="/WEB-INF/struts-bean.tld" prefix="bean" %>

<html>
<head>
    <title><bean:message key="display.title"/></title>
</head>
<body>
```

```
<h1> <bean:message key="display.title"/></h1>

<table cellspacing="0" cellpadding="0" border="0" width="50%" align="center">
<tr>
    <td><b><bean:message key="form.name.title"/></b></td>
    <td><bean:write name="testForm" property="name"/></td>
</tr>
<tr>
    <td><b><bean:message key="form.emailaddress.title"/></b></td>
    <td><bean:write name="testForm" property="emailAddress"/></td>
</tr>
<tr>
    <td><b><bean:message key="form.favsport.title"/></b></td>
    <td><bean:write name="testForm" property="favSport"/></td>
</tr>
<tr>
    <td><b><bean:message key="form.comments.title"/></b></td>
    <td><bean:write name="testForm" property="comments"/></td>
</tr>
</table>

</body>
</html>
```

Close this file and then add an appropriate entry for the new `display.title` message in the `messages.properties` file. Issue another `ant reload`, browse to the application, and enter valid details in all the form elements. Click the Submit button, and the results page should display all the values you entered.

All requirements have now been met. This simple example has used many of the Struts components and concepts described in this chapter:

❑   `DynaActionForm` use

❑   The Struts Validator

❑   Passing data from an action to the JSP page

❑   Using the actions to affect the flow of the application

❑   Struts Custom Tags

A real application would be immeasurably more complex, but it is easy to see how Struts has been designed to enable variance in the complexity of an application while still keeping the different components it provides relatively simple to use and easy to understand.

Summary

While a lot has been covered in this chapter, there are still more aspects of Struts that deserve attention, including the following:

- ❑ Data source specification
- ❑ More complex validation techniques using the Struts Validator
- ❑ More Struts Custom Tags
- ❑ Struts EL
- ❑ Struts modules
- ❑ Tiles

Unfortunately, these topics are beyond the scope of this chapter. For more information on Struts, you are encouraged to check out the voluminous documentation available at the Struts Web site (`http://jakarta.apache.org/struts/userGuide/index.html`) or refer to *Professional Jakarta Struts* (ISBN 0-7645-4437-3).

After working through this chapter, you should have an understanding of the following:

- ❑ The purpose of Struts with regard to its use as an MVC framework
- ❑ How Struts works and Validator configuration
- ❑ The role of Actions, form beans, and JSP files in a Struts application
- ❑ The different validation approaches available with Struts
- ❑ The many custom tags provided with Struts

Exercises

Further enhance the example application with the following exercises:

1. Add a new field to the form to collect the user's age, and add validation to the field requiring a valid numeric value that restricts the range of acceptable values to between 0 and 100, inclusive.

2. Add a login page to protect the application. An unauthenticated user should not be able to get to any page without being logged in.

Layout Management
with Tiles

This chapter introduces the Tiles framework and illustrates how it can provide structure and flexibility in presenting an interface to customers of your Web site. The chapter also demonstrates how to integrate Tiles with the Struts framework discussed in the last chapter.

This chapter covers the following topics:

❑   An introduction to Tiles

❑   Installing Tiles for use in a Web application

❑   Tiles definitions

❑   Tiles tags

❑   Advanced Tiles usage with parameters and inheritance

❑   The use of Tiles with Struts

Introduction to Tiles

Web developers have an awful habit of forgetting one of the most important concepts of software development: reuse. Why do something twice when you can do it once and use it everywhere? It has been said that some of the best software developers are essentially lazy souls who are always trying to ensure that they develop something only once, designing it flexibly enough so that *it*, whatever *it* is, can be used everywhere. Many of the techniques and tools explained in this book are created with this goal in mind. The Tiles framework is no different.

Tiles was first developed as a simple templating framework called *Components* by Cedric Dumoulin, and has since been renamed to Tiles to avoid the confusion that could result from using that word. Today, Tiles has been completely integrated into the Struts framework, although it can still be used independently.

What is the Tiles framework?

Pages that are displayed on Web sites often contain areas that are repeated in many places; menus, headers, and footers are typical examples. Web sites, therefore, are often designed in a layout or a number of layouts that don't change; only the content or what is actually displayed in those areas changes. Developers have traditionally tackled this challenge by using `jsp:include` invocations in an attempt to modularize these display elements. This approach, while achieving some degree of modularity, is limited because the included pages can become tightly bound to the pages in which they are used, with no way to define them, generally, across the application.

The Tiles framework enables a developer to use *templates* that contain common parts of an interface, without using includes. Tiles also organizes these templates into a series of reusable components that can be referenced from within the application.

For example, Figure 20-1 shows a very typical Web page layout. The separate areas have been shaded differently.

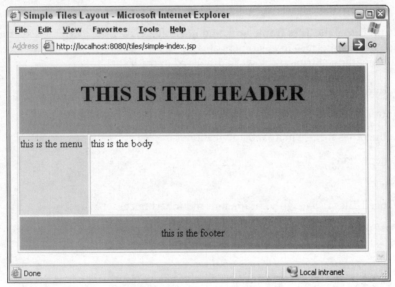

Figure 20-1: A simple Tiles template

The page displayed here uses a template (or *layout* in Tiles terminology) that defines four separate areas, or regions. In the Tiles framework, these regions are referred to as *tiles*. A tile in this context is a simple JSP page that displays some content: the header, some menu items, or the footer of a page. The layout that has been developed to show this page is a JSP file as well. It makes use of the tiles that have been provided and places them in the correct positions.

Figure 20-2 illustrates this structure of layouts and tiles being used to display a page.

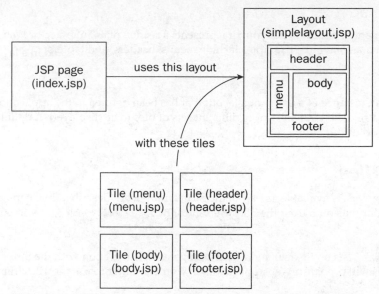

Figure 20-2: JSP page using a Tiles layout with certain Tiles pages

In this example, the `index.jsp` file defined which layout it will use and which tiles will be used in that layout. The tiles are passed to the layout as parameters. Note that the names defined in the layout page are consistent with the names of the tiles, such as `header`, `footer`, and `body`. When the tiles are passed to the layout, it uses these names to determine where each should be placed.

This *instance of usage* could also be defined as a *definition* and given a name that can be referenced in the application. Therefore, instead of the `index.jsp` file stipulating which tiles to use with the layout, and other pages having to do the same, it is defined centrally in an XML configuration file or another JSP file and called on by whatever pages require it. Each particular usage of this *definition* could then add special characteristics it requires. This second level of abstraction provided by tiles is enormously powerful.

Tiles terminology

This chapter uses terms that could become confusing if not understood in the correct context. This section defines the terms used in tiles to ensure that you understand the concepts presented in the rest of the chapter.

Layout

A *layout* is a JSP page that uses tiles to create an interface. An application can make use of many different layouts. A layout is simply a template for how a series of tiles can be placed together to form a view.

The term *layout* is used in this chapter instead of *template*, as it is consistent with Tiles terminology. In practice, the word *template* is equally correct.

Tile

A *tile* is an element or region of a layout; it represents a section of an interface or Web page that is likely to be reused in many layouts. Examples include menus, headers, and footers.

Definition

A *definition* is an instance of a usage of a layout that has been defined in the application. Separate definitions can take a single layout and apply different sets of tiles to be displayed. A definition can be given a name and reused throughout a site.

Installing Tiles

The Tiles framework is available as part of the Struts framework described in Chapter 19, "Struts Framework," or on its own from the Tiles Web site at http://www.lifl.fr/~dumoulin/tiles/index.html.

This chapter uses Tiles on its own and then investigates its integration with the Struts framework. The following steps will prepare a Web application on your computer to use the Tiles framework without using Struts:

1. Download the latest distribution from the Tiles Web site at www.lifl.fr/~dumoulin/tiles/index.html.

2. Extract the file you downloaded into a directory on your computer; in a Windows system this might be C:\tiles.

3. Copy the tiles.jar file from C:\tiles\lib into the WEB-INF/lib directory of your Web application.

4. Copy the struts-tiles.tld and tiles-config.dtd files from C:\tiles\lib into the WEB-INF directory of your Web application.

5. Tiles also requires some commons libraries from Jakarta (http://jakarta.apache.org/commons/). Download the following commons libraries and include the associated JAR files in the WEB-INF/lib directory:

    * Commons Digester: commons-digester.jar

    * Commons BeanUtils: commons-beanutils.jar

    * Commons Collections: commons-collections.jar

    * Commons Logging: commons-logging.jar

6. Although this step isn't compulsory for Tiles, the examples in this chapter use the JSTL. Place the jstl.jar and standard.jar files from the JSTL you have used in previous chapters in the /WEB-INF/lib directory

7. Make sure the WEB-INF/web.xml file in your Web application contains the following:

```
<?xml version="1.0" encoding="ISO-8859-1" ?>

<web-app xmlns="http://java.sun.com/xml/ns/j2ee"
         xmlns:xsi="http://www.w3.org/2001/XMLSchema-instance"
```

```
            xsi:schemaLocation="http://java.sun.com/xml/ns/j2ee
                http://java.sun.com/xml/ns/j2ee/web-app_2_4.xsd"
            version="2.4">

    <icon></icon>
    <display-name>Tiles Examples</display-name>
    <description>This is a Tiles Example</description>

  <servlet>
    <servlet-name>action</servlet-name>
    <servlet-class>org.apache.struts.tiles.TilesServlet</servlet-class>
    <init-param>
      <param-name>definitions-config</param-name>
      <param-value>/WEB-INF/tiles-defs.xml</param-value>
    </init-param>
    <load-on-startup>1</load-on-startup>
  </servlet>

  <servlet-mapping>
    <servlet-name>action</servlet-name>
    <url-pattern>*.do</url-pattern>
  </servlet-mapping>

  <welcome-file-list>
    <welcome-file>index.jsp</welcome-file>
  </welcome-file-list>
</web-app>
```

The servlet specified here is provided by the Tiles framework, and is required in order to initialize the Tiles factory with the specified configuration file (`tiles-defs.xml`). This configuration file will define the Tiles definitions available in the Web application. In addition to the `definitions-config` parameter, the following table describes the additional parameters that can be set.

Attribute	Description
definitions-config	Points to a Tiles configuration file or files. A comma should separate multiple values.
definitions-debug	Indicates the level of debugging that should be output from Tiles. Appropriate values here are 0, 1, or 2. A value of 2 will place Tiles in full debug mode.
definitions-parser-details	Similar to debug, but this parameter outputs detailed debugging information about parsing of the configuration file. Again, appropriate values are 0, 1, or 2.
definitions-parser-validate	Indicates that the tiles configuration file should be validated upon initialization. Values appropriate here are true and false.
definitions-factory-class	A developer can create a custom definition factory. In order for it to be initialized, this parameter would be used.

8. Create a file called `tiles-defs.xml` in the `WEB-INF` directory of your Web application. Note that the location matches the value of the `init-param` in the servlet definition in the previous step. Place the following content in the `tiles-defs.xml` file. This content doesn't actually do anything yet, but it will ensure that the file can be initialized properly when the servlet container loads it:

```
<!DOCTYPE tiles-definitions PUBLIC
        "-//Apache Software Foundation//DTD Tiles Configuration//EN"
        "http://jakarta.apache.org/struts/dtds/tiles-config.dtd">

<tiles-definitions>
</tiles-definitions>
```

Your application is now ready to use Tiles in the following Try It Out exercise. The examples in this chapter assume you are familiar with establishing an application in a servlet container such as Tomcat and applying changes as each example is discussed.

Try It Out   A Simple Tiles Example

In this example, you are going to create a page to show the view displayed in Figure 20-1. This will involve developing a simple layout and displaying various tiles within it.

Create a file called `simple-insert-index.jsp` in the root of your Web application. This is the file that will be invoked by the user of the site. Add the following to this new file:

```
<%@ taglib uri="/WEB-INF/struts-tiles.tld" prefix="tiles" %>

<tiles:insert page="/layout/simplelayout.jsp" flush="true">
  <tiles:put name="header" value="/tiles/simple-header.jsp" />
  <tiles:put name="menu" value="/tiles/simple-menu.jsp" />
  <tiles:put name="body" value="/tiles/simple-body.jsp" />
  <tiles:put name="footer" value="/tiles/simple-footer.jsp" />
</tiles:insert>
```

Tiles uses various JSP actions, which are made available by the `taglib` directive in the first line of this code fragment.

Now create a file called `simplelayout.jsp` in a subdirectory of the Web application called `layout`. This file will form the layout or template that will be used in this example. Add the following to `simplelayout.jsp`:

```
<%@ taglib uri="/WEB-INF/struts-tiles.tld" prefix="tiles" %>

<html>
  <head>
    <title>Simple Tiles Layout</title>
  </head>
<body bgcolor="white">

<table border="1" width="100%" height="100%" border="1">
<tr>
```

```
      <td colspan="2" height="100" bgcolor="gray">
          <tiles:insert attribute="header"/>
      </td>
    </tr>
    <tr>
      <td width="20%" valign="top" bgcolor="lightgrey">
          <tiles:insert attribute="menu"/>
      </td>
      <td valign="top"  align="left">
          <tiles:insert attribute="body"/>
      </td>
    </tr>
    <tr>
      <td colspan="2" height="50" bgcolor="gray">
          <tiles:insert attribute="footer"/>
      </td>
    </tr>
    </table>
    </body>
    </html>
```

This page defines the placement of each tile in the template.

You can now create the tiles themselves. Create corresponding JSP files for the four tiles that this template expects in a `tiles` subdirectory of your Web application:

❑   `/tiles/simple-menu.jsp`

❑   `/tiles/simple-header.jsp`

❑   `/tiles/simple-footer.jsp`

❑   `/tiles/simple-body.jsp`

For this example, these files can contain anything you want. In Figure 20-1, some text appears in each one to confirm that it is *that* tile that is being displayed. If you now send your browser to the `simple-insert-index.jsp` page in your Web application — for instance, `http://localhost:8080/<application name>/simple-insert-index.jsp` — you should see something like the view displayed in Figure 20-1. The source code for this and other examples is available from the Wrox Web site at `www.wrox.com`.

How It Works

Central to this example is the layout and the JSP page that uses it. The `simple-insert-index.jsp` page has used the `tiles:insert` tag to invoke a layout:

```
...
<tiles:insert page="/layout/simplelayout.jsp" flush="true">
...
</tiles:insert>
```

Nested within the `insert` tag are various `put` tags that define which tiles the layout will use. Each of these `put` tags defines a name for the tile with the `name` attribute and the file that is associated with that name in the `value` attribute:

```
...
<tiles:put name="menu" value="/tiles/simple-menu.jsp" />
...
```

We are effectively passing parameters into the layout page so that it knows which pages to use. These parameters are placed into the *tile scope* of the layout page, which you will learn more about later.

The layout page itself uses the tile values passed to it in order to display the correct tiles. Each place-holder for a tile uses the `insert` tag to display the page passed in the `put` tag from the invoking page:

```
...
<td><tiles:insert attribute="menu"/></td>
...
```

The attribute `menu` was passed to this layout page as an attribute that is now within its scope. The `insert` tag here inserts the content that the `menu` parameter represents: `simple-menu.jsp`.

From this simple example, you can see how the layout can be given various references for the tiles it expects to receive. These could even be determined dynamically, changing the behavior of the layout based on various conditions such as user preferences or internationalization settings.

Tile Scope

Throughout this book, you will have become familiar with the various scopes that are available from within JSP pages: `application`, `session`, `request`, and `page`. The Tiles framework introduces a new scope in order to avoid clashes with attributes that may appear in other scopes. This new scope is called *tile scope*. Internally, `tile` scope refers to a `Map` of objects placed within the existing page context. Some tags in the Tiles tag library allow you to copy values from the `tile` scope into the standard scopes you are already familiar with. From there, you can use the value just like other values in JSP pages.

As you will see in the following sections, when an attribute is passed to a layout tile or standard tile, it is placed within the `tile` scope of that tile only; it is not available to the other tiles that are being used. Developers must explicitly manage the scope and delegation of values from layout to tile and so on. This explicit declarative approach means that tiles will not become mistakenly reliant on an attribute unless it is deliberately made available. This enhances the decoupled nature of the components of the application.

Definitions

One limitation of the previous example is that the `simple-insert-index.jsp` page actually stipulates the tiles to be used, as well as the layout itself. What if this configuration were required from another page on the site? The same `insert` tag would be used, with the same parameters being passed. This is *duplication*, one of the many traps that Web applications fall into. Were a change to be made, such as the name of the `simple-menu.jsp` file, then each instance would have to be separately changed and tested. In a large system this is a serious problem, and in a smaller one it's just annoying.

Remember the comment that some of the best programmers are lazy? Making such a site-wide change could mean a lot of work. Thankfully, Tiles provides a way to define this instance of layout usage in a central place so that it can be used by the entire application and changed only in one place if the need arises.

This concept is the *definition* that was discussed earlier. Definitions can be stored centrally in two ways: within a JSP file that is included on pages within the site, or within an XML configuration file that resides in the `/WEB-INF/` directory of your Web application. Once a definition is specified, JSP pages can use the layout by using the `insert` tag in a slightly different way from the `simple-insert-index.jsp` page in the preceding example. If the definition were defined in a Tiles configuration file, the content of that page would appear as follows:

```
<%@ page language="java" %>
<%@ taglib uri="/WEB-INF/struts-tiles.tld" prefix="tiles" %>
<tiles:insert definition="simple.layout" flush="true" />
```

Note that there is no reference to the specific tiles used within the JSP page anymore. The following Try It Out exercise illustrates the use of a definition, as specified within a JSP page.

Try It Out   A JSP Page Definition

Create a file called `definitions.jsp` in a subdirectory called `definitions` in your Web application's root directory. This file will specify the definition that will be used, and will be included on the JSP page that is invoked. The content of this new file is as follows:

```
<%@ taglib uri="/WEB-INF/struts-tiles.tld" prefix="tiles" %>

<tiles:definition
            id="simple.include.layout"
            page="/layout/simplelayout.jsp"
            scope="request">
  <tiles:put name="header" value="/tiles/simple-header.jsp" />
  <tiles:put name="menu" value="/tiles/simple-menu.jsp" />
  <tiles:put name="body" value="/tiles/simple-body.jsp" />
  <tiles:put name="footer" value="/tiles/simple-footer.jsp" />
</tiles:definition>
```

Note that you have used the `definition` tag to specify this definition and it has been given a name: `simple.include.layout`, with the `id` attribute.

Now create a file called `simple-incdef-index.jsp` in the Web directory of your Web application. This is the file that will make use of the new definition. Enter the following code in this file:

```
<%@ page language="java" %>
<%@ include file="definitions/definitions.jsp"%>
<%@ taglib uri="/WEB-INF/struts-tiles.tld" prefix="tiles" %>
<tiles:insert beanName="simple.include.layout" beanScope="request"/>
```

This file uses the include directive to include the definitions.jsp file that has just been created, and calls the definitions it contains. (There's only one at the moment, but there could be as many as the application needs.) Note that the insert tag is used again, but this time it uses the name of the definition in the beanName attribute. If you now browse to your Web application's simple-incdef-index.jsp page, you should see the same screen shown in Figure 20-1.

Try It Out   XML Configuration File Definition

The same result can be achieved by defining the definition in the tiles-defs.xml file that was created when Tiles was first installed. To do so, add the following definition to this file (changes are highlighted):

```
<!DOCTYPE tiles-definitions PUBLIC
        "-//Apache Software Foundation//DTD Tiles Configuration//EN"
        "http://jakarta.apache.org/struts/dtds/tiles-config.dtd">

<tiles-definitions>
   <definition name="simple.xml.layout" path="/layout/simplelayout.jsp">
       <put name="header" value="/tiles/simple-header.jsp" />
       <put name="body"   value="/tiles/simple-body.jsp" />
       <put name="menu"   value="/tiles/simple-menu.jsp" />
       <put name="footer" value="/tiles/simple-footer.jsp" />
   </definition>
</tiles-definitions>
```

You can see that the syntax used here is similar to that used when declaring the definition in the JSP page, with the major exception of the put tag (tiles:put), which is replaced with the put XML element.

Now that this definition (simple.xml.layout) has been defined, it can be used in JSP pages on the site. Create a file called simple-xmldef-index.jsp in the root Web directory of your Web application. This file will make use of the configuration file's definition; it contains the following:

```
<%@ page language="java" %>
<%@ taglib uri="/WEB-INF/struts-tiles.tld" prefix="tiles" %>
<tiles:insert definition="simple.xml.layout" flush="true" />
```

This will also produce the same output as Figure 20-1. Note that while the insert tag has been invoked again, different attributes have been used.

This section has given you a brief introduction to definitions. Later in this chapter, we will expand on this to illustrate some of their more advanced features.

Tiles Tags

In the preceding examples, you saw the use of some of the Tiles tags that are available. This section introduces these and the remaining tags, and explains the attributes that can be used with them.

insert

You have seen the `insert` tag used in at least two capacities so far: First it was used within the nontile JSP pages so that a layout could be inserted and various tiles passed to it as parameters with the `put` tag. Second, it was used in the layout JSP page to display values it had been passed. The following table explains the attributes available for this tag.

Attribute	Description
attribute	The value for this attribute is the name of an attribute, such as the name of a tile or other component. This attribute corresponds to the `name` attribute in the `put` tag when the parameter is specified.
beanName	The name of a bean to be used. The `beanScope` attribute is used to define the scope in which this bean should be retrieved. The bean specified here could be a definition that has been declared.
beanProperty	Used in conjunction with the `beanName` attribute. Use of this attribute causes the value to be retrieved from this property of the bean specified.
beanScope	The scope used to retrieve the value specified in `beanName`. This attribute is optional; `page` scope is the default value.
component	Same as the `page` and `template` attributes. It represents the location of a tile or layout.
controllerClass	The Struts action class used before this insert tag is invoked. Only one of `controllerUrl` or `controllerClass` can be used.
controllerUrl	Used with Struts to specify an action used before this `insert` tag is invoked.
definition	Used to insert a definition defined in the `tiles-defs.xml` configuration file. The value of this attribute would be a definition id.
flush	Used to flush the body of the page to the output stream after this tag is invoked.
ignore	Used in conjunction with the `name` attribute. If the bean specified in the `name` attribute does not exist and the `ignore` attribute is set to `true`, no error is thrown and no value is displayed. When set to `false`, a runtime error would be displayed. The default value of this optional attribute is `false`.
name	Used to identify a bean to be inserted by this tag.
page	See `component`.
role	Used to specify the role that a user must have in order for this tag to be executed by the server.
template	See `component`.

definition

This tag is used to establish a definition as described earlier. A corresponding definition element in a tiles-defs.xml file performs the same basic function. This tag effectively creates a bean that can be used with the insert tag. This tag also supports more advanced usage whereby a new definition can inherit and add to the characteristics of another definition defined in the tiles-defs.xml file. You will see an example of this behavior in subsequent sections. The following table describes the attributes of the definition tag.

Attribute	Description
extends	The value of this optional attribute is the id of another definition defined in the tiles-defs.xml file. This allows the new definition to assume all the characteristics of the other definition.
id	The identifying name of this definition. Used by the insert tag to insert this definition into a page. Required.
scope	As this tag effectively creates a bean to be used, this attribute specifies the scope into which this bean will be placed. The default value of this optional attribute is page.
template	The value of this optional attribute is a path to a tile or layout to be used with this definition.
page	See template.
role	This optional attribute is used to specify the role that a user must have in order for this tag to be executed by the server.

put

This tag is used to pass parameters to components. You saw this tag used earlier where paths to tiles (JSP pages) were passed within the confines of a definition tag and where the insert tag was used to insert a layout for display. The put tag can only be used within the definition or insert tags.

Attribute	Description
beanName	This optional attribute defines the name of a bean to be passed. The beanScope attribute is used to define the scope in which this bean should be retrieved.
beanProperty	This optional attribute is used in conjunction with the beanName attribute. Using this attribute causes the value to be retrieved from this property of the bean specified.
beanScope	The scope used to retrieve the value specified in beanName. This attribute is optional; page scope is the default value. Valid values here include application, session, page, component, template, and tile. The last three are all the same.

Attribute	Description
content	Same as value.
direct	See type. Manipulates the way in which the tag handles the type attribute when it is missing. If the type attribute is used, this attribute has no effect. The documentation states that this is included for JSP template compatibility.
type	This defines the content type of the value being *put*. Valid values here are as follows: **string:** The value of the parameter is a text value and can be used directly (see direct). **page (template):** The value of the parameter is content retrieved from another file. With type set as one of these values, the value attribute is treated as a path, rather than as a value itself, or a definition. **definition:** Used where a definition is used as a parameter. The value here is the id or name of the definition being passed. The definition must have been defined in a definition factory, meaning it must have been added to the configuration XML file. If the type attribute is not used and the direct attribute is set to true, the value is implicitly used as though string were set here. If direct is specified as false, the value is implicitly treated as though page or template were used here. If the type attribute is not specified, but beanName is specified, then the object is treated as is, meaning as an object. See beanName, beanProperty, and beanScope. This is an optional attribute.
name	The name of this parameter. The value of this required attribute is used to reference the value this tag represents.
value	An object that is the value being *put*. The value of this attribute is entered either directly as a string value, or as the name of a bean that is available where this tag is being used. Optional, but one of beanName, value, or content must be used.
role	The role of users for which this tag will be used. If the user is not in the specified role, this tag is ignored. This attribute is optional.

putList

The putList tag, like put, defines a parameter to be passed to another Tiles component; however, putList creates a list of other objects as the value. This tag can be used only inside the definition or insert tags.

Internally, putList represents the data created as a java.util.List object. Elements are added to the object created by putList with nested add tags. You can use the attributes shown in the following table with putList.

Attribute	Description
name	The name of this parameter. The value of this required attribute is used to reference the value this tag represents.
role	This optional attribute defines the role of users for which this tag will be used. If the user is not in the specified role, this tag is ignored.

add

The add tag is used to add items to a surrounding putList tag. It cannot be used within any other tag. Its behavior is identical to that of the put tag described earlier (internally, the AddTag extends the PutTag class), except the values are added to the list being defined. All the parameters described in put apply to this tag, with the exception of the name attribute.

get

The get tag is used to retrieve a value that has been placed within the tile scope, and either print out its value (in the case of a string) or include it where this tag is called (in the case of a tile). Internally, the GetTag class extends the InsertTag class. The main difference between the get tag and the insert tag, other than the former having significantly fewer attributes, is the default value for the ignore attribute. The following table shows the attributes available for working with the get tag.

Attribute	Description
name	The name of the attribute or value on which the tag will act. This is a required attribute.
ignore	If the value specified in name does not exist, this attribute determines whether an error will be displayed. Valid values here are true and false. The default value of this optional attribute is true.
flush	Used to flush the body of the page to the output stream after this tag is invoked. The default value of this optional attribute is true.
role	The role of users for whom this tag will be used. If the user is not in the specified role, this tag is ignored. This attribute is optional.

getAsString

The getAsString tag basically invokes a toString() method on the object it is passed, and renders it via the JspWriter. It accepts the attributes shown in the following table.

Attribute	Description
name	This required attribute defines the name of the attribute or value on which the tag will act.
ignore	If the value specified in name does not exist, this attribute specifies whether an error will be displayed. Valid values here are true and false. The default value of this optional attribute is false.
role	The role of users for whom this tag will be used. If the user is not in the specified role, this tag is ignored. This attribute is optional.

useAttribute

The useAttribute tag is used to copy a value from the tile scope into a specified scope *and* the page scope. If the scope attribute is not specified, the value is only exposed to the page scope. There the value can be used like any other variable in the page. useAttribute accepts the attributes described in the following table.

Attribute	Description
id	The variable name with which the value can be referenced in the page and specified scopes. The default value of this optional attribute is the name of the value, its existing name (specified in the name attribute).
name	This required attribute specifies the name of the value to be acted on by this tag.
scope	In addition to the page scope, the value will also be placed in the scope specified by the value of this attribute. Possible values are application, session, request, and page. Due to this tag's behavior, specifying page scope here would be redundant. This attribute is optional.
ignore	If the value specified in name does not exist, this attribute specifies whether an error will be displayed. Valid values for this optional attribute are true and false. The default value is false.
classname	The class of the value being acted on by this tag. It has no impact on the behavior of the tag.

importAttribute

This tag is used to import a single value or all values in the tile scope into a specified scope. If the name attribute is not used, all values in the tile scope are imported. This tag accepts the attributes shown in the following table.

Attribute	Description
name	This required attribute specifies the name of the value to be acted on by this tag.
scope	This optional attribute specifies the scope into which the value is imported. The default is page scope.
ignore	This optional attribute is relevant only when importing a single value. If the value specified in name does not exist, this attribute indicates whether an error will be displayed. Valid values here are true and false. The default value is false.

initComponentDefinitions

The initComponentDefinations tag is used to initialize the definition factory with the specified XML configuration file. The following table describes the attributes this tag accepts.

Attribute	Description
file	This required attribute specifies the file that contains the definition elements.
classname	This optional attribute specifies the classname of the factory to initialize.

Passing Parameters to Tiles

Earlier in this chapter, you saw how parameters were passed within the body of the insert tag and definition tags. The parameters passed were pointers to tiles to be used in the template or layout tiles. It is also possible to pass other values to tiles components using the put and putList tags.

A simple example of this is where a string is passed to a layout as part of a definition and then used within the layout tile or a content tile. The following code fragment shows a definition tag being used to pass various parameters to the layout tile, including a string that will form the title of a page:

```
<tiles:definition
        id="simple.include.layout.title"
        page="/layout/simplelayout-title.jsp"
        scope="request">
  <tiles:put name="title" value="This is my New Title" />
  <tiles:put name="header" value="/tiles/simple-header-title.jsp" />
  <tiles:put name="menu" value="/tiles/simple-menu.jsp" />
  <tiles:put name="body" value="/tiles/simple-body.jsp" />
  <tiles:put name="footer" value="/tiles/simple-footer.jsp" />
</tiles:definition>
```

The parameters passed to this layout are placed in the `tile` scope of the layout; they are now accessible from within the `simplelayout-title.jsp` page using the `getAsString` tag (this tag only retrieves values from the `tile` scope). You have seen in the previous examples how most of these parameters can then be used. In the case of the `title` parameter, it can be displayed in the `simplelayout-title.jsp` page with the following code:

```
<%@ taglib uri="/WEB-INF/struts-tiles.tld" prefix="tiles" %>

<html>
  <head>
    <title>
      <tiles:getAsString name="title"/>
    </title>
  </head>
<body bgcolor="white">
...
```

This will display the value of the `title` parameter in the title of the Web page. What if you wanted to have the `title` parameter also within the scope of the `header` tile? The value would have to be specifically placed within the scope of that tile using the following addition to the `insert` tag of this tile in the `simplelayout-title.jsp` page:

```
...
  <td colspan="2" height="100" bgcolor="gray">
      <tiles:insert attribute="header">
          <tiles:put name="headerTitle" beanName="title"/>
      </tiles:insert>
  </td>
...
```

Now the value of the `title` parameter is within the `tile` scope of the `header` tile with an alias of `headerTitle`, and can be used in the same way. A `String` object suited our example here, but the same scope accessibility could be achieved with any Java object. What results from this of course is the capability to use the parameter within tiles that have been given access to it.

Advanced Tiles

The following sections build on the principles of tiles you have learned so far and introduce some advanced topics.

Definitions and inheritance

As discussed earlier, definitions are a powerful feature of the Tiles framework. Configuring various layout tiles, standard tiles, and other parameters under a common name enables them to be used everywhere in an application; reuse is a good thing.

Of course, there may be times when the definition used for 99 percent of a site doesn't suit the other 1 percent. For instance, in a members only area, a different menu tile might be presented, or the same tile with different parameters may be used. Your first approach might be to create another definition to suit this new situation, but then you would end up just replicating all the tiles and parameters that didn't change. All the brownie points you got for exercising reuse are gone.

Tiles provides an excellent solution to this and other scenarios in which certain characteristics of an existing definition need to be used in a new definition, a concept called *inheritance*. A cornerstone of object-oriented software development, inheritance means that one object inherits some or all of the characteristics of another object. The child entity may then override certain characteristics with its own version or even add new ones. Tiles uses the inheritance principle to allow definitions to inherit (or *extend* in Java speak) the characteristics of another definition. The application can then use the child definition in special situations. Note that you can implement as many *generations* of inheriting definitions as you want — that is, until it gets too complicated for you to understand. As always, features like this are often overused by eager developers who end up with something that is way too complicated for a human to understand and therefore becomes unmaintainable. Keep the structure of definitions simple and logical, even at the expense of some reuse if it keeps things clearer.

To illustrate, the following Try It Out exercise implements two definitions to be used in two different pages. The second page will use a definition that *extends* the first page by only changing some of its defined parameters.

Try It Out   Definition Inheritance

The first task is to define the parent definition and the parameters it will use. This example uses a mother/son combination to enforce the fact that inheritance is being used. Add the following mother definition to the `tiles-defs.xml` file discussed in the simple tiles example earlier:

```
<definition name="inh.mother.layout" path="/layout/inh-layout.jsp">
    <put name="header" value="/tiles/inh-header.jsp" />
    <put name="menu" value="/tiles/inh-mother-menu.jsp" />
    <put name="footer" value="/tiles/inh-footer.jsp" />

    <putList name="myMovies">
        <add value="The Bridges Over Madison County"/>
        <add value="Steel Magnolias"/>
        <add value="What Women Want"/>
        <add value="You've Got Mail"/>
        <add value="Sleepless in Seattle"/>
    </putList>
</definition>
```

As you can probably tell from the definition, the example will show `header`, `menu`, and `footer` tiles, as well as make use of a list of favorite movies to display. The movies listed here (some of my mother's favorites!) will be displayed on the layout tile defined by the `path` attribute of the definition element, `/layout/inh-layout.jsp`.

The son's definition will extend the mother's definition, making its own adjustments to suit the audience. In doing so, the list of movies will be changed to reflect the son's taste, and the menu tile will change to show a different menu. The remaining elements of the definition — the `header` and the `footer` tiles — will not need to be specified in the son's definition, as they are inherited from the mother's definition. This is a great demonstration of reuse. The son's definition should be added to the `tiles-defs.xml` file as follows:

```
<definition name="inh.son.layout"
            extends="inh.mother.layout">
    <put name="menu" value="/tiles/inh-son-menu.jsp" />

    <putList name="myMovies">
        <add value="The Matrix"/>
        <add value="The Return of The King"/>
        <add value="A Midnight Clear"/>
        <add value="Apocalypse Now"/>
        <add value="Tigerland"/>
        <add value="Spaced - Series 2"/>
    </putList>
</definition>
```

You might notice that the son's definition doesn't even include the `path` attribute to specify the name of the layout tile to use; this has been inherited as well. Perhaps more important, this characteristic could also be overridden by the son's definition, using a different layout tile completely.

Now that the definitions are established, we have a few more tasks to complete. First we need the layout tile to display the various tiles, and to list the `myMovies` list. The layout tile is similar to the one presented earlier, but this time we need to use the JSTL in order to iterate through the list and display each value. For this to work, we also have to use the `importAttribute` tag to copy the parameters passed to this tile from `tile` scope into `page` scope:

Create a new file called `inh-layout.jsp` in the `/layout/` directory of your Web application and enter the following code:

```
<%@ taglib uri="/WEB-INF/struts-tiles.tld" prefix="tiles" %>
<%@ taglib uri="http://java.sun.com/jsp/jstl/core" prefix="c"%>

<tiles:importAttribute />
<html>
  <head>
    <title>Inheritance Example</title>
  </head>
<body bgcolor="white">

<table border="1" width="100%" height="100%" border="1">
<tr>
  <td colspan="2" height="100" bgcolor="gray">
      <tiles:insert attribute="header"/>
  </td>
</tr>
<tr>
  <td width="20%" valign="top" bgcolor="lightgrey">
      <tiles:insert attribute="menu"/>
  </td>
```

```
    <td valign="top"  align="left">
<h3>Favorite Movies</h3>
    <ul>
<c:forEach items="${myMovies}" var="thisMovie">
              <li>${thisMovie}</li>
        </c:forEach>
      </ul>
  </td>
</tr>
<tr>
    <td colspan="2"><center><tiles:insert attribute="footer"/></center></td>
</tr>
</table>
</body>
</html>
```

In addition to the layout tile, we also need to establish common header and footer tiles that will be used by both definitions, as well as a separate menu tile for each.

First create two files called `inh-header.jsp` and `inh-footer.jsp` in the `/tiles/` directory of your Web application. These tiles will be common to the two definitions (the son's definition doesn't redefine these tiles with its own values). Add the following content to these two new files:

`inh-header.jsp`:

```
<center><h2>This is the header tile</h2></center>
```

`inh-footer.jsp`

```
<i>Mother and Son Web Sites Incorporated 2005</i>
```

Both these files will be used by both mother and son definitions. However, we require each definition to have its own menu tile.

Create a new file called `inh-son-menu.jsp` in the `/tiles/` directory of your Web application. This will be the menu used by the son's definition. Place the following in this file:

```
<h5>Son's Menu</h5>
<ul>
<li>War Movies</li>
<li>Books</li>
<li>Loud Music</li>
<li>Parties</li>
<li>College Website</li>
<li>Fast Cars</li>
</ul>
```

Now create a file called `inh-mother-menu.jsp` in the `/tiles/` directory of your Web application. This will be the menu used by the mother's definition. Place the following in this file:

```
<h5>Mom's Menu</h5>
<ul>
<li>Knitting</li>
<li>Tennis</li>
<li>Weekends Away</li>
<li>Pottery</li>
<li>Cooking Ideas</li>
</ul>
```

We now need some files to actually use these definitions. To achieve this, we will create two files, each to call a different definition. Create a file called `inh-mother-index.jsp` in the root directory of your Web application and add the following code:

```
<%@ page language="java" %>
<%@ taglib uri="/WEB-INF/struts-tiles.tld" prefix="tiles" %>
<tiles:insert definition="inh.mother.layout" flush="true" />
```

Create another file in the same directory called `inh-son-index.jsp` and add the following:

```
<%@ page language="java" %>
<%@ taglib uri="/WEB-INF/struts-tiles.tld" prefix="tiles" %>
<tiles:insert definition="inh.son.layout" flush="true" />
```

If you now point your browser to the son's definition index page, `inh-son-index.jsp`, you should see something similar to what is shown in Figure 20-3.

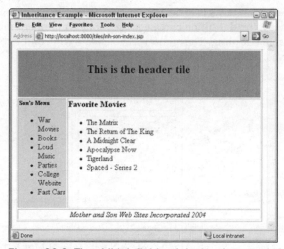

Figure 20-3: The child definition inherits characteristics from a parent definition.

As mentioned before, there is no limit to the number of generations of inherited definitions that can be defined (grandson definitions, etc.). And while this is powerful feature, overzealous use can quickly become unmanageable.

How It Works

The result of the `insert` tags in the `inh-son-index.jsp` and `inh-mother-index.jsp` is to display the relevant definition elements, with the desired effect that the son definition (`inh.son.layout`) includes all the elements of the mother definition (`inh.mother.layout`), except those that were overridden — namely, the `myMovies` list and the `menu` tile.

Nesting tiles

In previous examples, we used a definition to render a layout with certain tile and data attributes. This has only really defined a very simple layout pattern of two levels: the layout and the tiles used by it. Some Web sites use more complex layouts and have features or regions of a page that can themselves use a separate layout. To accommodate this, Tiles enables developers to insert a definition within a layout. It doesn't take long to appreciate the limitless combinations of tiles, definitions, and layouts that this provides.

The following Try It Out exercise illustrates the use of a new definition from within a layout.

Try It Out   Using a New Definition for the Menu

The new definition will use a new layout that defines only the specific region we are trying to represent. The definition will then be used inside one of the existing layouts we have already used in this chapter. The new layout will present a small list of menu items. The associated definition will therefore need to provide a title tile and body tile.

The best way to approach such tasks is to design the new layout in isolation from other definitions as much as possible; that way, the definition becomes a separate component that can be used in other definitions with a minimum of coupling. The menu we will create will comprise two regions, a small header and the list of menu items, as shown in Figure 20-4.

Figure 20-4: Planned layout for a menu definition

As the header will display only some text, we can probably live with this being output from the layout file itself, rather than from a separate tile. Therefore, the header will simply be a string value parameter passed to the layout. The menu list itself will be a separate tile. The menu tile will also need a list of items to display. This list forms the third parameter to send to the layout.

Now that we have a clear specification of the layout, create a new definition in the `tiles-defs.xml` file with the following content:

```
<definition name="menu"
            path="/layout/menu-layout.jsp">
  <put name="menuTitle" value="My Menu"/>
  <put name="menuTile" value="/tiles/menu-tile.jsp"/>
  <putList name="menuItems">
        <item value="Home Banking" link="http://somebank.com"/>
        <item value="Search" link="http://goggle.com"/>
        <item value="Java" link="http://java.sun.com"/>
  </putList>
</definition>
```

The syntax here should be familiar to you now. The `putList` encloses a series of `item` elements, rather than adding elements that were used in previous examples. Tiles provides this element when defining menu items in a definition. Under the covers, each `item` element here places a `org.apache.struts .tiles.beans.MenuItem` object in the list defined by `putList`. A `MenuItem` object contains values for `value` and `link` properties as used here, but also for `icon` and `tooltip`, which can be used in an interface. Very handy indeed!

The preceding definition places the three parameters (`menuTitle`, `menuTile`, and `menuItems`) within the tile scope of the layout tile `/layout/menu-layout.jsp`. With this in mind, we can now set about creating the layout itself. Remember that our goal here it to produce only the layout for the menu, nothing else.

Create a new file called `menu-layout.jsp` in the layout directory of your Web application. To display the layout presented in Figure 20-4, add the following code to this new file:

```
<%@ taglib uri="/WEB-INF/struts-tiles.tld" prefix="tiles" %>

<tiles:importAttribute/>

<table cellspacing="0" cellpadding="5" height="200" border="1">
<tr height="10">
    <td><font face="verdana" size="2"><b>
            <tiles:getAsString name="menuTitle"/>
        </b></font>
    </td>
</tr>
<tr>
    <td valign="top">
    <tiles:insert attribute="menuTile">
        <tiles:put name="menuList" beanName="menuItems" beanScope="tile"/>
    </tiles:insert>
    </td>
</tr>
</table>
```

All the parameters defined in the definition are represented here. First, the `menuTitle` attribute is output to the screen using the `getAsString` tag. Second, the `menuTile` tile is inserted in the appropriate place in the layout. Third, the `menuItems` bean is passed to the `menuTile` tile's tile scope as `menuList`. In order to have access to the `menuItems` bean, we used the `importAttribute` tag to place it within the page scope.

Note that there is no formatting where the `insert` tag places the `menu` tile. This is a good thing; it means that the menu's display is independent of other components. Of course, in a more complicated example where the items in the menu are provided by the Model layer of an application, the dependencies are more involved.

Now we can create the JSP page for the `menuTile` tile so that it can display the items in the `menuItems` bean, although it will see this value as `menuList`. The `menuTile` tile will make use of the JSTL tags to produce the output. The file `/tiles/menu-tile.jsp` is created with the following content:

```
<%@ taglib uri="/WEB-INF/struts-tiles.tld" prefix="tiles" %>
<%@ taglib uri="http://java.sun.com/jsp/jstl/core" prefix="c"%>

<tiles:importAttribute/>

<table cellspacing="0" cellpadding="0" border="0">
<c:forEach items="${menuList}" var="thisItem">
    <tr>
    <td><font face="verdana" size="2">
        <a href="${thisItem.link}">${thisItem.value}</a>
        </font></td>
    </tr>
</c:forEach>
</table>
```

Note that the `importAttribute` tag has been used again to place the `menuList` bean within the page scope of this tile. Once this is done, the items in the list can be iterated over, outputting the `link` and `value` properties of each.

So far, we have done nothing more than create a new, relatively simple definition, layout, and tile structure that is independent of the rest of the application. This structure can be verified independently as well. Simply create a new JSP page to use the new definition and it will display the new menu on its own. The new JSP file to display the definition would appear as follows:

```
<%@ page language="java" %>
<%@ taglib uri="/WEB-INF/struts-tiles.tld" prefix="tiles" %>
<tiles:insert definition="menu" flush="true" />
```

The output of this page should look like Figure 20-5.

Figure 20-5: New menu definition used in isolation

Our next task is to incorporate this definition inside another layout page. To achieve this, the new definition will serve to replace the `menu` tile in the inheritance example from earlier. In the `/layout/inh-layout.jsp` file, make the following adjustment (the change is highlighted):

```
...
<table border="1" width="100%" height="100%" border="1">
<tr>
  <td colspan="2" height="100" bgcolor="gray">
       <tiles:insert attribute="header"/>
  </td>
</tr>
<tr>
  <td width="20%" valign="top" bgcolor="lightgrey">
      <tiles:insert definition="menu"/>
  </td>
  <td valign="top"  align="left">
  <h3>Favorite Movies</h3>
      <ul>
          <c:forEach items="${myMovies}" var="thisMovie">
              <li>${thisMovie}</li>
          </c:forEach>
      </ul>
  </td>
</tr>
...
```

We have simply changed the `insert` tag to use a definition named `menu` instead of a tile attribute. In addition to the preceding change, you will have to remove the `menu` tile `put` element from the `inh.mother.layout` and `inh.son.layout` definitions. The mother definition in the `tiles-defs.xml` file should now appear as follows:

```
<definition name="inh.mother.layout" path="/layout/inh-layout.jsp">
  <put name="header" value="/tiles/inh-header.jsp" />
  <put name="footer" value="/tiles/inh-footer.jsp" />

  <putList name="myMovies">
    <add value="The Bridges Over Madison County"/>
    <add value="Steel Magnolias"/>
    <add value="What Women Want"/>
    <add value="You've Got Mail"/>
    <add value="Sleepless in Seattle"/>
  </putList>
</definition>
```

Note that the menu tile put element has been removed. This works because the inh-layout.jsp file inserts the new menu definition directly.

If you now browse to either the inh-mother-index.jsp or inh-son-index.jsp files from the inheritance example, the new menu definition output will be displayed, nested within the layout, as shown in Figure 20-6.

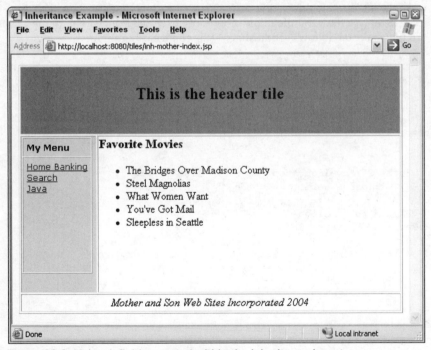

Figure 20-6: Menu definition nested within the inheritance layout

How It Works

This change we have made could be a little confusing. Let's step through the process again. Our goal was to replace the menus used by the mother and son definitions with a separate definition called `menu`, illustrating that a separate definition can be used from within a layout.

We first created a definition in the `tiles-defs.xml` file called `menu`. This new definition was given some data to display as menu items, defined within the definition entry of the `tiles-defs.xml` file. We then created a layout for the new definition to handle the layout for the menu itself. This new layout was provided with a new Tile called `menuTile` that displays the list of menu items. To verify that this worked, we displayed the menu on its own, as shown in Figure 20-5.

To make use of the definition properly, we then changed the `inh-layout.jsp` page to call on this new `menu` definition directly, meaning that both the mother and son definitions would now show the same menu. As a bit of cleanup, the menu `put` entry for the mother and son definitions in the `tiles-defs.xml` file was removed.

This is all well and good, but our layout JSP page will always display a menu in the left-hand region, and to change it we would have to modify the `inh-layout.jsp` file. Instead of inserting the definition directly in the layout file, the definition could be passed to the layout as just another attribute, configured as such in the configuration file. This is the goal of the next Try It Out exercise.

Try It Out   Passing a Definition as a Parameter

This change is relatively simple but will mean that the layout page we have created is almost entirely configurable, without touching any JSP code.

In the `tiles-defs.xml` file, modify the `inh-mother-layout` definition to now pass the `menu` definition as a parameter to the layout tile. The following listing shows the modification, with the changes highlighted:

```
<definition name="inh.mother.layout" path="/layout/inh-layout.jsp">
  <put name="header" value="/tiles/inh-header.jsp" />
  <put name="footer" value="/tiles/inh-footer.jsp" />
  <put name="movies" value="/tiles/inh-movies.jsp"/>
  <put name="menu.region" value="menu"/>

  <putList name="myMovies">
    <add value="The Bridges Over Madison County"/>
    <add value="Steel Magnolias"/>
    <add value="What Women Want"/>
    <add value="You've Got Mail"/>
    <add value="Sleepless in Seattle"/>
  </putList>
</definition>

<definition name="inh.son.layout"
            extends="inh.mother.layout">
  <putList name="myMovies">
    <add value="The Matrix"/>
    <add value="The Return of The King"/>
    <add value="A Midnight Clear"/>
```

```
        <add value="Apocalypse Now"/>
        <add value="Tigerland"/>
        <add value="Spaced - Series 2"/>
    </putList>
</definition>

    <definition name="menu"
                path="/layout/menu-layout.jsp">
...
```

Within the `inh-layout.jsp` page, the `insert` tag is used to display the parameter `menu.region`, just like any other tile parameter that the layout may be passed. Modify the `inh-layout.jsp` file to make use of this new parameter. Instead of appearing as

```
<tr>
    <td width="20%" valign="top" bgcolor="lightgrey">
        <tiles:insert definition="menu"/>
    </td>
    <td valign="top"  align="left">
    <h3>Favorite Movies</h3>
...
```

it should now appear as

```
<tr>
    <td width="20%" valign="top" bgcolor="lightgrey">
        <tiles:insert attribute="menu.region"/>
    </td>
    <td valign="top"  align="left">
    <h3>Favorite Movies</h3>
...
```

How It Works

In the preceding Try It Out example, we called the `menu` definition directly from the `inh-layout.jsp` file. The change in this section involved replacing this direct call with the use of a parameter that has been passed to the layout. This parameter just happened to be a definition, a definition to display the menu.

This is probably a good place to summarize the last few topics; we've made some real progress from some very humble beginnings.

We started with a simple mother/son definition inheritance in which a single layout was used but one definition was set up with certain parameters and another definition inherited some of these parameters, replacing the rest with its own version of things, such as the movie list and a menu.

We then decided that the menu itself was to be an important repeatable component and deserved its own definition along with some menu items. We used this new `menu` definition in the inheritance layout tile to show the menu in all circumstances. Now, with this latest change, the `menu` definition is passed as a parameter in the mother inheritance definition, which is therefore inherited by the son definition.

Tiles and Struts

Tiles has now become an integral part of the Struts framework described in Chapter 19. This section assumes you have read and understood the material presented in that chapter. If you haven't, it would be wise to do so now; you wouldn't want to miss out on this very powerful duo.

Configuring Tiles with Struts

In the first part of this chapter, we initialized Tiles in our application by registering the Tiles servlet. This initializes the definitions file, making the definitions available to the application. Within a Struts application, Tiles is configured slightly differently. The following steps will guide you through the addition of Tiles to an existing Struts application:

1. Ensure that the following commons JAR files are within the `/WEB-INF/lib` directory:

   ❑ **Commons Digester:** `commons-digester.jar`

   ❑ **Commons BeanUtils:** `commons-beanutils.jar`

   ❑ **Commons Collections:** `commons-collections.jar`

   ❑ **Commons Logging:** `commons-logging.jar`

2. Add the following plug-in entry to the `struts-config.xml` file:

```
...
<plug-in className="org.apache.struts.tiles.TilesPlugin" >
  <set-property property="definitions-config" value="/WEB-INF/tiles-defs.xml" />
  <set-property property="definitions-debug" value="2" />
  <set-property property="definitions-parser-details" value="2" />
  <set-property property="definitions-parser-validate" value="true" />
</plug-in>
...
```

   Note that the `set-property` elements within the plug-in set the same parameters used earlier to initialize the Tiles factory in the `TilesServlet`.

3. Create a `tiles-defs.xml` file within the `/WEB-INF/lib` directory along the same lines as before. There are no changes to the format of this file.

4. Ensure that the `/WEB-INF` directory contains the `struts-tiles.tld` file.

The Struts application should now be able to use Tiles as it has been used throughout this chapter.

Tiles definitions as action forwards

An action forward defined in the `struts-config.xml` file is typically given a name and a path that points to a JSP file or another action, as shown in the following example:

```
<action-mappings>
  <action path="/mypage"
          type="com.wrox.begjsp.ch20.struts.SomeAction"
          scope="request">
    <forward name="success" path="/somefile.jsp"/>
  </action>
</action-mappings>
...
```

The execute method of the action class then uses the name success to pass processing to the JSP file and, ultimately, to be displayed as a Web page. This is very powerful, as a layer of abstraction has been placed between the Controller portion of the application, the action, and the view portion, the JSP file.

When integrated with Tiles, a definition or tile name can be used as the value of the path attribute in the forward element. The preceding action mapping would appear as follows:

```
...
<action-mappings>
  <action path="/mypage"
          type="com.wrox.begjsp.ch20.struts.SomeAction"
          scope="request">
    <forward name="success" path="homepage"/>
  </action>
</action-mappings>
...
```

In the preceding code, homepage represents the name of a definition initialized by the Tiles factory (i.e., those definitions defined within the tiles configuration XML file, tiles-defs.xml).The following explanation will walk you through creating a very simple Struts action to display the inheritance example explained earlier.

The following listing shows a simple Struts action, much like the examples you have seen in the previous chapter. This action (HomePageAction) returns an ActionForward object, which has been given the name success:

```
package com.wrox.begjsp.ch20.struts;

import javax.servlet.http.HttpServletRequest;
import javax.servlet.http.HttpServletResponse;

import org.apache.struts.action.Action;
import org.apache.struts.action.ActionForm;
import org.apache.struts.action.ActionForward;
import org.apache.struts.action.ActionMapping;

public class HomePageAction extends Action
{
```

```
        public ActionForward execute(ActionMapping mapping,
                                ActionForm form,
                                HttpServletRequest request,
                                HttpServletResponse response)
        throws Exception
    {
        return mapping.findForward("success");
    }
}
```

Your first reaction might be, "Well, that's no different from all the other Struts examples!" I know, isn't it great! The action itself just knows it has to forward processing on to something called success; it is up to the view portion of the application, as well the application configuration, to determine exactly what that means.

The action mapping to invoke this action is configured in the struts-config.xml file with the following:

```
...
<action-mappings>
    <action path="/homepage"
            type="com.wrox.begjsp.ch20.struts.HomePageAction"
            validate="true"
            scope="request">
        <forward name="success" path="inh.mother.layout"/>
    </action>
</action-mappings>
...
```

Instead of a path to a JSP file, the path attribute of the forward element now refers to the definition described earlier (with my Mom's favorite movies). Now browsing to /homepage.do will present the same screen shown in Figure 20-6.

Passing values from Struts to Tiles

When an application uses Struts, typically the bulk of the data being used for content will come from a database or some other data source to which only the Model and Controller layers have access. While setting parameters inside configuration files is excellent for minor settings, they hardly suit the broad content demands of a sophisticated Web site. In Chapter 19, you saw examples of data being passed from the Controller layer to the View layer and being presented accordingly.

With Tiles, certain components (tiles, layouts, and so on) may be expecting elements of data, no matter what the source, to be in their tile scope. The following Try It Out exercise illustrates how data can be provided from a Struts action and used within the tiles of an application. To demonstrate the flexibility of tiles, the menu definition from a previous example will be used to display menu items provided by the action, rather than the definition, without changing any code.

Try It Out   **Providing Data from a Struts Action**

For this example, two new definitions will be created:

❑   **foo.bar:** This is the general layout for the page. It will use a new layout tile as well as provide for a header, footer, and menu tiles.

❑   **foo.bar.menu:** This definition will extend the previous menu definition and be used as the menu tile for foo.bar. The layout path and menuTile values will be inherited from its parent definition (menu), but all other characteristics will be overridden.

The action class for this example (FooBarAction) will provide the menu data for this application, as well as a list of movies to be displayed in the body of the page.

Create these two new definitions in the tiles-defs.xml file as follows (the additions have been highlighted). Note that the foo.bar.menu definition extends the menu definition:

```
...
<definition name="menu"
              path="/layout/menu-layout.jsp">
  <put name="menuTitle" value="My Menu"/>
  <put name="menuTile" value="/tiles/menu-tile.jsp"/>
  <putList name="menuItems">
    <item value="Home Banking" link="http://somebank.com"/>
    <item value="Search" link="http://goggle.com"/>
    <item value="Java" link="http://java.sun.com"/>
  </putList>
</definition>

<definition name="foo.bar"
              path="/layout/foobar-layout.jsp">
  <put name="header" value="/tiles/foobar-header.jsp" />
  <put name="footer" value="/tiles/foobar-footer.jsp" />
  <put name="foo.bar.menu.region" value="foo.bar.menu"/>
</definition>

<definition name="foo.bar.menu"
              extends="menu">
  <put name="menuTitle" value="My FooBar Menu"/>
  <putList name="menuItems"/>
</definition>
...
```

The foo.bar definition uses a new layout JSP page called foobar-layout.jsp. As with other layouts, this page will be responsible for general layout and passing on data for other tiles. When the Struts action is invoked, it will provide two values in the request scope:

❑   **animatedMovies:** A java.util.List of animated movie titles to display in the body of the layout

❑   **actionMenuItems:** A java.util.List of SimpleMenuItem objects to be displayed by the foo.bar.menu.region tile

The foo.bar definition references the foo.bar.menu definition as the value of its foo.bar.menu.region tile. The foo.bar.menu definition, listed above, extends the menu definition created earlier. The parent menu definition provides a number of parameters to this new subdefinition:

- ❑ **menuTitle:** This represents the title of the menu. It has been overridden with a new value in foo.bar.menu: My FooBar Menu.

- ❑ **menuTile:** A tile presenting the body of the menu's presentation. This will be used by the sub-definition and not overridden.

- ❑ **menuItems:** This list will be overridden by the foo.bar.menu definition and blanked out. The items to be presented in the menu will be provided by the Struts action.

Now that we know what needs to be done, we can create the new layout: open the foobar-layout.jsp file in the /layout/ directory of your Web application and enter the following code:

```
<%@ taglib uri="/WEB-INF/struts-tiles.tld" prefix="tiles" %>
<%@ taglib uri="http://java.sun.com/jsp/jstl/core" prefix="c"%>

<tiles:importAttribute />
<html>
  <head>
    <title>FooBar Example</title>
  </head>
<body bgcolor="white">

<table border="1" width="100%" height="100%" border="1">
<tr>
  <td colspan="2" height="100" bgcolor="gray">
      <tiles:insert attribute="header"/>
  </td>
</tr>
<tr>
  <td width="20%" valign="top" bgcolor="lightgrey">
      <tiles:insert attribute="foo.bar.menu.region">
          <tiles:put name="menuItems"
                    beanName="actionMenuItems" beanScope="request"/>
      </tiles:insert>
  </td>
  <td valign="top"  align="left">
  <h3>Animated Movies</h3>
      <ul>
          <c:forEach items="${requestScope.animatedMovies}" var="thisMovie">
              <li>${thisMovie}</li>
          </c:forEach>
      </ul>
  </td>
</tr>
<tr>
    <td colspan="2"><center><tiles:insert attribute="footer"/></center></td>
</tr>
</table>
</body>
</html>
```

Two particular areas of interest have been highlighted in the preceding code listing. The first represents placement of the `foo.bar.menu.region` tile. As discussed before, this needs to be treated just like the `menu` definition in a previous example, where the menu was first introduced as an independent definition. It needs some data to display. Previously, this was provided by some parameters using the `putList` and `item` elements within the `tiles-defs.xml` file. The source of the data is not important to this tile, however; it just knows it needs a list of `SimpleMenuItem` objects. The Struts action (`FooBarAction`) will provide just such a list and provide it within the `request` scope of this page; the highlighted section has then taken this list and placed it within the `tile` scope of the menu layout JSP page (`menu-layout.jsp`), under the name `menuItems`, the name it expects. From the JSP page's point of view, it's business as usual; there is no code change required.

The second highlighted area will list the `animatedMovies List` provided by the Struts action. It has to retrieve the value from the `request` scope.

The new footer and header tiles will display just static text.

Now that the view components have been established, we can turn our attention to the Struts action `FooBarAction`. This is another relatively simple action that will return an `ActionForward` pointing to our `foo.bar` definition. It will also provide the appropriate data for the `foo.bar.menu` and the list of movies to be displayed in the body of the page.

The following action mapping needs to be added to the `struts-config.xml` file in order to set up this new action:

```
<action path="/foobar"
        type="com.wrox.begjsp.ch20.struts.FooBarAction"
        scope="request">
  <forward name="success" path="foo.bar"/>
</action>
```

You should create a new file called `FooBarAction.java` in an appropriate package directory of your application. This file will contain the following:

```
package com.wrox.begjsp.ch20.struts;

import java.util.ArrayList;
import java.util.List;

import javax.servlet.http.HttpServletRequest;
import javax.servlet.http.HttpServletResponse;

import org.apache.struts.action.Action;
import org.apache.struts.action.ActionForm;
import org.apache.struts.action.ActionForward;
import org.apache.struts.action.ActionMapping;
import org.apache.struts.tiles.beans.MenuItem;
import org.apache.struts.tiles.beans.SimpleMenuItem;

public class FooBarAction extends Action
{
```

```
    public ActionForward execute(ActionMapping mapping,
                                 ActionForm form,
                                 HttpServletRequest request,
                                 HttpServletResponse response)
        throws Exception
    {
        request.setAttribute("actionMenuItems", getMenuItems());
        request.setAttribute("animatedMovies", getMovies());

        return mapping.findForward("success");
    }

    private List getMenuItems()
    {
        List menuItems = new ArrayList();
        menuItems.add(getMenuItem("http://java.sun.com/", "Java Home"));
        menuItems.add(getMenuItem("http://www.cnn.com/", "CNN"));
        menuItems.add(getMenuItem("http://slashdot.org/", "Slashdot"));
        return menuItems;
    }

    private MenuItem getMenuItem(String link, String value)
    {
        MenuItem item = new SimpleMenuItem();
        item.setLink(link);
        item.setValue(value);
        return item;
    }

    private List getMovies()
    {
        List movies = new ArrayList();
        movies.add("Shrek 2");
        movies.add("Finding Nemo");
        movies.add("Toy Story");
        movies.add("The Lion King");
        movies.add("Monsters Inc.");
        return movies;
    }
}
```

How It Works

As you can see, the menu data has been provided by two methods that construct a list of SimpleMenu
Item objects (these were discussed earlier). The movies are constructed by the getMovies() method.
The result of these methods is added to the request using the request.setAttribute method and
given the appropriate names that are expected in the foobar-layout.jsp file.

The result of this is to display a page not unlike others in this chapter, except this time the data has been
served by a Struts action and we have managed to reuse the characteristics of the menu definition that
was developed earlier. If you browsed to the action (/foobar.do), you would see a screen similar to the
one shown in Figure 20-7.

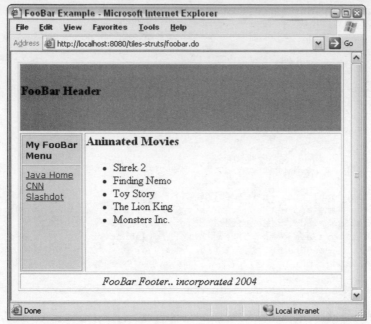

Figure 20-7: `FooBar` **example in a browser**

You can see how relatively easy it is to replace the data provided by one source with another. In a (much) more sophisticated application, the movie and menu data might come from a database; even so, the view components would be unaffected.

Summary

Although the full set of features and capabilities of the Tiles framework, as well as its integration with Struts, is beyond the scope of this chapter, the chapter has provided you with enough information to realize their power both separately and together and to use them in some capacity in your next Web application.

Some of the important features of Tiles that are not explained here include its capability to develop powerful portals, channels, and tabs, and the capability to integrate the `insert` tag with Struts controller classes, among others. Internationalization is also notably missing, but is featured in one of the exercises for this chapter.

Despite these omissions, this chapter has covered a lot of ground, including the following:

❑   A definition of Tiles

❑   Installing Tiles for use in a Web application

❑   Tiles definitions and tags

❑   Advanced Tiles usage with parameters and inheritance

❑   Using Tiles with Struts

The chapter began by introducing the need for a framework like Tiles. You learned the basic way in which Tiles is used and how its major concepts coordinate to add a level of abstraction between what is presented and how it is presented.

After installation of Tiles was covered, a simple example was introduced. This then led to configurations either using a JSP include file or via definitions in an XML configuration file. The intricacies of definitions were then explored, including inheritance and various ways in which parameters can be passed — as tiles, data, or even definitions themselves — to other components. The chapter then finished with two examples of Tiles integration with the Struts framework.

Exercises

1.   Create a simple definition inheritance example using three definitions. Ensure that at least one item is overridden by the child definitions.

2.   Using the Struts and Tiles resources on the Internet to help you, develop a one-page application using Struts that will display the result of a different definition based on different locale settings specified by the user.

JavaServer Faces

The last few chapters introduced you to the Model View Controller (MVC) design pattern and to the Struts, WebWork, and Spring frameworks that implement the pattern for Web-based applications. Struts has been around for some time, and is a proven framework for developing high-quality Web applications. However, the Java community has long desired a way to create components that can be used in Web applications in a manner similar to the way in which components are used in Swing or AWT-based applications. Enter the JavaServer Faces technology (JSF). Struts developers should feel comfortable with JSF because they share a number of similarities, as you will discover in this chapter. That is not an accident: One of the primary developers for Struts is also a primary developer for JSF. JSF may have one long-term advantage over Struts as a framework: JSF is to be included as part of a future J2EE standard. In this chapter, you will explore building Web applications using JSF.

In particular you will learn the following:

❑   How to configure a JSF project

❑   The JSF lifecycle

❑   How to validate data

❑   How to convert data

❑   How to handle events with listeners

Configuring a JSF Project

Because you will be working with a JavaServer Faces application right away, you will need to have a project set up with the correct directory structure, as shown in Figure 21-1.

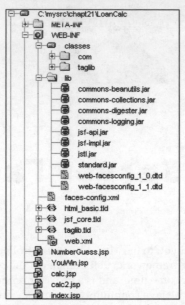

Figure 21-1: Directory structure for a JavaServer Faces application

The examples are based on using the JSF 1.1 reference version. You will also need the following files in the `lib` directory below `WEB-INF`:

- [ ] `commons-beanutils.jar`
- [ ] `commons-collections.jar`
- [ ] `commons-digester.jar`
- [ ] `commons-logging.jar`
- [ ] `html_basic.tld`
- [ ] `jsf_core.tld`
- [ ] `jsf-api.jar`
- [ ] `jsf-impl.jar`
- [ ] `jstl.jar`
- [ ] `standard.jar`
- [ ] `web-facesconfig_1_1.dtd`

The source code for the book includes a directory structure already configured with the correct files in place.

Getting Started with JSF

JSF is an implementation of the Model View Controller design pattern. Like Struts, JSF uses a single servlet that acts as a Controller. This servlet, known as the `FacesServlet`, must handle all HTTP requests for a JSF application. Rather than providing a complete overview at this time, let's start with a simple sample application.

Try It Out   Creating Hello JSF

Hello JSF is a simple application that prompts for a name and then simply renders a screen that says Hello. It is very simple and provides a good place to begin understanding JSF before more challenging topics are addressed. The first step we will take is to create the `web.xml` file.

As stated previously, JSF uses a single central servlet that handles all requests. This servlet needs to be configured in the `web.xml` as shown here:

```
<?xml version="1.0" encoding="UTF-8"?>
<!DOCTYPE web-app PUBLIC
    "-//Sun Microsystems, Inc.//DTD Web Application 2.3//EN"
    "http://java.sun.com/dtd/web-app_2_3.dtd">

<web-app>
    <context-param>
        <param-name>javax.faces.application.CONFIG_FILES</param-name>
        <param-value>/WEB-INF/faces-config.xml</param-value>
    </context-param>

    <servlet>
        <servlet-name>Faces Servlet</servlet-name>
        <servlet-class>javax.faces.webapp.FacesServlet</servlet-class>
        <load-on-startup>1 </load-on-startup>
    </servlet>
    <servlet-mapping>
        <servlet-name>Faces Servlet</servlet-name>
        <url-pattern>*.jsf</url-pattern>
    </servlet-mapping>
</web-app>
```

How It Works

The `servlet` element declares `FacesServlet` and then makes certain that it is loaded on startup. The servlet is mapped to any URL within the context that has a `.jsf` extension. A `context` parameter is provided so that `FacesServlet` will know where to find the `faces-config.xml` file. We will look at `faces-config.xml` in more detail shortly, but for now you just need to know that it is similar to the `struts-cfg.xml` file that you have seen in earlier chapters.

Try It Out   Creating the Pages

Our next step will be to create the two pages in this application. The first page collects the user's name. The second page responds with a personalized greeting. The pages we will create will be using custom tags provided by the JSF framework. Code the first page as follows and call it `hello.jsp`:

```
<%@ taglib uri="http://java.sun.com/jsf/html" prefix="h" %>
<%@ taglib uri="http://java.sun.com/jsf/core" prefix="f" %>
<html>
<head><title>HelloJSF</title></head>
<body>
    <f:view>
        <h:form id="helloForm">
            Please enter your name:
            <h:inputText id="name" value="#{HelloBean.name}" required="true"/>
            <h:commandButton action="#{HelloBean.action}" value="Go" id="submit" />
            <BR/>
            <h:messages />
        </h:form>
    </f:view>
</body>
</html>
```

The following lines, which also appear at the top of the JSP file, load the two required JSF tag libraries:

```
<%@ taglib uri="http://java.sun.com/jsf/html" prefix="h" %>
<%@ taglib uri="http://java.sun.com/jsf/core" prefix="f" %>
```

The last component to be discussed is the `messages` component. If the application has sent any error messages to the page, the `messages` component will display them. It is also possible to associate a message with an individual component. You will see how this is done in a later example.

Add the second JSP page as follows:

```
<%@ taglib uri="http://java.sun.com/jsf/html" prefix="h" %>
<%@ taglib uri="http://java.sun.com/jsf/core" prefix="f" %>
<html>
<head><title>JSF Greeting</title></head>
<body>
    <f:view>
        Hello <h:outputText value="#{HelloBean.name}"/><BR/>
    </f:view>
</body>
</html>
```

The only thing new here is the `outputText` component, which simply renders its value as text.

How It Works

The HTML tag library provides access to the standard HTML render kit. A *render kit* determines how the underlying components will be rendered within a specific implementation. In this case, the render kit renders the application's components into standard HTML tags. These tags can be found in the listing with the prefix h. Each custom tag represents a JSF component.

The core library is traditionally accessed using the f prefix (you may remember that c: is normally used for the JSTL core library). The core library provides tags that are used for *binding* objects with components. The only core tag used in the example is the <f:view> tag. This tag is required and must be the outermost tag of all JSF tags. In other words, all JSF tags within a JSP must be contained within the body of the view tag.

JSF maintains a tree-structured view of all of the components on a page. The view tag serves as the root of that tree. This is similar to the root element of an XML document. Therefore, the view tag is required if any JSF components are used.

Each of the tags with an h: prefix represents a JSF component. An example of two of these lines follows:

```
<h:inputText id="name" value="#{HelloBean.name}" required="true"/>
<h:commandButton action="#{HelloBean.action}" value="Go" id="submit" />
```

The inputText component is rendered as an HTML input element of type text. The commandButton component is rendered as an HTML input element of type submit. These are both contained within a form component, which simply renders as an HTML form element.

In the inputText component, the value is set to #{HelloBean.name}. This is a *value binding expression*. A value binding expression is used to associate the value of an attribute on a bean with the attribute of the component. A similar expression is seen on the commandButton component. In this case, the #{HelloBean.action} is a *method binding expression*. A method binding expression is used to associate the method of a class with a component. In this case, a method called action on an instance of HelloBean will be executed in response to the Submit button.

Binding expressions are similar in syntax to JSP EL expressions. Binding expressions use #{expression} instead of ${expression} and do not support EL functions.

Using backing beans

JSF uses ordinary JavaBeans to do most of the interesting work. These beans are called *backing beans* because they form the backbone of the application. One of the nice features of JSF is that simple Web applications can be easily created just by creating the pages and backing beans to support them. From the Struts point of view, a backing bean can be the action form and action class rolled into one.

The bean for our application needs to store the Name field and provide a means of navigation. The code for `HelloBean`, the action bean used in the current example, follows:

```
package com.wrox.jsp;

import javax.faces.application.FacesMessage;
import javax.faces.context.FacesContext;

public class HelloBean
{
  private String name = null;
  public HelloBean()
  {
  }
  public String getName()
  {
    return name;
  }
  public void setName(String anyname)
  {
    name = anyname;
  }

  public String action()
  {
    boolean success = true;
    FacesContext context = FacesContext.getCurrentInstance();
    if(name != null)
    {
      for(int i = 0; i < name.length();i++)
      {
        char c = name.charAt(i);

        if( !Character.isLetter(c) && !Character.isSpaceChar(c))
        {
          FacesMessage message = new FacesMessage(
            "Username must be all alphabetic characters.");
          context.addMessage("helloForm", message);
          success = false;
          break;
        }
      }
    }
    else
    {
      success = false;
    }
    return (success? "success" : "failure" );
  }
}
```

How It Works

The bean has a single attribute, name, with a supporting *getter* and *setter*. The bean also has an action method. The action method validates that the name is made up of all alphabetical characters and returns the word success or failure depending on the outcome. In the next section, you will see how this is used to control navigation between the pages of the application.

If the action method fails, it provides an error message that can be displayed by a message component on the JSP page. The message is added to the FacesContext. The FacesContext is created by the FacesServlet and provides access to all of the components that are current for the request being processed.

Managed beans

It is necessary to define the backing beans that will be used by the application. The way this is done is through a configuration file called faces-config.xml. This configuration file is similar in purpose to the struts-cfg.xml file used by Struts. The section used to define our bean is as follows:

```
<managed-bean>
    <managed-bean-name>HelloBean</managed-bean-name>
    <managed-bean-class>com.wrox.jsp.HelloBean</managed-bean-class>
    <managed-bean-scope>session</managed-bean-scope>
</managed-bean>
```

This entry names the bean HelloBean, which is how we reference the bean in the JSP pages, and associates the bean (or binds it) with the class com.wrox.jsp.HelloBean. The bean will be stored in or accessible from the session scope.

Controlling navigation

The action method of our bean returns one of two string values depending on the success or failure of the method. This return value is then used to determine which JSP will be used to render the response. This is accomplished through a configuration file called faces-config.xml. The section of the configuration file that controls the navigation is as follows:

```
<navigation-rule>
    <from-view-id>/hello.jsp</from-view-id>
    <navigation-case>
        <from-outcome>success</from-outcome>
        <to-view-id>/greeting.jsp</to-view-id>
    </navigation-case>
    <navigation-case>
        <from-outcome>failure</from-outcome>
        <to-view-id>/hello.jsp</to-view-id>
    </navigation-case>
</navigation-rule>
```

The `navigation-rule` element is first associated with a source page — in this case, `hello.jsp` — and comprises a number of navigation cases. The `navigation-case` element consists of two elements, `from-outcome` and `to-view-id`. The `from-outcome` element matches the string returned by the `action` method on the bean — in this case, success or failure. The `to-view-id` element describes where to go in each `navigation-case`.

Try It Out   Creating faces-config.xml

The two primary areas of the `faces-config.xml` file that are used for this application have been covered. The entire file follows:

```xml
<?xml version="1.0"?>
<!DOCTYPE faces-config PUBLIC
    "-//Sun Microsystems, Inc.//DTD JavaServer Faces Config 1.0//EN"
    "http://java.sun.com/dtd/web-facesconfig_1_0.dtd">

<faces-config>
    <navigation-rule>
        <from-view-id>/hello.jsp</from-view-id>
        <navigation-case>
            <from-outcome>success</from-outcome>
            <to-view-id>/greeting.jsp</to-view-id>
        </navigation-case>
         <navigation-case>
            <from-outcome>failure</from-outcome>
            <to-view-id>/hello.jsp</to-view-id>
         </navigation-case>
    </navigation-rule>

    <managed-bean>
        <description>Hello Bean Holder</description>
        <managed-bean-name>HelloBean</managed-bean-name>
        <managed-bean-class>com.wrox.jsp.HelloBean</managed-bean-class>
        <managed-bean-scope>session</managed-bean-scope>
    </managed-bean>

</faces-config>
```

As you can see, there isn't much here that hasn't already been discussed. Based on the `web.xml` file presented earlier, this file needs to be placed in the `WEB-INF` directory of the Web application.

Try It Out   Running the JSF Application

Now you should be ready to test the application. To run the application, use the following URL: `http://locahost:8080/hellojsf/hello.jsf`.

Figure 21-2 shows the first page of the application.

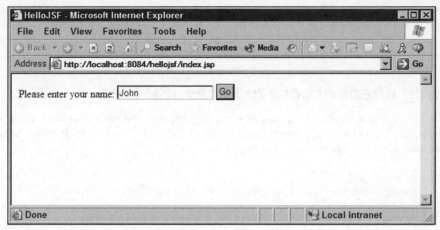

Figure 21-2: The first page of HelloJSF

If a name with non-alphabetic characters is entered, an error message is displayed, as shown in Figure 21-3.

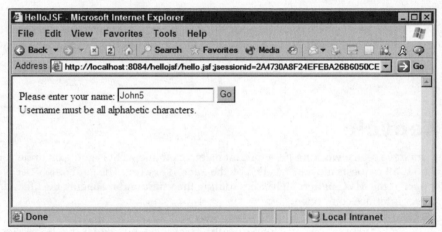

Figure 21-3: HelloJSF with an error message

The result of successfully entering the name John should simply be a screen that says "Hello John".

How It Works

When you access the application, you do not send the request to `hello.jsp`. This is because the `FacesServlet` must handle all requests. The `FacesServlet` has been configured in the `web.xml` file to handle all requests ending with a `.jsf` extension and will find `hello.jsp` when `hello.jsf` is requested.

The FacesServlet *must handle all faces requests before they are passed to a JSP. If you see an error message similar to "Cannot find FacesContext," this normally means that an attempt was made to access a faces JSP directly instead of through the servlet. This can be prevented by protecting the JSP with a security constraint in the* web.xml *file.*

Preventing direct access to Faces JSP files

As discussed in the previous section, all access must go through the FacesServlet. Because this is a requirement, it is a good idea to prevent direct access to JSP files. One way to do this is to add the following security constraint to the web.xml file:

```
<security-constraint>
    <display-name>Restricts access to JSP pages</display-name>
    <web-resource-collection>
        <web-resource-name>JSP Restriction</web-resource-name>
        <url-pattern>/hello.jsp</url-pattern>
        <url-pattern>/greeting.jsp</url-pattern>
    </web-resource-collection>
    <auth-constraint>
        <description>With no roles defined, no access granted</description>
    </auth-constraint>
</security-constraint>
```

Inserting this above the closing </web-app> tag in the web.xml file creates a security constraint requiring a user to be authorized before access is granted to the pages. No authorized users can access the pages directly because no roles are provided in the auth-constraint. The pages can still be accessed through the FacesServlet, which is the desired behavior.

JSF Lifecycle

Now that you have seen a working JSF application, let's examine what is going on under the hood. As you now know, all requests must be handled by the FacesServlet. The FacesServlet is the Controller part of the MVC pattern. It handles routing the traffic and managing the lifecycles of the beans and user interface components.

The UI components are organized in a tree structure. The root component is the UIViewRoot class and is represented in the JSP using the <f:view> tag. You should recall using the <f:view> tag on the page to establish this root element. Each component may be associated with the methods and attributes of a backing bean. While we did not use a validation method in the current example, each component may also be associated with a validation function or class.

As shown in Figure 21-4, a JSF request has six lifecycle phases:

❑   Restore view

❑   Apply request values

- ❑ Process validations
- ❑ Update model values
- ❑ Invoke the application
- ❑ Render the response

Each of these phases or stages may be executed in their entirety or the process may be short-circuited to handle errors, validation problems, or other special processing needs.

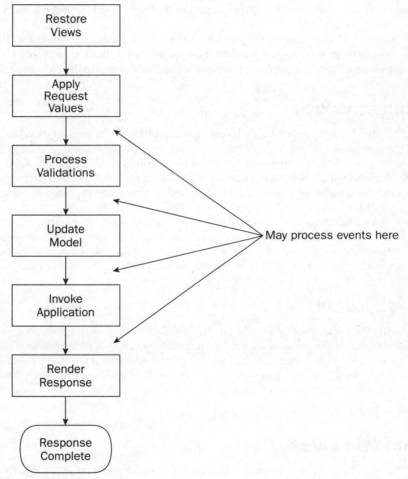

Figure 21-4: The JSF request lifecycle

The following paragraphs provide a brief explanation of each of the processing stages.

Restore view

The restore view phase associates a specific view with a request. The JSF application first determines whether a view already exists. A view may exist, for example, if the request came from a page that had previously been returned with validation errors or if the page posts to itself. The view itself is an instance of the class UIViewRoot. This is the root component for the component tree that makes up the JSF page. If a view does not exist, then one is created.

A mapping is performed on the requested URL to determine the URL to use for the view. In the case of the example hello program, the target URL containing hello.jsf is rewritten as hello.jsp to form the view. This is how the .jsf extension gets remapped so that the correct JSP page is found.

When the JSF implementation creates the view, it also makes the connections between the components and the various actions, validators, and converters associated with them. Finally, the view is stored in FacesContext along with all of the other information needed to handle the current request.

Apply request values

The apply request values stage enables each component within the view to set its value based on the values obtained in the request. These request values include request parameters, cookies, and request header items, for example. The values are converted to their final types. For example, if the form had included a field that was mapped to an integer type, the string content of the parameter would be converted to an integer at this time. If the conversion fails, then a message is placed in FacesContext.

Certain events may also be queued in this phase — for example, components that implement ActionSource (such as UICommand) may queue events. In general, these events are processed immediately after the stage has been completed. The FacesContext.responseComplete() method can be called here to shortcut the rest of the processing and jump directly to the render response phase.

Process validations

Each component on the tree may be associated with validation code. During the process validations phase, the validation code associated with each component is called. Validations that fail normally add a message to the FacesContext that can be displayed with the rendered page. If a failure occurs, the other phases are skipped and the processing jumps directly to the render response phase so that an input screen can be rerendered. Any events that are queued during this phase are processed at the completion of the phase.

Update model values

The update model values phase is reached when all of the components have had their values set and the data has been validated. At this point, the data should be correct and the underlying model may be updated to reflect the values in the components. The data is copied from the components in the view to their corresponding model components. In the hello example, the model is the backing bean. Data conversion may also occur here if the way in which the data is stored in the component differs from that of the model. If the conversion fails, then a message is added to FacesContext and the next phase is skipped and the render response phase is invoked instead. Again, any events that are queued are handled after the phase completes.

Invoke application

Any remaining events are fired and handled in the invoke application phase. In our application, the command associated with the Submit button is handled here. The action causes the "success" or "failure" event to be queued. There is a listener that handles this event by calling the default `NavigationHandler` with the navigation rules from the `faces-config.xml` file. This in turn determines which page is used for the render response phase.

Render response

The render response phase does two things: It renders the response to the client and saves the state of the response and the component tree to be used on subsequent requests. It renders the response by calling the methods and classes in the renderer that was loaded for the current render kit. The renderer is used to generate the required HTML for each component within the tree.

Validating Data

In the previous example, you saw one way of validating data for a JSF-created page. The backing bean in that example used the `action` method and navigation to validate that the name did not contain any non-alphabetic characters. If the name did have an illegal character, a message was added to `FacesContext` and the original form was redisplayed with the error message. This validation is actually being handled in the invoke application phase, a later stage of the response cycle than necessary. Validation can occur in the process validations phase by using a validator. The following section demonstrates some of the many ways that this can be done, but first you need a new example.

Try It Out   The Number Guess Example

The Number Guess program creates a random number between 1 and 10 and asks the user to try to guess the number. If the guess is incorrect, a message is provided that indicates how far off the guess was. If the guess is successful, then a success message is displayed and the user may play again. The game is based on the backing bean as shown here:

```
package com.wrox.jsp;

import java.util.Random;
import javax.faces.application.FacesMessage;
import javax.faces.context.FacesContext;

public class GuessBean
{
  private int number;
  private int guess;

  public GuessBean()
  {
    number = (new Random()).nextInt(9)+1;
  }

  public int getNumber()
```

```
  {
    return number;
  }

  public int getGuess()
  {
    return guess;
  }

  public void setGuess(int i)
  {
    guess = i;
  }

  public String replay()
  {
    number = (new Random()).nextInt(9)+1;
    return "success";
  }

  public String action()
  {
    if( guess == number )
    {
      return "success";
    }
    else
    {
      FacesContext context = FacesContext.getCurrentInstance();
      int delta = Math.abs(guess-number);
      String message = "You missed it by "+delta+". Try again.";
      context.addMessage("GuessForm", new FacesMessage(message));
    }
    return "failure";
  }
}
```

There are attributes for the number and the guess and two action methods, `action` and `replay`. The `faces-cfg.xml` file is shown next:

```
<?xml version="1.0"?>
<!DOCTYPE faces-config PUBLIC
  "-//Sun Microsystems, Inc.//DTD JavaServer Faces Config 1.0//EN"
  "http://java.sun.com/dtd/web-facesconfig_1_0.dtd">

<faces-config>
  <navigation-rule>
    <from-view-id>/NumberGuess.jsp</from-view-id>
    <navigation-case>
      <from-outcome>success</from-outcome>
      <to-view-id>/YouWin.jsp</to-view-id>
    </navigation-case>
    <navigation-case>
      <from-outcome>failure</from-outcome>
```

```
        <to-view-id>/NumberGuess.jsp</to-view-id>
      </navigation-case>
    </navigation-rule>

    <navigation-rule>
      <from-view-id>/YouWin.jsp</from-view-id>
      <navigation-case>
        <from-outcome>success</from-outcome>
        <to-view-id>/NumberGuess.jsp</to-view-id>
      </navigation-case>
    </navigation-rule>

    <managed-bean>
      <description>GuessBean</description>
      <managed-bean-name>GuessBean</managed-bean-name>
      <managed-bean-class>com.wrox.jsp.GuessBean</managed-bean-class>
      <managed-bean-scope>session</managed-bean-scope>
    </managed-bean>

</faces-config>
```

There are two navigation rules and a single managed bean. The managed bean is the GuessBean code that you have already seen. The first rule selects between NumberGuess.jsp and YouWin.jsp based on the result of the call to the action method of the GuessBean class. The second rule enables the game to be reset once it has been won, and returns the user back to NumberGuess.jsp. The code for NumberGuess.jsp follows:

```
<!-- name NumberGuess.jsp -->
<%@ taglib uri="http://java.sun.com/jsf/html" prefix="h" %>
<%@ taglib uri="http://java.sun.com/jsf/core" prefix="f" %>
<html>
  <head><title>Number Guess</title></head>
<body>
  I am thinking of a number between 1 and 10. Can you guess it?
  <f:view>
    <h:form id="GuessForm">
      <h:inputText id="number" value="#{GuessBean.guess}"  />
      <h:commandButton action="#{GuessBean.action}" value="Guess"/><BR/>
      <h:messages />
    </h:form>
  </f:view>
</body>
</html>
```

Currently, the JSP simply provides an inputText component for entering a number and a button for submitting the form to the action method. Shortly, you will be making changes to this file to demonstrate using standard validators. The final segment of code is the YouWin.jsp:

```
<!-- name YouWin.jsp -->
<%@ taglib uri="http://java.sun.com/jsf/html" prefix="h" %>
<%@ taglib uri="http://java.sun.com/jsf/core" prefix="f" %>
<html>
  <head><title>Number Guess</title></head>
```

```
<body>
  <f:view>
    <h:form id="GuessForm">
      You Win! 
      <h:commandButton action="#{GuessBean.replay}" value="Replay"/><BR/>
    </h:form>
  </f:view>
</body>
</html>
```

This JSP simply states "You Win!" and offers a replay. Calling the `replay` method on the backing bean generates a new random number and always returns success.

How It Works

The code as shown accepts any number entered into the field. If the value entered cannot be converted to a number, JSF automatically returns an error message for the component, indicating a conversion error. By adding the following as the first line of the action method, it can be shown that the action method is not even called when a conversion error occurs:

```
System.out.println("inside action method. guess="+guess+" number="+number);
```

Now an entry will be added to the logs if the action method is called. Try entering **abc** as the guess and you should see a response similar to the one shown in Figure 21-5.

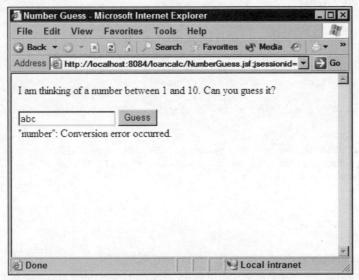

Figure 21-5: GuessNumber.jsp response when a number is not entered

Note that a log entry was not generated by the action method. This shows that the action method was not called.

Using standard validators

Our goal is to limit the valid user input to a number from 1 to 10. As it turns out, JSF provides a standard validator to do exactly this. The standard validators are as follows:

❑ **DoubleRangeValidator:** Determines whether the range of the component value is within the specified range. The value must be convertible to a double.

❑ **LengthValidator:** Determines whether the length of the component's value is within the specified range. The value must be a string.

❑ **LongRangeValidator:** Determines whether the value of the component falls within the specified integer range. The value must be convertible to a long.

You can use the standard validator by adding a tag to the JSP. In this case, the validator required is the LongRangeValidator and the code will be modified as follows. In NumberGuess.jsp, replace the line that reads

```
<h:inputText id="number" value="#{GuessBean.guess}"  />
```

with the following:

```
<h:inputText id="number" value="#{GuessBean.guess}" >
  <f:validateLongRange minimum="1" maximum="10" />
</h:inputText>
```

Now an attempt to enter 555 in the field returns the response shown in Figure 21-6.

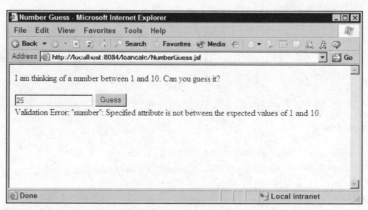

Figure 21-6: Number entered outside of allowed range

Creating your own validation

If one of the standard validators does not support your validation needs, it does not mean you are out of luck. JSF supports two different ways of adding your own validation code to support your application. You can create validation methods on the backing beans or you can create classes that implement the Validator interface.

Implementing the Validator Interface

You can create a custom validator by creating a class that implements the `Validator` interface. The `Validator` interface has one required method with the following signature:

```
void validate(
    javax.faces.context.FacesContext context,
    javax.faces.component.UIComponent component,
    java.lang.Object obj)
    throws ValidatorException
```

Try It Out   Creating a Validator

`FacesContext` has already been discussed. The `UIComponent` is the instance of the underlying JSF component whose value will be validated. The object is the value to be validated. An example validator that can be used with the Number Guess example follows (name this example `OneToTenValidator.java`):

```java
package com.wrox.jsp;

import javax.faces.application.FacesMessage;
import javax.faces.component.UIComponent;
import javax.faces.component.UIInput;
import javax.faces.context.FacesContext;
import javax.faces.validator.Validator;
import javax.faces.validator.ValidatorException;

public class OneToTenValidator implements Validator
{
  public OneToTenValidator()
  {
  }

  public void validate(FacesContext facesContext, UIComponent component, Object
obj)
  throws ValidatorException
  {
    boolean valid = false;
    String value = null;
    int i;
    if (!(component instanceof UIInput) || (obj == null))
    {
      return;
    }
    value = obj.toString();
    try
    {
      i = Integer.parseInt(value);
    }
    catch( NumberFormatException nfe )
    {
      FacesMessage message = new FacesMessage("Could not convert to int.");
      throw new ValidatorException(message);
    }
```

```
        if( (i < 1) || (i > 10) )
        {
            FacesMessage message =
                new FacesMessage("The guess must be between 1 and 10");
          throw new ValidatorException(message);
        }
        return;
    }


}
```

How It Works

The example simply ensures that the provided arguments are good, and then converts the object from a string into an integer and tests the integer to see if it is within range. If the test fails, an exception is thrown with the message that will be displayed on the form. To use this in your code, the line in NumberGuess.jsp that reads

```
<f:validateLongRange minimum="1" maximum="10" />
```

will need to be replaced with one that reads

```
<f:validator validatorId="OneToTenValidator"/>
```

The new validator needs to be registered in the faces-cfg.xml file. You do this by adding the following lines below the managed bean section of the faces-cfg.xml file:

```
<validator>
    <validator-id>OneToTenValidator</validator-id>
    <validator-class>com.wrox.jsp.OneToTenValidator</validator-class>
</validator>
```

When the application is executed and a number greater than 10 is entered, the result is as shown in Figure 21-7.

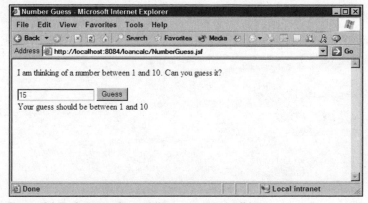

Figure 21-7: Output after adding a custom validator

Creating a custom validator tag

In the preceding example, the values for minimum and maximum were hard-coded in the custom validator. This enables the developer to use the validator tag to associate the validator with the control. For most applications this would be limiting because there is no way to pass parameters to the validator, so that validator must be preconfigured or hard-coded. This limitation can be overcome by creating a custom tag to configure the properties of the validator. The attributes of the tag correspond to the properties of the validator. The tag itself replaces the validator tag that was used in the code example. In order to demonstrate how this works, a new validator is needed, one that provides attributes that can be configured for the minimum and maximum values.

Try It Out   Creating a Custom Validator Tag

The code for this new IntRangeValidator follows:

```
package com.wrox.jsp;

import javax.faces.application.FacesMessage;
import javax.faces.component.UIComponent;
import javax.faces.component.UIInput;
import javax.faces.context.FacesContext;
import javax.faces.validator.Validator;
import javax.faces.validator.ValidatorException;

public class IntRangeValidator implements Validator
{
  private int min;
  private int max;
  private boolean minset = false;
  private boolean maxset = false;

  public IntRangeValidator()
  {
    System.out.println("IntRangeValidator built");
  }

  public void setMin(int m)
  {
    minset = true;
    min = m;
  }

  public int getMin()
  {
    return min;
  }

  public void setMax(int m)
  {
    maxset = true;
    max = m;
  }
```

```
  public int getMax()
  {
    return max;
  }

  public void validate(FacesContext facesContext, UIComponent component, Object
obj)
    throws ValidatorException
  {
    boolean valid = false;
    String value = null;
    int i;
    if (!(component instanceof UIInput) || (obj == null))
    {
      return;
    }
    value = obj.toString();
    try
    {
      i = Integer.parseInt(value);
    }
    catch( NumberFormatException nfe )
    {
      FacesMessage message = new FacesMessage("Could not convert to int.");
      throw new ValidatorException(message);
    }
    if( (minset && (i < min)) || (maxset && (i > max)) )
    {
      FacesMessage message =
      new FacesMessage("The entry must be between "+min+" and "+max);
      throw new ValidatorException(message);
    }
    return;
  }

}
```

In order to use this validator, a custom tag is needed that can set the min and max properties of the validator. The custom IntRangeTag extends the javax.faces.webapp.ValidatorTag class. The code for the tag follows:

```
package taglib;

import com.wrox.jsp.IntRangeValidator;
import javax.faces.validator.Validator;
import javax.faces.webapp.ValidatorTag;
import javax.servlet.jsp.JspException;

public class IntRangeTag extends ValidatorTag
{
  private int min = 0;
  private int max = 0;
```

```
  private boolean minset = false;
  private boolean maxset = false;

  public IntRangeTag()
  {
    super();
    super.setValidatorId("IntRangeValidator");
  }

  protected Validator createValidator()
  throws JspException
  {
    IntRangeValidator validator = null;
    validator = (IntRangeValidator) super.createValidator();
    if(validator == null)
    {
      System.out.println("null validator");
      return validator;
    }
    if( minset)
      validator.setMin(min);
    if( maxset )
      validator.setMax(max);
    return validator;
  }

  public void setMin(int m)
  {
    minset = true;
    min = m;
  }

  public int getMin()
  {
    return min;
  }

  public void setMax(int m)
  {
    maxset = true;
    max = m;
  }

  public int getMax()
  {
    return max;
  }
}
```

How It Works

Essentially, the tag provides attributes for min and max and tracks to see whether the attributes have been set. The constructor must also set the ValidatorId to the name as set in faces-cfg.xml. The changes to faces-cfg.xml will be examined in a few moments. The rest of the code is in the createValidator method, which is shaded in the code listing. This method creates an instance of the validator by calling the createValidator method on the superclass. Then it sets the min and max properties on the validator if needed.

Try It Out   Using the Tag Library

To use the tag library, a tag library descriptor (.tld) file is needed. The .tld file for this example follows:

```xml
<?xml version="1.0" encoding="UTF-8" ?>

<!DOCTYPE taglib
    PUBLIC "-//Sun Microsystems, Inc.//DTD JSP Tag Library 1.2//EN"
    "http://java.sun.com/dtd/web-jsptaglibrary_1_2.dtd">

<taglib>
   <tlib-version>1.0</tlib-version>
   <jsp-version>1.2</jsp-version>
   <short-name>taglib</short-name>
   <uri>/taglib</uri>
   <tag>
     <name>IntRangeValidator</name>
     <tag-class>taglib.IntRangeTag</tag-class>
     <body-content>empty</body-content>
     <display-name>IntRangeValidator</display-name>
     <attribute>
       <name>min</name>
       <required>false</required>
       <rtexprvalue>true</rtexprvalue>
       <type>int</type>
     </attribute>
     <attribute>
       <name>max</name>
       <required>false</required>
       <rtexprvalue>true</rtexprvalue>
       <type>int</type>
     </attribute>
   </tag>
</taglib>
```

The descriptor simply declares the new tag with optional min and max attributes. To use this tag, some changes are needed in the NumberGuess.jsp file. The new listing follows:

```jsp
<!-- name NumberGuess.jsp -->
<%@ taglib uri="http://java.sun.com/jsf/html" prefix="h" %>
<%@ taglib uri="http://java.sun.com/jsf/core" prefix="f" %>
<%@ taglib uri="/taglib" prefix="t" %>
<html>
  <head><title>Number Guess</title></head>
<body>
  I am thinking of a number between 1 and 10.  Can you guess it?
  <f:view>
    <h:form id="GuessForm">
```

```
      <h:inputText id="number" value="#{GuessBean.guess}" >
        <t:IntRangeValidator min="1" max="10" />
      </h:inputText>
      <h:commandButton action="#{GuessBean.action}" value="Guess"/><BR/>
      <h:messages />
    </h:form>
  </f:view>
</body>
</html>
```

The changes are shown with the shaded lines. The first change adds the reference to the new taglib and sets the prefix to t:. The second change uses the new tag to set the min and max values for the validator and associate it with the inputText component.

How It Works

The tag library descriptor (.tld file) provides the information that the container needs to know to use the tag in the JSP. The .tld file is referenced in the taglib directive in the JSP file that uses the tag. When the tag is encountered in the JSP, the Java code that implements the tag is passed the attributes and executed. This code in turn calls the validator class, IntRangeValidator, to validate that the values are within the desired range.

If you think this is a lot of effort for a simple range validation, you are right. This type of custom validator is warranted when it will be reused many times. There is still one more, much simpler way to add custom validation. A validation method can be added to a backing bean.

Using the backing bean

A backing bean can also have validation methods. A validation method for a backing bean has the same signature as the validation method in the Validator interface, except that the backing bean does not throw the ValidatorException; however, the validation method on the bean is often simpler. The listing for a validation method that can be added to the GuessBean.java class follows:

```
public void validate(FacesContext context, UIComponent component, Object obj)
{
  int i;
  String value = obj.toString();
  UIInput inputText = (UIInput)component;
  try
  {
    i = Integer.parseInt(value);
    if( (i < 1) || (i > 10) )
    {
      inputText.setValid(false);
      FacesMessage message =
          new FacesMessage("Your guess should be between 1 and 10");
      context.addMessage(component.getClientId(context),message);
    }
  }
  catch( Exception e )
  {
    inputText.setValid(false);
    FacesMessage message = new FacesMessage("Exception:"+e.getMessage());
```

```
        context.addMessage(component.getClientId(context),message);
    }
    return;
}
```

This method can be used by simply adding a `validator` attribute to the `inputText` tag as shown:

```
<h:inputText
    id="number"
    value="#{GuessBean.guess}"
    validator="#{GuessBean.validate}" />
```

There is no need for a `.tld` file or for changes to `faces-config.xml`.

Converting Data

When creating Web applications, all of the data entered into forms is initially available only as strings. These strings must be converted to the underlying data types used in our model. You'll often need to convert the strings into various types of numbers or dates, and vice versa. The data as represented in the model does not have to be in strings, but it should be represented in the format that is most convenient for how that data needs to be manipulated. For example, while it is possible to perform math calculations solely using strings (in Java, anyway), it is awkward and slow. Normally, we convert to the proper data type, perform the calculation, and then convert back to a string. In this section, you use a new code example that illustrates a simple loan payment calculator, with a simple twist. It will also show you how much you can borrow if you know what your payment should be. A screenshot of the application is shown in Figure 21-8.

Try It Out   Using the Backing Bean to Convert Data

The calculator consists of the JSP, a backing bean, and the `faces-config.xml` file. First, enter the source code for the backing bean:

```
package com.wrox.jsp;

public class LoanBean
{
    private double amount;
    private double payment;
    private double apr;
    private double periodic_rate;
    private double periods;

    public LoanBean()
    {
    }

    private double calcPayment( double amount, double iRate, double periods )
    {
        return amount * factor(iRate, periods);
    }
```

```
private double calcAmount( double payment, double iRate, double periods)
{
  return payment/factor(iRate, periods);
}

private double factor(double iRate, double periods)
{
  return (iRate * Math.pow((1.0 + iRate), (periods)))/(Math.pow((1.0+iRate),
periods)-1);
}

public String amount()
{
  LoanCalc calc = new LoanCalc();
  amount = this.calcAmount(payment, periodic_rate, periods );
  return "success";
}

public String payment()
{
  LoanCalc calc = new LoanCalc();
  payment = this.calcPayment(amount, periodic_rate, periods );
  return "success";
}

public double getAmount()
{
  return amount;
}

public void setAmount(double amount)
{
  this.amount = amount;
}

public double getApr()
{
  return apr;
}

public void setApr(double apr)
{
  this.periodic_rate = apr/1200.0;
  this.apr = apr;
}

public double getPayment()
{
  return payment;
}

public void setPayment(double payment)
{
  this.payment = payment;
}
```

```
public double getPeriodic_rate()
{
  return periodic_rate;
}

protected void setPeriodic_rate(double periodic_rate)
{
  this.periodic_rate = periodic_rate;
}

public double getPeriods()
{
  return periods;
}

public void setPeriods(double periods)
{
  this.periods = periods;
}
}
```

In the LoanBean class, normally you would expect the code for the methods calcPayment, calcAmount, and factor to appear in a separate helper class instead of being included in the backing bean. The methods are included as part of the backing bean in this example to improve the clarity of the example.

Now enter the navigation-rule and managed-bean elements of the faces-config.xml file as follows:

```
<navigation-rule>
    <from-view-id>/calc.jsp</from-view-id>
    <navigation-case>
        <from-outcome>success</from-outcome>
        <to-view-id>/calc.jsp</to-view-id>
    </navigation-case>
</navigation-rule>

<managed-bean>
    <description>LoanBean</description>
    <managed-bean-name>LoanBean</managed-bean-name>
    <managed-bean-class>com.wrox.jsp.LoanBean</managed-bean-class>
    <managed-bean-scope>session</managed-bean-scope>
</managed-bean>
```

Essentially, the application consists of a single page that always returns to itself. Enter the code for the page calc.jsp as follows:

```
<%@ taglib uri="http://java.sun.com/jsf/html" prefix="h" %>
<%@ taglib uri="http://java.sun.com/jsf/core" prefix="f" %>
<html>
  <head><title>Simple Loan Calculator</title></head>
  <body>
  <hr/>
```

```
If you select the Payment button, this application calculates
the payment on a standard commercial loan
given:
<li>the amount of the loan, </li>
<li>the annual percentage, </li>
<li>rate and the number of monthly payments.</li>
<br/><br/>
If the Amount button is selected then the application shows the amount of
money that can be borrowed when making the specified payment each month
for the specified number of months at the set interest rate.
<hr/>
<f:view>
  <h:form id="LoanForm">
    <table border='0' >
      <tbody>
        <tr>
          <td align='right'>Loan Amount:</td>
          <td>
            <h:inputText id="amount" value="#{LoanBean.amount}" >
              <f:convertNumber type="number" pattern="#,##0.00" />
            </h:inputText>
          </td>
        </tr>
        <tr>
          <td align='right'>Annual Percentage Rate:</td>
          <td>
            <h:inputText id="apr" value="#{LoanBean.apr}" >
              <f:validateDoubleRange minimum="0.0" maximum="25.0" />
              <f:convertNumber type="number" />
            </h:inputText>
          </td>
        </tr>
        <tr>
        <td align='right'>Months to Pay:</td>
        <td>
          <h:inputText id="periods" value="#{LoanBean.periods}" >
            <f:validateLongRange minimum="0" />
            <f:convertNumber integerOnly="true"/>
          </h:inputText>
        </td>
        </tr>
        <tr>
          <td align='right'>Payment:</td>
          <td>
            <h:inputText id="payment" value="#{LoanBean.payment}">
              <f:convertNumber type="number" pattern="#,##0.00"/>
```

```
              </h:inputText>
            </td>
          </tr>
        </tbody>
      </table>
      <br/>
      <h:commandButton
        action="#{LoanBean.amount}" value="Amount" id="AmountId" />
      <h:commandButton
        action="#{LoanBean.payment}" value="Payment" id="PaymentId" />
      <br/>
      <h:messages />
    </h:form>
  </f:view>
  </body>
</html>
```

Four lines are highlighted. For the first run, you will want to comment these lines out or delete them. When the application is run, you should see something similar to what is shown in Figure 21-8.

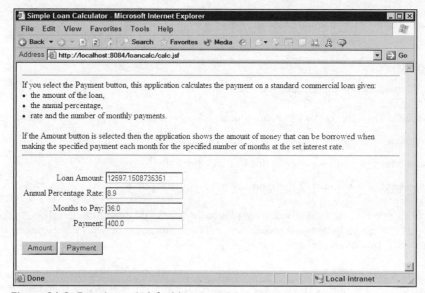

Figure 21-8: Running calc.jsf with conversion code removed

Notice how the currency values are represented as decimal numbers. When the lines are added back in, the screen looks like Figure 21-9.

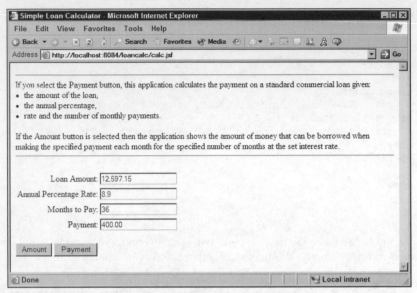

Figure 21-9: Running calc.jsf with conversion code active

How It Works

The application accepts four numeric values:

❑ **Amount:** The amount of a potential loan

❑ **APR:** The annual percentage rate of interest, in percent

❑ **Periods:** The numbers of months to repay the loan

❑ **Payment:** The amount of the monthly payment to repay the loan

The variable periodic_rate is divided by 12 months times 100 percent to get the actual rate used per period. The APR must be between 0 and 25 percent. Periods must be a positive integer, and Amount and Payment must be positive values.

There are two action methods: amount() and payment(). If amount is selected, then loan amount available for the provided monthly payment is calculated. If payment is selected, then the monthly payment to pay back the loan in the specified numbers of periods is calculated.

During the first run, when the f:convertNumber lines were commented out, the values were displayed without a fixed decimal point or any numeric formatting, as shown in Figure 21-8. Adding the formatting statements enabled the numbers to be rendered more correctly as integers or decimals, as shown in Figure 21-9.

This example makes use of one of the standard converters provided as a part of JSF, the numberConverter. The job of the converter is to convert things from strings to objects, and then from objects back to strings again. In the sample code, the numberConverter uses information passed in attributes of a custom tag to format the numbers. It also uses these formats to parse the numbers from strings to the correct type.

Standard converters

Just as there are standard validators, JSF provides a set of standard converters. The standard JSF implementation offers the following standard converters:

- ❏ `BigDecimalConverter`
- ❏ `BigIntegerConverter`
- ❏ `BooleanConverter`
- ❏ `ByteConverter`
- ❏ `CharacterConverter`
- ❏ `DateTimeConverter`
- ❏ `DoubleConverter`
- ❏ `FloatConverter`
- ❏ `IntegerConverter`
- ❏ `LongConverter`
- ❏ `NumberConverter`
- ❏ `ShortConverter`

The `NumberConverter` and the `DateTimeConverter` also provide custom tags to control the format of the conversions. If a component is bound to a backing, then the data is automatically converted to the type required by the property on the bean. Nothing further needs to be done. If you want to specify a specific converter to use and no parameters need to be provided to the converter, then the `converter` attribute of the component's tag can be used as shown.

```
<h:inputText
    id="number"
    value="#{GuessBean.guess}"
    converter="javax.faces.convert.IntegerConverter"/>
```

This might be useful, for example, if the backing bean supported a `long` but integer limits were desired.

Converting dates and times

The `DateTimeConverter` is accessed using a nested tag as shown:

```
<h:inputText id="number" value="#{InfoBean.BirthDate}" >
    <f:convertDateTime pattern="yyyy/mm/dd HH:mm:ss.SSS Z" />
</h:inputText>
```

In general, the patterns and attributes correspond to the patterns for `java.text.SimpleDateFormat`, and their attributes for the `java.text.DateFormat` classes. These patterns will be applied to both the input data and the output data. The following table describes the attributes supported by the `convertDateTime` tag.

Attribute	Type	Description
dateStyle	String	Valid values are default, short, medium, long, and full. Defines the format, as in DateFormat.getDateInstance(style).
locale	String or Locale	Determines the locale used for formatting. Defaults to the value returned by FacesContext.getLocale.
pattern	String	Custom formatting pattern used to determine how to format and parse the date. Patterns correspond to those supporting SimpleDataFormat.
timeStyle	String	Valid values are default, short, medium, long, and full. Defines the format, as in DateFormat.getTimeInstance(style).
timeZone	String or TimeZone	Sets the time zone to use for conversion.
type	String	Valid values are date, time, or both. Defaults to date. Determines if the string value will contain a date, a time, or both.

Converting numbers

The `NumberConverter` is accessed using a nested tag as shown:

```
<h:inputText id="amount" value="#{LoanBean.amount}" >
  <f:convertNumber type="number" pattern="#,##0.00" />
</h:inputText>
```

The attributes supported for the `convertNumber` tag are shown in following table.

Attribute	Type	Description
currencyCode	String	ISO4217 currency code.
currencySymbol	String	Currency symbol.
groupingUsed	boolean	If true, grouping separators are used in formatted output.
integerOnly	boolean	If true, then only the integer part of the value is parsed.
maxFractionDigits	int	Number of digits in the fractional part of the output.
maxIntegerDigits	int	Number of digits in the integer part of the output.
minFractionDigits	int	Minimum number of digits formatted in the fractional part of the output.

Attribute	Type	Description
minIntegerDigits	int	Minimum number of digits formatted in the integer part of the output.
locale	String	Locale whose styles are used to format or parse data.
pattern	String	Custom formatting pattern that determines how the number string is formatted and parsed. See NumberFormat class.
type	String	Values are number, currency, or percentage; defaults to number. Determines how the string value is parsed and formatted.

Implementing the Converter interface

What should you do if you need a custom conversion? The answer is simple: You create a class that implements the Converter interface and you bind it to the component. The interface supports two methods, getAsObject() and getAsString(). The first method takes a string and returns the appropriate object. The second method takes an object and converts it to a string.

Try It Out   Creating a Custom Converter

To demonstrate this, let's use the preceding example and add a custom converter for the Loan Amount field. When an amount is entered, we want the amount to be shown as currency, with the appropriate symbol and number of digits to the right of the decimal, but we do not want to have to enter the number this way. Therefore, a custom converter is needed. Here is the code for the custom converter:

```
package com.wrox.jsp;

import java.text.NumberFormat;
import javax.faces.application.FacesMessage;
import javax.faces.component.UIComponent;
import javax.faces.context.FacesContext;
import javax.faces.convert.Converter;
import javax.faces.convert.ConverterException;

public class NumberToCashConverter implements Converter
{
  public NumberToCashConverter()
  {
  }

  public Object getAsObject(
    FacesContext facesContext,
    UIComponent uIComponent,
    String str)
  {
    Double dbl = null;
    if ( str == null )
```

```
  {
    return null;
  }

  try
  {
    NumberFormat format = NumberFormat.getCurrencyInstance();
    if( format.getCurrency().getSymbol().charAt(0) == (str.charAt(0)))
    {
      Number num = format.parse(str);
      dbl = new Double( num.doubleValue() );
    }
    else
    {
      dbl = new Double(Double.parseDouble(str));
    }
  }
  catch (Exception e)
  {
    FacesMessage message =
      new FacesMessage("Conversion to Double failed! "+e.getMessage());
    throw new ConverterException(message);
  }
  return dbl;
}

public String getAsString(
  FacesContext facesContext,
  UIComponent uIComponent,
  Object obj)
{
  Double inputVal = null;
  String retVal = null;
  if ( obj == null )
  {
    return "";
  }
  // value must be of the type that can be cast to a String.
  try
  {
    inputVal = (Double)obj;
    //== strip $ character off but decimal
    NumberFormat format = NumberFormat.getCurrencyInstance();
    retVal = format.format(inputVal);
  }
  catch (Exception e)
  {
    FacesMessage message =
      new FacesMessage("Conversion to String failed! "+e.getMessage());
    throw new ConverterException(message);
  }
  return retVal;
  }
}
```

How It Works

In the `getAsObject()` method, the line that reads

```
if( format.getCurrency().getSymbol().charAt(0) == (str.charAt(0)))
```

determines whether the currency symbol of the current locale matches the first character of the string. If it does, then a currency conversion is performed by using the `parse` method of the `format` object. Otherwise, the string is parsed as a `double`.

Going the other direction should always give us a currency string by using the `format` object created with `NumberFormat.getCurrencyInstance()`.

To use the converter, we still have two more tasks. First we must register it by adding an entry to `faces-cfg.xml`. This is done by inserting the following lines before the closing `</faces-config>` tag:

```
<converter>
    <converter-id>NumberToCash</converter-id>
    <converter-class>com.wrox.jsp.NumberToCashConverter</converter-class>
</converter>
```

The final task is to bind the converter to the component in the JSP. This can be done by changing the lines in `calc.jsp` that read

```
<h:inputText id="amount" value="#{LoanBean.amount}" >
    <f:convertNumber type="number" pattern="#,##0.00" />
</h:inputText>
```

to the following:

```
<h:inputText id="amount" value="#{LoanBean.amount}"  converter="NumberToCash" />
```

Once this has been completed, run the application and observe the behavior of the Loan Amount field. Data rendered in the field is preceded with a $ in the US locale, but the data is converted correctly whether or not the $ is provided for the input.

Handling Events with Listeners

JavaServer Faces supports an event handling model that provides components with the capability to generate events, and for Listeners to be created to respond to those events. Three types of events are supported:

❑   action

❑   value-change

❑   data-model

`Action` events are generated by the `UICommand` component, which is the component behind the `<h:commandButton>` and `<h:commandLink>` tags.

Value-change events are generated when a user changes the value of a component represented by UIInput or one of its subclasses. These include the h:input and h:select series of tags.

Data-model events are related to the UIData component, which in turn is rendered by the h:dataTable tag. It is generated when a new row of the UIData component is selected.

Try It Out   Handling Value-Change Events

Value changes are generated when a value on a component changes. Value-change events can be handled in one of two ways — a method can be added to a backing bean, or a ValueChangeListener can be created. The following code demonstrates a ValueChangeListener called LogChange, which logs an entry to the standard output each time the value of the component changes:

```java
package com.wrox.jsp;

import javax.faces.event.AbortProcessingException;
import javax.faces.event.ValueChangeEvent;
import javax.faces.event.ValueChangeListener;

public class LogChange implements ValueChangeListener
{
  public LogChange()
  {
  }

  public void processValueChange(ValueChangeEvent event )
  throws AbortProcessingException
  {
    String id = event.getComponent().getId();
    String oldVal = event.getOldValue().toString();
    String newVal = event.getNewValue().toString();
    System.out.println("Component:"
      +id
      +" value changed from "
      +oldVal
      +" to "
      +newVal);
  }

}
```

How It Works

The LogChange class simply gets the component id and the old and new values and prints them to standard output. To use this in the calc.jsp example, we need to add the f:valueChangeListener tag inside of any of the h:inputText tags as shown:

```jsp
<h:inputText id="amount" value="#{LoanBean.amount}"  converter="NumberToCash" >
    <f:valueChangeListener type="com.wrox.jsp.LogChange" />
</h:inputText>
```

The `type` attribute of this tag needs to be the fully qualified class name of the class that implements the `ValueChangeListener` interface.

We hope that we've demonstrated the usefulness of general-purpose `ValueChangeListeners`. A value change event can also be handled by a backing bean. The backing bean needs to implement a method that accepts a `ValueChangeEvent` and returns void, just as the `processValueChange()` method of the sample listener does. Assuming that we were to add the `processValueChange()` method to the `LoanBean`, we would associate the method with the event in the JSP by making the following change to the `calc.jsp`:

```
<h:inputText id="amount" value="#{LoanBean.amount}"
    converter="NumberToCash"
    valueChangeListener="#{LoanBean.processValueChange}" />
```

This is all one tag and is broken across lines for clarity. The `valueChangeListener` attribute causes the method on the backing bean to be executed in response to the event.

Try It Out   Handling Action Events

`Action` events are generated when a command component is activated. An `action` event can be handled in one of two ways — a method that handles the event can be added to a backing bean or an `ActionListener` can be created. A sample `ActionListener` follows:

```
package com.wrox.jsp;

import javax.faces.event.AbortProcessingException;
import javax.faces.event.ActionEvent;
import javax.faces.event.ActionListener;
import javax.faces.event.PhaseId;

public class LogAction implements ActionListener
{
  public LogAction()
  {
  }

  public void processAction(ActionEvent event)
  throws AbortProcessingException
  {
    String id = event.getComponent().getId();
    String phase = event.getPhaseId().toString();
    System.out.println(
      "Component:"
      +id
      +" generated action event handled in phase "
      +phase);
  }

}
```

How It Works

The class implements the `ActionListener` interface. The `processAction` method handles the event. To use the handler, the following change needs to be made in `calc.jsp`. The line that reads

```
<h:commandButton
  action="#{LoanBean.amount}" value="Amount" id="AmountId" />
```

should be changed to add the `f:actionListener` tag as shown:

```
<h:commandButton
  action="#{LoanBean.amount}" value="Amount" id="AmountId" >
  <f:actionListener type="com.wrox.jsp.LogAction" />
</h:commandButton>
```

Now each time the Amount button is selected, a message will be logged to the standard output.

Again, the action can also be handled by the backing bean. To do this, simply add a method to the backing bean that accepts an `ActionEvent` and has no return value and then make the following change to the `h:commandButton` tag:

```
<h:commandButton
  action="#{LoanBean.amount}"
  actionListener="#{LoanBean.processAction}"
  value="Amount" id="AmountId" />
```

This assumes that you named the method `processAction`. The `actionListener` attribute causes the referenced method on the backing bean to be called in response to the event.

JSF versus Struts

Both JSF and Struts are implementations of the Model View Controller design pattern, and there are a number of similarities between them. That is to be expected because both projects were created by the same people. However, there are also a number of differences. The following list briefly compares Struts and JSF:

❑ Struts has been around longer; and through experience, a number of best practices have developed around Struts. JSF development is less mature.

❑ Several JSF constructs map to equivalent concepts in Struts, including the following:

  ❑ The JSF counterpart to the `struts-config.xml` file is the `faces-config.xml` file. These files describe the navigation between pages and the Java classes that are used to implement the code for the application.

  ❑ The JSF backing bean is similar to a Struts Action Form and Action class rolled into one.

❑ Struts is very page-focused. This can be addressed by using Tiles and tiles actions, but many developers are not familiar with these features of Struts. JSF, on the other hand, is designed to be component-focused. It is possible to create new, reusable JSF components that can be available for many applications. In this respect, it is similar to Swing and AWT.

❑ Finally, JSF is slated to become a part of the J2EE set of standards. While Struts is the current de facto standard for MVC frameworks, it remains to be seen what the effect of JSF becoming a part of the standard will have on Struts usage.

Fortunately, the two libraries are compatible and it is possible to use JSF within the context of a Struts application. That, however, is an advanced topic best left for another book.

Summary

This chapter introduced you to developing applications with JavaServer Faces technology. You learned about the following topics:

❑ JSF applications

❑ Backing beans

❑ Navigation

❑ The JSF lifecycle

❑ Data validation

❑ Data conversion

❑ Event handling

Along the way, you created several JSF applications and we hope you learned how to assemble the various parts of a JSF application into a working whole.

JSF is slated to become a standard part of the J2EE platform. Once this happens, vendors will incorporate better JSF tools and implementations into their development environments, and it is possible that JSF will become the dominant Web application development technology for the Java developer.

If you are looking for more JSF resources, a good place to start is the J2EE tutorial that can be found at http://java.sun.com/j2ee. A lot of useful documentation is also included with the JSF reference implementation that can be downloaded from http://java.sun.com/j2ee/javaserverfaces/download.html.

Exercises

1. Modify the Hello example to capitalize the first letter of each word in the name using a custom converter.

2. Modify the LoanBean in the calc example to log a message for value change events on the Payment field.

3. Modify the LoanBean to log messages for action events on both the Amount and Payment buttons.

JSP in J2EE

JSP is one of many components that make up the J2EE specification and technology stack. This chapter explores many of the aspects of the J2EE technologies, how these technologies work together, and the options that JSP developers have for working with the other J2EE technologies.

JSP is one of the important building blocks in the Java Web application development environment, and in this chapter the other components are examined. Additionally, the J2EE components most frequently used with JSP are examined in more detail.

After starting with an overview of the J2EE platform, this chapter moves on to more details about the components, the architecture, and some architectural options that JSP developers can use when building applications.

Finally, this chapter examines the J2EE technologies most important to the JSP developer, and provides a few examples.

In particular, this chapter

- ❏ Provides an overview of J2EE
- ❏ Discusses the benefits of J2EE
- ❏ Examines the components of J2EE
- ❏ Shows different JSP implementation scenarios
- ❏ Provides some examples of using the J2EE components

Overview of J2EE

Because this book focuses on JSP programming, this section provides a brief introduction to J2EE. In it you'll explore areas such as the concepts behind J2EE, its history, and some of the reasons why JSP developer might consider using a complete J2EE technology solution.

What is J2EE?

The Java 2 Enterprise Edition (J2EE) is a technology platform for building server-side applications. While primarily used for Web-centered applications, the platform is a general-purpose, enterprise-centric, server-side development and deployment environment.

The J2EE platform provides a standard development and deployment platform supporting core enterprise requirements, including the following:

- Transactions
- Security
- Scalability
- Integration with other systems

To take advantage of these capabilities, the J2EE platform contains a comprehensive set of APIs. Using this programming model along with the capabilities of the J2EE platform simplifies some of the complex aspects associated with applications developed outside the J2EE environment.

Instead of having to develop a system that handles threading, security, transactions, and interoperability with other systems, the J2EE environment provides these for the developer to build upon. That way, the developer can focus on solving the business problems, rather than building infrastructure.

The J2EE platform provides a multilayered approach to architecting solutions. Each of the layers is capable of scaling independently, providing a solution for even the most demanding applications. This *n-tier* approach to developing applications is covered in more detail in the following sections.

To support the multilayered approach, the J2EE platform provides a definition of four separate containers. These containers are runtime environments that have specific APIs defined for applications to utilize.

The following four containers are defined by the J2EE platform:

- Application Client container
- Applet container
- Web Component container
- Enterprise Java Bean container

All the containers use the J2SE (Java 2 Standard Edition) runtime as the engine to power the container, and some of the containers add additional functionality by way of additional libraries, which are exposed to the application as APIs. The libraries and APIs are covered in more detail in the following sections.

The Application Client container is a standard J2SE runtime, and for J2EE 1.4, it requires a J2SE 1.4 and later version of the Java runtime. An Application Client will communicate with the Web Component container via HTTP or HTTPS and with the Enterprise Bean container using RMI, or potentially using

SOAP/HTTP. An Application Client is normally known as a *fat client* (implemented in Swing or SWT) and has a rich user interface.

The Applet container also is a standard J2SE runtime, but generally will run in the context of a browser (such as Mozilla, Netscape, or Internet Explorer). Communication from the Applet container defined by the J2EE standard to the Web container is accomplished by using HTTP and HTTPS.

The Web Component container is traditionally thought of as *J2EE,* and this container defines the libraries and APIs for the JSP and servlets.

The final container is the Enterprise Bean container, which along with the Web Component container provides the final link in server-side development. The Enterprise Bean container defines the contracts for the Session and Entity beans used in distributed component development.

The Web Component and EJB containers are most commonly considered the J2EE platform, and this book focuses on the Web Component container, as this is the runtime environment for JSP.

These relationships are shown in Figure 22-1.

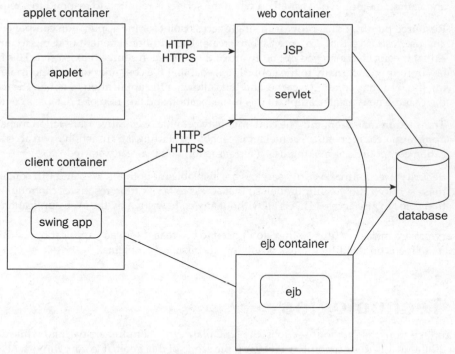

Figure 22-1: J2EE application container architecture

What does a container do?

A container in the J2EE architecture is used to provide a unified view of the underlying J2EE APIs to the application components. A J2EE application never directly interacts with other J2EE components; all these interactions are controlled and managed by the container.

To use the container, a developer needs to provide the application components and a deployment descriptor, which declares to the container the application components and what role those components are to be used for. For example, when creating a Web application, the application developer will create JSP files with an extension of `.jsp`, which is an implicit signal to the Web container that these files should be treated in a particular way. A further example is the use of a Java class file as a servlet. This class file is declared in the deployment descriptor, and a name is associated with the servlet so that it can be managed by the container, and accessed by external requests.

The container has contracts and interfaces to which the J2EE application developer conforms, to make use of the container. In return, the container can provide services such as the following:

❑ **Lifecycle management:** This involves starting and stopping the application components. If the application is a servlet, this will mean calling the `init()` method when the servlet is loaded, and calling the `service()` method when the servlet is required to respond to a request.

❑ **Resource pooling:** This provides a single access point for the application components to locate and use resources that are expensive to create. The additional benefit of using resource pooling is that the application need not be aware of the concrete resource that is used. This resource can be configured externally to the application, enabling the container to be responsible for obtaining the resource, creating a cache, and then allowing the application to obtain the resource from the cache. The typical example of this is the location and creation of a database connection pool.

❑ **Transaction management:** The container may provide declarative transaction management for application components. A container is capable of starting a transaction upon access to an application component or making use of a transaction that is already started.

❑ **Security:** Declarative security services are available for both the Web and EJB containers, and these services allow configuration so that access to application resources can require authentication prior to any access. This is all without any code written by the Web application developer.

These services are infrastructure, so they don't need to be created for each application, which enables developers to focus on the difficult task of solving the business problems.

J2EE Technologies

As you can see from the previous sections, the J2EE platform is comprehensive, and while detailed coverage of all the platform's capabilities is beyond the scope of this book, it is very important for JSP developers to understand the potential technologies available so they can be used effectively if required.

It is unlikely that many of the components of the J2EE platform would be part of the daily working life of the typical JSP developer (or server-side Java developer), but a good understanding will assist in integration and development efforts.

J2EE APIs

This section contains a brief description of all the APIs that a J2EE 1.4–compliant application server has to implement.

Because the J2EE runtime is based on using the J2SE runtime, some of the required J2EE APIs are based on APIs provided by J2SE 1.4. The following APIs are from J2SE:

- ❑ **Java IDL API:** Java IDL is a technology for distributed objects, similar to RMI, but for accessing CORBA-based objects. Unlike RMI, IDL allows objects using different languages to interoperate in invoking the distributed objects. More information on IDL can be found in the CORBA 2.3.1 specification.

- ❑ **JDBC API:** The Java Database Connection API provides a database-independent means for accessing a wide range of data sources, including relational databases, flat files, and tabular data.

- ❑ **RMI-IIOP API:** The RMI-IIOP subsystem allows the use of RMI, enabling objects with a defined RMI interface to be accessed via the IIOP protocol. This makes any enterprise bean (EJB) accessible via RMI-IIOP. More on this is defined in the CORBA 2.3.1 specification.

- ❑ **Java Naming and Directory Interface (JNDI API):** The JNDI API is for accessing a Naming and Directory service. Two similar services are offered. The first, for Naming, provides access to objects configured in the naming service context. An example of this is the `InitialContext` that is used to look up JDBC connection pools in a J2EE server.

  The second, for Directories, provides the functionality to view, create, and modify attributes for a directory object via a `DirContext`. An example is the information exposed by an LDAP-compliant server.

- ❑ **Java API for XML Processing (JAXP):** This API provides a means for applications to parse and transform XML documents in a manner that is independent of the implementation of the XML processing engine. JAXP also provides a means of substituting the XML processing engine. Some of the XML processing engines include Apache Xalan-J and the JAXP RI from Sun.

- ❑ **Java Authentication and Authorization Service (JAAS) API:** This API provides an interface for provider-based access to an authentication and authorization service. Like the JAXP API, the JAAS API allows for different implementations to be used, with the JAAS API providing a consistent way of using the functionality.

In addition to these, the following packages and APIs are required:

- ❑ **Enterprise Java Beans (EJB):** This standard extension specifies the J2EE application services for a distributed component server-side framework. EJB support is further specified in the EJB 2.1 specification. The most important result is that the J2EE platform has defined a consistent way of accessing the components, enabling the J2EE developer to build applications that will work with a wide variety of EJB containers.

- ❑ **Servlet:** This standard extension specifies the J2EE application services for building Web applications. Many of the JSP specifications are defined in the Servlet specification.

- ❑ **Java Server Pages (JSP):** This standard extension further develops the capabilities of a J2EE application server by introducing template-based scripting to the Web application platform.

725

❑ **Java Message Service (JMS):** The JMS provides reliable point-to-point and publish-subscribe protocols for use by the application. As with many of the J2EE platform components, the J2EE specification provides the capability to substitute the JMS implementation without affecting the APIs provided to the application.

❑ **Java Transaction API (JTA):** This API defines the interface to a UserTransaction that is used to control the lifecycle of a transaction under the control of the application. This lifecycle control consists of the capability to start, commit, and abort transactions.

❑ **JavaMail:** The JavaMail API provides a standard mechanism for accessing different implementations of mail transport protocols. These protocols include the implementation of message stores (such as a POP or IMAP mailbox) and the construction and delivery of MIME messages using SMTP.

The JavaMail APIs use the JavaBeans Activation Framework (JAF) for the MIME message-handling support.

❑ **JavaBeans Activation Framework (JAF):** The JAF APIs provide a series of objects for manipulation of MIME data types. This enables MIME-formatted data to be converted easily to Java objects.

❑ **J2EE Connector Architecture (JCA):** The JCA provides a standard interface to external systems that are used by the J2EE platform. These external systems normally take the form of an enterprise information system (EIS), but the external system can be something as simple as a file system.

Each external system provides a Resource Adapter that conforms to a defined set of interfaces loaded by the J2EE application server to access the resource.

The functionality provided by the Resource Adapter includes support for transactions, security, and connection pooling.

❑ **Java API for XML-Based RPC (JAX-RPC):** The JAX-RPC specification provides Web services interoperability between different platforms based on the use of SOAP over HTTP. The specification provides definitions for both the client invocation and server end-points of the protocol, using Web Services Description Language (WSDL) to enable clients and servers deployed on different platforms to interoperate smoothly.

The Web services end-points can be developed using either the Servlet or EJB component models, with the Web services deployed using the respective mechanisms.

❑ **SOAP with Attachments for Java (SAAJ):** This API provides a standard mechanism for sending XML documents. SAAJ is used by JAX-RPC to access the SOAP message in a JAX-RPC message handler.

SAAJ can also be used independently to create applications that produce and consume SOAP messages directly, without using JAX-RPC.

❑ **Java API for XML Registries (JAXR):** JAXR defines a standard interface for clients to access XML-based registries, including ebXML and UDDI.

❑ **J2EE Management 1.0:** The J2EE Management interface provides a means for tools to query the J2EE application server to examine internal information. This includes examining objects that identify the status of the application server, the applications deployed, the status of applications, and even collection of statistics to assist in performance monitoring.

The Management component is based on JMX, and identifies concrete object models that the J2EE application server will expose through a EJB known as the J2EE Management EJB Component.

❑ **Java Management Extensions (JMX):** The JMX support in the J2EE application server is required for the J2EE Management interface.

❑ **Java Authorization Contract for Containers (JACC):** The JACC specification defines a standard interface between a J2EE application server and an authorization policy provider. The specification includes definitions for how authorization policy providers are deployed, configured, and used in making access decisions.

J2EE platform architecture

Figure 22-2 shows a more detailed view of the J2EE platform architecture, focusing on the most common understanding of J2EE as a *thin client application,* with the user interface generated by a Web application, communicating to a business tier operating in the EJB container. It is worth noting that the Web container and EJB container shown in Figure 22-2 do not have to be installed in separate JVMs or even on separate machines. It is quite common for the Web and EJB containers to be running on the same JVM. The capability to distribute the Web and EJB containers across JVMs and hardware is evidence of the scalability of the J2EE architecture.

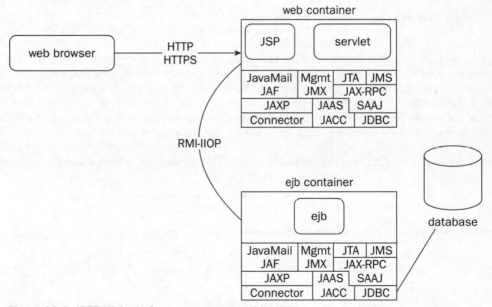

Figure 22-2: J2EE Web platform component architecture

It is important to understand that the J2EE architecture does not mandate the use of all the components when leveraging the J2EE platform. Many components are great for a mix-and-match opportunity, and selecting the appropriate components is one of the most important aspects of using the J2EE platform.

727

JSP development scenarios

The J2EE platform provides the opportunity to select a number of alternative architectures when developing a Web application. This section covers some of these alternatives, and provides some insight into what would be required during development of each of the scenarios.

The first scenario examined uses JSP for the entire application. This is well suited to simple applications and prototypes. The deployment of the JSP is simple: There is no need to compile additional Java classes, and the capability to change the functionality rapidly makes this a great alternative for working with customers to flesh out and clarify requirements.

Figure 22-3 shows the J2EE components used when using JSP only.

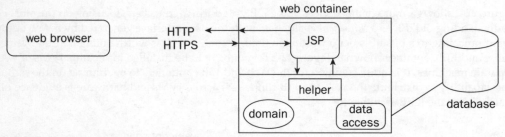

Figure 22-3: Web application using JSP only

The next scenario involves the use of JSP and servlets. This is one of the most common alternatives for general-purpose Web applications. The servlets are used to control the flow of the application and provide access to the domain information, and the JSPs are used to create the user interface. This model balances a need for rapid development and extensive multi-tier scalability. While the tiers within the application architecture can be appropriately layered, and transactions can be utilized, this scenario does require more work for a developer for more complex applications.

Figure 22-4 shows the J2EE components used when a Web application is built using JSP and servlets.

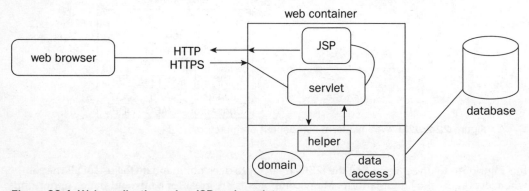

Figure 22-4: Web application using JSP and servlets

The final scenario involves both the Web and EJB containers, moving the domain and data access to the EJB tier. This alternative is the most complex, requiring deployment options and configuration not required for the Web application–only scenarios. This is most suitable for very complex applications, requiring high levels of scalability.

Figure 22-5 shows the J2EE components used when a Web application is built using JSP, servlets, and EJB components.

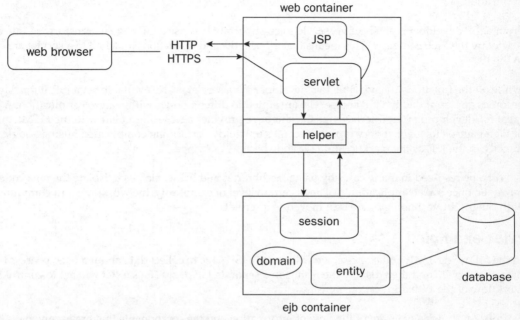

Figure 22-5: Web application using JSP, servlets, and EJB

As the previous section has shown, there is a variety of choices for developers building Web applications, but the one consistent element is the use of JSP.

Using JSP with J2EE Components

The previous sections have introduced a multitude of components the J2EE platform provides to application developers. This section describes in more detail some of the components a JSP developer is likely to need to interact with on projects, and includes a number of simple examples to illustrate their use.

Many of these J2EE components are covered in further detail, and with more comprehensive examples, in other chapters in the book.

Servlets

Servlets form the core of the server-side Web application development components. Servlets are used for a variety of functions, including processing user input, communicating with other J2EE technologies, such as JDBC and EJB, accessing the business domain classes, and generating responses.

At the most basic level, a servlet is a Java class that adds functionality to a Web application server. A servlet is installed in a Web container as part of a Web application and configured as part of that Web application.

From a JSP developer's perspective, servlets are important because a JSP page is transformed into a servlet by the Web container. This means that all benefits and restrictions attached to a servlet are carried to the JSP.

While all the functionality available to a developer via a servlet is also available via a JSP, it quickly becomes apparent that the JSP and servlet are suited to different roles within a Web application. A JSP is great for developing user interfaces, as the language provides a close alignment with the HTML markup of Web pages. However, it very rapidly becomes unwieldy performing complicated business logic directly in the JSP, as the markup and Java code become entwined.

This can be resolved in many cases by using tag libraries and helper classes to isolate the Java code; however, once a Web application reaches a certain level of complexity, the workflow and communication with other J2EE technologies are best moved to a servlet.

Servlet example

In the following Try It Out exercise, we will create a JSP page to collect data about a user, process the data in a servlet, and then display the results in a separate JSP page. The servlet will act to control the workflow of the Web application.

Figure 22-6 shows a diagram of the flow of information and the components that are involved.

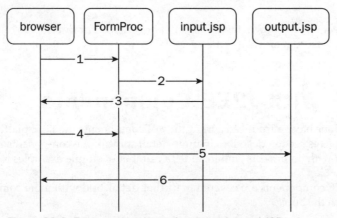

Figure 22-6: Form processing using a servlet and JSP

The steps involved in the processing are as follows:

1. The user browses to the form processing Web application, and the servlet `FormProc` is configured to intercept all the user requests.

2. The `FormProc` servlet forwards the user request to the `input.jsp` page.

3. The `input.jsp` page displays the form for the user to complete.

4. The user completes the form and submits the data.

5. The `FormProc` servlet processes the data, and then forwards the user request to the `output.jsp` page.

6. The `output.jsp` page displays the result for the user.

Try It Out   Building the Web Application

The Web application consists of the following files:

- ❑ `chapter22/src/com/wrox/begjsp/ch22/name/FormProc.java`
- ❑ `chapter22/web/WEB-INF/web.xml`
- ❑ `chapter22/web/input.jsp`
- ❑ `chapter22/web/output.jsp`
- ❑ `chapter22/chapter22.xml`

The following listing shows the contents of the form processing servlet, `FormProc.java`.

Create the file `FormProc.java` in the `src/com/wrox/begjsp/ch22/name` directory with the following contents:

```
package com.wrox.begjsp.ch22.name;

import java.io.IOException;
import java.util.Date;

import javax.servlet.RequestDispatcher;
import javax.servlet.ServletException;
import javax.servlet.http.HttpServlet;
import javax.servlet.http.HttpServletRequest;
import javax.servlet.http.HttpServletResponse;

public class FormProc extends HttpServlet
{
    private static final String INPUT_JSP  = "/input.jsp";
    private static final String OUTPUT_JSP = "/output.jsp";

    protected void service(HttpServletRequest request,
                           HttpServletResponse response)
            throws ServletException, IOException
    {
```

```java
        String userName = request.getParameter("userName");

        if ((userName == null) || (userName.length() == 0))
        {
            forwardToJSP(FormProc.INPUT_JSP, request, response);
        }
        else
        {
            request.setAttribute("user", userName);
            request.setAttribute("now", new Date());
            forwardToJSP(FormProc.OUTPUT_JSP, request, response);
        }
    }

    private void forwardToJSP(String target, HttpServletRequest request,
            HttpServletResponse response) throws ServletException, IOException
    {
        RequestDispatcher dispatcher = request.getRequestDispatcher(target);
        dispatcher.forward(request, response);
    }
}
```

Create the file `input.jsp` in the `src/web` directory with the following contents:

```html
<html>
  <head>
    <title> Enter Your Name </title>
  </head>
  <body>
    <h1> Name Entry </h1>
    <form action="name" method="post">
      <table>
        <tr>
          <td>Name: </td>
          <td>
            <input type="text" name="userName" />
          </td>
        </tr>
        <tr>
          <td> </td>
          <td>
            <input type="submit" value="submit" />
          </td>
        </tr>
      </table>
    </form>
  </body>
</html>
```

Create the file output.jsp in the src/web directory with the following contents:

```jsp
<%@ taglib prefix="fmt" uri="http://java.sun.com/jsp/jstl/fmt" %>
<%@ taglib prefix="c" uri="http://java.sun.com/jsp/jstl/core" %>

<jsp:useBean id="now" class="java.util.Date" scope="request" />
<jsp:useBean id="user" class="java.lang.String" scope="request" />
<html>
  <head>
    <title> Form Data </title>
  </head>
  <body>
    <h1> Form Data </h1>
    <table>
      <tr>
        <td>The name entered was: </td>
        <td>
          <b>
            <c:out value="${user}" />
          </b>
        </td>
      </tr>
      <tr>
        <td>Date processed: </td>
        <td>
          <fmt:formatDate value="${now}" type="both" />
        </td>
      </tr>
    </table>
    <p/>
    <a href="name">Try Again!</a>
  </body>
</html>
```

Create the file web.xml in the src/web/WEB-INF directory with the following contents:

```xml
<?xml version="1.0" encoding="ISO-8859-1"?>
<web-app version="2.4" uri="http://java.sun.com/xml/ns/j2ee" >
  <servlet>
    <servlet-name>FormProcServlet</servlet-name>
    <servlet-class>com.wrox.begjsp.ch22.name.FormProc</servlet-class>
  </servlet>
  <servlet-mapping>
    <servlet-name>FormProcServlet</servlet-name>
    <url-pattern>/name</url-pattern>
  </servlet-mapping>
  <welcome-file-list>
    <welcome-file>name</welcome-file>
  </welcome-file-list>
</web-app>
```

Finally, create the file `chapter22.xml` in the root directory with the following contents:

```
<?xml version='1.0' encoding='utf-8'?>
<Context docBase="/path/to/chapter22/web"
  path="/chapter22"
  reloadable="true"
  workDir="/path/to/chapter22/work">

</Context>
```

Make sure the attributes for `docBase` and `workDir` contain an absolute path to the location of the directories. Copy this file to `<Tomcat Installation Directory>` `conf/Catalina/localhost`, where it will be picked up by the Tomcat server.

After starting Tomcat, this Web application can now be accessed via the URL `http://localhost: 8080/chapter22/name`.

How It Works

`FormProc.java` is a very simple piece of Java. To be a servlet, the class must extend `HttpServlet` and then implement one of `doPost()`, `doGet()`, or `service()`. For this simple example, `service()` has been implemented.

In the `service()` method, the request parameter `userName` is checked to see if it exists, or if the length is not empty. If not, the flow of control is sent straight back to the input page (`input.jsp`). This flow is shown in Figure 22-6 as step 2.

If the `userName` is valid, then a small amount of processing is done. The `userName` is set as an attribute in the `request` object and is given the name `user`. In addition, the servlet creates a timestamp indicating when the processing occurs and stores this in the `request` object with the name `now`. Storing these objects in the `request` enables them to be used by the target of the forward. Finally, the flow of control is directed to the output page (`output.jsp`). This flow is shown in Figure 22-6 as step 5.

`input.jsp` is a simple page that contains an HTML form that will collect the value of `userName` and submit it to the target `name`. This flow is shown in Figure 22-6 as step 4.

`output.jsp` is another simple JSP that displays the information that was set in the `request` object by the `FormProc` servlet. The execution of this JSP is shown as step 6 in Figure 22-6.

The `web.xml` file configures the Web application, defining the Java class for the servlet, the URL to access the servlet, and the default resource to serve by the Web application via the `welcome-file-list`.

This simple Web application shows how servlet technologies can be used to work with the JSP and provide a means for controlling the page flow. Of course, this Web application is too simple to show the benefit of separating the concerns in this manner, but in Chapter 15, "JSP and Servlets," and the two project chapters (Chapters 27 and 28), more fully developed Web applications show how compelling this separation becomes.

More information on servlets and their interactions with JSP are covered in Chapter 15.

JNDI

The Java Naming and Directory Interface (JNDI) provides a general-purpose set of APIs to enable client applications to perform standard operations on a directory service, such as an LDAP-compliant directory.

However, within the context of J2EE applications, the main use of the JNDI APIs is to look up services provided by the J2EE container. It is this use that this section covers, as this is one of the most common tasks that a J2EE application developer (including JSP developers) will need to perform.

A JNDI service provides a namespace for the objects that it holds. These objects are then located by name, and can be retrieved as objects of the appropriate type. This is an advantage of a JNDI service — the information returned is in the form of an object, not just a piece of data, as would be found in a database.

The J2EE specification requires that a conforming J2EE container provide access to the following objects within the `java:` namespace:

❑   `EJBHome` objects

❑   JTA `UserTransaction` objects

❑   JDBC API `DataSource` objects using `java:comp/env/jdbc`

❑   JMS `ConnectionFactory` and `Destination` objects using `java:comp/env/jms`

❑   JavaMail `Session` objects using `java:comp/env/mail`

As well as these objects, the container provides JNDI access to the environment entries available from the application descriptors. These are the `<env-entry>` values, accessible via the `java:env/` namespace.

The following Try It Out exercise shows how to access the environment entries in the `web.xml` deployment descriptor. This first task is to modify the `web.xml` that was created for the servlet example.

Try It Out   Accessing the Environment Entries

The following listing contains a couple of simple environment entries as additions to `web.xml`.

Modify `web.xml` to include the additional environment entries as follows:

```
<?xml version="1.0" encoding="ISO-8859-1"?>
<web-app version="2.4" uri="http://java.sun.com/xml/ns/j2ee" >
  <env-entry>
    <env-entry-name>pageTitle</env-entry-name>
    <env-entry-type>java.lang.String</env-entry-type>
    <env-entry-value>JNDI Lookup Page</env-entry-value>
  </env-entry>
  <env-entry>
    <env-entry-name>versionNumber</env-entry-name>
    <env-entry-type>java.lang.Integer</env-entry-type>
    <env-entry-value>42</env-entry-value>
  </env-entry>
```

```
   <servlet>
     <servlet-name>FormProcServlet</servlet-name>
     <servlet-class>com.wrox.begjsp.ch22.name.FormProc</servlet-class>
   </servlet>
   <servlet-mapping>
     <servlet-name>FormProcServlet</servlet-name>
     <url-pattern>/name</url-pattern>
   </servlet-mapping>
   <welcome-file-list>
     <welcome-file>name</welcome-file>
   </welcome-file-list>
 </web-app>
```

The second task is to create a JSP page as web/jndi.jsp. The contents of jndi.jsp are as follows:

```
<%@ taglib prefix="c" uri="http://java.sun.com/jsp/jstl/core" %>
<%@ page import="javax.naming.Context" %>
<%@ page import="javax.naming.InitialContext" %>

<jsp:scriptlet>
  Context context = new InitialContext();
  Context applicationEnv = (Context)context.lookup("java:comp/env");
  String title = (String)applicationEnv.lookup("pageTitle");
  Integer version = (Integer)applicationEnv.lookup("versionNumber");

  pageContext.setAttribute("title", title);
  pageContext.setAttribute("version", version);
</jsp:scriptlet>

<html>
  <head>
    <title> <c:out value="${title}" /></title>
  </head>
  <body>
    <h1><c:out value="${title}" /></h1>
    <table>
      <tr>
        <td>This is version number: </td>
        <td>
          <b>
            <c:out value="${version}" />
          </b>
        </td>
      </tr>
    </table>
  </body>
</html>
```

The current version of jndi.jsp is really ugly, with all the scripting in the JSP. A quick modification to put the JNDI code into a helper class cleans this up nicely.

To perform these improvements, create the file web/jndi-neat.jsp with the contents shown here:

```
<%@ taglib prefix="c" uri="http://java.sun.com/jsp/jstl/core" %>

<jsp:useBean id="env" class="com.wrox.begjsp.ch22.jndi.JNDIHelper" />

<html>
  <head>
    <title> <c:out value="${env.title}" /></title>
  </head>
  <body>
    <h1><c:out value="${env.title}" /></h1>
    <table>
      <tr>
        <td>This is version number: </td>
        <td>
          <b>
            <c:out value="${env.version}" />
          </b>
        </td>
      </tr>
    </table>
  </body>
</html>
```

Create the file src/com/wrox/begjsp/ch22/jndi/JNDIHelper.java with the contents shown next:

```
package com.wrox.begjsp.ch22.jndi;

import javax.naming.Context;
import javax.naming.InitialContext;
import javax.naming.NamingException;

public class JNDIHelper
{
    private String _title;
    private Integer _version;

    public JNDIHelper()
    {
        try
        {
            Context context = new InitialContext();
            Context applicationEnv = (Context)context.lookup("java:comp/env");
            _title = (String)applicationEnv.lookup("pageTitle");
            _version = (Integer)applicationEnv.lookup("versionNumber");
        }
        catch (NamingException unexpected)
        {
            _title = "Unknown";
            _version = new Integer(0);
        }
    }
```

```
        public String getTitle()
        {
            return _title;
        }

        public Integer getVersion()
        {
            return _version;
        }
    }
```

Browse to `jndi-neat.jsp` and the results should be the same as the results from the `jndi.jsp`.

How It Works

Browsing to `http://localhost:8080/chapter22/jndi.jsp` displays the values of the environment entries from `web.xml`. The important elements for the JNDI lookup are the `Context` objects and the `lookup()` method. There is no need to break up the lookup, the title and version information could be located directly using the following:

```
String _title = (String)context.lookup("java:comp/env/pageTitle");
Integer version = (Integer)context.lookup("java:comp/env/versionNumber");
```

The introduction of the JNDI helper to the JSP makes the JSP far cleaner, without affecting its functionality.

Notice the change that removes the additional `<%@page import %>` statements from `jndi.jsp`, and the replacement of the `<jsp:scriptlet>` with the `<jsp:useBean>`. This cleans up the original JSP considerably. The functionality that existed in the `<jsp:scriptlet>` tag has now been moved to a helper class.

The maintainability of the new solution is vastly improved by the changes that were introduced.

This example shows the fundamentals of using the JNDI APIs for accessing the J2EE resources. Accessing other types of resources requires accessing the appropriate object in the namespace. The next section on using JDBC shows another example of looking up objects in the JNDI registry, the `DataSource` object.

JDBC

The J2EE specification mandates that support for a JDBC 3.0–compliant driver be made available to applications. One of the restrictions on an application is that it should not attempt to load the driver directly via the `Class.forName("com.company.jdbc.DriverName")`, but instead should rely on using the JNDI lookup for a `DataSource` object.

Some of the additional functionality that the J2EE specification requires JDBC support for is as follows:

- ❑ Metadata requests via `Connection.getMetaData()`
- ❑ Stored procedures
- ❑ Batch updates

The exact mechanism for setting up a JDBC `DataSource` in a J2EE application server depends on the server, but all follow similar principles. The JDBC Try It Out exercise that follows shows a simple example of setting up a JDBC connection, and then using the JSP tags provided by JSTL to query the database.

JDBC example

This example uses the popular MySQL database. This is freely available, and instructions on installation and general database configuration are covered in detail in Chapter 23, "Access to Databases."

As required by the J2EE specification, the MySQL driver will be configured as part of the JNDI namespace, and a `DataSource` will be located and used.

This example also uses the simplest possible approach to connecting JSP and a database. The JSTL includes the `<sql>` tags, which are used to connect and select data from the database. This approach works very well for a simple project or for prototyping, but it should be reiterated that this approach should not be considered best practice for all Web applications.

Try It Out   Setting Up the Environment

The first step is to configure the JNDI resource factory. This example uses the Tomcat application server, and configuration will be done via the Tomcat-specific application files.

The following listing shows the additions required to the `<Context>` configuration for this Web application.

Add the following to `chapter22.xml`:

```xml
<?xml version='1.0' encoding='utf-8'?>
<Context docBase="/path/to/chapter22/web"
  path="/chapter22"
  reloadable="true"
  workDir="/path/to/chapter22/work">

  <Resource name="jdbc/FootyDB"
      type="javax.sql.DataSource"
      auth="Container"
      />
  <ResourceParams name="jdbc/FootyDB">
      <parameter>
          <name>username</name>
          <value>footy</value>
      </parameter>
      <parameter>
          <name>password</name>
          <value>footy</value>
      </parameter>
      <parameter>
          <name>driverClassName</name>
          <value>com.mysql.jdbc.Driver</value>
      </parameter>
      <parameter>
          <name>url</name>
```

```
                <value>jdbc:mysql://localhost:3306/footydb?autoReconnect=true</value>
        </parameter>
    </ResourceParams>

</Context>
```

The next step is to declare the resource in the application web.xml:

```
<?xml version="1.0" encoding="ISO-8859-1"?>
<web-app version="2.4" uri="http://java.sun.com/xml/ns/j2ee" >
  <env-entry>
    <env-entry-name>pageTitle</env-entry-name>
    <env-entry-type>java.lang.String</env-entry-type>
    <env-entry-value>JNDI Lookup Page</env-entry-value>
  </env-entry>
  <env-entry>
    <env-entry-name>versionNumber</env-entry-name>
    <env-entry-type>java.lang.Integer</env-entry-type>
    <env-entry-value>42</env-entry-value>
  </env-entry>

  <resource-ref>
    <res-ref-name>jdbc/FootyDB</res-ref-name>
    <res-type>javax.sql.DataSource</res-type>
    <res-auth>Container</res-auth>
  </resource-ref>

  <servlet>
    <servlet-name>FormProcServlet</servlet-name>
    <servlet-class>com.wrox.begjsp.ch22.name.FormProc</servlet-class>
  </servlet>
  <servlet-mapping>
    <servlet-name>FormProcServlet</servlet-name>
    <url-pattern>/name</url-pattern>
  </servlet-mapping>
  <welcome-file-list>
    <welcome-file>name</welcome-file>
  </welcome-file-list>
</web-app>
```

Notice how the `<res-ref-name>` specified in web.xml matches the value defined in `<Resource name="....">`.

Create the file web/jdbc.jsp with the following contents:

```
<%@ taglib prefix="c" uri="http://java.sun.com/jsp/jstl/core" %>
<%@ taglib prefix="sql" uri="http://java.sun.com/jsp/jstl/sql" %>

<sql:setDataSource dataSource="jdbc/FootyDB" />
<c:set value="This Weeks Results" var="title" />

<html>
  <head>
```

```
      <title><c:out value="${title}" /></title>
    </head>
    <body>
      <h1><c:out value="${title}" /></h1>
      <table>
        <tr><th>Home Team</th><th>Away Team</th></tr>
        <sql:query var="results" scope="page">
          SELECT * from games
        </sql:query>
        <c:forEach items="${results.rows}" var="game" >
          <tr>
            <td <c:if test="${game.winner == 1}">bgcolor="yellow"</c:if>>
              ${game.home_team}
            </td>
            <td <c:if test="${game.winner == 2}">bgcolor="yellow"</c:if>>
              ${game.away_team}
            </td>
          </tr>
        </c:forEach>

      </table>
    </body>
</html>
```

How It Works

The `chapter22.xml` file contains the definitions of the resources required for the database, the security information, and the class name of the JDBC driver for the database. Depending on the J2EE container, this may be done slightly differently, but in general all of the same information will be required.

The `web.xml` file uses `resource-ref` to map the name used in the J2EE container configuration. This provides a name that can be used in a JNDI lookup to access the resource. In this example, the JNDI name is used in `jdbc.jsp` as the data source in the `<sql:setDataSource>` tag.

Finally, `jdbc.jsp` is a simple JSP that utilizes the JNDI data source, and then performs a simple query. The `forEach` tag is then used to iterate through the query results, displaying the data in the columns.

EJB

The final section in this chapter examines the role of EJB in the J2EE platform. Because this book is not a comprehensive guide to EJB or J2EE technologies, and does not cover how to develop an EJB, readers who are interested should check out Rod Johnson's *Expert One-on-One J2EE Design and Development* for further information.

To many developers, EJB is synonymous with J2EE. As shown in this chapter, the EJB components are a fairly small part of the J2EE platform, but EJB is certainly one of the technologies that has been around since the earliest versions of the J2EE specification.

A Java developer would not normally call an EJB directly from a JSP; however, a Web application would use a servlet to access the EJB components, storing data collected by a JSP, or retrieving data to be displayed by a JSP.

Benefits of EJB

An EJB is a Java-based component consisting of a number of classes and an XML descriptor defining the nature of the component. As discussed earlier in the chapter, an EJB runs in a J2EE EJB container. The container provides callback into the EJB to provide lifecycle management of the components, as well as the infrastructure for system-level services providing transactions, security, concurrency, and persistence.

An EJB is a reusable component. Historically, there has been some confusion about the best way to use the EJB components and architect solutions that take advantage of the powerful benefits that accrue from the use of EJBs.

The current wisdom when using EJB is to take a coarse-grained view of the EJB as a distinct high-level aggregated component providing a standard interface to a service. A developer can think of the EJB technology as a non-XML version of a Web service! This view is well founded, as in the current version of the EJB specification, a session bean can be exposed to clients as a Web service.

The EJB container presents a standard interface into the EJBs deployed in the container. This enables a variety of clients to access the EJBs. Some of the ways that EJBs can be accessed include the following:

❑ Remotely from a servlet or JSP in a Web container

❑ Locally by other EJBs in the same container

❑ Remotely by a Swing application on a different machine

❑ Remotely by a Web service client

Restrictions on EJB

Unfortunately, there is no such thing as a free lunch, and using EJBs is no exception. To gain the benefits associated with EJBs and the container-orchestrated functionality, some restrictions are placed on developers and what activities an EJB can perform.

In order to maintain portability of the developed EJB, the EJB specification defines certain activities as forbidden. That is, the EJB may well work on a particular EJB container, but it is not guaranteed to operate the same way across all J2EE-compliant containers, or indeed across different versions of the same vendor container supporting the same J2EE specification. Some of the most important restrictions on EJBs are as follows:

❑ **Writing to static fields:** All static fields in the EJB class should be declared as `final`, as there is no guarantee that all instances of a class are created in the same container. The EJB container may have a number of instances as part of a distributed configuration.

❑ **Manipulating threads:** No methods should use the `synchronized` keyword, or attempt to manage threads. The instances may be distributed, which will provide different threading semantics, and the management of threads is the responsibility of the container.

❑ **Using AWT for output, or obtaining input from a keyboard:** This is a server, so there is no guarantee of the existence of a display device or any input devices.

❑ **Using `java.io.*` to access the file system:** The server is responsible for accessing external services, so all the application components should obtain resources via a JNDI resource provider.

❑ **Listening to or accepting connections on a socket:** An EJB can be a network socket client, but not a server. If the EJB needs to service clients, the clients can access the EJB through the container-provided interfaces.

❑ **Performing certain functions with a `ClassLoader`:** The container is responsible for providing the loading of classes. Allowing an EJB to perform these functions could compromise the security of the container.

❑ **Using the value of `this` as an argument to a method, or a return value:** The container is responsible for intercepting calls to EJBs (to support the additional functionality) and as a result, returning `this` will subvert this mechanism. To return a reference to an EJB, or to use it as a method argument, the developer should use the `getEJBObject()` or `getEJBLocalObject()` methods available in the `SessionContext` and `EntityContext` interfaces.

This list is not exhaustive, and is refined as newer versions of the EJB specification are produced. Developers requiring detailed knowledge of the restrictions should read the EJB specification, which can be downloaded from the `java.sun.com` Web site.

Types of EJB

There are three major groups of EJBs:

❑ Session

❑ Entity

❑ Message-driven

Each of these forms of the EJB provides certain services for the J2EE platform, and each should be chosen to assist in different problem domains. As with the J2EE platform, choosing to use one particular entity bean does not force application developers to use all three. Many applications use session beans only to obtain the benefits of the transaction and security infrastructure, and then use a different persistence mechanism (such as Hibernate, an open-source Java persistence framework), rather than entity beans.

There is a fourth "type" of EJB, the Timer Service. This is not a distinct type of EJB, but more of an extension to the other three EJBs to provide a container-based scheduling system.

The architecture and requirements of the application should drive the choice of technologies used from the entire J2EE platform, and not the reverse. Sadly, many early J2EE projects failed spectacularly when naive developers implemented the technology "because it was there," rather than making well-considered judgments about what to include and what to leave out.

Session beans

A session bean is implemented to represent concepts such as workflow, business rule or, potentially, application state. A session bean can be stateless or stateful. The differences are obvious from their names — a stateless session bean cannot maintain any data between client requests, whereas a stateful session bean can.

One of the most important J2EE patterns to be identified is the use of the session bean as a front, or *facade*, to a client. This facade provides a coarse-grained interface to potentially many session and entity beans arranged to perform a service.

Following are two good reasons to use this pattern:

❑ **Reduced network traffic:** If a single entry point is provided to a client, then a single remote call encapsulates a high volume of interactions and data requests that stay within the EJB container. The session bean then marshals the responses to provide a single response to the client.

❑ **Correctly positioned business logic:** Creating a facade can force application architecture decisions to identify the appropriate layering of business logic. A facade can identify common business functionality and group it into a common interface. It can also identify areas of functionality that should be in a separate interface, or not exposed to a client at all. This decision-making process can aid in the reuse of components at a service level.

Entity beans

An entity bean represents an object-oriented view of some persistent data within the business domain of the application. The EJB container provides lifecycle support for entity beans to manage all the persistence functions associated with loading, saving, and updating data in a database.

The entity bean is a representation of the data within the database, and rather than a client directly accessing the data via JDBC and SQL, the entity bean acts as the interface. This enables clients of the entity beans (which are normally session beans) to use a more object-oriented view of the data, and obtain the benefits of this view.

Entity beans are not the only means of persisting data in a J2EE application, as the developer may use direct SQL via JDBC, or object-relational mapping (ORM) tools such as Hibernate or Toplink directly from session beans. Depending on the complexity of the data model and the data access requirements of the application, these might be viable options.

The advantage of using entity beans is the reduction of issues surrounding the mapping of data from an object model to a relational database, including the configuration that is concerned with that mapping.

Entity beans can be of two forms: container-managed persistence (CMP) or bean-managed persistence (BMP). A CMP bean delegates all the management of loading and storing data to the container, in contrast with a BMP bean, where the loading and saving is done via methods within the entity bean.

CMP entity beans are considered one of the major benefits of using J2EE in general, and EJB in particular, as they drastically reduce the development effort surrounding the management of the business data. The most common means to access data is via SQL. Writing SQL is a complex, time-consuming and error-prone process that gets more and more difficult as the complexity of the data model increases.

In the majority of cases, the container's support for CMP and the EJB specification that covers the querying capability of CMP is sufficient to persist the application data. For those cases that fall outside the support, there is BMP. BMP can enable developers to write persistence code that exists in the entity bean that specifically handles the needs of the application.

Using BMP was a reasonably common occurrence in older versions of the EJB implementations because of significant limitations in the CMP support. With the release of EJB 2.0, the CMP support has been greatly expanded, minimizing the need for developers to use BMP.

Unfortunately, using BMP means relinquishing many of the benefits of using entity beans for persistence, as the developer is back to using SQL as data access code.

Message-driven beans

The final member in the trio of EJBs is the message-driven bean (MDB). An MDB is a consumer of messages that will be invoked asynchronously by the container on receipt of a message. The MDB may use the Java Message Service (JMS) as the transport for the message, but may also support other types of messaging.

MDBs are stateless; the lifecycle is managed by the container. MDBs are also the simplest of all the EJBs.

A client cannot directly access an MDB because it has no client-accessible interfaces. Instead, it communicates by sending a message to a queue, indicating that the MDB is configured as the destination. MDB queue and message selection criteria are defined in the deployment descriptor, so the client access points are defined at deployment time.

Timer Service

Newly introduced in the EJB 2.1 specification, the Timer Service adds scheduling functionality to session, entity, and message-driven beans.

The Timer Service is intended to provide support for long-lived business processes, so the EJB specification requires that the container maintain the timer information and any associated EJB information over shutdown and restart of the container.

Timers can be associated only with entity beans, stateless session beans, and message-driven beans. Timers may not be associated with stateful session beans.

The Timer Service consists of the following components:

❑ **TimedObject:** This interface is implemented by the EJB that requires the scheduling functionality. The method ejbTimeout(Timer timer) is invoked by the container when the scheduled event occurs.

❑ **TimerService:** An instance of a TimerService is obtained from the EJBContext of the EJB. The TimerService is then used to register for notification of a schedule. The notification may be on a specific date, after a period of time, or at a recurring interval. The TimerService may also be used to obtain all the outstanding Timer events associated with the given EJB.

❑ **Timer:** A Timer represents a single notification event. A Timer can be used to cancel an upcoming scheduled event or to query information about the event.

A Timer that is associated with an entity bean is really associated with a specific instance of that entity bean and the data it represents. Using a Timer with an entity bean enables you to access the data associated with that identity. An example of using a timed entity bean is adjusting time-based reference data according to a schedule, such as decreasing prices on stock for a sale, and then increasing them after the sale has ended.

A Timer on a session bean should be associated only with a stateless session bean. Any available session bean will be notified when the scheduled time occurs. An example of the use of a timed stateless session bean is to validate that some workflow process has occurred within an appropriate timeframe. This might be especially relevant to a review phase, where a review must occur within a certain timeframe of a workflow step.

A Timer on a message-driven bean is similar to one on a stateless session bean. Given the asynchronous nature of an MDB, these are likely candidates to be activated via a timer, as well as external messaging.

Summary

This chapter has covered the fundamentals of the J2EE platform — what it is composed of, and the key technologies that a JSP developer should understand, including its structure, configuration, development, and deployment.

To conclude this chapter, let's review some of its key points:

❑   JSP is part of the J2EE platform.

❑   The J2EE platform provides infrastructure services for the development of applications.

❑   The J2EE platform is governed by a specification that mandates inclusion of certain technologies, such as JDBC, JTA, and JavaMail, for use by applications.

❑   The J2EE platform is architected as a number of containers, of which the Web and EJB container form the key server-side Java development components.

❑   A JSP developer can easily access the J2EE platform technologies through a standard set of APIs, gaining the benefit of application portability.

❑   A developer does not need to use all of the technology components provided by the J2EE platform to take advantage of the benefits provided by the services that are needed, and should ensure that the needs of the application drive the choice of technologies.

Exercises

1.   Develop a Web application to iterate through the `java:comp/env` namespace and display all the available objects.

2.   Develop a Web application that will enable the sending of an e-mail using the JavaMail J2EE component. The Web application should collect the To, Subject, and Body elements of the mail message.

Access to Databases

A database forms part of many enterprise applications, and Web applications are prime candidates for searching, displaying, and capturing data. Understanding how to use a database in a Web application is a very important part of a JSP developer's toolkit. Persistence of data is such a common requirement in modern applications that many developers consider not having any data storage or retrieval to be a mistake in the collection of requirements.

This chapter covers an introduction to databases and the standard means of accessing relational databases from Java, the JDBC API. It explores the different ways of accessing databases from a JSP, from using the `<sql>` tags provided by the JSTL for simple applications to more comprehensive approaches that are used as the complexity of the data model and data use increases. This exploration includes an examination of different types of common data access mechanisms using JDBC, as well as the issues associated with object-relational mapping (ORM).

Finally, the chapter looks at some other database access mechanisms, including object-relational mapping tools such as Hibernate and JDO.

This chapter covers the following topics:

❑   The fundamental components used in accessing databases from Java

❑   An introduction to the JDBC APIs

❑   Different techniques for accessing databases

❑   How to use direct JDBC calls to access a database

❑   How to use Hibernate to access a database

This chapter assumes a basic working knowledge of SQL syntax and the basic SQL commands required to set up and manage databases and tables, as well as SQL used for working with the data within the database and tables.

Introduction to Databases

A database can be considered a means of storing data; this may include relational databases, object databases, or even files in a directory. The most common form of database known to the majority of developers is a *relational database*. Examples of relational databases are Oracle, IBM's DB2, Microsoft's SQL Server, and the freely available MySQL, PostgreSQL, and Hypersonic.

Because of the overwhelming dominance of relational databases in the marketplace, this chapter focuses on solutions involving those technologies. Clearly, databases form a core part of an enterprise's IT assets, and the data they contain is often the reason why funding is allocated for development.

A database may be specific to a single Web application, but it is more common that the database is owned by the enterprise, and the Web application forms another access mechanism for the data. It is more complicated to build applications to access historical data than to start with a completely new application.

Many applications require the capability to save and recover information that may have to last for a long period of time. Usernames and passwords, user preferences, bulletin board postings, news articles, and even defect reports are all candidates for storage in a database.

Therefore, for all Java application developers, whether developing for the Web using J2EE or a standalone application, the skills that enable you to understand how to work with databases are an important set to have.

A database is such a common component in Web applications that the J2EE specification requires that an application server provide transparent access to databases for all the applications installed on the container. This capability is provided by a JNDI lookup to obtain a `DataSource` and configuration in the J2EE container. While a Web container is not required to provide this functionality, most of the currently available Web containers (such as Tomcat) have provided this, because of demand and a desire to enable applications to work on J2EE containers.

Therefore, after determining that your application needs to use a database, the next step is to consider which database to use. As an enterprise developer, this isn't generally something that is within the control of an individual application, but a decision that is made at a corporate level. However, when developing at home, or for pleasure, you can choose between a database and other means of persisting the data.

Different classes of relational databases are available, each providing different pros and cons. One set of databases consists of those likely to be found as enterprise solutions. These large-scale commercial offerings, such as Oracle and DB2, are traditionally complicated software products that require specialist skills to set up, manage, and maintain. They do offer the benefit of having the most comprehensive feature sets, but this comes at a cost, that of understanding how to work with them.

Fortunately, these systems are generally installed in large-scale commercial environments, so specialists are usually at hand to assist developers.

The next tier of databases includes the more developer-friendly systems such as MySQL and PostgreSQL. These databases are not lightweights; they contain the features required to develop robust and reliable Web applications, but they may lack some of the more comprehensive features provided in commercial offerings.

Finally, there are databases that are so lightweight they act as "in-memory" databases. HSQLDB is a Java-based version, with a JDBC driver that provides a subset of the SQL standard. This can be of great value during development and testing where setup and configuration of a "disk-based" database might be more complicated than is necessary, especially if the application, or testing requirements, are all based on reading data. Using a database like HSQLDB can provide a migration path as data requirements become more complicated. The JDBC standard provides interoperability between implementations, and supports a sufficiently large subset of the SQL standard. The JDBC driver implementation is conforming, so migration to other databases is a relatively straightforward process.

This book is not about databases, so this is a very general and highly subjective discussion of the databases. While there may be some merit in looking at databases from this angle, it is not within the scope of this book to perform a thorough analysis of different databases.

Because of the free availability of MySQL as a database platform, and the acceptance of MySQL in the developer community, coupled with the developer-friendly nature of the database, this chapter will test all code, and provide examples, using MySQL. There is no specific need to use MySQL to work through the code examples or exercises, but working with different database software may require changes to some of the database setup scripts and connection information, and some minor changes to keywords depending on the database you are using.

Connecting to a database

As discussed in the preceding section, Java has a standard set of APIs for connecting to a database. The JDBC APIs support accessing relational databases and other data sources such as flat files.

As an interesting aside, JDBC is a trademarked term and not an acronym. However, it is commonly considered to stand for Java Database Connectivity, or Java Database Connection.

The JDBC APIs define what is available to client software. To connect to any particular database, a JDBC-compatible driver must be provided by the database vendor, or a third party. Sun has provided a comprehensive (and probably database-backed) searchable list of currently available drivers at `http://servlet.java.sun.com/products/jdbc/drivers`.

This allows for searching for drivers based on a number of criteria. Obviously, searching by database is an option, but so is searching for the JDBC API driver version number, and the JDBC driver type.

One of the most important considerations for developers, apart from the JDBC API driver version, is the driver type. This determines, in general, how easy it will be to install and update the driver, and tends to indicate how recently the driver has been built, and how seriously the database vendor wishes to work with Java developers.

There are four basic types of drivers:

❑ A JDBC-ODBC bridge

❑ Native API/partly Java driver

❑ Net-protocol fully Java driver

❑ Native-protocol fully Java driver

Type 1: JDBC-ODBC bridge

The type 1 driver was one of the first available driver types supporting JDBC for database vendors. This is mostly due to the existing support and availability of ODBC drivers for databases, and the JDBC-ODBC bridge provides a unified API utilizing that support.

The main advantage that the JDBC-ODBC bridge had (which is now obsolete as a result of support for later, more comprehensive driver types across most database vendors) was the availability of ODBC drivers, which were already installed on the client machines that needed to use the database.

However, JDBC-ODBC bridge drivers suffer from a massive performance penalty because the JDBC call is routed through the bridge to the ODBC driver and then to the native database interface. When the database responds, the reverse occurs.

Another significant downside of the JDBC-ODBC bridge drivers is that for each new client machine that is installed, native support must be installed on each of those machines. This makes it much harder to deploy Java-only solutions.

Type 1 drivers are relatively uncommon now, having primarily been replaced by type 3 or type 4 drivers.

Type 2: Native API/Partly Java driver

The type 2 driver was a step up from the type 1 driver, where custom Java driver code was integrated with native database client code to provide a hybrid driver for communicating with the database.

Many type 2 drivers suffer from disadvantages similar to those of the type 1 client: low performance and the requirement for native code installation on the client. However, some of the type 2 drivers, notably the Oracle OCI drivers, have optimized native code for specific platforms, and so perform quite well.

The advantage that type 2 drivers have over type 1 drivers is an increase in performance. Like type 1 drivers, type 2 drivers represent a significant minority, especially for modern versions of the popular databases.

Type 3: Net Protocol/All Java driver

The type 3 driver is the first of all Java drivers available for JDBC access. A type 3 driver communicates with special database-specific middleware that converts JDBC calls to database-specific calls. The main advantage the type 3 driver provides is that the client code is all Java; no native client install is required, so distribution and configuration of Java applications is vastly simplified.

The middleware server can serve many different versions of databases and can act as a gateway to multiple database servers.

In general, the type 3 drivers are significantly faster than the type 1 or 2 drivers.

Type 4: Native Protocol/All Java driver

The type 4 driver, like the type 3 driver, provides an all-Java driver for the client. The main difference between the type 4 and type 3 drivers is that the type 4 driver communicates directly with the database, converting the JDBC calls to database-specific protocols within the JDBC driver.

One theoretical disadvantage of the type 4 drivers over type 3 is the need for specific drivers for each of the databases supported, whereas a type 3 driver could potentially serve many databases behind the middleware server. In practice, this isn't much of an issue.

Using a JDBC driver

Connecting to a database using JDBC can be performed in one of two ways. The first is to load the JDBC driver directly. The second is to use the J2EE container to provide an abstraction and obtain a DataSource object via JNDI.

The advantages of obtaining a DataSource from the container include the following:

❑ Configuration is not contained in client code, and is instead managed during deployment, allowing for substitution of drivers and databases.

❑ Additional features such as connection pooling can be implemented transparently to the application.

A Web container is not required to provide a JNDI resource pool containing a DataSource. Most do provide this facility, but to cover all the bases, the following examples highlight the differences between the two approaches. Both end up with a Connection object, and both examples are quite simple.

The following code fragment shows how to load a JDBC driver and obtain a Connection directly:

```
Connection conn = null;
try
{
    Class.forName("com.mysql.jdbc.Driver").newInstance();
    conn = DriverManager.getConnection("jdbc:mysql://localhost/mysql?params");
}
catch (SQLException unexpected)
{
    System.out.println("Error occurred obtaining connection");
    System.out.println(unexpected.getMessage());
}
. . .
```

The following code fragment shows how to locate a JDBC driver via a JNDI lookup, and obtain a Connection from the DataSource:

```
Connection conn = null;
try
{
    Context initialContext = new InitialContext();
    Context env = (Context) initialContext.lookup("java:comp/env");
    DataSource source = (DataSource) env.lookup("jdbc/FoolyDB");
    conn = source.getConnection();
}
catch (SQLException unexpected)
{
    System.out.println("Error occurred obtaining connection");
    System.out.println(unexpected.getMessage());
}
. . . .
```

Notice that the structure and layout of the code is almost identical. There's only a minor difference between the two approaches in obtaining a Connection.

At this point, not much can be done without setting up a database. The remaining examples assume that this setup and configuration are handled. This is not a comprehensive guide to setting up MySQL; for additional assistance, the MySQL Web site (www.mysql.org) provides very detailed instructions for installation and troubleshooting.

Downloading and Installing MySQL

The installation instructions vary slightly depending on the operating system that is used to run the database, and on the application server that is to be used.

Downloading MySQL

To download MySQL, go to www.mysql.org.

1. Download the latest production version of the MySQL database server. At the time of writing, this was 4.0.20.

   If MySQL is to be installed on a Linux system and the distribution supports the RPM format, then download the MySQL-server-VERSION.i386.rpm and MySQL-client-VERSION.i386.rpm. Otherwise, download the appropriate .tar.gz package.

2. Download the latest production version of the Connector/J driver. At the time of writing, this was 3.0.14

3. (Optional) Download the latest version of MySQL Control Center. This is a GUI tool that uses a cross-platform toolkit to run on both Windows and UNIX environments. This tool will make it easier to manage the installation of MySQL, create tables, and modify user permissions. MySQL Control Center can be downloaded from devmysql.com/products/mysqlcc/.

Installing MySQL

For Microsoft Windows:

1. Unzip the downloaded binary package.

2. Run the setup.exe program to begin the installation process.

3. The default options are appropriate for the examples. If the default options are not chosen, then additional configuration may be required after installation.

For Linux systems, the standard RPM tools will install the MySQL binaries and distribution to the appropriate places.

Installing the JDBC driver

The procedure for installing a JDBC driver depends on the application server that is installed for the examples. In general, it requires making the classes available to the application server so that they can be found and utilized by the server.

The Tomcat Web application server recommends placing the driver JAR file into `<Tomcat Installation Directory>/common/lib`; this enables it to take advantage of loading through the JNDI `DataSource`.

If there is no need or any interest in using the JNDI `DataSource` for locating and loading the driver, then the Connector/J JAR file can be packaged with the WAR during deployment.

All the following examples require that the driver JAR be installed with the application server, as the code will obtain a `DataSource` according to a JNDI lookup. This will enable the examples to be relatively independent of any database-specific setup or classes.

Starting MySQL

Starting MySQL is as simple as running `mysqld.exe` (Windows) or `safe_mysql` (UNIX). Using the RPM installation under Linux will create scripts to automatically start and stop the database when the system is started and shut down.

Windows users can install MySQL as a service, which provides the same lifecycle functionality.

JDBC APIs

The JDBC APIs consist of several packages that provide various services for application developers. Version 2.0 of the JDBC APIs contains two major parts: the JDBC 2.1 Core API (represented by classes in the `java.sql` packages) and the JDBC 2.0 Optional Package API (represented by classes in the `javax.sql` packages). In version 3.0 of the JDBC APIs, the two major parts have been combined into one, the JDBC API; in version 3.0, however the original package naming for all the classes still remains.

java.sql packages

This set of packages contains the core classes and interfaces that are necessary when dealing with databases. These elements relate to tasks such as the following:

- ❑ Making a connection to the database via the `DriverManager`
- ❑ Sending SQL statements to a database, including elements such as `Statement`, `PreparedStatement`, and `Connection`
- ❑ Dealing with responses and updates via the `ResultSet`
- ❑ Standard mapping of SQL types to classes and interfaces in the Java language, including elements such as `Array`, `Blob`, `Clob`, `Date`, `Time`, and `Timestamp`
- ❑ Obtaining metadata from a database via `DatabaseMetaData`, columns in a `ResultSet` via `ResultSetMetaData`
- ❑ Dealing with exceptions such as `SQLException`.

javax.sql

This set of packages contains the classes and interfaces that are used for server-side data source access. The `javax.sql` packages are now included in Java 1.4, but are also required as part of J2EE environments. The main inclusion as part of `javax.sql` is the `DataSource` provided as an alternative to

`DriverManager`. However, it also includes such things as connection pooling, distributed transactions, and the `RowSet` implementation.

JDBC connection and database access

The following table describes some of the more common classes and interfaces used to obtain database connections and perform queries on the database.

Class	Description
`java.sql.DriverManager`	This provides a basic service for managing JDBC drivers. In JDBC 2.0, this has been superceded by the use of the `javax.sql.DataSource`.
`javax.sql.DataSource`	This provides a *factory* for locating the object that provides an interface to the actual database connection. The `DataSource` is implemented by the JDBC driver author and may have the following results when the `getConnection()` method is invoked: ❑ Basic: Calls will return a standard `Connection` object. ❑ Connection pooling: Calls will produce a `Connection` object that automatically participates in a connection pool. ❑ Distributed transaction: Calls will produce a `Connection` object that may be used in a distributed transaction, and in most cases will be capable of participating in a connection pool.
`java.sql.Statement`	A `Statement` is used for executing a static SQL statement and returning the results. An important consideration is that only one `ResultSet` may be open for a `Statement` at any time. Applications that require multiple open `ResultSets` must create them from separate `Statement` objects.
`java.sql.PreparedStatement`	A `PreparedStatement` is a sub-interface of `Statement` that represents a precompiled SQL statement. This SQL statement may include parameters that can be changed for each call, without re-specifying the statement. An example of a parameterized statement is `"SELECT * from GAMES where round = ?"`
`java.sql.CallableStatement`	A sub-interface of `PreparedStatement`, `CallableStatement` provides a standard way to call stored procedures via JDBC in a database-independent manner. A `CallableStatement` may return one or more `ResultSet` objects.

Class	Description
java.sql.ResultSet	A ResultSet contains the rows returned from a Statement (including Prepared and Callable) querying the database. A ResultSet has a cursor that can be used to iterate through the results. Depending on the ResultSet, it may be scrollable in forward and reverse directions, and may be updateable.

JDBC data types

The following table describes the common Java data types that are needed to support the SQL data types. Using these Java classes may be required when obtaining information from a ResultSet.

Class	Description
java.sql.Array	Corresponds to an SQL ARRAY. A collection of SQL data types.
java.sql.Blob	Corresponds to an SQL BLOB.
java.sql.Clob	Corresponds to an SQL CLOB.
java.sql.Date	Corresponds to the SQL DATE. java.sql.Date extends the general purpose java.util.Date, and should be used in preference to java.util.Data in working with the SQL DATE data type.
java.sql.Time	Corresponds to the SQL type TIME. java.sql.Time also extends java.util.Date.
java.sql.Timestamp	Corresponds to the SQL type TIMESTAMP. A java.sql.Timestamp extends a java.util.Date and also includes support for nanoseconds.

Now that you are familiar with the descriptions of common components used when working with databases in Java, you can experiment with the following Try It Out example, which includes many of the concepts that have been covered.

Try It Out   Building an Application

This example represents a simple football roster management application. Football was chosen because you can modify the application to whatever football team is local to your country or region. Readers who aren't sports fans can pretend that they are building the application for a friend who is a fan.

The application (at this stage) will start with the following:

- ❑ A roster of teams that participate in a season
- ❑ A season that is split into a number of rounds
- ❑ A number of fixtures that occur on a round
- ❑ A pair of teams that play in each fixture at a venue

This is simple enough to start with, but also contains a rich enough set of functions to fully exercise the JDBC APIs to be used. This example provides functionality to add teams and set up rounds and fixtures.

Creating a database

The first steps in creating an application are to create the database and the tables that will hold the data. This can be done via JDBC or via an administrative tool. To keep things simple, it will be easiest to use an administrative tool to manage the creation of the database and tables.

To create the database, use the MySQL Control Center administration tool (`mysqlcc`). Downloading instructions are provided in a previous section of the chapter, "Downloading and Installing MySQL." Instructions for using the MySQL Control Center are located at the MySQL Web site (`www.mysql.org`).

Create the database using the following SQL, or `mysqlcc`:

```
CREATE DATABASE footydb;
```

Create a user and password to access the database using the following SQL, or create a user called `footy@localhost` with a password `footy`, with access to the `footydb` using `mysqlcc`:

```
GRANT ALL ON footydb.* TO footy@localhost IDENTIFIED BY 'footy';
```

Create the tables for the following entities: `roster`, `round`, `fixture`, and `venue`. Use either the following SQL or `mysqlcc` to create the tables:

```
CREATE TABLE `roster` (
  `id` int(11) NOT NULL auto_increment,
  `teamname` varchar(100) NOT NULL default '',
  PRIMARY KEY  (`id`)
) TYPE=MyISAM;

CREATE TABLE `round` (
  `id` int(11) NOT NULL auto_increment,
  `number` int(11) NOT NULL default '0',
  `startdate` date NOT NULL default '0000-00-00',
  `enddate` date NOT NULL default '0000-00-00',
  PRIMARY KEY  (`id`)
) TYPE=MyISAM;

CREATE TABLE `fixture` (
```

```
  `id` int(11) NOT NULL auto_increment,
  `roundid` int(11) NOT NULL default '0',
  `hometeam` int(11) NOT NULL default '0',
  `awayteam` int(11) NOT NULL default '0',
  `venueid` int(11) NOT NULL default '0',
  PRIMARY KEY  (`id`)
) TYPE=MyISAM;

CREATE TABLE `venue` (
  `id` int(11) NOT NULL auto_increment,
  `location` varchar(100) NOT NULL default '',
  PRIMARY KEY  (`id`)
) TYPE=MyISAM;
```

This has created a fresh database for the application, without any data. The next step is to build an application that will allow the addition of the teams to the `roster`.

Creating the roster administration

Figure 23-1 shows the components of the application that will be built to support the addition of teams to the `roster` table.

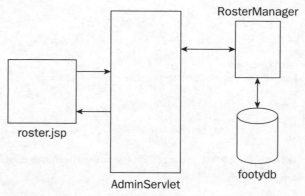

RosterManager

roster.jsp

AdminServlet

footydb

Figure 23-1: Roster administration

Web application directory setup

The Web application will follow the same structure as other Web applications in the book, so create an empty directory structure as follows:

```
chapter23/
        src/
        web/
            WEB-INF/
                lib/
```

Copy the `jstl.jar` and `standard.jar` used in earlier chapters into the `lib` directory.

Create the Tomcat context file `chapter23.xml` in the `chapter23` directory with the following contents:

```xml
<?xml version='1.0' encoding='utf-8'?>
<Context docBase="/path/to/chapter23/web"
  path="/chapter23"
  reloadable="true"
  workDir="/path/to/chapter23/work">

  <Resource name="jdbc/FootyDB"
      type="javax.sql.DataSource"
      auth="Container"
      />

  <ResourceParams name="jdbc/FootyDB">
      <parameter>
          <name>username</name>
          <value>footy</value>
      </parameter>
      <parameter>
          <name>password</name>
          <value>footy</value>
      </parameter>
      <parameter>
          <name>driverClassName</name>
          <value>com.mysql.jdbc.Driver</value>
      </parameter>
      <parameter>
          <name>url</name>
          <value>jdbc:mysql://localhost/footydb?autoReconnect=true</value>
      </parameter>
  </ResourceParams>

</Context>
```

The `/path/to` in `docBase` and `workDir` must match the full path to the `chapter23` directory. Under Windows this might look like the following:

```xml
<Context docBase="c:/dev/begjsp/chapter23/web"
```

Copy this file to `<Tomcat Installation Directory>/conf/Catalina/localhost`. This configuration enables Tomcat to find the `web` directory in the development directories, rather than needing to copy files when they are changed, or to work directly in the `<Tomcat Installation Directory>/webapps` directory.

The additional configuration required in this context fragment enables Tomcat to manage the database connection automatically. This removes all need for the Web application to understand how to connect, or even what database is used. This can make it easy to develop using lightweight databases, and to deploy using fully featured enterprise databases.

Finally, to set up the Web application, create the Web application deployment descriptor `web.xml` in the `web/WEB-INF` directory with the following contents:

```
<?xml version="1.0" encoding="ISO-8859-1"?>
<web-app version="2.4" uri="http://java.sun.com/xml/ns/j2ee" >

  <servlet>
    <servlet-name>AdminServlet</servlet-name>
    <display-name>Football administration servlet</display-name>
    <description>Football administration servlet</description>
    <servlet-class>com.wrox.begjsp.ch23.football.AdminServlet</servlet-class>
  </servlet>
  <servlet-mapping>
    <servlet-name>AdminServlet</servlet-name>
    <url-pattern>/admin</url-pattern>
  </servlet-mapping>

  <resource-ref>
    <res-ref-name>jdbc/FootyDB</res-ref-name>
    <res-type>javax.sql.DataSource</res-type>
    <res-auth>Container</res-auth>
  </resource-ref>

</web-app>
```

The `<resource-ref>` element providing the link to the `<Resource>` is defined in the `chapter23.xml` configuration for Tomcat.

Creating the administration servlet

Starting with the `AdminServlet`, this will perform a check on the method of calling, and if an HTTP GET is used to invoke the servlet, it will display the `roster.jsp`. `roster.jsp` will perform a few duties; these include providing a list of currently entered teams, deleting entered teams when necessary, changing the name of an existing team, or adding a new team.

It would not normally be a good idea to include so much responsibility in one page, but as the `roster` table is so simple and the operations to be performed on the data are not complex, it's not going to cause any major issues. Create the JSP code for `roster.jsp` in the `web` directory as follows:

```
<!--
<%@ taglib prefix="fmt" uri="http://java.sun.com/jsp/jstl/fmt" %>
<%@ taglib prefix="c" uri="http://java.sun.com/jsp/jstl/core" %>
-->
<jsp:useBean id="roster" class="java.util.ArrayList" scope="request" />
<jsp:useBean id="SERVLET_PATH" class="java.lang.String" scope="request" />
<c:set value="Team Roster Management" var="title" />
<html>
  <head>
    <script type="text/javascript" >
      function modifyTeam(id) {
      var roster = document.rosterlist;
      roster.ACTION.value="ROSTER_MODIFY";
      roster.teamid.value=id;
      var elementName = "teamname_"+id;
      var name = roster.elements[elementName].value;
```

```
      roster.teamname.value=name;
      roster.submit();
      }

      function deleteTeam() {
      document.rosterlist.ACTION.value="ROSTER_DELETE";
      document.rosterlist.submit();
      }
    </script>
    <title><c:out value="${title}" /></title>
  </head>
<body>
    <h1><c:out value="${title}" /></h1>
    <table border="1">
      <tr>
        <th>Team ID</th>
        <th>Team Name</th>
        <th>New Name</th>
        <th colspan="2"> </th>
      </tr>
      <form name="rosterlist" action="<c:out value="${SERVLET_PATH}" />"
           method="POST">
        <input type="hidden" name="ACTION" value="ROSTER" />
        <input type="hidden" name="teamid" value="" />
        <input type="hidden" name="teamname" value="" />

        <c:forEach var="team" items="${roster}" >
          <tr>
          <td>${team.id}</td>
          <td>${team.name}</td>
          <td><input id="teamname_${team.id}" type="text" size="20" /></td>
          <td><input type="button" value="Modify"
                     onclick="modifyTeam('${team.id}')" /></td>
          <td><input name="DELETE_LIST" type="checkbox" value="${team.id}" /></td>
          </tr>
        </c:forEach>
        <tr>
          <td align="right" colspan="4">Delete selected items</td>
          <td><input type="button" value="Delete Checked"
                     onclick="deleteTeam()" /></td>
        </tr>
      </form>
      <form action="<c:out value="${SERVLET_PATH}" />" method="POST">
      <input type="hidden" name="ACTION" value="ROSTER_ADD" />
      <tr>
        <td colspan="2"><b>Add new Team</b></td>
        <td><input name="teamname" type="text" size="20" /></td>
        <td><input name="ADD" type="submit" value="Add" /></td>
        <td> </td>
      </tr>
    </table>
  </body>
</html>
```

This first section (in the <head> tags) contains some functions that make operating the HTML a little easier. Because of a minor limitation on the way that HTML works, dual operations such as the Modify and Delete can be performed this way. The jsp:useBean for roster contains the results of the database query performed by the AdminServlet. The remainder of roster.jsp (the section in the <body>) is fairly standard, displaying the team id and team name in a list.

The next listing shows the AdminServlet that controls the inputs from the JSP page, determines what action to take, and then coordinates the results back to the JSP page. This is another example, a very simple example admittedly, of the Model View Controller (MVC) architecture covered in more detail in Chapter 17, "Model View Controller."

Create the file AdminServlet.java in the src/com/wrox/begjsp/ch23.football directory with the following contents:

```java
package com.wrox.begjsp.ch23.football;

import java.io.IOException;
import java.sql.SQLException;
import java.util.List;

import javax.naming.NamingException;
import javax.servlet.RequestDispatcher;
import javax.servlet.ServletException;
import javax.servlet.http.HttpServlet;
import javax.servlet.http.HttpServletRequest;
import javax.servlet.http.HttpServletResponse;

public class AdminServlet extends HttpServlet
{
    private static final String ROSTER_PAGE       = "roster.jsp";

    private static final String ACTION_TOKEN      = "ACTION";

    private static final String ACTION_ROSTER     = "ROSTER_LIST";
    private static final String ACTION_ROSTER_ADD = "ROSTER_ADD";
    private static final String ACTION_ROSTER_MOD = "ROSTER_MODIFY";
    private static final String ACTION_ROSTER_DEL = "ROSTER_DELETE";


    private FootyJDBCHelper      _jdbcHelper       = null;

    public void init() throws ServletException
    {
        try
        {
            _jdbcHelper = new FootyJDBCHelper();
        }
        catch (NamingException unexpected)
        {
            throw new ServletException("Cannot locate required database : " +
                                       unexpected);
        }
    }
}
```

```
public void doGet(HttpServletRequest request, HttpServletResponse response)
        throws ServletException, IOException
{
    doPost(request, response);
}

public void doPost(HttpServletRequest request, HttpServletResponse response)
        throws ServletException, IOException
{
    String action = findAction(request);

    if (ACTION_ROSTER_ADD.equals(action))
    {
        String newNameString = request.getParameter("teamname");
        if (isValidString(newNameString))
        {
            processRosterAdd(newNameString);
        }
    }
    else if (ACTION_ROSTER_DEL.equals(action))
    {
        String deleteIDs[] = request.getParameterValues("DELETE_LIST");
        if (deleteIDs != null)
        {
            for (int i = 0; i < deleteIDs.length; i++)
            {
                String idString = deleteIDs[i];
                int id = Integer.parseInt(idString);
                processRosterDelete(id);
            }
        }
    }
    else if (ACTION_ROSTER_MOD.equals(action))
    {
        String modIdString = request.getParameter("teamid");
        int modId = Integer.parseInt(modIdString);
        String modTeamName = request.getParameter("teamname");
        if (isValidString(modTeamName) && (modId > 0))
        {
            processRosterModify(new Team(modId, modTeamName));
        }
    }
    processRosterList(request);
    performRedirect(ROSTER_PAGE, request, response);
}


private void processRosterList(HttpServletRequest request)
{
    RosterManager manager = null;
    try
    {
        manager = getRosterManager();
        List teams = manager.getTeamsInRoster();
```

```java
            request.setAttribute("roster", teams);
        }
        catch (DataException unexpected)
        {
            log("Error processing roster list : " + unexpected);
        }
        finally
        {
            if (manager != null)
            {
                manager.releaseResources();
            }
        }
    }

    private void processRosterDelete(int teamId)
    {
        RosterManager manager = null;
        try
        {
            manager = getRosterManager();
            manager.deleteTeamFromRoster(teamId);
        }
        catch (DataException unexpected)
        {
            log("Error adding new team to roster : " + unexpected);
        }
        finally
        {
            if (manager != null)
            {
                manager.releaseResources();
            }
        }
    }

    private void processRosterAdd(String newTeam)
    {
        RosterManager manager = null;
        try
        {
            manager = getRosterManager();
            manager.addNewTeamToRoster(new Team(0, newTeam));
        }
        catch (DataException unexpected)
        {
            log("Error adding new team to roster : " + unexpected);
        }
        finally
        {
            if (manager != null)
            {
                manager.releaseResources();
            }
```

```
        }
    }

    private void processRosterModify(Team team)
    {
        RosterManager manager = null;
        try
        {
            manager = getRosterManager();
            manager.modifyTeamInRoster(team);
        }
        catch (DataException unexpected)
        {
            log("Error modifying team in roster : " + unexpected);
        }
        finally
        {
            if (manager != null)
            {
                manager.releaseResources();
            }
        }
    }

    private RosterManager getRosterManager() throws DataException
    {
        RosterManager manager;
        try
        {
            manager =
                RosterManagerFactory.createRosterManager(
                    _jdbcHelper.getConnection());
        }
        catch (SQLException connectionFailure)
        {
            throw new DataException(connectionFailure.getMessage());
        }
        return manager;
    }


    private boolean isValidString(String input)
    {
        return ((input != null) && (input.length() > 0));
    }

    private String findAction(HttpServletRequest request)
    {
        String action;
        if ((action = request.getParameter(ACTION_TOKEN)) == null)
        {
            action = ACTION_ROSTER;
        }
        return action;
```

```
        }

        private void performRedirect(String path, HttpServletRequest request,
                HttpServletResponse response) throws ServletException, IOException
        {
            if (path != null)
            {
                request.setAttribute("SERVLET_PATH", request.getContextPath()
                        + request.getServletPath());
                RequestDispatcher dispatch = request.getRequestDispatcher(path);
                dispatch.forward(request, response);
            }
        }
    }
```

How It Works

The `AdminServlet` is the coordination point for the application. It receives requests from the browser, checks for errors, and sends the request off to the appropriate method for processing.

The `init()` method creates an instance of the `FootyJDBCHelper()`. This object provides a simple means of looking up and getting database connections. The details for `FootyJDBCHelper` are shown in a later section of code.

The `doPost()` method identifies the appropriate action, and then calls the appropriate method to process the data from the browser. This works well for this simple example. More complicated applications with more actions and processes will find that an approach like this quickly becomes cumbersome. Jakarta Struts may be an appropriate framework to manage this complexity, and is described in detail in Chapter 19, "Struts Framework." However, Struts may be overkill for some applications, so a simplified mechanism for dealing with this complexity is shown in later sections.

`processRosterList()` is the first in a group of methods that are very similar. The all use an implementation of the `RosterManager` and a connection from the JDBC helper. The `RosterManager` provides an encapsulation of the database-specific code. `RosterManager` is an interface, and the reasons behind this choice will become more apparent as the chapter progresses. `processRosterDelete()`, `processRosterAdd()`, and `processRosterModify()` provide the additional methods that process the commands coming from the browser.

> *One of the advantages of using interfaces rather than concrete classes is that we can change the underlying implementation without changing the calling code. This chapter examines a number of different persistence techniques, each of which can create a specific implementation of* `RosterManager`.

A very, very important consideration when building code that works with databases is cleaning up the resources used with each database interaction. Not closing the connection in the manner shown previously can lead to resource starvation.

> *As an interesting exercise, remove the* `manager.releaseResources()` *from* `processRoster List()` *(or other methods) and then repeatedly access the Web application. Depending on the configuration of the application server, resource starvation may result as the database connections become exhausted.*

Management of externally located resources is an important consideration for Web application development. Correctly identifying the error paths and exception paths through code, and making sure that the resources are always cleaned up, is a time-consuming, but necessary activity.

Comprehensive unit testing can assist with locating issues like resource mismanagement, and Chapters 25, "Performance," and 26, "Best Practices and Tools," contain some additional tips on this topic for readers who are curious to explore this further.

The method `getRosterManager()` is worthy of a little explanation. This method could be implemented by just creating a specific implementation of a `RosterManager`, as shown here:

```java
private RosterManager getRosterManager()
{
    return new JDBCRosterManager(
                        _jdbcHelper.getConnection());
}
```

However, when the implementation changes to another mechanism — for example, a `HibernateRosterManager` — then it is necessary to change the `AdminServlet`. `RosterManagerFactory` implements all the logic for determining which version of the `RosterManager` will be used by the application.

This can be configured externally by an XML file, a properties file, or even by using deployment descriptor parameters. Not only can the application be installed on different application servers, it now can choose which mechanism it wants to use to persist the data, all of which is isolated in a couple of support classes, rather than scattered throughout the business logic of the application.

Some readers may consider this additional work excessive for small applications. The Web application shown here is about as small as it gets, and the additional work consisted of creating an interface and a very simple factory class to provide the concrete classes. When coupled with the testing advantages this approach provides, it should be considered a useful addition to even the smallest Web applications.

The remaining methods in `AdminServlet` are some utility methods for processing inputs and redirecting to an output page.

The final class to be entered is the most interesting in the context of database development. The `JDBCRosterManager` class contains all the JDBC-specific persistence code. This is where the application utilizes the JDBC objects for communicating with the database.

In the next section, this class is examined in more detail than the previous classes were because a number of new concepts are introduced.

Try It Out   JDBCRosterManager

The `JDBCRosterManager` class provides a single point in the application where all of the database-specific code is implemented

Create the file `JDBCRosterManager.java` in the `src/com/wrox/begjsp/ch23.football` directory with the following contents:

```
package com.wrox.begjsp.ch23.football;

import java.sql.Connection;
import java.sql.PreparedStatement;
import java.sql.ResultSet;
import java.sql.SQLException;
import java.sql.Statement;
import java.util.ArrayList;
import java.util.List;

public class JDBCRosterManager implements RosterManager
{
    private Connection _connection;

    public JDBCRosterManager(Connection connection)
    {
        _connection = connection;
    }
    public List getTeamsInRoster() throws DataException
    {
        List results = new ArrayList();
        Statement statement = null;
        try
        {
            statement = _connection.createStatement();
            ResultSet teams =
                    statement.executeQuery("SELECT * FROM roster ORDER BY id ASC");
            if (teams != null)
            {
                while (teams.next())
                {
                    int id = teams.getInt("id");
                    String name = teams.getString("teamname");
                    Team team = new Team(id, name);
                    results.add(team);
                }
            }
        }
        catch (SQLException unexpected)
        {
            throw new DataException(unexpected.getMessage());
        }
        finally
        {
            safeClose(statement);
        }
        return results;
    }
    private void safeClose(Statement statement)
    {
        try
        {
            if (statement != null)
            {
```

```
                statement.close();
            }
        }
    catch (SQLException unexpected)
    {
        // ignore this
    }
}

public void releaseResources()
{
    if (_connection != null)
    {
        try
        {
            _connection.close();
        }
        catch (SQLException unexpected)
        {
            // ignore this
        }
    }
}
public boolean addNewTeamToRoster(Team newTeam) throws DataException
{
    PreparedStatement statement = null;
    boolean result = false;
    try
    {
        statement = _connection.prepareStatement(
                "INSERT INTO roster (teamname) values (?)");
        statement.setString(1, newTeam.getName());

        result = statement.execute();
    }
    catch (SQLException unexpected)
    {
        throw new DataException(unexpected.getMessage());
    }
    finally
    {
        safeClose(statement);
    }
    return result;
}

public boolean modifyTeamInRoster(Team modifyTeam) throws DataException
{
    PreparedStatement statement = null;
    boolean result = false;
    try
    {
        statement = _connection.prepareStatement(
                "UPDATE roster set teamname = ? where id = ?");
```

```
                statement.setString(1, modifyTeam.getName());
                statement.setInt(2, modifyTeam.getId());

                result = statement.execute();
            }
            catch (SQLException unexpected)
            {
                throw new DataException(unexpected.getMessage());
            }
            finally
            {
                safeClose(statement);
            }
            return result;
        }

        public boolean deleteTeamFromRoster(int teamId) throws DataException
        {
            PreparedStatement statement = null;
            boolean result = false;
            try
            {
                statement = _connection.prepareStatement(
                        "DELETE from roster where id = ?");
                statement.setInt(1, teamId);

                result = statement.execute();
            }
            catch (SQLException unexpected)
            {
                throw new DataException(unexpected.getMessage());
            }
            finally
            {
                safeClose(statement);
            }
            return result;
        }
    }
```

How It Works

The constructor for `JDBCRosterManager` allows the `Connection` to be provided to the object. This gives the controlling code much greater scope for determining what capabilities `JDBCRosterManager` will provide. For example, in testing `JDBCRosterManager`, there is the capacity to provide a `Connection` that checks to see if it has been closed correctly. This helps to ensure that the code using `JDBCRosterManager` and the JDBC `Connection` will operate correctly in a production environment.

The method `getTeamsInRoster()` is used to process the request for the list of teams. The creation of the `Statement` from the `Connection` enables a SQL statement to be processed by the database. The results of the query are returned in a `ResultSet`. The data in the `ResultSet` is processed to return a `List` of `Team` objects.

It may be very tempting to just return the ResultSet and let the JSP extract the data required. While this might be an appropriate solution for an application of limited complexity, writing applications in this manner causes implementation details that affect the database structure to be reflected in the display logic of the application. This unnecessarily causes ripple effects when changes are made to the database during development, or enhancements are added to the application.

Creating a layer that deals with database access, and then produces results in terms of the business domain — in our case, the Team object — enables the persistence mechanism to be transparently changed without affecting the rest of the application.

In the section on Hibernate (another persistence mechanism), the benefits of this decision will become apparent, as it can be implemented, replacing the JDBCRosterManager, without changing the rest of the application.

The getTeamsInRoster() method completes with a call to safeClose(). This again follows the approach of releasing resources as soon as practical. Closing the Statement will also close the ResultSet that is associated with the Statement.

The safeClose() and releaseResources() methods ignore the SQLException that can be thrown by the close() methods. In general, ignoring a SQLException is not a good practice, but if the close fails, there is little the application can do to address the situation. In a more production-focused application, it would be worth logging the SQLException, as this might indicate more fundamental problems with the environment and assist with locating the issue.

Adding the logging code to this example would not add to our discussion here, and may end up obscuring the more important concepts in this section.

addNewTeamToRoster(), modifyTeamInRoster(), and deleteTeamFromRoster() all use the PreparedStatement for sending commands to the database.

The PreparedStatement enables precompilation of the SQL, and the use of parameters to allow for different values to be included as part of the processing.

> Note that when using a PreparedStatement, the parameters are specified by number. This process can be error prone, especially as the number of parameters increases. If changes to the database schema are likely, good testing of these methods is very important!

The final classes and interfaces for this Web application are included here for completeness. These are the RosterManager interface, and the RosterManagerFactory and FootyJDBCHelper classes.

Create the file RosterManager.java in the src/com/wrox/begjsp/ch23.football directory with the following contents:

```
package com.wrox.begjsp.ch23.football;

import java.util.List;

public interface RosterManager
{

void releaseResources();

    List getTeamsInRoster() throws DataException;
    boolean addNewTeamToRoster(Team newTeam) throws DataException;
    boolean modifyTeamInRoster(Team modifyTeam) throws DataException;
    boolean deleteTeamFromRoster(int teamId) throws DataException;
}
```
This interface will expand over time. After the teams, the venue, round and fixture access methods need to be added as more functionality is developed.

Create the file `RosterManagerFactory.java` in the `src/com/wrox/begjsp/ch23.football` directory with the following contents:

```
package com.wrox.begjsp.ch23.football;

import java.sql.Connection;

public class RosterManagerFactory
{
    public static final String JDBC_MANAGER     = "JDBC";
    public static final String HIBERNATE_MANAGER = "HIBERNATE";

    private static String      _currentManager  = JDBC_MANAGER;

    public static void setRosterManagerType(String type)
    {
        _currentManager = type;
    }

    public static RosterManager createRosterManager(Connection connection)
    {
        if (JDBC_MANAGER.equals(_currentManager))
        {
            return new JDBCRosterManager(connection);
        }
        throw new IllegalStateException(_currentManager +
                                        " persistence not implemented");
    }
}
```

The `RosterManagerFactory` provides a transparent means of selecting the persistence mechanism. At this stage of the application, the only choice is the `JDBCRosterManager`. Later in the application, development of an alternative persistence mechanism will be implemented.

Create the file `FootyJDBCHelper.java` in the `src/com/wrox/begjsp/ch23.football` directory with the following contents:

```java
package com.wrox.begjsp.ch23.football;

import java.sql.Connection;
import java.sql.SQLException;

import javax.naming.Context;
import javax.naming.InitialContext;
import javax.naming.NamingException;
import javax.sql.DataSource;

public class FootyJDBCHelper
{
    private DataSource _dataSource;

    public FootyJDBCHelper() throws NamingException
    {
        Context context = new InitialContext();
        Context applicationEnv = (Context)context.lookup("java:comp/env");
        _dataSource = (DataSource)applicationEnv.lookup("jdbc/FootyDB");
    }

    public Connection getConnection() throws SQLException
    {
        return _dataSource.getConnection();
    }
}
```

The `FootyJDBCHelper` provides a means to obtain a `Connection` from a JNDI `DataSource`, and is just a simple utility class to put the external lookup code in one place.

Running the application

To run the Web application, make sure the MySQL database is running, and that the Web application is deployed correctly to Tomcat, which is also running.

Browse to the following URL:

```
http://localhost:8080/chapter23/roster.jsp
```

This will display a page similar to Figure 23-2.

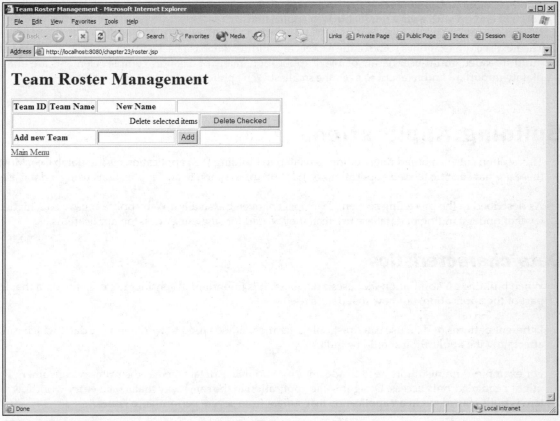

Figure 23-2: Roster management for football administration

It may seem that there was a lot of code written to perform a very simple Web input screen. The infrastructure code in the `AdminServlet` and the `JDBCRosterManager` provide a level of separation between the requests and responses to the Web front end and the loading and storing of data in the database. A small application does not do justice to the value of this separation; however, in later sections of this chapter, you will see the benefits of this separation as additional code is added to the Web application with a very small amount of effort.

This Web application uses a number of different JDBC classes and interfaces:

- ❑ **DataSource:** `FootyJDBCHelper` locates a `DataSource` via a JNDI lookup, and maintains a reference so that `Connection` objects can be obtained.

- ❑ **Connection:** `FootyJDBCHelper.getConnection()` returns a `Connection` so that it can be used by `JDBCRosterManager` to query the database.

- ❑ **Statement, PreparedStatement:** `JDBCRosterManager` uses a `Connection` to create `Statements` that execute SQL, which may return a `ResultSet`.

- ❑ **ResultSet:** `JDBCRosterManager.getTeamsInRoster()` loops through a `ResultSet` extracting the returned data and creating objects that will be used by the rest of the application.

Another important lesson is that database resources need to be managed carefully. If you fail to do this, you will end up with a very unreliable Web application.

The next section examines some of the aspects of building database-backed Web applications. Due to the multi-threaded, multi-user nature of a Web application, many of the more complex elements are immediately important and relevant to even the smallest Web application.

Building Applications

This section covers a broad range of topics related to building Web applications using databases. Most of these are not specific to Web applications or JSP, but are common to any applications using a database.

As described in the preceding section, developers of even the smallest Web applications need a higher level of understanding of database use than they would for single-user desktop applications.

Data characteristics

When building an application that uses a database, it is important to consider not only the data that is part of the application, but how that data is used.

Different patterns of data use can drastically alter the methods used to work with the data, which can affect how the application should be built.

For example, administrators need to add, modify, and delete data, whereas the primary consumers might need read-only access. Designing the application in the same way that a data entry workflow system is built may result in an application that suffers from severe performance issues.

Some of the questions that developers need to consider include the following:

❑ **How the data is used:** Are there many updates and not many reads, or vice versa? Does the application have an administration interface that requires strong transaction control? Is there a need to select large sets of data?

❑ **Concurrent updates:** Do most of the updates occur on the same sets of data, or are most updates likely to occur on completely different data? Examples of this are workflow applications compared to a bulletin board, or a Web site with personal data updated by individuals.

❑ **Stale data:** Does it matter if the data on the screen does not reflect the exact state of the database? In the content entry administration of a workflow application, this is probably very important, but in the display of the content to end users, probably less so. Due to the inherently stateless nature of the interactions with the Web browser, the possibility of stale data is worthy of extra consideration when you are building a Web application. The scope of this issue is broader than just the nature of the database transaction, but covers the entire end-to-end round-trip of the data from the database to the browser and back again.

❑ **Data history:** Is there a need to keep historical information about the data? Is there a versioning requirement? These requirements might lead to the concept of a *logical delete*, whereby the data is never removed from the database, but instead a flag is maintained on records to indicate its status. This will have profound implications on the manner in which data is not only maintained but queried.

❑ **Data migration:** Does data need to move from staging databases to production databases? Is backup and restoration of data needed? Using auto-incrementing identifiers or sequences are very convenient for generating primary keys for data, but when these are also moved or migrated to a different system, special consideration needs to be given to how this will be performed.

Many of the preceding points relate to how data will be managed during an update or query. This will directly influence the transaction strategy for the Web application. The next section covers transactions in more detail.

Transactions

A *transaction* is a unit of work whereby everything within the scope of the transaction must succeed or nothing will be allowed to succeed. It's an "all or nothing" situation. The most common example of a transaction is the transfer of funds from one bank account to another. If any error occurs during processing, then the state of the accounts must return to the state they were in before the transaction started. This property is known as *atomicity*.

Transactions are crucial for data integrity in a multi-user environment. When an application undergoes a transaction, it should move from one consistent state to the next. This property of a transaction is not directly under the control of the transaction and requires application support. For example, the transaction doesn't know that account balances cannot become negative; this is an application developer's responsibility. All the transaction can guarantee is that if the application data started in a valid state, it will end up in a valid state after the transaction has completed. This second property of a transaction is known as *consistency*.

The third property specifies that while the accounts are under the transaction, no external changes can be made. For example, in the bank accounts example, after it is determined that sufficient funds are available for transfer, another withdrawal may occur, causing the account to become overdrawn. This property is known as *isolation*.

The final property of a transaction specifies that the results of the transaction are permanently saved. Of course, another transaction might later change the data, but for each transaction, when complete, the changes are persisted. This property is known as *durability*.

These four properties of a transaction (atomicity, consistency, isolation, and durability) are known by the acronym *ACID*.

Transactions can be completed when they are committed, or rolled back. A committed transaction will make the results of the changes durable; and a rolled back transaction will return the application to the consistent state, prior to the application starting.

Effects of transactions

After discovering the power of the transaction to keep the data in the database and the application in a consistent, valid state, one might be tempted to use transactions everywhere. Again, there is no such thing as a free lunch, and transactions require careful use to avoid significant performance issues.

Imagine that for every read of the database, all of the data that was to be read was locked so no changes were possible. What benefit would that be for most applications? Certainly for a multi-user reporting application with no data updates, this would severely impact the performance, as each user has to wait for the previous user to complete the read.

The effects of isolation on a transaction can result in the application performing worse than it would without using transaction control at all. However, any JDBC query from a database will require a transaction. It appears that we've reached an impasse!

Luckily, there is a solution; the transaction isolation can be relaxed, lessening the constraints on the changes that can occur during the transaction. This relaxation, however, can produce other potential problems for the application:

❑ **Dirty reads:** A dirty read occurs when changes to data are visible to other transactions prior to the point at which the transaction making the changes has committed the changes. Dirty reads are generally okay in a read-only or read-mostly application, but will cause great difficulty when data integrity is paramount.

❑ **Nonrepeatable reads:** A nonrepeatable read occurs when an application, in the context of a transaction, reads some data, and then re-reads the same data and it has changed. This is different than the dirty read, in that the same transaction is interfered with by external changes.

❑ **Phantom read:** A phantom read is a close cousin of the nonrepeatable read. Instead of the data changing, new data is added. Therefore, an initial query and subsequent query will result in a different number of rows returned.

With these potential problems identified, JDBC supports four isolation levels, as well as support for no transactions, but databases are not required to support these isolation levels, or even indicate what level of support they provide.

These isolation levels (including no transactions) are as follows:

❑ **TRANSACTION_NONE:** This is the most relaxed isolation, and indicates that transactions are not supported. This is not normally supported by JDBC drivers, as a compliant driver requires transaction support. However, vendors may choose to support this as an option. This isolation level allows all three problems identified earlier to occur.

❑ **TRANSACTION_READ_UNCOMMITTED:** This isolation level allows for the reading of uncommitted data by other transactions. This level also allows all three problems to occur.

❑ **TRANSACTION_READ_COMMITTED:** This level prevents dirty reads because only committed changes to data are visible to the transaction. This level does not prevent nonrepeatable or phantom reads from occurring. This level is the most commonly supported, and often the default level for databases.

❑ **TRANSACTION_REPEATABLE_READ:** In addition to READ_COMMITTED, this level prevents other transactions from interfering with data that is being read by the transaction. This prevents the nonrepeatable read problem, and for most applications this isolation level provides sufficient data integrity.

❑ **TRANSACTION_SERIALIZABLE:** This is the most restrictive isolation level, and provides complete protection for the problems identified previously. Other transactions cannot read, update, or create new data in the data set for this transaction. Databases may have different mechanisms for performing this serialization, and applications need to understand how a specific database supports this facility.

The transaction isolation level is not set by the JDBC driver, but the default value is provided by the database, and can be updated by a call to `Connection.setTransactionIsolation()`.

Object-relational mapping

A relational database does a great job of storing the data and allowing languages such as SQL to provide access. Java, and by extension JSP, provide a fantastic object-oriented development environment with a robust set of capabilities for creating objects rich in functionality and for encapsulating data.

While the relational database data structure and the object class model are deceptively similar, the manner in which relationships between the data in the database and the data in the object model are handled by developers is quite different.

This difference and the requirements to persist the data managed by objects are known as the *object-relational impedance mismatch*. To resolve this mismatch, a series of tools have been developed. These tools are known as *object-relational mapping (ORM) tools*.

In the Java world, several commercial tools are available, such as TopLink and CocoBase. There is also the Java Data Objects (JDO) specification, led by the Java Community Process (JCP), which provides a standardized approach to object persistence.

The most commonly used ORM tool in Java today is Hibernate. Hibernate enjoys much of its success because it is simple, robust, and one of the best documented open-source products available. Hibernate is available from `www.hibernate.org`.

Hibernate is simple in the sense that it provides an API that is easy to work with, and there are no framework or infrastructure requirements for using Hibernate. This provides a very flat learning curve, with developers being able to start using the tool very quickly.

Another major benefit is that Hibernate is designed to work with plain Java objects. All the Java object needs to do in order for Hibernate to be able to persist it is to implement a JavaBean (not a Enterprise JavaBean) interface.

A later example uses Hibernate as the ORM layer in the application.

Different Types of Applications

One of the major benefits of the J2EE technology stack is the flexibility it offers developers in choosing between a very simple implementation and scaling up to a more complex implementation as the need demands. After carefully considering the contents of the preceding section, it still may be useful to build a simple, JSP-based Web application.

The following sections start with examples of building simple applications, and describe techniques for dealing with more complex applications. The more complex applications will still be quite simple, and it might be difficult to understand the value in implementing ORM mapping technologies such as JDO or Hibernate. Chapter 28, "JSP Project II: Shopping Cart Application," builds a more complete application using Hibernate, which should provide a better indication of the advantages to be found over using direct access to the database using JDBC.

Simple applications

Two characteristics that may result from building an application using simple techniques include the following:

❑ **Short life span:** An application that is developed only for a prototype or a "once-off" activity is often a good candidate for a simple implementation. The maintenance issues associated with building a database-backed Web application are negated by a Web application that has a short life.

❑ **Small scope:** The smaller the better! An application with many JSPs or complex data arrangements will very quickly become too cumbersome and prone to errors when building.

Two approaches that are suitable for building simple Web applications include the following:

❑ Have a JSP page connect directly to a database, using the `<sql:>` tags.

❑ Use simple JDBC-based helper classes with the JSP page to encapsulate the database functionality.

The characteristics and approaches identified here are not exhaustive but do illustrate the style of application and the solutions that may be appropriate. As with all software development activities, spending the appropriate time thinking about the problem and potential solutions will lead to a better result than blindly following advice written in a book!

Using JSP and JDBC

This part of the application will perform the data entry and viewing of information for the rounds table. Like the previous example of storing data in the roster table, this is a very simple part of the application. To contrast the development style, compare how the data entry and result display is performed in this section with the roster code.

The following Try It Out example uses the `<sql>` tags available in the JSTL to directly communicate with the database using JSP. The `<sql>` tags provide wrappers around the JDBC classes so they can be directly used by the JSP pages.

Try It Out   `<sql:>` Tags in JSP

The first JSP page lists the currently entered rounds, and then provides an input area to add new rounds; or, if the round number is the same as previous rounds, it updates the round information. There is no facility to delete rounds.

Create the file `round-input.jsp` in the `web` directory with the following contents:

```
<!--
<%@ taglib prefix="c" uri="http://java.sun.com/jsp/jstl/core" %>
<%@ taglib prefix="sql" uri="http://java.sun.com/jsp/jstl/sql" %>
-->
<c:set value="Round Management" var="title" />

<sql:query var="roundlist" dataSource="jdbc/FootyDB" >
```

```
    SELECT * from round
</sql:query>

<html>
  <head>
    <title><c:out value="${title}" /></title>
  </head>
  <body>
    <h1><c:out value="${title}" /></h1>
    <table border="1">
      <tr>
        <th>Round Number</th>
        <th>Start Date</th>
        <th colspan="2">End Date</th>
      </tr>
      <c:forEach var="round" items="${roundlist.rows}" >
        <tr>
          <td>${round.number}</td>
          <td>${round.startdate}</td>
          <td colspan="2">${round.enddate}</td>
        </tr>
      </c:forEach><tr>
        <form name="round-input" action="round-process.jsp" method="POST">
          <td><input name="round_number" type="text" size="20" /></td>
          <td><input name="round_startdate" type="text" size="20" /></td>
          <td><input name="round_enddate" type="text" size="20" /></td>
          <td><input type="submit" value="Update" /></td>
        </form>
      </tr>
    </table>

  </body>
</html>
```

The page is similar to the `roster.jsp` but with the addition of the `<sql:query>` tag at the start of the page to select the existing rounds. The use of the `dataSource` attribute enables the JSP to participate in the JNDI lookup for the `DataSource` of the same name. This is not required, but is definitely a good idea.

However, if the JSP is executing in a JSP container that does not provide JNDI support, then the alternative is to use an equivalent, as shown in the following JSP fragment:

```
<sql:query var="roundlist"
  dataSource="jdbc:mysql://localhost/footydb,com.mysql.jdbc.Driver,footy,footy">
  SELECT * from round
</sql:query>
```

There is a third means of obtaining a `dataSource` *that will be shown in* `round-process.jsp`.

The other section of JSP code that is important to consider is the `<c:forEach>` iterator, and the use of `roundlist.rows` to select the rows returned by the `<sql:query>`. It is very convenient that the database column names can be used to select the information directly from the returned rows. For a simple application, input and output screens can be developed very rapidly.

Create the file `round-process.jsp` in the `web` directory with the following contents:

```jsp
<!--
<%@ taglib prefix="c" uri="http://java.sun.com/jsp/jstl/core" %>
<%@ taglib prefix="sql" uri="http://java.sun.com/jsp/jstl/sql" %>
<%@ taglib prefix="fmt" uri="http://java.sun.com/jsp/jstl/fmt" %>
-->
<c:set value="Round Management" var="title" />

<sql:setDataSource dataSource="jdbc/FootyDB" />

<sql:query var="roundExists" >
  SELECT * from round
  WHERE number = ?
  <sql:param value="${param.round_number}" />
</sql:query>

<c:choose>
  <c:when test="${roundExists.rowCount != 0}">
    <sql:update>
      UPDATE round SET startdate = ?, enddate = ?
      WHERE number = ?
      <sql:param value="${param.round_startdate}" />
      <sql:param value="${param.round_enddate}" />
      <sql:param value="${param.round_number}" />
    </sql:update>
  </c:when>
  <c:otherwise>
    <sql:update>
      INSERT INTO round (number, startdate, enddate)
      VALUES (?, ?, ?)
      <sql:param value="${param.round_number}" />
      <sql:param value="${param.round_startdate}" />
      <sql:param value="${param.round_enddate}" />
    </sql:update>
  </c:otherwise>
</c:choose>
<c:redirect url="round-input.jsp" />
```

How It Works

To run the Web application, make sure the MySQL database is running, and that the Web application is deployed correctly to Tomcat, which is also running.

Browse to the following URL:

```
http://localhost:8080/chapter23/round-input.jsp
```

This will display a page similar to Figure 23-3.

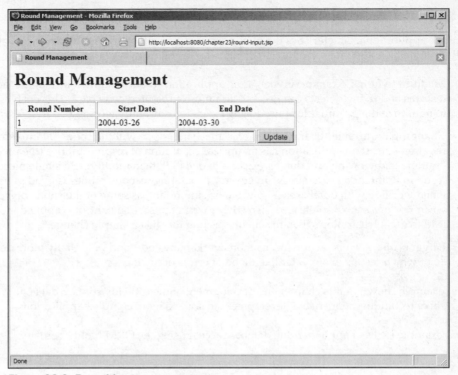

Figure 23-3: Round input management

Entering data in the input fields and clicking the Update button on `round-input.jsp` will post the form data to `round-process.jsp`. This provides an example of writing a Web application using no Java code at all.

The preceding code is very simple and took very little time to implement. There is limited checking of input data, and any data that isn't correctly formatted or of the correct value (for example, using xxx as the round number) produces erroneous results.

If we examine `round-process.jsp`, we see that it is possible to introduce logic to check the inputs for validity and redirect to error pages. However, the nature of writing more complex code in a JSP will rapidly lead to cumbersome pages that will become a maintenance nightmare over time. This is why it is recommended to use JSP for data capture and presentation, and servlets for the controlling logic for applications that have more complex requirements, and a longer active life.

Using this technique for developing Web applications is fantastic for prototyping and for working with customers or other developers to elicit further requirements. Rapid feedback of the visual interface, complete with realistic data, can assist in furthering the application's development.

More complex applications

Some of the application characteristics that may constrain a developer from building an application using the simple techniques shown previously include the following:

❑   **Medium to long life span:** As soon as an application enters a maintenance phase, adding new features and fixing defects can necessitate a more structured code base. This enables developers to minimize the potential for introducing errors into currently working code.

❑   **Changing requirements:** If requirements are changing, so will the code that implements the requirements. If an application has an unclear separation of responsibilities (the preceding example had viewing and database access in one JSP), then modifying a single piece of code can result in unintended side-effects. In general, separating responsibilities is good practice, but when working with databases it is even more important, as some of the subtle defects that occur when resources are not released correctly, or when transaction control is applied incorrectly, can lead to great frustration when the client is asking for "just a simple change."

❑   **Larger scope:** A larger scope means more work, more code, and potentially more developers, all of which results in a greater likelihood of errors occurring.

The first example shown in this chapter, the development of the code for `roster` data entry, demonstrates a set of techniques that enable development to scale to more complex applications.

The next example looks at implementing database access using the ORM tool Hibernate.

Using Hibernate

Hibernate is described by the Hibernate developers as "relational persistence for idiomatic Java." Hibernate provides a service for persisting plain Java objects (as opposed to a framework such as EJB) and a query language (HQL).

Using Hibernate enables a different approach to using JDBC to persist data. The use of the `RosterManager` shown earlier is a common pattern using JDBC. The `Manager` interface provides a service layer that will translate Java objects (such as the Team) and then use an SQL command to store or retrieve the data. This mapping layer becomes quite cumbersome as application complexity increases, especially when data relationships become involved.

However, using Hibernate (or JDO), the Java objects are used directly as part of the transaction. These objects can also contain collections of other objects, representing the data relationships that will also be persisted.

The following example uses Hibernate to select objects from a database:

```
Query allTeams = session.createQuery("from Team as team order by team.id asc");
List list = allTeams.list();
```

The returned `List` contains fully created and populated `Team` objects. The `session` object is used to maintain a conversation between the application and the database and is responsible for maintaining a cache of the persistent objects.

Compare this to the equivalent JDBC:

```
ResultSet teams = statement.executeQuery("SELECT * FROM roster ORDER BY id ASC");
while (teams.next())
{
    int id = teams.getInt("id");
    String name = teams.getString("teamname");
    Team team = new Team(id, name);
    results.add(team);
}
```

Not a huge difference for a query, but performing an insert or an update is where Hibernate's affinity with the Java language becomes apparent.

You can insert a new record using JDBC as follows:

```
Team newTeam = new Team(0, "New Town");
insertStmt = con.prepareStatement("INSERT INTO roster (teamname) values (?)");
insertStmt.setString(1, newTeam.getName());

result = statement.execute();
```

Unfortunately, this example isn't very "Java-like." Compare this to the Hibernate equivalent:

```
Team newTeam = new Team(0, "New Town");
Transaction tx = session.beginTransaction();
session.save(newTeam);
tx.commit();
```

To achieve this, Hibernate needs to be configured with a mapping between the objects and the relational data structures. This is done by an XML configuration file for each of the objects that are persisted.

An example of a mapping file is as follows:

```
<hibernate-mapping>
  <class name="com.wrox.begjsp.ch23.football.Team" table="roster">
    <id name="_id" column="id" access="field" type="integer" unsaved-value="0">
      <generator class="native" />
    </id>
    <property name="_name" column="teamname" access="field" type="string" />
  </class>
</hibernate-mapping>
```

The file consists of the name of the class and the table that contains the data. The next elements are the fields of the objects and the mapping to the columns in the database. The id element represents the primary key of the data in the table. It is conventional to place the metadata mapping files in the same directory as the Java objects that they configure.

As the preceding short fragments indicate, Hibernate is a fairly easy tool to work with — the following example elaborates on the capabilities of Hibernate, including relationships between objects.

Installing Hibernate

The first task is to download and install Hibernate. Download the latest version from www.hibernate.
org. At the time of this writing, this is version 2.1.4.

Installing Hibernate is a matter of uncompressing the downloaded hibernate-2.1.4 archive. The
archive contains all the Hibernate JAR files and all the Hibernate documentation.

To use Hibernate in the Web application, a number of libraries must be installed in the WEB-INF/lib
directory of the Web application.

The hibernate-2.1.4/lib directory contains a README.txt file that describes all the libraries provided by Hibernate, and which of them are required for the runtime. This example extends the football
roster application, so copy these files into the current WEB-INF/lib.

The files used are as follows:

- cglib-full-2.0.1.jar
- commons-collections-2.1.jar
- commons-logging-1.0.3.jar
- dom4j-1.4.jar
- ehcache-0.7.jar
- hibernate2.jar
- jta.jar
- odmg-3.0.jar

In the following series of Try It Out examples, you use Hibernate to build a Web application. This example builds the fixture and venue components for the football application. All the code for this example
is available for download from www.wrox.com. The complete application contains significant amounts
of code, so the following examples highlight the development activities involved in using Hibernate.

This is a fairly detailed walkthrough of using databases with Hibernate, and it contains several different
sections to make it easier to follow the steps required. Not all of the Try It Out examples create a working application. Where the Web application can be successfully operational, it will be mentioned in the
"How It Works" section.

Try It Out   Configuring a Persistent Object in Hibernate

As mentioned earlier, persistent objects in Hibernate are just plain Java objects. The first part of developing a Hibernate application is to create these objects.

Create the file Venue.java in the src/com/wrox/begjsp/ch23/football directory with the following contents:

```
package com.wrox.begjsp.ch23.football;

public class Venue
{
    private int    _id;
    private String _location;

    public Venue(int id, String location)
    {
        _id = id;
        _location = location;
    }

    public int getId()
    {
        return _id;
    }

    public String getLocation()
    {
        return _location;
    }

    public boolean equals(Object obj)
    {
        if (obj instanceof Venue)
        {
            Venue compare = (Venue)obj;
            return (_id == compare.getId());
        }
        return false;
    }

    public int hashCode()
    {
        return _location.hashCode();
    }

    public String toString()
    {
        return "[" + _id + "] : [" +_location + "]";
    }

    private Venue()
    {
        // required for hibernate
    }

    private void setId(int id)
    {
        _id = id;
    }

    private void setLocation(String location)
```

```
        {
            _location = location;
        }
    }
```

Create the file `Venue.hbm.xml` in the `src/com/wrox/begjsp/ch23.football` directory with the following contents:

```xml
<?xml version="1.0"?>
<!DOCTYPE hibernate-mapping PUBLIC
    "-//Hibernate/Hibernate Mapping DTD//EN"
    "http://hibernate.sourceforge.net/hibernate-mapping-2.0.dtd">

<hibernate-mapping>
  <class name="com.wrox.begjsp.ch23.football.Venue" table="venue">
    <id name="id" column="id" type="integer" unsaved-value="0">
      <generator class="native" />
    </id>
    <property name="location" column="location" type="string" />
  </class>
</hibernate-mapping>
```

How It Works

`Venue` is a standard-looking JavaBean, except for the provision of the `private` setters and the default no-argument constructor. The `Venue` objects are immutable, and Hibernate can work with objects such as these in two ways. The method used in `Venue.java` is to provide `private` setters. Hibernate can then use those setters to populate the objects. The second method is shown in the file containing the Hibernate XML for `Team.java` shown previously. Hibernate can directly manipulate the fields of the object when the XML configuration for the `property` includes the `access="field"` attribute and value, as shown in the following example:

```xml
<property name="_name" column="teamname" access="field" type="string" />
```

Hibernate's developers do not recommend using the `access="field"` attribute, but this is for reasons of encapsulation, rather than any underlying technical issue. The choice of which approach to take is left in the hands of the application developer.

The next Try It Out example uses the persistent object just configured to create, load, and update data stored in the database. This section introduces the simple API that Hibernate provides to perform these operations.

Try It Out	Creating, Loading, and Updating Data with Hibernate

To work with the persistent objects, we will create a Java class that provides an interface between the code manipulating the HTTP-specific parts of the data and the code for persistence.

This functionality is provided by the `HibernateRosterManager`. It contains the support code that initializes the Hibernate sessions, as well as the functionality for processing the requests. This code is the Hibernate equivalent of the `JDBCRosterManager` that was developed earlier in this chapter.

Modify the `RosterManager.java` interface to provide support for the new functionality as follows:

```java
package com.wrox.begjsp.ch23.football;

import java.util.List;

public interface RosterManager
{
    void releaseResources();

    List getVenuesInRoster() throws DataException;
    boolean addNewVenueToRoster(Venue venue) throws DataException;
    boolean deleteVenueFromRoster(int venueId) throws DataException;
    boolean modifyVenueInRoster(Venue venue) throws DataException;

}
```

This change has removed the previously available methods for the Team object management. This is to simplify the implementation steps. The Team object management will be added back into the RosterManager *interface later in the chapter.*

Create the file `HibernateRosterManager.java` in the `src/com/wrox/begjsp/ch23/football` directory with the following contents:

```java
package com.wrox.begjsp.ch23.football;

import java.sql.Connection;
import java.sql.SQLException;
import java.util.List;
import java.util.Properties;

import net.sf.hibernate.HibernateException;
import net.sf.hibernate.MappingException;
import net.sf.hibernate.Query;
import net.sf.hibernate.Session;
import net.sf.hibernate.SessionFactory;
import net.sf.hibernate.Transaction;
import net.sf.hibernate.cfg.Configuration;

public class HibernateRosterManager implements RosterManager
{
    private Connection      _connection;
    private SessionFactory _sessionFactory;
    private Session         _currentSession;

    public HibernateRosterManager(Connection connection)
    {
        _connection = connection;

        Configuration configuration = new Configuration();
        try
        {
            configuration.addClass(Venue.class);
```

```
        }
        catch (MappingException mappingFailure)
        {
            throw new IllegalArgumentException(
                    "Cannot find required object classes, check CLASSPATH : " +
                    mappingFailure);
        }
        Properties props = new Properties();
        props.put("hibernate.dialect", "net.sf.hibernate.dialect.MySQLDialect");
        props.put("hibernate.statement_cache.size", "0");
        configuration.setProperties(props);

        try
        {
            _sessionFactory = configuration.buildSessionFactory();
        }
        catch (HibernateException sessionFailure)
        {
            throw new IllegalArgumentException(
                    "Cannot build session factory, check configuration : " +
                    sessionFailure);
        }
    }
    /*-- getting objects --*/
    public List getVenuesInRoster() throws DataException
    {
        return getAllItems("from Venue as venue order by venue.id asc");
    }

    private List getAllItems(String query) throws DataException
    {
        initSession();
        List list = null;
        try
        {
            Query allItems = _currentSession.createQuery(query);
            list = allItems.list();
        }
        catch (HibernateException unexpected)
        {
            throw new DataException(unexpected.getMessage());
        }
        finally
        {
            flushSession();
        }
        return list;
    }
    /*-- adding and modifying objects --*/
    public boolean addNewVenueToRoster(Venue venue) throws DataException
    {
        addOrModifyVenue(venue, "ADD");
    }
```

```
public boolean modifyVenueInRoster(Venue venue) throws DataException
{
    addOrModifyVenue(venue, "MODIFY");
}

private boolean addOrModifyVenue(Venue venue, String action)
{
    initSession();
    Transaction tx = null;
    try
    {
        tx = _currentSession.beginTransaction();
        _currentSession.saveOrUpdate(venue);
        tx.commit();
    }
    catch (HibernateException cannotSaveOrUpdate)
    {
        try
        {
            tx.rollback();
        }
        catch (HibernateException cannotRollback)
        {
            // log this error
        }
        throw new DataException("Unable to "+action+" venue : "+
                             cannotSaveOrUpdate.getMessage());
    }
    finally
    {
        flushSession();
    }

    return false;
}
/*-- delete objects --*/
public boolean deleteVenueFromRoster(int id) throws DataException
{
    initSession();
    Transaction tx = null;
    try
    {
        tx = _currentSession.beginTransaction();
        Venue deleted = _currentSession.load(Venue.class, new Integer(id));
        _currentSession.delete(deleted);
        tx.commit();
    }
    catch (HibernateException cannotDelete)
    {
        try
        {
            tx.rollback();
        }
        catch (HibernateException cannotRollback)
```

```
        {
            // log this error
        }
        throw new DataException("Unable to delete venue ["+id+"]: "+
                                cannotDelete.getMessage());
    }
    finally
    {
        flushSession();
    }
    return false;
}

/*-- utility methods --*/
private void initSession()
{
    if (_currentSession == null)
    {
        _currentSession = _sessionFactory.openSession(_connection);
    }
}

private void flushSession()
{
    try
    {
        if (_currentSession != null)
        {
            _currentSession.flush();
        }
    }
    catch (HibernateException sessionFlushFailure)
    {
        // log this error
    }
}

public void releaseResources()
{
    if (_connection != null)
    {
        try
        {
            if (_currentSession != null)
            {
                _currentSession.connection().close();
                _currentSession.close();
                _currentSession = null;
            }
            _connection.close();

        }
        catch (HibernateException sessionCloseFailure)
        {
```

```
                    // log this error
            }
            catch (SQLException connectionCloseFailure)
            {
                    // log this error
            }
        }
    }
}
```

How It Works

The `HibernateRosterManager` file contains all the code required to set up a Hibernate connection, find the configuration for the persistent objects, and work with the objects. The constructor contains all the necessary code for setting up Hibernate ready for use.

There are two ways to configure Hibernate. In this Try It Out example, you implement the *programmatic method*. This involves creating a `Configuration` object and setting the appropriate properties. The most common method is to create a Hibernate configuration file that is loaded. Hibernate supports a `Properties` format file (`hibernate.properties`), as well as an XML format configuration file (`hibernate.cfg.xml`).

The configuration must include the objects that are to be persisted. You do this by specifying the classes (as shown previously), or by specifying the `hbm.xml` files. If the `hbm.xml` files are in the same location as the objects, then Hibernate will locate them and load the mapping correctly.

Finally, the specific configuration for the database is required. `hibernate.dialect` is used so that Hibernate will generate the correct SQL and use the correct sequence generators (if available) when communicating with the database. To maintain interface compatibility with the `JDBCRosterManager`, the `sessionFactory` creates sessions with a provided `Connection` object. The second configuration item prevents `PreparedStatements` from being cached. This is required when an external `Connection` object is used to create sessions. Session creation is handled by the `openSession()` method on a session factory; an example of this is found later in the `initSession()` method.

> *Building a session factory is a slow process, so this should be done as infrequently as possible. In this example, a session factory is created each time the `AdminServlet` processes a request. Because a `SessionFactory` is responsible for maintaining a configuration relating to a single database, it would be possible to initialize the servlet factory once on Web application initialization, and make the factory available to all servlets by placing it in the application scope of the Web application.*

To keep this example simple, the creation of the `SessionFactory` is included in the construction of the `HibernateRosterManager`.

The `Session` object created by the `SessionFactory` is used to perform all the actions on the persistent objects. This object provides the Hibernate methods to enable retrieval, addition, deletion, and modification of the data.

In the method `getVenuesInRoster()` is a call to a private method `getAllItems()`, with an appropriately structured query. The public interface for obtaining a list of `Venue` objects has been separated from the private implementation. This enables easy extension as more methods are added to the public interface, and allows the implementation to be changed if required without affecting the client code. This is an important concept when developing infrastructure so that other developers using the persistence layers do not have to continually update code as the persistence infrastructure matures

The methods `addNewVenueToRoster ()` and `modifyVenueInRoster ()` both use the same underlying private method `addOrModifyVenue()` to save or update the data. Hibernate provides a `saveOrUpdate()` method to deal with inserting new objects or updating existing object data. This reduces the amount of duplicated code that exists when using `save()` or `update()` methods independently. The second parameter to the public methods is only to provide additional information if the Hibernate methods fail.

Deleting objects is also simple and straightforward. The method `deleteVenueFromRoster` provides an example of how this is performed. The object is first loaded to confirm that it is exists; it would be a good idea to use additional error-checking prior to deleting a potentially nonexistent object. Then a call to the `delete()` method removes the object.

Best practices for using Hibernate include starting sessions and transaction management in servlet filters, and leaving the business code free of persistence infrastructure. This becomes very important as applications increase in size and complexity, but for this simple application it's more convenient to keep all the code together.

The methods `initSession()`, `flushSession()`, and `releaseResources()` are utility methods for dealing with the session and releasing resources as required. As with previous examples in this chapter, exceptions are caught and then ignored. This is not good practice, but for the sake of focusing on the important concepts in the example (the data interface), exception handling is deliberately ignored.

The next Try It Out example shows the data display and entry JSP for the venue data. This example ties together all the previous sections to create a working Web application.

Try It Out   Converting the Web Application to Hibernate

To make use of the persistent objects and the Hibernate interface to the database in the Web application, you need to create a JSP page for listing, creating, updating, and deleting the venue data.

Create the file `venue.jsp` in the `web` directory with the following contents:

```
<!--
<%@ taglib prefix="fmt" uri="http://java.sun.com/jsp/jstl/fmt" %>
<%@ taglib prefix="c" uri="http://java.sun.com/jsp/jstl/core" %>
-->
<jsp:useBean id="venues" class="java.util.ArrayList" scope="request" />
<jsp:useBean id="SERVLET_PATH" class="java.lang.String" scope="request" />
<c:set value="Team Venue Management" var="title" />
<html>
  <head>
    <script type="text/javascript" >
      function modifyVenue(id) {
      var venue = document.venuelist;
      venue.ACTION.value="VENUE_MODIFY";
      venue.venueid.value=id;
      var elementName = "venue_"+id;
```

```
            var name = venue.elements[elementName].value;
            venue.venuename.value=name;
            venue.submit();
            }
            function deleteVenue() {
            document.venuelist.ACTION.value="VENUE_DELETE";
            document.venuelist.submit();
            }
        </script>
        <title><c:out value="${title}" /></title>
    </head>
    <body>
        <h1><c:out value="${title}" /></h1>
        <table border="1">
          <tr>
            <th>Venue ID</th>
            <th>Venue Name</th>
            <th colspan="2"> </th>
          </tr>
          <form name="venuelist"
                action="<c:out value="${SERVLET_PATH}" />" method="POST">
            <input type="hidden" name="ACTION" value="VENUE" />
            <input type="hidden" name="venueid" value="" />
            <input type="hidden" name="venuename" value="" />
            <c:forEach var="venue" items="${venues}" >
              <tr>
                <td>${venue.id}</td>
                <td>${venue.location}</td>
                <td><input id="venue_${venue.id}" type="text" size="20" /></td>
                <td><input type="button"
                            value="Modify" onclick="modifyVenue('${venue.id}')" /></td>
                <td><input name="DELETE_LIST"
                            type="checkbox" value="${venue.id}" /></td>
              </tr>
            </c:forEach>
            <tr>
              <td align="right" colspan="4">Delete selected items</td>
              <td><input name="DELETE_BUTTON" type="button"
                            value="Delete Checked" onclick="deleteVenue()" /></td>
            </tr>
          </form>
          <form action="<c:out value="${SERVLET_PATH}" />" method="POST">
            <input type="hidden" name="ACTION" value="VENUE_ADD" />
            <tr>
              <td colspan="2"><b>Add new Venue</b></td>
              <td><input name="venuename" type="text" size="20" /></td>
              <td><input name="ADD" type="submit" value="Add" /></td>
              <td> </td>
            </tr>
        </table>
        <a href="menu.html">Main Menu</a>
    </body>
</html>
```

With both the persistence code and the user interaction code completed, the only task that remains is to provide the functionality to gather the requests from the Web browser and act on the request by issuing commands to the database using the Hibernate interface. The AdminServlet developed previously in the chapter performs this task, and in the following code has been enhanced significantly to cope with the additional requirements.

One of the goals of this chapter is to show how code can be transformed as more requirements are uncovered. The enhancements to AdminServlet coupled with the separation of responsibilities in the user interface and database manager classes show how this is possible.

The following code shows AdminServlet.java, significantly modified from the original shown earlier. As the code volume increases due to managing more data, it is important to structure the support infrastructure so that it will scale with the additional responsibilities, without becoming too cumbersome and prone to error.

Modify AdminServlet.java in the src/com/wrox/begjsp/ch23/football directory as follows:

```java
package com.wrox.begjsp.ch23.football;

import java.io.IOException;

import javax.naming.NamingException;
import javax.servlet.RequestDispatcher;
import javax.servlet.ServletException;
import javax.servlet.http.HttpServlet;
import javax.servlet.http.HttpServletRequest;
import javax.servlet.http.HttpServletResponse;

public class AdminServlet extends HttpServlet
{
    private static final String DEFAULT_PAGE     = "menu.html";

    private static final String ACTION_TOKEN    = "ACTION";

    private static final String VENUE_ACTIONS   = "VENUE";
    private FootyJDBCHelper      _jdbcHelper     = null;

    public void init() throws ServletException
    {
        RosterManagerFactory.
                    setRosterManagerType(RosterManagerFactory.HIBERNATE_MANAGER);
        try
        {
            _jdbcHelper = new FootyJDBCHelper();
        }
        catch (NamingException unexpected)
        {
            throw new ServletException("Cannot locate required database : " +
                                    unexpected);
        }
    }
```

```
    public void doGet(HttpServletRequest request, HttpServletResponse response)
            throws ServletException, IOException
    {
        doPost(request, response);
    }

    public void doPost(HttpServletRequest request, HttpServletResponse response)
            throws ServletException, IOException
    {
        String action = findAction(request);

        ProcessingCommand command = null;
        if (action != null)
        {
            if (action.startsWith(VENUE_ACTIONS))
            {
                command = new VenueProcessingCommand(_jdbcHelper);
            }

            if (command != null)
            {
                command.execute(request, response, action);
                return;
            }
        }
        RequestDispatcher menu = request.getRequestDispatcher(DEFAULT_PAGE);
        menu.forward(request, response);
    }

    private String findAction(HttpServletRequest request)
    {
        return request.getParameter(ACTION_TOKEN);
    }
}
```

To create the implementation for the ProcessingCommand interface easier, you can place a couple of utility methods in a parent class to be reused by the concrete classes. Create the file AbstractProcessingCommand.java in the src/com/wrox/begjsp/ch23/football directory with the following contents:

```
package com.wrox.begjsp.ch23.football;

import java.io.IOException;

import javax.servlet.RequestDispatcher;
import javax.servlet.ServletException;
import javax.servlet.http.HttpServletRequest;
import javax.servlet.http.HttpServletResponse;

public abstract class AbstractProcessingCommand implements ProcessingCommand
{
```

```
       public abstract void execute(HttpServletRequest request,
                                    HttpServletResponse response,
                                    String action)
    throws ServletException, IOException;

    public final boolean isValidString(String input)
    {
        return ((input != null) && (input.length() > 0));
    }

    public final void performRedirect(String path, HttpServletRequest request,
            HttpServletResponse response) throws ServletException, IOException
    {
        if (path != null)
        {
            request.setAttribute("SERVLET_PATH", request.getContextPath()
                    + request.getServletPath());
            RequestDispatcher dispatch = request.getRequestDispatcher(path);
            dispatch.forward(request, response);
        }
    }

}
```

Create the file `VenueProcessingCommand.java` in the `src/com/wrox/begjsp/ch23/football` directory with the following contents:

```
package com.wrox.begjsp.ch23.football;

import java.io.IOException;
import java.sql.SQLException;
import java.util.List;

import javax.servlet.ServletException;
import javax.servlet.http.HttpServletRequest;
import javax.servlet.http.HttpServletResponse;

import org.apache.log4j.Logger;

public class VenueProcessingCommand extends AbstractProcessingCommand
{
    private static final Logger LOG = Logger.getLogger(
                                    VenueProcessingCommand.class);

    private static final String VENUE_PAGE       = "venue.jsp";
    private static final String VENUE_LIST_TOKEN = "venues";

    private static final String ACTION_VENUE_ADD = "VENUE_ADD";
    private static final String ACTION_VENUE_MOD = "VENUE_MODIFY";
    private static final String ACTION_VENUE_DEL = "VENUE_DELETE";

    private FootyJDBCHelper      _helper         = null;
```

```java
public VenueProcessingCommand(FootyJDBCHelper helper)
{
    _helper = helper;
}

public void execute(HttpServletRequest request,
                    HttpServletResponse response, String action)
    throws ServletException, IOException
{
    if (ACTION_VENUE_ADD.equals(action))
    {
        String newNameString = request.getParameter("venuename");
        if (isValidString(newNameString))
        {
            processVenueAdd(newNameString);
        }
    }
    else if (ACTION_VENUE_DEL.equals(action))
    {
        String deleteIDs[] = request.getParameterValues("DELETE_LIST");
        if (deleteIDs != null)
        {
            for (int i = 0; i < deleteIDs.length; i++)
            {
                String idString = deleteIDs[i];
                int id = Integer.parseInt(idString);
                processVenueDelete(id);
            }
        }
    }
    else if (ACTION_VENUE_MOD.equals(action))
    {
        String modIdString = request.getParameter("venueid");
        int modId = Integer.parseInt(modIdString);
        String modVenue = request.getParameter("venuename");
        if (isValidString(modVenue) && (modId > 0))
        {
            processVenueModify(new Venue(modId, modVenue));
        }
    }
    processVenueList(request);
    performRedirect(VENUE_PAGE, request, response);
}
private void processVenueModify(Venue venue)
{
    RosterManager manager = null;
    try
    {
        manager = getRosterManager();
        manager.modifyVenueInRoster(venue);
    }
    catch (DataException unexpected)
    {
```

```java
                LOG.error("Error modifying venue : " + unexpected);
        }
        finally
        {
            if (manager != null)
            {
                manager.releaseResources();
            }
        }
    }

    private void processVenueDelete(int teamId)
    {
        RosterManager manager = null;
        try
        {
            manager = getRosterManager();
            manager.deleteVenueFromRoster(teamId);
        }
        catch (DataException unexpected)
        {
            LOG.error("Error deleting venue : " + unexpected);
        }
        finally
        {
            if (manager != null)
            {
                manager.releaseResources();
            }
        }
    }

    private void processVenueAdd(String newVenue)
    {
        RosterManager manager = null;
        try
        {
            manager = getRosterManager();
            manager.addNewVenueToRoster(new Venue(0, newVenue));
        }
        catch (DataException unexpected)
        {
            LOG.error("Error adding new venue : " + unexpected);
        }
        finally
        {
            if (manager != null)
            {
                manager.releaseResources();
            }
        }
    }

    private void processVenueList(HttpServletRequest request)
```

```
{
    RosterManager manager = null;
    try
    {
        manager = getRosterManager();
        List venue = manager.getVenuesInRoster();
        request.setAttribute(VENUE_LIST_TOKEN, venue);
    }
    catch (DataException unexpected)
    {
        LOG.error("Error processing venue list : " + unexpected);
    }
    finally
    {
        if (manager != null)
        {
            manager.releaseResources();
        }
    }
}

private RosterManager getRosterManager() throws DataException
{
    RosterManager manager;
    try
    {
        manager = RosterManagerFactory.createRosterManager(
                                _helper.getConnection());
    }
    catch (SQLException connectionFailure)
    {
        throw new DataException(connectionFailure.getMessage());
    }
    return manager;
}
}
```

The final piece of the application is the menu.html page described in the AdminServlet. This is the index page for the application.

Create the file menu.html in the web directory with the following contents:

```
<html>
  <head>Football Administration Menu</head>
  <body>
    <ul>
      <li><a href="round-input.jsp">Round</a></li>
      <li><a href="admin?ACTION=VENUE_LIST">Venue</a></li>
    </ul>
  </body>
</html>
```

How It Works

The first part of the servlet defines some constants for working with the different requests from the Web browser. Notice how the definitions of the ROSTER_ACTIONS and VENUE_ACTIONS are strings that represents the first part of the group of actions for that type of data. The venue.jsp has a number of actions such as VENUE_ADD and VENUE_DELETE, which are used in the AdminServlet.doPost() method to determine which operation to perform. A very simple HTML-based menu called menu.html has been created and is used to select between the various administration tasks.

The actions that are specific to each particular data-entry screen have been removed from the AdminServlet and moved to classes that will process the data-entry requirements for each data-entry area. This is an important step in keeping complexity under control; imagine how large the AdminServlet would become if there were ten different data-entry screens, each having a list, add, modify, and delete action.

The code in AdminServlet.doPost() replaces all the previous roster processing code and also includes the venue processing code. As more processing is required, implementations of ProcessingCommand can be provided for each group of actions. This enables the AdminServlet to focus on determining which command to execute, with the commands themselves containing the processing code.

AdminServlet.findAction() has been simplified in this version to identify when a request is made without supplying an action. In this case, the method will return null to indicate that status and is handled by the AdminServlet.doPost() method by redirecting to the menu page. It would have been possible to create a NullProcessingCommand() to deal with this option, but this was simpler.

The ProcessingCommands are now responsible for processing each of the groups of actions for a particular set of data. The example of the VenueProcessingCommand shows a template for how the remaining ProcessingCommands should be implemented.

The VenueProcessingCommand now contains all the constants that were defined in the AdminServlet specific to the processing of requests relating to the venue data. This enables the AdminServlet to focus on coordination and the ProcessingCommand to work with the required data.

The changes to the code are long, but are reasonably simple; the code that was in AdminServlet.doPost() has been moved to the VenueProcessingCommand.execute() method. The AdminServlet selects a command to run and then invokes a method to run the command. The remaining methods are the workers that perform the tasks for the identified actions, finding a persistence manager and then calling the appropriate method.

Browse to the following URL:

```
http://localhost:8080/chapter23/menu.html
```

This will display the simple menu available. Click the link for Venue and after a short delay while the database connection is established and the Hibernate mapping files are processed, this should display a page similar to the one shown in Figure 23-4.

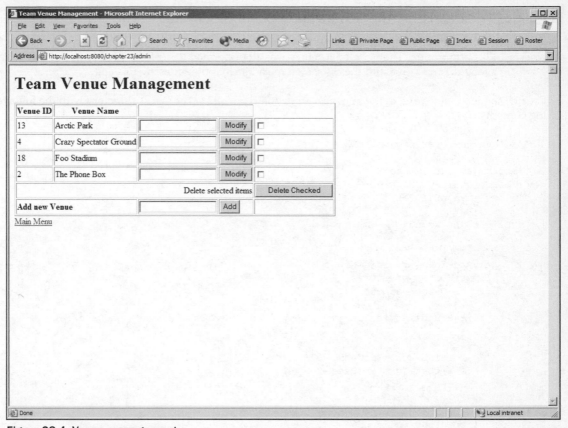

Figure 23-4: Venue management

Managing object relationships with Hibernate

The final component in this example is the creation of the `fixture` data entry. This is slightly different than the elements created previously, as there are relationships between the `fixture`, `round`, `venue`, and `roster` tables. Using JDBC, it rapidly becomes a difficult proposition to query the different tables and then later match up the foreign keys.

Using Hibernate, the relationships can be managed in the same way that Java code manages relationships. The `Round`, `Roster`, and `Venue` objects are created and added to the `Fixture` object representing the match to be played. It's easier and cleaner and requires much less code than the equivalent JDBC approach.

The following Try It Out example creates the `fixture` data-entry screens and objects for the Web application.

Try It Out   Persisting the Fixture Data Using Hibernate

To get the `fixture` entry to work successfully with Hibernate, the first task is to create some missing objects and configuration. The `round` data entry was all performed using SQL directly from a JSP, so `Round.java` and `Team.java` and the associated metadata mapping files are missing.

Create the file `Round.java` in the `src/com/wrox/begjsp/ch23/football` directory with the following contents:

```
package com.wrox.begjsp.ch23.football;

import java.util.Date;
import java.util.HashSet;
import java.util.Set;

public class Round
{
    private int  _id;
    private int  _roundNumber;
    private Date _startDate;
    private Date _endDate;

    public Round(int id, int roundNumber, Date startDate, Date endDate)
    {
        _id = id;
        _roundNumber = roundNumber;
        _startDate = startDate;
        _endDate = endDate;
    }

    public int getId()
    {
        return _id;
    }

    public Date getStartDate()
    {
        return _startDate;
    }

    public int getRoundNumber()
    {
        return _roundNumber;
    }

    public Date getEndDate()
    {
        return _endDate;
    }

    public boolean equals(Object obj)
    {
```

```
        if (obj instanceof Round)
        {
            Round compare = (Round)obj;
            return (_id == compare.getId());
        }
        return false;
    }

    public int hashCode()
    {
        int hash = 7;
        hash = 31 * hash + _id;
        hash = 31 * hash + _roundNumber;
        return hash;
    }

    public String toString()
    {
        return getClass() + "[" + _id + "] : [" + _roundNumber + "]";
    }

    private Round()
    {
        // required for hibernate
    }

    private void setEndDate(Date endDate)
    {
        _endDate = endDate;
    }

    private void setRoundNumber(int roundNumber)
    {
        _roundNumber = roundNumber;
    }

    private void setStartDate(Date startDate)
    {
        _startDate = startDate;
    }

    private void setId(int id)
    {
        _id = id;
    }
}
```

The Round object contains the round number, start and end date, and the auto-generated primary key. The Round.hbm.xml metadata mapping file is similar to the previous files. Create this also in the src/com/wrox/begjsp/ch23/football directory:

```xml
<?xml version="1.0"?>
<!DOCTYPE hibernate-mapping PUBLIC
    "-//Hibernate/Hibernate Mapping DTD//EN"
    "http://hibernate.sourceforge.net/hibernate-mapping-2.0.dtd">

<hibernate-mapping>
  <class name="com.wrox.begjsp.ch23.football.Round" table="round">
    <id name="id" column="id" type="integer" unsaved-value="0">
      <generator class="native" />
    </id>
    <property name="roundNumber" column="number" type="int" />
    <property name="startDate" column="startdate" type="date" />
    <property name="endDate" column="enddate" type="date" />
  </class>
</hibernate-mapping>
```

Create the file `Team.java` in the `src/com/wrox/begjsp/ch23/football` directory with the following contents:

```java
package com.wrox.begjsp.ch23.football;

public class Team
{
    private int    _id;
    private String _name;

    public Team(int id, String name)
    {
        _id = id;
        _name = name;
    }

    public int getId()
    {
        return _id;
    }

    public String getName()
    {
        return _name;
    }

    public boolean equals(Object obj)
    {
        if (obj instanceof Team)
        {
            Team compare = (Team)obj;
            return (_id == compare.getId());
        }
        return false;
    }

    public int hashCode()
```

```
    {
        return _name.hashCode();
    }

    public String toString()
    {
        return getClass() + "[" + _id + "] : [" + _name + "]";
    }

    private Team()
    {
        // required for hibernate
    }

    private void setId(int id)
    {
        _id = id;
    }

    private void setName(String name)
    {
        _name = name;
    }
}
```

Again, create the file `Team.hbm.xml` in the `src/com/wrox/begjsp/ch23/football` directory with the following contents:

```
<?xml version="1.0"?>
<!DOCTYPE hibernate-mapping PUBLIC
    "-//Hibernate/Hibernate Mapping DTD//EN"
    "http://hibernate.sourceforge.net/hibernate-mapping-2.0.dtd">

<hibernate-mapping>
  <class name="com.wrox.begjsp.ch23.football.Team" table="roster">
    <id name="id" column="id" type="integer" unsaved-value="0">
      <generator class="native" />
    </id>
    <property name="name" column="teamname" type="string" />
  </class>
</hibernate-mapping>
```

Let's move to the more interesting components; the first is the `Fixture.java` class. Enter the following code in the `src/com/wrox/begjsp/ch23/football` directory:

```
package com.wrox.begjsp.ch23.football;

public class Fixture
{
    private int    _id;
    private Round _round;
    private Team  _homeTeam;
```

```
    private Team   _awayTeam;
    private Venue _venue;

    public Fixture(int id, Round round, Team homeTeam, Team awayTeam, Venue venue)
    {
        _id = id;
        _round = round;
        _homeTeam = homeTeam;
        _awayTeam = awayTeam;
        _venue = venue;
    }

    public Team getAwayTeam()
    {
        return _awayTeam;
    }

    public Team getHomeTeam()
    {
        return _homeTeam;
    }

    public int getId()
    {
        return _id;
    }

    public Round getRound()
    {
        return _round;
    }

    public Venue getVenue()
    {
        return _venue;
    }

    public boolean equals(Object obj)
    {
        if (obj instanceof Fixture)
        {
            Fixture compare = (Fixture)obj;
            return (_id == compare.getId());
        }
        return false;
    }

    public int hashCode()
    {
        int hash = 7;
        hash = 31 * hash + _id;
        hash = 31 * hash + (_round == null ? 0 : _round.hashCode());
        hash = 31 * hash + (_homeTeam == null ? 0 : _homeTeam.hashCode());
        hash = 31 * hash + (_awayTeam == null ? 0 : _awayTeam.hashCode());
```

```
        hash = 31 * hash + (_venue == null ? 0 : _venue.hashCode());
        return hash;
    }

    public String toString()
    {
        return getClass() + "[" + _id + "]";
    }

    private Fixture()
    {
        // required for hibernate
    }

    private void setAwayTeam(Team awayTeam)
    {
        _awayTeam = awayTeam;
    }

    private void setHomeTeam(Team homeTeam)
    {
        _homeTeam = homeTeam;
    }

    private void setId(int id)
    {
        _id = id;
    }

    private void setRound(Round round)
    {
        _round = round;
    }

    private void setVenue(Venue venue)
    {
        _venue = venue;
    }
}
```

When examining the structures in the Fixture class, it isn't obvious how this class can ever be persisted. The class contains no keys or relationship information. The secret is in the following file.

The following Fixture.hbm.xml file contains the relationship mapping information. The Java objects are used directly as relationships. Create this file also in the src/com/wrox/begjsp/ch23/football directory:

```
<?xml version="1.0"?>
<!DOCTYPE hibernate-mapping PUBLIC
    "-//Hibernate/Hibernate Mapping DTD//EN"
    "http://hibernate.sourceforge.net/hibernate-mapping-2.0.dtd">
```

```
<hibernate-mapping>
  <class name="com.wrox.begjsp.ch23.football.Fixture" table="fixture">
    <id name="id" column="id" type="integer" unsaved-value="0">
      <generator class="native" />
    </id>
    <many-to-one name="round" column="roundid" />
    <many-to-one name="homeTeam" column="hometeam" />
    <many-to-one name="awayTeam" column="awayteam" />
    <many-to-one name="venue" column="venueid" />
  </class>
</hibernate-mapping>
```

To allow for the processing of the Fixture objects, create the file FixtureProcessingCommand.java in the src/com/wrox/begjsp/ch23/football directory with the following contents:

```java
package com.wrox.begjsp.ch23.football;

import java.io.IOException;
import java.sql.SQLException;
import java.util.List;

import javax.servlet.ServletException;
import javax.servlet.http.HttpServletRequest;
import javax.servlet.http.HttpServletResponse;

import org.apache.log4j.Logger;

public class FixtureProcessingCommand extends AbstractProcessingCommand
{
    private static final Logger LOG = Logger.getLogger(
                                        FixtureProcessingCommand.class);

    private static final String FIXTURE_PAGE        = "fixture.jsp";

    // for the dropdown menus
    private static final String ROUND_LIST_TOKEN    = "rounds";
    private static final String TEAM_LIST_TOKEN     = "teams";
    private static final String VENUE_LIST_TOKEN    = "venues";
    private static final String FIXTURE_LIST_TOKEN  = "fixtures";

    private static final String ACTION_FIXTURE_ADD = "FIXTURE_ADD";
    private static final String ACTION_FIXTURE_DEL = "FIXTURE_DELETE";

    private FootyJDBCHelper      _helper              = null;

    public FixtureProcessingCommand(FootyJDBCHelper helper)
    {
        _helper = helper;
    }

    public void execute(HttpServletRequest request,
                    HttpServletResponse response, String action)
```

```
            throws ServletException, IOException
{
    if (ACTION_FIXTURE_ADD.equals(action))
    {
        String roundIdString = request.getParameter("round_id");
        String awayTeamIdString = request.getParameter("away_team_id");
        String homeTeamIdString = request.getParameter("home_team_id");
        String venueIdString = request.getParameter("venue_id");

        processFixtureAdd(Integer.parseInt(roundIdString),
                    Integer.parseInt(awayTeamIdString),
                    Integer.parseInt(homeTeamIdString),
                    Integer.parseInt(venueIdString));
    }

    else if (ACTION_FIXTURE_DEL.equals(action))
    {
        String deleteIDs[] = request.getParameterValues("DELETE_LIST");
        if (deleteIDs != null)
        {
            for (int i = 0; i < deleteIDs.length; i++)
            {
                String idString = deleteIDs[i];
                int id = Integer.parseInt(idString);
                processFixtureDelete(id);
            }
        }
    }
    processFixtureList(request);
    performRedirect(FIXTURE_PAGE, request, response);
}

private void processFixtureDelete(int fixtureId)
{
    RosterManager manager = null;
    try
    {
        manager = getRosterManager();
        manager.deleteFixtureFromRoster(fixtureId);
    }
    catch (DataException unexpected)
    {
        LOG.error("Error deleting fixture : " + unexpected);
    }
    finally
    {
        if (manager != null)
        {
            manager.releaseResources();
        }
    }
}
```

```java
private void processFixtureAdd(int roundId, int homeTeamId,
                              int awayTeamId, int venueId)
{
    RosterManager manager = null;
    try
    {
        manager = getRosterManager();

        Round round = manager.getRoundById(roundId);
        Team homeTeam = manager.getTeamById(homeTeamId);
        Team awayTeam = manager.getTeamById(awayTeamId);
        Venue venue = manager.getVenueById(venueId);

        manager.addNewFixtureToRoster(new Fixture(0, round,
                                      homeTeam, awayTeam, venue));
    }
    catch (DataException unexpected)
    {
        LOG.error("Error adding new fixture : " + unexpected);
    }
    finally
    {
        if (manager != null)
        {
            manager.releaseResources();
        }
    }
}

private void processFixtureList(HttpServletRequest request)
{
    RosterManager manager = null;
    try
    {
        manager = getRosterManager();

        List venues = manager.getVenuesInRoster();
        List teams = manager.getTeamsInRoster();
        List rounds = manager.getRoundsInRoster();
        List fixtures = manager.getFixturesInRoster();

        request.setAttribute(FIXTURE_LIST_TOKEN, fixtures);
        request.setAttribute(TEAM_LIST_TOKEN, teams);
        request.setAttribute(ROUND_LIST_TOKEN, rounds);
        request.setAttribute(VENUE_LIST_TOKEN, venues);
    }
    catch (DataException unexpected)
    {
        LOG.error("Error processing fixture list : " + unexpected);
    }
    finally
    {
        if (manager != null)
```

```
            {
                manager.releaseResources();
            }
        }
    }


    private RosterManager getRosterManager() throws DataException
    {
        RosterManager manager;
        try
        {
            manager = RosterManagerFactory.createRosterManager(
                                    _helper.getConnection());
        }
        catch (SQLException connectionFailure)
        {
            throw new DataException(connectionFailure.getMessage());
        }
        return manager;
    }
}
```

First modify RosterManager.java to include the new functionality as follows:

```
package com.wrox.begjsp.ch23.football;

import java.util.List;

public interface RosterManager
{
    void releaseResources();

    List getTeamsInRoster() throws DataException;
    boolean addNewTeamToRoster(Team newTeam) throws DataException;
    boolean modifyTeamInRoster(Team modifyTeam) throws DataException;
    boolean deleteTeamFromRoster(int teamId) throws DataException;

    List getVenuesInRoster() throws DataException;
    boolean addNewVenueToRoster(Venue venue) throws DataException;
    boolean deleteVenueFromRoster(int venueId) throws DataException;
    boolean modifyVenueInRoster(Venue venue) throws DataException;

    List getFixturesInRoster() throws DataException;
    boolean addNewFixtureToRoster(Fixture fixture) throws DataException;
    boolean deleteFixtureFromRoster(int fixtureId) throws DataException;
    boolean modifyFixtureInRoster(Fixture fixture) throws DataException;

}
```

Now modify `HibernateRosterManager.java` to include the new Hibernate persistent objects, as well as the additional public methods to perform the actions and remain compatible with the `RosterManager` interface. The modified code sections are shown as follows:

```java
package com.wrox.begjsp.ch23.football;

import java.sql.Connection;
import java.sql.SQLException;
import java.util.List;
import java.util.Properties;

import net.sf.hibernate.HibernateException;
import net.sf.hibernate.MappingException;
import net.sf.hibernate.Query;
import net.sf.hibernate.Session;
import net.sf.hibernate.SessionFactory;
import net.sf.hibernate.Transaction;
import net.sf.hibernate.cfg.Configuration;

public class HibernateRosterManager implements RosterManager
{
    private static final String ADD_DATA_ACTION    = "ADD";
    private static final String MODIFY_DATA_ACTION = "MODIFY";

    private Connection          _connection;
    private SessionFactory      _sessionFactory;
    private Session             _currentSession;

    public HibernateRosterManager(Connection connection)
    {
        _connection = connection;

        Configuration configuration = new Configuration();
        try
        {
            configuration.addClass(Team.class);
            configuration.addClass(Venue.class);
            configuration.addClass(Round.class);
            configuration.addClass(Fixture.class);
        }
        catch (MappingException mappingFailure)
        {
            throw new IllegalArgumentException(
                    "Cannot find required object classes, check CLASSPATH : " +
                    mappingFailure);
        }

        Properties props = new Properties();
        props.put("hibernate.dialect", "net.sf.hibernate.dialect.MySQLDialect");
        props.put("hibernate.statement_cache.size", "0");
        configuration.setProperties(props);

        try
        {
```

```
                _sessionFactory = configuration.buildSessionFactory();
        }
        catch (HibernateException sessionFailure)
        {
            throw new IllegalArgumentException(
                "Cannot build session factory, check configuration : " +
                sessionFailure);
        }
    }
```

```
    /*-- getting objects --*/
    public List getTeamsInRoster() throws DataException
    {
        return getAllItems("from Team as team order by team.name asc");
    }

    public List getVenuesInRoster() throws DataException
    {
        return getAllItems("from Venue as venue order by venue.location asc");
    }

    public List getRoundsInRoster() throws DataException
    {
        return getAllItems("from Round as round order by round.roundNumber asc");
    }

    public List getFixturesInRoster() throws DataException
    {
        return getAllItems("from Fixture as fixture order by fixture.id asc");
    }

    private List getAllItems(String query) throws DataException
    {
        initSession();
        List list = null;
        try
        {
            Query allTeams = _currentSession.createQuery(query);
            list = allTeams.list();
        }
        catch (HibernateException unexpected)
        {
            throw new DataException(unexpected.getMessage());
        }
        finally
        {
            flushSession();
        }
        return list;
    }

    /*-- adding and modifying objects --*/
    public boolean addNewTeamToRoster(Team team) throws DataException
    {
```

```
        return addOrModifyObject(team, ADD_DATA_ACTION);
    }

    public boolean addNewVenueToRoster(Venue venue) throws DataException
    {
        return addOrModifyObject(venue, ADD_DATA_ACTION);
    }

    public boolean modifyTeamInRoster(Team team) throws DataException
    {
        return addOrModifyObject(team, MODIFY_DATA_ACTION);
    }

    public boolean modifyVenueInRoster(Venue venue) throws DataException
    {
        return addOrModifyObject(venue, MODIFY_DATA_ACTION);
    }

    public boolean addNewFixtureToRoster(Fixture newFixture) throws DataException
    {
        return addOrModifyObject(newFixture, ADD_DATA_ACTION);
    }

    public boolean modifyFixtureInRoster(Fixture fixture) throws DataException
    {
        throw new UnsupportedOperationException(
                "Modify a Fixture not supported, use delete, then add");
    }

    private boolean addOrModifyObject(Object object, String action)
    throws DataException
    {
        initSession();
        Transaction tx = null;
        try
        {
            tx = _currentSession.beginTransaction();
            _currentSession.saveOrUpdate(object);
            tx.commit();
        }
        catch (HibernateException cannotSaveOrUpdate)
        {
            try
            {
                tx.rollback();
            }
            catch (HibernateException cannotRollback)
            {
                // log this error
            }
            throw new DataException("Unable to " + action + " : " +
                                    cannotSaveOrUpdate.getMessage());
        }
```

```
        finally
        {
            flushSession();
        }

    return false;
}

/*-- loading by id --*/
public Round getRoundById(int id) throws DataException
{
    return (Round)loadObjectById(Round.class, id);
}

public Team getTeamById(int id) throws DataException
{
    return (Team)loadObjectById(Team.class, id);
}

public Venue getVenueById(int id) throws DataException
{
    return (Venue)loadObjectById(Venue.class, id);
}

public Fixture getFixtureById(int id) throws DataException
{
    return (Fixture)loadObjectById(Fixture.class, id);
}

private Object loadObjectById(Class clazz, int id) throws DataException
{
    initSession();
    Object rv = null;
    try
    {
        rv = _currentSession.load(clazz, new Integer(id));
    }
    catch (HibernateException unexpected)
    {
        throw new DataException(unexpected.getMessage());
    }
    finally
    {
        flushSession();
    }
    return rv;
}

/*-- delete objects --*/
public boolean deleteTeamFromRoster(int id) throws DataException
{
    return deleteObject(Team.class, id);
}
```

```java
public boolean deleteVenueFromRoster(int id) throws DataException
{
    return deleteObject(Venue.class, id);
}

public boolean deleteFixtureFromRoster(int id) throws DataException
{
    return deleteObject(Fixture.class, id);
}

private boolean deleteObject(Class clazz, int id) throws DataException
{
    initSession();
    Transaction tx = null;
    try
    {
        tx = _currentSession.beginTransaction();
        Object aboutToBeDeleted = loadObjectById(clazz, id);
        _currentSession.delete(aboutToBeDeleted);
        tx.commit();
    }
    catch (HibernateException cannotDelete)
    {
        try
        {
            tx.rollback();
        }
        catch (HibernateException cannotRollback)
        {
            // log this error
        }
        throw new DataException("Unable to delete  : " +
                                cannotDelete.getMessage());
    }
    finally
    {
        flushSession();
    }
    return false;
}

/*-- utility methods --*/
private void initSession()
{
    if (_currentSession == null)
    {
        _currentSession = _sessionFactory.openSession(_connection);
    }
}

private void flushSession()
{
    try
```

```
        {
            if (_currentSession != null)
            {
                _currentSession.flush();
            }
        }
        catch (HibernateException sessionFlushFailure)
        {
            // log this error
        }
    }

    public void releaseResources()
    {
        if (_connection != null)
        {
            try
            {
                if (_currentSession != null)
                {
                    _currentSession.connection().close();
                    _currentSession.close();
                    _currentSession = null;
                }
                _connection.close();

            }
            catch (HibernateException sessionCloseFailure)
            {
                // log this error
            }
            catch (SQLException connectionCloseFailure)
            {
                // log this error
            }
        }
    }
}
```

As with the other data management components, a JSP page is created to provide the user interface. Create the file fixture.jsp in the web directory with the following contents:

```
<!--
<%@ taglib prefix="fmt" uri="http://java.sun.com/jsp/jstl/fmt" %>
<%@ taglib prefix="c" uri="http://java.sun.com/jsp/jstl/core" %>
-->
<jsp:useBean id="fixtures" class="java.util.ArrayList" scope="request" />
<jsp:useBean id="teams" class="java.util.ArrayList" scope="request" />
<jsp:useBean id="rounds" class="java.util.ArrayList" scope="request" />
<jsp:useBean id="venues" class="java.util.ArrayList" scope="request" />
<jsp:useBean id="SERVLET_PATH" class="java.lang.String" scope="request" />
```

```
<c:set value="Team Fixture Management" var="title" />
<html>
  <head>
    <title><c:out value="${title}" /></title>
  </head>
  <body>
    <h1><c:out value="${title}" /></h1>
    <table border="1">
      <tr>
        <th>Fixture ID</th>
        <th>Round #</th>
        <th>Home Team</th>
        <th>Away Team</th>
        <th>Venue</th>
        <th colspan="2"> </th>
      </tr>
      <form name="fixturelist" action="<c:out value="${SERVLET_PATH}" />"
            method="POST">
        <input type="hidden" name="ACTION" value="FIXTURE_DELETE" />
        <c:forEach var="fixture" items="${fixtures}" >
          <tr>
            <td>${fixture.id}</td>
            <td>${fixture.round.roundNumber}</td>
            <td>${fixture.homeTeam.name}</td>
            <td>${fixture.awayTeam.name}</td>
            <td>${fixture.venue.location}</td>
            <td><input name="DELETE_LIST" type="checkbox"
                 value="${fixture.id}" /></td>
          </tr>
        </c:forEach>
        <tr>
          <td align="right" colspan="5">Delete selected items</td>
          <td><input name="DELETE_BUTTON" type="submit"
               value="Delete Checked" /></td>
        </tr>
      </form>
      <form action="<c:out value="${SERVLET_PATH}" />" method="POST">
      <input type="hidden" name="ACTION" value="FIXTURE_ADD" />
      <tr>
        <td> </td>
        <td>
          <select name="round_id">
            <c:forEach var="round" items="${rounds}" >
              <option value="${round.id}">${round.roundNumber}</option>
            </c:forEach></select>
        </td>
        <td>
          <select name="home_team_id">
            <c:forEach var="homeTeam" items="${teams}" >
              <option value="${homeTeam.id}">${homeTeam.name}</option>
            </c:forEach>
          </select>
        </td>
```

```
      <td>
        <select name="away_team_id">
          <c:forEach var="awayTeam" items="${teams}" >
            <option value="${awayTeam.id}">${awayTeam.name}</option>
          </c:forEach>
        </select>
      </td>
      <td>
        <select name="venue_id">
          <c:forEach var="venue" items="${venues}" >
            <option value="${venue.id}">${venue.location}</option>
          </c:forEach>
        </select>
      </td>
      <td><input name="ADD" type="submit" value="Add Fixture" /></td>
    </tr>
  </table>
  <a href="menu.html">Main Menu</a>
  </body>
</html>
```

Finally, perform a minor modification to the `web/menu.html` file to enable the fixture administration to be selected:

```
<html>
  <head>Football Administration Menu</head>
  <body>
    <ul>
      <li><a href="round-input.jsp">Round</a></li>
      <li><a href="admin?ACTION=VENUE_LIST">Venue</a></li>
      <li><a href="admin?ACTION=FIXTURE_LIST">Fixture</a></li>
    </ul>
  </body>
</html>
```

How It Works

The Web application has grown to a reasonably complex application, with a significant proportion of the functionality required to manage the data for the football roster implemented. The fixture data management shows how Hibernate can manage relationships between objects in a very convenient way for the Web application developer without having to resort to cumbersome and repetitive SQL. Under the covers of the Hibernate libraries, SQL is still issued to the database via the JDBC interfaces. The Hibernate team has done a comprehensive job of shielding the developer from needing to understand the complexity of the underlying SQL.

Notice how the `Fixture` class is very "Java-like." It's an object, and it contains other objects. It was difficult to see this in previous parts of the example, as the other objects map very closely to their relational database representations with only simple fields. The persistence of different types of objects with relationships between objects is where Hibernate shines.

819

In many projects, the `Fixture` class would be implemented with the following fields:

```
private int   _id;
private int   _roundId;
private int   _homeTeamId;
private int   _awayTeamId;
private int   _venueId;
```

This would make it very easy to map to a database and avoid much of the complicated JDBC code normally found with hand-built ORM, but it sacrifices the advantages of using Java as the programming language.

Hibernate removes the complication, enabling Java developers to express their business objects in a far more expressive and natural manner.

The `Fixture.hbm.xml` mapping file should appear quite familiar, except for the new element, `many-to-one`, that has been introduced. The choice of the `many-to-one` element may seem a little unusual. However, that's the relationship that `Fixture` has with `Round` (or `Team` and `Venue`), a *unidirectional many-to-one association*. The relationship is only one way (from `Fixture` to `Round`) and the column `roundid` in the `fixture` table is a foreign key for the primary key column for the `Round` object.

Notice how the `<many-to-one>` elements specify only the field (`round`, `homeTeam`, and so on) that contains the object. Hibernate uses runtime reflection to determine the actual class name, locates the appropriate mapping file, and then performs the appropriate mapping for the foreign key. How cool is that!

The `class` attribute can be used in the `<many-to-one>` mapping to make the relationship more explicit:

```
<many-to-one name="homeTeam" class="Team" column="hometeam" />
```

Browse to the following URL:

```
http://localhost:8080/chapter23/menu.html
```

This will display the simple menu available. Click the link for Fixture. This should show a screen similar to the one shown in Figure 23-5.

Similar to the other JSP output shown previously, the table contains the list of existing fixtures, with check boxes for the deletion of fixtures and addition of new fixtures. However, unlike other JSP examples the fixtures are all added via drop-down lists of currently available records.

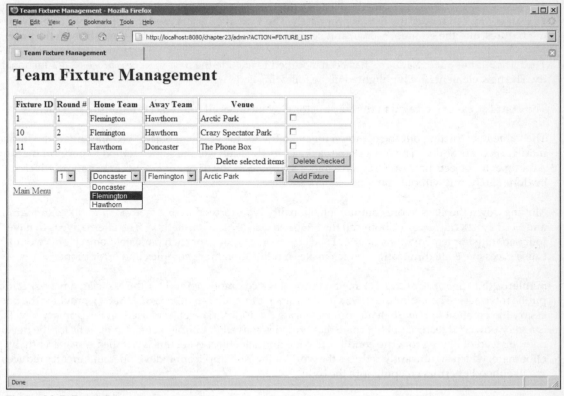

Figure 23-5: Team fixture management

The adding of fixtures is done by using existing data created by other screens. The drop-down menus contain lists of data that are chosen to create the fixture. The Fixture processing is managed in a symmetrical way to the Venue processing, via the implementation of a ProcessingCommand.

The FixtureProcessingCommand is very similar to the existing VenueProcessingCommand, converting the parameters contained in the HttpServletRequest into the correct values and invoking the appropriate RosterManager methods.

The Strings defined at the start of the class are used by fixture.jsp to load lists of data obtained from the database.

The add action occurs when the action parameter equals the constant ACTION_FIXTURE_ADD, obtaining the parameters from the fixture.jsp POST and converting it into objects that represent the foreign key values. In a production quality system, better checking of the input values would be mandatory, but for this example they are skipped for clarity.

To add the new Fixture, the processFixtureAdd() method is called, and the parameters obtained from the Web application are used to load the objects from the database. Again, this would be a good place to add some error-checking to ensure that the objects returned exist prior to adding the new Fixture.

The processFixtureList() method loads a number of collections of objects into request scope so the fixture.jsp can render the lists appropriately. The fixtures list is used to display the currently existing fixtures, and the venues, teams, and rounds are used to display the drop-down lists on the page.

The HibernateRosterManager has been modified to include the new fixture processing functionality. The new elements are highlighted in the following code.

The configuration created in the constructor now includes all four objects requiring persistence.

The value in extracting out the common functionality for the query of objects becomes more apparent as more objects are added. The getXXXInRoster() methods all call the same method to perform the work. Adding extra objects now only requires minor additions to the HibernateRosterManager, which can be done safely and without spending significant time.

Moving down the class, more common functionality is performed in one method: addXXXToRoster() and modifyXXXInRoster() both call the addOrModifyObject() method. The alternative is to have four separate implementations of addOrModifyObject(), one for each persistent object. This would cause excessive code duplication, which makes modification more complex and error prone.

Similarly, the loadObjectById() method provides a common method for the associated type-specific public interfaces. The use of the Class as a parameter to _currentSession.load() provides the necessary information to Hibernate to correctly locate the appropriate object based on the primary key. This is a very powerful feature of Hibernate that provides convenient implementation options for the developer. Instead of having to write conditional code for each object type, this is handled transparently by Hibernate, which significantly reduces the work of the Web application developer and greatly reduces the likelihood of errors creeping into the code.

The pattern repeats for the deleteObject() method. However, to obtain the appropriate object to delete, the loadObjectById() method is called. This will find the object to be deleted to ensure that it exists. This is a slightly different pattern from the other methods, and at first glance seems very strange. Why create an object just for the purpose of deleting it?

The alternative is to create an identity object holding just the id in the deleteXXXXFromRoster() methods. However, that may require the addition of a specific constructor that takes only the id as a parameter, as shown here:

```
deleteObject(new Team(id));
```

Alternatively, you can relax the error-checking in the constructor, allowing null values to be passed into the object:

```
deleteObject(new Team(id, null);
```

Finally, you can enable the construction of temporary objects specifically for deletion:

```
deleteObject(new Team(id, "deleteMe"));
```

While these options are possible, none of them are particularly clean; and with more complex objects, they start to look far less attractive:

```
deleteObject(new Fixture(id, (Round)null, (Team)null, (Team)null, (Venue)null));
```

The downside of creating an identity object is that these techniques make it impossible for the rest of the application to now rely on the consistent state of the persistent objects. Creating an identity object might be appropriate for very short-lived objects that exist only in the persistence management layer of the application. However, another developer may choose to use one of the identity object creation methods in another part of the application, causing major errors to occur. It is not a good idea to create objects that exist in an illegal state under most circumstances, especially when there are alternatives.

Hibernate will work with any of the preceding options, but these are generally considered a workaround to enable persistence, and it is a better idea to load the object prior to deletion.

> Some developers may dismiss the load and then delete strategy for performance reasons, arguing that the load from the database will adversely affect the application too greatly. The good news is that the Hibernate session cache will generally have these objects available in the cache ready for loading without needing to perform a database access. Yet again, Hibernate provides functionality to enable Java developers to work with the objects in a natural way without penalty.

The `fixture.jsp` is similar to the previous JSP, but the use of the collections of objects to create the drop-down lists is something not shown before. Nonetheless, it's a very common feature to be found in Web applications accessing databases. Single and multiple selections of data from lists drive many Web user interfaces.

When developing the Web application, remember that even though the data from the database was used to create the initial lists, there is no guarantee that when the form data is sent back to the server the information represented by the keys exists. The data may have been deleted or the user may be maliciously trying to cause errors. This is another good reason to be vigilant about checking the data coming from Web browsers, and validating the use of that data within the Web application.

The Hibernate example shown in this chapter only scratches the surface of the power available to the developer using this tool. Additionally, Hibernate provides support for collections of data, lazy-loading of child objects to prevent a cascade of objects from loading with the parent object, and many-to-many relationships. The Hibernate Query Language (HQL) also provides extensive means for working with selecting complex graphs of objects.

Developers with a further interest in this topic should read *Professional Hibernate* by Eric Pugh and Joseph Gradecki (Wrox, 2004).

Summary

This chapter has covered Web application development using a database. The coverage included directly communicating to a database via a JSP using the JSTL tags, using raw JDBC with a persistence layer, and using the open-source ORM tool Hibernate.

To conclude this chapter, let's review some of its key points:

❑ Database access is commonly required in Web applications.

❑ Incorrectly implementing database access can lead to excessive complexity.

❑ Ignoring important considerations such as resource cleanup and transaction management will lead to an unstable Web application.

❑ The database connection and management is best handled as a separate layer to the business objects.

❑ Checking of data for validity and properly handling error conditions will assist in building a robust and reliable Web application. Failing to adequately address unexpected situations or erroneous input can lead to crashes and embarrassing errors.

❑ ORM mapping tools such as Hibernate can provide a more natural mechanism for persisting rich Java objects than hand-built JDBC.

Security

This chapter looks at one of the more challenging areas in Web application development, that of securing the Web application.

The chapter begins by examining security in general, and includes a breakdown of the term "security" into a number of different areas that can be addressed independently depending on the requirements of the Web application.

Next you will examine examples of how these security areas can be implemented using the Tomcat JSP and servlet container, and examples of use in JSP. This covers technologies such as SSL, and implementing different J2EE support authentication techniques such as basic, form, and client-certificate.

Finally, the chapter concludes with some examples of using programmatic authorization.

In particular, this chapter

❑   Provides a general discussion about Web application security

❑   Shows how to configure Tomcat with SSL

❑   Shows examples of the J2EE-supported authentication types

❑   Shows examples of programmatic authorization

Areas of Security

The security of Web applications is covered by a number of different areas. These areas will generally relate to different requirements for the Web application and the data that is used by the Web application. The sorts of questions that can be used to identify how and what should be secured are as follows:

❑   Who is allowed to access the Web application?

❑   How will you identify the users?

❑ Are there any restrictions on where the application is accessed from?

❑ Is any of the application data private?

❑ Who can add/modify/delete data?

These questions look very much like additional requirements for a Web application. This is how security should be viewed. A common error in building software of all types, not only Web applications, is to try to build the functionality of the software (what it does) and then try to add security later. Failing to identify and incorporate the security requirements as business requirements can lead to fragile and error-prone implementations.

This is a path that will lead to much toil and trouble for both the developer and the user. It is very important to consider the security requirements as part of exactly the same process as the functionality requirements, and design and build the Web application with all the requirements in mind from the beginning. This method also helps to identify areas early that might require additional resources (such as obtaining server certificates) or hardware environments for testing that are often left until far too late in the project cycle for sufficient testing or deployment.

The four main areas relating to security requirements are as follows:

❑ Authentication

❑ Authorization

❑ Data integrity

❑ Confidentiality

These areas are covered in more detail in the following sections.

Authentication

Authentication is the proof of identity. The most well-known form of authentication in computer applications is the username and password, although having a personal key pair and certificate is starting to become more common with the introduction of smart cards to securely hold the keys. Widespread adoption of this means of authentication, however, is likely to be many years away due to cost and inconvenience.

Authentication is used by many applications to relate an identity to a HTTP session that is accessing some resource in a Web application. This resource may be protected in some manner, and authentication is used to validate whether the identity is authorized to access the resource. An example of this is Internet banking or Web-based e-mail. In these circumstances, the identity is related to a real person, and access probably depends on some proof of that identity during creation of the authentication parameters.

For some applications, the resources are not protected and the authentication is used to apply personalization or provide identity validation for submitted information. Examples of this use include Web-based information services such as Slashdot (www.slashdot.org) or Java Blogs (javablogs.com). There is no real requirement to relate a real-world identity to the login credentials; these sites don't care about real-world relationships.

The Servlet specification provides support for the container to perform authentication via the security-constraint element in the web.xml file.

The forms of authentication specified in the Servlet specification and provided by servlet containers such as Tomcat are as follows:

❑   HTTP basic authentication

❑   HTTP digest authentication

❑   Form-based authentication

❑   SSL client certificate authentication

Another option is to implement a custom authentication solution that manually accesses a user database directly after obtaining user credentials from a form or HTTP request. This can be done as part of the core Web application or implemented as a filter that controls access to resources based on the requests. Additionally, Web frameworks such as WebWork (www.opensymphony.com/webwork/) or using an open-source solution such as Seraph (http://opensource.atlassian.com) can be leveraged to provide authentication solutions depending on the complexity of the requirements.

This chapter focuses on the container-provided security and authentication mechanisms, as this is the most likely scenario for the majority of JSP developers.

HTTP basic authentication is the simplest method for a Web application to support. No other resources are required to be provided by the Web application (other than configuration of the user database); and if the requirement is merely to protect a resource, then this provides a quick method for the Web application deployer.

There are three considerable drawbacks with using HTTP basic authentication. The first is that the security of the transmitted information is very poor. The username and password are transferred by the browser for every request and are "protected" by a BASE-64 encoding of the information.

The second drawback is that the visual aspects of the authentication dialog are quite basic, and do not fit in well with the style of many Web applications.

The third drawback is that the use of basic authentication is controlled by the browser, and there is no way to "log out" the user other than to shut down the browser. This is generally not an acceptable option.

HTTP digest authentication is a similar approach to HTTP basic authentication, the difference being that the information transmitted from the browser to the server does not contain the password, but a *digest* consisting of the password and some random values. HTTP digest authentication is not commonly used because of lack of support by browsers.

Form-based authentication provides advantages over HTTP basic authentication. The first and most significant is from a visual point of view: Form-based authentication uses an HTML FORM element that can be styled to suit a Web application. The second advantage is that form-based authentication is implemented using some form of server-side session tracking, so the session can be invalidated and the user can "log out," often a very desirable feature.

The final option available is SSL client-certificate authentication. This is not just configuring SSL on the server, but actually having the servlet container verify the authenticity of the client-presented certificates. This is generally not a very attractive option as it requires the users of the system to create and install certificates to use the Web application. In certain specific circumstances (such as an extranet application for which the user base is managed by the Web application owners), it may be a worthwhile authentication mechanism.

It is a very useful technique to implement HTTP basic authentication or form-based authentication over HTTPS, as this will secure the credentials passed between the browser and the container.

Authorization

Authorization is also known as access control. Whereas authentication provides the identity of the user accessing the resource, authorization determines whether the user has the permissions to access the resource.

In the Servlet specification, the authorization model is role-based. This means that a user is assigned one or more roles, and resources can be accessed by authenticated users with the specified role. Roles are a convenient means of providing a set of users with the same access rights. Users can be added or removed from a particular role to change the resources that can be accessed. If new resources are added to the Web application (such as new functionality), then all users who are currently assigned to a particular role can access the new resource with a single change. This is a preferable option to modifying the access rights of each and every user.

The group of users and roles for a particular authentication policy is known as a `Realm`.

The implementation of the authorization mechanism for a J2EE or JSP/servlet container is not defined by the Servlet specification, so implementation, or even a range of implementations, is specific to the container.

Tomcat supports a number of different implementations of an authorization realm, such as an XML file, a relational database, and an LDAP connector. To the JSP developer, all provide the same service, so the choice does not affect the Web application implementation, but it does affect configuration of the system as a whole.

Authorization of access to resources can be performed in two ways: *declarative* or *programmatic*. In declarative authorization, the application developer provides elements in the Web application deployment descriptor (`web.xml`) to specify resources that are protected. This is the `security-constraint` element, which provides a URL mapping specifying the resource that is protected and the role required to access the resource.

The declarative security model is based only on client-initiated requests. Any use of the `RequestDispatcher` *to invoke* `forward` *or* `include` *methods to resources is not processed by the servlet container and may be used to access otherwise "protected" resources.*

As the Web application developer has complete control over the use of these methods to access resources within the Web application, selecting the appropriate mechanisms to implement the Web application's security is an important design consideration.

The following example illustrates the `security-constraint` element and the corresponding user and role configuration:

```
(in web.xml)
<security-constraint>
      <display-name>Administrators Only</display-name>
      <web-resource-collection>
          <web-resource-name>
              Administration
          </web-resource-name>
          <url-pattern>/admin/*</url-pattern>
          <http-method>GET</http-method>
          <http-method>POST</http-method>
      </web-resource-collection>
      <auth-constraint>
          <role-name>administrators</role-name>
      </auth-constraint>
      <user-data-constraint>
          <transport-guarantee>
              NONE
          </transport-guarantee>
      </user-data-constraint>
  </security-constraint>

(in conf/tomcat-users.xml)
<?xml version='1.0' encoding='utf-8'?>
<tomcat-users>
  <role rolename="administrators"/>
  <user username="jon" password="secret" roles="administrators"/>
</tomcat-users>
```

As you can see from the configuration, the declarative security is controlled at a high level with a very coarse-grained approach to authorizing access to a resource. In many situations this may be suitable, but where authorization forms part of business rules, an alternative mechanism is required.

An example of authorization forming part of the business rules of a system might be preventing access to a resource out of your internal network, or having roles with fine-grained rights such as "can view the staff information and modify personal details, but not add or delete new staff."

To facilitate these requirements, the second security model for authorization is available. As the name suggests, this *programmatic* security requires the Web developer to explicitly write code to implement the authorization rules.

> *Programmatic security requires the implementation of rules within the Java code of the Web application, but still uses the servlet security framework for authentication of the users. If the* security-constraint *elements are not used within the Web application, then the following APIs will not contain useful values.*

The following methods are used to obtain user and role information when developing programmatic security solutions:

- ❑ **String getRemoteUser():** Returns the username that is currently authenticated, or `null` if the user is not authenticated.

- ❑ **boolean isUserInRole(String role):** Returns `true` if the currently authenticated user is in the specified role.

- ❑ **Principal getUserPrincipal():** Returns a `Principal` object representing the currently authenticated user, or `null` if the user is not authenticated. The `Principal` object can then be queried using `principal.getName()` to return the current username.

Data integrity

Data integrity is often a forgotten aspect of security. Data integrity is the property that prohibits changes from occurring in the data during transmission. Basically, whatever the client or server sends, the recipient gets exactly as sent. If not, it can be detected that a change has been made.

A Web application developer can do little to affect data integrity of information, as it is a servlet container responsibility and is provided when HTTPS/SSL connections are used.

Confidentiality

Confidentiality is generally the only part that most people consider when thinking about security. Confidentiality is the aspect of security that keeps private data private during transmission, and it is implemented by encrypting the data. Servlet containers provide this functionality by implementing an HTTPS/SSL connection to be used by the Web application.

Confidentiality for many Web applications is not enough, as the data may be transmitted secretly but if there is no authentication or authorization, anybody can access the original data! The converse is certainly true as well. If the authentication information can be easily examined during transmission between the client and server, then authentication is severely compromised.

The confidentiality configuration is performed as part of the declarative security model and is often outside of the control of the Web application developer. This may pose a problem if the Web application developer requires data to be transmitted confidentially. The `ServletRequest` object provides a method `isSecure()` that returns `true` if the request was made over a secure channel.

The Web developer can implement code within a Web application — either as a filter or as code within a servlet — that can prohibit access to resources unless the request has been performed over a secure channel.

Data Integrity and Confidentiality

While authentication and authorization are very important concepts, the most commonly implemented security components in Web applications are those relating to data integrity and confidentiality. All Web applications requiring some degree of security will generally implement HTTPS to protect the data transferred between the client and the server.

Even without the need to authenticate individuals, transferring data privately is a very common requirement for Web applications. Online stores, bill payments, and delivery addresses are all important data to protect from modification and prying eyes.

Implementing these security areas is simply a matter of implementing SSL in the Web container. The following examples use Tomcat as the target Web container, but many of these steps will be common to any J2EE server.

Implementing SSL

Implementing SSL in a J2EE server requires the following steps:

1. Obtain the Java Secure Socket Extension (JSSE).
2. Create keys and certificates.
3. Configure the J2EE server to use the keys.
4. Configure the SSL connector in the J2EE server.

Obtaining JSSE

JSSE is a Java implementation of the Secure Sockets Layer (SSL) and Transport Layer Security (TLS) protocols. JSSE contains all the functionality required to implement data integrity and confidentiality through encryption and server authentication.

JSSE is bundled with the standard Sun JRE 1.4. Users that are still using JRE 1.3 should download and install JSSE from Sun. JSSE is available from `http://java.sun.com/products/jsse`.

Comprehensive installation documentation is also available at the same location, and with the JSSE download.

Creating keys and certificates

Using SSL requires the creation of public and private keys, and information about the server requires signing by a third party to create a certificate. This certificate is then used to verify the details of the server by the client browser authenticating the server.

Normally the creation of the certificate is performed by a trusted third party called a *certificate authority (CA)*. Because of the requirements involved in becoming a CA, this small market has been dominated by VeriSign and Thawte. Recently, a number of smaller CAs have entered the global market, although the dominance of VeriSign and Thawte continues, particularly because their root certificates are distributed with browsers and the JVM.

However, it is not necessary to use a third party to create the certificate; this can be done using open-source tools such as EJBCA (`ejbca.sourceforge.net`), a Java-based CA. There is even a simpler option available to Java developers. The Java `keytool` provides a means for creating self-signed certificates and storing them in a keystore. This is a perfect option for testing our security.

For simplicity and ease of configuration, place the keystore created in the following Try It Out section into the root directory of the Tomcat installation. Either copy the keystore after creation, or create it directly in the target directory.

In the following Try It Out example, you learn to create a certificate.

Try It Out   Creating a Certificate

To create a new keystore in the current directory containing a self-signed certificate using the RSA algorithm, use the following command:

```
keytool -genkey -alias localhost -keyalg RSA -keystore ./keystore
```

The keytool *is in the* bin *directory of the Java distribution. Make sure this directory is included in the PATH, or specify the full path to the* keytool *command.*

This will run the keytool, which asks a series of questions as follows:

```
Enter keystore password:
```

Answer with **secret.**

```
What is your first and last name?
```

Answer with **localhost.**

It is very unlikely that any name actually is localhost, *but this certificate is for the server, and not for a person. If the server has a real name (like* darkmatter.com), *then this can be used.*

The next group of questions asked is purely demographic. Either use the default value provided (Unknown), enter information that is specific to the server, or use the information provided in the following steps. This is purely presentation, and has no bearing on the validity of the generated certificate.

Of course, when generating a non-test certificate, this is the information that would link a digital identity to a real-world identity, so third-party CAs are very strict about this information, and generally require proof of correctness before creating the certificate. You'll have to respond to the following prompts:

```
What is the name of your organizational unit?
```

Answer with **Beginning JSP.**

```
What is the name of your organization?
```

Answer with **Wrox.**

```
What is the name of your City or Locality?
```

Answer with **Melbourne.**

```
What is the name of your State or Province?
```

Answer with **Victoria.**

```
What is the two-letter country code for this unit?
```

Answer with **AU**.

The last question validates the entered information:

```
Is CN=localhost, OU=Beginning JSP, O=Wrox, L=Melbourne, ST=Victoria, C=AU correct?
   [no]:
```

Answer with **yes**.

The final question asks for the password to be used for the key. Using this keystore with Tomcat requires that the keystore password and key password be the same. This is a limitation of the Tomcat implementation, and it may be different on other J2EE servers.

```
Enter key password for <localhost>
        (RETURN if same as keystore password):
```

Answer this by just accepting the default and pressing Return.

How It Works

That's it. The keystore created in the current directory contains the newly created keys and certificate. Type in the following to list the entries:

```
keytool -list -v -keystore ./keystore -storepass secret
```

This should result in a listing similar to the following:

```
Keystore type: jks
Keystore provider: SUN

Your keystore contains 1 entry

Alias name: localhost
Creation date: 2/09/2004
Entry type: keyEntry
Certificate chain length: 1
Certificate[1]:
Owner: CN=localhost, OU=Beginning JSP, O=Wrox, L=Melbourne, ST=Victoria, C=AU
Issuer: CN=localhost, OU=Beginning JSP, O=Wrox, L=Melbourne, ST=Victoria, C=AU
Serial number: 4136f771
Valid from: Thu Sep 02 20:35:29 EST 2004 until: Wed Dec 01 21:35:29 EST 2004
Certificate fingerprints:
        MD5:  54:55:03:A8:EE:0B:E7:44:A5:3F:B5:1E:56:0F:E7:2E
        SHA1: 0B:97:9A:92:8C:4F:C8:C3:FD:79:BE:75:8C:4E:F4:3D:F7:1C:16:9B
```

Configuring Tomcat

The server.xml file contains the configuration of the different options for Tomcat. The Connector elements are used to configure the HTTP and HTTPS connectors for the server. To enable SSL, a new connector element needs to be activated so the Tomcat server can accept connections using the SSL protocol.

The default installation of Tomcat has an SSL connector preconfigured in server.xml. By default, it is enclosed in comments to prevent activation during startup. The server.xml file can be found in the conf subdirectory of the root install directory for Tomcat. In the following Try It Out example, you modify server.xml and test your connector.

Find the following connector:

```
<!--
    <Connector port="8443"
               maxThreads="150" minSpareThreads="25" maxSpareThreads="75"
               enableLookups="false" disableUploadTimeout="true"
               acceptCount="100" debug="0" scheme="https" secure="true"
               clientAuth="false" sslProtocol="TLS" />
-->
```

Remove the HTML comments from above <!-- and below -->. Add the following highlighted lines to the end of the element:

```
<Connector port="8443"
           maxThreads="150" minSpareThreads="25" maxSpareThreads="75"
           enableLookups="false" disableUploadTimeout="true"
           acceptCount="100" debug="0" scheme="https" secure="true"
           clientAuth="false" sslProtocol="TLS"
           keystoreFile="/path/to/keystore"
           keystorePass="secret" />
```

The value for keystoreFile is the full path to the keystore created above. For example, under Windows this will look something like the following:

```
keystoreFile="c:\tomcat\keystore"
```

Under UNIX, it will look as follows:

```
keystoreFile="/usr/local/tomcat/keystore"
```

The path depends on where the keystore was created.

Finally, test the modified configuration by starting Tomcat and then browsing to the following URL:

```
https://localhost:8443/
```

This should result in a screen similar to the one shown in Figure 24-1.

Before this page was displayed, the browser would have displayed a dialog box alerting the user that although the certificate provided was valid and matched the host displaying the page (localhost), the certificate was not issued by a company that the browser trusts.

These dialog boxes should look similar to what is shown in Figure 24-2 for Mozilla/Firefox, or Figure 24-3 for Internet Explorer.

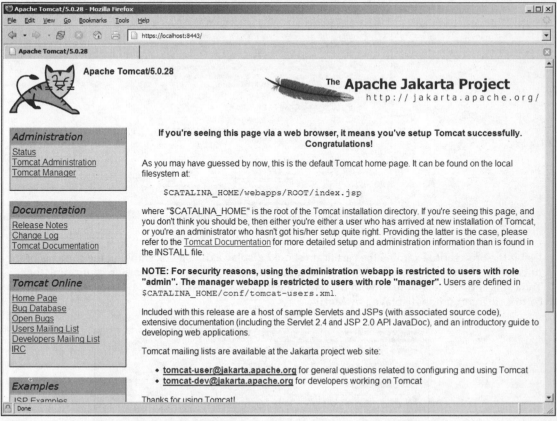

Figure 24-1: Default Tomcat page viewed over SSL

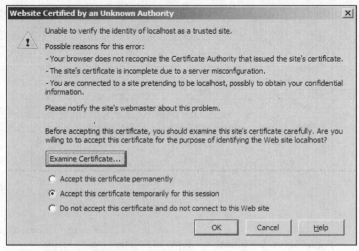

Figure 24-2: Mozilla warning dialog

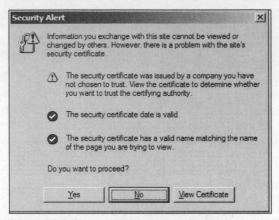

Figure 24-3: Internet Explorer warning dialog

Using the browser to examine the certificate should display a dialog box showing the contents of the certificate. The fields indicate that they contain the same information entered earlier, confirming that Tomcat is correctly configured with the certificate that was created. Figure 24-4 shows an example of the certificate information displayed by Mozilla.

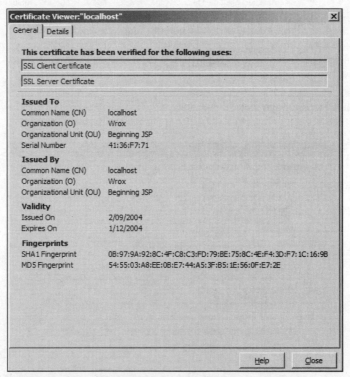

Figure 24-4: Certificate contents dialog box from Mozilla

How It Works

The introduction of the keystore and the configuration of the connector in Tomcat have activated the HTTPS protocol on the server. The use of the `https` prefix and the `8443` port number in the browser URL has enabled a connection to the SSL connector. The browser has validated the connection, and in this case alerted the user that not everything is 100 percent satisfactory.

The alert occurs because of the use of the self-signed certificate. If the certificate was issued by VeriSign or Thawte, the connection would occur without any problems, but there is no reduction in security in this approach, just an additional step when accessing the site.

After the user accepts the connection, the browser displays the Web page and displays the "closed lock" icon, identifying the page as having been encrypted and sent to the browser.

Authentication

Encrypting the data from the server to the browser is only the first step in ensuring that the users of the Web application can store personal information and keep that information private.

The next step, arguably the most important, is identifying the user and ensuring that the user is providing the appropriate credentials. In the simplest terms, this is providing the username and password to access the Web application.

As you will see in subsequent examples, there are other means of proving identity suitable for authentication.

HTTP BASIC authentication

This is the simplest form of authentication available to Web applications. However, it is the least customizable and the most clumsy for users to interact with.

Try It Out   **Creating the Web Application**

Create the following directory structure:

```
chapter24/
        src/
        web/
            private/
            public/
            WEB-INF/
                    lib/
```

Copy the `jstl.jar` and `standard.jar` files used in earlier chapters into the `lib` directory.

Create the Tomcat context file `chapter24.xml` in the `chapter24` directory with the following contents:

```
<?xml version='1.0' encoding='utf-8'?>
<Context docBase="/path/to/chapter24/web"
  path="/chapter24"
```

```
    reloadable="true"
    workDir="/path/to/chapter24/work">
</Context>
```

The /path/to in docBase and workDir must match the full path to the chapter24 directory. Under Windows this might look like the following:

```
<Context docBase="c:/dev/begjsp/chapter24/web"
```

Copy this file to <Tomcat Installation Directory>/conf/Catalina/localhost. This configuration enables Tomcat to find the web directory in the development directories rather than needing to copy files when they are changed, or work directly in the <Tomcat Installation Directory>/webapps directory.

Modify the <Tomcat Installation Directory>/conf/tomcat-users.xml file to add the following role and user:

```
<?xml version='1.0' encoding='utf-8'?>
<tomcat-users>
  <role rolename="manager"/>
  <role rolename="admin"/>
  <role rolename="chapter24" />
  <user username="manager" password="manager" roles="manager"/>
  <user username="admin" password="admin" roles="admin,manager"/>
  <user username="user24" password="secret" roles="chapter24" />
</tomcat-users>
```

Create a web.xml file in the web/WEB-INF directory with the following contents:

```
<?xml version="1.0" encoding="ISO-8859-1"?>

<web-app version="2.4" uri="http://java.sun.com/xml/ns/j2ee" >

  <security-constraint>
    <web-resource-collection>
      <web-resource-name>Everything Private</web-resource-name>
      <url-pattern>/private/*</url-pattern>
    </web-resource-collection>
    <http-method>GET</http-method>
    <http-method>POST</http-method>
    <user-data-constraint>
      <transport-guarantee>CONFIDENTIAL</transport-guarantee>
    </user-data-constraint>

    <auth-constraint>
      <role-name>chapter24</role-name>
    </auth-constraint>

  </security-constraint>

  <login-config>
    <auth-method>BASIC</auth-method>
    <realm-name>Private Realm</realm-name>
  </login-config>
```

```
    <security-role>
      <role-name>chapter24</role-name>
    </security-role>

</web-app>
```

Create the file `public-page.jsp` in the `web/public` directory with the following contents:

```
<!--
<%@ taglib prefix="c" uri="http://java.sun.com/jsp/jstl/core" %>
-->
<c:set value="Public Page" var="title" />
<html>
  <head>
    <title>
      <c:out value="${title}" />
    </title>
  </head>
  <body>
    <h1>
      <c:out value="${title}" />
    </h1>
    This is a public page ! <p/>
    The request is from : <b>${pageContext.request.remoteAddr}</b> <p/>
    Is the request secure ? : <b>${pageContext.request.secure}</b>

  </body>
</html>
```

Create the following file `private-page.jsp` in the `web/private` directory:

```
<!--
<%@ taglib prefix="c" uri="http://java.sun.com/jsp/jstl/core" %>
-->
<c:set value="Private Page" var="title" />
<html>
  <head>
    <title>
      <c:out value="${title}" />
    </title>
  </head>
  <body>
    <h1>
      <c:out value="${title}" />
    </h1>
    This is a private page ! <p/>
    The request is from : <b>${pageContext.request.remoteAddr}</b> <p/>
    Is the request secure ? : <b>${pageContext.request.secure}</b> <p/>

    Hello Remote User : <b>${pageContext.request.remoteUser}</b> <p/>

    Hello Principal : <b>${pageContext.request.userPrincipal.name}</b>

  </body>
</html>
```

How It Works

Start by browsing to `http://localhost:8080/chapter24/public/public-page.jsp`. This should display a page similar to the one shown in Figure 24-5.

This page is not secured and doesn't require authentication, as the URL doesn't match the specification in the `web.xml` file. The relevant section is as follows:

```
<web-resource-collection>
  <web-resource-name>Everything Private</web-resource-name>
  <url-pattern>/private/*</url-pattern>
</web-resource-collection>
```

Now browse to `http://localhost:8080/chapter24/private/private-page.jsp`. This is within the configuration of a secured page.

This should result in a page similar to the one shown in Figure 24-6.

Entering **user24** for the user name and **secret** for the password and clicking OK should result in a screen similar to the one shown in Figure 24-7.

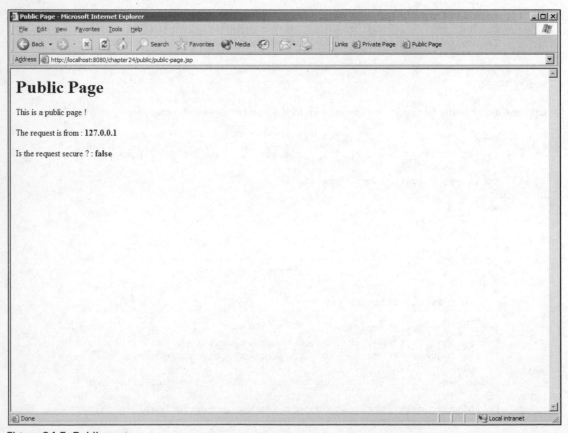

Figure 24-5: Public page

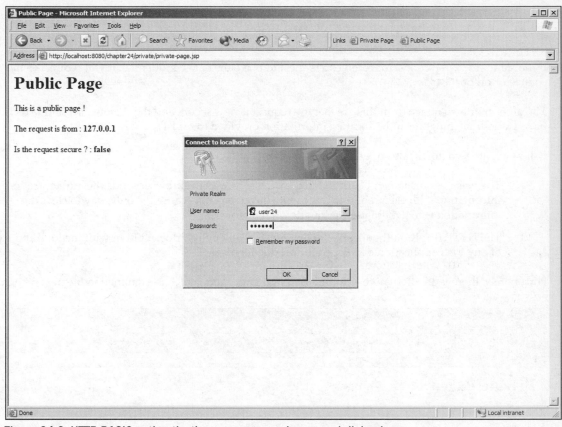

Figure 24-6: HTTP BASIC authentication username and password dialog box

Notice how the URL is now `https://localhost:8443/chapter24/private/private-page.jsp`.
The servlet container has redirected the input URL to use HTTPS. This was achieved by the setup of the
Tomcat connectors. If you look at `<Tomcat Installation Directory>/conf/server.xml`, the impor-
tant attribute is in the first of the two connectors, the `redirectPort`:

```
<Service name="Catalina">
    <Connector port="8080"
            maxThreads="150" minSpareThreads="25" maxSpareThreads="75"
            enableLookups="false" redirectPort="8443" acceptCount="100"
            debug="0" connectionTimeout="20000"
            disableUploadTimeout="true"
            compression="on"
            compressionMinSize="2048"
            noCompressionUserAgents="gozilla, traviata"
            compressableMimeType="text/html,text/xml" />


    <Connector port="8443"
            maxThreads="150" minSpareThreads="25" maxSpareThreads="75"
            enableLookups="false" disableUploadTimeout="true"
            acceptCount="100" debug="0" scheme="https" secure="true"
```

```
                clientAuth="false" sslProtocol="TLS"
                keystoreFile="c:\tomcat\keystore"
                keystorePass="secret" />
```

If the standard HTTP connector receives a request to make the data confidential, it will redirect to the connector on port 8443.

The other points to notice from this are that the request is now secure and the remote user and principal have values matching the authentication information provided (user24).

Following are two downsides of using BASIC authentication:

❑ The user session cannot be invalidated by the server, as the browser sends the authentication information with each request. This can be inconvenient because the only way to clear this information is to get the user to shut down the browser.

❑ The HTTP BASIC authentication dialog box is really ugly. It doesn't fit in with the look and feel of any Web application developed for production use.

Fortunately, there is an alternative — form-based authentication, which is examined in the next section.

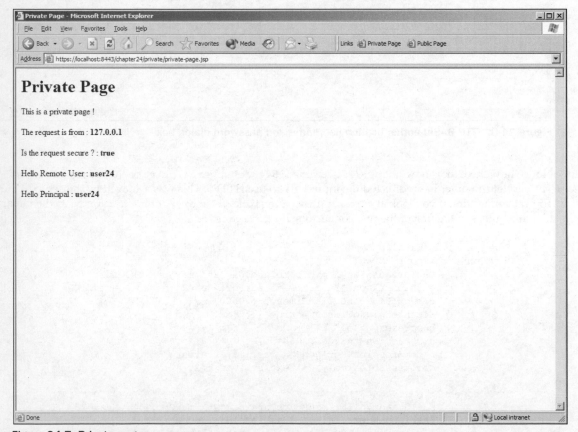

Figure 24-7: Private page

Form-based authentication

Form-based authentication is another type of authentication supported by the J2EE specification. As discussed previously, it provides some advantages over the HTTP BASIC authentication scheme, and it is the most widely implemented of the authentication schemes. In the next Try It Out example, you learn about implementing form-based authentication.

Try It Out   Implementing Form-Based Authentication

The first thing to modify is the `web.xml` file to specify FORM rather than BASIC authentication. Change the `login-config` stanza to the following:

```
<login-config>
  <auth-method>FORM</auth-method>
  <form-login-config>
    <form-login-page>/login.html</form-login-page>
    <form-error-page>/login-error.html</form-error-page>
  </form-login-config>
</login-config>
```

Create the following `index.html` file in the `web` directory:

```
<!DOCTYPE HTML PUBLIC "-//W3C/DTD HTML 4.01 Transitional//EN">
<html>
  <head>
    <title>Chapter 24 Web Application</title>
  </head>
  <body>
    <h1>Chapter 24 Web Application</h1>
    <table>
      <tr>
        <td><a href="public/public-page.jsp">Public Page</a></td>
      </tr>
      <tr>
        <td><a href="private/private-page.jsp">Private Page</a></td>
      </tr>
    </table>
  </body>
</html>
```

To support the form login, create a `login.html` file in the `web` directory with the following contents:

```
<!DOCTYPE HTML PUBLIC "-//W3C/DTD HTML 4.01 Transitional//EN">
<html>
  <head>
    <title>Private Area Login Page</title>
  </head>
  <body>
    <h1>Warning: Authorised Users Only</h1>
    <form action="j_security_check" method="post">
      <table>
        <tr>
          <td>User Name</td>
```

843

```
            <td><input type="text" name="j_username"></td>
          </tr>
          <tr>
            <td>Password</td>
            <td><input type="password" name="j_password"></td>
          </tr>
          <tr>
            <td align="right">
              <input type="submit" value="login">
            </td>
            <td align="left">
              <input type="reset">
            </td>
          </tr>
        </table>
      </form>
    </body>
</html>
```

Finally, create the `login-error.html`, also in the web directory:

```
<!DOCTYPE HTML PUBLIC "-//W3C/DTD HTML 4.01 Transitional//EN">

<html>
  <head>
    <title>Private Area Login Error</title>
  </head>

  <body>
    <h1>Warning: Authorised Users Only</h1>

    An error occurred during login.
    <p/>
    This is probably due to an incorrect username and/or password.
    <p/>
    Click on the link below to try again.
    <p/>
    <a href="../index.html">Return to the Index Page</a>
  </body>
</html>
```

For convenience, create an `index.html` file in the web directory. This will make it easier to browse the public and private pages. This file should contain the following contents:

```
<!DOCTYPE HTML PUBLIC "-//W3C/DTD HTML 4.01 Transitional//EN">
<html>
  <head>
    <title>Chapter 24 Web Application</title>
  </head>
  <body>
    <h1>Chapter 24 Web Application</h1>
    <table>
      <tr>
```

```
      <td><a href="public/public-page.jsp">Public Page</a></td>
    </tr>
    <tr>
      <td><a href="private/private-page.jsp">Private Page</a></td>
    </tr>
  </table>
</body>
</html>
```

How It Works

Start by browsing to `http://localhost:8080/chapter24/index.html`. This should display the page shown in Figure 24-8.

When you select the Private Page link, you should be redirected by the browser to the login form shown in Figure 24-9.

You enter the same credentials as before, a user name of **user24** and a password of **secret**. When you click the Login button, you see the same page shown in Figure 24-7.

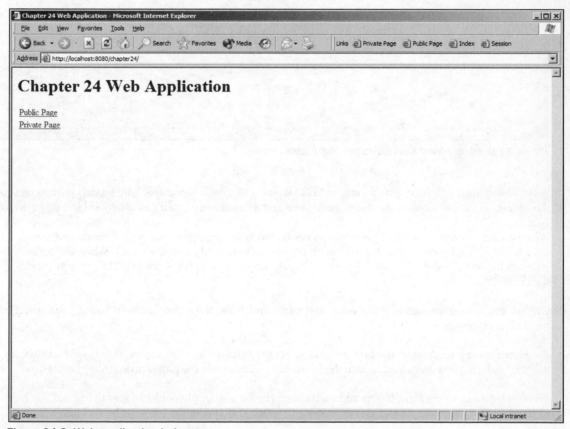

Figure 24-8: Web application index page

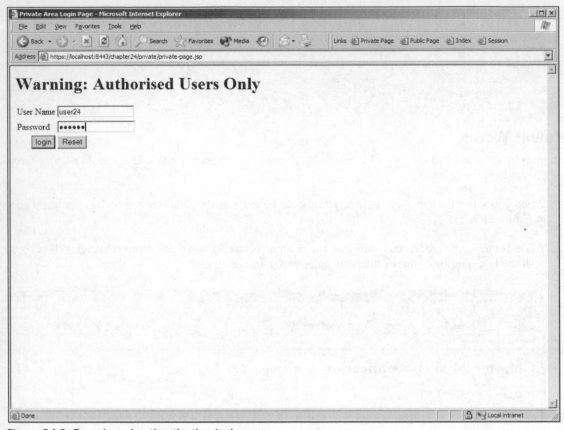

Figure 24-9: Form-based authentication login page

Form-based authentication uses a standard HTML form to submit some specially named parameters to the server. These parameters are the `j_username` and `j_password` input fields defined in `login.html`.

When a user requests a secured page, the server redirects the request to the page defined in `form-login-page`. This page contains a form with the specially named parameters, and when the user submits the form to the `j_security_check` target, the server intercepts the HTTP POST and checks the credentials.

On success, the server redirects to the secured page; on failure, the server redirects to the page specified in `form-error-page`.

To see the error page, restart the browser and select the Private Page link again. This time, just click login without entering any information into the form. This will display the page shown in Figure 24-10.

The final change to the form-based authentication scheme is to implement a means to log out, as shown in the next Try It Out example. Such functionality is not available to the basic authentication scheme.

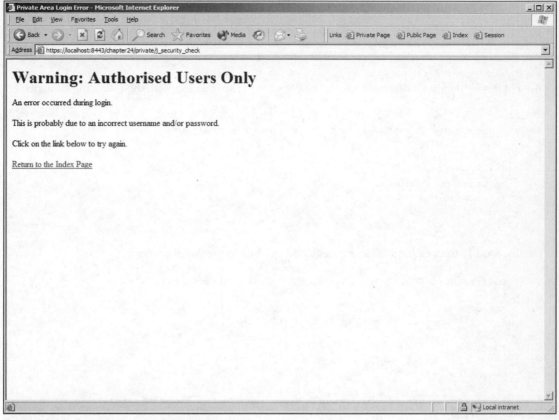

Figure 24-10: Error page from form login

Try It Out   Implementing a Logout

In the web/public directory, create the file session.jsp with the following contents:

```
<!--
<%@ taglib prefix="c" uri="http://java.sun.com/jsp/jstl/core" %>
-->
<c:set value="Show Session Information" var="title" />
<html>
  <head>
    <title>
      <c:out value="${title}" />
    </title>
  </head>
  <body>
    <h1>
      <c:out value="${title}" />
    </h1>
    The current session is : <b>${pageContext.request.session.id}</b> <p/>
```

```
      <a href="kill-session.jsp">Logout</a> <p/>
      <a href="../index.html">Back to index page</a>

   </body>
</html>
```

Also in the web/public directory, create the file kill-session.jsp with the following contents:

```
<!--
<%@ taglib prefix="c" uri="http://java.sun.com/jsp/jstl/core" %>
-->

<jsp:scriptlet>
  session.invalidate();
</jsp:scriptlet>

<c:redirect url="../index.html" />
```

Finally, modify the web/index.html file to add in a link to the session.jsp:

```
<!DOCTYPE HTML PUBLIC "-//W3C/DTD HTML 4.01 Transitional//EN">
<html>
  <head>
    <title>Chapter 24 Web Application</title>
  </head>
  <body>
    <h1>Chapter 24 Web Application</h1>
    <table>
      <tr>
        <td><a href="public/public-page.jsp">Public Page</a></td>
      </tr>
      <tr>
        <td><a href="private/private-page.jsp">Private Page</a></td>
      </tr>
      <tr>
        <td><a href="session.jsp">Show Session Information</a></td>
      </tr>
    </table>
  </body>
</html>
```

Browse to the URL http://localhost:8080/chapter24/index.html and select the Private Page link. The user will be redirected to a page similar to the one shown in Figure 24-9. Enter the username and password used previously in this chapter and click login. The screen should look like Figure 24-7.

Now, browse to different URLs in the public and private directories; the user is not required to re-authenticate as browsing continues.

Browse to the URL http://localhost:8080/chapter24/index.html and click the Show Session Information link. This screen should look like the one shown in Figure 24-11.

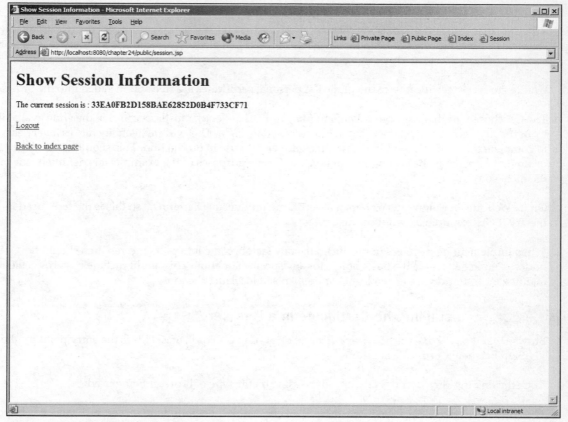

Figure 24-11: Showing session information

Click the Logout link. This should direct you back to `index.html` and display the screen shown in Figure 24-8, with the additional Show Session Information link. Click the Private Page link, and at this point you will be forced to re-authenticate via the `login.html` page shown in Figure 24-9.

How It Works

The session information is stored by the server, and a cookie is stored in the browser to maintain the session's validity. The `session.invalidate()` method in `kill-session.jsp` deletes the session on the server, and the user is forced to re-authenticate because the cookie in the browser is now no longer linked to a valid, authenticated session.

Client-certificate authentication

The final form of authentication supported by the J2EE container is client-certificate authentication. This scheme is the least frequently used, primarily because of the inconvenience it poses to the end users, making it unsuitable for general-purpose Internet applications. The client certificate is a good fit for intranet or extranet applications in which a higher degree of confidence in the identity of the user is needed.

Personal certificates

There are many different ways to obtain a user certificate. Like the server certificate created earlier in the chapter, a user certificate can be manually generated and installed, or you can use a variety of certificate authorities (CA) that provide personal certificates.

Unlike the server certificates, many of the CA personal certificates are free and installed into the browser.

The CA chosen for this example is VeriSign (`www.verisign.com`), mostly because of the wide availability of the root certificates pre-installed in browsers and the JVM. This wide availability makes it very easy to complete this example, and in practice makes it easy to use in production. This should not be taken to mean that VeriSign is the best or only option, but for the purposes of the example, it is definitely one of the most convenient.

On its Web site, VeriSign calls its personal certificate product a "Digital ID," so this is the term used in the Try It Out example to avoid confusion.

When implementing a system in production, many factors come into play, and research should be undertaken to determine the best choices for any specific situation. This might include cost, convenience, maintenance, support, and even legal requirements of local jurisdictions.

Try It Out   Installing the Certificate in a Browser

Browse to `https://digitalid.verisign.com/client/enroll.htm`. This is the entry point for the VeriSign Personal Certificate sign-up.

Click the link for Microsoft or Netscape, depending on the type of browser being used.

This presents a page with some fields to be filled out. Unlike generating the server certificate, it is important to fill in this information accurately. Of critical importance is the e-mail address — in order to complete the VeriSign enrollment, an e-mail is sent to this address, so ensure that this is a valid and accessible e-mail address.

There is no need to purchase the Digital ID; select the "60-day trial Digital ID for free" option, and leave the "Billing Information" section blank.

Select either 2048 (High Grade) or 1024 (Medium Grade) Encryption Strength; it isn't particularly important for the example which one is used. Selecting the Medium Grade strength will be slightly faster.

Click the Accept button after reading the Subscriber Agreement. This will generate a key and VeriSign will send an e-mail message to the address specified previously.

When the e-mail message from VeriSign arrives, it will have a subject line of "Trial Class 1 VeriSign Digital ID Installation Instructions." Follow the instructions in the e-mail message to install the Digital ID in the browser.

To see the installed Digital ID under Internet Explorer, select Tools ➪ Internet Options ➪ Content, and click the Certificates button under the Certificates section. This should show a dialog box similar to the one shown in Figure 24-12.

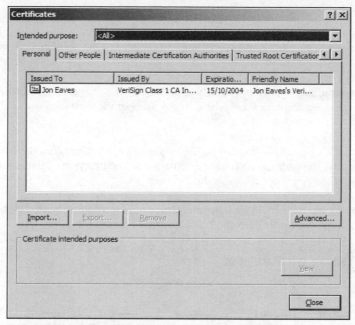

Figure 24-12: Internet Explorer Certificates dialog box

Double-clicking the certificate opens another dialog box that shows detailed information about the certificate. This should resemble the dialog box shown in Figure 24-13.

Figure 24-13: Certificate Information dialog box

How It Works

This process created a private key and a public key, and the public key was signed by a CA, creating a certificate. This certificate can be used to identify the holder of the certificate when accessing Web resources.

Unlike a username and password, the identity is proved by the user actually holding the private key. Our next challenge is determining what to use in our Web application to allow or disallow a user with a certificate.

The following Try It Out example shows you the process of configuring Tomcat to accept client certificates and authenticate the user based on those certificates. The first part of the example provides some helper code to show the client certificate in the browser.

The capability to display the certificate is very useful, as the configuration of the client certificate mapping in Tomcat is somewhat primitive and has a few traps for the unwary.

Try It Out   Testing with Tomcat

Modify the `server.xml` HTTPS connector so that the `clientAuth` value is want:

```
<Connector port="8443"
        maxThreads="150" minSpareThreads="25" maxSpareThreads="75"
        enableLookups="false" disableUploadTimeout="true"
        acceptCount="100" debug="0" scheme="https" secure="true"
        clientAuth="want" sslProtocol="TLS"
        keystoreFile="/path/to/keystore"
        keystorePass="secret" />
```

Create the following `find-certinfo.jsp` file in the `private` directory:

```
<!--
<%@ taglib prefix="c" uri="http://java.sun.com/jsp/jstl/core" %>
<%@ taglib prefix="fn" uri="http://java.sun.com/jsp/jstl/functions" %>
-->
<c:set value="Find Certificate Info" var="title" />
<html>
  <head>
    <title>
      <c:out value="${title}" />
    </title>
  </head>
  <body>
    <h1>
      <c:out value="${title}" />
    </h1>
    <table border=1>
      <c:forEach var="cert"
          items="${requestScope['javax.servlet.request.X509Certificate']}" >
        <c:set var="subject" value="${cert['subjectDN']}" />
        <c:set var="expiry" value="${cert['notAfter']}" />
        <c:set var="quote" value="\"" />
        <tr>
```

```
              <td>SubjectDN</td><td>${fn:replace(subject, quote, '&amp;quot;')}</td>
          </tr>
          <tr>
              <td>Expiry</td><td>${expiry}</td>
          </tr>
      </c:forEach>
    </table>
  </body>
</html>
```

Start Tomcat, and browse to `http://localhost:8080/chapter24/private/find-certinfo.jsp`. This should result in the form-based authentication method as displayed in Figure 24-9. Enter the username and password used previously in the chapter and press login.

This should result in a screen similar to the one shown in Figure 24-14.

The certificate information has been partially processed by the JSP to enable it to be directly copied into the Tomcat configuration file `tomcat-users.xml`. Create a new user in the `tomcat-users.xml` file with a copy of the contents of the table cell starting with the EMAILADDRESS attribute. In this example, this is the first certificate.

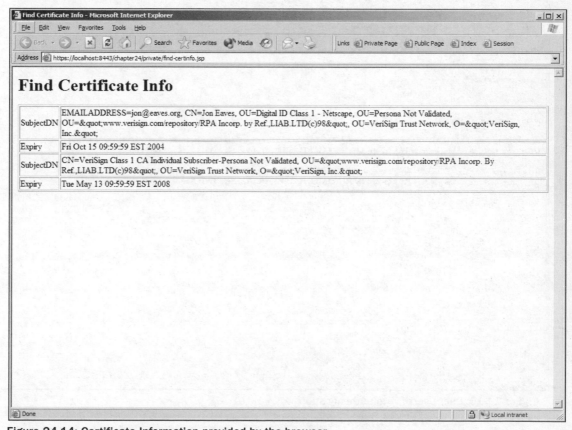

Figure 24-14: Certificate Information provided by the browser

853

This should be copied, creating a user, as follows:

```
<user username="EMAILADDRESS=jon@eaves.org, CN=Jon Eaves, OU=Digital ID Class 1 -
Netscape, OU=Persona Not Validated, OU=&quot;www.verisign.com/repository/RPA
Incorp. by Ref.,LIAB.LTD(c)98&quot;, OU=VeriSign Trust Network, O=&quot;VeriSign,
Inc.&quot;" password="null" roles="chapter24" />
```

The text inside the `username` *attribute must be on a single line in the* `tomcat-users.xml` *file.*

Modify the `login-config` element in `web.xml` to use `CLIENT-CERT` authentication as follows:

```
<login-config>
   <auth-method>CLIENT-CERT</auth-method>
   <realm-name>Private Realm</realm-name>
</login-config>
```

Browse to the URL `http://localhost:8080/chapter24/private/private-page.jsp`. This should display a page similar to the one shown in Figure 24-15.

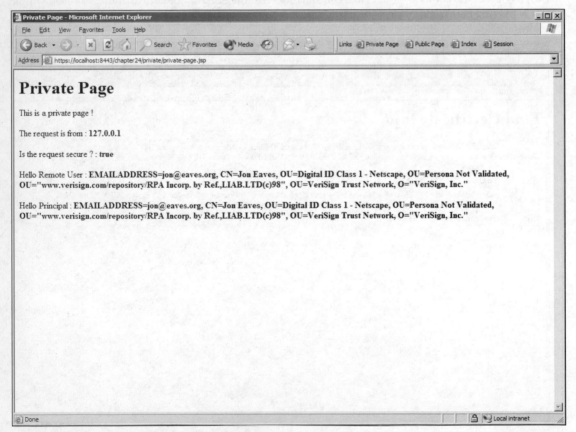

Figure 24-15: Client certificate authentication

How It Works

The configuration of the connector requests the browser to send a certificate if it has one available, and the `find-clientinfo.jsp` page is used to display the contents of the certificate. In a production environment, it would be necessary to have two Web applications, as only one authentication realm may be active at any time. This prevents the need to swap between the FORM and CLIENT-CERT login configurations.

> Note the substitution performed by the client-certificate information JSP. All instances of the double-quote (") are replaced by with the XML-safe equivalent ("). This is required to prevent Tomcat from having difficulties loading the `tomcat-users.xml`. This might not be required depending on the servlet container used.

As with all the other authentication schemes, the programmer is unaware of the type of authentication scheme used. In each case, the JSP uses the remote user to get the information provided by the container.

Authorization

The role of authorization in the Web application is strongly linked with authentication. Authorization generally needs a confirmed identity to perform the activity, but not always. For example, access to a resource might be restricted by time (business hours, Monday to Friday) or location (within the company intranet).

Container

All the examples in the authentication section are examples of container-based declarative security. These provide a restriction based on coarse-grained role-based access to resources. For example, there is no means of declaratively creating a policy that "users in the manager role can access the payroll details for their own staff, but not for any other staff." This functionality is implemented using programmatic authorization.

Programmatic

Programmatic authorization puts the control of authorization implementation in the hands of the developer. This offers the developer a more detailed level of control over the decisions that are possible but with the added burden of developing and testing the code.

The most common forms of programmatic authorization are data-related functionality, where depending on the identity of the user, certain operations are allowed or denied on sets of the data. For example, whereas declarative authorization would deny access to the "view payroll" page, programmatic authorization would allow users to see their own data on that page, and potentially the payroll details for all of the staff.

The second form of authorization is less common, but still relevant in the role of enterprise development. This is authorization based not on data, but on some other factor, such as time or location. Access to certain resources might be limited to business hours, or within a certain network. This can also be coupled with the data-related functionality, creating very complex business rules around access to sensitive resources.

In most cases of Web application development, authentication is managed by the container over a broad range of resources (such as the administration application), while authorization about what data is to be shown is managed by code implemented in the Web application using the identity provided by the container. In the next Try It Out example, you learn how to implement programmatic authorization.

Try It Out   Implementing Programmatic Authorization

Add two new users and a new role to `tomcat-users.xml` as follows:

```
<role rolename="example1" />
<user username="staff1" password="staff1" roles="staff" />
<user username="staff2" password="staff2" roles="staff" />
```

Modify the `web.xml` file to include a new `security-constraint`, a new `filter` configuration, an updated `login-config`, and a new `security-role` as follows:

```
<?xml version="1.0" encoding="ISO-8859-1"?>

<web-app version="2.4" uri="http://java.sun.com/xml/ns/j2ee" >

  <security-constraint>
    <web-resource-collection>
      <web-resource-name>Everything Private</web-resource-name>
      <url-pattern>/private/*</url-pattern>
    </web-resource-collection>
    <http-method>GET</http-method>
    <http-method>POST</http-method>
    <user-data-constraint>
      <transport-guarantee>CONFIDENTIAL</transport-guarantee>
    </user-data-constraint>

    <auth-constraint>
      <role-name>chapter24</role-name>
    </auth-constraint>
  </security-constraint>
```

```
  <security-constraint>
    <web-resource-collection>
      <web-resource-name>Staff Roster</web-resource-name>
      <url-pattern>/roster/*</url-pattern>
    </web-resource-collection>
    <http-method>GET</http-method>
    <http-method>POST</http-method>
    <user-data-constraint>
      <transport-guarantee>CONFIDENTIAL</transport-guarantee>
    </user-data-constraint>

    <auth-constraint>
      <role-name>staff</role-name>
    </auth-constraint>
  </security-constraint>

  <filter>
```

```
      <filter-name>SecurityFilter</filter-name>
      <filter-class>com.wrox.begjsp.ch24.roster.SecurityFilter</filter-class>
   </filter>

   <filter-mapping>
      <filter-name>SecurityFilter</filter-name>
      <url-pattern>/roster/*</url-pattern>
   </filter-mapping>

   <login-config>
      <auth-method>FORM</auth-method>
      <form-login-config>
        <form-login-page>/login.html</form-login-page>
        <form-error-page>/login-error.html</form-error-page>
      </form-login-config>
   </login-config>

   <security-role>
      <role-name>chapter24</role-name>
      <role-name>staff</role-name>
   </security-role>

</web-app>
```

Create a servlet filter, `SecurityFilter`, in `src/com/wrox/begjsp/ch24/roster` with the following:

```java
package com.wrox.begjsp.ch24.roster;

import java.io.IOException;
import java.util.HashMap;
import java.util.Map;

import javax.servlet.Filter;
import javax.servlet.FilterChain;
import javax.servlet.FilterConfig;
import javax.servlet.ServletException;
import javax.servlet.ServletRequest;
import javax.servlet.ServletResponse;
import javax.servlet.http.HttpServletRequest;

public class SecurityFilter implements Filter
{
    private Map _roster = new HashMap();

    public void init(FilterConfig config)
    {
        _roster.put("staff1", "Monday");
        _roster.put("staff2", "Tuesday");
    }

    public void doFilter(ServletRequest request,
                         ServletResponse response,
                         FilterChain chain)
```

```
                throws IOException, ServletException
    {
        if (request instanceof HttpServletRequest)
        {
            HttpServletRequest httpRequest = (HttpServletRequest)request;

            httpRequest.setAttribute("staffRoster", _roster);
            boolean isAdmin = httpRequest.isUserInRole("manager");
            httpRequest.setAttribute("isAdmin", Boolean.valueOf(isAdmin));
        }

        chain.doFilter(request, response);
    }

    public void destroy()
    {
        // do nothing
    }
}
```

Finally, create a new JSP file called `staff-roster.jsp` in a new `roster` subdirectory:

```
<!--
<%@ taglib prefix="c" uri="http://java.sun.com/jsp/jstl/core" %>
-->
<html>
  <head>
    <title>
      <c:out value="${title}" />
    </title>
  </head>
  <body>
    <h1>
      <c:out value="${title}" />
    </h1>

    <c:set var="user" value="${pageContext.request.remoteUser}" />
    <c:set var="workDay" value="${staffRoster[user]}" />

    Welcome  <b>${user}</b> <p/>

    You are rostered to work on <b>${workDay}</b> <p/>

    <a href="../public/kill-session.jsp">Logout</a> <p/>
  </body>
</html>
```

Browse to the URL `http://localhost:8080/roster/staff_roster.jsp`. The form-based authentication will intercept the request and display the form login screen shown in Figure 24-9. Enter the username **staff1** and the password **staff1** into the form and press login.

This will display the screen shown in Figure 24-16.

Browse around to the public page (`http://localhost:8080/chapter24/public/public-page.jsp`) and then back to the roster page. Notice how the same user is still logged in. Press the Logout link and browse to the roster page again.

Again, the form-based authentication interceptor will intervene. This time enter the username as **staff2** and the password as **staff2**. The screen should now look like the one shown in Figure 24-17.

How It Works

This is a very simple example of how J2EE authentication can be used with programmatic authorization. The `HashMap` is used in the `SecurityFilter` to simulate a database access for the same information.

Once the J2EE authentication has been performed, the value of the remote user can be used for any purpose. In this case, it is used to look up user-specific data to be displayed.

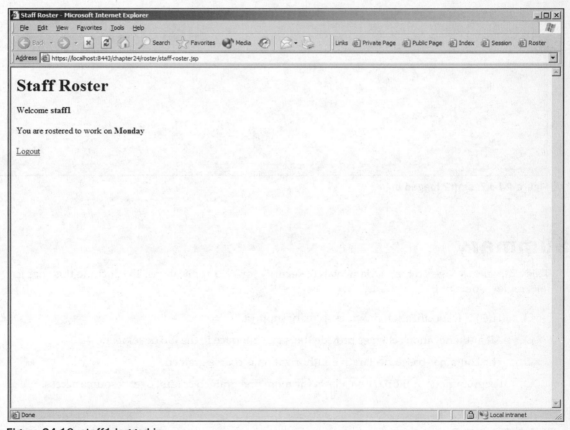

Figure 24-16: staff1 logged in

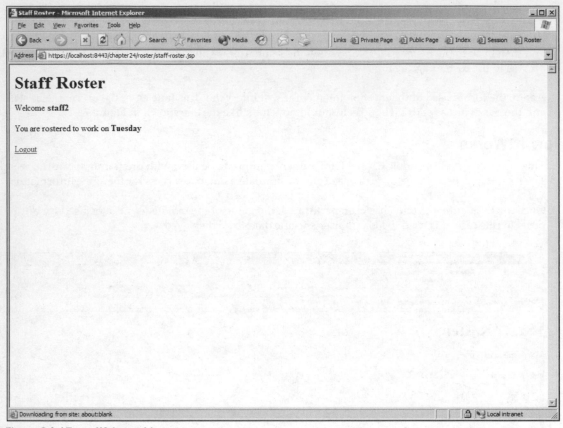

Figure 24-17: staff2 logged in

Summary

This chapter has covered the fundamentals of security for Web applications. To conclude this chapter, let's review some of its key points:

- ❑ The J2EE specification provides security support.
- ❑ All authentication schemes provide the same interface to the JSP developer.
- ❑ The container-based declarative authorization is coarse-grained.
- ❑ Programmatic authorization allows for more fine-grained control over resource access.

Exercises

1. Modify the roster JSP page such that it will let the role of `"manager"` access the page and display all the staff roster information.

2. Extend exercise 1 so that the authorization allows staff to access the roster JSP page during business hours (9:00 A.M. to 6:00 P.M.) and managers at any time.

Performance

Performance is very important for Web applications. Even if your application has a lot of useful functionality and an elegant user interface, your users may still not use it if they have to wait a long time for a Web page to load.

This chapter covers the following issues relating to the performance of Web applications:

❑ The meaning of performance as it applies to a Web application

❑ Measuring the performance of a Web application.

❑ Investigating the reasons behind performance bottlenecks in your Web application

❑ Some common mechanisms to improve performance

Performance tuning is a complex area. For a Web application deployed in an enterprise, many of the factors that affect performance are often outside the application itself. These factors may include the network configuration and hardware platform characteristics, the operating system settings, Java virtual machine parameters, database tuning parameters, and the architecture of the Web application itself.

Naturally, everything that affects performance cannot be covered here. The objective of this chapter is to introduce you to performance measurement and tuning concepts, give you a hands-on feel for some of the tools used for performance measurement, and cover those areas of JSP development and deployment that affect performance.

Performance Concepts

What does performance mean for a Web site? From a user's perspective, the performance of a Web site boils down to how fast (or how slow) the Web pages load. As a Web developer, you need precise ways to quantify the performance of your Web site.

In the following subsections, you will first learn how you can quantify the performance of your Web site, rather than using imprecise terms such as "fast" or "slow." You will then be shown some techniques to obtain this performance measurement. Finally, after you complete performance testing, you will be introduced to ways in which you can analyze causes of poor performance.

What to measure

There are two important properties that you should measure to quantify the performance of your Web site:

❑ Response time

❑ Scalability

The *response time* is the time it takes for one user to perform an operation. For example, in a storefront Web site, after the customer puts items in a shopping cart and clicks the Buy button, the time it takes to process the order and for the checkout screen to appear is the response time for the checkout Web page. Typically, you would test this operation multiple times, and note the *average response time*. Different operations on your Web site (listing items in stock, adding items to a cart, checkout) might have different response time values. You can add these to get the *total transaction time* for the user. In this case, for a "buy item" transaction, you would add the time for listing items, adding items to a cart, and checking out to get the total transaction time. Is this how long a user will have to wait every time while buying items? Not really: The response time varies depending on the load on the Web site.

Scalability, in the context of Web applications, refers to the ability of your Web site to handle multiple users at the same time. Naturally, the response time for your application usually increases as multiple users access your Web site at the same time. To measure scalability, you note the response time as the load on the Web site (increased number of users, users doing complex transactions, and so on) increases. At some point, things just break: Either the response gets unreasonably slow, or users start seeing errors caused by the Web site — refusing connections, database connection unavailability, or a host of other reasons. The number of users that the Web site can support with a reasonable response time is a measure of its scalability.

Another property of your Web site, related to its response time and scalability, is *throughput*. Throughput is the number of transactions that can occur in a given amount of time. The throughput is usually measured in *transactions per second (tps)*.

However, before you start any performance testing, you should be clear about what kind of performance is expected from the Web site, as reflected in the following questions:

❑ How long should a Web transaction take?

❑ How long should a user wait before a page loads?

❑ How many users should the Web site support?

❑ What kind of user traffic are you expecting? Is it *bursty* (meaning does it have periods of low activity and high activity)?

Understanding what kind of Web traffic is expected is important while designing performance test cases.

The user's perspective

The beginning of this section talked about the user's perspective on performance. Often, a factor in this is how the user accesses the Web site. Naturally, a user accessing the Web site over a slow network connection, such as a dial-up modem, will not see the same kind of performance as a user accessing it over a high-speed network, or the local LAN. Some features of your Web site — such as graphics-intensive Web pages, applets embedded inside a Web page, and so on — might even load so slowly on dial-up connections that the user experiences timeouts from the Web browser.

Another issue that affects performance from a user's perspective is *server proximity*. If a server is located in California, a user accessing the Web site from Korea might not see the same performance because of network-related issues, such as multiple network *hops* to reach the server.

It is important to design performance tests that simulate these different kinds of user experiences. Many of the performance monitoring tools listed later in the chapter enable you to do this.

How to measure performance

You can perform several tests to determine the performance characteristics of your Web site under user load. The kinds of tests you can do fall broadly into three categories:

❑ Load testing

❑ Stress testing

❑ Continuous hours of operation testing

The terms *load testing* and *stress testing* are often uses interchangeably. The confusion is caused by the fact that they are done in a somewhat similar manner. In both tests, the system (in this case, the Web application) is subjected to multiple concurrent users. What is different in the two tests is the objective of the tests.

In *load testing*, the Web application is subjected to a "normal" amount of load. You would start with a low number of users accessing the Web application and then increase the number of users incrementally until you reach a "high load" on the application. During this process, the response time is measured as the number of concurrent users increases. At the end of the load test, you have data on how well (or badly) the Web site scales with increased load, and if it can provide a reasonable response time at peak load.

The objective of *stress testing* is simply to break the system. You subject the Web application to an unreasonable amount of load — perhaps 5,000 or 10,000 concurrent users, for instance — and continue increasing the load until something crashes. The kind of errors you would get might result from the Web server refusing connections, the JVM running out of memory or other resources, new database connections failing, or just about anything else. Basically, you are looking for answers to the following:

❑ What kind of load would break the system?

❑ What bugs in the Web application show up in such extreme conditions?

The bugs that you should be concerned about relate to data corruption. For example, in a banking Web site, a crash during stress testing should not leave the bank accounts being modified at that time in an inconsistent state.

You should remember that the load to which the Web application is subjected in the stress test is something out of the ordinary. Therefore, you don't have to, in most cases, go back and improve performance so that it can handle this load. All you need to do is ensure that harmful bugs (data corruption, etc.) do not occur in situations of extreme load. In addition, if possible, you should handle such conditions gracefully on the Web site, such as by displaying an error message asking users to try again later.

Finally, in *continuous hours of operation (CHO)* testing, you would leave your Web application running for a few days and simulate normal user traffic on your Web site. You would then monitor the response time, as well as the system's characteristics. The system's characteristics include memory and CPU usage. Tools such as `top` (on Linux/UNIX) and the Task Manager (on Windows) can be used for this purpose.

CHO tests are useful in detecting subtle problems that are often not detected by other forms of testing. These problems could relate to resources not being released properly, such as memory leaks, database connections, and other connection pool resources not being freed. For instance, an increase in memory usage by the Web server or container over time might be an indication of a memory leak. This kind of testing doesn't strictly fall under the category of performance testing, however, as it is targeted toward detecting problems in the code.

Running these kinds of tests requires automated tools, as it is not feasible (or cost effective!) to get a large number of users to access your Web site manually over extended periods of time. Several such automated test tools are available, and some popular ones are listed in the following table.

Performance Tool	Company	URL	Licensing
JMeter	Apache Software Foundation	`http://jakarta.apache.org/jmeter/`	Open Source, Apache License
Flood	Apache Software Foundation	`http://httpd.apache.org/test/flood/`	Open Source, Apache License
LoadRunner	Mercury Interactive	`www.mercury.com/`	Commercial
Silk Performer	Segue Software	`www.segue.com/`	Commercial
Rational Performance Tester	IBM	`www.306.ibm.com/software/awdtools/tester/performance/index.html`	Commercial
WebLOAD	Radview Software	`www.radview.com/`	Commercial

The first tool listed in the preceding table, JMeter, is covered briefly later in the chapter.

After you have determined the performance characteristics for your Web site for the first time, you can use them as a *baseline* for comparison purposes. When you make changes to the Web application for functionality or performance reasons, you can rerun your tests to see how the performance changes relative to the baseline.

Some of the changes you make to improve performance include changing the way your Web applications work, how they are deployed, or even throwing more system resources at the problem — more hardware, more memory for servers, changing the operating system or network parameters, changing database parameters, and so on.

Before you start making changes for this, you must analyze the reasons for your performance — or the lack of it.

What to do after performance testing

After you complete the initial performance testing and find that your Web application is very slow or cannot handle the expected user load, you might be tempted to rush in with a solution, redo parts that seem slow, throw more hardware at the problem, and so on. Don't!

It is important to analyze the reasons why your application is slow and identify the bottlenecks. Following are some of the steps that you can perform to identify the root causes of your performance problem:

❑ Log your system information, such as the memory and CPU utilization on your server. Using tools such as `top` on UNIX/Linux and the Task Manager on Windows are some of the ways you can do this.

❑ *Instrument* your code to trace the areas of poor application performance. Instrumenting your Web application for performance analysis means adding additional code to your Web application that tracks and records the amount of time it takes to perform certain tasks. Typically, this is in the form of logging statements that output the amount of time taken for operations. For example, you would add such statements around database invocations, calls to remote methods, and so on. In Chapter 14, "JSP Debugging Techniques," you saw how Log4j or the Java Logging API can be used for logging from Web applications.

❑ Use profiling tools to analyze your applications, draw visual representations of the behavior under load, and show *call graphs* with the time taken in each module. The call graph is a diagram that identifies the modules of a system and shows which module calls another. Some popular profiling tools are shown the following table.

Profiling Tool	Company	URL	Licensing
JProbe	Quest Software	www.quest.com/jprobe/index.asp	Commercial
OptimizeIt	Borland	www.borland.com/optimizeit/	Commercial
JProfiler	EJ Technologies	www.ej-technologies.com/products/jprofiler/overview.html	Commercial

The objective of using these profiling tools or instrumenting your Web application code is to identify the performance bottlenecks in your application and to address those specifically.

As mentioned before, these performance bottlenecks can often be caused by external components. For instance, if a database call from your Web application takes a long time, you could explore whether the SQL query can be made more efficient, or use a database stored procedure call, or tune database parameters, and so on.

Measuring Performance Using JMeter

Several tools for performance testing are available—both open source (such as Apache JMeter) as well as popular commercial ones such as LoadRunner and Silk Performer. This section looks at using JMeter for testing a Web application.

Installing JMeter

JMeter can be downloaded from `http://jakarta.apache.org/site/binindex.cgi#jmeter_binaries`. It comes as a zip file (`tar.gz` for Linux/UNIX), and all you need to do is extract it in a directory of your choice. Other than that, JMeter requires JDK version 1.4 or later to run, and your `JAVA_HOME` should be set to the JDK 1.4 install directory.

JMeter concepts

JMeter runs in three modes:

❑   As a standalone GUI application

❑   Non-interactively, through the command line, or using Ant scripts

❑   In a server mode, for distributed testing

The standalone mode is the most common way to use JMeter. To run JMeter in this mode, run the `jmeter.bat` batch file (the `jmeter` shell script for Linux/UNIX) located under `<JMETER_HOME>/bin`. This starts up a Swing-based GUI application, as shown in Figure 25-1.

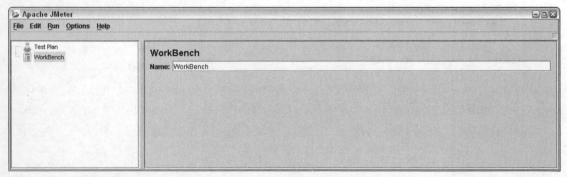

Figure 25-1: JMeter GUI

JMeter can be used to test not only a Web site/Web application, but also a database server, LDAP server, or a Web service. This section focuses on just the Web site testing.

If the machine you are running JMeter from accesses the Web site using a proxy server, you can specify the proxy host/port to the JMeter batch file or shell script using the −H and −P command-line parameters as shown:

```
jmeter -H proxy_host -P proxy_port
```

To start testing, you first have to define a test plan, and then execute it to view the results. You can also save a test plan so that the performance testing can be repeated later. This is a good idea, for typically you would run performance tests, then make changes in the Web application or its deployment, and then rerun the tests to see how performance is affected. As mentioned earlier, the results obtained in the initial runs can be used as a *baseline* for future testing.

Building a test plan in JMeter for Web testing involves the following steps:

1. **Add users for testing:** In this step, you configure the number of users that would be simulated, how many requests are sent by each user, and the delay between requests as they start up. You can also specify if the users support cookies or not.

2. **Configure the Web server properties:** Next, you specify the Web server properties, such as the hostname, port, and so on.

3. **Specify the requests to be sent to the Web server:** Here, you list all the requests sent to the server (GET and POST requests, and file uploads).

4. **Define a listener to store the results of the test:** Finally, you define a listener that stores the results of a test run and presents it visually. A listener is a JMeter component that stores and processes test results. Some examples of listeners are Graph Listener (shows results in a graph) and Mailer Visualizer (sends out an e-mail).

The test plan can be saved and run at a later time. Rerunning the test plan can be done either through the JMeter GUI, or even non-interactively. Some form of performance testing can be included as a part of a build and release procedure to track how code changes affect performance. For running JMeter non-interactively, you can use the command-line options shown here:

```
jmeter -n -t test_plan -l log_file
```

Here, the −n option indicates that JMeter is being run non-interactively, the −t option specifies the test plan to be run, and the −l option indicates the log file to which sample results should be sent.

JMeter can even be run from Ant build scripts. A third-party library that implements Ant support for JMeter can be downloaded from programmerplanet.org/ant-jmeter/. Apache Ant is covered in greater detail in Chapter 26, "Best Practices and Tools."

JMeter also has a lot of other features that enable you to simulate users more realistically, and thus perform better testing:

❑ **Timer:** A timer enables you to introduce delays between user requests. JMeter supports constant timers (a constant delay between each request), constant throughput timers (constant number of requests per minute), as well as random timers that simulate the random real-world traffic to your Web site.

❑ **Logic controller:** Manages the execution flow of the test plan.

❑ **Assertions:** Validates the data returned from the Web server.

❑ **HTTP proxy server:** The proxy server can record the traffic between the Web browser and the server, and this can be played back as performance test cases.

❑ **Distributed load testing:** JMeter can also run in a server mode, controlled by one JMeter client. This enables you to do distributed load testing, especially if you are trying to test the effect of *server proximity* on performance.

Server load testing with JMeter is covered in more detail in *Professional Apache Tomcat 5* by Vivek Chopra, et al. (Wrox Press; ISBN 0764559028).

In the following Try It Out exercise, you develop a performance test plan for one of the Web applications developed earlier in this book. In your test, you will do a load test, and increase the number of users to observe how the application scales.

Try It Out　Developing a Performance Testing Plan

The Web application described in Chapter 18, "Web Frameworks," will be used in this example. The example assumes that the Web application is deployed in Tomcat, and can be accessed at the URL `http://localhost:8080/webwork-skeleton`.

The first thing you need to do is define the number of users for the Web application. In this example, initially ten users are defined. In later tests, you can increase this number.

In the JMeter GUI, right-click the Test Plan node, select the Add option, and select `Thread Group`, as shown in Figure 25-2.

A `Thread Group` corresponds to a group of simulated users. The characteristics of these users can be modeled using the Thread Group parameters, as shown in Figure 25-3. Specify the parameters for the Thread Group as shown in the figure. Set the `Number of Threads` parameter to 10, the `Ramp-Up Period` to 1, and `Loop Count` to forever.

Figure 25-3 shows a test with ten users that run requests at one-second intervals.

You can similarly define other thread groups with 20, 30, 40 users and so on.

Next, specify the Web server properties. Right-click the thread group (10 users) you just created, and select Add ⇨ Sampler ⇨ HTTP Request, as shown in Figure 25-4.

Figure 25-5 shows the HTTP request called `Post to form`, which posts the parameters of user, age, and comments to the form URL specified in the `Path` parameter (`http://localhost:8080/webwork-skeleton/formtest.action`).

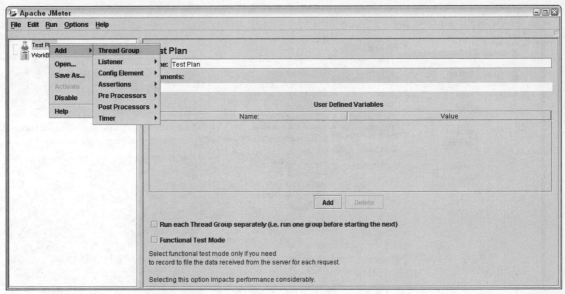

Figure 25-2: Adding a thread group

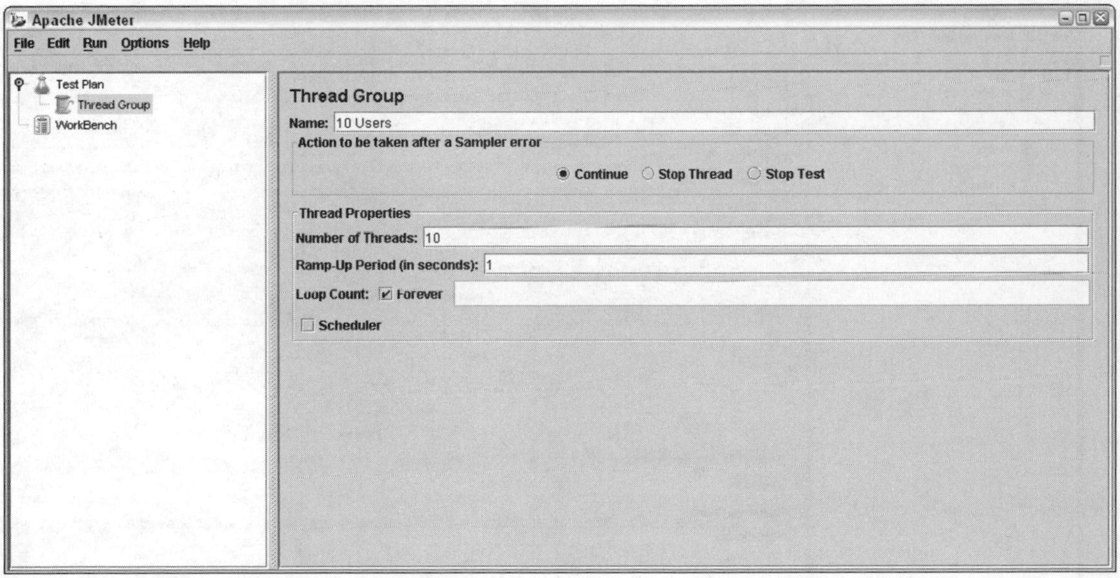

Figure 25-3: Adding ten users

You can see another HTTP request called `Get form` just above the `Post to form` request: This gets the `http://localhost:8080/webwork-skeleton/formtest!default.action` Web form.

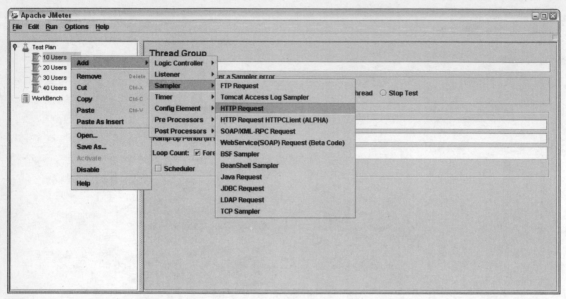

Figure 25-4: Creating an HTTP request

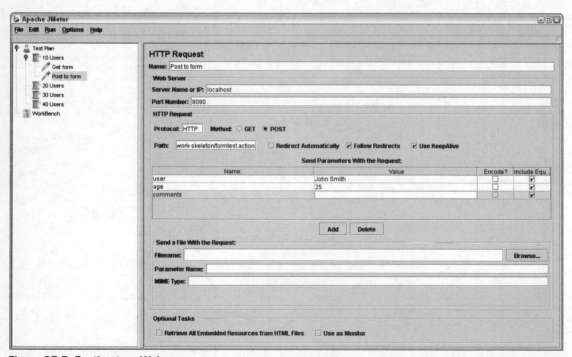

Figure 25-5: Posting to a Web page

The final step before being able to run the tests is to add listeners. In this example, an `Aggregate Report` listener is set up by clicking the Add ⇨ Listener ⇨ Aggregate Report menu options. This listener provides a concise summary of the test data in a tabular form (see Figure 25-6).

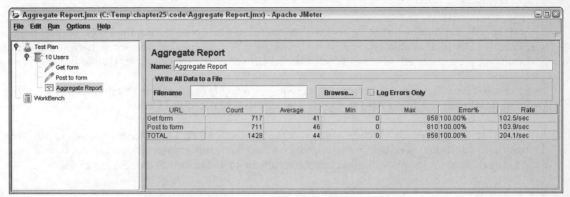

Figure 25-6: Test results in an Aggregate Report listener

To run the test, click Run from the Start menu. Because you earlier configured the tests to run indefinitely (see Figure 25-3), you have to use Run ⇨ Stop to stop it. Figure 25-6 shows the aggregated test results, including the request count, the minimum, the maximum, the average request, the error rate, and the *throughput*.

You can then repeat this test, increasing the number of users and tracking the change in throughput.

How It Works

As you saw in the Try It Out example, the minimal setup required for JMeter to simulate user load on a Web site involves the following:

❑ Configure users

❑ Configure Web server properties

❑ Configure HTTP request properties

❑ Configure listeners

As mentioned earlier, configuring users involves configuring the `Thread Group` element. A `Thread Group` corresponds to a group of simulated users, and has a number of configurable parameters, including the following:

❑ **Number of Threads:** This parameter indicates the number of threads to be started. Each thread simulates a user.

❑ **Ramp-Up Period:** The `Ramp-Up Period` controls the time after which each thread (i.e., user) in the thread group is started. A `Ramp-Up Period` of 0 starts all at once; a `Ramp-Up Period` of 1 starts a user every 1 second until the `Number of Threads` is reached.

❑ **Loop Count:** The Loop Count determines how many times this whole set of users will execute their requests; it defaults to forever.

❑ **Scheduler:** Finally, there is a Scheduler that can be used to start or stop the users at a particular time.

You can specify the parameters to be sent with the request, while configuring the HTTP request properties. The HTTP request enables you to configure Web server attributes such as server name or IP address, port number, protocol, method (GET/POST), and the URL to which user requests should be sent.

This can also be configured as a default for all requests, using HTTP Request Defaults (select your thread group and right-click to select Add ➪ Config Element ➪ HTTP Request Defaults).

After a test is run, the results of the test are processed by the listener. The listener component can store the result, do additional processing if required, visualize the result graphically, and so on. In this case, the Aggregate listener shows a summary of the results in a tabular format (see Figure 25-6).

Performance Tuning Tips

Because performance tuning is a complex topic, it isn't possible to address everything that affects performance in one chapter. This section will first give you a feel for what can affect the performance of a Web application, and then address areas specific to JSP development and deployment.

Broadly, things that affect performance can be addressed at three stages:

❑ Design time

❑ Development time

❑ Deployment time

Decisions made at design time often have the greatest impact on performance. The design includes both the software as well as the system architecture. The software architecture is concerned with issues such as design of software modules, data structures, and so on. The system architecture, on the other hand, would also address issues such as the following:

❑ Is there load balancing to handle a large volume of requests?

❑ Are there clustering/failover capabilities to handle situations when a Web server or any another component of the Web site goes down?

This chapter does not address these kinds of issues. The development and deployment-time issues specific to JSP programming are covered next.

Development-time measures

Following are some JSP coding practices that developers can use to positively affect performance:

❑ Do not create sessions for JSPs if they are not required.

❑ Do not store large objects in your session.

❏ Time out sessions quickly, and invalidate your sessions when you are done with them.

❏ Use the right scope for objects.

❏ Use connection pooling for improving performance.

❏ Cache static data.

❏ Use transfer objects to minimize calls to remote services.

❏ Minimize logging from Web applications, or use simple logging formats.

The following sections examine each of these practices in more detail.

Avoid creating sessions for JSPs if not required

As you learned earlier in the book, HTTP is a stateless protocol. The servlet container, however, provides session support for servlets and JSP pages. This enables you to keep track of users and the state of the application across multiple requests from the Web browser. This session is internally implemented using cookies. If cookies aren't supported, URL rewriting is used.

For example, if you have a JSP page that shows the contents of a shopping cart, having a session enables you to know which user's cart to display.

However, not all JSP pages need to have a session. A JSP page that shows the same information to each user — for example, the stock quote for a company — may not need to know user-specific information.

Using sessions in a JSP page adds overhead to it, and if a session isn't required for a page, it should not be used.

You can avoid creating sessions by adding the following JSP directive at the top of the JSP page:

```
<%@ page session="false"%>
```

Session objects should be small in size

The objects that you store in your session should be as small as possible. Having large objects in your session negatively affects your application's scalability.

For example, even though you might store 500K of Java objects in your session, it adds up if you have multiple concurrent sessions — 0.5GB for 1,000 sessions, 1GB for 2,000, and so on — and that is just the session data!

Time out sessions quickly

For similar scalability reasons, session timeouts should be kept low. You can change this value during the configuration of the container, or even programmatically.

The following lines from the deployment descriptor (web.xml) file show the default setting of session timeouts (30 minutes). You can change it here, or modify it programmatically in your application.

```
<session-config>
    <session-timeout>30</session-timeout>
</session-config>
```

The following code fragment shows how the session timeout can be configured programmatically from within your servlet or JSP page:

```
// Set timeout to 1800 seconds
httpSession.setMaxInactiveInterval(1800);
```

However, a low session timeout value might cause timeout errors for users if they are inactive for a while, or if the Web transaction takes a long time to complete.

Use the right scope for objects

As you know by now, there are four levels of scope: page, request, session, and application.

The following shows a JavaBean declaration in session scope:

```
<jsp:useBean id="currency" class="Currency" scope="session"/>
```

The scope attribute determines the lifetime of the object: A bean declared with session scope will live for the duration of the session; a bean with application scope will be around as long as the Web application remains loaded. A request scoped bean, on the other hand, will be created for every request.

The scope should be used as appropriate. A JavaBean required only for the request should be declared with request scope; otherwise, it will stay around for the entire session, retaining the memory allocated for it.

Use connection pooling for performance

Your Web application should use connection pooling for any kind of remote calls, including calls to databases.

Typical database connection pooling mechanisms, such as Jakarta DBCP (http://jakarta.apache .org/commons/dbcp/), allocate a pool of connections at startup time. A request for a database connection is met from this pool, and connections are returned to it when the database call is over. This avoids the overhead of creating a connection for every new database call.

Cache data

Static data used across JSP calls should be cached for performance. Typically, such caching is useful for commonly accessed database records, results of complex processing, or data retrieved from remote sites.

Use transfer objects

Your Web application often has to access remote applications or processes to get data. This could include databases, LDAP registries, other Web applications, or even another layer of the same Web application. Making several network calls to access data is expensive and should be minimized. A collection of data items should be returned in each call, rather than individual items. For example, if a Web application needs the username, the user's account information, and his or her customizable options, they should be retrieved in one single *user profile* object instead of using multiple calls.

This kind of object that is used to transfer data between layers is called a *data transfer object (DTO),* or sometimes just *transfer object.* Using a DTO is a common design pattern while building enterprise applications. Chapter 27, "Project I: Personalized Portal," illustrates the use of transfer objects.

Minimize logging

Logging is important, as you can log runtime errors, and even cause alerts to be sent in abnormal situations. It can also be used to trace the behavior of Web applications and help debug complex problems. However, excessive logging can be expensive as far as performance is concerned.

Log4j is the most widely used logging framework, even though the JDK 1.4 comes with another logging mechanism called the Java Logging API. Both these frameworks are covered in Chapter 14, "JSP Debugging Techniques." Some of the ways in which you can get the benefits of logging without affecting performance too much are listed here:

❑ **Minimize the amount of information being logged:** Both Log4j and the Java Logging API support multiple logging levels. For example, Log4j has debug, info, warn, error, and fatal levels. The debug and info levels are useful for development environments and can be turned off for production deployments. Using the different logging levels enables you to screen out most of the messages and leave only the critical logging in place. The log level for an application can be configured via a configuration file, or even programmatically.

❑ **Use efficient logging formats:** Both logging mechanisms allow for configurable logging formats. In Log4j, for instance, you can opt for a plain string format, choose from more complex formats with date and time embedded, or even log in an HTML or XML format. However, the more elaborate formats are expensive in terms of performance. Again, these settings can be set (or changed) via a configuration file. This enables you to have a more verbose or easier-to-read log format for development, and have a compact and efficient one for production deployment.

❑ **Add conditional code before logging statements:** If you have logging statements in your code for informational or debug messages, and you turn those logging levels off, those messages will not be logged. However, a method invocation will still occur, with the associated cost of constructing the parameters to the method. To get around this cost, you could add code to check for a particular logging level.

In other words, instead of an unadorned debug message log as shown here

```
logger.debug ("Info:" + infoMessage);
```

you should first determine whether the debug logging level is enabled:

```
if (logger.isDebugEnabled())
{
    logger.debug ("Info:" + infoMessage);
}
```

Deployment-time measures

In the previous section, you learned some of the things that you can do to improve performance while developing your Web applications.

After a Web application is developed, it is deployed on a server. This section covers some of the deployment-time considerations that affect performance. This section covers four measures:

❑ Precompiling your JSP pages

❑ Disabling your container from checking for JSP modifications

❑ Enabling pooling of your custom tags

❑ Using a Web server, such as Apache or IIS, to serve static content

In addition to these performance measures, there are a host of other deployment-time measures related to tuning the parameters of the Application server or the container itself, the Java Virtual Machine (JVM), the database to which the Web application connects, the operating system on which this runs, and so on. These are not covered in this chapter, which examines only those deployment-time considerations that are specific to JSPs.

Precompile JSPs

The first request for a JSP is handled differently from subsequent requests. When a browser requests a JSP page for the first time, the following set of tasks happens behind the scenes:

1. The container translates the JSP to Java code. This Java class is actually a servlet.

2. This servlet is compiled into Java bytecode, and this class file is kept in a file system location specific to the container.

3. The servlet class file is then loaded into memory.

4. The container calls an initialization method for the servlet.

5. Finally, the *service* method of this servlet is called. The service method handles the incoming request and generates the response that is eventually sent back to the user's browser.

For every subsequent call to the JSP page, all of the following steps need to be performed:

1. The container first determines whether the JSP file has changed since the last time it was compiled. This is typically done by comparing the timestamps on the files.

2. If there was a change, the container would, as before, first translate the JSP to corresponding servlet Java code, and then compile it to a class file.

3. If nothing was changed in the JSP file, the container determines whether the servlet class corresponding to the JSP page has been loaded into memory.

4. If the servlet class is not in memory, the container loads and initializes it.

5. Finally, as before, the service method of this servlet is called. The service method handles the incoming request and generates the response that is eventually sent back to the user's browser.

This lifecycle of JSPs is summarized in Figure 25-7.

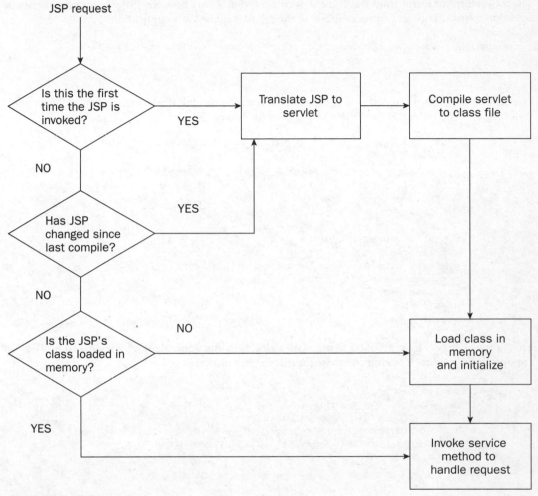

Figure 25-7: JSP lifecycle

The difference between the first invocation (when the JSP is translated and then compiled into bytecode) and subsequent invocations is quite evident; the first time the JSP is called, the response is noticeably slower than all other times.

This overhead can be avoided if the JSP is *precompiled*. Precompiling JSPs involves manually doing the tasks that the container does for first-time invocation of JSPs:

1. Translating JSPs to Java code

2. Compiling the Java code

3. Copying the class files to a location where they can be loaded along with the rest of the Web application classes

The following Ant script from the Tomcat documentation shows how the JSP precompilation can be done for Tomcat. This script precompiles all the JSP files in the Web application:

```
<project name="Webapp Precompilation" default="all" basedir=".">

<target name="jspc">
```

The script first defines the Ant task (jasper2) for converting a JSP file to the equivalent Java code. This task uses Jasper 2, which is the JSP page compiler for Tomcat 5:

```
<taskdef classname="org.apache.jasper.JspC" name="jasper2" >
  <classpath id="jspc.classpath">
    <pathelement location="${java.home}/../lib/tools.jar"/>
    <fileset dir="${tomcat.home}/bin">
      <include name="*.jar"/>
    </fileset>
    <fileset dir="${tomcat.home}/server/lib">
      <include name="*.jar"/>
    </fileset>
    <fileset dir="${tomcat.home}/common/lib">
      <include name="*.jar"/>
    </fileset>
  </classpath>
</taskdef>
```

The jasper2 task is then invoked to translate all JSP files into equivalent Java source code. These classes are output in the directory pointed to by the outputDir attribute:

```
<jasper2
        validateXml="false"
        uriroot="${webapp.path}"
        webXmlFragment="${webapp.path}/WEB-INF/generated_web.xml"
        outputDir="${webapp.path}/WEB-INF/src" />

</target>
```

Finally, the Java code is compiled to class files using Ant's built-in javac task, as shown in the following code. The class files are output in the <web application path>/WEB-INF/classes directory, as specified by the destdir attribute of the javac task:

```
<target name="compile">

  <mkdir dir="${webapp.path}/WEB-INF/classes"/>
  <mkdir dir="${webapp.path}/WEB-INF/lib"/>

  <javac destdir="${webapp.path}/WEB-INF/classes"
         optimize="off"
         debug="on" failonerror="false"
         srcdir="${webapp.path}/WEB-INF/src"
         excludes="**/*.smap">
    <classpath>
      <pathelement location="${webapp.path}/WEB-INF/classes"/>
```

```
            <fileset dir="${webapp.path}/WEB-INF/lib">
              <include name="*.jar"/>
            </fileset>
            <pathelement location="${tomcat.home}/common/classes"/>
            <fileset dir="${tomcat.home}/common/lib">
              <include name="*.jar"/>
            </fileset>
            <pathelement location="${tomcat.home}/shared/classes"/>
            <fileset dir="${tomcat.home}/shared/lib">
              <include name="*.jar"/>
            </fileset>
            <fileset dir="${tomcat.home}/bin">
              <include name="*.jar"/>
            </fileset>
          </classpath>
          <include name="**" />
          <exclude name="tags/**" />
        </javac>

    </target>

    <target name="all" depends="jspc,compile">
    </target>

</project>
```

Ant is covered in more detail in Chapter 26, "Best Practices and Tools."

In the next Try It Out example, you will see for yourself how much overhead is introduced if a JSP page is to be translated and compiled.

Try It Out Precompiling JSP Pages

Tomcat stores the translated servlet code and the compiled class files under the <Tomcat Installation Directory>\work\Catalina\<virtual host name> directory. For the default Tomcat configuration, this would be <Tomcat Installation Directory>\work\Catalina\localhost\<web application name>. Change to this directory and remove all the files under the ch09 Web application.

Now start your browser and access the URL http://localhost:8080/ch09/example1/. Note the delay before the page actually appears in the browser. Now start another browser window, and browse to the same URL; the page loads a lot faster the second time.

> *Remember to clear out your browser's cache before you perform this test, or you might get spurious results.*

JSP modification-time checks

The JSP lifecycle in the preceding section showed how each time there is a request for a JSP, the container first checks to see if it has been modified. This feature is useful for a development environment, as it saves you the overhead of doing a compile and deploy every time you want to try out the effect of changes.

However, in a production environment, this can affect the performance of JSP pages. Often in such environments, this JSP modification-time check is disabled.

The following excerpt is from the global Web application configuration file (`<Tomcat Installation Directory>/conf/web.xml`); it shows how this parameter can be tuned for the Jasper servlet. The Jasper servlet, as mentioned earlier, invokes the JSP page compiler.

The two attributes that control the JSP compilation behavior in Tomcat are `development` and `reloading`. If you don't want the JSP pages to be checked for modification each time there is a request, you should set `development` to `false`.

In the following settings, the `reloading` attribute is also set to `false`. Had `reloading` been `true`, background compiles would have been enabled. The background compile option would cause the container to check and compile JSPs after a period of time. Another configurable parameter, called `checkInterval`, determines how frequently the compiles are triggered.

In the current Tomcat default setting, both `development` and `reloading` are set to `true`, and `checkInterval` is set to `300 seconds`.

```
<servlet>
    <servlet-name>jsp</servlet-name>
    <servlet-class>org.apache.jasper.servlet.JspServlet</servlet-class>
    <init-param>
        <param-name>fork</param-name>
        <param-value>false</param-value>
    </init-param>

    <init-param>
        <param-name>development</param-name>
        <param-value>false</param-value>
    </init-param>

    <init-param>
        <param-name>reloading</param-name>
        <param-value>false</param-value>
    </init-param>

    ...

</servlet>
```

The two techniques described previously are among the reasons why JSP development is so popular. The modification-time check feature enables you to use JSPs as a scripting tool in development environments. In these environments, you can make changes to JSP files and immediately see the effect.

When you are finally ready for production, you can simply turn this off and precompile the code for better performance.

Custom tag pooling

Throughout this book, you have been taught that good JSP design means keeping Java code out of JSPs, and that using a tag library (JSTL or custom) makes for more maintainable code.

A clean and maintainable design does not come without some costs, however, and excessive use of customs tags affects performance. When you are facing the trade-off between a maintainable design and squeezing out a little bit more performance, a maintainable design should be chosen — it pays off in the long run in terms of programmer productivity.

Jasper (the JSP-to-Java translator for Tomcat) addresses the issue of tag performance to some extent by supporting custom tag pooling. The Java objects instantiated for the custom tags are now pooled and reused, which boosts the performance of JSP pages.

The following is an excerpt from the global Web application deployment descriptor (TOMCAT_HOME\conf\web.xml), which has defaults for all the Web applications. The settings below are for the JspServlet that handles all requests for JSP pages. The enablePooling attribute specifies whether the pooling of Tag library classes is to be enabled (true) or not (false). This attribute is enabled by default, so you don't have to do anything here. In case you are using another application server, you need to check its documentation to see if this feature is supported, and if so, how to enable it.

```
<servlet>
    <servlet-name>jsp</servlet-name>
    <servlet-class>org.apache.jasper.servlet.JspServlet</servlet-class>
    <init-param>
        <param-name>fork</param-name>
        <param-value>false</param-value>
    </init-param>

    <init-param>
        <param-name>enablePooling</param-name>
        <param-value>true</param-value>
    </init-param>
    ...
</servlet>
```

Using Web servers for static content

Web sites contain both static and dynamic content. The static content includes HTML pages, images, and style sheets (.css files), while the dynamic content includes JSPs and servlets.

All the examples in this book have been shown running within a servlet container (Tomcat). While this is fine for development time, for production deployments, often a Web server is used in addition to a servlet container or a J2EE application server. In such deployments, the Web server — for example, Apache or IIS — serves up the static content to Web browsers. When there is a request for a JSP or a servlet, a special configuration at the Web server end tells it how to send the request to the servlet container. The servlet container then processes the request and returns the result to the Web server, and finally to the user's browser.

Figure 25-8 shows a typical deployment.

The primary reason for using a Web server in addition to a servlet container is performance. Servlet containers and J2EE application servers are typically written in Java and do not perform as well as native Web servers do.

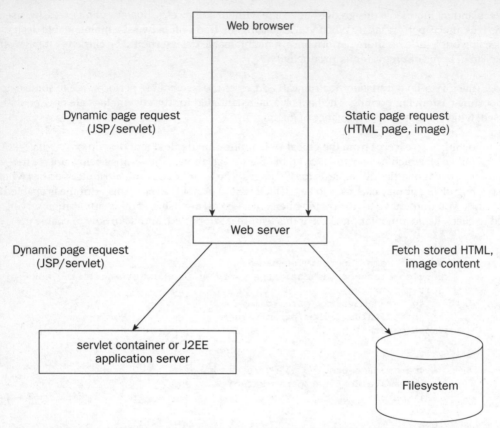

Figure 25-8: Using a Web server in addition to a servlet container or J2EE application server

Some other reasons for using a Web server include the following:

❑ **Stability:** Such a configuration is more stable than a standalone one involving just a servlet container; Web servers such as Apache are typically a lot more robust. If the servlet container crashes, for instance, the rest of the Web site that contains static content is still available to users.

❑ **Legacy support:** Web sites sometimes have legacy modules implement in other languages such as Perl, Python, and so on. Using a Web server front end such as Apache enables you to continue using their functionality.

The steps for configuring a Web server such as Apache or IIS to work as a front end to Tomcat are beyond the scope of this book. For more information, see Vivek Chopra's *Professional Apache Tomcat 5* (Wrox, 2004) or visit the Tomcat Web site at `http://jakarta.apache.org/tomcat/`.

Summary

Performance tuning a Web application requires knowledge of not just Web development concepts, but also databases, network configurations, and operating system tuning, among other things. This chapter gave you a feel for some of these issues, focusing on those aspects of JSP development that affect performance.

To summarize the important points of this chapter:

❑ You should decide what you are going to measure, and develop a performance test plan before you start. The test plan typically includes the desired performance (e.g., how many concurrent users to support, expected response time, expected throughput), as well as the testing methodology (e.g., load test, stress test) and their details.

❑ The test plan should also include the user transactions being simulated, the load being tested, and the environment for testing.

❑ You should determine a baseline measure the first time you test, and use that to compare against after making changes.

❑ Tools such as JMeter, LoadRunner, and Silk Performer help automate testing.

❑ After performance testing is completed, analyzing the test results helps determine the root causes of poor performance. This should be done before attempting any changes for performance.

❑ Some JSP-related measures for improving performance include precompiling JSP pages, not using sessions when not required, and invalidating sessions sooner. Often, however, the cause of poor performance might lie outside your Web application, related to such issues as database access or deployment.

The next chapter covers programming methodologies, best practices, and developer tools.

Best Practices and Tools

Building reliable software is not easy. In the preceding chapters, you learned several techniques for developing Web applications, and best practices while using them. These techniques are important, but even more important is learning how to develop software well. This skill is applicable to all programming domains, whether you are developing Web applications or writing operating system code.

This chapter covers a range of topics, from development methodologies to tools used for Web development and best practices. It starts off by briefly explaining some of the popular development methodologies that are relevant today, and provides a tutorial introduction to tools that should be in every Web developer's tool box. Finally, the chapter summarizes the best practices that were used throughout the book. This is the last chapter prior to the project chapters, so it covers what you need to know, in addition to JSP programming, to be a professional Web developer.

This chapter contains the following important topics:

❑ Popular development methodologies

❑ A range of tools for development, version control, building and deployment, testing, and performance metrics for Web applications

❑ How to work with the CVS version control system

❑ How to write an Ant script to build and deploy Web applications

❑ How to use JUnit and HttpUnit for unit and regression testing

❑ The importance of coding standards and conventions, and some tools that can help enforce these standards

❑ Best practices that relate to Web programming in general, and JSP development in particular

As you can see, that's a long list of tools and techniques, not all of which can be covered in detail in a single chapter. This chapter provides a brief tutorial-style introduction to these tools and techniques, and provides references (i.e., Web sites, books) where further information can be found.

Development Methodologies

A development methodology refers to way in which the software development process is carried out. Several development methodologies aim to help you develop reliable software, and sometimes they differ in their approach to software development.

This chapter doesn't advocate any one particular methodology, and besides, these methodologies are often set by company policy. What is important is that you follow a consistent development approach that is suitable for your application domain.

Although several methodologies exist, they broadly fall under two categories:

❑ Waterfall methodologies

❑ Iterative methodologies

Waterfall and iterative methodologies

Many of the design methodologies in use in the past few decades were variations of the *waterfall methodology*. This design methodology borrows from traditional engineering disciplines in its approach to developing software, with distinct stages:

❑ *Define* the requirement.

❑ *Design* the software components.

❑ *Code* the software.

❑ *Test* the software.

❑ *Implement* the solution for the customer. This stage would also include training and documentation.

These methodologies are called waterfall methodologies because there is no moving backward in the process. They are also characterized by a structured approach to developing software, with a defined set of activities and deliverables from each stage. For example, the deliverable from the requirements definition stage is the requirements document, from the design stage it is the design document, and so on.

As opposed to this, the *iterative methodologies* have multiple iterations over the design ➪ code ➪ test stages of the project, often with customer feedback, until the final solution is ready for implementation.

In recent years, a new set of iterative methodologies, called *agile methodologies,* has become very popular. Another term for these is *adaptive methodologies,* as opposed to traditional waterfall methodologies, which are termed *predictive methodologies*. These recent methodologies are called adaptive because they can adapt to a changing set of requirements. Yet another term for agile methodologies is *lightweight methodologies*, as traditional methodologies have a larger amount of procedure and documentation requirements.

Some of the agile methodologies include the following:

- ❏ Extreme programming
- ❏ Test-driven development
- ❏ Crystal methodologies
- ❏ Feature-driven development

These methodologies claim that traditional, structured, and waterfall methodologies have inherent risks, such as the following:

- ❏ Requirements are often not defined properly.
- ❏ Requirements change.
- ❏ Late integration of software exposes incompatibilities when the modules have already been written.
- ❏ Design flaws are sometimes not detected until the testing phase, by which time all the code is already written.

These methodologies all deal with code in small "bite-size" portions and place emphasis on continuous integration and testing of the code, and continuous *refactoring*.

> **Refactoring is a term that you'll see a lot while reading about agile methodologies — it refers to not only rewriting code, but also to making improvements on the design of a software module. Martin Fowler, a renowned proponent of these methodologies, defines it as follows:**
>
> *"Refactoring is a disciplined technique for restructuring an existing body of code, altering its internal structure without changing its external behavior. Its heart is a series of small behavior-preserving transformations. Each transformation (called a "refactoring") does little, but a sequence of transformations can produce a significant restructuring. Because each refactoring is small, it's less likely to go wrong. The system is also kept fully working after each small refactoring, reducing the chances that a system can get seriously broken during the restructuring."*
>
> **You can get more information on refactoring from the `refactoring.com` Web site.**

You can get additional information on agile development methodologies from the following Web sites:

- ❏ **Extreme programming Web sites:** `xprogramming.com` and `extremeprogramming.org`
- ❏ **Crystal methodologies:** `http://alistair.cockburn.us/crystal/crystal.html`
- ❏ **Feature-driven development:** `featuredrivendevelopment.com`
- ❏ **Finally, the principles of agile software development:** The Agile Manifesto at `agilemanifesto.org/principles.html`

Rational Unified Process

Rational Unified Process (RUP) is a software methodology created by the Rational Corporation (now IBM). It adheres to the following broad guidelines:

❑ Develop software iteratively.

❑ Determine management requirements. RUP defines how design decisions and functionality should be documented.

❑ Use component-based architecture.

❑ Visually model software. RUP recommends using Unified Modeling Language (UML) to model and document the software design.

❑ Verify software quality.

❑ Control changes to software, and track and monitor changes.

Even though RUP advocates an iterative approach to software development, it has a much more formally defined process than many of the agile methodologies.

Extreme Programming

Extreme Programming (XP) is the most widely known agile methodology. It defines a set of practices (described later in this section) and emphasizes testing as the foundation of development and continuous integration and build throughout the development cycle. XP has programmers writing test code along with production code, instead of having a separate group of people writing tests.

XP practices are grouped around the tasks of planning, designing, coding, and testing. Some of these are covered in the following list. A more complete list of rules and practices and additional information can be found at `extremeprogramming.org/rules.html`.

Planning practices:

❑ Write *user stories*. User stories are similar to use cases, and are written by the customer. They often drive the *acceptance testing* of the product. Acceptance testing, and other forms of testing, are described later in the chapter in the "Testing tools" section.

❑ Make frequent releases of small pieces of functionality.

❑ Divide the project into iterations.

Designing practices:

❑ The design should be simple.

❑ Use a consistent and easy-to-understand convention for naming classes and methods.

❑ Involve the entire project team in the design.

❑ Add extra functionality later.

❑ Refactor often.

❑ Run acceptance tests often and publish the results.

Coding practices:

- ❑ The customer should always be available to the development team.
- ❑ Code must be written to agreed standards.
- ❑ The unit test code must be written before production code.
- ❑ All production code should be written by teams of two programmers.
- ❑ Only one programming pair integrates code at a time.
- ❑ Integration should be done often.
- ❑ Code ownership should be collective.
- ❑ Optimizations should be left until the end.

Testing practices:

- ❑ All code must have unit tests.
- ❑ All code must pass all unit tests before release.
- ❑ When a bug is found, a new unit test must be created.
- ❑ Acceptance tests are run often and results are published.

Two major proponents of XP are Kent Beck and Ward Cunningham. Kent has also been involved with a related methodology called test-driven development.

Test-driven development

Test-driven development (TDD) proposes a model of development centered on writing test cases for the code. The process involves the following steps for incremental amounts of code:

1. Write the test before writing the code.
2. Write the code to satisfy the test.
3. Run tests to check the code.
4. Make changes in the code until the test succeeds.
5. Refactor the code to remove duplicates.
6. Repeat for the next piece of code you have to write.

The chief proponent of test-driven development (TDD), Kent Beck, is also one the authors of the *JUnit* testing framework. This is not a coincidence, as JUnit and similar frameworks (collectively called *xUnit* testing frameworks) are at the core of test-driven development. Two of these frameworks — JUnit and *HttpUnit* — are covered later in the chapter.

TDD often involves writing more test code than production code. In addition, after your entire software is complete, you still have to do more testing; the test code is usually made up of *functional* and *regression* tests. You still need to test for performance and usability of the complete software.

Feature-driven development

Feature-driven development (FDD) defines a project as a list of features and functions, and plans development based on these features. FDD believes in short iterations of development, each of about two weeks duration.

FDD defines five processes; the first three are done at the beginning of the project, and the last two within each of the iterations. Each of these processes is broken down into tasks, with verification criteria. These processes are as follows:

1. Develop an overall model of the system.
2. Build a list of features.
3. Plan by feature.
4. Design by feature.
5. Build by feature.

Development Tools

Tools are important to all these development methodologies. Tools help programmers do their job in a predictable way, and help minimize the risks in software development. These tools can be broadly divided into the following categories:

❑ Tools that help in developing software — these include editors, integrated development environments (IDEs), and build environments.

❑ Tools that keep track of different versions of the software.

❑ Tools that help validate the software: These include frameworks that help in unit testing, regression testing, performance testing and profiling, as well as mechanisms to output log information.

This section looks at an assortment of tools that are extremely useful for software developers in general, and Web programmers in particular.

Version-control tools

Version-control tools keep track of different versions of the software and enable teams of programmers to work together without the risk of overwriting someone else's code. The most popular version-control tools in use are the open-source Concurrent Versions System (CVS) as well as commercial products such as Rational Clearcase (now IBM) and Microsoft's Visual SourceSafe. CVS is covered is some detail later in this chapter.

Build tools

Build tools not only compile the source code, but can also build distributable versions of the software. The most commonly used build tool for Java and Web projects is Apache Ant. Ant is covered later in the chapter. Build tools can be automatically invoked from within an IDE such as Eclipse, JBuilder, Netbeans, or IntelliJ, or from the command line.

Testing tools

Testing is a broad area and includes, among others, the following aspects:

❑ **Unit testing:** Testing of individual units of the program, often with knowledge of the internal functioning of the program (i.e., *white box* testing)

❑ **Regression testing:** Testing carried out to ensure that the new code doesn't break earlier code

❑ **Acceptance testing:** Testing that covers anything of value to the customer

❑ **Functional testing:** Testing of specific functionality in the program

❑ **System testing:** Testing of the entire system as a whole

❑ **Performance and load testing:** Testing the performance of the software and its behavior under a large user load

Some of these areas require custom test plans and approaches, but the testing areas for which you can find numerous tools to automate the process are unit, regression, and performance testing.

The xUnit set of testing frameworks (JUnit, HttpUnit, NUnit, Cactus, etc.) are commonly used for unit and regression testing, especially by practitioners of agile development methodologies. JUnit and HttpUnit are covered later in the chapter.

Performance and load testing tools include open-source tools such as jMeter (covered in Chapter 25, "Performance"), as well as commercial tools such as LoadRunner.

Logging tools

Adding log statements to your Web applications is a common way to debug them, or to trace the behavior of a long-running Web application. However, adding such statements to your code affects its performance and increases the code size. Not only that, turning logging on or off often requires you to change the Web application code.

Logging frameworks and APIs such as Log4j and the Java Logging API (standard in J2SE 1.4) address both these issues—they allow for a standard, configurable way to add log statements to your code, and can be turned on or off without requiring code modification. Log4j is the older of the two, and a widely used mechanism for logging. Both these logging mechanisms are covered in Chapter 14, "JSP Debugging Techniques."

Tools for enforcing coding standards

Coding conventions are important for improving the readability of code, especially because the maintainers of the code are often not the developers. Well-designed code conventions can also prevent common programming mistakes at development time.

The most well-known coding convention for Java programming is that defined by Sun (`http://java .sun.com/docs/codeconv/html/CodeConvTOC.doc.html`). Coding conventions are often the subject of debates between programmers, but having and following a consistent convention is often more important than which one you follow.

Two open-source tools that can ease the task of following coding conventions are Jalopy and Checkstyle.

Jalopy (`http://jalopy.sourceforge.net`) is a code formatter that can convert code to a user-specified formatting style. Checkstyle (`http://checkstyle.sourceforge.net`) is an even more comprehensive tool; in addition to code style issues, it can also catch incorrect use of Javadoc comments, naming conventions, and common coding problems.

The following sections cover some of these tools — Ant, CVS, JUnit, and HttpUnit — in more detail.

Apache Ant

Ant was designed to be a tool to build Java code, but it has become a lot more than that. One reason for its popularity is the capability it provides for developers to extend Ant via custom tasks. For example, Tomcat has custom Ant tasks that enable you to deploy and undeploy Web applications from within your Ant build script. This means that not only can you build the Web application using the Ant build script, you can also go a step further by installing, removing, or reloading the application while running Tomcat.

This section provides a brief introduction to the features of Ant, including the following:

❑ A tutorial introduction to Ant

❑ A sample Web application and its associated Ant build script, which is used to compile the application and get it ready for deployment to a Tomcat instance

❑ References to additional information on Ant

Installing Ant

Apache Ant can be downloaded from `http://ant.apache.org`. This chapter uses the latest release available at the time of writing (Ant 1.6.1).

Installing Ant is simple:

1. Download Ant from `http://ant.apache.org/bindownload.cgi` and unzip it in a directory of choice. For the remainder of the chapter, $ANT_HOME will be used as the environment variable that points to the installation directory of Ant.

2. Add $ANT_HOME/bin to your system PATH.

Ant often is used to do additional tasks, other than building Java code. Typically, this requires copying JAR files for these custom tasks into $ANT_HOME/lib.

For example, when Ant is to be used to manage Web applications, you need to copy the `catalina-ant`
`.jar` file that contains Tomcat's Ant tasks from the `<Tomcat Installation Directory>/server/`
`lib` directory to `$ANT_HOME/lib`.

Ant concepts

As a developer, you might have used other tools to build code (`make`, for instance). So why is another
build tool required?

Ant is built around the following central ideas:

❑　Implement the build tool in Java, and use XML to store the build information. This results in a
platform-independent build tool.

❑　Allow for extensibility of the tool. Developers can extend Ant by writing Java classes, and thus,
develop custom tasks. An example of this kind of integration is the capability to run JUnit test
cases from Ant build scripts, using the optional `<junit>` task.

Ant uses an XML file to store build information, and this file contains the list of tasks to be performed.
The general structure of an Ant build file is shown in Figure 26-1.

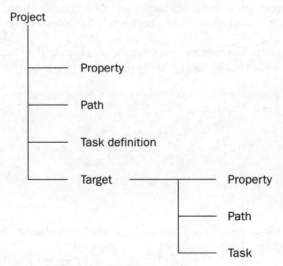

Figure 26-1: Ant build file structure

A *project* consists of a number of *properties*, *targets*, *paths*, and *task definitions*. Properties at the project level
are name-value pairs that are available throughout the project and to each target.

A target consists of a series of tasks. A target can define its own set of properties, which override the
global project properties. A target can depend on other targets, which means that all targets on which it
depends will execute first, before running the tasks associated with it. Ant comes with several built-in
tasks that can be called. Some of the built-in tasks include creating directories, copying files, compiling
Java source files, and so on.

You can also define path elements at both the project level and target level. A path is used to include or exclude certain files and directories. For example, you can construct a path element to contain the directories/JAR files that comprise the classpath.

Consider the following simple Ant file (`mybuild.xml`). This build file creates a directory and then copies a file to that directory.

First, the `<project>` element must be specified:

```
<project name="MyAntProject" basedir="." default="copyfile">
```

The `name` attribute in the `<project>` element is set to the name of the project (`MyAntProject`, in this case). The `basedir` attribute indicates the root directory, which will be used as a reference for all the tasks present in this project. The `default` attribute indicates the target that will be executed by default if none is specified while running Ant.

Next, the properties for the project are defined:

```
<property name="dir.name" value="${basedir}/mydir"/>
<property name="file.name" value="file1.txt"/>
```

Here, two global properties are defined: `dir.name` and `file.name`. The `dir.name` property specifies the name of the directory to be created, and `file.name` is the file to be copied.

After this, the targets to be performed are specified. In this project, these include creating a directory (`mydir`) and copying the file (`file1.txt`) into the newly created directory:

```
<target name="makedirectory" description="Create directory mydir">
  <mkdir dir="${dir.name}"/>
</target>

<target name="copyfile" depends="makedirectory" description="Copy files">
  <copy file="${file.name}" todir="${dir.name}"/>
</target>

</project>
```

In these two targets, `makedirectory` and `copyfile`, note that the target `copyfile` is made dependent on `makedirectory`. So even if you specify the `copyfile` target, Ant will make sure that all the dependencies are run first, and `makedirectory` will be executed irrespective of the situation.

The target `makediretory` creates the directory. Note how the directory name is referenced via the `${dir.name}` property. The built-in tasks `<mkdir>` and `<copy>` are used to perform the functions of making a directory and copying the file. The syntax of the Ant command is as follows:

```
ant -buildfile <filename> <target-name>
```

If the `buildfile` option is not used, Ant will look for a file named `build.xml` file in the directory from which the Ant command was issued. If the target name is not specified, Ant will look for the default target to execute as specified by the `default` attribute of the root `<project>` element.

The following code shows the Ant command being run with the `mybuild.xml` build file:

```
$ ant -buildfile mybuild.xml

Buildfile: mybuild.xml

makedirectory:
    [mkdir] Created dir: /home/tomcat/ch26/mydir

copyfile:
    [copy] Copying 1 file to /home/tomcat/ch26/mydir

BUILD SUCCESSFUL
Total time: 1 second
```

Ant tasks

Ant includes a number of predefined tasks for performing operations such as copying files; creating directories, zip files, and JAR files; compiling Java code; and interacting with CVS repositories. Ant's core tasks are described listed in the following table.

Task Name	Description
ant	Run Ant on a build file. This task can be used to build subprojects.
antcall	Call another target within the same build file.
antstructure	Generate a Document Type Definition (DTD) for Ant build files.
apply	Execute a system command. This task has an optional os parameter that specifies the operating system on which the command should be run.
available	Set a property if a resource (file, directory, class, JVM system resource) is available at runtime.
basename	Determine the basename of a specified file. Also see dirname.
buildnumber	Used to track build numbers.
bunzip2	Unzip a file using the BZip2 algorithm.
bzip2	Compress a file using the BZip2 algorithm.
checksum	Generate a checksum for a file.
chmod	Change permissions of file(s).
concat	Concatenate a file or series of files to a file or console.
condition	Set a property if a condition is true.
copy	Copy a file or set of files to new location.
cvs	Handle CVS modules.

Table continued on following page

Task Name	Description
cvschangelog	Generate a CVS Changelog in XML format.
cvspass	Add entries to the CVS .cvspass file (same effect as doing a cvs login).
cvstagdiff	Generate a diff between two CVS tags (or dates).
delete	Delete a file, a set of files, or a directory.
dependset	Manage arbitrary dependencies between files.
dirname	Determine the directory path of a specified file.
ear	An extension of the jar task for handling Enterprise ARchive (EAR) files.
echo	Echo a message to a logger or a listener (the default is to echo to the console).
exec	Execute an OS-specific system command.
fail	Exit the current Ant build.
filter	Set up a token filter. These filters are used by file copying tasks.
fixcrlf	Adjust a text file for local OS conventions.
genkey	Generate a key in a keystore.
get	Get a file from a URL.
gunzip	Uncompress a file using the Gzip protocol.
gzip	Compress a file using the Gzip protocol.
input	Prompt for input from the user.
jar	Create a JAR file.
java	Execute a Java class within the same virtual machine.
javac	Compile a Java source tree.
javadoc	Run javadoc to create project documentation.
loadfile	Load a text file into a property.
loadproperties	Load Ant properties from a file.
mail	Send e-mail.
manifest	Create a manifest file (used in JAR files).
mkdir	Create a directory.
move	Move a file, a set of files, or a directory to a new location.
parallel	Execute a set of tasks in parallel. Each task executes in its own thread.

Task Name	Description
patch	Apply a diff file patch to the original file.
pathconvert	Used for converting representations of a path from one form to another.
property	Set a property.
record	Listener to the current build process that records the output to a file.
replace	Replace a string with another string in a text file.
rmic	Runs the rmic compiler.
sequential	Specify a set of tasks to be run in sequence. Typically used for grouping inside a nested parallel task.
signjar	Sign a JAR or ZIP file using the signjar command.
sleep	"Sleep" for a specified amount of time.
sql	Execute a SQL statement via JDBC.
style	Process a set of documents using XSLT.
tar	Create a TAR archive.
taskdef	Add a task definition for new (optional) tasks.
tempfile	Set a property to the name of a temporary file.
touch	Change the modification time of a file.
tstamp	Set the timestamp-related properties in the build file.
typedef	Specify a new type definition for the project.
unjar/untar/unwar/unzip	Extract a JAR/TAR/WAR or ZIP file.
uptodate	Set a property if a target file (or set of files) is more current than a source file (or set of files).
waitfor	Block until a certain condition is true. Often used in conjunction with the parallel task.
war	An extension of the JAR task for handling WAR files
xmlproperty	Load properties from an XML file.
xslt	Process a set of documents using XML Stylesheet Transforms (XSLT).
zip	Create a ZIP file.

In addition to these core tasks, Ant has a number of optional tasks. More details on these core and optional tasks can be found in the Ant manual at http://ant.apache.org/manual/index.html.

Try It Out   Using Ant

This section demonstrates how to build a sample Web application with Ant. The steps include compiling the files and creating the appropriate directory structure for the WAR file to get the application ready for deployment.

Let's start with a sample development-time directory structure for a Web application project, as shown in Figure 26-2.

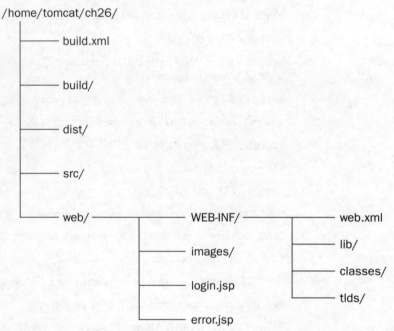

Figure 26-2: Sample development-time directory structure for a Web application

This directory structure consists of the following:

❑   The main build file (build.xml).

❑   A directory (src) containing all the Java source files of the Web application (for example, all the servlet classes).

❑   A directory (web) containing the HTML and JSP files. In addition, it contains any other resource directories — for example, images. It also contains the WEB-INF directory with the deployment descriptor (web.xml). The WEB-INF directory also has a lib directory that contains any third-party JAR files.

❑   A directory (build) in which the compiled Java classes would be built and the expanded WAR structure created. This directory is to be created by the build script.

❑   And finally, a directory (dist) in which the WAR file is generated from the build directory. This directory is also created by the build script.

The `build.xml` build file is shown here—you can create this in any editor of your choice. The default target is the `compile` target.

```
<!-- Ant build file for Sample Web Application -->
<project name="myWebapp" default="compile" basedir=".">
```

The next section shows how the global properties that are used throughout the build file are initialized. Note that you might have to change some of these properties to suit your environment. For example, the `catalina.home` property should point to the root directory of your Tomcat installation.

```
<property name="catalina.home"
                              value="/usr/tomcat/jakarta-tomcat-5.0.15"/>
<property name="app.name"     value="myWebapp"/>
<property name="app.path"     value="/${app.name}"/>
<property name="src.home"     value="${basedir}/src"/>
<property name="web.home"     value="${basedir}/web"/>
<property name="docs.home"    value="${basedir}/docs"/>
<property name="build.home"   value="${basedir}/build"/>
<property name="dist.home"    value="${basedir}/dist"/>
<property name="war.file"     value="${dist.home}/${app.name}.war"/>
```

In this build file, the properties are included in the file itself for the sake of simplicity. A good programming practice is to move them to a separate properties file that contains the name-value property pairs. This enables you to use the same build script for different deployment environments. The property file can then be specified via a command-line option:

```
ant -buildfile <filename> <target-name> -propertyfile <propertyfilename>
```

The `clean` target deletes the `build` and `dist` directories and all subdirectories within them. This target is useful if you want to clean all the files generated by a build.

```
<!-- ====== Clean Target ====== -->
  <target name="clean"
          description="Deletes the build and dist directories">
    <delete dir="${build.home}"/>
    <delete dir="${dist.home}"/>
  </target>
```

The `prepare` target creates the expanded WAR directory structure and copies the static Web files from `web` and its subdirectories:

```
<!-- ====== Prepare Target ====== -->

  <target name="prepare">
    <mkdir  dir="${build.home}"/>
    <mkdir  dir="${build.home}/images"/>
    <mkdir  dir="${build.home}/WEB-INF"/>
    <mkdir  dir="${build.home}/WEB-INF/classes"/>
```

```
      <!-- Copy static content of this web application -->
      <copy todir="${build.home}">
        <fileset dir="${web.home}"/>
      </copy>

  </target>
```

The `compile` target compiles all the Java source files present in the `src` directory. The destination directory for the class files is `./build/WEB-INF/classes`:

```
<!-- ====== Compilation  ====== -->
    <target name="compile" depends="prepare">

        <javac srcdir="${src.home}"
               destdir="${build.home}/WEB-INF/classes"
               debug="true"
               deprecation="true">
           <classpath>
              <fileset dir="${web.home}/WEB-INF/lib">
                 <include name="*.jar"/>
              </fileset>

            <pathelement location="${catalina.home}/common/classes"/>
              <fileset dir="${catalina.home}/common/endorsed">
                 <include name="*.jar"/>
              </fileset>

              <fileset dir="${catalina.home}/common/lib">
                 <include name="*.jar"/>
              </fileset>

              <pathelement location="${catalina.home}/shared/classes"/>

              <fileset dir="${catalina.home}/shared/lib">
                 <include name="*.jar"/>
              </fileset>

           </classpath>
        </javac>

        <!-- Copy application resources -->
        <copy  todir="${build.home}/WEB-INF/classes">
             <fileset dir="${src.home}" excludes="**/*.java"/>
        </copy>
        <copy  todir="${build.home}/WEB-INF/lib">
             <fileset dir="${web.home}/WEB-INF/lib"/>
        </copy>
    </target>
```

The `dist` target creates a WAR file out of the expanded WAR directory structure present in the `build` directory:

```
<!-- ====== Dist Target ====== -->

    <target name="dist" depends="compile"
            description="Create WAR file">

        <!-- Create WAR file -->
        <mkdir dir="${dist.home}"/>
        <jar jarfile="${war.file}"  basedir="${build.home}"/>
    </target>
```

The `all` target runs all the targets. Ant will run each target once in the order specified in the `depends` attribute for this target:

```
<!-- ====== All Target ====== -->

    <target name="all"
            depends="clean, prepare, compile, dist"
            description="Builds the web application and war file"/>

</project>
```

Let's run the different targets now to make sure that our environment is set up to run Ant correctly. To execute the Ant script, type the Ant command followed by the target name.

Open the console window and go to the `/home/tomcat/ch26` directory and run the `clean` target as shown here. Note that if you run the `clean` target after running the `compile` or `dist` targets, you will find the `build` and `dist` directories getting cleared in the `clean` target:

```
$ ant clean
Buildfile: build.xml

clean:
   [delete] Deleting directory /home/tomcat/ch26/build
   [delete] Deleting directory /home/tomcat/ch26/dist

BUILD SUCCESSFUL
Total time: 2 seconds
```

The `dist` target is responsible for generating the WAR file. Because this target depends on the `compile` target, by running it you ensure that not only will the files be compiled and copied into an expanded WAR directory structure, but that the WAR file is also generated:

```
$ ant dist
Buildfile: build.xml

prepare:
    [mkdir] Created dir: /home/tomcat/ch26/build
    [mkdir] Created dir: /home/tomcat/ch26/build/images
    [mkdir] Created dir: /home/tomcat/ch26/build/WEB-INF
    [mkdir] Created dir: /home/tomcat/ch26/build/WEB-INF/classes
    [mkdir] Created dir: /home/tomcat/ch26/build/WEB-INF/lib
     [copy] Copying 4 files to /usr/tomcat/ch26/build
     [copy] Copied 1 empty directory to /usr/tomcat/ch26/build

compile:
    [javac] Compiling 1 source file to /home/tomcat/ch26/build/WEB-INF/classes

dist:
    [mkdir] Created dir: /home/tomcat/ch26/dist
      [jar] Building jar: /home/tomcat/ch26/dist/myWebapp.war

BUILD SUCCESSFUL
Total time: 5 seconds
```

Now that you have the expanded WAR directory structure for the Web application as well as the .war file, you are ready to deploy it. This Web application can be deployed in a number of ways:

❑ Copy the WAR file to the <Tomcat Installation Directory> /webapps directory.

❑ Create a context for the Web application by making a directory within <Tomcat Installation Directory> /webapps — for example, <Tomcat Installation Directory> /webapps/ myWebapp — and copy the expanded WAR directory structure in the build directory to <Tomcat Installation Directory> /webapps/myWebapp.

❑ Use the Manager Web application GUI to deploy the application.

❑ Use the Ant interface to the Manager application.

In addition to the simple examples covered here, Ant can be used to construct very elaborate build environments that perform a range of tasks:

❑ Checking in or checking out code from version-control systems such as CVS. More details on CVS, and CVS's Ant task, are covered later in the chapter.

❑ Running test cases (when coupled with JUnit, and Ant's JUnit-specific tasks).

❑ Building installable packages.

❑ Deploying applications (for example, using Tomcat's Ant tasks to deploy a Web application).

❑ E-mailing the status of the test cases or the build to developers.

❑ Formatting code according to an organization's coding standards. Earlier in the chapter you were introduced to formatting tools such as Jalopy and Checkstyle. These come with Ant tasks too, enabling you to add commands to format code from within your build script. See `http://jalopy.sourceforge.net/plugin-ant-usage.html` for details on Jalopy's Ant task and `http://checkstyle.sourceforge.net/anttask.html` for Checkstyle's Ant task.

Additional resources

More information on Apache Ant (including a list of Ant tasks) is available at the Ant Web site at `http://ant.apache.org/manual/index.html`. Another good resource is *Professional Java Tools for Extreme Programming* by Richard Hightower, et al (Wrox Press; ISBN 0764556177).

CVS

Concurrent Versions System (CVS) is an open-source version-control system that is the de facto versioning tool used by most open-source projects. Even if you use another version-control system at work, such as Clearcase, Perforce, or SourceSafe, knowing how to use CVS is useful. If you need to get the latest version (or a specific version) of your favorite open-source software, such as the Apache HTTP server, Tomcat, or Struts, you might have to get it from their CVS repository. Many open-source projects post only the last few released versions on their Web site.

Installing CVS

The installation and administration of the CVS server is beyond the scope of this book. Moreover, as developers, you will usually need to use only the CVS client.

The CVS client comes as a part of most Linux distributions if you have the development tools installed. For other UNIX platforms, such as SunOS, HP-UX, and AIX, you can download either the source code distribution of CVS or binary versions from `cvshome.org/downloads.html`.

For Windows, you can either install a GUI version of the CVS client, called WinCVS (`wincvs.org`), or get the Cywin development environment (`cygwin.com`) that provides most UNIX command-line tools for Windows.

CVS concepts

CVS is a version-control system that enables you to maintain different versions of your file (called *revisions*). It also enables groups of people to work on files at the same time — hence, the name *Concurrent Versions System*.

CVS has a safekeeping place called a *repository* for holding groups of files. A related group of files is called a *module*. Developers can *checkout* a module or specific files within a module and make changes in it. Once they are done, they can *commit* (i.e., check in) the files back into the repository for others to access. CVS has mechanisms such that developers can either prevent others from making changes while a file is checked out (*reserved checkout*), or not (*unreserved checkout*, the default). If a file has been checked out with an unreserved checkout, then two or more people can be modifying the same file at the same time. CVS has tools to help merge code in such cases.

You can create a code *branch* from the main code *trunk*. A branch refers to a version of code that has been forked out from the main development version. For example, if sequential versions of the source code are labeled as 1.0, 1.1, 1.2, and so on, you could take out a branch from the 1.1 version, label it 1.1.1 and continue development on that line. You might do this if you wanted to work on adding specific features to your software without disturbing the primary work going on. The latest versions of the code on the main trunk are called *top of trunk*, and the latest version of any branch or trunk is called the *head* of that branch/trunk. CVS has the capability to merge changes from a branch onto the main trunk. This is illustrated in Figure 26-3.

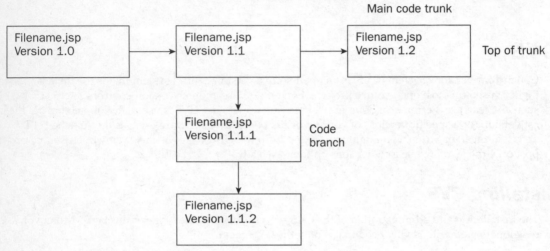

Figure 26-3: A sample source code tree in CVS

Once a module has been developed, it can be released to users. Before doing so, it is a good practice to put a *tag* on the module, such as `release_1-0`. A tagged release consists of a snapshot of the files in a module at a given point in time, and these files often have different versions. Tagging a release helps keep track of any issues with a specific release. For example, if after some months a bug is reported by your users, you can get the specific version of code released to them from the CVS repository, and fix the problem.

Connecting to a CVS server

Information on which CVS server to connect to is passed though an environment variable called CVSROOT. Usually, you would get this information from your system administrator.

A typical CVSROOT variable setting for Linux/UNIX is as follows:

```
$ CVSROOT=":pserver:username@host.domain.com:/home/cvs/modulename"; export CVSROOT
```

Here, pserver indicates the authentication protocol used for connecting to the CVS server. The most common protocol is pserver, and other protocols include rhosts, ssh, and ntserver. The username and host.domain.com should be replaced by the username and hostname for the CVS server. Finally, the path (/home/cvs/modulename) indicates the file system path to your code module. If you are going to be connecting to this CVS server often, you should add this to your login startup scripts, such as .kshrc, .bashrc, and so on.

Once the CVSROOT variable is specified, you need to log in to the CVS server using the cvs login command. You may be prompted for a password depending on your authentication settings.

```
$ cvs login
```

In the WinCVS GUI, use the Admin->Preferences->General option to set CVSROOT, and then use Admin->Login to log in to the CVS server. Figure 26-4 shows the CVS settings in WinCVS for anonymously retrieving code from the Apache Jakarta Project.

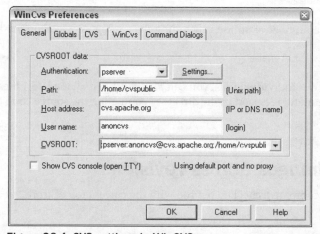

Figure 26-4: CVS settings in WinCVS

Once you have logged in, depending on your setting, you don't have to log in each subsequent time. The login information is kept in an internal configuration file, and the CVS client logs you in automatically.

Checking in code

To check in a module for the very first time, change to the directory in which the source code is located and issue the cvs import command as shown:

```
$ cd code-directory
$ cvs import -m "message here" modulename vendorname release
```

Here, modulename is the name of the module, vendorname is a string that identifies you or your company, and release is a tag for identifying the latest version of the files. The message specified after the -m flag is for documentation purposes.

In the WinCVS client, the same can be done using the Remote->Import module option.

Once the module is checked in, you must check it out (see the "Checking out code" section next) before you can start using it.

To check in individual files, use the `cvs ci` command as shown:

```
$ cvs ci filename
```

You will be asked to enter a comment while checking in a file. This comment is used for documenting the changes made in the file.

Checking out code

Checking out the latest version (i.e., the top of trunk) can be done using the `cvs co` command:

```
$ cvs co filename
```

This command has a number of options, including the `-r` flag for checking out a specific version of a file:

```
$ cvs co -r 1.0 filename
```

Instead of checking out individual files, you can also check out all the latest files using the `cvs update` command. This command is issued in the directory containing the source code to be updated:

```
$ cvs update .
```

Comparing changes across revisions

With CVS, you can compare a checked out file with the current top of trunk, or compare two specific versions of a file.

The following code compares a checked out file with the current top of trunk in CVS:

```
$ cvs diff -wb filename
```

This code compares two version of the file:

```
$ cvs diff -r 1.1 -r 1.2 -wb filename
```

The `-wb` option is one of the many `cvs diff` options. This particular option ignores whitespace characters while doing the comparison.

Managing code versions through Ant scripts

These CVS commands can also be executed through your Ant build script. This powerful feature enables you to build, test (as you shall see in the next section), and check in a final release version of your code—all from your build script.

More details on the CVS task in Ant can be found at
`http://ant.apache.org/manual/CoreTasks/cvs.html`.

Additional resources

This CVS tutorial contained only a handful of the commands required to work with a CVS repository. A complete list of CVS commands is documented in the CVS manual, which can be found online at `cvshome.org/docs/manual/`.

JUnit

JUnit is a framework for writing unit and regression tests in Java. This framework has become extremely popular, especially with practitioners of agile programming methodologies, such as test-driven development (TDD). JUnit, written by Erich Gamma and Kent Beck, is a simple and small test framework, but it implements very useful testing patterns. To quote Martin Fowler, "Never in the field of software development was so much owed by so many to so few lines of code."

JUnit has also inspired a number of other testing frameworks, including the following:

- ❑ **cppunit:** A testing framework for C++ code (`http://cppunit.sourceforge.net/`)
- ❑ **NUnit:** A testing framework for .NET languages (`nunit.org/`)
- ❑ **HttpUnit:** A framework for testing Web applications (`http://httpunit.sourceforge.net/`)
- ❑ **Cactus:** A framework for testing server-side Java code (`http://jakarta.apache.org/cactus/index.html`)

These and other testing frameworks are listed on the `http://www.xprogramming.com/software.htm` Web site. This section provides a tutorial introduction to JUnit.

Installing JUnit

JUnit can be downloaded from `junit.org`. The version used in this section (3.8.1) was the latest available at the time of writing.

After you download the zip file (typically named `junitx.y.z`, where `x.y.z` is the version number), extract it to a directory of your choice. This contains JAR files and documentation. All you need to do is add `junit.jar` in your classpath, and you are ready to go.

On Windows, type the following at the command prompt:

```
C:\> set CLASSPATH="%CLASSPATH%;C:\junit3.8.1\junit.jar
```

On Linux/UNIX, type the following:

```
$ CLASSPATH="$CLASSPATH:/home/me/junit3.8.1/junit.jar"; export CLASSPATH
```

JUnit concepts

As mentioned earlier, JUnit provides a framework for building unit and regression tests. The framework includes a Java class (`junit.framework.TestCase`) that all test cases extend. This class has methods for test case initialization and cleanup, and a mechanism to write and run tests.

A summary of the steps for writing a test suite is as follows:

1. Implement a subclass of the `junit.framework.TestCase` class.

2. Perform initialization for the test case by overloading the `setUp()` method. This usually involves initializing instance variables that store the state of the test.

3. Write individual tests.

4. Perform cleanup after the test by overloading the `tearDown()` method.

A testing term that you'll see often in JUnit documentation is *fixture* — this is just another name for a test setup.

Developing an individual test involves writing code that performs operations with the Java class it has to test, and then uses assert method calls to confirm that the Java class is in the desired state.

For example, writing a test for a `debit()` method of a Bank Account class would involve the following steps:

1. Debit a certain amount from the bank account, say $100.

2. Assert that the current bank balance is less than the original bank balance by $100.

This example is shown in more detail in the JUnit example in the next section.

Once the tests are written, the following line in the `main()` method of your test suite will execute all test cases:

```
public static void main (String[] args)
{
    junit.swingui.TestRunner.run (BankAccountTest.class);
}
```

The `junit.swingui.TestRunner` class used in the preceding code is a Swing-based test runner. There are other test runners too, such as the non-GUI `junit.textui.TestRunner`. The approach shown previously dynamically runs all tests defined in the `BankAcccountTest` test class.

You can also selectively run specific tests, as shown here:

```
public static Test suite()
{
    TestSuite suite= new TestSuite();

    // add test method testCredit() and testDebit() to the
    // test suite
```

```
        suite.addTest (new BankAccountTest ("testCredit"));
        suite.addTest (new BankAccountTest ("testDebit"));
         return suite;
    }


    public static void main (String[] args)
    {
        // Run selected tests in the suite using the non-GUI test runner
        junit.textui.TestRunner.run (suite());
    }
```

Try It Out   **Writing a JUnit Test**

This example creates a test for a simple Java class (BankAccount) that models a bank account. First take a look at the code for the BankAccount.java class for which we are writing this test:

```
package com.wrox.begjsp.ch26;

public class BankAccount
{
```

The class has an accountId that is an identification number for the bank account, an accountType that can be either checking or savings, and the current balance in the account (currentBalance). These fields are not important for our example — the currentBalance, shown here, is:

```
public static final int   CHECKING_ACCOUNT      = 0;
public static final int   SAVINGS_ACCOUNT       = 1;

/* Unique ID for bank account */
private long  accountID;
/* Type of account- CHECKING_ACCOUNT or SAVINGS_ACCOUNT */
private int    accountType;
/* Account balance */
private float currentBalance;

public BankAccount (long accountID, int accountType, float currentBalance)
{
    this.accountID     = accountID;
    this.accountType   = accountType;
    this.currentBalance = currentBalance;
}
```

Note that the debit() method doesn't allow you to overdraw money from your bank account. If debit succeeds, it returns true; otherwise, it returns false:

```
public boolean debit (float debitAmount)
{
    /* No overdraft allowed */
    if (debitAmount > currentBalance)
        return false;
```

```
        currentBalance -= debitAmount;
        return true;
    }

    public boolean credit (float creditAmount)
    {
        currentBalance += creditAmount;
        return true;
    }
```

The `transferFrom()` method simply debits one bank account with the appropriate amount and credits the other account with the same amount. You probably noticed that there is no check to determine whether the bank account from which the amount has been debited has the required amount—well, that is what we'll be testing for:

```
    public boolean transferFrom (BankAccount account, float amount)
    {
        account.debit (amount);
        this.credit (amount);
        return true;
    }
```

Finally, the `getCurrentBalance()` method returns the current balance in the account:

```
    public float getCurrentBalance ()
    {
        return currentBalance;
    }
}
```

The first step in writing a test case for the `BankAccount` class is deciding what we want to test. In this example, it is simple—we want to test if we can successfully debit and credit a bank account and if the `transferFrom()` method correctly transfers money. We perform tests that transfer valid amounts of money, as well as money that doesn't exist in an account.

The next step is to write a test class that is, by convention, called `BankAccountTest`. Notice that it is in the same package as the class we are testing—this, too, is a convention, and it helps the test code to access data private to a package. `BankAccountTest` extends the `junit.framework.TestCase` class.

```
package com.wrox.begjsp.ch26;

import junit.framework.Assert;
import junit.framework.Test;
import junit.framework.TestSuite;
import junit.framework.TestCase;

public class BankAccountTest extends TestCase
{
```

The `account1` and `account2` variables are the instance variables that store the state of the test. They are initialized in the `setUp()` method and accessed in the test cases:

```
private BankAccount account1;
private BankAccount account2;
```

In the `setup()` method for the test, we initialize the two bank accounts (`account1` and `account2`) with some money. There is no need for a `tearDown()` method in this case, as there are no resources that need to be released. If, for instance, we had established a database connection in the test, then code to release it back to the database pool would have been placed in the `tearDown()` method:

```
protected void setUp ()
{
    account1 = new BankAccount (1, BankAccount.CHECKING_ACCOUNT, 1000);
    account2 = new BankAccount (2, BankAccount.SAVINGS_ACCOUNT,  1000);
}
```

Our first test case, `testDebit()`, debits $100 from the bank account and then verifies the transaction using an assert statement showing that the account contains $100 less. As you can see in the example, a JUnit test is a method with no parameters and has a prefix, `test`:

```
public void testDebit ()
{
    float balance = account1.getCurrentBalance();
    account1.debit (100);
    Assert.assertEquals (balance-100, account1.getCurrentBalance(),0);
}
```

The `testCredit()` method, similarly, adds $100 to the account and checks the current balance:

```
public void testCredit ()
{
    float balance = account1.getCurrentBalance();
    account1.credit (100);
    Assert.assertEquals (balance+100, account1.getCurrentBalance(),0);
}
```

Next, we test the functionality to transfer money between bank accounts. We try transferring varying amounts, some of which are valid (such as $10 and $100), and some of which are not (such as $10,000). What is important is that accounts should not be left in an inconsistent state — the receiving account should not be credited money if there are insufficient funds in the sending account.

```
public void testTransferFrom ()
{
    float transferAmount[] = {10, 100, 1000, 10000};

    for (int i = 0; i < transferAmount.length; i++)
    {
```

```
            float balance1 = account1.getCurrentBalance();
            float balance2 = account2.getCurrentBalance();
            boolean transferSuccess = account1.transferFrom (account2,
                                                      transferAmount[i]);
            if (transferSuccess)
            {
              Assert.assertEquals (balance1+transferAmount[i],
                              account1.getCurrentBalance(),
                              0);
              Assert.assertEquals (balance2-transferAmount[i],
                              account2.getCurrentBalance(),
                              0);
            }
            else /* transfer of money between bank accounts failed */
            {
              Assert.assertEquals (balance1, account1.getCurrentBalance(),0);
              Assert.assertEquals (balance2, account2.getCurrentBalance(),0);
            }
        }
    }
```

Finally, we have the test runner, which specifies that all tests in the BankAccountTest class should be run. JUnit enables you to run specific tests, too, instead of all tests in a suite, as you saw earlier in the "JUnit concepts" section.

```
    public static void main (String[] args)
    {
        junit.swingui.TestRunner.run (BankAccountTest.class);
    }
}
```

The test can be run as shown:

```
$ java com.wrox.begjsp.ch26.BankAccountTest
```

The test for the transfer account fails, as shown in Figure 26-5.

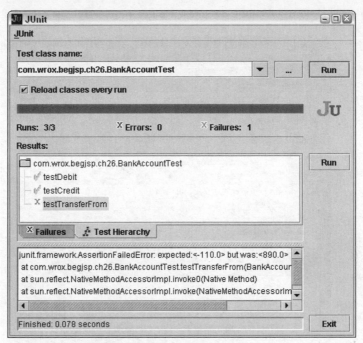

Figure 26-5: JUnit test indicating failure

The cause is indicated by the failure message and is not hard to trace—we did not confirm that the sending bank account had enough money before crediting the receiving account. The following code from BankAccount class shows the fix:

```
public boolean transferFrom (BankAccount account, float amount)
{
     // Check if we have money in account
     if (account.debit (amount))
         return this.credit (amount);

     // If we reach here, then debit() failed-
     // therefore transferFrom() fails too
     return false;
}
```

After recompiling the class and rerunning the test, we get a successful test run, as shown in Figure 26-6.

Figure 26-6: JUnit test indicating success

Running JUnit tests from Ant scripts

JUnit tests can also be started from Ant scripts. This is a powerful feature, as it enables you to add unit tests to your development process. For example, these unit tests could be executed each time you rebuild your code, thus catching any errors introduced by your changes. This kind of testing, whereby you check to see if your new changes affect existing functionality, is called *regression testing*.

To be able to do this, you have to copy the JUnit JAR file (`junit.jar`) in a location where Ant can find it. This can either be in your classpath or conveniently copied to `$ANT_HOME/lib`.

Once this is done, you can add a JUnit task to your Ant script, as shown in the following excerpt:

```
<junit>
  <formatter type="brief" usefile="false"/>
  <test name="com.wrox.begjsp.ch26.BankAccountTest"/>
</junit>
```

Here the `test` element specifies the test class, and the `formatter` element specifies the format of the result. The result in this case is being printed in the `brief` format and is output to the console and not a file (`usefile` set to `false`).

The JUnit task is an optional task. To get more information on this task, see `http://ant.apache.org/manual/OptionalTasks/junit.html`.

Additional resources

You can find additional documentation about JUnit at `http://junit.sourceforge.net/#Documentation`. Another useful resource is *Professional Java Tools for Extreme Programming* (ISBN 0764556177).

HttpUnit

HttpUnit is an open-source unit and regression testing framework for Web applications. It is based on JUnit and emulates the behavior of a Web browser for automating testing. It handles most things that a browser does — form submission, JavaScripts, HTTP-BASIC authentication, cookies, and page redirection. The response from a Web page can be handled in tests as text, an XML document, or even Java representations for forms, tables, and links. It also has a simulated servlet container for isolating and testing individual servlets.

HttpUnit is different from other Web application testing tools that are based on *record-and-playback*. HttpUnit actually parses the HTML response from the Web pages, so it is not as "brittle" as tools that depend upon the layout of a Web page. However, building a test case in HttpUnit may take longer than such tools.

Installing HttpUnit

HttpUnit can be downloaded from the `http://httpunit.sourceforge.net` Web site. It is available as a zip file named `httpunit-x.y.z.zip`, where `x.y.z` is the version number. The version used in this section is HttpUnit 1.5.4. Installing HttpUnit is a simple matter of extracting the zip file in a directory of your choice.

Once HttpUnit is installed, the Java classpath has to be changed to include the JUnit and HttpUnit JAR files, as well as the supporting JAR files that help process the HTTP requests and responses. These JAR files are included with the HttpUnit download.

A Windows script for setting the classpath is shown here. In the script, `HTTPUNIT_HOME` is the location where HttpUnit is installed:

```
set HTTPUNIT_HOME=d:\software\httpunit-1.5.4
set
CLASSPATH=%CLASSPATH%;%HTTPUNIT_HOME%\lib\httpunit.jar;%HTTPUNIT_HOME%\jars\Tidy.ja
r;%HTTPUNIT_HOME%\jars\js.jar;%HTTPUNIT_HOME%\jars\junit.jar;%HTTPUNIT_HOME%\jars\n
ekohtml.jar;%HTTPUNIT_HOME%\jars\servlet.jar;%HTTPUNIT_HOME%\jars\xercesImpl.jar;%H
TTPUNIT_HOME%\jars\xmlParserAPIs.jar;.
```

The corresponding setting for UNIX/Linux is shown here:

```
HTTPUNIT_HOME=/home/username/httpunit-1.5.4
CLASSPATH=$CLASSPATH:$HTTPUNIT_HOME/lib/httpunit.jar:$HTTPUNIT_HOME/jars/Tidy.jar:$
HTTPUNIT_HOME/jars/js.jar:$HTTPUNIT_HOME/jars/junit.jar:$HTTPUNIT_HOME/jars/nekohtm
l.jar:$HTTPUNIT_HOME/jars/servlet.jar:$HTTPUNIT_HOME/jars/xercesImpl.jar:$HTTPUNIT_
HOME/jars/xmlParserAPIs.jar:.
```

HttpUnit concepts

HttpUnit tests follow the same pattern as JUnit tests:

1. Set up the test fixture using the `setUp()` method.

2. Write individual tests.

3. Write cleanup code in the `tearDown()` method.

4. Run all tests or specific tests in a `TestSuite` using either the `junit.textui.TestRunner` or the `junit.swingui.TestRunner` test runners.

The reason for this similarity is that HttpUnit builds upon the JUnit code base. What HttpUnit provides in addition is a complete HTTP client that performs the same tasks that a browser does — form submission, JavaScripts, HTTP-BASIC authentication, cookies, and page redirection.

The most important class here is `WebConversation`. This class models a Web browser, and is used to request a resource from a Web site, as shown here:

```
WebConversation wc = new WebConversation ();
WebRequest     req = new GetMethodWebRequest("http://www.wrox.com");
WebResponse    resp = wc.getResponse (req);
```

The response from the Web site (the `WebResponse` object) can then be manipulated in the test code in three ways:

❑ **As plain text:** The `getText()` method of the `WebResponse` class returns a string representation of the entire Web page.

❑ **As an XML document:** The `getDOM()` method of the `WebResponse` class returns an XML representation of the entire Web page.

❑ **As Java object representations of HTML elements:** These can be forms (`getForms()` method), tables (`getTables()` method), links (`getLinks()` method), images (`getImages()` method), and so on.

Try It Out   **Writing an HttpUnit Test**

In this example, we will write a test case for the `webwork-skeleton` Web application introduced in Chapter 18, "Web Frameworks." In order to run this test, you have to install the application as specified in the chapter. The Web application, once installed, should be accessible at `http://localhost:8080/webwork-skeleton/formtest!default.action`. If there is a change to this, you have to modify the `FORM_URL` constant in the code appropriately.

The first step in the test is similar to JUnit—extend the `junit.framework.TestCase` class:

```
package com.wrox.begjsp.ch26;

import com.meterware.httpunit.*;
import junit.framework.*;


/**
 * An example of testing servlets using HttpUnit
 **/
public class FormTest extends TestCase
{
```

As mentioned earlier, the `FORM_URL` contains the URL of the Web form to be tested:

```
    public static final String FORM_URL = "http://localhost:8080/webwork-
skeleton/formtest!default.action";
```

The HttpUnit test runner shown here is the same as in JUnit:

```
    public static void main(String args[])
    {
        junit.textui.TestRunner.run (suite());
    }

    public static Test suite()
    {
        return new TestSuite (FormTest.class);
    }
```

The first test is a sanity check to see if the form exists and has the required parameters—user, age, and comments:

```
    /**
     * Verifies that the web page has exactly one form, with
     * three parameters- user, age and comments.
     **/
    public void testForm() throws Exception
    {
        WebConversation     conversation = new WebConversation();
        WebRequest request = new GetMethodWebRequest(FormTest.FORM_URL);

        WebResponse response = conversation.getResponse (request);
        WebForm forms[] = response.getForms();
        assertEquals (1, forms.length);
        assertEquals (3, forms[0].getParameterNames().length);
        assertEquals ("user", forms[0].getParameterNames()[2]);
        assertEquals ("age", forms[0].getParameterNames()[1]);
        assertEquals ("comments", forms[0].getParameterNames()[0]);
    }
```

Next, we check for an invalid age input. This should result in the error message "Age cannot be less than 18." If this is true, the test passes. If not, the test fails with an `Incorrect age does not flag` error message:

```
/**
 * Verifies that submitting the form with an invalid
 * age value fails with an error message.
 */
public void testIncorrectAge() throws Exception
{
    WebConversation     conversation = new WebConversation();
    WebRequest  request = new GetMethodWebRequest (FormTest.FORM_URL);

    WebResponse response = conversation.getResponse (request);
    WebForm form = response.getForms()[0];
    request = form.getRequest();
    request.setParameter ("user", "John Doe");
    request.setParameter ("age", "17");
    response = conversation.getResponse (request);
    assertTrue ("Incorrect age does not flag error",
        response.getText().indexOf ("Age cannot be less than 18") != -1);
}
```

Finally, we check for a valid age input. This should result in a success status from the Web application, and some information is presented to the user. The test checks this by confirming that the response Web page contains the `Advice` string. If this is true, the test passes. If not, the test fails with a "Correct age limit not accepted" message:

```
/**
 * Verifies that submitting the form with a valid
 * age value works fine.
 */
public void testCorrectAge() throws Exception
{
    WebConversation     conversation = new WebConversation();
    WebRequest  request = new GetMethodWebRequest (FormTest.FORM_URL);

    WebResponse response = conversation.getResponse (request);
    WebForm form = response.getForms()[0];
    request = form.getRequest();
    request.setParameter ("user", "Jane Doe");
    request.setParameter ("age", "18");
    response = conversation.getResponse (request);
    assertTrue ("Correct age limit not accepted",
      response.getText().indexOf ("Advice") != -1);
}

}
```

To compile and run the test, the classpath has to include the JUnit and HttpUnit JAR file, as well as the supporting JAR files that help process the HTTP requests and responses. The section "Installing HttpUnit" shows how this can be done.

Once the classpath is set, the test can be run as shown in Figure 26-7.

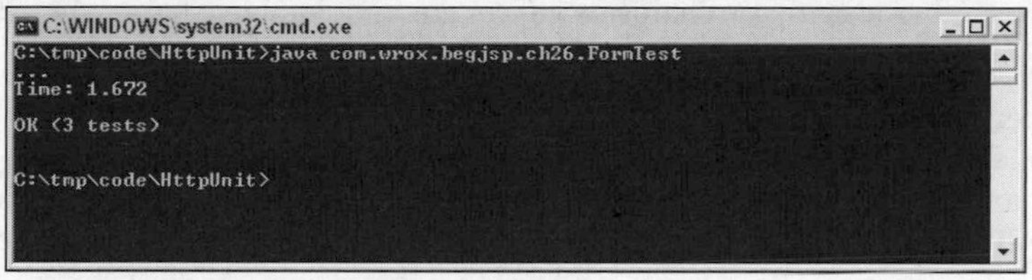

Figure 26-7: Running the HttpUnit test

Additional resources

Further documentation on HttpUnit is available at the HttpUnit Web site (http://httpunit. sourceforge.net). Another resource is *Professional Java Tools for Extreme Programming* (ISBN 0764556177).

Best Practices for Web Development

Now that you are almost at the end of the book, you have seen a range of best practices in use in the various chapters. The most important of these best practices are summarized in this section.

Follow good JSP coding practices

Earlier in the book, you were introduced to a range of best practices related to JSP coding, including the following:

❑ Use the simplest HTML to prototype your application before adding in style and layout. See Chapter 2, "JSP Basics 1: Dynamic Page Creation for Data Presentation," for more details on this.

❑ Separate JSP development from HTML layout and formatting if possible. Again, refer to Chapter 2 for more details.

❑ Avoid the use of Java scriptlets in JSP; use EL or tag libraries instead. This is described further in Chapter 5, "JSP and EL," and Chapter 6, "JSP Tag Libraries and JSTL." An example of what not to do, e.g., use Java scriptlets, is demonstrated in Chapter 3, "JSP Basics 2: Generalized Templating and Server Scripting."

❑ Use stylesheets for the layout and fonts of your JSP pages. Chapter 4, "CSS, JavaScript, VBScript, and JSP" has examples of dynamically creating stylesheets.

❑ Use the JSP inclusion mechanism to avoid redundant code. Examples of the include directive in action can be seen in Chapter 7, "JSP Directives."

❑ Use JavaBeans to pass data between the business logic and the presentation. This is introduced in Chapter 9, "JSP and JavaBeans," and formally covered as a design pattern in Chapter 27, "JSP Project I: Personalized Portal."

❑ Handle errors in your Web application gracefully and yet log enough information so that the cause of the error can be debugged. Error handling is discussed in Chapter 10, "Error Handling," and logging mechanisms are covered in detail in Chapter 14, "JSP Debugging Techniques."

❑ Consider developing internationalized Web pages. Even if your Web site is currently only in one language, you may at some time in the future want to support multiple languages. Chapter 13, "Internationalization and Localized Content," explains the JSTL support for internationalization, and Chapters 19 and 27 show an alternative mechanism using Struts' tag library.

Separate application logic and presentation

Any application-related logic, relating to both any business logic as well as control flow in your Web site, should be kept separate from your presentation. See Chapter 17, "Model View Controller," for a recommended architecture for your Web applications.

Use design patterns where appropriate

Many of the problems that you solve as a software developer have already been faced by others before you. Instead of repeatedly reinventing a new way to solve a certain class of problems, it is wiser to use a tried and tested solution. A *design pattern* is a solution to a type of a problem.

Some of the patterns that have been used in this book are listed as follows. Note that this is not an exhaustive list of patterns and is not organized in any particular manner.

❑ **Factory:** The factory pattern is used create an object at runtime. Examples of the factory pattern are shown in Chapter 23, "Access to Databases," and Chapter 27, "JSP Project I: Personalized Portal."

❑ **Facade:** A facade provides a unified interface to a subsystem. The facade pattern is used in Chapter 23.

❑ **Transfer Object/Data Transfer Object:** This is an object that carries data across layers in an application, to minimize the number of method calls. This is especially useful if the layer in question is a remote layer. The transfer object is used in Chapter 9 and Chapter 27.

❑ **Data Access Object (DAO):** A Data Access Object encapsulates all access to a persistent store, such as a database. The DAO is used in Chapters 23 and 27.

❑ **Model View Controller (MVC):** The MVC pattern separates the user interface into three roles: the Controller (the part that responds to user requests), the Model (the data model of the application), and the View (the actual presentation). This pattern is described extensively in Chapter 17, "Model View Controller," and examples of its use can be seen in Chapter 18, "Web Frameworks," Chapter 19, "Struts Framework," and Chapter 21, "JavaServer Faces."

❑ **Front controller:** The front controller is a single interface point for handling all requests to a Web site; examples of this can be seen in Chapter 9, "JSP and JavaBeans," and Chapter 12, "Advanced Dynamic Web Content Generation."

❑ **Remote proxy:** The proxy object is used to control access to a remote object. This is illustrated in Chapter 27.

❑ **Service locator:** The service locator, as the name suggests, does any lookup that is required for a service. This pattern is used in Chapter 27.

Use frameworks for developing applications

Chapter 18, "Web Frameworks," lists a number of frameworks, including those for Web development, testing, persistence, and templating, among others.

Frameworks are good for the same reason design patterns are good — they implement solutions to common problems faced by developers in an application domain, they provide a structure for your solutions, and they leave you to focus on the business problem at hand. Not only that, a framework typically has been used by a lot of developers before you, and thus provides you with a mature and stable platform to build upon.

The frameworks covered in this book include the following:

- ❑   **MVC frameworks:** Struts (Chapter 19), Spring and WebWork (Chapter 18)
- ❑   **Templating frameworks:** Tiles (Chapter 20)
- ❑   **Logging frameworks:** Log4j and Java Logging API (Chapter 14)
- ❑   **Persistence frameworks:** Hibernate (Chapter 23)

Early testing and integration

Earlier in the chapter you were introduced to agile methodologies, which focus on writing test cases before beginning development, and the benefits of early integration. Even if you don't follow such methodologies rigorously, the benefits of early testing and integration while developing complex applications cannot be stressed enough. This chapter introduced you to two tools that help you build test cases: JUnit and HttpUnit. You were also introduced to the Apache Ant build tool, which as you saw in its support for other tools, such as CVS, JUnit, and so on, is a lot more than just a build tool.

Summary

This chapter covered a range of development methodologies and the best practices they espouse. It also introduced you to commonly used software tools. To be a good Web programmer, it is not enough to be able to code JSPs and develop Web applications. It is also important to be aware of the different programming methodologies and be armed with a set of tools to handle complex customer requirements. It is hoped that this chapter was a good starting point to that end.

To summarize what we covered:

- ❑   Traditional waterfall methodologies take an engineering approach to software development. They are predictive and freeze the requirements and design before beginning development.
- ❑   Iterative methodologies are more adaptive to changing customer requirements.
- ❑   Agile methodologies are relatively lightweight and emphasize writing tests before the actual code. They encourage iterative development, dealing with smaller code portions, continuous integration, and continuous refactoring.
- ❑   Version-control systems, such as CVS, enable the tracking of different versions of the code and are essential for projects involving teams of engineers.

# Chapter 26

❏ Build tools such as Ant help automate the software build and deploy process.

❏ Unit and regression testing tools such as JUnit are central to iterative/agile software development.

❏ Performance and load testing can be automated using tools such as jMeter.

❏ Logging can be added in a standard and configurable manner using logging frameworks such as Log4j or the Java Logging API.

❏ Coding standards are important, and tools such as Jalopy and Checkstyle help enforce them.

Exercises

1. Write a JUnit test for the Authentication service used in Chapter 27, "JSP Project I: Personalized Portal."

Part III: Spreading Your New Wings: Applying JSP in the Real World

JSP Project I: Personalized Portal

The first two parts of this book covered JSP development and introduced you to a lot of other areas in Enterprise Java in general and Web development technologies in particular. In this, the third and final part of the book, you will see how these technologies are brought together into two projects. These projects are complete by themselves yet simple enough to demonstrate important concepts.

This first project, a personalized portal, builds on many of the concepts covered earlier, and specifically from the following chapters:

- ❏ Chapter 5, "JSP and EL"
- ❏ Chapter 6, "JSP Tag Libraries and JSTL"
- ❏ Chapter 14, "JSP Debugging Techniques"
- ❏ Chapter 17, "Model View Controller"
- ❏ Chapter 19, "Struts Framework"
- ❏ Chapter 20, "Layout Management with Tiles"
- ❏ Chapter 26, "Best Practices and Tools"

By the end of these projects, you will be able to piece together different concepts taught in the book and apply them in complete, real-world Web applications.

The Portal Project

This project demonstrates a personalized portal. It enables users to register and customize their preferences. Based on these preferences, the portal gathers news and other content from different Web sites and aggregates it for the user. This is done using the *RSS* news syndication technology.

In addition, the portal retrieves information about books and (potentially) other items that match the user's interest, and presents them as advertisements on the customized news page. Presenting such *targeted* items increases the chance that the user will buy them, and thus helps pay for the cost of hosting the portal. These items are pulled in from Amazon.com using their *Web service* API.

This book is about JSPs and Web development, and not Web services or RSS. However, because they are used in this project, the following section provides a brief introduction.

Introduction to RSS

RSS is an XML *content syndication* format invented by Netscape in 1999. Many Web sites today fall under the category of content providers. Some of these include traditional news sites such as CNN, BBC, or Wired. Even non-news Web sites offer RSS feeds — for example, the iTunes music store has customizable RSS feeds for new songs released.

What is an RSS feed? RSS is a format for describing metadata about news content. For example, the news at a certain point in time from Slashdot (`www.slashdot.org`), a popular technology Web site, has the following items:

❑   Stress Costs U.S. $300 Billion a Year

❑   Mozilla Usage Doubles in 9 Months

Slashdot also publishes metadata about this content as an RSS file, available from `http://slashdot.org/index.rss`. The content of this file for these news items is listed here:

```
<rdf:RDF>
  <channel rdf:about="http://slashdot.org/">
    <title>Slashdot</title>
    <link>http://slashdot.org/</link>
    <description>News for nerds, stuff that matters</description>
    <dc:language>en-us</dc:language>
    <dc:rights> Copyright 1997-2004, OSTG - Open Source Technology Group, Inc.  All
Rights Reserved.</dc:rights>
    <dc:date>2004-09-05T03:13:13+00:00</dc:date>
    <dc:publisher>OSTG</dc:publisher>
    <dc:creator>pater@slashdot.org</dc:creator>
    <dc:subject>Technology</dc:subject>
  </channel>

  <item rdf:about="http://slashdot.org/article.pl?sid=04/09/04/219248">
    <title>Stress Costs U.S. $300 Billion a Year</title>
    <link>http://slashdot.org/article.pl?sid=04/09/04/219248</link>
    <description>
        jburroug writes "A new study, as reported in the New York Times claims that
the stress of the modern always-on work environment is taking a far greater toll on
the health of workers than previously believed, to the tune of $300 billion in lost
productivity and increased health care costs in the U.S. alone."
    </description>
    <dc:creator>michael</dc:creator>
    <dc:subject>science</dc:subject>
    <dc:date>2004-09-05T03:08:00+00:00</dc:date>
    <slash:section>science</slash:section>
  </item>
```

```
<item rdf:about="http://slashdot.org/article.pl?sid=04/09/04/1825227">
  <title>Mozilla Usage Doubles in 9 Months</title>
  <link>http://slashdot.org/article.pl?sid=04/09/04/1825227</link>
  <description>
      TheBadger writes "Thanks to the success of Firefox, Mozilla now appears to
have 14.9% of the browser share, double that of 9 months ago. Let this be a lesson
in complacency."
  </description>
  <dc:creator>michael</dc:creator>
  <dc:subject>mozilla</dc:subject>
  <dc:date>2004-09-04T23:44:00+00:00</dc:date>
  <slash:section>mainpage</slash:section>
</item>
</rdf:RDF>
```

This listing has been edited for clarity, and is not a complete RSS document. However, even if you don't know RSS (or even much XML), you can gather what this document contains. It has information about the content provider, such as the following:

- The name (Slashdot)
- Web site URL (`http://slashdot.org`)
- A description of the Web site (News for nerds, etc.)
- Copyright
- Language for the content
- Date
- Publisher
- Subject

Then, for each news item on the Web site, it contains the following metadata:

- Title
- URL for the full news article
- Description
- Date
- Creator of article
- Subject

An application that "subscribes" to the content from this Web site will periodically grab the latest RSS file at the `http://slashdot.org/index.rss` URL, and display information about any new news items. This is possible because each article "item" has date and time information as a part of the metadata.

A content provider such as Slashdot doesn't have to manually generate the RSS file. In most cases, the software that runs the Web site generates an updated RSS file every time a new article is posted on it.

RSS is a badly fragmented standard; there are seven different versions of this standard proposed by rival groups. In addition, there is an alternative look-alike standard called Atom that has similar features. In fact, even the abbreviation RSS has multiple expansions; the three commonly used ones are *Rich Site Summary*, *RDF Site Summary*, and *Really Simple Syndication*. When people cannot agree on what the abbreviation stands for, it is no wonder that they don't agree on the standards! However, you don't have to worry too much about this; most RSS clients and API implementations handle RSS feeds in multiple formats.

Finally, RSS does not restrict you to news content. For example, CVS checkin logs, Web site revision information—in short, just about anything that needs to be communicated to a larger audience—can be published as RSS content.

The Importance of RSS

Even though RSS has been around for a while now, its recent spike in popularity is due to its adoption by Weblogs. RSS enables you to aggregate content from different providers. This can be done using RSS *readers* that can either work as standalone programs (e.g., BlogExpress, Straw, FeedDemon, NetNewsWire, to name a few) or be integrated with your browser (e.g., Sage, RSS Reader Panel, Aggreg8, NewsMonster) or Mail reader (e.g., NewsGator, intraVnews, Genecast). The proliferation of RSS readers gives you some idea of how popular RSS has become. Figure 27-1 shows one such RSS reader.

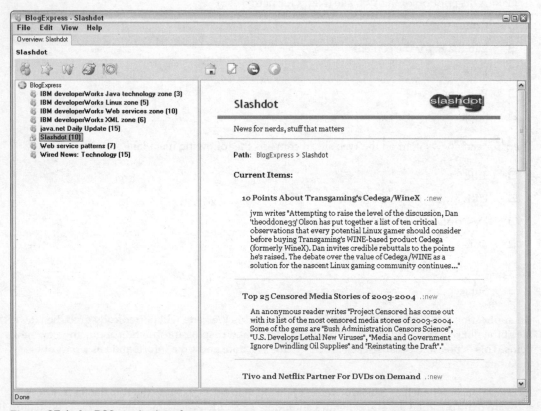

Figure 27-1: An RSS reader interface

With an RSS reader, you don't have to visit several Web sites every day, or every few hours, to check for updated news. All you have to do is add the RSS feed URL to your reader and it will fetch new content from these Web sites periodically. You can specify how frequently the reader should poll for content.

Another way to consume RSS content is using an online *RSS aggregator*. This is a Web site that aggregates RSS content from different content providers. This way, you can visit just one Web site instead of many to get information. The personalized portal covered in this chapter is an example of an RSS aggregator.

Introduction to Web services

Distributed computing has been around for a few decades now, with a number of technologies such as RPC (remote procedure call), CORBA, DCE, and COM. What Web services brought into this mix was *loose coupling* between services and clients, better cross-platform support, and most important, support across all vendors. The initial Web services specifications came from IBM, Microsoft, and others, but has since been adopted by most companies.

Although there are several Web service specifications and technologies, such as those that deal with security and transactions, for instance, we are going to look at just two of these in this chapter: SOAP and WSDL. These are, in fact, the core Web service technologies on which everything else builds.

The first concept to understand is that of a *service*. A service is a software component that implements some business logic and has a well-defined interface. For example, a weather service would take the name of a city or a postal code as input and return the current temperature and humidity.

In order for your service to be used by client applications, you would need to describe its interface in some form and ensure that even if the implementation of the service changes, it is transparent to the client applications. In the Java world, you do this by defining an *interface* and then writing an implementation for that interface. Client classes will then code to the interface and not the implementation. This is what is meant by the term *loose coupling* that was introduced in the first paragraph of this section. The Web service equivalent of this is called *WSDL* or *Web Service Definition Language*. WSDL is an XML format for describing the interface provided by a service, defining the input and output parameter types, as well as, optionally, the *end point* for the service.

When a service is invoked, the message from and to the client can move along several alternative transports — HTTP, JMS, SMTP, or even a bare-bones TCP socket. The network end point the service listens on, such as the URL, is called the *end point* of the service. The format of the message is important — it needs to be platform- as well as language-independent, as the client and server can be on heterogeneous platforms, and be implemented in different languages. For this reason, an XML format was chosen for the messages. This format is called *SOAP*, or *Simple Object Access Protocol*.

A *Web service*, therefore, is a service whose interface is described using a WSDL definition, and can be invoked using a SOAP message. Typically, a service provider would implement a Web service, describe it using WSDL, and then announce this WSDL to users either by listing it in registry, or by some other ad-hoc mechanism. For example, `xmethods.net` is a Web site that lists many Web services and their WSDL descriptions.

While developing Web services or writing client that invoke a Web service, in most cases you don't have to deal with the XML representations of either the SOAP message or the WSDL interface. Several software tools can handle the XML formats, leaving you free to develop the application logic in your language of choice. In practice, however, some understanding is useful, especially while debugging tricky problems. In this chapter, you will look at a simple application and will be spared detailed XML listings.

The Importance of Web services

Why are Web services so important? There are many places where Web services can be used, but to illustrate their importance, consider the following two areas where they play an invaluable role:

❑ Enterprise Application Integration (EAI)

❑ Web sites as applications

Enterprise application integration

A company usually has a lot of applications, with useful data spread all across them. Some of these applications, such as spreadsheets, run on PCs. Others, such as payroll systems and supply chain systems, may run on UNIX systems, NT servers, or even mainframes. Even applications running on the same system (for example, Solaris) might well be from different vendors, with different data formats, APIs, and implementation languages. Web services ease the task of integrating across applications and prevent your enterprise data from being locked up in isolated application silos.

Web sites as applications

In the last decade, Web sites have evolved from being brochure-ware to serious e-commerce applications. In fact, many of the popular Web sites in use today, such as eBay, Amazon, PayPal, and Google, are conceptually applications with a browser interface. Web services take this a step further and enable you to expose these application interfaces in a standard manner. Thus, other companies, such as resellers and partners, can incorporate this functionality into their own Web sites and applications. For example, using the Google Web service API, you can add Google search functionality into your applications. Similarly, using Amazon's API, you can provide a customized list of products on your Web site and thus earn a commission each time someone buys these products from your site. In fact, the project covered later in the chapter demonstrates this very example.

This does not mean that Web services are a "golden hammer" suitable for each and every task. As a developer, you should choose your tools based on the task at hand. For example, situations in which all applications share the same platform, such as Java or .NET, or for which there are performance and high data volume considerations, may be better served by using other more conventional technologies.

Project Features

The first step in developing a software application is *requirement analysis*. In this phase, the software analysts sit down with the intended users to understand their requirements.

Often, users are not able to precisely state their requirements. Hence, a very useful technique in this stage is creating *use cases*. Use cases demonstrate how the user interacts with the system and are an effective way of capturing the functional requirements of the system. In addition, use cases can be translated very easily into test cases and can form the basis for *acceptance testing* of the application.

A detailed requirement analysis process is beyond the scope of this chapter, so the use cases are enlisted as a lightweight substitute for a formal requirements document.

Use cases

The use cases for the system are listed here:

1. The user should be able to register with the system and specify preferences. These preferences include the following:

   a. The username and password for logging in

   b. The user's display name

   c. A list of publishers that the user is interested in reading news from

   d. Any interests that the user has, specified by keywords. Examples of keywords could be Java, XML, or even poetry.

2. The user should be able to log on to the portal using a username and password configured during the registration phase.

3. The user should be able to change his preferences, including the password, the display name, the list of publishers, and interest items.

4. On logging in to the portal, users should be presented with a personalized page with news items and other content from all the publishers that they have subscribed to.

5. The user should also be presented with advertisements for items that match his profile as specified in his "interests" keywords.

6. On clicking a book advertisement link, the user should be taken to Amazon's Web page to purchase it. Because these links contain the partner id (the "Amazon Associates id") of the portal, any purchase would pay a commission.

7. Finally, the user should be able to log off from the portal.

Initial analysis

Based on the use cases, we can come up with a list of entities in this system, and the relationship between them. This constitutes what is called the *domain model* of the system. The entities of the domain model are as follows:

❏ **User profile:** The user profile contains information that identifies the user, such as the user name, display name and password, as well as the user preferences. These preferences include a list of publishers and the news feeds to which the user has subscribed, and a list of keywords that identify what the user is interested in. These keywords are entered by the user in this project, but they can also be automatically "learned." For example, if the user subscribes to sports news, the sports can be added to his list of interests. This learning can also occur based on the user's interaction with the system, such as the news items the user actually reads (if he reads basketball-related news more than any other news item, then we can add basketball to his interest list). Many popular e-commerce Web sites, such as Amazon.com, use these and related techniques to suggest new items to the user, thus increasing the likelihood of selling them. This being a simple project, we are going to restrict ourselves to asking the user to enter his interests in a Web form, rather than inferring it from his interaction with the Web site.

❑ **News source:** A source of news from which the user can choose. The information that we keep for a news source includes the name of the news provider, a short description, the category it falls under, and finally and most important, the URL of the RSS feed for this news source.

❑ **News feed:** The news feed from a news source. This consists of the title of the feed (e.g., "Yahoo! News–Sports"), a brief description, and a group of news items.

❑ **News item:** A news item is contained in a news feed. This consists of the headline, a description of the news item, and the URL for the actual news story.

❑ **Advertisement feed:** Similar to the news feed, an advertisement feed would have the name of the feed (e.g., "Java books from Amazon.com") and a group of advertised items.

❑ **Advertised item:** An advertised item has the name of the item, a URL to the picture of the item, and finally a URL from where it can be purchased. This URL, as mentioned earlier, contains embedded information that enables the portal to earn a commission for each sale.

From this domain model and the use case, you can now proceed to design the persistent store/database and the application and to develop each of the components.

The Application Design

The application design section covers the following topics:

❑ Designing the persistent store

❑ Designing the key entity objects

❑ Designing the Web site control flow

Of these, the first two topics correspond to the Model layer in a typical MVC architecture, and the last corresponds to the Controller layer. The Controller layer is covered in more detail later in the chapter.

Designing the persistent store

Every application has some data that needs to live on across application runs. This data is called *persistent data*, as it persists even when the application does not. Typically, it is stored in a relational database, such as Oracle, Sybase, SQL Server, DB2, or mySQL. For very simple Web applications, the data can also be stored on the file system. However, what you gain in terms of simplicity by using files, you lose in terms of functionality. Chapter 23, "Access to Databases," introduced you to the benefits of databases, such as a powerful query mechanism and transaction support.

After mentioning all this, we now backtrack and use a file-based mechanism for persisting data on our portal Web application! However, the following code shows a *factory* design pattern that makes the database access mechanism transparent to the Web application code. This enables you to change the implementation from a file-based mechanism to a relational database with minimal-to-no code change.

The actual change to a database-based implementation is left as an exercise for you, though a solution is provided at the end of the book. Chapter 26, "Best Practices and Tools," introduces design patterns briefly, and lists those that are used in this book.

First, let's look at the data being persisted — the user profile and the publishers. The user profile consists of the following:

- ❏ User name
- ❏ User password
- ❏ Display name
- ❏ Subscriptions for the user (a multi-valued field)
- ❏ User's interests (a multi-valued field)

The publisher's object is simpler — it consists of multiple rows of the following:

- ❏ Publisher name
- ❏ Publisher description
- ❏ Category of the news feed
- ❏ RSS URL of the news feed

Access to the persistent data is through a *factory* (`com.wrox.begjsp.ch27.dal.DBFactory`). The factory is a design pattern that enables us to create an object, with the exact type of the object decided at runtime. For example, the `DBFactory` class shown next returns instances of file-based implementations (`UserProfileDBMemoryImpl`, `PublisherDBMemoryImpl`) but could easily be changed to return any other implementation. The client code accesses these implementations using interfaces (`UserProfileDB`, `PublisherDB`). As you will see later in the exercise, this enables us to swap out the memory-based implementation with a relational database–based one without affecting client code:

```
package com.wrox.begjsp.ch27.dal;

/**
 * Returns instances of Database Access Objects
 */
public class DBFactory
{
    public static PublisherDB getPublisherDB()
    {
        return PublisherDBMemoryImpl.getInstance();
    }

    public static UserProfileDB getUserProfileDB()
    {
        return UserProfileDBMemoryImpl.getInstance();
    }
}
```

The Java package structure (com.wrox.begjsp.ch27.dal) shown in the code is explained in the "Directory structure" section, later in the chapter.

The interface for the UserProfileDB is listed next. The UserProfileDBMemoryImpl implements this interface and any relational database–based implementation will have to do the same.

```java
package com.wrox.begjsp.ch27.dal;

import com.wrox.begjsp.ch27.dto.UserProfile;


/**
 * Interface for the database access layer for UserProfile objects
 */
public interface UserProfileDB
{
    public UserProfile getUserProfile(String username)
        throws DatabaseException;

    public void updateUserProfile(UserProfile userProfile)
        throws DatabaseException;

    public void insertUserProfile(UserProfile userProfile)
        throws DatabaseException;

    public void deleteUserProfile(String username) throws DatabaseException;
}
```

The same applies for the PublisherDB interface listed next. The PublisherDBMemoryImpl implements this interface, and any relational database–based implementation will have to do the same.

```java
package com.wrox.begjsp.ch27.dal;

import com.wrox.begjsp.ch27.dto.Publisher;

import java.util.List;


/**
 * Interface for the database access layer for Publishers
 */
public interface PublisherDB
{
    public List getPublishers() throws DatabaseException;

    public Publisher getPublisher(String feedUrl) throws DatabaseException;
}
```

Another design pattern in use here is the *Data Access Object*, or the *DAO*. The DAO abstracts out the implementation details of the database access and has find, insert, replace, or delete methods that act on the database.

The classes that implement the `PublisherDB` and `UserProfileDB` interface are examples of DAOs. These include the file-based implementations `PublisherDBMemoryImpl` and `UserProfileDBMemory Impl` mentioned earlier, as well as the MySQL database–based implementations `PublisherDBMySQL` and `UserProfileDBMySQLImpl` discussed in the exercises at the end of the chapter.

Defining the key entity objects

A complex online system has multiple layers. Traditionally, there are at least three: a *database layer* (or *database access layer*), a *business layer*, and a *presentation layer*, and each might have further granularity. Passing data between different layers and processes is expensive. To reduce the number of calls across layers and processes, more data should be transferred in each call. For example, to serve up advertisements, instead of making multiple calls for each advertised item, all the items should be fetched at the same time.

This kind of object that is used to transfer data between layers is called a *data transfer object (DTO)*, or just a *transfer object*. A DTO is a common design pattern that is used while building enterprise applications.

In our simple example, the transfer objects and the database look identical as far as the data in them is concerned. However, in most real-life systems, they are not the same — a transfer object has only that piece of information that is required by a specific application layer. Transfer objects are also closely tied to the use case being implemented and may pull together data from different sources and organize it in a way required by the application.

The following six data transfer objects are used in our application:

❑ **`com.wrox.begjsp.ch27.dto.UserProfile`**: Models the user's profile

❑ **`com.wrox.begjsp.ch27.dto.Publisher`**: A news provider, which can provide one or more news feeds

❑ **`com.wrox.begjsp.ch27.dto.NewsFeed`**: A related group of news items from the publisher/ news provider

❑ **`com.wrox.begjsp.ch27.dto.NewsItem`**: An individual news item

❑ **`com.wrox.begjsp.ch27.dto.ItemFeed`**: A related set of advertisements (for books)

❑ **`com.wrox.begjsp.ch27.dto.InterestItem`**: An individual (advertised) item that a user might be interested in

More information on the Java package structure (`com.wrox.begjsp.ch27.dto`) is provided in the section "Directory structure," later in the chapter.

The code for the `UserProfile` is listed here. As you can see, it contains the following data elements:

❑ **`userName`:** Used to uniquely identify a user.

❑ **`password`:** Secures a user's account from unauthorized access.

❑ **`displayName`:** The name to display on a user's account.

❑ **subscriptions:** A group of news feeds (as indicated by RSS feed URLs) to which the user subscribes.

❑ **interests:** The interests of the user. This is indicated by a group of keywords indicating the interest topics.

❑ **status:** Used by the Web application to manage the state of a user's profile.

```java
package com.wrox.begjsp.ch27.dto;

import java.io.Serializable;

/**
 * User Profile
 */
public class UserProfile implements Serializable
{
    /* The values of the status codes */
    final public static int STATUS_ERROR            = -1;
    final public static int STATUS_INVALID_USER      = 1;
    final public static int STATUS_INVALID_PASSWORD = 2;
    final public static int STATUS_LOGGED_IN         = 3;
    final public static int STATUS_NOT_LOGGED_IN     = 4;

    /* Status of a user- used to indicate invalid,logged in or not
     * logged in users
     */
    private int status;

    /* The username for logging in */
    private String userName;

    /* The password for logging in */
    private String password;

    /* The display name on account, defaults to userName */
    private String displayName;

    /* The news feeds the user has subscribed to */
    private String[] subscriptions;

    /* A list of keywords indicating user's interests */
    private String[] interests;

    public String getDisplayName()
    {
        return displayName;
    }

    public String[] getInterests()
    {
        return interests;
    }
```

```java
    public String getPassword()
    {
        return password;
    }

    public int getStatus()
    {
        return status;
    }

    public String[] getSubscriptions()
    {
        return subscriptions;
    }

    public String getUserName()
    {
        return userName;
    }

    public void setDisplayName(String string)
    {
        displayName = string;
    }

    public void setInterests(String[] strings)
    {
        interests = strings;
    }

    public void setPassword(String string)
    {
        password = string;
    }

    public void setStatus(int i)
    {
        status = i;
    }

    public void setSubscriptions(String[] strings)
    {
        subscriptions = strings;
    }

    public void setUserName(String string)
    {
        userName = string;
    }
}
```

Following is the code for the `NewsFeed`. It contains the following data elements:

- ❑ **title:** The title for the news feed
- ❑ **description:** A short description
- ❑ **items:** A group of news items in this feed

```java
package com.wrox.begjsp.ch27.dto;

import java.io.Serializable;

/**
 * A news feed from a publisher that the user has subscribed to
 */
public class NewsFeed implements Serializable
{
    /* The name/title of the news provider */
    private String title;

    /* A short description for the news provider */
    private String description;

    /* A group of news items from this news provider */
    private NewsItem[] items;

    public String getDescription()
    {
        return description;
    }

    public String getTitle()
    {
        return title;
    }

    public NewsItem[] getItems()
    {
        return items;
    }

    public void setDescription(String string)
    {
        description = string;
    }

    public void setTitle(String string)
    {
        title = string;
    }

    public void setItems(NewsItem[] newsItem)
    {
```

```
            items = newsItem;
        }
    }
```

The code for the NewsItem is listed next. It contains the following data elements:

❑   **headline:** The headline for this news item

❑   **description:** A short description of the news item

❑   **newsURL:** The URL for the actual news item

```java
package com.wrox.begjsp.ch27.dto;

import java.io.Serializable;

/**
 * A news item
 */
public class NewsItem implements Serializable
{
    /* The headline for the news item */
    private String headline;

    /* A short description for the news item */
    private String description;

    /* The URL for the complete news item */
    private String newsURL;

    public String getDescription()
    {
        return description;
    }

    public String getHeadline()
    {
        return headline;
    }

    public String getNewsURL() {
        return newsURL;
    }

    public void setDescription(String string)
    {
        description = string;
    }

    public void setHeadline(String string)
    {
        headline = string;
    }
```

```
    public void setNewsURL(String string) {
        newsURL = string;
    }
}
```

The code for the `Publisher` is listed next. As explained earlier, it contains the following data elements:

❑   **name:** The name of the publisher/news provider.

❑   **description:** A short description.

❑   **category:** The category under which this news feed can be classified.

❑   **feedUrl:** The URL for the RSS feed. The actual feed is modeled by the `NewsFeed` and `NewsItem` objects discussed earlier.

```java
package com.wrox.begjsp.ch27.dto;

import java.io.Serializable;

/**
 * A publisher entry registered with the portal Web site
 */
public class Publisher implements Serializable
{
    /* Name of the publisher */
    private String name;

    /* Description of the news feed */
    private String description;

    /* The RSS URL for the news feed */
    private String feedUrl;

    /* The category this news feed can be classified under */
    private String category;

    public Publisher()
    {
        // Do nothing
    }

    public Publisher(String name, String description, String category,
        String feedUrl)
    {
        this.name = name;
        this.description = description;
        this.category = category;
        this.feedUrl = feedUrl;
    }
```

```
    public String getCategory()
    {
        return category;
    }

    public String getDescription()
    {
        return description;
    }

    public String getFeedUrl()
    {
        return feedUrl;
    }

    public String getName()
    {
        return name;
    }

    public void setCategory(String string)
    {
        category = string;
    }

    public void setDescription(String string)
    {
        description = string;
    }

    public void setFeedUrl(String string)
    {
        feedUrl = string;
    }

    public void setName(String string)
    {
        name = string;
    }
}
```

The code for the `ItemFeed` is listed next. As explained earlier, it models a group of related items being advertised to the user and consists of the following:

❑   **itemFeedName:** The name for this feed

❑   **interestItem:** The related group of items being advertised

```
package com.wrox.begjsp.ch27.dto;

import java.io.Serializable;

/**
 * A group of items that the user might be interested in
 */
public class ItemFeed implements Serializable
{
    /* A descriptive name for the set of items */
    private String itemFeedName;

    /* The group of items the user might be interested in */
    private InterestItem[] interestItem;

    public InterestItem[] getInterestItem()
    {
        return interestItem;
    }

    public String getItemFeedName()
    {
        return itemFeedName;
    }

    public void setInterestItem(InterestItem[] items)
    {
        interestItem = items;
    }

    public void setItemFeedName(String string)
    {
        itemFeedName = string;
    }
}
```

Finally, you have the source code for the InterestItem. This models an item that is being advertised to the user and contains the following data elements:

- **itemName:** The name for this item
- **imageUrl:** An image of this item, specified by a URL
- **itemUrl:** A URL for a Web page from which the item can be purchased

```
package com.wrox.begjsp.ch27.dto;

import java.io.Serializable;

/**
 * Items that the user might be interested in
 */
public class InterestItem implements Serializable
{
    /* The URL to the image for the item */
    private String imageUrl;

    /* The name of the item */
    private String itemName;

    /* The URL to the item */
    private String itemUrl;

    public String getImageUrl()
    {
        return imageUrl;
    }

    public String getItemName()
    {
        return itemName;
    }

    public String getItemUrl()
    {
        return itemUrl;
    }

    public void setImageUrl(String string)
    {
        imageUrl = string;
    }

    public void setItemName(String string)
    {
        itemName = string;
    }

    public void setItemUrl(String string)
    {
        itemUrl = string;
    }
}
```

As you can see from the preceding code listings, DTOs are JavaBeans with simple GET/SET methods, and don't contain any business logic.

Designing the Web site control flow

The next step in designing the Web site is describing the control flow. This control flow can be validated against the use cases. One technique used for describing the control flow is a *sequence diagram*. Figure 27-2 shows what happens when a user tries to log in.

First the logon form is presented. This captures the username and password and passes it to the logon action. The action invokes an authentication service to verify the username and password. The authentication service returns a user profile if it succeeds and an error indicator if it fails. The user profile contains the user's subscriptions and interests. The logon action can use this to invoke the News and Advertising services, respectively, and pass this collected information to the portal page to display.

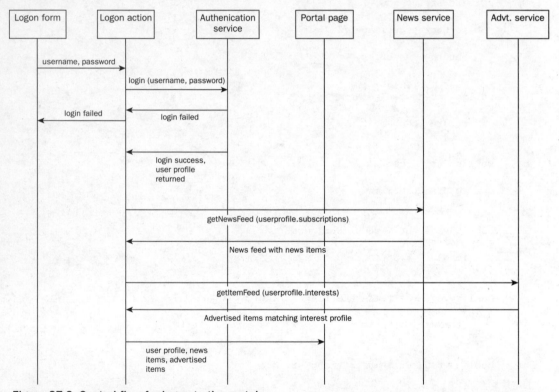

Figure 27-2: Control flow for logon to the portal

Where do service invocations fit in an MVC architecture? Chapter 17, "Model View Controller," looked at MVC architecture in detail. These invocations update the data in the Model, as shown in Figure 27-3. Notice that the Web service call is behind an additional Web service proxy layer. This insulates the Advertisement/Item service from any changes in Web service implementation.

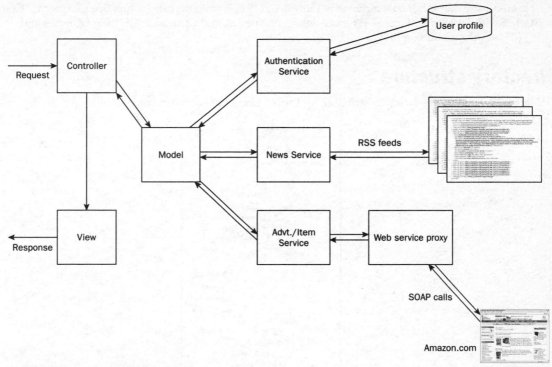

Figure 27-3: Accessing external services

Now that the key entities of the system and the control flow through the different components have been designed, we can look at the development environment and setup required for the Web application.

The Development Environment

This section covers the development environment setup, the installation of third-party components, as well as any additional setup that is required.

This includes the following:

- ❑ Directory setup for the development and build environment
- ❑ JSTL setup
- ❑ Struts setup
- ❑ The build script for the application
- ❑ Log4j installation and configuration
- ❑ The Rome RSS library used for getting news content
- ❑ The Apache Axis library used for making SOAP calls to Amazon's Web services

A prerequisite that is not covered here is Tomcat and JSTL installation and setup. See Chapter 1, "Getting Started with JavaServer Pages," for more details on Tomcat, and Chapter 6, "JSP Tag Libraries and JSTL," for information on JSTL.

Directory structure

Figure 27-4 shows the directory structure for the development environment.

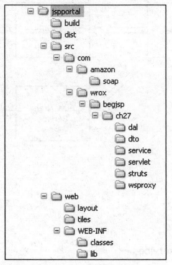

Figure 27-4: Directory structure

Note the following important directories:

- ❑ **src:** This contains all the Java code for the Web application, including that of the DTOs, the servlets, and the Struts action classes.

- ❑ **web:** The web directory contains all the JSP pages and configuration files. Its directory structure is identical to that of the WAR file. This is no accident — the build script shown in the next section will copy the structure into the `build` directory as a first step towards creating a deployable WAR file.

- ❑ **build:** This directory is created by the build script and contains all the compiled Java classes as well as the copied contents of the web directory. After a successful compile, the build directory contains the extracted version of a Web application.

- ❑ **dist:** The dist directory is also created by the build script to store the deployable WAR file.

The `src` directory contains all the Java source code for the Web application. As you can see, the package structure consists of the following:

- ❏ **com.amazon.soap:** This consists of the client-side stubs/proxies to invoke the Amazon Web services. This code is generated from the WSDL definition of the Web services. The "Apache Axis" section later in the chapter explains more about this.

- ❏ **com.wrox.begjsp.ch27.dal:** This is the code for the *data access layer*. The data access layer contains all the details for accessing the data, including the data access objects (DAOs). This enables you to make changes in the way you access this data (for example, from being stored in a file to being stored in a relational database) without affecting the rest of the code.

- ❏ **com.wrox.begjsp.ch27.dto:** These are the *data transfer objects* that were discussed earlier in the section "Defining the key entity objects."

- ❏ **com.wrox.begjsp.ch27.service:** This is the code for accessing remote services for RSS news feeds, advertised items, and the authentication service. The authentication service is not a remote service, but using a service interface for it enables us to potentially use one in the future. An example of a remote authentication service could be using a corporate directory service, or even the Microsoft Passport service to authenticate users in the system.

- ❏ **com.wrox.begjsp.ch27.servlet:** All servlets used in the application. These servlets, as you shall see later, are used for initializing resources such as the logging system.

- ❏ **com.wrox.begjsp.ch27.struts:** This is all the Struts-specific code, such as the Struts action classes.

- ❏ **com.wrox.begjsp.ch27.wsproxy:** These are the client-side Web service proxy classes. Why do you need this when you already have the generated proxy classes (i.e., com.amazon.soap)? Using an additional proxy class enables you to decouple any code specific to Apache Axis from the application. In the future, if you move to another Web service implementation, all the Axis-specific code would be localized to the proxy classes.

Build scripts

The Ant-based build script shown next creates a WAR file for the Portal Web application. This WAR file can then be deployed in a servlet container, such as Tomcat. If you haven't already installed Ant, you can download it from `http://ant.apache.org`. More details on Ant installation and the syntax of Ant build scripts are covered in Chapter 26, "Best Practices and Tools."

The first step in the Ant script is to set all the properties required in the script. This includes the Tomcat install directory (`catalina.home`), the location of the source code to be compiled (`src.home`), the location of the JSP and configuration files that are copied as is to the Web application (`web.home`), and the location where the WAR file (`war.file`) is to be created (`dist.home`). After this, all the targets for the build script are specified.

```
<!   Ant build file for JSP Project I Web Application -->

<project name="jspportal" default="compile" basedir=".">
  <property name="catalina.home" value="D:\\software\\tomcat\\jakarta-tomcat-
5.0.25"/>
  <property name="app.name"      value="ch27"/>
  <property name="app.path"      value="/${app.name}"/>
  <property name="src.home"      value="${basedir}/src"/>
  <property name="web.home"      value="${basedir}/web"/>
  <property name="docs.home"     value="${basedir}/docs"/>
  <property name="build.home"    value="${basedir}/build"/>
  <property name="dist.home"     value="${basedir}/dist"/>
  <property name="war.file"      value="${dist.home}/${app.name}.war"/>
```

Next, the prepare target creates the required directory structure with the build and dist directories, and copies the JSP files, along with all configuration files, into the build directory:

```
<!-- ====== Prepare Target ====== -->
<target name="prepare">
  <mkdir  dir="${build.home}"/>
  <mkdir  dir="${build.home}/WEB-INF"/>
  <mkdir  dir="${build.home}/WEB-INF/classes"/>

  <!-- Copy static content of this web application -->
  <copy todir="${build.home}">
    <fileset dir="${web.home}"/>
  </copy>
</target>
```

The compile target compiles all Java code into the build directory. Notice the CLASSPATH settings for the compilation — it includes all JAR files in the WEB-INF/lib directory, as well as Tomcat's common JAR files (${catalina.home}/common/lib). The former includes all the third-party JAR files for the Web application (for instance, for Axis, the Rome RSS library, Struts, Tiles, and so on), and the latter includes the servlet API JAR files required for compiling your servlets.

```
<!-- ====== Compilation  ====== -->
<target name="compile" depends="prepare">
  <javac srcdir="${src.home}"
         destdir="${build.home}/WEB-INF/classes"
         debug="true"
         deprecation="true">

    <classpath>
      <fileset dir="${web.home}/WEB-INF/lib">
        <include name="*.jar"/>
      </fileset>
      <pathelement location="${catalina.home}/common/classes"/>
      <fileset dir="${catalina.home}/common/endorsed">
        <include name="*.jar"/>
      </fileset>
      <fileset dir="${catalina.home}/common/lib">
        <include name="*.jar"/>
      </fileset>
```

```
      <pathelement location="${catalina.home}/shared/classes"/>
      <fileset dir="${catalina.home}/shared/lib">
        <include name="*.jar"/>
      </fileset>
    </classpath>
  </javac>

  <!-- Copy application resources -->
  <copy  todir="${build.home}/WEB-INF/classes">
    <fileset dir="${src.home}" excludes="**/*.java"/>
  </copy>
  <copy  todir="${build.home}/WEB-INF/lib">
    <fileset dir="${web.home}/WEB-INF/lib"/>
  </copy>
</target>
```

The dist target takes the contents of the build directory and creates a deployable WAR file out of it:

```
<!-- ====== Dist Target ====== -->
<target name="dist" depends="compile"
        description="Create WAR file">
  <!-- Create WAR file -->
  <mkdir dir="${dist.home}"/>
  <jar jarfile="${war.file}" basedir="${build.home}"/>
</target>
```

The clean target removes all compiled files and generated WAR files, along with the directories:

```
<!-- ====== Clean Target ====== -->
<target name="clean" description="Deletes the build and dist directories">
  <delete dir="${build.home}"/>
  <delete dir="${dist.home}"/>
</target>
```

Finally, the all target invokes the clean, prepare, compile, and dist targets, respectively:

```
<!-- ====== All Target ====== -->
<target name="all"
        depends="clean, prepare, compile, dist"
        description="Builds the web application and war file"/>
</project>
```

Struts

Struts installation and configuration is explained in detail in Chapter 19, "Struts Framework." In brief, the following steps are involved:

1. Download Struts from http://struts.apache.org and extract it in a directory of choice.

2. Copy the Struts JAR files from <Struts installation directory>/lib into WEB-INF/lib.

3. Configure the Action servlet in the deployment descriptor (`WEB-INF/web.xml`) as shown:

```
<!-- Action Servlet Configuration -->
<servlet>
  <servlet-name>action</servlet-name>
  <servlet-class>org.apache.struts.action.ActionServlet</servlet-class>
  <init-param>
    <param-name>config</param-name>
    <param-value>/WEB-INF/struts-config.xml</param-value>
  </init-param>
  <load-on-startup>3</load-on-startup>
</servlet>
```

4. Write a Struts configuration file (`struts-config.xml`). The Struts configuration file contains the action mappings that drive the control flow of the Web application. This control flow is derived from the use cases, as described in the section "Designing the Web site control flow," earlier in the chapter. The Struts configuration file and the action classes for the mapping are explained in more detail in the "Controller" section, later in the chapter.

Tiles

Tiles installation and configuration is explained in detail in Chapter 20, "Layout Management with Tiles." In brief, the following steps are involved:

1. Tiles is available from `www.lifl.fr/~dumoulin/tiles/index.html`. However, Tiles is also packaged with Struts, so you don't have to download it explicitly.

2. Create a Tiles definition file. The following definition file for the project (`tiles-defs.xml`) defines the portal layout (`portal.layout`):

```
<!DOCTYPE tiles-definitions PUBLIC
        "-//Apache Software Foundation//DTD Tiles Configuration//EN"
        "http://jakarta.apache.org/struts/dtds/tiles-config.dtd">

<tiles-definitions>
  <definition name="portal.layout" path="/layout/portal-layout.jsp">
      <put name="header" value="/tiles/portal-header.jsp" />
      <put name="body"   value="/tiles/portal-body.jsp" />
      <put name="advt"   value="/tiles/portal-advt.jsp" />
      <put name="footer" value="/tiles/portal-footer.jsp" />
  </definition>
</tiles-definitions>
```

3. Finally, configure the Tiles servlet in `web.xml` and specify the Tiles definition file:

```
<!-- Tiles Servlet Configuration -->
<servlet>
<servlet-name>tilesaction</servlet-name>
<servlet-class>org.apache.struts.tiles.TilesServlet</servlet-class>
<init-param>
```

```
                    <param-name>definitions-config</param-name>
                    <param-value>/WEB-INF/tiles-defs.xml</param-value>
                </init-param>
                <load-on-startup>4</load-on-startup>
            </servlet>
```

You are now ready to start using Tiles and designing layouts for your Web pages. See the "View" section later in the chapter for more details on the layout design for the portal Web pages.

Log4j

Chapter 14, "JSP Debugging Techniques," explains how Log4j can be installed and configured. The installation here is pretty much the same, except that the Log4j JAR file (in this case, `log4j-1.2.8.jar`) should be copied into the `\WEB-INF\lib` directory so that it becomes a part of the Web application's runtime.

Next, configure the Log4j settings as shown in the `\WEB-INF\log4j.properties` file listed here. Notice that even though the logging level for the root logger has been set to WARN, (i.e., no DEBUG and INFO messages are to be printed), this can be overruled on a per package or class basis. The `log4j.logger.com.wrox.begjsp.ch27.struts=All` line at the end shows how this is done:

```
# Set root logger level to DEBUG and its only appender to ConsoleOut.
log4j.rootLogger=WARN, ConsoleOut

# ConsoleOut is set to be a ConsoleAppender.
log4j.appender.ConsoleOut=org.apache.log4j.ConsoleAppender

# ConsoleOut uses PatternLayout.
log4j.appender.ConsoleOut.layout=org.apache.log4j.PatternLayout
log4j.appender.ConsoleOut.layout.ConversionPattern=%-4r [%t] %-5p %c - %m%n

# Set logging levels, or turn specific logging on or off for
# selective packages or classes
log4j.logger.com.wrox.begjsp.ch27.struts=All
```

The `log4j.properties` property file needs to be loaded, which the `com.wrox.begjsp.ch27.servlet.WroxLogServlet` does for us, as shown next. The name of the Log4j properties file is read from the `log4jconfig` property.

```
package com.wrox.begjsp.ch27.servlet;

import javax.servlet.*;
import javax.servlet.http.*;
import java.io.*;
import java.util.*;
import org.apache.log4j.PropertyConfigurator;

public class WroxLogServlet extends HttpServlet {

    public void init()
    throws ServletException {
```

```
        // Get Fully Qualified Path to Properties File
        String config = getServletContext().getRealPath("/") +
getInitParameter("log4jconfig");
        System.out.println("*** LoggingServlet Initialized using file :" + config);

        // Initialize Properties for All Servlets
        PropertyConfigurator.configure(config);
    }


    ....
}
```

This servlet in turn has to be started up at Web application startup time. This is done by the following configuration in \WEB-INF\web.xml. Note the log4jconfig parameter that specifies the name and path of the Log4j properties file and the load-on-startup element that causes this servlet to be loaded when the Web application starts up:

```
    <!-- Log4j Configuration -->
    <servlet>
      <servlet-name>WroxLogServlet</servlet-name>
      <servlet-class>com.wrox.begjsp.ch27.servlet.WroxLogServlet</servlet-class>
      <init-param>
        <param-name>log4jconfig</param-name>
  <param-value>/WEB-INF/log4j.properties</param-value>
      </init-param>
      <load-on-startup>1</load-on-startup>
    </servlet>
```

Now you are all set to use Log4j. The logger initialization (Logger.getLogger()) gets the logger specific to this class, and the logger.debug() call logs a debug statement. Note the logger.isDebugEnabled() check. This ensures that the debug statement is not even evaluated when the logger is set to a level above DEBUG. You might remember this performance tip from Chapter 25, "Performance."

```
public final class LogonAction extends Action
{
    private Logger logger = Logger.getLogger(LogonAction.class.getName());
    ...
    public ActionForward execute(ActionMapping mapping, ActionForm form,
        HttpServletRequest request, HttpServletResponse response)
        throws Exception
    {
        ...
        if (logger.isDebugEnabled())
        {
            logger.debug("Attempting to log in " + username);
        }
```

To summarize our steps:

1. Copy `log4j-1.2.8.jar` into the `\WEB-INF\lib` directory.

2. Configure the Log4j properties in `\WEB-INF\log4j.properties`.

3. Load the properties using a servlet (`com.wrox.begjsp.ch27.servlet.WroxLogServlet`).

4. Configure the deployment descriptor to load the `WroxLogServlet` when the Web application starts up.

5. Add log statements to Java files.

Rome

Rome ("All feeds lead to Rome") is an open-source RSS library that can be downloaded from `https://rome.dev.java.net`. It supports all RSS versions, as well as the Atom syndication standard. The first installation step is to copy the Rome JAR file (`rome.jar`) into `/WEB-INF/lib`. The version of Rome used in this application is 0.3.

Rome depends on the JDOM XML parsing library, and you would need to copy the JDOM JAR files into `/WEB-INF/lib`, too. All dependencies of Rome can be downloaded from `http://wiki.java.net/bin/view/Javawsxml/Rome`.

The code (`com.wrox.begjsp.ch27.service.NewsServiceImpl`) that uses the Rome RSS library to get and parse the RSS feed is shown next. The `getNewsFeed()` method takes as input the RSS URL and reads its content into a `SyndFeedI` object, which is a Rome-specific class for representing an RSS feed. You then extract specific fields from `SyndFeedI` into your NewsFeed DTO and return that to the calling program:

```
package com.wrox.begjsp.ch27.service;

import com.wrox.begjsp.ch27.dto.NewsFeed;
import com.wrox.begjsp.ch27.dto.NewsItem;

import com.sun.syndication.feed.synd.SyndEntry;
import com.sun.syndication.feed.synd.SyndFeedI;
import com.sun.syndication.io.FeedException;
import com.sun.syndication.io.SyndFeedInput;


...

/**
 * An implementation of the NewsService
 */
public class NewsServiceImpl implements NewsService
{
    ...
```

```
    public NewsFeed getNewsFeed(String subscription) throws WroxServiceException
    {
        NewsFeed newsFeed = new NewsFeed();
        URL channelUrl = null;

        try
        {
            channelUrl = new URL(subscription);
        }
        catch (MalformedURLException e)
        {
            throw new WroxServiceException("Invalid RSS feed URL " + subscription,
e);
        }

        SyndFeedInput input = new SyndFeedInput();

        SyndFeedI feed = null;

        try
        {
            feed = input.build(getFeedReader(channelUrl));
        }
        catch (IllegalArgumentException e)
        {
            ...
        }

        newsFeed.setTitle(feed.getTitle());
        newsFeed.setDescription(feed.getDescription());

        List entries = feed.getEntries();

        ListIterator listIterator = entries.listIterator(0);
        NewsItem[] newsItems = new NewsItem[entries.size()];

        int i = 0;

        while (listIterator.hasNext())
        {
            SyndEntry entry = (SyndEntry) listIterator.next();
            NewsItem item = new NewsItem();
            item.setHeadline(entry.getTitle());

            item.setDescription((entry.getDescription()).getValue());
            item.setNewsURL(entry.getLink());
            newsItems[i] = item;
            i++;
        }

        newsFeed.setItems(newsItems);

        return newsFeed;
    }
```

```
        private static Reader getFeedReader(URL feedUrl) throws IOException
        {
            ...
        }
    }
```

Finally, the Web application accesses the `NewsServiceImpl` functionality through a service locator interface, as shown here:

```
newsService = WroxServiceLocator.getNewsService();
NewsFeed newsFeed = newsService.getNewsFeed(subscription);
```

This *service locator* is a design pattern that is used when you want to consolidate all lookup operations for services in one place and also hide the implementation details of the lookup. The code listing for the service locator (`com.wrox.begjsp.ch27.service.WroxServiceLocator`) is shown next. As you can see, it returns instances of not only the news service, but also the authentication and item (advertisement) services:

```
package com.wrox.begjsp.ch27.service;


/**
 * Returns instances of the services
 */
public class WroxServiceLocator
{
    public static AuthenticationService getAuthenticationService()
        throws WroxServiceException
    {
        return new AuthenticationServiceImpl();
    }

    public static ItemService getItemService() throws WroxServiceException
    {
        return new ItemServiceImpl();
    }

    public static NewsService getNewsService() throws WroxServiceException
    {
        return new NewsServiceImpl();
    }
}
```

You can find additional details about the Rome RSS library, including Javadocs, at its Web site (`https://rome.dev.java.net/`).

To summarize our steps.

1. Download the Rome RSS library and JDOM.
2. Copy all JAR files into the `/WEB-INF/lib` directory.
3. Use the Rome API to get and parse the RSS news feeds.

Apache Axis

Apache Axis can be downloaded from `http://ws.apache.org/axis`. Download and extract it in a directory of your choice. Add all the classes under `AXIS_HOME/lib` to your Java `CLASSPATH`; you will need that for generating the client-side stubs for invoking Amazon's Web service API.

Next, you need to get a developer token from Amazon. This can be done from the `http://soap.amazon.com/` Web site. This Web site also has a developer's toolkit. You don't need it for this example, but you can download it to look at example code.

Next, generate the client-side stubs using the following command:

```
java org.apache.axis.wsdl.WSDL2Java http://soap.amazon.com/schemas3/
AmazonWebServices.wsdl
```

The WSDL2Java program takes an interface definition of a Web service (defined as a WSDL file) and generates client-side stubs. These stubs expose the Web service API as a Java API and contain all the code required to take Java objects, convert them to their XML representation, make a SOAP method call, and finally take the XML response and convert it back into Java for us. Client programs can then simply invoke these client-side stubs and avoid dealing with any SOAP or XML details.

This command presumes that all JAR files under `AXIS_HOME/lib` are in your `CLASSPATH`. When this command executes successfully, you will see a lot of Java classes generated under the `com.amazon.soap` package hierarchy in your current directory.

Copy all the JAR files from `AXIS_HOME/lib` into `WEB-INF/lib` and copy all the generated classes to the `src` directory. You are now all set to start invoking Amazon's Web service API.

The following code listing shows how the generated Axis code can be used for making a Web service call. This class has a `searchByKeyword()` method that takes a keyword and returns items from Amazon.com's inventory that match the keyword. The things to note here are as follows:

❑ The end point specified in `AMAZON_ENDPOINT` is the network end point where Amazon's Web services listen for client requests.

❑ The associate's id (`ASSOCIATE_ID`) is like a username that enables any purchases to be credited to your account. In case you don't have an Amazon associate's id, you can use the anonymous id `webservices-20` as shown.

❑ The developer token (`DEVELOPER_TOKEN`) is necessary — you need to get this before any examples can be run.

❑ The mode indicates what items categories to search under. It is currently set to `books`.

```java
package com.wrox.begjsp.ch27.wsproxy;

import com.amazon.soap.AmazonSearchPort;
import com.amazon.soap.AmazonSearchService;
import com.amazon.soap.AmazonSearchServiceLocator;
import com.amazon.soap.Details;
import com.amazon.soap.KeywordRequest;
import com.amazon.soap.ProductInfo;
```

```java
import com.wrox.begjsp.ch27.dto.InterestItem;
import com.wrox.begjsp.ch27.dto.ItemFeed;

import java.net.MalformedURLException;
import java.net.URL;

import java.rmi.RemoteException;

import javax.xml.rpc.ServiceException;


/**
 * Proxy class for retrieving data from Amazon.com's Web store
 */
public class AmazonStore implements WebserviceStore
{
    /* The Web service end point */
    private final static String AMAZON_ENDPOINT =
"http://soap.amazon.com/onca/soap3";

    /* The Amazon associate id */
    private final static String ASSOCIATE_ID = "webservices-20";

    /* The developer token from Amazon */
    private final static String DEVELOPER_TOKEN = "<Your developer token here>";

    /* The page number to retrieve */
    private final static String PAGE_NUMBER = "1";

    /* Search for books */
    private final static String MODE = "books";

    /* Amount of information to return- 'lite' mode or 'heavy' */
    private final static String TYPE = "lite";

    /* Web service version to invoke */
    private final static String VERSION = "1.0";

    /* Axis SOAP objects for making Web service call */
    private AmazonSearchService service;
    private AmazonSearchPort port;

    public AmazonStore() throws MalformedURLException, ServiceException
    {
        service = new AmazonSearchServiceLocator();
        port = service.getAmazonSearchPort(new URL(AMAZON_ENDPOINT));
    }

    public InterestItem[] searchByKeyword(String keyword)
        throws RemoteException
    {
        KeywordRequest request = new KeywordRequest();
```

```
                /* Set search parameters */
                request.setKeyword(keyword);
                request.setPage(PAGE_NUMBER);
                request.setMode(MODE);
                request.setTag(ASSOCIATE_ID);
                request.setType(TYPE);
                request.setDevtag(DEVELOPER_TOKEN);


                //request.setVersion(VERSION);
                ProductInfo productInfo = port.keywordSearchRequest(request);

                Details[] details = productInfo.getDetails();
                int productCount = details.length;
                InterestItem[] items = new InterestItem[productCount];

                for (int i = 0; i < productCount; i++)
                {
                    InterestItem item = new InterestItem();
                    item.setItemName(details[i].getProductName());
                    item.setImageUrl(details[i].getImageUrlSmall());
                    item.setItemUrl(details[i].getUrl());
                    items[i] = item;
                }

                return items;
        }
    }
```

Extensive documentation for Apache Axis is available at http://ws.apache.org/axis/java/index.html.

To summarize the steps:

1. Download Apache Axis and copy all JAR files into WEB-INF/lib.

2. Get a developer token for Amazon's Web service API. You can also download the toolkit to look at examples.

3. Use the WSDL2Java class to generate client-side stubs for Amazon's Web service API.

4. Use the stubs to make Web service calls to get Amazon's catalog information or to place orders in Amazon's shopping cart. The Amazon associates id and developer token will be passed along with the order, ensuring that you get paid a commission on purchases.

The Application

The previous sections covered the design of the Web site and the control flow ("Project Features" section), the model used in the Web site along with the transfer objects ("Defining the Key Entities" section), and finally the services — the News service, Authentication service, and Advertisement/Item service — that are invoked by the model.

In this section, you look at the View and Controller portions of the application.

View

In the Struts configuration explained earlier in the chapter, you saw how the Action servlet was configured and the Struts configuration file (`/WEB-INF/struts-config.xml`) passed to it as a parameter. The Struts configuration has form bean definitions as shown:

```
<!-- ========== Form Bean Definitions ==================================== -->
<form-beans>

  <!-- Logon form bean -->
  <form-bean        name="logonForm"
                    type="org.apache.struts.validator.DynaValidatorForm">
    <form-property name="username" type="java.lang.String"/>
    <form-property name="password" type="java.lang.String"/>
  </form-bean>

  <form-bean        name="registrationForm"
                    type="com.wrox.begjsp.ch27.struts.RegistrationForm"/>

</form-beans>
```

These form beans have their values set to what the user fills out in the form and are then passed to an appropriate action for further processing. Let's start with the first form (`logon.jsp`) that the users see when they browse to the portal application.

Note the following in the HTML form:

❑   The text shown on the form page is internationalized. Note the `bean:message` tags; they specify which text message should be displayed using `key` attributes. The actual messages are picked up from a property file (`ApplicationResources.properties`) that is configured in `struts-config.xml` as follows. Chapter 13, "Internationalization and Localized Content" explains the concepts behind internationalization and shows how it can be accomplished using JSTL tags. This is similar to that but uses the Struts bean tag library instead of JSTL.

```
<message-resources
    parameter="com.wrox.begjsp.ch27.ApplicationResources"/>
```

The content of the `ApplicationResources.properties` properties file that corresponds to the messages shown in this form is as follows:

```
# -- logon page --
welcome.title=Beginning JavaServer Pages Portal Project
welcome.heading=Welcome to your portal!
welcome.message=Please log in to your portal
welcome.logon=Login
welcome.newuser=Please register if you are a new user
```

❑   Note the `username` and `password` properties. What the user enters here is filled in the LogonForm bean.

❑   When the user submits the form, the result is sent to the logon action as specified in the Struts configuration. This is discussed later in the chapter in more detail.

❑   Finally, note the `editRegistration.do` link for creating a new user. This triggers the edit registration action, which uses the `registration.jsp` form to accept user preferences.

Figure 27-6 (later in the chapter) shows what this form looks like when it is rendered by the browser. The JSP code for the form is listed here:

```
<%@ page contentType="text/html;charset=UTF-8" language="java" %>
<%@ taglib uri="/WEB-INF/struts-bean.tld" prefix="bean" %>
<%@ taglib uri="/WEB-INF/struts-html.tld" prefix="html" %>

<html:html locale="true">
<head>
<title><bean:message key="welcome.title"/></title>
<html:base/>
</head>
<body bgcolor="white">
<h3><bean:message key="welcome.heading"/></h3>
<strong><font color="red">${error}</font></strong>
<strong><font color="blue">${ok_message}</font></strong>
<html:form action="/logon">
  <table width="100%" border="0">
    <tr>
      <td width="38%"><bean:message key="prompt.username"/></td>
      <td width="62%"><html:text property="username" size="16"
maxlength="18"/></td>
    </tr>
    <tr>
      <td><bean:message key="prompt.password"/></td>
      <td><html:password property="password" size="16" maxlength="18"
                  redisplay="false"/>
      </td>
    </tr>
    <tr>
      <td> </td>
      <td>
    <html:submit>
          <bean:message key="welcome.logon"/>
      </html:submit>
  </td>
    </tr>
    <tr>
      <td> </td>

    <td> </td>
    </tr>
    <tr>
      <td><html:link page="/editRegistration.do"><bean:message
key="welcome.newuser"/></html:link></td>
      <td> </td>
    </tr>
  </table>
</html:form>
</body>
</html:html>
```

The next JSP page shown is `registration.jsp`, mentioned earlier. This simple form enables users to enter their username, password, and interests, and select news feeds from a set of publishers:

```
<%@ page contentType="text/html;charset=UTF-8" language="java" %>
<%@ taglib uri="http://java.sun.com/jsp/jstl/core" prefix="c" %>
<%@ taglib uri="/WEB-INF/app.tld"     prefix="app" %>
<%@ taglib uri="/WEB-INF/struts-bean.tld" prefix="bean" %>
<%@ taglib uri="/WEB-INF/struts-html.tld" prefix="html" %>
<%@ taglib uri="/WEB-INF/struts-logic.tld" prefix="logic" %>
<html:html>
<head>
  <title><bean:message key="registration.title.create"/></title>
<html:base/>
</head>
<body bgcolor="white">

<html:errors/>

<html:form action="/saveRegistration">
<html:hidden property="action"/>
<table border="0" width="100%">

  <tr>
    <th align="right">
      <bean:message key="registration.username"/>:
    </th>
    <td align="left">
        <html:text property="userName" size="16" maxlength="16"/>
    </td>
  </tr>

  <tr>
    <th align="right">
      <bean:message key="registration.password"/>:
    </th>
    <td align="left">
      <html:password property="password" size="16" maxlength="16"/>
    </td>
  </tr>

  <tr>
    <th align="right">
      <bean:message key="registration.displayName"/>:
    </th>
    <td align="left">
      <html:text property="displayName" size="50"/>
    </td>
  </tr>

  <tr>
    <th align="right">
```

```
      <bean:message key="registration.interests"/>:
    </th>
    <td align="left">
      <html:text property="interests" size="50"/>
    </td>
  </tr>

  <tr>
    <th align="right">
      <bean:message key="registration.subscription"/>:
    </th>
    <td align="left">
      <html:select property="subscriptions" multiple="true">
        <c:forEach items="${publisher_info}" var="a_publisher">
            <jsp:useBean id="a_publisher"
type="com.wrox.begjsp.ch27.dto.Publisher"/>
            <html:option value="${a_publisher.feedUrl}">[${a_publisher.name}]
${a_publisher.description}</html:option>
        </c:forEach>
      </html:select>
    </td>
  </tr>

  <tr>
    <td align="right">
      <html:submit>
        <bean:message key="button.save"/>
      </html:submit>
    </td>
    <td align="left">
      <html:reset>
        <bean:message key="button.reset"/>
      </html:reset>
    </td>
  </tr>

</table>
</html:form>

</body>
</html:html>
```

As you can see in the registration JSP, no validation checks are being performed. See the exercises at the end of the chapter — this is left for you to do. Solutions are provided in Appendix D, "Exercise Solutions."

We finally come to the most important JSP page in the application, the portal page itself. This page is designed using Tiles. Figure 27-5 shows the layout of this page.

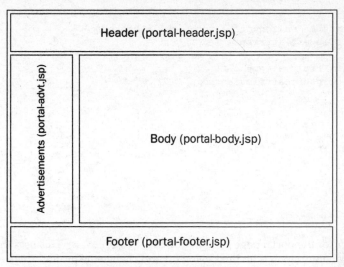

Figure 27-5: Tiles layout for the portal page

The JSP code for this page (`portalPage.jsp`) is shown here. As you can see, it simply includes its layout from `portal.layout`:

```
<%@ page language="java" %>
<%@ taglib uri="/WEB-INF/struts-tiles.tld" prefix="tiles" %>
<%@ taglib uri="/WEB-INF/app.tld" prefix="app" %>

<app:checkLogon/>
<tiles:insert definition="portal.layout" flush="true" />
```

You saw earlier in `tiles-def.xml` how `portal.layout` maps to the `layout/portal-layout.jsp` JSP file. This file is listed next and as the name suggests, defines the layout of the portal page. Compare how this corresponds to Figure 27-5.

```
<%@ taglib uri="/WEB-INF/struts-tiles.tld" prefix="tiles" %>
<%@ taglib uri="/WEB-INF/struts-bean.tld" prefix="bean" %>


<html>
  <head>
    <title><bean:message key="portalPage.title"/></title>
  </head>
<body bgcolor="white">

<table border="1" width="100%" height="100%" border="1">
<tr>
  <td colspan="2" height="100" bgcolor="gray">
      <tiles:insert attribute="header"/>
  </td>
</tr>
</tr>
```

```
<tr>
  <td width="20%" valign="top" bgcolor="lightgrey">
      <tiles:insert attribute="advt"/>
  </td>
  <td valign="top" align="left">
      <tiles:insert attribute="body"/>
  </td>
</tr>
<tr>
  <td colspan="2" height="50" bgcolor="gray">
      <tiles:insert attribute="footer"/>
  </td>
</tr>
</table>
</body>
</html>
```

Next is the header for the portal page (`tiles/portal-header.jsp`). This uses the bean profile to show the user's display name, along with links to log off and change the profile. This bean is loaded into the session by the logon action, as you will see later in the chapter.

```
...
<table width="100%" border="0">
  <tr>
    <td width="25%"> </td>
    <td width="50%"><h1 align="center"><bean:message
key="portalPage.heading"/></h1></td>
    <td width="25%"> </td>
  </tr>
  <tr>
    <td><div align="left"><bean:message key="portalPage.greetings"/>
<jsp:getProperty name="profile" property="displayName"/></div></td>
    <td> </td>
    <td><div align="right">[<html:link page="/editProfile.do"><bean:message
key="portalPage.registration"/></html:link>|<html:link
forward="logoff"><bean:message key="portalPage.logoff"/></html:link>]</div></td>
  </tr>
</table>
```

The body of the portal page (`tiles/portal-body.jsp`) shows all news items stored in the `news` bean. This bean is loaded into the request by the logon or save profile actions, as you will see later in the chapter. Note also the `c:catch` JSTL tag surrounding the JSP code. This catches any exceptions that occur during the execution of the page and prints an error message.

```
...
<c:catch var="exception">
  <c:forEach items="${news}" var="publishers">
    <jsp:useBean id="publishers" type="com.wrox.begjsp.ch27.dto.NewsFeed"/>

    <table width="100%" border="0">
      <tr>
        <td bgcolor="#CCCCCC"><div align="center"> <strong>
        <jsp:getProperty name="publishers" property="title"/>
```

```
            </strong> :
            <jsp:getProperty name="publishers" property="description"/>
            </div></td>
        </tr>
      <c:forEach items="${publishers.items}" var="newsitem">
        <jsp:useBean id="newsitem" type="com.wrox.begjsp.ch27.dto.NewsItem"/>
        <tr>
          <td><div align="left"><a href="${newsitem.newsURL}"
target=_blank>${newsitem.headline}</a></div></td>
        </tr>
        <tr>
          <td><div align="left"><em>${newsitem.description}</em></div></td>
        </tr>
        <tr>
          <td> </td>
        </tr>
      </c:forEach>
      </table>
  </c:forEach>
</c:catch>
<c:if test="${not empty exception}">
  Sorry, no news. The RSS feeds are down. Cause: ${exception}
</c:if>
```

Next are the advertisements that are shown on the sidebar (tiles/portal-advt.jsp). This JSP uses the items bean to display the advertisements. This bean is also loaded into the request by the logon or save profile actions. Again, the c:catch JSTL tag catches any exceptions that occur during the execution of the page and prints an error message.

```
<c:catch var="exception">
  <c:forEach items="${items}" var="itemgroups">
    <jsp:useBean id="itemgroups" type="com.wrox.begjsp.ch27.dto.ItemFeed"/>

  <table width="100%" border="0">
    <tr>
      <td bgcolor="#CCCCCC"><div align="center"> <strong>
          <jsp:getProperty name="itemgroups" property="itemFeedName"/>
          </strong>
          </div></td>
    </tr>
    <c:forEach items="${itemgroups.interestItem}" var="interestitem">
    <jsp:useBean id="interestitem" type="com.wrox.begjsp.ch27.dto.InterestItem"/>
      <tr>
        <td><div align="left"><a href="${interestitem.itemUrl}" target=_blank><img
src="${interestitem.imageUrl}"/></a></div></td>
      </tr>
      <tr>
        <td> <div align="left"><em><a href="${interestitem.itemUrl}"
target=_blank>${interestitem.itemName}</a></em></div></td>
      </tr>
      <tr>
        <td> </td>
      </tr>
    </c:forEach>
```

```
      </table>
    </c:forEach>
</c:catch>
<c:if test="${not empty exception}">
  Sorry, the store is closed. Cause: ${exception}
</c:if>
```

Controller

In the Struts configuration explained earlier in the chapter, you saw how the Action servlet was config-ured and the Struts configuration file (/WEB-INF/struts-config.xml) passed to it as a parameter. The Struts configuration file has the following action mappings defined:

```
<!-- ========== Global Forward Definitions ============================== -->
<global-forwards>
    <forward   name="logon"              path="/logon.do"/>
    <forward   name="logoff"             path="/logoff.do"/>
</global-forwards>


<!-- ========== Action Mapping Definitions ============================== -->
<action-mappings>

  <!-- Process a user logoff -->
  <action    path="/logoff"
             type="com.wrox.begjsp.ch27.struts.LogoffAction">
    <forward name="success"              path="/logon.jsp"/>
  </action>


  <!-- Process a user logon -->
  <action    path="/logon"
             type="com.wrox.begjsp.ch27.struts.LogonAction"
             name="logonForm"
             scope="session"
             input="logon">
    <forward name="success"     path="/portalPage.jsp"/>
    <forward name="failure"     path="/logon.jsp"/>
  </action>


  <!-- Edit user registration -->
  <action    path="/editRegistration"
             type="com.wrox.begjsp.ch27.struts.EditRegistrationAction"
        attribute="registrationForm"
          scope="request"
        validate="false">
    <forward name="success"              path="/registration.jsp"/>
  </action>
```

```
    <!-- Save user registration -->
    <action    path="/saveRegistration"
               type="com.wrox.begjsp.ch27.struts.SaveRegistrationAction"
               name="registrationForm"
             scope="request"
             input="registration">
        <forward name="success"    path="/logon.jsp"/>
        <forward name="failure"    path="/logon.jsp"/>
    </action>

    <!-- Edit profile -->
    <action    path="/editProfile"
               type="com.wrox.begjsp.ch27.struts.EditProfileAction"
         attribute="registrationForm"
             scope="request"
          validate="false">
      <forward name="success"                   path="/editProfile.jsp"/>
    </action>

    <!-- Save profile -->
    <action    path="/saveProfile"
               type="com.wrox.begjsp.ch27.struts.SaveProfileAction"
               name="registrationForm"
             scope="request"
             input="registration">
        <forward name="success"    path="/portalPage.jsp"/>
        <forward name="failure"    path="/logon.jsp"/>
    </action>

</action-mappings>
```

These action mappings can also be mapped to the control flow defined in the use cases. For example, in use case 1, the user registering with the system maps to the /editRegistration and /saveRegistration action mappings (editRegistration.do ⇨ registration.jsp ⇨ saveRegistration.do). Similarly, a user logging in as specified in use case 2 maps to /logon (logon.jsp ⇨ logon.do ⇨ portalPage.jsp).

Let's look at the code for the logon action (com.wrox.begjsp.ch27.struts.LogonAction) first:

```
package com.wrox.begjsp.ch27.struts;
...

/**
 * Implementation of an Action that authenticates a user and pulls up
 * the user profile
 */
public final class LogonAction extends Action
{
```

The first thing to note in the code is how the Log4j logger is initialized with the logger of the class. This enables you to turn on/off logging at the class level:

```
    private Logger logger = Logger.getLogger(LogonAction.class.getName());

    ...
    public ActionForward execute(ActionMapping mapping, ActionForm form,
        HttpServletRequest request, HttpServletResponse response)
        throws Exception
{

    HttpSession session = request.getSession();

    // Is there a currently logged on user?
    UserProfile userProfile = (UserProfile)
session.getAttribute(WebappConstants.PROFILE_OBJECT);

    String username = null;

    if (userProfile == null)
    {
        String error = null;
```

The code then grabs the username and password that was entered in the logon.jsp form. Based on this, the authentication service is called and the user profile is pulled up:

```
        username = (String) PropertyUtils.getSimpleProperty(form, "username");

        String password = (String) PropertyUtils.getSimpleProperty(form,
                "password");

        if (logger.isDebugEnabled())
        {
            logger.debug("Attempting to log in " + username);
        }

        try
        {
            userProfile = authenticateUser(username, password);

            if ((userProfile == null) ||
                    (userProfile.getStatus() != UserProfile.STATUS_LOGGED_IN))
            {
                error = (userProfile.getStatus() ==
UserProfile.STATUS_INVALID_USER)
                        ? "Invalid user" : "Invalid password";
                logger.info("Logon for user " + username +
                    " failed. Reason: " + error);
            }
        }
        catch (WroxServiceException e)
        {
            logger.error("Error accessing Authentication service " +
                e.getLocalizedMessage());
            error = "Portal unavailable";
        }
```

If the login call fails, perhaps due to an incorrect username/password, then an appropriate error is returned:

```
        // Report any errors
        if (error != null)
        {
            request.setAttribute(WebappConstants.ERROR_INFO, error);

            return (mapping.findForward("failure"));
        }
```

On a successful login, the profile object is saved in the session. You also get the news subscriptions for the user, along with the matching advertisements, and store them in the request. These objects (news, advertised items) are required only for the next page (portalPage.jsp), so it doesn't make sense to store them in the session. Storing a lot of information in the session is bad for Web site scalability. This and other performance tips can be found in Chapter 25, "Performance."

```
        // Save our logged-in user in the session
        session.setAttribute(WebappConstants.PROFILE_OBJECT, userProfile);
    }

    // Get the news subscriptions for the user, and save them in the request
    ArrayList news = ServiceHelper.getSubscriptions(userProfile, logger);
    request.setAttribute(WebappConstants.NEWS_OBJECT, news);

    // Get the items matching the user interest and save them in the request
    ArrayList items = ServiceHelper.getItems(userProfile, logger);
    request.setAttribute(WebappConstants.ITEMS_OBJECT, items);

    if (mapping.getAttribute() != null)
    {
        if ("request".equals(mapping.getScope()))
        {
            request.removeAttribute(mapping.getAttribute());
        }
        else
        {
            session.removeAttribute(mapping.getAttribute());
        }
    }

        if (logger.isDebugEnabled())
        {
                logger.debug("User " + username + " logged in.");
        }

    // Forward control to the specified success URI
    return (mapping.findForward("success"));
}

...
private UserProfile authenticateUser(String username, String password)
    throws WroxServiceException
```

```
        {
            AuthenticationService authService =
    WroxServiceLocator.getAuthenticationService();
            UserProfile userProfile = authService.login(username, password);

            return userProfile;
        }
    }
```

Next you have the two actions that help register a new user. The first one (`com.wrox.begjsp.ch27.`
`struts.EditRegistrationAction`) is called before the registration form (`registration.jsp`) is
shown. This initializes the form and loads the publisher list bean into the request. This bean is used by
`registration.jsp` to show details on the publishers and enables the user to choose one or more
of them.

```
package com.wrox.begjsp.ch27.struts;
...
public final class EditRegistrationAction extends Action
{
    private static Logger logger =
Logger.getLogger(EditRegistrationAction.class.getName());
    ...
    public ActionForward execute(ActionMapping mapping, ActionForm form,
        HttpServletRequest request, HttpServletResponse response)
        throws Exception
    {
        if (logger.isDebugEnabled())
        {
            logger.debug("EditRegistration invoked");
        }

        form = new RegistrationForm();
        request.setAttribute(mapping.getAttribute(), form);

        // Save a new transaction token in the user's profile
        saveToken(request);

        List publisherList = DBFactory.getPublisherDB().getPublishers();

        request.setAttribute(WebappConstants.PUBLISHER_INFO_OBJECT,
            publisherList);

        return (mapping.findForward("success"));
    }
}
```

The second action (`com.wrox.begjsp.ch27.struts.SaveRegistrationAction`) is called after the
registration form (`registration.jsp`) is shown. This does the following:

❑ Checks whether the username entered in the form is unique. If not, an error is returned.

❑ If the username is unique, then the user's profile is saved to the database and a success message
is returned.

```
package com.wrox.begjsp.ch27.struts;
...

/**
 * Processes the user registration information entered by the user.
 */
public final class SaveRegistrationAction extends Action
{
    private Logger logger =
Logger.getLogger(SaveRegistrationAction.class.getName());

    ...
    public ActionForward execute(ActionMapping mapping, ActionForm form,
        HttpServletRequest request, HttpServletResponse response)
        throws Exception
    {
        HttpSession session = request.getSession();
        RegistrationForm regform = (RegistrationForm) form;
        UserProfile userProfile = new UserProfile();

        String username = regform.getUserName();

        // Check for duplicate user name; flag error
        UserProfile checkProfile =
(DBFactory.getUserProfileDB()).getUserProfile(username);

        if ((checkProfile != null) &&
            (username.equals(checkProfile.getUserName())))
        {
            // Duplicate user!
            String errorMessage = "User " + username + " already exists";
            logger.error(errorMessage);
            request.setAttribute(WebappConstants.ERROR_INFO, errorMessage);

            return (mapping.findForward("failure"));
        }

        if (logger.isDebugEnabled())
        {
            logger.debug("Create user called for " + username +
                " with interests " + regform.getInterests() +
                " and subscription [" + regform.getSubscriptions() + "]");
        }

        userProfile.setUserName(username);
        userProfile.setPassword(regform.getPassword());
        userProfile.setDisplayName(regform.getDisplayName());

        String interestString = regform.getInterests();
        StringTokenizer tokenizer = new StringTokenizer(interestString, ",");
        String[] interests = new String[tokenizer.countTokens()];

        int i = 0;
```

```
        while (tokenizer.hasMoreTokens())
        {
            interests[i] = tokenizer.nextToken();
            i++;
        }

        userProfile.setInterests(interests);

        userProfile.setSubscriptions(regform.getSubscriptions());

        session.setAttribute(WebappConstants.PROFILE_OBJECT, userProfile);

        (DBFactory.getUserProfileDB()).insertUserProfile(userProfile);

        // Remove the obsolete form bean
        if (mapping.getAttribute() != null)
        {
            if ("request".equals(mapping.getScope()))
            {
                request.removeAttribute(mapping.getAttribute());
            }
            else
            {
                session.removeAttribute(mapping.getAttribute());
            }
        }

        // Forward control to the specified success URI
        request.setAttribute(WebappConstants.SUCCESS_INFO,
            "User account for " + regform.getUserName() +
            " created. Please log in.");

        return (mapping.findForward("success"));
    }
}
```

The edit profile (com.wrox.begjsp.ch27.struts.EditProfileAction) action that is invoked when the user is already logged in is similar to the edit registration, except for two differences:

❑   If the user's session has expired, the user is redirected to the logon page.

❑   The registration form is populated with the contents of the profile. This enables the edit profile form (editProfile.jsp) to show existing values, and enables the user to change them if desired.

The code for edit profile is shown next, with the changes highlighted:

```
public final class EditProfileAction extends Action
{
    private static Logger logger =
Logger.getLogger(EditProfileAction.class.getName());

    ...
```

```java
public ActionForward execute(ActionMapping mapping, ActionForm form,
    HttpServletRequest request, HttpServletResponse response)
    throws Exception
{
    HttpSession session = request.getSession();

    ...

    UserProfile userProfile = (UserProfile) session.getAttribute
(WebappConstants.PROFILE_OBJECT);

        // If we can't find the user profile object, then send to logon page
        if (userProfile == null)
        {
            logger.error("Session for user expired; redirecting to logon page");

            return (mapping.findForward("logon"));
        }

        // Populate the user profile
        if (form == null)
        {
            form = new RegistrationForm();
        }

        /* Populate the registration form */
        RegistrationForm regform = (RegistrationForm) form;

        regform.setUserName(userProfile.getUserName());
        regform.setPassword(userProfile.getPassword());
        regform.setDisplayName(userProfile.getDisplayName());

        String interestStr = "";
        String[] interests = userProfile.getInterests();

        for (int i = 0; i < interests.length; i++)
        {
            if (i == 0)
            {
                interestStr = interests[0];
            }
            else
            {
                interestStr += ("," + interests[i]);
            }
        }

        regform.setInterests(interestStr);
        regform.setSubscriptions(regform.getSubscriptions());

        request.setAttribute(mapping.getAttribute(), form);

    List publisherList = DBFactory.getPublisherDB().getPublishers();
    request.setAttribute(WebappConstants.PUBLISHER_INFO_OBJECT,
```

```
            publisherList);

        return (mapping.findForward("success"));
    }
}
```

The save profile (`com.wrox.begjsp.ch27.struts.SaveProfileAction`) action is similar in intent to the save registration, but has many differences:

❑   It is invoked for a logged on user, so if the session has expired, the user should be directed to the logon page instead of executing the rest of the action.

❑   You don't have to check for duplicate usernames, as you do a save profile only on an existing user.

❑   You do an update of an existing user's information, instead of inserting a new user.

❑   Finally, because this page forwards to the portal page (`portalPage.jsp`), and not the logon page like the save registration action, you would need to get fresh advertisements and news subscriptions and load them in the `request` scope.

These differences are highlighted in the following code:

```
public final class SaveProfileAction extends Action
{
    ....
    public ActionForward execute(ActionMapping mapping, ActionForm form,
        HttpServletRequest request, HttpServletResponse response)
        throws Exception
    {
        HttpSession session = request.getSession();
        RegistrationForm regform = (RegistrationForm) form;
        String action = regform.getAction();

        // Is there a currently logged on user
        UserProfile userProfile = (UserProfile)
session.getAttribute(WebappConstants.PROFILE_OBJECT);

        if (userProfile == null)
        {
            String errorMessage = "Trying to edit profile when session does not
exist";
            logger.error(errorMessage);
            request.setAttribute(WebappConstants.ERROR_INFO, errorMessage);

            return (mapping.findForward("failure"));
        }

        userProfile.setUserName(regform.getUserName());
        userProfile.setPassword(regform.getPassword());
        userProfile.setDisplayName(regform.getDisplayName());
        userProfile.setStatus(UserProfile.STATUS_LOGGED_IN);

        String interestString = regform.getInterests();
```

```
    if (interestString != null)
    {
        StringTokenizer tokenizer = new StringTokenizer(interestString, ",");
        String[] interests = new String[tokenizer.countTokens()];

        int i = 0;

        while (tokenizer.hasMoreTokens())
        {
            interests[i] = tokenizer.nextToken();
            i++;
        }

        userProfile.setInterests(interests);
    }

    String[] subscriptions = regform.getSubscriptions();

    if ((subscriptions != null) && (subscriptions.length != 0))
    {
        userProfile.setSubscriptions(regform.getSubscriptions());
    }

    session.setAttribute(WebappConstants.PROFILE_OBJECT, userProfile);

    (DBFactory.getUserProfileDB()).updateUserProfile(userProfile);

    // Get the news subscriptions for the user, and save them in the request
    ArrayList news = ServiceHelper.getSubscriptions(userProfile, logger);
    request.setAttribute(WebappConstants.NEWS_OBJECT, news);

    // Get the items matching the user interest and save them in the request
    ArrayList items = ServiceHelper.getItems(userProfile, logger);
    request.setAttribute(WebappConstants.ITEMS_OBJECT, items);
    ...
    // Forward control to the specified success URI
    request.setAttribute(WebappConstants.SUCCESS_INFO,
        "User account for " + regform.getUserName() + " modified.");

    return (mapping.findForward("success"));
}
```

Running the portal application

Now that the application has been developed, it's time to try it out. Run the Ant script to create the WAR file. You should see output on your screen similar to the following:

```
D:\work\chapter27\jspportal>ant all
Buildfile: build.xml

clean:

prepare:
```

```
    [mkdir] Created dir: D:\work\chapter27\jspportal\build
    [mkdir] Created dir: D:\work\chapter27\jspportal\build\WEB-INF
    [mkdir] Created dir: D:\work\chapter27\jspportal\build\WEB-INF\classes
     [copy] Copying 63 files to D:\work\chapter27\jspportal\build

compile:
    [javac] Compiling 98 source files to D:\work\chapter27\jspportal\build\WEB-
INF\classes
     [copy] Copying 1 file to D:\work\chapter27\jspportal\build\WEB-INF\classes

dist:
    [mkdir] Created dir: D:\work\chapter27\jspportal\dist
      [jar] Building jar: D:\work\chapter27\jspportal\dist\ch27.war

all:

BUILD SUCCESSFUL
Total time: 43 seconds
```

Deploy the WAR file (ch27.war) in Tomcat as explained in Chapter 1. Browse to the URL http://
localhost:8080/ch27/ and you should see the initial logon form, as shown in Figure 27-6.

*The following steps assume that the machine on which the Web application runs can connect to the
Internet directly. Check your browser settings (for example, Tools ⇨ Internet Options ⇨ Connections ⇨
LAN Settings in Internet Explorer) to verify this. If you are running on a machine behind a proxy
server, you need to pass that information to the JVM. This can be done by editing the Tomcat startup
script (<Tomcat Installation Directory>\bin\catalina.bat or catalina.sh), adding
the following lines at the beginning of the script:*

For catalina.bat:

set CATALINA_OPTS=%CATALINA_OPTS% -Dhttp.proxySet=true

set CATALINA_OPTS=%CATALINA_OPTS% -Dhttp.proxyHost=<proxy_host>

set CATALINA_OPTS=%CATALINA_OPTS% -Dhttp.proxyPort=<proxy_port>

For catalina.sh:

CATALINA_OPTS="${CATALINA_OPTS} -Dhttp.proxySet=true -Dhttp.proxyHost=
<proxy_host> -Dhttp.proxyPort=<proxy_port>"

*These settings are required because your Web application connects to other sites (e.g., for RSS feeds, for
Amazon Web services) internally.*

Another useful property to note here is http.nonProxyHosts. *You don't have to set it this time, but
if your application was accessing some services in an internal network, then you would specify those
hosts as nonproxy hosts because the proxy server might not be able to resolve them.*

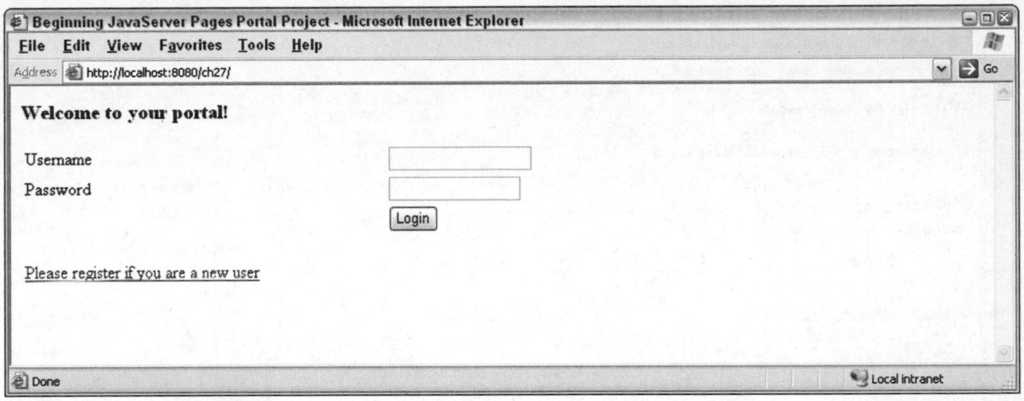

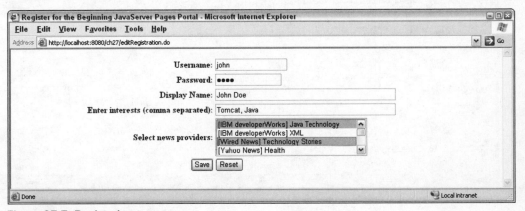

Figure 27-6: Logon form

Click the Please Register If You Are a New User link, and enter your profile information as shown in Figure 27-7. Here you create a user with interests in Tomcat and Java, and who wishes to subscribe to news content from IBM developerWorks and Wired News.

Figure 27-7: Registering a new user

Upon successfully creating a user, you are directed back to the logon page with a success message, as shown in Figure 27-8.

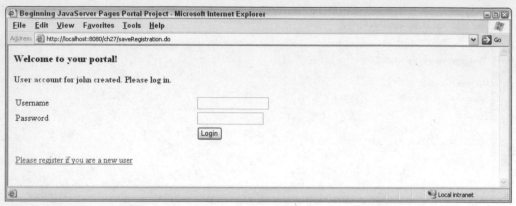

Figure 27-8: Account successfully created

If you try creating a user that already exists (the username should be unique), then you see the "User already exists" error message instead, as shown in Figure 27-9.

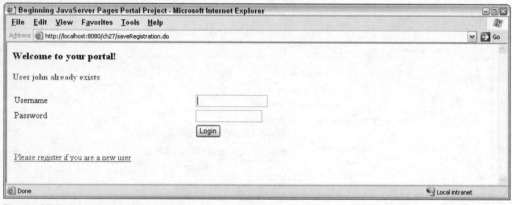

Figure 27-9: Trying to create a user that already exists

Finally, when you log in, you are shown your portal page (see Figure 27-10), with news from the publishers that you configured, and advertisements for books that match your interest profile.

If you don't like what you see, you can click the Edit Profile link, and edit your profile as shown in Figure 27-11. Here, the user chooses just one news provider (XML news from IBM developerWorks) and enters XML as the sole interest area.

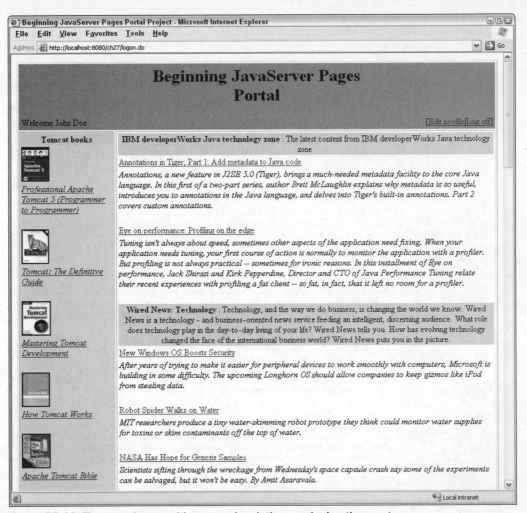

Figure 27-10: The portal page with news subscriptions and advertisements

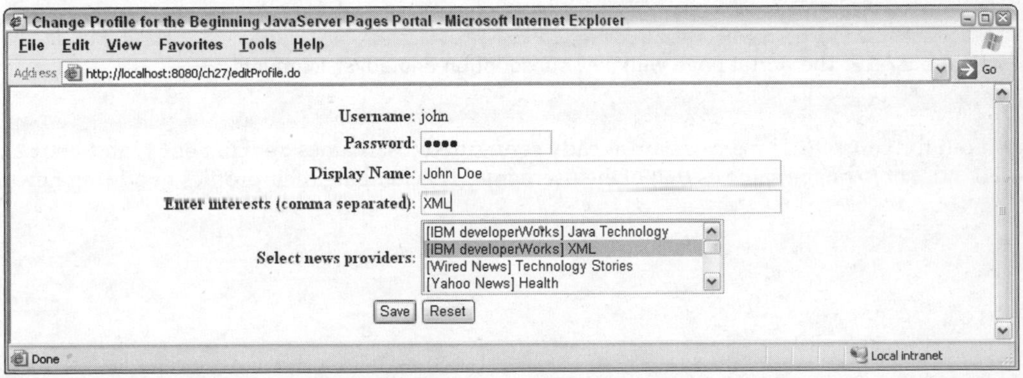

Figure 27-11: It's easy to modify a profile.

When this profile is saved, the user is returned to the portal page (see Figure 27-12), with the new profile in effect. Notice the new content from the IBM developerWorks XML zone, and also the different books being advertised to the user.

Figure 27-12: The portal page with new subscription and advertisements

Try it out for yourself! Three users are already configured (usernames test0, test1, and test2), with passwords set to be the same as that of the username. Try changing their profiles or adding new users.

Summary

This project, which exposed you to several concepts described in previous chapters, was designed to be a refresher to the earlier chapters. These concepts included the MVC architecture, Struts, Tiles, Log4j, Ant, and JSTL among others. The project also touched upon more complex areas, such as design patterns and concepts from enterprise Java. It is difficult to cover a complete JSP-based project that illustrates good design principles yet avoid mentioning or using common design patterns. That said, this is not a design pattern book, or an enterprise Java book, but rather lays the foundations from which you can move on to that stage.

The complete code for this project can be downloaded from the Wrox Web site (www.wrox.com).

Exercises

1. Replace the memory database implementation with one that uses a relational database, minimizing code changes to the portal.

2. Add validation to the registration and change profile Web forms.

28

JSP Project II: Shopping Cart Application

Welcome to the final chapter of the book! You've come a long way since the humble beginnings of Chapter 1. This chapter, together with Chapter 27, applies some of the tools and techniques that have been covered in the preceding 26 chapters and illustrates them in the context of a real-world application. In addition to the general JSP usage explained in the book, this chapter focuses on the concepts covered in the following chapters for building an application:

❑   Chapter 11, "Building Your Own Custom JSP Tag Library"

❑   Chapter 17, "Model View Controller"

❑   Chapter 19, "Struts Framework"

❑   Chapter 20, "Layout Management with Tiles"

❑   Chapter 23, "Access to Databases"

❑   Chapter 26, "Best Practices and Tools"

You should make yourself familiar with the content of these chapters before embarking on this one. By the end of this chapter, you should have a much better understanding of how the tools and techniques explained in this book will help you develop your own applications.

This chapter is progressive. First the features of the application are discussed, much like a customer would describe them. The chapter then describes the design approach the application will take, examining the database schema and the key entities and objects involved. The development environment is then described, enabling you to replicate it on your own computer. Note that the source code of the application described in this chapter can be downloaded from the Wrox Web site at www.wrox.com.

Once the development environment is established, the functional areas of the application are examined individually, enabling you to gain an understanding of how the different components and entities interact to fulfill the requirements.

The Bookstore Project

The shopping cart application presented in this chapter will use an online bookstore as its implementation but could be easily adapted to sell a range of products to customers. Applications, even simple ones like this one, can have massive requirements, and because of the limited space of a single chapter, we can present only a subset of the implementation required for a full-scale online inventory and sales system. You could use this project as a basis for your own implementations if you were so inclined.

Project features

The features of the bookstore project are presented here in a brief, informal use-case type format. Use cases are simply one way of describing the interaction of the user of a system with the system itself. They do not specify the implementation because this is typically not something the customer needs (or wants) to know about. Use cases are designed to capture the specific requirements of a system without clouding the user with technical detail. As developers, however, we are technical people, so it is therefore our job to read the use cases and translate their implications into some sort of workable product that will accurately deliver the functionality desired by the customer. This is sometimes easier said than done. Because project management and business analysis are not our main concerns here, we've gone easy on you and made the requirements fairly explicit and clear.

There are entire books, even careers, devoted to the techniques and strategies of collecting and presenting customer requirements. A use case is only one of these techniques. They are used here in a very informal manner.

Use cases

The application has the following requirements:

1. The user browses to the application and is presented with a list of book categories.

2. The user selects a book category and is presented with a list of books that are within the selected category.

3. The user clicks a link to add a book to the shopping cart. If a selected item is already in the shopping cart, the quantity in the cart will be incremented by one, rather than being added as a new item.

4. The user clicks a menu link to view the current contents of the shopping cart. This page, the Manage Cart page, presents a list of the shopping cart items, along with the quantity and price of each. At the bottom of the list is the total value of the cart. The quantity of each item is presented in a form that the user can modify to change the quantity in the cart. At the bottom of the list is an Update button that refreshes the page and updates the user's shopping cart with the new quantities. If a value of zero is entered as the quantity of a shopping cart item, that item will be removed from the cart.

5. If the user goes to the Manage Cart page and there are no items, a message will be displayed indicating that there are no items in the cart.

6. From the Manage Cart page, the user can select to clear the entire cart, removing all items. When the user selects this link, all items are removed from the cart and the user is presented with the catalogue list, as in use case 1.

7. The user selects a Checkout button from the menu and is presented with a form that collects personal and credit cart number information. The form ensures that all values are entered, and appropriate validation is performed against the zip code field and the credit card number. At the base of the form, the current content and value of the order are again displayed.

8. If the user selects to checkout when there are no items in the shopping cart, the form will not be displayed. A message will indicate that there are no items to check out.

9. Once all values are entered into the checkout form, the user clicks a Checkout button and the order is submitted to the system. If the credit card purchase is approved, the user is presented with a confirmation screen and the current shopping cart is emptied. If the credit cart purchase is declined, the user is presented with a message inviting them to try again or contact their bank. In the decline scenario, the shopping cart is not emptied.

10. The customer needs to keep track of declined orders, so even though an order is declined it should be recorded and marked as declined.

11. On all pages in the application, a small discrete area will display the current number of unique items in the shopping cart and its current value.

12. The system should ensure that a price change for a book does not affect the cost of orders that have previously been recorded or the cost of books that users have already added to their shopping cart. Customers are understandably unhappy when they add an item to a shopping cart at one price and find out that the item is suddenly more expensive when they check out.

Initial analysis

Looking over this list of requirements and behaviors, it is often good practice to identify the major entities, or domain concepts, that the system uses. It is hoped that you will have identified the following:

❑ **Shopping Cart:** A temporary receptacle for the user's pending order. This contains shopping cart items of various quantities.

❑ **Category:** A logical grouping of books.

❑ **Book:** The product the user intends to purchase from the system. A book has a price.

❑ **Order:** A purchase order recorded in the system containing customer details and items that are purchased by the customer in various quantities.

❑ **Order Status:** Whether an order was approved or declined.

❑ **Shopping Cart item:** An item that might be ordered by the user and has been added to the shopping cart. A shopping cart item has a property representing the quantity of the book it represents.

Based on this list, you can make some important decisions. It is clear that an item in a shopping cart is related to, but distinct from, a simple book, the product. First of all, a shopping cart item can represent many copies of the same book. Its value, therefore, is not simply the value of the book, but the value of the book multiplied by the quantity requested. A book, however, is the basic product itself, with a per-unit price.

Use case 12 tells us that the prices of books in recorded orders and in shopping carts should not be affected by price changes made to books in the system. We will need to record the unit price of the book when an item is added to the user's shopping cart. This unit price will be separate from the unit price that the system holds for each book.

An order is closely related to a shopping cart; both have a collection of items with various quantities. The differences are that the order contains customer information and is a permanent record, whereas a shopping cart is a temporary entity. Once the user completes an order successfully, or leaves the site, the shopping cart ceases to exist. Figure 28-1 represents the process of creating an order in the system.

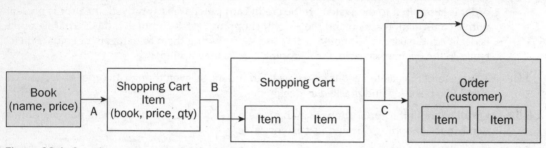

Figure 28-1: Creating a new order in the system

Tracing the steps of the diagram in Figure 28-1, step A represents a user selecting a book and creating a shopping cart item. This item is then placed in the shopping cart in step B. Step C shows the customer committing to an order. Step D represents a customer abandoning a shopping cart. The gray boxes highlight parts of the system that are persistent: a book with its own name and unit price, and an order, along with its customer details and collection of items. There are other parts of the system that we will need to persist, but these are the most important areas for this discussion.

Now that we have a clear understanding of the relationships that exist in the shopping cart system, the design process can move on to the database and define the important objects that will exist in the system.

Application Design

In this section, we will determine the broad structure of some of the key entities in the application and how some of these will be represented in the database.

Database design

Our initial design discussion led to the discovery of some important *things* that need to be represented in the application. Some of these are temporary, and only live as long as the duration of the user's session on the application; others need to be recorded in the database.

The diagram in Figure 28-1 and the requirements illustrate that the following entities need to be persisted in some way (for us this will be using a relational database):

❏   Customer order

❏   Order status

❏   Shopping cart item

❏   Book

❏   Category

By the time a shopping cart item is persisted, it is no longer related to the shopping cart itself, but to the order. A shopping cart item's sole purpose is to be associated, eventually, with an order. Therefore, it makes sense to call it an order item instead, even though it is initially created in a shopping cart. From now on we will refer to this entity as an order item.

The driving force behind designing any relational database is, as the name suggests, the relationships that exist between the entities. In this application, the relationships are very easy to illustrate. They can be summarized as follows: A category has many books; a book has one category. An order item has one book; a book has many order items. An order can have many order items; an order item has one order. An order has one order status. An order status can have many orders.

These relationships become clearer when we present the associated entity relationship diagram (ERD), as shown in Figure 28-2.

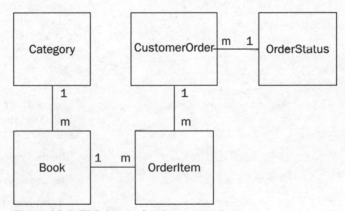

Figure 28-2: ERD for the bookstore application

An ERD is a very powerful diagram that is fairly ubiquitous with relational database design. You read the diagram much like the text description earlier: A category has many books; a book has one category, and so on. The *1* and *m* represent the *one* and *many* sides of the relationship. ERDs are capable of representing far more complicated relationships than these, but our application doesn't require them

These entities represent the tables in our database. Each table will have a number of columns that will record the required information for each row. The following table shows the columns for each of these.

Name	Type	Description
category		
id	int, primary key, auto increment	Unique identifier for categories.
name	varchar(100)	The name of the category.
description	varchar(200)	A description of the category.
book		
id	int, primary key, auto increment	Unique identifier for books.
name	varchar(100)	The name of the book.
description	varchar(200)	A description of the book.
unitprice	float	The unit price of each copy of this book.
category	int, foreign key	Foreign key to the id field of the category table. Represents the relationship between a book and a category.
customerorder		
id	int, primary key, auto increment	Unique identifier for customer orders. Will also represent the reference number received by the customer.
firstname	varchar(100)	The first name of the customer.
lastname	varchar(100)	The last name of the customer.
address	varchar(100)	The address of the customer.
zipcode	varchar(10)	The Zip code of the customer's address.
orderdate	datetime	The date and time of the order.
status	int, foreign key	Foreign key to the id field of the orderstatus table. Represents the relationship between a customer order and order status.
cardnumber	varchar(20)	The credit card number of the customer.

Name	Type	Description
orderstatus		
id	int, primary key	Unique identifier for customer orders.
name	varchar(20)	The name of the order status (approved or declined).
orderitem		
id	int, primary key, auto increment	Unique identifier for customer orders.
bookid	int, foreign key	Foreign key to the id field of the book table. Represents the relationship between an order item and a book.
ordered	int, foreign key, allow null	Foreign key to the id field of the customerorder table. Represents the relationship between a customerorder and an orderitem.
unitprice	float	The price of the book at the time of purchase.

This database structure will satisfy the requirements of the application. Additional requirements, such as customer accounts, stored shopping carts, and other products, would require additional changes to be made.

Defining the key entity objects

In a simplistic application such as this one, typically the database entities are shadowed by corresponding programmatic objects. For instance, all the tables listed in the previous section will have associated objects representing important business concepts.

The mapping between the database entities and the object entities will be managed by Hibernate. Hibernate enables you to treat your interactions with persistent objects in an object-oriented manner, rather than piecing together objects from unique identifiers. This way, your objects can have rich references to other objects, rather than an integer id reference. For example, the CustomerOrder object will need a reference to an OrderStatus. Rather than simply having a private int member variable as a reference to the ID of the appropriate row of the orderstatus table, our CustomerOrder object can actually have an OrderStatus as the member variable. This has the effect of making our application code more about the relationships between objects, rather than the relationships between database tables.

Not all of the key entity objects will be persisted. The ShoppingCart object, for instance, will represent the collection of items the customer *might* buy; it will reside in the session of the user but will not be persisted when an order is made. Instead, a new `CustomerOrder` representing its contents and the details of the customer will be created and saved to the database.

The following discussion defines each of these key entities and provides their source code.

BaseEntity

`BaseEntity` is an abstract object that will act as a superclass for objects that are managed and persisted by Hibernate. `BaseEntity` also provides a member variable, the `int id`, as well as associated getter and setter methods that the subclasses can inherit. Having this `BaseEntity` available will be convenient when implementing the class that will manage the persistence of objects. The source code for the `BaseEntity` class is as follows:

```
package com.wrox.begjsp.ch28.bookstore;

public abstract class BaseEntity
{
    private int _id = 0;

    public int getId()
    {
        return _id;
    }

    public void setId(int id)
    {
        _id = id;
    }
}
```

This class is declared `abstract` as it is not intended to be instantiated in the application; rather, it is used as a core type for other entities so that they can be referenced in a more general manner.

CustomerOrder

A `CustomerOrder` object extends `BaseEntity` and represents a completed order in the system. Its member variables include a collection of `OrderItem` objects and details of the customer who created the order. `CustomerOrder` objects will also have a reference to an `OrderStatus` indicating if the order was approved or declined.

```
package com.wrox.begjsp.ch28.bookstore;

import java.sql.Date;
import java.util.Iterator;
import java.util.Set;

public class CustomerOrder extends BaseEntity
{
    private String _firstName;
    private String _lastName;
    private String _address;
    private String _zipCode;
    private Date _orderDate;
```

```java
private OrderStatus _status;
private String _cardNumber;
private Set _orderItems;

public String getAddress()
{
    return _address;
}

public void setAddress(String address)
{
    _address = address;
}

public String getFirstName()
{
    return _firstName;
}

public void setFirstName(String firstName)
{
    _firstName = firstName;
}

public String getLastName()
{
    return _lastName;
}

public void setLastName(String lastName)
{
    _lastName = lastName;
}

public Date getOrderDate()
{
    return _orderDate;
}

public void setOrderDate(Date orderDate)
{
    _orderDate = orderDate;
}

public OrderStatus getStatus()
{
    return _status;
}

public void setStatus(OrderStatus status)
{
    _status = status;
}
```

```
        public String getZipCode()
        {
            return _zipCode;
        }

        public void setZipCode(String zipcode)
        {
            _zipCode = zipcode;
        }

        public String getCardNumber()
        {
            return _cardNumber;
        }

        public void setCardNumber(String cardNumber)
        {
            _cardNumber = cardNumber;
        }

        public Set getOrderItems()
        {
            return _orderItems;
        }

        public void setOrderItems(Set orderItems)
        {
            _orderItems = orderItems;
        }

        public float getValue()
        {
            Iterator it = _orderItems.iterator();
            float result = 0.0f;

            while (it.hasNext())
            {
                OrderItem item = (OrderItem) it.next();
                result += item.getValue();
            }

            return result;
        }
    }
```

In addition to the set and get methods for each of the member variables, a getValue method has been added. This method provides us with the total value of the items represented by this order. It uses the getValue method of each of its OrderItem objects in order to calculate it.

OrderItem

The OrderItem extends BaseEntity and represents an item in a customer's order. Rather than an order being made up of an individual item for each individual product purchased, the OrderItem will represent the book, a unit price, and a quantity that the customer has ordered. Recording the unit price separately from the book ensures that our model supports the price changes requirement discussed earlier.

If a customer purchases ten copies of a book, it will be represented by one corresponding OrderItem object with a quantity of ten, and a value that reflects the product of unit price and quantity. Because of the structure of this object, it makes sense to use it in the temporary phases of an order's creation. When a customer adds a new item to the shopping cart, the system will represent this by adding an appropriate OrderItem. This is consistent with the diagram in Figure 28-1, but we've renamed the shopping cart item to OrderItem.

An OrderItem, therefore, has a reference to the book the customer has ordered, the unit price at the time the OrderItem was selected, and a quantity of this item in the order. The source code for the OrderItem class is as follows:

```java
package com.wrox.begjsp.ch28.bookstore;

public class OrderItem extends BaseEntity
{
    private Book _book;
    private CustomerOrder _order;
    private int _qty = 0;
    private float _unitPrice = 0.0f;

    public OrderItem()
    {
    }

    public Book getBook()
    {
        return _book;
    }

    public String getBookDescription()
    {
        return _book.getDescription();
    }

    public int getBookId()
    {
        return _book.getId();
    }

    public String getBookName()
    {
        return _book.getName();
    }

    public CustomerOrder getOrder()
    {
        return _order;
    }
```

```
    public int getQty()
    {
        return _qty;
    }

    public float getUnitPrice()
    {
        return _unitPrice;
    }

    public float getValue()
    {
        return _unitPrice * _qty;
    }

    public void setBook(Book book)
    {
        _book = book;
    }

    public void setOrder(CustomerOrder order)
    {
        _order = order;
    }

    public void setQty(int qty)
    {
        _qty = qty;
    }

    public void setUnitPrice(float unitPrice)
    {
        _unitPrice = unitPrice;
    }

    public int hashCode()
    {
        return getBook().getId();
    }

    public boolean equals(Object o)
    {
        OrderItem i = (OrderItem) o;
        return _book.equals(i.getBook());
    }
}
```

Note in this class how the default equals method has been overridden. The system will equate two OrderItem objects (consider them the same) if they represent the same book.

OrderStatus

OrderStatus extends BaseEntity and represents the success or failure of the order with respect to payment. There are only two possible values of OrderStatus: approved and declined. This simple object will have a name field. The source code for the OrderStatus class is as follows:

```
package com.wrox.begjsp.ch28.bookstore;

public class OrderStatus extends BaseEntity
{
    private String _name;

    public String getName()
    {
        return _name;
    }

    public void setName(String name)
    {
        _name = name;
    }
}
```

Category

The Category object extends BaseEntity and represents a logical collection of books. The Category object will have a reference to a collection of Book objects, that being the books in this category. In addition, the Category object will have a name and description so that it can be referenced and displayed.

```
package com.wrox.begjsp.ch28.bookstore;

import java.util.List;

public class Category extends BaseEntity
{
    private List _books;
    private String _description;
    private String _name;

    public Category()
    {
    }

    public int getBookCount()
    {
        return _books.size();
    }

    public List getBooks()
    {
        return _books;
    }
```

```
public String getDescription()
{
    return _description;
}

public String getName()
{
    return _name;
}

public void setBooks(List books)
{
    _books = books;
}

public void setDescription(String description)
{
    _description = description;
}

public void setName(String name)
{
    _name = name;
}
}
```

Book

A Book object extends BaseEntity and represents the product in the system that customers intend (hopefully!) to buy. A Book has a reference to its associated Category. Additionally, the Book object will have a name, a description, and a unit price. The source code is shown here:

```
package com.wrox.begjsp.ch28.bookstore;


public class Book extends BaseEntity
{
    private Category _category;
    private String _description;
    private String _name;
    private float _unitPrice;

    public Book()
    {
    }

    public Category getCategory()
    {
        return _category;
    }

    public String getDescription()
    {
```

```
        return _description;
    }

    public String getName()
    {
        return _name;
    }

    public float getUnitPrice()
    {
        return _unitPrice;
    }

    public void setCategory(Category category)
    {
        _category = category;
    }

    public void setDescription(String description)
    {
        _description = description;
    }

    public void setName(String name)
    {
        _name = name;
    }

    public void setUnitPrice(float price)
    {
        _unitPrice = price;
    }

    public int hashCode()
    {
        return getId();
    }

    public boolean equals(Object o)
    {
        Book b = (Book) o;

        if (getId() == b.getId())
        {
            return true;
        }

        return false;
    }
}
```

ShoppingCart

The ShoppingCart object reflects the collection of items that the customer may purchase and has a life-cycle extending from the customer's first arrival at the site to her departure or completion of an order. The lifecycle of this object is not really our concern here; this will be managed by the controller structure we implement. This is covered later in the chapter in more detail.

The ShoppingCart object must be structured in such a way that it can store a list of unique OrderItem objects that represent products in quantities before they are purchased. In addition to storing data in a certain fashion, it must also provide behavior to manipulate that data as the application requires.

Internally, the ShoppingCart will maintain a java.util.Set of items. Implementations of the Set interface (such as java.util.HashSet) guarantee a unique collection of items such that no objects in the Set are equal (using the object's equals method). This suits our purposes perfectly, as we want to ensure that when a customer adds an item to her shopping cart and that item is already there, the quantity is only incremented rather than a separate new item being added. We can use the behavior of the Set interface to help us enforce this business rule.

The ShoppingCart also needs to expose methods that will enable the application to manipulate the contents of the cart, such as adding items, replacing items, and removing items. The source code for the ShoppingCart object is as follows:

```
package com.wrox.begjsp.ch28.bookstore;

import java.util.HashSet;
import java.util.Iterator;
import java.util.Set;

public class ShoppingCart
{
    private Set items = null;

    public ShoppingCart()
    {
        items = new HashSet();
    }

    public void addOrIncrementItem(OrderItem toAdd)
    {
        OrderItem existing = getItemForBook(toAdd.getBook());

        if(existing != null)
        {
            removeItem(existing);
            int qty = existing.getQty();
            toAdd.setQty(toAdd.getQty() + qty);
        }
        addItem(toAdd);
    }

    public void replaceItem(OrderItem toReplace)
    {
```

```java
        OrderItem existing = getItemForBook(toReplace.getBook());

        if(existing != null)
        {
            removeItem(existing);
        }
        addItem(toReplace);
    }

    private void addItem(OrderItem item)
    {
        items.add(item);
    }

    public void removeItem(OrderItem  item)
    {
        items.remove(item);
    }

    public void clear()
    {
        items.clear();
    }

    public Set getItems()
    {
        return items;
    }

    public int getItemCount()
    {
        return items.size();
    }

    private OrderItem getItemForBook(Book book)
    {
        Iterator it = items.iterator();

        while(it.hasNext())
        {
            OrderItem item = (OrderItem) it.next();
            if(item.getBook().equals(book))
                return item;
        }
        return null;
    }

    public float getValue()
    {
        Set items = getItems();
        float result = 0.0f;

        Iterator it = items.iterator();
```

```
        while (it.hasNext())
        {
            OrderItem i = (OrderItem) it.next();
            result += i.getValue();
        }

        return result;
    }
}
```

The ShoppingCart class exposes methods that enable its contents to be manipulated, such as addOrIncrementItem(OrderItem), which will either add an item that doesn't exist already in the ShoppingCart or increase the quantity of that item as appropriate. If the item does exist, then its quantity is added to the existing items. replaceItem(OrderItem) ignores the quantity of the existing item (if any) and simply replaces it. A getValue() method in this class enables the total value of its contents to be retrieved.

Note from the preceding discussion that none of these objects is aware of the environment in which they will be used. This includes knowledge of the persistence mechanism to be used (Hibernate), or the MVC framework that will organize and present data stored in these structures to the customer (Struts/Tiles). These objects represent key components of the Model layer of our application; keeping them decoupled as much as possible from other layers and the infrastructure is an important goal to achieve.

Persistence management design

Hibernate will be used to persist most of the objects described in the preceding section. This will be achieved with the implementation of an EntityManager object whose role is to manage the saving, updating, and retrieving of these entities to and from the database. The EntityManager object will be instantiated with the class that it is responsible for managing (i.e., OrderItem.class). This means that the single EntityManager object can be used to manage all the Hibernate mapped classes in the application. To make the instantiation of the EntityManager easier, an EntityManagerFactory object is used to create an EntityManager object for the desired class. For the EntityManager to be useful, it needs access to a Hibernate session object. This is the job of the SessionProvider.

SessionProvider

The EntityManager will use a SessionProvider object as a source of the Hibernate session. The Hibernate session represents a conversation between the application and the persistence mechanism. This session will be used in the EntityManager to save, update, and retrieve data in the database. It manages the important line between the relational world of the database and the object-oriented world of the application. Importantly, the application does not need to be explicitly aware of the semantics of the database that is managed by Hibernate.

A Hibernate session is derived from a SessionFactory that is configured according to the demands of the application — classes to persist with object mappings, database connections, and database dialects, just to name a few. As you learned in Chapter 23, "Access to Databases," creating a SessionFactory is an expensive task in terms of performance, so it makes sense that the application creates it only once. The SessionProvider will therefore have a static reference to the SessionFactory that is instantiated when the SessionProvider is first invoked. There are countless ways to manage this, static and non-static, but the implementation illustrated here is used as much for clarity as anything else.

The Hibernate session itself is instantiated from the `SessionFactory` and stored in the confines of a static `ThreadLocal` object. The semantics of `ThreadLocal` are beyond the scope of this discussion. It is only important to understand that each thread that accesses the `ThreadLocal` variable is provided with its own copy of the Hibernate session. If you wish to learn more about `ThreadLocal`, there is a good explanation from IBM developerWorks (www-106.ibm.com/developerworks/java/library/j-threads3.html). The source code for the `SessionProvider` is as follows:

```java
package com.wrox.begjsp.ch28.bookstore.persist;

import net.sf.hibernate.FlushMode;
import net.sf.hibernate.HibernateException;
import net.sf.hibernate.Session;
import net.sf.hibernate.SessionFactory;
import net.sf.hibernate.cfg.Configuration;

public class SessionProvider
{
    private static final SessionFactory sessionFactory;
    public static final ThreadLocal session = new ThreadLocal();

    static
    {
        try
        {
            Configuration config = new Configuration();
            config = config.configure("/hibernate.cfg.xml");
            sessionFactory = config.buildSessionFactory();
        }
        catch (HibernateException ex)
        {
            throw new RuntimeException("Exception building SessionFactory: " +
                ex.getMessage(), ex);
        }
    }

    public static Session currentSession() throws HibernateException
    {
        Session s = (Session) session.get();

        // Open a new Session, if this Thread has none yet
        if (s == null)
        {
            s = sessionFactory.openSession();
            s.setFlushMode(FlushMode.COMMIT);
            session.set(s);
        }

        return s;
    }

    public static void closeSession() throws HibernateException
    {
        Session s = (Session) session.get();
```

```
        session.set(null);

        if (s != null)
        {
            s.close();
        }
    }
}
```

This is probably the most complicated class in this application. Its job is to provide the application with Hibernate sessions (as the name suggests). It can provide this session because the SessionFactory that provides the sessions has been configured appropriately. This configuration can be seen in the static{} initializer at the top of the code sample. Here, the default configuration file (a file called hibernate.cfg.xml that you will see later) is used to configure the SessionFactory only once when the SessionProvider class is first instantiated. This code explicitly specified the hibernate.cfg.xml file when using the configure method of the Configuration object for clarity, but strictly speaking you wouldn't have to; Hibernate will look for a file by this name if one is not specified.

The currentSession method shown previously will be used from the EntityManager object to retrieve the current session. If one is not available, a new session will be created and added to the ThreadLocal instance. This session will then be used to save, update, and retrieve persistent objects in the EntityManager. The closeSession method will be called at the conclusion of each request in the application.

EntityManager and EntityManagerFactory

The EntityManager is the interface into Hibernate and object persistence used by the rest of the application. The EntityManager provides a series of simple methods to save, update, and retrieve items from and to the data store as the application demands.

Some of the operations in the EntityManager need to know which persistent object is being worked on. For instance, if you retrieve a list of all items of something, the EntityManager needs to know that you in fact mean to retrieve a complete list of CustomerOrders, or one of the other Hibernate-managed classes. The EntityManager will therefore take a Class in its sole constructor when being set up for relevant operations. Some of the operations within EntityManager don't rely on this class object; for instance, the saveOrUpdate method takes a BaseEntity object as its only parameter. It knows which class it needs to persist; it can determine this from the parameter itself. It would therefore be possible to persist a CustomerOrder object with an EntityManager set up to manage Category objects; ugly, but possible. The full source code of the EntityManager is shown here:

```
package com.wrox.begjsp.ch28.bookstore.persist;

import java.util.ArrayList;
import java.util.List;

import net.sf.hibernate.Criteria;
import net.sf.hibernate.HibernateException;
import net.sf.hibernate.Query;
import net.sf.hibernate.Session;
import net.sf.hibernate.Transaction;
```

```
import com.wrox.begjsp.ch28.bookstore.BaseEntity;

public class EntityManager
{
    private Class _cl;

    protected EntityManager(Class cl)
    {
        _cl = cl;
    }

    public List findAll() throws HibernateException
    {
        List rv = new ArrayList();

        Session session = SessionProvider.currentSession();
        Criteria criteria = session.createCriteria(_cl);
        rv = criteria.list();

        return rv;
    }

    public BaseEntity findById(int id) throws HibernateException
    {
        Session session = SessionProvider.currentSession();
        BaseEntity rv = (BaseEntity) session.get(_cl, new Integer(id));

        return rv;
    }

    public BaseEntity saveOrUpdate(BaseEntity entity) throws HibernateException
    {
        Session session = SessionProvider.currentSession();
        Transaction tx = session.beginTransaction();
        session.saveOrUpdate(entity);
        tx.commit();

        return entity;
    }
}
```

The EntityManager contains the following key methods for manipulating values in the database.

findAll()

This method retrieves a list of all the values in the database for this object mapping. A simple Hibernate Criteria object is established with the Class object that was used when this EntityManager was established. The returning value will be a list of the objects represented by the mapped class.

findById(int id)

This method retrieves a single value based on the `Class` this `EntityManager` has been configured with and the `id` parameter. The method creates a `Query` object with the appropriate Hibernate SQL (HSQL) and retrieves a list containing a single item. The `load()` method of the Hibernate session is used to instantiate the value required. If the value doesn't exist, a `HibernateException` is thrown.

saveOrUpdate(BaseEntity entity)

This method creates new persistent values or updates existing values. Hibernate determines which action to perform based on the value of the `id` field. A value of 0, the default value as defined in the `BaseEntity` class, ensures that Hibernate creates a new value. Any other value for the `id` field will cause Hibernate to perform an update. The *unsaved value*, 0 in this case, is defined in the Hibernate configuration files discussed later. Note in this method that the operation is performed within a transaction. Hibernate uses the underlying JDBC transaction management to ensure proper transactional integrity of such operations.

Note that the `EntityManager` has a constructor with protected access. This means that only objects within the `com.wrox.begjsp.ch28.bookstore.persist` package (or their subclasses) can instantiate this class as an object. So how does the rest of the application use this important class? Instantiations of the `EntityManager` are retrieved from the `EntityManagerFactory`. The `Entity ManagerFactory` has a retrieval method for each of the persistent objects in the application that require direct management: `CustomerOrder`, `OrderStatus`, `Category`, and `Book`. These methods return `EntityManager` instances instantiated with the appropriate class. The source code is as follows:

```
package com.wrox.begjsp.ch28.bookstore.persist;

import com.wrox.begjsp.ch28.bookstore.Book;
import com.wrox.begjsp.ch28.bookstore.Category;
import com.wrox.begjsp.ch28.bookstore.CustomerOrder;
import com.wrox.begjsp.ch28.bookstore.OrderStatus;

public class EntityManagerFactory
{
    public static EntityManager getBookManagerInstance()
    {
        return new EntityManager(Book.class);
    }

    public static EntityManager getCategoryManagerInstance()
    {
        return new EntityManager(Category.class);
    }

    public static EntityManager getOrderManagerInstance()
    {
        return new EntityManager(CustomerOrder.class);
    }

    public static EntityManager getOrderStatusManagerInstance()
    {
        return new EntityManager(OrderStatus.class);
    }
}
```

Using this factory is simple. Suppose you wanted to manage `CustomerOrder` objects in some way. The following example code uses the factory to create an appropriate manager and then perform some function with the manager:

```
EntityManager orderManager = EntityManagerFactory.getOrderManagerInstance();
CustomerOrder order = (CustomerOrder) orderManager.findById(3);
```

As the `findById(int)` method of the `EntityManager` returns the generic `BaseEntity` object, (`CustomerOrder` is a `BaseEntity`), the value needs to be cast to a `CustomerOrder`.

Controller object design

So far, we have discussed entities and objects that form the model layers of the application, i.e., where the specific business relationships are defined and used. In Controller object design, you are more concerned with how to structure the Struts actions that will control and manage the presentation of the application to a browser.

You know from the requirements of the application that various actions need to be implemented. You can also tell that these actions will need to perform various functions that other actions may also need to perform. It makes sense therefore that the actions in this application should extend a common action that you can control, rather than the typical Struts `Action` class, which you have no control over because you don't want to change Struts. Having a common parent class Controller means that the common operations can be defined in one place that all actions can access, thereby reducing code duplication. Figure 28-3 shows the hierarchy of Struts actions in the application.

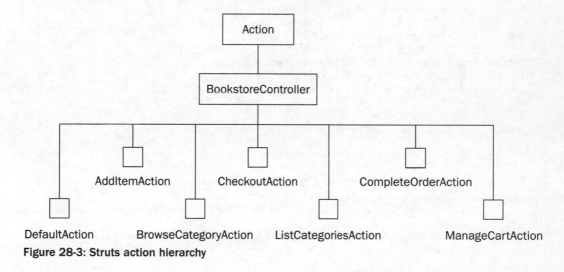

Figure 28-3: Struts action hierarchy

The parent Controller is called `BookstoreController` and performs two important functions for the application:

❑ It exposes methods that are used by more than one subclass action.

❑ It manages the lifecycle of a user request through the application such that operations can be executed before and after the subclass action has been executed.

The BookstoreController is able to provide these capabilities for two reasons:

❑ It extends the Struts Action class, which all Struts actions must extend. All actions in this application will use the BookstoreController as their superclass.

❑ It implements the execute method that Struts actions must implement. This method implementation calls a doAction method found in all of its subclasses. Subclasses are forced to implement the doAction method because it is declared abstract in the BookstoreController. This capability to call the doAction method of the subclass from the execute method of BookstoreController allows us to intervene and perform logic that will apply to all the subclass actions before and after the call to doAction.

The source code for the BookstoreController is as follows:

```
package com.wrox.begjsp.ch28.bookstore.controller;

import com.wrox.begjsp.ch28.bookstore.Category;
import com.wrox.begjsp.ch28.bookstore.OrderItem;
import com.wrox.begjsp.ch28.bookstore.ShoppingCart;
import com.wrox.begjsp.ch28.bookstore.persist.SessionProvider;

import net.sf.hibernate.HibernateException;

import org.apache.struts.action.Action;
import org.apache.struts.action.ActionForm;
import org.apache.struts.action.ActionForward;
import org.apache.struts.action.ActionMapping;

import java.util.List;

import javax.servlet.http.HttpServletRequest;
import javax.servlet.http.HttpServletResponse;
import javax.servlet.http.HttpSession;


public abstract class BookstoreController extends Action
{
    private final static String CART_NAME = "cart";

    public abstract ActionForward doAction(ActionMapping mapping,
        ActionForm form, HttpServletRequest request,
        HttpServletResponse response) throws Exception;

    public ActionForward execute(ActionMapping mapping, ActionForm form,
        HttpServletRequest request, HttpServletResponse response)
        throws Exception
    {
        intialize(request);

        ActionForward fwd = doAction(mapping, form, request, response);
        cleanUp();

        return fwd;
    }
```

```java
    protected void cleanUp() throws HibernateException
    {
        SessionProvider.closeSession();
    }

    protected void intialize(HttpServletRequest request)
    {
        getOrCreateCart(request);
    }

    protected ShoppingCart getOrCreateCart(HttpServletRequest request)
    {
        HttpSession session = request.getSession(true);
        ShoppingCart cart = (ShoppingCart) session.getAttribute(CART_NAME);

        if (cart == null)
        {
            cart = new ShoppingCart();
            session.setAttribute(CART_NAME, cart);
        }

        return cart;
    }

    protected void addItemToCart(HttpServletRequest request, OrderItem item)
    {
        ShoppingCart cart = getOrCreateCart(request);
        cart.addOrIncrementItem(item);
    }

    protected void removeItemFromCart(HttpServletRequest request, OrderItem item)
    {
        ShoppingCart cart = getOrCreateCart(request);
        cart.removeItem(item);
    }

    protected void clearCart(HttpServletRequest request)
    {
        ShoppingCart cart = getOrCreateCart(request);
        cart.clear();
    }

    protected void prepareForBrowseCategory(HttpServletRequest request,
        Category cat)
    {
        List books = cat.getBooks();
        request.setAttribute("category", cat);
        request.setAttribute("books", books);
        request.setAttribute("bookCount", String.valueOf(books.size()));
    }
}
```

Of particular interest in this class is the implementation of the `execute` method and the use of the `doAction` method in the subclasses. The `execute` method is implicitly called by Struts when the action is invoked:

```
public ActionForward execute(ActionMapping mapping, ActionForm form,
    HttpServletRequest request, HttpServletResponse response)
    throws Exception
{
    intialize(request);

    ActionForward fwd = doAction(mapping, form, request, response);
    cleanUp();

    return fwd;
}
```

The `initialize` method is called to ensure that there is a `ShoppingCart` in the user's HTTP session. If other preconditions are required, they can be added to this method. To ensure this, a method called `getOrCreateCart(..)` will attempt to retrieve the `ShoppingCart` object from the HTTP session via an attribute name. If one does not exist, it is created for the session and returned. This process from `execute` method to `initialize` to `getOrCreateCart` ensures that every visitor to the site is guaranteed to have a `ShoppingCart` object available in their HTTP session.

The subclass's `doAction` method is then invoked with the same parameters as the `execute` method. From this invocation, an `ActionForward` is retrieved that represents the forward this action will pass control to. Once the `ActionForward` is retrieved, a `cleanUp` method is called. The `cleanUp` method is able to process any final operations before control is passed to the action forward resource. In this application, the `cleanUp` method will call the `closeSession` method on the `SessionProvider`.

You will also notice another method in the `BookstoreController` called `prepareForBrowseCategory`. The significance of this will be shown later; for now it is enough to know that this is an example of the `BookstoreController` providing functionality to two subclasses.

The Development Environment and Its Configuration

Now that you have defined the major objects in the application, you should define the exact structure of the development environment required as well as the various configuration files that go with it. Java applications these days can turn into a maze of XML configuration files, so it's important to stand back and account for each of them in turn. This section therefore explains the location and function of the following:

❑ **Ant build file:** `build.xml`

❑ **Hibernate configuration file:** `hibernate.hbm.xml`

❑ **Hibernate mapping files:** `CustomerOrder.hbm.xml` etc

❑ **Struts configuration file:** `struts-config.xml`

❑ **Tiles definitions file:** `tiles-defs.xml`

❑ **Web application descriptor:** `web.xml`

❑ **Validation file:** `validation.xml`

Quite a list and somewhat confusing for the uninitiated! Rest assured that most newcomers to the Java Web application world are overwhelmed by the volume of important XML-based configuration files, so you're not alone.

If you are going to get this application working in your own environment, you can download the source code from the Web site for this book. You will then need to ensure that your environment follows the structure defined in the following sections. You should pay particular attention to the Tomcat, MySQL, and Ant sections. All the configuration files and the directory structure are included in the download.

Directory structure

The directory structure described here assumes that the application will be compiled and viewed from within Tomcat in a kind of "development mode." That is, no WAR files will be used. Instead, Tomcat will reference a part of this directory structure as the document root. This description has been included because it is how you would actually set about creating your own application.

The directory structure of this application should be thought of in two parts: the first is where the basic source code and configuration files live (the development home), and the second is where the source code has been compiled and all other files have been placed in appropriate positions as a standard Web application (the build home). The build home will be generated automatically for you through Ant. The following instructions assume that the application will live in a directory named as follows:

```
c:\bookstore
```

Beneath this directory is where the entire application will reside: both development and build homes. Figure 28-4 displays the entire directory structure fully expanded.

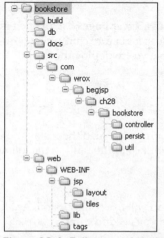

Figure 28-4: Fully expanded directory structure

The elements in the directory structure contain the following information:

- ❑ **c:\bookstore:** This directory contains the build.xml file for Ant usage.

- ❑ **c:\bookstore\src:** Beneath this directory is the location of all Java source code for the application within the package structure. Other files such as messages.properties and Hibernate configurations will also be stored here.

- ❑ **c:\bookstore\web:** This directory stores the WEB-INF directory along with all of its configuration and Jar files.

- ❑ **c:\bookstore\web\WEB-INF\jsp:** All JSP files will be stored within this directory structure. Storing the JSP files beneath the WEB-INF directory ensures that they cannot be invoked directly by a browser; however, Tiles and Struts components can still access and reference them.

- ❑ **c:\bookstore\build:** When the application is compiled from within Ant, this directory will represent the properly structured Web application and will be referenced by Tomcat as the root directory. For instance, Java source files will be compiled and placed in the directory c:\bookstore\build\WEB-INF\classes.

Packages

The directory structure illustrated here shows the package structure of the Java classes for this application:

- ❑ **com.wrox.begjsp.ch28.bookstore:** Stores the core objects for the application, such as CustomerOrder, etc.

- ❑ **com.wrox.begjsp.ch28.bookstore.persist:** Stores the objects involved in persisting objects in the database

- ❑ **com.wrox.begjsp.bookstore.util:** Utility classes for special requirements

- ❑ **com.wrox.begjsp.bookstore.controller:** Actions and other Struts-related classes

Tomcat

Chapter 1, "Getting Started with JavaServer Pages," explained how Tomcat could be set up on your computer; you should follow those steps before continuing with this section. Once Tomcat is set up, the following section on Ant will enable you to deploy the download from this book into Tomcat to get up and running.

Ant

Chapter 26, "Best Practices and Tools," explained the installation of Apache Ant. The following material assumes you have set up Ant on your computer and in the following directory:

```
c:\apache-ant-1.6.2
```

When building this application, you will use some custom Ant tasks that can communicate with Tomcat. For these tasks to work effectively, you need to copy c:\Tomcat 5.0\server\lib\catalina-ant.jar into the c:\apache-ant-1.6.2\lib directory.

Tomcat provides an excellent example Ant script to use when building and deploying applications. This section explains the customization of this script for use with your application. The `build.xml` file that results from this explanation is stored and invoked from the `c:\bookstore` directory.

The `build.xml` file customized here can be copied from the `c:\Tomcat 5.0\webapps\tomcat-docs\appdev\sample` directory. In its raw form, this file contains a set of Ant tasks that can be used to perform certain actions on the application and to communicate with Tomcat.

If you are using the version included with the download for this chapter, you will need to modify the following properties to suit your environment:

- ❑ **Project name attribute:** The name of project (bookstore).
- ❑ **app.name:** The name of the project (bookstore).
- ❑ **catalina.home:** The location of Tomcat on your computer.
- ❑ **manager.username:** The administrator username for Tomcat.
- ❑ **manager.password:** The administrator password for Tomcat.
- ❑ **hibernate.home:** The location of Hibernate on your computer.
- ❑ **struts.home:** The location of Struts on your computer.
- ❑ **mysqljdbc.home:** The location of the MySQL JDBC driver on your computer.
- ❑ **jstl.home:** The location of JSTL on your computer. We have used the JSTL release from Jakarta. The build file included with this application assumes you have as well.

The following instructions assume you are adapting the original file copied from Tomcat.

Properties customization

The `build.xml` file described here uses certain properties to find libraries, locate Tomcat, and so on. If you open the default file, the first change to make concerns the name of the project, which is defined in the project element of the Ant script:

```
<project name="bookstore" default="compile" basedir=".">
```

After the project element is a set of properties that defines the various important locations relevant to this application:

```
<property name="app.name"       value="bookstore"/>
<property name="app.path"       value="/${app.name}"/>
<property name="app.version"    value="0.1-dev"/>
<property name="build.home"     value="${basedir}/build"/>
<property name="catalina.home"  value="c:/Tomcat 5.0"/>
<property name="dist.home"      value="${basedir}/dist"/>
<property name="docs.home"      value="${basedir}/docs"/>
<property name="manager.url"    value="http://localhost:8080/manager"/>
```

```
<property name="manager.username" value="admin"/>
<property name="manager.password" value="password"/>
<property name="src.home"        value="${basedir}/src"/>
<property name="web.home"        value="${basedir}/web"/>
```

Two properties have been added to this list: `manager.username` and `manager.password`. They represent the username and password you nominated for the admin user when you installed Tomcat. Other changes to this list have been highlighted. You should change the `catalina.home`, `manager.url`, `manager.username`, and `manager.password` properties to match your environment.

Your application also needs to know where Hibernate and Struts are located so that the required library files can be used in compiling the application, and for its deployment. Therefore, add the following properties beneath those just described:

```
<property name="hibernate.home" value="c:/hibernate-2.1"/>
<property name="struts.home"    value="c:/jakarta-struts-1.2.4"/>
<property name="mysqljdbc.home"
        value="f:/java/tools/mysql-connector-java-3.0.14-production"/>
<property name="jstl.home"      value="c:/jakarta-taglibs"/>
```

These home locations will be used to specify the required JAR files in their respective directories. You should modify these properties to match the equivalent locations on your computer. These JAR file references will be used to compile the application and for the JAR files to be copied into the `/WEB-INF/lib` directory when the application is deployed.

Property references will be made for the following JAR files:

Struts

❑ `struts.jar`

❑ `commons-beanutils.jar`

❑ `commons-collections.jar`

❑ `commons-digester.jar`

❑ `commons-validator.jar`

❑ `commons-logging.jar`

Hibernate

❑ `hibernate2.jar`

❑ `cglib-full-2.0.1.jar`

❑ `dom4j-1.4.jar`

❑ `ehcache-0.7.jar`

❑ `jta.jar`

JSTL

❏ standard.jar

❏ jstl.jar

MySQL driver

❏ mysql-connector-java-3.0.14-production-bin.jar

The following entries create property aliases inside the build.xml file so that these JAR files can be referenced in the compile classpath and the prepare target:

```
<property name="struts.jar" value="${struts.home}/lib/struts.jar"/>
<property name="commons-beanutils.jar"
        value="${struts.home}/lib/commons-beanutils.jar"/>
<property name="commons-collections.jar"
        value="${struts.home}/lib/commons-collections.jar"/>
<property name="commons-digester.jar"
        value="${struts.home}/lib/commons-digester.jar"/>
<property name="commons-validator.jar"
        value="${struts.home}/lib/commons-validator.jar"/>
<property name="commons-logging.jar"
        value="${struts.home}/lib/commons-logging.jar"/>
<property name="hibernate2.jar" value="${hibernate.home}/hibernate2.jar"/>
<property name="cglib-full-2.0.1.jar"
        value="${hibernate.home}/lib/cglib-full-2.0.1.jar"/>
<property name="dom4j-1.4.jar"
        value="${hibernate.home}/lib/dom4j-1.4.jar"/>
<property name="ehcache-0.7.jar"
        value="${hibernate.home}/lib/ehcache-0.7.jar"/>
<property name="jta.jar"
        value="${hibernate.home}/lib/jta.jar"/>
<property name="odmg-3.0.jar"
        value="${hibernate.home}/lib/odmg-3.0.jar"/>
<property name="jstl.jar" value="${jstl.home}/standard/lib/jstl.jar"/>
<property name="standard.jar" value="${jstl.home}/standard/lib/standard.jar"/>
<property name="mysqljdbc.jar"
        value="${mysqljdbc.home}/mysql-connector-java-3.0.14-production-bin.jar"/>
```

Classpath

The Ant build.xml script builds a list of directories and files it needs to add to the classpath for compilation. By default, the build.xml script includes references to the JAR files provided by Tomcat; this ensures that J2EE-specific resources are included when you compile. As this application also has dependencies on other resources, some of the properties defined in the preceding section also need to be referenced when building the classpath.

These references are added with the following addition to the path element used for the classpath:

```
<path id="compile.classpath">
    <pathelement location="${struts.jar}"/>
    <pathelement location="${hibernate2.jar}"/>

    <!-- Include all elements that Tomcat exposes to applications -->
    <pathelement location="${catalina.home}/common/classes"/>
    <fileset dir="${catalina.home}/common/endorsed">
      <include name="*.jar"/>
    </fileset>
    <fileset dir="${catalina.home}/common/lib">
      <include name="*.jar"/>
    </fileset>
    <pathelement location="${catalina.home}/shared/classes"/>
    <fileset dir="${catalina.home}/shared/lib">
      <include name="*.jar"/>
    </fileset>
</path>
```

Note that only `struts.jar` and `hibernate.jar` are required for compilation. The remaining JAR files are required for the application to run.

Runtime resources

The Ant script also needs to be customized to ensure that all the JAR files referenced earlier are copied from their respective homes into the `/WEB-INF/lib` directory when the application is deployed. It also needs to copy the appropriate `*.tld` and `validation-rules.xml` files from Struts into the `WEB-INF/` directory. To ensure this occurs, make the following addition to the `prepare` target in the `build.xml` file:

```
<copy todir="${build.home}/WEB-INF/lib" file="${struts.jar}"/>
<copy todir="${build.home}/WEB-INF/lib" file="${commons-beanutils.jar}"/>
<copy todir="${build.home}/WEB-INF/lib" file="${commons-collections.jar}"/>
<copy todir="${build.home}/WEB-INF/lib" file="${commons-digester.jar}"/>
<copy todir="${build.home}/WEB-INF/lib" file="${commons-logging.jar}"/>
<copy todir="${build.home}/WEB-INF/lib" file="${commons-validator.jar}"/>
<copy todir="${build.home}/WEB-INF/lib" file="${hibernate2.jar}"/>
<copy todir="${build.home}/WEB-INF/lib" file="${cglib-full-2.0.1.jar}"/>
<copy todir="${build.home}/WEB-INF/lib" file="${dom4j-1.4.jar}"/>
<copy todir="${build.home}/WEB-INF/lib" file="${ehcache-0.7.jar}"/>
<copy todir="${build.home}/WEB-INF/lib" file="${jta.jar}"/>
<copy todir="${build.home}/WEB-INF/lib" file="${odmg-3.0.jar}"/>
<copy todir="${build.home}/WEB-INF/lib" file="${mysqljdbc.jar}"/>
<copy todir="${build.home}/WEB-INF/lib" file="${jstl.jar}"/>
<copy todir="${build.home}/WEB-INF/lib" file="${standard.jar}"/>

<copy todir="${build.home}/WEB-INF/">
    <fileset dir="${struts.home}/lib">
        <include name="*.tld"/>
        <include name="validator-rules.xml"/>
    </fileset>
</copy>
```

Targets

The changes described so far are the only ones required to be made to the sample `build.xml` file from Tomcat. If you have downloaded the sample application and have the Hibernate, Tomcat, and Struts properties configured properly, you should be in a position to build the application and communicate with Tomcat from a command line.

Various targets in the aforementioned `build.xml` file will help you during development or deployment of the application. Here's a brief summary of each:

❑ **all:** Runs the following targets in order: `clean`, `compile`.

❑ **clean:** Removes all items from the build directory (`C:\bookstore\build`).

❑ **compile:** Compiles all Java files and copies all files to the `build` directory in the correct locations.

❑ **dist:** Creates a binary distribution of the application into the `dist` directory. This task also creates Javadoc files for the application.

❑ **install:** Installs the application into Tomcat.

❑ **list:** Communicates with Tomcat to list all the applications installed in Tomcat.

❑ **reload:** Reloads the application (when an application has been installed or the context is available in Tomcat via another method), enabling Tomcat to incorporate any Java class or configuration file changes. This target also runs the `compile` target so that the changes are placed in the build directory.

❑ **remove:** Uninstalls the application from Tomcat.

The communication with Tomcat is especially convenient when developing such applications. You can use the `install` target to make your application immediately available within Tomcat. Once executed, you can browse to `http://localhost:8080/bookstore` and the application will appear. If you make changes to the source code, simply run the `reload` target and the changes will be incorporated and the application reloaded. Behind the scenes, the `install` ant target creates a `bookstore.xml` context file in the `c:\Tomcat5.0\conf\Catalina\localhost` directory. This is Tomcat's configuration file to find the application.

If you are running this application in your own environment, first ensure that all the components in this section are configured accordingly, including Tomcat, MySQL, and Ant. You can then call the `install` target using Ant. This can be done from the command line in the same directory as the `build.xml` file, `c:\bookstore`, with the following command:

```
c:\bookstore> ant install
```

The application will be compiled and deployed to the `c:\bookstore\build` directory, and the context XML file will be deployed to Tomcat. The application would now be available at `http://localhost:8080/bookstore`.

Database

This application will use MySQL to store data. MySQL was briefly introduced in Chapter 23, and this chapter assumes you have set up MySQL appropriately. For this application to function, a new database needs to be created and various SQL commands need to be run. For convenience, a complete SQL file capable of creating the database and all the tables, and inserting some test data, has been included in the download for this chapter. The following instructions explain how to complete this task using the command line.

Assuming you have extracted the download for this chapter into the `c:\bookstore` directory, the relevant SQL file can be found at `c:\bookstore\db\bookstore.sql`.

1. Start up a command prompt and type **mysql**. If you have not changed the default permissions for the root user, this should log you into MySQL immediately. If not, you will have to use the following syntax to log you in with a username and password you have specified:
   `mysql -u <username> -p`

2. Type the following command: source c:\bookstore\db\bookstore.sql

The new database will be created and all the tables and some example data will be installed.

You could also specify specialized user permissions for this database as per the instructions in Chapter 26. In this chapter, the application will communicate with MySQL using the following administrator username and password details:

❑ **Username:** root

❑ **Password:** password

This may be different in your environment depending on how you set up MySQL.

In order for the application to communicate properly with the database, it must be provided with a MySQL JDBC driver. This driver must reside in the classpath of the application at runtime. In the next section, Hibernate's configuration uses the `Driver` class from the MySQL JDBC driver.

The MySQL driver will reside in the `WEB-INF/lib` directory of our application. The MySQL JDBC driver can be downloaded from the MySQL site at `mysql.com/products/connector/j/`. The `build.xml` file described earlier will reference this JAR file and place it in the required location along with all the other JAR files. You should only need to adjust the `build.xml` file to point the `mysqljdbc.home` property to the location on your computer where the driver was installed.

The version used in this application is 3.0.14.

Hibernate

As you learned in Chapter 26, Hibernate manages the persistence of objects in a relational database. This mapping between the object-oriented world of your application and the relational world of the database is defined by a set of Hibernate configuration files that reside in the classpath of the application. These files are referenced centrally in the configuration file that was referenced in the `SessionProvider` object discussed earlier — `hibernate.cfg.xml`. This file resides in the root of the package tree (c:\bookstore\src\hibernate.cfg.xml), along with the other Hibernate configuration files that relate to each object being managed.

The hibernate.cfg.xml file can be used for many configurable elements of Hibernate, most of which are out of the scope of this chapter. However, for our purposes this file has been used as follows:

❑ To inform Hibernate from where and with what parameters it can retrieve database connections

❑ To provide the name of specific configuration files for objects that will be managed

The contents of the hibernate.cfg.xml file are as follows:

```xml
<?xml version='1.0' encoding='utf-8'?>
<!DOCTYPE hibernate-configuration
    PUBLIC "-//Hibernate/Hibernate Configuration DTD//EN"
    "http://hibernate.sourceforge.net/hibernate-configuration-2.0.dtd">

<hibernate-configuration>
    <session-factory>
        <!-- datasource -->
        <property name="dialect">net.sf.hibernate.dialect.MySQLDialect</property>
        <property
          name="hibernate.connection.driver_class">
            com.mysql.jdbc.Driver
        </property>
        <property name="hibernate.connection.url">
          jdbc:mysql://localhost:3306/bookstore
        </property>
        <property name="hibernate.connection.username">root</property>
        <property name="hibernate.connection.password">password</property>
        <property name="show_sql">true</property>

        <!-- Mapping files -->
        <mapping resource="Book.hbm.xml"/>
        <mapping resource="OrderStatus.hbm.xml"/>
        <mapping resource="CustomerOrder.hbm.xml"/>
        <mapping resource="OrderItem.hbm.xml"/>
        <mapping resource="Category.hbm.xml"/>
    </session-factory>
</hibernate-configuration>
```

The first section (with the comment datasource above it) tells Hibernate everything it needs to know about connecting to the MySQL database and using this database to manage your objects. If you are at all familiar with connection parameters to a database using straight JDBC, you will see some similarities with some of these parameters.

Various sets of properties can be used in this capacity in the hibernate.cfg.xml file. With these, Hibernate can be configured to connect to data sources provided in a number of ways, such as JNDI lookup and connection pooling. In this application, you have used a basic configuration. If you wished to implement a more robust data source management routine, it would simply be a matter of changing this file appropriately.

You should also notice in the preceding file that a dialect has been specified. The value of this property is a Hibernate-provided class that tells Hibernate the rules it should abide by when communicating with a particular database. Dialect class files are available for many of the more popular relational databases.

The second section of the `hibernate.cfg.xml` file, entitled `Mapping files`, specifies the mapping files for each of the objects you expect Hibernate to manage. The following sections briefly describe these mapping files and highlight the relationships that are fulfilled.

Book.hbm.xml

If you recall the description of the `Book` object, it represented a product in the system that could be purchased. In this configuration file, you need to map the fields of the object with the columns in the database and, if necessary, specify the nature of the relationship a field may have with another object, something you can facilitate with the use of a foreign key. You can see this in the listing of `Book.hbm.xml`:

```xml
<?xml version="1.0"?>
<!DOCTYPE hibernate-mapping
    PUBLIC "-//Hibernate/Hibernate Mapping DTD//EN"
    "http://hibernate.sourceforge.net/hibernate-mapping-2.0.dtd">

<hibernate-mapping>
    <class name="com.wrox.begjsp.ch28.bookstore.Book" table="book">
        <id name="id" type="int" column="id" unsaved-value="0">
            <generator class="identity"/>
        </id>
        <property name="name">
            <column name="name" sql-type="varchar(100)" not-null="true"/>
        </property>
        <property name="description">
            <column name="description" sql-type="varchar(200)" not-null="true"/>
        </property>
        <property name="unitPrice">
            <column name="unitprice" sql-type="float" not-null="true"/>
        </property>
        <many-to-one column="category"
                     name="category"
                     class="com.wrox.begjsp.ch28.bookstore.Category"
                     not-null="true"/>
    </class>
</hibernate-mapping>
```

This file first specifies the class that is represented by this configuration as well as the associated database table. Within the class element is a list of properties that define the member variables of the object and maps them to columns in the database table. In some cases, such as `category`, these fields are defined in terms of their relationships with other objects in the application. If you quickly refer to the source code for the `Book` object, you will note that the `category` member variable is in fact a `Category` object. This mapping means that when a `Book` object is retrieved from Hibernate, the associated `Category` object will be available by calling the `getCategory()` method. Under the covers, Hibernate performs some extensive SQL in order for this relationship to be appropriately object-oriented at the application level. This mapping is defined in Hibernate as a `many-to-one` mapping; a book has one category and a category can have many books. This is consistent with the relationship between these two entities discussed earlier. You will see examples of other types of relationships in other mapping files.

Note the `id` element of this file that maps the `id` field of the `Book` object with the `id` field of the `book` table. The `unsaved-value` attribute tells Hibernate how to distinguish between objects that have been persisted and those that are new. This is important in the context of the `saveOrUpdate` method of the `EntityManager` object discussed earlier.

Category.hbm.xml

A category object is associated with a list of book objects. This relationship is defined in the `Category.hbm.xml` file:

```xml
<?xml version="1.0"?>
<!DOCTYPE hibernate-mapping
    PUBLIC "-//Hibernate/Hibernate Mapping DTD//EN"
    "http://hibernate.sourceforge.net/hibernate-mapping-2.0.dtd">

<hibernate-mapping>
    <class name="com.wrox.begjsp.ch28.bookstore.Category" table="category">
        <id name="id" type="int" column="id" unsaved-value="0">
            <generator class="identity"/>
        </id>
        <property name="name">
            <column name="name" sql-type="varchar(100)" not-null="true"/>
        </property>
        <property name="description">
            <column name="description" sql-type="varchar(200)" not-null="true"/>
        </property>
        <bag name="books" table="book" lazy="false" inverse="false"
                cascade="save-update">
          <key column="category"></key>
          <one-to-many class="com.wrox.begjsp.ch28.bookstore.Book"/>
        </bag>
    </class>
</hibernate-mapping>
```

Note the `<bag..>` element that informs Hibernate of the relationship a Category has with its associated Book objects. The `<bag>` element defines the one-to-many relationship this object has. The `key` reference to the `category` column of the `book` table maps the relational binding between these two entities. Note the reversed relationship perspective between this and the `Book` mapping file.

CustomerOrder.hbm.xml

A `CustomerOrder` has a set of `OrderItem` objects. From the `CustomerOrder` object's perspective, this is a one-to-many relationship. This object also has a many-to-one relationship with `OrderStatus`. The remaining fields are simple `id` and `varchar` column mappings:

```xml
<?xml version="1.0"?>
<!DOCTYPE hibernate-mapping
    PUBLIC "-//Hibernate/Hibernate Mapping DTD//EN"
    "http://hibernate.sourceforge.net/hibernate-mapping-2.0.dtd">

<hibernate-mapping>
    <class name="com.wrox.begjsp.ch28.bookstore.CustomerOrder"
           table="customerorder">
        <id name="id" type="int" column="id" unsaved-value="0">
            <generator class="identity"/>
        </id>
        <property name="firstName">
            <column name="firstname" sql-type="varchar(100)" not-null="true"/>
        </property>
        <property name="lastName">
            <column name="lastname" sql-type="varchar(100)" not-null="true"/>
        </property>
        <property name="address">
            <column name="address" sql-type="varchar(100)" not-null="true"/>
        </property>
        <property name="zipCode">
            <column name="zipcode" sql-type="varchar(10)" not-null="true"/>
        </property>
        <property name="orderDate">
            <column name="orderdate" sql-type="datetime" not-null="true"/>
        </property>
        <property name="cardNumber">
            <column name="cardnumber" sql-type="varchar(20)" not-null="true"/>
        </property>
        <set name="orderItems" cascade="save-update">
            <key column="orderid"/>
            <one-to-many class="com.wrox.begjsp.ch28.bookstore.OrderItem"/>
        </set>
        <many-to-one column="status"
                     name="status"
                     class="com.wrox.begjsp.ch28.bookstore.OrderStatus"
                     not-null="true"/>
    </class>
</hibernate-mapping>
```

OrderItem.hbm.xml

OrderItem is a central object in the model of this application. It has important relationships with both the CustomerOrder and Book objects. These are defined by two many-to-one mappings that enable an OrderItem to provide its associated CustomerOrder and Book objects. Remember that the orderitem table had two foreign keys to the customerorder and book tables.

```xml
<?xml version="1.0"?>
<!DOCTYPE hibernate-mapping
    PUBLIC "-//Hibernate/Hibernate Mapping DTD//EN"
    "http://hibernate.sourceforge.net/hibernate-mapping-2.0.dtd">
```

```
<hibernate-mapping>
    <class name="com.wrox.begjsp.ch28.bookstore.OrderItem" table="orderitem">
        <id name="id" type="int" column="id" unsaved-value="0">
            <generator class="identity"/>
        </id>
        <property name="qty">
            <column name="qty" sql-type="int" not-null="true"/>
        </property>

        <property name="unitPrice">
            <column name="unitprice" sql-type="float" not-null="true"/>
        </property>

        <many-to-one column="bookid" name="book"
                     class="com.wrox.begjsp.ch28.bookstore.Book"
                     not-null="true"/>
        <many-to-one column="orderid" name="order"
                     class="com.wrox.begjsp.ch28.bookstore.CustomerOrder"
                     not-null="false"/>
    </class>
</hibernate-mapping>
```

Take note of the relationships here, especially between this object and the CustomerOrder. The order mapping allows a null value (and a corresponding allowable null on the database column). This enables Hibernate to persist a new CustomerOrder with a set of new OrderItem objects all in one transaction. This will be illustrated later.

OrderStatus.hbm.xml

An OrderStatus object represents the success or failure of a CustomerOrder with regard to payment. Only two values are defined in the database for this object, approved and declined. It is included in this example to show a simple many-to-one mapping from the CustomerOrder object:

```
<?xml version="1.0"?>
<!DOCTYPE hibernate-mapping
    PUBLIC "-//Hibernate/Hibernate Mapping DTD//EN"
    "http://hibernate.sourceforge.net/hibernate-mapping-2.0.dtd">

<hibernate-mapping>
    <class name="com.wrox.begjsp.ch28.bookstore.OrderStatus" table="orderstatus">
        <id name="id" type="int" column="id" unsaved-value="0">
            <generator class="identity"/>
        </id>
        <property name="name">
            <column name="name" sql-type="varchar(20)" not-null="true"/>
        </property>
    </class>
</hibernate-mapping>
```

So where do all these Hibernate configuration files reside? They typically reside in the classpath either alongside their associated objects Java file or in the root of the classpath at the top of the package structure. In the context of the directory structure used in this chapter, they would sit at c:\bookstore\src\; the top of the package structure and the ant compile target will copy them into the appropriate c:\bookstore\build\WEB-INF\classes directory.

Struts, Validator, and Tiles

The bookstore application makes heavy use of the Struts framework described in Chapter 19, "Struts Framework." Each functional section of the site makes use of at least one Struts action in order to interface with the model components and pass them to appropriate resources for the view. These Struts actions are configured in the struts-config.xml file that resides in the /WEB-INF/ directory.

Two HTML forms in the application are managed by Struts and rely on the coordination between Struts and its inbuilt Validator framework to provide simple validation. The rules for validating these forms are defined in the validation.xml file in the /WEB-INF/ directory. Messages referenced by these validation rules are defined in the messages.properties file that resides in the classpath of the application.

The result of most of the actions in the application is the presentation of a Web page managed via the Tiles framework. As discussed in Chapter 20, "Layout Management with Tiles," Tiles and Struts coordinate to enable Tiles definitions to be referenced as the corresponding ActionForward for display purposes. The application uses a series of Tiles definitions to represent the various views the application presents. These are all defined within the tiles-defs.xml file that resides in the /WEB-INF/ directory.

Two types of Tiles definitions are used in this application. The bulk of definitions present the screen display for the user. A further definition, used by the others, is for the presentation of a simple menu. The contents of this menu are also provided by this definition.

The details of each of the Struts actions, forms, action forwards, and Tiles definitions will be illustrated as each piece of functionality is explained. However, the Tiles and Validator plug-ins are declared within the struts-config.xml file with the following:

```
<?xml version="1.0" encoding="ISO-8859-1" ?>

<!DOCTYPE struts-config PUBLIC
        "-//Apache Software Foundation//DTD Struts Configuration 1.1//EN"
        "http://jakarta.apache.org/struts/dtds/struts-config_1_1.dtd">

<struts-config>
    <form-beans>
      ...
    </form-beans>
    <global-forwards>
      ...
    </global-forwards>
    <action-mappings>
      ...
    </action-mappings>
    <message-resources parameter="messages" null="false"/>
```

```
        <plug-in className="org.apache.struts.validator.ValidatorPlugIn">
            <set-property property="pathnames"
                       value="/WEB-INF/validator-rules.xml,
                              /WEB-INF/validation.xml"/>
        </plug-in>
        <plug-in className="org.apache.struts.tiles.TilesPlugin" >
          <set-property property="definitions-config"
                       value="/WEB-INF/tiles-defs.xml" />
          <set-property property="definitions-debug" value="2" />
          <set-property property="definitions-parser-details" value="2" />
          <set-property property="definitions-parser-validate" value="true" />
        </plug-in>
</struts-config>
```

You can see that the Tiles and Validator plug-ins nominate their respective configuration files residing in the /WEB-INF/ directory of the application. The contents of these files will be explained alongside each corresponding piece of functionality. As you would have noticed in the Ant section, the JAR, TLD, and XML files appropriate for Struts are copied from the Struts installation directory to the /WEB-INF/ directory of the deployment.

web.xml

The application would not be complete without a web.xml file. As you learned in Chapter 19, the web.xml file defines the Struts Controller servlet and specifies the location of the struts-config.xml file. The contents of web.xml are as follows:

```
<web-app xmlns="http://java.sun.com/xml/ns/j2ee"
    xmlns:xsi="http://www.w3.org/2001/XMLSchema-instance"
    xsi:schemaLocation="http://java.sun.com/xml/ns/j2ee
http://java.sun.com/xml/ns/j2ee/web-app_2_4.xsd"
    version="2.4">
    <icon></icon>
    <display-name>Bookstore</display-name>
    <description>Chapter 28 Online Bookstore</description>
    <servlet>
        <servlet-name>action</servlet-name>
        <servlet-class>org.apache.struts.action.ActionServlet</servlet-class>
        <init-param>
            <param-name>config</param-name>
            <param-value>/WEB-INF/struts-config.xml</param-value>
        </init-param>
        <load-on-startup>1</load-on-startup>
    </servlet>
    <servlet-mapping>
        <servlet-name>action</servlet-name>
        <url-pattern>*.do</url-pattern>
    </servlet-mapping>
    <welcome-file-list>
      <welcome-file>index.jsp</welcome-file>
    </welcome-file-list>
</web-app>
```

With the environment and configuration now explained, you can move on to the implementation of each piece of functionality the site will offer. Along the way, corresponding entries in the struts-config.xml, tiles-defs.xml and validation.xml files will also be explained.

The Application

This section will detail the implementation of each unit of functionality within the application, with particular focus on the Controller and View components.

Application layout: Tiles

Chapter 20 explained the power of template management through the use of the Tiles framework. Tiles is used in this application for the presentation of each interface. One central layout tile is used to represent the page structure, as shown in Figure 28-5.

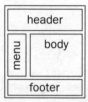

Figure 28-5: Tiles layout

The menu tile will contain a simple list of links within the application. These links will be defined within the Tiles definition for the menu component itself. The header will contain a cart status display panel to show customers the value of their shopping cart. The body will show whatever content the current view focuses on, and the footer tile will show a simple copyright message.

This central layout tile (/WEB-INF/jsp/layout/standard-layout.jsp) contains the following:

```
<%@ taglib uri="/WEB-INF/struts-tiles.tld" prefix="tiles" %>

<html>
  <head>
    <title>Online Bookstore</title>
  </head>
<body bgcolor="white">

<table border="1" width="100%" height="100%" border="1">
<tr>
  <td colspan="2" height="100" bgcolor="gray">
      <tiles:insert attribute="header"/>
  </td>
</tr>
<tr>
```

```
    <td width="20%" valign="top" bgcolor="lightgrey">
        <tiles:insert attribute="menu"/>
    </td>
    <td valign="top"  align="left">
        <tiles:insert attribute="body"/>
    </td>
</tr>
<tr>
    <td colspan="2" height="50" bgcolor="gray">
        <tiles:insert attribute="base"/>
    </td>
</tr>
</table>
</body>
</html>
```

As you can see, a standard HTML table organizes the component tiles into the structure illustrated in Figure 28-5.

Within the `tiles-defs.xml` file, this layout is used to define a definition that will be used, or extended, by most of the other definitions in the application. Its associated entry in the `tiles-defs.xml` file is as follows:

```
<definition name="view.abstract" path="/WEB-INF/jsp/layout/standard-layout.jsp">
    <put name="header"      value="/WEB-INF/jsp/tiles/header.jsp" />
    <put name="menu"        value="bookstore.menu" />
    <put name="base"        value="/WEB-INF/jsp/tiles/base.jsp" />
</definition>
```

This definition is called `view.abstract` because it will not be directly invoked by the application for layout purposes. Instead, subdefinitions use its features as a basis for their own. Note that it does not define a `body` tile; this is provided by the subdefinitions.

Menu tile definition

The code fragment in the preceding section showing the `tiles-defs.xml` entry for the `view.abstract` definition used another definition to represent the value of the menu tile `bookstore.menu`. The `bookstore.menu` definition is defined in the `tiles-defs.xml` files as follows:

```
<definition name="bookstore.menu" path="/WEB-INF/jsp/layout/menu-layout.jsp">
    <put name="menuTile"       value="/WEB-INF/jsp/tiles/menu.jsp"/>
    <putList name="menuItems">
      <item value="Book Categories" link="listcategories.do"/>
      <item value="View Cart" link="managecart.do"/>
      <item value="Checkout" link="checkout.do"/>
    </putList>
</definition>
```

This definition includes a reference to a separate layout for just this definition. A menu tile (`menuTile`) is put within the menu layout along with the list entitled `menuItems`. The contents of the `menu-layout.jsp` tile layout are as follows:

```
<%@ taglib uri="/WEB-INF/struts-tiles.tld" prefix="tiles" %>

<table cellspacing="0" width="100%" cellpadding="5" border="0">
<tr>
    <td valign="top">
    <tiles:insert attribute="menuTile">
        <tiles:put name="menuList" beanName="menuItems" beanScope="tile"/>
    </tiles:insert>
    </td>
</tr>
</table>
```

This simple, self-contained layout just presents the contents of the `menuTile`, along with the list it has been passed, `menuList`. The `menuTile` tile will iterate over the contents of this list and present the menu to the customer. As you can tell from the `bookstore.menu` definition, the menu tile JSP page itself resides in the `/WEB-INF/jsp/tiles` directory as `menu.jsp`. Its contents are as follows:

```
<%@ taglib uri="/WEB-INF/struts-tiles.tld" prefix="tiles" %>
<%@ taglib uri="http://java.sun.com/jsp/jstl/core" prefix="c"%>

<tiles:importAttribute/>

<table cellspacing="0" cellpadding="0" border="0">
<c:forEach items="${menuList}" var="thisItem">
    <tr>
    <td><a href="${thisItem.link}">${thisItem.value}</a></td>
    </tr>
</c:forEach>
</table>
```

Tiles implicitly creates a collection of `org.apache.struts.tiles.beans.SimpleMenuItem` objects to represent the menu items presented on the page, so the properties `link` and `value` can be accessed via EL.

Cart status

Within the header tile, a cart status panel is presented. This panel will show the current user's `ShoppingCart` object. Remember that all visitors to the site are guaranteed to have a `ShoppingCart` object in their HTTP session. The role of this panel is to present the dollar value and number of unique items in it to the customer. This is the perfect job for a custom tag file. The problem is simple enough that a Java-based custom tag is not required, yet this is a piece of functionality that may need to be reused elsewhere.

To satisfy this functionality, a tag file called `cartstatus.tag` is found in the `/WEB-INF/tags` directory. This tag file is called from the `header` tile, `header.jsp`, with the following:

```
<%@ taglib prefix="begjsp" tagdir="/WEB-INF/tags" %>
<table cellspacing=0 cellpadding=0 width="100%">
<tr>
    <td width="100%"><h1>BOOKSTORE</h1></td>
    <td><begjsp:cartstatus/></td>
</tr>
</table>
```

The `cartstatus.tag` file itself contains the following:

```
<%@ tag body-content="empty" %>
<%@ taglib prefix="c" uri="http://java.sun.com/jsp/jstl/core" %>
<%@ taglib prefix="fmt" uri="http://java.sun.com/jsp/jstl/fmt" %>
<jsp:useBean id="cart" scope="session"
            class="com.wrox.begjsp.ch28.bookstore.ShoppingCart"/>

<table width="200" height="100%" bgcolor="white"
        cellspacing="2"
        cellpadding="2" border="0">
<thead>
<tr>
    <th colspan="2"><a href="managecart.do">Shopping Cart</a></th>
</tr>
<tbody>
<tr>
    <td width="100%" colspan="2">
    There are ${cart.itemCount} items in the cart
    </td>
</tr>
<tr>
    <td><b>Value:</b></td>
    <td width="50%"><fmt:formatNumber value="${cart.value}" type="currency"/></td>
</tr>
</table>
```

At the start of the tag, the `ShoppingCart` object guaranteed to be available is retrieved from the `session` scope using the name it is given in the `BookstoreController`, `cart`. Once the object is available, two of its properties can be used. If you refer to the `ShoppingCart` object presented earlier in the chapter, you will notice the `getValue` and `getItemCount` methods that make the calls in this tag file possible. The value returned from the `ShoppingCart` object is formatted using the JSTL `formatNumber` tag.

What results from this use of Tiles and custom tags is an interface that can handle all the requirements for the application. Figure 28-6 shows the entry page of the application with the menu and cart status panel. The body of the interface shows the result of the next piece of functionality, a list of categories.

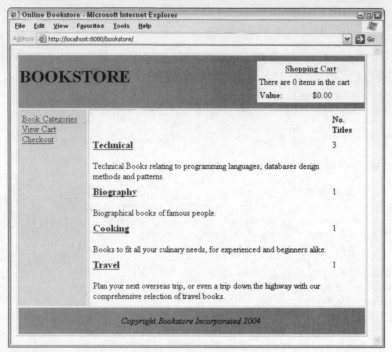

Figure 28-6: Bookstore interface showing the menu and cart status panel

Presenting a list of categories

Figure 28-6 displays the result of this area of functionality — a list of book categories with a brief description and a total of the number of books within each. The heading of each category will link to a list of the associated books.

To display this list, a Struts action `ListCategoriesAction` has been implemented. This action retrieves a list of `Category` objects and passes them on to the appropriate `ActionForward` resource for display. The JSP page then iterates over the list and presents the output you see in Figure 28-6. The `ActionForward` resource reference returned from the `ListCategoriesAction` points to a Tiles definition defined in the `tiles-defs.xml` file.

The `ListCategoriesAction` is configured in the `struts-config.xml` file with the following entry:

```
<action path="/listcategories"
        type="com.wrox.begjsp.ch28.bookstore.controller.ListCategoriesAction"
        scope="request">
    <forward name="success" path="list.categories"/>
</action>
```

The `ListCategoriesAction` is therefore invoked when the following URL is called: `http://localhost:8080/listcategories.do`. This source code for this action is as follows:

```
package com.wrox.begjsp.ch28.bookstore.controller;

import com.wrox.begjsp.ch28.bookstore.persist.EntityManager;
import com.wrox.begjsp.ch28.bookstore.persist.EntityManagerFactory;

import org.apache.struts.action.ActionForm;
import org.apache.struts.action.ActionForward;
import org.apache.struts.action.ActionMapping;

import java.util.List;

import javax.servlet.http.HttpServletRequest;
import javax.servlet.http.HttpServletResponse;


public class ListCategoriesAction extends BookstoreController
{
    public ActionForward doAction(ActionMapping mapping, ActionForm form,
        HttpServletRequest request, HttpServletResponse response)
        throws Exception
    {
        EntityManager manager = EntityManagerFactory.getCategoryManagerInstance();
        List categories = manager.findAll();
        request.setAttribute("categories", categories);

        return mapping.findForward("success");
    }
}
```

The ListCategoriesAction class extends the BookstoreController and therefore must implement a doAction(ActionMapping, ActionForm, HttpServletRequest, HttpServletResponse) method. This method is called via the execute method defined in the BookstoreController class.

The doAction method simply creates an EntityManager object via the EntityManagerFactory class. This ensures that the EntityManager is aware of which Hibernate-mapped class it is to work with. The findAll() method is then called, which returns a List of Category objects from the data source. Remember that each Category object also has a reference to a List of the Book objects that it contains. This enables the number of books in each category to be displayed, another requirement of this interface.

Once the List has been retrieved, it is set as an attribute in the request so that the JSP page will have access to it, under the alias categories. The action then returns an ActionForward from its action mapping entry called success.

The action forward success, defined in the /listcategories action mapping, refers to a Tiles definition in its path attribute, list.categories. This definition is defined in the tiles-defs.xml file as follows:

```
<definition name="list.categories"  extends="view.abstract">
  <put name="body"         value="/WEB-INF/jsp/tiles/category-list.jsp" />
</definition>
```

The list.categories definition extends the view.abstract definition described earlier, and therefore it only needs to provide a value for the body tile that the layout expects. The body tile nominated for this definition is implemented in the JSP file /WEB-INF/jsp/tiles/category-list.jsp. This JSP file iterates over the List of Category objects added to the request as an attribute under the name categories. With each iteration, the name of the Category is printed, along with a link to enable browsing the books in that Category. The getBookCount() method of each Category object is also called in order to display the number of books each Category holds. The content of this file is as follows:

```
<%@ taglib uri="http://java.sun.com/jsp/jstl/core" prefix="c"%>

<table cellspacing=3 cellpadding=3 width="100%">
<tr>
    <td></td>
    <td><b>No. Titles</b></td>
</tr>
<c:forEach items="${categories}" var="thisItem">
<tr>
        <td valign="top"><h3>
          <a href="browsecategory.do?cat=${thisItem.id}">${thisItem.name}</a>
        </h3>${thisItem.description}</td>
        <td valign="top">${thisItem.bookCount}</td>
</tr>
</c:forEach>
</table>
```

What results from this processing is the output shown in Figure 28-6. Notice that each Category name in the list links to a further action called browsecategory.do. This is the subject of the next piece of functionality.

Presenting a list of books

As per the requirements listed previously, when customers click a category name in the category list, they are presented with a list of the books in that category.

As you saw from the link for each category in the category-list.jsp file, a parameter named cat is sent with the request to the browsecategory.do action. The value of this parameter is the unique id of the category selected. This value will be used in the BrowseCategoryAction class in order to retrieve the correct Category object from the persistence layer.

The resulting list of books is displayed to the customer. It is from this list that a book can be added to the customer's shopping cart. The interface for this screen is illustrated in Figure 28-7.

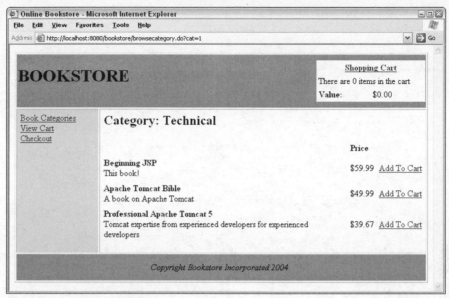

Figure 28-7: Browse category screen

The Struts action for this functionality, /browsecategory, is defined in the struts-config.xml file as follows:

```
<action path="/browsecategory"
        type="com.wrox.begjsp.ch28.bookstore.controller.BrowseCategoryAction"
        scope="request">
    <forward name="success" path="view.category"/>
</action>
```

This action mapping's corresponding class, BrowseCategoryAction, is passed a parameter called cat from the Category list when a category is selected. Its job is to retrieve the corresponding Category object from the persistence layer. This category, and its list of book objects, is then passed to the View layer for display. As the list is displayed via this Struts action, and also via the AddItemAction, it makes sense to move some of the logic to the BookstoreController class to reduce duplication. The source code for the BrowseCategoryAction class is as follows:

```
package com.wrox.begjsp.ch28.bookstore.controller;

import com.wrox.begjsp.ch28.bookstore.Category;
import com.wrox.begjsp.ch28.bookstore.persist.EntityManager;
import com.wrox.begjsp.ch28.bookstore.persist.EntityManagerFactory;
import com.wrox.begjsp.ch28.bookstore.util.NumericUtil;

import org.apache.struts.action.ActionForm;
import org.apache.struts.action.ActionForward;
import org.apache.struts.action.ActionMapping;
```

```
import javax.servlet.http.HttpServletRequest;
import javax.servlet.http.HttpServletResponse;


public class BrowseCategoryAction extends BookstoreController
{
    public ActionForward doAction(ActionMapping mapping, ActionForm form,
        HttpServletRequest request, HttpServletResponse response)
        throws Exception
    {
        String category = request.getParameter("cat");

        if (!NumericUtil.isInteger(category))
        {
            return mapping.findForward("home");
        }

        int categoryId = NumericUtil.getInt(category);
        EntityManager manager = EntityManagerFactory.getCategoryManagerInstance();

        Category cat = (Category) manager.findById(categoryId);
        prepareForBrowseCategory(request, cat);

        return mapping.findForward("success");
    }
}
```

Note that a class called NumericUtil is used to ensure that the value of the cat parameter is numeric, and for the conversion from String to int. Its implementation is not important within this discussion, so if you're really interested, have a look at this class in the downloaded source code.

Once the cat parameter has been converted into a usable int, an EntityManager is instantiated and the specific Category is retrieved via the findById(..) method. As this method returns a BaseEntity object, it must be cast to the specific class we are expecting. The requested Category object is then used to prepare for the display of the Book list. As mentioned earlier, the common functionality required for preparation of this list has been encapsulated in a method called prepareForBrowseCategory(..) in the BookstoreController class. To save you the trouble of referring back to the BookstoreController listing, here's the method again:

```
protected void prepareForBrowseCategory(HttpServletRequest request,
    Category cat)
{
    List books = cat.getBooks();
    request.setAttribute("category", cat);
    request.setAttribute("books", books);
    request.setAttribute("bookCount", String.valueOf(books.size()));
}
```

It simply adds the category and its associated list of Book objects into the request. A bookCount attribute is also passed to the request so that the JSP page can readily determine if the list of Book objects has any values.

The `struts-config.xml` mapping for this action references a Tiles definition for its `success` `ActionForward` outcome: `view.category`. This is defined in the `tiles-defs.xml` file with the following entry:

```xml
<definition name="view.category"  extends="view.abstract">
  <put name="body"         value="/WEB-INF/jsp/tiles/category-browse.jsp" />
</definition>
```

The `category-browse.jsp` page presents a list of books, each with an associated price and Add to Cart link, enabling a single unit of the item to be placed in the `ShoppingCart` object for this user. The source for the `category-browse.jsp` file is as follows:

```jsp
<%@ taglib uri="http://java.sun.com/jsp/jstl/core" prefix="c"%>
<%@ taglib prefix="fmt" uri="http://java.sun.com/jsp/jstl/fmt" %>

<table cellspacing=3 cellpadding=3 width="100%">
<tr>
    <td><h2>Category: ${category.name}</h2></td>
</tr>
<c:choose>
    <c:when test="${bookCount gt 0}">
        <tr>
            <td></td>
            <td><b>Price</b></td>
            <td></td>
        </tr>
        <c:forEach items="${books}" var="thisItem">
        <tr>
            <td>
                <b>${thisItem.name}</b><br>
                ${thisItem.description}
            </td>
            <td><fmt:formatNumber value="${thisItem.unitPrice}"
                              type="currency"/></td>
            <td><a href="additem.do?book=${thisItem.id}">Add To Cart</a></td>
        </tr>
        </c:forEach>
    </c:when>
    <c:otherwise>
    <tr>
        <td colspan="3">There are no books in this category</td>
    </tr>
    </c:otherwise>
</c:choose>
</table>
```

This JSP page presents a list of the books for the chosen category. If there are no books in the chosen category, an appropriate message is displayed to the user.

Adding a book to the shopping cart

The list of books presented in the preceding section also provided a link so that each book can be added to the customer's ShoppingCart. The Add to Cart link invokes the AddItemAction and passes it an id (as parameter book) of the corresponding Book to add. This action is configured in struts-config.xml with the following:

```
<action path="/additem"
        type="com.wrox.begjsp.ch28.bookstore.controller.AddItemAction"
        scope="request">
    <forward name="success" path="view.category"/>
</action>
```

Note that the success forward configured here points to the view.category definition; this is the same screen from which this action is being invoked. This means that when a customer clicks the link to add the item to the cart, the item is added and then the same list is re-presented. This will also have the effect of incrementing the values presented in the Shopping cart status panel.

The source code for AddItemAction is as follows:

```
package com.wrox.begjsp.ch28.bookstore.controller;

import com.wrox.begjsp.ch28.bookstore.Book;
import com.wrox.begjsp.ch28.bookstore.Category;
import com.wrox.begjsp.ch28.bookstore.OrderItem;
import com.wrox.begjsp.ch28.bookstore.persist.EntityManager;
import com.wrox.begjsp.ch28.bookstore.persist.EntityManagerFactory;
import com.wrox.begjsp.ch28.bookstore.util.NumericUtil;

import org.apache.struts.action.ActionForm;
import org.apache.struts.action.ActionForward;
import org.apache.struts.action.ActionMapping;

import javax.servlet.http.HttpServletRequest;
import javax.servlet.http.HttpServletResponse;


public class AddItemAction extends BookstoreController
{
    public ActionForward doAction(ActionMapping mapping, ActionForm form,
        HttpServletRequest request, HttpServletResponse response)
        throws Exception
    {
        String book = request.getParameter("book");

        if (!NumericUtil.isInteger(book))
        {
            return mapping.findForward("home");
        }

        int bookId = NumericUtil.getInt(book);
        EntityManager manager = EntityManagerFactory.getBookManagerInstance();
        Book bookToAdd = (Book) manager.findById(bookId);
        OrderItem item = getOrderItem(bookToAdd, 1);
```

```
                addItemToCart(request, item);

                Category category = bookToAdd.getCategory();
                prepareForBrowseCategory(request, category);

                return mapping.findForward("success");
        }

        private OrderItem getOrderItem(Book book, int qty)
        {
                OrderItem item = new OrderItem();
                item.setBook(book);
                item.setQty(qty);
                item.setUnitPrice(book.getUnitPrice());

                return item;
        }
}
```

Obviously, this is a much more involved action than we have seen previously. After using the
NumericUtil class to ensure that book parameter is a number, the associated Book object is retrieved
from an appropriately created EntityManager. This Book is then used to create a new OrderItem by
calling the getOrderItem(..) method with a given quantity. Of course, this new OrderItem is not
persisted; the value of its id property will be zero.

Once the OrderItem is returned from the getOrderItem method, the addItemToCart method of the
BookstoreController is called to add the OrderItem to the ShoppingCart object in the customer's
HTTP session. To save you the trouble of referring back to the BookstoreController listing, here is the
addItemToCart method:

```
protected void addItemToCart(HttpServletRequest request, OrderItem item)
{
    ShoppingCart cart - getOrCreateCart(request);
    cart.addOrIncrementItem(item);
}
```

First the cart is retrieved (or created, if the HTTP session has expired), and the OrderItem is passed to
the ShoppingCart's addOrIncrementItem method:

```
public void addOrIncrementItem(OrderItem toAdd)
{
    OrderItem existing = getItemForBook(toAdd.getBook());

    if(existing != null)
    {
        removeItem(existing);

        int qty = existing.getQty();
        toAdd.setQty(toAdd.getQty() + qty);
    }

    addItem(toAdd);
}
```

This method will either add the new `OrderItem` to the `ShoppingCart` or increment the quantity of the item in the `ShoppingCart` if it already exists. The increment amount is equal to the amount of the new `OrderItem` being passed to the method. In this case, it is only 1.

Once the new item has been added to the customer's `ShoppingCart`, the `AddItemAction` then prepares the request to represent the browse category page. It can do this using the `prepareForBrowseCategory` method described earlier, passing it the `Category` of the `Book` that has just been added. Once this is done, the success `ActionForward` of this action is returned, again presenting the `view.category` definition.

Managing the shopping cart

At any time in their shopping experience (!), customers can select View Cart from the menu, or the Shopping Cart link from the Cart status panel, and display the contents of the shopping cart, its value, as well as an input field for each item's quantity so that this can be changed. If the customer chooses to change a value in a quantity input field, the Update button needs to be clicked to record the change in the shopping cart. When the Update button is clicked, the page will simply refresh, displaying the new values, subtotals, and the total value of the cart. Figure 28-8 shows this page after the quantity of the second item in the cart has been changed to two and the Update button has been clicked.

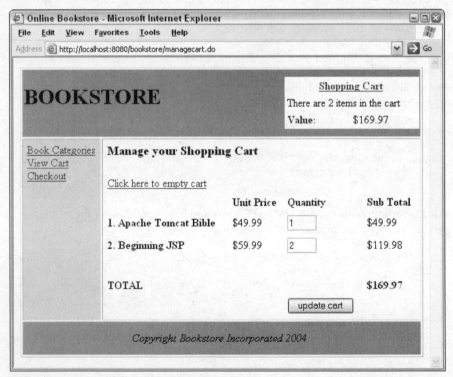

Figure 28-8: Manage Your Shopping Cart screen

Notice that this page also includes a link to empty the cart completely. If this link is clicked, the `ShoppingCart` object in the session is cleared of `OrderItem` objects and the customer is taken to the List Category page.

Probably the most challenging aspect of this interface is the dynamic nature of the Struts form. Remember that customers can have any number of items in their shopping cart; therefore, the size of the form must be able to grow and shrink as the case may be. To address this issue, a `Map`-backed Struts form has been used. This enables one or many items to be represented, rather than using a static form in which a fixed number of form elements are displayed.

The `struts-config.xml` entry to define this action is as follows:

```
<action path="/managecart"
        type="com.wrox.begjsp.ch28.bookstore.controller.ManageCartAction"
        scope="request"
        validate="false"
        name="cartForm">
    <forward name="success" path="manage.cart"/>
</action>
```

The action presented here will also make use of a global-forward called `home`, which denotes the front page of the site, the List Categories page:

```
<global-forwards>
    <forward name="home" path="/default.do"/>
</global-forwards>
```

Unlike the preceding actions in this application, a form has been nominated with the `name` attribute. `cartForm` represents the Map-backed form that will be displayed on this screen.

The `Action` class, `ManageCartAction`, will first display the current content of the shopping cart, and when the form is submitted, it will manipulate the content of the cart accordingly, redisplaying the screen with the new values. This action also handles cases in which the customer selects to clear the cart completely.

The source code for the `ManageCartAction` is as follows:

```
package com.wrox.begjsp.ch28.bookstore.controller;

import com.wrox.begjsp.ch28.bookstore.OrderItem;
import com.wrox.begjsp.ch28.bookstore.ShoppingCart;
import com.wrox.begjsp.ch28.bookstore.util.NumericUtil;

import org.apache.struts.action.ActionForm;
import org.apache.struts.action.ActionForward;
import org.apache.struts.action.ActionMapping;

import java.util.ArrayList;
import java.util.Iterator;
import java.util.List;
import java.util.Map;
import java.util.Set;
```

```
import javax.servlet.http.HttpServletRequest;
import javax.servlet.http.HttpServletResponse;


public class ManageCartAction extends BookstoreController
{
    public ActionForward doAction(ActionMapping mapping, ActionForm form,
        HttpServletRequest request, HttpServletResponse response)
        throws Exception
    {
        ManageCartForm cartForm = (ManageCartForm) form;
        String command = cartForm.getCommand();

        if ("update".equals(command))
        {
            updateCart(request, cartForm);
        }
        else if ("clear".equals(command))
        {
            clearCart(request);

            return mapping.findForward("home");
        }

        ShoppingCart cart = getOrCreateCart(request);

        initializeForm(cartForm, cart);

        return mapping.findForward("success");
    }

    private void updateCart(HttpServletRequest request, ManageCartForm form)
    {
        ShoppingCart cart = getOrCreateCart(request);
        Map values = form.getValues();
        Set items = cart.getItems();
        List itemsArr = new ArrayList(items);
        Iterator it = itemsArr.iterator();

        while (it.hasNext())
        {
            OrderItem item = (OrderItem) it.next();
            String newQty = (String) values.get(String.valueOf(item.getBookId()));

            if (NumericUtil.isInteger(newQty))
            {
                int qty = Integer.parseInt(newQty);

                if (qty > 0)
                {
                    item.setQty(qty);
                    cart.replaceItem(item);
                }
                else
                {
```

```
                    cart.removeItem(item);
                }
            }
        }
    }

    private void initializeForm(ManageCartForm form, ShoppingCart cart)
    {
        Set items = cart.getItems();
        Iterator it = items.iterator();

        while (it.hasNext())
        {
            OrderItem item = (OrderItem) it.next();
            form.setValue(String.valueOf(item.getBookId()),
                new Integer(item.getQty()));
        }
    }
}
```

The imports for this class have been truncated to allow for its size.

The initializeForm method is first called; this method takes the ShoppingCart and sets up the values in the Map-backed form, ManageCartForm. Each item from the ShoppingCart is represented as a corresponding item in the form's Map property using the Book object's id as a key. As no Book can appear in the ShoppingCart more than once, this is guaranteed to be unique. The value for each item in the Map is, of course, the current quantity.

You will see the Map itself when the ManageCartForm is explained next.

ManageCartForm is defined in the struts-config.xml file as follows:

```
<form-bean      name="cartForm"
                type="com.wrox.begjsp.ch28.bookstore.controller.ManageCartForm">
</form-bean>
```

ManageCartForm is a very simple class with only two properties: a Map to store the value pairs for the items in the form, and a String called command to track the task with which the user is invoking the form: update or clear. It also includes methods to manipulate these values. The source code for this class is included here:

```
package com.wrox.begjsp.ch28.bookstore.controller;

import java.util.HashMap;
import java.util.Map;

import org.apache.struts.action.ActionForm;

public class ManageCartForm extends ActionForm
{
    private Map values = new HashMap();
    private String command = "";
```

```
    public String getCommand()
    {
        return command;
    }

    public void setCommand(String value)
    {
        command = value;
    }

    public void setValue(String key, Object value)
    {
        values.put(key, value);
    }

    public Object getValue(String key)
    {
        return values.get(key);
    }

    public Map getValues()
    {
        return values;
    }
}
```

Once the form is initialized, the number of items in the cart is also added to the request under the alias cartSize, so that the JSP page can more easily determine whether to display the form, or a message, to the customer.

The success ActionForward from the ManageCartAction is then returned. success for this action is to present the manage.cart Tiles definition, as per the entry in tiles-defs.xml:

```
<definition name="manage.cart"  extends="view.abstract">
  <put name="body"          value="/WEB-INF/jsp/tiles/manage-cart.jsp" />
</definition>
```

The manage-cart.jsp page is presented as the body tile for this action. manage-cart.jsp either displays the contents of the shopping cart as well as the associated form or presents a message to the customer if the shopping cart is empty. manage-cart.jsp is a rather long page, so we'll look at it in stages. The head of the JSP page simply sets up the resources required:

```
<%@ taglib uri="http://java.sun.com/jsp/jstl/core" prefix="c"%>
<%@ taglib uri="http://java.sun.com/jsp/jstl/fmt" prefix="fmt"%>
<%@ taglib uri="/WEB-INF/struts-html.tld" prefix="html" %>
```

The following section presents a heading for the page and the form content if there is more than one item in the shopping cart:

```
<table cellspacing=3 cellpadding=3 width="100%">
<tr>
    <td colspan="5"><h3>Manage your Shopping Cart</h3></td>
</tr>
<c:choose>
    <c:when test="${cart.itemCount gt 0}">
        <html:form action="managecart.do">
        <html:hidden property="command" value="update"/>
        <tr>
            <td colspan="3">
              <a href="managecart.do?command=clear">
                Click here to empty cart
              </a>
            </td>
        </tr>
        <tr>
            <td></td>
            <td><b>Unit Price</b></td>
            <td><b>Quantity</b></td>
            <td><b>Sub Total</b></td>
        </tr>
        <c:forEach items="${cart.items}" var="thisItem" varStatus="status">
          <c:set value="${thisItem.book}" var="book"/>
        <tr>
            <td>
                <b>${status.count}. ${book.name}</b>
            </td>
            <td><fmt:formatNumber
                    value="${thisItem.unitPrice}" type="currency"/>
            </td>
            <td><html:text size="3" property="value(${thisItem.bookId})"/></td>
            <td><fmt:formatNumber value="${thisItem.value}"
                                    type="currency"/>
              </td>
        </tr>
        </c:forEach>
        <tr>
            <td colspan="4"> </td>
        </tr>
        <tr>
            <td colspan="3"><b>TOTAL</b></td>
            <td><b><fmt:formatNumber value="${cart.value}"
                                    type="currency"/></b>
            </td>
        </tr>
        <tr>
            <td colspan="2"></td>
            <td><html:submit value="update cart"/>
            <td></td>
        </tr>
        </html:form>
    </c:when>
```

The Struts form presents all the current values from the `ManageCartForm` that was initialized in the `ManageCartAction`. The contents of the cart are then iterated over, printing out the unit price and total value for each item. The highlighted entry highlights the form element that represents the quantity of each item in the cart. The value of the `property` attribute here might look a bit confusing, but it is recognized by the Struts framework as a call to the `getValue(String key)` method of the `ManageCartForm`. This ensures that the correct quantity is displayed for each item in the Map (remember that the `Book` object's id was used as the key in the Map). When the list of items is completed, the total value of the cart's contents is displayed. At the top of the form, the `command` property is assigned the value `update`. This will indicate to the `ManageCartAction` that the form has been submitted and trigger the manipulation of the quantities of the items in the cart.

The final section of the `manage-cart.jsp` page is the alternate content to the above and is displayed when there are no items in the customer's `ShoppingCart` object:

```
    <c:otherwise>
        <tr>
            <td colspan="5">Your shopping cart is empty.</td>
        </tr>
    </c:otherwise>

</c:choose>
</table>
```

When the form presented in `manage-cart.jsp` is submitted, the `ManageCartAction` is again invoked. This time, there is a recognized value in the `command` property of the form, `update`. With this value, the `updateCart` method of the `ManageCartAction` is called and passed the HTTP request and the submitted form. The `updateCart` method iterates over the `OrderItem` objects in the `ShoppingCart` object and updates the associated quantity of each with the corresponding value retrieved from the form. If a retrieved quantity is not numeric, the new quantity is ignored and the existing value will remain. If the new quantity is less than 1, it is removed from the cart. Once the Shopping cart update is completed, the `initializeForm` method is called again, and the `manage-cart.jsp` page is again displayed with the new values. Because the value of the `ShoppingCart` in the session has changed, the Cart status panel will reflect the new values.

Note that there was no interaction with the persistence layer in this functionality. The `OrderItem` objects in the cart are not persisted, as the customer hasn't committed to an order yet. When the customer actually checks out and makes a purchase, the `OrderItem` objects in the `ShoppingCart` will be saved as part of an order.

Checkout

When the customer has selected a book to purchase, and hopefully used the Manage Cart form to increase its quantity, we hope that the next step will be to make a purchase. The functionality explained in this section enables customers to do just that.

From the menu on the left-hand side of the screen, the customer can select the Checkout link. This presents a simple form on which the customer can enter some basic details, including name, address, and credit card number. Validation will therefore be required for all of these details, using the Struts Validator framework discussed in Chapter 19. This functionality will also highlight the persistence of the new `CustomerOrder`, together with its `OrderItems`.

Two Struts actions will be presented here: `CheckoutAction`, which will present the form to the customer, and `CompleteOrderAction`, which will receive a successfully completed order form, approve or decline the credit card payment, and save the order to the persistence layer. A page will then be displayed informing the customer of the validation results. If the payment is approved, the shopping cart will be cleared; if the payment is declined, the cart will be left intact in case the customer wishes to try again.

These actions are defined within Struts with the following entries to the `struts-config.xml` file:

```
<action path="/checkout"
        type="com.wrox.begjsp.ch28.bookstore.controller.CheckoutAction"
        scope="request"
        validate="false"
        name="checkOutForm">
    <forward name="success" path="view.checkout"/>
</action>

<action path="/completeorder"
        type="com.wrox.begjsp.ch28.bookstore.controller.CompleteOrderAction"
        scope="request"
        validate="true"
        input="/checkout.do"
        name="checkOutForm">
    <forward name="success" path="view.checkout.completed"/>
</action>
```

The form mentioned in both these entries under the `name` attribute, `checkOutForm`, is a `DynaValidatorForm` provided by Struts. Unlike the `ManageCartForm` presented in the preceding section, this form is dynamically instantiated using its configuration entry in the `struts-config.xml` file rather than a concrete class. The entry for this form is as follows:

```
<form-bean      name="checkOutForm"
                type="org.apache.struts.validator.DynaValidatorForm">
  <form-property name="firstName" type="java.lang.String"/>
  <form-property name="lastName" type="java.lang.String"/>
  <form-property name="address" type="java.lang.String"/>
  <form-property name="zipCode" type="java.lang.String"/>
  <form-property name="cardNumber" type="java.lang.String"/>
</form-bean>
```

These properties match those of the `CustomerOrder` object presented earlier.

The `CheckoutAction` is invoked when a customer selects to checkout their shopping cart and commit to an order. The source code for this action is presented here:

```
package com.wrox.begjsp.ch28.bookstore.controller;

import org.apache.struts.action.ActionForm;
import org.apache.struts.action.ActionForward;
import org.apache.struts.action.ActionMapping;

import javax.servlet.http.HttpServletRequest;
import javax.servlet.http.HttpServletResponse;
```

```
public class CheckoutAction extends BookstoreController
{
    public ActionForward doAction(ActionMapping mapping, ActionForm form,
        HttpServletRequest request, HttpServletResponse response)
    {
        return mapping.findForward("success");
    }
}
```

The `ActionForward` `success` returned from this action corresponds to the Tiles definition `view.checkout`. This definition is defined in the `tiles-defs.xml` file as follows:

```
<definition name="view.checkout"  extends="view.abstract">
  <put name="body"         value="/WEB-INF/jsp/tiles/checkout.jsp" />
</definition>
```

Once again, the definition for our view only has to implement the `body` tile with the JSP page `/WEB-INF/jsp/tiles/checkout.jsp`.

The `checkout.jsp` page presents two sections to the customer: the checkout form and a summary of the items being purchased. You can see both these elements in Figure 28-9.

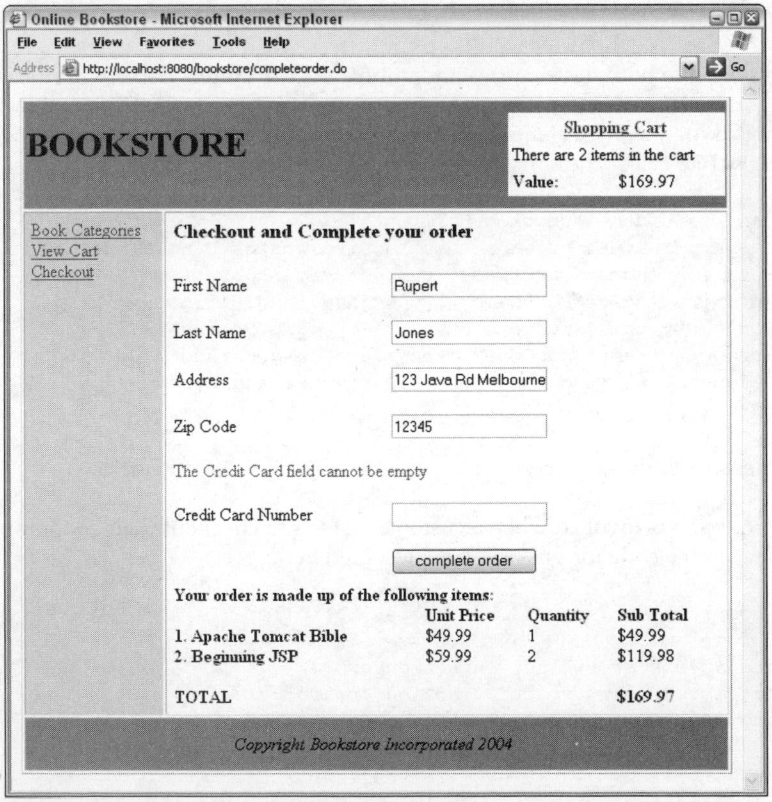

Figure 28-9: Checkout form with order items

Anticipating that it will be used elsewhere in the site, the list of items is displayed using a custom tag file. The custom tag, listitems, takes a Set of OrderItem objects as its only attribute. This tag file is implemented in a file called /WEB-INF/tags/listitems.tag. Implementing a tag file in this way means that with minimal effort, the contents of the cart can be displayed in a predefined format wherever we like. The source code for this tag file is as follows:

```
<%@ tag body-content="empty" %>
<%@ taglib prefix="fmt" uri="http://java.sun.com/jsp/jstl/fmt" %>
<%@ taglib prefix="c" uri="http://java.sun.com/jsp/jstl/core" %>
<%@ attribute name="items" required="true" type="java.util.Set" %>

<table cellspacing=0 cellpadding=0 width="100%">
<tr>
    <td></td>
    <td><b>Unit Price</b></td>
    <td><b>Quantity</b></td>
    <td><b>Sub Total</b></td>
</tr>

<c:forEach items="${items}" var="thisItem" varStatus="status">
    <c:set value="${total + thisItem.value}" var="total"/>
    <c:set value="${thisItem.book}" var="book"/>
<tr>
        <td><b>${status.count}. ${book.name}</b></td>
        <td><fmt:formatNumber value="${thisItem.unitPrice}" type="currency"/></td>
        <td>${thisItem.qty}</td>
        <td><fmt:formatNumber value="${thisItem.value}" type="currency"/></td>
</tr>
</c:forEach>
<tr>
    <td colspan="4"> </td>
</tr>
<tr>
    <td colspan="3"><b>TOTAL</b></td>
    <td><b><fmt:formatNumber value="${total}" type="currency"/></b></td>
</tr>
</table>
```

As you can see, the tag displays a simple table of the set provided, with a total of the items displayed at the end. Note that the output of the tag file is a complete table with minimal formatting. This provides the greatest flexibility to any surrounding display code that may make use of the tag.

This tag is used at the base of the form presented in the checkout.jsp page. Once again, the presentation of the form, and the list provided by the preceding custom tag, is dependent on the number of items in the ShoppingCart in the customer's session. If there are no items, it doesn't make any sense to allow the customer to proceed to checkout. The checkout.jsp page is rather lengthy, so it will be presented here piece by piece.

The first section of the checkout.jsp page simply prepares the resources that the rest of the page may need:

```
<%@ taglib uri="http://java.sun.com/jsp/jstl/core" prefix="c"%>
<%@ taglib uri="/WEB-INF/struts-html.tld" prefix="html" %>
<%@ taglib uri="/WEB-INF/struts-logic.tld" prefix="logic" %>
<%@ taglib prefix="begjsp" tagdir="/WEB-INF/tags" %>
```

In the preceding code, you can see directives for the tag libraries that are required for the rest of the page; note the begjsp entry so we can access the listitems.tag tag file. The checkout.jsp page then has to determine whether the form and items list can be presented based on the size of the cart. The cart can be referenced directly as it is in the session scope:

```
<table cellspacing=3 cellpadding=3 width="100%">
<tr>
    <td><h3>Checkout and Complete your order</h3></td>
</tr>
<c:choose>
    <c:when test="${cart.itemCount gt 0}">
    <tr>
        <td>
```

Much like the Manage Cart page presented earlier, the Checkout page will show the form and items list if there are, in fact, items ready to purchase. The Struts form is presented next, along with appropriate entries to output validation errors should they occur upon form submission. The listing here has been truncated to show the errors for only the first field, firstName:

```
<html:form action="completeorder.do">
<table cellspacing=0 cellpadding=0>
<logic:messagesPresent property="firstName">
<tr>
        <td colspan=2>
            <font color="red">
                <html:errors property="firstName"/>
            </font>
        </td>
</tr>
<tr>
        <td colspan="2"> </td>
</tr>
</logic:messagesPresent>
<tr>
        <td width="200">First Name</td>
        <td><html:text property="firstName"/></td>
</tr>
 ...
<tr>
        <td>Last Name</td>
        <td><html:text property="lastName"/></td>
</tr>
 ...
<tr>
        <td>Address</td>
        <td><html:text property="address"/></td>
</tr>
```

```
        ...
        <tr>
                <td>Zip Code</td>
                <td><html:text property="zipCode"/></td>
        </tr>
        ...
        <tr>
                <td>Credit Card Number</td>
                <td><html:text property="cardNumber" /></td>
        </tr>
        <tr>
                <td> </td>
                <td><html:submit value="complete order"/></td>
        </tr>
        </html:form>
        </table>
```

The form will present each property provided to cartForm in an identical element. Errors that are displayed through validation will appear, in red, above each. The rest of checkout.jsp presents the list of items in the ShoppingCart through the listitems.tag and the message to display if a customer attempts to checkout when there are no items in her cart:

```
        </td>
    </tr>
    <tr>
        <td>
            <table cellspacing=0 cellpadding=0 width="100%">
            <tr>
                <td colspan="4"><b>
                 Your order is made up of the following items:
                </b></td>
            </tr>
            <tr>
            <td>
                <begjsp:listitems items="${cart.items}"/>
            </td>
            </tr>
            </table>
        </td>
    </tr>
    </c:when>
    <c:otherwise>
        <tr>
            <td>There are no items in your shopping cart</td>
        </tr>
    </c:otherwise>
</c:choose>
</table>
```

Because of the flexibility of the layout provided within the listtags custom tag, it can be placed within the structure of this page easily.

Validation

This form has a variety of values that need to be entered by the customer, some with specific validation needs. All the fields in this form are required, and some need to be only numeric or have a required length. The credit card field has all of these requirements in addition to being a real credit card number. This represents a significant amount of logic. Thankfully, the validation framework provided with Struts handles all of this for us with a minimum of configuration.

The message actually displayed when one of these errors occurs is one of four types: missing, integer, length, or card number. Instead of having a specific message for each error for each field, the validation framework enables you to nominate a template for each error message type. The template for each message will include a field name, and may include other specific values, such as the minimum and maximum length, so that, for example, the Zip code field can display the following error:

```
The Zip Code field must be between 5 and 6 characters in length
```

Zip Code, 5, and 6 are values simply given to the length message template when it is displayed. To accomplish this, the following entries are added to the message.properties file that resides at the top of the package structure (C:\bookstore\src\messages.properties) and will therefore be available to the application:

```
checkout.error.missing = The {0} field cannot be empty
checkout.error.integer = The {0} field must only contain numbers
checkout.error.length = The {0} field must be between {1} and {2} characters long
checkout.error.cardNumber = The credit card entered was invalid
```

The {0}, {1}, and {2} are placeholders for values to be placed in each message template. The field names in these templates ({0}) are provided by the following entries, also in the messages. properties file:

```
checkout.field.address = Address
checkout.field.firstName = First Name
checkout.field.lastName = Last Name
checkout.field.zipCode = Zip Code
checkout.field.cardNumber = Credit Card
```

So where is all this used? As you learned in Chapter 19, the validation framework is configured to provide validation for this form via entries in the WEB-INF/validation.xml file. Each field is provided with an entry that nominates its specific validation requirements and uses the preceding message structure to allocate the correct notification to the customer. Let's look at each field of the checkOutForm in turn.

The First Name field needs to be entered by the user, so this field has to be assigned the required validation:

```
<form-validation>
  <form name="checkOutForm">
    <field property="firstName" depends="required">
      <msg name="required" key="checkout.error.missing"/>
      <arg0 key="checkout.field.firstName"/>
    </field>
    ...
```

The start of the `form` element has been shown here to provide some context. The `firstName` field *depends* on being `required`, and an associated message is assigned with the `msg` element. This message template takes a single parameter, the form element's friendly name from the `messages.properties` file, which you can nominate using its key.

The `lastName` and `address` fields are also required:

```
<field property="lastName" depends="required">
    <msg name="required" key="checkout.error.missing"/>
    <arg0 key="checkout.field.lastName"/>
</field>

<field property="address" depends="required">
    <msg name="required" key="checkout.error.missing"/>
    <arg0 key="checkout.field.address"/>
</field>
```

The same message template, `checkout.error.missing`, is used for these fields, each passing its appropriate key for the field's name.

The `zipCode` field is a special case. Zip codes need to be numeric, of a certain length, and of course they are `required`. The entry for `zipCode`, therefore, needs to cover all these requirements and provide appropriate messages:

```
<field property="zipCode" depends="required,integer,minlength,maxlength">

    <msg name="required" key="checkout.error.missing"/>
    <msg name="integer" key="checkout.error.integer"/>
    <msg name="minlength" key="checkout.error.length"/>
    <msg name="maxlength" key="checkout.error.length"/>

    <arg0 name="minlength" key="checkout.field.zipCode"/>
    <arg1 name="minlength" key="${var:minlength}" resource="false"/>
    <arg2 name="minlength" key="${var:maxlength}" resource="false"/>

    <arg0 name="maxlength" key="checkout.field.zipCode"/>
    <arg1 name="maxlength" key="${var:minlength}" resource="false"/>
    <arg2 name="maxlength" key="${var:maxlength}" resource="false"/>

    <arg0 name="required" key="checkout.field.zipCode"/>
    <arg0 name="integer" key="checkout.field.zipCode"/>

    <var>
      <var-name>minlength</var-name>
      <var-value>5</var-value>
    </var>
    <var>
      <var-name>maxlength</var-name>
      <var-value>6</var-value>
    </var>
</field>
```

Note how the `maxlength` and `minlength` validation messages reference the `var` values defined at the bottom of this listing. These `var` values are required for the `minlength` and `maxlength` validation mechanisms to work.

The final field to validate here is the Credit Card number field. This field is not only required but must also conform to the requirements of most credit card numbers. The validation framework provides for this as well:

```
                <field property="cardNumber" depends="required,creditCard">
                  <msg name="required" key="checkout.error.missing"/>
                  <arg0 name="required" key="checkout.field.cardNumber"/>
                  <msg name="creditCard" key="checkout.error.cardNumber"/>
                </field>
          </form>
          </formset>
       </form-validation>
```

If you are interested in credit card number validation and how it is done, use your favorite search engine to search for the *Luhn Formula*, which most credit card numbers comply with. If you are working with the completed application and don't have a credit card to test with, try using 4111111111111111. This is a test credit card number that complies with the Luhn Formula.

If you refer back to the `struts-config.xml` file entry for this section, you will notice that the `validate` attribute on the `checkout.do` action was `false`. This ensures that the validation presented here is not executed when the customer first loads the Checkout page. However, the `completecheckout.do` action has its `validate` attribute as `true`; therefore, the form submission, which will invoke this action, will fire off all these validation rules.

To summarize the validation infrastructure set up for this application, let's walk through the configuration steps once more:

1.   Include the validate plug-in entry in the `struts-config.xml` file.

2.   Ensure that the `validation-rules.xml` file will be available in the WEB-INF directory when the application is run.

3.   Ensure that the `commons-validate.jar` file is within the application's classpath (WEB-INF/lib) when the application is run.

4.   The form is defined as an appropriate Validator type form in the `struts-config.xml` file.

5.   Ensure that the form has appropriate validation rules set up in the `validation.xml` file, which should also be in the WEB-INF directory.

6.   Ensure that the form page has appropriate message placeholders for each field.

What results is a very clean and convenient method of providing the validation for our checkout form.

Saving the order

We're in the home stretch now. Once the customer has entered the form information that satisfies the validation criteria, the system will save the details as a `CustomerOrder` with a set of `OrderItem` objects in the database. This is the function of the `CompleteOrderAction` configured earlier. Because of the length of this class, it will be explained piece by piece. The declarations and `doAction` method are as follows:

```
package com.wrox.begjsp.ch28.bookstore.controller;

import com.wrox.begjsp.ch28.bookstore.BookstoreConstants;
import com.wrox.begjsp.ch28.bookstore.CustomerOrder;
import com.wrox.begjsp.ch28.bookstore.OrderStatus;
import com.wrox.begjsp.ch28.bookstore.ShoppingCart;
import com.wrox.begjsp.ch28.bookstore.persist.EntityManager;
import com.wrox.begjsp.ch28.bookstore.persist.EntityManagerFactory;

import net.sf.hibernate.HibernateException;

import org.apache.struts.action.ActionForm;
import org.apache.struts.action.ActionForward;
import org.apache.struts.action.ActionMapping;
import org.apache.struts.validator.DynaValidatorForm;

import java.sql.Date;

import java.util.Calendar;

import javax.servlet.http.HttpServletRequest;
import javax.servlet.http.HttpServletResponse;


public class CompleteOrderAction extends BookstoreController
{
    public ActionForward doAction(ActionMapping mapping, ActionForm form,
        HttpServletRequest request, HttpServletResponse response)
        throws Exception
    {
        DynaValidatorForm validForm = (DynaValidatorForm) form;
        CustomerOrder order = getOrder(request, validForm);
        setCreditDecision(order);
        order = saveOrder(request, order);

        clearCartWhenApproved(request, order);

        request.setAttribute("order", order);

        return mapping.findForward("success");
    }
```

This action first instantiates `ActionForm` as a `DynaValidatorForm` so that the appropriate accessor methods will be available. A new `CustomerOrder` object is then created with a call to the `getOrder(..)` method:

```
private CustomerOrder getOrder(HttpServletRequest request,
    DynaValidatorForm form)
{
    Calendar cal = Calendar.getInstance();
    ShoppingCart cart = getOrCreateCart(request);
```

```
        String firstName = (String) form.get("firstName");
        String lastName = (String) form.get("lastName");
        String address = (String) form.get("address");
        String zipCode = (String) form.get("zipCode");
        String cardNumber = (String) form.get("cardNumber");

        CustomerOrder newOrder = new CustomerOrder();
        newOrder.setFirstName(firstName);
        newOrder.setLastName(lastName);
        newOrder.setAddress(address);
        newOrder.setZipCode(zipCode);
        newOrder.setCardNumber(cardNumber);
        newOrder.setOrderItems(cart.getItems());
        newOrder.setOrderDate(new Date(cal.getTimeInMillis()));

        return newOrder;
    }
```

The getOrder(..) method retrieves the ShoppingCart object for this customer using the getOrCreateCart method in BookstoreController. The details the customer entered are then retrieved from the DynaValidatorForm object. A new CustomerOrder object is then populated with these values as well as the OrderItem objects from ShoppingCart. Finally, the new CustomerOrder object is returned to the doAction method.

Once the CustomerOrder has been instantiated, it is passed to the setCreditDecision method, where the order is either approved or declined:

```
    private void setCreditDecision(CustomerOrder order)
        throws HibernateException
    {
        EntityManager statusManager =
            EntityManagerFactory.getOrderStatusManagerInstance();
        OrderStatus declined = (OrderStatus)
            statusManager.findById(BookstoreConstants.DECLINED_ID);
        OrderStatus approved = (OrderStatus)
            statusManager.findById(BookstoreConstants.APPROVED_ID);

        if (order.getCardNumber().equals("4111111111111111"))
        {
            order.setStatus(approved);
        }
        else
        {
            order.setStatus(declined);
        }
    }
```

This method simulates the function that a credit card payment approval service might perform. In this example, we have ensured that the only credit card number that will be approved is the test credit card number mentioned earlier. You can try other test credit card values to simulate a decline decision. Another test credit card number is 4012888888881881.

The OrderStatus objects for approve and declined decisions are retrieved from the persistence layer using an appropriate EntityManager instantiation. Once the decision has been set in the CustomerOrder object, the method completes and the CustomerOrder within the doAction method now has a decision.

Now the new CustomerOrder object, and its OrderItem values, can be saved to the persistence layer. Remember that the CustomerOrder, and all the OrderItem objects, have id values of 0. The Hibernate configurations for these objects nominated 0 as the unsaved-value. This indicates to Hibernate that all these items should be saved with an INSERT SQL statement, rather than an UPDATE statement.

The source code for the saveOrder method is as follows:

```
private CustomerOrder saveOrder(HttpServletRequest request,
    CustomerOrder order) throws HibernateException
{
    EntityManager orderManager = EntityManagerFactory.getOrderManagerInstance();
    order = (CustomerOrder) orderManager.saveOrUpdate(order);

    return order;
}
```

Note that the CustomerOrder can be saved directly, not as an order and then as individual OrderItem values. Because of the mappings configured between the CustomerOrder object and the OrderItem object, Hibernate will recognize the relationship and cascade the save down to the individual OrderItem values.

The SQL operation required of Hibernate to complete this task is tricky. It must save the OrderItem objects, yet the orderId column in the orderitem table requires a value so it can be linked to an appropriate customerorder record. However, the CustomerOrder has no such id value yet. This is the very reason we deliberately set the orderId column of the orderitem table to allow null values. Hibernate cleverly deals with this problem by saving the CustomerOrder and OrderItem objects, and then performing an update on the orderitem table to ensure that these new values have correct orderId's set. To create a CustomerOrder with just one OrderItem, Hibernate will issue the following SQL statements when it performs the save:

```
insert into customerorder (firstname, lastname, address, zipcode, orderdate,
cardnumber, status) values (?, ?, ?, ?, ?, ?, ?)
insert into orderitem (qty, unitprice, bookid, orderid) values (?, ?, ?, ?)
update orderitem set orderid=? where id=?
```

Once the CustomerOrder is saved to the persistence layer, the action determines whether it can clear the ShoppingCart of values with the clearCartWhenApproved(...) method:

```
private void clearCartWhenApproved(HttpServletRequest request,
    CustomerOrder order)
{
    if (order.getStatus().getId() == BookstoreConstants.APPROVED_ID)
    {
        clearCart(request);
    }
}
```

This method simply calls the `clearCart` method found in `BookstoreController` if the new `CustomerOrder` has an approved status.

Once all the processing is completed here, the new `CustomerOrder` is added to the request so that the JSP page presented to the customer can correctly convey the results. The `success ActionForward` returned from the `doAction` method refers to the `view.checkout.completed` Tiles definition defined in the `tiles-defs.xml` file:

```
<definition name="view.checkout.completed"  extends="view.abstract">
  <put name="body"         value="/WEB-INF/jsp/tiles/checkoutcompleted.jsp" />
</definition>
```

Once again, the body tiles are simply populated with an appropriate JSP page to display the results: `checkoutcompleted.jsp`.

The JSP page determines whether to display the approve or decline details based on the success of the order:

```
<%@ taglib uri="http://java.sun.com/jsp/jstl/core" prefix="c"%>
<%@ page import="com.wrox.begjsp.ch28.bookstore.BookstoreConstants"%>
<c:set value="<%=String.valueOf(BookstoreConstants.APPROVED_ID)%>" var="approved"/>

<c:choose>
    <c:when test="${order.status.id eq approved}">
        <table cellspacing=3 cellpadding=3 border=0 width=500>
        <tr>
            <td><h3>Order Completed</h3></td>
        </tr>
        <tr>
            <td>Your order has been approved.<p>
                For your reference the order number is: ${order.id}.<P>
                The goods will be shipped to the following address as soon as
                possible:
            </td>
        </tr>
        <tr>
            <td>${order.firstName} ${order.lastName}<br>
                ${order.address}<br>
                ${order.zipCode}</td>
        </tr>
        </table>
    </c:when>
```

The approved value is equated with the `APPROVED_ID` constant stored in the `BookstoreConstants` class. This class is simply a convenient way to access certain unchanging values in the system, such as approved and declined `OrderStatus` id values. The values are static, enabling them to be referenced in this way.

If the order is approved, a comforting message is displayed, confirming the delivery details of the order. If the value is declined, a less pleasant message informs the customer of steps they can take, including trying again. Remember that the `ShoppingCart` in the customer's HTTP session is still intact:

```
    <c:otherwise>
         <table cellspacing=3 cellpadding=3 border=0 width=500>
        <tr>
            <td><h3>There was a problem</h3></td>
        </tr>
        <tr>
            <td>Your order has been declined by your credit card's financial
                institution.<p>
                For your reference the order number is: ${order.id}.
                <P>
                If you would like to try again please click
                <a href="javascript:history.back(-1)">here</a>.
                If the problem continues, please contact you bank as soon as
                possible.
                </td>
        </tr>
        </table>
    </c:otherwise>
</c:choose>
```

Summary

This chapter has walked you through almost every facet of the code and decision-making that went into creating this application. Our goal was to meet the customer's requirements while ensuring an appropriate architecture and implementation along the way. Numerous tools and techniques have been discussed and applied, and we hope that this exercise has provided you with some additional context with which to understand the concepts and tools presented throughout the book.

Remember that you can download the entire application from the Wrox Web site. While the walkthrough presented here will help in many ways, working directly with the code and configuration settings will enhance your understanding immeasurably.

Exercises

1. Create a sales report for the application. This report, accessible via a menu item, should list all the orders placed in the system — approved orders first and then declined orders. Each order listed should include the customer details entered (but not the credit cart number!), as well as a list of the individual order items, their quantity, and the total value.

2. Internationalize the checkout form, i.e., make it potentially multi-lingual. Ensure that the labels come from the messages.properties file.

Part IV: Appendixes

Appendix A: JSP Syntax Reference

Appendix B: JSP Expression Language Reference

Appendix C: JSTL Reference

Appendix D: Exercise Solutions

JSP Syntax Reference

This book has covered a lot of ground. Every fundamental concept in JSP was discussed, and the example code presented important programming techniques. However, in order to maintain a reasonable flow in the text, the syntactical details of many JSP elements were not fully explored.

This appendix captures, at one location, all of the JSP elements that are covered in the text, and provides a more detailed syntax description. It should serve as a useful reference resource during your daily JSP programming activities.

JSP pages are text files composed of the following components:

- ❑ **Template text:** Template text is any text that is not a JSP element. Template text is static and does not change between invocations of the same JSP.

- ❑ **JSP elements:** Many JSP elements result in the dynamic generation of Web content. Because template text can be any static text, a JSP element can contain template text that is in any format. Two of the most common formats are HTML and XML.

JSP elements can be composed of the following components:

- ❑ Directives
- ❑ Actions
- ❑ Scripting elements

Directives are typically enclosed in <%@ .... %>. For example, a JSP page directive may look like the following:

```
<%@ page language="java" %>
```

Actions are specified in standard XML notation. For example, an occurrence of the `<jsp:useBean>` action with a nested occurrence of the `<jsp:setProperty>` action may appear as follows:

```
<jsp:useBean id="newsfeed" class="com.wrox.begjsp.ch2.NewsFeed" scope="request" >
  <jsp:setProperty name="newsfeed"  property="topic" value="weather"/>
</jsp:useBean>
```

While directives are not in XML format, there exists an equivalent XML form for all directives. This means that any JSP can be represented in an XML-compatible format. In practice, this is important only for tools and automated management of JSPs.

Scripting elements provide a mechanism to include raw Java code in-line within the body of a JSP page, as shown in the following example:

```
<%!
  private static String EXAMPLE = "/example1";

  private  String dispPrice( String price)
  {
      int len = price.length();
      if (len <= 2)
          return price;
      else
          return "$" + price.substring(0,len -2) + "." + price.substring(len-2);
  }
%>
```

Scoping

When an object is created within a JSP page, it is always associated with a *scope*. The scope dictates when and where the created object may be accessible. The scope also dictates when the object will be released, and therefore is no longer available. The four available scopes are `page`, `request`, `session`, and `application`.

page scope

Attributes attached to the `pageContext` implicit object are in the `page` scope. These attributes are accessible only within the JSP page in which they are created. This means that these attributes are no longer available after a response has been generated and sent back to the client. This also means that the attributes are no longer available if the request is forwarded to another JSP (or other Web resources such as a servlet). These attributes are automatically released after a response is sent, or when the request is forwarded to another JSP.

The following JSP code creates a JavaBean in the `page` scope. Because `page` scope is the default, there is no need to use the scope attribute of the `<jsp:useBean>` standard action.

```
<jsp:useBean id="newsfeed" class="com.wrox.begjsp.ch02.NewsFeed" />
```

Using JSTL, the following JSP code creates a scoped variable in the page scope. The page scope is the default with the <c:set> JSTL action:

```
<c:set var="selectedCat" value="${param.catid}"/>
```

request scope

Attributes attached to the request implicit object are in the request scope. These attributes are accessible from all the JSP pages that are used in processing the request in which the attribute is created. This means that if the request is forwarded between a set of JSP pages, all the pages will have access to these attributes. This also means that the attributes will no longer be accessible after a response is sent back to the client. These attributes are automatically released after a response is sent to the client.

The following JSP code creates a JavaBean in the request scope:

```
<jsp:useBean id="reqtime" class="java.util.Date " scope="request" />
```

Using JSTL, the following JSP code creates a scoped variable in the request scope:

```
<c:set var="selectedItem" value="${param.item}" scope="request" />
```

session scope

Attributes attached to the session implicit object are in the session scope. A session object can be associated with multiple requests. Not all requests have sessions associated with them. The <%@page %> directive can be used to control whether a JSP page will create a session associated with incoming requests. The attributes in session scope are accessible across all requests associated with the session in which they are created. This means that the attributes may be accessible for multiple incoming requests and multiple JSP pages servicing those requests. The attributes are automatically released when the session ends (usually from a timeout, but sometimes from explicitly ending — i.e., user logout).

The following JSP code creates a JavaBean in the session scope:

```
<jsp:useBean id="loginUser" class="com.wrox.begjsp.ch11.UserIdentity"
  scope="session" />
```

Using JSTL, the following JSP code creates a scoped variable in the session scope:

```
<c:set var="memberDiscount" value="${user.discount}" scope="session" />
```

application scope

Attributes attached to the application implicit object are in the application scope. The application implicit object is a ServletContext instance. This is a truly global scope. Attributes that are created in the application scope are available to all incoming requests for that application, across all the JSP pages that may be servicing those requests. Once created, these attributes will remain available as long as the application remains deployed. It may be necessary in some applications to explicitly remove these attributes. The attributes will be automatically released only if the `ServletContext` is destroyed (only when the application is restarted or undeployed).

The following JSP code creates a JavaBean in the `application` scope:

```
<jsp:useBean id="newsItems" class="com.wrox.begjsp.ch12.StanardNewsItems"
  scope="application" />
```

Using JSTL, the following JSP code creates a scoped variable in the `application` scope:

```
<c:set var="cats" value="${wxshop:getCats()}" scope="application" />
```

Implicit Objects

Implicit objects in JSP are objects that are immediately usable within a JSP page, without your explicit creation or declaration.

The request object

The `request` object represents the request currently being processed. In Web applications, it is usually of the type `javax.servlet.http.HttpServlet.Request`. Attributes created in the `request` scope are attached to this object. Some very useful properties of this object are shown in the following table.

Property	Description
request.queryString	The part of the URL that is used to carry request parameters when an HTTP GET method is used to submit form data.
request.remoteUser	The name of the user if the browser-managed authentication has occurred; or null otherwise.
request.requestURI	The part of the request URL up to the query string.
request.servletPath	The portion of the request URL that called the servlet. Always starts with a backslash (/). May be an empty string if the URL pattern (in the web.xml file servlet mapping) /* matched the servlet.
request.method	The HTTP method used in the request. It can be GET, POST, or PUT.

The response object

This represents the response being sent back to the browser. In Web applications, it is usually of the type `javax.servlet.http.HttpServletResponse`. While this object has properties that control the content type and the locale of the generated response, attributes of the `<@% page %>` directive should be used to set these values in most cases. Several useful properties of this object are shown in the following table.

Property	Description
response.committed	Indicates whether the response is committed (i.e., the status code and headers are already written)
response.bufferSize	The preferred size of the buffer used by the container

The pageContext object

The pageContext object represents the current JSP instance being executed during the processing of the current request. It is always of the type javax.servlet.jsp.PageContext. Attributes created in the page scope are attached to this object. Once the request is forwarded to another JSP page, or if a response is sent back to the client, this object instance is destroyed. This object does not survive across multiple requests. This object maintains references to all of the implicit objects associated with the page. The container will actually use this object to obtain the implicit objects. As a JSP author, however, it is more convenient to use the implicit objects provided. The useful properties of this implicit object are shown in the following table.

Property	Description
pageContext.page	Same as the page implicit object
pageContext.request	Same as the request implicit object
pageContext.response	Same as the response implicit object
pageContext.session	Same as the session implicit object
pageContext.servletConfig	Same as the config implicit object
pageContext.servletContext	Same the application implicit object

The session object

This represents the current HTTP user session maintained by the server. Usually, a cookie is sent to the user's browser and returned with every request in the session. On browsers that do not support cookies, URL rewriting may be used to keep track of sessions (by attaching a session ID to all URLs). This object is always of the type javax.servlet.http.HttpSession. A session survives multiple requests and is valid across all the JSP pages that service the requests within the session. Attributes that are created in the session scope are attached to this implicit object. Some interesting properties in the session object are shown in the following table.

Property	Description
session.new	True if the client has not yet joined the session (i.e., the first request returning a cookie has not yet been received).
session.id	A unique string containing the session identifier.

Table continued on following page

Property	Description
session.creationTime	The creation time of the session. The value is a long value representing milliseconds since midnight January 1, 1970 GMT. This is a standard long-valued representation of date/time in Java and is very convenient for time comparisons.

The application object

This represents the servlet context associated with this Web application. This object is always of the type javax.servlet.ServletContext. Attributes created in the application scope are attached to this object. These attributes are essentially global across all sessions, requests, and JSPs being processed within this application. Several interesting properties of this object are shown in the following table.

Property	Description
application.majorVersion	The major version number of the Servlet API that is supported by the container. For example, this is "2" for the Servlet 2.4 API.
application.minorVersion	The minor version number of the Servlet API supported by the container. For example, this is "4" for the Servlet 2.4 API.
application.serverInfo	The name of the application server, with version information.
application.servletContextName	The name of the Web application, specified by the <display-name> element in the web.xml deployment descriptor file.

The out object

The out object represents the output stream of the current JSP page. It is used implicitly in composing the response to the current request. There is usually no need to address this object directly, as any generated output is automatically sent via this output stream. This object is always of the type javax.servlet.jsp.JspWriter, and is in the page scope, meaning that a new instance is available for each JSP instance used in processing a request. The following table describes a few properties of this object that are accessible within a JSP page and perhaps useful in some debugging situations.

Property	Description
out.bufferSize	The size of the buffer used by the JspWriter object
out.remaining	The available space remaining in the buffer of the JspWriter object

Property	Description
out.autoFlush	True if the JspWriter object is auto-flushing, meaning that buffer flushing is managed by the JspWriter object itself

The config object

This represents a servlet configuration object, always of the type javax.servlet.ServletConfig. This object is in the page scope, and can be used to access initialization parameters that may be supplied in the deployment descriptor (web.xml file) for a JSP page. Directly working with this implicit object is typically reserved for code that has embedded scriptlets (i.e., embedded Java coding). However, using the implicit object called initParam in EL (see Appendix B), these values can be easily accessed within a JSP without using scripting elements. The only interesting property on this object to a JSP author is shown in the following table.

Property	Description
config.servletName	The name of the servlet instance

The page object

This object represents the instance of a JSP page that is currently being used to process the current request. It is a subclass of java.lang.Object. Usually, it is an instance of the Java class that is generated after the JSP container has translated the JSP code into Java code. This means that it is almost always a servlet. There are no interesting properties on this implicit object.

The exception object

This implicit object is made available only in the error-handling page. The error handling page must be specified using a <%@page %> directive, as in the following:

```
<%@page isErrorPage="true" %>
```

This object is always a subtype of java.lang.Throwable. The exception implicit object contains the actual exception that caused the error-handling page to display. Some useful properties of this object are shown in the following table.

Property	Description
exception.message	Description of the exception.
exception.localizedMessage	Localized version of the exception description.
exception.cause	Sometimes exceptions are wrapped around other exceptions. In these cases, this property may be used to access the "inner" Throwable. For example, you may need to use exception.cause.message to obtain the actual cause of the exception.

Directives

Directives in JSP are hints and directions for the container. Directives, unlike actions, typically do not generate any dynamic output. One can consider directives as a way to customize and configure behaviors of the container down to a very fine granular level — that of a JSP page. Directives are handled during translation time, not at request time.

The page directive

The page directive is used to set attributes that affect the translation, compilation, and execution of the current JSP page. The page directive has the following general syntax:

```
<%@page [... attributes...] %>
```

The available optional attributes are described in the following table.

Attribute Name	Description
language	Specifies the scripting language used when (and if) scripting elements are used within the JSP. This defaults to Java.
extends	Specifies the superclass that the container will use in generating the servlet Java code, representing the JSP page, during the translation phase.
import	Specifies the library classes that will be used within the JSP page by the scripting elements. Fully qualified (full names) library class names are separated by commas.
session	Specifies whether the container should create a session for the JSP page (if not already in a session) during request time. The default value is true.
buffer	Either a number of kilobytes in size for the buffer or none. Any numeric value must have suffix kb. Default is 8kb or more, depending on the container.
autoFlush	Specifies whether the buffer should be flushed automatically once filled. The default is true. If set to false, a buffer full condition will cause an exception to be thrown.
isThreadSafe	The default is true. If set to false, requests that the container generates code that operates in the SingleThreadModel. This model is deprecated in Servlet 2.4, and will not be available in the future. Do not alter the setting of this attribute.
info	Supplies information about the page. Any value you specified here is made available to JSP developer tools.
errorPage	If true, tells the container that this JSP page is used by other JSP pages to handle errors.
isErrorPage	If true, tells the container that this JSP page is used by other JSP pages to handle errors. If this is the error page, an implicit object called exception will be available to the page when it is executed. The default is false.

Attribute Name	Description
contentType	Specifies the MIME type and, optionally, character encoding used in the JSP page. The default is text/html.
pageEncoding	Specifies the page character encoding used for the JSP page. See Chapter 13, "Internationalization and Localized Content," for some commonly used IANA names for character encodings.
isELIgnored	Specifies that EL expressions in the page should (false) or should not (true) be evaluated. This defaults to false—i.e., EL will be evaluated.

The taglib directive

The taglib directive is used to include tag libraries for use within a JSP page. It is also used to specify a prefix to all the tags in a tag library. The general syntax of the taglib directive is as follows:

```
<%@ taglib { uri="...URI..." | tagdir="...dir..." } prefix="..prefix.." %>
```

If tagdir is specified instead of the uri attribute, the tag library is implemented in the form of tag files. Tag files enable JSP developers to store commonly used segments of JSP code in their own tag libraries.

The attributes in the taglib directive are enumerated in the following table.

Attribute Name	Description
uri	Used by the container to locate a TLD file that describes the tag library. The URI can be absolute, as in http://java.sun.com/jsp/jstl/core, or relative, as in /tags/core. The URI is just used as a unique identifier for mapping and is not accessed directly. TLD can be mapped using a taglib map element within the web.xml file.
tagdir	Specifies the actual directory that contains the tag files containing the implementation of the tag library. For JSP 2.0, this should always start with /WEB-INF/tags.
prefix	The prefix to be used within this JSP page, before every tag from the tag library specified with this <%@ taglib %> directive.

The include directive

The include directive provides a translation-time inclusion mechanism. Using this directive tells the container to "pull in" the included content before the resulting JSP is translated into Java code. The JSP code being included is not executed, but merely included in-line at the position of the directive. Coinciding with JSP translation, the inclusion is typically performed only once. Once the JSP is translated into Java code and compiled, only the compiled image is kept around. Note that this is very different from the include action, which performs the inclusion of resources at request processing time for each and every request. The general syntax for the include directive is as follows:

```
<%@ include file="....  URL specification .... " %>
```

The URL specification should be relative to the directory of the location of the current JSP.

Tag file directives

Several JSP directives are used exclusively within tag files. Tag files provide a way to create a tag library using JSP. In addition to the directives in the following sections, the taglib and include directives are also available within tag files.

The tag directive

The tag directive is used to provide directions and information to the container or development tool regarding the tag. Typically, a development tool may use some of these attributes in determining how to display a specific tag to the developer. Its purpose is similar to the <%@ page %> directive for regular JSP pages. The general syntax of this directive is as follows:

```
<%@ tag .... attributes.... %>
```

The available attributes for this directive are described in the following table.

Attribute Name	Description
display-name	A name to be displayed by a development tool accessing this tag. The default is the name of the tag file.
body-content	The default is scriptless. The choices are scriptless, tagdependent, or empty. scriptless means that no embedded Java code is allowed within the body, empty means that there can be no body content, and tagdependent means that scripts are allowed in the body.
dynamic-attributes	Used to implement a tag that allows for a flexible and changing set of attributes, determined only during runtime. This is an advanced JSP topic and beyond the scope of this appendix. This attribute should not be specified if the tag does not support dynamic-attributes (the default).
small-icon	Path to a small icon to represent the tag. Typically used by developer tools.
large-icon	Path to a large icon to represent the tag. Typically used by developer tools.
description	A textual description of the tag. Typically used by developer tools.
example	A string that shows how to use this tag. Typically used by developer tools.

Attribute Name	Description
language	Same as the `language` attribute of the `<%@ page %>` directive.
import	Same as the `import` attribute of the `<%@ page %>` directive.
pageEncoding	Same as the `pageEncoding` attribute of the `<%@ page %>` directive.
isELIgnored	Same as the `isELIgnored` attribute of the `<%@ page %>` directive.

The attribute directive

The `attribute` directive is used to declare an attribute for the tag in a tag file. The general syntax for this directive is as follows:

```
<%@ attribute name="...attr name..."   .... more attributes ..... %>
```

The allowed attributes for this directive are described in the following table.

Attribute Name	Description
name	The name of the attribute.
required	Indicates if this attribute is a mandatory attribute for the tag. The default is `false`.
fragment	Indicates to the container if this attribute should be processed by the container first (`false`) or passed to the tag handler first (`true`). The default is `false`.
rtexprvalue	Indicates if the attribute value may contain a scriptlet expression. The default is `true`.
type	Specifies the runtime type of this attribute. The default is a `String`.
description	Specifies a description of the attribute. Typically used by developer tools.

The variable directive

The `variable` directive is used to expose a variable that can be accessed within the JSP page containing the tag. The general syntax of this directive is as follows:

```
<%@ variable { name-given="... name ..." |  name-from-attribute="...name..."}
.... more attributes.... %>
```

The attributes of this directive are described in the following table.

Attribute Name	Description
name-given	Specifies the name of a scripting variable that will be defined in the JSP containing this tag.
name-from-attribute	Specifies the name of an attribute whose value at translation time will be used to create a scripting variable in the JSP containing the tag.
alias	Must be used in conjunction with name-from-attribute. Will create a locally scoped attribute to hold the value of the variable.
variable-class	Defaults to String. Specifies the Java type of this variable.
declare	The default value is true. Specifies if the variable is declared within this tag file.
scope	The scope of the scripting variable, determining when the container will perform synchronization of values. Can be AT_BEGIN, AT_END, or NESTED. The default is NESTED.
description	A description of the variable. Typically used by development tools.

Actions

Actions are often called tags in JSP. While the `<%@taglib %>` directive can add custom actions via tag libraries, JSP has a set of built-in, ready-to-use tags. These built-in tags are called *standard actions*.

Standard actions

Standard actions haven't evolved much since earlier versions of JSP. Therefore, you are likely to see many of these tags used in legacy code that you may be maintaining.

The <jsp:useBean> action

The `<jsp:useBean>` action can be used to create a new instance of a JavaBean or to make an existing instance of a JavaBean (perhaps created using scripting elements) visible to the JSP page. The general syntax of `<jsp:useBean>` is as follows:

```
<jsp:useBean id="......"  scope="...."  type="...." />
```

The following table describes the attributes that can be used with `<jsp:useBean>`.

Attribute Name	Description
id	The name of the JavaBean instance to look for. It is also the name used to refer to the new JavaBean instance if one is created. You cannot have two `<jsp:useBean>` standard actions using the same id attribute. This is a mandatory attribute.

Attribute Name	Description
class	This is the full Java class name of the JavaBean. It is used to create a new instance if the named bean cannot be found. This is an optional attribute, but one of the class or type attributes (or both) must be specified.
type	This is a Java interface that the JavaBean instance implements or a superclass that the JavaBean instance extends. This type is used in the generation of Java source code during the translation phase. This is an optional attribute, but one of the class or type attributes (or both) must be specified.
scope	Specifies the scope in which the standard action will attempt to create the JavaBean. This is an optional attribute. The default value when not specified is the page scope.

The <jsp:setProperty> action

This standard action is used to set a property value on a JavaBean instance. The general usage form of this standard action is as follows:

```
<jsp:setProperty name=".. JavaBean name..." property=".. property name ..."   [
value="..value to set.." | param="... parameter name..."] />
```

This standard action does not support a body.

The following can be used to set the value(s) of a JavaBean via the <jsp:setProperty> standard action:

❑ A string constant

❑ A request parameter

❑ An EL expression

The attributes of this standard action are described in the following table.

Attribute Name	Description
name	Specifies the name used to search through the four scopes for an attached attribute, a JavaBean, with the same name. If the attribute cannot be found, an exception will be raised.
property	Specifies the property of the JavaBean to be set (not a read-only property). It can also contain the special * notation. This will cause the container to match each request parameter against the properties of the JavaBean and to perform an assignment for each property with an identical name to a request parameter.

Attribute Name	Description
param	Specifies the request parameter whose value will be used in the assignment. Only one of param or value may be specified.
value	Specifies the value to be used in the assignment. Only one of param or value may be specified.

The <jsp:getProperty> action

The <jsp:getProperty> standard action is used to render the property value of a JavaBean. The general form is as follows:

```
<jsp:getProperty name="...javabean name..." property="...property name..." />
```

The two attributes of this tag are shown in the following table.

Attribute Name	Description
name	Specifies the name of the JavaBean whose property is to be rendered. This is typically made available by an earlier <jsp:useBean> standard action.
property	The name of the property to render.

The <jsp:include> action

The <jsp:include> standard action is a request-time action that will include the output of another JSP at the location of the tag within the calling JSP. The general syntax for this standard action is as follows:

```
<jsp:include page="...url.." flush="true or false"/>
```

The tag can optionally contain a body:

```
<jsp:include page="...url..." flush="true or false">
  <jsp:param ..../>
</jsp:include>
```

In this second usage, there are one or more <jsp:param> standard actions within the body of <jsp:include>. These <jsp:param> standard actions specify additional request parameters that will be available within the JSP whose output is being included.

The attributes of this standard action are shown in the following table.

Attribute Name	Description
page	A URL that is relative to the current JSP page at request time
flush	Specifies if the buffer for the output should be flushed immediately before the included page's output

The <jsp:forward> action

This standard action forwards the requests to another JSP or Web resource. The processing of the current JSP will be terminated. The basic syntax of the `<jsp:forward>` standard action is as follows:

```
<jsp:forward page="...url..." />
```

The following code shows an alternative form whereby a body can consist of `<jsp:param>` standard actions:

```
<jsp:forward page="..url...">
  <jsp:param ..../>
</jsp:forward>
```

This second form can be used to add parameters to the request that will be available within the JSP to which the request is being forwarded. The attribute available for this standard action is described in the following table.

Attribute Name	Description
page	A relative URL to which the request will be forwarded. The URL is a request-time evaluated URL and may be mapped by entries in the deployment descriptor (`web.xml` file).

The <jsp:params> action

The `<jsp:params>` standard action can occur only within the body of the `<jsp:plugin>` tag. It is used to group a set of `<jsp:param>` entries. Its basic syntax is as follows:

```
<jsp:params>
  <jsp:param ..../>
  <jsp:param ..../>
  ....
</jsp:params>
```

There can be any number of `<jsp:param>` standard actions in the body of the `<jsp:params>` tag. Each will be translated to a parameter for the applet and/or bean embedded on the Web page.

The <jsp:param> action

This standard action can appear in the body of `<jsp:include>` and `<jsp:forward>` standard actions. It can also be used within the `<jsp:params>` standard action. The general syntax of the `<jsp:param>` standard action is as follows:

```
<jsp:param name="..name..." value="...value..."/>
```

Each `<jsp:param>` creates a parameter that has a name and a value. Exactly how these parameters will be used depends on the tag for which the parameters are used.

For example, in both of the `<jsp:include>` and `<jsp:forward>` cases, these parameters are request parameters available for the JSP page being included (or being forwarded to).

The <jsp:plugin> action

The <jsp:plugin> standard action will generate the HTML code to embed a Java object on the page. This is typically a Java applet. The general syntax of the <jsp:plugin> standard action is as follows:

```
<jsp:plugin type="... applet or bean..."  code="..." codebase="..." archive="..."
....>
  ...
</jsp:plugin>
```

The body of this standard action can contain a <jsp:params> and a <jsp:fallback> standard action. The attributes of this standard action are shown in the following table.

Attribute Name	Description
type	Either applet or bean; specifies the type of Java object that will be embedded on the HTML page.
other attributes	Any attributes for the HTML <OBJECT> or <EMBED> tags can be specified. See an HTML reference for the possible attributes.

The <jsp:fallback> action

The <jsp:fallback> standard action can be used only within the body of the <jsp:plugin> tag. This standard action specifies the HTML that will be rendered (or the JSP code that will be executed) if the browser does not support the plugin. The basic syntax for <jsp:fallback> is as follows:

```
<jsp:fallback>
  ... HTML or JSP that will be rendered if the browser does not support plugin ...
</jsp:fallback>
```

Other JSP standard actions

There are several other standard JSP actions that are only used in the creation of tag files. They are listed here but are not covered in this reference. See the JSP 2.0 specification available at http://java.sun.com/products/jsp/reference/api/index.html if you need the detailed syntax of these actions:

- ❑ <jsp:attribute>
- ❑ <jsp:body>
- ❑ <jsp:invoke>
- ❑ <jsp:doBody>
- ❑ <jsp:element>
- ❑ <jsp:text>
- ❑ <jsp:output>

Scripting Elements

Scripting elements are embedded non-templating code within JSP pages. This code is typically in the Java programming language. Scripting elements can take one of three forms:

- ❑ Declarations
- ❑ Scriptlets
- ❑ Expressions

Declaration scripting elements

Declaration scripting elements are Java code that is used to declare variables and methods. The general syntax is as follows:

```
<%!  ... Java declaration goes here... %>
```

The following example declares a Java constant and a Java method:

```
<%!
  private static String EXAMPLE = "/example3";

  private  String dispPrice( String price)
  {
      int len = price.length();
      if (len <= 2)
          return price;
      else
          return "$" + price.substring(0,len -2) + "." + price.substring(len-2);
  }
%>
```

Scriptlets

Scriptlets contain arbitrary Java code segments. The general syntax is as follows:

```
<%      ... Java code goes here ...     %>
```

The following example generates dynamic output by writing directly to the out JSP implicit object:

```
<%
  if  (state.isLocal())
    out.print(totalCost * localTax);
  else
    out.println(totalCost);
%>
```

Expression scripting elements

Expressions are Java code that yield a resulting value and generate dynamic output when the JSP is executed. The resulting value is converted to a text string and placed at the location of the scripting element. The general syntax is as follows:

```
<%=    ... Java expression goes here ... %>
```

The following example renders a product name and pricing within an HTML table:

```
<table>
  <tr>
    <td><%= curItem.getName() %></td>
    <td><%= dispPrice(String.valueOf(curItem.getPrice()))  %></td>
  </tr>
</table>
```

While scripting elements offer powerful extension possibilities to JSP developers, they also encourage the mixing of presentation-level code and business-logic code. This can result in highly convoluted JSP pages that are difficult to maintain. Modern software design principles mandate that JSP should be used only for templating or presentation purposes. Business logic should be implemented in another tier outside of JSP using technology such as Enterprise Java Beans (EJBs), or other alternative mechanisms.

JSP Expression Language Reference

This appendix captures, at one location, the syntactical details of the Expression Language (EL) in JSP 2. It serves as a quick reference for resolving usage questions as you apply EL in your JSP programs.

EL Expressions

EL is a language that complements JSTL, enabling the creation of completely scriptless JSPs. As its name implies, EL is a language that revolves around the evaluation of expressions. EL expressions provide powerful access to JavaBeans, Java collections, Java maps, and Java arrays. This capability eliminates the need to perform access through Java coding from within scripting elements. An EL expression is always dynamically evaluated at request time. All EL expressions are contained in the following notation:

```
${.... EL expression..... }
```

El expressions may appear in two distinct locations in a JSP page:

- ❑   In-line with template data
- ❑   Within attribute values of tags (for example, JSTL tags)

EL expressions in-line with template data

An EL expression can be used to render a textual string in-line with template data — for example, as a constant EL arithmetic expression:

```
<b>There are ${5 + 1} bears in the cave.</b>
```

Another example demonstrates the use of EL to address a property of nested JavaBeans:

```
<b>The total cost for this order is ${order.totals.afterTax}.</b>
```

EL expressions in attribute values

EL expressions are also used for the attribute values of certain tags. Namely, EL expressions are frequently found in the attribute values of tags in the JSTL. For example, the `<c:if>` JSTL tag uses an EL logical expression for its `test` attribute value:

```
<c:if test="${salary > 100000}">
<b>Rich cousin!</b><br/>
</c:if>
```

Accessing Arrays, Maps, Object Properties, and Collections

The most powerful aspect of EL is the ease with which it can be used to access Java arrays, maps, object properties, and collections. Access to all of these types is unified via the dot (`.`) or `[ ]` (square brackets) notation. The rules of access are designed in such a way that the most "obvious" way of accessing an element, given that you're familiar with Java programming, will work as intended.

Object properties access

To access the `minQual` property of a Java object called `member`, for example, use the following EL:

```
<b>You must earn ${member.minQual} points to maintain your membership.</b>
```

You can also use the equivalent `[]` notation:

```
<b>You must earn ${member["minQual"]} points to maintain your membership.</b>
```

The `getMinQual()` getter method of the object will be invoked to obtain the value to be rendered.

Array member access

To access the ninth element in a Java array named `callHistory`, you can use the following EL:

```
<b>In the most recent call to the customer, ${callHistory[8]} is discussed .</b>
```

Java map access

A Java `Map` typed object provides mapping between a set of keys and a set of values. Using EL, as long as the key values can be converted to strings, the elements in the `Map` can be directly accessed using EL.

For example, to access the value associated with the key "Mumbai" in a `HashMap` (a concrete implementation of a Java `Map`) called temperature, the following EL can be used:

```
<b>The temperature now is ${temperature.Mumbai}.  </b>
```

The following code is equivalent to the preceding code:

```
<b>The temperature now is ${temperature["Mumbai"]}.  </b>
```

Java collection access

EL can readily work with any Java Collection object (i.e., objects that implement the `java.util` `.Collection` interface). Iterative access is achieved in collaboration with JSTL's `<c:forEach>` tag (see Appendix C, "JSTL Reference"). Individual elements of a `List`-based collection can be accessed via the following EL:

```
<tr><td>${memberList[3]} </td></tr>
```

The preceding code will call the `memberList.get(3)` method and coerce the result to a string for rendering. The fourth element in the list will be displayed.

Elements of EL Expressions

EL expressions are composed of named variables, literals, operators, and functions.

Named variables

Any named variables within EL expressions are first checked against the available EL implicit objects (see the "Implicit Objects" section later in this appendix). If the named variable does not correspond to any implicit object, the EL runtime will search through the different scopes for an attribute with the specified name. It will search the scopes in the order of page ➪ request ➪ session ➪ application.

Literals

Literals are constants that can be used within EL. The following table shows the different types of literals available in EL.

Literal Type	Description
Boolean	The value `true` or `false`
Integer	An integer numeric value
Floating point	A floating-point numeric value
String	A string within either double or single quotes
Null	The value `null`

Operators

Operators fall into four categories:

❑   Arithmetic operators

❑   Logical operators

❑   Comparison operators

❑   The empty prefix operator

Arithmetic operators

All the basic arithmetic operators that you are familiar with are available within EL expressions. This includes addition, subtraction, multiplication, division, and modulus. The following table lists these operators.

Operator	Symbol
Addition	+
Subtraction	–
Multiplication	*
Division	/ or div
Modulo	% or mod

Logical operators

In EL, logical operators can be used to combine multiple boolean-valued sub-expressions. The logical operators supported by EL are shown in the following table.

Operator	Symbol
And	&& or and
Or	|| or or
Not	! or not

Comparison (relational) operators

EL supports a range of comparison operators found in most programming languages. Each of the operators has a symbolic form and an abbreviated textual form. The following table enumerates the available comparison operators.

Operator	Symbol
Greater than	`>` or `gt`
Greater than or equal to	`>=` or `ge`
Less than	`<` or `lt`
Lesser than or equal to	`<=` or `le`
Equal to	`==` or `eq`
Not equal to	`!=` or `ne`

The empty operator

The empty operator is a unary operator that can be used to test certain conditions. The conditions tested will depend on the type of the actual operand. The following table shows the empty values for the different operand types.

Operand Data Type	Empty Value
String	`""`
Any named variable	Null
Array	No elements
Map	No elements
List/Collection	No elements

Operator precedence

As with most programming languages, parentheses `( )` can be used to control the exact precedence of the operators.

Otherwise, the precedence follows this order:

1. `[]` and `.` ; cannot be overridden by parentheses
2. `()`
3. Unary operators (`-`, `!`, `empty`)
4. `*` `/` `%`
5. `|`
6. `<` `>` `<=` `>=`
7. `==` `!=`

8. `&&`
9. `||`
10. `? :`

Functions

Functions can be used within EL to transform values of variables or other expressions. The general syntax to call a function within EL is as follows:

```
xx:fname( arg1, arg2, ..... )
```

Here, `xx` is the prefix of a tag library that contains the EL function, `fname` is the name of the function, and `arg1`, `arg2`, `....` is a list of arguments for the function.

EL functions must be packaged as part of a tag library.

Namespace and EL functions

EL functions use the same namespace concept that custom tags use. They must be defined within the Tag Library Descriptor (TLD).

For example, for an EL function called `rankOf()`, you may use the following EL expression:

```
${wf:rankOf(name, level)}
```

Before using the preceding EL expression, the `wf` namespace/prefix must be defined in a `<%@ taglib %>` directive earlier — in this case, a `<%@ taglib %>` directive similar to the following:

```
<%@ taglib prefix="wf" uri="http://www.wrox.com/begjsp/el-functions-taglib" %>
```

EL function implementation: static methods of a Java class

EL functions are implemented in the Java programming language. They must be defined as static methods in a Java class. They can return a value of any data type, although `String` return types are most useful when rendering in EL expressions.

An EL function implemented as a static method can also have any number of arguments. The TLD must describe the return data type and the arguments' data type.

For example, the following TLD fragment describes a `rankOf()` EL function that returns a `String`, and takes a `String` and an `int` as arguments:

```
<function>
  <description>Function to determine a member's rank</description>
  <name>rankOf</name>
  <function-class>com.wrox.begjsp.ch15.ElFuncs</function-class>
  <function-signature>String rankOf(String,  int )</function-signature>
</function>
```

Type Conversions

To make programming in EL as simple as possible, EL has a set of type conversion rules that tries to "do the right thing" under most circumstances. This set of rules governs what happens when operands or arguments of an inappropriate type are supplied in expressions.

Coercion: automatic type conversion

Coercion, or automatic type conversion, occurs when the input type does not match the required type. For example, the attribute of a tag may require an integer value, but the input value is a string. Before this conversion can happen, EL will always first "box" a primitive type, as explained next.

Boxing and unboxing

Boxing is simply the action of creating an associated Java object from a primitive type. The following table shows the common primitive types and their boxed form. Unboxing refers to the action of creating a primitive typed value from the associated Java object.

Primitive Type	Boxed Type
int	Integer
long	Long
double	Double
char	Character
boolean	Boolean

Coercion to String

Variable values are coerced to a `String` type as follows:

1. First box the variable if it is primitive.

2. Use the `toString()` method of the wrapping object to obtain the `String` equivalent.

Null values are returned as an empty string, `""`. An error will result if the call to `toString()` throws an exception.

Coercion to Number

Number types include `short`, `int`, `float`, `double`, and their boxed types.

Variables of any type are coerced to a number type by first boxing them if necessary, and then taking one of the following actions:

❑ If the type is `String`, use the `valueOf()` method to get its value; `""` empty string will return `0`.

❑ If the type is `Character`, use `new Short((short) v.charValue())`, assuming the `Character` variable is called `v`.

❑ Unbox the variable if necessary.

Null values are returned as 0. If the type is a `Boolean`, an error will result. Numbers can always be converted successfully among themselves (for example, `Integer` to `Float`). If the call to `valueOf()` throws an exception, an error will result.

Coercion to Character

Variable values are coerced to `Character` type in the following manner:

❑ If the type is a Number type, first it is coerced to the type Short, and then a `Character` is returned that is numerically equivalent to the short value.

❑ If the type is `String`, the method `charAt(0)` is used to obtain the `Character`. This is essentially the first character of the string.

Coercing a null value causes `(char) 0` to be returned as the result. A `Boolean` incoming type will cause an error.

Implicit Objects

Implicit objects are built-in objects that can be used within any EL expression. This concept is similar to implicit objects in JSP. In fact, EL can be used to access equivalent JSP implicit objects through the `pageContext` implicit object.

However, accessing JSP implicit objects is unnecessary because the set of EL implicit objects makes accessing relevant values substantially easier.

There are 11 EL implicit objects, which can be classified into five major categories:

❑ **JSP implicit object:** `pageContext`

❑ **Convenience scoping access:** `pageScope`, `requestScope`, `sessionScope`, `applicationScope`

❑ **Convenience parameter access:** `param`, `paramValues`

❑ **Convenience header access:** `header`, `headerValues`, `cookies`

❑ **Convenience initialization parameter access:** `initParam`

The pageContext implicit object

This is the same as the JSP implicit object of the same name. The properties of this implicit object can be used to access the various JSP implicit objects.

For example, `pageContext.request` is the same as the `request` JSP implicit object, and `pageContext.servletContext` is the same as the JSP `application` implicit object. For more details on the available properties, see a description of the `pageContext` JSP implicit object in Appendix A.

The pageScope implicit object

The pageScope implicit object provides a map of all the available attributes in the page scope. In EL, values of a Map can be accessed via the [] notation or the . notation.

For example, to render the value of an attribute named selectedRow in the page scope, the following EL can be used:

```
${pageScope.selectedRow}
```

The following EL is equivalent:

```
${pageScope["selectedRow"]}
```

The requestScope implicit object

The requestScope implicit object provides a map of all the available attributes in the request scope. In EL, values of a map can be accessed via the [] notation or the dot (.) notation.

For example, to render the value of an attribute named currentCert in the request scope, the following EL can be used:

```
${requestScope.currentCert}
```

The following EL is equivalent:

```
${requestScope["currentCert"]}
```

Note that in some cases, if the incoming request is originating from another Web resource (for example, a PERL script), the name of the attribute may actually contain embedded dot (.) characters. In this case, you must use the second EL syntax shown above—the [] notation to access the value of the attribute.

The sessionScope implicit object

The sessionScope implicit object provides a Map of all the available attributes in the session scope. In EL, values of a Map can be accessed via either the [] notation or the dot (.) notation.

For example, to render the value of an attribute named orderTotal in the session scope, the following EL can be used:

```
${sessionScope.orderTotal}
```

The following EL is equivalent:

```
${sessionScope["orderTotal"]}
```

The applicationScope implicit object

The `applicationScope` implicit object provides a map of all the available attributes in the `application` scope. In EL, values of a map can be accessed via the `[]` notation or the dot (`.`) notation.

For example, to render the value of an attribute named `productCategories` in the `application` scope, the following EL can be used:

```
${applicationScope.productCategories}
```

The following EL is equivalent:

```
${applicationScope["productCategories"]}
```

The param implicit object

The `param` implicit object is a map containing all the incoming request parameters. The keys of the map are the names of the parameters, and the values are the corresponding values. In EL, values of a map can be accessed via the `[]` notation or the dot (`.`) notation.

For example, to render the value of a request parameter named `address1`, the following EL can be used:

```
${param.address1}
```

The following EL is equivalent:

```
${param["address1"]}
```

The paramValues implicit object

The `paramValues` implicit object is a map providing access to all multivalued incoming request parameters. The keys of the map are the names of the parameters, and the values are arrays of strings (`String[]`) with the corresponding values. In EL, values of a map can be accessed via the `[]` notation or the dot (`.`) notation.

For example, to access the values in a multivalued request parameter named `itemsPurchased`, the following EL can be used. Of course, you are likely to use `<c:forEach>` to iterate through the resulting array value.

```
${paramValues.itemsPurchased}
```

Equivalently, the following EL can also be used obtain the array:

```
${paramValues["itemsPurchased"]}
```

The header implicit object

The `header` implicit object is a `Map` containing all the HTTP headers. The keys of the `Map` are the names of the headers, and the values are the corresponding header values. In EL, values of a `Map` can be accessed via the `[]` notation or the dot (`.`) notation.

For example, to render the value of the HTTP header `User-Agent`, the following EL can be used:

```
${header["User-Agent"]}
```

The headerValues implicit object

The `headerValues` implicit object is a `Map` providing access to all multivalued HTTP request headers. The keys of the `Map` are the names of the headers, and the values are arrays of strings (`String []`) with the corresponding values. In EL, values of a `Map` can be accessed via the `[]` notation or the dot (`.`) notation.

For example, to access the values in a multivalued HTTP header named `Accept-Encoding`, the following EL can be used. Of course, you are likely to use `<c:forEach>` to iterate through the resulting array.

```
${header["Accept-Encoding"]}
```

The cookies implicit object

The `cookies` implicit object is a map containing all the values from available HTTP cookies with the request. The keys of the map are the names of the cookies, and the values are the corresponding values. In EL, values of a map can be accessed via either the `[]` notation or the dot (`.`) notation.

For example, to render the value of a cookie named `lastLoginName`, the following EL can be used:

```
${cookies.lastLoginName}
```

Equivalently, the following EL can also be used:

```
${cookies["lastLoginName"]}
```

Multiple cookies with the same name are not well supported by the implementation and should be avoided.

The initParam implicit object

The `initParam` implicit object is a `Map` containing all the values from initialization parameters for the current `ServletContext` (specified through the `web.xml` deployment descriptor; see Chapter 15, "JSP and Servlets," for more details). The keys of the map are the names of the initialization parameters, and the values are the corresponding values. In EL, values of a map can be accessed via either the `[]` notation or the dot (`.`) notation.

For example, to render the value of an initialization parameter named `localOffice`, the following EL can be used:

```
${initParam.localOffice}
```

The following EL is equivalent:

```
${initParam["localOffice"]}
```

JSTL Reference

The Java Standard Tag Library (JSTL) is a standardized collection of custom tags. It has a number of tags for common tasks such as iterating through lists, interacting with databases, handling XML data, formatting data, and much more.

The latest version of JSTL (at the time of writing) is 1.1. An implementation of JSTL can be downloaded from the Apache Jakarta Web site (http://jakarta.apache.org/).

JSTL consist of four sets of tags and a library of functions, grouped according to their functionality:

❑ JSTL core tags
❑ JSTL XML tags
❑ JSTL formatting tags
❑ JSTL SQL tags
❑ JSTL functions

JSTL Core Tags

The JSTL core tag library contains tags that deal with flow control in JSP pages, iterating over collections, evaluating expressions, and importing resources.

Before using the core tag library, the following directive needs to be added to the JSP page:

```
<%@ taglib prefix="c" uri="http://java.sun.com/jsp/jstl/core" %>
```

The equivalent XML syntax for this directive is as follows:

```
<jsp:directive.taglib prefix="c" uri="http://java.sun.com/jsp/jstl/core" />
```

The following table summarizes the JSTL core tags.

Tag Name	Description
catch	Catches any Throwable exception that occurs in the body of the tag
choose	Provides conditional operation and allows for choosing between mutually exclusive options
if	Provides conditional operation
import	Imports a resource specified by a URL and exposes it to the page, variable, or reader
forEach	Iterates over collections
forTokens	Iterates over tokens
out	Outputs expressions to the Web page
otherwise	A conditional operation tag for choosing between mutually exclusive options. This tag is a subtag of the choose tag.
param	Used along with the import, redirect, or url tags to add a parameter to a URL
redirect	Redirects to a new URL
remove	Removes a variable from a scope
set	Sets the value of an attribute
url	Creates a URL
when	A conditional operation tag that includes its body when an expression evaluates to true. This tag is a subtag of the choose tag.

catch

The catch tag is used to catch any java.lang.Throwable exception in the body of the tag. The syntax of the catch tag is as follows:

```
<c:catch [var="variable_name"]>
    JSP body content
</c:catch>
```

The catch tag has one attribute:

❏ **var:** Name of the variable that is set to the thrown exception. This is an optional attribute.

An example of the catch tag is listed here:

```
<c:catch var="exp">
  <c:import url="http://www.foobar.com/stuff.html"/>
</c:catch>
<c:if test="${not empty exp}">
  Sorry, unable to import from URL, got exception <c:out value="${exp}" />
</c:if>
```

choose

The `choose` tag is used to provide conditional operation, and allows for choosing between mutually exclusive options. The actual selection is done using its subtags: `when` and `otherwise`. The syntax of the `choose` tag is shown here:

```
<c:choose>
  <c:when test="expression">
    JSP body content
  </c:when>
  ...
  <c:otherwise>
    JSP body content
  </c:otherwise>
</c:choose>
```

An example of the `choose` tag is as follows:

```
<c:choose>
  <c:when test="${userrole} == 'admin'}">
    Welcome admin. Proceed to your admin page <a href="/admin">here</a>
  </c:when>
  <c:when test="${userrole} == 'member'}">
    Welcome member. Proceed to your home page <a href="/memberhome">here</a>
  </c:when>
  <c:otherwise>
    Welcome guest. Log in <a href="/login">here</a>.
  </c:otherwise>
</c:choose>
```

if

The `if` tag evaluates a test condition. If it is true, it processes its body. If the test condition is false, the body is ignored. The syntax of the `if` tag is shown here:

```
<c:if test="test condition>
    [var="variable name"]
    [scope="page|request|session|application"]>
  JSP body content
</c:if>
```

The `if` tag has three attributes:

❑ **test:** The test condition that determines whether the body of the tag is to be processed. This is a mandatory attribute.

❑ **var:** Variable that holds the result (`true` or `false`) of the test condition evaluation. This variable can be used for future test conditions (depending on the scope of the variable), thus avoiding reevaluation of the test condition. This is an optional attribute.

❑ **scope:** Scope of the variable specified in the `var` attribute. This can be `page`, `request`, `session`, or `application`, and defaults to `page` if not specified. This is an optional attribute.

An example of the if tag is listed here:

```
<c:if test="${not empty exp}">
   Sorry, unable to import from URL, got exception <c:out value="${exp}" />
</c:if>
```

import

The import tag imports a resource specified by a URL and exposes it to the page, variable, or reader. It is similar to the <jsp:include> directive, but with more features. The body of the import tag can have param tags for adding parameters to the URL. The syntax for the tag is shown here:

```
<c:import url="resource URL"
          [var="variable name"]
          [scope="page|request|session|application"]
          [varReader="variable name"]
          [context="context name"]
          [charEncoding="character encoding"]>
     JSP body content
</c:import>
```

The import tag has six attributes:

❑   **url:** The relative or absolute URL of the resource being imported. This is a mandatory attribute.

❑   **var:** The variable in which the content retrieved from the specified URL should be stored. This is an optional attribute.

❑   **scope:** Scope of the variable specified in the var attribute. This can be page, request, session, or application, and defaults to page if not specified. This is an optional attribute.

❑   **varReader:** Name of the Reader for the URL resource. This is an optional attribute.

❑   **context:** When the URL being imported is a relative URL in another context, the context name is specified in this attribute. This is an optional attribute.

❑   **charEncoding:** The character encoding of the content at the specified URL. This is an optional attribute.

An example of the import tag is listed here:

```
<c:import url="http://www.foobar.com/stuff.html"/>
```

forEach

The forEach tag is used for iteration over collections. The syntax of the forEach tag is shown here:

```
<c:forEach [items="collection of items"]
           [begin="begin index"]
           [end="end index"]
           [step="step size"]
           [var="variable name"]
```

```
                [varStatus="status variable name"]>
          JSP body content
     </c:forEach>
```

The forEach tag has six attributes:

- ❑ **items:** The collection of items to iterate over. The collection can be any Java object of type java.util.Collection or java.util.Map. This is an optional attribute.

- ❑ **begin:** The start index for the iteration. This is an optional attribute.

- ❑ **end:** The end index for the iteration. This is an optional attribute.

- ❑ **step:** The size of the index increment while iterating over the collection. The iteration will process every step item of the collection, starting from the begin index (or first item, if begin is not specified). For example, if step is 5, the index is incremented by 5 every iteration. This is an optional attribute.

- ❑ **var:** The name of the variable in which the current item in the iteration is stored. This is an optional attribute.

- ❑ **varStatus:** The name of the variable in which the status of the iteration is stored.

An example of the forEach tag is listed here:

```
<ul>
    <c:forEach items="${list}" var="listItem" varStatus="status">
        <li><c:out value="${listItem}"/></li>
    </c:forEach>
</ul>
```

forTokens

The forTokens tag is used for iterating over tokens separated by a delimiter. The syntax of the forTokens tag is shown here:

```
<c:forTokens items="string of tokens"
             delims="delimiter characters"
             [begin="begin index"]
             [end="end index"]
             [step="step size"]
             [var="variable name"]
             [varStatus="status variable name"]>
       JSP body content
   </c:forTokens>
```

The forTokens tag has seven attributes:

- ❑ **items:** The string of tokens to iterate over. This is a mandatory attribute.

- ❑ **delims:** The set of characters that separate the tokens in the string (i.e., delimiters). This is a mandatory attribute.

❑ **begin:** The start index for the iteration, which defaults to 0. This is an optional attribute.

❑ **end:** The end index for the iteration. This is an optional attribute.

❑ **step:** The size of the index increment while iterating over the tokens. The iteration will process every step token, starting from the begin index (or first item, if begin is not specified). This is an optional attribute.

❑ **var:** The name of the variable in which the current item in the iteration is stored. This is an optional attribute.

❑ **varStatus:** The name of the variable in which the status of the iteration is stored.

An example of the forTokens tag is listed here:

```
<ul>
    <c:forTokens items="${list}" delims =":" var="listItem" varStatus="status">
        <li><c:out value="${listItem}"/></li>
    </c:forTokens>
</ul>
```

out

The out tag is used to output the result of an expression. It functions similarly to the <%= ... => JSP syntax. The syntax of the out tag is shown here:

```
<c:out value="expression"
        [default="default expression value"]
        [escapeXml="true|false"]>
    JSP body content
</c:out>
```

The out tag has three attributes:

❑ **value:** The expression to be evaluated. The result of the expression is output to the page. This is a mandatory attribute.

❑ **default:** The default value of the expression in case it results in a null. This is an optional attribute.

❑ **escapeXml:** Determines whether the <, >, " and ' characters in the resultant string should be converted to their corresponding character entity codes. This is an optional attribute and defaults to true.

An example of the out tag is listed here:

```
<ul>
    <c:forTokens items="${list}" delims =":" var="listItem" varStatus="status">
        <li><c:out value="${listItem}"/></li>
    </c:forTokens>
</ul>
```

otherwise

The otherwise tag is used for conditional evaluation of its body. It is a subtag of the choose tag and executes only if none of the when tags evaluate to true. The syntax of the otherwise tag is shown here:

```
<c:otherwise>
    JSP body content
</c:otherwise>
```

An example for the otherwise tag is listed here:

```
<c:choose>
  <c:when test="${userrole} == 'admin'}">
    Welcome admin. Proceed to your admin page <a href="/admin">here</a>
  </c:when>
  <c:when test="${userrole} == 'member'}">
    Welcome member. Proceed to your home page <a href="/memberhome">here</a>
  </c:when>
  <c:otherwise>
    Welcome guest. Log in <a href="/login">here</a>.
  </c:otherwise>
</c:choose>
```

param

The param tag is used along with the import, redirect, or url tags to add a parameter to a URL. The syntax of the param tag is shown here:

```
<c:param name="parameter name" [value="parameter value"]>
    JSP body content
</c:param>
```

The param tag has two attributes:

❑ **name:** The name of the parameter. This is a mandatory attribute.

❑ **value:** The value for the parameter. This is an optional attribute.

An example for the param tag is listed here. This generates a URL of the form http://www.google.com/search?q=<search term>.

```
<c:url value="http://www.google.com/search">
  <c:param name="q" value="${searchTerm}"/>
</c:url>
```

redirect

The redirect tag redirects the user to a new URL. The body of the redirect tag can have param tags for adding parameters to the URL. The syntax for the tag is shown here:

```
<c:redirect url="resource URL>
            [context="context name"]>
    JSP body content
</c:redirect>
```

The `redirect` tag has two attributes:

❏ **url:** The relative or absolute URL of the resource being imported. This is an optional attribute.

❏ **context:** When the URL to which one is being redirected is a relative URL in another context, the context name is specified in this attribute. This is an optional attribute.

An example of the `redirect` tag is listed here:

```
<c:catch var="exp">
  <c:import url="http://www.foobar.com/stuff.html"/>
</c:catch>
<c:if test="${not empty exp}">
  <c:redirect url="/error.jsp"/>
</c:if>
```

remove

The `remove` tag removes a variable from a scope. The syntax of the `remove` tag is shown here:

```
<c:remove var="variable name"
          [scope="page|request|session|application"] />
```

The `remove` tag has two attributes:

❏ **var:** The variable to be removed. This is a mandatory attribute.

❏ **scope:** Scope of the variable specified in the `var` attribute. This can be `page`, `request`, `session`, or `application`, and defaults to `page` if not specified. This is an optional attribute.

An example of the `remove` tag is listed here:

```
<c:remove var="foobar"/>
```

set

The `set` tag sets a variable or a property to the value of an expression. The syntax of the `set` tag is shown here:

```
<c:set    [var="variable name"]
          [value="expression"]
          [target="JavaBean or Map object name"]
          [property="target property name"]
```

```
            [scope="page|request|session|application"] >
      JSP body content
</c:set>
```

The set tag has five attributes:

- ❑ **var:** The variable that is set to the value of the expression. This is an optional attribute.

- ❑ **value:** The expression to be evaluated. This is an optional attribute.

- ❑ **target:** The target object (JavaBean or Map object) whose property will be set.

- ❑ **property:** Name of the property to be set in the target attribute.

- ❑ **scope:** Scope of the variable specified in the var attribute. This can be page, request, session, or application, and defaults to page if not specified. This is an optional attribute.

An example of the set tag is listed here:

```
<c:set var="index" value="1" scope="page" />
```

url

The url tag creates a URL. The body of the url tag can have param tags for adding parameters to the URL. The syntax for the tag is shown here:

```
<c:url   [var="variable name"]
         [scope="page|request|session|application"]
         [value="url"]
         [context="context name"]>
      JSP body content
</c:url>
```

The url tag has four attributes:

- ❑ **var:** The variable that contains the processed URL.

- ❑ **scope:** Scope of the variable specified in the var attribute. This can be page, request, session, or application, and defaults to page if not specified. This is an optional attribute.

- ❑ **value:** The URL to be processed. This is an optional attribute.

- ❑ **context:** When the URL is a relative URL in another context, the context name is specified in this attribute. This is an optional attribute.

An example of the url tag is listed here:

```
<c:url value="http://www.google.com/search">
  <c:param name="q" value="${searchTerm}"/>
</c:url>
```

when

The when tag is used for conditional evaluation of its body. It is a subtag of the choose tag, and its body is included only if the test condition is true. The syntax of the otherwise tag is shown here:

```
<c:when test="test condition" >
    JSP body content
</c:when>
```

The when tag has one attribute:

❑   **test:** The test condition that determines whether the body of the tag is to be processed. This is a mandatory attribute.

An example of the when tag is listed here:

```
<c:choose>
  <c:when test="${userrole} == 'admin'}">
    Welcome admin. Proceed to your admin page <a href="/admin">here</a>
  </c:when>
  <c:when test="${userrole} == 'member'}">
    Welcome member. Proceed to your home page <a href="/memberhome">here</a>
  </c:when>
  <c:otherwise>
    Welcome guest. Log in <a href="/login">here</a>.
  </c:otherwise>
</c:choose>
```

JSTL XML Tags

The JSTL XML tag library has custom tags for interacting with XML data. This includes parsing XML, transforming XML data, and flow control based on XPath expressions.

XPath is a syntax for addressing parts of an XML document. It allows for both relative and absolute paths to a XML element or attribute. For example, child::foo *refers to an XML element called* foo *that is a child of the current XML node, and* /employee/dependent *refers to all XML elements called* dependent *that are children of the root element* employee.

For more information on XPath, XSL, and other XML technologies, refer to Beginning XML, 2nd Edition (ISBN 0-7645-4394-6).

Before using the XML tag library, the following directive needs to be added to the JSP page:

```
<%@ taglib prefix="x" uri="http://java.sun.com/jsp/jstl/xml" %>
```

The equivalent XML syntax for this directive is as follows:

```
<jsp:directive.taglib prefix="x" uri="http://java.sun.com/jsp/jstl/xml" />
```

The following table summarizes the JSTL XML tags.

Tag Name	Description
choose	Provides conditional operation and allows for choosing between mutually exclusive options.
forEach	Iterates over collections based on XPath expressions.
if	Provides conditional operation based on XPath expressions.
otherwise	A conditional operation tag for choosing between mutually exclusive options. Subtag of the choose tag.
out	Outputs expressions to the Web page.
param	Used along with the transform tag to add a parameter to the XML transformer.
parse	Parses XML content.
set	Evaluates an XPath expression and sets the value of an attribute to it.
transform	Applies an XSLT stylesheet to XML data.
when	A conditional operation tag that includes its body when an expression evaluates to true. Subtag of the choose tag.

choose

The choose tag is used to provide conditional operation and allows for choosing between mutually exclusive options. The actual selection is made using its subtags: when and otherwise. The syntax of the choose tag is shown here:

```
<x:choose>
  <x:when test="XPath expression">
    JSP body content
  </x:when>
  ...
  <x:otherwise>
    JSP body content
  </x:otherwise>
</x:choose>
```

An example of the choose tag is listed here:

```
<x:choose>
  <x:when select="message[.= 'warning']">
    An error occurred.
  </x:when>
  <x:when select="message[.= 'fatal']">
    A fatal error occurred.
  </x:when>
  <x:otherwise>
    Welcome guest. Log in <a href="/login">here</a>.
  </x:otherwise>
</x:choose>
```

forEach

The forEach tag is used for iterating over collections. The syntax of the forEach tag is shown here:

```
<x:forEach select="XPath expression"
           [begin="begin index"]
           [end="end index"]
           [step="step size"]
           [var="variable name"]
           [varStatus="status variable name"]>
    JSP body content
</x:forEach>
```

The forEach tag has six attributes:

- ❑ **select:** The XPath expression to be evaluated. This is a mandatory attribute.

- ❑ **begin:** The start index for the iteration. This is an optional attribute.

- ❑ **end:** The end index for the iteration. This is an optional attribute.

- ❑ **step:** The size of the index increment while iterating over the collection. The iteration will process every step item of the collection, starting from the begin index (or first item, if begin is not specified). This is an optional attribute.

- ❑ **var:** The name of the variable in which the current item in the iteration is stored. This is an optional attribute.

- ❑ **varStatus:** The name of the variable in which the status of the iteration is stored.

An example of the forEach tag is listed here:

```
<x:forEach select="$rssDocument//*[name()='item']">
  <li>
     <a href="<x:out select="./*[name()='link']"/>">
     <x:out select="./*[name()='title']" escapeXml="false"/>
     </a>
  </li>
</x:forEach>
```

if

The if tag evaluates a test XPath expression; if it is true, it processes its body. If the test condition is false, the body is ignored. The syntax of the if tag is shown here:

```
<x:if select="XPath expression"
      [var="variable name"]
      [scope="page|request|session|application"]>
    JSP body content
</x:if>
```

The `if` tag has three attributes:

- ❑ **select:** The test XPath expression that determines whether the body of the tag is to be processed. This is a mandatory attribute.

- ❑ **var:** Variable that holds the result (`true` or `false`) of the test condition evaluation. This variable can be used for future test conditions (depending on the scope of the variable), thus avoiding reevaluation of the test condition. This is an optional attribute.

- ❑ **scope:** Scope of the variable specified in the `var` attribute. This can be `page`, `request`, `session`, or `application`, and defaults to `page` if not specified. This is an optional attribute.

An example of the `if` tag is listed here:

```
<x:if select="message[.= 'warning']">
    An error occurred.
</x:if>
```

otherwise

The `otherwise` tag is used for conditional evaluation of its body. It is a subtag of the `choose` tag and executes only if none of the `when` tags evaluates to `true`. The syntax of the `otherwise` tag is as follows:

```
<x:otherwise>
    JSP body content
</x:otherwise>
```

An example of the `otherwise` tag is listed here:

```
<x:choose>
  <x:when select="message[.= 'warning']">
    An error occurred.
  </x:when>
  <x:when select="message[.= 'fatal']">
    An fatal error occurred.
  </x:when>
  <x:otherwise>
    Welcome guest. Log in <a href="/login">here</a>.
  </x:otherwise>
</x:choose>
```

out

The `out` tag is used to output the result of an XPath expression. It functions similarly to the `<%= ... =>` JSP syntax. The syntax of the `out` tag is shown here:

```
<x:out select="XPath expression"
       [escapeXml="true|false"] />
```

The out tag has two attributes:

❑ **select:** The XPath expression to be evaluated. The result of the expression is output to the page. This is a mandatory attribute.

❑ **escapeXml:** Determines if the <, >, ", and ' characters in the resultant string should be converted to their corresponding character entity codes. This is an optional attribute and defaults to true.

An example of the out tag is listed here:

```
<x:out select="./*[name()='title']" escapeXml="false"/>
```

param

The param tag is used along with the transform tag to add a parameter to the transformer. The syntax of the param tag is shown here:

```
<x:param name="parameter name" [value="parameter value"]>
    JSP body content
</x:param>
```

The param tag has two attributes:

❑ **name:** The name of the parameter. This is a mandatory attribute.

❑ **value:** The value for the parameter. This is an optional attribute

An example of the param tag is listed here:

```
<x:transform xml="${xmlDoc}" xslt="${styleSheet}">
    <param name="id" value="${idvalue}" />
</x:transform>
```

parse

The parse tag is used to parse XML data specified either via an attribute or in the tag body. The syntax of the parse tag is shown here:

```
<x:parse [var="variable name"]
        [varDom="variable name"]
        [scope="page|request|session|application"]
        [scopeDom="page|request|session|application"]
        [doc="XML document"]
        [systemId="system identifier URI"]
        [filter="filter"]>
    JSP body content
</x:parse>
```

The parse tag has seven attributes:

- **var:** A variable that contains the parsed XML data. The type of this data is implementation dependant.

- **varDom:** A variable that contains the parsed XML data. The type of this data is org.w3c.dom.Document.

- **scope:** Scope of the variable specified in the var attribute. This can be page, request, session, or application, and defaults to page if not specified. This is an optional attribute.

- **scopeDom:** Scope of the variable specified in the varDom attribute. This can be page, request, session, or application, and defaults to page if not specified. This is an optional attribute.

- **doc:** XML document to be parsed

- **systemId:** The system identifier URI for parsing the document

- **filter:** The filter to be applied to the source document

The parse tag also has an attribute called xml, which has been deprecated; the doc attribute should be used instead.

An example of the parse tag is listed here:

```
<c:import var="rssFeed" url=" "http://www.theserverside.com/rss/theserverside-
servletsjsp-rss2.xml"/>
<x:parse var="rssDocument" xml="${rssFeed}"/>
```

set

The set tag sets a variable to the value of an XPath expression. The syntax of the set tag is shown here:

```
<x:set    var="variable name"
          [select="XPath expression"]
          [scope="page|request|session|application"]/>
```

The set tag has three attributes:

- **var:** A variable that is set to the value of the XPath expression. This is a mandatory attribute.

- **select:** The XPath expression to be evaluated. This is an optional attribute.

- **scope:** Scope of the variable specified in the var attribute. This can be page, request, session, or application, and defaults to page if not specified. This is an optional attribute.

An example of the set tag is listed here:

```
<x:set var="firstTitle"
       select="$rssDocument//*[name()='channel']/*[name()='title'][1]}"/>
```

transform

The `transform` tag applies an XSL transformation on a XML document. The syntax for the tag is shown here:

```
<x:set    [var="variable name"]
          [scope="page|request|session|application"]
          [result=""]
          [doc=""]
          [docSystemId=""]
          [xslt=""]
          [xsltSystemId=""]>
JSP body content
</x:set>
```

XSL (Extensible Style Sheet) is a stylesheet language for XML. XSLT (XSL Transformation) is an XML language that describes the rules for transforming an XML document into another XML document.

The `transform` tag has seven attributes:

❑   **var:** The `org.w3c.dom.Document` variable that is set to the transformed XML document. This is an optional attribute.

❑   **scope:** Scope of the variable specified in the `var` attribute. This can be `page`, `request`, `session`, or `application`, and defaults to `page` if not specified. This is an optional attribute.

❑   **result:** The result object that captures or processes the transformation result. This is an optional attribute.

❑   **doc:** The XML document to be transformed. This is an optional attribute.

❑   **docSystemId:** The system identifier URI for parsing the XML document. This is an optional attribute.

❑   **xslt:** The stylesheet, which is specified as a `String`, `Reader`, or `Source` object. This is an optional attribute.

❑   **xsltSystemId:** The system identifier URI for parsing the XSLT stylesheet. This is an optional attribute.

The `transform` tag also has attributes called `xml` and `xmlSystemId` that have been deprecated; `doc` and `docSystemId` should be used instead.

An example of the `transform` tag is listed here:

```
<c:import var="rssFeed" url=" "http://www.theserverside.com/rss/theserverside-
servletsjsp-rss2.xml"/>
<c:import var="rssToHtml" url="/WEB-INF/xslt/rss2html.xsl"/>
<x:transform xml="${rssFeed}" xslt="${rssToHtml}"/>
```

when

The when tag is a subtag of choose, and it evaluates its body when the expression used in it is true. The syntax for the tag is shown here:

```
<x:when    select="XPath expression">
  JSP body content
</x:when>
```

The when tag has one attribute:

❑ **select:** The XPath expression to be evaluated. This is a mandatory attribute.

An example of the when tag is listed here:

```
<x:when select="message[.= 'warning']">
  An error occurred.
</x:when>
```

JSTL Formatting Tags

The JSTL formatting tag library provides support for internationalization (i18n); that is, it enables the formatting of data (dates, numbers, time) in different locales.

Before using the formatting tag library, the following directive needs to be added to the JSP page:

```
<%@ taglib prefix="fmt" uri="http://java.sun.com/jsp/jstl/fmt" %>
```

The equivalent XML syntax for this directive is as follows:

```
<jsp:directive.taglib prefix="fmt" uri="http://java.sun.com/jsp/jstl/fmt" />
```

The following table summarizes the JSTL formatting tags.

Tag Name	Description
bundle	Loads a resource bundle
formatDate	Formats date and time
formatNumber	Formats a numeric value as a number, currency, or a percentage
message	Outputs a localized string
param	Supplies an argument to a containing message tag
parseDate	Parses a string representation of date/time
parseNumber	Parses a string representation of a number, currency, or a percentage

Table continued on following page

Tag Name	Description
requestEncoding	Sets the request character encoding
setBundle	Loads a resource bundle and stores it in a named variable
setLocale	Stores the locale in a named variable
setTimeZone	Stores the time zone in a named variable
timeZone	Specifies the time zone for formatting or parsing date/time data

bundle

The bundle tag loads a resource bundle for the body of the tag. The body usually contains a nested fmt:message tag to display a localized message. The syntax of the tag is shown here:

```
<fmt:bundle  basename="resource bundle basename"
             [prefix="message key prefix"]>
    JSP body content
</fmt:bundle>
```

The bundle tag has two attributes:

❑ **basename:** The basename of the resource bundle. This is a mandatory attribute.

❑ **prefix:** The prefix to be applied to the message key for any nested fmt:message tags. This is an optional attribute.

An example of the bundle tag is listed here:

```
<fmt:bundle basename="com.wrox.webapps.ErrorBundle">
    <fmt:message key="com.wrox.webapps.ErrorBundle.loginError"/>
</fmt:bundle>
```

formatDate

The formatDate tag formats date and time data according to a specified style and pattern. The syntax of the tag is shown here:

```
<fmt:formatDate  value="string representation"
                 [type="date|time|both"]
                 [dateStyle="formatting style"]
                 [timeStyle="formatting style"]
                 [pattern="formatting pattern"]
                 [timeZone="timezone"]
                 [var="variable name"]
                 [scope="page|request|session|application"] />
```

The `formatDate` tag has eight attributes:

❑ **value:** The date/time to be formatted. This is a mandatory attribute.

❑ **type:** Specifies if the data to be formatted contains a date, time, or both.

❑ **dateStyle:** Formatting style used for dates. The valid style values are defined by the `java.text.DateFormat` class (i.e., default, short, medium, long, and full). Valid only if the type attribute is `date` or `both`.

❑ **timeStyle:** Formatting style used for time values. The valid style values are defined by the `java.text.DateFormat` class (i.e., default, short, medium, long, and full). Valid only if the type attribute is `time` or `both`.

❑ **pattern:** Custom formatting pattern for dates and times. The patterns are specified by the `java.text.SimpleDateFormat` class. Some examples include `MM/dd/yyyy` for dates and `h:mm a` for time.

❑ **timeZone:** Time zone to be used for the time information.

❑ **var:** Variable containing the parsed date/time value. This variable is of type `java.util.Date`.

❑ **scope:** Scope of the `var` variable. This optional attribute can be `page`, `request`, `session`, or `application`.

An example of the `formatDate` tag is listed here:

```
The job posting time is <fmt:formatDate value="${timeValue}" pattern="h:mm a zz"/>.
```

formatNumber

The `formatNumber` tag formats a numeric value as a number, currency, or a percentage in a locale-specific manner. The syntax of the tag is shown here:

```
<fmt:formatNumber    [value="numeric value"]
                     [type="number|currency|percentage"]
                     [pattern="pattern"]
                     [currencyCode="currency code"]
                     [currencySymbol="currency symbol"]
                     [groupingUsed="true|false"]
                     [maxIntegerDigits="max integer digits"]
                     [minIntegerDigits="min integer digits"]
                     [maxFranctionDigits="max fractional digits"]
                     [minFractionDigits="min fractional digits"]
                     [var="variable name"]
                     [scope="page|request|session|application"]>
        JSP body content
</fmt:formatNumber>
```

The `formatNumber` tag has 12 attributes:

❑ **value:** The numeric value to be formatted.

❑ **type:** Specifies if the numeric value is to be formatted as a number, currency, or a percentage, and defaults to a number if not specified.

- ❑ **pattern:** Custom formatting pattern. The patterns are as specified by the `java.text.DecimalFormat` class (for example, "#,###").

- ❑ **currencyCode:** Currency codes as defined by the ISO 4217 standard (`www.iso.ch/iso/en/prods-services/popstds/currencycodes.html`). This is applicable only when the `type` attribute is `currency`.

- ❑ **currencySymbol:** Symbol to use for currency. This is applicable only when the `type` attribute is `currency`. `currencySymbol` is not generally required and can be used to override the defaults.

- ❑ **groupingUsed:** Specifies if the output format contains any grouping separators. These grouping are usually done using commas in English language locales (e.g., one thousand is 1,000.00) or using a period in some non-English locales (e.g., one thousand is 1.000,00). The `groupingUsed` attribute defaults to `true`.

- ❑ **maxIntegerDigits:** Maximum number of digits in the integer portion of the formatted output.

- ❑ **minIntegerDigits:** Minimum number of digits in the integer portion of the formatted output.

- ❑ **maxFractionDigits:** Maximum number of digits in the fractional portion of the formatted output.

- ❑ **minFractionDigits:** Minimum number of digits in the fractional portion of the formatted output.

- ❑ **var:** Variable that contains the formatted numeric value as a string.

- ❑ **scope:** Scope of the `var` variable. This is an optional attribute, and can be `page`, `request`, `session`, or `application`.

An example of the `formatNumber` tag is listed here:

```
This item costs <fmt:formatNumber value="1000" type="currency"/>.
```

message

The `message` tag displays a localized message. The body can contain a nested `fmt:param` tag to pass parameterized values to the message. The syntax of the tag is shown here:

```
<fmt:message [key="message key"]
             [bundle="localization bundle where key is looked up"]
             [var="variable that stores localized message"]
             [scope="page|request|session|application"]>
    JSP body content
</fmt:message>
```

The `message` tag has four attributes:

- ❑ **key:** The message key corresponding to the message. This is an optional attribute.

- ❑ **bundle:** The localization context in which the message key is looked up. This is an optional attribute.

❑   **var:** The variable that stores the localized message. This is an optional attribute.

❑   **scope:** Scope of the var variable. This is an optional attribute and can be page, request, session, or application.

An example of the message tag is listed here:

```
<fmt:bundle basename="com.wrox.webapps.ErrorBundle">
    <fmt:message key="com.wrox.webapps.ErrorBundle.loginError"/>
</fmt:bundle>
```

param

The param tag is nested within a fmt:message tag to pass parameterized values to the message. The syntax of the tag is shown here:

```
<fmt:param    [value="argument value"] >
    JSP body content
</fmt:param>
```

The param tag has one attribute:

❑   **value:** Value used for parametric replacement in the fmt:message tag. This is an optional attribute.

An example of the param tag is listed here:

```
<fmt:message key="com.wrox.webapps.Messages.helloMessage">
    <fmt:param value="${user.Name}"/>
</fmt:message>
```

parseDate

The parseDate tag parses string representations of date and time specified either via an attribute or in its body content. The syntax of the tag is shown here:

```
<fmt:parseDate    [value="string representation"]
                  [type="date|time|both"]
                  [dateStyle="formatting style"]
                  [timeStyle="formatting style"]
                  [pattern="formatting pattern"]
                  [timeZone="timezone"]
                  [parseLocale="locale"]
                  [var="variable name"]
                  [scope="page|request|session|application"]>
    JSP body content
</fmt:parseDate>
```

The parseDate tag has nine attributes:

- ❑ **value:** The string to be parsed.

- ❑ **type:** Specifies if the value is to be parsed; contains a date, time, or both.

- ❑ **dateStyle:** Formatting style used for the date. The valid style values are defined by the java.text.DateFormat class (i.e., default, short, medium, long, and full). Valid only if the type attribute is date or both.

- ❑ **timeStyle:** Formatting style used for time values. The valid style values are defined by the java.text.DateFormat class (i.e., default, short, medium, long, and full). Valid only if the type attribute is time or both.

- ❑ **pattern:** Custom formatting pattern for date and time strings. The patterns are specified by the java.text.SimpleDateFormat class. Some examples are MM/dd/yyyy for dates and h:mm a for time.

- ❑ **timeZone:** Time zone to be used for the time information.

- ❑ **parseLocale:** Locale to be used for formatting date and time values.

- ❑ **var:** Variable that contains the parsed date/time value. This variable is of type java.util.Date.

- ❑ **scope:** Scope of the var variable. This is an optional attribute and can be page, request, session, or application.

An example of the parseDate tag is listed here:

```
<c:set var="dateString">1/1/05 12:00 PM</c:set>
<fmt:parseDate value="${dateString}" parseLocale="en_US" type="both"
               dateStyle="short" timeStyle="short" var="usDate"/>
```

parseNumber

The parseNumber tag parses a string representation of a number, currency, or a percentage specified either via an attribute or in its body content. The syntax of the tag is shown here:

```
<fmt:parseNumber    [value="string representation"]
                    [type="number|currency|percentage"]
                    [pattern="pattern"]
                    [parseLocale="locale"]
                    [integerOnly="true|false"]
                    [var="variable name"]
                    [scope="page|request|session|application"]>
    JSP body content
</fmt:parseNumber>
```

The parseNumber tag has seven attributes:

- ❑ **value:** The string to be parsed.

- ❑ **type:** Specifies whether the value is to be parsed as a number, currency, or a percentage, and defaults to a number if not specified.

- ❑ **pattern:** Custom formatting pattern for parsing the value attribute. The patterns are specified by the `java.text.DecimalFormat` class (for example, "#,###").

- ❑ **parseLocale:** Locale to be used for parsing.

- ❑ **integerOnly:** Specifies that only the integer part needs to be parsed.

- ❑ **var:** Variable that contains the parsed numeric value.

- ❑ **scope:** Scope of the `var` variable. This is an optional attribute and can be `page`, `request`, `session`, or `application`.

An example of the `parseNumber` tag is listed here:

```
<fmt:parseNumber value="${salePrice}" parseLocale="en_US" type="currency"/>
```

requestEncoding

The `requestEncoding` tag sets the character encoding for the request. The syntax of the tag is shown here:

```
<fmt:requestEncoding  [value="character encoding name"] />
```

The `requestEncoding` tag has one attribute:

- ❑ **value:** The name of the character encoding for the request. Examples of request encodings include UTF-8, ISO-8859-1, JIS_C6220-1969-jp, and so on. A complete list of encodings can be found at `www.iana.org/assignments/character-sets`. This is an optional attribute.

An example of the `requestEncoding` tag is listed here:

```
<fmt:requestEncoding value="UTF-8"/>
```

setBundle

The `setBundle` tag loads a resource bundle for a specified scope (as compared to the `bundle` tag, which loads it only for its body). The syntax of the tag is shown here:

```
<fmt:setBundle  basename="resource bundle basename"
          [var="Localization context variable"]
          [scope="page|request|session|application"] />
```

The `setBundle` tag has three attributes:

- ❑ **basename:** The basename of the resource bundle. This a mandatory attribute.

- ❑ **var:** The name of the localization context variable (`javax.servlet.jsp.jstl.fmt.LocalizationContext`). This is an optional attribute.

- ❑ **scope:** Scope of the localization context variable. This is an optional attribute, and can be `page`, `request`, `session`, or `application`.

An example of the `setBundle` tag is listed here:

```
<fmt:setBundle basename="com.wrox.webapps.ErrorBundle"/>
```

setLocale

The `setLocale` tag sets the locale value in the locale configuration variable. The syntax of the tag is shown here:

```
<fmt:setLocale  value="Locale string"
                [variant="Vendor or browser specific variant"]
                [scope="page|request|session|application"]
                />
```

The `setLocale` tag has three attributes:

❑   **value:** The name of the character encoding for the request. Examples of request encodings include UTF-8, ISO-8859-1, JIS_C6220-1969-jp, and so on. A complete list of encodings is at `www.iana.org/assignments/character-sets`. This is a mandatory attribute.

❑   **variant:** This is a vendor/browser-specific value. Examples of the variants are WIN (for Windows), MAC (for Macintosh), and POSIX (for POSIX).

❑   **scope:** Scope of the locale configuration. This is an optional attribute, and can be `page`, `request`, `session`, or `application`.

An example of the `setLocale` tag is listed here:

```
<fmt:setLocale value="en"/>
```

setTimeZone

The `setTimeZone` tag sets the time zone value in the time zone configuration variable for a specified scope (as compared to the `timeZone` tag, which sets it only for its body content). The syntax of the tag is shown here:

```
<fmt:setTimeZone  value="Time Zone string"
                  [var="time zone variable"]
                  [scope="page|request|session|application"]
                  />
```

The `setTimeZone` tag has three attributes:

❑   **value:** The name of the time zone. This can be specified as a custom time zone ID ("GMT+8") or as a time zone supported by Java ("America/Los_Angeles"). This is a mandatory attribute.

❑   **var:** Name of the time zone variable. This is an optional attribute.

❏ **scope:** Scope of the time zone variable configuration. This is an optional attribute and can be `page`, `request`, `session`, or `application`.

An example of the `setTimeZone` tag is listed here:

```
<fmt:setTimeZone value="GMT-8"/>
```

timeZone

The `timeZone` tag specifies the time zone for any time formatting in its body content. The syntax of the tag is shown here:

```
<fmt:timeZone  value="time zone">
    JSP body content
</fmt:timeZone>
```

The `timeZone` tag has one attribute:

❏ **value:** The time zone value for the body content. This can be specified as a custom time zone ID ("GMT+8") or as a time zone supported by Java ("America/Los_Angeles"). This is a mandatory attribute.

An example of the `timeZone` tag is listed here:

```
<fmt:timeZone value="GMT-8">
    ...
</fmt:timeZone>
```

JSTL SQL Tags

The JSTL SQL tag library provides tags for interacting with relational databases (RDBMSs) such as Oracle, mySQL, or Microsoft SQL Server. The tags are designed for rapid prototyping of applications or for developing simple Web applications; any serious database use in an enterprise application should be through a database tier, as described in Chapter 23, "Access to Databases," and demonstrated in Chapter 28, "JSP Project II: Shopping Cart Application."

Before using the SQL tag library, the following directive needs to be added to the JSP page:

```
<%@ taglib prefix="sql" uri="http://java.sun.com/jsp/jstl/sql" %>
```

The equivalent XML syntax for this directive is as follows:

```
<jsp:directive.taglib prefix="sql" uri="http://java.sun.com/jsp/jstl/sql" />
```

The following table summarizes JSTL SQL tags.

Tag Name	Description
dateParam	Sets a parameter in a SQL statement to a specified java.util.Date value
param	Sets a parameter in a SQL statement to a specified value
query	Executes a SQL query
setDataSource	Specifies a data source for the database connection
transaction	Provides one connection to all nested database actions so that they can be executed as a transaction
update	Executes a SQL update

dateParam

The dateParam tag is embedded in the body of a query or update tag. It is used to pass java.util.Date parameters to a SQL statement. The syntax of the tag is shown here:

```
<sql:dateParam  value="date parameter value"
                [type="date|time|timestamp"] />
```

The dateparam tag has the following attributes:

❑   **value:** The parameter value for the SQL statement. This can be a date, time, or timestamp. This is a mandatory attribute.

❑   **type:** The type of parameter. This can be date, time, or timestamp. This is an optional attribute.

An example of the dateParam tag is listed here:

```
<sql:query sql="select * from employee where join_date > ?">
  <sql:dateParam value="${cutoff_date}" type="date"/>
</sql:query>
```

param

The param tag is embedded in the body of a query or update tag. It is used to pass parameters to a SQL statement. The syntax of the tag is shown here:

```
<sql:param [value="parameter value"]>
    JSP body content
</sql:param>
```

The param tag has one attribute:

❑   **value:** The parameter value for the SQL statement

An example of the `param` tag is listed here:

```
<sql:query sql="select * from employee where salary > ?">
  <sql:param value="${min_salary}"/>
</sql:query>
```

query

The `query` tag executes an SQL query statement specified either via an attribute or embedded in the body of the tag. A `query` tag can have nested `param` tags to pass parameters to the SQL statement. The syntax of the tag is shown here:

```
<sql:query  var="variable name"
            [scope="page|request|session|application"]
            [sql="SQL query statement"]
            [startRow="starting row"]
            [maxRows="maximum number of rows"]
            [dataSource="DataSource"]>
    JSP body content
</sql:query>
```

The `query` tag has six attributes:

❑   **var:** This specifies the variable that contains the result of the SQL query statement. This is a mandatory attribute.

❑   **scope:** Scope of the variable defined in the `var` attribute. This is an optional attribute, and can be `page`, `request`, `session`, or `application`.

❑   **sql:** The SQL query statement to execute. This is an optional attribute.

❑   **startRow:** The starting row for the returned results. This is an optional attribute and defaults to zero.

❑   **maxRows:** The maximum number of rows to return. This is an optional attribute and defaults to -1 (i.e., no maximum limit) if not specified.

❑   **dataSource:** The DataSource for the database to be accessed. This is an optional attribute; if not specified, the default JSTL DataSource is used.

An example of the `query` tag is listed here:

```
<sql:query sql="select * from employee where salary > ?">
  <sql:param value="${min_salary}"/>
</sql:query>
```

Another example is as follows:

```
<sql:query var="roundlist"
  dataSource="jdbc:mysql://localhost/footydb,com.mysql.jdbc.Driver,footy,footy">
  SELECT * from round
</sql:query>
```

setDataSource

The setDataSource tag creates a DataSource for connecting to the database. The syntax for this tag is shown here:

```
<sql:setDataSource [var="variable name"]
                   [scope="page|request|session|application"]
                   [driver="JDBC driver"]
                   [url="JDBC URL for database"]
                   [user="Username to connect to the database"]
                   [password="Password to connect to the database"]
                   [dataSource="DataSource"]/>
```

The setDataSource tag has seven attributes:

❑   **var:** This specifies the variable that contains the specified DataSource. This is an optional attribute.

❑   **scope:** Scope of the variable defined in the var attribute. This is an optional attribute, and can be page, request, session, or application.

❑   **driver:** JDBC driver class name.

❑   **url:** JDBC URL for the database.

❑   **user:** Username to connect to the JDBC database.

❑   **password:** Password to connect to the JDBC database.

❑   **dataSource:** The DataSource for the database to be accessed. This is an optional attribute, and if not specified, the default JSTL DataSource is used.

An example of the setDataSource tag is listed here:

```
<sql:setDataSource  url="jdbc:mysql:///taglib"
                    driver="org.gjt.mm.mysql.Driver"
                    user="admin"
                    password="secret"/>
<sql:query sql="select * from employee where salary > ?">
  <sql:param value="${min_salary}"/>
</sql:query>
```

transaction

Other SQL tags are nested within a transaction tag. The tag provides them with a shared connection object and allows all the nested tags to run as one transaction. The syntax of the transaction tag is shown here:

```
<sql:transaction [dataSource="DataSource"]
       [isolation="read_committed|read_uncommitted|repeatable_read|serializable"] >
    JSP body content
</sql:transaction>
```

The transaction tag has two attributes:

❑   **dataSource:** The DataSource for the database to be accessed. This is an optional attribute, and if not specified, the default JSTL DataSource is used.

❑   **isolation:** Isolation level for the transaction. This can be read_committed, read_uncommitted, repeatable_read, or serializable. This is an optional attribute and defaults to the DataSource isolation level.

An example of the transaction tag is listed here:

```
<sql:transaction>
  <sql:update sql="update employee set salary = ? where emp_id = ?">
    <sql:param value="${new_salary}"/>
    <sql:param value="${empId}"/>
  </sql:update>
  <sql:update sql="update employee set salary_deductions = ? where emp_id = ?">
    <sql:param value="${new_deductions}"/>
    <sql:param value="${empId}"/>
  </sql:update>
</sql:transaction>
```

update

The update tag executes an SQL update statement specified either via an attribute or embedded in the body of the tag. An update tag can have nested param tags to pass parameters to the SQL statement. The syntax of the tag is shown here:

```
<sql:update [var="variable name"]
            [scope="page|request|session|application"]
            [sql="SQL update statement"]
            [dataSource="DataSource"]>
     JSP body content
</sql:update>
```

The update tag has four attributes:

❑   **var:** This specifies the variable that contains the result of the SQL update statement. This is an optional attribute.

❑   **scope:** Scope of the variable defined in the var attribute. This is an optional attribute and can be page, request, session, or application.

❑   **sql:** The SQL update statement to execute. This is an optional attribute.

❑   **dataSource:** The DataSource for the database to be accessed. This is an optional attribute, and if not specified, the default JSTL DataSource is used.

An example of the update tag is listed here:

```
<sql:update>
  UPDATE round SET startdate = ?, enddate = ?
  WHERE number = ?
  <sql:param value="${param.round_startdate}" />
  <sql:param value="${param.round_enddate}" />
  <sql:param value="${param.round_number}" />
</sql:update>
```

JSTL Functions

The JSTL function library contains a number of string manipulation functions. These include functions for splitting and concatenating strings, returning substrings, determining whether a string contains a specified substring, and many others.

Before using the function library, the following directive needs to be added to the JSP page:

```
<%@ taglib prefix="fn" uri="http://java.sun.com/jsp/jstl/functions" %>
```

The equivalent XML syntax for this directive is as follows:

```
<jsp:directive.taglib prefix="fn" uri="http://java.sun.com/jsp/jstl/functions" />
```

The following table summarizes the JSTL functions.

Tag Name	Description
contains	Tests whether an input string contains the specified substring. This is a case-sensitive search.
containsIgnoreCase	Tests whether an input string contains the specified substring in a case-insensitive way.
endsWith	Tests whether an input string ends with the specified suffix.
escapeXml	Escapes characters that could be interpreted as XML markup.
indexOf	Returns the index within a string of the first occurrence of a specified substring.
join	Concatenates all elements of an array into a string.
length	Returns the number of items in a collection or the number of characters in a string.
replace	Returns a string that results from replacing in an input string all occurrences of a "before" string into an "after" substring.
split	Splits a string into an array of substrings.

Tag Name	Description
startsWith	Tests whether an input string starts with the specified prefix.
substring	Returns a subset of a string.
substringAfter	Returns a subset of a string following a specific substring.
substringBefore	Returns a subset of a string before a specific substring.
toLowerCase	Converts all of the characters of a string to lowercase.
toUpperCase	Converts all of the characters of a string to uppercase.
trim	Removes white spaces from both ends of a string.

contains

The `contains` function determines whether an input string contains a specified substring. The syntax of the function is shown here:

```
boolean contains(java.lang.String, java.lang.String)
```

An example of the `contains` function is listed here:

```
<c:if test="${fn:contains(theString, searchString)}">
```

containsIgnoreCase

The `containsIgnoreCase` function determines whether an input string contains a specified substring. The syntax of the function is shown here:

```
boolean containsIgnoreCase(java.lang.String, java.lang.String)
```

An example of the `containsIgnoreCase` function is listed here:

```
<c:if test="${fn:containsIgnoreCase(theString, searchString)}">
```

endsWith

The `endsWith` function determines whether an input string ends with a specified suffix. The syntax of the function is shown here:

```
boolean endsWith(java.lang.String, java.lang.String)
```

An example of the `endsWith` function is listed here:

```
<c:if test="${fn:endWith (theString, suffix)}">
```

escapeXml

The `escapeXml` function escapes characters that can be interpreted as XML markup. The syntax of the function is shown here:

```
java.lang.String escapeXml(java.lang.String)
```

An example of the `escapeXml` function is listed here:

```
${fn:escapeXml(xmlContainingText)}
```

indexOf

The `indexOf` function returns the index within a string of a specified substring. The syntax of the function is shown here:

```
int indexOf(java.lang.String, java.lang.String)
```

An example of the `indexOf` function is listed here:

```
${fn:indexOf(theString, searchString)}
```

join

The `join` function concatenates all the elements of an array into a string with a specified separator. The syntax of the function is shown here:

```
String join (java.lang.String[], java.lang.String)
```

An example of the `join` function is listed here:

```
Your Path settings should be ${fn:join(filenamesArray, ";")}.
```

length

The `length` function returns the string length or the number of items in a collection. The syntax of the function is shown here:

```
int length(java.lang.Object)
```

An example of the `length` function is listed here:

```
There are ${fn:length(shoppingCart.items)} items in your shopping cart.
```

replace

The `replace` function replaces all occurrences of a string with another string. The syntax of the function is shown here:

```
boolean replace(java.lang.String, java.lang.String, java.lang.String)
```

An example of the `replace` function is listed here:

```
The CLASSPATH for Windows is ${fn:replace(classpathString, ":", ";")}.
```

split

The `split` function splits a string into an array of substrings based on a delimiter string. The syntax of the function is shown here:

```
java.lang.String[] split(java.lang.String, java.lang.String)
```

An example of the `split` function is listed here:

```
${fn:split(theString, delimiterString)}
```

startsWith

The `startsWith` function determines whether an input string starts with a specified substring. The syntax of the function is shown here:

```
boolean startsWith(java.lang.String, java.lang.String)
```

An example of the `startsWith` function is listed here:

```
<c:if test="${fn:startsWith(theString, prefixString)}">
```

substring

The `substring` function returns a subset of a string specified by `start` and `end` indices. The syntax of the function is shown here:

```
java.lang.String substring(java.lang.String, int, int)
```

An example of the `substring` function is listed here:

```
${fn:substring(theString, beginIndex, endIndex)}
```

substringAfter

The `substringAfter` function returns the part of a string after a specified substring. The syntax of the function is shown here:

```
java.lang.String substringAfter(java.lang.String, java.lang.String)
```

An example of the `substringAfter` function is listed here:

```
${fn:substringAfter(theString, substring)}
```

substringBefore

The `substringBefore` function returns the part of a string before a specified substring. The syntax of the function is shown here:

```
java.lang.String substringBefore(java.lang.String, java.lang.String)
```

An example of the `substringBefore` function is listed here:

```
${fn:substringBefore(theString, substring)}
```

toLowerCase

The `toLowerCase` function converts all the characters of a string to lowercase. The syntax of the function is shown here:

```
java.lang.String toLowerCase(java.lang.String)
```

An example of the `toLowerCase` function is listed here:

```
${fn:toLowerCase(theString)}
```

toUpperCase

The `toUpperCase` function converts all the characters of a string to uppercase. The syntax of the function is shown here:

```
java.lang.String toUpperCase(java.lang.String)
```

An example of the `toUpperCase` function is listed here:

```
${fn:toUpperCase(theString)}
```

trim

The `trim` function removes white space from both ends of a string. The syntax of the function is shown here:

```
java.lang.String trim(java.lang.String)
```

An example of the `trim` function is listed here:

```
${fn:trim(theString)}
```

Exercise Solutions

Chapter 1 Exercises

Exercise 1

To modify the index.jsp file in the third example to display a page similar to Figure 1-17, create a index1.jsp page containing the following code:

```
<%@ taglib prefix="wroxtags" tagdir="/WEB-INF/tags" %>
<html>
  <head>
    <title><wroxtags:bookTitle/></title>
  </head>
  <body>
    <h1><wroxtags:bookTitle/></h1>
    <p><i>published by <wroxtags:publisher/></i></p>
    <p><small>Note: You will need <wroxtags:containerName/> to use this
book.</small></p>
        </body>
</html>
```

Exercise 2

There is a tag called showBrowser.tag in the WEB-INF/tags directory. You will need to use this tag in creating index2.jsp:

```
<%@ taglib prefix="wroxtags" tagdir="/WEB-INF/tags" %>
<html>
  <head>
    <title>Book Information</title>
  </head>
  <body>
    <h1>Book Information</h1>
```

```
    <hr>
    <p>The name of this book is <i><wroxtags:bookTitle/></i>.</p>
    <p>It is published by <wroxtags:publisher/>.</p>
    <p>The server used in all the examples is <wroxtags:containerName/>.</p>
    <p>The browser you are using is <wroxtags:showBrowser/>.</p>
    </body>
</html>
```

Chapter 2 Exercises

Exercise 1

Create a showportal.jsp file that contains the following:

```
<%@ taglib prefix="c" uri="http://java.sun.com/jsp/jstl/core" %>
<html>
  <head>
   <link rel=stylesheet type="text/css" href="portal.css">
    <title>New Portal</title>
  </head>
  <body>
      <jsp:include page="news.jsp" >
       <jsp:param name="mode" value="standalone"/>
       </jsp:include>
      <jsp:include page="weather.jsp" >
          <jsp:param name="mode" value="standalone"/>
       </jsp:include>

      <jsp:include page="entertain.jsp" >
         <jsp:param name="mode" value="standalone"/>
       </jsp:include>

  </body>
</html>
```

Exercise 2

Modify news.jsp to the following:

```
<%@ taglib prefix="c" uri="http://java.sun.com/jsp/jstl/core" %>
<c:choose>
<c:when test="${param.mode != 'standalone'}">
<head>
<link rel=stylesheet type="text/css" href="portal.css">
<title>News Portal</title>
</head>
<body>
</c:when>
<c:otherwise/>
</c:choose>
```

```
<table class="mainBox" width="600">
<tr><td class="boxTitle" >
Welcome to the News Portal!
</td></tr>
<tr><td>
<span class="headLine">
<jsp:useBean id="newsfeed" class="com.wrox.begjsp.ch2.NewsFeed" scope="request" >
<jsp:setProperty name="newsfeed"  property="topic" value="news"/>
<jsp:getProperty name="newsfeed" property="value"/>
</jsp:useBean>
</span>
<span class="newsText">
<jsp:include page="dummytext.html" />
</span>
</td></tr>
</table>
```

Modify weather.jsp to contain the following:

```
<%@ taglib prefix="c" uri="http://java.sun.com/jsp/jstl/core" %>
<c:choose>
<c:when test="${param.mode != 'standalone'}">
<head>
<link rel=stylesheet type="text/css" href="portal.css">
<title>Weather Portal</title>
</head>
<body>
</c:when>
<c:otherwise/>
</c:choose>

<table class="mainBox" width="600">
<tr><td class="boxTitle" >
You Get the Latest Weather!
</td></tr>
<tr><td>
<jsp:useBean id="newsfeed" class="com.wrox.begjsp.ch2.NewsFeed" scope="request" />
<jsp:setProperty name="newsfeed"  property="topic" value="weather"/>

<table>
  <c:forEach items="${newsfeed.values}" var="row" >
    <tr><td class="tableCell" width="200">  ${row.city}  </td>
        <td> ${row.temp}</td>
    </tr>
  </c:forEach>
</table>
</td></tr>
</table>
```

Modify entertain.jsp to contain the following:

```
<%@ taglib prefix="c" uri="http://java.sun.com/jsp/jstl/core" %>
<c:choose>
<c:when test="${param.mode != 'standalone'}">
```

```
<head>
<link rel=stylesheet type="text/css" href="portal.css">
<title>Weather Portal</title>
</head>
<body>
</c:when>
<c:otherwise/>
</c:choose>
<table class="mainBox" width="600">
<tr><td class="boxTitle" >
Entertainment News Just for You!
</td></tr>
<tr><td>
<span class="headLine">
<jsp:useBean id="newsfeed" class="com.wrox.begjsp.ch2.NewsFeed" scope="request" >
<jsp:setProperty name="newsfeed"  property="topic" value="entertainment"/>
<jsp:getProperty name="newsfeed" property="value"/>
</jsp:useBean>
</span>
<span class="newsText">
<jsp:include page="dummytext.html" />
</span>
</td></tr>
</table>
```

Chapter 3 Exercises

Exercise 1

Modify shopcart.jsp as follows to add sales tax calculations. The changes are highlighted:

```
<%@ page language="java"
import = "com.wrox.begjsp.ch03.*,java.util.*" session="true" %>


<%!
private static String EXAMPLE = "/example3";
private static String SHOP_PAGE = "/estore.jsp";
private static String CART_PAGE = "/shopcart.jsp";

private  String dispPrice( String price) {
   int len = price.length();
   if (len <= 2)
         return price;
   else
      return "$" + price.substring(0,len -2) + "." + price.substring(len-2);
}
%>


<html>
<head>
<title>Wrox Shopping Mall - Shopping Cart</title>
```

```
</head>
<body>

<%
  ArrayList items = (ArrayList) session.getAttribute("lineitems");
  String action =  request.getParameter("action");
  String sku = request.getParameter("sku");
  Product prod = null;
  if (sku != null)
    prod = EShop.getItem(sku);

  if (items == null) {  // add first item
    items = new ArrayList();
    items.add(new LineItem(1,sku,prod.getName(),
                prod.getPrice() ));
    session.setAttribute("lineitems", items);
    }
  else  if (action.equals("clear")) {
        items.clear();
    }
  else {
     boolean itemFound = false;
     // check to see if sku exists
     for (int i=0; i<items.size(); i++) {
        LineItem curItem = (LineItem) items.get(i);
        if (curItem.getSku().equals(sku))  {
            itemFound = true;
            curItem.setQuantity(curItem.getQuantity() + 1);
            break;
        }  // of if
      } //of for

    if (!itemFound)
        items.add(new LineItem(1,sku,prod.getName(),
                prod.getPrice() ));

  } // of final else

  long total = 0;
%>
<table width="600">
<tr>
<td>
<h1></h1>
<table border="1" width="600">
<tr><th colspan="5">Your Shopping Cart</th></tr>
<tr><th align="left">Quantity</th><th align="left">Item</th><th
align="right">Price</th>
<th align="right">Extended</th>
<th align="left">Add</th></tr>

<%
  for (int i=0; i< items.size(); i++)  {
    LineItem curItem = (LineItem) items.get(i);
```

```
        int quan = curItem.getQuantity();
        long price = curItem.getPrice();
        long extended = quan * price;
        total += extended;

%>

<tr>
    <td><%= quan %></td>
    <td><%= curItem.getDesc()    %></td>
    <td align="right"><%= dispPrice(String.valueOf(price)   %></td>
    <td align="right"><%= dispPrice(String.valueOf(extended)   %></td>
    <td>
<a href="<%= request.getContextPath() + EXAMPLE + CART_PAGE + "?action=inc&sku=" +
curItem.getSku() %>">
        <b>Add 1</b></a>
    </td>
</tr>
<%
    }
    long tax = total / 100 * 8 ; // 8 % sales tax
    total = tax + total;
%>
<tr>
<td colspan="5">  
</td>
</tr>


<tr>
<td colspan="3" align="right"><b>Sales Tax (8%):</b></td>
<td align="right"><%= dispPrice(String.valueOf(tax)) %></td>
<td> </td>
</tr>


<tr>
<td colspan="3" align="right"><b>Total:</b></td>
<td align="right"><%= dispPrice(String.valueOf(total)) %></td>
<td> </td>
</tr>


<tr>
<td colspan="5">
<a href="<%= request.getContextPath() + EXAMPLE + CART_PAGE + "?action=clear" %>">
Clear the cart</a>
</td>
</tr>


<tr>
<td colspan="5">
<a href="<%= request.getContextPath() + EXAMPLE + SHOP_PAGE %>">
Return to Shopping</a>
</td>
</tr>
```

```
</table>
</body>
</html>
```

Exercise 2

Modify shopcart.jsp, in the third Try It Out example. Add a link on each line item to subtract 1 from the displayed quantity. Make the changes as highlighted:

```
<%@ page language="java"
import = "com.wrox.begjsp.ch03.*,java.util.*" session="true" %>


<%!
private static String EXAMPLE = "/example3";
private static String SHOP_PAGE = "/estore.jsp";
private static String CART_PAGE = "/shopcart.jsp";

private  String dispPrice( String price) {
   int len = price.length();
   if (len <= 2)
          return price;
   else
      return "$" + price.substring(0,len -2) + "." + price.substring(len-2);
}
%>

<html>
<head>
<title>Wrox Shopping Mall - Shopping Cart</title>
</head>
<body>

<%
  ArrayList items = (ArrayList) session.getAttribute("lineitems");
  String action =  request.getParameter("action");
  String sku = request.getParameter("sku");
  Product prod = null;
  if (sku != null)
    prod = EShop.getItem(sku);

  if (items == null)  {  // add first item
    items = new ArrayList();
    items.add(new LineItem(1,sku,prod.getName(),
                prod.getPrice() ));
    session.setAttribute("lineitems", items);
    }
  else  if (action.equals("clear")) {
        items.clear();
      }
  else {
     boolean itemFound = false;
     // check to see if sku exists
```

```
          for (int i=0; i<items.size(); i++) {
              LineItem curItem = (LineItem) items.get(i);
              if (curItem.getSku().equals(sku))  {
                  itemFound = true;
                if (action.equals("inc")) {
                  curItem.setQuantity(curItem.getQuantity() + 1);
                        } else {
                     if (curItem.getQuantity() > 0)
                        curItem.setQuantity(curItem.getQuantity() - 1);
                     }
                  break;
              }  // of if
          } //of for

       if (!itemFound)
          items.add(new LineItem(1,sku,prod.getName(),
                    prod.getPrice() ));

    } // of final else

   int total = 0;
%>
<table width="600">
<tr>
<td>
<h1></h1>
<table border="1" width="600">
<tr><th colspan="5">Your Shopping Cart</th></tr>
<tr><th align="left">Quantity</th><th align="left">Item</th><th
align="right">Price</th>
<th align="right">Extended</th>
<th align="left">Add</th></tr>

<%
   for (int i=0; i< items.size(); i++)  {
     LineItem curItem = (LineItem) items.get(i);
     int quan = curItem.getQuantity();
     long price = curItem.getPrice();
     long extended = quan * price;
     total += extended;
%>

<tr>
   <td><%= quan %></td>
   <td><%= curItem.getDesc()   %></td>
   <td align="right"><%= dispPrice(String.valueOf(price))  %></td>
   <td align="right"><%= dispPrice(String.valueOf(extended))  %></td>
   <td>
<a href="<%= request.getContextPath() + EXAMPLE + CART_PAGE + "?action=inc&sku=" +
curItem.getSku() %>">
         <b>Add 1</b></a>
<a href="<%= request.getContextPath() + EXAMPLE + CART_PAGE + "?action=dec&sku=" +
curItem.getSku() %>">
         <b>Subtract 1</b></a>
```

```
      </td>
    </tr>
<%
     }
%>
<tr>
<td colspan="5">  
</td>
</tr>
<tr>
<td colspan="3" align="right"><b>Total:</b></td>
<td align="right"><%= dispPrice(String.valueOf(total)) %></td>
<td> </td>
</tr>

<tr>
<td colspan="5">
<a href="<%= request.getContextPath() + EXAMPLE + CART_PAGE + "?action=clear" %>">
Clear the cart</a>
</td>
</tr>


<tr>
<td colspan="5">
<a href="<%= request.getContextPath() + EXAMPLE + SHOP_PAGE %>">
Return to Shopping</a>
</td>
</tr>

</table>
</body>
</html>
```

Chapter 4 Exercises

Exercise 1

Modify index.jsp to create index2.jsp. The changes are highlighted:

```
<html>
<head>
  <link rel=stylesheet type="text/css" href="portal.css">
  <title>Select Your Portal</title></head>
<body>
  <table class="mainBox" width="400">
    <tr><td class="boxTitle" colspan="2">
      Wrox JSP Portal Selector
    </td></tr>
    <tr><td colspan="2"> </td></tr>
    <tr><td>
```

```
<form  action="showportal2.jsp" method="get">
  <table>
    <tr>
      <td width="200">
        Your First Name: </td>
      <td><input name="username" type="text" size="25"/></td>
    </tr>
    <tr>
      <td width="200">Color Theme</td><td>
        <select name="color">
          <option>blue</option>
          <option>red</option>
          <option>green</option>
        </select>
      </td>
    </tr>

    <tr>
      <td width="200">Font</td><td>
        <select name="font">
          <option>sans-serif</option>
          <option>serif</option>
        </select>
      </td>
    </tr>

    <tr>
      <td width="200">Style</td><td>
        <select name="style">
          <option>normal</option>
          <option>italic</option>
        </select>
      </td>
    </tr>

    <tr>
      <td width="200">Portal Selection</td><td>
        <select name="portchoice">
          <option>news</option>
          <option>weather</option>
          <option>entertainment</option>
        </select>
      </td>
    </tr>
    <tr><td colspan="2"> </td></tr>
    <tr><td colspan="2" align="center">
      <input type="submit" value="Select"/>
    </td></tr>
  </table>
</form>
</td></tr>
</table>
</body>
</html>
```

Modify `showportal.jsp` to create `showportal2.jsp`. The changes are highlighted:

```
<%@ taglib prefix="c" uri="http://java.sun.com/jsp/jstl/core" %>
<html>
<head>
<c:choose>
    <c:when test="${param.color == 'blue'}">
        <c:set var="selcolor" value="blue"/>
    </c:when>
    <c:when test="${param.color == 'red'}">
        <c:set var="selcolor" value="red" />
    </c:when>
    <c:when test="${param.color == 'green'}">
        <c:set var="selcolor" value="green" />
    </c:when>
</c:choose>

<c:choose>
    <c:when test="${param.font == 'sans-serif'}">
        <c:set var="selfont" value="Verdana, Geneva, Arial, Helvetica, sans-
serif"/>
    </c:when>
    <c:when test="${param.font == 'serif'}">
        <c:set var="selfont" value="'Times New Roman',Times,serif" />
    </c:when>
</c:choose>

<style>
.tableCell
{
 font-family : ${selfont};
 font-size : 16;
 font-weight : bold;
 font-style: ${param.style};
 color : #0f7fcf;
 background-color: #ffffff;
}

.valueCell
{
 font-family : ${selfont};
 font-size : 16;
 color : #000000;
 background-color: #fefefe;
}
.headLine
{
 font-family : ${selfont};
 font-size : 18;
 font-weight : bold;
 font-style: ${param.style};
 color: #000000;
}
```

```
.newsText
{
 font-family : ${selfont};
 font-size : 10;
 color: #000000;
}
.boxTitle
{
 font-family : ${selfont};
 font-size : 22;
 font-weight : bold;
 font-style: ${param.style};
 color : #ffffff;
 background-color: ${selcolor};

}
.mainBox
{
 font-family : ${selfont};
 font-size : 12;
 color : #ffffff;
 background-color: #eeeeee;
}

</style>

 <c:choose>
    <c:when test="${param.portchoice == 'news'}">
      <jsp:include page="news.jsp" >
          <jsp:param name="user" value="${param.username}"/>
      </jsp:include>
    </c:when>
    <c:when test="${param.portchoice =='weather'}">
      <jsp:include page="weather.jsp" >
          <jsp:param name="user" value="${param.username}"/>
      </jsp:include>
    </c:when>
    <c:when test="${param.portchoice == 'entertainment'}">
      <jsp:include page="entertain.jsp" >
          <jsp:param name="user" value="${param.username}"/>
      </jsp:include>
    </c:when>
    <c:otherwise>
      <head><title>System Portal</title></head>
      <body>
      <h1>Application logic problem detected!</h1>
      </body>
    </c:otherwise>
</c:choose>
</body>
</html>
```

Exercise 2

Modify weather.jsp to create the new weather.jsp. The changes are highlighted:

```
<%@ taglib prefix="c" uri="http://java.sun.com/jsp/jstl/core" %>
  <title>Weather Portal</title>
</head>
<body>
  <script language="JavaScript" src="menu.js"></script>
  <script language="JavaScript">
    function showToolbar()
    {
      menu = new Menu();

      <c:choose>
        <c:when test="${param.menuchoice == 'news-only'}">
          menu.addItem("newsportalid", "News Portal", "News Portal", null, null);
          menu.addItem("otherportalid", "Other Portals", "Other Portals",
            null, null);
          menu.addSubItem("newsportalid", "World News", "World News",
            "http://localhost:8080/ch04/example2/","");
          menu.addSubItem("newsportalid", "American News", "American News",
            "http://localhost:8080/ch04/example2/","");
          menu.addSubItem("newsportalid", "UK News", "UK News",
            "http://localhost:8080/ch04/example2/","");

          menu.addSubItem("otherportalid", "Yahoo News", "Yahoo News",
            "http://localhost:8080/ch04/example2/","");
          menu.addSubItem("otherportalid", "CNN News", "CNN News",
            "http://localhost:8080/ch04/example2/","");
        </c:when>
        <c:when test="${param.menuchoice == 'all'}">
          menu.addItem("newsid", "News", "News", null, null);
          menu.addItem("weatherid", "Weather", "Weather", null, null);
          menu.addItem("entid", "Entertainment", "Entertainment", null, null);
          menu.addItem("lotid", "Lotteries", "Lotteries", null, null);

          menu.addSubItem("newsid", "World News", "World News",
            "http://localhost:8080/ch04/example2/","");
          menu.addSubItem("newsid", "American News", "American News",
            "http://localhost:8080/ch04/example2/","");
          menu.addSubItem("newsid", "UK News", "UK News",
            "http://localhost:8080/ch04/example2/","");

          menu.addSubItem("newsid", "Yahoo News", "Yahoo News",
            "http://localhost:8000/ch04/example2/","");
          menu.addSubItem("newsid", "CNN News", "CNN News",
            "http://localhost:8080/ch04/example2/","");

          menu.addSubItem("weatherid", "Accurate Weather", "Accurate Weather",
            "http://localhost:8080/ch04/example2/","");
          menu.addSubItem("weatherid", "Weather Central", "Weather Central",
            "http://localhost:8080/ch04/example2/","");
```

```
        menu.addSubItem("entid", "E Motion", "E Motion",
            "http://localhost:8080/ch04/example2/","");

        menu.addSubItem("entid", "Hollywood on the Run", "Hollywood on the Run",
            "http://localhost:8080/ch04/example2/","");

        menu.addSubItem("lotid", "Lucky 9", "Lucky 9",
            "http://localhost:8080/ch04/example2/","");

        menu.addSubItem("lotid", "Mega Fortune", "Mega Fortune",
            "http://localhost:8080/ch04/example2/","");

      </c:when>
    </c:choose>
    menu.showMenu();
    }

    showToolbar();
    function UpdateIt()
    {
      if (ie&&keepstatic&&!opr6)
        document.all["MainTable"].style.top = document.body.scrollTop;
      setTimeout("UpdateIt()", 200);
    }
    UpdateIt();
  </script>
  <br/>
  <br/>

  <table class="mainBox" width="600">
    <tr><td class="boxTitle" >
      You Get the Latest Weather, ${param.user}!
    </td></tr>
    <tr><td>
      <jsp:useBean id="newsfeed" class="com.wrox.begjsp.ch2.NewsFeed"
        scope="request" >
        <jsp:setProperty name="newsfeed"  property="topic" value="weather"/>
      </jsp:useBean>
      <table>
        <c:forEach items="${newsfeed.values}" var="row" >
          <tr><td class="tableCell" width="200">  ${row.city}  </td>
            <td> ${row.temp}</td>
          </tr>
        </c:forEach>
      </table>
    </td></tr>
  </table>
```

Modify entertain.jsp to create the new entertain.jsp. The changes are highlighted:

```
<%@ taglib prefix="c" uri="http://java.sun.com/jsp/jstl/core" %>
  <title>Weather Portal</title>
</head>
```

```
<body>
  <script language="JavaScript" src="menu.js"></script>
  <script language="JavaScript">
    function showToolbar()
    {
      menu = new Menu();

      <c:choose>
      <c:when test="${param.menuchoice == 'news-only'}">
        menu.addItem("newsportalid", "News Portal", "News Portal", null, null);
        menu.addItem("otherportalid", "Other Portals", "Other Portals",
          null, null);
        menu.addSubItem("newsportalid", "World News", "World News",
          "http://localhost:8080/ch04/example2/","");
        menu.addSubItem("newsportalid", "American News", "American News",
          "http://localhost:8080/ch04/example2/","");
        menu.addSubItem("newsportalid", "UK News", "UK News",
          "http://localhost:8080/ch04/example2/","");

        menu.addSubItem("otherportalid", "Yahoo News", "Yahoo News",
          "http://localhost:8080/ch04/example2/","");
        menu.addSubItem("otherportalid", "CNN News", "CNN News",
          "http://localhost:8080/ch04/example2/","");
      </c:when>
      <c:when test="${param.menuchoice == 'all'}">
        menu.addItem("newsid", "News", "News", null, null);
        menu.addItem("weatherid", "Weather", "Weather", null, null);
        menu.addItem("entid", "Entertainment", "Entertainment", null, null);
        menu.addItem("lotid", "Lotteries", "Lotteries", null, null);


        menu.addSubItem("newsid", "World News", "World News",
          "http://localhost:8080/ch04/example2/","");
        menu.addSubItem("newsid", "American News", "American News",
          "http://localhost:8080/ch04/example2/","");
        menu.addSubItem("newsid", "UK News", "UK News",
          "http://localhost:8080/ch04/example2/","");

        menu.addSubItem("newsid", "Yahoo News", "Yahoo News",
          "http://localhost:8080/ch04/example2/","");
        menu.addSubItem("newsid", "CNN News", "CNN News",
          "http://localhost:8080/ch04/example2/","");

        menu.addSubItem("weatherid", "Accurate Weather", "Accurate Weather",
          "http://localhost:0000/ch04/example2/","");
        menu.addSubItem("weatherid", "Weather Central", "Weather Central",
          "http://localhost:8080/ch04/example2/","");


        menu.addSubItem("entid", "E Motion", "E Motion",
          "http://localhost:8080/ch04/example2/","");

        menu.addSubItem("entid", "Hollywood on the Run", "Hollywood on the Run",
          "http://localhost:8080/ch04/example2/","");
```

```
        menu.addSubItem("lotid", "Lucky 9", "Lucky 9",
          "http://localhost:8080/ch04/example2/","");

        menu.addSubItem("lotid", "Mega Fortune", "Mega Fortune",
          "http://localhost:8080/ch04/example2/","");

    </c:when>
  </c:choose>
  menu.showMenu();
  }

  showToolbar();
  function UpdateIt()
  {
    if (ie&&keepstatic&&!opr6)
      document.all["MainTable"].style.top = document.body.scrollTop;
    setTimeout("UpdateIt()", 200);
  }
  UpdateIt();
</script>
<br/>
<br/>
```

```
<table class="mainBox" width="600">
  <tr><td class="boxTitle" >
    Entertainment News Just for You, ${param.user}!
  </td></tr>
  <tr><td>
    <span class="headLine">
      <jsp:useBean id="newsfeed" class="com.wrox.begjsp.ch2.NewsFeed"
        scope="request" >
      <jsp:setProperty name="newsfeed"  property="topic"
        value="entertainment"/>
      <jsp:getProperty name="newsfeed" property="value"/>
      </jsp:useBean>
    </span>
    <span class="newsText">
      <jsp:include page="dummytext.html" />
    </span>
  </td></tr>
</table>
```

Chapter 5 Exercises

Exercise 1

Create a form for entry of the number, called index1.jsp:

```
<html>
<head>
  <title>Multiplication Table</title>
```

```
</head>
<body>

  <h1>Enter a Number</h1>

  <form action="multtab.jsp" method="get">
    <b>Number:</b><input name="mult" size="10">
    <br/>
    <input type="submit" value="See multiplication table" />
   </form>
</body>
</html>
```

Create `multtab.jsp` to render the multiplication table:

```
<%@ taglib prefix="c" uri="http://java.sun.com/jsp/jstl/core" %>

<html>
<head>
  <title>Multiplication Table</title>
</head>
<body>
  <c:set var="op" value="${param.mult}"/>

  <h1>Multiplication Table for ${op}</h1>

  ${op} times 1 is ${op * 1}.<br/>
  ${op} times 2 is ${op * 2}.<br/>
  ${op} times 3 is ${op * 3}.<br/>
  ${op} times 4 is ${op * 4}.<br/>
  ${op} times 5 is ${op * 5}.<br/>
  ${op} times 6 is ${op * 6}.<br/>
  ${op} times 7 is ${op * 7}.<br/>
  ${op} times 8 is ${op * 8}.<br/>
  ${op} times 9 is ${op * 9}.<br/>
  ${op} times 10 is ${op * 10}.<br/>

</body>
</html>
```

Exercise 2

Modify the `WEB-INF/jsp/function-taglib.tld` file to add the functions, highlighted here:

```
<?xml version="1.0" encoding="UTF-8" ?>

<taglib xmlns="http://java.sun.com/xml/ns/j2ee"
  xmlns:xsi="http://www.w3.org/2001/XMLSchema-instance"
  xsi:schemaLocation="http://java.sun.com/xml/ns/j2ee web-jsptaglibrary_2_0.xsd"
  version="2.0">
  <description>A taglib to define some EL accessible functions.</description>
  <tlib-version>1.0</tlib-version>
  <short-name>ELFunctionTaglib</short-name>
```

```xml
  <uri>/ELFunctionTagLibrary</uri>
  <function>
    <description>Exposes the abs() function from java.lang.Math
package</description>
    <name>abs</name>
    <function-class>java.lang.Math</function-class>
    <function-signature>int abs( int )</function-signature>
  </function>

  <function>
    <description>Exposes the round() function from java.lang.Math
package</description>
    <name>round</name>
    <function-class>java.lang.Math</function-class>
    <function-signature>int round( double )</function-signature>
  </function>

  <function>
    <description>Exposes the integer min() function from java.lang.Math
package</description>
    <name>min</name>
    <function-class>java.lang.Math</function-class>
    <function-signature>int min( int, int )</function-signature>
  </function>

  <function>
    <description>Exposes the integer max() function from java.lang.Math
package</description>
    <name>max</name>
    <function-class>java.lang.Math</function-class>
    <function-signature>int max( int, int )</function-signature>
  </function>
  <function>
    <description>Exposes the sin() function from java.lang.Math
package</description>
    <name>sin</name>
    <function-class>java.lang.Math</function-class>
    <function-signature>double sin( double )</function-signature>
  </function>
  <function>
    <description>Exposes the cos() function from java.lang.Math
package</description>
    <name>cos</name>
    <function-class>java.lang.Math</function-class>
    <function-signature>double cos( double )</function-signature>
  </function>
  <function>
    <description>Exposes the sqrt() function from java.lang.Math
package</description>
    <name>sqrt</name>
    <function-class>java.lang.Math</function-class>
    <function-signature>double sqrt( double )</function-signature>
  </function>
</taglib>
```

Create a test JSP for the functions called `index2.jsp`:

```jsp
<%@ taglib prefix="wf" uri="http://www.wrox.com/begjsp/el-functions-taglib" %>

<html>
<head>
  <title>New EL Functions</title>
</head>
<body>
  <h1>New EL Functions</h1>

  min(10, 5)  is ${wf:min(10,5)}<br/>
  max(10, 5)  is ${wf:max(10,4)}<br/>
  sin(3.14) is ${wf:sin(3.14)}<br/>
  cos(3.14) is ${wf:cos(3.14)}<br/>
  sqrt(49) is ${wf:sqrt(49)}<br/>
</body>
</html>
```

Chapter 6 Exercises

Exercise 1

The `estore2.jsp` page is a modified version of `estore.jsp`, with the changes highlighted here:

```jsp
<%@ taglib prefix="c" uri="http://java.sun.com/jsp/jstl/core" %>
<%@ taglib prefix="fmt" uri="http://java.sun.com/jsp/jstl/fmt" %>
<%@ taglib prefix="wxshop" uri="http://www.wrox.com/begjsp/eshop-functions-taglib"
%>

<%@ page session="true" %>
<c:if test="${empty cats}">
  <c:set var="cats" value="${wxshop:getCats()}" scope="application"/>
</c:if>

<html>
<head>
  <title>Wrox Shopping Mall</title>
  <link rel=stylesheet type="text/css" href="store.css">
</head>
<body>
  <table width="600">
    <tr><td colspan="2" class="mainHead">Wrox JSTL Web Store</td></tr>

    <tr>
      <td width="20%">
      <c:forEach var="curCat" items="${cats}">
        <c:url value="/example1/estore2.jsp" var="localURL">
          <c:param name="catid" value="${curCat.id}"/>
        </c:url>
```

```
            <a href="${localURL}" class="category">${curCat.name}</a>
          </br>
        </c:forEach>
      </td>
      <td width="*">
        <h1></h1>
        <table border="1" width="100%">
          <tr><th align="left">Item</th><th align="left">Price</th><th
align="left">Order</th></tr>
            <c:set var="selectedCat"  value="${param.catid}"/>
            <c:if test="${empty selectedCat}">
              <c:set var="selectedCat"  value="1"/>
            </c:if>
            <c:forEach var="curItem" items="${wxshop:getItems(selectedCat)}">
              <tr>
                <td>
                  <c:url value="/example1/product.jsp" var="localURL">
                    <c:param name="sku" value="${curItem.sku}"/>
                  </c:url>
                  <a href="${localURL}">${curItem.name}</a>
                </td>
                <td align="right">
                  <fmt:formatNumber value="${curItem.price / 100}" type="currency"/>
                </td>
                <td>
                <c:url value="/example1/shopcart2.jsp" var="localURL">
                    <c:param name="action" value="buy"/>
                    <c:param name="sku" value="${curItem.sku}"/>
                  </c:url>
                  <a href="${localURL}"><b>BUY</b></a>
                </td>
              </tr>
            </c:forEach>
        </table>
      </td>
    </tr>
  </table>

</body>
</html>
```

The `product.jsp` page is a newly created JSP:

```
<%@ taglib prefix="c" uri="http://java.sun.com/jsp/jstl/core" %>
<%@ taglib prefix="fmt" uri="http://java.sun.com/jsp/jstl/fmt" %>
<%@ taglib prefix="wxshop" uri="http://www.wrox.com/begjsp/eshop-functions-taglib"
%>

<%@ page session="true" %>

<c:set var="EXAMPLE" value="/example1"/>
<c:set var="SHOP_PAGE" value="/estore2.jsp"/>
<c:set var="CART_PAGE" value="/shopcart2.jsp"/>
```

```
<html>
<head>
  <title>Wrox Shopping Mall - Product Page</title>
  <link rel=stylesheet type="text/css" href="store.css">
</head>
<body>
  <c:if test="${!(empty param.sku)}">
    <c:set var="prod" value="${wxshop:getItem(param.sku)}"/>
  </c:if>

  <table width="640">
    <tr><td class="mainHead">Wrox JSTL Web Store</td></tr>
    <tr>
      <td>
        <h1></h1>
        <table border="1" width="640">
          <tr>
            <th>
              ${prod.name}
            </th>
          </tr>

          <tr>
            <td>
              <img src="prodfoto.gif" width="320" height="240"/>
              <p>
                This is a great product, and the detailed product
                description should go here. In a real e-commerce
                system, this information will be retrieved from
                a relational database.
              </p>
            </td>
          </tr>

          <tr>
            <td><h2>Only  <fmt:formatNumber value="${prod.price / 100}"
type="currency"/>  </h2>
            </td>
          </tr>

          <tr>
            <td>
              <c:url value="${EXAMPLE}${CART_PAGE}" var="localURL">
                <c:param name="sku" value="${prod.sku}"/>
                <c:param name="action" value="buy"/>
              </c:url>
              <a href="${localURL}"><h3>Buy Now</h3></a>
            </td>
          </tr>


          <tr>
            <td>
              <c:url value="${EXAMPLE}${SHOP_PAGE}" var="localURL"/>
```

```
                <a href="${localURL}">Return to Shopping</a>
              </td>
            </tr>
          </table>
        </td>
      </tr>
    </table>
  </body>
</html>
```

Exercise 2

The modified version of shopcart.jsp that performs tax and shipping charge calculations is shown next, with the modifications highlighted. This JSP file is saved as shopcart2.jsp.

```
<%@ taglib prefix="c" uri="http://java.sun.com/jsp/jstl/core" %>
<%@ taglib prefix="fmt" uri="http://java.sun.com/jsp/jstl/fmt" %>
<%@ taglib prefix="wxshop" uri="http://www.wrox.com/begjsp/eshop-functions-taglib"
%>

<%@ page session="true" %>

<c:set var="EXAMPLE" value="/example1"/>
<c:set var="SHOP_PAGE" value="/estore2.jsp"/>
<c:set var="CART_PAGE" value="/shopcart2.jsp"/>


<html>
<head>
  <title>Wrox Shopping Mall - Shopping Cart</title>
  <link rel=stylesheet type="text/css" href="store.css">
</head>
<body>
  <c:if test="${!(empty param.sku)}">
    <c:set var="prod" value="${wxshop:getItem(param.sku)}"/>
  </c:if>

  <jsp:useBean id="lineitems" class="java.util.ArrayList" scope="session"/>

  <c:choose>
    <c:when test="${param.action == 'clear'}">
      ${wxshop:clearList(lineitems)}
    </c:when>

    <c:when test="${param.action == 'inc' || param.action=='buy'}">
      <c:set var="found" value="false"/>

      <c:forEach var="curItem" items="${lineitems}">

        <c:if test="${(curItem.sku) == (prod.sku)}">
          <jsp:setProperty name="curItem" property="quantity"
value="${curItem.quantity + 1}"/>
          <c:set var="found" value="true" />
        </c:if>
      </c:forEach>
```

```
      <c:if test="${!found}">
        <c:remove var="tmpitem"/>
        <jsp:useBean id="tmpitem" class="com.wrox.begjsp.ch03.LineItem">
          <jsp:setProperty name="tmpitem" property="quantity" value="1"/>
          <jsp:setProperty name="tmpitem" property="sku" value="${prod.sku}"/>
          <jsp:setProperty name="tmpitem" property="desc" value="${prod.name}"/>
          <jsp:setProperty name="tmpitem" property="price" value="${prod.price}"/>
        </jsp:useBean>
        ${wxshop:addList(lineitems, tmpitem)}
      </c:if>
    </c:when>
  </c:choose>


  <c:set var="total" value="0"/>
  <table width="640">
    <tr><td class="mainHead">Wrox JSTL Web Store</td></tr>
    <tr>
      <td>
        <h1></h1>
        <table border="1" width="640">

        <tr><th colspan="5" class="shopCart">Your Shopping Cart</th></tr>
        <tr><th align="left">Quantity</th><th align="left">Item</th><th
align="right">Price</th>
          <th align="right">Extended</th>
          <th align="left">Add</th>
        </tr>
        <c:forEach var="curItem" items="${lineitems}">
          <c:set var="extended" value="${curItem.quantity * curItem.price}"/>
          <c:set var="total" value="${total + extended}"/>
          <tr>
            <td>${curItem.quantity}</td>
            <td>${curItem.desc}</td>
            <td align="right">
              <fmt:formatNumber value="${curItem.price / 100}" type="currency"/>
            </td>
            <td align="right">
              <fmt:formatNumber value="${extended / 100}" type="currency"/>
            </td>
            <td>

              <c:url value="${EXAMPLE}${CART_PAGE}" var="localURL">
                <c:param name="action" value="inc"/>
                <c:param name="sku" value="${curItem.sku}"/>
              </c:url>
              <a href="${localURL}"><b>Add 1</b></a>
            </td>
          </tr>
        </c:forEach>

        <c:set var="rtax" value="${(total * 0.07)/100}"/>
        <c:set var="ftax" value="${(total * 0.08)/100}"/>

        <tr>
```

```
          <td colspan="3" align="right">Regional tax (7%):</td>
          <td align="right" >
            <fmt:formatNumber value="${rtax}" type="currency"/>
          </td>
          <td> </td>
        </tr>


        <tr>
          <td colspan="3" align="right">Federal tax (8%):</td>
          <td align="right" >
            <fmt:formatNumber value="${ftax}" type="currency"/>
          </td>
          <td> </td>
        </tr>


        <tr>
          <td colspan="5">  
          </td>
        </tr>
        <tr>
          <td colspan="3" align="right"><b>Total:</b></td>
          <td align="right" class="grandTotal">
            <fmt:formatNumber value="${total / 100 + rtax + ftax}"
type="currency"/>
          </td>
          <td> </td>
        </tr>

        <tr>
          <td colspan="5">
            <c:url value="${EXAMPLE}${CART_PAGE}" var="localURL">
              <c:param name="action" value="clear"/>
            </c:url>
            <a href="${localURL}">Clear the cart</a>
          </td>
        </tr>

        <tr>
          <td colspan="5">
            <c:url value="${EXAMPLE}${SHOP_PAGE}" var="localURL"/>
            <a href="${localURL}">Return to Shopping</a>
          </td>
        </tr>

      </table>
    </td>
  </tr>
  </table>
</body>
</html>
```

Chapter 7 Exercises

Exercise 1

The modified `xindex.jsp` with an all XML syntax is listed here:

```
<jsp:root
  xmlns:jsp="http://java.sun.com/JSP/Page"
  version="2.0">
  <jsp:directive.page language="java"  contentType="text/html"  />
  <html>
    <head>
    </head>
    <body>
      <h1> This is an HTML page. </h1>
      <table border="1">
        <tr>
          <td>This is a HTML table.</td>
        </tr>
      </table>
    </body>
  </html>
</jsp:root>
```

Exercise 2

In `web.xml`, add the `<include-prelude>` element as shown:

```
<jsp-property-group>
  <url-pattern>/example3/index.jsp</url-pattern>
  <include-prelude>/WEB-INF/jspf/pre2.jspf</include-prelude>
</jsp-property-group>
```

Create the JSP fragment file in the `WEB-INF/jspf` directory; call it `pre2.jspf`:

```
<%@ taglib prefix="c" uri="http://java.sun.com/jsp/jstl/core" %>
```

Delete the `<%@ taglib %>` directive from `index.jsp`, resulting in the following:

```
<html>
<head>
</head>
<body>

  <c:choose>
    <c:when test="${param.pg == 'news'}">
      <%@ include file="news.jsp" %>
    </c:when>
    <c:otherwise>
      <%@ include file="data.jsp" %>
```

```
        </c:otherwise>
      </c:choose>
  </body>
  </html>
```

Chapter 8 Exercises

Exercise 1

Make the following changes in index1.jsp:

```
<%@ taglib prefix="c" uri="http://java.sun.com/jsp/jstl/core" %>
<%@page import="com.wrox.begjsp.ch03.*" %>
<html>
<head>
   <%
     pageContext.setAttribute("myCats", EShop.getCats());
   %>
</head>
<body>
   <jsp:useBean id="myProduct" class="com.wrox.begjsp.ch03.Product">
     <jsp:setProperty name="myProduct" property="sku" value="12345"/>
     <jsp:setProperty name="myProduct" property="name" value="DSL Modem"/>
   </jsp:useBean>

   <jsp:useBean id="myCats" class="java.util.ArrayList"/>

   <table border="1">
     <tr>
       <td>Sku:</td><td><%= myProduct.getSku() %></td>
     </tr>
     <tr>
       <td>Name:</td><td>${myProduct.name}</td>
     </tr>
   </table>

   <jsp:useBean id="myMap"  class="java.util.HashMap" />
   <jsp:useBean id="myMap2"  class="java.util.HashMap"  type="java.util.Map"/>


   <table border="1">
     <tr>
       <th>ID</th><th>Category</th></tr>
     </tr>
     <c:forEach var="curcat" items="${myCats}">
       <tr>
         <td>${curcat.id}</td><td>${curcat.name}</td>
       </tr>
     </c:forEach>
   </table>
</body>
</html>
```

Examining the generated code at `<Tomcat Installation Directory>/work/Catalina/localhost/ch08/org/apache/example1/jsp/index1_jsp.java`, you can see that the `myCats` Java variable generated by the `<jsp:useBean>` standard action is of type `java.util.ArrayList`. This is shown in the following line from `index1_jsp.java`:

```
java.util.ArrayList myCats = null;
```

Exercise 2

Make the following modifications to `index.jsp`, creating `index2.jsp`:

```html
<html>
<head>
  <title>Product Information Entry</title>
<style>
  .label { font-weight: bold; }
</style>
</head>
<body>
  <h1> Enter Product Information</h1>
  <form  action="procprod2.jsp" method="post">
    <table border="1">
      <tr>
        <td class="label">SKU:</td>
        <td><input name="sku" type="text" width="40"/> </td>
      </tr>

      <tr>
        <td class="label">Name:</td> <td><input name="name" type="text"
          width="40"/> </td>
      </tr>
      <tr>
        <td class="label">Description:</td> <td><input name="desc" type="text"
          width="40"/> </td>
      </tr>
      <tr>
        <td class="label">Price:</td> <td> <input name="price" type="text"
          width="40"/></td>
      </tr>

      <tr>
        <td class="label">Format:</td>
        <td>
          <select name="docformat">
            <option>html</option>
            <option>xml</option>
          </select>
        </td>
      </tr>

      <tr>
        <td colspan="2"> <input type="submit"/></td>
      </tr>
```

```
      </table>
    </form>
  </body>
</html>
```

The replacement of `procprod.jsp` (`procprod2.jsp`) just performs the forwarding as shown:

```jsp
<%@ taglib prefix="c" uri="http://java.sun.com/jsp/jstl/core" %>
<c:choose>
  <c:when test="${param.docformat == 'xml'}">
    <jsp:forward page="prodxml.jsp"/>
  </c:when>
  <c:otherwise>
    <jsp:forward page="prodhtml.jsp"/>
  </c:otherwise>
</c:choose>
```

The `prodxml.jsp` JSP is used to render the product information in XML format:

```jsp
<%@ taglib prefix="fmt" uri="http://java.sun.com/jsp/jstl/fmt" %>
<%@page contentType="text/xml" %>
<product>
  <jsp:useBean id="localProd" class="com.wrox.begjsp.ch03.Product" />
  <jsp:setProperty name="localProd" property="*" />
  <sku>
    <jsp:getProperty name="localProd" property="sku"/>
  </sku>
  <name>
    <jsp:getProperty name="localProd" property="name"/>
  </name>
  <desc>
    <jsp:getProperty name="localProd" property="desc"/>
  </desc>
  <price>
    <fmt:formatNumber value="${localProd.price / 100}" type="currency"/>
  </price>
</product>
```

Finally, `prodhtml.jsp` is used to render the product information in HTML format, and its code is taken from the old `procprod.jsp` file:

```jsp
<%@ taglib prefix="fmt" uri="http://java.sun.com/jsp/jstl/fmt" %>
<%@page contentType="text/html" %>
<html>
<head>
  <title>Processing Product Information</title>
  <style>
    .label { font-weight: bold; }
  </style>
</head>

<body>
  <jsp:useBean id="localProd" class="com.wrox.begjsp.ch03.Product" />
```

```
      <jsp:setProperty name="localProd" property="*" />
      <h1>Information Received</h1>
      <table border="1">
        <tr>
          <td class="label" >SKU:</td> <td><jsp:getProperty name="localProd"
            property="sku"/> </td>
        </tr>

        <tr>
          <td class="label">Name:</td> <td><jsp:getProperty name="localProd"
            property="name"/> </td>
        </tr>
        <tr>
          <td class="label">Description:</td> <td><jsp:getProperty name="localProd"
            property="desc"/> </td>
        </tr>
        <tr>
          <td class="label">Price:</td>
          <td>
            <fmt:formatNumber value="${localProd.price / 100}" type="currency"/>
          </td>
        </tr>
      </table>
    </body>
  </html>
```

Chapter 9 Exercises

Exercise 1

Modify index.jsp to create index1.jsp. The changes are highlighted:

```
<%@ taglib prefix="c" uri="http://java.sun.com/jsp/jstl/core" %>
<c:choose>
  <c:when test="${empty param.action}">
    <jsp:forward page="enterbid1.jsp"/>
  </c:when>
  <c:when test="${param.action eq 'bid'}">
    <jsp:useBean id="bidinfo" class="com.wrox.begjsp.ch09.Bid" scope="request">
      <jsp:setProperty name="bidinfo" property="*"/>
    </jsp:useBean>


    <c:if test="${(param.price <= 0) ||  (param.price >= 999)}">
      <jsp:useBean id="biderror" class="com.wrox.begjsp.ch09.BidError"
scope="request">
        <jsp:setProperty name="biderror" property="msg" value="Sorry, your bid is
not in range. Please enter again."/>
      </jsp:useBean>
      <jsp:forward page="enterbid1.jsp"/>
    </c:if>
```

```
        <jsp:forward page="showbid.jsp"/>
      </c:when>
    </c:choose>
```

Modify `enterbid.jsp` to `enterbid1.jsp`:

```jsp
<%@ taglib prefix="c" uri="http://java.sun.com/jsp/jstl/core" %>
<html>
<head>
  <link rel=stylesheet type="text/css" href="auction.css">
  <title>Enter Your Bid</title></head>
<body>
  <table class="mainBox" width="400">
    <tr>
      <td class="boxTitle" colspan="2">
        Wrox JSP Auction
      </td>
    </tr>
    <c:if test="${!(empty biderror)}">
    <tr>
      <td class="errorText" colspan="2">
        ${biderror.msg}
      </td>
    </tr>
    </c:if>

    <tr><td colspan="2"> </td></tr>
    <tr><td>
      <form  action="index1.jsp" method="get">
        <table>
          <tr>
            <td width="200">Item to bid on</td>
            <td>
              <select name="item">
                <option
                  <c:if test="${!(empty biderror)}">
                    <c:if test="${bidinfo.item eq '27 inch TV'}">
                     selected
                    </c:if>
                  </c:if>
                >27 inch TV</option>
                <option
                  <c:if test="${!(empty biderror)}">
                    <c:if test="${bidinfo.item eq 'DVD Player'}">
                     selected
                    </c:if>
                  </c:if>
                >DVD Player</option>
                <option
                  <c:if test="${!(empty biderror)}">
                    <c:if test="${bidinfo.item eq 'Digital Camera'}">
                     selected
                    </c:if>
                  </c:if>
```

```
            >Digital Camera</option>
          </select>
          <input type="hidden" name="action" value="bid"/>
        </td>
      </tr>
      <tr>
        <td
          <c:if test="${!(empty biderror)}">
            class="redLabel"
          </c:if>
          >Bid Price:</td>
        <td><input name="price" type="text" width="10"
          <c:if test="${!(empty biderror)}">
            value="${bidinfo.price}"
          </c:if>

          />
        </td>
      </tr>
      <tr><td colspan="2"> </td></tr>
      <tr>
        <td colspan="2" align="center">
          <input type="submit" value="Bid now!"/>
        </td>
      </tr>
    </table>
  </form>
</td></tr>
</table>
</body>
</html>
```

Add the following to auction.css:

```
.redLabel
{
  font-family : Verdana, Geneva, Arial, Helvetica, sans-serif;
  font-size : 18;
  color : #ff0000;
  background-color: #ffffff;
}
```

Exercise 2

Modify index.jsp to index1.jsp as shown in the highlighted changes:

```
<%@ taglib prefix="c" uri="http://java.sun.com/jsp/jstl/core" %>
<c:choose>
  <c:when test="${empty param.action}">
    <jsp:forward page="enterbid1.jsp"/>
  </c:when>
  <c:when test="${param.action eq 'bid'}">
```

```
    <jsp:useBean id="bidinfo" class="com.wrox.begjsp.ch09.Bid" scope="request">
      <jsp:setProperty name="bidinfo" property="*"/>
    </jsp:useBean>
    <c:if test="${param.price > 1000}">
      <jsp:forward page="winner.jsp"/>
    </c:if>


    <!-- validation code -->
    <c:if test="${param.price <= 0}">
      <jsp:useBean id="biderror" class="com.wrox.begjsp.ch09.BidError"
scope="request">
          <jsp:setProperty name="biderror" property="msg" value="Sorry, your bid is
not in range. Please enter again."/>
      </jsp:useBean>
      <jsp:forward page="enterbid1.jsp"/>
    </c:if>
    <!-- data validated -->


    <!-- perform bidding -->
    <jsp:useBean id="bidder" class="com.wrox.begjsp.ch09.Bidder" scope="request">
      <jsp:setProperty name="bidder" property="item"/>
      <jsp:setProperty name="bidder" property="price"/>
    </jsp:useBean>
    <c:set var="bidresult" value="${bidder.result}" scope="request"/>


    <jsp:forward page="showbid.jsp"/>
  </c:when>
</c:choose>
```

Modify `enterbid.jsp` to `enterbid1.jsp`:

```
<%@ taglib prefix="c" uri="http://java.sun.com/jsp/jstl/core" %>
<html>
<head>
  <link rel=stylesheet type="text/css" href="auction.css">
  <title>Enter Your Bid</title></head>
<body>
  <table class="mainBox" width="400">
    <tr>
      <td class="boxTitle" colspan="2">
        Wrox JSP Auction
      </td>
    </tr>
    <c:if test="${!(empty biderror)}">
    <tr>
      <td class="errorText" colspan="2">
        ${biderror.msg}
      </td>
    </tr>
    </c:if>
```

```
        <tr><td colspan="2"> </td></tr>
        <tr>
          <td>
            <form  action="index1.jsp" method="get">
              <table>
                <tr>
                  <td width="200">Item to bid on</td>
                  <td>
                    <select name="item">
                      <option>27 inch TV</option>
                      <option>DVD Player</option>
                      <option>Digital Camera</option>
                    </select>
                    <input type="hidden" name="action" value="bid"/>
                  </td>
                </tr>
                <tr>
                  <td>Bid Price:</td>
                  <td><input name="price" type="text" width="10"/>
                  </td>
                </tr>
                <tr><td colspan="2"> </td></tr>
                <tr>
                  <td colspan="2" align="center">
                    <input type="submit" value="Bid now!"/>
                  </td>
                </tr>
              </table>
            </form>
          </td>
        </tr>
      </table>
    </body>
    </html>
```

Add the new winner.jsp:

```
<%@ taglib prefix="c" uri="http://java.sun.com/jsp/jstl/core" %>
<html>
<head>
  <link rel=stylesheet type="text/css" href="auction.css">
  <title>Enter Your Bid</title></head>
<body>
  <table class="mainBox" width="400">
    <tr><td class="boxTitle" colspan="2">
      Wrox JSP Auction
    </td></tr>
    <c:if test="${!(empty biderror)}">
      <tr>
        <td class="errorText" colspan="2">
          ${biderror.msg}
        </td>
      </tr>
    </c:if>
```

```
        <tr><td colspan="2"> </td></tr>
        <tr>
          <td>
            <form  action="index1.jsp" method="get">
              <table>
                <tr>
                  <td width="200">Item to bid on</td>
                  <td>
                    <select name="item">
                      <option>27 inch TV</option>
                      <option>DVD Player</option>
                      <option>Digital Camera</option>
                    </select>
                    <input type="hidden" name="action" value="bid"/>
                  </td>
                </tr>
                <tr>
                  <td>Bid Price:</td>
                  <td><input name="price" type="text" width="10"/>
                  </td>
                </tr>
                <tr><td colspan="2"> </td></tr>
                <tr>
                  <td colspan="2" align="center">
                    <input type="submit" value="Bid now!"/>
                  </td>
                </tr>
              </table>
            </form>
          </td>
        </tr>
      </table>
  </body>
</html>
```

Chapter 10 Exercises

Exercise 1

Modify index.jsp to create index1.jsp, as shown in the highlighted changes:

```
<%@ taglib prefix="c" uri="http://java.sun.com/jsp/jstl/core" %>
<html>
<head>
  <jsp:useBean id="errgen" class="com.wrox.begjsp.ch10.ErrorGenerator" />

  <title>Error Generating page</title>
</head>
<body>
  <h1>Page to Generate Error</h1>
```

```
<table>
  <tr>
    <td><h3>
      <c:catch var="localerr">
        ${errgen.divideByZero}
      </c:catch>
      <c:if test="${localerr.rootCause.class eq
        'class java.lang.ArithmeticException'}">
        Do not divide by zero!
      </c:if>
      <c:if test="${localerr.rootCause.class eq
        'class java.lang.ArrayIndexOutOfBoundsException'}">
        Fix array index!
      </c:if>
    </h3></td>
  </tr>
</table>


</body>
</html>
```

Note that the `<%@ page %>` directive with the `errorPage` attribute has been removed.

To test for array index out of range errors, replace the line

```
${errgen.divideByZero}
```

with the line

```
${errgen.outOfRange}
```

Exercise 2

Modify `index.jsp` from the third Try It Out example to form `index1.jsp`:

```
<%@page language="java" errorPage="disperr.jsp" %>
<html>
<head>
  <title>Error in JSP directives and actions</title>
</head>
<body>
  <h1>Page with error in JSP directive and actions</h1>

  <jsp:include page="nosuch.jsp"  />
  <jsp:setProperty name="errobj" property="nosuch" value="This is invalid" />

</body>
</html>
```

Note that the JSTL `taglib` directive and the `<c:catch>` tags have been removed.

Create a new `disperr.jsp` page containing the following:

```
<%@page isErrorPage="true" %>

<html>
<head>
  <title>Page to Display Error Information</title>
</head>
<body>
  <h1>Error Information</h1>
  <table width="600" border="1">

    <tr valign="top">
      <td ><b>Error:</b></td>
      <td>${pageContext.exception.rootCause}</td>
    </tr>

    <tr valign="top">
      <td><b>URI:</b></td>
      <td>${pageContext.errorData.requestURI}</td>
    </tr>


    <tr valign="top">
      <td><b>Status code:</b></td>
      <td>${pageContext.errorData.statusCode}</td>
    </tr>
  </table>

</body>
</html>
```

The thing to note in the preceding code is the use of `${pageContext.exception.rootCause}` to print the actual error.

Chapter 11 Exercises

Exercise 1

First, the JSP page (`exercise-randomnumber.jsp`) that uses the random number generator tag is shown:

```
<%@ taglib prefix="beginjsp" tagdir="/WEB-INF/tags" %>


<beginjsp:randomnumber max="100"/>

Random Number: ${randomNumber}
```

The implementation of the random number tag (randomnumber.tag) is listed next:

```
<%@ tag import="java.util.Random" body-content="empty" %>

<%@ attribute name="max" type="java.lang.Integer" required="true" %>
<%@ variable name-given="randomNumber" variable-class="java.lang.Integer"
scope="AT_BEGIN"%>

<%
    Random rand = new Random();
    int result = rand.nextInt(max.intValue());
    jspContext.setAttribute("randomNumber", new Integer(result));
%>
```

Exercise 2

The JSP page (exercise-calformat.jsp) that uses the calendar tag is as follows:

```
<%@ page import="java.util.Calendar" %>
<%@ taglib prefix="beginjsp" tagdir="/WEB-INF/tags" %>

<%
    Calendar cal = Calendar.getInstance();
    String pattern = "EEEE d MMMM yyyy G";

    pageContext.setAttribute("cal", cal);
    pageContext.setAttribute("pattern", pattern);
%>

<beginjsp:calformat calendar="${cal}"
                    pattern="${pattern}"/>
```

The implementation of the calendar tag (calformat.tag) is as follows:

```
<%@ tag body-content="empty"
        import="java.util.Calendar,java.text.SimpleDateFormat" %>

<%@ taglib prefix="core" uri="http://java.sun.com/jsp/jstl/core" %>
<%@ taglib prefix="function" uri="http://java.sun.com/jsp/jstl/functions" %>

<%@ attribute name="calendar" required="true" type="java.util.Calendar" %>
<%@ attribute name="pattern" required="true" %>

<%
    SimpleDateFormat formatter = new SimpleDateFormat(pattern);
    String result = formatter.format(calendar.getTime());
    out.println(result);
%>
```

Chapter 12 Exercises

Exercise 1

Modify index.jsp to create index1.jsp:

```
<%@ taglib prefix="c" uri="http://java.sun.com/jsp/jstl/core" %>
<c:choose>
  <c:when test="${empty param.action}">
    <jsp:forward page="bidform.jsp"/>
  </c:when>

  <c:when test="${param.action eq 'bidsubmit'}">
    <jsp:forward page="procbid.jsp"/>
  </c:when>
</c:choose>
```

Create bidform.jsp:

```
<%@ taglib prefix="my" tagdir="/WEB-INF/tags/wroxtags" %>
<html>
<head>
  <title>Auction Bidding</title>
  <my:validateFunctions>
    <my:checkField name="name" type="alphanum"/>
    <my:checkField name="item" type="digits"/>
    <my:checkField name="bid" type="digits"/>
  </my:validateFunctions>
</head>
<body>
  <h1>Enter Your Bid Information</h1>
  <form  name="prodform" action="index1.jsp" method="post"
    onsubmit="return validateForm()">
  <table border="0" >
    <tr>
      <td>Name:</td>
      <td>
        <input name="name" type="text" width="40"/>
        <my:validateErrMsg name="name"
          msg="<-- please enter alphabet letters only"/>
      </td>
    </tr>

    <tr>
      <td>Item Number:</td>
      <td>
        <input name="item" type="text" width="40"/>
        <my:validateErrMsg name="item"
          msg="<-- please enter numeric digits only"/>
      </td>
    </tr>
```

```
      <tr>
        <td>Bid Price:</td>
        <td>
        <input name="bid" type="text" width="40"/>
        <my:validateErrMsg name="bid"
          msg="<-- please enter price in dollars only, do not enter cents"/>
        </td>
      </tr>

      <tr>
        <td colspan="2"> <input type="submit" value="Bid now!" />
          <input type="hidden" name="action" value="bidsubmit"/>
        </td>
      </tr>


    </table>
    </form>
  </body>
</html>
```

Create the new `procbid.jsp`:

```
<html>
  <head>
    <title>Processing Bid Information</title>
  </head>
  <body>
    <h1>Bid Information Received</h1>
    <table border="1">
      <tr>
        <td>Name:</td> <td>${param.name}</td>
      </tr>

      <tr>
        <td>Item Number:</td> <td>${param.item}</td>
      </tr>
      <tr>
        <td>Bid Price:</td> <td> ${param.bid}</td>
      </tr>

    </table>
  </body>
</html>
```

After you complete this exercise, you should realize that the tag library is not yet ready for general use. Namely, it still has two interdependencies with the source:

❑   The form must be called `prodform`.

❑   The `onsubmit` handler of the form still refers to a JavaScript method called `validateForm()`.

Exercise 2

Modify `index1.jsp` from the third Try It Out example to create `index2.jsp`:

```
<%@ taglib prefix="fn" uri="http://java.sun.com/jsp/jstl/functions" %>
<%@ taglib prefix="my" tagdir="/WEB-INF/tags/wroxtags" %>
<%@page contentType="text/xml" %>
<?xml version="1.0"?>
<entry>
  <my:getInfo/>

  <name>
    ${fn:escapeXml(name)}
  </name>
  <comment>
    ${fn:escapeXml(comment)}
  </comment>
  <code>
    ${fn:escapeXml(code)}
  </code>
</entry>
```

Chapter 13 Exercises

Exercise 1

The first step in internationalizing for French is to create a GIF file for the selection of the French language, called `french.gif`.

Next, modify the `index.jsp` file to create an `index1.jsp` file containing the changes highlighted:

```
<%@ taglib prefix="c" uri="http://java.sun.com/jsp/jstl/core" %>
<html>
<head>
  <title>Select a language</title>
</head>
<body>
  <h1>Please select a language:</h1>
  <c:url value="en/application.jsp" var="engURL"/>
  <a href="${engURL}">
    <img src="english.gif"/>
  </a>
  <br/>
  <br/>
  <c:url value="zh/application.jsp" var="chineseURL"/>
  <a href="${chineseURL}">
    <img src="chinese.gif"/>
  </a>
  <br/>
  <br/>
```

```
    <c:url value="fr/application.jsp" var="frenchURL"/>
    <a href="${frenchURL}">
      <img src="french.gif"/>
    </a>

  </body>
</html>
```

Create a localized `fr` directory, and modify `application.jsp` to create `fr/application.jsp`:

```
<%@ taglib prefix="c" uri="http://java.sun.com/jsp/jstl/core" %>
<html>
<head>
  <meta http-equiv="Content-Type" content="text/html;charset=utf-8" >
  <title>Formulaire de Demande</title>
</head>
<body>
  <h1>Formulaire de Demande</h1>
  <br/>
  <c:url value="procform.jsp" var="actionURL"/>
  <form action="${actionURL}" method="post">
    <table>
      <tr>
        <td>Prénom</td>
        <td><input type="text" name="lastname" size="40"/></td>
      </tr>

      <tr>
        <td>Nom</td>
        <td><input type="text" name="firstname" size="40"/></td>
      </tr>

      <tr>
        <td>Code postal</td>
        <td><input type="text" name="postcode" size="40"/></td>
      </tr>

      <tr>
        <td>Mot de passé</td>
        <td><input type="password" name="pass" size="40"/></td>
      </tr>

      <tr>
        <td colspan="2" align="center">
        <input type="submit" value="Valider"/></td>
      </tr>

    </table>
  </form>
</body>
</html>
```

Create an en/procform.jsp file, containing the following:

```html
<html>
<head>
  <meta http-equiv="Content-Type" content="text/html;charset=utf-8" >
  <title>L'information de demadeur</title>
</head>
<body>
  <h1>L'information de demadeur</h1>
  <br/>

  <table border="1">
    <tr>
      <td>Prénom</td>
      <td>${param.lastname}</td>
    </tr>

    <tr>
      <td>Nom</td>
      <td>${param.firstname}</td>
    </tr>

    <tr>
      <td>Code postal</td>
      <td>${param.postcode}</td>
    </tr>

    <tr>
      <td>Mot de passé</td>
      <td>${param.pass}</td>
    </tr>

  </table>
</body>
</html>
```

Exercise 2

Copy the french.gif from the first Try It Out example into the solution directory.

Modify the second Try It Out example's index.jsp to create index1.jsp:

```jsp
<%@ taglib prefix="c" uri="http://java.sun.com/jsp/jstl/core" %>
<html>
<head>
  <title>Select Language</title>
</head>
<body>
  <h1>Please select language:</h1>
  <c:url value="application.jsp" var="engURL">
    <c:param name="locale" value="en_US"/>
  </c:url>
```

```
<a href="${engURL}">
  <img src="english.gif"/>
</a>
<br/>
<br/>
<c:url value="application.jsp" var="chineseURL">
  <c:param name="locale" value="zh_HK"/>
</c:url>

<a href="${chineseURL}">
  <img src="chinese.gif"/>
</a>
<br/>
<br/>
<c:url value="application.jsp" var="frenchURL">
  <c:param name="locale" value="fr_FR"/>
</c:url>

<a href="${frenchURL}">
  <img src="french.gif"/>
</a>


</body>
</html>
```

Create an `app_fr.properties` file in the `WEB-INF/classes` directory:

```
newTitle=Formulaire de Demande
lastName=Pr\u00e9nom
firstName=Nom
postalCode=Code postal
password=Mot de pass\u00e9
submitForm=Valider
appInfo=L\u2019information de demadeur
```

Chapter 14 Exercises

Exercise 1

The answer is found in the file `FilterByNdc.java` in the package `com.wrox.book.chapt14`:

```
package com.wrox.book.chapt14.log4j;
public class FilterByNdc extends org.apache.log4j.spi.Filter
{
    private boolean allowOnMatch = true; // blocks if false
    private String match = null;

    public FilterByNdc()
    {
    }
```

```
    public int decide(org.apache.log4j.spi.LoggingEvent loggingEvent)
    {
        String ndcValue = loggingEvent.getNDC();
        // null matches everything
        if(( match == null ) || (ndcValue == null))
        {
            return allowOnMatch ? ACCEPT : DENY;
        }
        if((match.equals(ndcValue)))
        {
            return allowOnMatch ? ACCEPT : DENY;
        }
        return allowOnMatch ? DENY : ACCEPT;
    }

    boolean getAllowOnMatch()
    {
        return allowOnMatch;
    }

    void setAllowOnMatch(boolean allow)
    {
        this.allowOnMatch = allow;
    }

    String getMatch()
    {
        return match;
    }

    void setmatch(String matchVal)
    {
        this.match = matchVal;
    }
}
```

Exercise 2

The solution is found in the class `com.wrox.book.chapter14.NdcIpFilter`:

```
package com.wrox.book.chapt14;

import java.io.IOException;
import javax.servlet.*;
import org.apache.log4j.NDC;


public class NdcIpFilter implements Filter
{
    private FilterConfig filterConfig = null;

    public NdcIpFilter()
    {
```

```
    }

    public void init(FilterConfig fc)
    {
        filterConfig = fc;
    }


    public void doFilter(
ServletRequest request,
ServletResponse response,
FilterChain chain)
    throws IOException, ServletException
    {
        // adds the Ip Address to the NDC
        String ip = request.getRemoteAddr();
        NDC.push(ip);
        chain.doFilter(request, response);
        NDC.pop();
    }

    public void destroy()
    {
    }
}
```

Exercise 3

The solution is found in the file Exercise3.jsp:

```
<%@page contentType="text/html"%>
<%@page pageEncoding="UTF-8"%>
<%@page import="org.apache.log4j.Logger" %>
<%@taglib prefix="c" uri="http://java.sun.com/jsp/jstl/core" %>
<%@taglib prefix="log" uri="http://jakarta.apache.org/taglibs/log-1.0" %>
<html>
<head><title>Debugger Exercise</title></head>
<body>
<%
    Logger logger = Logger.getLogger(this.getClass().getName());
    int dice = 0;
    java.util.ArrayList imageNames = new java.util.ArrayList(5);
    java.util.Random rnd = new java.util.Random();
    for (int i = 0; i < 5; i++)
    {
        dice = rnd.nextInt(6)+1;
        imageNames.add( new String("dice128_"+dice+".gif"));
        logger.debug( imageNames.get(i) );
    }
    pageContext.setAttribute("dice", imageNames);
%>
<c:set var="logCat" value="${pageContext.page.class.name}" scope="page" />
<table>
```

```
        <tbody align="center">
            <tr>
            <c:forEach var="imageName" items="${dice}" >
                <td><img src='${imageName}'/></td>
                <log:info category="${logCat}" message="${imageName}" />
            </c:forEach>
            </tr>
        </tbody>
        </table>
    </body>
    </html>
```

Chapter 15 Exercises

Exercise 1

Modify the deployment descriptor (web.xml) to add the servlet declaration and the servlet mappings (new code highlighted):

```
<?xml version="1.0" encoding="ISO-8859-1"?>

<web-app xmlns="http://java.sun.com/xml/ns/j2ee"
  xmlns:xsi="http://www.w3.org/2001/XMLSchema-instance"
  xsi:schemaLocation="http://java.sun.com/xml/ns/j2ee
http://java.sun.com/xml/ns/j2ee/web-app_2_4.xsd"
  version="2.4">

  <description>
    Wrox Beginning JavaServer Pages Examples - Chapter 15
  </description>
  <display-name>Chapter 15 Example (Wrox Beginning JavaServer Pages)</display-name>

  <servlet>
    <servlet-name>BasicServlet</servlet-name>
    <servlet-class>com.wrox.begjsp.ch15.servlet.BasicServlet</servlet-class>
  </servlet>

  <servlet>
    <servlet-name>ControllerServlet</servlet-name>
    <servlet-class>com.wrox.begjsp.ch15.servlet.ControllerServlet</servlet-class>

    <init-param>
      <param-name>hot</param-name>
      <param-value>/example2/red.jsp</param-value>
    </init-param>
    <init-param>
      <param-name>cool</param-name>
      <param-value>/example2/blue.jsp</param-value>
    </init-param>
  </servlet>
```

```xml
<servlet>
  <servlet-name>MessageServlet</servlet-name>
  <servlet-class>com.wrox.begjsp.ch15.servlet.MessageServlet</servlet-class>

  <init-param>
    <param-name>message</param-name>
    <param-value>Hello, world!</param-value>
  </init-param>
</servlet>

<servlet-mapping>
  <servlet-name>BasicServlet</servlet-name>
  <url-pattern>/</url-pattern>
</servlet-mapping>

<servlet-mapping>
  <servlet-name>ControllerServlet</servlet-name>
  <url-pattern>*.do</url-pattern>
</servlet-mapping>

<servlet-mapping>
  <servlet-name>MessageServlet</servlet-name>
  <url-pattern>/talktomeplease</url-pattern>
</servlet-mapping>

</web-app>
```

Create a `MessageServlet.java` file in the `WEB-INF\classes\com\wrox\begjsp\ch15\servlet` directory:

```java
package com.wrox.begjsp.ch15.servlet;
import javax.servlet.*;
import javax.servlet.http.*;

public class MessageServlet extends HttpServlet
{
    private String msg;

    public void init(ServletConfig config) throws
      ServletException
    {
        super.init(config);
        msg = config.getInitParameter("message");
    }

    public void destroy()
    {
    }

    protected void processRequest(HttpServletRequest request,
      HttpServletResponse response)
      throws ServletException, java.io.IOException
    {
        try
```

```
        {
            response.setContentType("text/html");
            java.io.PrintWriter out = response.getWriter();
            out.write("<html>\n");
            out.write("<head>\n");
            out.write("<title>Message Servlet</title>\n");
            out.write("</head>\n");
            out.write("<body>\n");
            out.write("<h1>" + msg + "</h1>\n");
            out.write("</body>\n");
            out.write("</html>");
            out.close();
        }
        catch(Exception e)
        {
            throw new ServletException(e);
        }
    }

    protected void doGet(HttpServletRequest request,
        HttpServletResponse response)
        throws ServletException, java.io.IOException
    {
        processRequest(request, response);
    }

    protected void doPost(HttpServletRequest request,
        HttpServletResponse response)
        throws ServletException, java.io.IOException
    {
        processRequest(request, response);
    }
}
```

Compile the servlet using the `compile.bat` file under the `WEB-INF/classes` directory.

Exercise 2

Modify the deployment descriptor (`web.xml`) to add new initialization parameters for the `ControllerServlet`. The new code is highlighted:

```
<?xml version="1.0" encoding="ISO-8859-1"?>

<web-app xmlns="http://java.sun.com/xml/ns/j2ee"
    xmlns:xsi="http://www.w3.org/2001/XMLSchema-instance"
    xsi:schemaLocation="http://java.sun.com/xml/ns/j2ee
http://java.sun.com/xml/ns/j2ee/web-app_2_4.xsd"
    version="2.4">

    <description>
        Wrox Beginning JavaServer Pages Examples - Chapter 15
    </description>
    <display-name>Chapter 15 Example (Wrox Beginning JavaServer Pages)</display-name>
```

```
<servlet>
  <servlet-name>BasicServlet</servlet-name>
  <servlet-class>com.wrox.begjsp.ch15.servlet.BasicServlet</servlet-class>
</servlet>

<servlet>
  <servlet-name>ControllerServlet</servlet-name>
  <servlet-class>com.wrox.begjsp.ch15.servlet.ControllerServlet</servlet-class>

  <init-param>
    <param-name>hot</param-name>
    <param-value>/example2/red.jsp</param-value>
  </init-param>
  <init-param>
    <param-name>cool</param-name>
    <param-value>/example2/blue.jsp</param-value>
  </init-param>
  <init-param>
    <param-name>warm</param-name>
    <param-value>/example2/message.jsp</param-value>
  </init-param>
  <init-param>
    <param-name>message</param-name>
    <param-value>Hello, world!</param-value>
  </init-param>

</servlet>

<servlet-mapping>
  <servlet-name>BasicServlet</servlet-name>
  <url-pattern>/</url-pattern>
</servlet-mapping>

<servlet-mapping>
  <servlet-name>ControllerServlet</servlet-name>
  <url-pattern>*.do</url-pattern>
</servlet-mapping>

</web-app>
```

Modify the second example's `ControllerServlet.java` to add the highlighted code:

```
package com.wrox.begjsp.ch15.servlet;
import javax.servlet.*;
import javax.servlet.http.*;

import java.util.HashMap;

public class ControllerServlet extends HttpServlet
{
    private HashMap forwards;
    private final static String HOT="hot";
    private final static String COOL="cool";
```

```
private final static String WARM="warm";
private String msg;

public void init(ServletConfig config) throws
  ServletException
{
    super.init(config);
    forwards = new HashMap();
    forwards.put(HOT, config.getInitParameter(HOT));
    forwards.put(COOL, config.getInitParameter(COOL));
    forwards.put(WARM, config.getInitParameter(WARM));
    msg = config.getInitParameter("message");

}

public void destroy()
{
}

protected void processRequest(HttpServletRequest request,
  HttpServletResponse response)
  throws ServletException, java.io.IOException
{
    try
    {
        //forward request to the associated page
        ServletContext context = getServletContext();
        String logicalName = request.getServletPath();
        String physicalURL = "/";
        logicalName= logicalName.substring(logicalName.lastIndexOf('/') + 1,
          logicalName.indexOf('.'));

        if (logicalName.equals(HOT))
            physicalURL= (String) forwards.get(HOT);

        if (logicalName.equals(COOL))
            physicalURL= (String) forwards.get(COOL);

        if (logicalName.equals(WARM))
            physicalURL= (String) forwards.get(WARM);

        request.setAttribute("msg", msg);

        RequestDispatcher dispatcher =
          context.getRequestDispatcher(physicalURL);
        dispatcher.forward(request, response);
    }
    catch(Exception e)
    {
        throw new ServletException(e);
    }
}
```

```
      protected void doGet(HttpServletRequest request,
        HttpServletResponse response)
        throws ServletException, java.io.IOException
    {
        processRequest(request, response);
    }

      protected void doPost(HttpServletRequest request,
        HttpServletResponse response)
        throws ServletException, java.io.IOException
    {
        processRequest(request, response);
    }

  }
```

Compile the preceding servlet using the `compile.bat` batch file in the `WEB-INF/classes` directory.

Add a `message.jsp` file to the `example2` directory:

```
<html>
<head>
  <title>Message Page</title>
</head>
<body>
  <h1>${msg}</h1>
</body>
</html>
```

The message is attached as an attribute, named `msg`, to the request by the `ControllerServlet`. This attribute is subsequently rendered by an EL expression within `message.jsp`.

Chapter 16 Exercises

Exercise 1

The goal of exercise 1 is to add header and footer elements to each JSP page served by the Web application.

Create the header and footer fragment files in the `web` directory as follows:

`header.htmlf`

```
<div class="header">
<hr/>
This is the header of all the pages
<hr/>
</div>
```

`footer.htmlf`

```
<div class="footer">
<hr/>
This is the footer of all the pages
<hr/>
</div>
```

Edit the web.xml file to include the jsp-config element as follows:

```
<web-app version="2.4" uri="http://java.sun.com/xml/ns/j2ee"

  <jsp-config>
    <jsp-property-group>
      <url-pattern>*.jsp</url-pattern>
      <include-prelude>/header.htmlf</include-prelude>
      <include-coda>/footer.htmlf</include-coda>
    </jsp-property-group>
  </jsp-config>

  <security-role>
    <role-name>chapter16role</role-name>
  </security-role>

  <security-constraint>
    <web-resource-collection>
      <url-pattern>/showDate.jsp</url-pattern>
    </web-resource-collection>
    <auth-constraint>
      <role-name>chapter17role</role-name>
    </auth-constraint>
  </security-constraint>

  <login-config>
    <auth-method>BASIC</auth-method>
    <realm-name>Chapter 16 Realm</realm-name>
  </login-config>

</web-app>
```

Browse to the showDate.jsp page. Note that index.html does not have header and footer elements added to the page.

Exercise 2

The goal of exercise 2 is to use pages with an html extension as JSP pages and add some dynamic content to the current index.html. For this exercise, implement a counter that increases each time the index.html page is viewed since the Web application has been started.

Edit the web.xml file to include the jsp-property-group:

```
<?xml version="1.0" encoding="ISO-8859-1"?>

<web-app version="2.4" uri="http://java.sun.com/xml/ns/j2ee" >
```

```xml
    <jsp-config>
      <jsp-property-group>
        <url-pattern>*.jsp</url-pattern>
        <include-prelude>/header.htmlf</include-prelude>
        <include-coda>/footer.htmlf</include-coda>
      </jsp-property-group>

      <jsp-property-group>
        <url-pattern>*.html</url-pattern>
      </jsp-property-group>
    </jsp-config>

    <security-role>
      <role-name>chapter16role</role-name>
    </security-role>

    <security-constraint>
      <web-resource-collection>
        <url-pattern>/showDate.jsp</url-pattern>
      </web-resource-collection>
      <auth-constraint>
        <role-name>chapter16role</role-name>
      </auth-constraint>
    </security-constraint>

    <login-config>
      <auth-method>BASIC</auth-method>
      <realm-name>Chapter 16 Realm</realm-name>
    </login-config>

  </web-app>
```

Edit `index.html` as follows:

```jsp
<%@ taglib prefix="c" uri="http://java.sun.com/jsp/jstl/core" %>
<c:set var="count" scope="application" value="${count + 1}" />
<html>
  <head>
    <title> Chapter 16 Exercises </title>
  </head>
  <body>
    <h1> Chapter 16 Exercises </h1>
    <ol>
        <li> Exercise 1 - Creating and deploying the simplest web application
        <li> Exercise 2 - <a href="showDate.jsp">Adding a JSP page</a>
        <li> Exercise 3 - Securing the JSP page
        <li> Exercise 4 - Adding headers and footers
        <li> Exercise 5 - Dynamic HTML pages
    </ol>
    <hr/>
    <center>
      Page Count:  <c:out value="${count}" />
    </center>
    <hr/>
  </body>
</html>
```

Exercise 3

The value of the page counter in exercise 2 will continue to be incremented until the Web application is restarted. Modify the Web application so the page counter is linked to each user session.

Edit index.html as follows:

```
<%@ taglib prefix="c" uri="http://java.sun.com/jsp/jstl/core" %>
<c:set var="count" scope="session" value="${count + 1}" />
<html>
  <head>
   <title> Chapter 16 Exercises </title>
  </head>
  <body>
  <h1> Chapter 16 Exercises </h1>
    <ol>
      <li> Exercise 1 - Creating and deploying the simplest web application
      <li> Exercise 2 - <a href="showDate.jsp">Adding a JSP page</a>
      <li> Exercise 3 - Securing the JSP page
      <li> Exercise 4 - Adding headers and footers
      <li> Exercise 5 - Dynamic HTML pages
    </ol>
    <hr/>
    <center>
      Page Count:  <c:out value="${count}" />
    </center>
    <hr/>
  </body>
</html>
```

Chapter 17 Exercises

Exercise 1

Following is the addition to displayCustomer.jsp:

```
<%@ taglib prefix="c" uri="http://java.sun.com/jsp/jstl/core" %>

<c:set var="customer" value="${requestScope.customer}"/>
<html>
<head>
    <title>Display Customer</title>
</head>
<body>

<table cellspacing="3" cellpadding="3" border="1" width="60%">
<tr>
    <td colspan="2"><b>Customer:</b>
     ${customer.firstName}    ${customer.lastName}
```

```
            </td>
        </tr>
        <tr>
            <td><b>Id</b></td>
            <td>${customer.id}</td>
        </tr>
        <tr>
            <td><b>First Name</b></td>
            <td>${customer.firstName}</td>
        </tr>
        <tr>
            <td><b>Last Name</b></td>
            <td>${customer.lastName}</td>
        </tr>
        <tr>
            <td><b>Address</b></td>
            <td>${customer.address}"</td>
        </tr>
        <tr>
            <td colspan="2">
                <a href="controller?action=editcustomer&id=${customer.id}">
                Edit This Customer
                </a>
            </td>
        </tr>
    </table>
    </body>
    </html>
```

Here is the addition to the SimpleController servlet:

```
else if ("displaycustomer".equals(action))
{
        String id = request.getParameter("id");
        CustomerManager manager = new CustomerManager();
        Customer customer = manager.getCustomer(id);
        request.setAttribute("customer", customer);

        jspPage = "/displayCustomer.jsp";
}
else if ("editcustomer".equals(action))
{
        String id = request.getParameter("id");
        CustomerManager manager = new CustomerManager();
        Customer customer = manager.getCustomer(id);
        request.setAttribute("customer", customer);

        jspPage = "/editCustomer.jsp";
}

dispatch(jspPage, request, response);
}
```

Following is the new JSP page, editCustomer.jsp:

```
<%@ taglib prefix="c" uri="http://java.sun.com/jsp/jstl/core" %>

<c:set var="customer" value="${requestScope.customer}"/>
<html>
<head>
    <title>Edit Customer</title>
</head>
<body>
<form action="controller?action=editcustomerexe">
<table cellspacing="3" cellpadding="3" border="1" width="60%">
<input type="hidden" name="id" value="${customer.id}">
<tr>
    <td><b>First Name:</b>
  <td><input type="text" name="firstname" value="${customer.firstName}"></td>
</tr>
<tr>
    <td><b>Last Name:</b>
  <td><input type="text" name="lastname" value="${customer.lastName}"></td>
</tr>
<tr>
    <td><b>Address:</b>
  <td><input type="text" size="50" name="lastname"
            value="${customer.address}"></td>
</tr>
<tr>
    <td colspan="2"><input type="submit" value="edit customer"></td>
</tr>
</table>
</form>
</body>
</html>
```

Chapter 18 Exercises

Exercise 1

Following are the additions to /WEB-INF/spring-servlet.xml:

```
<?xml version="1.0" encoding="UTF-8"?>
<!DOCTYPE beans PUBLIC "-//SPRING//DTD BEAN//EN"
"http://www.springframework.org/dtd/spring-beans.dtd">

<beans>
  <bean id="testFormValidator"
        class="com.wrox.begjsp.ch18.spring.TestFormValidator"/>

  <bean id="testFormController"
        class="com.wrox.begjsp.ch18.spring.TestFormController">
    <property name="sessionForm"><value>false</value></property>
```

```xml
      <property name="validateOnBinding"><value>true</value></property>
      <property name="bindOnNewForm"><value>false</value></property>
      <property name="commandName"><value>testForm</value></property>
      <property name="commandClass">
        <value>com.wrox.begjsp.ch18.spring.TestForm</value>
      </property>
      <property name="validator"><ref bean="testFormValidator"/></property>
      <property name="formView"><value>form</value></property>
    </bean>

    <bean id="testDataListController"
          class="com.wrox.begjsp.ch18.spring.TestDataListController"/>

    <bean id="messageSource"
          class="org.springframework.context.support.ResourceBundleMessageSource">
      <property name="basename"><value>messages</value></property>
    </bean>

    <bean id="urlMapping"
          class="org.springframework.web.servlet.handler.SimpleUrlHandlerMapping">
      <property name="mappings">
        <props>
          <prop key="/form.htm">testFormController</prop>
          <prop key="/data.htm">testDataListController</prop>
        </props>
      </property>
    </bean>

    <bean id="viewResolver"
          class="org.springframework.web.servlet.view.ResourceBundleViewResolver">
      <property name="basename"><value>views</value></property>
    </bean>
</beans>
```

Make sure that the TestForm object implements Serializable. Change the TestForm class to appear as follows:

```java
public class TestForm implements Serializable
{
...
```

Here are the modifications to TestFormController.java:

```java
package com.wrox.begjsp.ch18.spring;

import org.springframework.validation.BindException;

import org.springframework.web.servlet.ModelAndView;
import org.springframework.web.servlet.mvc.SimpleFormController;

import java.util.ArrayList;
import java.util.HashMap;
import java.util.List;
import java.util.Map;
```

```java
import javax.servlet.ServletException;
import javax.servlet.http.HttpServletRequest;
import javax.servlet.http.HttpSession;


public class TestFormController extends SimpleFormController
{
    public ModelAndView onSubmit(Object object)
    {
        TestForm form = (TestForm) object;
        Map items = new HashMap();
        items.put("testForm", form);

        return new ModelAndView("success", items);
    }

    protected Map referenceData(HttpServletRequest request)
                        throws ServletException
    {
        Map refData = new HashMap();
        List ages = new ArrayList();

        for (int i = 0; i <= 100; i++)
        {
            ages.add(new Integer(i));
        }

        refData.put("ages", ages);

        return refData;
    }


    protected void onBindAndValidate(HttpServletRequest request, Object object,
                                BindException errors)
                        throws Exception
    {
        if (!errors.hasErrors())
        {
            TestForm form = (TestForm) object;
            HttpSession session = request.getSession(true);
            List formList = (List) session.getAttribute("dataList");

            if (formList == null)
            {
                formList = new ArrayList();
            }

            formList.add(form);
            session.setAttribute("dataList", formList);
        }
    }
}
```

The new Controller class (`TestDataListController.java`) is as follows:

```java
package com.wrox.begjsp.ch18.spring;

import org.springframework.web.servlet.ModelAndView;
import org.springframework.web.servlet.mvc.Controller;

import java.util.ArrayList;
import java.util.List;

import javax.servlet.http.HttpServletRequest;
import javax.servlet.http.HttpServletResponse;
import javax.servlet.http.HttpSession;


public class TestDataListController implements Controller
{
    public ModelAndView handleRequest(HttpServletRequest request,
                                      HttpServletResponse response)
                          throws Exception
    {
        HttpSession session = request.getSession(true);
        List data = (List) session.getAttribute("dataList");

        if (data == null)
        {
            data = new ArrayList();
        }

        request.setAttribute("dataList", data);

        return new ModelAndView("datalist");
    }
}
```

Following is the addition to `views.properties`:

```
form.class=org.springframework.web.servlet.view.JstlView
form.url=/WEB-INF/jsp/form.jsp

success.class=org.springframework.web.servlet.view.JstlView
success.url=/WEB-INF/jsp/success.jsp

datalist.class=org.springframework.web.servlet.view.JstlView
datalist.url=/WEB-INF/jsp/data.jsp
```

The new view (`/WEB-INF/jsp/data.jsp`) is as follows:

```jsp
<%@ taglib prefix="fmt" uri="http://java.sun.com/jsp/jstl/fmt" %>
<%@ taglib prefix="c" uri="http://java.sun.com/jsp/jstl/core" %>

<html>
<head>
```

```
    <title><fmt:message key="datalist.title"/></title>
</head>
<body>

<h1><fmt:message key="datalist.title"/></h1>

<a href="form.htm">Back to Form</a>
<p>

<table cellspacing="0" cellpadding="0" border="1" width="60%">
<tr>
  <td></td>
  <td><b><fmt:message key="datalist.colheading.name"/></b></td>
  <td><b><fmt:message key="datalist.colheading.age"/></b></td>
  <td><b><fmt:message key="datalist.colheading.comments"/></b></td>
</tr>
<c:forEach items="${requestScope.dataList}" var="thisElement" varStatus="status">
  <tr>
    <td>${status.count}</td>
    <td>${thisElement.name}</td>
    <td>${thisElement.age}</td>
    <td>${thisElement.comments}</td>
  </tr>
</c:forEach>
</table>
</body>
</html>
```

Following are the additions to `messages.properties`:

```
form.title=Test Form

form.error.heading=Please fix all the errors!
form.error.name.missing=The name field is missing
form.error.comments.missing=The comments field is missing
form.error.age.value=Age cannot be less than 18
form.error.novalue=Value required

form.name.title=Name
form.comments.title=Comments
form.age.title=Age

success.title=Success Page
```

```
datalist.title = Data
datalist.colheading.name = Name
datalist.colheading.age = Age
datalist.colheading.comments = Comments
```

Additions to `messages_fr.properties` are as follows:

```
form.title=Examinez La Forme

form.error.heading=Veuillez fixer toutes les erreurs!
form.error.name.missing=La zone d'identification est absente
```

```
form.error.comments.missing=Le champ de commentaires est absent
form.error.age.value=Le champ d'âge ne peut pas être moins de 18
form.error.novalue=La valeur a exigé

form.name.title=Nom
form.comments.title=Commentaires
form.age.title=Âge

success.title=Page De Succès

datalist.title = Données
datalist.colheading.name = Nom
datalist.colheading.age = Âge
datalist.colheading.comments = Commentaires
```

Chapter 19 Exercises

Exercise 1

The following code shows the new field added to the testForm definition in struts-config.xml, with changes highlighted:

```
...
<form-bean        name="testForm"
                  type="org.apache.struts.validator.DynaValidatorForm">
  <form-property name="name" type="java.lang.String"/>
  <form-property name="emailAddress" type="java.lang.String"/>
  <form-property name="age" type="java.lang.String"/>
  <form-property name="favSport" type="java.lang.String"/>
  <form-property name="comments" type="java.lang.String"/>
</form-bean>
...
```

This code shows the new field added to form.jsp, with changes highlighted:

```
...
<logic:messagesPresent property="emailAddress">
<tr>
      <td colspan=2><html:errors property="emailAddress"/></td>
</tr>
</logic:messagesPresent>
<tr>
    <td><bean:message key="form.emailaddress.title"/></td>
    <td><html:text altKey="form.emailaddress.title" property="emailAddress"
                  size="30"/></td>
</tr>
<logic:messagesPresent property="age">
<tr>
      <td colspan=2><html:errors property="age"/></td>
</tr>
</logic:messagesPresent>
<tr>
```

```
        <td><bean:message key="form.age.title"/></td>
        <td><html:text altKey="form.age.title" property="age" size="30"/></td>
    </tr>
    ...
```

The following code shows the validation added to validation.xml for the new field, with changes highlighted:

```
...
<field property="emailAddress" depends="required,email">
  <msg name="required" key="form.error.emailaddress.missing"/>
  <msg name="email" key="form.error.emailaddress.invalid"/>
</field>
<field property="age" depends="required,integer,intRange">
  <msg name="required" key="form.error.age.missing"/>
  <msg name="intRange" key="form.error.age.range"/>
  <msg name="integer" key="form.error.age.invalid"/>
  <arg0 name="intRange" key="${var:min}" resource="false"/>
  <arg1 name="intRange" key="${var:max}" resource="false"/>
  <var>
      <var-name>min</var-name>
      <var-value>0</var-value>
  </var>
  <var>
      <var-name>max</var-name>
      <var-value>100</var-value>
  </var>
</field>
...
```

Here are the new properties added to messages.properties:

```
...
form.error.age.missing=You must enter your age
form.error.age.range=Age can must be a number between {0} and {1}
form.error.age.invalid=Age must be a number
form.age.title=Age
...
```

Exercise 2

Following is the new class for LoginAction:

```
package com.wrox.begjsp.ch19.struts;

import org.apache.struts.action.Action;
import org.apache.struts.action.ActionForm;
import org.apache.struts.action.ActionForward;
import org.apache.struts.action.ActionMapping;

import javax.servlet.http.HttpServletRequest;
import javax.servlet.http.HttpServletResponse;
```

```
public class LoginAction extends Action
{
    public ActionForward execute(ActionMapping mapping, ActionForm form,
        HttpServletRequest request, HttpServletResponse response)
        throws Exception
    {
        return mapping.findForward("success");
    }
}
```

This code shows the new class for `LoginExeAction`:

```
package com.wrox.begjsp.ch19.struts;

import org.apache.struts.action.Action;
import org.apache.struts.action.ActionForm;
import org.apache.struts.action.ActionForward;
import org.apache.struts.action.ActionMapping;
import org.apache.struts.action.DynaActionForm;

import javax.servlet.http.HttpServletRequest;
import javax.servlet.http.HttpServletResponse;
import javax.servlet.http.HttpSession;


public class LoginExeAction extends Action
{
    public ActionForward execute(ActionMapping mapping, ActionForm form,
        HttpServletRequest request, HttpServletResponse response)
        throws Exception
    {
        HttpSession session = request.getSession();

        if (authenticated(form))
        {
            session.setAttribute("loginKey", "admin");

            return mapping.findForward("success");
        }

        return mapping.findForward("failure");
    }

    private boolean authenticated(ActionForm form)
    {
        DynaActionForm loginForm = (DynaActionForm) form;
        String userName = (String) loginForm.get("username");
        String password = (String) loginForm.get("password");

        if ("admin".equals(userName) && "password".equals(password))
        {
            return true;
        }
```

```
            return false;
    }
}
```

The changes to `FormAction` are highlighted here:

```java
package com.wrox.begjsp.ch19.struts;

import org.apache.struts.action.Action;
import org.apache.struts.action.ActionForm;
import org.apache.struts.action.ActionForward;
import org.apache.struts.action.ActionMapping;
import org.apache.struts.util.LabelValueBean;

import java.util.ArrayList;
import java.util.List;

import javax.servlet.http.HttpServletRequest;
import javax.servlet.http.HttpServletResponse;
import javax.servlet.http.HttpSession;


public class FormAction extends Action
{
    public ActionForward execute(ActionMapping mapping, ActionForm form,
        HttpServletRequest request, HttpServletResponse response)
        throws Exception
    {
        HttpSession session = request.getSession();
        String loginValue = (String) session.getAttribute("loginKey");

        if ((loginValue == null) || !loginValue.equals("admin"))
        {
            return mapping.findForward("forcedout");
        }

        request.setAttribute("sports", getSports());

        return mapping.findForward("success");
    }
    ...

}
```

The changes to `TestAction` are highlighted here:

```java
package com.wrox.begjsp.ch19.struts;

import org.apache.struts.action.Action;
import org.apache.struts.action.ActionForm;
import org.apache.struts.action.ActionForward;
import org.apache.struts.action.ActionMapping;
```

```
import javax.servlet.http.HttpServletRequest;
import javax.servlet.http.HttpServletResponse;
import javax.servlet.http.HttpSession;


public class TestAction extends Action
{
    public ActionForward execute(ActionMapping mapping, ActionForm form,
        HttpServletRequest request, HttpServletResponse response)
        throws Exception
    {
        HttpSession session = request.getSession();
        String loginValue = (String) session.getAttribute("loginKey");

        if ((loginValue == null) || !loginValue.equals("admin"))
        {
            return mapping.findForward("forcedout");
        }

        return mapping.findForward("success");
    }
}
```

Following are the highlighted changes to index.jsp:

```
<%@ taglib uri="/WEB-INF/struts-logic.tld" prefix="logic" %>
<logic:redirect page="/login.do"/>
```

Here is the code showing the new form-bean entry for loginForm in the struts-config.xml file:

```
...
<form-bean       name="loginForm"
                 type="org.apache.struts.validator.DynaValidatorForm">
  <form-property name="username" type="java.lang.String"/>
  <form-property name="password" type="java.lang.String"/>
</form-bean>
...
```

The new global-forward entry in the struts-config.xml file is as follows:

```
...
<global-forwards>
    <forward name="forcedout" path="/login.do"/>
</global-forwards>
...
```

Here are the new action-mapping entries in struts-config.xml for login and loginExe:

```
...
<action path="/login"
        type="com.wrox.begjsp.ch19.struts.LoginAction"
        scope="request">
        <forward name="success" path="/login.jsp"/>
</action>
```

```
<action path="/loginExe"
        type="com.wrox.begjsp.ch19.struts.LoginExeAction"
        scope="request"
        name="loginForm"
        input="/login.do">
        <forward name="success" path="/form.do"/>
        <forward name="failure" path="/login.jsp"/>
</action>
...
```

Chapter 20 Exercises

Exercise 1

New definitions for grandparent, child, and grandchild in the `tiles-defs.xml` file are as follows:

```
<definition name="grandparent" path="/layout/inheritance.jsp">
  <put name="title" value="Grandparent Page"/>
  <put name="body" value="/tiles/grandparentbody.jsp"/>
</definition>

<definition name="child" extends="grandparent">
  <put name="title" value="Child Page"/>
</definition>

<definition name="grandchild" extends="child">
    <put name="title" value="Grandchild Page"/>
    <put name="body" value="/tiles/grandchildbody.jsp"/>
</definition>
```

Here is the new layout JSP page, `inheritance.jsp`:

```
<%@ taglib uri="/WEB-INF/struts-tiles.tld" prefix="tiles" %>
<%@ taglib uri="http://java.sun.com/jsp/jstl/core" prefix="c"%>

<html>
  <head>
    <title>Inheritance Example</title>
  </head>
<body bgcolor="white">

<table border="1" width="100%" height="100%" border="1">
<tr>
  <td height="100" bgcolor="gray">
        <tiles:getAsString name="title"/>
  </td>
</tr>
<tr>
  <td valign="top"  align="left">
        <tiles:insert attribute="body"/>
```

```
      </td>
    </tr>
  </table>
  </body>
  </html>
```

Following are new tiles for grandparentbody.jsp and grandchildbody.jsp. There is no childbody.jsp, as the body value is inherited from the grandparent definition:

grandparentbody.jsp:

```
<p>
<center><h5>grand parent body page</h5></center>
```

grandchildbody.jsp:

```
<p>
<center><h5>grand child body page</h5></center>
```

Exercise 2

The solution lies in the creation of a tiles-defs.xml file for each locale that the application will support. For instance, in the example solution, the following locales have been provided:

- ❑ Default: tiles-defs.xml
- ❑ Spanish [es]: tiles-defs_es.xml
- ❑ French [fr]: tiles-defs_fr.xml
- ❑ Italian [it]: tiles-defs_it.xml

All these files are placed within the /WEB-INF/ directory of the Web application and configured in the Struts configuration file with the following plug-in:

```
<plug-in className="org.apache.struts.tiles.TilesPlugin" >
  <set-property property="definitions-config" value="/WEB-INF/tiles-defs.xml" />
  <set-property property="definitions-debug" value="2" />
  <set-property property="definitions-parser-details" value="2" />
  <set-property property="definitions-parser-validate" value="true" />
</plug-in>
```

There is no specific reference to the locale-based configuration files. The value for the definitions-config property determines the naming pattern for the international versions — for example, *_<locale>.xml. If the locale of the user is not supported, the default configuration file is used.

The locale of the user is passed in the request object (specified by the browser setting) to the Struts application and interpreted by the framework to provide the appropriate configuration file.

Each configuration file will then define the definitions in their own particular way. For instance, the default definition is as follows:

```
    <definition name="homepage" path="/layout/homepage.jsp">
        <put name="header" value="/tiles/header.jsp" />
        <put name="footer" value="/tiles/footer.jsp" />
        <put name="body" value="/tiles/body.jsp"/>
        <put name="menu" value="/tiles/menu.jsp"/>
    </definition>
```

This resides in the `tiles-defs.xml` file. The French version is as follows:

```
    <definition name="homepage" path="/layout/homepage.jsp">
        <put name="header" value="/tiles/fr/header.jsp" />
        <put name="footer" value="/tiles/fr/footer.jsp" />
        <put name="body" value="/tiles/fr/body.jsp"/>
        <put name="menu" value="/tiles/fr/menu.jsp"/>
    </definition>
```

It resides in the `tiles-defs_fr.xml` file. Note that the name of the definition is the same as the default version. This is important, as the Struts action configuration will reference this name as its action forward. In order to provide different content based on locale, the `header.jsp`, `footer.jsp`, `body.jsp`, and `menu.jsp` JSP pages for French visitors are in the `/tiles/fr/` directory.

The Struts configuration for the action to be invoked is as follows:

```
<action-mappings>
  <action path="/page"
          type="com.wrox.begjsp.ch20.exercises.InternationalAction"
          scope="request">
    <forward name="success" path="homepage"/>
  </action>
</action-mappings>
```

The `InternationalAction` class is very simple; it actually does nothing specific for the locale:

```
package com.wrox.begjsp.ch20.exercises;

import javax.servlet.http.HttpServletRequest;
import javax.servlet.http.HttpServletResponse;

import org.apache.struts.action.Action;
import org.apache.struts.action.ActionForm;
import org.apache.struts.action.ActionForward;
import org.apache.struts.action.ActionMapping;

public class InternationalAction extends Action
{
    public ActionForward execute(ActionMapping mapping,
                                 ActionForm form,
                                 HttpServletRequest request,
                                 HttpServletResponse response)
        throws Exception
    {
        return mapping.findForward("success");
    }
}
```

In order to actually select a locale — for example, if a user elects to see the Web page in a language other than their default value — the new locale value can be set with

```
setLocale(request, new Locale("fr"));
```

inside the `execute` method of the action. This code would force the French version to be displayed, regardless of the default value.

If you want to try out the solution in your own environment, and can't afford the ticket to Paris to use a French browser, then simply follow these steps for setting the default language in Microsoft Internet Explorer 6.0:

1. Select Tools from the menu.

2. Select Internet Options.

3. Click the Languages button.

4. Click the Add button.

5. Select the desired locale and then click OK.

6. Ensure that the locale you selected now appears at the top of the Locale list. If it isn't, select it and then click the Move Up button on the right-hand side until it is.

7. Click OK on all the open windows.

8. Close your browser.

9. Visit the page in a new browser window.

Chapter 21 Exercises

Exercise 1

Starting with the Hello example, there are three steps to this solution:

1. You create a class that implements the `javax.faces.converter.Converter` interface.

2. You register the class in `faces.xml`.

3. You change `hello.jsp` to use the converter.

An example of an appropriate converter class is shown in the class `TitleConverter`, which follows:

```
package com.wrox.jsp.solutions;
import javax.faces.application.FacesMessage;
import javax.faces.component.UIComponent;
import javax.faces.context.FacesContext;
import javax.faces.convert.Converter;
import javax.faces.convert.ConverterException;

public class TitleConverter implements Converter
{
```

```
        public TitleConverter()
        {
        }

        public Object getAsObject(FacesContext facesContext,
            UIComponent uIComponent, String str)
        {
            return titleCase(str);
        }

        public String getAsString(FacesContext facesContext,
            UIComponent uIComponent, Object obj)
        {
            return titleCase(obj.toString());
        }

        private String titleCase(String s)
        {
            if( s == null || "".equals(s))
            {
                return s;
            }

            StringBuffer sb = new StringBuffer(s.length());
            boolean isSpace = true;
            for( int i = 0; i < s.length();i++)
            {
                char c = s.charAt(i);
                if(Character.isSpaceChar(c))
                {
                    isSpace = true;
                }
                else
                {
                    if((isSpace && Character.isLowerCase(c)))
                    {
                        c = (Character.toUpperCase(c));
                    }
                    isSpace = false;
                }
                sb.append( c );
            }
            return sb.toString();
        }

    }
```

To register this class as a converter, add the following four lines to `faces-config.xml` immediately after the `<managed-bean>` closing tag:

```
<converter>
    <converter-id>TitleConverter</converter-id>
    <converter-class>com.wrox.jsp.solutions.TitleConverter</converter-class>
</converter>
```

Finally, modify the line in `hello.jsp` that reads

```
<h:inputText id="name" value="#{HelloBean.name}"/>
```

so that it reads

```
<h:inputText id="name" value="#{HelloBean.name}" converter="TitleConverter"/>
```

Exercise 2

The chapter demonstrates adding a value change listener on the `amount` field. This time, you want to add the listener to the payment field. To do this, you need to simply insert the following tag into the `<h:inputText>` tag for the payment field in `calc.jsp`:

```
<f:valueChangeListener type="com.wrox.jsp.LogChange" />
```

This changes the code from

```
<h:inputText id="payment" value="#{LoanBean.payment}">
    <f:convertNumber type="number" pattern="#,##0.00"/>
</h:inputText>
```

to

```
<h:inputText id="payment" value="#{LoanBean.payment}">
    <f:convertNumber type="number" pattern="#,##0.00"/>
    <f:valueChangeListener type="com.wrox.jsp.LogChange" />
</h:inputText>
```

Exercise 3

The text within the chapter demonstrates how to use an `ActionListener` to log an event when the Amount button is selected. To add the event to the Payment button, the simplest solution is to change the `<h:commandButton>` tag for the Payment button from

```
<h:commandButton
    action="#{LoanBean.payment}" value="Payment" id="PaymentId" />
```

to

```
<h:commandButton
    action="#{LoanBean.payment}" value="Payment" id="PaymentId" >
    <f:actionListener type="com.wrox.jsp.LogAction" />
</h:commandButton>
```

Chapter 22 Exercises

Exercise 1

The goal of this exercise is to list all the objects available to the application in the JNDI service:

```
<!--
<%@ taglib prefix="c" uri="http://java.sun.com/jsp/jstl/core" %>
<%@ taglib prefix="fn" uri="http://java.sun.com/jsp/jstl/functions" %>
-->

<jsp:useBean id="namespace"
class="com.wrox.begjsp.ch22.example1.JNDINamespaceHelper" />
<c:set var="title" value="Listing the JNDI Namespace" />

<html>
  <head>
    <title> <c:out value="${title}" /></title>
  </head>
  <body>
    <h1><c:out value="${title}" /></h1>
    <table border="1" width="90%">
      <tr>
        <th>Context</th>
        <th>Object Name</th>
        <th>Object Class</th>
        <th width="50%">Object Value</th>
      </tr>
      <c:forEach items="${namespace.namespace}" var="element" >
        <tr>
          <td> <c:out value="${element.contextName}" /></td>
          <td> <c:out value="${element.name}" /></td>
          <td> <c:out value="${element.className}" /></td>
          <td> <c:out value="${fn:replace(element.object, ',', ', ')}" /></td>
        </tr>
      </c:forEach>
    </table>
  </body>
</html>

package com.wrox.begjsp.ch22.example1;

import java.util.ArrayList;
import java.util.List;

import javax.naming.Binding;
import javax.naming.Context;
import javax.naming.InitialContext;
import javax.naming.NamingEnumeration;
import javax.naming.NamingException;

public class JNDINamespaceHelper
{
```

```java
    public List getNamespace() throws NamingException
    {
        Context context = new InitialContext();
        return getNamespaceElements(context, "java:comp/env");
    }

    private List getNamespaceElements(Context context, String contextName)
    throws NamingException
    {
        Context newContext = (Context)context.lookup(contextName);
        NamingEnumeration enum = newContext.listBindings("");
        List results = new ArrayList();
        while (enum.hasMore())
        {
            Binding binding = (Binding)enum.next();
            if ((binding.getObject() instanceof Context))
            {
                String subContextName = binding.getName();
                List subContextElements = getNamespaceElements(context,
                                        contextName + "/" + subContextName);
                results.addAll(subContextElements);
            }
            else
            {
                JNDIElement element = new JNDIElement(contextName, binding);
                results.add(element);
            }
        }
        return results;
    }

}

package com.wrox.begjsp.ch22.example1;

import javax.naming.Binding;

public class JNDIElement
{
    private String  _contextName;
    private Binding _binding;

    public JNDIElement(String contextName, Binding binding)
    {
        _contextName = contextName;
        _binding = binding;
    }

    public String getClassName()
    {
        return _binding.getClassName();
    }

    public Object getObject()
```

```
        {
            return _binding.getObject();
        }

        public String getContextName()
        {
            return _contextName;
        }

        public String getName()
        {
            return _binding.getName();
        }
}
```

Exercise 2

The goal of this exercise is to create a Web application that will enable the sending of an e-mail using the JavaMail J2EE component. The Web application should collect the To, Subject, and Body elements for the mail message:

```
<!--
<%@ taglib prefix="c" uri="http://java.sun.com/jsp/jstl/core" %>
<%@ taglib prefix="sql" uri="http://java.sun.com/jsp/jstl/sql" %>
-->
<jsp:useBean id="SERVLET_PATH" class="java.lang.String" scope="request" />
<jsp:useBean id="ERROR_MESSAGE" class="java.lang.String" scope="request" />
<jsp:useBean id="SENT_MESSAGE" class="java.lang.String" scope="request" />
<c:set value="Send an Email" var="title" />
<html>
  <head>
    <title><c:out value="${title}" /></title>
  </head>
  <body>
  <h1><c:out value="${title}" /></h1>
  <c:if test='${!empty ERROR_MESSAGE}' >
    <h4> <font color="red">${ERROR_MESSAGE}</font> </h4>
  </c:if>
  <c:if test='${!empty SENT_MESSAGE}' >
    <h4> <font color="green">${SENT_MESSAGE}</font> </h4>
  </c:if>
  <table border="1">
    <form name="email-input" action="${SERVLET_PATH}" method="POST">
      <input type="hidden" name="ACTION" value="MAIL_SEND" />
      <tr><td><b>To</b></td><td><input name="email_to" type="text" size="40"
/></td></tr>
      <tr><td><b>Subject</b></td><td><input name="email_subject" type="text"
size="80" /></td></tr>
      <tr><td><b>Message</b></td><td><textarea name="email_message" cols="60"
rows="10" ></textarea></td></tr>
      <tr><td colspan="2" align="center" ><input name="SEND" type="submit"
value="Send Email" /></td></tr>
    </form>
```

```
    </table>
    <p/>
</html>

package com.wrox.begjsp.ch22.example2;

import java.io.IOException;
import java.util.Properties;

import javax.mail.Message;
import javax.mail.MessagingException;
import javax.mail.Session;
import javax.mail.Transport;
import javax.mail.internet.AddressException;
import javax.mail.internet.InternetAddress;
import javax.mail.internet.MimeMessage;
import javax.servlet.RequestDispatcher;
import javax.servlet.ServletException;
import javax.servlet.http.HttpServlet;
import javax.servlet.http.HttpServletRequest;
import javax.servlet.http.HttpServletResponse;

public class MailServlet extends HttpServlet
{
    private static final String DEFAULT_PAGE    = "example2/mail.jsp";

    private static final String ACTION_TOKEN    = "ACTION";

    private static final Object SMTP_HOST = "localhost";
    private static final String SMTP_FROM = "example2-chapter22-begjsp@wrox.com";

    public void doGet(HttpServletRequest request, HttpServletResponse response)
            throws ServletException, IOException
    {
        doPost(request, response);
    }

    public void doPost(HttpServletRequest request, HttpServletResponse response)
            throws ServletException, IOException
    {
        String action = findAction(request);

        if (action != null)
        {
            String toAddress = request.getParameter("email_to");
            String subject = request.getParameter("email_subject");
            String emailMessage = request.getParameter("email_message");

            boolean messageSent = false;
            if (isValidString(toAddress))
            {
                messageSent = sendEmail(toAddress, subject, emailMessage);
                if (!messageSent)
                {
```

```
                    request.setAttribute("ERROR_MESSAGE",
                        "Unable to send message : check logs for error messages");
            }
            else
            {
                request.setAttribute("SENT_MESSAGE",
                    "Message sent to : "+toAddress);
            }
        }
        else
        {
            request.setAttribute("ERROR_MESSAGE",
                "An email address is mandatory");
        }
    }
    performRedirect(DEFAULT_PAGE, request, response);
}

private boolean sendEmail(String toAddress, String subject,
                          String emailMessage)
{
    Properties props = new Properties();
    props.put("smtp.host", SMTP_HOST);
    Session session = Session.getDefaultInstance(props, null);

    Message message = new MimeMessage(session);

    InternetAddress inetToAddress = null;
    InternetAddress inetFromAddress = null;
    try
    {
        inetToAddress = new InternetAddress(toAddress);
        inetFromAddress = new InternetAddress(SMTP_FROM);
    }
    catch (AddressException addressError)
    {
        log("Cannot create email addresses : "+ addressError);
        return false;
    }

    try
    {
        message.addRecipients(Message.RecipientType.TO,
                new InternetAddress[] { inetToAddress });
        message.setFrom(inetFromAddress);
        message.setSubject(subject);
        message.setContent(emailMessage, "text/plain");
    }
    catch (MessagingException headerError)
    {
        log("Cannot construct email message : "+ headerError);
        return false;
    }
```

```
        try
        {
            Transport.send(message);
        }
        catch (MessagingException sendError)
        {
            log("Cannot send email message : "+ sendError);
            return false;
        }

        return true;
    }

    private boolean isValidString(String paramString)
    {
        return (paramString != null && (paramString.length() > 0));
    }

    private String findAction(HttpServletRequest request)
    {
        return request.getParameter(ACTION_TOKEN);
    }

    private void performRedirect(String path, HttpServletRequest request,
            HttpServletResponse response) throws ServletException, IOException
    {
        if (path != null)
        {
            request.setAttribute("SERVLET_PATH", request.getContextPath()
                    + request.getServletPath());
            RequestDispatcher dispatch = request.getRequestDispatcher(path);
            dispatch.forward(request, response);
        }
    }
}
```

Chapter 24 Exercises

Exercise 1

Confirm that the following exists in Tomcat users.xml:

```
<role rolename="manager" />
<user username="manager" password="manager" roles="manager" />
```

Modify web.xml as follows:

```
<?xml version="1.0" encoding="ISO-8859-1"?>

<web-app version="2.4" uri="http://java.sun.com/xml/ns/j2ee" >
```

```xml
<security-constraint>
  <web-resource-collection>
    <web-resource-name>Everything Private</web-resource-name>
    <url-pattern>/private/*</url-pattern>
  </web-resource-collection>
  <http-method>GET</http-method>
  <http-method>POST</http-method>
  <user-data-constraint>
    <transport-guarantee>CONFIDENTIAL</transport-guarantee>
  </user-data-constraint>

  <auth-constraint>
    <role-name>chapter24</role-name>
  </auth-constraint>
</security-constraint>

<security-constraint>
  <web-resource-collection>
    <web-resource-name>Roster</web-resource-name>
    <url-pattern>/roster/*</url-pattern>
  </web-resource-collection>
  <http-method>GET</http-method>
  <http-method>POST</http-method>
  <user-data-constraint>
    <transport-guarantee>CONFIDENTIAL</transport-guarantee>
  </user-data-constraint>

  <auth-constraint>
    <role-name>staff</role-name>
    <role-name>manager</role-name>
  </auth-constraint>
</security-constraint>

<filter>
  <filter-name>SecurityFilter</filter-name>
  <filter-class>com.wrox.begjsp.ch24.roster.SecurityFilter</filter-class>
</filter>

<filter-mapping>
  <filter-name>SecurityFilter</filter-name>
  <url-pattern>/roster/*</url-pattern>
</filter-mapping>

<login-config>
  <auth-method>FORM</auth-method>
  <form-login-config>
    <form-login-page>/login.html</form-login-page>
    <form-error-page>/login-error.html</form-error-page>
  </form-login-config>
</login-config>

<security-role>
  <role-name>chapter24</role-name>
  <role-name>staff</role-name>
```

```
    <role-name>manager</role-name>
  </security-role>

</web-app>
```

Modify `staff-roster.jsp` as follows:

```
<!--
<%@ taglib prefix="c" uri="http://java.sun.com/jsp/jstl/core" %>
-->
<c:set value="Staff Roster" var="title" />
<html>
  <head>
    <title>
      <c:out value="${title}" />
    </title>
  </head>
  <body>
    <h1>
      <c:out value="${title}" />
    </h1>
    <c:set var="user" value="${pageContext.request.remoteUser}" />
    <c:set var="workDay" value="${staffRoster[user]}" />
    Welcome  <b>${user}</b> <p/>
    <c:choose>
      <c:when test="${isAdmin}">
        <table border="1">
          <tr><th>Staff Member</th><th>Rostered Day</th></tr>
          <c:forEach items="${staffRoster}" var="staff" >
            <tr><td>${staff.key}</td><td>${staff.value}</td></tr>
          </c:forEach>
        </table>
      </c:when>
      <c:otherwise>
        You are rostered to work on <b>${workDay}</b> <p/>
      </c:otherwise>
    </c:choose>
    <a href="../public/kill-session.jsp">Logout</a> <p/></body>
</html>
```

Modify `SecurityFilter.java` as follows:

```
package com.wrox.begjsp.ch24.roster;

import java.io.IOException;
import java.util.HashMap;
import java.util.Map;

import javax.servlet.Filter;
import javax.servlet.FilterChain;
import javax.servlet.FilterConfig;
import javax.servlet.ServletException;
import javax.servlet.ServletRequest;
```

```
import javax.servlet.ServletResponse;
import javax.servlet.http.HttpServletRequest;

public class SecurityFilter implements Filter
{
    private Map _roster = new HashMap();

    public void init(FilterConfig config)
    {
        _roster.put("staff1", "Monday");
        _roster.put("staff2", "Tuesday");
    }

    public void doFilter(ServletRequest request,
                         ServletResponse response,
                         FilterChain chain)
            throws IOException, ServletException
    {
        if (request instanceof HttpServletRequest)
        {
            HttpServletRequest httpRequest = (HttpServletRequest)request;

            httpRequest.setAttribute("staffRoster", _roster);

            boolean isAdmin = httpRequest.isUserInRole("manager");
            httpRequest.setAttribute("isAdmin", Boolean.valueOf(isAdmin));
        }

        chain.doFilter(request, response);
    }

    public void destroy()
    {
        // do nothing
    }

}
```

Exercise 2

Modify staff-roster.jsp as follows:

```
<!--
<%@ taglib prefix="c" uri="http://java.sun.com/jsp/jstl/core" %>
-->
<c:set value="Staff Roster" var="title" />
  <html>
    <head>
      <title>
        <c:out value="${title}" />
      </title>
    </head>
    <body>
      <h1>
```

```
        <c:out value="${title}" />
    </h1>

    <c:set var="user" value="${pageContext.request.remoteUser}" />
    <c:set var="workDay" value="${staffRoster[user]}" />

    Welcome  <b>${user}</b> <p/>

    <c:choose>
      <c:when test="${isAdmin}">
        <table border="1">
          <tr><th>Staff Member</th><th>Rostered Day</th></tr>
          <c:forEach items="${staffRoster}" var="staff" >
            <tr><td>${staff.key}</td><td>${staff.value}</td></tr>
          </c:forEach>
        </table>
      </c:when>
      <c:otherwise>
        <c:choose>
          <c:when test="${isBusiness}">
            You are rostered to work on <b>${workDay}</b> <p/>
          </c:when>
          <c:otherwise>
            Outside business hours, please try again later
          </c:otherwise>
        </c:choose>
      </c:otherwise>
    </c:choose>

    <p/><a href="../public/kill-session.jsp">Logout</a> <p/>
  </body>
</html>
```

Modify SecurityFilter.java as follows:

```
package com.wrox.begjsp.ch24.roster;

import java.io.IOException;
import java.util.Calendar;
import java.util.HashMap;
import java.util.Map;

import javax.servlet.Filter;
import javax.servlet.FilterChain;
import javax.servlet.FilterConfig;
import javax.servlet.ServletException;
import javax.servlet.ServletRequest;
import javax.servlet.ServletResponse;
import javax.servlet.http.HttpServletRequest;

public class SecurityFilter implements Filter
{
    private Map _roster = new HashMap();
```

```
public void init(FilterConfig config)
{
    _roster.put("staff1", "Monday");
    _roster.put("staff2", "Tuesday");
}

public void doFilter(ServletRequest request,
                     ServletResponse response,
                     FilterChain chain)
    throws IOException, ServletException
{
    if (request instanceof HttpServletRequest)
    {
        HttpServletRequest httpRequest = (HttpServletRequest)request;

        httpRequest.setAttribute("staffRoster", _roster);

        boolean isAdmin = httpRequest.isUserInRole("manager");
        httpRequest.setAttribute("isAdmin", Boolean.valueOf(isAdmin));

        Calendar timeNow = Calendar.getInstance();
        int hour = timeNow.get(Calendar.HOUR_OF_DAY);

        boolean isBusiness = ((hour >= 9) && (hour <= 17));
        httpRequest.setAttribute("isBusiness", Boolean.valueOf(isBusiness));
    }

    chain.doFilter(request, response);
}

public void destroy()
{
    // do nothing
}

}
```

Chapter 26 Exercises

Exercise 1

The code for the test case for the Authentication service is listed here. The Authentication service, which is covered in Chapter 27, logs in a user to the portal Web application. The following code sets up the test case (setUp() method) with three users: one with a correct username and password, one with a correct username but incorrect password, and finally one with both the username and password incorrect. The test case (testLogin() method) tries each one in turn, and compares the status returned in each of the cases with the expected status:

```
package com.wrox.begjsp.ch27.service;

import com.wrox.begjsp.ch27.dto.UserProfile;
import junit.framework.*;
```

```java
public class AuthenticationServiceTest extends TestCase
{
    private UsernamePassword testAccount[]    = null;
    private AuthenticationService authService = null;

    protected void setUp ()
    {
        // Set up test accounts

        testAccount     = new UsernamePassword[3];
        // A login account with correct username/password
        testAccount[0] = new UsernamePassword ("test0", "test0");
        // A login account with correct username, incorrect password
        testAccount[1] = new UsernamePassword ("test1", "invalid");
        // A login account with incorrect username
        testAccount[2] = new UsernamePassword ("invalid", "invalid");

        // Get instance of Authentication Service
        try
        {
            authService = WroxServiceLocator.getAuthenticationService();
        }
        catch (WroxServiceException e)
        {
            e.printStackTrace();
        }
    }

    public void testLogin()
    {
        UserProfile profile;
        try
        {
            // A login account with correct username/password
            profile = authService.login (testAccount[0].getUsername(),
testAccount[0].getPassword());
            Assert.assertEquals ("Unable to log in user with correct credentials",
UserProfile.STATUS_LOGGED_IN,profile.getStatus());
            // A login account with correct username, incorrect password
            profile = authService.login (testAccount[1].getUsername(),
testAccount[1].getPassword());
            Assert.assertEquals ("Invalid password error not returned",
UserProfile.STATUS_INVALID_PASSWORD,profile.getStatus());
            // A login account with incorrect username
            profile = authService.login (testAccount[2].getUsername(),
testAccount[2].getPassword());
            Assert.assertEquals ("Invalid user error not returned",
UserProfile.STATUS_INVALID_USER,profile.getStatus());
        }
        catch (WroxServiceException e)
        {
            e.printStackTrace();
        }

    }
```

```
        public static void main (String[] args)
        {
            junit.swingui.TestRunner.run (AuthenticationServiceTest.class);
        }

        class UsernamePassword
        {
            private String username;
            private String password;

            public UsernamePassword (String username, String password)
            {
                this.username = username;
                this.password = password;
            }

            public String getUsername ()
            {
                return username;
            }

            public String getPassword ()
            {
                return password;
            }
        }
    }
```

Chapter 27 Exercises

Exercise 1

Did you notice earlier in the chapter how we used a factory class (DBFactory.java) to return instances of the database access classes (PublisherDBMemoryImpl.java and UserProfileDBMemoryImpl.java)?

The rest of the code only interacted with the database using the interfaces defined for the two database classes (PublisherDB.java and UserProfileDB.java). The following code from SaveProfileAction.java illustrates this use:

```
(DBFactory.getUserProfileDB()).updateUserProfile(userProfile);
```

Due to this architecture, changing to an implementation that involves a real database requires only the following:

❑ Create implementations of the PublisherDB.java and UserProfileDB.java classes that access databases. For example, we might decide to use MySQL, and hence write MySQL-based implementations, PublisherDBMySQL.java and UserProfileDBMySQL.java, respectively.

❑ Get the factory class (DBFactory.java) to return these new implementations.

That's it. No other modification of the application code is required, and the fact that we have moved to a relational database is transparent to the application.

The entire solution is too verbose to include here, so representative portions are listed. For example, the PublisherDBMySQL.java implementation might look like the following:

```java
public class PublisherDBMySQLImpl extends GenericDB implements PublisherDB
{
    ...
    public List getPublishers() throws DatabaseException
    {
        ArrayList list = null;
        Statement statement = null;

        try
        {
            statement = connection.createStatement();

            ResultSet resultSet = statement.executeQuery(
                    "select * from publishers");

            while (resultSet.next())
            {
                String name        = resultSet.getString("name");
                String description = resultSet.getString("description");
                String rssurl      = resultSet.getString("rssurl");
                String category    = resultSet.getString("category");
                Publisher publisher = new Publisher(name, description, category,
                                                    rssurl);
                list.add(publisher);
            }
        }
        catch (SQLException e)
        {
            throw new DatabaseException("Unable to access publisher table", e);
        }
        finally
        {
            try
            {
                statement.close();
            }
            catch (SQLException e)
            {
                /* ignore */
            }
        }

        return list;
    }
}
```

These classes would also require a database schema to be created, as shown in the following SQL script:

```
create table profile {
    username varchar (10) not null,
    password varchar (10) not null,
    displayname varchar(50) not null,
    interests varchar (100) not null,
    primary key (username)
}

create table subscriptions {
    username varchar (10) not null,
    rssurl   varchar(100) not null,
    primary key (username, rssurl)
}

create table publishers {
    name varchar (20) not null,
    description varchar(256),
    rssurl varchar(100) not null,
    category varchar(100),
    primary key (rssurl)
}
```

The change to DBFactory.java is shown next:

```
public static PublisherDB getPublisherDB()
{
    //return PublisherDBMemoryImpl.getInstance();
    return PublisherDBMySQLImpl.getInstance();
}

public static UserProfileDB getUserProfileDB()
{
    //return UserProfileDBMemoryImpl.getInstance();
    return UserProfileDBMySQLImpl.getInstance();
}
```

In fact, even this code change can be avoided if the factory class picked up the implementation from a configuration file instead of being hard-coded.

Exercise 2

The next project explains how validation can be done in Struts. Another approach, more appropriate for simpler types of validation, is using plain JavaScript. The following is a modified version of registration.jsp with JavaScript-based validation added:

```
<%@ page contentType="text/html;charset=UTF-8" language="java" %>
<%@ taglib uri="http://java.sun.com/jsp/jstl/core" prefix="c" %>
<%@ taglib uri="/WEB-INF/app.tld"     prefix="app" %>
<%@ taglib uri="/WEB-INF/struts-bean.tld" prefix="bean" %>
<%@ taglib uri="/WEB-INF/struts-html.tld" prefix="html" %>
<%@ taglib uri="/WEB-INF/struts-logic.tld" prefix="logic" %>
```

```
<script Language="JavaScript">

function validRequired(formField,fieldLabel)
{
        var result = true;
        if (formField.value == "")
        {
                alert('Please enter a value for the "' + fieldLabel +'" field.');
                formField.focus();
                result = false;
        }

        return result;
}

function validateForm(theForm)
{
        if (!validRequired(theForm.userName,"Name"))
                return false;

        if (!validRequired(theForm.password,"Password"))
                return false;

        if (!validRequired(theForm.displayName,"Display Name"))
                return false;

        if (!validRequired(theForm.interests,"Interests"))
                return false;

        if (!validRequired(theForm.subscriptions,"Subscriptions"))
                return false;

        return true;
}
</script>
```

```
<html:html>
<head>
  <title><bean:message key="registration.title.create"/></title>
<html:base/>
</head>
<body bgcolor="white">

<html:errors/>

<html:form action="/saveRegistration" onsubmit="return validateForm(this)">
<html:hidden property="action"/>
<table border="0" width="100%">
...
</table>
</html:form>

</body>
</html:html>
```

The code shown adds a check to prevent users from submitting forms without entering anything in the form fields. The same check can be added to editProfile.jsp. As you learned earlier in Chapter 12, "Dynamic Web Content Generation and Web Services," and Chapter 19, "Struts Framework," validation can be done on either the client side (using JavaScript) or the server side. This exercise solution demonstrates a very simple client-side validation approach.

Chapter 28 Exercises

Exercise 1

Following is the sales report addition to the struts-config.xml file:

```
<action path="/salesreport"
        type="com.wrox.begjsp.ch28.bookstore.controller.SalesReportAction"
        scope="request">
    <forward name="success" path="view.salesreport"/>
</action>
```

Here is the SalesReportAction class:

```
package com.wrox.begjsp.ch28.bookstore.controller;

import com.wrox.begjsp.ch28.bookstore.persist.EntityManager;
import com.wrox.begjsp.ch28.bookstore.persist.EntityManagerFactory;

import org.apache.struts.action.ActionForm;
import org.apache.struts.action.ActionForward;
import org.apache.struts.action.ActionMapping;

import java.util.List;

import javax.servlet.http.HttpServletRequest;
import javax.servlet.http.HttpServletResponse;

public class SalesReportAction extends BookstoreController
{
    public ActionForward doAction(ActionMapping mapping, ActionForm form,
        HttpServletRequest request, HttpServletResponse response)
        throws Exception
    {
        EntityManager manager = EntityManagerFactory.getOrderManagerInstance();
        List orders = manager.findAllOrdered("status", true);
        request.setAttribute("orders", orders);

        return mapping.findForward("success");
    }
}
```

The following code shows the new method added to the `EntityManager` to retrieve the ordered `CustomerOrder` object list:

```
public List findAllOrdered(String orderBy, boolean desc)
    throws HibernateException
{
    String direction = (desc ? "desc" : "asc");
    Session session = SessionProvider.currentSession();
    String qry = "from " + _cl.getName() + " as e order by e." + orderBy +
        " " + direction;
    Query q = session.createQuery(qry);
    List result = q.list();

    return result;
}
```

Here is the new Tiles definition for the report:

```
<definition name="view.salesreport" extends="view.abstract">
  <put name="body"             value="/WEB-INF/jsp/tiles/salesreport.jsp"/>
</definition>
```

The following code shows the addition to the menu definition for the new menu item:

```
<definition name="bookstore.menu" path="/WEB-INF/jsp/layout/menu-layout.jsp">
  <put name="menuTile"        value="/WEB-INF/jsp/tiles/menu.jsp"/>
  <putList name="menuItems">
      <item value="Book Categories" link="listcategories.do"/>
      <item value="View Cart" link="managecart.do"/>
      <item value="Checkout" link="checkout.do"/>
    <item value="Sales Report" link="salesreport.do"/>
  </putList>
</definition>
```

Here is the `salesreport.jsp` file to present the report:

```
<%@ taglib uri="http://java.sun.com/jsp/jstl/core" prefix="c"%>
<%@ taglib prefix="begjsp" tagdir="/WEB-INF/tags" %>

<table cellspacing=3 cellpadding=3 width="100%">
<tr>
    <td><h2>Sales Report</h2></td>
</tr>
<c:forEach items="${orders}" var="thisOrder">
    <c:set value="${thisOrder.orderItems}" var="orderItems"/>
<tr bgcolor="lightgrey">
        <td><b>Order Number: ${thisOrder.id}</b></td>
        <td>Customer Name: ${thisOrder.firstName} ${thisOrder.lastName}<br>
            Address: ${thisOrder.address} ${thisOrder.zipCode}
</tr>
<tr bgcolor="lightgrey">
        <td colspan="2">Decision: ${thisOrder.status.name}</td>
```

```
    </tr>
    <tr>
        <td colspan="2">
            <begjsp:listitems items="${orderItems}"/>
        </td>
    </tr>
    </c:forEach>
    </table>
```

Exercise 2

Following are the additions to the `messages.properties` file:

```
checkout.message.orderContent = Your order is made up of the following items
checkout.message.orderContentEmpty = There are no items in your shopping cart
checkout.message.title = Checkout and Complete your order
```

Direct text labels are then replaced with key references, such as the following:

```
<tr>
    <td><bean:message key="checkout.field.cardNumber"/></td>
    <td><html:text property="cardNumber" /></td>
</tr>
```

Index

T

tabbedpane **WebWork tag, 556**
table **WebWork tag, 557**
tag. *See also* **JSTL (JavaServer Pages Standard Tag Library)**
  action
    attribute role in passing value to action, 345
    including tag in, 242
    relation to tag, 34, 242
    tag file action, 242
  alias, 357
  attribute
    action, role in passing value to, 345
    dynamic, 336, 354–355
    fragment attribute, 338, 348, 350, 1069
    tag file, 337–338, 345
    XML tag, 34
  body, 34, 341–344
  Calendar object display, formatting using, 360
  custom, 342–344, 345–348, 359–360
  directive, 335–336, 354, 1068–1069
  directory, 224, 225
  empty, 22, 34
  file
    action, tag file, 242
    attribute, 337–338, 345
    date-display tag file, 330–331, 336–337
    described, 329–330
    directive, using, 215, 335–336
    directory, 184, 224, 225, 330
    implicit object, invoking, 334–335
    include directive, 337
    JAR file, packaging in, 355–359
    modularity, role in creating, 331
    namespace, 27
    packaging flexibility, 332
    reusing, 331
    scope, 332–335
    separation of concerns application design, 331–332
    simplicity, 332
    variable directive, 339–341
  HTML, embedding in, 28
  icon, associating with, 336
  language, specifying, 336
  library
    choose JSTL tag, using with, 226, 228
    container instruction provided by, 214, 223–224
    include construct, accessing using, 229–230
    index.jsp file, 226, 227–228

    JSF, 684, 685, 703–704
    JSTL declaration, 152, 190
    logging using, 460–464
    namespace information conveyed in, 22, 27, 152, 173, 183
    path, 22, 224, 330
    prefix, 43, 182, 225, 337, 1067
    Struts tag library, 607
    thread-safe, 494
    URI, 357
    validation, using in client-side, 382–386
    version, 357
    Webwork Custom Tag Library, 556–557
  location, 224, 225
  name, 34, 357
  namespace, 22, 27, 43
  number, generating random using, 359
  pooling custom tags, optimizing performance via, 880–881
  prefix, 43, 182, 225, 337, 1067
  table, generating using custom, 345–348
  template, placement within, 22
  text, searching and replacing, 342–344
  XML, 34
.tag **files, 28, 224**
Tag Library Descriptors (TLD), 173–174, 182–183, 355–356
tagdir taglib **directive attribute, 225, 1067**
taglib **directive**
  choose JSTL tag, using with, 226, 228
  container instruction provided by, 214, 223–224
  described, 21–22
  function-taglib.tld file, 176–177
  include construct, accessing using, 229–230
  index.jsp file, 226, 227–228
  JSTL declaration, 152, 190
  logging setup, 461
  namespace information conveyed in, 22, 27, 152, 173, 183
  path, 22, 224, 330
  prefix attribute, 43, 182, 225, 337, 1067
  syntax, 33, 1067
  tagdir attribute, 225, 1067
  uri attribute, 43, 176, 183, 191, 224–225
  web.xml file taglib element, 176, 183, 514
  XML, converting to, 238–239
taglib-uri web.xml **file element, 514**
taglibuser.tag **file, 337**
Taiwan, localizing for, 400
Tapestry framework, 553